# Contemporary
# Literary Criticism

# Guide to Gale Literary Criticism Series

| For criticism on | Consult these Gale series |
| --- | --- |
| Authors now living or who died after December 31, 1999 | **CONTEMPORARY LITERARY CRITICISM (CLC)** |
| Authors who died between 1900 and 1999 | **TWENTIETH-CENTURY LITERARY CRITICISM (TCLC)** |
| Authors who died between 1800 and 1899 | **NINETEENTH-CENTURY LITERATURE CRITICISM (NCLC)** |
| Authors who died between 1400 and 1799 | **LITERATURE CRITICISM FROM 1400 TO 1800 (LC)** <br> **SHAKESPEAREAN CRITICISM (SC)** |
| Authors who died before 1400 | **CLASSICAL AND MEDIEVAL LITERATURE CRITICISM (CMLC)** |
| Authors of books for children and young adults | **CHILDREN'S LITERATURE REVIEW (CLR)** |
| Dramatists | **DRAMA CRITICISM (DC)** |
| Poets | **POETRY CRITICISM (PC)** |
| Short story writers | **SHORT STORY CRITICISM (SSC)** |
| Black writers of the past two hundred years | **BLACK LITERATURE CRITICISM (BLC)** <br> **BLACK LITERATURE CRITICISM SUPPLEMENT (BLCS)** |
| Hispanic writers of the late nineteenth and twentieth centuries | **HISPANIC LITERATURE CRITICISM (HLC)** <br> **HISPANIC LITERATURE CRITICISM SUPPLEMENT (HLCS)** |
| Native North American writers and orators of the eighteenth, nineteenth, and twentieth centuries | **NATIVE NORTH AMERICAN LITERATURE (NNAL)** |
| Major authors from the Renaissance to the present | **WORLD LITERATURE CRITICISM, 1500 TO THE PRESENT (WLC)** <br> **WORLD LITERATURE CRITICISM SUPPLEMENT (WLCS)** |

ISSN 0091-3421

Volume 151

# Contemporary Literary Criticism

Criticism of the Works
of Today's Novelists, Poets, Playwrights,
Short Story Writers, Scriptwriters, and
Other Creative Writers

**Jeffrey W. Hunter**
SENIOR EDITOR

**Tom Burns**
ASSOCIATE EDITOR

GALE GROUP

THOMSON LEARNING

Detroit • New York • San Diego • San Francisco
Boston • New Haven, Conn. • Waterville, Maine
London • Munich

# STAFF

Janet Witalec, Lynn M. Zott, *Managing Editors, Literature Product*
Kathy D. Darrow, Ellen McGeagh, *Content-Product Liaisons*
Jeffrey W. Hunter, *Senior Editor*
Mark W. Scott, *Publisher, Literature Product*

Rebecca J. Blanchard, Tom Burns, Madeline S. Harris, Ron Morelli, *Associate Editors*
Jenny Cromie, *Technical Training Specialist*
Deborah J. Baker, Joyce Nakamura, Kathleen Lopez Nolan, *Managing Editors*
Susan M. Trosky, *Director, Literature Content*

Maria L. Franklin, *Permissions Manager*
Kim Davis, *Permissions Associate*
Sharon Toth, *Permissions Assistant*

Victoria B. Cariappa, *Research Manager*
Sarah Genik, *Project Coordinator*
Tamara C. Nott, Tracie A. Richardson, *Research Associates*
Nicodemus Ford, *Research Assistant*

Dorothy Maki, *Manufacturing Manager*
Stacy L. Melson, *Buyer*

Mary Beth Trimper, *Manager, Composition and Electronic Prepress*
Carolyn Roney, *Composition Specialist*

Michael Logusz, *Graphic Artist*
Randy Bassett, *Imaging Supervisor*
Robert Duncan, Dan Newell, Luke Rademacher, *Imaging Specialists*
Kelly A. Quin, *Editor, Image and Multimedia Content*

---

Since this page cannot legibly accommodate all copyright notices, the acknowledgments constitute an extension of the copyright notice.

While every effort has been made to secure permission to reprint material and to ensure the reliability of the information presented in this publication, the Gale Group neither guarantees the accuracy of the data contained herein nor assumes any responsibility for errors, omissions or discrepancies. Gale accepts no payment for listing; and inclusion in the publication of any organization, agency, institution, publication, service, or individual does not imply endorsement of the editors or publisher. Errors brought to the attention of the publisher and verified to the satisfaction of the publisher will be corrected in future editions.

This publication is a creative work fully protected by all applicable copyright laws, as well as by misappropriation, trade secret, unfair competition, and other applicable laws. The authors and editors of this work have added value to the underlying factual material herein through one or more of the following: unique and original selection, coordination, expression, arrangement, and classification of the information.

All rights to this publication will be vigorously defended.

Copyright © 2002 Gale Group, Inc.
27500 Drake Road
Farmington Hills, MI 48331-3535

All rights reserved, including the right of reproduction in whole or in part in any form.

Gale Group and Design is a trademark used herein under license.

---

Library of Congress Catalog Card Number 76-46132
ISBN 0-7876-5851-0
ISSN 0091-3421
Printed in the United States of America

10 9 8 7 6 5 4 3 2 1

# Contents

Preface vii

Acknowledgments xi

Literary Criticism Series Advisory Board xv


**Ana Castillo 1953-** .................................................................................................... 1
*American novelist, poet, essayist, editor, playwright, short story writer, and children's writer.*

**Atom Egoyan 1960-** ............................................................................................... 121
*Canadian screenwriter and director.*

**Donald Hall 1928-** ................................................................................................. 178
*American poet, essayist, memoirist, children's writer, short story writer, editor, playwright, and critic.*

**Kathryn Harrison 1961-** ....................................................................................... 237
*American novelist and memoirist.*

**Maureen Howard 1930-** ....................................................................................... 259
*American novelist, memoirist, editor, and short story writer.*

**Amy Tan 1952-** ...................................................................................................... 293
*American novelist, screenwriter, and children's writer; entry devoted to the novel* The Joy Luck Club *(1989).*


Literary Criticism Series Cumulative Author Index 355

Literary Criticism Series Cumulative Topic Index 441

*CLC* Cumulative Nationality Index 449

*CLC-151* Title Index 463

# Preface

Named "one of the twenty-five most distinguished reference titles published during the past twenty-five years" by *Reference Quarterly,* the *Contemporary Literary Criticism* (*CLC*) series provides readers with critical commentary and general information on more than 2,000 authors now living or who died after December 31, 1999. Volumes published from 1973 through 1999 include authors who died after December 31, 1959. Previous to the publication of the first volume of *CLC* in 1973, there was no ongoing digest monitoring scholarly and popular sources of critical opinion and explication of modern literature. *CLC,* therefore, has fulfilled an essential need, particularly since the complexity and variety of contemporary literature makes the function of criticism especially important to today's reader.

## Scope of the Series

*CLC* provides significant passages from published criticism of works by creative writers. Since many of the authors covered in *CLC* inspire continual critical commentary, writers are often represented in more than one volume. There is, of course, no duplication of reprinted criticism.

Authors are selected for inclusion for a variety of reasons, among them the publication or dramatic production of a critically acclaimed new work, the reception of a major literary award, revival of interest in past writings, or the adaptation of a literary work to film or television.

Attention is also given to several other groups of writers—authors of considerable public interest—about whose work criticism is often difficult to locate. These include mystery and science fiction writers, literary and social critics, foreign authors, and authors who represent particular ethnic groups.

Each *CLC* volume contains individual essays and reviews taken from hundreds of book review periodicals, general magazines, scholarly journals, monographs, and books. Entries include critical evaluations spanning from the beginning of an author's career to the most current commentary. Interviews, feature articles, and other published writings that offer insight into the author's works are also presented. Students, teachers, librarians, and researchers will find that the general critical and biographical material in *CLC* provides them with vital information required to write a term paper, analyze a poem, or lead a book discussion group. In addition, complete biographical citations note the original source and all of the information necessary for a term paper footnote or bibliography.

## Organization of the Book

A *CLC* entry consists of the following elements:

- The **Author Heading** cites the name under which the author most commonly wrote, followed by birth and death dates. Also located here are any name variations under which an author wrote, including transliterated forms for authors whose native languages use nonroman alphabets. If the author wrote consistently under a pseudonym, the pseudonym will be listed in the author heading and the author's actual name given in parenthesis on the first line of the biographical and critical information. Uncertain birth or death dates are indicated by question marks. Single-work entries are preceded by a heading that consists of the most common form of the title in English translation (if applicable) and the original date of composition.

- A **Portrait of the Author** is included when available.

- The **Introduction** contains background information that introduces the reader to the author, work, or topic that is the subject of the entry.

- The list of **Principal Works** is ordered chronologically by date of first publication and lists the most important works by the author. The genre and publication date of each work is given. In the case of foreign authors whose works have been translated into English, the English-language version of the title follows in brackets. Unless otherwise indicated, dramas are dated by first performance, not first publication.

- Reprinted **Criticism** is arranged chronologically in each entry to provide a useful perspective on changes in critical evaluation over time. The critic's name and the date of composition or publication of the critical work are given at the beginning of each piece of criticism. Unsigned criticism is preceded by the title of the source in which it appeared. All titles by the author featured in the text are printed in boldface type. Footnotes are reprinted at the end of each essay or excerpt. In the case of excerpted criticism, only those footnotes that pertain to the excerpted texts are included.

- A complete **Bibliographical Citation** of the original essay or book precedes each piece of criticism.

- Critical essays are prefaced by brief **Annotations** explicating each piece.

- Whenever possible, a recent **Author Interview** accompanies each entry.

- An annotated bibliography of **Further Reading** appears at the end of each entry and suggests resources for additional study. In some cases, significant essays for which the editors could not obtain reprint rights are included here. Boxed material following the further reading list provides references to other biographical and critical sources on the author in series published by Gale.

# Indexes

A **Cumulative Author Index** lists all of the authors that appear in a wide variety of reference sources published by the Gale Group, including *CLC*. A complete list of these sources is found facing the first page of the Author Index. The index also includes birth and death dates and cross references between pseudonyms and actual names.

A **Cumulative Nationality Index** lists all authors featured in *CLC* by nationality, followed by the number of the *CLC* volume in which their entry appears.

A **Cumulative Topic Index** lists the literary themes and topics treated in the series as well as in *Literature Criticism from 1400 to 1800, Nineteenth-Century Literature Criticism, Twentieth-Century Literary Criticism,* and the *Contemporary Literary Criticism* Yearbook, which was discontinued in 1998.

An alphabetical **Title Index** accompanies each volume of *CLC*. Listings of titles by authors covered in the given volume are followed by the author's name and the corresponding page numbers where the titles are discussed. English translations of foreign titles and variations of titles are cross-referenced to the title under which a work was originally published. Titles of novels, dramas, nonfiction books, and poetry, short story, or essay collections are printed in italics, while individual poems, short stories, and essays are printed in roman type within quotation marks.

In response to numerous suggestions from librarians, Gale also produces an annual cumulative title index that alphabetically lists all titles reviewed in *CLC* and is available to all customers. Additional copies of this index are available upon request. Librarians and patrons will welcome this separate index; it saves shelf space, is easy to use, and is recyclable upon receipt of the next edition.

# Citing *Contemporary Literary Criticism*

When writing papers, students who quote directly from any volume in the Literary Criticism Series may use the following general format to footnote reprinted criticism. The first example pertains to material drawn from periodicals, the second to material reprinted from books.

Alfred Cismaru, "Making the Best of It," *The New Republic* 207, no. 24 (December 7, 1992): 30, 32; excerpted and reprinted in *Contemporary Literary Criticism,* vol. 85, ed. Christopher Giroux (Detroit: The Gale Group, 1995), 73-4.

Yvor Winters, *The Post-Symbolist Methods* (Allen Swallow, 1967), 211-51; excerpted and reprinted in *Contemporary Literary Criticism,* vol. 85, ed. Christopher Giroux (Detroit: The Gale Group, 1995), 223-26.

## Suggestions are Welcome

Readers who wish to suggest new features, topics, or authors to appear in future volumes, or who have other suggestions or comments are cordially invited to call, write, or fax the Managing Editor:

Managing Editor, Literary Criticism Series
The Gale Group
27500 Drake Road
Farmington Hills, MI 48331-3535
1-800-347-4253 (GALE)
Fax: 248-699-8054

# Acknowledgments

The editors wish to thank the copyright holders of the excerpted criticism included in this volume and the permissions managers of many book and magazine publishing companies for assisting us in securing reproduction rights. We are also grateful to the staffs of the Detroit Public Library, the Library of Congress, the University of Detroit Mercy Library, Wayne State University Purdy/Kresge Library Complex, and the University of Michigan Libraries for making their resources available to us. Following is a list of the copyright holders who have granted us permission to reproduce material in this volume of *CLC*. Every effort has been made to trace copyright, but if omissions have been made, please let us know.

## COPYRIGHTED MATERIAL IN *CLC*, VOLUME 151, WAS REPRODUCED FROM THE FOLLOWING PERIODICALS:

*Agni,* v. 47, 1998. Reproduced by permission.—*American Poetry Review,* v. 18, January/February, 1989. Copyright © 1989 by World Poetry, Inc. Reproduced by permission of the author.—*Americas Review,* v. 20, Spring 1992; v. 21, Fall-Winter 1993; v. 22, Spring-Summer, 1994. Arte Público Press–University of Houston. All reproduced by permission.—*Aztlan,* v. 24, Fall, 1999, UCLA Chicano Studies Research Center. Reprinted with permission of The Regents of the University of California. Not for further reproduction.—*Belles Lettres,* v. 8, Spring 1993; v. 9, Fall, 1993. Both reproduced by permission.—*The Bloomsbury Review,* v. 15, July/August, 1995. Copyright © by Owaissa Communications Company, Inc. 1995. Reproduced by permission of the author.—*Book World–The Washington Post,* May 24, 1984 for "The Lure of the Bright Lights" by Noel Perrin./May 11, 1986 for "Maureen Howard: Satire and Sympathy" by Jonathan Yardley./November 22, 1992 for "Lost in Bridgeport" by Noel Perrin. March 7, 1993 for "Shooting His Daughter" by Wendy Smith./May 31, 1993 for "Battling with Magic" by James Polk./September 1, 1996 for "Love Among the Golden Cockroaches" by Louise Titchener./December 25, 1997 for "Sweet Hereafter: A Cry for Hope" by Stephen Hunter./February 8, 1998, for "Stormy Weather" by Susan Dooley./November 19, 1999 for "Felicia's Journey: Soup to Nut" by Stephen Hunter. © 1984, 1986, 1992, 1993, 1996, 1997, 1998, 1999 Washington Post Book World Service/Washington Post Writers Group. All Reproduced by permission of the respective authors.—*Chicago Tribune Books,* October 25, 1992 for "Circling Back to Bridgeport: Maureen Howard's Unconventional Saga of a Family and City" by Carol Anshaw./June 4, 1995, for "Love and Death, High and Low" by Judith Dunford./April 20, 1997 for "Novelist Kathryn Harrison's Memoir of Her Affair with Her Father" by Joanne Kaufman./September 26, 1999 for "Ana Castillo's Story of a Woman Who Seeks to Understand Her Past and Imagine Her Future" by Manuel Luis Martinez. © 1992, 1995, 1997, 1999. All rights reserved. All reproduced by permission of the respective authors.—*The Christian Century,* v. 110, March 3, 1993; v. 115, February 18, 1998. Both reproduced by permission.—*Christian Science Monitor,* December 14, 1992 for "Novel Strains for Effect" by Merle Rubin. © 1992 The Christian Science Publishing Society. All rights reserved. Reproduced by permission of the author.—*Cineaste,* v. 23, Spring, 1997; v. 25, Winter 1999. Copyright © 1997, 1999 by Cineaste Publishers, Inc. Both reproduced by permission.—*Commonweal,* v. 120, February 12, 1993; v. 120, September 14, 1993; v. 121, January 14, 1994; v. 125, March 27, 1998. Copyright © 1993, 1994, 1998 Commonweal Publishing Co., Inc. All reproduced by permission of the Commonweal Foundation.—*Feminist Studies,* v. 19, Fall, 1993 for "Daughter-Text/Mother-Text: Matrilineage in Amy Tan's Joy Luck Club," by Marina Heung. Reproduced by permission of Feminist Studies, Inc., Department of Women's Studies, University of Maryland, College Park, MD 20724.—*Film Comment,* v. 25, November-December, 1989 for "Memories of Overdevelopment: Up and Atom" by Amy Taubin./v. 29, November-December, 1993 for "Ruined" by Chris Chang. Copyright © 1989, 1993 by Film Comment Publishing Corporation. Reproduced by permission of the respective authors.—*Film Quarterly,* v. 48, Spring, 1995.© 1995 by the Regents of the University of California. Reprinted from Film Quarterly.—*Genders,* Winter, 1992. Copyright © 1992 by the University of Texas Press. Reproduced by permission.—*Harper's Magazine,* v. 299, September, 1999. Copyright © 1999 by *Harper's Magazine*. All rights reserved. Reproduced from the September issue by special permission.—*The Hudson Review,* v. 51, Winter, 1999. Copyright © 1999 by The Hudson Review, Inc. Reproduced by permission.—*Journal of Aging and Identity,* v. 3, June, 1993. Copyright 1998 by Human Sciences Press. Reproduced by permission of the publisher and the author.—*The Journal of the Midwest Modern Language Association,* v. 30, Spring 1997 for "Queering Chicano/a Narratives: Lesbian as Healer, Saint and Warrior in Ana Castillo's So Far From God" by Colette Morrow. Copyright 1997 by The Midwest Modern Language Association. Reproduced by permission of the publisher and the author.—*Los Angeles Times,* March 12, 1995; November 23, 1997. Copyright 1995, 1997 *Los Angeles Times*. Both reproduced by permission.—*Los Angeles Times Book Review,* May 18, 1986; October 25, 1992; February 14, 1993; May 16, 1993; June 18, 1995; August 25, 1996; January 25, 1998. Copyright 1986, 1992, 1993, 1995, 1996, 1998, *Los Angeles Times*. All reproduced by permission.—*Maclean's Magazine,* October 3, 1994; September 8, 1997; September 13, 1999; November 15, 1999. © 1994, 1997, 1999 by *Maclean's Magazine*. All reproduced by permission.—*The Massa-*

chusetts Review, v. 39, Winter, 1998/1999. Reproduced from *The Massachusetts Review,* The Massachusetts Review, Inc. by permission.—***MELUS,*** v. 18, Spring, 1993; v. 19, Spring, 1994; v. 22, Fall, 1997; v. 23, Spring 1998; v. 24, Summer, 1999; v. 25, Summer, 2000. Copyright, MELUS: The Society for the Study of Multi-Ethnic Literature of the United States, 1993, 1994, 1997, 1998, 1999, 2000. All reproduced by permission.—***Michigan Quarterly Review,*** v. 30, Fall, 1991 for "Donald Hall's Old and New Poems" by Lawrence Joseph. Copyright © The University of Michigan, 1991. All rights reserved. Reproduced by permission of the author./v. 35, Fall, 1996 for "The Harvard Advocate" by Laurence Goldstein. Copyright © The University of Michigan, 1996. All rights reserved. Reproduced by permission of the author.—***The Nation,*** New York, January, 1998. © 1998 *The Nation* magazine/The Nation Company, Inc. Reproduced by permission.—***New Criterion,*** v. 15, May, 1997 for "Devouring Love" by Brooke Allen. Copyright © 1997 by The Foundation for Cultural Review. Reproduced by permission of the author.—***The New Leader,*** v. 75, December 14, 1992. © 1992 by The American Labor Conference on International Affairs, Inc. Reproduced by permission.—***The New Republic,*** v. 207, November 9, 1992. © 1992 The New Republic, Inc. Reproduced by permission of *The New Republic.*—***New Statesman & Society,*** v. 1, October 7, 1988; v. 8, July 28, 1995; v. 126, August 15, 1997. © 1988, 1997, 1995 Statesman & Nation Publishing Company Limited. Reproduced by permission.—***The New York Review of Books,*** December 3, 1992; September 25, 1997; July 16, 1998. All reprinted with permission from *The New York Review of Books.* Copyright © 1992, 1997, 1998 NYREV, Inc.—***The Observer,*** April 13, 1997. Reproduced by permission of The Observer Limited, London.—***The Ohio Review,*** Spring, 1990. Copyright © 1990 by the Editors of *The Ohio Review.* Reproduced by permission.—***Partisan Review,*** v. LX, 1993, for the review of *Natural History* by Pearl K. Bell. Copyright © 1993 by the author. Reprinted by permission of the author.—***Ploughshares,*** v. 17, Spring, 1991 for an interview with Donald Hall about *The One Day* by George Myers, Jr. Reproduced by permission of the author.—***Poetry,*** v. 73, February, 1999 for "Review of Without" by Leslie Ullman. © 1999 by the Modern Poetry Association. Reproduced by permission of the Editor of *Poetry* and the author.—***Poets & Writers,*** v. 28, March-April 2000. Reproduced by permission.—***Publishers Weekly,*** v. 239, June 29, 1992; v. 240, March 1, 1993; v. 243, August 12, 1996; v. 245, March 23, 1998. Copyright 1992, 1993, 1996, 1998 by Reed Publishing USA. All reproduced from *Publishers Weekly,* published by the Bowker Magazine Group of Cahners Publishing Co., a division of Reed Publishing USA., by permission.—***Quill and Quire,*** v. 61, May, 1995 for a review of *Lucy's Summer* by Joanne Schott. Reproduced by permission of the author.—***The Review of Contemporary Fiction,*** v. 17, Spring, 1997. Copyright, 1997, by John O'Brien. Reproduced by permission.—***Salmagundi,*** Winter, 1990. Copyright © 1990 by Skidmore College. Reproduced by permission.—***Saturday Night,*** v. 113, April, 1998 for "The Sweet Here and Now" by Patricia Pearson. Copyright © 1998 by *Saturday Night.* Reproduced by permission of the author.—***Sewanee Review,*** v. 102, Summer, 1994; v. 104, January, 1996. Copyright © 1994, 1996 by The University of the South. Both reproduced with permission of the editor.—***Sight & Sound,*** v. 2, June, 1992; v. 5, May, 1995; v. 7, October, 1997. All reproduced by permission.—***Studies in Short Fiction,*** v. 27, Winter, 1990. Copyright 1990 by Newberry College. Reproduced by permission.—***Style,*** v. 30, Fall 1996 for "No Country to Call Home: A Study of Castillo's *Mixquiahuala Letters*" by Tanya Long Bennett. Copyright © *Style,* 1996. All rights reserved. Reproduced by permission of the publisher and the author.—***The Spectator,*** v. 278, March 19, 1997; v. 278, April 19, 1997. Copyright © 1997 by *The Spectator* Both reproduced by permission of *The Spectator.*—***The Times Literary Supplement,*** no. 4774, September 30, 1994; no. 4812, June 23, 1995; no. 5067, May 12, 2000. © The Times Supplements Limited 1994, 1995, 2000. All reproduced from *The Times Literary Supplement* by permission.—***The University of Toronto Quarterly,*** v. 64, Winter, 1994. © University of Toronto Press 1994. Reproduced by permission of University of Toronto Press Incorporated.—***The Women's Review of Books,*** v. VI, September, 1989 for "Many-colored Poets" by Margaret Randall./v. 10, December, 1992 for "Tale of Two Cities" by Gail Pool./v. 10, July, 1993, for "When Fiction Meets Fact" by Jeffrey Ann Goudie./v. 14, May, 1997 for "Divinely Subversive" by Jane Caputi./v. 14, July, 1997 for "Blaming the Victim" by Lisa Alther. All reprinted by permission of the respective authors.—***Voice Literary Supplement,*** v. 42, No. 13, April 1, 1997. Reproduced by permission of the *The Village Voice.*

## COPYRIGHTED MATERIAL IN *CLC*, VOLUME 151, WAS REPRODUCED FROM THE FOLLOWING BOOKS:

Alarcon, Norma. From "The Sardonic Powers of the Erotic in the Work of Ana Castillo," in **Breaking Boundaries: Latina Writing and Critical Readings.** Edited by Asuncion Horno-Delgado and Others. The University of Massachusetts Press, 1989. Copyright © 1989 by The University of Massachusetts Press. All rights reserved. Reproduced by permission.—Bower, Ann. From **Epistolary Responses: The Letter in 20th-Century American Fiction and Criticism.** The University of Alabama Press, 1997. Copyright © 1997 by Ann Bower. All rights reserved. Reproduced by permission of the publisher.—Ghymn, Esther Mikyung. From "Mothers and Daughters," in **Images of Asian American Women by Asian American Women Writers.** Peter Lang AG, 1995. Copyright © Esther Mikyung Ghymn 1995. All rights reserved. Reproduced by permission of the publisher.—Ho, Wendy. From "Swan Feather Mothers and Coca-Cola Daughters: Teaching Amy Tan's *The Joy Luck Club,*" in **Teaching American Ethnic Literatures.** Edited by John R. Maitino and David R. Peck. University of New Mexico Press, 1996. Copyright © John R. Maitino and David R. Peck 1996. All rights reserved. Reproduced by permission of the publisher.—Li, David Leiwei. From "Genes, Generation, and Geospiritual (Be)longings," in *Imagining the Nation: Asian American Literature and Cultural Consent.* Stanford University Press, 1998. Copyright © 1998 by David Leiwei Li. All rights reserved. Reprinted by permission of the publisher.—Quintana, Alvina E. From *Criticism in the Borderlands: Studies in Chicano Literature, Culture, and Ideology.* Edited by Hector Calderon and Jose David Saldivar. Duke University Press, 1991. Copyright © 1991 by Duke University Press, Durham, NC. Reproduced by permission.

**PHOTOGRAPHS AND ILLUSTRATIONS APPEARING IN *CLC,* VOLUME 151, WERE RECEIVED FROM THE FOLLOWING SOURCES:**

Castillo, Ana, photograph. Arte Publico Press Archives, University of Houston. Reproduced by permission.—Egoyan, Atom, Cannes, France, 1997, photo by Lionel Cironneay. AP/Wide World Photos. Reproduced by permission.—Hall, Donald, photograph by Steven W. Lewis. Reproduced by permission of Donald Hall.—Harrison, Kathryn, photograph. © Jerry Bauer. Reproduced by permission.—Howard, Maureen, John Cheever, Garry Wills (each holding their 1978 National Book Critics Circle Awards), 1979, photograph. AP/Wide World Photos. Reproduced by permission.—Tan, Amy Ruth (holding book), photograph. Archive Photos, Inc. Reproduced by permission.

# Literary Criticism Series Advisory Board

The members of the Gale Group Literary Criticism Series Advisory Board—reference librarians and subject specialists from public, academic, and school library systems—represent a cross-section of our customer base and offer a variety of informed perspectives on both the presentation and content of our literature criticism products. Advisory board members assess and define such quality issues as the relevance, currency, and usefulness of the author coverage, critical content, and literary topics included in our series; evaluate the layout, presentation, and general quality of our printed volumes; provide feedback on the criteria used for selecting authors and topics covered in our series; provide suggestions for potential enhancements to our series; identify any gaps in our coverage of authors or literary topics, recommending authors or topics for inclusion; analyze the appropriateness of our content and presentation for various user audiences, such as high school students, undergraduates, graduate students, librarians, and educators; and offer feedback on any proposed changes/enhancements to our series. We wish to thank the following advisors for their advice throughout the year.

**Dr. Toby Burrows**
Principal Librarian
The Scholars' Centre
University of Western Australia Library

**Steven R. Harris**
English Literature Librarian
University of Tennessee

**Mary Jane Marden**
Literature and General Reference Librarian
St. Petersburg Jr. College

**Catherine Palmer**
Instructional Services Librarian and
English and Comparative Literature Librarian
University of California, Irvine

**Patricia Sarles, MA, MLS**
Canarsie High School Library
Brooklyn, New York

**Mark Schumacher**
Jackson Library
University of North Carolina at Greensboro

**Gwen Scott-Miller**
Humanities Department Manager
Seattle Public Library

**Ann Marie Wiescinski**
Central High School Library
Bay City, Michigan

# Ana Castillo
## 1953-

(Full name Ana Hernandez Del Castillo) American novelist, poet, essayist, editor, playwright, short story writer, and children's writer.

The following entry presents an overview of Castillo's career through 2000.

## INTRODUCTION

Castillo is a highly respected contemporary Chicana writer. Her poetry sheds light on the struggles of victimized people, but at the same time highlights the simple joys and dreams of the downtrodden. Her novels and essays focus on the plight of Chicana women and challenge patriarchal societies that fail to recognize women's individuality. Castillo's strong beliefs in feminist and Chicana issues are reflected in her writings, which are noted as constituting socio-political demands for fairness and equality.

## BIOGRAPHICAL INFORMATION

Castillo was born on June 15, 1953 in Chicago, Illinois, to Raymond Castillo and Raquel Rocha Castillo. Her parents were struggling working-class Mexican Americans. Castillo began writing poems at the age of nine, following the death of her grandmother. She attended public schools and during her childhood was constantly aware of her ethnic roots, which stood in contrast to Chicago's caucasian mainstream society. In high school, Castillo became active in the Chicano movement, utilizing her writing skills to compose protest poetry. She attended a secretarial high school, but soon realized that a career as a secretary held no promise for her. After attending Chicago City College for two years, she transferred to Northeastern Illinois University, where she received a B.A. in liberal arts in 1975. Castillo then moved to California, where she taught ethnic studies for a year at Santa Rosa Junior College. In 1977, she returned to Chicago, where she served as writer-in-residence for the Illinois Arts Council. Castillo's first chapbook of poems, *Otro Canto,* was published in 1977. In 1979, Castillo earned an M.A. in Latin-American and Caribbean studies from the University of Chicago. From 1980 to 1981, she served as poet-in-residence for Urban Gateways of Chicago, and in 1985, Castillo returned to California to teach at San Francisco State University and to serve as an editor for Third Woman Press. Her first novel, *The Mixquiahuala Letters,* was published in 1986 and received the Before Columbus Foundation's American Book Award. Castillo was honored by the Women's Foundation of San Francisco for "pioneering excellence in literature" in 1987. Castillo taught Chicano humanities literature at Sonoma State University in 1988, creative writing and fiction at California State University from 1988 to 1989, and Chicana feminist literature at the University of California at Santa Barbara as a dissertation fellow/lecturer for the Chicano Studies Department. Castillo received a California Arts Fellowship for fiction in 1989 and a National Endowments for the Arts Fellowship in 1990. She received her Ph.D. in American studies from the University of Bremen in 1991, writing her dissertation on "Xicanisma," a term she created to describe Chicana feminism. This dissertation was published as *Massacre of the Dreamers: Essays on Xicanisma* (1994) and received the Gustaves Myers Award. Castillo's third novel, *So Far from God* (1993), won the Carl Sandburg Literary Award in fiction in 1993 and the Mountains and Plains Booksellers Award in 1994. Castillo subsequently received a second National Endowment for the Arts Fellowship in 1995. In April 2000, a historical mural featuring Castillo and other notable Chicagoans was unveiled on the 103rd floor of the skydeck of the Sears Tower building in Chicago, Illinois.

## MAJOR WORKS

Castillo began her literary career as a poet. Her first three published collections, *Otro Canto, The Invitation* (1979), and *Women Are Not Roses* (1984), are filled with poems that focus on women's issues. She embraces a woman's desire for identity and sexuality, traits that the Mexican male-dominant society and the Catholic church fail to recognize. Castillo continued to explore these ideas in her first novel, the epistolary *Mixquiahuala Letters*. This work examines the relationship between two women, Teresa and Alicia, solely through correspondence. The letters are in no certain order, and Castillo invites the reader to read these letters in three different arrangements to gain different insights: Conformist, Cynic, and Quixotic. The insights into the protagonists' personalities and beliefs remain the same, but with each different reading, the outlook of the novel changes. Castillo's next novel, *Sapogonia* (1990), features a male protagonist, Máximo Madrigal. Máximo fits Castillo's definition of an anti-hero, a man who believes his actions are above reproach and is a hero in his own mind. His abuse of and control over women is self-justified, and at times, even beneath his notice. He becomes obsessed with Pastora Aké, who refuses to be controlled by him, a defiance that he cannot allow and subsequently leads him to murder her. In 1993, *So Far from God* was published and became Castillo's first widely read and reviewed work. The novel follows the life of a strong Chicana woman, Sofi, and her four daughters, Esperanza, Fe, Caridad, and La Loca. All of the women endure numerous trials and tribulations stemming from the male-dominated culture, the Catholic Church, and white American society. The four daughters each die unusual and untimely deaths, yet the novel emphasizes the importance of women taking control of their destinies. Castillo stresses the peace that may be realized by seizing control of one's life and underscores the underlying inherent magical properties of being a woman. In 1994, Castillo published her doctoral dissertation, *Massacre of the Dreamers: Essays on Xicanisma*. Xicanisma is a word that Castillo coined to encompass feminist and Chicana issues. In the essays, she attempts to uncover sexual and gender-based discrimination and describes how white feminism has had little effect on the liberation of the Chicana. *Loverboys* (1996) is a collection of short stories that explore the dynamics of heterosexual and homosexual relationships. Several stories return to themes of discrimination, including an examination of the biases against homosexuality and overt sexual behavior by women. In *Peel My Love like an Onion* (1999), Castillo returned to the novel format. The protagonist of the book, Carmen, is a woman who is obsessed with becoming a flamenco dancer even though one of her legs is afflicted by polio. Her selfish and insensitive family is unsupportive of her endeavors and constantly ridicule her dreams. *My Daughter, My Son, the Eagle, the Dove* (2000) is a work consisting of two long poems based on Aztec and Nahuatal instructions to youths facing rites of passage. The poems relate teachings from Castillo's ancestry that are several hundred years old, yet are still applicable to the modern world. *I Ask the Impossible* (2001) is a new collection of poems, several of which focus on Castillo's young son as he grows and matures.

## CRITICAL RECEPTION

Critical reception to Castillo's work has been largely favorable. Critics have recognized Castillo's efforts to shed light on feminist and Chicana concerns in her poetry and prose. Commentators have complimented her poems for being lyrical, straightforward, and successful in capturing the essence of a proud Chicana woman in a society dominated by white males. Reviewers have consistently noted Castillo's natural poetic abilities that many claim are apparent in her fiction. Her first novel, *The Mixquiahuala Letters,* received wide critical praise. The technique of offering three different courses of reading has been lauded as insightful and thought to contribute to a deeper understanding of the characters. Critics were divided over Castillo's third novel, *So Far from God*. While a handful of reviewers found the novel's magical realism unoriginal and a detraction from the overall message, others have praised the book for its important empowerment themes and believe this work to be Castillo's most important novel to date.

# PRINCIPAL WORKS

*i close my eyes (to see)* (poetry) 1976
*Otro Canto* (poetry) 1977
*The Invitation* (poetry) 1979; revised edition, 1986
*Clark Street Counts* (play) 1983
*Women Are Not Roses* (poetry) 1984
*The Mixquiahuala Letters* (novel) 1986
*My Father Was a Toltec: Poems* (poetry) 1988; revised edition, 1995
*This Bridge Called My Back: Writings by Radical Women of Color* [editor with Cherríe Moraga] (poetry, essays, and short stories) 1988; also published as *Este puente, mi espalda: Voces de mujeres tercermundistas en los Estados Unidos,* 1988
*Sapogonia: An Anti-Romance in 3/8 Meter* (novel) 1990
*The Sexuality of Latinas* [editor with Norma Alarcón and Cherríe Moraga] (essays, short stories, and poetry) 1993
*So Far from God* (novel) 1993
*Chicago Poetry* [editor with Heiner Bus] (poetry) 1994
*Massacre of the Dreamers: Essays on Xicanisma* (essays) 1994
*Goddess of the Americas: Writings on the Virgin of Guadalupe* [editor] (essays, poetry, and short stories) 1996; also published as *La Diosa de las Américas,* 2000
*Loverboys* (short stories) 1996
*Peel My Love like an Onion* (novel) 1999

*My Daughter, My Son, the Eagle, the Dove* (juvenilia) 2000
*I Ask the Impossible: Poems* (poetry) 2001

---

# CRITICISM

**Norma Alarcón (essay date 1989)**

SOURCE: "The Sardonic Powers of the Erotic in the Work of Ana Castillo," in *Breaking Boundaries: Latina Writing and Critical Readings,* University of Massachusetts Press, 1989, pp. 94–107.

[*In the following essay, Alarcón analyzes Castillo's writing in the context of male/female relationships and the politics of women's sexuality.*]

Ana Castillo, a native of Chicago, first made an impact on the Chicano writers' community with the publication of her chapbook, *Otro Canto* (1977). Written mostly in English (as is almost all of Castillo's work), it ensured her reputation as a "social protest" poet at a time when it was difficult to be anything else. As a result, some of the ironic tones already present in the early work have been easily over-looked in favor of the protest message, which in fact is re-doubled by irony. It can be argued that irony is one of Castillo's trademarks. Irony often appears when experience is viewed after-the-fact or in opposition to another's subjectivity. In this essay, I would like to explore the ironically erotic dance that Castillo's speaking subjects often take up with men. Thus, my exploration will follow the trajectory of the traditional heterosexual, female speaking subjects in Castillo's published works: *Otro Canto, The Invitation* (1979), *Women Are Not Roses* (1984), and *The Mixquiahuala Letters* (1986).[1]

*Otro Canto* portrayed the burdens of the urban poor through the voice of a young woman who had learned the bitter lessons of disillusionment early in life. Thus, in the poem **"1975,"** we hear a sigh of relief when all those "proletarian talks"—the nemesis of many a left-wing activist—are finally translated into action. The speaker underscores the repetitiveness of mere talk by starting off every stanza with the line, "talking proletarian talks," which subsequently opens the way for details that give rise to such talk. We are not relieved from this tactical monotony "until one long / awaited day— / we are tired / of talking" (pp. 49–51). Though in **"1975"** the speaker is not gendermarked but is revealed as being in a "we-us" speaking position within a Marxist revolutionary stance, that speaker is transformed into a "we-us" who makes **"A Counter-Revolutionary Proposition."** In this poem we are called upon to make love and "forget / that Everything matters" (*Women Are Not Roses,* p. 63). Given the litany of the things that matter in the stanza preceding the call, however, the poem urges me to ask if the speaker is wryly alluding to the well-known Anglo counterculture slogan of the sixties: "Make Love, Not War." As the poem notes, what matters to the proletarian (i.e., Marxist) revolutionary speaker is the struggle to overcome class oppression, a struggle that is spoken through a supposedly non-gendered we. However, juxtaposing the poem's title, **"A Counter-Revolutionary Proposition,"** with the implicit allusion to the slogan "Make Love, Not War," may help us to unravel a story with a difference for the underclass female speaker who addresses her partner, "Let's forget . . ." (p. 63).

Notwithstanding the recent involvement of women in revolutionary struggles (i.e., Cuba and Nicaragua), it is still the case that in opposition to the erotic, a revolution or a war is especially marked with a traditional male subjectivity that awaits analysis. In order for a female speaker to recover the full meaningful impact of herself, she still must address how that self figures in the "heterosexual erotic contract," revolutions not excepted. Within this contract, the female body continues to be the site of both reproduction and the erotic; despite class position, a speaker and her gendered social experience are imbricated in that age-old contract. Thus, **"A Counter-Revolutionary Proposition"** may now be understood as a call to explore the politics of the erotic. Let us actively explore the neo-revolutionary implications of erotic relations that have been constantly displaced, undervalued, and even erased by masculine-marked militancy, or at best rendered passively by the male poet, with the woman as the muse, the wife, the mother.

From this point of view, the poem's title acquires a polyvalence that goes beyond the private, where the erotic has often been held "hostage," and is placed in the political arena. In a sense, then, "Let's 'make love'" is taken from the lips of an Anglo, male, left-wing activist by the most unexpected of speakers—Ana Castillo's poetic persona. In retrospect, Castillo's early work stands out as one of her first attempts to appropriate the erotic and its significances for the female speaker, with ironic repercussions. Given the assumed class position of the speaker herself, affirming the erotic, as she takes pause from the class struggle, is tantamount to speaking against herself, or so her "brother/lover" may attest. The implicit suggestion that the erotic and the class struggle may be incompatible in a patriarchal world, when both are made public, places the underclass female in a double bind, since she may be forced to choose between areas of life that, for her, are intertwined or indivisible. In my view, the speakers in Castillo's work refuse to make such choices. Choosing one or the other splits the subject into the domains that heretofore have been symbolically marked feminine or masculine.

In the seventies, Chicanas and other women of color had a difficult time within their fraternal group when they insisted that feminist politics, with its commitment to the exploration of women's sexuality and gendered identities, also applied to them. The supposed contradictory position of women of color, one that was between a male-identified class liberation struggle and a middle- or upper-class, white, female-identified sexual liberation struggle, forced women of color to walk a tightrope in their quest for an exploration of gender.[2] Thus, a poem such as **"A Counter-Revolutionary Proposition"** was politically risky, as the speaker addresses another, ostensibly male, and asks that he forget that "Everything matters." Yet, it is only within this apparent self-contradictory situation that such a speaker may be able to claim sexuality for herself and explore the significance of the female body that is always, and already, sexually marked. Such a "proposition" simultaneously opens up a gap between the fact of economic oppression and the desire for erotic pleasure and significance that faces us when we perceive the separation between the first and the second stanzas in the poem.

In *The Invitation* (1979), a chapbook-length collection of erotic poems and vignettes, Castillo's speaker no longer requests that her interlocutor forget that "everything matters" but pursues, instead, a sustained exploration of her erotic, at times bisexual, desires. The appropriation of the erotic for the female speaker is again a motivating force. The emphasis, however, is not so much on the speaker's uneasy conjunction with "proletarian politics" as it is with "textual politics." That is, the appropriative process resonates respectively against, and with, two important books of our time: Octavio Paz's *The Labyrinth of Solitude* (1950), and Maria Teresa Horta, Maria Isabel Barreno, and Maria Velho da Costa's *The Three Marias: New Portuguese Letters* (1975).[3] Consider, for example, that in the second chapter of his book, Paz affirms women's dormant and submissive sexuality that awaits discovery through male efforts, while "The Three Marias" reject this view throughout their book and protest women's political bondage that, at the core, is based on their sexuality. Notwithstanding the different approaches that each of "The Three Marias" would take to liberate women, there is very little doubt that they agree that male perception of women's sexuality pervades all levels of women's existence.

The erotic thematics of *The Invitation* openly declare the influence of those two books (pp. iii, 9). Castillo's text, when viewed in their light, becomes a purposefully glossed negation of Paz's view and an extension of the authors' own erotic vision. It is as if the relative absence of any sociopolitical debate of the Chicana/Mexicana's sexuality had made it imperative that Castillo explore instead her speaker's desire in the light of a textual milieu. Moreover, reading Castillo's work in this fashion enables us to clarify her struggle to place her erotic thematics and voices in the interstice of both her sociopolitical and textual experiences. In other words, if, due to her social position, the underclass female is called upon to address her class oppression with a ready-made, class struggle rhetoric, attempting to address her sexual/erotic oppression forces her to see it in relation to texts. Her own response to those texts enables her to give voice to her experience and make it public. If she does not make an effort to bring out that voice herself, it will remain muted, as she is forced to align herself with the heretofore masculine-marked class voice. Thus, she is reconfirming, from another angle, Gilbert and Gubar's call in *The Madwoman in the Attic* for our critical need to explore "the metaphor of experience" (in **"1975"** and **"A Counter-Revolutionary Proposition"**) and "the experience of metaphor" (in *The Invitation*).[4] The speaker/writer and the critic must discern, insofar as it is possible, between the metaphors female speakers create to represent our sociopolitical and erotic experience and the metaphors these speakers inherit and that *a priori* inscribe our potential experience. Thus, a writer/speaker can unwittingly live out the experiences that the metaphors call upon her to duplicate (i.e., Paz's description of female sexuality) or she can struggle to lay them bare and thus reinscribe her evolving position (i.e., "The Three Marias" struggle to reinscribe women's sexuality).

Paz's work, as well as *The Three Marias* and *The Invitation* itself, are, in a sense, all glossed over in Castillo's epistolary narrative, *The Mixquiahuala Letters* (1986), which more closely approximates the sociopolitical images of *Otro Canto*. In a sense, *Letters* is more aggressive in its conjugation of "the experience of metaphor" and "the metaphor of experience" as it pertains to the erotic, for it is yet another link in Castillo's exploration of sexuality and its significance for women. If in *Letters,* however, the negation of Paz's view of women's sexuality is continued, even as it is ironically reconfirmed by some of the males represented in the text, the work of "The Three Marias" is honored by adapting its epistolary form. However, the letters of "The Three Marias" are also supplemented by Castillo's Anglo-American political and sexual angle of vision. Castillo's sole speaking protagonist—Teresa ("Tere")—takes up the position, initially, of a free agent, while the narrative web of *The Three Marias* starts out by recognizing that women are not free agents in any sense whatsoever. Moreover, as Darlene Sadlier's essay makes clear, "The Three Marias" did not have the political freedom to explore women's sexual oppression or question its nature even textually, let alone in practice.[5] As a result, they were placed on trial for publishing their book. Ironically, the trial itself corroborated their point; women have not been free to express an uncensored subjectivity. Ana Castillo's *Letters* supplements "The Three Marias" insofar as her protagonist projects a subjectivity, free to express and practice her sexuality, but still imprisoned by an intangible heterosexist ideology, a heterosexist ideology for which we may posit Paz's view as the model. Thus, in *Letters* we have a protagonist who, by virtue of North American political practices and feminist influence, had "forgotten" what it is like to live in the world of "The Three Marias" or even in Paz's world. As a result, Tere, the main speaker in *Letters,* undergoes a trial by fire when Mexico's cultural configuration is put into play. She is forced to recall that she is not as free as she thought. Since Teresa is a woman of Mexican descent (a Chicana), she should not have forgotten but, insofar as she wants to be a freer agent, she would want to forget. The complexities of her diverse levels of consciousness may be located in the push and pull of divergent political countries, i.e., the United States and Mexico. As Gloria Anzaldúa states in "La Conciencia de la Mestiza: Towards a New Consciousness":

> Within us and within *la cultura chicana,* commonly held beliefs of the white culture attack commonly held beliefs of the Mexican culture, and both attack commonly held beliefs of the indigenous culture. . . . In a constant state of mental nepantlism, an Aztec word meaning torn between ways, *la mestiza* is a product of the transfer of the cultural and spiritual values of one group to another . . . and in a state of perpetual transition, the *mestiza* faces the dilemma of the mixed breed: which collectivity does the daughter of a darkskinned mother listen to?[6]

Indeed, this may explain the rationale behind addressing the letters to Alicia, who was Tere's traveling companion and ought to have known what they experienced. Nevertheless, the technique enables Tere to bring out, through Alicia, the Anglo-American cultural influence that, in any case, does not save either of them in the face of the erotic, as we shall see.

Before further consideration of **The Mixquiahuala Letters,** however, other important points must be brought up that will clarify its social and literary importance as well as my necessarily complex critical approaches. The critical conjugation of "the metaphor of experience" and "the experience of metaphor" is as complex as its literary elaboration.

Selections from both chapbooks, **Otro Canto** and **The Invitation,** as well as sixteen new poems, have been made available to a wider audience in Castillo's book, **Women Are Not Roses.** As happens in "selections" books, the evolution of a writer's work is often cut short in favor of the "best" that a writer has produced, a factor that is the prerogative of editors. As a result, **Women Are Not Roses** does not provide the reader with many clues to the intertextual observations made above. Theorists of the text, of course, have taught us that one does not need to have recourse to direct intertextual sources for the pursuit of such considerations. However, it is also the case that writers do respond consciously to their textual milieus and effect a revisionary dialogue. As such, it is of paramount political importance to identify the textual milieu of culturally marginalized writers such as Chicanas, as well as to clarify the appropriative strategies at work in the struggle to construct and reconstruct an identity despite its instability, lest a writer appear to speak in a vacuum. Moreover, writers and critics often rely on a textual milieu and an actual experience, insofar as that milieu assists with the verbal translation of our cultural experience. In this fashion, a variety of discourses can be negated, supplemented, modified, and repeated, though it may not always be possible, or even necessary, to make clear-cut source identifications.[7]

**Women Are Not Roses** does not provide any clues to Castillo's appropriative strategies and experimentations, though the word "roses" in the title points to, and plays upon, the masculine textual production in which women are represented as flowers/nature. In this book, however, there are at least two poems that resonate intertextually and intratextually, and their examination may also help us in the reading of **The Mixquiahuala Letters.**

Both **"An Idyll"** (pp. 8–10) and **"The Antihero"** (p. 24) warrant a closer look because they not only evoke the Western romantic tradition that has underpinned women's erotic image within patriarchy but also, in this instance, further the female speaker's appropriation of that tradition to explore her sexuality and revise the image. Moreover, since Tere, the letter-writing protagonist of **Letters,** does not explicitly speak of her erotic illusions and ideals but instead reconstructs, from a ten-year distance, a period of her life that she calls a "cesspool" (Letter #2), a consideration of these two poems may help us come to terms with the nature of her failed erotic quest. Though **Letters** represents sexual encounters with men, Tere often assumes a sarcastic, pragmatic, and even distant tone that contrasts sharply with whatever illusions and ideals may have led her (Letter #1) and her friend Alicia to actively explore their sexuality. This is an exploration that falls short of erotic bliss, to say the least: hence, the label "cesspool." In a sense, the expectations of heterosexual erotic bliss constitute the partially repressed aspects of **Letters,** which on occasion contains such startling confessions as "i was docile" (p. 113) or "i believed i would be placed in the little house and be cared for . . ." (p. 118).[8] These occasional confessions are barely audible. They tend to get lost in Tere's latter-day, after-the-fact sardonic anger. As we shall see, she has been framed *a priori* by certain "semantic charters,"[9] and Castillo mocks her further by framing her with the "reading charts" offered to the reader.

**"An Idyll"** and **"The Antihero"** reinscribe two aspects of the erotic/romantic hero—the god-like and the demonic—from the point of view of a female speaker. Their representation, however, is complicated by the different spatiotemporal positions that the speaker takes, consequently putting into question how one translates and interprets (writes/reads) the experience. Since **"The Antihero"** is a significant inversion of the hero in **"An Idyll,"** the speaker's relational position to each becomes very important, adding another dimension to their inscription. A speaker's position in relation to such monumental and heroic figures cannot be all that simple. The speaker is probing not only a relationship to the symbolic, that is, how the romantic hero has figures in textual tradition, but her social experience as well, that is, how she has lived her sexuality in, and through, such figurations.

In these two poems, the speaker filters her position through an intricate use of the first- (**"An Idyll"**) and third- (**"The Antihero"**) person pronouns in combination with temporal distance and proximity, respectively. These spatiotemporal, positional techniques are employed in **Letters** as well; though most of the letters are first-person accounts, Letters #21 and #32 are examples of speaker shifts. **"An Idyll"** is a first-person narration of past experience, punctuated by contemporaneous evaluations of that experience that is represented in fantastic terms, a virtual parody of male literary figurations:

> now
> i can tell
> of being swept b
> y a god a michael
> angelo's david a
> man of such phys
> ical perfection,
> one could not be
> lieve him human.
>
> (P. 8)

In this poem, the very columnar shape points to a phallic symmetry that distorts the potential plasticity of language for its own sake. It takes a very well-programmed machine to reproduce that form. It is akin to a divine hierarchical account that only "now," by stepping outside of it, can be apprehended. The narrator, who only "now" can represent her enthrallment with the beautiful stony hero, assesses that erotic dance as "truer" because it was satisfying, in some measure. Enthrallment itself may have its own temporary erotic rewards. The romantic interlude—an idyll—as a symbolic fantasy may be spellbinding, but the effort to transform it into a social reality literally enslaves her:

> i ate
> with it slept wi
> th it made its b
> ed in the mornin
> g when it disapp
> eared . . . i waited
> for its return—
> each night.
>
> (P. 9)

Indeed, like language, she is immobilized and transfixed by "it," a god-like man. "It" has turned her into a robot. The murder of this fantastic being is due to her almost sudden awareness that her union with him, despite its insane and masochistic pleasures, is tantamount to her own self-destructive collusion. In the poem, his murder is anonymous, perhaps collective. As a crowd gathers to demand his expulsion, one of them shoots him when he refuses to leave:

> until one of us c
> ould not stand it
> any longer and
> shot him.
>
> (P. 10)

Now that the fantasy, with its perverse truth, is over, the first-person speaker is free to recall her delusion. Indeed, it is the newer, after-the-fact consciousness that makes it possible to see the enthrallment as a delusion. The one who narrates, however, is distanced from the one who lives the fantasy, that distance itself muting the emotional charge of the actual experience that was once lived as true and is now viewed through the lens of fabulous fiction. It is as if there was something inherently ironic in an experience recollected from the now-distant point of a changed consciousness. This is precisely the ironic tone effected in many of the letters (see, for example, Letter #16 where Tere's attraction to Alvaro is later viewed as a weakness). Tere mocks her initial enthrallment. She "Believed that beneath his rebellion was a sensitive human being with an insight that was unique and profound" (p. 48). Years later, however, either Tere's narrative hindsight or that of an unidentified narrator reports, "This is a woman conditioned to accept a man about whom she has serious doubts . . ." (p. 48).

The ironies of **"An Idyll"** take a more cruel turn in **"The Antihero,"** who exhibits a reckless disregard for his partner's erotic desires: "the antihero / always gets the woman / not in the end / an anticlimax instead" (p. 24). If the heterosexual dance in **"An Idyll"** is paradoxically viewed as a true fiction by the first-person narrator, the lyrical speaker of **"The Antihero"** views him as purposely playing his partner false. He obfuscates erotic desire by rendering sexual experience anticlimactic, as against pleasure and dénouement. He manipulates her desire so as "to leave her yearning lest / she discover that is all" (p. 24). She is double-crossed by the anticlimactic ruse into continuing to conflate desire with him. It is clear, as Luce Irigaray comments in another context, that "man's desire and woman's are strangers to each other."[10] If she discovered the infinite power of her own desire, then certainly the cruel dance would undergo a transformation or come to a stop. The poem presents the anticlimactic sexual event in the present-tense lyrical mode, through the lens of the third person. The couple is objectified in the present tense to suggest an ongoing, unsatisfactory scenario of desire that brings them together, yet keeps them apart. Thus, contrary to the dictates of the lyric, which calls for a personal account of sensual experience, the poem switches the speaker's position to suggest a model of contemporaneous behavior that distorts erotic desire. For Castillo, then, angles of perception, which may be both spatial and/or temporal, are sites for discrete eruptions of meaning that may be subsequently juxtaposed, thus effecting additional meanings. In a sense, the significance of any one thing is highly unstable and much depends on the angle of vision.

Conventionally, the letter form has shared at least two important features with the lyric, notwithstanding the fact that the first is prose and the second is poetry.[11] Both reveal the intimate events in the life of the speaker, *combined* with the speaker's emotional response to them, thus exploring the personal states of mind at the moment of the event or with respect to it. It should be noted, in passing, that **Letters** is a mixture of poetic and prosaic forms, but the speaker, who may not always be identified with Tere, does not feel bound by conventions. This disruption of conventions signals, in my view, a pursuit of narrative approaches that may be beyond Tere's simple "i." In a sense, she is undergoing an inquisition that makes her both the subject of her narrative and the object of someone else's.

Consider how, in recalling events shared with Alicia, her sole interlocutor, Tere almost consistently shifts to a third-person, present narration to explore emotional responses to an event. Letter #21 is an example of such an instance, an account telling of Tere's breakdown as a result of her misalliance with Alexis:

> After a while, she adapts to neglecting herself more than he can. Her nails are bitten to the quick. She forgets to eat or eats when she's not hungry. Her inability to sleep makes her face droop like the jowls of an old hound dog. She is twenty-six years old. With nervous gestures, she tears an invisible thread from the edge of her slip. If she doesn't watch out, she will quietly go mad and no one will have noticed.
>
> (P. 112)

As in **"An Idyll,"** enthrallment again leads to a slavish madness, but it cannot be stated in the first person. Who narrates? An older Tere, who fears to re-enter that period of insanity with a personal "i"? Also, as in **"The Antihero,"** the speaker shifts to the third-person account, thus creating distance with regard to speaking positions, but not to time. As a narrator of her own letters, Tere reveals that she occasionally shifts personae to "create distance with the use of a personal 'i'" (p. 64). As such, it would appear to be an admission that, emotionally, events have a dangerous, contemporaneous power that must be objectified, displaced to a "she/her." Often, Tere can only *re*-present what has lost the power to hurt her. Romantic love, however, cannot be spoken of, intimately or directly. As she—or is it she?—coldly says; "Love? In the classic sense, it describes in one syllable all the humiliation that one is born to and pressed upon to surrender to a man" (p. 111). In our time, "the classic sense" of love is the erotically romantic one that has been popularized *ad nauseam* through romance novels or, in the case of Mexico and Latin America, *fotonovelas*—as Tere knows (p. 50). It is a genre that cuts across classes and makes many women, regardless of their economic status, sisters under the skin, daughters of patriarchy. In fact, it is the erotic quest that holds Tere and Alicia's friendship together. The true closeness of the friendship is placed in question when we read Letter #13, in which Tere emphasizes her occasional loathing of Alicia. The wedge between them is Alicia's privilege, color, and worldly wise airs. Clearly, Tere and Alicia's relationship requires further scrutiny. However, what keeps them together is their shared relationship to the romantic. Letter #40 serves to additionally reiterate the erotic common ground.

In Letter #33, to further explore her relations with Alexis, Tere again shifts speaking positions. On this occasion, she switches to her fantasy of his voice. When Tere encounters Alexis five years after the breakup, she imagines what he should be thinking upon seeing her. This is the end to the affair that pleases her (p. 114). The poem, entitled "Epilogue" and attributed to Alexis, is a tribute to Tere's unequaled charms, a testimonial to his lingering affection for Tere, despite the passage of time and his subsequent involvements with other women: "It was *her.* / . . . *She* / was there, in the same room . . ." (p. 115). Tere is effectively converted into his Muse, the one still capable of stirring him into poetic reverie. Indeed, she reveals that being the object of his desire is something in which she is well trained, so well in fact, that she can even write poems about that object, *herself,* and assume his voice. Even as this version of the end pleases her more than the actual reported sordid end of their affair, Tere's self-conscious posing parodies the experience of the romantic metaphor: *She,* the muse, the love object that truly moves him; *He,* the desiring lover/poet. In Tere's relationship with Alexis, the gap between the metaphor of experience, insanity and abandonment, and the experience of metaphor, the enchanting muse, provides us with a variation of the chords struck in **"The Antihero"** and **"An Idyll"** (see Letter #28 for Tere's initial response to Alexis). As Janice A. Radway has told us in *Reading the Romance,*[12] romantic/erotic bliss is the salient promise that Western patriarchy holds out to women, a bliss that constantly eludes our hapless heroines. Why? I can only conjecture that, while both Tere and Alicia are quite adept at posing as the object of desire, they find it impossible to carry through the subsequent social actualization of that objectification, primarily because it is not an option at all. It spells the death of their subjectivity. Ironically, that is their near-unconscious discovery. The patriarchal promise of romantic/erotic bliss, re-presented in all manner of popular literature, is an ideological maneuver to kill their subjectivity and any further exploration of their own desire.

The understated, failed quest for romantic/erotic bliss effects a blisteringly sardonic tone in the *Letters,* which are an exercise in hindsight. If, in fact, *Letters* represents the struggle to move beyond the quest, the irony is Tere's inability to succeed. In part, this is due to the fact that both the women and their string of men are still operating under a romantic/erotic heterosexist ideology that is hard to shake, notwithstanding Tere's latterday awareness that this is so. Consider what she says ten years after the quest for "womanhood": "Destiny is not a metaphysical confrontation with one's self, rather, society has knit its pattern so tight that a confrontation with it is inevitable" (p. 59). The quest for "womanhood" is still socially defined in sexual terms under the popular emblem of the romantic/erotic. Both Tere and Alicia are pressed to fulfill the pattern. In a sense, *Letters* offers us a different version of the so-called "star-crossed" lovers. Destiny, as such, is a socially enforced misrecognition under the guise of love that places Tere in a double bind: on the one hand, a desire for her own sexual definition, and on the other, an overly determined script in which she takes part. Tere, in short, is bitter over her unwitting, yet unavoidable, folly. The appropriation of the erotic, as enjoyed and desired in the more symbolic book, *The Invitation,* is betrayed in *Letters. Letters* makes evident the possibility that an appropriation of the erotic in a heterosexist society may only end up being revealed as a misappropriation.

Castillo's experimentations with shifting pronouns and appropriative techniques for the purpose of exploring the romantic/erotic does not stop with Tere's letters, however. If we return to the "real beginning" of **Letters,** we must note that the first letter is to the reader, penned by Castillo. We are directed to undertake a variety of unconventional readings—"The Conformist," "The Cynic," and "The Quixotic"—each tailored to our reading needs. We are also given the option to read each of the forty letters separately, as if they were short fiction. We are alerted that we are in for a variety of ironic and parodic plays but we are ignorant of what they might be. In short, the book brings into question our own reading practices, for the apparently unconventional suggested readings actually lead to resolutions that are more conventional than the handful of letters attributed to Tere. Insofar as each suggested reading by Castillo presents us with a resolution, we are handed an ideological nexus (i.e., The Conformist-idyllic conjugal life) that forces us to reconstruct the meaning of Tere's letters as always and already leading in that direction.[13] Was that Tere's desired end, or is it The Quixotic, or The Cynic's? If, as readers, we play along with the suggested charts, we are forced to come to terms with the notion that Tere is very much trapped by a variety of ideological nexus that she, and we, need to question and disrupt.

But it is not only our reading and interpretive practices that are in question; Tere's are, too. She constantly shifts voices in an effort to "read" and interpret her own experiences. Which one of the various selves that she explores is she? Is she the vampish one, the docile one, the clever one, the fearful one, the liberated one, or the oppressed one? Insofar as each is connected with her sexuality, she is all of them, and more. Above all, I think she is betrayed by a cultural fabric that presses its images of her upon her, and her response (as well as Castillo's) is to give them all back to us, albeit sardonically. Tere is no longer a sitting duck, as Paz or even "The Three Marias" would have it, but she still inhabits a shooting gallery in which she must wear many a mask to survive and to understand where she has been.

*Notes*

1. Ana Castillo, *Otro Canto* (Chicago: n.p., 1977); *The Invitation* (Chicago: n.p., 1979; 2d. ed. n.p., 1986) (may be obtained by writing: P.O. Box 163, 3309 Mission St., San Francisco, Calif. 94110); *Women Are Not Roses* (Houston: Arte Público Press, 1984); *The Mixquiahuala Letters* (Binghamton, N.Y.: Bilingual Review Press, 1986). All cited pages are from *Women Are Not Roses* and *The Mixquiahuala Letters* and shall be indicated in body of text.

2. For testimonials regarding this predicament, one of the most accessible books is *This Bridge Called My Back: Writings by Radical Women of Color,* 2d. ed., ed. Cherríe Moraga and Gloria Anzaldúa (New York: Kitchen Table Press, 1983). Leftist feminists in Latin America encounter similar predicaments when working in a framework of "grassroots" feminism. See Magaly Pineda, "Feminism and Popular Education: A Critical but Necessary Relationship," *Isis International,* no. 6 (1986): 111–13.

3. For the purposes of this essay I have used *The Labyrinth of Solitude,* trans. Lysander Kemp (New York: Grove Press, 1961); and *The Three Marias: New Portuguese Letters,* trans. Helen R. Lane (New York: Doubleday, 1975).

4. Sandra M. Gilbert and Susan Gubar, *The Madwoman in the Attic: The Woman Writer and the Nineteenth-Century Literary Imagination* (New Haven: Yale University Press, 1979), xiii. Sigrid Weigel makes a similar suggestion in her essay "Double Focus: On the History of Women's Writing," in *Feminist Aesthetics,* ed. Gisela Ecker, trans. Harriet Anderson (Boston: Beacon Press, 1986), 59–80.

5. For an excellent discussion of both the political problems and the narrative modes of this book, see Darlene Sadlier, "Form in Novas Cartas Portuguesas," *Novel* 19:3 (Spring 1986): 246–63.

6. Gloria Anzaldúa, "La Conciencia de la Mestiza: Towards a New Consciousness," in *Borderlands: La Frontera, The New Mestiza* (San Francisco: Spinster/Aunt Lute, 1987), 77–91.

7. I am specifically referring to the work of Julia Kristeva, *Revolution in Poetic Language,* trans. Margaret Waller, intro. Leon S. Roudiez (New York: Columbia University Press, 1984), 59–60; and *Desire in Language,* ed. Leon S. Roudiez, trans. Thomas Gora, Alice Jardine, and Leon S. Roudiez (New York: Columbia University Press, 1980), 15; as well as the work of M. M. Bakhtin, *The Dialogic Imagination,* ed. Michael Holquist, trans. Caryl Emerson and Michael Holquist (Austin: University of Texas Press, 1981), 259–422.

8. The use of the small "i" pronoun throughout *Letters* is disturbing but something other than an affectation. Weigel suggests that to use the "I" in public, women will have to learn to speak "without having first to acknowledge the male definition of their gender role" (see note 4).

9. Pierre Maranda suggests that "Semantic charters condition our thoughts and emotions. They are culture specific networks that we internalize as we undergo the process of socialization." Moreover, these charters or signifying systems "have an inertia and a momentum of their own. There are semantic domains whose inertia is high: kinship terminologies, the dogmas of authoritarian churches, the conception of sex roles" (184–85). See his essay "The Dialectic of Metaphor: An Anthropological Essay on Hermeneutics," in *The Reader in the Text: Essays on Audience and Interpretation,* ed. Susan R. Suleiman and Inge Corsman (Princeton: Princeton University Press, 1980), 183–204.

10. Luce Irigaray, *This Sex Which Is Not One,* trans. Catherine Porter with Carolyn Burke (Ithaca, N.Y.: Cornell University Press, 1985), 27.

11. Ruth Perry discusses at length the enactment of "a self-conscious and self-perpetuating process of emotional self-examination," as well as the history of the epistolary genre, in her book, *Women, Letters, and the Novel* (New York: AMS Press, 1980), 117.

12. Janice A. Radway, *Reading the Romance: Women, Patriarchy, and Popular Literature* (Chapel Hill: University of North Carolina Press, 1984).

13. Fredric Jameson's commentary on "the kind of reading which attaches itself to finding out how everything turns out in the end" provides a helpful perspective for understanding Castillo's parodic plots. See "The Ideology of the Text," *Salmagundi* 31–32 (Fall 1975/Winter 1976): 225.

## Margaret Randall (review date September 1989)

SOURCE: "Many Colored Poets," in *Women's Review of Books*, Vol. 6, No. 12, September, 1989, pp. 29–31.

[*In the following review, Randall explores the similarities of style and theme among the poems of Paula Gunn Allen, Chrystos, and Castillo.*]

> . . . only you, unblessed conqueror,
> father of my son, remained ignorant,
> boastful of a power you would never own.
> You stride the continents of your fool's
>     pride
> not knowing why it is I, Malinche, whose
>     figure
> looms large above the tales of your con-
>     quests . . .
>
> (from "Malinalli, La Malinche, to Cortes, Conquistador,"
>                           by Paula Gunn Allen)

> . . . In the scars of my knees you can see
> children torn from
> their families bludgeoned into govern-
>     ment schools . . .
> Our sacred beliefs have been made into
>     pencils
> names of cities gas stations
> My knee is wounded so badly that I
>     limp constantly
> Anger is my crutch I hold myself
>     upright with it
>     My knee is wounded
>         see
>             How I Am Still Walking
>
> (from "I Walk in the History of My People," by Chrystos)

> . . . Men try to catch my eye. i talk to them
> . . . And they go away.
> But women stay. Women like stories.
> They like thin arms around their
>     shoulders . . .
> Because of the seductive aroma of mole
> in my kitchen, and the mysterious
>     preparation
> of herbs, women tolerate my cigarette
> and cognac breath, unmade bed,
> and my inability to keep a budget—
> in exchange for a promise . . .
> Oh Daddy, with the Chesterfields
> rolled up in a sleeve,
> you got a woman for a son.
>
> (from "**Daddy with Chesterfields in a Rolled Up Sleeve**,"
>                           by Ana Castillo)

Paula Gunn Allen, recently 50, is a Laguna Pueblo/Sioux/Lebanese woman whose critical work as well as her poetry and fiction have reached a powerful maturity. Born in 1939, she was raised on a Spanish land grant in New Mexico. Her life and work move back and forth between the landscapes of her growing, her culture in its traditions, and the scholarship that has made that heritage a documented resource for us all.

Allen is best known for *The Sacred Hoop: Recovering the Feminine in American Indian Traditions* (Beacon Press, 1985). Before that there was the volume of critical essays and course designs she edited, *Studies in American Indian Literature*, published in 1983. Her novel, *The Woman Who Owned the Shadows* (Spinsters' Ink, 1984) reminds us of her great richness with words. *Skins and Bones* is her sixth book of poems; previous volumes go back to 1975. Allen teaches Native American Studies at the University of California in Berkeley.

Only seven years younger, Chrystos nevertheless probably belongs to the next full generation as this is measured in the literary context. Her work is younger, sung to a different beat. *Not Vanishing* is her first book of poems. She is also Native American—tribe or tribes unspecified in her book—but unlike Allen, who grew up in a rural landscape, hers is the urban ghetto experience. "I was not born on the reservation," she warns in a prefatory note, "but in San Francisco, part of a group called 'Urban Indians' by the government. I grew up around Black, Latin, Asian & white people . . . Don't admire what you perceive as our stoicism or spirituality—work for our lives to continue in our own Ways. Despite the books which still appear, even in radical bookstores, we are not Vanishing Americans."

In some interesting ways, Chrystos' and Allen's lives have moved in opposite directions: Chrystos left the life of a cityscape ghetto for Bainbridge Island in the state of Washington, where she's been living and writing for the past ten years. Allen traveled from the land grant country of northern New Mexico to California's Bay Area.

Ana Castillo, slightly younger than Chrystos (though not by enough writing years to constitute a different generation), comes from a Chicago tradition similar to the one that produced the wonderful Mexican-American writer Sandra Cisneros. Castillo's several previous books of verse go back to 1977 (***Otro Canto***), and her novel ***The Mixquiahuala Letters*** (1966) brought her critical acclaim as "a leading Chicana voice." Like Cisneros, she writes powerfully out of the Mexican-American culture of her youth. Her use of Spanish, however, is a much more central element in her work.

Two poets from two very different American Indian backgrounds and one Mexican-American from Chicago, all three women share a lesbian identity. Although the current crop of strong women writers are certainly not all lesbians, I would argue that lesbians are authoring a particularly powerful and often cohesive cultural creativity. In the three books under review, the explicitly sexual lesbian identity is forceful in Chrystos' work, an underlying presence in Castillo's, and simply a part of the fabric of Allen's world view.

These are all poems of identity: moving back in time, conjuring, inventing, reclaiming memory and using it powerfully. And these are statements of identity by three important women poets of color. These poets' voices are as different as Williams' is from Eliot's, and it is distressing that they will probably be lumped by more than one promoter of our many-peopled culture under the category "women of color."

In "Of Color: What's in a Name?" (*Sojourner,* February, 1989), Vivienne Louise reminds us that "women . . . classified under the term 'of color' are members of distinct ethnicities. We are African, Asian, Latin, Native Americans . . . to align simply along lines of oppression is weak glue for self-affirmation." Ana Castillo illustrates Louise's point. In **"We Would Like You to Know"** she writes

> we are not all brown.
> Genetic history has made
> some of us blue eyed as any
> German immigrant
> and as black as a descendant
> of an African slave.
> We never claimed to be
> a homogeneous race . . .
> We are not all victims, all loyal to one
>     cause,
> all perfect; it is a
> psychological dilemma
> no one has resolved . . .

**("We Would Like You to Know,"** pp. 67–68)

Or from Chrystos' "I Am Not Your Princess":

> Sandpaper between two cultures which
>     tear
> one another apart I'm not
> a means by which you can reach
>     spiritual understanding or even
> learn to do beadwork . . .
> Look at me
> See my confusion loneliness fear
>     worrying about all our
> struggles to keep what little is left for us
> . . . I'm scraped
> I'm blessed with life while so many I've
>     known are dead
> . . . See my simple cracked hands which
>     have washed the same things
> you wash . . .

(pp. 66–67)

In this poem, like many in *Not Vanishing,* there is righteous anger and a plea for a common meeting place.

In her moving effort to retrieve a spurned history, Paula Gunn Allen begins her collection with "Songs of Tradition" and moves through "Songs of Colonization" and "Songs of Generation." We have learned to expect such attention to history from this author of *The Sacred Hoop.* I found the poems in the first section, "C'koy'u, Old Woman," the most provocative and exciting. They comprise a deeply female journey in the tradition of Muriel Rukeyser, Jane Cooper and Adrienne Rich, whose work has brought so many of our foremothers to life. Allen's sense of history also moves along a road cleared by the likes of Uruguayan Eduardo Galeano in his trilogy *Genesis of Fire.*

And Allen takes on difficult foremothers. She explores complex figures like La Malinche, Pocahontas and Sacagawea, by beginning with images of their lives prefaced by short passages from more often heard male voices. Then her renditions take off on their own, free of sweetened metaphor or an urge to turn it all to right. Listen to these lines, from "Molly Brant, Iroquois Matron, Speaks":

> . . . But
> we had forgotten the Elder's Plan.
> So it was we could not know
> a Council Fire would be out,
> . . . We had not counted on fate—
> so far from the Roots of our being
> had we flown . . .
> That's how it is with revolutions.
> Wheels turn. So do planets.
> Stars turn. So do galaxies.
> Mortals see only this lifetime
> or that. How could we know,
> bound to the borders we called home,
> the Revolution we conspired for
> would turn us under
> like last year's crop? . . .
> I speak now because I know
> the Revolution has not let up.
> Others like my brother and like me
> conspire with other dreams,
> argue whether or not
> to blow earth up, or poison it mortally
> or settle for alteration . . .
> Still, let them obliterate it, I say.
> What do I care?
> What have I to lose,
> having lost all I loved so long ago?
> Aliens, aliens everywhere,
> and so few of the People
> left to dream. All that is left
> is not so precious after all—
> great cities, piling drifting clouds
> of burning death, waters that last drew
>     breath
> decades, perhaps centuries ago,
> fourleggeds, wingeds, reptiles all
> drowned in bloodred rivers of an alien
>     dream
> of progress. Progress is what

they call it. I call it cemetery,
charnel house, soul sickness,
artificial mockery
of what we called life.

(pp. 10–13)

*Skins and Bones* is filled with lost history, wisdom and humor. Poems like "Eve the Fox," "Taking a Visitor to See the Ruins" and "Teaching Poetry at Votech High, Santa Fe, the Week John Lennon Was Shot" offer a particular mix of American Indian humor with the raw context from which it emerges; and the joke only superficially provides a cover for the serious statement even as it salts our lips for more.

The ruins of the second poem are not ancient Indian dwellings but Allen's family:

> Joe, I said when we'd gotten inside the
> chic apartment,
> I'd like you to meet the old Indian ruins
> I promised.
> My mother, Mrs. Francis, and my
> grandmother, Mrs. Gottlieb.
> His eyes grew large, and then he
> laughed . . .

(p.22)

Ana Castillo's use of Spanish, Chicago street lingo and English in *My Father Was a Toltec* is exciting and—forerunners notwithstanding—absolutely new. **"Electra Currents"** reads in full:

> Llegué a tu mundo
> sin invitación
> sin esperanza
> me nombraste por
> una canción.
> Te fuiste
> a emborrachar.

(p. 4)

I would translate this: "I came to your world / without invitation, / without hope / You named me for a song. / You went out and got drunk." In Castillo's book there is no translation, as there is none for much of the new Hispanic poetry. I can only assume that this is because these poets wish we would make the effort, in deciphering their work, that millions of Spanish speakers in this country must make to read our English texts.

Energy: if I were limited to one, perhaps that's the word I would use to define Castillo's voice. Much of Castillo's energy—the impulse that infuses her poetry—comes, I think, from her intense movement through language and languages. Like Allen, she uses history—a much more recent history, to be sure—in the organization of these poems. The Toltecs was a street gang to which Castillo's father belonged. The book's first section is called "The Toltec," and the poet's identity is assumed and redefined within it. In the sections "La Heredera" and "Ixtacihuatl Died in Vain," Castillo searches for fore-mothers. And the book ends with the poems of "In My Country," where the various threads pull together.

Castillo's snapshot images are wonderful: **"Saturdays,"** all that goes into **"Daddy with Chesterfields in a Rolled Up Sleeve." "Woman of Marrakech," "Encuentros," "Mi Comadre Me Aconseja," "Traficante, Too"** and many more. From **"A Christmas Gift for the President of the United States, Chicano Poets, and a Marxist or Two I've Known in My Time,"** the following is for me the perfect response to the Alan Blooms who would crush literary relevance:

> Rape is not a poem.
> Incest does not rhyme.
> Nor the iridescent blue labor
> of the placenta that follows
> giving birth. These are not thoughts
> great books have withstood time for,
> so unlike the embellishment of war
> or man's melancholy at being
> neither earth nor heaven bound.
> My verses have no legitimacy.
> A white woman inherits
> her father's library,
> her brother's friends. Privilege
> gives language that escapes me.
> Past my Nahua eyes
> and Spanish surname, English syntax
> makes its way to my mouth
> with the grace of a clubbed foot.

(pp. 52–53)

From the masterful long work, **"For Jean Rhys"**:

> . . . He talked throughout the night, gave
>     300 pages
> of his unwritten memoir:
> the stint
> in military school,
> narrow escape
> from the Jesuits,
> the uncle sent to Siberia,
> and the present wife,
> whom he first loved
> in dreams.
> She hardly edged in a word
> like the last body in the metro
> before the train goes off.
> She smoked his cigarettes and
> drank the bordeaux,
> all the while, not losing sight
> (in that practical manner
> he so obviously detests)
> that she was only there
> due to circumstances.
> At last, calculated sighs, even tears
> punctuated with a "Well?"
> to heighten the drama.
> "Well what?" she replies.
> "Well, will you have sex
> with me or not?"
> Well,

>     she could have gone to a park
>     sought asylum in a police station:
>     "I've been robbed."
>     100 report forms, the sun up
>     she'd go out to mix with the crowd.
>     All she needs is sleep,
>     in a safe place . . .
>
>                                    (pp. 30–31)

Of the three poets, Chrystos' range of inquiry and denunciation/annunciation is the broadest. With Castillo, she shares a mixing of Spanish and English, and although Castillo's exploration of linguistic possibilities is more inventive, Chrystos also sometimes virtually creates another language born of her particular use of both. The organization of *Not Vanishing* is very different from the other two books; as the table of contents announces, the poems are "arranged in roughly chronological order, in the pace of one of my readings."

"You Can't Get Good Help These Daze," "I Walk in the History of My People," "The Silver Window," "Bag Lady," "White Girl Don't" and "Water" are among the truly memorable pieces in this book. "Yesterday He Called Her a Pig" is a love poem:

>     he's a white man / she's Black
>     she's his boss / he was egged on by some
>         politically correct
>     white lesbians
>     it's better to avoid the subject of colors
>     Today I swept her floor  washed her
>         sheets
>     cleaned her kitchen  bought food
>     arranged a bouquet of bright
>     red carnations
>     I love her  want to be an eraser for her
>     Bear her insult  more insults
>     I let in light
>     put her books in a careful stack beside
>         the bed
>     brought flowers
>     it didn't help.
>
>                                          (p.22)

Much of Chrystos' attention is aimed at the system's quick catalogue artist or the well-meaning liberal. She deflates our faulted conclusions with deep insight:

> They call Indians & Negroes a thief. Now one of these people they stole from their own country & the other one they stole their own country from. Now you tell me who is the thief? WHO is the thief? & lazy! HA! I never seen nothing lazier than a white man. Even built a machine to sharpen knives. Ridiculous. Some spit & a stone is all you need. Listen, I've cleaned white houses since I was 15 & I'll tell you nobody is lazier. They'll vomit in a sink & not even bother to rinse it down. Wait for the cleaning woman to come. I spit at them. Yes I do. Sit everyday on Fifth & Pine & I spit at them going by. They ACT like I'm not there but you'll notice they stay out of my range . . .
>
>                              ("Bag Lady," p. 64)

It's an honor to be able to review and recommend books like these three. We need these voices like our old/new world, as we need air, struggle, change.

## Alvina E. Quintana (essay date 1991)

SOURCE: "Ana Castillo's *The Mixquiahuala Letters*: The Novelist as Ethnographer," in *Criticism in the Borderlands: Studies in Chicano Literature, Culture, and Ideology*, Duke University Press, 1991, pp. 73–83.

[*In the following essay, Quintana finds* The Mixquiahuala Letters *to be a study of the cultural liberation of Chicanas.*]

> *Personal narrative mediates this contradiction between the engagement called for in fieldwork and the self-effacement called for in formal ethnographic description, or at least mediates some of its anguish, by inserting into the ethnographic text the authority of the personal experience out of which the ethnography is made.*—Mary Louise Pratt (1986)

In recent years the academy has been shaken by a significant shift in scholarly concerns which raises provocative questions regarding the politics of representation. By addressing problems in the Western intellectual tradition, cultural critics have uncovered what has come to be thought of as a crisis in representation. Giving rise to such subjects as the objectification of women and other minorities, their debates challenged theories of interpretation. Mary Louise Pratt's quote resonates with a self-critical mode characteristic of the present moment in history, a moment in which dominant ideas and assumptions are problematized because of their ideological implications. While illustrating how questions raised in this time of reassessment have been appropriated by modern anthropological discourse, Pratt also reveals how some anthropologists have begun to question their own practices. She is, in fact with her treatise, deconstructing the ethnographic process, as she sharpens her focus on the concept of ethnographic authority, questioning the notion of objectivity. When we consider Pratt's assertions concerning personal narrative and formal ethnographic description, it becomes evident that we must also reevaluate the authority of personal experience. For in classical anthropological terms:

> Ethnography is a research process in which the anthropologist closely observes, records, and engages in the daily life of another culture—an experience labeled as the fieldwork method—and then writes accounts of this culture, emphasizing descriptive detail. These accounts are the primary form in which fieldwork procedures, the other culture, and the ethnographer's personal and theoretical reflections are accessible to professionals and other readerships.
>
>                              (Marcus and Fischer 1986, 18)

Pratt's voice is but one of many which have begun to question ethnographic authority, reflecting on the relationship between personal narrative and "formal ethnographic description." We can view her approach as one which developed in dialectical relationship to a re-envisioning process that was initiated by Clifford Geertz's *The Interpretation of Cultures* (1973). What Geertz called for in his text was a reassessment of the ethnographic field-work process—a process he still thinks of as objective, though symbolic and interpretive in nature. Pratt, on the other hand, suggests that the representation of culture involves a creative and interpretive mode of writing which reflects the subjective experiences of the ethnographer.

Although Geertz and Pratt connect the symbolic and interpretive quality of ethnographic writing, it is Pratt who implies that ethnographies are never simply ethnographies but rather "ethnographies for," written in the interest of the dominant culture. But as dominant culture is a value-laden term which signifies a point of view that has been traditionally dominated by a male perspective, as both the tradition of novel writing by men and traditional ethnography have functioned to systematically marginalize or "other" women, we begin to see the ideological limitations of both of these narrative forms. And once we apprehend that ethnographies are merely interpretations, we must determine the extent to which these interpretations or detailed descriptions can qualify as factual and objective documentations. Following this line of inquiry brings forth an interesting paradox concerning the creative, interpretive process. Is it possible to develop a discourse that is both interpretive and objective? Because the relationship between interpretation and subjectivity is a blurred one, it would seem that the anthropologist's method for observing and documenting the "daily life of another culture" could easily be viewed as subjective literary production. In George Marcus's and Michael Fischer's terms (1986) ethnography becomes a personal and imaginative vehicle by which anthropologists provide cultural critiques rather than objective representations.

What becomes evident at this point in our inquiry is the relationship between imaginary writing and ethnography as a written product. Both forms of writing reflect limited ways of seeing the world; both are influenced by social conditions and the ideology of a particular historical moment. In this light it is interesting to think about feminist writers of fiction, who, much like an anthropologist, might focus on microcosms within a culture, unpacking rituals in the context of traditional symbolic and social structures of subjugation. Yet unlike both the conventional anthropologist and the classical Chicano writer of fiction, the Chicana feminist is also interested in scrutinizing the assumptions that root her own cultural influences, unpacking so-called tradition and political institutions that shape patriarchal ways of seeing. Even though the Chicano narrative has always had some cultural context, focusing on the ethnic identification process by redefining past traditions as the work of Tomás Rivera, Américo Paredes, and Oscar Zeta Acosta illustrates, it has for the most part overlooked issues that revolve around female gender identification.

*The Mixquiahuala Letters* (1986) is a postmodernist, Chicana feminist novel that reflects the historical forces of the eighties, as well as an incredible diversity of concerns, literary and otherwise, from what has been previously recognized and legitimized by canonical structures. What I want to explore is not so much the pervasive ramifications of an American literary canon, which serves to reify social injustice and inequality as it suppresses the nature and development of the experiences of people of color, but rather how a close reading of *The Mixquiahuala Letters* reveals Ana Castillo's attempt to retaliate, by striking out against the limitations created by canonical structures. Castillo's novel functions as an oppositional feminist discourse that challenges the limitations inherent in both Anglo-American and Mexican culture. Certainly, feminist literary criticism has helped to expose the limitations of a canon which fails to equitably represent the nature and development of "white" women in America. But when we consider how mainstream feminist theory has likewise, because of its failure to appraise race and class oppression, helped to perpetuate white middle-class values, it seems to me that we can deem Chicana feminist creative writings as emancipatory cultural formations, that are either in alternative or oppositional relationship to Anglo-American feminist discourse.

Chicano culture draws on two external forces and has been labelled by anthropologists as a "creole culture" because it is one which draws on two or more origins: (1) a long-standing culture one is born into, and (2) a culture in terms of its social and political forces in the immediate environment. Both of these points of origin are limiting for Chicanas in that neither addresses gender issues. The Chicana writer is thus engaged in mediating and negotiating between two cultural systems, constructing a cultural and feminist identity as she works to deconstruct the predominantly male cultural paradigms that have worked to suppress a female perspective. Following this train of thought, Chicana literature functions as a bold cultural intervention, which ironically enough resembles what we have come to respect as interpretive or experimental ethnography. I want to begin my study by juxtaposing the words of two cultural critics, Clifford Geertz and Ana Castillo:

> There is no such thing as human nature independent of culture.
>
> (Geertz 1973)

> There was a definite call to find a place to satisfy my yearning spirit, the Indian in me that had begun to cure the ails of humble folk distrustful of modern medicine; a need for the sapling woman for the fertile earth that nurtured her growth.
>
> (Castillo 1986)

Geertz and Castillo, though utilizing different discourses directed to different audiences, raise similar issues concerning culture and human nature. Geertz's comments are drawn from his rather elaborate discussion on culture in chapter 1 of *The Interpretation of Cultures*. He contends that humans are like animals suspended in the "webs of significance" they themselves have spun. An analysis of these webs should not be viewed as an experimental science in search of law but rather as an interpretative search for meaning. If humans are suspended within cultural webs, it seems obvious that "there can be no such thing as human nature independent of culture." Geertz's ideas, taken out of their anthropological context, seem innocent enough, but we must remember that he is speaking as an ethnographer, speaking in terms of "the Other" and so-called "primitive culture." If we consciously avoid the subtle trappings of this hierarchical way of seeing, his metaphor can also be used to describe the self-fashioning process marginal ethnic groups undertake in the United States, as they attempt to create an existence, drawing from not one but two distinct cultural systems. It is important to note that Geertz's views on culture and his notion of interpretive analysis (thick description as he calls it) have been appropriated by many feminist scholars, since the feminist analysis of women's culture also involves decoding and interpreting many of the same systems with which traditional anthropologists are concerned (i.e., gender relations, kinship, sexuality, taboos, etc.).

Castillo's words are different than Geertz's in that they are taken from a work of fiction—*The Mixquiahuala Letters*. She makes no claims of factualism, but states rather explicitly early on that her text is fiction, and that "Any resemblance it may have to actual persons or incidents is co-incidental" (Introduction, n.p.). Even so, it is clear in the above passage that as a creative writer, she, like Geertz, is grappling with the influence of an elusive, but powerful, cultural force. It becomes clear to Castillo's readers that her protagonist's existential well-being is dependent on culture. When we carry forward Geertz's semiotic concept of culture and evaluate the ethnographic writings of traditional anthropologists as representations based on individual interpretations, it becomes difficult to qualify them as objective, factual accounts of reality. Once we admit that these cultural representations should also be viewed as a mixture of descriptive and interpretive modes of discourse, the gap between imaginary and ethnographic writing shrinks before our eyes as both forms of writing are reduced to a particular way of seeing the world. And as such, we can see that Castillo, like Geertz, is involved in the process of describing and interpreting culture.

But aside from what appears to be a somewhat natural affinity, these two quotes are also interesting because on a broader level, they illustrate the vast difference in objective and subjective writing. Geertz, in the straightforward language of an "authority," states that all human nature is influenced by culture. In contrast, Castillo's language, more personal in tone, elaborates on Geertz's comments regarding the significance of culture. As they bring to life a rather academic yet direct observation, her words seem to embroider Geertz's by illustrating why or how his thoughts might be applied in the real world of subjective experiences. With her words she has in effect grounded his theory in practice. In the final analysis it is evident that each quote seems to grow in insight when juxtaposed to the other. This grounding of theory with practice becomes relevant when we begin to consider the rather abstract subject: the Chicana writers' quest for self-definition.

Put simply, the process of fashioning any kind of marginal identity (whether it be Chicana, feminist, or hyphenated American) involves a series of negotiations and mediations between the past and the future—a past and a future which for the Chicana is culturally explosive in terms of women's experiences and historical implications because, at this point in history, she attempts to define herself as she maneuvers between two opposing realities that fail to acknowledge her existence. Chicanas are not represented, but instead fall into the category of structured absences in both Chicano and Anglo feminist ideologies. Because of the Chicana's positioning between the Chicano and Anglo feminist postures, she is faced with the task of formulating an ideology, an identity out of two plans: the nostalgic plan of the past and the stereotypical Anglo feminist plan for the future. The nostalgic past refers to the idealization of old customs, largely a patriarchal interpretation of Mexican cultural traditions and history. The limitations of this plan are obvious when compared to the barriers created by an Anglo-American feminist movement which has, for the most part, failed to acknowledge female differences based on culture and ethnicity. It is because of this movement's failure to acknowledge differences that Anglo-American feminist theory has provided Chicanas with more of a mirage than a vehicle for understanding or change. *The Mixquiahuala Letters* illustrates Chicanas caught between these two polarities, moving closer to self-discovery by drawing and synthesizing usable aspects from both Anglo and Mexican cultures, weaving a complicated present out of the past and future options. The novel centers on the marginal experiences of two friends, Teresa and Alicia, as they live and travel through Mexico and the United States. By representing the daily activities of these two women, Castillo is able to reveal exactly what is at risk when an invisible entity attempts to define itself out of the structured omissions of two oppositional ideologies.

Stephen Greenblatt's *Renaissance Self-Fashioning* (1980) is useful for conceptualizing the Chicana's self-definition process. Although his discussion focuses on self-fashioning in Renaissance literature, it provides a workable method for analyzing the Chicana's struggle for self-identification. It is because of the clear distinctions he makes between self-fashioning in upper and marginal classes that his approach becomes useful to our inquiry. He states that for marginal classes:

> Self-fashioning is achieved in relation to something perceived as alien, strange, or hostile . . . ; self-fashioning always involves some experience of threat some effacement or undermining, some loss of self . . . ; we may say that self-fashioning occurs at the point of encounter between an authority and an alien, that what is produced in this encounter partakes of both the authority and the alien that is marked for attack, and hence that way achieved identity always contains within itself the signs of its own subversion or loss.
>
> (1980, 9)

Greenblatt's discourse emphasizes the issues involved when marginals ("aliens" as he calls them) seek to obtain an autonomous status created by self-identification. When we consider Greenblatt's analysis, we can see how the Chicanas' self-fashioning "always involves some experience of threat" or "some loss of self." Castillo's protagonist, Teresa, speaks of such a loss when she reflects on her relationship to Mexico in letter number nineteen: "Mexico. Melancholy, profoundly right and wrong, it embraces as it strangulates. Destiny is not a metaphysical confrontation with one's self rather, society has knit its pattern so tight that a confrontation with it is inevitable" (59). Teresa's words reveal that she understands that her destiny as a woman is not determined through a confrontation with herself, but rather through a confrontation with a society that holds the very real threat of restricting, silencing, and marginalizing women. In letter number thirteen, Teresa refers to another threat, while at the same time revealing her attitudes about Anglo women. She writes to Alicia:

> why i hated white women and sometimes didn't like you:
> Society had made them above all possessions the most desired. And they believed it.
> My husband admitted feeling inferior to them. . . .
> i hated
> white women who took black pimps
> everyone knows savages have bestial members
> i hated
>
> white women who preferred Latins and Mediterraneans because of the fusion of hot and cold blood running through the very core of their erections and nineteenth-century romanticism that makes going to bed with them much more challenging than with WASP men who are only good for making money and marrying.
>
> (43)

Teresa's thoughts communicate how she, as an individual, perceives white women as a threat. But when we consider this letter as a symbolic representation of cultural attitudes, it tells us something basic about the Chicana woman's experience. Yet her reference to her husband's admission of feeling inferior to them illustrates how the threat created by white women moves beyond gender distinctions. With this letter Castillo has unmasked one of the ideological limitations of Anglo feminist theory, a feminism with little concern for issues of race, class, or culture. It becomes apparent in Teresa's letter that the subordination and control of "women of color" is further complicated when white women are elevated to the status of "most desirable": as a backlash to this white privilege, women of color, regardless of their gender, are relegated to a subordinate position with respect to white women, simply because the standards for desirability are based on light skin beauty. And once we consider the structured absences in feminist theory, Chicana autonomy becomes a critical issue that cannot be overlooked.

For Greenblatt autonomy, though important, does not represent the central issue. What is crucial here is the power one has to impose a shape upon oneself, a power to control one's identity. He, like Geertz and, for that matter, many Chicano writers, argues that the interplay between external forces is what determines self-fashioning. His discussion reinforces the need to understand the external forces that will ultimately affect the Chicana's self-fashioning process. If we are to carry this discussion further, then we must consider these "external forces" and the implications involved whenever Chicanas attempt to define themselves in cultural and feminist terms. The issues I wish to address, therefore, focus specifically on how *The Mixquiahuala Letters* negotiates and mediates between the external forces which encompass time and space as well as the past and future.

Chicana critic Norma Alarcón conceives of Chicana poets as "umpires" mediating between a past Chicano patriarchal interpretation of culture, which holds the potential for locking them into "crippling traditional stereotypes," and a future that can be equally limiting within an "Anglo-American feminist promise" (1985). In *The Mixquiahuala Letters,* Ana Castillo has moved beyond her role as poet "umpire" into the position of modern (experimental) ethnographer, as she has produced a personal narrative which mediates between objective and subjective narratives, thereby overcoming what James Clifford has identified as anthropology's "impossible attempt to fuse objective and subjective practices" (1986, 109). The significance of Clifford's point becomes clearer when we consider Eric Wolf's thoughts on fieldwork in *Europe and the People Without History* (1982):

> Fieldwork—direct communication with people and participant observation of their on-going activities . . . became a hallmark of anthropological method. Fieldwork has proved enormously fruitful in laying bare and correcting false assumptions and erroneous descriptions. It has also revealed hitherto unsuspected connections among sets of social activities and cultural forms. Yet the very success of the method lulled its users into a false confidence. It became easy for them to convert merely heuristic considerations of method into theoretical postulates about society and culture.
>
> (13)

Indeed, if we consider *The Mixquiahuala Letters* as a personal narrative that mediates between objective and subjective practices, we can envision—as I have argued elsewhere (1988)—examining the social sciences and literature together to set the stage for a more inclusive type of theorizing. In other words, once we make one minor adjustment and move toward an interdisciplinary approach, anthropology's impossibilities appear to become possibilities. Likewise, when we consider Castillo's text as a mediation between objective and subjective practices, the imaginary, fictive content of this novel seems to transcend its form. Once we are able to make this leap in consciousness, opening rather than closing our respective discourses, the limitations created by our fragmented visions quickly begin to dissipate.

Because Castillo's epistolary novel consists of letters that systematically observe, record and describe experiences that take place in the daily life of Mexican and American culture—a process we have previously described as the fieldwork method—we can read it as a parody of modern ethnographic and travel writing. It is interesting to note that Castillo's process of textual production is somewhat suggestive of Linda Hutcheon's *A Theory of Parody* (1985). Drawing from the double etymology of the prefix *para* she concludes: "on a pragmatic level parody was not limited to producing a ridiculous effect [para as 'counter' or against], but that the equally strong suggestion of complicity and accord [para as 'beside'] allowed for an opening up of the range of parody. This distinction between prefix meaning, has been used to argue for the existence of both comic and serious types of parody" (53).

As a parody of modern ethnography, Castillo's text becomes an enterprise that provides the voices and experiences involved in growing up Chicana, revealing in Wolf's words "unsuspected connections among sets of social activities and cultural forms." Like an ethnographer, Castillo uses the voice of her informant, Teresa, to focus on what is at risk when a Chicana attempts to fashion an identity in response to two opposing cultures. In letter number four, Teresa foregrounds the Catholic church's enormous influence on young women as the institution molds individual Mexican/Chicana identity into a cultural model that promotes women's passivity and guilt. She writes:

> Alicia,
>
> Do you know the *smell* of a church? Not a storefront, praise the Lord, hallelujah church, or a modest frame building with a simple steeple projecting to the all heavens, but a CATHEDRAL, with doors the height of two very tall men and so heavy that when you pull one open to enter you feel as small as you are destined.
>
> You were never led by the hand as a little girl by a godmother, or tugged by the ear by a nun whose dogmatic instruction initiated you into humility which is quite different from baptism when you were anointed with water as a squirming baby in the event that you should die and never see God face-to-face because you had not been cleansed of the sin of your parents' copulation.
>
> It smells of incense, hot oils, the wax of constant burning candles, melting at a vigilant pace, the plaster of an army of saints watching with fixed glass eyes, revered in exchange for being mediators and delivering your feeble prayers. It smells of flowers and palms that precede Easter. It smells of death. The last time i went to CHURCH, genuflecting my way to the confessional, i was eighteen years old.
>
> i was a virgin, technically speaking, a decent girl, having been conditioned to put my self-respect before curiosity. This did not satisfy the priest, or should i say, stimulate his stagnant duty in that dark closet of anonymity and appointed judgement.
>
> He began to probe. When that got him no titillating results, he suggested, or more precisely, led an interrogation founded on gestapo technique. When i didn't waiver under the torment, although feeling my knees raw, air spare, he accused outright: "*Are you going to tell me you haven't wanted to be with a man? You must have let one do more than . . . than what?*"
>
> i ran out of the booth in tears and in a rage, left the CHURCH without waiting to hear my penance for absolution of my unforgivable sins.
>
> (24–25)

Her emotional narrative describes religious rituals that have limited the development of a feminist political consciousness. Her thoughts on religion also resonate with the powerful words of Chicana feminist and social activist Cherríe Moraga:

> Women of color have always known, although we have not always wanted to look at it, that our sexuality is not merely a physical response or drive, but holds a crucial relationship to our entire spiritual capacity. Patriarchal religions—whether brought to us by the colonizer's cross and gun or emerging from our own people—have always known this. Why else would the female body be so associated with sin and disobedience? Simply put, if the spirit and sex have been linked in our oppression, then they must also be linked in the strategy toward our liberation.
>
> (1983, 132)

Castillo uses the epistolary form as a vehicle, enabling her to move freely from one issue to another, from one country to another as she describes the relationship between the sexes. But more importantly, it is the epistolary from which gives her the flexibility to describe the differences between the way women are viewed in the United States and Mexico. In an entry devoted to recollections about her experiences in Veracruz, Teresa recalls a conversation she had with Ponce, a Mexican engineer:

> He began, "I think you are a 'liberal woman.' Am I correct?" His expression meant to persuade me that it didn't matter what I replied. In the end he would win. He would systematically strip away all my pretexts, reservations, and defenses, and end up in bed with me.
>
> In that country, the term "liberated woman" meant something other than what we had strived for back in the United States. In this case it simply meant a woman who would sleep nondiscriminately with any man who came along. I inhaled deeply from the strong cigarette he had given me and released the smoke in the direction of his face which diminished the sarcastic expression.
>
> (73)

In postmodernist fashion Castillo provides her readers with a pastiche of what has been a nearly invisible section of Chicano culture. Her fragmented approach is a powerful tool that enables her to negotiate and mediate as she probes the female psyche. Her style reflects the influence and power of many of Latin America's greatest writers. And because of this it comes as no surprise that she dedicates her novel "in memory of the master of the game, Julio Cortázar" (Introduction, n. p.).

Following Cortázar, Castillo is also a mistress of play, an author who seems to intuitively understand the issues at stake when providing a puzzlelike narrative. The text comes to life as a series of games revolving around courtship, wit, and women. In the opening letter to the reader, Castillo playfully suggests three proposed readings of her novel: "It is the author's duty to alert the reader that this is not a book to be read in the usual sequence. All letters are numbered to aid in following any one of the author's proposed options: For the Conformist; For the Cynic; For the Quixotic" ("Dear Reader," n. p.). She closes by including a message "For the reader committed to nothing but short fiction, all the letters read as separate entities. Good luck whichever journey you choose!" Castillo forces her readers to select a sequence; the interpretation of an itinerary through her text is in fact left open to them. By taking this step she has managed to release her readers from what could be referred to as her personal biases or subjective interpretations. Castillo's narrative strategy aimed at releasing her readers from a prescribed reading, encourages them to become active participants in her text. Umberto Eco's concept of the "open work" is reminiscent of Castillo's process of textual production.

> [i] "open works," insofar as they are in movement, are characterized by the invitation to make the work together with the author and [ii] on a wider level [as a subgenus in the species "work in movement"] there exist works, which though organically completed, are "open" to a continuous generation of internal relations which the addressee must uncover and select in his act of perceiving the totality of incoming stimuli. [iii] Every work of art, even though it is produced by following an explicit poetics of necessity, is effectively open to a virtually unlimited range of possible readings, each of which causes the work to acquire a new vitality in terms of one particular taste, or perspective, or personal performance.
>
> (1979, 63)

Castillo's use of the "open work" structure allows her to become an active participant in her own novel. She is in this way not only mediating between "personal narrative" and "objective description," but also between her role as author and her role as reader. It is through this mediation process, as an aside to the reader, that she raises questions regarding the issue of authority and interpretation, an issue which has become problematic in the disciplines of history and anthropology. We could very easily think of Castillo's text as meta-ethnography.

Thus Castillo's novel functions as a linguistic artifact that does more to inform readers about the Chicana's struggle for self-definition than many of the contemporary theoretical efforts, which because of their failure to consider race, ethnicity, and class as variables have produced ineffective, one-dimensional paradigms. In *The Mixquiahuala Letters* Castillo attempts to retaliate against social injustice and inequality by documenting what is at risk when the Chicana defies authority in order to break away from the stagnant traditions and ideals that smother and suppress female desire. She explores the female psyche—the unspeakable, unveiling secrets and taboos in language that are profound and whimsical, perverse and waggish. Ultimately, the text can be read as a revolt against order, which eloquently illustrates why it is essential for feminists to expose and thereby destroy the power of any outside or foreign "authority" by creating a space for themselves. The novel reveals how subjective experiences provide relevant strands of information, which are essential to creating a space that is fundamental to the Chicana's self-definition process. In this way Castillo's epistolary novel (like mainstream feminist theory) is effective in simultaneously marking out women as special selves and claiming, in Marilyn Strathern's words, "that knowledge of the self as such can come only from acknowledging this special nature" (1984, 22).

### Yvonne Yarbro-Bejarano (essay date Spring 1992)

SOURCE: "The Multiple Subject in the Writing of Ana Castillo," in *Americas Review,* Vol. 20, No. 1, Spring, 1992, pp. 65–72.

[*In the following essay, Yarbro-Bejarano comments on the three perspectives often used in Castillo's works. Castillo writes alternately in first-, second-, and third-person perspective, but because of her experiences in a multi-ethnic world, her first-person writing style has a myriad of voices.*]

In her book *Borderlands/La frontera: The New Mestiza,* Gloria Anzaldúa speaks of the political reality of the U.S./Mexican border and also of the psychological, sexual and spiritual borderlands that form "wherever two or more cultures edge each other, where people of different races occupy the same territory, where under, lower, middle and upper classes touch, where the space between two individuals shrinks with intimacy."[1] These borderlands are not only external but internal, marking out the rifts and splits of our "shifting and multiple identity." My use of the term "borderlands" to refer to the multiple subjectivity constructed in Castillo's texts responds to a need to delve into the writings of Chicanas themselves for the theoretical tools with which to analyze their work. As we enter the 1990's, we are faced with the appropriation and misappropriation of the discourse on difference. Some ramifications of this mis-appropriation are the use of the term "difference" or "women of color" as a euphemism for culture which erases differences of power and experiences of racism that led to the political identification of women of color as women of color in the first place. Or the proliferation of differences, for example including "career choice" or "individuality" among race, class, culture and sexual practice, as if any difference is as good or innocent as any other difference. This collapsing of orders of difference in such a way as to depoliticize it, this talk of difference with no talk of racism or power makes the term function as a synonym for the Other, other and different because not the same, the same as white people. For this reason it is important to search for alternative strategies to "difference," ones that will not reinscribe women of color in a relationship of otherness to the dominant Same.

In her article "The Theoretical Subject(s) of *This Bridge Called My Back* and Anglo-American Feminism," Norma Alarcón theorizes the construction of the Chicana subject across and through a multiplicity of discourses in relation to the unified female subject of much white feminist theory.[2] My project here is to explore the artistic strategies that construct this multiple subject in three texts by Ana Castillo. Castillo's subjects enact the "border" or "mestiza consciousness" of which Anzaldúa speaks. Her texts open up what Homi Bhabha calls a space of "translation," "neither the one nor the Other," a third space of flux and negotiation between colonized and colonizer.[3] These subjects speak from a multiplicity of positions that at times compliment and at times contradict one another. Their subjectivity is a weave of differences, contradictory and potentially transformative.

While this multiple subject recalls that of postmodern theory, Guillermo Gómez Peña of the Border Arts Workshop noted its historical specificity when he said "we've always had postmodern, only ours was involuntary." As Alarcón points out, many of the positions from which the Chicana subject speaks are occupied in relation to racial, class and cultural conflicts and divisions. Aida Hurtado, in her article "Relating to Privilege: Seduction and Rejection in the Subordination of White Women and Women of Color," reminds us that the median income for women of Mexican descent in the U.S. is $4,556, that of white women $15,575.[4] In Castillo's writing Chicanas struggle to understand themselves in relation to what Alarcón calls a "multiplicity of others"—the individual women and men of their culture and of other cultures as well as entire racial, class and cultural groups. To see the consciousness of these subjects as what Alarcón calls "the site of multiple voicings" is necessarily to see their establishment in a context of domination and resistance.

The three texts I would like to consider are the epistolary novel *The Mixquiahuala Letters,* 1986; Castillo's second novel *Sapogonia,* 1990; and her latest book of poetry *My Father Was a Toltec,* 1988. Although *Sapogonia* appeared in print after *Toltec,* it was finished long before work on *Toltec* was completed, and this is the order in which I prefer to discuss the texts.[5]

The speaking/writing subject of *The Mixquiahuala Letters* occupies the borderlands between the U.S. and Mexico, the third space of translation and negotiation Chicanos inhabit between the violence of racism in the U.S. and the violence of rejection as "pochos" in Mexico. While the journey to Mexico as idealized homeland appears in other Chicano narratives. Castillo's text reveals the gender specificity of this experience. Not only is Teresa viewed as a "pocha," she is perceived as sexually available, as whore, because she is traveling "alone" (that is, in the company of another woman, Alicia).

The text also explores the borderlands of sexuality and gender between women and women, and women and men, focusing on the nature of the bond between Teresa and Alicia. Much of their bonding, both positive and negative, is established through their relationships with men and their internalization of various discourses on femininity and sexuality. They compete for men, Alicia perceiving Teresa to be at an advantage as the more traditionally attractive of the two; both are loyally there for the other when one relationship after the other fails. Teresa struggles with the limits set on their relationship by the internalized and real devaluation of women. She saves Alicia from threatened rape, in spite of her knowing "there is little in the end i can do. i have a vagina too" (78). She would like to convince Alicia of her beauty, which she praises in the homoerotic Letter 14, but knows hearing it from Teresa would not help: "They were only the words of another woman" (46).

Although their relationship is described as a "love affair," not devoid of homoerotic attraction, other barriers rise up in the borderlands of race, culture and class and combine with those related to gender and sexuality to prevent the establishment of real intimacy between the two women. Letter 13 begins "Alicia, why i hated white women and sometimes didn't like you" (43), and ends with the balancing of Alicia's class- and skin-privilege against her perceived inferiority in physical attractiveness. The contradictory positioning of Teresa's subjectivity is seen in the juxtaposition of these two letters. In one she loves Alicia's beauty; in the other she hates her for her privilege and assigns herself superiority on the basis of attractiveness to men.

Teresa feels betrayed by Alicia's ignorance of Mexican culture that places the women at times in physical jeopardy, as in Letter 23. Teresa's betrayal of Alicia also has to do with cultural difference. Teresa "lies" to Alicia, letting her believe that men are more attracted to her for her body, while she knows that it is because she is docile. In spite of her rebellious independence and even hostile indifference to men, she struggles with the internalization of maternal and cultural discourses on submissive femininity. After she has been left by Alexis, the one man she allowed herself to open up to, she frames a picture she has drawn "of a woman whose eyes bulge comically and whose hair is aflame, but who sits with hands restrained on her lap. She wears a rebozo . . . and the face is her own Indian one" (113).

While the text uses the image of the mirror to speak of the relationship between the two women, their mirroring of each other works paradoxically against their identification, due at times to the inaccuracy of the representation. In the other each sees the reflection of her own need and dependence from which she must avert her gaze. Yet they love each other more than men, and are "driven to see the other improved in her own reflection" (23).

Just as Teresa's subjectivity is multiple and cannot be reduced to any one of a number of contradictory positionings, the text itself insists on polyvalency and resists the closure of dominant narrative. The reader is presented with a multiplicity of endings: the author informs us Cortázar-style at the beginning that the letters may be read on their own or in any order, and offers three possible combinations. As published, the ending foregrounds the bonding between the two women through failed relationships with men. On discovering that her lover has killed himself, Alicia cries out Teresa's name (although we must remember the writing subject's control of the narrative event, i.e., Teresa reconstructs the event in this way). The other endings, labeled the conformist, the cynic, and the quixotic, represent other possible ways of living out different strands of Teresa's subjectivity—the confirmation of maternal and cultural dictates in the conformist, safely recuperated within the traditional, extended Mexican family; the confirmation of women's betrayal of women in the cynic, as Alicia takes off for Puerto Rico with Teresa's boyfriend; and the quixotic preparations for yet another trip to Mexico in the version that ends with the first letter, in spite of or perhaps because of all they have learned. The text's meaning is in no one of these endings and in all.

The epistolary form, in which Teresa as writing subject seeks self-understanding through the sifting and reconstructing of experience, opens up a space for other genres, such as poetry, and also for other points of view. By including a poem from Alexis' point of view, Teresa practices a kind of "textual revenge." Having spurned her, he is forced to witness her dazzling entrance into a club on the arm of a dashing escort (115–17).

*Sapogonia* presents a similar project of negotiation with and translation of male narrative form and male point of view. The text offers a plurality of narrative positions: a selectively omniscient third-person narrator, a second-person narrator and the "I" of the male subject, Máximo Madrigal. The parodic intent of the text is visible in the definition of the anti-hero offered by the female character of the novel, Pastora Velásquez Aké, before the novel even begins. In this definition, the anti-hero is indistinguishable from the hero: "1. In mythology and legend, a man who celebrates his own strength and bold exploits. 2. Any man who notes his special achievements. 3. The principal male character in a novel, poem, or dramatic work" (3).

The text executes a series of maneuvers that position women readers to not identify with Máximo, yet Pastora is only partially available for identification. Her multiple and contradictory subjectivity is at once revealed and concealed by the narrative. Although she and Máximo share an imaginary shaped by *mestizo* culture and history, they are very differently positioned in relation to that culture and history as political subjects and as woman and man. Máximo's subjectivity is constructed in opposition to Woman as inaccessible enigma and *vagina dentata*. His masculinity is defined contradictorily in relation to his desire for primordial unity, imaged by the textual fusion of Pastora and Coatlicue, pre-Columbian goddess of the union of opposites, and his terror of the absorption of his identity in that unity. A visual example of this particular dynamic of masculine identity in Chicano culture is David Ávalos' hubcap sculpture "Straight-Edge Razor Taco," depicting female genitalia whose labia are represented by a razor.[6] Máximo needs to see Pastora in this way to maintain a fixed sense of identity; paradoxically, she is threatening to him if she does represent wholeness and threatening to him if she does not. Castillo's text recognizes the potential violence towards women that lies just beneath the surface of this scenario: the feared and desired razor can easily be turned against the woman. The novel begins and ends with Máximo's murder of Pastora. The final episode is presented as a dream, but at the beginning of the novel Máximo had revealed that in his life the boundaries between dream and reality are blurred, and that his dreams are of two kinds: those that reflect his present and those that are prophetic (11).

Certain passages in the novel and especially the Epilogue that closes it reveal Pastora's complicity with the objectification of woman necessary for this construction of masculine identity. Although various alternative narratives are available to her—for example, what is perceived by others as her lesbian life with Perla, an alternative that recurs in an explicitly sexual relationship with Mary Lou while Pastora is in prison—she is deeply attracted by her relationship with Máximo, hooked on her own objectification as enigma and object of desire. As female subject, she both desires the Other and desires to be desired as Other. Her enigmatic opacity also functions as a shield from intimacy in ways that remind the reader of Teresa—both contemptuously independent of men and dependent on them.

Her attraction to an opposite kind of life with Eduardo, the political activist, culminates in the stable marriage complete with male son idyllically presented in the Epilogue, In an ironic writer like Castillo, this scene reads almost like a parody of the Holy Family (Eduardo is even a carpenter). And there is a snake in this paradise. Pastora knows that sooner or later Máximo will call again and sooner or later "it would all begin again" (311). She will continue being his "celluloid fantasy," his Coatlicue. Of course the reader is privy to Máximo's prophetic dream and knows the dangers involved for Pastora in playing this role. *Sapogonia* is a fascinating text that explores male fantasy, its potential for violence against women and the female subject's struggle to interpret herself both within and outside of this discourse on femininity.

As Alarcón points out, the linguistic status of the speaking subject of much Anglo-American theory is taken for granted. The silencing of women of color writers involves the enforcement of dominant linguistic conventions. *Toltec*'s bilingual format—not code-switching but a mix of monolingual poems in English or in Spanish—is part of Castillo's struggle for interpretive power, reclaiming the space of literary authority.

Even more than in *Letters* or *Sapogonia,* in *Toltec* the multiple "I" is apprehended in various positions of racial and economic dominance that create a sense of group identity based on shared culture and historical oppression.

As Hurtado remarks, in much writing by women of color, "the (white) Man" is visible mostly in different state apparatuses. The poem **"Me and Baby,"** chronicling a futile wait in the welfare office, reveals the economic conditions that break down the dichotomy between public and private for poor women. Hurtado points out that, "the American state has intervened constantly in the private lives and domestic arrangements of the working class . . . There is no such thing as a private sphere for people of color except that which they manage to create and protect in an otherwise hostile environment" (849). This is quite different from certain white and middle-class feminist projects of projecting private issues into the public sphere (850).

As desiring and speaking subject, the "I" of the poetic texts explores a subjectivity of marginalization—what it means to be poor; what it means to be hated by others for no reason of unique self-hood, but only because of skin color and culture; what it means to be the daughter o-pub-f a Mexican woman and a Mexican man. This exploration takes the reader through the first section, "The Toltec," focusing on what was received and rejected from father and mother, through the second section, "La Heredera," pursuing that inheritance in the ways heterosexual desire and the heterosexual woman have been culturally defined, and through the third section, "Ixtacihuatl Died in Vain," in which female bonding and lesbian desire are presented as non-utopian possibility.

The final poem of this section, **"I Am the Daughter / Mother Who Has Learned,"** reveals the poetic project of self-understanding and self-naming as neither one nor the other but multiple: as daughters/mothers/lovers to unlearn what has been learned about gender and sexuality and open up the space for women loving women: "Released to nowhere, / we can return / to each other / baptized with new names / like nuns sanctified / by virtue of / having named ourselves" (49).

As in the other two texts, narrative structuring adds to the play of multiple subjectivity. The book is divided into four sections culminating in "In My Country," which is made up of poems of social protest. This structure privileges the positioning of the multiple female subject in the collective struggle of a group against racial, cultural and economic domination. At the same time, the production of the collective "we" of the third section, for example in the poem **"We Would Like You to Know,"** seems to depend on the prior accounting of self in the first three sections, including the self as gendered through different cultural discourses and including the lesbian self. Besides the collective "we" denouncing stereotypes of Mexicans in **"We Would Like You to Know,"** there is the male "I" of **"Tomás de Utrera's First Day of Spring"** meditating on death in Amerika, very different from the parodic construction of Máximo's "I" in **Sapogonia** or from the textual revenge visible behind Alexis' "I" in **Letters.**

The book ends with the title poem of the final section, **"In My Country,"** a utopian vision of a world that has put an end to multiple oppressions. The final lines of this poem read "In my world the poet sang loud / and clear and everyone heard / without recoiling. It was sweet / as harvest, sharp as tin, strong / as the western wind, and all had / a coat warm enough to bear it" (75). This final text privileges another aspect of the multiple subject of *Toltec*: the writer who pens the texts and constructs the collective "we" and the other "I"'s—female and male. In **"A Christmas Gift for the President of the United States, Chicano Poets, and a Marxist or Two I've Known in My Time,"** the Chicana writing subject identifies literary authority with male and white-skin privilege. The poem underlines the difference Hurtado examines between women of color and white women in relational position to the source of power. While white women are subordinated through seduction, they at least occupy what Hurtado calls the "spectator's seat"; the Chicana and her language, subordinated through rejection, are "barred from all public discourse" (848):

> My verses have no legitimacy.
> A white woman inherits
> her father's library,
> her brother's friends. Privilege
> gives language that escapes me.
> Past my Nahua eyes
> and Spanish surname, English syntax
> makes its way to my mouth
> with the grace of a clubbed foot.
>
> (53)

The appropriation of literary production and authority as male, white and privileged cancels the Chicana as subject; the Chicana who writes does not exist: "so these are not poems, i readily admit, / as i grapple with non-existence, / making scratches with stolen pen . . . / Rape is not a poem. / Incest does not rhyme" (52–53).

**"Christmas Gift"** and **"Esta mano"** capture the psychic and material violence done to women of color, as well as what is necessary to overcome the opposition to a Chicana writing. In **"Christmas Gift,"** the writing subject declares: "Something inherent resists / the insistence that i don't exist" (53). The poem **"Esta mano"** undermines the dichotomy of the body and writing in ways that are very different from the *jouissance* of some French feminist writers, showing rather the pain of the process: "¿poemas? / no tengo / poemas / tengo / esta mano que / escribe" (71). Language fragments under the strain of writing this particular *mestiza* body which is self and other at once: ". . . este verso sería / de ella—*la otra* / . . . Su cuerpo que es / su petate, piso, caja, cárcel, casa, / canasta, campo, columpio, costal, co / mal, tamal, topacio, tan tin tan / to que aguantar tendrá que brotar / poemas, llorar poemas, vomitar y orinar poemas (71–72).

Writing the Chicana "I" questions the authority of dominant discourses, and resists the appropriation of the knowing subject either male or female that "forgets" race and class oppression. Chicana writers', like Castillo's, struggle to claim the "I" of literary discourse is inseparable from their struggle for empowerment in the economic, social and political spheres.

*Notes*

1. (San Francisco: Spinsters/Aunt Lute, 1987): vii.

2. *Making Face, Making Soul/Haciendo Caras. Creative and Critical Perspectives by Women of Color*, Gloria Anzaldúa, ed. (San Francisco: Aunt Lute, 1990): 356–69.

3. "The Commitment to Theory," *New Formations* 5 (Summer 1988): 10–11.

4. *Signs* 14:4 (Summer 1989): 836.

5. *The Mixquiahuala Letters* (Binghamton, NY: Bilingual Press, 1986); *My Father Was a Toltec* (Albuquerque: West End Press, 1988); *Sapogonia* (Binghamton, NY: Bilingual Press, 1990).

6. In the catalogue for his show "Café Mestizo" at Intar Gallery, in which the piece is reproduced, the artist refers to it as "the management's impersonation of *La Malinche*" (*Café Mestizo*. New York: Intar Gallery, 1989, inside front cover.)

**Irene Campos Carr (review date Spring 1993)**

SOURCE: "Flicker, Flame, Butterfly Ablaze," in *Belles Lettres*, Vol. 8, No. 3, Spring, 1993, pp. 19–20.

[*In the following positive review of* The Mixquiahuala Letters, *Carr examines the tragedy of Teresa, the protagonist, who is doomed to unhappiness because of social and personal beliefs.*]

Ana Castillo's first novel, **The Mixquiahuala Letters,** originally published by Bilingual Press in 1986, has reached the mainstream. A Chicana native to Chicago, Castillo has been well-known in the Latino academic community as a poet and writer. The recent and sudden "discovery" of Mexican American literature by critics and publishing houses is bringing greater visibility to Castillo and other Latina writers.

A well-crafted epistolary novel, **Mixquiahuala** [pronounced Mēxkēäwälä; indigenous name of a village in Mexico] relates the story of the long and intimate friendship of Teresa and Alicia. In the letters Teresa writes to Alicia, she reminisces about the critical moments in their lives. Each letter brings back a memory, a story revealing a particular experience the two friends shared—new perspectives found in retrospect.

Although the book starts with Letter One and concludes with Letter Forty, the numbered sequence does not represent a time-ordered chronology. Castillo plays games with the reader by suggesting in her preface that the letters may be read in alternative sequences and proposes three different options (a literary device borrowed from Julio Cortazar, the Argentine author to whom she dedicates her book). In effect, the author provides the reader with some suspense by carefully offering a missing piece of a puzzle with each successive letter as she moves back and forth in time, ending with the explosive last letter.

Writing to Alicia, Teresa reflects on their friendship, the focal point of the narrative: "[We were] passion bound / by uterine comprehension. In sisterhood. In solidarity. . . . We were not to be separated. A fine edged blade couldn't have been wedged between our shared consciousness, like two huge slabs of stone placed adjacent with inexplicable precision by the Incas."

The two young women, Teresa, a Mexican American poet from Chicago, and Alicia, an Anglo American artist from New York, meet in Mexico City as students at a language and culture institute. Teresa was part of the Mexican culture that would not allow her to separate. She writes,

> *i was the flicker, flame, butterfly ablaze, my husband's bride who wanted to fly in search of mythical rainbows beyond the rain. . . . It was apparent i was no longer prepared to face a mundane life of need and resentment, accept monogamous commitments and honor patriarchal traditions, and wanted to be rid of the husband's guiding hand . . . led by a contradicting God.*

Restless, they demonstrate their independence, and their break with traditional norms, by traveling together—and separately—searching for adventure and love.

For Teresa, rebelling against the sexual repression imposed on women by Mexican tradition means enjoying open-ended heterosexual affairs. Expressing her sexuality is important to her. Yet neither Teresa nor Alicia find their "prince charming" in their various romantic adventures in Mexico, the United States, or other more exotic places. Both women are invariably emotionally abused and abandoned by their men ("Love? in the classic sense, it describes in one syllable all the humiliation that one is born to and pressed upon to surrender to a man.") Only their mutual love endures.

> *When i say ours was a love affair, it is an expression of nostalgia and melancholy for the depth of our empathy. We weren't free of society's tenets to be convinced we could exist indefinitely without the demands and complications one aggregated with the supreme commitment to a man.*

Discussing the relationship of Alicia and Teresa, Castillo has said that only the reader can decide whether the women are in love with each other, since the protagonists' state of denial prevents the full realization of their love. She feels that as a Chicana writer she must reflect the unhappy reality of women not often opting for women lovers.

Writing in a lyrical prose that often becomes poetry, Castillo interweaves the sounds, the words, the nuances that create a Mexican American ambiance. I have taught this book for three years and never tire of it. Every time I read it, I savor the beautiful prose, become absorbed in the inevitable conflicts, and find new insights in the reflections of a woman who is caught between her desire to be free of societal expectations and her own internalized constrictions.

### Barbara Kingsolver (review date 16 May 1993)

SOURCE: "Lush Language: Desert Heat," in *Los Angeles Times Book Review,* May 16, 1993, pp. 1, 9.

[*Barbara Kingsolver is a best-selling novelist and essayist. In the following review, she praises Castillo's* So Far from God, *finding it to be a well-written and humorous novel that encompasses both parody and social commentary.*]

*So Far from God* could be the offspring of a union between *One Hundred Years of Solitude* and "General Hospital" a sassy, magical, melodramatic love child who won't sit down and—the reader can only hope—will never shut up.

This delightful novel is the third from Ana Castillo, who won an American Book Award for ***The Mixquiahuala Letters,*** and like much of her other work it is set in the cultural borderlands of the U.S. Southwest. Castillo's terrain is not the New Mexico that recently had its 15 minutes of fame in trendy galleries, it is the enduring land of enchantment, of *curanderas* and Pueblo rain dances, of drought-stricken chile fields and a Spanish-speaking people whose tenure on that land precedes the arbitrary titles of "United States" and even "Mexico." It is also a land of modern complications: polluted canals, food stamps, unemployment and wide-screen TVs, which promise so much more, and so much less, than real life has to offer.

*So Far from God* is the story of the matriarch Sofi, her wayward husband Domingo ("That marriage had a black ribbon on its door from the beginning") and their four daughters, none of whom is ever more than two steps away from God, the grave or some catastrophe involving a man. The youngest, La Loca, dies on Page 1 and promptly undergoes a dramatic resurrection, but is never quite right again; she spends her life shunning people in favor of the company of animals and the visitations of sundry dead relatives. The eldest sister, Esperanza, first and only member of her family to go through college, earns a master's in communications and becomes a newscaster; but she finds that these accomplishments plunge her into "transitional years where she felt like a woman with brains was as good as dead for all the happiness it brought her in the love department."

Caridad, the beauty, is equally unlucky in the love department, though tending toward the opposite extreme: "At about the time that her sister, who was definitely not prettier . . . but for sure had more brains, was on the 10 o'clock nightly news, you could bet that Caridad was making it in a pickup off a dark road with some guy whose name the next day would be as meaningless to her as yesterday's headlines were to Esperanza la newscaster."

Even the "normal" sister, Fe, known to all as an efficient and hard-working employee of the Savings and Loan, falls into a year-long screaming trance after returning one day from her fitting at Bernadette's Bridal Gowns to find a "Dear Juana" letter from her fiance. Like a good *telenovela*—a Mexican soap opera—the plot of this novel meanders at breakneck pace as each sister moves toward her disastrous, glorious and highly individual destiny.

The chapter titles alone are a worthy read: Chapter 12, for example, is called "Of the Hideous Crime of Francisco el Penitente, and His Pathetic Calls Heard Throughout the Countryside as His Body Dangled from a Piñon like a Crow-Picked Pear; and the End of Caridad and Her Beloved Emerald, Which We Nevertheless Will Refrain from Calling Tragic."

It's a fact that a good deal is given away by the table of contents, but finding out who lives or dies here is not exactly the point. The story is driven by such a charming and jocular voice, it's simply a joy ride to follow along as the narrative strays down one side road after another, offering the reader practical advice, ever-useful miracle cures, and recipes for wedding cookies.

By far the most entertaining character here (and that is saying a lot) is the narrator herself, who is never identified, but who sounds like some sort of omniscient nosy neighbor—perhaps La Señora God. Anonymous though she is, the narrator does not refrain from expressing opinions about everything, from the dangers of nuclear power to the foolhardiness of allowing husbands to have the last word. One of the later chapters is bluntly entitled, "La Loca Santa Returns to the World via Albuquerque Before Her Transcendental Departure; and a Few Random Political Remarks from the Highly Opinionated Narrator."

The ingenuous tone works a miracle here, for it never feels any more pointed than the spicy lectures of a beloved, batty grandmother—but in fact the "Political Remarks" are not random at all. As Sofi and her remarkable daughters keep us swooning with high drama, the subtext of the story lays out the terms of brutal poverty and discrimination that confront Hispanic and indigenous people in the rural Southwest. Castillo's characters are caught between two cultures: an old one that is both reverent and exploitative of women; and a new one that views them mainly as a cheap labor force to be used up and abandoned. Sofi's daughters are touched poignantly by miracles, occupational illness, sainthood and boyfriend problems, and, to their eternal credit, they never seem to take the easy way out.

Like Sandra Cisneros's acclaimed *House on Mango Street* and *Woman Hollering Creek,* Castillo's writing is seasoned with Mexican aphorisms and the rich symbolism of a culture whose pantheon includes the Virgin Mary, Pancho Villa and Aztec goddesses. With her unabashed prescriptions for social change, however, Castillo has taken her subject a step farther into the domain of North American magic realism, a tentative genre descended from the politically astute masterpieces of Gabriel Garcia Márquez and Isabel Allende, and placed surely on our own map by the likes of John Nichols and Linda Hogan.

*So Far from God* is one of the most engaging contributions yet, distinguishing itself from its South American predecessors by its chatty, accessible *Norteño* language and relentless good humor. Give it to people who always wanted to read *One Hundred Years of Solitude* but couldn't quite get through it. This one has levitating children and birds dropping out of the sky, too, but it's as readable as a teen-aged sister's secret diary—and as impossible to resist.

**James Polk (review date 31 May 1993)**

SOURCE: "Battling with Magic," in *Washington Post,* May 31, 1993, p. D6.

[*In the following mixed review, Polk gives a positive assessment of* So Far from God's *plot, but finds the magical-realism format to be overused and unoriginal.*]

Have we had enough of the magical yet? Is there still room on the world's bookshelves for another Hispanic novel set in a dusty town where life and death coexist, and where the marvelous is commonplace?

The trouble with *So Far from God,* no matter how frequently engaging and well crafted it may be—and it is both—is that it strikes too many familiar chords. From the opening, when Sofi's 3-year-old daughter suffers a seizure and dies only to rise up at her own funeral and fly to the roof of the church in the impoverished New Mexican hamlet of Tome, we can hear the echoes.

That's a shame because Ana Castillo, a poet and author of a fine epistolary novel, **The Mixquiahuala Letters,** here assembles a lively cast of characters and situations and unleashes them on a solid plot. By the end of the novel, we know these people.

After the youngest returns from her excursion to the nether world with the announcement that she has been sent back to pray for Tome and its citizens, she withdraws from human contact ("only her mother and the animals were ever unconditionally allowed to touch her") and begins routinely performing miracles of the most unexpected sort. From then on the girl is known as Loca, though with considerable respect.

Her three sisters also undergo peculiar transformations. Caridad wins and then loses her high school sweetheart, has several pregnancies and several abortions, and is finally mangled and left for dead by an unknown assailant. After being restored to her former beauty by one of Loca's casual wonders ("I prayed real hard"), she likewise distances herself from affairs of human commerce.

While her sister's unworldly experience binds her to home, Caridad follows her "Holy Restoration" by striking out on her own—actually, she's accompanied by a horse—and settles into a trailer park near Albuquerque. There, under the guidance of Felicia, the ancient manager of the place, she begins to master the healing arts, develops second sight and lives a spiritual life.

At first Fe, Sofi's third daughter, seems headed for a conventional destiny. She works at a bank, has a boyfriend and does not understand how her mother and sisters can be "so self-defeating, so unambitious." Suddenly, just before their wedding, Tom backs out and Fe breaks down. For weeks on end, she fills every waking moment with screams until the noise becomes such a part of life's normal background that not even the animals bother to stir.

The eldest, Esperanza, goes to college, falls in and out of love with Ruben, a sort of new age Chicano (they spend quality time in sweat lodges), becomes a news reporter on local TV and then a network correspondent. What is strange about this otherwise uplifting tale of one woman's rise from poverty is that there seems no driving ambition behind it.

Without particularly wanting to, Esperanza becomes the first of her family to get an education and leave Tome. Neither she nor anyone else wonders much about this easy climb from her origins, just as no one wonders that none of the others shares her inclinations. It's just the way things are.

At the center of this world of extraordinary women is their extraordinary mother. Sofi endures the hurly-burly of her daughters' bizarre lives with considerable aplomb; nor is she much shaken by the appearances and disappearances of her husband, a compulsive gambler, who shows up to raid the family coffers when in need of a new stake. Defeated, she stands taller at the end, when her daughters have departed for various spiritual planes and her husband has deserted her yet again, than at the beginning. Her strength is at the heart of Castillo's novel.

In many ways, *So Far from God* is a hymn to the endurance of women, both physical and spiritual. Sofi and her daughters do continual battle against the incursions of men who haven't a clue; that they come out whole at the end (which is not to say alive and well, exactly) is a singular tribute to their clear-sighted perseverance.

The author tells an important story and she tells it with inventiveness and verve. If she had told it in a more original voice, the result would be memorable.

**Irene Campos Carr (review date Fall 1993)**

SOURCE: "Faith, Hope, Charity—and Sophia," in *Belles Lettres*, Vol. 9, No. 1, Fall, 1993, pp. 52–53.

[*In the following positive review of* So Far from God, *Carr argues that although Castillo's writing sounds forced at times, the novel itself is thoroughly enjoyable.*]

In this amusing and often farcical tragicomedy, the central characters, Sofia and her four daughters, Esperanza (Hope), Fe (Faith), Caridad (Charity), and la Loca (the crazy one) suffer many "misfortunes" during their lives in the small town of Tome, New Mexico. The opening lines of the book are appropriately melodramatic:

> La Loca was only three years old when she died. Her mother Sofi woke at twelve midnight to the howling and neighing of five dogs, six cats, and four horses, whose custom it was to go freely in and out of the house. Sofi got up and tiptoed out of her room. The animals were kicking and crying and running back and forth with their ears back and fur standing on end, but Sofi couldn't make out what their agitation was about.

The little girl was having convulsions and appears to die. However, at her funeral she comes to life; that is, she resurrects and mystically rises to the roof of the church, where she speaks to a crowd who drop to their knees. The unbeliever, of course, might prefer the author's additional explanation: When the anxious mother subsequently takes the child to an Albuquerque hospital, la Loca is diagnosed as a probable epileptic. One of her older sisters "highly suspected that such a thing as her little sister flying up to the church rooftop had never happened." The miraculous resurrection, nonetheless, is a more appealing version to those who "came from all over the state in hopes of receiving her blessing or of her performing of [sic] some miracle for them."

For the rest of her life, la Loca behaves in a peculiar fashion, repelled by human smell, averse to the physical closeness of anyone except her mother, possessed of a special affinity to animals, a child who becomes a woman without ever leaving the area surrounding her house. In a different milieu, she might have been called autistic—a psychological word devoid of the mythical connotations and extraordinary powers attributed to la Loca.

The lives and destinies of the other three daughters are as strange as that of their youngest sister. Nevertheless, Sofia faces her many tribulations with strength, patience, humor, ingenuity, and the wisdom her name implies. The story of this woman, her daughters, her "wayward husband," and a large cast of peripheral characters catches the reader in a net of surprises as the narrator carefully details folklore, New Mexican recipes, home remedies, and more.

In this novel, Castillo changes her narrative voice, replacing the lyrical prose of her first work of fiction, *The Mixquiahuala Letters*, with the colloquial style of the oral tradition. Castillo brings to life the memories of a people whose history was controlled by the Spaniards in the colonial period and the United States in the postcolonial years. "So far from God—so near the United States," observed Porfirio Diaz, Mexico's president and dictator from 1877 to 1911. It was the United States that swallowed in one gulp more than a million square miles of Mexican territory, its people, and its culture—the price exacted by the United States after its military victory in the Mexican-American War in 1848. For centuries, the Mexican territory that became New Mexico had had a land system of large holdings and extensive communal estates where sheep were raised. The Hispanos/as (a self-designated term for many years) have remained noticeably proud of their heritage and their land.

*So Far from God* is written in the regional speech of the Hispano/a of New Mexico: English interspersed with Spanish words and phrases and assorted Spanish anglicisms. Without a doubt, much of the storytelling fun is related to the meaning of Spanish words interjected by the narrator as she smoothly moves from one language to the other (code switching). On the other hand, the attempt to imitate the oral discourse of a plain-speaking storyteller does not always make smooth reading: "Even if Loca was not someone she would for any reason go to for instruction about nothing, it was Loca whom she had gone to see that afternoon specifically, to ask her for cooking classes." At other times, the storyteller's style implicitly adds to the comedy. Making fun of Hispanos' desire to appear Spanish, the narrator describes Caridad:

> Unlike the rest of the women in her family who, despite her grandmother's insistence that they were Spanish, descendants of pure Spanish blood, all shared the flat butt of the Pueblo blood undeniably circulating through their veins, Caridad had a somewhat pronounced ass that men were inclined to show their unappreciated appreciation for everywhere she went.

Nevertheless, the author's tendency to try to include *everything* in this book seems forced, and at times becomes intrusive—if this is possible in a story that swerves in two dozen different directions. For instance, when Castillo wants to address her political concerns, she allows the narrator to become didactic and cleverly announces it in the chapter heading: "La Loca Santa Returns to the World via Albuquerque Before Her Transcendental Departure; and a Few Random Political Remarks from the Highly Opinionated Narrator." It should be added that the lengthy chapter headings imitate the particular custom of Cervantes in *Don Quixote* and add another amusing aspect to the novel.

Castillo immerses the reader in *el ambiente* of New Mexico as she races through *cuentos y leyendas* and the lives of *las mujeres*. *So Far from God* makes entertaining reading. Enjoy the book, and if you cannot understand what is so funny, ask a Mexican-American friend to explain it. *Talvez te dice*.

**Heiner Bus (essay date Fall–Winter 1993)**

SOURCE: "'i too was of that small corner of the world': The Cross-Cultural Experience in Ana Castillo's *The Mixquiahuala Letters* (1986)," in *Americas Review*, Vol. 21, Nos. 3–4, Fall–Winter, 1993, pp. 128–38.

[*In the following essay, Bus explores the cultural attitudes and the journey of self-discovery that Teresa and Alicia undertake in* The Mixquiahuala Letters, *and how these issues affect their constantly changing relationship.*]

Ana Castillo's first novel, ***The Mixquiahuala Letters***[1] consists of 40 letters the Chicana Teresa writes to her friend Alicia. The letters take an inventory of "the cesspool twirl of our 20s" (17) immediately preceding the time of their composition. Teresa tries to set this decade into perspective," to gather the pieces of the woman who was my self." (108), in particular. The emphasis is on "was."

Applying the terminology of Clifford Geertz's *The Interpretation of Cultures* (1973), the critic Alvina E. Quintana said that in ***The Mixquiahuala Letters*** the "protagonist's existential well-being is dependent on culture."[2] We have to add that for two women with mixed ethnic backgrounds extensively traveling within the U.S. and Mexico this means defining themselves with and against two or even three cultures in which the role of women is either restricted or largely ambiguous at best. In the novel this effort is closely connected with the ups and downs of Teresa's and Alicia's relationship as told in Teresa's monologues disguised as dialogues. The two women live somewhat emancipated from their social contexts. They share a Hispanic background but they also exhibit major differences. Teresa once calls Alicia "the privileged girl of the suburbs" (42) and "some WASP chick or JAP from Manhattan's west side" (44), while she herself takes pride in being "a peona by birthright comfortable without chair or table but squatted" (44).

Letter One drives in some of the signposts of this friendship and of Teresa's character both by deliberate portrayal and by 'uncontrolled' self-revelation. The subsequent thirty-nine letters explain, confirm, modify and develop this initial information on the last ten years by documenting many individual efforts to come to terms with various aspects of this period by applying different perspectives, by employing prose, poetry, dream and myth, by making new beginnings and eventually asking the reader to draw his/her own conclusions about the nature of the cross-cultural experience. Thus the mode of presentation reflects the difficulties involved in this search for meaning, its fragmentary character, its diversity and subjectivity.[3]

Teresa introduces herself as a thirty-year-old intelligent, experienced, eloquent, corny and resourceful Chicana who, as a kind of benevolent mentor wants to introduce Alicia to the standards by which she and any other female will be measured by her Mexican-American family in California. After the imminent encounter the two plan to go to Mexico. Alicia emerges from this letter as a fairly naive outsider who needs assistance like the well-intentioned liberal Anglo reader even farther removed from the clash of cultures under investigation. This fairly passive role designed for Alicia is slightly impaired by Teresa's wish for an emancipated conspirator once in a while spoiling the smooth interplay of male-dominated challenges and responses both in the U.S. and in Mexico. But as much as she wants to shape Alicia as a replica of her own role, she also warns her against total rejection of the other culture, especially of the courageous struggle and suffering of women in it. This comprises her own efforts to establish an honest balance between detachment and closeness. Thus, from the outset she gives Alicia a marginal, yet significant place in a system of power structures to be forever tested and hopefully rearranged here and there.

The topics discussed in Letter One mainly refer to the restricted role of women in Teresa's extended family in which some spaces open up whenever the males cannot temporarily exert their power because of their physical or mental absence, or when they considerably violate the traditional codes of behavior as demonstrated by the five male role models given. Teresa systematically exposes these violations to the outsider with the fairly mean intention of using her family for her own ends. At the same time she anxiously guards her people from an overbearing Alicia whose cross-cultural inexperience could create confrontations and also question vital segments of Teresa's identity.

The period concluded in Letter One and recorded in detail in the subsequent thirty-nine letters started with a fundamental crisis triggering off a search for new values together with Alicia. They met when they "enrolled at a North American institution in Mexico City for a summer to study its culture and language" (18) including a weekend in Mixquiahuala,

> a pre-Columbian village of obscurity, neglectful of progress, electricity notwithstanding. Its landmark and only claim to fame were the Toltec ruins of Tula, monolithic statues in tribute to warriors and a benevolent god in self-exile who reappeared later on Mayan shores, and again, on the back of a four-legged beast to display his mortal fallibilities.[4]
>
> (19)

For Teresa this trip did not mean an easy exchange of one culture for another, a miraculous homecoming, as her mother imagined,[5] but rather a complicated effort of gaining a new perspective not only on the temporary actual environment but also on her life in the U.S.: "Life [in Mexico] is balanced. Even New York makes sense" (17).[6]

From the outset Mexico reveals itself as a fairly slippery terrain for two women suffering from the oppressions of U.S. society. Teresa chose this country as her home after the separation from her husband, when she felt "a definite call to find a place to satisfy my yearning spirit, the Indian in me; . . . a need for the sapling woman for the fertile earth that nurtured her growth" (46). In another letter she is more precise:

> i sometimes saw the ancient Tenochtitlán, home of my mother, grandmothers, and greatmother, as an embracing bosom, to welcome me back and rock my weary body and mind to sleep in its tumultuous, over populated, throbbing, ever pulsating heart.
>
> (92)

Generally, Teresa portrays two aspects: The first one comprises exotic, idyllic small town scenes e.g. in Mixquiahuala pervaded by a sense of timelessness but also of the perpetual immediacy and extreme closeness of life and death, destruction and recreation.[7] Alvina E. Quintana has described this as follows: "The nostalgic past refers to the idealization of old customs, largely a patriarchal interpretation of Mexican cultural traditions and history."[8]

Among the ruins of ancient civilizations Teresa also feels an "intense devotion to the culture that had preceded European influence" (49), of being "transposed back in time" (48). In a dream she draws the picture of an archaic community in a Mexican provincial town where

> The people were of mixed blood, people of the sun and earth . . . i too was of that small corner of the world. i was of that mixed blood, of fire and stone, timber and vine, a history passed down from mouth to mouth since the beginning of time when God, finding Himself lonely one eon of a day, decided to make a companion out of clay.[9]
>
> (95–96)

The person thus created of course is "brown, firm, and strong" (96), giving the dreamer "a sensation of pride and belonging" (96). The scene is rudely interrupted by troops approaching to destroy the pastoral setup which the soldadera Teresa rushes to defend with the gun in her hand. This letter is introduced by her confession "i too suffer from dreams." (95), underlining the pains of such image making and role playing.

The second aspect of Teresa's Mexico is related to the experience of the two women never acknowledged as insiders rather as "two snags in its pattern. Society could do no more than snip us out" (59). Above all the fact that Teresa and Alicia are traveling without male companions stigmatizes them as transgressors who are even refused the protective measures Mexican culture offers as poor reward for a fairly low status.[10] Mexican women are described as readers of cheap romances denying them individuality and confirming "the unrelenting customs of the fierce people who never gave in" (58). Still, Teresa does not stop relating herself to such patterns of behavior. She e.g. "tolerated the inexplicable obstinacy," (49) or, though she does not admit this to her friend, she knows that it is not her physical appearance that makes her more attractive than Alicia for Mexican men but her docility as part of her heritage,[11] because "i was part of that culture that wouldn't allow me to separate" (21).

Such cautious self-acceptance occurs among a whole series of disappointments, of "myth[s] involving Mexican tradition dissipated before our eyes" (93). She once locates herself "in the midst of decadence and absurdity, destitution drawing ever near" (74)[12] and before leaving the country she sighs: "i'd had enough of the country where relationships were never clear and straightforward but a tangle of contradictions and hypocrisies" (54). But against all odds Mexico keeps the status of a homeland, though quite a paradoxical one: "Mexico. Melancholy, profoundly right and wrong, it embraces as it strangulates" (59).[13] Significantly enough, the novel takes its title from the pastoral small town of Mixquiahuala.

This accommodative tendency complies with Teresa's temporary return to her husband, the birth of their son Vittorio, and her intention to take them all to Mexico for a visit,[14] though only five letters later she leaves her husband again.[15] As an alternative to Alicia's detachment[16] Teresa formulates her attitude towards Mexico and life in general:

> you resented me enough for having an edge on society's contradictions by admitting to their enforced power over us, and you didn't need to believe i also had an edge with something as irrational as ghosts, demons, and God Himself by virtue of my own admittance, . . .[17]
>
> (86)

As indicated earlier Teresa's quest for identity and a home is closely connected both with the image of Mexico and the evolution of her friendship with Alicia. In Letter Thirty-Six Teresa assesses a distinct change in their relationship: "For the first half of the decade we were an objective one, a single entity, nondiscriminate of the other's being" (122). And here again, Mexico functions prominently, this time as a sort of catalyst, when she characterizes Alicia's present situation as ". . . what I found was the carrion of what vultures in Mexico had discarded" (122). Consequently, with the progress of the letter writing Alicia's Hispanic background is more and more disregarded whereas her European roots are emphasized.[18] At this point we have to keep in mind that all the information we get on her is from Teresa. So it might well be that Alicia is deliberately shaped as a person such as Teresa needs to serve her purposes in her own search, though she maintains that she is writing "to stir your memory" (47).

In Mexico Alicia's strong, but sometimes inconsistent feminist convictions close the doors to a large section of experience[19] and, above all, neglect Teresa's urgent desire for a sense of belonging. Alicia's merely superficial and romantic fascination with Mexico, "her paradise niche" (29), ends in exchanges of stereotypical responses[20] which she easily compensates and shrugs off in an artist's exorcism, a disturbing mixed-media show of angry papièr maché dolls.[21] Teresa once complains "You refused to have your shield penetrated" (58). And one of the most bitter accusations against this free-wheeling life style is included in Letter Thirty-Five devoted to Alicia's strategy to get a cheap abortion at the age of seventeen by going to a clinic with the welfare card of a friend of a friend "posing as the Puerto Rican woman who had already borne fatherless children." (120) and being sterilized consequently. Teresa exposes her art not as emancipatory but as "a personal statement of violation and fear" (121) and sardonically closes this episode: "Maybe that Puerto Rican woman with the five children went on to have yet another child? Who knows?" (121). This is far from the kindness Teresa demonstrates when speaking about her rather quaint Mexican friend Alvaro Pérez Pérez, though here her irony cannot be suppressed either:

> We were drawn to each other by the Indian spirit of mutual ancestors . . . and finally i believed that beneath this rebellion was a sensitive human being with an insight that was unique and profound. (This is a woman conditioned to accept a man about whom she has serious doubts concerning his legitimate status with the human race.)
>
> (48)

The novel ends with the reinstitution of Teresa as Alicia's "self-appointed guardian" (78). Alicia has become totally dependent on her pathetic lover Abdel who eventually commits suicide in her apartment after she threatened to leave him. Oddly enough Teresa reconstructs Alicia's confrontation with this death as if she had been a witness dictating Alicia's emotional responses, a desperate curse and a call for help: "MOTHER OF GOD, HELP! TERESA? . . . ABDEL, YOU SON OF A BITCH! Motherfucker, why didn't you just leave?" (132). Teresa has shaped herself a new/old companion for the fourth decade of her life to be re-introduced into the cross-cultural experience because "at the end of a journey, one comes home for one purpose: to start over" (128). Now Letter One can be composed to prepare yet another trip to Mexico[22] starting the next cycle of cross-cultural encounters with the potential of another record in letter or book form.

Let us now return to the nature of the cross-cultural experience in *The Mixquiahuala Letters*. It is not a fusion of cultures and certainly not a locus amoenus as Teresa indicates when she compares her Mexico to that of other people:

> . . . were they *happy* because they had no need to question irregularities in the way they were treated? Had they survived the summer in Mexico by not becoming part of its heart-wrenching/spirit-drenching madness?
>
> (22)

The cross-cultural experience is non-prescriptive and not easily transferable as in the novel it is bound to a distinct and strong personality and her evolving many-faceted relationship with another character.

The letter form stresses its fragmentary and dynamic qualities in a constant interplay of opposites and recurrent cycles of closeness and detachment called by the late Dieter Herms the "dialectics of attraction and repulsion."[23] and by Gloria Anzaldúa in her *Borderlands/La Frontera* "one's shifting and multiple identity and integrity"[24] Norma Alarcón has related these features to post-modern phenomenology by pointing out:

> In a sense, the significance of any one thing is highly unstable and much depends on the angle of vision . . . she is undergoing and inquisition that makes her both the subject of her narrative and the object of someone else's.[25]
>
> (102)

It is not chic, but a very tough form of existence, not of one's own choice but imposed upon a person by the social pressure of the monologic myths of uniformity and symmetry, of purity and unambiguousness, combining with the human urge for self-exploration, requiring a permanent emotional and intellectual alertness, the ability and readiness to construct and deconstruct one's own position. This also includes the defense of individual choice against overdetermination by the collective. Such efforts ask for a forceful character willing to struggle with ambiguities and to accept painful defeats. Gloria Anzaldúa has said that "It's not a comfortable territory to live in, this place of contradictions. Hatred, anger and exploitation are the prominent features of this landscape."[26]

In Teresa's letters an attitude of ironic detachment, of objectifying the past, of taking control[27] predominates turning her into a somewhat lonely, monologic person though as the ideal mediator who is versed in more than one culture, she lives in one but has her home elsewhere, always striving for the dialogue. For Teresa hers is both a position of pride and humbleness to resist the temptations of an elitist attitude. She feels "driven to see the other improved in her own reflection" (23). The final plan of going to Mexico again is suggested after Alicia's assumed break with an affair denying her individuality and potential growth through new experience. Teresa once comments on the last ten years with Alicia: "So much was possible then" (27). Mexico promises a challenge for a multiplicity of human faculties, an opportunity for a new cycle of essential encounters, an escape from "the critical accusations of the word dealers" (97), and the renewal of their friendship to carry them through the fourth decade of their lives in a U.S. American social context.

And because the novel does not argue in favor of a fusion, we should not neglect the American components of Teresa's and Ana Castillo's ideology.[28] Among the virtues needed to bear the cross-cultural life we find Calvin's or Kant's moral imperative and the lessons of Benjamin Franklin, James Baldwin, Malcolm X, and the rugged individualist Theodore Roosevelt implied in the text. Finally we can also once in a while hear Woody Guthrie singing a medley of "Ain't Got No Home," "Hard Ain't It Hard," "I Ain't Going to Be Treated This Way," "I See a Better World A'Comin', Yes I Know."

*Notes*

1. Ana Castillo. *The Mixquiahuala Letters* (Binghamton, N.Y.: Bilingual Press, 1986). All subsequent quotes

in the text have been taken from this edition. Ana Castillo published two more novels, *Sapogonia* (1990) and *So Far from God* (1993), dealing with the major themes of the work of 1986 from different perspectives. Basic information on the author is available in Patricia de la Fuente, "Ana Castillo (15 June 1953–)," in F. A. Lomelí and C. R. Shirley, eds. *Chicano Writers. Second Series* (Detroit, 1992), 62–65 and in Wolfgang Binder, ed. *Contemporary Chicano Poetry II: Partial Autobiographies* (Erlangen, 1985), 28–38.

2. "Ana Castillo's *The Mixquiahuala Letters*: The Novelist as Ethnographer," in H. Calderón and J. D. Saldívar, eds. *Criticism in the Borderlands* (Durham and London, 1991), 75.

3. In her preface Ana Castillo even suggests alternative readings of the novel for the conformist, the cynic, and the quixotic by changing the sequence of the letters. The book is dedicated to the "memory of the master of the game, Julio Cortázar," the Argentinian experimental surrealist writer (1914–1984) and his rejection of the conventional linear plot structure as best practised and denominated in *Rayuela* (1963).

4. Unfortunately the quite promising motif of the God moving through various cultures is not further explored in the novel. Mixquiahuala forms a stark contrast to the "extroverted and ultramodern metropolis" (69) Veracruz which Teresa also calls "Babylonia with its vestiges of doom with every encounter" (85).

5. Cf. 93.

6. In Letter Twelve she will call New York City one of these "cities infamous for alienation of the human heart." (42) and later in the novel "that eclectic city of yours" (117). One principle of her approach to the various phenomena is formulated in Letter Thirty-Nine referring to her changing attitudes towards her son Vittorio: "There are days when i want to shout for all to see the miracle. i confess, they carry me through those when i want to deny his existence" (128). Teresa repeatedly expresses her desire to relate to any one of her local and social contexts: "The truth is i just like to get into my environment" (13). But this rather cautious, more or less matter-of-fact justification of closeness clearly distinguishes itself from her comment in the same Letter One on her retarded but thoroughly amiable cousin Peloncito who does things not only "because it's what the others are doing" but because "he wants to belong" (13). In Letter Fifteen Teresa comments on her and Alicia's perception and evaluation of Mexico: "Wearily, you muttered, never having been able to pull apart its entanglement in your memory. You sensed, in the end, it all had to have meant something, that, if we were able to analyze, it would be pertinent, not just to benefit our lives, but womanhood. i nodded, alert, having already begun to open the sealed passages to those months. 'i'm writing about it,' i confessed. You shuddered, went to bed" (47).

7. Cf. 49.

8. A. E. Quintant, op.cit., 76. Teresa uses the terms "nostalgic" and "nostalgia" (cf. e.g. 59 and 84).

9. Note the very similar creation myths in Afro-American folklore!

10. Cf. 59: "We would have hoped for respect as human beings, but the only respect granted a woman is that which a gentleman bestows upon a lady. Clearly, we were no ladies."

11. Cf. 113.

12. Also "in the homeland of spiritual devastation" (55). In Letter Thirty-Four Teresa complains about "our miserable experience across the land of beauty and profound intrigue" (118).

13. Mexico is still a reality to be preserved and protected from overreactions: "We were timid because of our foreignness and tried our best to remain as inconspicuous as possible, as if our presence suddenly discovered might cause our new surroundings to vanish" (69). Cf. also Juan Bruce-Novoa, "Mexico in Chicano Literature," *Revista de la Universidad de Mexico* 29:5 (1975), 13–18; reprinted in *RetroSpace* (Houston, 1990), 52–62.

14. Cf. 62 and 119.

15. In this letter she concedes that even her feelings for her child underlie considerable fluctuations. Cf. 128.

16. Cf. e.g. 81.

17. In Letter Thirty-Seven she combines this statement with her permanent existential search of identity: "i want to take my ghosts, Alicia, confront them face to face, snarl at them, stick out my tongue, wiggle my fingers from the sides of head, nya-nya!" (124).

18. Towards the end of the novel Teresa hopes that her friend's European trip "will lead you to a place you'll want to go back to and call home too" (119). This expectation follows Teresa's description of the abortion of the child from her Spanish lover Alexis, "not a man conflicted with mestizo blood and inferiority complexes of the evident sort" (104), and her bitter revenge in Letter Thirty-Three featuring a scene of humiliation in her poem "Epilogue" presented in his conquered perspective (cf. 114–117).

19. One of aspects demonstrating this is Chicano/Mexican Catholicism (cf. e.g. 24–25, 70, and 82–84). Cf. also ". . . not concealing your intolerance of the indulgences of others . . . what was clearly your unsociable spirit." (87) and her statement that she "felt betrayed by your ineptitude to grasp that in the lion's den one doesn't play by one's own rules" (78). For Alicia the encounter with Mexico was obviously less essential and existential than for Teresa. Cf. e.g. the imagined symbolical New York scene after her return from Mexico with two bags of souve-

nirs: "Your legs and arms were useless and the bags dropped like anchors on the unwashed linoleum, the pattern of which had faded a generation before" (43). Because, on one hand, Alicia in unison with Teresa sought "approval from man through sexual meetings" (39), and, on the other, denies men (cf. 79) and feels alienated from them (cf. 105), Teresa openly criticizes her feminist concepts with reprimands like "All you had sought in Babylonia was a good time at a man's expense." (78) or "your curiosity of the laws that guide men" (40). For some basic definitions of white and Chicana feminism consult Norma Alarcón, "Chicana's Feminist Literature: A Re-Vision through Malintzin/or Malinche: Putting Flesh Back on the Object," in Ch. Moraga and G. Anzaldúa, eds. *This Bridge Called My Back* (New York, 1983), 182–190 and "The Theoretical Subjects(s) of *This Bridge Called My Back* and Anglo-American Feminism," in H. Calderón and J. D. Saldívar, eds. *Criticism in the Borderlands* (Durham and London, 1991), 28–39. María Linda Apodaca, "A Double Edge Sword: Hispanas and Liberal Feminism," *Crítica* 1:3 (1986), 96–114. Marta Cotera, "Feminism: The Chicana and Anglo Versions," in M. B. Melville, ed. *Twice a Minority* (St. Louis, 1980), 217–234, Dieter Herms, "La Chicana: Dreifache Diskriminierung als Drittweltfrau," *Gulliver* 10 (1981), 79–93, and Consuelo Nieto, "The Chicana and the Women's Rights Movement," *La Luz* 3:6 (September 1974), 10–11 and 32. A direct reference to the U.S. feminist movement can be found in letter Twenty-Five (cf. 86).

20. Cf. her affair with Adán, the Indian caretaker, Acapulco (cf. 26–30) and her image of Mexico: "oceans, casitas, dreams and follies of gringas and suave Latin lovers" (118). Cf. also how Teresa describes the fading out of Alicia's acknowledgment of her gypsy background which could provide interesting fields of contact with Teresa's idea of Mexico: "You told me that gypsies are an oppressed dark people who nevertheless live celebrating death through life. That was all you knew about gypsies . . . Your parents had never wanted anything to do with that mongrel race, the lost tribe, and fought in America for American ideals" (25).

21. Cf. 117–119.

22. Cf. 124: "Maybe we can plan a visit, a visit to make a new plan."

23. Developments in the Chicana Cultural Movement and Two Works of Chicana Prose Fiction in 1986: Estela Portillo's Trini and Ana Castillo's *Mixquiahuala Letters*," in W. Karrer and H. Lutz, eds. *Minority Literatures in North America: Contemporary Perspectives* (Frankfurt am Main, 1990), 153. Cf. also his comments on the novel in his *Die zeitgenössische Literatur der Chicanos (1959–1988)* (Frankfurt am Main, 1990), 180–189. In letter Twenty-Two Teresa refers to the dangers of extreme detachment: "Months of miles of moving continuously away from the familiar had worked their evil on our minds and emotions" (69).

24. "Preface" to *Borderlands/La Frontera*: The New Mestiza (San Francisco, 1987).

25. In a round table discussion Guillermo Gómez Peña has stated: ". . . we've always had postmodern, only ours was involuntarily." (As quoted in Yvonne Yarbo-Bejarano, "The Multiple Subject in the Writing of Ana Castillo" (66).

26. "Preface" to *Borderlands/La Frontera*. G. Anzaldúa's book has been recognized as a major text describing 'the border' as "a specific place of hybridity and struggle, policing and transgression" (cf. James Clifford, "Traveling Cultures," in L. Grossberg, C. Nelson, P. Treichler, eds. *Cultural Studies* (New York, 1992, 109; also Hector A. Torres, "Experience, Writing, Theory: The Dialectics of Mestizaje in Gloria Anzaldúa's *Borderlands/La Frontera: The New Mestiza*," in J. Trimmer and T. Warnock, eds. *Cultural and Cross-Cultural Studies and the Teaching of Literature* (New York, 1991), Ada Savin, "Course and Discourse in Gloria Anzaldúa's *Borderlands/La Frontera*: The New Mestiza" in G. Fabre, ed. *Parcours Identitaires* (Paris, 1994), 110–120 and Alfred Artega, "Beasts and Jagged Strokes of Color: The Poetics of Hybridization on the U.S./Mexican Border," in A. Artega, ed. *An Other Tongue: Nation and Ethnicity in the Linguistic Borderlands* (Durham, 1994). Since Teresa's identity in considerably determined by her transgression of borders much of *The Mixquiahuala Letters* can be understood as an illustration of Gloria Anzaldúa's book.

27. This is certainly a result of her idea: "To be rid of it, i must create distance . . ." (64).

28. For a discussion of the interaction between ethnic and mainstream concepts cf. Robert Coles, "Minority Dreams, American Dreams," *Daedalus* 60 (1981), 29–41.

## Ana Castillo with Elsa Saeta (interview date 1993–1994)

SOURCE: "A MELUS Interview: Ana Castillo," in *MELUS*, Vol. 22, No. 3, Fall, 1997, pp. 133–49.

[*In the following excerpt, compiled from interviews and conversations between Saeta and Castillo between 1993 and 1994, Castillo explains how her Chicana background, feminist beliefs, and other Latin American writers influence her writing.*]

Over the last three decades, Chicano literature has experienced its own renaissance. Many of the voices in that literary renacimiento belong to women—by the 1990s, nearly two-thirds of the contemporary literature was being written by women. Firmly committed to challenging and redefining the gender, race, culture, and class distinctions which have historically defined Chicanos/as in the United States, Chicana writers have become "conscious transmitters of literary expression . . . excavators of our common culture, mining legends, folklore, and myths for our own metaphors" (Ana Castillo *Massacre of the Dreamers*). Writing can dream and invent new possibilities. It is the utopian space where the long-silenced Other begins to speak heretofore unheard things—where authority is questioned, tradition subverted, privilege challenged. One of the most articulate, powerful voices in contemporary Chicana literature belongs to author Ana Castillo whose work has long questioned, subverted, and challenged the status quo.

An internationally recognized poet, novelist, essayist, and editor, Castillo first published her poetry in the chapbooks, *Otro Canto* (1977) and *The Invitation* (1979). Frequently anthologized, her early poetry ensured her reputation as a social protest poet. Her first collection, *Women Are Not Roses* (1984), was followed by the critically acclaimed *My Father Was a Toltec* (1988). An expanded edition of that collection—*My Father Was a Toltec and Selected Poems, 1973–1988* was published in 1995. The recipient of numerous fellowships, grants, and awards, Castillo has published three novels—the classic *The Mixquiahuala Letters* (1986, 1992), *Sapogonia* (1990, 1994) and the acclaimed *So Far from God* (1993). Her collection of critical essays, *Massacres of the Dreamers: Essays on Xicanisma* (1994), has been described as an unorthodox blend of cultural criticism, social sciences, and creative literature. In this collection, Castillo reissues her invitation to engage in a much needed dialogue on racism, sexism, and classicism, on sexuality and spirituality, on mothering and motherhood.

In this extended excerpt from interviews and conversations between March 1993 and October 1994, Castillo focuses on her prose discussing her development as a writer, the background of her fictional works, and the development as a writer, the background of her fictional works, and the philosophical backdrop of her critical works.

[Saeta:] *Ana, when did you decide to be a writer?*

[Castillo:] It was not something I ever intended to do. And it's very difficult for me even now to regard it as a profession or career. I started out very much wanting to be a visual artist in an environment in Chicago in which that would not have been considered a real profession for me. I was sent to business school—rather a secretarial girls high school—when I was a teenager. That was what I was supposed to be according to my family and my background—be a file clerk. I suppose I couldn't have been a secretary because I'm a lousy typist and I've always had this aversion to authority, so I knew that I wouldn't get far in that atmosphere.

But I loved to draw—I always loved to draw and I always liked to write. I've written since I was very little. I wrote poetry and wrote stories and drew on whatever I could, painted on whatever I could—anything, any piece of paper that was around. So when I got to college age, I started to send myself to school: first to junior college, and then to a regular college. During the mid 70s, the extent of the racism and the sexism of the university in a city like Chicago discouraged me to such a degree that by the time I was finishing my B.A.—and it took a lot of work to get scholarships and grants to get through the university system—I was really convinced that I had no talent. I couldn't draw and I had no right to be painting. And, I couldn't draw anymore—I literally did not draw or paint anymore. What I started to do about my third year of school was to write poetry. I worked very hard in the community in terms of organizing other artists. I had a lot of political consciousness. When I started to write, I got a lot of feedback and encouragement from those friends. When I was twenty and I was still in college, I did my first public reading of my poetry. By the time I was twenty-one and just finishing college I was being published. So with that kind of encouragement I thought "Well, that's the way to go." I decided that I would never take courses with anybody or any university—we didn't have the kinds of programs and alternatives or models in universities that we have now—because I was so afraid that I would be discouraged and told that I had no right to be writing poetry, that I didn't write English well enough, that I didn't write Spanish well enough. After twenty years on my own, I've learned to have an eye for what I want to do in my work.

For myself, as an artist, I had conviction, I had desire and perseverance. I was going to do this; despite the fact that I had to work twenty different types of jobs to make a living. I continued writing my poetry and stories. I studied other things so that I could earn a living doing something else. It's just been, as a I said, with the popularity and the success of my work that people consider it a career, a profession.

*You've said that you did not participate in writing workshops, you read. What writers would you say have influenced you the most?*

I think the writers that have influenced many of us of my generation are among the ones that taught me to write. When I was a teenager, I did begin to read Latin American writers because we didn't have many U.S. Latino writers. Very few people were being published at that time. This was during the early 70s, not that long ago in the history of our literature in this country. So what I did was I looked for writers that somehow spoke to my experience. For me, that had to do with the Latin American experience, the Latino, Mexican, Spanish. I also read a lot of African American writers, of course, especially the women, Toni Morrison for example. I did not read white women because white women derive from a different literary tradition which is Anglo or English. Instead I read women, for example, like Anais Nin, who is still white but had Spanish ancestry and Latin influence with French and Spanish in her language. And she was Catholic. Those things were very important to me. I stopped following the Catholic Church when I was eighteen, but Catholicism is embedded in our culture, in our psyche . . . so she was a great teacher for me. Fifty years before I was writing, she was writing in the 1930s about issues that were very similar to the issues that I was writing about in the context of being Mexican.

Among the other influences were Gabriel Garcia-Marquez, later Jorge Amado. I studied Portuguese in graduate school and was a big fan of a lot of the Brazilian culture as well as the literature. As a young woman, I read anything that somehow spoke to the experience here and that was who I was learning to write from. The book that I always cite as the most inspiring for me is *The Three Marias* by the great Portuguese writers that I read when I was around 19, 20, 21. You see that influence in **The Mixquiahuala Letters**—the communication, the challenging of the church, the sexuality—all of those things come from *The Three Marias*. They were punished, castigated in Portugal for doing those things. When that book came out they were jailed and these were successful middle class journalists. I could identify with that as a Catholic, as a person from a Catholic culture. I used to think it was very strange that I loved to read fiction, but I didn't like to read poetry very much and yet I was a poet for eight to ten years. In 1980, I made a commitment to the fiction writing—to start practicing fiction writing, and now you see where all those early influences have come in. That early training was there; it was just in dormancy while I was training myself by writing free form verse.

*I've always wanted to ask you about your dedication of* **The Mixquiahuala Letters** *to Julio Cortazar . . . was he an influence in terms of your experimentation with form?*

When I decided to write **The Mixquiahuala Letters** I was twenty-three. I had all of these stories that I wanted to tell and I started to write them down. I didn't know how to, but I had very grandiose ideas about how I wanted to do it. So I decided I was going to play with time, I was going to do time shift, tense shift, all this kind of stuff. In the meantime, I continued to write poetry. One day I was talking with a friend about what I was going to do with this project and he said, "That's already been done." He took me to the library and pulled *Rayuela* off the shelf and I thought "Oh my God, I've already been plagiarized! Twenty years before, when I was five years old, my idea was already taken."

As the years went on—it took me seven years to get to the point where I finished **The Mixquiahuala Letters**—I continued writing poetry and I started to write other short stories practicing that genre. The year that I finished it, in 1984 just as I finished it, he died. It was not because I saw the book, or read the book, or was influenced directly by Julio Cortazar that I dedicated that book to him, but because he was another person that I felt was the master in the particular form of writing that I was aspiring to. He had done it and had been brilliant. I have heard once or twice that some critics make note of the fact that I give credit in what they call a feminist novel to Julio Cortazar. Unfortunately, all of the classics and much of the literature done by men is up for scrutiny in that sense—whether if s valid or not—because of the sexism that's there in that perspective. Again, that had nothing to do with the story, what it had to do for me was the ability to play with language and structure. In fact, I was enroute—I was on a plane from Chicago to Houston for the reception of **Women Are Not Roses** when I read in a magazine like *Time* or *Newsweek* that he had died. I had the completed manuscript in my possession since I was submitting it to Bilingual Press and I saw that and thought "This means something to me." So I gave him the dedication. Obviously people would at some point see the association and wonder about it. So I think it's better to be up front and acknowledge the credit. That's why I acknowledged it.

*Sandra Cisneros has spoken about the influence of contemporary Chicana writers on one another—"things that Cherrie says, things that Ana says, make me feel like going to my typewriter and responding." Do you feel a similar reaction? To whose work?*

Cherrie Moraga and I co-edited two publications within a period of three years. We traveled extensively in our readings promoting our books and we had the great privilege at that time to be in constant dialogue. I think that was a very exciting and important time for me as a writer. There was also the time in which I was talking with Norma Alarcon—we all lived on the same street—Lucha Corpi, Yvonne Yarbro-Bejarano, Cherrie Moraga, and myself. Within those three years we were always in dialogue about feminism, Chicana politics, Chicanos. In terms of theory and thought, that was very important. When I was working on **Massacre of the Dreamers**—the book on Xicanisma [Chicano feminism] recently published by the University of New Mexico Press, I did a great deal of reading of what other Chicanas are writing to try to find some common ground: to find how we come to conclusions, how we live our lives, what decisions we make, why, what alternatives we have if we have any. So in that sense, I think in the comment that Sandra's making is interesting. She mentions Cherrie and myself because she has always acknowledged that both of us and Gloria Anzaldua are among the writers who do a lot of "theorizing."

As far as style is concerned, style to me is a combination of influences and I am always inspired or charged up when I read something that speaks to me, is exciting to me. I think there are many fine and talented Chicanas and because we are speaking about the same subjects we can't help but influence each other. Mary Helen Ponce recently published her autobiography—now she's about 15 years older than we are—but when I was reading her manuscript it was very parallel to my own childhood. I'm telling those stories in very different ways in **So Far from God** and **Massacre of the Dreamers.** We do, of course, sometimes elicit memories and that's another way of influencing each other—saying "Yeah, I remember when my mother used to say that to me when I was a child" or "I had an aunt that was like that." So I think in that sense that the fantastic thing for us as Chicanas in print is that we have this wealth of background that we can explore and manifest in so many ways in fiction, non-fiction, poetry, theory. Now what I try to do and what Gloria and Cherrie have also done is ask "Can we make theory out of this?" That's the next step. It can be a truism in poetry, but can you state it in a critical essay? Can we say that all Chicanas come to the same conclusion or have the same experience? So that's another challenge . . . another way in which we inform each other.

*We've been talking about Chicana literature, Chicana criticism, the Chicana community, yet the term "Chicana" can apply to such a broad range of experiences—New Mexico is not Texas is not Michigan is not California . . . Are there dangers in attempting to generalize those varied experiences?*

I think the advantages are much greater than any danger you can place on it. The term Chicana or Chicano as such is already a political term. It was an attempt in the last twenty years to label or categorize a politically conscious person of Mexican descent and sometimes of Latino descent in the U.S. So already it's a political term. Even back in the 70s or late 60s, it was always used only by people with that kind of conscientizacion. The advantage of it is that it attempts to bring together what might be loosely described as the Chicano or Chicana Diaspora on this land. And so, if you're looking at the dilemma of Chicano existence you have to bring together all of these populations in the U.S. So I think the advantage is much greater than the danger. The danger is only one that comes when you start to do a much more intense investigation and you start to make assumptions about Chicanas from Chicago or Chicanas from New Mexico or Chicanas from California.

*How do you define your term?*

To begin with, the term Chicana or Chicano that came out of the late 60s to mid 70s had political connotations. Today in 1993, when we have what is called Chicana literature, the term has become much broader. Chicana literature is something that we as Chicanas take and define as part of U.S. North American literature. That literature has to do with our reality, our perceptions of reality, and our perceptions of society in the United States as women of Mexican descent or Mexican background or Latina background. I don't object to a U.S.-born Latina who has been in close association within Mexican culture calling herself Chicana. I wouldn't think that she'd necessarily have to be called Chicana, but if she were, she would have to have a very acute understanding of what that experience is. She doesn't have to be a feminist necessarily, she doesn't have to be very gung-ho politically or really on the left, but she probably will not ever be on the right and call herself Chicana. I think we have had the unfortunate experience in our history during the 1980s in which we have whole lot of people, mostly under the age of thirty, who, having bought the Republican administration's ideals of assimilation into American society, reject the term Chicana and call themselves Hispanic.

*And that labeling allows you to maintain a safe connection to your culture . . .*

You use your roots only in as much as they are not politically threatening to the status quo. Yes, it's okay to be bilingual, it's okay to be proud of your Mexican heritage, it's okay to go out and celebrate the Mexican Independence Day parade, it's okay to love eating Mexican food—the whole premise of diversity, but that doesn't threaten changing society. And inadvertently, that's what makes you a consciously political individual. But by not wanting to threaten society, you are still doing something very political and I think the person who calls herself Hispanic is, of course, a political individual by virtue of her acts and by virtue of the fact that she refuses to make any kind of conscious challenges of society.

*Given the diversity of the Chicano community, how do you see your role as a writer in relationship to that community?*

I started out writing when I was in college and that was in the early to mid 70s—this was perhaps the height of the Chicano/Latino movement—so I started out very consciously as a Latina poet, a political poet, or what is sometimes called a protest poet talking about the economic inequality of Latino people in this country. And I don't think I've changed that much. I still have that commitment. How do I think I play a part in the Latino community? One, by my existence—by being a Chicana writer, or by being a Latina writer—and two, by the things that I say and do. And that means again that I'm not a Hispanic writer; I'm not just proud of my heritage. I acknowledge that racism is a dynamic of our society, that sexism is a dynamic of our society that in fact the particular society that we live in depends on racism, and on sexism, and on classism. And those things come out in my work too. Some people are very proud when they see me make appearances: "Oh, we're so proud to see this Mejicana, this Mexican American, this Hispanic writer" and they feel that I've made it like Richard Rodriguez has made it. They don't stop to think about how we have "made it" in very, very different ways and we're being acknowledged by very different sectors. So I play a part by my person and by my name and my presence, and also in terms of what I say in my work about our reality.

*Some of those people who are proud of your achievements as a writer, do you get the feeling that they sometimes don't listen to what you're saying?*

Oh yeah, of course, they may even be a little disturbed by what I'm saying and they wince a little when I say "Chicana" or if I talk about lesbian or gay issues. They'd rather I not move out of the realm of cultural identification. That is exactly the reason why a person like Richard Rodriguez—I don't want to sound like I'm using him as my target—but that is why he gets that kind of attention that he gets and I've gotten the kind of attention that I've gotten from two entirely different audiences for the most part.

*Yes, his audience is much more mainstream, whereas your audience tends to be more political. But I believe that you've deliberately addressing different audiences.*

I think that the question as to who your audience is or who the audience is that a writer has in mind when she sits down to write is a very difficult one for everybody. Most people usually say "Well, I wasn't really thinking about anybody when I was writing this." And what I usually say is that "When I'm writing, I'm thinking about a woman who is very much like me reading it." Because that is the void that we have had in literature: a void in the representation in the literature of women who look and think and feel like me and who have had similar experiences in society. I wanted to fill that void. Why should I want to write about characters that are all too familiar to American literature? They're there already: somebody else has done it and somebody else has done a much better job of it than I can because I haven't experienced that. All I can do, in the most convincing and powerful way that I know how, is to write from what is true to me. When I think about who I would like to read what I write I think about another Chicana very similar to me.

*You've probably characterized your ideal audience as "another woman of color" or more specifically as a "friend who was a budding feminist . . . had some consciousness . . . and needed to work things out." Is that still your ideal audience?*

I still think so. If I focus on my perspective and what I feel I've needed to explore as a social being, as an entity in this society, that guides me on what I write. For example, in **Massacre of the Dreamers,** a book about Chicano and Mexican women, I have that focus. I said in the introduction that when I spoke of men and women, I was specifically talking about Mexican men and Mexican women unless otherwise specified. My editor, my agent, and my publisher—all said, "You know, Ana, although you are directing yourself to this woman, there are a lot of people who are interested and will be using that work." I would like to think that anybody in my time right now will pick up my work and say "there's something in there for me." People have been asking me for the past 5 years, white students at universities for example, "I really identify with your poetry or with *The Mixquiahuala Letters,* does that bother you?" and I always respond "No that doesn't bother me. I'm very delighted that you enjoyed it and that it speaks to you." So, now I'm much clearer on the importance of acknowledging that there is a wider audience in the country and abroad. In fact, I welcome it because by welcoming it—it's not that I personally get accepted, but that we are communicating as a culture to other people. That's making it acceptable to other people instead of historically being foreign and strange and therefore something they could reject.

*Although you're not always overtly political, there is a great deal which is subversive or revolutionary in your work.*

It's implicit in the work. Obviously, one does not only undermine the status quo by stating it, but you undermine it by virtue of the language that you're chosen to write in, and by your acts. I started out self-publishing my poetry, and I have always had Spanish in my works—so I think that I've been an insurgent structurally, but also in terms of the language that I use. My language is not white standard English. It doesn't matter if you claim to be Chinese American or Mexican American or African American and put in all the familiar cultural motifs if you're still using the language that is acceptable by the status quo. And I've not done that. In **So Far from God,** one of the important aspects of the narrative, of the story that is being told, is the narrator. The same thing happens in **Sapogonia**; you have a Sapogon, he's pretentious, English is his second language, and you can see that in the narrative of **Sapogonia.** You have a very different narrator in **The Mixquiahuala Letters**; she is a Chicana, who is a radical poet and she uses the small "i" and she uses verse whenever she feels like it. So inherent in the content is also the language. I was just thinking of Luce Irigaray . . . she's an example of someone causing a revolution in her profession and in writing just by virtue of the language that she used. I was thinking of her book, *Speculum of the Other Woman,* try to read that! She was attacking white, male writing—she broke all the rules in the French language to do that.

*In an essay in* **Massacre of the Dreamers,** *you say that the language is a living language and we have to use it, to make it suitable to our moment in history. It was in the passage where you were talking about not using the flourishes of the culture like Oaxacan paper cuts.*

Yes, that it's not a cultural motif like the Oaxacan paper cuts that you string from beam to beam and the audience responds "Oh how beautiful, how wonderful, how lovely, she's a Latina . . . our new Hispanic writer." But what's important is that you have to see everything that we are—everything that we are which to this date people have not wanted to see. And that means if s not just the pretty or the clever or what is embellished by romance and poetry. I believe that you cannot not be political. Even stating that you're not political is a political act. Refusing to participate is a political act. What you're doing is not that you're not participating, it's that you're joining in with the mainstream or you're joining in with the status quo. And that is a political act. So, we are political by virtue of the decisions we make in participating in society. The kind of political person that I am, of course, is one who does challenge racism in society, who does challenge sexism and economic inequality for the majority of the people. I do that in my work and I do that by the way that I live my life, too. As we were saying before the interview started, with fame does not necessarily come money. That comes from the kind of writing that I've chosen to devote myself to and that will probably be, for the most part, the way that it will be for me as a writer.

*So that you've made a conscious decision about your work. From your experience does the literature—especially that written by Chicanas—reexamine, question, subvert, or reinforce the values of the dominant society?*

When I was reading the question and thinking about the prominent Chicana writers of our generation and what their goals are and what their writings is like, I thought about what the word "values" means and what we got shoved down our throats during the 80s by the Republican administration. Somehow people's values supposedly changed. In contemporary society, whether you are African American and work in a gas station and that's how you support your family, or whether you're a Chicana who calls herself Hispanic and helps support her family by working in an office downtown in a city, or whether you're a white person who works in a university setting—hopefully the value is to lead a life in which you're not suffering physically, where you can eat well, where your children get a "decent" education, where you can live in a clean environment. So I think all of us in the United States share the same values. I think that as a mother, for example, I share the same values that a white woman in Tennessee who is a mother of an eleven-year old child has: she wants her child to grow up in a safe and clean world and to have a decent education and then hopefully to have a fulfilling life. That's the kind of life we can all have.

I think we all have many of the same values, so the way that a Chicana writer—a self-defined Chicana writer—challenges society is by introducing the particular dilemmas of what it is to be Chicana, a brown person. Let me just use specific examples: Cherrie Moraga, who has been instrumental in creating Chicana literature and whose work I have been familiar with, and Sandra Cisneros, who is also a prominent Chicana writer. These are two self-defined Chicanas—one from Chicago and one from southern California—who have similar, but not exactly the same goals in what they do when they write. And that's because one was also identified as a lesbian and as a feminist from very early on and wanted to challenge, truly wanted to challenge, to subvert American literature and white feminism. So those were her goals in the 80s. And then we have Sandra Cisneros who wanted to reflect—in my opinion—rather than to overtly challenge. The fact that she writes does challenge the white mainstream literature but what she was wanting to do for example in *The House On Mango Street* was to reflect the reality of a young Latina growing up in Chicago. I'm using their differences as an example, but I could say the same thing for example about Helena Viramontes, whom I also respect and admire, and her talent and her goal as a writer and as a woman who calls herself a Chicana of our generation. We're going to see Chicanas who are under the age of thirty putting out novels in the next few years and they're going to be reflecting the realities of the 80s and the 90s in a very different way than we can ever do because they'll have different goals. They will start their writing careers with a recognition of Chicana literature in the publishing world already in existence and hopefully, move on from there.

I do know that as Chicanas we are reexamining, we are questioning, we are subverting, we are reinforcing the values of the American ideal—democracy. But what we're doing is we are also giving first voice witness to our particular dilemmas and our particular perspective. And they're not the same: Cherrie Moraga is not the same as Sandra Cisneros; Sandra Cisneros is not the same as Helena Viramontes; Helena Viramontes is not the same as Mary Helen Ponce; and Mary Helen Ponce is not the same as the next woman. . . . We can't say at any point that any white woman—or to be more politically correct—any Euro-American woman writer between the ages of 35 and 45 who is writing today is going to be reflecting and examining American society the way the next one will. They come from their own perspectives and so do we. But what we have shared—the common thread for us—is that we're all coming from the Chicana reality.

*Although we recognize the individual perspectives of many writers, we tend to see each Chicana writer as being a spokesperson for the whole perspective.*

That tendency is very real. When Cherrie Moraga or Gloria Anzaldua would address a predominantly white audience in 1985, or when Sandra Cisneros would address an almost all white audience in 1991—the reason why these Chicanas would be looked upon and be weighted down by that pressure is because we are so under-represented. But once we start to see the range of our voices we begin to understand that of course there isn't one exclusive, politically correct Chicana literature.

*Going back to your work specifically, both the novels* **Sapogonia** *and* **So Far from God** *originated in short story form—*Sapogonia *in "Antihero" and* So Far from God *in "Loca Santa." Is that a typical pattern for your novels?*

When you have three novels, I guess you can start to establish a pattern. As I've always said, being a self-taught writer I do things rather pragmatically. I didn't have a mentor or someone to say "This is how you start to work. . . ." But fortunately I think I did have some sense about it. How did I start learning to write prose was by doing small things, sketches, trying to construct a short story. It would have been very defeating for me between the ages of twenty-three and twenty-five to say "I'm going to write a novel" and never have studied with anybody, never have conferred with anybody about how you do this. In fact, I do remember Sandra Cisneros, who did go to the Iowa Writers Workshop, saying in reference to her own training that you have to start with constructing a short story and then you start to work toward a bigger project. So that's part of it. Another part of it is getting to know your characters. I did a lot of little sketches—there were little poems of Maximo Madrigal and there were sketches that never got to the public—besides the **"Antihero"** story. It took me about two to three years before I could know that character well enough in my head. Could I do him? Did I know him well enough? So I think the other part of doing the short stories is you start to get a feeling for your characters. It's about alchemy. It's about acting, projecting yourself into another reality.

*You've created a number of unique characters. Do you have one that particularly stands out in your mind?*

Last year, I started doing sketches on a new character. Her name is Miss Rose and I like her a lot. My editor at Norton saw my short stories and asked my agent if in fact Miss Rose was going to be a novel. You can tell. You may have three pages and then three more pages of another little story with Miss Rose and you can already tell that this character wants to be big—a big project. She is a kind of mysterious character in the Southwest desert; she's black—I don't know if she's African American—she's a hoodoo woman and she's lesbian. She says and does all kinds of things that are very egocentric. Two other characters that are related to her are two Chicanas from Mexicali—so far they're from Mexicali, I'm still not sure—and they're also very different. Miss Rose just does all kinds of things; she's very much into her own world. I enjoy her a lot. So for right now, I'd really like to be able to get my grasp on her and explore that character and grow with that. It's a trilogy because it's this woman plus these two other women and all of them are very much in tune with their psyches. I think that has a great deal to do with my own interests right now—my personal interests. These characters are able to manifest that. That's what all characters are really—it's just like a dream—everyone in your dreams is you and everyone in your novel is you. That character is calling something in you that you want to explore. So she's someone—Miss Rose—she's someone that I'm really fascinated by. In *So Far from God,* I have a tenderness for La Loca, but again I believe it was like the splitting of an atom of all my different sides that came out in these different women. And then, you have to remember that the novels are written over a number of years and so you live with those people and while you're with them that's when they seem to be most special to you. So I think my newest characters are like the newest baby in the family wanting all the attention. And the other ones, they're here, they've manifested themselves, they may get stubborn and make appearances and not want to go away—they're part of the whole body of work, but it's the baby that wants the attention. That's why I can say it's Miss Rose. We'll see what happens to her.

*That's a perfect lead in to our next question. Your novels are often linked by the cameo appearances of characters— Tere and Alicia in **Sapogonia** and Pastora in **So Far from God**. Which of the characters from **So Far from God** is going to show up in the next novel?*

In the next novel? I don't know. But I do know that somebody has to go through that desert obviously . . . someone has to work in there and appear in there. Since I don't have the next novel planned, I can't tell you. But I do have it in mind that that is my way of still being faithful to my children—I want them to know that in that strange world of literature, they will always have a place in my writing. They can come there and make a little appearance.

*Critics have often commented on your ironic sense of humor. The subject matter of some of your work is potentially very tragic. How do you use the humor in your work?*

I have a very sardonic sense of humor and if I let myself go I can see everything like that. I would like to examine that more and more. That's something you don't see in poetry. Some people can do funny poetry, not everyone. So when I do the fiction, you see immediately that I have this sense of humor. And, I also would like to be able to think that in cultures like the Hispanic culture of New Mexico, the Mexican culture—my own background—that we love to play with language. If we can't laugh or find joy, which is one of our greatest strengths, it would be a tragedy. Because we do have to live, in addition to living with the environmental issues, the economic destitution we have children to raise, we have celebrations, we have our rituals, and if we didn't find joy and humor we would have long been gone. We're not drones. We may be perceived as being drones in society, but we are not drones. It seems weird to see somebody trying to be funny about it, but that is the way that we move on from generation to generation by seeing the irony. It's not a laughing, vacant joke humor; it's humor that is pointing out the contradictions—always. That's being done more than anything in *So Far from God.*

*Aren't you having a little fun in the poem "Not Just Because My Husband Said"?*

There you see the irony again. It's the very careless reader that will see something and say "Well, she really means that." And of course, I'm always saying things with tongue in cheek. I believe that if we see the irony and the contradictions in the institutions that we are given that is part of our ability not only to survive them but to contribute to a change. If you don't see it, if you don't point it out—"Yes, we have to accept this now, but look what it's doing to us" then you can't laugh and say "So, now what do I do about it so that we can move on? What I did in *So Far from God* was that I did give the ending a hopeful note because otherwise it would have been quite tragic with all of the characters dying off because of environmental issues and so forth. I projected it into the future where there will always be problems, but people are always trying to work them out.

*You're right, if that last chapter had not been there it would have been a Greek tragedy . . .*

In the mythology, the early Christian medieval mythology, they've taken Sofia who is the Greek goddess, and her daughters and turned them into martyrs. At the very ending of that story, Sofia is on the grave crying for her three martyred daughters. So that's how I originally ended my story. But my agent who was reading the manuscript commented that "Well, this is very depressing. You know, you promised Norton a happy ending." So I thought, "what would she [Sofia] do to change that, particularly as a religious figure. What would she do?" She takes over. She doesn't submit to that point in history when patriarchy took over her authority.

*To follow up, in an essay in* **Massacre of the Dreamers** *you say that the Mexican-Indian women writers have become "excavators of our culture mining our own metaphors, legends, folklore, myths . . ."*

That quote is from my essay on the poetics of conscientizacion. It follows the line of thinking of an American writer studying in an English department, reading Chaucer, reading Homer as his informants or her informants for writing today going into the 21st century in the United States—a country that didn't exist the way it does now but has derived from the Greek tradition philosophically and the English tradition linguistically. It is the same thing that we did—that we were doing—we were looking for our link because definitely we didn't have a direct link to Europe in that sense. Since we're from the Americas, we looked for our parallels. Once we got into college and we were dealing with this great opposition to our presence, then we went and started digging up "Who does speak to me? If this model doesn't speak to me, where is one that does?"

*The poem* **"Zoila Lopez"** *is a powerful poem about a heroic woman who normally would simply be overlooked or ostracized by society. Not letting those women be forgotten seems an important concern in your work.*

I think that the poetry provides glimpses into things that I expand later in prose. In **Massacre of the Dreamers** that's exactly what I talk about. Think about a person like that—and that's one of the biggest messages that I keep repeating when people talk to me about that project. Think about a person like Zoila Lopez—who gets up in the morning, who puts her lipstick on, who washes her hair—she's dark, short, squat—everything esthetically that this society says is no good—she's wearing a used polyester dress, and yet she kisses her husband, and they make love, and she has a baby. Think about it. In all that, she'll walk down the street with her head up high and she'll look straight at people. Think of that kind of character. That's a formidably courageous, strong, and knowledgeable . . . a very wise woman. Sometimes they don't think about it because they say "Well, I'm just trying to survive." But survival just means you exist and we're not just survivors. We are women who go way beyond survival. We don't just exist. We have great faith and optimism in the future. She's the perfect example of what I talk about. If you think about how we look in the media, they say "Well, you don't have a great job, you don't have an education, you're not 5'7"

and blonde, you don't weigh 120 pounds, you don't have a house with a two car garage." All the things that are put to us in this society as measures of success and beauty. And, then you've got somebody who doesn't have any of that and still gets up and thinks of herself as a heck of a person—that is someone that we can learn from. And that's my biggest message in **Massacre of the Dreamers.**

When people wonder "Well, with so much, Ana, don't you feel defeated or don't women feel defeated?" My response is "No, we don't feel defeated. Look at us." just look at us. There's a lot of secrets that we're holding to ourselves. My projection of our future is that it's not so much for us to assimilate and be accepted by society, but for us to bring society to the fold, bring the dominant society, bring men of all backgrounds, to our way of thinking because we have in our psyches, and in our bodies, and in our memories, and in our histories . . . everything possible to make a different world. That's why I believe it's about bringing society to us not for us to be accepted and become part of a civilization and a society that is marching very quickly on its way to destruction.

I'd like to explain where the title, **Massacre of the Dreamers,** came from. When I was doing my research for the book and doing a lot of reading on pre-conquest Mexico, I read that Montezuma had some idea about the coming of the Spaniards and the doom of the empire. He had been told and it was written in the Codices. As part of his fear, he sent out emissaries throughout Tenochtitlan, the empire, to find people who had dreamed about the fall of the empire. As it turns out, the emissaries found thousands of people who had dreamt about it. He had them brought to the palace. They all foretold doom. He was filled with so much despair and felt so hopeless that he had them all massacred. Thousands of dreamers were killed and it was known in the Codices as the "massacre of the dreamers." What is important about that incident is that afterward no one in the empire would tell their dreams. No one would talk about their dreams for fear, of course, of what would happen. But "what would happen" did happen anyway.

And so **Massacre of the Dreamers** for me is us if we're afraid to dream . . . if we're afraid to have a vision . . . if we're afraid to speak up. In other words, if we submit ourselves to apathy, it is not going to stop the inevitable doom of our society, of our civilization, of our globe. So we have to do something. We have to have a vision. We have to believe in our intuitions. We have to speak up locally and nationally. That's the message of **Massacre of the Dreamers**: to have a vision and not be afraid to speak that vision.

**Ilan Stavans (review date 14 January 1994)**

SOURCE: "And So Close to the United States," in *Commonweal*, Vol. 121, No. 1, January 14, 1994, pp. 37–38.

[*In the following mixed review, Stavans expresses disappointment with* So Far from God, *finding Castillo's earlier work to be more original and vastly superior.*]

The recent renaissance of Latino letters is led by a number of very accomplished women. This, of course, is good news. It has, after all, taken far too long to find Hispanic women a room of their own in the library of world literature. With the exception of Sor Juana Ines de La Cruz, a seventeenth-century Mexican nun who astonished the Spanish-speaking world with her conceptual sonnets and philosophical prose (Octavio Paz wrote a spellbinding biography, *SorJuana: Or, The Traps of Faith,* [see *Commonweal* January 27, 1989]), women have rarely been read and discussed by mainstream Latino culture. Rosario Castellanos, Isabel Allende, Elena Poniatowska, and Gabriela Mistral—the latter received the 1945 Nobel Prize—are a few of the better known women authors. Prominent among the new wave of Latino writers in English are Sandra Cisneros, Julia Alvarez, and Cristina Garcia. In opening a window across gender lines, each revisits the Hispanic's innermost fears and hopes.

On the very same list is Ana Castillo, a veteran novelist, poet, translator, and editor whose previous books were published by small presses in Arizona, Texas, and New Mexico. Unfortunately, Castillo remains relatively unnoticed by the media. She is the most daring and experimental of Latino novelists, and as American novelists Robert Coover and William Gaddis well know, experimentalism has its costs. Born in 1953 in Chicago and now living in Albuquerque, Castillo was educated at Northern Illinois University and the University of Chicago. She is the author of **Sapogonia: An Anti-Romance in 3/8 Meter,** published in 1989, and of the poetry collections **Women Are Not Roses, The Invitation,** and **My Father Was a Toltec.** Her most memorable work, to my mind, is **The Mixquiahuala Letters,** an avant garde epistolary novel published in 1986 and recently reissued by Anchor-Doubleday. **Letters** received a Before Columbus Foundation's American Book Award.

The novel concerns the friendship of two independent Hispanic women, Alicia and Teresa, whom we accompany, through the device of introspective letters, from their youthful travels to Mexico to their middle-years in the United States. Stylistically **Letters** is a tribute to Julio Cortazar, the Argentine master responsible for Hopscotch, a novel typical of the sixties' French nouveau roman, and is designed as a labyrinth in which the writer suggests at least two possible sequences for reading—two possible ways of ordering the chapters. Similarly, Castillo's book offers three alternative reading s: one for the conformist, another for the cynic, and the last for the Quixotic. Among the very few people I know who have read **The Mixquiahuala Letters,** none (including me) has had the patience to attempt each of the three possibilities.

While Castillo's experimental spirit, much like Carlos Fuentes's, often strikes me as derivative and academically fashionable, her desire to find creative alternatives and to take risks is admirable. An accomplished parodist, Castillo's obsession, it seems, is to turn popular and sophisticated genres upside down—to revisit their structure by decomposing them. In recent years, however, her avant-garde ambitions seem to be fading. Lately, she has become a client of Susan Bergholtz, a powerful New York literary agent whose list includes such Latino writers as Cisneros, Alvarez, and Rudolfo A. Anaya. In many ways, Bergholtz is occupying a role similar to that of Carmen Balcells in Barcelona, who launched the careers of south-of-the-border luminaries such as Gabriel Garcia Marquez and Mario Vargas Llosa. Bergholtz is convincing major publishing houses to put big bucks into novels by and about Hispanics. Moving from the periphery to the center necessarily entails sacrifice, however. **So Far from God** is a case in point: the experimental spirit is absent here.

The novel's intent is original: to parody the Spanish-speaking telenovela, e.g., the popular television soap operas that enchant millions in Mexico and South America. Framed by two decades of life in Tome, a small hamlet in central New Mexico, the novel tells the story of a Chicana mother, Sofia, and her four daughters: Fe, Esperanza, Caridad (their names, as Spanish speakers can testify, recall a famous south-of-the-border melodrama), and La Loca. The terrain is overtly sentimental and cartoonish. Magic realism is combined with social satire: whores, miracles, prophecies, resurrections, and a visit to the Chicano activism of the late sixties intertwine.

Melodrama is indeed the key word here. Castillo is involved in a dramatic embroidery characterized by heavy reliance on suspense, sensational episodes, and romantic sentiment. Any parody works through a tacit agreement between writer and reader, who share the knowledge of the genre parodied and understand the rules of the game. Unfortunately, with an overabundance of stereotypes and its crowded cast of theatrical characters, **So Far from God** stumbles from the outset. Castillo loses control of her marionettes. Even more disturbing, Castillo is never quite sure whether to ridicule her characters or idealize them in spite of their superficiality. As a result, the novel is uneven, conventional, and often annoying.

Still, we must pay attention to Ana Castillo. In due time, her creativity will match her passion to experiment and the outcome will be formidable. In fact, of all the Hispanic writers in the firmament of the current Latino renaissance, she strikes me as the most intellectually sophisticated and thus might end up producing the most intriguing books. Unlike most of her colleagues, a sense of tradition can be found in Castillo's approach to the novel. She is a deeply committed reader whose art, I'm afraid, is not necessarily for the masses. Her tastes are singular, but she has yet to write the book that will display her talent in its full splendor.

## Ibis Gómez-Vega (essay date Spring–Summer 1994)

SOURCE: "Debunking Myths: The Hero's Role in Ana Castillo's *Sapogonia*," in *Americas Review,* Vol. 22, Nos. 1–2, Spring–Summer, 1994, pp. 244–58.

[*In the following essay, Gómez-Vega examines the character traits that define* Sapogonia's *anti-hero, Máximo Madrigal, and the true hero(ine), Pastora.*]

The characters in Ana Castillo's *Sapogonia* evolve out of a cultural mind set defined by sexual identity. In this novel, Castillo creates Máximo Madrigal, the "anti-hero," a character who functions within an intrinsically male-identified culture in order to expose his lack of human connectedness as the direct result of his living by a male myth that values the mythological male hero's separation from the community as an individual rather than his fusion into the whole. Through this man's eyes, Castillo presents Pastora Velásquez Aké, a woman who epitomizes the Latin male's "myth" of the female. She is seen as an aloof, distant, unattainable beauty, as a castrating bitch who demands male sacrifices, and as a passive sexual object who nevertheless can destroy the man who dares to enter her. However, even as she is defined by Máximo Madrigal's dehumanizing view of women, Pastora emerges as the antagonist who questions the anti-hero's values and as the feminine force who forges connections with other people as the only answer to the male anti-hero's inability to connect.

One of the first male "myths" addressed by *Sapogonia* is Octavio Paz's claim in *El laberinto de la soledad* that "el hombre es nostalgia y búsqueda de comunión (man is nostalgia and search for communion)" (175). Castillo provides in Máximo Madrigal an anti-hero as the novel's apparent hero, a man who represents neither nostalgia nor the search for communion. In fact, Máximo's journey through the novel can be seen as a journey away from communion into solitude, and at the core of this journey lies his inability to see women, especially Pastora, as individuals with whom communion is achieved not only through sexual intercourse but also through human intercourse. From the moment he leaves his family home without regard for his family's safety to the time towards the end of the novel when he leaves his wife, Máximo Madrigal is clearly a man who cannot sustain any human connections. Although his journey seems to assume a purpose when he goes in search of his father, what he finds is a man who, like himself, lives a random, disconnected life.

Máximo's search for his father reveals Castillo's commentary on the story of La Malinche and the Mexican man's complex feelings about her. Máximo, like Pastora, springs from a mixture of Spanish and Indian people. His grandfather on his mother's side conquers an Indian wife by first assaulting her, perhaps even raping her, and then later returning to marry her. The chapter in which the grandfather conquers the "indita" reveals a collapsing in Máximo's mind of his grandfather's and his father's behavior towards women. While Máximo claims to be telling his grandfather's story as the grandfather and a friend stop at the spot where "Mayan virgins were once drowned as offerings to the gods" (106), he says "it was here that my *father* [my italics] and his friend stopped" (106). He inadvertently says "father" rather than "grandfather," an indication that in this man's life the roles of all men collapse into almost stereotypical sexually defined male behavior.

The story of the Indian girls' conquest, as told by Máximo, becomes a matter-of-fact account of the events without regard for the girls' feelings. One is told that "the young women had been virgins," which not only indicates that they had not known sex, but that they had not been touched by non-Indian hands. In the grip of the Spaniards, however, the Indian girls submit. Máximo says that "the one my grandfather had, tried to run, but seeing she was done for, submitted without a whimper or complaint" (106). The only comment one gets of the Indian girl's feelings concerning the rape relates entirely to the worth of a deflowered virgin in a male-dominated society. Although the grandfather does not understand what the Indian girl is telling him "half in Quechua and half in Spanish," he gets the general drift that "because she was no longer a virgin, she had lost her worth" (106). However, whether the deflowered Indian girl's lack of worth is part of her Indian culture or part of what the Spaniard understands from what he hears is a debatable issue. In a male-dominated world, a woman's worth is defined by how she is seen by the men around her, just as La Malinche's basic act of survival has been traditionally interpreted by Mexican males as an act of betrayal, an act that devalues her. The young Spaniard interprets the woman's grief through his own cultural interpretation of women's worth, which assumes that a deflowered virgin has lost her value.

The Spanish young man later returns to marry "his Mayan lover by the customs of her people, and then [takes] her south to his father's house where he then [marries] her by the Church" (107). Like the original conquered Indian woman, La Malinche, the "indita," must submit her body and mind to the conquering Spaniard, and this pattern of conquering women that begins with this grandfather becomes the standard by which men in this family behave. Máximo will repeat his grandfather's deed when he uses Pastora, a mestiza like himself, exclusively as a sexual object. His own father also repeats the deed when he uses Máximo's mother as a sexual object and then leaves her behind so that he can return to Spain. The pattern of abuse and misuse of women is a cultural legacy that runs deep in Máximo's blood.

Pastora, Máximo's female counterpart, seems to personify Octavio Paz's version of the Mexican woman who "simplemente no tiene voluntad (simply has no will of her own)." In her relationship with Máximo, Pastora appears to represent the male myth of the woman whose "cuerpo duerme y solo se enciende si alguien lo despierta (body sleeps and only awakes if someone awakens it)." She seems to be the passive woman who "nunca es pregunta, sino respuesta, materia fácil y vibrante que la imaginación y la sensualidad masculina esculpen (is never a question but an answer, an easy and vibrant matter that masculine imagination and sensuality sculpt)" (*El laberinto* 33). It is no coincidence that, in *Sapogonia,* Máximo Madrigal has become a sculptor by the time he meets Pastora. His most important work throughout the novel seems to be his creation of the myth of Pastora as a woman who accepts him, unquestioningly, physically and emotionally, without making demands on him. This is the Pastora whom the reader sees through Máximo's eyes. Without Máximo, however,

Pastora can be seen as a vibrant, fully committed individual who risks her own life to help others.

Pastora, when Máximo first sees her, is described to him as a lesbian, as a woman who "in the next minutes . . . [yanks] off [Máximo's] testicles, figuratively speaking" (25). Máximo's first perception of Pastora becomes the myth through which one must judge her. He tells the story through which the woman's life is presented. The reader who chooses to believe Máximo's definition of Pastora as a man-eater must ignore the life she presents for herself through the omniscient narrator's story and through her own narrative when she is in jail. Máximo automatically sees her in sexual terms as someone "with a terrific aloofness" who is capable of castrating "a man with a glance" (25) or as a lesbian who has no need of men like him. Both views reveal his inherent inability to recognize the woman as an individual separate from her sexual function, but the reader cannot ignore the fact that, although Máximo is the most predominant narrator in this novel, his perception of Pastora is not totally reliable. As a Sapogonian male, Máximo cannot see beyond the myth of the female propagated by Paz and embraced by other men of his ilk. His version of a woman's character is nothing more than an extension of the female myth being exposed by Castillo.

Close examination of Pastora's character reveals that she is, in fact, not a passive woman. In her involvement with Máximo, she is fully aware that "they were each sources of destruction for the other" (110), but she chooses to maintain the connection with Máximo as disconnected as it is. She chooses not to play the role of the female who clings but to allow this man to come and go in her life without any discernible boundaries. During the duration of their relationship,

> there were times when one, in the pit of loneliness, utilized the telephone to call the other, but it ended there. Neither spoke of the wish that the other might satisfy his/her need of consolation. During such brief communication, it was certain that the receiver of the call would put the other off. 'I have work.' 'I was asleep.' Then silence, as redundant as the hum on the telephone line when the call ended.
>
> (110)

Pastora's relationship with Máximo is defined by its lack of connection, by the casual consistency in its inconsistency, because she seems to know without being told that Máximo is not capable of connection. He comes in and out of her life at will, and she seems to play the role of the passive female who waits for her man and accepts what he has to offer on whatever terms.

Passivity, however, is hardly the term used by Castillo to define Pastora's reaction to Máximo. According to Castillo, in this relationship,

> each went her/his own way, parted without the vulgar promises and gestures of tentative lovers. No one knew when the next contact would be, neither dated to sug-

> gest it. It all depended on the other's will to resist. These were lovers who, instead of surrendering to the physical heat each felt for the other, engaged in mutual submission to the intrigue, which could only be sustained by the refusal of each to reveal more than one or two secrets with each sporadic meeting.
>
> (110)

Pastora's relationship with Máximo is not a passive one, but it is an unemotional, almost intellectual one; it is also one of "mutual submission," which implies that, like Máximo, Pastora does indeed have a choice when she chooses to submit. She provides to him the same lack of connection that he expects from her because, for her, the "attraction to Máximo lay at times more in their capacity to share their knowledge and the drive for such. On this level, their souls were equal" (110).

When Castillo justifies Pastora's relationship with Máximo as an examination of "their capacity to share their knowledge and the drive for such," she is referring to carnal knowledge, which is in fact the only knowledge shared by Máximo and Pastora. As an active participant in this sharing of "knowledge," Pastora shatters the myth of the passive female whose sexuality must be defined by men. She goes against the grain of what is expected of her in the Sapogonian/Latin culture that allows sexual freedom for the male but denies it to the female. She in fact defies cultural taboos and chooses to share the knowledge and the drive for this knowledge as any male character would, and this is something that many critics (who may be far more influenced by the "myth" of female sexual passivity than they realize) find objectionable.

In "The Multiple Subject in the Writing of Ana Castillo," Yvonne Yarbro-Bejarano argues that Pastora relates to Máximo on his terms, as if she were his toy, his sexual object, and that she allows this relationship to define her. Yarbro-Bejarano therefore accuses Pastora of "complicity with the objectification of woman necessary for this construction of masculine identity" because she is "deeply attracted by her relationship with Máximo" and "hooked on her own objectification as enigma and object of desire. As female subject, she both desires the Other and desires to be desired as Other" (69). Yarbro-Bejarano, however, provides no evidence that Pastora is an accomplice in her own objectification. What she sees of Pastora is the vision offered by Máximo of the woman who is capable of castrating "a man with a glance" (25) or capable of swallowing him. Pastora herself offers an answer to Yarbro-Bejarano's accusation when she tells Perla that

> Latino men always thought that a woman who allowed herself to be thought of sexually and denied any reason to feel shameful of it and had none of the inhibitions or insecurities with relation to commitments as it was considered women should—had to be a witch.
>
> (125)

Her point is that men who could not understand a woman who chose to be sexual simply called her names. They interpreted her difference as a social and cultural transgression, and basically placed the burden of difference on her. Like those men, Yarbro-Bejarano places the burden of complicity in the creation of female objectification on Pastora when her only sin seems to be that she accepts Máximo's sexual offerings for what they are, disconnected encounters.

Pastora recognizes that "Madrigal . . . always had and always would prefer that she remain a mystery, a personification of sensual fantasy" (*Sapogonia* 215), but this does not mean that Pastora herself is a mystery. She is only a mystery to the man who does not care to know her, the man who acknowledges women only through his own vision, much like the vision offered by the short love poems that his name represent. The "madrigals" idealized women. They spoke poetically of the love of women who lived in the poet's imagination, women who probably never existed and therefore emerged as mysteries. Likewise, Máximo's version of Pastora is his own creation, but it is a creation based on little knowledge of its subject. Although their encounters run the length of the novel, Máximo "had only made love to [Pastora], at best, a dozen times" (267). But through the years,

> He had to continue returning to explore her, knowing with each cycle he would never fully create her. It was Máximo alone who concocted Pastora and he did not ever want to know the formula.
>
> (311)

Not wanting to know the formula, Máximo never learns about the two years that Pastora spends in jail nor about the vision of his Mayan grandmother that she has while she is in prison. He knows practically nothing about her life, and he criticizes what little he knows about her music. By the end of the novel, he does not even know if Pastora's son is his child or her husband's child.

The problem created by Yarbro-Bejarano's interest in Máximo's objectification of Pastora and what she calls Pastora's "complicity" in this objectification is that it victimizes the woman. It assumes that, because Pastora refuses to question Máximo's objectification of women, she accepts it. This argument does not acknowledge that Pastora has very little control over Máximo's objectification of her. She cannot determine how he looks at her; what she can do is recognize his behavior for what it is. As a Sapogonian, a Latin, she knows the socio-cultural background from which he springs. She knows what it is to be the máximo madrigal, the most objectifying man, and she chooses to let him into her life. However, whether or not she is an object, she is still the one who chooses to be an object. Máximo's Mayan Mamá Grande has no such control. Her life is decided for her by one man's actions. Pastora not only opens the door of her bedroom to Máximo, but leads an independent life without him. The objectification of women examined in *Sapogonia* is an integral part of the message inherent in Castillo's novel about the meaning of myths created by men like Máximo, whether they come in the guise of madrigal poets or philosophers like Octavio Paz.

Yarbro-Bejarano concludes her article by saying that "*Sapogonia* is a fascinating text that explores male fantasy, its potential for violence against women and the female subject's struggle to interpret herself both within and outside of this discourse on femininity" (69). The problem with Yarbro-Bejarano's article is that it neglects the novel to make a political statement. *Sapogonia*'s female character is not struggling to define herself. If anything can be said about Pastora, it is that she seems to have a firm grasp of who she is and what she wants. And by the end of the novel she has chosen not only to be politically active, but emotionally involved with the man who fathers her child. Pastora's choices make some people uncomfortable because she chooses community rather than individuality. She chooses to mother a child rather than dedicate herself to "the struggle," whatever that may be in the critic's mind, but her choices are quite consistent with the expectations of a people who value community over individuality.

Máximo's choices in *Sapogonia* are considerably more questionable than Pastora's choices could ever be. In his erratic, sometimes incomprehensible behavior, he represents the traditional Latin male whom popular culture has come to recognize as the type of man who "loves them and leaves them" without ever getting too emotionally involved. Although he lives with several women through the novel, he does it for convenience, to further his career. In his forward motion from woman to woman, he is in fact repeating the pattern of disconnected sexual encounters begun by his grandfather without bothering to assume the kind of personal, moral responsibility that his grandfather assumes. Máximo does not want human connections or responsibilities; he wants simply to play the sexual game that he started as a young man of conquering the woman who does not want him. He even admits to being conscious of "the constant thrill Pastora [gives] his relentless ego by not allowing herself to be the conquest" (173) that other women have been. Pastora, the female recipient of his sexual favors, has learned to accept his detachment and use it as her own. She turns the female passivity of which Paz speaks into such an aggressive act that Máximo feels compelled to murder her with her own scissors.

Pastora's definition of the anti-hero at the beginning of *Sapogonia* provides the background against which her own character must be judged. It defines the anti-hero in terms previously used to define a hero as "a man who celebrates his own strength and bold exploits" as "any man who notes his special achievements," and as "the principal male character in a novel, poem, or dramatic work" (3). In Castillo's poem by the same name published in *Women Are Not Roses*, another dimension is added to the anti-hero's character. He is not only the man who brags about his exploits, but he is also the man who

> always gets the woman
> not in the end
> an anticlimax instead
> in the end
> spits on her

stretched out body
a spasmodic carpet
yearning still
washes himself

doesn't know why
it is that way searching
not finding finding
not wanting wanting more
or nothing
in the end the key is
to leave her yearning lest
she discovers that is all.

(24)

The anti-hero in Castillo's poem is a man who is not in a "búsqueda de comunión (search for communion)" as Octavio Paz suggests in *El laberinto de la soledad*. Instead, he is a man who can only offer sexual intercourse and does so with the fear that the women whom he favors with his gift will one day find out that there is more to life than what he can give. That is the reason why Máximo's first introduction to Pastora as a lesbian becomes a significant footnote to the relationship that develops between these two characters. Whatever misconceptions the reader may have about lesbians, the one constant is that, sexually, lesbians have no need of men. When sex is all that Máximo can offer, one must wonder not about the objectification of women but about the myth of who needs whom in male/female relationships.

Since Pastora, who has no need of Máximo but still plays a significant role in his life, is the antagonist to his "anti-hero," one must conclude that she is the "hero" of the novel. In *The Feminization of Quest-Romance*, Dana A. Heller examines the role of the female hero in contemporary literature as she defines "heroism from a female perspective" (9). Heller acknowledges the feminist critics' awareness that "women's images have not been shaped by women themselves but by men," and she argues that

> As soon as a female protagonist becomes the subject of the quest, she sacrifices this man-made aspect of her identity. Her feminized search requires an authentic 'private image,' an image that will ultimately benefit both the individual woman and a society where men and women hold equal power.
>
> (12–13)

The most prominent image of Pastora provided to the reader in *Sapogonia* is the one created by Máximo, but that image is the stereotypical one of the female who passively accepts the male's definition of who she is. The subversive image presented by Pastora herself, through her life, reflects Dana A. Heller's concept of the female hero, the hero whose quest embodies "the opposite impulses of separation and connection." Unlike Máximo's detached anti-hero who severs connections as soon as the connections become too close for comfort, Pastora's version of the hero is one "who enables self-discovery through the forming of nurturant, reciprocal bonds with others" (Heller 13).

The first three chapters in *Sapogonia* provide important information about Máximo Madrigal, the principal male character, anti-hero, and occasional narrator of the novel. Chapter one provides a clear example of the extremes to which this man will go in order to keep from connecting with people, an act that Pastora, his antagonist, holds dear. The novel in fact opens as Máximo admits that he has stabbed a woman to death with a pair of scissors. The woman, unknown to the reader at that point, is Pastora, whom Máximo compares to an alley cat who has "conditioned" (8) him to act a certain way. After Máximo stabs the woman, "the yellow spotted cat leaps out at him" (9) and attacks him. The implication created by the analogy between the woman and the yellow cat is that Máximo has come to need the woman more than she needs him. Castillo explains that

> Once, he lured a yellow spotted cat into his house with a fish fillet. He left the kitchen window open all summer. At the same hour every day the yellow spotted cat would jump through and have its dinner, leaving without so much as a thank you. But if he happened to be sitting at the table, he was allowed to reach a hand out with ever so much finesse and pet its thick coat, causing the cat to stretch its back into a hump and close its eyes for three intimate seconds. Then it jumped out the window. His Five-Minute Cat he called it.
>
> By the end of the summer, he had been conditioned to have the cat's fillet waiting, and he sitting quietly at the table, if he were to stroke it at all.
>
> (8)

Like the cat, the woman has somehow conditioned the man to need her, and Máximo cannot accept such a need in him. His solution to such a problem is to kill her. However, through this ritualized killing of his antagonist, Máximo provides the concluding act in what Northrop Frye defines in *Anatomy of Criticism* as "the passage from struggle through a point of ritual death to a recognition scene discovered in comedy" (187) that is also an integral part of romance. Unknown to Máximo, Pastora has lived through a social and emotional struggle and through the recognition scene provided by his grandmother's apparition in a dream sequence. The ritual death confirms the cycle that enhances the reader's understanding of Pastora as the real hero of *Sapogonia*.

Although the relationship between Máximo and Pastora is not as simple as the analogy of the yellow spotted cat implies, his essential urge to not need her is simple and somehow related to his paternal line. In this man's family, seamstresses play a peculiar feminine role. His father's name is Pio de la Costurera (Pio of the Seamstress), which means that, for some reason, there is no male last name associated with the father, who, by Máximo's own admission, "was not present at [his] birth" (9). The father's name also influences the son through one of the meanings of the word Pio, which is "an ardent desire that one has for something," a meaning which relates the father's name to the son's story as Máximo desires Pastora, a sometime seamstress, whose name associates her with his father's mother and later in the novel with his own mother, who by the end of the novel has moved to Chicago and has also become a seamstress. Thus Máximo, the grandson of the seamstress, stabs Pastora, a sometime seamstress herself, with her own scissors. The man who, like Máximo, wants to disconnect himself from his female source must kill Pastora, the woman who embodies the womanly link, the connection.

Chapter two records Máximo's Mamá Grande's assertion that Máximo's "life was merely a series of dreams" (12) which are understood by Máximo as "dreams of revelation and prophecy, and those dreams that manifest [his] present" (11). The dreams reveal Máximo's connection to his Mamá Grande, and in a bizarre twist they also reveal Pastora's connection to Máximo when Mamá Grande appears to her three times. Even before Máximo knows what has happened to his grandparents, Pastora, in jail, has three dreams in which an Indian woman appears to her. After the third dream in which the old woman's "cotton nightgown was blood soaked" (196), Pastora realizes that she will never see the old woman again. Máximo, however, sees his grandmother when he visits the ranch. Her visit with him at that point is not a dream but an apparition through which the woman tells him what to do about the bodies rotting in the bed-room. The old woman returns to set her lands in order.

Chapter three reveals, in a matter-of-fact narrative, Máximo's admission that he "forces" himself upon a girl who does not want him and that he tries to strangle his girl friend when she tells him, "Your friend is much better than you" (14) at sex. When Máximo examines the reason why he forces himself on the girl, two of the basic ingredients that make up his character are revealed. The first one is his obvious lack of connection with people. He simply acts without concern for others. The second one is that he is insulted by knowing that a woman does not want him. He admits that

> In all honesty, I hardly know why I took that girl by force. It wasn't as if I couldn't have had any other girl that I wanted without a struggle, but somehow it occurred to me to choose this one and once I realized that she didn't love me, that she didn't even like me, it was too late. I was committed to having her.
>
> (13–14)

Máximo concludes his telling of the rape story by stating his belief that his "grandfather understood this and I believe so did her brothers" (14). The "this" which needs no explanation in Máximo's male culture is his flimsy justification for his violent behavior toward women and a direct result of his second basic character trait. Máximo rapes the girl when he realizes that she does not love him, that she does not even like him, but he acts upon this knowledge knowing that men understand and accept this behavior. The fact that the girl admits to not liking him negates his existence, his self-worth, and, to him, her total negation of his person is a serious insult punishable by making that self felt.

Having committed the rape, Máximo is beaten by the girl's "brothers [who] were like mad dogs when they caught up with him" (13). As the brothers beat him, his own grandfather interferes and saves him from being killed, but leaves him "half drowned on the river bank" (13). The irony of this little anecdote is that the rape becomes something to be settled among men. In a culture that values women as extensions of the men behind whom they stand, what the girl thinks or feels is never mentioned; it is not important. Even the Mamá Grande, when Máximo gets home and is being cared for by his mother, comments not on the rape that he commits but on the fact that her earlier prophecy concerning his having drowned in a previous life or his having drowned somebody ("A mí me parece que en una de tus vidas te ahogaste . . . o si no, tú ahogaste a alguien") has come to pass. "You see? I told you" (13), she tells him. It is his story that matters, not the girl's story, and Mamá Grande's earlier statement that Máximo is a very old soul ("tú eres un alma mu-uuy vieja") links Máximo's story of violence against women with other men's stories, especially that of his own grandfather who, one later learns, assaults his own wife the first time he sees her. Thus, Máximo has every reason to believe that his "grandfather understood this" (14), the Sapogonian male's way of dealing with women.

In "The Multiple Subject in the Writing of Ana Castillo," Yvonne Yarbro-Bejarano continues her social commentary on the works of Chicana writers when she argues that "as we enter the 1990's, we are faced with the appropriation and mis-appropriation of the discourse of difference" (65). She refers to the uses of terms like "difference" and "women of color" as euphemisms "for culture which erases differences of power and experiences of racism that led to the political identification of women of color as women of color in the first place" (65). She adds that

> this collapsing of orders of difference in such a way as to depoliticize it, this talk of difference with no talk of racism or power makes the term function as a synonym for the Other, other and different because not the same, the same as white people. For this reason it is important to search for alternative strategies to 'difference,' one that will reinscribe women of color in a relationship of otherness to the dominant Same.
>
> (65)

From her politically focused interpretation of human relations and her concept of the "Other," Yarbro-Bejarano examines how Ana Castillo defines her "subjects," the characters in her texts, and especially in *Sapogonia*. She argues that "Castillo's subjects enact the 'border' or mestiza consciousness' of which Anzaldúa speaks" (65) in *Borderlands*. She claims that Castillo's "texts open up what Homi Bhabha" in "The Commitment to Theory" "calls a space of 'translation,' 'neither the one nor the Other,' a third space of flux and negotiation between colonized and colonizer. These subjects speak from a multiplicity of positions that at times compliment and at times contradict one another" (qtd. in Yarbro-Bejarano 65–66).

Without actually registering an opinion about Castillo's use of this multiplicity of positions, Yarbro-Bejarano says that "*Sapogonia* presents a . . . project of negotiation with and translation of male narrative form and male point of view," and she adds that "the text offers a plurality of narrative positions; a selectively omniscient third-person narrator, a second-person narrator and the 'I' of the male subject, Máximo Madrigal" (68), but the reader is left wondering how the "negotiation with" and the "translation of" the male point of view actually function within the novel or what they actually negotiate or translate. Yarbro-Bejarano simply slips into her next point, the political argument concerning Máximo's and Pastora's ancestry, when she claims that "although [Pastora Velásquez Aké] and Máximo share an imaginary (sic) shaped by *mestizo* culture and history, they are very differently positioned in relation to that culture and history as political subjects and as woman and man" (68).

The explanation provided by Yarbro-Bejarano focuses on the notion that "Máximo's subjectivity is constructed in opposition to Woman as inaccessible enigma and *vagina dentata*," the notion that a woman's vagina has teeth that chew on the man who enters it, and that "his masculinity is defined contradictorily in relation to his desire for primordial unity, imaged by the textual fusion of Pastora and Coatlicue, pre-Columbian goddess of the union of opposites, and his terror of the absorption of his identity in that unity" (68). However, it is Máximo's terror of his absorption into Pastora's vagina, her world, that provides the most insight into his character. Although Máximo tells Pastora, "Sometimes, I believe I am Huizilopochtli, 'Sun of the Aztecs'!" (*Sapogonia* 121), he acts more like a victim than a sun king. The day he admits to Pastora that he imagines himself a sun king, he suffers chest pains. As he suffers from chest pains, the specific part of the anatomy which the Aztecs made hollow and set on fire, Máximo prays to Xalaquia, the maiden who is sacrificed to Coatlicue. At his moment of weakness, when he feels that Pastora "had swallowed him in his entirety and left him to suffocate inside her entrails" (122), Máximo identifies with a sacrificial victim rather than with the victimizer, although his male legacy, his lineage, has prepared him to identify with power rather than with weakness.

Pastora's choices throughout *Sapogonia,* unlike Máximo's choices, involve making connections. As a hero of a feminine quest defined by Dana Heller in *The Feminization of Quest-Romance,* "her specific ties to community, family, and loved ones empower—rather than restrict—her capacities" (13). From the first time she appears, she is said to be "consumed" by the depression caused by her inability to restrain "herself from reflecting on the child she would have had that spring" (17). Unlike Máximo, who seems to have no emotion other than self-preservation, Pastora mourns the lost connection. Later, it is Pastora who invites "Perla over and [lets] her into her life" (21). The relationship between the two women is so close that others around them perceive it as a lesbian one even when it is not.

Pastora also chooses to connect when she not only agrees to perform on behalf of Nicaraguan immigrants, but to help transport "illegal" aliens to safe houses. For her commitment to the cause, she serves two years in jail after she is caught transporting Eduardo's wife, an undesirable, into the city. While in jail, she befriends Mary Lou and maybe becomes her lover. She also keeps in touch with Yvonne, an old friend, and returns to Eduardo after she is out of jail and he is no longer married. Eventually, she bears a child and completes the cycle begun when the novel opens and she is seen mourning the loss of another child. For Pastora, life is a series of connections, although the man who attempts to define her says that she "was tall and slender, with a terrific aloofness" (25). Clearly, in *Sapogonia,* "aloofness" is defined along gender lines. Máximo sees aloofness in a woman who is totally defined by her connections to other people.

Vernon E. Lattin, in "The Quest for Mythic Vision in Contemporary Native American and Chicano Fiction," argues that contemporary Native-American and Mexican-American writers are "rejecting the phenomonological limitation of writers like Becket and Kafka, where the dissolution of the hero's quest is the form" and are creating instead a fiction in which "the protagonist [returns] to wholeness and mythic vision and [transcends] the limitations of both society and time" (639). If this is the case, the hero of Ana Castillo's *Sapogonia* can be no other than Pastora, the one who creates connections and thereby debunks many of the myths that men like Máximo create about women like her. It is Pastora who, by choosing to marry Eduardo, creates a connection that, unlike any of Máximo's marriages, bears fruit. Máximo, the anti-hero, after finally finding his father and learning thereby very little about himself (because he fails to recognize the importance of the women, the seamstresses, in his life), seems to have no purpose other than to keep alive in his own mind the myth of Pastora as a man-eating, sexual object who wants him.

*Works Cited*

Castillo, Ana. *Sapogonia.* Tempe, AZ: Bilingual Press/Editorial Bilingüe, 1990.

———. *Women Are Not Roses.* Houston: Arte Público Press, 1984.

Frye, Northrop. *Anatomy of Criticism.* New Jersey: Princeton UP, 1957.

Heller, Dana A. *The Feminization of Quest Romance.* Austin: U of Texas P, 1990.

Lattin, Vernon E. "The Quest for Mythic Vision in Contemporary Native American and Chicano Fiction." *American Literature* 50.4 (1979): 625–40.

Paz, Octavio. *El laberinto de la soledad.* México: Fondo de Cultura Económica, 1959.

Yarbro-Bejarano, Yvonne. "The Multiple Subject in the Writing of Ana Castillo." *The Americas Review* 20.1 (1992): 65–72.

**Tanya Hellein (review date 30 September 1994)**

SOURCE: "Simply a Question of Belief," in *Times Literary Supplement*, No. 4774, September 30, 1994, p. 25.

[*In the following positive review, Hellein finds* So Far from God *to be a well-written novel full of magic realism and humor.*]

Ana Castillo *So Far from God* creates the illusion of a story told orally, in strong Latin American accents. As in the best tradition of folktales, an informal tone preserves the nuances of spoken narrative and a local flavour is added by a generous sprinkling of Latino-Hispanic words and local lore. Magic is not merely an accoutrement, but it is firmly rooted at the novel's heart and alters the lives of the principal characters; Sofia and her four daughters.

The quarter of daughters, a mixture of the ethereal and the earthly, all Chicana Latin Americans of Spanish descent, are a strange hybrid of Catholic and native spirituality. Sofi's youngest daughter, La Loca, becomes a visionary when, at the age of three, she is wrongly believed dead after an epileptic fit, emerging from her coffin at the funeral service. Thereafter, she develops an allergic reaction to people, whose odour she claims reminds her of her brief visit to hell. Her sister, Caridad, is miraculously restored to her former beauty after an attack leaves her mutilated, and she exchanges her libertine life for that of a hermetic healer. Even Esperanza, the pragmatic journalist, becomes a devotee of mystical native meetings.

Like Laura Esquivel, in *Like Water for Chocolate,* Castillo mixes stories with recipes—native remedies for such diverse ailments as the evil eye and stress, for Castillo marries beliefs from the Old World and New. Francisco el Penitente, the godson of Dona Felicia, Caridad's friend and mentor, is a "santero"—a man who according to native tradition carves the faces of saints brought from the Old World. Caridad's attack is by a "malogra," a creature of native myth, and she commits suicide in response to a call from two Mexican goddesses, while La Loca received the news of Esperanza's death from La Lorona, the mythical announcer of death. The surreal effect achieved by such mythology is epitomized by a comment on the death of Fe, Sofi's non-visionary daughter, whose sole peculiarity was to scream for a year after being jilted:

> After she died, she did not resurrect as La Loca did at age three. She also did not return ectoplasmically like her tenacious earth bound sister, Esperanza. . . . And when someone dies that plain dead, it is hard to talk about.

In *So Far from God,* both life and death are so strange that normality itself becomes an aberration.

Fe's story also shows an awareness of the practical costs of life. She is killed by cancer, developed after using a lethal chemical in a factory, and had earlier suffered a miscarriage because of the same chemical. Her younger sister, La Loca, contracts AIDS. Castillo's women are, for the most part, unfortunate in their choice of men. Esperanza is deserted by her lover, Ruben; Caridad's husband continues to visit his old girlfriend after their marriage; and Fe is jilted by her fiancé, Tom, who, as La Loca divines, sees marriage as being comparable to "having lunch with the devil." Sofi's husband, the charming but feckless Don Domingo, gambles their house away on his return after twenty years. Domingo is the only man apart from Francisco el Penitente who is sharply drawn. The other men flit vaguely and unreliably in and out of the narrative like migrating swallows. The women's lives mirror the vicissitudes of the Chicana as a whole, lamenting their decline, a lament expressed powerfully in a religious procession at every station of which are spoken not prayers but litanies on the destruction of lives and land. Yet the novel ends on a light note with a description of the "Disneyfication" of the Society of Martyrs and Saints, which is founded by the remarkably resilient Sofia in tribute to her last daughter.

Such an ending is appropriate to the novel, which glimmers throughout with Castillo's exuberant humour. The more magical episodes are infused with glimpses of semi-comic realism, such as the canny opportunism of Domingo who uses his daughters' gift got prophecy to win a fortune at gambling. Even the names are humorous—Francisco dislikes the nickname "Chico" which he was given in Vietnam, because in his native tongue it means a roasted corn or hard kernel. Two of the characters, Maria and Helena, name their cats Artemis, Athena and Xochitl. Occasionally, the humour turns into farce, as when Fe's husband is described as having a genetic tendency to bleat owing to 300 years of ancestral shepherding. Castillo is also wryly ironic at the expense of the Catholic Church, particularly on the reaction of the local priest, Father Jerome, to La Loca's miraculous resurrection. The title itself is ironic, because *So Far from God* is about faith—in amalgamated Latino beliefs, in Dona Felicia's remedies and in oneself.

**Ana Castillo with Samuel Baker (interview date 12 August 1996)**

SOURCE: "Ana Castillo: The Protest Poet Goes Mainstream," in *Publishers Weekly*, August 12, 1996, pp. 59–60.

[*In the following interview, Castillo discusses her formative years, inspirations for her writing, and her upcoming projects.*]

The road from the nearest el stop to Ana Castillo's North Side Chicago home curves for several blocks alongside the solemn, deserted expanse of historic Graceland Cemetery and then enters an offbeat shopping district that features a fortune-teller's storefront, a shuttered nightclub and a Mexican restaurant incongruously named Lolita's. Far from seeming out of place, these picturesque locations mesh perfectly with the bustling everyday Chicago life that surrounds them. Such harmonies between the romantic and the mundane, manifest in Castillo's neighborhood, also resonate in the adventurous chords of her art—as heard most recently in the story collection *Loverboys* (Forecasts, July 8), out this month from Norton.

Castillo lives halfway down a side-street full of lush lawns and profuse sprinklers, in the ground-floor apartment of a tidy brick two-flat. Her son, Marcel, just out of seventh grade, ushers PW into a modest combination livingroom and study. Decorated in a subtle Southwestern style, the room is dominated by a series of striking paintings of Castillo—self-portraits, it turns out. Literary quarterlies share space on the coffee table with an issue of *USA Weekend* that features a Castillo story, **"Juan in a Million."**

The day has been a scorcher. When Castillo herself enters the room, however, her bold features set off by her long black hair and simple white sun dress, she appears totally imbued with cool. As she begins to hold forth, a wry sense of humor catalyzes energy together with reserve; she couches passion for life and work in gentle ironies. One of the most prominent Latina writers in the U.S., Castillo is already the author of three novels, several volumes of poetry and an essay collection. Today, however, our conversation starts with the latest events in her fast-moving career: the publication of her story in *USA Weekend,* with its circulation of nearly 40 million, and her appearances at the just-concluded 1996 Chicago ABA, where she did an autograph session and served on the Booksellers for Social Responsibility panel.

Talk of the ABA sparks an account of Castillo's interest in the independent bookstore scene. In the title story in *Loverboys,* Castillo draws on her experience with, and affinity for, booksellers to create a narrator who "runs the only bookstore in town that deals with the question of the soul." This protagonist handsells a volume of Camus to a philosophically inclined customer, who subsequently emerges as the main "loverboy" of the piece.

No particular store served as her model, but Castillo has long depended on independent bookstores to nurture her public. When she wrote **"Loverboys"** she was living in Albuquerque, writing her novel *So Far from God* (Norton, 1993) and organizing occasional events at the Salt of the Earth bookstore. Castillo extols Salt of the Earth for its support of the writers' community in Albuquerque and across the country and laments its demise this past year. Owner John Randall originally coordinated the Booksellers for Social Responsibility panels at the ABA.

"As a writer whose books were published with small presses," Castillo says, "it was a natural for me to talk about the importance of bookstores." She speaks in rapid cadences of full sentences, given a musical lilt by her warm voice. "The kind of literature I write is not directed for the mainstream, although *So Far from God* did very well, and I'm hoping that we're entering a new era now where it will be more and more the case that writers from the fringes occupy the mainstream."

If *Loverboys* bids to occupy the mainstream of contemporary fiction, it nonetheless retains strong connections to Castillo's tremendously varied, and often quite radical, previous body of work. Born and raised in Chicago, Castillo began publishing poetry in the mid-1970s, when she was a college student. Norton's recent edition of her poetry, **My Father Was a Toltec and Selected Poems, 1973–1988** (1995), collects work from the period when writing was her calling, but not yet a career. It includes selections from two self-published chapbooks, *Otro Canto* (1977) and *The Invitation* (1979), together with many poems from **Women Are Not Roses** (Arte Publico, 1984) and all of **My Father Was a Toltec** (West End Press, 1988). Castillo's verse moves freely between English and Spanish, interlacing unvarnished accounts of her life, her family and her friends with boldly erotic passages and matter-of-fact political statements.

Castillo links her impulse to write to idealism. "In the mid-'70s, the idea was to work towards social change. The call of the day for young people everywhere of all colors and backgrounds was to contribute in some way to a more just society. Being of Mexican background, being Indian-looking, being a female, coming from a working-class background, and then becoming politicized in high school, that was my direction. I was going to be an artist, a poet. Never once did I think of it as a career. I certainly never thought I could possibly earn a dime writing protest poetry. So all those years I went around like a lot of young poets—and a lot of old poets—going anywhere I could find an audience, getting on a soapbox and reading. I was a Chicana protest poet, a complete renegade—and I continue to write that way."

Even as Castillo continues to write as a renegade, however, her work—in particular, her fiction—has found a home with the reading public. Her first novel, **The Mixquiahuala Letters,** was published by Bilingual Review Press in 1986. It brought Castillo critical acclaim, an American Book Award from the Before Columbus Foundation and steady sales. Without consulting Castillo, Bilingual Review sold the rights to that novel and to Castillo's subsequent effort, **Sapogonia,** to Doubleday/Anchor, which brought them out in paperback in 1992 and 1994, respectively. This annoyed Castillo, who would have liked to have had more involvement in the publication (she eventually was able to make some revisions to **Sapogonia**). Her chief comment on the matter now is to urge young writers to have their contracts vetted, no matter how small and friendly the press.

## Prospering at Norton

In the wake of the success of her first fiction efforts, Castillo signed up with agent Susan Bergholz, of whom she speaks warmly. Bergholz, Castillo says, played a key role in the genesis of what would become Castillo's debut publication with Norton, the novel *So Far from God.* In an emotionally bleak period during her sojourn in New Mexico, Castillo had happened upon an edition of *The Lives of the Saints.* Reading its spiritual biographies inspired her to write a story about a modern-day miracle that happens to a little girl known as La Loca. After dying, La Loca does not only rise from the dead: she ascends to the roof of the church that had been about to house her funeral and reproves the Padre for attributing her resurrection to the devil. Upon reading this story, Bergholz suggested that Castillo develop it into a novel.

"So I wrote two more chapters," she recalls; she sent it out and eventually Gerald Howard took it at Norton. The story grew to encompass the lives of four sisters, martyrs in different ways to the modern Southwest, and of their mother, Sofia, who turns her bereavements to positive account by organizing the community politically and by working to reconfigure the Catholic religion. Castillo speaks very highly of Howard's editing.

"When *So Far from God* came out," Castillo declares, "I started looking at writing as a career, because indeed, after 22 years, I began to earn my living from it." Having settled back into the very same apartment where, more than a decade ago, she wrote *The Mixquiahuala Letters,* she now plans to write full-time in Chicago, forgoing the itinerant writer-in-residence life that took her in recent years to colleges from Chico State in California to Mount Holyoke in Massachusetts.

Castillo has made forays into writing cultural criticism, collected in *Massacre of the Dreamers: Essays on Xicanisma* (Univ. of New Mexico Press, 1994), which earned her a Ph.D. from the University of Bremen. While she speaks positively of the resident-writer experience, she is disdainful of fiction-writing workshops. This sentiment has its roots in her own formation. "By no means had I, as many young writers do these days, gone for an M.F.A. and said 'well, I want to be a writer,'" Castillo says. "I had wanted to be a painter, but I was discouraged in college. And so I thought, I'm not going to go through that with my writing." For Castillo, a more idiosyncratic, personal path is best.

Castillo does have a strong investment in pedagogy, however, a commitment currently finding its most direct expression in a children's book project, *My Daughter, My Son, the Eagle, the Dove.* This manuscript consists of two long poems based on Aztec and Nahuatal instructions to youths facing rites of passage. "These poems are teachings from my ancestry," she says, "hundreds of years old, from the time of the conquest of the Americas, and yet applicable today—we're going to package them with contemporary illustrations."

Also underway is a new novel, *Peel My Love like an Onion.* In this project, Castillo focuses on the Chicago gypsy community, for which a good friend serves her as native informant. Uncomfortable with the idea of fully assuming gypsy character in narrating this work, Castillo currently has the novel narrated by a Chicana woman who speaks with a gypsy.

Clearly, Castillo's social conscience continues to inform the choice and development of her projects. Forthcoming in October from Riverhead is *Goddess of the Americas,* an essay collection which she has edited on the Virgin of Guadalupe, beloved patron of the oppressed peoples of Latin America. Castillo's good friend Sandra Cisneros is one contributor; others include Elena Poniatowska and Luis Rodríguez. The idea for the book originated with its editor at Riverhead, Julie Grau. When Grau "asked if I was interested," says Castillo, "I couldn't say no to the Virgin of Guadalupe—I saw that as a discreet message to me." While Castillo herself is not a practicing Catholic, she feels that celebrating the Virgin can help redress the sad fact that "what we could call the feminine principle is too absent from—is too denigrated by—Western society."

"I don't particularly care if people want to worship the Virgin of Guadaloupe," she continues, "if they get the message that we need to respect the things that we call female, which we don't. You know, we put so much pressure on mothering, and as a single mother I understand that, but how much support and respect do we really give mothers in our society?" Castillo is not afraid to provoke controversy. "One of my goals in life is to get an encyclical from the church—if not from the pope, then from the bishops—to ban the book. I think that would be the best advertisement for the book, if a cardinal or someone would say that it definitely should not be read by any good Catholic in the world."

It might seem that Castillo's new offerings, *Loverboys* and *Goddess of the Americas,* separate sexuality and spirituality into distinct packages. But this is not the case. For Castillo, "spirituality is a manifestation of one's energy, and that energy includes who you are as a total being"— including your sexuality. She sees the propinquity of the two publications as a clear message that "these are not two separate issues for me, but one issue for us to consider."

The spiritual epiphanies that sexual desires and experiences bring in *Loverboys* occur not as religious visions but rather as aesthetic fulfillment. Sometimes characters recognize such fulfillment themselves. More often, they remain confused, even lost, even while Castillo's rendering of their lives into stories touches them with grace. This grace works whether the story be a tragic one or more essentially comic. This graceful touch of Castillo's is a powerful and unique gift—as many readers of hers already know, and as many more readers will soon discover.

**Sandra Scofield (review date 25 August 1996)**

SOURCE: "An Antidote for Women Who Get Bitten," in *Los Angeles Times Book Review,* August 25, 1996, p. 8.

[*In the following review, Scofield offers a negative assessment of* Loverboys, *voicing her disappointment with the short and repetitive stories.*]

The most astonishing tale in Ana Castillo's new book, a collection of stories, is the last, called **"By Way of Acknowledgment."** An itinerant writer, "scattered by the wind" that surrounds her fate, suddenly gets money out of nowhere, suddenly gets a contract for a book she hasn't yet written. She races back to "Chi-town," where there are her *comadres*, with their faith and passion and generosity, with their space and discipline and vodka, to make it all happen. Her talent and luck and ethnicity pay off. She finishes her stories, calls the book *Loverboys*. Of course, this story is true.

I'm not from Chicago, and I'm not Latina and I don't have so many friends, but I do know what a loverboy is. He thinks he's hot, and he thinks you're hot but he's full of promises he can't keep. "His eyes are succulent as oranges and very black. . . ." He slips in and out of your bed and your life and he's a moving target for your anger and sarcasm but also for your once-in-awhile nostalgic sigh. He makes you think of your papi, who jerked your mother around for years and scorned your independent spirit, but then bragged about your books. He calls you from pay phones. . . .

And damned if you can keep from talking about him and telling him how much better women are, how much better you are. He's a thorn in your side, he can go straight to hell, but he is something to write about.

*Loverboys* is an antidote for women who still let themselves get bitten. It's a plate full of tight little taquitos to warm up on the morning after. It's exuberant, gutsy, arrogant (dare you to mind!), passionate. It's in your face.

*Loverboys* is all about attitude.

The brightest thread running through the 22 stories doesn't actually have to do with men in any "classic" sense. Some women love them, but like as not the women are bisexual and glad of it, and the men were lapses of good sense.

In the title story, the narrator Carmen talks the way someone might who just met you in a bar or on a bus who thinks she'll like you. She tells you about her business—a metaphysical bookstore—and her drinking and her history with Rosie. This story, like most of them, is short on specifics and event. It's more a circle, a kind of Latin Grace Paley story, with ideas linking the way children's notions do—strung together loosely but adding up to an effect.

Besides, Carmen shows up again in the end, in the longest, funniest of the tales, **"La Miss Rose,"** in which she and her pal Stormy take up with a West Indian gypsy witch and rollick their way to good luck.

In between, there are pieces so slight they are more sliced than shaped, with the feel of tossed-off ideas. There's a lot of talk about writing and writers, with a running subtext of resentment against those who don't pass the narrator's political litmus tests.

In **"Vatolandia,"** one big-hipped mama calls out her anger-turned-humor in put-downs of arrogant, rude, strutting, snakeskin-boot-wearing "sad-butt bag boys." In **"A Lifetime,"** there's actually tenderness when a woman visits her dying ex in the hospital. And pathos in **"Foreign Market,"** when an immigrant girl makes too much of an Arab fruit vendor's one night of romance. I liked **"Subtitles"** next best after **"La Miss Rose,"** "I have lived my life in a foreign film," the narrator begins. It's an original story, and it stands out for its use of images.

Some pieces are too little or too much of the same ol' same ol'. **"Who Was Juana Gallo?"** is like a shaggy dog story, despite its reference to the Mexican Revolution. **"Again, Like Before"** says it all in the title. **"A Kiss Errant"** reads like juvenilia.

In short, this is an uneven, often self-indulgent collection, with its lusty touches and its good moments of insight and humor. It's short on character and story. (I don't think "plot" would even be an appropriate word to use for evaluation here.) There is an appealing sense of Bohemia; many women will love the earthy, gusty voice. But all in all, despite Ana Castillo's good luck, she'd have done better to take more time and give us a few more real stories. She's a writer with a great range. I know she can do it.

## Louise Titchener (review date 1 September 1996)

SOURCE: "Love among the Golden Cockroaches," in *Washington Post Book World,* Vol. XXVI, No. 35, September 1, 1996, p. 6.

[*In the following mixed review of* Loverboys, *Titchener states that the short stories display skillful characterizations, but are lacking in plot.*]

WARNING: I prefer stories with sympathetic or, at least, engaging protagonists. I regard a clear conflict with a satisfying resolution at the story's end as important plot elements. I subscribe to the "show-don't-tell" theory of storytelling and love to watch characters come to life on a page by means of action and dialogue. Unfortunately for me and for readers who share my literary tastes, Ana Castillo's short story collection, *Loverboys,* rarely satisfies these desires. Love is the central theme in Castillo's short stories. She presents love in its many guises—lustful, yearning, romantic, parental, sanctioned and illicit. But love disappointed and disillusioned is the star of her show. The first story in Castillo's collection is a soliloquy, an artfully self-conscious mode she favors. The narrator, a Hispanic owner of a lesbian bookstore, languishes in a bar bemoaning the desertion of her young male lover. She theorizes that he left her because "his brothers started ragging him about running around with a lesbian . . . who plays soccer and who knows how to do her own tune-ups and oil change." Since the only realized character in this claustrophobic narrative is the narrator herself, some readers risk feeling trapped with a personality they'd prefer to know less intimately. Yet on the one occasion when Castillo allows herself to dramatize a cast of characters, she demonstrates real skill. In the book's final story, **"La Miss Rose,"** Castillo introduces us to a memorable lesbian voodoo priestess. Miss Rose whisks a pair of young Hispanic women off to Chicago, where she charms them (and the reader) with her spells, snakes, ceremonies, humor and intriguing view of life. **"La Miss Rose,"** like so many other stories in *Loverboys,* is weak on plot and doesn't conclude with anything resembling a satisfying resolution of the various cloudy issues raised in the narrative. But since Castillo dramatizes her characters in this story so effectively, readers will keep turning pages. Alas, this is not the case with many of her other tales. **"Who Was Juana Gallo?,"** the second story in the collection, is a dreary lecture extolling the virtues of a Mexican heroine. The narrator's disembodied voice achieves some color only when he mentions at the conclusion of his lecture that he was in love with Juana Gallo. **"If Not for the Blessing of a Son"** is another less than riveting exercise in telling instead of showing. In this distanced, third-person omniscient account of a dysfunctional Hispanic-American family the narrator hints at incest. But since none of the characters in the story is developed in such a way as to pique our interest and the incest issue is not resolved or even raised until the story's end, the story reads like a shapeless third-hand account from an untrustworthy gossip. **"Christmas Story of the Golden Cockroach"** does have an engaging plot element. In an entrepreneurial effort unlikely to mollify the anti-immigration faction in California, Paco and Rosa import their cockroach collection to the United States in hopes of breeding golden cockroaches. "I've been aware of the belligerence of the roaches in Paco and Rosa's house and how they don't worry a bit over the possibility of disgusting company," the narrator muses. Unfortunately, for every golden cockroach the Mexicans produce, many thousands of ordinary ones are spawned. "The tenants in the rest of the building are outraged over the recent infestation. They are sending bomb threats to the realty office that manages the building for the landlord." In **"Conversations with an Absent Lover on a Beachless Afternoon,"** Castillo displays the skill that her self-conscious narrative technique demands. In this soliloquy she advises her runaway lover, "We believe we are moving in a straight line when in fact we travel in spirals all our lives—so wide, at first, that for a long time we've thought we were heading forward. But after years, decades perhaps, the spirals have begun to narrow, finally becoming ringlets of memory. "That is when you will come back—a man in a ringlet of fire." This collection, like most, is a mixture of disappointments, revelations and nice surprises. If its goal is to highlight the quirky, painful and unpredictable nature of love, it succeeds. But we already knew that love was quirky, painful and unpredictable.

**Tanya Long Bennett (essay date Fall 1996)**

SOURCE: "No Country to Call Home: A Study of Castillo's *Mixquiahuala Letters,*" in *Style,* Vol. 30, No. 3, Fall, 1996, pp. 462–78.

[*In the following essay, Bennett provides an in-depth study of the dynamics of the relationship between Teresa and Alicia in* The Mixquiahuala Letters.]

> I cannot say I am a citizen of the world as Virginia Woolf, speaking as an Anglo woman born to economic means, declared herself; nor can I make the same claim to U.S. citizenship as Adrienne Rich does despite her universal feeling for humanity. As a mestiza born to the lower strata, I am treated at best, as a second class citizen, at worst, as a non-entity. I am commonly perceived as a foreigner everywhere I go, including in the United States and in Mexico.
>
> Ana Castillo, *Massacre of the Dreamers*

In Ana Castillo's *The Mixquiahuala Letters,* the narrator struggles with the problem that Castillo describes as being without a home, the problem of having no clearly defined identity to call one's own. As a result, the narrator not only reflects upon her self in the novel, but also, ultimately, recognizes the constructedness of her self. *The Mixquiahuala Letters* is made up of letters written by a young mestiza woman, Teresa, to her friend Alicia, concerning Teresa's and Alicia's friendship and the forces that work upon both women during their travels in Mexico and the United States. Some features of Castillo's novel are notably postmodern, for example, its particular form of epistolary narrative, the structure of which may only be determined by the reader, and the narrator's reference to herself as "i." The letters that make up the novel are numbered, but Castillo suggests that their arrangement is arbitrary and that the reader's own preference for the novel's outcome should determine their order. In giving such a flexible structure to the novel, Castillo creates a text that cannot be defined by any unified ideology. Similarly, her choice of "i" as pronoun for her self undermines the notion of the authorial "I" in that it refuses to indicate the authority representing dominant discourses. Yet in saying "i," Teresa, through her letters, can voice a self, a fragmented self that resists ideological definition.

Teresa is, from the outset, aware of the conflicting identities encompassed by her self. As a mestiza, she is U.S. American (from Chicago), Mexican, and Native-American, or "Indian."[1] Further, she is Catholic, a religion that includes not only Christian superstition but also that of her Native-American heritage, much of which has been absorbed by the Catholic tradition in the mestiza culture; and she is intellectual, a quality that requires her to disregard her superstitions. In addition, to complicate the relationships among these identities, she is a woman. Teresa writes her letters roughly between the ages of twenty and thirty, as a way to "make sense" of both her own and Alicia's experiences. By writing the letters, she is able to gain some distance from both her experiences and her feelings, as she expresses here:

> i doubt if what i'm going to recall for both our sakes in the following pages will coincide one hundred percent with your recollections, but as you make use of my determination to attempt a record of some sort, to stir your memory, try not to look for flaws or inaccuracies.
>
> Rather, keep the detachment you've strived for since knowing, if you kept it close, it would go on hurting. This isn't a tale of our experiences, but of two women.
>
> (53)

The act of writing these letters is often disturbing for Teresa, and once having written them, she is not necessarily any more at peace than she was before. As she notes in letter 16, "when one is confronted by the mirror, the spirit trembles" (55). Yet, there is a need to write. Although what Teresa learns by looking in the mirror/writing her letters is not comforting, it allows her a new sense of agency. This agency comes primarily from her observation that reality is constructed, that is, the act of writing gives her a medium, first for deconstructing oppressive ideologies, and then for constructing her own reality, including her self. The constructedness of things is emphasized by the structural play Castillo sets up in the text itself, demanding the reader's recognition of its nature as a construct and participation in the construction of her/his own reality.

As for Alicia's role as recipient of the letters, Teresa is clearly aware of the pitfalls of such a position, thus her acknowledgement that Alicia will undoubtedly have her own version of the narrated events. Anne Lieberman Bower suggests that "Tere's [Teresa's] persistent effort to rewrite the past for herself and for Alicia could be termed, to borrow a phrase from Nancy K. Miller, an effort 'to unwrite the text which keeps her prisoner'" (105). Yet simply to rewrite the past for Alicia would be to reenact conventions that would imprison her in yet another narrative that is not her own. Erlinda Gonzales-Berry explores *The Mixquiahuala Letters* in light of a conventional effect of epistolary fiction: the establishment of the subject-object or master-slave hierarchy. This hierarchy results from the control that the writer usually exercises over the narrative, authorizing experience and sending it to the receiver/object of correspondence. Yet, as Gonzales-Berry states, while on a certain level Teresa writes to convey information and feelings to Alicia, Castillo also complicates the conventional paradigm to subvert "traditional trappings" (231). First, she reverses the qualities of the friends so that Teresa, who as writer would traditionally be superior, exhibits traditionally inferior qualities—she is "morena" (brown) with "round fleshy contours" and "Indian Ancestry" (231)—while Alicia's qualities would traditionally be considered superior: she is "fair skinned" with "thin muscular contours" and "Anglo-Spanish Ancestry" (231). Second, Teresa writes, at least to a certain extent, to herself. As Gonzales-Berry states, "The very conventions of the genre which traditionally have marked the boundaries between self and other [dates, clear pronouns, greetings, farewells, and signatures] begin to disappear and ambiguity shows her tantalizing face" (233). While Lieberman Bower's point that Teresa desires a renewal of the bond between herself and Alicia is well-taken, Gonzales-Berry suggests that the very notion of subject/object is broken down in the novel and that the two women begin to merge through "difference—plural, fluid, fragmentary" (234). In spite of this merging, however, Teresa does not intend to absorb Alicia's own narrative, as is evident in her suggestion that their "recollections" will differ. In Teresa's words, Alicia will "make use of [Teresa's] determination to attempt a record of some sort, to stir [Alicia's] memory" rather than simply adopting Teresa's narrative as her own (53; emphasis added). Thus, while Teresa does rewrite her experience, she suggests in her letters to Alicia that her version of those experiences is only that, one version among many others.

The tension between Teresa's conflicting identities and her desire to establish a liberated self that is unconstricted by ideological constructs, including the notion of binary oppositions, is the force that drives the novel. Language, metaphor, and form are the most apparent forums for this tension; the epistolary novel is, of course, a prime genre for developing such tension. By using the epistolary novel, widely considered a conventional women's form (Perry ix), by developing tension through language and metaphor, and by manipulating form to show the nature of Teresa's fragmentation, Castillo places readers—and Teresa—somewhere between a perspective that acknowledges ideology and one that rejects ideological dominance. This fluctuation reflects the impossibility of taking any permanent position and foregrounds the resulting fragmentation of Teresa's self.

As suggested above, it is by no means easy to categorize the elements of Teresa's identities. In her language, both Spanish and English, at times both formal and informal, often venturing even into the poetic, Teresa continually conveys the internal conflict she experiences as a "countryless woman" (*Massacre* 21). The letters are written primarily in English, and, typical of correspondence to friends, their tone is often informal. Further, Teresa uses idiomatic and slang phrases to create a tone of familiarity in keeping with the conventions of informal letter-writing. For instance, to describe her Tia Filomena, she consistently uses Spanish to describe familial relationships. She says, "She took in laundry, children of working-out-of-the-home-mothers and whipped out some mean drapes on an old pedestal Singer" (17). Of Tia Filomena's oldest son, she says, "Eddie is now Edie—if you get my drift" (18). She uses words like "cool" for Tia Filomena, who does not mind Teresa's sunbathing (17), and "hot" to describe what Eddie/Edie is not, since he has become a woman (18). Though many of the letters are more formal or poetic than letter 1, written usually to reflect and/or to examine rather than to request action from Alicia, idiom and slang appear from time to time throughout the collection. For example, in a parenthetical note to Alicia/the reader in letter 25, Teresa writes, "Years later, only hindsight causes us to look upon the engineers' proposition as ludicrous, but we are not those of then, and if anyone else happens to read this account and would like to give us the benefit of the doubt, i warn him/her not to put money on it" (94). In letter 37, she states, again idiomatically, "i want to take my ghosts, Alicia, confront them face to face, snarl at them, stick out my tongue, wiggle my fingers from the sides of my head, nya-nya!" (130).

On the other hand, there are times when Teresa takes a more formal or, according to white American academic standards, "sophisticated" tone. For example, in letter 11, she offers an explanation of the complex relationship she shares with Alicia: "We weren't free of society's tenets to be convinced we could exist indefinitely without the demands and complications one aggregated with the supreme commitment to a man" (45). In a similar tone in letter 14, she tries to clarify her definition of Alicia's beauty: "i'm not referring to that inner beauty one goes on about with diplomacy and discretion as consolation for the absence of external attributes, ever critical to women beings" (51). Interestingly, following this passage, Teresa moves into a more poetic expression to reveal what she does mean by beauty: "You keep your virgin hair long, long, a snake hung by its tail down the narrow ripples of your vertebrae. Putting antiquated values regarding feminine beauty aside, it is lovely. You know that. That's why you keep it, brushing fastidiously nightly like a weaver of precious silk" (51). Teresa, then, moves repeatedly between formal English, necessary for being heard by a "mainstream" audience, and informal English, which might be more commonly associated with a lower-strata, mestiza culture, and in doing so, she generates poetic expression that draws attention to the power of language itself, the power to produce vision and perspective and/or to explode those things.

Similarly, she shifts between English and Spanish, both factors of her complex identity. While she does not have access to the language of her Native American ancestors, she expresses herself readily in Spanish, even sometimes turning an English word into a Spanish-sounding one, like the substitution of "Nuyorquina" (18) for New Yorker. She relates Spanish dialogue from episodes with her relatives, friends, and acquaintances (for example, "Y traeme una para mi y el nino, hija,' tia Filo said, coming around the house with Peioncito by the hand" [19]), and includes Spanish words and phrases in her poetry as well, such as "Un cuento sin ritmo / Time is Fluid" (70). Her use of the languages associated with her various identities becomes, in fact, something of a collage, a collection of fragments brought together to make a powerful expression of who she is. The shifts in tone and/or dialect and between English and Spanish generate an awareness for the reader that Teresa cannot be defined by any one of these languages, though each one shapes her in some way as we will see, and that the medium of letters accommodates her fragmented identity.

The metaphors that Teresa uses in her letters reveal the same tension as does her use of multiple languages. These metaphors typically address the conflict between the desire for essentialism, for a sense that "home" has a particular and definable essence, and the flaws in the notion that the systems that describe reality can accurately represent such an essence. For example, the religious representations are double-edged. For Teresa, the Catholic religion is inescapable; the church points to life that might be condemned by an almighty, all-knowing God. Teresa asks Alicia in letter 4, "Do you know the smell of a church? . . . a CATHEDRAL, with doors the height of two very tall men and so heavy that when you pull one open to enter you feel as small as you are destined" (30). Teresa's memory of her past is steeped in the experience of this kind of church: "It smells of incense, hot oils, the wax of constant burning candles, melting at a vigilant pace, the plaster of an army of saints watching with fixed glass eyes, revered in exchange for being mediators and delivering your feeble prayers. It smells of flowers and palms that precede Easter. It smells of death" (30). Here, the church is revealed to be both wonderful and terrifying. Even though at 18 she ran out of the confession box and never returned to church, she cannot disregard its place in her life. When she gives birth to a son, she has him baptized; as she explains in letter 40, "It's been said once a Catholic, always a Catholic. Perhaps it was a superstitious idiosyncracy that provoked me to want Vittorio baptized" (134). Although her early experience in the confession box temporarily drove her away from her religious life, she writes in letter 24 that her regard for her spiritual heritage serves as a liberating force when she and Alicia are threatened by bad spirits while staying for a few days at the home of the young engineers in Mexico. Since Alicia has no belief in spiritual matters, and thus no spiritual power, it is up to Teresa to protect them from the "massive rolling of energy blacker than the darkness in the room" (88): "Clutching the crystal-beaded rosary in my hands and winding it around your fingers against my chest. i whispered with an exorcist's will in your ear . . . Our Father Who art in heaven . . ." (88; ellipses and emphasis in original).

Yet, some of Teresa's letters reveal her recognition of the limiting effects of Christianity as well. Even in light of her bad experience in the confessional, she writes in letter I that she was married not in the church but in a park by a Hare Krishna. She reflects back on this when her Madrina warns her of the consequences of divorce: "According to the Church, even if you get a divorce, you'll always be married and you'll live in sin with any other man, Teresita. . . . We didn't even get married in a church, i added" (22). Likewise, in letter 27, she describes a dream in which she visits a village, one not yet destroyed by a world of "progress." This village "didn't seek to change the world but lived in good faith and prayer offered to an imposing God" (103). Of course, in light of the impositions of God and of "the world," this village has no future. Its imposing God will put a stranglehold on it that will allow its absorption by European culture and lead to its virtual annihilation. The metaphors of the death-smell of the church and the dream-village are mitigated, however. For instance, she writes in letter 3 of the Toltec ruins, which are symbols of gods who, for Teresa, pre-existed the Christian God: "monolithic statues in tribute to warriors and a benevolent god in self-exile who reappeared later on Mayan shores, and again, on the back of a four legged beast to display his mortal fallibilities" (25). Even this benevolent vision includes only men, however, and it is still a monolith, a system in which truth is fixed, imposed and imposing. While both Christianity and the system of religion that preceded it ostensibly offer Teresa sources of strength, in actuality they both deny her a "home."

The essentialist system of patriarchal rule, both in the United States and in Mexico, is represented ambivalently as well in metaphors that reveal its snake-like abilities to embrace as well as to choke. When Alicia joins a women's group in order to become independent enough to pursue her career, the group imposes celibacy as a requirement for membership (111). The problems Alicia encounters after joining the group result from "the absence of what [she] couldn't pinpoint to anything but nature yielding [her] body and spirit despite society's obstacles. Men and women belonged together" (112). Alicia wants a family, someone with whom to share the responsibilities and joys of life. She ends up sharing her apartment with a Viet Nam veteran, Abdel. Teresa has acknowledged in letter 11 that what Alicia seems to be filling in this episode is the need "to seek approval from man through sexual meetings" (45). Yet, Teresa has also betrayed the movement by returning to her husband. Even after she has left him again, Teresa suggests in letter 30 that to commit to celibacy would be "biting your nose off to spite your face" (111). Although the feminist movement of this period succeeds in generating an awareness for women, and for some men, of the inequities experienced in U.S. society, the movement itself is not a saving entity for Alicia or for Teresa. As many have noted, one of the movement's biggest obstacles is the difficulty of effecting separatism in a world in which heterosexuality is dominant. Teresa feels the impossibility of such a thing as separatism, for instance, in the context of Alicia's and her experience. Yet, in letter 30, even as she empathizes with Alicia's desire for a relationship with a man, Teresa describes being choked by her relationship with Alexis, the flamenco artist: "[I]t was a period in which all those ideals were twisted and made perverse by the man who held me rumpled, like composition sheets, in his tight grip" (112).

This image of a hand holding her trapped is enhanced by the snake metaphor used to describe the relationship between men and women. Teresa writes in letter 10 that having rejected men for just a little while, Alicia, Teresa, and her childhood friend, who had left her husband "to find herself" (44) lived together, seeking strength from one another: "We were obsessed / with visions of snakes that threatened / to wind themselves around our yearning hearts . . ." (44). Although letter 21 describes from a third person point of view either her or Alicia's fascination with snakes as representative of Coatlicue, a version of the Mother Earth,[2] this symbol is a complex one. As Teresa and Alicia walk along the Yucatan beach, "[o]ne picked up a dead branch and lingeringly drew something in the sand. She drew a snake. S. She draws another snake. S. Two snakes. S. S. She was obsessed with snakes. The snake woman, Coatlicue" (72). This snake image is of an empowered female, yet it is also an image that depends upon the patriarchy's dominant position for its power. In ***Massacre of the Dreamers,*** Castillo explains that by the time the Mother Earth figure evolved into Coatlicue in the sixteenth century,

> [t]he death aspect of the dual power of Mother—fertility and death—had taken over. Around her neck a necklace of men's hearts and hands was symbolic of her insatiable thirst for human sacrifice. Let's keep in mind that that image of Coatlicue was created in the context of a war-oriented, conquest-driven society, that of the Aztecs.
>
> (11)

Thus, the snake image in Teresa's letters is an ambivalent one, ultimately reflecting the patriarchy. In letter 19, in a description of Mexico, Teresa expresses her ambivalence toward the place she would like to call her homeland but which rejects her as "revolting" since "the only respect granted a woman is that which a gentleman bestows upon a lady. Clearly, we were no ladies" (65). She also describes this "homeland" using the snake-like image: "Mexico. Melancholy, profoundly right and wrong, it embraces as it strangulates" (65).

The image of self that she has constructed from the internalization of these historical value systems and legends, while it is based on essential systems that pose as unified ones, does not, of course, hold up. As a fundamental proponent of truth, the Church fails. As a mythical homeland with the potential for reestablishment, the pre-Columbian culture of Mexico fails as well. And pervasive in the modern cultures of both the U.S. and Mexico is the deceptive system of the strangulating patriarchy, ostensibly promoting yet actually oppressing individualism. The metaphors for the Church, the Toltec world, and modern-day patriarchy reveal them to be essentialist and frightening. The cathedral with its big heavy doors and the ruins with their monoliths are imposing, limiting even as they claim essential, fixed truth. The patriarchal rule, resting upon the power established by these traditions and on its power to seduce, traps and ultimately destroys.

The ambivalence Teresa feels about all of these ideologies results, then, from her constant movement between conflicting essentialist perspectives. Just as her metaphors of religious and political monoliths function to reveal that ambivalence, the form she chooses, letters, serves as a metaphor for that movement as well. Metaphorically, the letters function as a mirror: not only may they ostensibly reflect an image, but, more accurately, they may also deconstruct/construct an image. When Teresa meets Alvaro Perez in the central square of a small Mexican town, she sees in him a reflection of herself as a result of "the Indian spirit of mutual ancestors" (54). Teresa comments that "[w]hen one is confronted by the mirror, the spirit trembles" (55). Yet Teresa's and Alvaro's different perspectives on the world soon send them on their separate ways, the differences in their views caused mostly by their different genders in a culture that labels a woman travelling without a man a "tramp" (57). The ideal of her Native American ancestral heritage as a "home" does not mirror her fully, so she opts for a mirror that is more fragmented and fluctuating, her letters.

In letter 19, Teresa makes the following statement: "Destiny is not a metaphysical confrontation with one's self, rather, society has knit its pattern so tight that a confrontation with it is inevitable" (65). Although her identity encompasses the tradition of Hispanic Catholicism and its own inheritance of Native-American religious superstitions, including ideas of transcendent spirituality, this statement hits upon the inescapable fact of constructed reality. While the ideal that one has a metaphysical self that exists in a pure form outside of the influences of reality might be interesting, and even feasible in some other realm, in the end, in this realm, reality shapes the way one sees one's very self. For instance, Yvonne Yarbro-Bejarano addresses the notion that Teresa and Alicia mirror one another:

> While the text uses the image of the mirror to speak of the relationship between the two women, their mirroring of each other works paradoxically against their identification, due at times to the inaccuracy of the representation. In the other each sees the reflection of her own need and dependence from which she must avert her gaze. Yet they love each other more than men, and are "driven to see the other improved in her own reflection."
>
> (67)

Teresa's letters exhibit the same subjectivity as a mirror image. Although at various points in the novel Teresa and Alicia achieve what Teresa perceives as a state of oneness, performing "cranelike movements in slow motion one and its mirror" (128), each is actively working to shape the other. As Teresa understands it, "We needled, stabbed, manipulated, cut, and through it all we loved, driven to see the other improved in her own reflection" (29). This comment is interesting in light of the suggestion in the previous quote that Teresa is Alicia's reflection and Alicia is Teresa's. Not only does each seek to improve the other, but each also needles, stabs, manipulates, and cuts at herself, longing to improve the reflection of the other—in other words, her self. Yet for each, the agency she can achieve in trying to shape her self is often frustrated by the pattern society has knit in the shape of herself. What does this fact say about the letters themselves?

Teresa writes the letters as a way to get to know her self, and this purpose gives the letters an essential quality, a reflexive one. Similarly, Teresa's reality as reflected in her letters might seem to be passed on to Alicia as well as to us, just as one might wish to pass on the truth, whole and material. Yet, several things contradict this essential quality traditionally attributed to the written word. First, in referring to her self as "[i]," Teresa reveals that she is not only reflecting her self but also creating her self in the letters. Yarbro-Bejarano notes that

> [w]riting the Chicana "I" questions the authority of dominant discourses, and resists the appropriation of the knowing subject either male or female that "forgets" race and class oppression. Chicana writers', like Castillo's, struggle to claim the "I" of literary discourse is inseparable from their struggle for empowerment in the economic, social and political spheres.
>
> (72)

While Teresa is empowered by her ability to speak in the first person, she resists the tendency to become the authorial "I," instead calling her self "[i]." In her unconventional choice of pronoun for her self, she forces the reader to recognize her role yet at the same time exercises control over the narrative voice. Further, as Teresa suggests, there is no essential Teresa to create that self; rather it is she, whose shape is at least partly molded by society, who is constructing the letters. Thus, it is impossible for her to free her self entirely from what surrounds and constructs her, thwarting, for good or for ill, the idea of total individualism and the benefits attributed to it, including the American dream, are impossible.

Yet, in an act of agency—of a self/empowered by the knowledge that ideologies are only that, ideologies—Teresa/Castillo designs a postmodern text whose shape is not predetermined by her. Barbara Brinson Curiel addresses the postmodern quality of Castillo's text, focusing on the way in which Castillo crosses boundaries between genres. In a discussion of the heteroglossia set up by Castillo's suggested readings of the novel, Curiel describes in particular Castillo's distinction between appearance and reality. She notes that, for example, there are "strong intertextual links between *The Mixquiahuala Letters* and Miguel de Cervantes's *Don Quixote*," revealed most overtly by the suggestion of a Quixotic reading of *The Mixquiahuala Letters*. She points out that "[b]oth are metafictions, fictions about fictions" (15). Curiel argues further that in setting up this connection, Castillo chooses

> to present the range of viewpoints on issues such as gender roles, courtship, and marriage, aspects of contemporary life which are in a supreme state of flux, and so has created a space for her own vision, presented with all of its living conflicts and contradictions. She has created, instead of a monoglot and closed narrative unity, a "dynamic unity which is uniquely capable of representing a conflicting and evolving cultural and social life.
>
> (21)

Curiel suggests that in blurring the boundaries between the novel employing a conventional ending and those lacking a fixed ending, *The Mixquiahuala Letters* yields a more honest, albeit unresolved, commentary on its subject. Not only does Castillo refuse to provide a traditional fixed ending for her novel, but she forces the reader into an awareness that he/she helps determine his/her experience of reading the novel. Instead of simply reading an account of Teresa's and Alicia's experiences, the reader helps to construct that narrative. Further, Castillo forces the reader to acknowledge that social constructs will influence, perhaps even determine, the way the reader will "choose" to read the narrative. With labels like "cynic," "conformist," and "quixotic" to choose from, the reader must ask by what influence she/he leans toward a particular way of reading the narrative. For example, for the conformist Castillo suggests that the story end with Teresa in confronting the memories of her rejection in Mexico and putting to rest (we assume) her resentments of that country. Conversely, the cynic would choose to arrange the letters so that the novel ends with an angry letter in which Teresa chastises her friend for "stealing" an old lover. Regardless of the reader's biases, Teresa's/Castillo's form brings the reader into an awareness of those choices and of the influence of those choices.[3] It is this awareness, she suggests, that can effect some agency over one's experience.

In addition, the structural play she sets up raises some questions about dominance and control. As Alvina E. Quintana notes, in the context of her letters, Teresa/Castillo mediates between ethnography and conventional fiction. Quintana argues that Chicana literature in general "functions as a bold cultural invention, which ironically enough resembles what we have come to respect as interpretive or experimental ethnography" (74–75). She suggests that rather than serving strictly as an "objective" account of cultural habits, traditions, and values, as proposed by a conventional ethnographical study or as a fictive account of personal experience, detached from social and cultural forces, *The Mixquiahuala Letters* does both. Quintana notes, "as a parody of modern ethnography [which would employ the voice of objective authority], Castillo's text becomes an enterprise that provides the voices and experiences involved in growing up Chicana, revealing in [Eric] Wolf's words 'unsuspected connections among sets of social activities and cultural forms'" (80). This issue of objective authority versus subjective participant overlaps with the issue of Anglo dominance. Although Teresa has no real space in which to create her self, she refuses to repeat the oppressive act of the ethnographer by taking on the voice of authority. Rather, she unravels the objective, ordered account of her experiences and makes it entirely a subjective but nevertheless an important comment on cultural, social, and gender differences.

The main effect of Castillo's use of language, metaphor, and form to exhibit the problems of essentialism is an undermining of dominant ideologies as systems by which one may be fully defined. Within what has historically been accepted by the patriarchy as a "women's form," Castillo examines patriarchal rule as a factor in the shaping of all facets of society. The variety of contradictory subject positions that Teresa experiences reveals, in turn, her problems of identity under the influence of the patriarchal system. She is not accepted as an orthodox member either of her ancestral religion or of Catholicism since she chooses to pose as a free agent, leaving her husband, travelling through Mexico with "only" another woman as her companion, and calling herself a poet. Here, Teresa faces another problem of identity: she seeks the acceptance and the affirmation of her Mexican roots, yet the more "liberal" definition of her sexuality clashes with cultural ones. Norma Alarcon describes well the conflict for a woman between commitment to cultural revolution and expression of her sexuality, specifically the erotic:

> Given the assumed class position of the speaker herself, affirming the erotic, as she takes pause from the class struggle, is tantamount to speaking against herself, or so her "brother/lover" may attest. The implicit suggestion that the erotic and the class struggle may be incompatible in a patriarchal world, when both are made public, places the underclass female in a double bind, since she may be forced to choose between areas of life that, for her, are intertwined or indivisible. In my view, the speakers in Castillo's work refuse to make such choices.
>
> (95–96)

Teresa's refusal to choose presupposes an awareness of the gap between her sexual liberation and her Mexican roots. Yet she refuses to reject her Mexican heritage since it is an important fragment of her world that may be of use to her.

In fact, in some ways Teresa seems to have an easier time of it in Mexico than she does in the United States since in "the old world," the odds she is up against are overt and therefore more easily challenged. For example, when Alicia is almost raped twice in one evening, Teresa has seen it coming, for she knows that "in the lion's den one doesn't play by one's own rules" (84). She knows that for a woman to dance freely with men in this country is for her to "admit" promiscuity. Although she realizes her own vulnerability in coming to her friend's defense since she has "a vagina too" (84), she hurls words into the air anyway in an attempt to overcome the "spell" the men are under. Significantly, the words are "LEAVE HER ALONE YOU SON OF A GOD-DAMNED FATHERLESS BITCH OR . . ." (84). The very words she uses to break the spell confirm woman's inferior position in this society: as fatherless, woman is condemned. Yet Teresa's acknowledgement, her understanding of this system, serves her well in such situations. Unlike Alicia, who does not understand the system, she has "an edge on society's contradictions by admitting to their enforced power over us" (92). The advantage Teresa holds while in familiar territory parallels the agility she exhibits in the epistolary mode. Her letters to Alicia, in a "women's form," offer her space within which to express her fragmented self without being as vulnerable as she might be in other circumstances.

In contrast to her experience in Mexico, in the United States, Teresa does not hold such advantages. She realizes that "[w]omen in the United States could rally around government buildings, flash placards at media cameras, write letters of complaint to their congressmen (or congresswomen if that were the case)" (92); as a result of the women's movement, both Teresa and Alicia have a sense of the attainability of freedom for women in the United States. Yet, the idea of this newfound freedom is in some ways deceptive, for even in the United States both Alicia and Teresa find themselves demeaned in relationships with men, even in the United States, because of their status as women. For instance, Alicia's relationship with Ahmad leaves her drained: "The man/who lived with you was like a mean draft to one in the last phases of pneumonia. He spent the food allowance on smoke and beer. He brought unsavory types to hang out in the apartment. The plants withered" (129). Although it is not only Alicia who suffers in this relationship—Ahmad commits suicide in the end, aware that he does not fit society's definition of a man—what makes her vulnerable to this kind of relationship is her understanding that without a man she is not enough.

Similarly, even in the United States Teresa takes a submissive role in her relationships. Her husband, Libra, subjects her to humiliation even after she has left him once and then returned. After Teresa travels with her husband, his partner Melvin, and Melvin's girlfriend Cristina to visit a farm in the country and see a horse that is for sale, Melvin tells the women to hitch a ride back to town so the men can talk about "business" (41). When Teresa appears shocked at his suggestion, he charges her, "c'mon woman. Don't give Libra a hard time now. You always talkin' 'bout being equal to men, being able to do anything a man can do, don't tell us you afraid of hitching home!" (41). Even after Teresa leaves Libra following this episode, she falls into the role of submissive partner to men. She automatically grants the gay poet who becomes her roommate the superior role as artist even though Teresa considers herself a poet. Yet, at least he does not dominate her in other ways. She explains, "I deferred humbly to his talent and as he was homosexual, he wasn't interested in making me a conquest" (109). As a gay man, he is sensitive to her need to have "someone's approval of [her] existence" (109). But when Alexis moves in, they both submit to him. She explains, "then the fire of Alexis spread, not just throughout our souls that ached for understanding, protection, approval, but to our minds and it manifested in petty jealousies and competitions for his attention" (110). Though Teresa ultimately triumphs in the contest for Alexis, the relationship ends in trauma after she aborts the child that results from the affair. Exhibiting some control over her experience, she has the abortion because "he would never have been out of my life if i'd had his child" (116), but she does not escape without some major scars—she has loved him. After he screams at her, "you bitch!," tries and fails to injure her physically, and accuses her of "never think[ing] of anyone but [her]self!" (115), she orders him out of her house. Yet, determined to wrest back control over the relationship, control that she has stolen in having the abortion, Alexis refuses to leave "when i wanted him to go" (116). Rather, it is when she is "up and about, able to cook, do his laundry, that he decided to leave" (116). Further, while Teresa exhibits some agency in this episode, she has trouble recovering. She writes Alicia, "i'm much better now and will be up and around soon to gather the pieces of the woman who was my self" (114).

In letter 32, she offers Alicia her definition of love: "In the classic sense, it describes in one syllable all the humiliation that one is born to and pressed upon to surrender to a man" (117). Perhaps it is her failure to understand that in the United States the system oppresses her just as it does in Mexico that makes her vulnerable to this kind of humiliation. In Mexico, her recognition of the inequity of the system gives her an edge. In the U.S., she is deceived into thinking that she is an equal with the men of her society, and this belief keeps her from having any advantages. She writes Alicia, "you had been angry that i never had problems attracting men. You pointed out the obvious, the big breasts, full hips and thighs, the kewpie doll mouth. Underlining the superficial attraction men felt toward me is what you did not recognize. i was docile" (119).[4]

Perhaps the most striking effect of patriarchal control over these women's experience is that, both in Mexico and in the United States, it keeps them from sharing a homosexual relationship. Although both have been treated badly, even by men with good intentions, Alicia and Teresa never sever sexual ties with men. Ultimately, they need men in order to be defined and approved of in a patriarchal system. Yet, they have also shared an intimacy and, in some ways, an understanding that they never experienced with any of the men they have known. They have been like beacons to one another: "By candlelight we each found our way to a room for the night, like phantoms, called to each other out of the blackness to give a point of destination" (32). Although it has not involved sex, Teresa defines their relationship as a "love affair": "When i say ours was a love affair, it is an expression of nostalgia and melancholy for the depth of our empathy" (45). And while it is true that they have "never been lovers," they have shared not just emotional but physical intimacy as well:

> It is true we slept together curled up on the rickety Mexican bus that wound its way through the nocturnal roads from one strange place to another; a soft shoulder served as a pillow for the other's head. . . .
>
> It is true
>
> we bathed together
>
> in the most casual sense, scrubbed each other's back, combed out one another's wet hair, braided it with more care than grandmothers who invariably catch it on broken tooth combs. We pierced each other's ears.
>
> For the first half of the decade we were an objective one, a single entity, nondiscriminate of the other's being.
>
> (127–28)[5]

There is a paradox, then, in the formation of this intimate relationship: while the patriarchy promotes it, the patriarchy also limits it.

Teresa acknowledges that what has brought her and Alicia so close is struggling with the problems caused them by their status as women. She explains, "our thoughts had been synchronized. The closeness we had felt for each other had been heightened by our desire to survive during our travels that had been filled with unpredictable dilemmas" (98). Thus, it is not biological essentialism that has generated their "uterine comprehension" (24); rather, it is their common experience as women. Teresa explains that "our sticking together had become a habit born of preventative measures" (87). But the patriarchal society has taken measures to keep its control over even such a relationship. The dynamics of Teresa's and Alicia's friendship are altered by the fact that women are defined in such a society by their relationships with men, relationships with other women not being important enough. Even though Teresa describes them as "being one," they are never completely synchronized because of tension between them with regard to men. Alicia resents Teresa for having a body that men desire. Teresa resents Alicia because she is white: "Society had made them [white women] above all possessions desired. And they believed it" (49). When they seek comfort from the danger and pain they have experienced in Mexico and in the United States at the hands of the men they have known, they turn again to men: "We licked our wounds with the underside of penises and applied semen to our tender bellies and breasts like Tiger's balm" (106). Teresa's partner in this process is Alexis, who ends up hurting her worse, perhaps, than any of her other lovers. Although she and Alicia are compassionate companions to each other, society makes them feel that this relationship is inferior to that between man and woman: "The assumption here is that neither served as a legitimate companion for the other" (66).

This feeling, the result of their own insecurities, leads to bickering between the two friends. When they visit the Zapotec ruins and meet up with a local artist, a native of the area, they mistake his initial interest in Alicia's art for romantic interest. When he begins instead to show romantic interest for Teresa, Alicia becomes jealous and resentful. Back at the hotel, Teresa, anxious to reconcile, speaks aloud of her weariness of men, but this does not break down the barrier that the episode has created between them. Alicia cries, "lifting [her] face to the dull mirror, 'You . . . just . . . don't . . . understand . . . Do . . . you . . . ?'" Teresa's answer, a lie, is "No!" (64). Even in her attempts to reconcile with Alicia, Teresa cannot admit her own part in the system, a part she later characterizes as docility. Again, in letter 38, Teresa chastises Alicia for stealing a former lover, Vicente, from her: "How long did you think i would tolerate your growing pains?" (131). Not particularly connected to the letters around it, it lies a fragment among fragments, evidence of the element in the two women that is complicit with the patriarchal system to the extent that they cannot be "one." Teresa's description of Alicia's art seems to describe their relationship: "one angry doll inside the house, before a lopsided table with real, miniature copper utensils and clay vessels. The other drowns in the ocean, visible from the window of the little house" (124). In spite of the apparent merging that took place between them during their experiences, as Gonzales-Berry suggests, their state of oneness has been temporary, if periodic, since patriarchal standards are a force neither woman can ignore.

But the epistolary form does allow a sort of agency. Carl Gutierrez-Jones argues that while in Teresa's failure to transfer her understanding of this ideology's workings to Alicia she fails to transcend patriarchal control over her relationship to men and to Alicia, through her letters, she "challenges the power [of the oppressor] as well as the process of gender construction and its goal of perpetuating silent acceptance" (115). She does what Ramon Saldivar suggests feminism is capable of doing: "pluraliz [ing] meaning by violating the taboos erected by the classist, racist, sexist ruling-order by opening her lips, politicizing the word, and proclaiming its revolutionary force" (198–99). One taboo that has been violated through this form involves the relationship between Teresa and Alicia. Here, in her letters, Teresa can call it a "love affair." Here, the patriarchy does not keep her from acknowledging the significance of the relationship or its superiority over those Teresa and Alicia have with their male lovers.

In addition, the epistolary form allows Teresa to be all the fragments that make up her self. Her greetings and signatures show the fluctuation in that self. Her addresses to Alicia vary from "My sister, companion, my friend" (24) to "Poor Alicia" (34), "So Alicia, as you may reluctantly recall" (52), "Mi agridulce Alicia" (134), to no greeting at all. Her closures vary also, from "Always, Teresa" (38), to "i'm sorry, Alicia, T." (64), "just another pretty face" (70), "Amen" (90), "Always, Tere" (125), to no signature at all. At one moment a self who cannot admit to Alicia that she understands the effects of male rejection on her friend, she is in another moment, another letter, a self who can and does: "i wouldn't deny to you again that i understand why you hated yourself" (119). And not only is Teresa a composite of fragments, but she also seems aware of this, that she is like "a collage of imaginary realities" (120). Her description of Alicia's art can also be applied to Teresa's letters: "There are traces of Frida Kahlo and postmortem praise, her exposed heart as a blood pumping organ rather than the romantic metaphor expressing emotional rejection" (127). Teresa's metaphors are not romantic; rather, they serve to deconstruct romantic ones. In addition, she is able through her letters to reconstruct a fragmented self rather than an ostensibly unified one, and, in doing so; to construct a new metaphor of that kind of self.

By choosing the form she does, a collection of fragments that may be organized in any way the reader chooses, Teresa/Castillo suggests that the limits that keep Teresa and Alicia from the full benefits of their relationship can be deconstructed only after they are recognized. Teresa wrestles with the ideologies that shape her view of the world, never achieving a complete escape. The process of constructing the mirror image, however, in which she may view, somewhat objectively, her self, her experiences, is what gives her a certain amount of agency over the definition of her self. Since constructing the self is a process,

Castillo infers that it must be a continual activity. Further, the reader is in a state of self-examination immediately upon opening this text and must attempt to organize it according to his/her own preferences, simultaneously beginning a process of deconstruction/construction as well. This process, Castillo suggests, is the only avenue that leads away from the traps of ideological perspective.

*Notes*

1. In *Massacre of the Dreamers,* Castillo comments about her heritage: "The woman in the United States who is politically self-described as Chicana, mestiza in terms of race, and Latina or Hispanic in regards to her Spanish-speaking heritage, and who numbers in the millions in the United States cannot be summarized nor neatly categorized" (1). She later terms herself a "mestiza Amerindian woman" (1). While she does not use the term "Indian" by itself to refer to the Native American, she uses the word "indio" in reference to the indigenous populations of the Americas (2). With respect for Castillo's careful description of her background, I attempt, in this chapter, to use her terminology as scrupulously and as accurately as possible.

2. Castillo, *Massacre of the Dreamers* 11.

3. In an interview with Castillo, Mitchell, et al. ask about a story that parallels *The Mixquiahuala Letters* in its lack of a conventional plot: "Does that in any way reflect the 'limbo' that maybe the Chicano person has to deal with, in regards to identifying himself or herself?" Castillo answers, "I know you don't want that responsibility as a reader, but you got it" (154).

4. Alarcon points out the contradictions between the "docile" Teresa and the more assertive and angry Teresa. While these contradictions are apparent and offer key evidence of the multiplicity of Teresa's identity, Alarcon's suggestion that Castillo "mocks" Teresa's submissiveness seems misguided. She comments that "confessions [of docility and complicitous hopes] are barely audible. They tend to get lost in Tere's latter-day, after-the-fact sardonic anger" (100). Teresa does mock herself, as Alarcon notes. Rather than mocking Teresa, however, Castillo seems to be generating for the reader a way of sympathizing with Teresa by constructing a narrative in which one can see the nature of her multiplicity. As Alarcon herself argues earlier in her essay, Castillo seems to refuse to commit either to her culture or to feminism to the exclusion of the other. The indication seems, rather, that, for Teresa, separating her culture from the oppressive roles it has set up is an impossibility. It is only the recognition of that fact that seems to liberate Teresa to some extent.

5. Teresa employs a somewhat poetic format in this passage that I have tried to preserve.

*Works Cited*

Alarcon, Norma. "The Sardonic Powers of the Erotic in the Work of Ana Castillo." *Breaking Boundaries: Latina Writing and Critical Readings.* Ed. Asuncion Horno-Delgado, et al. Amherst: U of Massachusetts P, 1989. 94–107.

Bower, Anne Lieberman. "Rewriting the Self, Writing the Other: An Investigation of Recent American Epistolary Novels." Diss. West Virginia U, 1990.

Castillo, Ana. *The Mixquiahuala Letters.* New York: Doubleday, 1986.

———. *Massacre of the Dreamers: Essays on Xicanisma.* Albuquerque: U of New Mexico P, 1994.

Curiel, Barbara Brinson. "Heteroglossia in Aria Castillo's *The Mixquiahuala Letters.*" Discurso: Revista de Estudios Iberoamericanos 7 (1990): 11–23.

Gonzales-Berry, Erlinda. "*The* (Subversive) *Mixquiahuala Letters*: An Antidote for Self-Hate." *L'lci et ailleurs.* Ed. Jean Beranger, et al. Talence Cedex: PU de Bordeaux, Centre de Resetches sur S'Amerique Anglophone, 1991. 227–40.

Gutierrez-Jones, Carl. *Rethinking the Borderlands: Between Chicano Culture and Legal Discourse.* Berkeley: U of California P, 1995.

Mitchell, Jacqueline, et al. "Entrevista a Aria Castillo." *Mester* 20.2 (1991): 145–56.

Perry, Ruth. *Women, Letters, and the Novel.* New York. AMS, 1980.

Quintana, Alvina E. "Ana Castillo's *The Mixquiahuala Letters*: The Novelist as Ethnographer." *Criticism in the Borderlands: Studies in Chicano Literature, Culture, and Ideology.* Ed. Hector Calderon and Jose David Saldivar. Durham: Duke UP, 1991. 72–83.

Saldivar, Ramon. *Chicano Narrative: The Dialectics of Difference.* Madison: U of Wisconsin P, 1990.

Yarbro-Bejarano, Yvonne. "The Multiple Subject in the Writing of Ana Castillo." *The Americas Review: A Review of Hispanic Literature and Art of the USA* 20 (1992): 65–72.

**Anne Bower (essay date 1997)**

SOURCE: "Remapping the Territory: Ana Castillo's *The Mixquiahuala Letters*," in *Epistolary Responses: The Letter in 20th-Century American Fiction and Criticism,* University of Alabama Press, 1997, pp. 132–50, 194–95.

[*In the following essay, Bower explores Teresa's relationship with herself, Alicia, and the other characters in* The Mixquiahuala Letters.]

Epistolary novels place primacy on the acts of writing and reading. I have contended that as they write to others of various events, feelings, and thoughts and as they read others' responses to their letters, characters in these novels rewrite or redefine themselves. In addition, they offer to themselves and others the possibilities of rereadings. That is, the epistolary heroine may use the letter as a place to solve mysteries, undo misconceptions, and perceive patterns previously hidden from her view, discovering new interpretations of past happenings that she can present to herself and others. We might call this use of the epistolary response site *remapping,* for it takes ground that has been gone over and changes the way characters and readers see it. This term seems apropos for *The Mixquiahuala Letters* because its letters recount adventures and trips in many locations. The term *remapping* also appeals to me because it responds to the historic link between conquest of land and conquest of the female body that has characterized patriarchal societies.

Ana Castillo's epistolary novel[1] features only one letter writer: the poet, Teresa. Undated letters address her close friend, Alicia, but we know nothing of that artist friend's reading and little of her writing, for Teresa seldom refers to communication from her. Teresa's letters, as succinctly explained by one reviewer, "reflect on [the two women's] experiences in order to confront the ghosts that often haunt women" (Lawhn 1392). Those ghosts, however, are as much internalized attitudes and approaches as external elements of the patriarchal society in which Teresa dwells, as Castillo's epigraph hints: "I stopped loving my father a long time ago. What remained was the slavery to a pattern." This epigraph, a quote from Anaïs Nin (*Under a Glass Bell*), who was famous for her ground-breaking personal diaries, forecasts that Castillo's novel will also use a personal writing style to explore troubled relationships with male figures and that it will investigate conformity and nonconformity and the concept of pattern—in art and consciousness itself. The poet/writer heroine and her sketching/painting correspondent must use their arts, both public and private, to repattern or remap the land of former assumptions. Letters function well in such a revisionary effort, but clearly Castillo sees them as but one method.

The responses documented in this particular epistolary novel then are not redefinitions or restorations or regenerations of the protagonist's self. Rather, at the level of story, the letters encompass a search for new ways Teresa and Alicia can perceive, understand, and live with their continuing, conflicted, and known selves. In addition, as Teresa explains to Alicia, this personal effort may serve others: it may become "pertinent, not just to benefit our lives, but womanhood" (47). For this study of pattern, Castillo chooses a highly patterned form—the letter novel—and enacts her call for change by playing with that form.

Castillo reinforces the importance of pattern with introductory material that provides three tables of contents for reading the novel's letters, telling us to decide which plan to follow. Labeled "For the Conformist," "For the Cynic," and "For the Quixotic," these lists leave out certain letters, rearrange their sequence, or both. Of course they also ask that the external reader label herself, thus setting up the expectation that part of Castillo's project is to question the reader's role. What label applies to the reader who, because of the cover-to-cover reading habit, reads letters one through forty in that order, a pattern Castillo does not recommend? Is such a reader to see herself as the ultimate conformist or, in this particular case, relative to the author's instructions, a nonconformist? After providing the three labeled reading strategies, the author also advises us that each letter is a short story in and of itself, and she opens the door to our own participation by wishing us well no matter what pattern of reading we select: "Good luck whichever journey you choose!" Regardless of which path one follows, an initial letter focuses on journeying. In letter 1, Teresa plots the complications of a trip the two women hope to take to Mixquiahuala, Mexico; in letter 2, she refers to a trip to Mexico ten years earlier; in letter 3, she details the two women's first meeting during a summer culture and language course in Mexico City. Thus the notion of pattern becomes intertwined with trips south of the border.

This is very much a quest novel, subsequent letters leading us on various journeys and visits to Mexico, New York, California, and Chicago, but with form and explanation taking us into the women's emotional and artistic searches. The quest here is not for a grail of selfhood, but for a way to live out that selfhood. Eliana Ortega and Nancy Saporta Sternbach assert that Latina writers, when depicting a "search," usually do so in terms of "a search for the *expression* or *articulation* of that identity, but not for . . . identity itself" (3). Indeed, Castillo's heroine never expresses doubts about her sexuality, desires, pleasures, her mestizo background, or her career choice. Her letters demonstrate, however, that she does struggle with discovering the writing self's best modes of expression, questing for more suitable patterns (in writing and living) than the ones the past has cut.

Castillo's prefatory ploy emphasizes the difference between story and novel because, as Barbara Dale May explains, each approach yields "a very different resolution and interpretation of each life" (314). Castillo's strategy also calls into question the whole notion of letters' verisimilitude and forces the external reader to question his or her own reasons for and ways of reading the novel. Reading as quest (and for what?), reading as linear journey (and to where?) enter the situation, and again Castillo comments on reading processes through introductory material, for her book is dedicated "In memory of the master of the game, Julio Cortázar." If reading and, by implication, writing are games, then they amuse, they have rules, but they also can leave behind losers and winners. For these games, the winning strategies, I believe Cortázar and Castillo would agree, are those that open up self-awareness and choice.[2]

In this highly self-reflexive novel, strangely enough, the relationship between experience and language goes largely unquestioned. The narrative's Chicana protagonist seems to accept experience as the precursor to language and language as an adequate transmitter of that experience. Castillo however, undercuts this conviction somewhat through the work's epistolary form and through her postmodern tactic of alternative orderings for the letters. No matter what a letter novel is about ostensibly, its letter quality makes it about giving and withholding information, about language's ability to transmit thoughts and feelings or to mask them, and about how we construct or misconstruct meaning from language and how we are constructed or misconstructed by language. In the conventional epistolary novel, pen-wielders write "to the moment," providing their addressees with incomplete, new, fragmentary sections of experience. In this novel however, Alicia knows most of what Teresa writes. The communication focuses not on passing information but on reworking that information, making new sense out of it. Also, if one does not perceive that Teresa seeks new responses to old patterns—that this goal is at the heart of *The Mixquiahuala Letters*—then its epistolary format will seem very strange. One puzzled anonymous reviewer wrote: "What is not clear is why anyone would write such elaborate letters simply to retell, without analysis, what the recipient already knows" (*Rocky Mountain Review* 128). Analysis does exist, however. The reviewer neglects the highly reflective quality of the content, along with the possibility that writing here functions to reexamine the experiences, cultural norms, and selves with which the two women have lived. Castillo's heroine participates in the integrative process Ortega and Sternbach claim for Latina writers, in their particular bicultural situation: "She [the Latina writer] accomplishes this integrity by the act of writing itself. This process constitutes an affirmation, and then definition, of that inter-cultural self and serves as her way of returning to the community those stories they have collectively and historically shared with her, recreating them now into new imaginary worlds" (17). In a way, Teresa writes for a small community—that of herself and her best friend—but she also blazes a trial for others.[3]

The affirmative work of *The Mixquiahuala Letters* documents the woman writer's ability to overcome patriarchally imposed conformity and quiescence of women, particularly minority women. Writing itself becomes a way to reach understanding of both the near past, involving unresolved jealousies and needs these two women experienced during their twenties, and the farther past, involving their separate youths and family backgrounds. Letter writing also affirms a bond between these two women in a society where, typically, women's friendship is seen as a pallid substitute for marriage or heterosexual relationship. Teresa writes that society decrees a woman should be satisfied by male sustenance: "Her needs had to be sustained by him. If not, she was to keep her emptiness to herself" (29). Nevertheless, for the two women in this novel, unsatisfied by their relationships with men (yet very much involved in heterosexual pursuits), writing can fill some of the emptiness. Teresa creates letters and poems; Alicia prefers visual arts. Words and artwork alike trace new patterns, new understandings, and new supportive lifelines between them.

The self-reflexivity typical of all letter novels is especially strong in *The Mixquiahuala Letters*. Because, as James Watson reminds us, a letter is always about writing as much as anything else (8), and because Teresa herself is also a professional writer, her letters not only interrogate the stories of her own and her confidante's pasts but also question the telling of those stories. The letter form's particular claim to authenticity—as a document of the writer's heart, as fiction that is nonfiction, as private confession—all of this is questioned in the complex of recollections, imaginings, stories, poems, and diatribe produced by Teresa. For some letter-writing characters, writing is a way to uncover or reveal the truth about an idea or event; for others it is a way to imagine it. As Barbara Hardy observes in her study of narration, any kind of narrative can be compounded of "lies, truths, boasts, gossips, confessions, confidences, secrets, jokes" (7). Castillo and her heroine run the gamut.

In *The Mixquiahuala Letters,* Teresa goes over experience (her own, her friend's, their shared times) to try to discover what did happen. The character occasionally questions the probability that this process will yield truth. For example, recounting a time when she rescued Alicia from aggressive males, assuming that her friend would be grateful, Teresa admits that her perception of Alicia's reaction may have been off the mark. Perhaps Alicia did not really want to be rescued: "perhaps, you hated me too" (79). However, such expression of doubt is rare in the protagonist. It is primarily Castillo who questions the difficulty of ascertaining the truth, signaling her doubts through the novel's game plan. Norma Alarcón finds that "Castillo mocks [Teresa] . . . by framing her with the 'reading charts' offered to the reader" (100).

Although Castillo's format takes potshots at the notion of some knowable, fixable truth, this author is clearly dedicated to the idea that writing clears paths to experiences otherwise unavailable, for her protagonist can write herself into new understandings and into others' experiences.[4] For instance, letter 4 recounts for Alicia material about Teresa's relationship to the Catholic Church, giving the addressee a specific event to experience as her own; letter 5 recounts Alicia's background, clearly unnecessary information for Alicia but presumably an exercise in which the writer is wondering whether her comprehension of her friend's past is accurate. Letter 33 includes a poem Teresa writes from the point of view of an old lover, Alexis, expressing his reactions to seeing Teresa after five years, and in letter 40 Teresa imagines what Alicia must have seen and felt at her lover's suicide. In this exploratory, imaginative use of writing, the character and her author seem fully agreed, confident that the writing act is a powerful transformative enactment of desire and subjectivity, a way to create and maintain human bonds.

Epistolary characters will transmit the belief either that writing is a direct way to express emotion or that it is a way to master emotion. In discussing Jane Austen's novel-in-letters, *Lady Susan,* Patricia Meyer Spacks sorts out the two ways epistolary characters write emotion. The traditional emotive and sentimental character, whose emotions are represented as overwhelming, supposedly transfers emotional content directly to the letter's recipient. The nontraditional, aggressive character, whose emotions are elements to be mastered or disguised, uses writing as an artifice by which to manipulate the recipient (64–67). In Castillo's novel, the protagonist, although never manipulative of her addressee, takes both the traditional and nontraditional roles in relationship to the letters' emotionalism.

One way Teresa exorcises remembered events and their pain is by writing. She can explain and reflect on Alicia's and her own conflicts over a particular man or over their ways of dealing with strangers. Expression of feelings is sometimes unbearable, however; exploring a shared experience in Yucatan, Teresa explains to Alicia that "to be rid of it, i must create distance" (64). Recounting events is a way to control the emotions that would otherwise overwhelm her. Yet, at times she reaches an impasse and has to admit loss of control: "i don't want to go on with this story. You know the rest" (68). Sometimes story, in the classic sense of beginning, middle, and end, is more than Teresa can, or perhaps wants to, impose on experience and emotion.[5] In such instances Castillo allows her poet-protagonist to shift (within the letters) into other forms: dreams, poems, third-person fiction, and reporting of uninterrupted dialogue. Here we find Castillo extending the epistolary format, crossing genres to repattern the discourse form itself and the content it represents. She exploits the form's power to communicate emotion, modifying the protagonist's letter content and writing style, so that either can communicate changing motives, states of mind, and so on. As has been noted in earlier chapters, the formal aspects of writing can represent complex emotional relationships even when the relationships themselves are not the precise content of the letters: "to write a letter is to map one's coordinates—temporal, spatial, emotional, intellectual—in order to tell someone else where one is located at a particular time and how far one has traveled since the last writing" (Altman *Epistolarity* 119).

Emotional conflicts can also be implied in terms of the materials and circumstances of writing itself. This inscription has a long history. In *Clarissa,* for instance, Lovelace's ability to control the heroine's access to pen and paper, his easy interception and reading of her correspondence to others, and his forging of letters all represent his control of her body and his power to control the relationship (Castle 22–23). Teresa's dedication to the writing act and the lack of letters from her addressee imply a conflict over much of how the two women understand the past, a conflict Teresa wants to resolve because she continually asks Alicia to "recall" and "remember" the past. These letters form a bond, one Teresa insists she can create in spite of the men who come and go in both their lives, in spite of the miles between them.

Teresa's letters to Alicia, undated, but covering we are told at least a ten-year period, clearly demonstrate the writer's desire to affirm and continue a relationship. A variety of closings indicate a wide range of feelings. "Amen" closes a letter that recounts a night in a haunted house during which Teresa's background of mixed Catholic and folk faiths assisted the two women (84). A letter that delves into the difficult topic of how women attract men and confesses her own docility before men is signed with an unassuming "T" (113), whereas a letter hopeful about the future of both women inscribes futurity with "Always, / Tere" (119).

The letters' salutations similarly encode a variety of emotional ties, moving within three letters, for example, from nothing at all to "Querida Alicia" to "A—" (104–11). Not only is the emotional tone of the letters subject to fluctuation; presumably silences or nonverbal responses (such as the drawings or small gifts Alicia reportedly sends) are tenable parts of the relationship as well. Although the emotional content of Teresa's letters may vary, their steadfast commitment to retelling the past and clarifying it for both women is indicated by the fact that none of the letters is a note: each entails a substantial allocation of space and time. Teresa's persistent effort to rewrite the past for herself and for Alicia could be termed, to borrow a phrase from Nancy K. Miller, an effort to "unwrite the text which keeps her prisoner" (*The Heroine's Text* 95). Miller finds that the early "feminocentric novel in letters . . . is the locus of an exchange of desires unauthorized by the fathers" (150). Certainly this generalization about earlier texts applies to Castillo's novel, for it is the world of their fathers which both characters struggle against and which Teresa attempts to rewrite.

Of Teresa's biological father we hear nothing, other than that he was "a migrant worker or a laborer in the North" (21)—her uncertainty is a comment in and of itself. Another father, the priest to whom she confesses, interrogates her, probing suggestively, and providing no guidance or comfort (24). Alicia's father plays no part in the story. The art instructor under whom Teresa and Alicia study in Mexico City is "an adequate instructor, could be charming," but teaches them little and flirts with the blonde students (20). Rather than actual fathers or father figures, what Castillo's heroine rails against are authoritarian, male-dominated social systems that constantly threaten women's autonomy and freedom. Thus she writes that in Mexico "society has knit its pattern so tight that a confrontation with it is inevitable" (59), and the confrontations there with men young and old, college educated or street smart, seldom yield anything but pain. America is no better: a place where women's lives and hopes are constantly at risk. Husbands and lovers are ineffective at best, brutish or self-destructive at worst. Thus, although both women crave "a family, to share life with a steady man, children to sit around the table together, hold fast to each other during winters, and to go out to play in better days, always as one unit" (106), each must find another life pattern, one that does not revolve around male figures, to satisfy their needs for community and communion.

Castillo's novel gives us a body of letters addressed to one individual, in a pattern typical of much epistolary fiction.

By frequently positioning personal correspondence within a broader social context this novel also accepts epistolary tradition. The social (and political, economic, and historic) commentary in letter novels, as Spacks and others have pointed out, can subvert given social norms or contribute to their inculcation, or it can critique some aspects of society while accepting others.[6] It can also explore an individual's ideas and feelings about social freedoms.

For the protagonist of Castillo's novel, social and personal freedoms must be wrested from the patriarchal power system, a system she evidently presumes will endure. Teresa is a young Chicana who has experienced the so-called liberation of the sixties and seventies and yet not found herself freed of psychological or social burdens, and because her sole correspondent is another woman of similar experience (though of Spanish, not Mexican, descent), this novel's letters are very much a critique of the patriarchy. Repeated incidents detail the psychological and physical freedoms men take with women, liberties patterned into both the American and the Mexican social systems. Yet the letters always return to the personal, focusing on the protagonist's relationship to her correspondent Alicia, who can be seen as both an alter ego and an Other with whom the writer experiences conflict.

Depending on how one reads this novel, the letters resolve the writer's relationship to herself and to her friend in different ways. If one ends with letter 1 (the "quixotic" route) one sees the letters as working toward a new resolve and maturity, but facing an unknown outcome. The two women seem to be planning a new trip to Mexico, a place of past adventures. However, Teresa seems to accept her own situation: "At thirty, i feel like i'm beginning a new phase in life: adulthood" (15). At the same time, she wonders if the reason that the women seem not to have reached their idealistic goals is that they "were not furious enough" (16).

If one ends with letter 34 (the path recommended for "the conformist") one is left with the picture of both women entering new phases of their lives with determination and assurance. Alicia has just had her first one-woman art show, a show Teresa praises for the works' power to perform "the exorcism of the artist's rite" (118). The artist-friend has survived the past and become capable of expressing her anger at and rejection of the existing social power structure. Teresa, meanwhile, has chosen a different path. She announces to her friend that she is "going home" to Mexico, where she and her son will be enveloped in the love and acceptance of the boy's grandparents and where Teresa's husband (from whom she has had long separations) will play a vaguely benevolent nonthreatening role (119). Teresa will teach, but mentions nothing about her poetry. This version of the story is for the conformist because it plots a divided womanhood: either one is the artist or one is the domestic, as so often in the past. The alter ego splits off. Alicia goes to Europe, to art; Teresa turns to motherhood, teaching. This is the plot that women have known for years.

If one follows the "cynic" track of this novel, then letter 8 closes the story. In this angry letter Teresa asks Alicia, "How long did you think i would tolerate your growing pains?" (125). Teresa is jealous of Alicia's flirtation with Vicente, once her own companion. Here is another trapping plot: the one that says a man will always come between women.

In letter 40, placed at the end of the physical novel, Teresa recounts the christening of her son and Alicia's participation in that ritual. This letter, written after the suicide of Alicia's lover, includes a second narrative of participation, for in it Teresa creates an account of the events surrounding the suicide, events she, Teresa, never witnessed. In this writing, Teresa makes herself into Alicia and demonstrates to Alicia her empathic understanding of the friend's terrifying experience. The telling of the story is the making or proving of the relationship. Writing becomes a way the correspondent creates herself and her friend and their importance to each other.

The internal reader in **The Mixquiahuala Letters** is the nonwriting painter friend Alicia. Yet one realizes that the other internal reader of Teresa's letters is Teresa herself. These recountings of the past are as much self-directed as other-directed. For this protagonist (as for many other epistolary protagonists), writing a letter is an opportunity to read herself, an "interpretive rereading" (Irigaray 75). Thus both of the posited readers in this text assume that reading a text can change the way one sees the events reported in that text and, consequently, can change one's beliefs or actions. Castillo, in spite of her metafictional and postmodern stance, seems to have considerable faith that language can reconstruct reality.

The third letter in the novel states that the two women's earliest letters were "passion bound by uterine comprehension" (18), associating friendship with a maternal bond. Sexuality and physical action are inscribed in the letter too, for Teresa refers to their then correspondence as a way they could know each other and themselves: "We needled, stabbed, manipulated, cut and through it all we loved, driven to see the other improved in her own reflection" (23). Reading is here intimately tied to writing, and both acts are metaphors for physical violence and love. Verbal acts are also related by Teresa to the exchange of other items: jewelry, poems, and sketches (23). The metonymy of the letter as a piece of the self is as strong for the reader/receiver as for the writer/sender. Teresa and Alicia serve various roles for each other: friend, quasi-lover (one might say a sexless lesbianism), colearner, sister, confidante, guide, guardian (in the case of Teresa, who sees herself as rescuer of the more delicate Alicia), rival, alter ego. Castillo here follows a model common to Latina artists. As Ortega and Sternbach explain: "In Latina writing, the entire extended family of women—mothers, daughters, sisters, aunts, cousins, godmothers, lovers, neighbors, fortune-tellers, *curanderas* (healers), midwives, teachers, and friends, especially girlhood friends—makes up a cast of characters" (12). Teresa's mother, other female friends, her grandmother, and Alicia in a multitude of roles fill out that circle of female characters. Latina "writers have often displaced a central patriarchal figure, replacing it with a woman-headed and woman-populated household" (Ortega and Sternbach 12). Yet Castillo is clear on the heterosexuality of the two women, their desires for and interest in men, even as she establishes the two women's distrust of particular men and anger at a male-dominated society.

In spite of her discursive strength, Teresa worries that a woman's words can never make enough difference to another woman. When she frets that her attempts to help Alicia see herself as beautiful have failed because they are not a man's words (45), is she not casting doubts on the whole project of convincing Alicia of anything? Here she questions the power of her woman's voice to use society's language to dismantle that society, a questioning she shares with many feminists. Although Teresa seems content that she can reread the world around her, she fears that Alicia will not be able to do so. These doubts do not deter her, however; she continues to write, "fighting" (127).

It seems logical for Teresa to place her most intimate trust in another woman. Although Alicia may not read Teresa's texts with complete accuracy, and although Alicia is capable of keeping secrets and deceiving her, still this old friend is more likely to understand Teresa's experience (and her own) than any man. Castillo gives her protagonist the implicit belief that, as Judith Fetterley puts it, "Women can read women's texts because they live women's lives; men can not read women's texts because they don't lead women's lives" ("Reading about Reading" 149). Throughout *The Mixquiahuala Letters* men are depicted as imposing egotistical or sexual needs on women, and they do not perceive the women as separate or distinctive from themselves. Teresa reports a simple instance of this in a scene between herself and her uncle Chino early in the novel: "i said i was going in to get a beer as an excuse to get away. He said, no thanks, he already had one. i said, it wasn't for him, but for me. The look i got could've stopped a charging bull" (13). Chino, like most of the other men both Alicia and Teresa have known, is incapable of perceiving that women have their own needs—their own stories. The men here are like the men in Susan Glaspell's "A Jury of Her Peers." As Fetterley explains, "It is not simply that the men can not read the text that is placed before them. Rather, they literally can not recognize it as a text because they can not imagine that women have stories" ("Reading about Reading" 147–48). For Castillo, women have many stories, and, presumably, other women will best understand them.

In *The Mixquiahuala Letters* both the pleasure of the quest and the pleasure of the text are deliberately frustrated by the author's refusal to create a plot of conquest or a set timeline. In addition, tension arises because of confusion the external reader will probably experience concerning the possibility of a lesbian relationship between the two women. Various letters suggest such a bond, but at one point Teresa pointedly denies it, affirming to Alicia that "you and I had never been lovers" (121). What to conclude? The external reader may discover that he or she becomes complicit with a culture that refuses the possibilities of intimacy or sensuality without genital sexuality.

With its content-level focus on the ways women interpret the actions of men and women, *The Mixquiahuala Letters* forces reflection on how women readers respond to texts by women versus texts by men (and, consequently, how men respond to male-and female-authored texts). Castillo's novel encourages us to think about whether we read for mastery and knowledge or for intimacy and the sharing of experience. Castillo incorporates her own theory of reading that highlights indeterminacy, multiple interpretations, and the need for re-readings. Then too, as Patrocinio Schweickart explains about feminist reading in general, this text heightens one's awareness of how the woman's text exists in its social context. What Schweickart says of feminist reading is true of this feminist text: it stresses "the difference between men and women, . . . the way the experience and perspective of women have been systematically and fallaciously assimilated into the generic masculine, and . . . the need to correct this error" (39).

Nonetheless, although *The Mixquiahuala Letters* presents a woman-centered reading of society, it does so while also situating that reading within the specifics of place and history. To read this novel is necessarily to delve into how one reads individual women affected by their class, race, ethnicity, education, and roles as artists, teachers, mothers, and so on. Because Teresa's letters are preponderantly retellings of past events and fastidiously rooted in the particulars of places and times, Castillo does not seem to dictate to each reader what she should think about women in general. Rather, she asks each of us to read as we wish. We can take each letter as a short story, follow one of the three patterns the author recommends, or read from cover to cover. The hope of recovering the personal past to re-pattern the future will still exist. Reading Teresa's letters could encourage one's own act of redefinition, but would ask that we consistently confront stereotypes with particular experiences, just as Teresa does.

The letters in this novel permit us to see that Teresa can read herself and Alicia in different ways, just as society can interpret either woman's actions in different ways. To see with one's own eyes becomes not only the goal of the artist but also the goal of the socially and personally responsible individual who wants to move past sexism and prejudice of all kinds. Yet, reading this epistolary novel, as Alarcón notes, "brings into question our own reading practices, for the apparently unconventional suggested readings actually lead to resolutions that are more conventional than the handful of letters attributed to Tere" (105). Alarcón believes that each of the suggested reading maps provided by the author actually provides "an ideological nexus . . . that forces us to reconstruct the meaning of Teresa's letters as always and already leading in that direction," thus countering the notion of play and choice that her introduction apparently introduced. That is, each of us carries textual reading patterns in our heads that we need to question, just as Teresa carries patterns for "reading" relationships which she very much wishes to question.

*The Mixquiahuala Letters* uses various techniques to repattern our assumptions about the epistolary novel. The most obvious, certainly, is the "hopscotch" possibility of alternative reading routes. Just as important is Castillo's demonstration that letters need not contain "news." Kauffman notes that "it may seem quixotic to study 'epistolarity' . . . when letter writing has practically become a lost art, supplanted by telephones, fax machines, computers, camcorders and tape cassettes" *Special Delivery* xiv).[7] Yet we see here that the letter form retains specific helpful properties not provided by newer technologies. The writer of a personal letter requires no special equipment or special training. Letters can be adapted to the needs of the individual (formal, informal, including poems, sketches, and so forth); they pass from writer to reader, carrying the touch of one individual to the other, and they can be kept and reread. No other means of communication combines these particular qualities and is so readily available to the poor and rich, the itinerant and the stay-at-home, the radical and the conservative. For Castillo's protagonist what other means would do?

Whether we see Teresa's struggle for a new life pattern as successful or not, we will necessarily focus on the sources of accepted or considered patterns. Alarcón refers to the protagonist being "framed by certain 'semantic charters,' using terminology borrowed from Pierre Maranda (100).[8] Such charters exist within each of us, but, if we follow Castillo, the hope exists that they can be restructured. Through the writing act, which entails also acts or rereading the self, others, and experiences, we may discover new maps of understanding, new patterns of greater freedom. To adapt DuPlessis's well-known book title, we could engage in *reading* as well as "writing beyond the ending."

When I began working on Castillo's novel, I wrote to her with various questions, inviting her to respond with a letter that would then form part of this chapter. Among the topics I suggested she might explore were the way that Teresa uses writing to retell her own and her friend's experiences and how the character of Alicia functions—did Castillo see her mostly as Teresa's construction or as her alter ego or as her friend? I also asked what influenced Castillo to choose the epistolary form. The letter I received, echoing *The Mixquiahuala Letters*' use of narrative as a reflective tool, tells a story of its own.

> Yes, dear critic, there really is an Alicia:
>
> The last time I saw her—head bobbing just above the crowd, predictably slender, Alicia was taking brisk New Yorker strides towards me. I was standing kattycorner from Washington Square Park in front of my hotel. We spotted each other and smiled what could be said to have been sad smiled, then we each looked away. She was hardly recognizable, not only to me, she remarked later, but to everyone who knew her. Her hair, which as long as I had known her, she had always kept waist length, was now in a crew-cut.

The color of that hair, which matches her shiney coal black eyes, comes from her father's side, the Andalusian gitana grandmother, the one who retired in a trailer park in Pensacola and who called herself "exotic," who knew a rosary of men after the brief marriage to Alicia's grandfather in New York, after she disappeared one day, leaving husband, children behind and emerging decades later in that peninsula of exiles, Florida. Eyes and hair and tannable skin, all made my friend the non-fit of her mother's family that came from Eastern European stock. Alicia, the foreign-looking child whose blood must surely be darker. She remembered a family member remarking once, as dark as a monkey's, the relative joked at a family gathering. Alicia's mother did not laugh—her mother and her Czech grandmother who never learned English very well and therefore had not understood the "joke."

On her own Alicia would never have cut that straight sheet of dark hair, never. That was the Latina side of her, the one tell-tale betrayal to her feminism, keeping her hair so long because men loved it so much. Maybe it was the Eastern European side of her, too, inherited from her mother's mother, the one who hid her flaxen braids under babushkas when she cleaned houses in Queens in the early decades of this century, wrapped tight and covered like Alicia does when she is at the potter's wheel and the way she looked the very first time I saw her in Mexico, studying art in a gringo summer program, nearly two decades ago.

We were having orientation and all the students were sitting outside on metal fold-out chairs beneath the sheathed Mexico City sun. A little restless, maybe bored, for sure already disappointed in the summer program I had worked so hard and traveled so far for and had dreamed of attending for so long, I turned all the way around, to take a glance at my soon-to-be classmates, who had turned out to be mostly all gringas, and my gaze fell on her who later was to become known to me—and to you, as Alicia. Her chiseled cheekbones, the bandanna tied around her slender head, black eyes and lashes, in a Georgia O'Keefe kind of way, she was utterly stunning. That Stieglitzian image has been locked permanently in my memory bank. That is, that young woman who was at that moment a stranger to me had, not the kind of beauty that turns heads on the street, but a photographable remarkableness, chiaroscuro, black and white, hung in galleries later where you might find yourself staring, wondering, *what was she like?* I asked myself that question that afternoon, twenty years ago. And not long after that, perhaps starting that same afternoon, because of the fusion fomented by an instant friendship, I was no longer wondering. She was funny. She was difficult—an incorrigible Yo-Se-Todo. She was too frugal for my comfort. (She'd rather wait at night for a bus in the pouring rain than spring for a cab for us.) And she was formidably talented. At not quite twenty-one years of age she was—compared to my urban provincialism—well travelled—from art school in Rome to pottery classes on a Navajo reservation. She could find her way around New York like I, a young renegade Mexican-American wife, knew my way around my apartment kitchen in Chicago. She was sharp as a tack. And after that summer, I loved her for years.

Ronnie, a good friend, having known me for many years said he had observed that I invent myself as I do the characters in my novels, or rather transform my image: stylish vintage in Chicago, fluorescent beachwear in Southern California and yes, Tony Lamas in New Mexico. And once, this same poet friend told a third party when I had taken up residence in San Francisco and having seen me go through these various stylistic reincarnations living in different cities, "Ana is like a chameleon, she blends right into any environment she inhabits."

But Alicia, to my knowledge, is not a chameleon. You, above all the readers of *The Mixquiahuala Letters* I think, would agree to that. She was born in New York and has never lived elsewhere. Her life is a constant, the daughter of New York liberals, she was raised a vegetarian, as a child with her mother walked the UFW picket lines, growing up as an only child, studied karate and guitar and for a long time, as a young adult, lived alone. She is the product of an American city that belongs to the world. A Manhattanite through and through, she is anything but American and everything American. She has been an artist her whole life and although she has never been terribly ambitious, over the years she made a name for herself around town—a town where no doubt to make your mark as an artist is nothing to sneeze at. She still loves to dance as she did in dancehalls and nightclubs from Puerto Rico to Puebla, Mexico, merengueing from Santo Domingo to San Francisco, although as she settled into her thirties, she did less and less of it. Her art, the man who stayed who does not dance and is also an artist: her life, mostly a quiet one. For complicated reasons, no children, because of allergies no pets and as a matter of preference perhaps rather than economics, her life became a stable affair, unfettered by the kind of spontaneity that is usually attributed to the artist's nature.

Alicia and I embraced and then walked to find a café open for lunch. She immediately took note of my postmodern sunglasses, asked to take a look at them and said she didn't like them. I inquired about her health. Alicia, as I've already mentioned, has always eaten organic; she has never smoked cigarettes not even tolerated cigarette smoking in her living quarters. She never cared for the taste of alcohol, not even a glass of champagne on New Year's Eve. A glass of sparkling apple cider at the stroke of midnight and then off to bed. She has never been into caffeine, no café au laits, no Cokes, nothing but herbal teas for our Alicia. But she still breathed New York City pollution all her life. And she still drank New York City tap water, at least on occasion, I would guess. In short, she was a product of this neo-civilization of ours and like one out of every four U.S. residents today, she got cancer. The crew-cut was one of the results of recent chemotherapy treatments. "You lose *all* your hair," she said to me sardonically, over lunch, "everywhere."

Four years after the publication of *The Mixquiahuala Letters* Alicia was fighting cancer, my friend Ronnie— who I met the day after Reagan was first elected— tested HIV positive, and I was grateful to be biting the heels of "almost 40" with both breasts, uterus and ovaries intact, no surgical scars, no "positive results" on any of my annual tests. So far a virtual model of good health. Considering the odds, a miracle in itself.

There are certain almost perfunctory questions I am always asked concerning my first novel, *The Mixquiahuala Letters*. The most common one usually comes from students, those poor innocents whom I always fear will be turned off to my writing altogether because of having to develop a critical eye for interpretation, being prodded to find hidden meaning in the text in order to satisfy academia rather than simply enjoying or not enjoying the stories I enjoyed (as well as in some passages did not enjoy) telling. The most popular question concerning that text has to do with the use of the lower case "i" for the personal pronoun. Although the letters are not dated, one letter does clearly set the time of the novel which is in the mid-seventies. As you may know, the use of the lower case "i" for poets was at that time a trademark of protest poetry. Teresa saw herself as a political activist and hoped to become a poet.

Different languages do not give different names for the same thing, they give different names for very different things. In Teresa's other language, Spanish, the personal pronoun is not capitalized. However the abbreviated formal "you," *Ud.,* is. You,—Ud.—are important, i—yo—am no one, simply your humble servant— Spanish, baroque and elegant, a tango of reflexive verbs and reversed syntax, perhaps falsely humble but provocative and charming nevertheless, a veritable concert of courtesies. The Spanish yo of the poor, the agricultural pickers and factory workers was a we—at least then, at least in spirit, at least in our stories.

The second most common question refers to the authenticity of the events told in the novel. In other words, is *The Mixquiahuala Letters* autobiographical? My standard answer is that approximately forty per cent of the novel is based on actual occurrences; however, it is up to the reader to decide for her/himself what in the novel comprises autobiography and what is only and always possibility.

As to the ingenuous opinion of one of your colleagues, who wrote in a review that it is "unclear as to why anyone would write such elaborate letters simply to retell, without analysis, what the recipient already knows," I would have to suggest for that scholar to do as he most surely demands of his students and that is to kindly take the time for a more careful reading of the text.

To my knowledge, Alicia herself has never read *The Mixquiahuala Letters*. I never asked why or if I did she did not answer. She told me that afternoon over lunch that she kept the copy I sent her in a closet, hidden from view.

After lunch Alicia gave me a small gift of a pair of pastel flowered socks. I picked up the tab. We hugged, arms wound tight around each other, breasts to breasts, and then let go. As we parted in front of the restaurant I remembered to give her *saludos* from Teresa, who still lives in Chicago. "Oh yeah," Alicia replied, smiling a bit and seeming suddenly to be caught up in private reflection, "By the way, is she still gaining weight?" she asked.

"Oh no!" I said, as usual a little put off by Alicia's bluntness and this unshakable feeling that she can be, for all her political correctness, catty. "The last time I saw her, Teresa looked fantastic—beautiful, in fact—as always!" I added. Alicia shrugged her shoulders, or maybe it was a reflex, and waved good-bye and turning around, was immediately sucked into the mesh of the Manhattan lunchtime crowd.

Another question I have frequently been asked regarding the book is what I think about what critics think about it. Well, for a long time, I didn't. But increasingly there is a tendency for that entity known as the critic to split and multiply; and with time, appear in all manner of shapes, tones and sizes everywhere I go. There are critics who believe that without them my work has no meaning. I am sure, dear critic, that you are not one of them.

Franz Capra in his book *The Tao of Physics,* states ". . . In atomic physics, we can never speak about nature without, at the same time, speaking about ourselves." Likewise, no matter how sure of himself or herself a critic may feel behind the illusion of an empirical argument, I think the critic cannot speak on a text without revealing him/herself. Susan Sontag, critic and novelist, in her essay, "Against Interpretation," states that ultimately all thought is interpretation. Therefore, I feel that even my own comments here on my novel several years after its publication are very likely interpretations of others' interpretations of **The Mixquiahuala Letters,** rather than untainted reflections of my own. I can only add that the writing process was an experience that I would like to remember as being one of unselfconsciousness, having been a self-taught and relatively unknown poet at the time that I completed the second version of the manuscript and with not so much as a presumption about my first novel's potential publication. I close with a simple thanks for your interest in my work.

*Te deseo mucha suerte con tu proyecto—Siempre,*

Ana Castillo

July 18, 1992 / 'Burque, Nuevo Méjico

y June 6, 1995, Gainesville, Florida

## Notes

1. The novel was published in 1986 and won the 1987 American Book Award. Published originally by Bilingual Press, the book is now more widely available in a paperback edition from Doubleday.

2. One of the strongest statements I have ever read about reading strategies comes from Patrocinio P. Schweickart, discussing feminist approaches. "The point is not merely to interpret literature in various ways; the point is to *change the world.* We cannot afford to ignore the activity of reading, for it is here that literature is realized as *praxis.* Literature acts on the world by acting on its readers." Reading and writing are critical aspects of "interpreting the world in order to change it" (39).

3. Although Teresa's primary community for her writing is herself and her best friend, the letters' content mentions other outlets. Because both Teresa and Alicia actively produce art (Teresa teaches and writes, although she does not mention publishing; Alicia meets with success as a visual artist), their artistic products can influence others. Teresa also selfconsciously and humorously notes the possibility of others reading the letters (88).

4. Given Alicia's art, Castillo presumes that nonverbal and verbal processes can yield new insight. Alicia's one-woman exhibit (described by Teresa in letter 34, the final letter for "the conformist" reader, but absent for "the cynic" and "the quixotic") contains a project titled *La casita*—mixed media pieces that analyze stereotypes of domestic women (118).

5. Norma Alarcón analyzes the way this distancing is linked to the emotions surrounding "romantic love" that "cannot be spoken of, intimately or directly" (103).

6. Spacks contends that most epistolary novels have "reinforced the status quo by assuming it. Declaring in their reliance on epistolary form their concern only with 'private' matters, women novelists apparently accepted the necessity of the system under which they suffered" (75). Janet G. Altman also finds that little epistolary fiction of the past "overtly challenged the privilege accorded to male conqueror figures" ("Graffigny's Epistemology" 173). Like Jane Austen, whose epistolary Lady Susan is a "female character capable of play and mastery through play" (Spacks 75), Castillo invents a heroine who uses word play and verbal mastery to explore a range of public and private issues.

7. Note, however, that fax machines, e-mail, and computers still often use the basic letter form. One difference is the speed of the letter's transmission. Video and audio recording devices certainly depart radically from the letter format, especially the first, which (especially when edited) can become nonlinear and contains different ways of reflecting on or analyzing

8. Maranda proposes that "semantic charters condition our thoughts and emotions. They are culture specific networks that we internalize as we undergo the process of socialization" and "have an inertia and a momentum of their own" (qtd. in Alarcón, 106).

## Brian Evenson (review date Spring 1997)

SOURCE: A review of *Loverboys,* in *Review of Contemporary Fiction,* Vol. 17, No. 1, Spring, 1997, p. 201.

[*In the following review, Evenson offers a mixed assessment of certain stories in* Loverboys, *but overall receives the collection favorably.*]

As one of the more accomplished of Latina writers, Castillo is often able to paint a vivid image of characters and the way in which they are affected by their sense of who they are and what their cultures tell them to be. Nevertheless, despite the fact that many of its individual stories are successful, *Loverboys* is interesting less for the stories taken separately than for the resonances that begin to become established between stories.

As intriguing as the book's culture depictions is the complex way in which gender and desire are figured and refigured from story to story. We have desire of all types, heterosexual and homosexual, from women who flirt with other women despite feeling themselves largely heterosexual, to the lesbian in the title story who finds herself drawn irresistibly to a young man. With the stories often showing passage from gay to straight relationships or vice versa, with the characters often torn between different desires, sexuality is envisioned as fluid. Sometimes this is echoed culturally when characters seem to experience similar fluidity in terms of possessing a social identity that makes multiple claims on the individual.

In addition to providing a number of stories that fit fairly snugly into our sense of what a conventional story is or does, Castillo also offers some that quietly test the boundaries. The three paragraph **"A Kiss Errant,"** for instance, reduces a relationship to a single gesture. Others, like **"Crawfish Love,"** seem to break off just as the story is beginning. **"If Not for the Blessing of a Son"** ends where it begins, the story cyclic in a way that suggests its enormous hidden secret. While some of the stories stumble—such as **"Who Was Juana Gallo?"** which telegraphs its ending or **"A Lifetime"** which risks sentimentality—few fall on their faces, and the other, stronger stories keep the collection moving forward.

**Colette Morrow (essay date Spring 1997)**

SOURCE: "Queering Chicano/a Narratives: Lesbian as a Healer, Saint and Warrior in Ana Castillo's *So Far from God*," in *Midwest Modern Language Association*, Vol. 30, Nos. 1–2, Spring, 1997, pp. 63–80.

[*In the following essay, Morrow examines the character Caridad in* So Far from God, *and how Caridad's lesbianism is a liberating factor in the male-dominant Mexican culture.*]

One of the most conspicuous features of Mexican-American liberatory and feminist discourses is their radicalization of traditional narratives for the purpose of social reform.[1] These discourses were constructed by Chicana/o rights activists in the 1960s and Chicana feminists in the 1970s and 1980s. Both civil rights and feminist discourses contextualized historic Mexican-American models of communal and individual identities in late-twentieth-century terms. Such revisionist pre-Columbian, colonial and postcolonial narratives argued for programs of ethnic and gender empowerment. Much of their appeal to Mexican-American audiences derived from their cultural familiarity. Contemporary ideas were framed in the conventions and icons used by old stories, for example, about Aztlán, the Aztec homeland, and Malinche/Malintzin, the sixteenth-century Aztec noblewoman who is said to have given birth to the first Mexicans and Mexican-Americans. Recently, as various discourse communities in the United States are discussing LesBiGay civil rights with increasing seriousness, this strategy of politicizing traditional narratives has been revived in Chicana fiction. Notably, Ana Castillo's 1993 novel *So Far from God* revises narratives commonly used to socialize Chicanas into traditional gender roles in order to refute a belief widely held among Mexican-Americans that lesbianism constitutes *ethnic* as well as sexual deviance, that lesbianism is a product and problem of Euro-American social values. Hence, in *So Far from God* an empowered lesbian subject assumes the roles of healer, virgin-saint, and warrior, the commonplaces for female identity in traditional Mexican and Native American discourses. This represents lesbianism as one of many culturally indigenous identities available to Mexican-American women rather than a betrayal, a "selling out" to the dominant culture.

Historic Mexican-American narratives have been invoked in service of social change since the civil rights movement of the 1960s when traditional stories and symbols were re-read from the perspective of contemporary liberation politics. For instance, during this period, the idea of Aztlán, a Chicano/a homeland, was used to establish a much needed sense of political solidarity among Mexican-Americans. Such solidarity, critical to the success of the civil rights movement, had been impeded by at least two factors. Mexican-Americans are dispersed throughout the United States, complicating attempts to organize a national effort. Moreover, they constitute a population group whose origins and identity lie in a broader experience of cultural diaspora.

In *Borderlands/La Frontera: The New Mestiza* Gloria Anzaldúa uses the metaphor of frontier borderlands, the strip of land where Mexico adjoins the United States, to describe this experience. She explains that the Chicano/a diaspora is a consequence of cultural formation that occurs "between the borders" of other ethnic and national populations rather than in a discrete geo-national unit.

> *Nosotros los* [We the] Chicanos straddle the borderlands. . . . We don't identify with the Anglo-American cultural values and we don't totally identify with the Mexican cultural values. We are a synergy of two cultures with various degrees of Mexicanness or Angloness. I have so internalized the borderland conflict that sometimes I feel like one cancels out the other and we are zero, nothing, no one. *A veces no soy nada ni nadie* [Sometimes I am neither nothing nor nobody].
>
> (62–63)

The idea of Aztlán, the Aztec homeland featured in pre-Columbian discourses, was revived during the Chicano/a rights movement to remedy the feeling of ethnic "nothingness" experienced by Anzaldza and others. The rhetoric of Aztlan played an important role in establishing a Chicano/a national sensibility and fostered Chicano/as' self-conscious identification of themselves as a 'people.' Aztlan supplied Chicano/as a symbolic space in which a communal identity could be forged and answered the need for a sense of unity among Mexican-Americans: *"Aztlán simboliza la unión espiritual de los chicanos, algo que se lleva en el corazón, no importa dónde se viva o se encuentre* [Aztlán symbolizes the spiritual union of the Chicanos, something that lifted up the heart, no matter where they lived or were encountered]" (Leal 22–23).

Furthermore, attempts to locate Aztlán in a specific geography, most often identified as the territory Mexico ceded to the United States in the 1848 Treaty of Guadalupe Hidalgo, supported claims of Chicano/a socio-economic entitlement. For example, the "Plan Espiritual de Aztlán," the Chicano/a rights manifesto drafted in 1969, figured twentieth-century Mexican-Americans as the political, spiritual, and material heirs of the Aztecs. This authorized the manifesto's argument that Mexican-American farm workers were entitled to a greater share of the economic benefits from the lands they farmed, the same lands that had been taken from their indigenous ancestors by the governments of Mexico and the United States.

While this rhetoric of Aztlán and other rhetorics of empowerment described and denounced Mexican-Americans' experience of disenfranchisement in the United States, they also perpetuated traditional, misogynous attitudes toward women, as Alma García recounts in "The Development of Chicana Feminist Discourse, 1970–1980." Such attitudes are epitomized in the traditional biography of La Malinche or Malintzin, perhaps the most popular Mexican and Mexican-American narrative of ethnic origin. According to this traditional version of her life's story, Malinche/Malintzin, an Aztec noblewoman, was responsible for Western Europeans' subordination of the indigenous peoples of Mexico. Malinche/Malintzin was the slave and mistress of the Spanish conqueror, Hernán Cortés. The children she bore him were "mixed-blood," the first *mestizas* and *mestizos*—Mexicans and Mexican-Americans. Hence, Malinche is blamed for giving birth to a "bastard" or hybrid "race," Octavio Paz tells us in *The Labyrinth of Solitude.* Paz represents Malinche acquiescing to sexual violation, a representation that suggests Malinche was a whore who betrayed her children to the conqueror even as she conceived them. Explaining how *chingada* [the female who is fucked] became a synonym for Malinche/Malintzin, Paz reveals how her story circulates in the Mexican and, we can infer, the Mexican-American social imagination: "The *Chingada* is the Mother forcibly opened, violated, deceived. . . . In effect, every woman—even when she gives herself willingly—is torn open by the man, is the *Chingada* . . ." (80).

Chicana feminists began to reread and rewrite such narratives when it became clear that "traditional gender roles . . . limited [Chicanas'] participation and acceptance within the Chicano movement" and that gender equity was not included in the civil rights agenda (García 221). As disenfranchised by a patriarchal cultural ethic as by the dominant Euro-American ideology, Chicanas constructed "alternate mythical and even historical accounts of women" (Ordóñez 19). For example, Norma Alarcón, in "Chicana's Feminist Literature: A Re-Vision Through Malintzin/or Malintzin: Putting Flesh Back on the Object," imputed pejorative representations of Malinche/Malinztin to male authorship: "The male myth of Malintzin is made to seem betrayal first of all in her very sexuality, which makes it nearly impossible at any given moment to go beyond the vagina as the supreme site of evil . . ." (183). Other feminist accounts, such as those by Juana Armanda Alegría in *Psicologma de las mexicanas* and Marta Cotera in *Diosa y Hembra,* provided new perspectives on Malinche/Malintzin by reconsidering her relationship with Cortés (Cotera 30–35; Alegría 65–79). Emphasizing that she was sold into the service of Western Europeans by her own family, they showed that she was betrayed rather than a betrayer. These feminist revisions contended that Malinche/Malintzin, fluent in Spanish as well as several dialects, was Cortés's advisor and translator. They depicted her as intelligent and authoritative rather than colluding in her own sexual violation or implicated in the subjugation of her descendants. Her role in the Spanish conquest, explained Cordelia Candelaria, was a model for Chicanas resisting traditional gender roles: "La Malinche embodies those personal characteristics—such as intelligence, initiative, adaptability, and leadership—which are most often associated with Mexican-American women unfettered by traditional restraints against public achievement" (qtd. in Fox 22). For three decades such revisionist narratives both reshaped and embodied the "personal and collective identity" of Mexican-American women (Ordóñez 19). They participated in revising traditional models of identity, offered women alternative subjective formulae, and involved writers and readers in radical acts of subject constitution whose scope was both individual and communal.

One of the reasons both these revisionist rhetorics—feminist and Chicano/a rights—appealed to Mexican-American audiences is that the programs they advanced were phrased in traditional, culturally familiar narratives. The trope of Aztlán as an idyllic homeland stolen from the heirs of the Aztecs supported the political mobilization of Mexican-Americans. Narratives recasting La Malinche as a model of leadership and resistance rather than submission and sexual surrender argued the cultural appropriateness of feminism. This strategy, slightly modified, is repeated in Ana Castillo's ***So Far from God*** in order to refute a belief widely held among Mexican-Americans that lesbianism constitutes ethnic deviance, that lesbianism is a troubling manifestation of Euro-American socio-sexual mores.

Lesbianism almost unanimously is designated a category of ethnic and class alterity by an otherwise ideologically diverse Mexican-American population. Colloquially labeled a "white" or "Anglo thing" by Mexican-Americans whose political and religious beliefs range from traditional to radical, lesbianism is excluded from culturally appropriate identities. As Carla Trujillo explains in her insightful essay, "Chicana Lesbians: Fear and Loathing in the Chicano Community," a woman cannot be both lesbian and Mexican-American unless she is a *vendida*—a sellout or ethnic traitor. This belief was well summarized by a young woman attending the 1993 conference of the National Association of Chicano Studies (NACS) in San Diego. During a session on the future of lesbian and gay studies in NACS, she said:

> I'm a heterosexual and I'm really surprised actually to be here in a place where there's 50 to 60 Chicanos and Chicanas and they say this is an issue in our community. . . . I'm really surprised because to me this is an Anglo thing and I'm not trying to be racist or anything.

Asked "what's an Anglo thing?" by another audience member, she continued: "I mean to be homosexual. . . . To me it's just so different because I never thought it was in our community. . . . It's something from another race, another culture. I'm really surprised." Such a response to lesbianism, argues Trujillo, originates in a sexist as well as homophobic/heterosexist ethic: "Chicana lesbians are perceived as a greater threat to the Chicano community because their existence disrupts the established order of male dominance, and raises the consciousness of many Chicanas regarding their own independence and control" (255).

This ethic, writes Cherríe Moraga in a series of essays in *The Last Generation,* caused lesbians and gays to be excluded from psychological and spiritual citizenship in the Chicano/a nation/union conceived during the civil rights movement: "When 'El Plan Espiritual de Aztlán' was conceived a generation ago, lesbians and gay men were not envisioned as members of the 'house'; we were not . . . counted as members of the 'bronze continent'" (159). Lesbians and gays subsequently were left out of the Chicano/a rights movement because it was organized on the model of the traditional Chicano family:

> The preservation of the Chicano *familia* became the *Movimiento*'s mandate and within this constricted *"familia"* structure, Chicano politicos ensured that the patriarchal father figure remained in charge both in their private and political lives. . . . In the name of this "culturally correct" *familia,* certain topics were censored both in cultural and political spheres as not "socially relevant" to Chicano and not typically sanctioned in the Mexican household. These issues included female sexuality generally and male homosexuality and lesbianism specifically. . . . In the process, the Chicano Movement forfeited the participation and vision of some very significant female and gay leaders and never achieved the kind of harmonious Chicano *"familia"* they ostensibly sought.
>
> (Moraga 158)

**So Far from God** attempts to redress such exclusion of lesbians and gays by countering charges that "lesbian" is an ethnically alien model of identity for Mexican-American women and by attacking patriarchal cultural institutions that perpetuate those charges. Set in the *Sangre de Cristo* [Blood of Christ] Mountains of New Mexico, where historically sheepherding was the primary economic enterprise, **So Far from God** chronicles two decades in the lives of Sofi and her four daughters, Fe [Faith], Esperanza [Hope], Caridad [Charity], and la Loca [the Crazy One]. Their stories are told in Castillo's trademark style, a conspicuously ironic form of magical realism that in this book facilitates a lesbianization of Mexican, Mexican Catholic and Native American discourses.

This lesbianization of traditional discourses is brought about through the figure of Caridad who, unexpectedly falling in love with a woman, eventually occupies each of the principal models of female identity offered by these discourses. Caridad first experiences lesbian desire when she undertakes a Lenten Week pilgrimage to *el Santuario de Chimayo* [the Chimayo shrine] as part of her training in *curanderismo,* the arts of spiritual, psychological and physical healing that originated in pre-Columbian Latin America. At the shrine, a chapel built on lands sacred to Native Americans where a statue of Christ had been found in the nineteenth century, Caridad becomes infatuated at her first sight of another pilgrim, a woman.

The setting and circumstances of this moment clearly foreground it in multiple spiritual and religious traditions. As an apprentice *curandera,* a practitioner of *curanderismo,* Caridad embodies a pre-Columbian model of female identity while participating in a Mexican Catholic ritual at a site considered holy by Mexican and Roman Catholics and Native Americans. Caridad's response to her desire for a woman and, in turn, the community's response to Caridad lends a lesbian inflection to these traditions and their discourses.

Caridad is so affected by the woman, literally and metaphorically idolizing her, that she disappears from her community and for a year lives in a mountain cave. When discovered, Caridad resists returning to society, is beatified in local legend, and becomes a media icon venerated as the "handmaiden of Christ" (87). Consecrated by popular acclaim, Caridad comes to embody a feminist version of a second model of female identity—saint—that was introduced to Latin America by Spanish colonizers. When Caridad's story circulates further, among Native American Yaquis, she embodies yet a third identity, for she is said to be the ghost of Lozen, a legendary female Apache warrior. This convergence of three subjective forms in the figure of Caridad, brought about through the agency of lesbian desire, demonstrates that *lesbianismo* [Chicana lesbianism] is culturally authentic and profoundly transformational. Moreover, lesbian desire is portrayed as a force empowering Chicanas to resist sexist/heterosexist forms of control.

In her role as *curandera,* Caridad receives, preserves, and exercises a form of knowledge, *curanderismo,* that emerged from the synthesis of fifteenth-century Spanish and Latin American medical practices. Fifteenth-century Spanish medical theories, combining the ideas of Galen,

Aristotle and Hippocrates, were brought to Latin America by Spanish friars. These theories were especially compatible with the beliefs of indigenous populations, as Ari Kiev explains in *Curanderismo: Mexican-American Folk Psychiatry.* In Mexico, the two knowledge paradigms intermixed, fused by *curandero/as* into an integrated set of medical practices which have remained intact through the twentieth century (Kiev 22–30).

Both traditionally and in contemporary practice, the *curandera* mediates multiple domains—spiritual, temporal and cultural—for the community because she is understood as simultaneously occupying the borders of the natural and supernatural. This unique position endows the power of spiritual, psychological and physical healing on the *curandera,* whose cures typically reflect the belief that health is a composite of all three categories.

In addition to fulfilling her role as healer, the *curandera* often negotiates large-scale social changes for the community. Trained in an ancient form of knowledge but practicing in present day United States, the Mexican-American *curandera* mediates two historical times and three cultures—Mexican, Mexican-American, and Euro-American. As Kiev explains, she "represents a link with Mexican traditions and can interpret contemporary problems and conflicts with a time-tested . . . ideology" that continues to hold meaning for the community (38). Therefore, in the figure of the *curandera,* unlike the lesbian, alterity betokens authority, and the *curandera*'s position at the borders of her community is cause for centrality within it. *Curanderas* are greatly revered, and in Latin America some achieve considerable fame as healers and mystics. For instance, "La Madre María," a *curandera* who practiced in Buenos Aires, is remembered as a saint because her cures were effected through her great faith, Raul Ortelli tells us in *Brujos y curanderas,* describing widespread popular devotion to Madre Maria which continued years after her death.[2]

In *So Far from God,* however, Caridad initially is better known for her frequent and energetic sexual encounters with men than for her healing powers. These encounters began when she discovered that her husband, Memo, had impregnated another woman. The community interpreted Caridad's sexual energy as promiscuity. Therefore, when she is viciously raped and mutilated by the *malogra,* the evil wool spirit of local legend, it is widely understood as the natural consequence of promiscuity, an interpretation that embroiled her father in numerous fights: "Domingo had heard many insulting stories about his daughter and had defended her honor more than once in Valencia County bars when it was suggested that she had for all intents and purposes 'asked for it' when she was attacked" (83).

Disparaged by the community, Caridad's sexual energy is transformed into healing power after she miraculously recovers from the *malogra* attack. Chapter four, "Of the Telling of Our Clairvoyant Caridad Who After Being Afflicted with the Pangs of Love Disappears and Upon Discovery is Henceforth Known as *La Armitaña,*" relates how Caridad fell in love with a woman. The ironic voice of the narrator explains that in the eyes of doña Felicia, a *curandera* of many years' experience, Caridad's sexual energy was an abundance of heart that made her ideally suited to study the mystical arts of healing:

> It was a funny thing because you might figure that after what happened to her not only with Memo, but especially because of that nightmarish night in Caridad's life, she might have become an embittered woman, who hated men for having served little purpose in her life but to bring her misery and shame. But she didn't. Caridad was incapable of hating anyone or anything, which is why doña Felicia had elected her heiress to her healing legacy. Hating came quite easy in this life of injustices, doña Felicia figured, but having an abundant heart took the kind of resiliency a curandera required.
>
> (77)

Caridad acquires the functions and authority of the *curandera* when she begins her apprenticeship with doña Felicia. Applying Kiev's description of the *curandera*'s social role to Caridad allows us to see her as a link with tradition, a character who keeps ancient practices and forms of knowledge alive. When she experiences the sexual energy that qualified her to become a *curandera* as lesbian desire, an oral tradition that *curanderas* often are lesbians is textualized.[3] Such textualization of this oral tradition *explicitly* represents lesbianism as central to Mexican-American culture because the *curandera* occupies a central position in it. Lesbianism is portrayed as being within rather than alien to Mexican-American culture. Hence, the figure of Caridad interprets lesbian identity as a culturally indigenous subjective possibility for Mexican-American women just as previous revisions of the male myth of Malintzin provided a cultural context for feminist agendas.

Framing Caridad's initial experience of lesbian desire in Mexican Catholic rituals, iconography and discourses also argues that lesbianism is a culturally appropriate identity. Roman Catholicism was imposed upon the indigenous populations of Latin America in the Spanish Conquest and remains a dominant socio-cultural construct. Historically, its ideologies have organized multiple aspects of Mexican and Mexican-American culture, especially gender relationships. Contextualizing a lesbian love story in the forms and practices of Mexican Catholicism claims a central cultural position for homosexuality.

One such practice exercised by New Mexican Catholics living in the region where the novel is set is a Holy Week procession to *el Santuario de Chimayo.* Significantly, the history of this chapel is linked intertextually with Native American, Mexican colonial, and New Mexican Catholic religious narratives. Before the arrival of Spanish Catholics in New Mexico, Native Americans attributed healing powers to the land on which the chapel sits. Early in the nineteenth century, an incarnation of Christ known as *Nuestro Señor de Esquipulas, el Cristo Negro* [Our Lord of Esquipulas, the Black Christ] came to be worshipped by New Mexican Catholics living in the region. *Nuestro Señor de Esquipulas,* according to Stephen F. Borhegyi in his history of *El Santuario de Chimayo,* is a statue that was used by sixteenth-century Spaniards to convert the indigenous population of Esquipulas, Guatemala, to Christianity. Carved from a dark wood, this image was more appealing to native Guatemalans than Eurocentric likenesses of Christ. A chapel honoring *Nuestro Señor de Esquipulas* was built at a site in Esquipulas where, like Chimayo, the soil is thought to have curative properties. Borhegyi speculates that someone transferred worship of *Nuestro Señor de Esquipulas* to New Mexico because of this connection between the otherwise disparate places. Other explanations are articulated in local legend.[4] The most widely known, cited by Castillo in **So Far from God,** is that during Holy Week a Penitente brother, a member of a Mexican Catholic fraternity, who was performing penances in the *Sangre de Cristo* hills saw a light coming out of the ground. Digging, he found a statue of *Nuestro Señor de Esquipulas* near the Santa Cruz river. The statue, identical to the Guatemalan Christ except that it is not black, was installed at the Santuario de Chimayo. This spot continues to play a prominent role in the spiritual practices of regional Mexican and Roman Catholics as well as Christian and non-Christian Native Americans. Annually, thousands of pilgrims honor *Nuestro Señor de Esquipulas* by journeying to the *Santuario* which the archbishop of New Mexico, Michael J. Sheehan, S.T.L., J.C.D., recently described as "*un centro de fe tricultural* [a tri-cultural center of faith]."[5]

During such a pilgrimage to *el Santuario* Caridad falls in love with a lesbian: "She was dark. Indian or Mexican. Black, black hair. Big sturdy thighs" (79). Caridad first sees the woman on Good Friday when she and doña Felicia reach the *Santuario* after a three-day journey on foot:

> It was then . . . that she stopped short at the sight of the most beautiful woman she had ever seen sitting on the adobe wall that surrounds the sanctuary. At that moment the woman also turned toward Caridad, but since she was wearing sunglasses, Caridad wasn't sure whether her gaze was being returned. "Come on, come on," doña Felicia summoned Caridad the way one does with children. Caridad, completely overwhelmed by the sight of the woman, blushed and followed doña Felicia into the church without a word.
>
> (76)

This and subsequent passages detailing Caridad's feelings for the beautiful Chicana lesbian are framed in the conventions of Roman and Mexican Catholic apparitional narratives relating encounters with a divine or sanctified figure, often the Virgin Mary. Clearly, the tale recounting the discovery of the statue of *Nuestro Señor de Esquipulas* at Chimayo is a variant of such narratives, but the most influential Mexican Catholic apparitional narrative is the archetypal story of Juan Diego's encounter with the *Virgen de Guadalupe.*[6] In fact, it provides one of the behavioral models traditionally prescribed Chicanas, the virgin-saint.

Although each apparitional story differs in detail, such accounts share a number of distinctive narrative conventions. Vision recipients are astonished when they first see a divine figure. Sometimes they doubt the vision's authenticity, thinking that it is a hallucination caused by a debilitating physical condition such as illness. The divine figure provides a variety of proofs to reassure them and to persuade others that the vision is authentic. Vision recipients characteristically assume a posture that signifies respect and awe for the divine figure. Frequently, their eyes are averted from the vision because it is too majestic to be seen by mortals. Vision recipients inevitably are transformed by the encounter, a transformation that often is consummated by gazing directly on the divine figure. Usually, a miraculous event or healing marks vision recipients' transformation. Such miracles almost always cause the community to recognize vision recipients' transformation as beatifying. As in the story of Juan Diego's encounter with the *Virgen de Guadalupe,* vision recipients *and* the divine figure subsequently become objects of veneration, the divine figure often known by the place where the apparition occurred. The Virgin Mary, for example, is variously identified as Our Lady of Lourdes, Our Lady of Fatima, Our Lady of Knock, etc., because she appeared at these locations.

Such narratives are composed within the patriarchal cultures of Roman and Mexican Catholicism and long have been critiqued by feminists for socializing women into traditional, limiting gender roles. For example, the story of the *Virgen de Guadalupe,* according to Trujillo's analysis, has been employed to exercise control over Chicanas by mandating motherhood and, further, by teaching that passive suffering renders the experience of motherhood redemptive:

> Religion, based on the tradition of patriarchal control and sexual, emotional, and psychological repression, has historically been a dual means of hope for a better afterlife and social control in the present one. Personified by the *Virgen de Guadalupe,* the concept of motherhood and martyrdom go hand in hand in the Catholic religion.
>
> (258)

The figure of the Virgin Mother, Mary, has been so important in perpetuating this and related beliefs regulating Mexican American women that they are referred to as *marianismo* by behavioral scientists. *Marianismo,* according to Rosa Maria Gil and Carmen Inoa Vazquez in *The Maria Paradox: How Latinas Can Merge Old World Traditions with New World Self-Esteem,* masks women's subordination to men as veneration and adoration. In general terms, *marianismo* inhibits women's self-realization: "The noble sacrifice of self (the ultimate expression of *marianismo*) is the force which has for generations prevented Hispanic women from even entertaining the notion of personal validation" (7–8). Specifically, female sexuality is the object of *marianismo* regulation. Olivia Espín writes that women's sexual repression is the consequence of the mother/martyr mandate embodied in the figure of the Virgin Mother.

> To shun sexual pleasure and to regard sexual pleasure as an unwelcome obligation toward her husband a nec-

essary evil in order to have children may be seen as a manifestation of virtue. In fact, some women even express pride at their own lack of sexual pleasure or desire.

(qtd. in Castillo, *Massacre* 125)

Castillo shows, moreover, that the belief that women's sexual pleasure is evil is problematic when internalized by Mexican American women, especially lesbians:

> The Mexican Catholic lesbian, rejected by family and ostracized by her immediate community, may find it painful and even impossible to acknowledge a direct connection between her faith and the rejection she suffers as a woman who loves women because Catholicism is so much a part of her sense of self.

(*Massacre* 139)

The "choice" this ethic forces on Mexican Catholic lesbians, Castillo suggests, is to reject their culture and religion or to reject themselves.

Offering a representation of lesbian desire as empowering and *sanctifying*, **So Far from God** repudiates the sexist/heterosexist belief that it is evil for women to claim their sexuality and take pleasure in it. This representation is constructed by using the narrative conventions of apparitional literature to organize Caridad's performance of lesbian desire in her encounters with the beautiful woman. In initial encounters, the woman occupies the position of the divine figure while Caridad operates as the vision recipient. This configuration is suggested by Caridad's astonishment at her first sight of the woman. Summoned into the chapel by doña Felicia, Caridad "could do nothing but think of the woman on the wall" (76). Unconvinced that the sight of a woman could induce such overwhelming desire, Caridad ascribes her feelings to the affects of the hot sun: "Maybe she had sunstroke and had just imagined her. She was exhausted and nearly dehydrated and surely she could not have experienced what she felt throughout her entire body just from the sight of a woman!" (76). A second vision of the beautiful woman, however, offers proof that the woman is real and that Caridad's desire is authentic:

> But as soon as they were outside, coming around from the back of the church, she saw the woman in question, more real than before, still on the wall. Moreover, the woman on the wall was looking over her shoulders in Caridad's direction!
>
> . . . . .
>
> All the while, Caridad kept sneaking glances over at the woman on the wall who, as far as she could tell, was unabashedly staring at her as well.

(76)

Significantly, the two women's gazes intersect, a moment that parallels the juncture in apparitional narratives when the vision recipient looks directly at the divine figure. This intersection of the women's gazes catalyzes a multivalenced set of transformations that have far reaching consequences in terms of character and plot development and as a response to the idea that lesbian identity and desire constitute cultural betrayal.

Having her gaze reciprocated by the lesbian is crucial to Caridad's development as a character and the telling of her life's story. Like vision recipients in Roman and Mexican Catholic apparitional narratives, Caridad is transformed. Gazing upon the lesbian and having her gaze returned is healing, for it restores her ability to love. It cures Caridad of the heartsickness caused by male transgression, her betrayal and abandonment by her husband, Memo, that had led to so many loveless sexual encounters with men: "for the first time in years, since way before the attack, her heart was renewed, moved by another human being" (79).

Caridad's recovery, literally a recovery of desire, leads to another transformation, her sanctification, for Caridad is beatified by popular acclaim at the end of a year-long pilgrimage that she is prompted to undertake by the sight of the lesbian. When she returns, Caridad is venerated as *la Santa Armitaña*.[7] The spectacular nature of these transformations, miraculous healing and sanctification, suggests that the intersection of lesbian gazes is analogous to the exchange of gazes featured in apparitional narratives—it has supernatural force. Likewise, lesbian desire is shown to have parallel consequences to encountering a divine being. On one hand, the beautiful Chicana lesbian is herself divinized, both in Caridad's perception and by the narrative devices framing the story. On the other hand, Caridad plays a role in the community reminiscent of Juan Diego's and vision recipients in other more conventional apparitional narratives.

In spite of its spectacular motivation and ending, Caridad's pilgrimage has an ordinary enough beginning. Seeking to understand her inexplicable desire for a woman, Caridad sets out to meet her. She asks doña Felicia to approach the woman: "Will you go up to that woman for me and ask her where she thinks she knows me from . . . if that's why she keeps looking at me?" (78). However, the woman has disappeared from the wall. When doña Felicia points out that the crowd of worshippers at the *Santuario* makes it impractical to seek out and speak with the woman, Caridad prostrates herself in prayer-like despair:

> Caridad sat back down. Her whole body was affected by a stranger and she couldn't explain why. And now the woman on the wall was lost to her in the thick of the crowd. In total despair, sitting on the ground with her legs tucked beneath her, she threw her body forward, arms stretched out, and let out a deep sigh of despair like a prayer.

(78)

Significantly, this despairing, full-body genuflection honors the beautiful Chicana lesbian rather than Our Lord of Esquipulas. The woman clearly has replaced the Black Christ and Chimayo's healing earth as the object of Caridad's attention, of her adoration. That Caridad literally as well as metaphorically worships the lesbian is confirmed for the reader when the narrator refers to the beautiful Chicana as "Woman-on-the-wall." Later, this appellation is expanded to "Woman-on-the-wall-now-on-a-hill" and "Woman-on-the-wall-later-woman-on-a-hill-with-someone-else." Like the titles given divine figures in apparitional literature, these names for the lesbian are derived from the site(s) where she appeared.

Despairing but undeterred, Caridad sets out to find the beautiful woman. Spotting her on a hill, Caridad climbs toward her and greets the woman and her companion. Caridad falls in love when the lesbian returns her greeting which, says the narrator, becomes "the most dramatic moment in Caridad's life thus far" (80). Overwhelmed, Caridad retreats down the hill and, accompanied by doña Felicia, leaves *el Santuario*. Once home, Caridad is obsessed by the memory of Woman-on-the-wall. Unable to sleep, she cleans house without cessation. Intervening, doña Felicia suggests that she pray for enlightenment. Caridad prays until she passes out two days later. Revived by doña Felicia but still unenlightened, Caridad sets out for a mineral bath at *Ojo Caliente* [Hot Eye] but never arrives there. Instead, she retreats to an isolated cave in the *Sangre de Cristo* mountains where she first felt lesbian desire.

Despite a search effort and the prayers of doña Felicia, it is a year before Caridad is discovered by doña Felicia's godson, Francisco el Penitente, who, as his name indicates, is a member of the same fraternity as the man who found the statue of *Nuestro Señor de Esquipulas* at Chimayo. Francisco and three of his fellow *Penitentes* spot Caridad as they are riding horseback in the mountains. What follows is a feminist-lesbian miracle, for Caridad emerges from her cave empowered to resist the ecclesiastical, patriarchal control embodied in Francisco and his fellow *Penitentes*:

> "You're coming with us!" one of the brothers said sternly. . . .
>
> Caridad shook her head. The man dismounted from his Arabian steed and went over to her to pull her firmly toward his horse. She resisted and let herself drop on the ground. He bent down to take her up in his arms, figuring she would be even easier to get on the horse without any resistance but he couldn't lift her. "What the . . . !" he said, dumbfounded at how heavy she was although she was only half his size.
>
> The other man joined him and finally Francisco el Penitente and yet the young woman could not be budged. The first brother, irate that his strength seemed no match for such a slight person, motioned to yank her along by the hair.
>
> (86–87)

Francisco piously interprets Caridad's strength as a sign of holiness: "Stop," he calls, "It is not for us to bring this handmaiden of Christ back. . . . Can't you all see that? It is not our Lord's will" (87). But Caridad is nothing like any "handmaiden of Christ" depicted in Roman and Mexican Catholic discourses. In fact, Caridad's refusal to obey the men radically revises the model of female obedience and submission to patriarchal authority personified in the female saints and virgins who populate Roman and Mexican Catholic apparitional narratives.[8] Caridad resists the men rather than surrendering to them and is miraculously strengthened because of it.

The news "that a woman hermit was living in a cave . . . and that she resisted with passive yet herculean strength three men who tried to carry her home" spreads quickly. Revised in the repetition, the dimensions of Caridad's resistance are amplified to the extent that she is portrayed as a female warrior before whom men bow in supplication:

> The three men whom Caridad resisted by making herself into lead weight turned into a score of men as the story spread. Francisco's humble gesture of delivering a prayer for her well-being became the act of many men brought to their knees before the holy hermit, all begging forgiveness for their audacious attempt at manhandling her. It was said that she lifted the very horse that the *hermano* [brother] had tried to force her to mount—with him on it—but out of benevolence brought it back down safely without so much as spooking the horse with her defiant magic.
>
> (87–88)

A series of exaggerations and embellishments thus amplifies the challenge to male authority depicted in the story of Caridad's "rescue": Caridad's strength is magnified; the number of men is increased; and the men are depicted begging for forgiveness. In addition, Caridad's original gesture of passive resistance—refusing to mount the horse—is portrayed as the more aggressive act of lifting the horse and rider. Rather than merely adding detail to the story, this revision is a play on the commonplace sexual metaphor in which riding signifies heterosexual intercourse. Not only does Caridad refuse to mount (ride), but she mounts (lifts up) the horse with its male rider still in the saddle. When read in the context of the embedded sexual innuendo, Caridad's *active* resistance to the male rider bespeaks a woman in control of her own sexuality, a control that she gained through the agency of lesbian desire. This representation of a physically and sexually empowered woman contrasts radically with the community's belief, revealed when she was attacked by the *malogra*, that Caridad colluded in her own sexual violation by men. Hence, the story of Caridad's "rescue" replaces this image of Caridad with the vision of a woman defying traditional heterosexist constructions of gender.

The farther this story of female empowerment spreads, the greater impact it has on the community. During Holy Week the local population forsakes their churches to make pilgrimages to Caridad's cave:

> [H]undreds of people made their way up the mountain to La Caridad's cave in hopes of obtaining her blessing and just as many with hopes of being cured of some ailment or another. Not only the *nuevo mejicano*-style Spanish Catholics went to see her but also Natives

from the pueblos, since for more than a year Caridad's disappearance had been a mystery through the state and her spartan mountain survival alone seemed incredible.

(87)

Significantly, traditional religious practices in the region are disrupted by the spectacle of a woman successfully living outside patriarchal society for a year and subsequently defying male attempts to re-impose control over her. Caridad's cave replaces the *Santuario de Chimayo* and local churches as sites of worship. Caridad is sanctified by the community's application to her for blessing and healing just as recipients of divine visions and extraordinary *curanderas* are popularly venerated. In Caridad's case, however, her transformation is achieved through the agency of lesbian desire.

This phenomenon attracts media attention. By the time the story is reported in the newspapers, Caridad's beatification for feminist resistance to male authority is consummated in the imagination of the community:

> [T]he daily newspapers had reported the pilgrimage to her mountain with "eyewitnesses" who had supposedly seen her. Some claimed to have been touched and blessed by her and still some others insisted that she had cured them! One man said that when he laid eyes on her, he saw a beautiful halo radiate around her whole body, like the *Virgen de Guadalupe,* and that she had relieved him of his drinking problem. One woman showed the press a small scrap of cloth that she said she had torn from *la Santita Armitaña's* robe.
>
> (90)

These reports shift Caridad from the position of vision recipient to divine figure. Caridad, the reports claim, miraculously cures physical and social ills. She, like the *Virgen de Guadalupe,* is said to emanate a gold, glowing light. The Mexican Catholic community subsequently borrows traditional forms and practices used to venerate the *Virgen de Guadalupe* and *Nuestro Señor de Esquipulas* and adapts them to its worship of Caridad. Hence, commonplace items associated with Caridad are treated as sacred relics just as the faithful collect and cherish saints' artifacts and other articles such as holy medals, prayer cards, statues, etc. As a result, veneration of a feminist, lesbian *curandera* replaces worship of figures such as *Nuestro Señor de Esquipulas* and the *Virgen de Guadalupe* whose sanctity is licensed by ecclesial authority. This revision of religious iconography, discourses and practices argues that Mexican Catholic forms of spirituality and lesbianism are compatible rather than oppositional. Consequently, Mexican Catholic lesbians need not feel compelled choose between religion/culture and self.

In addition to being designated a feminist-style saint in the tradition of Mexican and Roman Catholicism, Caridad comes to be associated with a legendary female warrior, Lozen, figured in New Mexican, Native American discourses. When her story circulates beyond the immediate area of Chimayo to Sonora where, the narrator tells us, the Yaqui live, Caridad is acclaimed as the ghost of Lozen, an "Apache mystic woman warrior." Lozen, according to the narrator, was the sister of chief Victorio "who had vowed 'to make war against the white man forever'" (88). The only woman among thirty-eight male warriors, Lozen alerted the company when the enemy approached: "being warned herself first by the tingling of her palms and her hands turning purple" (88). Like Caridad, Lozen is said to have travelled through the wilderness alone. Lozen's strength during this journey was derived from her spirituality: "When left by herself, Lozen turned toward the four directions and sang to her god Ussen to guide her through the wilderness" (88). Learning of Caridad's similar, year-long sojourn in the mountains, the Yaqui attribute her ability to resist Francisco and his fellow Penitentes to being Lozen's spirit-memory rather than the handmaiden of Christ.

The appropriation of Caridad's story by each of these discourses clearly executes a multi-directional parody of various social and discursive conventions. Framing a lesbian love story in the conventions of Roman and Mexican Catholic apparitional literatures satirizes these discourses and the social practices associated with them. Likewise, ironically exaggerating—burlesquing—the hyperbole that marks media and oral storytelling parodies these discourses as well.

Nevertheless, serious claims about subject constitution are articulated in the passages dedicated to Caridad's first lesbian love and its consequences for her and the community. The story of Caridad in ***So Far from God*** revises/lesbianizes images of women proffered by three discursive traditions: Mexican/Mexican-American *curanderismo,* Mexican Catholic *marianismo,* and Native American accounts of resistance against Euro-American aggression. It textualizes the oral tradition that some *curanderas* are lesbian. It revises Mexican Catholic narratives used to socialize Chicanas into traditional gender roles by projecting the spectacle of a feminist/lesbian saint. Finally, it lesbianizes the model of female identity articulated in Native American discourses by figuring Caridad the spirit of the Apache warrior Lozen. Consequently, multiple and diverse subjective modes available to Chicanas—the *curandera,* the saint, and warrior—are conflated in the figure of Caridad through the agency of lesbian desire. As a fictional character, therefore, Caridad actualizes Castillo's contention "that lesbians can "remain true to a . . . Mexican/Chicana/Latina/India/Mestiza . . . socio-political identity" while exploring their "erotic selves" (***Massacre*** 45). This, in turn, demonstrates that lesbianism and Mexican-American identity are overlapping categories, mutually inclusive rather than exclusive and refutes the idea that homosexuality constitutes ethnic betrayal. Hence, ***So Far from God*** makes a space for lesbians in the Mexican American community.

*Notes*

1. I wish to make explicit my position in relation to Chicano/a scholarship and literature. I am a Euro-American feminist and lesbian rearing a Mexican-

American daughter. Hence, my critical perspective is shaped by the anomalous experience of being simultaneously inside and outside Chicano/a culture.

This paper is written primarily for a non-Chicano/a audience unfamiliar with Chicano/a discourses. Consequently, translations from Spanish to English are provided in the text.

I also wish to thank my colleagues, Jane Campbell, Theresa Carilli, Julie Hagemann, Janet Jackson, Zenobia Mistri, and Robert Selig, for their generous assistance on this project. Their insightful comments have contributed significantly to my reading of Ana Castillo's *So Far from God*.

2. Such veneration of *curandero/as* is not uncommon. They are commonly considered holy figures and, as Ortelli explains, can be revered as saints. Consequently, some theologians think of *curanderismo* as competing with institutional religions for devotees. In contrast, most practitioners of curanderismo consider themselves collaborating with institutional religions to sustain the good health and spirituality of their clients. For most, *curanderismo* is a vocation to which they are called by God. A variety of studies show that consulting *curandero/as* about both spiritual and physical concerns is commonplace because, in part, *curanderismo* is grounded in the premise that spirituality and materiality are integrally linked.

3. I refer to the belief that some *curanderas* are lesbians as primarily an oral tradition because only once have I seen it explicitly stated in Chicana fiction, critical scholarship, or in sociological studies of *curanderismo*. Moraga, in *The Last Generation*, includes *curanderas* in a list of lesbian and gay Chicano/as who play a significant role in the community: "*Somos activistas, académicos y artistas, parteras y políticos, curanderas y campesinos* [We are activists, academics and artists, midwives and politicians, healers and farm workers]" (164–65). The healer, of course, is a prominent figure in contemporary lesbian culture, and lesbian and gay social histories such as Judy Grahn's *Another Mother Tongue: Gay Words, Gay Words* give healers a central place in the "mythic/spiritual/religious aspects of Gay culture" (120). Grahn identifies lesbian and gay healers and rituals in contemporary and historic cultures: ancient Greek, Celtic, Native American, African, Caribbean, etc.

4. The ironic explanation offered by the narrator of *So Far from God* is that with the appearance of *Nuestro Señor de Esquipulas* at Chimayo, "the Catholic Church endorsed as sacred what the Native peoples had known all along since the beginning of time" (73).

5. *El Santuario de Chimayo* also is featured in one of the poems, "La Despedida" ["The Final Verse"], in Moraga's *Last Generation*. In this poem, *El Santuario* is described as a place of healing and renewal where spiritual rebirth is made possible by the holy earth: "*Soy la santa* [I am the saint] / five feet of human / dimension and heart. / I birth electric / from the flames of the faithful. / Their burnt offerings singe / my cracked desert lips. Holy water / *lagrinas* [tears] stain my ashen cheeks" (48).

6. The following version of the story of Juan Diego and the *Virgen de Guadalupe* is taken from *A Woman Clothed with the Sun: Eight Great Appearances of Our Lady in Modern Times*, edited by John J. Delaney. According to an account written in Nahuatl (c. 1560), in December 1531 the *Virgen de Guadalupe* appeared to an Aztec-Mexican field worker named Juan Diego at Tepeyac, a hill where a temple dedicated to the Aztec mother-goddess formerly had stood. Speaking in Juan Diego's dialect, the Virgin charged him with petitioning the Spanish Bishop-elect of Mexico City, Juan de Zumarraga, to build a church at Tepeyac in her honor. When Zumarraga refused, the Virgin again appeared to Juan Diego, instructing him to repeat the request. This time, Zumarraga asked for a sign from the Virgin. When the Virgin appeared a third time, she caused exotic Castilian roses to grow on the cold, barren hill and simultaneously appeared to his dying uncle, Juan Bernardino, curing him and announcing her name. Furthermore, her image was imprinted on the *tilma* [an Aztec-style cape] in which Juan Diego carried the roses to Zumarraga. A chapel and a hermitage for Juan Diego were built on the hill at Tepeyac; eight million Native Mexicans were baptized between 1532 and 1538. Until his death in 1548, Juan Diego received pilgrims at the hermitage where he recounted his story and displayed the *tilma*. Juan Diego continues to be honored in celebrations venerating the *Virgen de Guadalupe*, who has been named the patron of the Americas by the Roman Catholic church.

7. This term conflates two words, *arma* and *ermitaña/o*. *Arma* translates as weapon or arm while *ermitaña/o* is a hermit. Consequently we can understand *La Santa Armitaña* as a play on words that refers to Caridad's pilgrimage as well as to the physical strength (symbolic of her empowerment) that she acquires during this year.

8. Female martyrs who died rather than renounce their faith or acquiesce to sexual aggression, of course, did engage in acts of resistance, but in order to obey, fulfill, and perpetuate the teachings of ecclesial authorities.

*Works Cited*

Alarcón, Norma. "Chicana's Feminist Literature: A Re-Vision Through Malintzin/or Malintzin: Putting Flesh Back on the Object." *This Bridge Called My Back: Writings by Radical Women of Color*. Ed. Cherríe Moraga and Gloria Anzaldúa. Watertown, Massachusetts: Persephone, 1981. 182–90.

Alegría, Juana Armanda. *Psicología de las Méxicanas.* Asia 29; Serie: Cuarta Dimensión. Coyoan, México: Editorial Samo, 1974.

Anzaldúa, Gloria. *Borderlands/La Frontera: The New Mestiza.* San Francisco: Spinsters/Aunt Lute, 1987.

Castillo, Ana. "La Macha: Toward a Beautiful Whole Self." *Massacre of the Dreamers: Essays on Xicanisma.* Albuquerque: U of New Mexico P, 1994.

———. *So Far from God.* New York: Norton, 1993.

Cotera, Martha P. *Diosa y Hembra: The History and Heritage of Chicanas in the United States.* Rptd. from *Profile on the Mexican American Woman.* Austin: Information Systems Development, 1976.

de Borhegyi, Stephen F. *El Santuario de Chimayo.* Santa Fe: Ancient City, 1956.

Delaney, John J., ed. *A Woman Clothed with the Sun: Eight Great Appearances of Our Lady in Modern Times.* 1961. New York: Doubleday, 1990.

Fox, Linda C. "Obedience and Rebellion: Re-Vision of Chicana Myths of Motherhood." *Women's Studies Quarterly* 11.4 (1983): 20–22.

Gárcia, Alma M. "The Development of Chicana Feminist Discourse, 1970–1980." *Gender and Society.* 3.2 (1989): 217–38.

Grahn, Judy. *Another Mother Tongue: Gay Words, Gay Worlds.* 1984. Boston: Beacon, 1990.

Kiev, Ari. *Curanderismo: Mexican-American Folk Psychiatry.* New York: Free, 1968.

Leal, Luis. *Aztlán y Mexico: perfiles literarios e historicos.* Binghampton: Bilingual Press/Editorial Bilingue, 1985.

Moraga, Cherríe. *The Last Generation.* Boston: South End, 1993.

Ordoñez, Elizabeth. "Sexual Politics and the Theme of Sexuality in Chicana *Poetry.*" *Women in Hispanic Literature: Icons and Fallen Idols.* Ed. Beth Miller. Berkeley: U of California P, 1983. 316–39.

Ortelli, Raul. *Brujos y curanderas.* Mercedes, Argentina, 1966.

Paz, Octavio. *The Labyrinth of Solitude.* New York: Grove, 1961.

Sanchez, Rosaura. *Chicano Discourse: Socio-historic Perspectives.* Houston: Arte Publico, 1994.

Sheehan, Michael J. Television interview. Chicago. 27 June 96.

Trujillo, Carla. "Chicana Lesbians: Fear and Loathing in the Chicano Community." *Chicana Lesbians: The Girls Our Mothers Warned Us About.* Ed. Carla Trujillo. Berkeley: Third Woman, 1991.

## Jane Caputi (review date May 1997)

SOURCE: "Divinely Subversive," in *Women's Review of Books,* Vol. 14, No. 8, May, 1997, pp. 16–17.

[*In the following review of* Goddess of the Americas: Writings on the Virgin of Guadalupe, *Caputi shows appreciation for the provocative essays in the collection, but criticizes the brief annotations and the lack of a concluding essay.*]

My Italian immigrant grandmother, Margaret, was extremely religious, but not the variety I had experienced in Church. She practiced a folk Catholicism that entailed petitions to specific saints and special devotion to the Blessed Virgin. Her bedroom housed scores of statues of these saints as well as many Madonnas. I would sit there for hours, awed. Perhaps that was where I first learned to make altars of my own, always to the Mother, and in my case always outdoors. At the same time, the Church brought out in me a lifelong propensity to rebel. By early adolescence, deeply and finally frustrated with the emptiness of the spiritual experience that was offered by the institution, I quit.

This early intuition of female cosmic powers never left me. Now living in New Mexico, I recognize, though I have not actively participated in, a popular tradition of Goddess worship in the reverence accorded the Virgin of Guadalupe. Her image, from sacred high art to votive candles, tattoos and T-shirts, is ubiquitous in Mexican and Mexican American cultures. She appears not only in these religious and popular cultural contexts but also in overtly political ones. Her image mobilized and guided the movement to gain Mexican independence from Spain and, more recently, graced the banner of the United Farmworkers Union. Contemporary Chicana artists such as Esther Hernández and Yolanda Lopez reclaim her as a radically unsubmissive, indigenous, simultaneously ancient and utterly modern Goddess.

*Goddess of the Americas* begins with a prayer. Indeed, its overall purpose is a reverent one: to pay "homage to Our Mother, at the end of this century and the end of a millennium of migrations, miscegenation, conquests, and endless hope and prayer." Essays in the collection range over the history of the *Virgen de Guadalupe*; her significance to Mexicans, Mexican Americans and others; the subversive powers of her iconography, particularly her special relationships with the indigenous, with women, and with the poor; her sexuality; her relationship to divine and folk figures from other traditions; and her mystery.

The anthology includes a diverse range of voices, political stances and beliefs: the message seems to be that Guadalupe is for all of us. As Chicana novelist, poet and essayist Ana Castillo notes in her preface, all contributors—believers and nonbelievers, Catholics and Jews, Mexicans, Mexican Americans and others, feminists and non-feminists, women and men—are bound "by common respect for Her and Her power over the spiritual life of millions." Any of us can embrace her and, Castillo believes, we should: "These writings also all serve as impassioned testimony of the need for recognition of the Mother in a world that is hanging by a thin thread of hope."

The history of Our Lady of Guadalupe is told most completely by F. Gonzalez-Crussi in "The Anatomy of a Virgin." Her story begins with attempted deicide. "When the Spaniards first arrived at the sacred hill of Tepeyacac . . . they encountered, on top of a low hill, the temple to the goddess Tonantzin, meaning 'Our Mother.'" Her image scandalized the Spaniards, who deemed it indecent, and they ordered her demolition and replacement by a cross. Tonantzin was linked then and continues to be linked to the "Snake Woman" goddesses, Cihuacoatl and Coatlicue, and the "sex goddesses" Tlazolteotl and Totzin.

Guadalupe was the name of a child-holding Madonna from Extremadura, Spain, and the Spaniards soon installed her in Tonantzin's site. Yet, as Gonzalez-Crussi reads it, the chthonic Tonantzin, gaining strength from her burial in the earth, effects a means to indigenize the imported Virgin. According to the "rationalist" account of her origins, soon after the conquest an anonymous Indian painter transferred the features of the Virgin onto a fabric made of agave fibers. She now wears a *rebozo*-like mantle, holds her palms in an Indian gesture of prayer and is framed by the sun while her feet rest upon a crescent moon. Her complexion is bronze, as is that of the angel beneath her.

In the far more widely accepted "apparitionist tradition," the Virgin appeared on December 12th, 1531, several times to an Indian, Cuautlatóhuac, known also as Juan Diego, imprinting her image on his cloak and giving him roses in the midst of winter to prove the miracle to a doubting bishop. A great festival commemorating this event is celebrated in Mexico each December.

Clearly, the phenomenon of Guadalupe-Tonantzin facilitated the conversion of the Indians to Catholicism, yet it is the belief of all the contributors to this volume that her cult transcends and powerfully subverts that form of colonization, working eventually not only to absorb Catholicism into Indian spirituality but to revitalize a people who, through conquest, were "spiritually dead, abandoned by their gods." Her "coming restored the people's reason to live and to hope." Gonzalez-Crussi points out that the shade of her skin and her features mark her not as an Indian but a "mestizo woman . . . her physiology is prophetic, announcing the foundation of a new race."

The Guadalupe's power to instill devotion is remarkable. She is, as Gloria Anzaldúa writes,

> the single most potent religious, political and cultural image of the Chicano/mexicano . . . She is the symbol of the *mestizo* true to his or her Indian values . . . Because Guadalupe took upon herself the psychological and physical devastation of the conquered and oppressed *indio*, she is our spiritual, political and psychological symbol. As a symbol of hope and faith, she sustains and insures our survival. The Indian, despite extreme despair, suffering and near genocide, has survived. To Mexicans on both sides of the border, Guadalupe is the symbol of our rebellion against the rich, upper and middle class; against their subjugation of the poor and the *indio*.
>
> (pp. 53–54)

This theme resounds throughout the anthology. Pilgrimages to Guadalupe take the supplicant to Mexico City on December 12th, and to the "immigration jail." Chicano activist Reubén Martinez names her the "Undocumented Virgin." Through her, he claims, we can learn of a national connectedness relevant to the current debate over the "illegal" immigration of people to the America that is now dominated by immigrant European peoples. As Martinez sees it, European-American deification of individualism would probably make the togetherness of the annual Mexican festival of *la Virgen* incomprehensible if not distasteful. Yet, "what Americans misunderstand about Mexicans is precisely what they need the most. Americans need to embrace themselves. I've found in Mexico, through Guadalupe-Tonantzin, what I'd lost in Prop 187, three-strikes-you're-out California."

Guadalupe is also the guardian of gang members, the Mother figure who through ritual can lead men away from violence and into rebirth. She is "an exhorter to social action" on behalf of the poor and homeless. And she is the face and body of female divinity, empowering women to honor ourselves and resist the oppressions of patriarchy.

Ana Castillo tells a powerful story of the way her *abuelita* (grandmother) and other women honor the *Virgen,* protect themselves and aid the young through a secret abortion rite for a teenage member of the family. Luisah Teish, the feminist activist, storyteller and priestess in the Yoruba Lucumi tradition, links Guadalupe to African and African American traditions and offers one of her unfailingly potent rituals to be performed for the Guadalupe during times of strife in women's communities.

Cherríe Moraga pays tribute to the Moon Goddess Coyolxauhqui, the divine being who is recognized in patriarchal culture only through such acceptable representatives as the Catholicized Virgin of Guadalupe. In Mexico, Moraga attends a ceremony marking the moon's eclipse of the sun: "During those six minutes of darkness . . . I understood for the first time the depth and wonder of the feminine, although I confess I have been awed by it before, as my own female face gazes upon its glory and I press my lips to that apex in the woman I love."

Also reclaiming the associations with the female divine with sex is Sandra Cisneros, in an exquisitely impudent essay, "Guadalupe, the Sex Goddess." Cisneros details the ways in which Latinas' bodies are rendered taboo, forbidden zones even to themselves, and the dangers to which this profound silencing exposed her as a young adult. At first, in her rebellion against this personal oppression, she understood Guadalupe only as a "goody goody," pointing the way to the living death of patriarchal marriage and motherhood. But as she matured as a feminist she realized an alternate presence—"Guadalupe the sex goddess, a goddess who makes me feel good about my sexual power, my sexual energy . . . My *Virgen de Guadalupe* is not the mother of God. She is God."

Cisneros writes of a horrifying image from a porn movie:

> The film star's *panocha*—a tidy, elliptical opening, pink and shiny like a rabbit's ear. To make matters worse, it was shaved and looked especially childlike and unsexual . . . my own sex has no resemblance to this woman's. My sex, dark as an orchid, rubbery and blue as *pulpo*, an octopus, does not look nice and tidy, but otherworldly . . . When I see *la Virgen de Guadalupe* I want to lift her dress as I did my dolls' and look to see if she comes with *chones* [underwear], and does her *panocha* look like mine, and does she have dark nipples too? Yes, I am certain she does. She is not neuter like Barbie. She gave birth. She has a womb. *Blessed art thou and blessed is the fruit of thy womb* . . . Blessed art thou, Lupe, and, therefore blessed am I.
>
> (p. 51)

Cisneros and many of the other activist-authors here are testifying to and accomplishing a type of contemporary myth-making, what performance artist Guillermo Gomez-Peña describes as a radical and empowering popular revision and use of a mythically charged mainstream symbol. In his experience in Mexico, Guadalupe was used as a "demagogic tool of control." But in the States, Chicanas and Chicanos "had expropriated it, reactivated it, recontextualized it, and turned it into a symbol of resistance"—an anti-racist warrior goddess and muse who "in the Chicano feminist Olympus . . . stood defiant and compassionate as a symbol of female strength, right next to *la Malinche*, Frida, Sor Juana, and more recently, Selena."

Reading this, I was surprised to find, a few pages later, Octavio Paz's "The Sons of La Malinche," a 1950 essay which many Chicanas have pointed to as troubling if not misogynist because of its identification of the "feminine condition" with "Nothingness" and its projection of woman's alleged psychological and biological "openness," leading inevitably to passivity, submission and an utter lack of agency. Here some editorial commentary or contextualization would have been especially helpful.

Anthologies—even ones that, like **Goddess of the Americas,** grace their readers with insight and passion—frequently mete out such frustrations. In general I would have welcomed a greater presence from the editor, Ana Castillo, in more extensive introductions to the individual contributions, as well as a concluding essay reflecting on Guadalupe from the vantage-point of the diverse perspectives the reader experiences as she reads the essays. The homage is to Our Mother at the end of a millennium; but what does She tell us about the next?

**Carmela Delia Lanza (essay date Spring 1998)**

SOURCE: "Hearing the Voices: Women and Home and Ana Castillo's *So Far from God,*" in *MELUS,* Vol. 23, No. 1, Spring, 1998, pp. 65–80.

[*In the following essay, Lanza examines both the physical and the abstract idea of "home" in* So Far from God.]

> I tie up my hair into loose braids, and trust only what I have built with my own hands.
>
> —Lorna Dee Cervantes

In the nineteenth century, Louisa May Alcott made subjects of objects when she wrote her domestic novel *Little Women,* which centered on four sisters and their mother during the American Civil War. Alcott created a *home* for the March girls that was removed from the world of war and male supremacy. In the twentieth century most critics who have devoted their attention to *home* space and domestic ritual have concentrated on white, middle-class homes (Matthews xvi). It is necessary, however, to begin including working-class homes and the homes of women of color in this dialectic. The subject of *home* space has not gone unnoticed by some women of color, like cultural theorists bell hooks and Gloria Anzaldua, and novelist Toni Morrison. Each of these writers is re-visioning the *home* space and its significance regarding gender roles, racism and spirituality in the homes of working-class women of color. For example, in her essay, "Homeplace: a Site of Resistance," bell hooks is not interested in further exploration of the "white bourgeois norms (where *home* is conceptualized as politically neutral space)" (47). Instead, she uses her theory to examine the "homeplace" of African American women, a space she defines as a "site of resistance and liberation struggle" (43).

Bell hooks's theory on "the homeplace" can be used to explore the domestic world that Ana Castillo has created in her novel, **So Far from God.** In this novel, Castillo, like hooks and other women writers of color, constructs the *home* as a "site of resistance" for the woman of color living in a racist and sexist world. Deconstructing physical, political and spiritual boundaries, Castillo takes on the role Gloria Anzaldua describes in her book, *Borderlands/La Frontera,* as "the new mestiza' (79). With its playful and ironic style, and its insistence on ambiguity and contradictions, **So Far from God** offers a postmodern inversion of Alcott's *Little Women.* Both works are American novels dealing with the primary relationships of four sisters; however, Castillo's novel is concerned with four Chicana sisters and a mother living a working class life in Tome, New Mexico. According to Cordelia Chavez Candelaria, Castillo is "one of the earliest Chicana voices to articulate a sexual politics through textual poetics" (146), and this is clearly seen in **So Far from God.** Unlike Alcott's created *home* space that for the most part is politically neutral, the home space in Castillo's novel is infused with political resistance. It is a place where women of color have an "opportunity to grow and develop" spiritually and politically, which is not always possible or allowable in a "culture of white supremacy" (hooks 42).

The daughters in *So Far from God* are dealing with power relations that the March girls in nineteenth century middle class America did not even have to think about. The March girls, despite their own oppression in a patriarchal culture and their own sympathy for the poor and destitute, were part of the hegemony of white culture. The sisters in *So Far from God,* on the other hand, must construct a *home* space that will offer them sustenance, security and spirituality in order to move into a white world as subjects. This is crucial, for according to hooks, "when a people no longer have the space to construct homeplace, we cannot build a meaningful community of resistance" (47). The daughters in *So Far from God* are given the opportunity to "reconceptualize ideas of homeplace, once again considering the primacy of domesticity as a site for subversion . . ." (hooks 48).

I am sitting at my kitchen table, thinking about the anger in Ana Castillo's novel—and how it is masked in humor. A narrator's voice disguising rage with flippancy, telling the story of four daughters who cannot live their entire lives in their mother's *home,* womb, female space. My baby starts to cry—he is angry because he's hungry, and I have to stop thinking about why Caridad is wearing Fe's wedding gown when she floats across the room in her healing vision. I get a bottle for the baby and it is love in action; it is a political act; it is a moment when my private sphere, my *home* space is directly connected to the growth of another human being. I think about what Louise Erdrich said regarding mothering and how that relates to my *home,* my so-called private life:

> One reason there is not a great deal written about what it is like to be the mother of a new infant is that there is rarely a moment to think of anything else besides that infant's needs. Endless time with a small baby is spent asking, "What do you want? What do you want?"
>
> (38)

It is the opposite of war. The ego is put aside; ideas, philosophies, theories all shrink down in the chthonic force of sustaining life—feeding another person.

It is in this continuous state of childbirth, moving into grace with all my resistance that I want to say, "Leave me alone, I'm busy." But I don't. According to Clarissa Pinkola Estes "There is a saying, 'You can't go *home* again.' It is not true. While you cannot crawl back into the uterus again, you can return to the soul-*home*. It is not only possible, it is requisite" (284). I wash and sweep within the four walls and create stories; and like Ana Castillo, Toni Morrison, Gloria Anzaldua, and Louise Erdrich, I want to give voice to the "cultural silence of the domestic sphere" (Wright 113). Writing a poem while writing a poem in my *home* space.

In the first chapter of *So Far from God,* the voice of the matriarchy is clearly heard through the mother, Sofi, when her daughter, La Loca, comes back from the dead. After Loca awakens from her other state of consciousness (whether she actually dies or suffers from epilepsy is irrelevant), opens her coffin and flies up to the church roof, the priest immediately declares his judgement by asking, "'Are you the devil's messenger or a winged angel?'" (23). He is embodying the voice of institutions—Christianity, patriarchy. La Loca can either be a devil or an angel, a virgin or a whore according to his linear thinking. Sofi, however, will not allow this destructive language of dichotomy to continue. She demands in the voices of Coatlicue, Hestia, Demeter, Guadalupe:

> 'Don't you dare! . . . Don't you dare start this about my baby! If our Lord in this heaven has sent my child back to me, don't you start this backward thinking against her; the devil doesn't produce miracles! And this is a miracle, an answer to the prayers of a broken-hearted mother . . .'
>
> (23)

Sofi is the head of her *home,* a *home* she has created for her daughters. For one daughter, Loca, the *home* is the only space she can call her own. She stays *home,* not playing the role of angel or devil, and is "without exception, healing her sisters from the traumas and injustices they were dealt by society—a society she herself never experienced firsthand" (27). As for the other daughters, they "had gone out into the world and had all eventually returned to their mother's *home*" (25). They become trapped in the "quest-pattern that has dominated Western literature" (Romines 7). They are unwilling to accept what Kathryn Allen Rabuzzi describes in her book about spirituality and domesticity, *The Sacred and the Feminine: Toward a Theology of Housework,* as the "positive face of chaos, a letting go into possibilities that freedom from externally fixed routine allows" (153) and that external routine is the world of male domination and the world of racism. In the novel, the daughters can only face chaos when they re-enter their mother's *home* and re-discover their identity, their spirituality, and their strength. Eventually all of the daughters, including La Loca, experience loss in the collision of their need to create a *home* space with the destructive forces outside.

> where I am born, I fall
>
> in the snow you and I cannot open our mouths
> to the ice house of rules and minutes,
> quick thoughts of before buildings and I
> feel muscles in every brick, steel girder,
> I cannot breathe and try to explain what it feels
> like to live in a world as an alien.
>
> What is our place in the universe at a time
> that goddess and poet have both made their excuses
> leaving us biting our nails in the dark trying to
> turn the highway into a bowl,
> melting another iceberg with our tongues,
> "Suck on this,"

"housework doesn't suck
because if it did, men would love it,"*

*From a greeting card that was given to a friend.

We wait inside Emily's poem,
the freezing people walking in circles
making our tombstone from a home and we can no
   longer
resign or revision or remember our honey moon.

The first daughter to move away from the *home* and into the perilous and destructive outside world is Esperanza. She enters her "quest-pattern" when she chooses to leave *home* and work as a television anchorwoman in Washington, D.C. On the surface, her decision appears sensible: ". . . it was pretty clear to her that there was no need of her on the homefront. Her sisters had recovered" (46) from their encounters with physical and emotional abuse. Esperanza also believes her mother no longer needs her because her father has returned *home* years after abandoning the family. Esperanza, however, misjudges her own position and the source of power within her family. In turning away from her *home,* her mother, her sisters, she is turning away from "the great and terrifying mother earth from whom all life emerges, but to whom it likewise all returns" (Rabuzzi 51). Her sisters continue to need her and her father is as ineffective now as he has always been. Esperanza is deceived by the male values that dominate the outside world in the novel; in turning from the female world of her *home* space (which her mother and sisters created) to the male world of war, she is moving towards self-destruction and can only return *home* after she is dead, in the form of a spirit. At first she speaks through La Llorona, who is described in the novel as "a loving mother goddess" (163). La Llorona is a messenger who informs La Loca (they were on a "first-name basis" [163]) that Esperanza has died. After that, Esperanza is seen by all the members of the family including the father who is a bit disturbed by his "transparent daughter" (163). Sofi sees Esperanza as a little girl who "had had a nightmare and went to be near her mother for comfort" (163). Caridad has one-sided conversations with Esperanza talking mostly about politics, and La Loca sees and talks to her by the river behind their *home.*

As a spirit, Esperanza returns to the *home* space to be comforted by her mother and sisters and to also teach them. Once Esperanza becomes a spirit, she is no longer a victim or an object of the white world. She belongs to a world that Anzaldua boldly asserts exists, a spiritual world that "the whites are so adamant in denying" (38). It is no accident that the dead Esperanza communicates with La Llorona, "a woman who had been given a bad rap by every generation of people since the beginning of time . . ." (Castillo 162–63). While she lived, Esperanza was also given a "bad rap." But in death, La Llorona is revisioned and so is Esperanza. Both are liberated from the boundaries of white culture. Both can finally return *home*—and the *home* can be a river or a mother's arms.

After Esperanza accepts her job in Washington, D.C., she is assigned to Saudi Arabia, a place about to erupt in war. Esperanza accepts this fate because she desires to move away from the *home* where the "mothers are the ones who actually have to change, feed, and connect with children for all their bodily functions," and move towards the "male saviors" whose "relative absence . . . from homelife automatically places them in a privileged position" (Rabuzzi 19). It is ironic (or maybe not so ironic) that Esperanza, in choosing the male hero as her model—leaving *home,* participating in a patriarchal institution, war, because "'it's part of my job'" (48)—is really choosing torture and death. Esperanza is experiencing what Anzaldua aptly describes in *La Frontera* as "shutting down" (20). She is living with the fear of rejection from the outside culture and she is also living with the fear of losing her *home,* her mother, "La Raza" (20). Esperanza experiences this psychic paralysis. She is a woman of color who is:

> Alienated from her mother culture, 'alien' in the dominant culture, the woman of color does not feel safe with the inner life of her Self. Petrified, she can't respond, her face caught between los intersticios, the spaces between the different worlds she inhabits.
>
> (20)

It is only after Esperanza has died that she can return to her "mother culture."

> Smoothing the sheets down on the bed,
> stroking a window pane,
> carrying a book to the table
> and I think of hands making him soup,
> carrying dirty underwear to the washing machine,
> ripping lettuce under cold water,
> stretching the chicken legs apart,
> slamming the ice tray against the table,
> holding, pushing, patting, kneading,
> punching the pillow down under my stomach and
> looking at the light spilling out to the street,
> "you are not my mother and you never will be,"
> tasting my blood with honey
> on my finger, around the corners of my mouth
> and I wonder how I have lasted another moon cycle
> in this place.

Fe is another one of the daughters in *So Far from God* who chooses a patriarchal institution that moves her away from her *home* space and eventually destroys her. Fe chooses marriage and in a literal and symbolic way, it poisons her to death.

The daughter who chooses marriage, chooses to create a new domestic environment echoes the myth of Demeter and Persephone. Persephone does leave her mother but she eventually returns to her for at least some of the year's cycle:

> Persephone therefore has two homes: her home of origins with her mother and her present adult home with her husband. Because the story is told from the perspective of her mother, Persephone's homecoming is her ascent to Demeter, not her descent to Hades.
>
> (Rabuzzi 135)

Anzaldua discusses her own separation and return to her origins which involves the dance of rebelling, celebrating, and defending aspects of her own Chicana culture. She asserts that it was necessary for her to leave *home* in order "to live life on my own." Yet she concludes, "in leaving *home* I did not lose touch with my origins because lo mexicano is in my system. I am a turtle, wherever I go I carry 'home' on my back" (21). Fe, in marrying Casimiro and moving to the land of "the long-dreamed-of automatic dishwasher, microwave, Cuisinart and the VCR" (171), is trying in her own way to return to her mother but she cannot truly find her way back because of her inability to view her *home* and her culture in all of its complexity. She can only look at her mother's *home* and her sisters as a source of embarrassment or pity:

> As it was, while Fe had a little something to talk to Esperanza about, she kept away from her other sisters, her mother, and the animals, because she just didn't understand how they could all be so self-defeating, so unambitious.
>
> (28)

Fe wants desperately to re-vision her mother's *home* by making it sterile, shiny, closer to the definition of *home* by mainstream white culture. She cannot see the spiritual richness in her *home*. In fact, Fe describes one of her sisters, La Loca, as "a soulless creature" (28) because she always wears the same clothes and doesn't bother with shoes. For herself, Fe insists on imitating the mainstream culture with a considerable amount of effort: "Fe was beyond reproach. She maintained her image above all—from the organized desk at work to weekly manicured fingernails and a neat coiffure" (28). Anzaldua points out that fear is the cause of this denial of *home,* a kind of "homophobia." She states:

> We're afraid of being abandoned by the mother, the culture, la Raza, for being unacceptable, faulty, damaged . . . To avoid rejection, some of us conform to the values of the culture, push the unacceptable parts in the shadows. Which leaves only one fear—that we will be found out and that the Shadow-Beast will break out of its cage.
>
> (20)

At the beginning of the novel, Fe embraces mainstream white culture; she wants to be like the white women she works with. She chooses "three gabachas" from her job to be her bridesmaids instead of her sisters (29). But instead of gaining any power, she ends up wrapped in the shower curtain, screaming her way back to the matriarchal circle of her mother and sisters. Her first boyfriend, Tom, decides he isn't ready for intimacy and commitment. And it is her mother and her sisters who become the healers and nurse, who clean and pray over Fe. Fe loses her voice as a result of her constant screaming yet she still does not learn how to integrate her *home* space with the world outside. Eventually, Fe marries one of her cousins, Casimiro. She still desires to live in a suburb in a house that does not smell the way her mother's house smells.

Fe's journey does end back at *home* and she is finally able to see her *home* as a source of comfort, wisdom and spirituality but it is only after the outside world has done its best to destroy her. After being exposed unknowingly to a very toxic chemical, Fe goes *home* to die:

> A year from the time of her wedding, everything ended, dreams and nightmares alike, for that daughter of Sofi who had all her life sought to escape her mother's depressing home—with its smell of animal urine and hot animal breath and its couch and cobijas that itched with ticks and fleas; where the coming and goings of the vecinos had become routine because of her mom's mayoral calling . . . Despite all this and more, Fe found herself wanting to go nowhere else but back to her mom and La Loca and even to the animals to die just before her twenty-seventh birthday. Sofia's chaotic home became a sanctuary from the even more incomprehensible world that Fe encountered that last year of her pathetic life.
>
> (171–72)

In Fe's chase for the American Dream, she only finds infertility, deception, and ultimately a death that unlike her sisters' deaths, offers no spiritual transformation or resurrection: "Fe just died. And when someone dies that plain dead, it is hard to talk about" (186).

Caridad, the other sister who leaves, like Fe and Esperanza also finds violence and ultimate destruction in the world outside the *home*. Early in the novel Caridad is physically attacked. It is a brutal sexual invasion, an attack on the female body:

> Sofi was told that her daughter's nipples had been bitten off. She had also been scourged with something, branded like cattle. Worst of all, a tracheotomy was performed because she had also been stabbed in the throat.
>
> (33)

Caridad's attack is treated by her society as merely a cause for prayer, because "the mutilation of the lovely young woman was akin to martyrdom" (33). And it is treated with contempt by the police department who felt she deserved what she got because of her sexual promiscuity. In the end Caridad is "left in the hands of her family, a nightmare incarnated" (33). Caridad's attack is an attack on the female, on what is closest to *home*—death, birth, blood. According to Anzaldua in *Borderlands/La Frontera*:

> The female, by virtue of creating entities of flesh and blood in her stomach (she bleeds every month but does not die), by virtue by being in tune with nature's cycles, is feared. Because, according to Christianity and most major religions, woman is carnal, animal, and closer to the undivine, she must be protected. Protected from herself. Woman is the stranger, the other. She is man's recognized nightmarish pieces, his Shadow-Beast. The sight of her sends him into a frenzy of anger and fear.
>
> (17)

Caridad becomes "the stranger, the other" when she is attacked, and she is only healed through her sisters and mother at *home*. She floats through the living room wearing Fe's wedding gown and is beautiful again; her wounds all vanish because La Loca prays for her. She moves into a transcendent world by no longer existing as an object for the world. Instead, Caridad meets an older woman, Dona Felicia, a surrogate mother who teachers her to become a healer. Dona Felicia is the one who points out the power that Caridad and her family possess:

> All they did at the hospital was patch you up and send you home, more dead than alive. It was with the help of God, heaven knows how He watches over that house where you come from. . . .
>
> (55)

Therefore, it is through the rituals of the *home* that Caridad enters into a spiritual life. Caridad's renewed life "became a rhythm of scented baths, tea remedies, rubdowns, and general good feeling" (63). She makes particular chores like dusting her altar and her statues and pictures of saints, taking baths, and cleaning her incense brazier part of her spiritual life. She takes on the role of a priestess, who "enacts her purification rites primarily for her own benefit" (Rabuzzi 114).

In the outside dominant culture where "We've been taught that the spirit is outside our bodies or above our heads somewhere up in the sky with God" (Anzaldua 36), Caridad's actions may be perceived as "cultlike" or even superstitious. But for women of color, her actions not only contradict what hooks identified as "white bourgeois norms (where *home* is conceptualized as politically neutral space)" (47), they re-connect and remember the *home* to the body to the spirit.

Caridad's mentor, Dona Felicia, creates a *home* in her trailer that is overflowing with the smells of beans cooking and incense burning. She is creating in her *home* "the spiritual life and ceremonies of multi-colored people" (Anzaldua 69) and is moving out of the "consciousness of duality" (Anzaldua 37). There is nothing neutral about her *home* (as there is nothing neutral about Sofi's *home*, filled with the smells of animals). They do not imitate the white culture with the "white sterility they have in their kitchens, bathrooms, hospitals, mortuaries and missile bases" (Anzaldua 69). Instead, Caridad and Dona Felicia's homes echo Anzaldua's words on institutionalized religions and *home*:

> Institutionalized religion fears trafficking with the spirit world and stigmatizes it as witchcraft. . . . In my own life, the Catholic Church fails to give meaning to my daily acts, to my continuing encounters with the 'other world.' It and other institutionalized religions impoverish all life, beauty, pleasure.
>
> (37)

Anzaldua also writes about her own *home* rituals and how they are strongly connected to her creative and spiritual life:

> I make my offerings of incense and cracked corn, light my candle. In my head I sometimes will say a prayer—an affirmation and a voicing of intent. Then I run water, wash the dishes or my underthings, take a bath, or mop the kitchen floor.
>
> (67)

Despite Caridad's rejection of institutionalized religions and her attempts to create a protective *home* space for herself, whether it is in a trailer or in a cave, she is again terrorized by the outside world. The woman she loves, Esmeralda, is raped by Francisco, a man who is obsessed with Caridad. Because of this man's desire to own a woman at any cost, because of his "machismo," which Anzaldua defines as a need to "put down women and even to brutalize them" (83) (a concept which Anzaldua connects to racism and shame), Caridad and Esmeralda both commit suicide at Acoma. They go to Acoma after Esmeralda's attack, and when Caridad realizes that Esmeralda was violated, and that Francisco followed them, they hold hands and jump off the mesa and are taken by Tsichtinako, "the Invisible One who had nourished the first two humans, who were also both females" (211). This spirit leads both women back to the womb, back to a safe *home*:

> not out toward the sun's rays or up to the clouds but
>    down, deep
>      within
> the soft, moist dark earth where Esmeralda and Caridad would be
> safe and live forever.
>
> (211)

> we cannot talk,
> it is better to only hear
> the water running in the kitchen sink
> dreaming of rooms and you sitting
> across from me saying "yes, yes
> I will defend you, I know exactly what I will say"
> but after you leave your words change,
> you lie and eat food my dead grandmother prepares and
> I know I must change all my poems now,
> throwing books at you in front of my parents' house
> and you laugh and hold your breath waiting
> for the hysterical woman to stop so you can
> go on walking down the street,
> so you can go on driving in the car,
> so you can go on your horse
> to another town and fuck another woman
> with your words, your money and your gun.

As long as woman is put down, the Indian and the Black in all of us is put down. The struggle of the mestiza is above all a feminist one. As long as los hombres think they have to chingar mujeres and each other to be men, as long as men are taught that they are superior and therefore culturally favored over la mujer, as long as to be a vieja is a thing of derision, there can be no real healing of our psyches. We're halfway there—we have such love of the Mother, the good mother. The first step is to unlearn the puta/virgin dichotomy and to see Coatlapopeuh-Coatlicue in the Mother, Guadalupe. (Anzaldua 84)

The two women in the novel who do not leave *home* are the mother, Sofi, and one daughter, La Loca. Both women look to their *home* space as a source for spiritual growth and as a reconnection between their own culture and the outside dominating culture. Neither Sofi nor Loca desire the objects, the static role or the sterile, domestic environment of mainstream white culture. They are rooted in their own history and at the same time, they accept their world in its playful state of constant change, and contradictions. This tension between rootedness and flexibility is observed by Anzaldua in *Borderlands/La Frontera*:

> Los Chicanos, how patient we seem, how very patient . . . We know how to survive. When other races have given up their tongue, we've kept ours. We know what it is to live under the hammer blow of the dominant norteamericano culture. But more than we count the blows, we count the days the weeks the years the centuries the eons until the white laws and commerce and customs will rot in the deserts they've created, lie bleached. Humildes yet proud, quietos yet wild, nosotros los mexicanos-Chicanos will walk by the crumbling ashes as we go about our business. Stubborn, persevering, impenetrable as stone, yet possessing a malleability that renders us unbreakable, we, the mestizas and mestizos, will remain.
>
> (63–64)

Sofi was married to a gambler, Domingo, who was:

> little by little betting away the land she [Sofi] had inherited from her father, and finally she couldn't take no more and gave him his walking papers. Just like that, she said, Go, hombre, before you leave us all out on the street!
>
> (214)

Domingo returns years later and attempts to win back Sofi's affection but she has no desire to share a life with him again. She will no longer accept his perceptions as law: "'And don't call me 'silly Sofi no more neither.' . . . 'Do I look like a silly woman to you, Domingo?'" (109–10). Sofi is participating in what Norma Alarcon describes as "the ironically erotic dance that Castillo's speaking subjects often take up with men" (94); however, Sofi is no longer allowing herself to be victimized by the dance.

Domingo makes the mistake of losing Sofi's house in a gambling bet and that is one mistake Sofi cannot forgive, for her identity, her history is her house:

> But the house, that home of mud and straw and stucco and in some places brick—which had been her mother's and father's and her grandparents', for that matter, and in which she and her sister had been born and raised—that house had belonged to her.
>
> (215)

Domingo's insensitivity and carelessness concerning this loss is what finally pushes Sofi to file divorce papers. She also manages to hold on to her house. Like the matriarchal goddess, Hestia, who will not allow any god to "share her strictly matriarchal province," and who nurtures a fire in the hearth that was "the center of the earth," (Walker 400), Sofi cannot let the fires in her *home* go out or let the fires consume her in rage. In her book, *The Sacred and the Feminine*, Rabuzzi describes this balancing act of the housewife who must carefully dance between her own *home* rituals, which includes spirituality, and outside influence:

> . . . all the domestic rites a housewife performs are designed to maintain Hestia's fire properly. If she allows the fire to go out, her house is no longer a home . . . if a homemaker allows the fire to rage out of control, her home will vanish along with its physical embodiment.
>
> (Rabuzzi 95)

Sofi balances her dedication to her *home,* her duty to "La Loquita, her eternal baby" and her devotion to herself when she decides to finally bring closure to her failed marriage. Sofi does not act in a fit of rage; in fact with a charitable and flexible nature, she offers him a small house in Chimayo (which was built for Caridad). She may not want to be married to Domingo but she refuses to see him homeless.

This balancing act is also evident when Sofi, despite the fact that her own grandparents built the house, accepts an arrangement with the judge who won the house in a cockfight. He allows Sofi to "reside in her own *home* after she agreed to pay him a modest rent" (216).

Like her mother, La Loca uses the *home* space as a source of spiritual nourishment and a source of strength. Loca does all her work, whether it is healing her sisters or talking to La Llorona, within the domestic sphere. While living in her mother's *home,* Loca becomes a mythic force in her own right. She becomes a player in a scene far older and larger than her individual self. No longer does she participate in profane historical time; instead she is participating in mythic time (Rabuzza 96). Loca visits hell, heals her sisters Fe and Caridad, and can smell other people's agony. She participates in a "mortal collision between the rituals of a house" (Romines 198) when she describes to Sofi how she can smell her father's spiritual pain:

> 'Mom,' La Loca said, 'I smell my dad. And he was in hell, too. . . . Mom, I been to hell. You never forget that smell. And my dad . . . he was there, too.' 'So you think I should forgive you dad for leaving me, for leaving us all those years?' Sofi asked. 'Here we don't forgive, Mom. . . . Only in hell do we learn to forgive and you got to die first. . . . Mom, hell is where you go to see yourself. This dad out there, sitting watching T. V., he was in hell a long time.'
>
> (41–42)

Loca, like Hestia, is a virgin who is "the representative of pure homelife" (Rabuzzi 95). Since her experience of death and resurrection at age three, Loca never leaves *home,* and she only allows her mother to come close to her. She never went to school, to mass, to any social activity. Her entire world is the house, the stalls, and the river by the house. She does not attempt to assimilate into the dominant culture like her sisters, Fe and Esperanza. She plays the violin without having to go to a teacher outside the *home*; she just learns using her own ability and talent. Loca doesn't rely on mainstream institutions for anything, whether it be to gain knowledge or spirituality in her life.

Yet the world comes to Loca in the shape of a disease, AIDS. Castillo does not explain how Loca contracts the disease, which adds to Loca's role in the novel as a character who is larger than her own self (Rabuzzi 96). The disease, which Castillo describes as the "Murder of the Innocent" (243), seeks Loca out.

In the end, like Caridad, Loca is taken away by a female deity, the Lady in Blue who is wearing a horsehair vest under her habit. The lady can be Guadalupe, La Llorona, "My-Mother-Who-Gives" Coatlicue—all aspects of the goddess who was "usurped of ancient feminine prerogatives" (Walker 526) by the outside culture but has found a voice within the *home* space. Loca, within her domestic sphere, is still disrupted by the racism and sexism of the patriarchy. She is the representative feminist healer and speaker operating from within the *home*. She is also the queer that Anzaldua speaks about when she says, "People, listen to what your joteria is saying" (85). And because of the disease she contracts, a disease of the postmodern world, she, like her sisters, Esperanza, Fe and Caridad, is a representative victim of the patriarchy. For only Sofi remains at the end of the novel, as the president of Mothers of Martyrs and Saints, an organization that worships another symbol of the *home,* the womb.

> I wanted to write about this dream and call it
> "peeling garlic" smelling my fingers
> hours after I cooked
> and no, I do not believe women would start a war
> because they are not looking
> at the beginning or the end

What is *home?* Is it "the space in which you feel secure enough to be most fully yourself" (Rabuzzi 139)? Is domestic ritual only a private act? "I am writing a book, performing a public act that seems a far cry from my turkey dressing," writes Romines (293). Is it? What do women learn in the *home?* Is the "place where all that truly mattered in life took place—the warmth and comfort of shelter, the feeding of our bodies, the nurturing of our souls. There we learned dignity, integrity of being; there we learned to have faith" (hooks 41–42). Anzaldua writes, "I am a turtle, wherever I go I carry *home* on my back" (21). I stand outside, bleeding. I watch the lunar eclipse, a heavy moon pulling on my womb; the moon is slowly disappearing above my house, and I hear my baby breathing under my skin. Five months ago, *home* for him was my body. I want to join the voices of the private and public that will not look at what is done in the home as disconnected to what is done outside the *home,* that will not disconnect the female body from the female spirit. I want to join the force "making a new culture—una cultura mestiza—with my own lumber, my own bricks and mortar and my own feminist architecture" (Anzaldua 22).

*Works Cited*

Alarcon, Norma. "The Sardonic Powers of the Erotic in the Work of Ana Castillo." *Breaking Boundaries: Latina Writing and Critical Readings.* Amherst: U of Massachusetts P, 1989. 94–107.

Anzaldua, Gloria. *Borderlands/La Frontera: The New Mestiza.* San Francisco: Aunt Lute, 1987.

Candelaria, Cordelia Chavez. "Latina Women Writers: Chicana, Cuban American and Puerto Rican Voices." *Handbook of Hispanic Cultures in the United States.* Vol. 4. Ed. Francisco Lomeli. Houston: Arte Publico, 1993. 134–162.

Castillo, Ana. *So Far from God.* New York: Norton, 1993.

Erdrich, Louise. "A Woman's Work." *Harper's,* May 1993: 35–46.

Estes, Clarissa Pinkola. *Women Who Run with the Wolves: Myths and Stories of the Wild Woman Archetype.* New York: Ballantine, 1992.

hooks, bell. "Homeplace: A Site of Resistance." *Yearning: Race, Gender and Cultural Politics.* Boston: South End, 1990. 41–49.

Matthews, Glenna. "Just a Housewife": *The Rise and Fall of Domesticity in America.* New York: Oxford UP, 1987.

Rabuzzi, Kathryn Allen. *The Sacred and the Feminine: Toward a Theology of Housework.* New York: Seabury, 1982.

Romines, Ann. *The Home Plot: Women, Writing and Domestic Ritual.* Amherst: U of Massachusetts P, 1992.

Walker, Barbara G. *The Woman's Encyclopedia of Myths and Secrets.* New York: Harper Collins, 1983.

Wright, Wendy M. *Sacred Dwelling: A Spirituality of Family Life.* New York: Crossroad, 1989.

## Roland Walter (essay date Spring 1998)

SOURCE: "The Cultural Politics of Dislocation and Relocation in the Novels of Ana Castillo," in *MELUS,* Vol. 23, No. 1, Spring, 1998, pp. 81–97.

[*In the following essay, Walter analyzes how characters in Ana Castillo's novels are often subjected to struggles for identity and for freedom from oppression.*]

> Now, I-woman am going to blow up the Law . . . in language.
>
> (Cixous "The Laughing Medusa" 887)
>
> By creating a new mythos—that is, a change in the way we perceive reality, the way we see ourselves, and the ways we behave—*la mestiza* creates a new consciousness.
>
> (Anzaldúa *Borderlands/La Frontera* 80)

Ever since the initial success of vanguard Chicana writers such as Lorna Dee Cervantes, Estela Portillo-Trambley, Gina Valdés, Bernice Zamora, Lucha Corpi and Alma Villanueva in the late 1970s and early 1980s and throughout the boom of Chicana literary output from the mid 1980s until now, Chicana writers have used the written word in order to *"reveal"* and *"change,"* that is, they have been engage writers in one way or another.[1] According to María Hererra-Sobek, Chicana writers have been making "daring inroads into 'new frontiers' . . . exploring new vistas . . . and new perspectives" which reveal "new dimensions" for both Chicano and mainstream American literatures (10–11). Focusing upon Ana Castillo's novels, *The Mixquiahuala Letters, Sapogonia,* and *So Far from God,* this essay addresses the politics of dislocation and relocation as a key aspect of the interacting social and cultural practices and ideological discourses that constitute the narrative's signifying process.

In *Borderlands/La Frontera* Gloria Anzaldúa describes the border space as "a vague and undetermined place created by the emotional residue of an unnatural boundary," a space "in a constant state of transition" (3). Those who live in the Chicano borderlands, this interstitial cross-cultural space, are "plagued by psychic restlessness . . . torn between ways . . . a product of the transfer of the cultural and spiritual values of one group to another" (78). I want to suggest that Castillo's characters, male and female, are border subjects *positioned* between cultures and in search of an alternative to their lived "nepantla" state of invisibility and transition.[2] In terms of her female characters, this state is aggravated by what Castillo calls in *Massacre of the Dreamers* "double sexism, being female and indigenous," that is, by the Chicana's identity as man's *specularized Other,*[3] a subject-position conditioned by racism and misogyny. Castillo, I want to demonstrate, uses writing to reveal and change the mestiza's imposed "subject-position," which, according to JanMohamed, can be defined only "in terms of the effects of economic exploitation, political disenfranchisement, social manipulation, and ideological domination on the cultural formation of minority subjects and discourses" (9). In this process her narrative problematizes the "ethos" and "worldview" of Chicano and Anglo-American cultures through the aesthetic creation of a new mestiza consciousness, a *repositioning* of the marginalized subject by means of a counter-hegemonic discourse that establishes what Göran Therborn has called a narrative "alterideology" (*Identity of Power* 28): a narrative "dialectic of difference"[4] as socially symbolic act with an ideological utopian function intent on finding imaginary solutions to existing social conflicts. This utopian function—an impulse of liberation and salvation—embraces the relation between both the individual and the collective and life as it is lived and experienced imaginatively. Hence, I want to argue that Ana Castillo's narrative instantiates counter-hegemony (culture/ideology) as a substance of Chicana/o thinking and is therefore, in Frederic Jameson's terms, "informed by . . . a political unconscious . . . a symbolic meditation on the destiny of community" (*The Political Unconscious* 70). It becomes, as it creates, what Bhabha based on Jacques Lacan has termed the place of "the signifying time-lag of cultural difference" (*The Location of Culture* 237).

In *The Mixquiahuala Letters* Castillo describes a Chicana's search for identity in the borderlands by foregrounding "the psychic restlessness" which characterizes the protagonist's endeavors to deconstruct her imposed identity as man's Other and create an authentic consciousness. The novel, an indignant outcry against the Chicana's fragmented and alienated existence in a racist, patriarchal order—an outcry that characterizes the narrative style, structure, and theme—centers on the experiences of two Chicanas, Teresa and Alicia, living and traveling in the United States and Mexico. Playing Julio Cortázar's game without sticking to his rules, Castillo uses a fragmented epistolary style—40 letters written by Teresa—and invites the reader to read in different, nonchronological ways.[5] This device, the use of multiple perspectives and a protean, lyrical prose revealing both the conscious and unconscious levels of Teresa's mental life break with the chronological *order* of the narrative and connote *free choice* and *otherness*. Style and structure furthermore intimate the implicit author's renunciation of authority and, based on the theme, suggest a radical deconstruction of the symbolic order as a solution to Teresa's identity crisis and search for selfhood. This mode of presentation reflects two basic interacting "structures of feeling"[6]: the confusion / anxiety / crisis of being "torn between ways" that characterizes life in the shifting space of the borderlands and the desire to transcend this state, to put the fragmented pieces of one's colonized identity together—structures conditioned by what Erlinda Gonzales-Berry has described as "the discrepancies between women's desires to act and define themselves and the world's reception and suppression of those desires" (237).

Teresa experiences a cultural crisis of dislocation which I propose to read within the context of the following questions: who am I-Chicana living in the United States? How do I-woman relate to the other, male and female? Teresa "was no longer prepared to face a mundane life of need and resentment, accept monogamous commitments and honor patriarchal traditions and wanted to be rid of the husband's guiding hand, holidays with family and in-laws, led by a contradicting God, society . . ." (22–23). The novel's epigraph, taken from Anais Nin's *Under the Glass Bell,* introduces Castillo's outcry against a system that reduces women to objects of men's will: "I quit loving my father a long time ago. What remained was a slavery to a pattern." Father, church, husband, the three pillars of a system that stifles Teresa's self-determination, are on trial in the novel. In several letters Teresa denounces what Luce Irigaray has described as "the natural substratum" of "the [hierarchically structured] patriarchal social body," namely, "woman-as-other": (*Je, tu, nous* 45).

> A woman takes care of the man she has made her life with, cleans, cooks, washes his underwear, does as if he were her only child, as if he had come from her womb. In exchange, he may pay her bills, he may not.

> He may give her acceptance into society by replacing her father's name with his, or he may choose to not. He may make her feel like a woman, or rather, how she has been told a woman feels with a man or he may not.
>
> (112)

The narrative initiates Teresa's redefinition of selfhood as growth in consciousness from this subaltern position, this "periphery of authorized power and privilege," (Bhabha 2) in a deconstructive process; a process that reveals and challenges her experience of otherization and thereby opens an in-between space—a space separating the I-woman from the 'woman-as-other'—that gradually becomes a place of emergence, a terrain for insurrection, an interstice where Teresa's new mestiza consciousness is negotiated as a strategy of representation. The necessity for this redefinition, which implies a renegotiation of culture, ideology and society, is nowhere better expressed than in the following statement: "In rage, i tore open the worn shirt to reveal flesh: 'i was a woman,' i shouted, 'but i was first human'"(97). One could argue that this exclamation is an emblem of the novel's politics of dislocation and relocation: a Chicana who through writing reveals the psychic wounds inflicted upon her by a racist, sexist and classist order, turning her into a stranger, into man's and society's "Shadow-Beast," (Anzaldúa *Borderlands* 17) and "speak[s] from the cracked spaces . . . *con voz del abismo* . . . to subvert the status quo," employing her voice as a strategy of resistance to hegemonic cultural constructions (Anzaldúa "*Haciendo caras, una entrada*" xxii–xxv). By using her voice in a gesture of defiance, insisting upon her right of self-determination, Teresa moves from silence into speech, from invisibility into visibility: an act of cultural revision intent on transforming the "abismo," this unhomely liminal space, into a home.

Unable to find a satisfactory solution to her double dislocation, Teresa, together with her friend Alicia, travels to Mexico, the mythical homeland which she has only known from stories told by her grandmother, in order to satisfy her "yearning spirit, the Indian in me that had begun to cure the ails of humble folk distrustful of modern medicine; a need for the sapling woman for the fertile earth that nurtured her growth."[7] Mexico, however, as Teresa gradually realizes after two journeys, embraces her with its indigenous roots—"i sometimes saw the ancient Tenochtitlan, home of my mother, my grandmothers and greatmother, as an embracing bosom, to welcome me back . . . people of the sun and earth . . . i too was of that small corner of the world, i was of that mixed blood, of fire and stone . . . " (92, 95–96)—and strangles her with its machismo at the same time. While the journeys to Mexico do not provide her with clear-cut answers, the mere fact of moving within nepantla signifies a radical change from mere interrogation to initiation. Traveling and writing about this experience enable Teresa to rethink and renegotiate individual and collective cultural values of the Chicano border experience. In this process, she creates her own migratory in-between space in which self-definition is initiated in an ambivalent way and no definite answers and solutions are found. Female bonding—one of the principal messages of Castillo's poetry[8]—and relationships with men are problematized and render the shifting and multiple forms of existence in the borderlands. The "dialectics of attraction and repulsion"[9] characterizing the friendship between Teresa and Alicia as well as their relationships with men, reflect the "struggle of . . . Self amidst adversity and violation" (Anzaldúa *Borderlands* Preface) and refract the social and psychic dislocation from which the possibilities of consciousness-raising and reconstruction of identity emerge. A possible solution to the gender war, hinted at in the short moments of sexual pleasure shared with *emancipated* men—"We licked our wounds with the underside of penises and applied semen to our tender bellies and breasts like Tiger's balm" (100)—resides in the education of boys (in this specific case Teresa's son) and/or the re-education of men: ". . . he should be taught to look after himself, mend his own clothes, cook, clean up and do his share. He should be allowed to do whatever it was that little boys liked to do but he should also be sensitive . . . Vittorio must learn . . . to grow up to be a decent companion to a woman" (130). I am inclined, then, to read this alternative as a counter-hegemonic utopian move intent on changing what Lacan termed the Symbolic Order.

In terms of what Edward Said has described as "being at home in a place" (*The World* 8). Teresa's problem remains unresolved. A vision, expressed via dreams and imagination, however, hints at a utopian solution to her existence-in-crisis: in line with Anzaldúa's survival strategies in the borderlands, Teresa is depicted as becoming "a crossroads" where her individual struggle transcends the horizon of Chicano culture and conjoins the one of the oppressed, marginalized people "of mixed blood, people of the sun and earth" (*Borderlands* 95). Even though Teresa feels empowered by this dream, the roads to be traveled as well as the destinations to be reached are undefined, vaguely recognizable. Given the fragmentary character of style and structure and the narrative's undecidability—that is signification exists as meaning-possibilities in an unresolved, ambiguous state[10]—***The Mixquiahuala Letters*** can be seen as the aesthetic creation of a strategical interstitial space-in-process that instantiates counter-hegemony as cultural politics of dislocation and relocation from the margin with the intention of facilitating a renegotiation of ideological and cultural values. In this sense, the novel supports Frantz Fanon's claim that the process of decolonization and liberation is always initiated in a "zone of occult instability," an atmosphere of crisis and anxiety. The novel's importance, therefore, does not so much reside in the ways and outcome of the liberatory struggle, but rather in the fact that such a struggle is necessary and, as Teresa's case demonstrates, that one has to become conscious of its necessity. Hence, the image of the 'opaque window' and the 'weapon' illustrates "the need to know what one's needs are."[11]

In ***Sapogonia*** Castillo succeeds in broadening the issues of gender and race in the borderland experience. By focusing on Máximo, a sculptor from Sapogonia (a fictitious country somewhere in the Americas), and his affairs with women, Castillo delves into the male and female psyche in order to reveal and problematize not only the difficulties of survival in the borderlands but also, and most importantly, effects of a borderland existence on individuals. Máximo could be seen as Teresa's male counterpart insofar as he is another border subject experiencing an existential crisis. Máximo, who leaves his country torn by civil war, begins his migratory odyssey in Europe and finally comes to the United States, establishing himself as a successful artist. Yet Castillo emphasizes the underside of this success story, namely, the alienated and fragmented psyche of a man who sells his soul to the American Dream, (ab)uses women and denies his indigenous roots. Throughout the narrative Máximo is delineated as a reified antihero, a symbol of postmodern *man* who, on account of his attitude and way of thinking, contributes to the perpetuation of the patriarchal order and the implicit objectification of woman's existence. Furthermore, Castillo uses this male protagonist and his experience to render an image of the border subject's estrangement from his natural roots, from a wholesome cosmic relation to nature and reality, or to use Cixous's phrase, his "lacking earth and flesh."[12] Unlike Teresa, who by shouting "i was a woman . . . i was first human" reclaims her womanhood and humanness in an act of renaming and possession, Máximo internalizes the value system of the dominant culture—the frenzy for commodities, money, fame and individual recognition based on a highly competitive spirit—and thereby accentuates what Castillo called the "spiritual split in his collective psyche."[13]

Castillo sets Máximo's "spatial and social confusion"[14] against an alternative mode of thinking, living and relating, a mode personified by Mamá Grande, Máximo's grandmother, and Pastora, a Joan Baez-type singer and activist. Earthy women with a cosmic worldview, they embody the potential for change. Mamá Grande familiarizes Máximo with the mytho-magical worldview of his indigenous ancestors, a cyclical worldview based upon "the inborn awareness of equality with other living things on earth,"[15] and warns him not to "deceive woman . . . not to use woman like an animal" (104). Mamá Grande, a woman who has visions, sees into the future, and appears after her death as a living spirit, exists in a timeless, mythical present. In these passages of the novel, Castillo uses a magico-realist discourse to express a worldview that goes beyond the rational empirical categories of reality, including the visualized ones, those categories in which dreams are transformed into a visible and tangible reality. This type of *weltanschauung* is characterized by a harmonious and dynamic relationship between man and his surroundings; a relationship in which man plays an active role and in which significations can constantly assume new dimensions.[16] This dynamic harmony is carried by a discourse that naturalizes the supernatural categories of reality, that is, both levels of the discourse, the natural and the supernatural, are harmoniously intertwined, producing what Roland Barthes termed an *"effet de réel"* (*Le bruissement de la langue* 174). Throughout the episodes in which Mamá Grande's spirit appears to Máximo and Pastora this naturalization is achieved by three principal devices, namely, a matter-of-fact style, authorial reticence and the characters' reaction; neither the characters nor the narrator show signs of hesitation and / or surprise with regard to the supernatural categories, accepting them as vital parts of their belief system: "'¿Mamá Grande?' I uttered. It was an eerie meeting from the start. She didn't move any closer, but stood where she was. . . . 'How good that you came back, son,' she said. Yes it was the voice of Mama Grande, but she remained still as if her feet were dug in the ground where she stood. She wrapped her shawl tighter about her little body as if she were cold. 'I knew you would come back soon'" (220). This magico-realist texture signifies, on the one hand, the transcendence of binary oppositions characterizing the rational and patriarchal Western metaphysics of presence and, on the other, a revaluation of the indigenous worldview as an integral element of Chicano culture.

This indigenous mytho-magical worldview with its sense of fluidity, its harmony between the material and the spiritual, is further personified by Pastora. Paradoxically it is Máximo who, while denying his own indigenous roots, calls her "Coatlicue"; Coatlicue, the Aztec snake goddess, the symbol of fused opposites, "the eagle and the serpent, heaven and the underworld, life and death, mobility and immobility, beauty and horror" (*Borderlands* 47). It is through Pastora-Coatlicue, a woman who 'gives and takes' life, that Castillo re-creates the Aztec goddess as an incarnation of contradictory cosmic processes. Máximo, who describes Pastora's supernatural powers as witch-type magic, is enchanted, irresistibly attracted and repelled by her beauty and sensuality, that is, he experiences what Anzaldúa has termed "the Coatlicue State," a contradictory sensation, a nepantla death-in-life and life-in-death existence/crisis:

> Pastora was a witch, an unequivocal bruja who'd undoubtedly used her wicked powers to hex him. . . . Somehow, she had managed to take something so vital and potent from his being, like the umbilical cord his grandmother had severed with her teeth the dawn he was born. . . . Pastora Ake had severed something in him with her bare teeth, like a savage monster acting upon a primal female instinct, because what bound him to her was unquestionably physical, . . . .
>
> (172)

Like Fanon in *The Wretched of the Earth* and Bhabha in *The Location of Culture,* Anzaldúa in *Borderlands/La Frontera* delineates this space/sensation/state of betweenness and transition as a possible place of emergence, "a prelude of crossing" from darkness to light, invisibility to visibility, confusion to "knowing," in short, as a place where strategies of representation, empowerment, and change can (and are necessary to) be developed. It is in this sense that I read Máximo's incapacity to make meaning out of his experience: "When I made love to Pastora, I wasn't even on earth. . . . I lost my substance, became the molecules of which my body was made and became formless and erratic, unlike with the women with whom I felt I could challenge anything. I was Goliath . . . with them, and the clever David did not exist. With Pastora I was only a man" (296). Pastora's matriarchal powers provoke Máximo's fear and confusion, a feeling of "vulnerability" (296), precisely because they undermine his image of male conquistador. Relishing his patriarchal inheritance as Spanish Goliath while denying not only his indigenous roots but also his willingness to be "only a man," Máximo fails to cross from confusion to knowledge, or as Gayatri Spivak would say, to deconstruct his textuality, and is lead to destruction. Máximo's *possible* rebirth is thwarted by his inability to undo the patriarchal effects of power, as Michel Foucault would say, which constitute him and act through him.[17] By dividing Pastora-Coatlicue's contradictory powers and foregrounding her life-taking forces, Máximo deprives himself of a possible recreation through her: "Awesome Coatlicue. . . . She was the blood that appeared on your penis the first time you entered a woman who was menstruating and you feared it would curse you. She was the breast that, without milk, still comforted. She was the dark tunnel through which you passed and began your first memory of this world" (312).[18]

The implicit deconstruction of the patriarchal order, which appears as the novel's political unconscious in the temporal/spatial break in between the signs, the said and the unsaid, this caesura that reveals Máximo's disjunctive experience and is the place of a possible utopian counter hegemonic revision, is based on female agency, a (mythical) revaluation of woman's life-giving powers, a rendering visible of the female body and mind as text, as discourse that reclaims the indigenous matriarchal social structure and way of thinking and asserts/demands a radically new male and female consciousness and subject-position. The strong images of the two earthy women suggest not only that a new mestiza consciousness has already emerged but also, and most importantly, that this consciousness carries a potential for change—a change of ideology and culture, that is, lived hegemony.[19]

Whereas **Sapogonia** and **The Mixquiahuala Letters** emphasize the postmodern alienation and fragmentation of individuals in the borderlands, their dislocation in an interstitial cross-cultural nepantla space, **So Far from God** can be regarded as an aesthetic attempt at tracing a state of selfhood that involves *collective* self-definition, a place among one's people. In this process, Castillo uses a counter-hegemonic worldview and mestiza consciousness as imaginary solution to what Norma Alarcón has called "the crisis of meaning as women" and, I would add, to the postmodern crisis of meaning as human beings, the *"desyoización"* of the individual.[20]

In **So Far from God** Castillo creates community—defined by Tomas Rivera as "place, values, personal relationships, and conversation"[21]—by means of a "speakerly"[22] magico-realist narrative texture. The driving forces of this process are women: women who think, dream, act and relate in what Anzaldúa has called a "pluralistic mode," transcending binary oppositions, a rational "dualistic thinking in the individual and collective consciousness," in an effort to heal "the split that originates in the very foundation of our lives, our culture, our languages, our thoughts" (*Borderlands* 80). The keyword of this worldview, carried as in **Sapogonia** by a discourse in which the natural and supernatural categories of reality are harmoniously intertwined, is faith: a faith that facilitates a dynamic relationship between human beings and their surroundings and an implicit magico-realist conception of the world in which the imaginary is regarded as factual reality.[23] Faith is the fundamental principle which underlies La Loca's resurrection, Caridad's miraculous recovery and predictions, Felicia's holistic treatments, and the appearance of living (mythical) spirits. This peculiar type of faith, which is revised and actualized through female *agency*,[24] is the driving force behind the collective activism and the implicit alternative mode of living and relating outlined in the novel; a counter-hegemonic mode conceived as possible solution to the postmodern fragmentation and dislocation experienced in the borderlands.

This magico-realist worldview, whose fundamental essence resides in "the interconnectedness of things" (242), is expressed by means of a "speakerly" texture in which a *skaz*-like discourse, being at work in and acting on the actual discourse, an unnamed narrator, who as a storyteller represents both a communal and an individual voice, and the use of multiple points of view and perspectives recreate and interweave individual and collective experiences as the novel's political unconscious. A telling example of this fluid dialogical texture is the episode in which Sofi, La Loca's mother, announces to a comadre her plan to run for mayor of Tome. On entering Sofi's house, just before the actual dialogue between the two women, the comadre, whose namelessness suggests her collective identity, is lost in thoughts about Sofi and her family. Introduced by the phrase, ". . . for when she repeated the story later to the other comadres . . ." (133), her reflections take on a highly oral tone: she seems to speak to herself and the community at the same time. Phrases such as "You know, la pobre Sofi . . . ," "But everyone understood . . ." (133), "Everybody still remembered . . . ," and "nobody . . . had been able to explain . . ." (135), lend an oral coating to this interior monologue, a "speakerly" texture in which the above-mentioned rhetorical devices exist not only "as representations of oral narration" but also "as integral aspects of plot and character development."[25] By means of this polyphonic discourse the community of Tome is created in a time-space continuum in which a condensation and a concretization of the temporal and spatial indexes constitute a radical *present*-ation of time in space and space in time. The effect upon plot and character development can be called accretive insofar as Sofi's decision to run for mayor is accompanied and, as the unfolding story shows, supported by the rest of the female population and leads to the construction of an alternative, economically self-sufficient community (146–48). In other words, women are the driving force behind the creation of an alternative space of living, thinking and relating based on justice and equality; a process made possible by a worldview whose accretive dynamics are created and expressed on the level of discourse by orality and the mode of magical realism.

Influenced by her children—La Loca's and Caridad's faith in an expanded reality, Esperanza's rebellious restiveness, and Fe's suicidal materialist attitude—Sofi becomes the emblem of female activism. Her daughters show her that it is possible and necessary to make choices in life and that life itself should be "defined as a state of courage and wisdom and not an uncontrollable participation in society" (250). While the possibility of change is articulated and actualized through a culturally specific faith in an expanded reality, its necessity is made explicit through what Sartre called *"dévoiler,"* that is, the revelation of past and present Chicano experience in New Mexico: the encroachment of Anglo culture and its devastating impact on the Chicano way of life, the loss of land and identity. The necessity for activism, then, is a matter of survival as is demonstrated by Fe's selling out to the American way of life and thinking[26] and by the factory workers' ignorance of "what was going on around them" (189). Against this background of ongoing cultural imperialism (aggravated by internalization) and the ensuring fragmentation of the individual, I read Castillo's creation of community—the collective activism that results in progressive change symbolized by "the sheep-grazing" and "wool-weaving cooperative," selling "hormone-free meat" to food co-ops run by and for the benefit of the people of Tome (147–48)—as a utopian solution to the loss of identity, assimilation and the spread of Anglo culture.[27]

I want to suggest that this is not only community but also "cultural revolution" in the making. The counterhegemonic discourse that Castillo employs in her three novels—a rhetoric that deconstructs the marginal position of the mestiza in the Chicano borderlands and recreates, via *concrete* utopia,[28] a new mestiza consciousness as an organic process of interrelated individual and collective experiences—is a discourse of radical cultural liberation: it does not only "blow up the Law" (Cixous) and create a "new mythos" (Anzaldúa) but redefines relationships, lifestyles, and the conception of reality from a Chicana perspective.[29] While **The Mixquiahuala Letters** and **Sapogonia** initiate what Spivak has called "subaltern insurgency,"[30] **So Far from God** adds to the initial moment of *negation,* an individual existence in a state of crisis, one of *affirmation,* a communal existence in the borderlands. The three novels can be seen as examples of liberating fiction precisely because they offer a *humanizing* vision by attempting explanations, interpretations, and alternative solutions to the postmodern nepantla existence in the Chicano borderlands without glossing over the "intracultural conflict."[31] The journey from **The Mixquiahuala Letters** to **So Far from God,** a movement form interrogation (dislocation) to initiation (relocation), stages the search for selfhood as an examination of self through both individual and collective history, linking it to a search for place among one's people.

If, according to Said, the word culture suggests "an environment, process, and hegemony in which individuals (in their private circumstances) and their works are embedded," if it "is in culture that we can seek out the range of meanings and ideas conveyed by the phrases *belonging to* or *in* a place, being *at home in* a place," and if culture "is used to designate not merely something to which one belongs but something that one possesses" (*The World* 8–9), then this search for selfhood in Castillo's novels implies a revolutionary cultural redefinition; a redefinition that aims, on the one hand, at what Foucault has described as "the insurrection of subjugated knowledge," the rediscovery and rectification of knowledge and experience suppressed by the dominant system and its ideology (*Power/Knowledge* 81) and, on the other, at a radical transformation of our sense of being, living and thinking. The politics of dislocation and relocation, seen as the political unconscious of the novels, instantiate counterhegemony in the Chicano borderlands through an affirmation of otherness—an otherness not imposed but recreated: an identity based on difference with the capacity to relocate, a "differential consciousness"—whose nature shifts from individual separateness to collective multiplicity—that posits no "ultimate answers, no terminal utopia . . . no predictable final outcomes"[32] but transcends hegemony via *concrete* utopia, a strategic use of deconstructive différance that traces the *necessity* for change and anticipates the *possibility* of an alternative lifestyle. By locating the agency of change in the mestiza—the re-creation of woman as creator who has a vision, is not "afraid to speak that vision" (Saeta Interview), and, most importantly, acts accordingly. And by restoring their indigenous roots, Castillo invests her female characters with a historicized and politicized consciousness—a nonessentialized consciousness based on a radical mestiza subjectivity, that is, a subversive position of intelligibility and mode of knowing necessary for the transformation of cultural practices—as strategy of empowerment and liberation.[33] For that reason I read her politics of dislocation and relocation as resistance Xicanisma that envisions the mestiza consciousness as "a crossroads sin fronteras," (*Borderlands* 195) a "locus of possibility" (Sandoval 14), a motivating force behind "the development of an alternative social system" (Castillo **Massacre** 22). The deconstructive nature of this undertaking resides in the revelation of the necessity for insurgency/activism[34] without legitimating the envisioned results as transcendental truths: a "talking back" whose echoes do not spiral down into *abyme* but create a "real state of emergency" (Benjamin 257) that carries the possibility of "new life and new growth," (hooks 211) or to use Heidegger's phrase, *"something begins its presencing"* in the Chicano borderlands (Bhabha 1).

*Notes*

1. Jean-Paul Sartre, *Qu'est-ce que la litterature* (Paris: Gallimard, 1948) 30: "L'ecrivain engagé sait que *dévoiler* c'est *changer* et qu'on ne peut dévoiler qu'en projetant de changer."

2. Rosario Castellanos translated the Aztec expression 'nepantla' as "terra intermediária . . . terra de ninguém." See Gunter W. Lorenz, *Diálogo coma America Latina* (Sao Paulo: EPU, 1973) 194.

3. See Luce Irigaray, *Speculum de l'autre femme* (Paris: Minuit, 1974).

4. See Ramon Saldivar, "A Dialectic of Difference. Towards a Theory of the Chicano Novel," *MELUS* 6.3 (Fall 1979): 73–92.

5. Umberto Eco called this type of novel "open work." See Umberto Eco, *The Role of the Reader: Explorations in the Semiotics of Texts* (Bloomington: Indiana UP, 1979) 63.

6. Raymond Williams, *Problems in Materialism and Culture* (London: Verso, 1997) 22–27. See also Edward Said, *Culture and Imperialism* (New York: Vintage, 1994) 14, 52.

7. Ana Castillo, *The Mixquiahuala Letters* (Binghampton, NY: Bilingual Press, 1986) 46. All further references will be included in the text.

8. See also Castillo's statements in *Partial Autobiographies, Interviews with Twenty Chicano Poets,* ed. Wolfgang Binder (Erlangen: Palm & Enke, 1985) 37.

9. Dieter Helms, "Developments in the Chicana Cultural Movement and Two Works of Chicana Prose Fiction in 1986: Estela Portillo's *Trini* and Ana Castillo's *The Mixquiahuala Letters*," *Minority Literatures in North America: Contemporary Perspectives,* eds. W. Karrer and H. Lutz (Frankfurt: Vervuert, 1990) 153.

10. This narrative fragmentation and undecidability has been described by Heiner Bus as "a constant interplay of opposites and recurrent cycles of closeness and detachment." See Heiner Bus, "'i too was of that small corner of the world': The Cross-Cultural Experience in Ana Castillo's *The Mixquiahuala Letters* (1986)" 11 (Manuscript presented at the Conference of the Association for the Study of the New Literatures in English, Munich, Germany 1993).

11. Terry Eagleton, "Nationalism: Irony and Commitment," in *Nationalism, Colonialism, and Literature,* ed. Seamus Deane (Minneapolis: U of Minnesota P, 1990) 29.

12. Helene Cixous, "The Place of Crime, the Place of Forgiveness," in *The Hélène Cixous Reader,* ed. Susan Sellers (London/New York: Routledge, 1994) 152.

13. Castillo, *Massacre* 169. She argues that "the alienation of" man's "own connection to living matter" set in with the "dominance of man over woman's psyche" and is one of the basic constitutive elements of "man's view of woman as 'other.'"

14. Fredric Jameson, *Postmodernism, or, the Cultural Logic of Late Capitalism* (Durham: Duke UP, 1991) 54. In the era of late capitalism when geographical and cultural borders give way to globalism, transnationalism, and transmigrational borderlands, in our postmodern mass-mediatized world, human emotions are walled up. This, I would say, is one of the principal implicit messages underlying Máximo's role in the novel.

15. Ana Castillo, *Sapogonia* (Tempe: Bilingual, 1990) 16. Further references will be given in the text. According to Castillo it is natural that women represent this *weltanschauung* and that it is translated into their writing because "nosotras las mujeres no pensamos *linearly*. We think in the spiral, or . . . in circles . . . that's the only way that I could think of writing." Jacqueline Mitchell et al., "Entrevista a Ana Castillo," *Mester* 20.2 (Fall 1991): 155.

16. For a detailed analysis of this topic see my *Magical Realism in Contemporary Chicano Fiction* (Frankfurt: Vervuert, 1993) 13–21 and 129–37.

17. Castillo links his state of confusion and resultant attitude to the collective male profanation of Coatlicue, a process that began when, according to Anzaldúa, "the male-dominated Aztec-Mexica culture drove the powerful female deities underground by giving them monstrous attributes and by substituting male deities in their place." Gloria Anzaldúa, *Borderlands* 27. Máximo continues this tradition and the novel shows how he does not only *other* Pastora-Coatlicue through his attitude but himself too.

18. Unlike Sixo in Morrison's *Beloved,* Máximo, unable to *share* love, does not regard Pastora as a friend of his mind, a woman capable of gathering the pieces of his fragmented identity and giving them back to him "in all the right order." See Toni Morrison, *Beloved* (New York: Signet, 1989) 335.

19. Norma Alarcon, "Making *Familia* From Scratch: Split Subjectivities in the Work of Helena María Viramontes and Cherrie Moraga," in *Chicana Creativity and Criticism: Charting New Frontiers in American Literature,* eds. Maria Hererra-Sobek and Helena María Viramontes 157.

20. Carlos Fuentes used the term to describe the "disintegration of the human personality." See John King, "Carlos Fuentes: An Interview," in *Modern Latin American Fiction: A Survey,* ed. John King (London: Faber and Faber, 1987) 142.

21. Tomas Rivera, "Chicano Literature: The Establishment of Community," in *A Decade of Chicano Literature (1970–1979). Critical Essays and Bibliography,* eds. Luis Leal et al. (Santa Barbara: La Causa, 1982) 9–17.

22. For the definition of a "speakerly text" see Henry Louis Gates, Jr., "Zora Neale Hurston and the Speakerly Text," in *Southern Literature and Literary Theory,* ed. Jefferson Humphries (Athens: U of Georgia P, 1990) 150.

23. On the role of faith in a magico-realist worldview see Alejo Carpentier, *El reino de este mundo* (La Habana: Letras Cubanas, 1984) 7 and Mircea Eliade, *Mito y realidad* (Madrid: Guadarrama, 1968) 19. On the imaginary as factual reality see Paula Gunn Allen, *The Sacred Hoop* (Boston: Beacon, 1992) and Miguel Angel Asturias' statements in Lorenz, *Diálogo* 256–257.

24. See, for example, the episode in which La Loca's actions and statements challenge Father Jerome's patriarchal Christian notion of faith (22–25), or the scene in which Felicia says to Caridad, ". . . you healed yourself by pure will" (55). Ana Castillo, *So Far from God* (New York: Plume, 1994). Further references will be given in the text.

25. The fundamental difference between *Their Eyes Were Watching God* and *So Far from God* lies in the interplay of orality and magical realism that characterizes the creation of community in Castillo's novel—a difference which serves as the basis for my elaboration on Gates' definition.

26. Fe is the emblem of reification, the transformation of all human functions into commodities, and her role in the novel stresses what Lukács described as the "dehumanized and dehumanizing function of the commodity relation." See Georg Lukacs, *History and Class Consciousness* (London: Merlin, 1971) 83.

27. It could be argued, then, that Castillo rewrites faith—the fundamental principle of this process—as a political force of subversion and a strategy of subaltern representation and empowerment as it is the faith in an enlarged reality—a magico-realist worldview—that functions as the in-between space which provides the terrain for an articulation of cultural difference.

28. Ernst Bloch, in *Das Prinzip Hoffnung* (Frankfurt: Suhrkamp, 1985) 163–65, defines a "concrete utopia" as being based on "imaginary ideas which extend existing things to the future possibilities of their difference and betterment in an anticipatory way." According to Bloch, this type of utopia, unlike abstract utopias, expresses hope based on reality. My translation.

29. Kenneth Burke called this rhetoric "negativism," that is, the creation of counter-values through a process of negation as ideological struggle on the discursive level. See Kenneth Burke, *Counter-Statement* (Berkeley: U of California P, 1968) 111.

30. Defined by her as "an effort to involve oneself in representation, *not* according to the lines laid down by the official institutional structures of representation." Gayatri Spivak, "Subaltern Talk," in *The Spivak Reader,* eds. Donna Landry and Gerald MacLean (London: Routledge, 1996) 306.

31. Bruce-Novoa argues that Chicana writers of the first two decades of contemporary Chicano literature have revealed "the fissures in the interior circle." "The dialogue between the sexes" used by contemporary Chicana writers to problematize their invisibility and articulate the problems of self-representation (and the implicit necessity to refashion themselves and society), continues to play an important role in Castillo's creative work as is attested by her stories in *Loverboys* (1996). Juan Bruce-Novoa, "Dialogical Strategies, Monological Goals: Chicano Literature," in *An Other Tongue,* ed. Alfred Arteaga (Durham: Duke UP, 1994) 240.

32. Chela Sandoval, "U.S. Third World Feminism: The Theory and Method of Oppositional Consciousness in the Postmodern World," *Genders* 10 (Spring 1991): 23.

33. A strategy that moves from what Williams called an "alternative practice" in *The Mixquiahuala Letters* and *Sapogonia* to an "oppositional practice" in *So Far from God.* See Raymond Williams, *Problems in Materialism and Culture* (London: Verso, 1997) 41–42.

34. This necessity, which is the core of what Castillo calls "*concientizacion*" (*Massacre* 10; 220) and constitutes one of the basic subtexts of her novels, is maybe best expressed in the following remark by the narrator in *So Far from God*: "Every single step of launching off the cooperative took a lot of effort, a lot of time, and mostly a lot of not only changing everyone's minds about why not to do it but also changing their whole way of thinking so that they *could* do it" (146).

*Works Cited*

Allen, Paula Gunn. *The Sacred Hoop*. Recovering the Feminine in American Indian Traditions. Boston: Beacon, 1992.

Anzaldúa, Gloria. *Borderlands/La Frontera*. San Francisco: Spinsters Aunt Lute, 1987.

———. ed. *Making Face, Making Soul/Haciendo Caras: Creative and Critical Perspectives by Feminists of Color*. San Francisco: Spinsters/Aunt Lute, 1990.

Barthes, Roland. *Le bruissement de la langue*. Paris: Seuil, 1984.

Benjamin, Walter. *Illuminations*. New York: Schocken, 1969.

Bhabha, Homi M. *The Location of Culture*. New York: Routledge, 1994.

Binder, Wolfgang, ed. *Partial Autobiographies,* Interviews with Twenty Chicano Poets. Erlangen: Palm & Enke, 1985.

Bloch, Ernst. *Das Prinzip Hoffnung*. Frankfurt: Suhrkamp, 1985.

Bruce-Novoa, Juan. "Dialogical Strategies, Monological Goals: Chicano Literature." *An Other Tongue*. Ed. Alfred Arteaga. Durham: Duke UP, 1994. 225–45.

Burke, Kenneth. *Counter-Statement*. Berkeley: U of California P, 1968.

Bus, Heiner. "'i too was of that small corner of the world': The Cross-Cultural Experience in Ana Castillo's *The Mixquiahuala Letters* (1986): Manuscript, 1993.

Carpentier, Alejo. *El reino de este mundo.* La Habana: Letras Cubanas, 1984.

Castillo, Ana. *Sapogonia.* Tempe: Bilingual, 1990.

———. *So Far from God.* New York: Plume, 1994.

———. *Massacre of the Dreamers.* Albuquerque: U of New Mexico P, 19.

———. *The Mixquiahuala Letters.* Binghamton, NY: Bilingual, 1986.

Cixous, Hélène. "The Laugh of the Medusa." *Signs* 1.4 (Summer 1976): 875–93.

———. "The Place of Crime, the Place of Forgiveness." *The Hélène Cixous Reader.* Ed. Susan Sellers. London: Routledge, 1994. 149–56.

Deane, Seamus, ed. *Nationalism, Colonialism, and Literature.* Minneapolis: U of Minnesota P, 1990.

Derrida, Jacques. "Differance." *The Continental Philosophy Reader.* Eds. Richard Kearney and Mara Rainwater. London: Routledge, 1996. 441–64.

Eco, Umberto. *The Role of the Reader: Explorations in the Semiotics of Texts.* Bloomington: Indiana UP, 1979.

Eliade, Mircea. *Mito y realidad.* Madrid: Guadarrama, 1968.

Foucault, Michel. *Power/Knowledge.* Ed. Colin Gordon. New York: Pantheon, 1980.

Gonzales-Berry, Erlinda. "*The* (Subversive) *Mixquiahuala Letters*: An Antidote for Self-Hate." *L'ici et l'ailleurs: Multilinguisme et multiculturalisme en Amerique du Nord.* Ed. Jean Beranger. Bordeaux: Presses de l'Universite de Bordeaux, 1991. 227–40.

Hererra-Sobek, Maria, and Helena Maria Viramontes, eds. *Chicana Creativity and Criticism: Charting New Frontiers in American Literature. Americas Review* 15. 3–4 (1987).

hooks, bell. "Talking Back." *Making Face, Making Soul/Haciendo Caras.* Ed. Gloria Anzaldúa. San Francisco: Aunt Lute, 1990. 207–11.

Humphries, Jefferson, ed. *Southern Literature and Literary Theory.* Athens: U of Georgia P, 1990.

Fanon, Frantz. *The Wretched of the Earth.* New York: Penguin, 1967.

Geertz, Clifford. *The Interpretation of Cultures.* New York: Basic, 1973.

Irigaray, Luce. *Je, tu, nous. Toward a Culture of Difference.* London: Routledge, 1993.

———. *Speculum de l'autre femme.* Paris: Minuit, 1974.

Jameson, Fredric. *Postmodernism, or, the Cultural Logic of Late Capitalism.* Durham: Duke UP, 1991.

———. *The Political Unconscious: Narrative as a Socially Symbolic Act.* Ithaca: Cornell UP, 1981.

JanMohamed, Abdul R., and David Lloyd, eds. *The Nature and Context of Minority Discourse.* New York: Oxford UP, 1990.

Karrer, Wolfgang, and H. Lutz, eds. *Minority Literatures in North America: Contemporary Perspectives.* Frankfurt: Vervuert, 1990.

King, John, ed. *Modern Latin American Fiction: A Survey.* London: Faber and Faber, 1987.

Lentricchia, Frank. *Criticism and Social Change.* Chicago: U of Chicago P, 1985.

Lorenz, Gunter W. *Diálogo coma América Latina.* São Paulo: EPU, 1973.

Lukacs, Georg. *History and Class Conscience.* London: Merlin, 1971.

Mitchell, Jacqueline, et al. "Entrevista a Ana Castillo." *Mester* 20.2 (Fall 1991): 145–56.

Morrison, Toni. *Beloved.* New York: Signet, 1989.

Rivera, Tomas. "Chicano Literature: The Establishment of Community." *A Decade of Chicano Literature (1970–1979). Critical Essays and Bibliography.* Eds. Luis Leal, Fernando de Necochea, Francisco Lomeli and Roberto G. Trujillo. Santa Barbara: La Causa, 1982. 9–17.

Saeta, Elsa. "A *MELUS* Interview: Ana Castillo. *MELUS* 22.3 (Fall 1997): 133–49.

Said, Edward W. *The World, the Text, and the Critic.* Cambridge: Harvard UP, 1983.

———. *Culture and Imperialism.* New York: Vintage, 1994.

Saldivar, Ramon. "A Dialectic of Difference: Towards a Theory of the Chicano Novel." *MELUS* 6.3 (Fall 1979): 73–92.

Sandoval, Chela. "U.S. Third World Feminism: The Theory and Method of Oppositional Consciousness in the Postmodern World." *Genders* 10 (Spring 1991): 1–24.

Sartre, Jean-Paul. *Qu'est-ce que la litterature.* Paris: Gallimard, 1948.

Spivak, Gayatri. "Subaltern Talk: Interview with the Editors." *The Spivak Reader.* Eds. Donna Landry and Gerald MacLean. New York: Routledge, 1996. 287–308.

Therborn, Goran. *The Ideology of Power and the Power of Ideology.* London: NLB, 1980.

Walter, Roland. *Magical Realism in Contemporary Chicano Fiction.* Frankfurt: Vervuert, 1993.

Williams, Raymond. *Marxism and Literature.* Oxford: Oxford UP, 1977.

———. *Problems in Materialism and Culture.* London: Verso, 1997.

**Manuel Luis Martinez (review date 26 September 1999)**

SOURCE: "Ana Castillo's Story of a Worn Woman Who Seeks to Understand Her Past and Imagine Her Future," in *Chicago Tribune Books,* September 26, 1999, pp. 1, 3.

[*In the following review, Martinez offers a positive assessment of* Peel My Love like an Onion *and commends Castillo's ability to create compelling stories.*]

Carmen Santos suffers, and we learn from it. The wise and able self-styled "crippled" flamenco dancer of Ana Castillo's latest novel, *Peel My Love like an Onion,* takes us on a journey through a subculture so esoteric it seems as strange as the men who love and leave and love Carmen, and yet is made familiar by the stirring recollections of peculiar but recognizable inner life.

On the surface the novel covers old ground: a love triangle involving an older, married man who discovers and then shapes a young, beautiful girl with a tragic physical flaw, and a later emotional entanglement with a handsome, talented younger man who happens to be the older man's protege. But the seemingly inevitable, agonizing choice we expect never quite materializes, and we find, surprisingly, that this is not so much a well-wrought romance as it is the stoic memoir of one of the bravest and most intelligent narrators in recent memory.

We find Carmen living with her aging, somewhat insensitive mother and a father and set of brothers who are distant and not particularly interested in her travails. Fearing that her childhood polio has returned, Carmen hobbles back and forth to work at an airport cafe as she tries to understand how she has ended up so destitute. "Time in and of itself does not shape you forever," she reflects, "but incidents, people, a single place can. Something happens and suddenly you look around and you don't recognize anything, not even yourself." Thus the novel is fueled not by its familiar romantic elements so much as by a worn woman's desire to recount and then reconcile herself to her past, and in so doing, to perhaps imagine a future.

Introduced by a kind and inspiring high school teacher to Agustin, the Cleveland-born gypsy leader of a flamenco troupe, the teenage Carmen begins to dance professionally. Agustin is domineering and ruthless, and yet Carmen finds that she gains strength in his refusal to see her as disabled:

> "A good lover will . . . see something worthwhile in you that you never knew was there. And when there's something you don't like to see in yourself a good lover won't see it either."

A stormy, 17-year love affair begins. As the relationship peters out, Manolo, Agustin's god-son, captures Carmen's affections.

Young Manolo is impetuous, handsome, passionate and deeply in love with Carmen. But he is also loyal to his godfather and unwilling to take Carmen from him, even though Agustin is unwilling to commit wholly to her. All three must deal with conflicting desire and loyalty. Meanwhile Carmen's physical condition begins to deteriorate and she finds an unlikely source of comfort and strength in her estranged mother, who is suffering from a heart condition. Reconciliation emerges as the dominant and compelling theme in this complex novel.

In lesser hands, the plot could easily devolve into melodrama. But Castillo has shown in her past novels, especially in her last, *So Far from God,* that drama and romance are still excellent vehicles for serious, if not downright philosophic, contemplation. Castillo defies stereotypes even while she evokes them: Gypsies, romantic Latinos, sultry dancers, Chicago Chicanas, domineering mothers and spunky drag queens populate the novel, all the while being drawn in ways that successfully reconsider all the characters in all their flawed, empathic, comic humanity. "If you believe one thing to be true about a people, the very opposite will also be true," Carmen says. Castillo's novel gives proof to that observation, paring away the vellum her characters hide beneath in order to reveal the multifaceted personas lurking there.

Carmen, of course, is the center of this thoughtful and engaging novel. She is in many ways the novel personified, a compelling work through which we are willing to peel away page after page in order to come to a comprehensible core, And Carmen is a compelling character: beautiful, funny, intelligent and articulate. She invites the reader to listen to her story of love, betrayal, incredible affliction and heart-rending sorrow. Survival, however, is the main subject of this novel, and Carmen is too smart and too strong to wallow in self-pity.

In a world where one must name and then claim one's own redemption, Carmen is wise enough to know that one must learn to love one-self. For her that means accepting her atrophied leg, understanding her flawed lovers and coming to terms with a willful, sometimes cruel mother.

Carmen knows that achieving these goals is not a matter of coming to some sudden Jamesian moment of clarity, but is a matter of painful, life-long lessons and observations:

> "[S]ometimes you have to look real close for the tiniest sign of something green. Like a lotus that has grown out of the mud underneath water and blossoms when it reaches light and a new life unfolds."

In reading, we are fortunate not only to witness Carmen's observations, but to come to a few of our own.

Carmen has suffered, and she tells us all about it. Along the way we remember our own pain, be it caused by old, half-remembered lovers, siblings and parents only half-conscious of the pain they inflict, or our own treacherous bodies breaking down in the face of relentless time or oblivious disease. We all hurt, we all strive to survive.

Reading *Peel My Love like an Onion* reminds us of our own small but glorious victories. Ana Castillo has written her best novel to date, one that ministers to the pain of love and the self-knowledge and self-acceptance that suffering, in all hope, engenders.

**Maya Socolovsky (essay date Fall 1999)**

SOURCE: "Borrowed Homes, Homesickness, and Memory in Ana Castillo's *Sapogonia*," in *AZTLAN: A Journal of Chicano Studies*, Vol. 24, No. 2, Fall, 1999, pp. 73–94.

[*In the following essay, Socolovsky highlights the contradictory elements of Máximo Madrigal, the anti-hero of* Sapogonia: *hero versus antihero, power versus loss of control, exile versus tourist, memories of the past versus the present, and Madrigal's homesickness for his fatherland versus his yearning for a motherland.*]

> We pretend that we are trees and speak of roots. Look under your feet. You will not find gnarled growths sprouting through the soles. Roots, I sometimes think, are a conservative myth designed to keep us in our place.
>
> —Salman Rushdie, *Shame*

In this paper, I examine the formation of home through ideas of tourism and exile, homesickness, and houses, in Ana Castillo's second novel, *Sapogonia*. I claim that the protagonist of the novel, Máximo Madrigal, manipulates and borrows others' spaces to form a memory of a myth which might serve as a remnant of home from the past. I show that for Máximo, home as a migrant concept consists not only of a moving place but also of moving memories that "ground" that place.

As a starting point, it is useful to interrogate two models of home and houses offered by Alfred Arteaga in *Chicano Poetics: Heterotexts and Hybridities* (1997) and by Gaston Bachelard in *The Poetics of Space* (1994). Much has been written on the impact of Bachelard's writing on Sandra Cisneros's work;[1] allegedly Cisneros was driven to write her first novel, *The House on Mango Street,* in answer to a seminar discussion of Bachelard's *Poetics*. Cisneros writes, in response to *Poetics,* "what did I know except third-floor flats. Surely my classmates knew nothing about that. That's precisely what I chose to write: about third floor flats, and fear of rats, and drunk husbands sending rocks through windows, anything as far from the poetic as possible" (1987, 73). Cisneros's statement can be seen as a call to critics to recognize not the lack of the poetic in her work, but the way in which her writing, and the writing of other Chicana and minority women in America, redefine the poetics of home and memory as a migrant one. Furthermore, the statement shows the need for the Chicana writer to articulate her own theory of home and space. I choose to develop this theory of home as one that is in opposition to Bachelard's writing, combined with elements of Arteaga's discussion of Aztlán and the borderlands.

Arteaga offers a precise model of two alternating and opposing conceptions of space for the Chicano/a people. Aztlán, as the mythical home of the Aztecs, is located as the ancient homeland: "to be a Chicano and to live in Aztlán is to have historical precedence over Anglos in the Southwest; it is to declare a historical fact of descent" (Arteaga 1997, 9). The "Plan Espirituel de Aztlán," drawn up in 1969 in the first Chicano National Conference in Denver, declared Aztlán as the Chicano homeland, pointing out that it answers the "call of our blood" and evoking a rural existence: "Aztlán belongs to those who plant the seeds, water the fields, and gather the crops, and not to the foreign Europeans" (Arteaga 1997, 12). The Aztlán represented here speaks to the male Chicano, the "brotherhood," and locates itself within American political borders, so that what is called for is a cultural nationalism rather than a political one: "The conceived homeland is ambiguous enough to arouse passion, yet not mandate revolution" (Arteaga 1997, 14).[2] What I would like to take from the concept of Aztlán as a homeland is its understanding that the notion of a "return" to it is not needed because one is already there, and the idea that "it functions as the national myth in a manner similar to the myths of any people" (Arteaga 1997, 14). We can see elements of racial memory and pride being sown here, however, that will be appropriated by Chicana and Latina writers later on, such as Castillo, and interrogated, as she constructs, in *Sapogonia,* a hero and heroine unable to "settle at home" anywhere.

For Arteaga, the borderlands, in contrast to Aztlán, offer a "poorer conception of homeland because one never knows where the real borderland ends and the metaphoric one begins" and although Aztlán is a myth, "the borderlands is an argument" (Arteaga 1997, 18). Yet it is the combination of myth and argument developed from this that precisely offers a fertile ground for beginning to consider ideas of home and memory for Chicanas and other minority women writers in America. The state of relations and differences that the borderlands represent indicates the need for movement-as-home, but the myth that a homeland offers represents the importance of belief and of storytelling that come to make up a nation. To combine argument with myth in the formation of a homeland is to leave all myths of that homeland constantly open to reinterpretation and reappropriation, and Castillo's portrayal of Pastora in the text demonstrates an alternative response to such myths, that Chicana and Latina writers attempt to subvert. To build one's own myths is, therefore, akin to being the architect of one's own home in the here and now, and the impossibility of return to a country that one is in exile from is resolved when that return becomes represented by the movement of that country to the present location and time, through memory. As Iain Chambers has suggested, once we are led away from nostalgic dreams of going home to a mythic, metaphysical location, we enter the realm of theorizing a way of "being at home" that accounts for "the myths we know to be myths yet continue to cling to, cherish and dream" (Chambers 1990, 104). If the community clinging to the myth has also been active in building and renewing that myth, an understanding of home will be found in migrancy and displacement.

In *Sapogonia,* Ana Castillo has created a metaphorical country set in Latin America, from which all mestizos originate. The story follows the travels of an expatriate of Sapogonia, Máximo Madrigal, who moves from his hometown to Paris, from there to Barcelona and Madrid, and then to various locations in North America. During this time, he meets and comes to know his father in Spain, travels in America, and becomes obsessed with Pastora Ake, an American woman of Spanish and Native American blood who tries to escape all his attempts to control her. The text alternates between a first-person and a third-person narration of events, a process which is, I will argue, significant in demonstrating Max's vacillating position as both an exile and a traveling tourist. In this reading of the text, I suggest that Máximo Madrigal needs to be seen as a dual tourist-exile figure who narrates his own heroic adventures only to have his narration and invented heroism constantly interrupted by pangs of exilic homesickness, both for his homeland Sapogonia and inspired by his disturbing relationship with Pastora. He is thus positioned as a lighthearted tourist who gets struck by intense and melancholy homesickness. Max wavers on the line between exile and tourist, and through his narrative, a rewritten myth of home and memory is created.[3] I begin with a discussion of Sapogonia—the country—itself, and from that develop a reading of Max's tourism, his promiscuity as a tourist, the relevance of the text's various slippages between first- and third-person narrators, and its definition of the "antihero." I then turn to an analysis of Max's relationship to the land, both in terms of his personal relations to his grandfather and father, and his consideration of father/mother lands. Finally, I trace the ways in which he becomes homesick for a woman and a country, and briefly look at the ways in which Pastora herself breaks various cycles of myth.

### The Sapagonian Tourist-Exile

What is significant in Castillo's creation of Sapogonia is that as a homeland based on a borderland consciousness, it merges the mythical Aztlán with the contemporary and argumentative borderlands. Described as "a distinct place in the Americas where all mestizos reside, regardless of nationality, individual racial composition, or legal residential status" (1), Sapogonia represents a situation where, as Saldívar writes, "culture is understood in terms of material hybridity, not purity" (Saldívar 1997, 19). In Sapogonia, Castillo has not only housed people of mixed European and Native Central or South American blood but has also distinguished them as natives of the country. That is, the borderland mestizo no longer originates from more than one place, but instead has a single and pure place of origin: Sapogonia. But that pure origin of Sapogonia is itself based in hybridity, so that hybridity becomes the origin of one's race. In a brief description of Sapogonia's history, the reader learns that the country has undergone slavery, genocide, immigration, and civil uprising, and Max's first departure from Sapogonia occurs alongside his anticipation and fear of another civil overthrow. On his return to Sapogonia halfway through the text, Max notices the markings of civil dispute and unrest, saying, "what was new to my eyes, the eyes of a new generation of adults, was the foreboding presence of the military among civilians" (86). Thus, Max abroad represents the duality of the tourist-exile figure. Although on his initial departure from Sapogonia he leaves with his friend El Tinto in disguise and escapes the mounting political tension, he himself is not at any personal risk. El Tinto, whose brother has just enacted the ancient myth of becoming *un desaparesido* due to his involvement with the university periodical, is perhaps more at risk, but Max, as the protagonist, performs a borrowing of El Tinto's exilic status and mingles it with his own tourism. His tourist self delegitimates his self-imposed exilic despair and homesickness, reminding us both that his exile is self-imposed, and that the comparative luxury of his bohemian lifestyle in Europe is financed by his grandfather in Sapogonia. Thus, he remains a visitor even while he is a migrant in that he borrows and chooses the lifestyle of the immigrant, lives among immigrants, but always with a touristic awareness of the self-imposed exile he has undertaken, with some of the privileges of choice.

As a country that asserts itself as home to mestizos, Sapogonia locates the ambiguities and difficulties of living on the border, both metaphorically and politically within its own borders. It is a borderland Aztlán, a mythical country that creates a diasporic homeland. Thus, the creation of Sapogonia can be seen as an attempt both to demythologize the distant Aztlán that remains fixed in a specific historical heritage and cultural past, and to mythologize the arguments and differences of Arteaga's borderlands to give rise to an active political nation that functions like any other through its own myths and imagined communities. As far as the ruling metaphor of this nation is that it locates hybridity as its origin, it also performs the impossibility of a static home that is fixed to a particular place, and with the figure of Máximo Madrigal, sets up the possibility of a migrant and moving existence as the only ultimate home. *Sapogonia,* set in the homeland of the migrant Máximo, acts as a rewriting of the traditional Aztlán myth, in which the specificity of a return to a location is interrogated and demythologized.

Against this backdrop of his homeland, two layers are at work in the text. First, Máximo's double narrative represents the dual nature of his tourist-exile status, and interrogates both his relationship to home, and to his homeland Sapogonia. The third-person narrative situates Máximo Madrigal as the quintessential roaming traveler, a blundering and arrogant hero figure on a vaguely articulated quest that alternates between sometimes attempting to find himself, his father, or Pastora, but at other times not looking for anything in particular. He eventually settles down more or less temporarily in America and becomes a considerably well-known sculptor. The switches between the first- and the third-person narratives demonstrate a particular edginess to this travel narrative, in that the hero is simultaneously the narrator of his own heroic escapades and the participating hero in them. This, as I will go on to demonstrate, has significant implications for the construction of the tourist exile as an antiheroic figure. As Caren Kaplan has argued, tourism has been seen to stress the mystique surrounding exile and modes of travel associated in the nineteenth and early twentieth centuries, and Máximo, in his authoring of himself, self-consciously poses as an artist in exile, a state of displacement which allows for considerable "aesthetic gain through exile" (Kaplan 1996, 36).

Interrupting and thus delegitimizing this lighthearted travel narrative is the second layer in the text: that of the homesick exile. The homesickness, which works against the grain of the tourism, incorporates both what could be read as traditional longings for a distant homeland, and a more disturbing and affective sickness that is located around and inspired by Max's relationship with Pastora Ake. Positioned as a lighthearted tourist who is nevertheless struck by intense and melancholy homesickness, Máximo Madrigal wavers constantly on the line between the two, and through his experiences, a rewriting of the myth of home emerges. In the following section I examine the idea of Max as a tourist and as a travel writer, before I go on to look at how this is interrupted by the homesickness latent in the text.

### The Promiscuous Tourist: Narrating Anti-heroism

As a traveler, Máximo becomes the promiscuous tourist who performs a search for home, and for the articulation of the American dream. After deciding to go to North America, he imagines how "he would arrive, get lost in the Romanesque arena of anonymous characters and freaks found in the streets of Manhattan, and . . . concentrate on seeking that promised fortune" (62). Kaplan says that the tourist aims "to realize fantasies of erotic freedom," (Kaplan 1996, 54) but Kristeva has written that "the shattering of repression is what leads one to cross a border and find oneself in a foreign country," and that "tearing oneself away from family, language and country in order to settle down elsewhere is a daring action accompanied by sexual frenzy . . ." (Kristeva 1991, 30). Máximo Madrigal's borrowing of homes is based on his determination to cease all attachment to his past. Through his promiscuity, he performs a "shattering of the former body" that Kristeva also describes as part of the exilic process (Kristeva 1991, 30), legitimating himself as a traveler who constantly leaves behind his past and cannot live in any time but the present tense. For example, he is able to leave his girlfriend Hilda easily because of this particular disassociation between past and present:

> already he thought of [Hilda] as something that had been rather than still existing somewhere else . . . To Max, Hilda was nonexistent. All that Max left behind ceased to exist, was unreal, like the celluloid on which a whole story was told; it was all imaginary, pictures contrived and pieced together for the sake of entertainment.
>
> (74–75)

In the text, what would be devastating events for the exile, are instead articulated by the lighthearted tourist as mere excursions and diversions. For example, when Max is suddenly deported while working in a restaurant in Los Angeles, he writes that he "was deported to Tijuana and . . . stayed to sight-see for a few days" (82). This is the jaunty tone of an unperturbed narrator who is unconcerned for the real safety of his character because of the innate certainty that as a hero nothing can go wrong for him. This persists throughout, so that when Max decides to return to the United States with a valid student visa and consequently has to undergo much red tape and bureaucracy, we learn that "undaunted in the face of perpetual obstacles, our principal character in this tale made two trips to the capital before he was issued a passport" (111). On his way to America, Max has to spend time in Mexico where he gets his papers organized and works at a temporary job. Even at this point, on the threshold of a migrancy that could determine the status of his exile, he becomes distracted and spends a few months on the beach, "unable to resist the fabulous beaches, outdone only by the European and American beauties basking on white shores. Máximo stayed on in the peninsula for a month" (112).

The way in which the tourist-status of Máximo is undermined and thwarted by his inevitable self-exile can be demonstrated through the definition of an antihero at the start of the book. It is Pastora who describes the antihero, and this is significant in that it is ultimately Pastora who, in representing homesickness for Max, makes it impossible for Max to be a hero in the travel-narrative sense of the word, and indeed, later on explicitly refuses to see him as one, saying to him "you are less of a god than you think" (148–49). Pastora describes the antihero as someone who "in mythology and legend, [is] a man who celebrates his own strength and bold exploits." That is, rather than defining the antihero as a person who lacks heroic qualities, Pastora turns the antithesis of hero into someone who celebrates those qualities himself. What is negated is not the presence of specific qualities but the presence of an audience and perspective of outsiders and followers. An antihero is thus a man who establishes himself as a mythical figure, a legend, and Max becomes the embodiment of the antihero every time his first-person narrator slips into the third-person; that is, every time Max's "I" decides to tell a story about himself in the third person, he positions himself as a hero in his own narrative. The question of origins is also pertinent here; in slipping between the first and third person, Max succeeds in being both the hero and thus the central origin and source within the legend, and the narrator of that legend; he is the author and originating storyteller of the myth.

This simultaneous authoring of and participation in his own legend becomes the only way for the exile to tell his own story, because running against the desire to be a hero, and to narrate his travels (to be different), is the need to remain invisible (to assimilate). At one point in the text, Máximo is waiting at the bus station when he notices two immigration officials who stop two women (who we, together with Max, learn are Pastora and her friend Perla) and ask for documentation. The women arouse suspicion because they are dressed in their native garb as a contrast to Max who fears being found un-documented but is pale and "dressed in denim pants and his sheepskin coat" (76). As an illegal immigrant and a tourist, he has achieved a third status, that of an anonymous native of the place in which he stands at that present moment. Max is presented as chameleon-like throughout: "Máximo changed with his environment as the chameleon became the color of the leaf or a rock to protect it from being detected easily by a predator" (80). The officials attract his attention by calling him "buddy" and returning his ticket to him, which he had accidentally dropped on the floor. The moment in which he turns and responds to the interpolation "buddy" is also the moment he realizes that "he had been able to get past the immigration officials, right below their noses, without arousing the least suspicion" (76). The interpolation embeds him in a discursive matrix where "hey buddy" means "you're one of us."[4] As long as he remains silent and does not reveal his "foreign" accent—he responds to the returned ticket with a nod of his head—he can perform both the nationality and camaraderie that the officials impose on him and demonstrate his exilic status. After this, Max feels "a curious sense of freedom . . . that came to the person whose identity had been completely erased" (76) and he watches the immigration officials hound a "small man with a mane of black hair . . . his collar up, as if wishing he were invisible" (77). Max, who needs this anonymity and invisibility, is forced to limit the audience of his heroic tales to only himself. In other words, the only way to reconcile being a hero with being anonymous and invisible is to become the antihero that Pastora describes, in which he narrates his exploits to himself. Pastora, who meets Max in the second part of the book, disrupts his antiheroic performance because the homesickness she inspires in him makes him wish for visibility, for a past and for an affective memory of that past. She thus destroys the fine line he has been able to maintain between being a travel narrator describing his own touristic exploits and a native of Sapogonia undergoing self-imposed political exile.

### The Attachment to Land

Max also compares his own touristic antiheroism with his stately and heroic grandfather, and his absent and much built up father. When young, Max believed his father to be "a grand man in or about Galicia, Spain, an enchanted place way across the body of massive water that separated us" (8). The search for his father begins with a self-consciously heroic and epic tone: "I bought a train ticket to Madrid the next morning, and a few days later I was on my way in the dramatic search for my father" (43). Of his grandfather Max says, "I adored my grandfather . . . I often thought he was larger than life, a man whom I could never replace on the ranch, nor would I have wanted to" (54). Throughout the text his grandfather is carefully located in one place, the ranch, and an inextricable connection is made between the land and heroism.[5] We learn that even as a young man, his grandfather "preferred to return to his country . . . so that he might learn the business of running the ranch. He wanted to have his hands blackened with the soil of the land" (99). As an advocate for a rural existence, much like the *Plan Espiritual de Aztlán,* his grandfather represents the filial link to the land, and an origin that Máximo rejects in favor of travel and tourism. His grandfather says to him "you, I can tell, have no intentions of staying . . . the earth is not in your blood" (93). To fight for the land, as Max's dead uncle did, or to feel an intimacy toward it, is to demonstrate a heroism that Max cannot copy.

Máximo's intimate love for the land does eventually emerge, however, and is translated into the migrant's reappropriation of the traveling tourist-exile. As a sculptor in Chicago, Max sends for the sculptures he made while in Sapogonia and on their arrival, he finds that they are completely ruined. But the loss, he explains, would have been overwhelming if the sculptures had been lost because, he says, "I had used wood from my grandfather's land" (265). Max thus rewrites the myth of an attachment to land by quite literally transplanting that land, and setting it down elsewhere. His use of the ranch's wood for his artwork demonstrates the way in which the place follows the migrant, rather than the migrant returning to the place and calling it home. The notion of a return home is thus reworked; as for this native of the borderland, a return comes to mean an uprooting and transplanting of the land, a change for the land, rather than a return, through nostalgic flashbacks to the past, to an unchanged terrain. The "place" of Sapogonia becomes raw material for varying artistic production and creativity, rather than a fixed source of previously given meaning. The migrant thus refuses to leave the past as having "passed" through this transplanting of place, and the understanding of time as a separation of past and present is collapsed. Time is renegotiated so that the present is able to become familiar through the presence of an object from the past (the wood from the ranch in Sapogonia), and the memory inspired by looking at the sculpture challenges the onset of nostalgia because it is focused on an object that is simultaneously old and new: the old wood has a new form. The familiar, or the home, is thus translated as a place in being brought forward in time and space to the present.

*Sapogonia* is also partly an examination of the workings of one's relationship to the home country as alternately paternal and maternal. The text progresses to show Máximo moving from an attachment to his homeland as his fatherland—whereby he focuses mostly on the patriarchs in his family—to an attachment to Sapogonia as a motherland, a mother and a home, through his possessive obsession with Pastora. By the end, when Pastora herself becomes a mother and bears a son, she and Max both perform a denial of parenthood, in refusing to interpolate themselves as "mother" and "father." As Pastora says to Max, "my son is not a continuation of you or me, who've considered ourselves exceptional individuals among the species, but a continuity of the species, a simple and humble fact" (304). She then adds, "there are no mothers and no fathers" (304). Alongside Pastora's rejection of an origin linked to lineage, Max states that it is his goals that are "a way of preserving his notion of immortality, much more than a son, who grows to become a stranger, or worse, betrays you, your ideals" (305). Máximo himself, as a tourist, has demonstrated this same strangeness that alienates him from his grandfather's Sapogonia. One's native home, in this context, becomes foreign to its own children, and one's children become strangers to their home (their parents and/or their land). The myth of homeland and heroism is thus rewritten as one of travel and rootlessness, in which the origin is always and only traceable as far back as its narrative origin, that is, its authorial voice. The origin, the primary source and beginning of something, the location of ancestry or parentage, is translated into a hybridity of narration.

In his work as a sculptor, Max authors and shapes forms based on an original, yet locates himself as the creator and father of that work of art. In this way, he is able to position himself both as an origin who provides a home for his art, and as a traveler who finds a home in the art. Like the first person Max who provides a place and home for the legend of his third person Max, he is both parent and child, demonstrating the freedom of being an exile and "a foreigner . . . from nowhere, from everywhere, citizen of the world . . ." (Kristeva 1991, 30). For the migrant tourist, home comes from positioning the self temporarily as an origin, and from positioning that self as representative of a beginning. The hybridity that makes up Max's origins allows the hierarchy of origins to break down. That is, there is no longer a prior attachment or right to a particular place, history, or parent. Instead, every element of the tourist exile is in itself an origin, a beginning, and an end.

As a traveler and anonymous wanderer, Max is a borrower and trespasser of homes, women, and land, and in being a borrower, he finds that returning the home is easy because he has refused it a place in memory. The happiness that comes with the freedom of invisibility is based on the lack of origins to weigh him down from the past, and the knowledge that as his own creator, he can simply speed on into a future and make more homes. Two episodes illustrate his borrowing of origins and the ease with which he returns them to the past. First, after bidding his father farewell in Spain, Max goes to America, where he tracks down Hilda, a girl who fell in love with his father Pío twenty years earlier, did not consummate her love for him, and who continues to send him Christmas and birthday cards each year. Max begins a relationship with Hilda that clearly originates in an unrequited relationship from the past. Hilda has been "given" to Max by his father as a specific gift: "One night Pío made another gift to me, the gift of a woman," and Pío assures Max that "when she sees you, she'll love you with the same adulation that she showed me twenty years ago" (59–60). Eventually however, Hilda's "adulation" develops into a "possessiveness [which] was no longer guised in caring or protectiveness over a naive foreigner. The obsession that motivated the string of cards sent to a man she had not seen in more than twenty years lapsed over to the fear of losing the surrogate" (69).

In her relationship with Max, Hilda herself performs a homesickness for the home (Pío) she was never allowed to know, and demonstrates the making of a home as possession. Prior to his escape from Hilda, Max is the possession in a borrowed home, both the imagined fatherland and the child of that land.

The second instance of borrowed origins occurs when Max arrives in New York. There, he describes seeing his father's face "on every face on New York City streets, every hustler, every immigrant worker in the subway . . ." (60). In doing this, he constructs a father figure in every immigrant's face, creating the immigrant class as a part of his own lineage, and constructing a sense of origin that enables him to feel less strange in a foreign land because every stranger's face is in fact his father's face. This "homing" of his foreign environment is a temporary laying down of roots, a borrowing of the immigrant status of migrancy for his own origins. This constructed origin of immigration is, importantly, a hybrid one, in that "Asian-faced or East Indian" (60) they are all his father. Finally, in seeing Pío's face everywhere, Max repeats the act of fathering over and over again, and the act of making himself a "son" to that father(land) in the streets of New York, thus inventing himself again as a hero in a legendary myth. This performance of fathering and of making an origin occurs only in the "now," making the telling of a nation's story or history particular to the present and making it work against the possibility of recording it in memory. It only exists through myth and retelling, where it is always subject to change. Hybridity, once again, replaces the purity of origin. Max is told the story of the hero for light entertainment, and the erasure of the past allows for extensive tourism and borrowing of homes. The "whole story" that Max imagines, with himself as the central hero, illustrates his construction of origins that leave no impressions, and of the past as always entirely "passed." His determination to experience time only in the present is a denial of nostalgia, but it is also an intricate denial of home, because the erasing of past events and history means an erasing of memory. Without memory to make associations between the past and present, the here and elsewhere, there is nothing to make the present time or place familiar in any way, and it is ultimately the familiarity which presents itself in the form of Pastora that makes Max susceptible to homesickness.

### Homesickness and Myth

Kaplan, in writing on the exile and the tourist, says that "the exile is homesick at home or away," and despite being a carefree tourist, Max experiences occasional pangs of homesickness that seem nostalgic and focus on the familiar: either Sapogonia (that is, a specific place), or Pastora, a woman whom he reads as a metaphor for his motherland. His particular longing for a home is filtered retrospectively, through memory. For example, during his stay in Sapogonia after his grandparents' funeral he says that "I'd begun to refer to Sapogonia as my country for the first time in my life. Home as represented by a territory set off by political borders became Sapogonia when it not only gave to me, but took away" (255). Typically, he knows Sapogonia to be his home only when it can represent itself as a loss and an absence. This retrospective nostalgia, in which he mourns the loss of knowledge of home, as well as the loss of a home never experienced in the present tense, also occurs when, at the beginning of his travels, Max sleeps with Catherine, the daughter of a woman that he and El Tinto stay with on their arrival in Paris. He writes, "I felt nostalgia for the virgin after penetration. Why couldn't I love her and let her remain whole, as she had been loved by the mother? Why in the process of loving woman, did man have to nullify something so profound that it was no longer physical?" (32).[6] Here, Max experiences the presence of something only after its absence and loss. The wholeness and purity he describes as having been there before penetration signifies a beginning, reminiscent of the origins of motherly love. Catherine's body is described as being "trespassed" on (32), and Max is the tourist who treads all over someone else's motherland or home.

With Pastora, Max's homesickness emerges as that of the exile that he realizes is always within him. Although he mistreats her, she mistreats him too, diluting the stereotyped "macho" paradigm of their relationship. Ibís Gómez-Vega, in her analysis of the text, claims that Max is not capable of making connections, and that Pastora is, breaking the myth that Max has of her as a typically passive Latina woman. I read Max's relationship with the past, however, as one of struggle (with nostalgia, homesickness, and rootlessness), rather than of complete absence or diffidence. He continually experiences and makes connections between his exilic state (in New York, for example) and his memories of his parents and grandparents, between Pastora's music and his childhood in Sapogonia. Although it is true to say that a great deal of Pastora and Max's relationship is based on carnal knowledge, the text suggests other connections between them. For example, connections on a mystical level are implied when Pastora, during her time in jail, has visions of Max's dead grandmother. The fact that she is unable to tell Max about this does not signify a lack of intuitive connection between them as much as a difficulty in communication.[7] Max refers to Pastora as a disease: "Everything was going well again in my life when . . . I got the symptoms: Pastora was festering beneath my skin once again" (285). For Max, Pastora *is* Sapogonia, and to enter a relationship with her is to enter a homely and uncanny relationship with an unfamiliar space that is also home. In his courting of Pastora, Max nurtures a familiarity with her that is unlike all his previous conquests of women: "I saw her a good many times so that finally I felt I had never seen her for the first time at all, but had always been aware of Pastora on the periphery of my existence. It seemed her name had come to me in veiled fragments, perhaps in dreams or conversations I'd overheard" (135).[8] From the start, then, Pastora takes on an unusual temporal significance for Max in that she seems to exist both in his past and in his present. Once they are together, they each reveal themselves as a history of familiar territory for the other: "intimate childhood memories easing from a half-conscious state . . . all so familiar to the other as to call up . . . a momentary recognition" (157). Later on, Max differentiates between Pastora and other women, saying that with other women he feels he can challenge anything: "I was Goliath himself with them" but "with Pastora I was only a man" (336). Importantly, Pastora will not let Máximo sustain his heroism because around her he desires visibility: "I tried to make myself visible" (135). Pastora's initial refusal to notice him, and her subsequent refusal to need him all work to undo his heroism. By then, however, his invisibility and anonymity are destroyed, and his home becomes the constant and nagging presence of homesickness that is Pastora, both in her absence and her presence.

Just as Max's previous relationships with women defied memory, the one with Pastora precisely roots itself more in memory than in the present moment. In trying to cure himself of her, Max "escaped from her to every woman as unlike her as he could find. . . . Meanwhile, he remembered her. He remembered her especially when he worked, when he welded, when he stared at what might be no more than the beginning of a wall, a crosspiece in an iron fence, and in his mind's eye saw it take form" (6). Memory invokes Pastora even through difference (Max seeks women "unlike her"), a sense of beginnings and origins is created, and of their physical relationship only "the recollection would remain the trophy" (157). Memory defines a performance that is sustainable only in the present, and inspires their time together with a constellation of past and future absences and presences. Along with memory, Pastora brings to Max the experience of affectiveness that works to make whichever place he is in at that moment into a home. Pastora's music reminds him of Sapogonia without the nostalgia of loss, but with the embrace and touch of a home transplanted to the present in that moment: "her performance . . . had carried him to heights and depths he had only recalled during his childhood in Sapogonia, the thrill of riding bare horseback, when his grandfather took him out to deer hunt" (145). The familiarity of home, which is only appreciated in retrospect, after its loss, can in this way be reenacted in the present.

Pastora is also depicted through images of edifices and houses. For Max, in her haughtiness, she seems to exist behind some kind of a wall, and he determines that "he was about to defy that opaque wall from which behind she observed the world and all its inhabitants" (146). Max constructs Pastora as living in a separate building, as entering and exiting, and as being permitted or denied access. Thus, entering Pastora, in the sexual and emotional sense, also means entering a house that might serve as an actual home. Although he entertains the notion of wondering "what would life be, packing his bags, showing up at her door, surrendering once and for all?" (192); the "surrender" of himself to any definite house or place is something he fears too much. He fears Pastora's basement apartment "where one had to reach out to the cold walls in the dark descent of the cement steps to her door" (184). Max, we learn "was afraid of stairs. He had always been afraid of stairs, especially this kind that led to attics and creaked when no one else was around" (176, emphasis in original text). The explanation given for this fear is that as a child, Max's friend Mario told him of an incident when Mario's brother Guillermo saw the ghost of their dead grandmother going up the stairs and crying out to him. The uncanny connotations that stairs carry for Max are based on his uncertainty about what realm they lead to, and the extent to which the place to which they lead will remain unchanged. The dual nature of Pastora's familiarity and strangeness leads Max to fear settling in a home that is uncanny in its homesickness.

Although Pastora's body and land is something Max has to "surrender" to, he is otherwise the "Cortés of every vagina he crosses" (160). The image of a woman's body as a territory to be conquered and as a home space to be borrowed while visiting takes on a political edge. For example, Max needs a green card to stay in America, and he acquires this green card by marrying Laura Marie Jefferson, a woman who has helped his career take off due to her contacts at the Museum of Progressive Art.[9] The metaphor of Cortés conquering land and women is enacted by Máximo's ability to gain citizenship through marital and sexual relations with a woman. Her body becomes the geography of the land he adopts as home, and which in turn nourishes him as a son. Pastora's body, however, which seems to defy frequent trespassing, is portrayed as mythical due to the parallels drawn between herself and the goddess Coatlicue. It thus exists beyond the confines of a geographical nation with politically drawn borders. At one level she becomes a reworking of the Chicana temptress/seductress figure who is impossible to conquer and who consumes men. Anzaldúa writes that "Coatlicue is a rupture in our everyday world. As the Earth, she opens and swallows us, plunging us into the underworld . . ." (Anzaldúa 1987, 46) while Tey Diana Rebolledo describes Coatlicue as both a goddess and a monster who, when portrayed as a decapitated earth goddess, comes to resemble land.[10] Jésus, Max's acquaintance, says of Pastora, "I think she's a witch" (143), and later on, Max similarly mythologizes her: "Coatlicue, he said to himself, tonight she was a goddess incarnated . . . tonight Pastora was dust particles and ether" (144). When he dreams of Pastora as Coatlicue with her face painted red and yellow, and he wakens to ask "are you Coatlicue as I've dreamt?," Pastora responds "have you been so conceited as to believe Coatlicue your mother? You are less of a god than you think" (148–49). To imagine himself as Coatlicue's son is to imagine himself located within a particular legend that is told and retold, and to imagine himself as an offshoot of that myth. Pastora as Coatlicue offers Max a way of placing his attempt at a heroism that is based on a legend rather than on the travel narrative myth that cannot find expression for the homesickness he has encountered through Pastora. Later on, Pastora's marriage to Eduardo, and her motherhood, makes even this placement in the Coatlicue myth unsustainable for Max. He has particular difficulty in coming to terms with a deity giving birth to a mortal and

thinks, "Pastora ceased to be the exalted celestial being. Pastora now labored and toiled like every woman" (300–301). Pastora has rewritten the Coatlicue myth in that she represents a corporeal Coatlicue, who is subordinate to the experiences of the flesh. She undoes the specific traditional myth of a celestial being and instead makes mythological the concept of a real woman. That is, the myth can now represent a corporeal toiling woman like Pastora.

To bring all the issues I have discussed together, I see the text as one that begins as a travel narrative in which Max performs the role of the antihero, telling the story of the invisible but heroic exile. In Part 2, however, this travel narrative is interrupted through Max's meetings with Pastora. The myth of antiheroism is destroyed because Pastora demands visibility and constantly cuts down his attempts at both mythologizing her, and through his proximity and familiarity with her, mythologizing himself. Demythologizing thus occurs at the level of storytelling; and parenting, origins, and father/mother lands are further demythologized when Max and Pastora together, at the end of the book, come to believe in no fathers and no mothers, and to deny "place" as a location for setting down roots. Instead, they see themselves as a species that travels and dislocates itself continually. In this way, Max and Pastora are true hybrid Sapogonians.

As Tey Diana Rebolledo says, "Mythology often functions as a collective symbolic code that identifies how we should live. Cultures use myths and the stories of heroines and heroes to create role models" (Rebolledo 1995, 49). The particular transported and renewed myths of these borderland migrants dissolve the rigid paradigms of role models through their translation into other locations and other cultures. They work against nostalgic dreams of going home to a mythic location, and instead, theorize a way of being at home in which it is the arrival of the past place to the present which replaces the migrant's return to place through nostalgia and longing. Homesickness, for this borderland consciousness, is thus not a question of longing for a lost home or the realization of the construct of that home.[11] Instead, homesickness is the underlying familiarity of the always-borrowed "home-space" in the present, because it incorporates not a reminder of loss, but a manifestation of a new and purposefully built structure or edifice. The incorporation of old and new is in effect the rewriting of an old myth, or the appropriation of an old legend for new purposes. The myths, transportable, are carried by migrants, and come to represent both homesickness (as a borrowed familiarity rather than disease) and renewal.

*Notes*

1. Among others, Ellen McCracken (1989), and Julian Olivares (1996).

2. Gloria Anzaldúa develops a space that is a queer Aztlán: queering the queer so that Aztlán no longer exists in an impossible past nor in the never-here future, but in the here-and-now present. Three years after the conference, the Aztlán plan was written down in a more gender-sensitive way.

3. Critics have read *Sapogonia* in various ways that tend to focus mostly on Max's "badness" and machismo. Juan Antonio Perles Rochel considers the narrative switches of the text when he states that Castillo draws, in Max, "a rootless Latino immigrant in search of an impossible identity, the picture of pathological masculinity, and thus does not wish easy identification with the character" and he considers Pastora eventually "the true heroine and model of empowered femininity" (Rochel 1997, 130). Ibíz Gómez-Vega's reading (Gómez-Vega 1994) also sees Pastora as the heroine of the text, and Max as failing in this role because he lacks the ability to make connections to the past. Although Gómez-Vega offers an excellent analysis of the text, I see a gap precisely in her declaration that Max cannot experience nostalgia: my interpretation of the text finds nostalgia and memory in Max's character. Her reading also depends on seeing Pastora and Max's relationship as a purely carnal one, a slippage which I shall attend to later on in this section. A last important element of the text is that of the level of dream versus reality along which the events function. Elsa Saeta draws attention to the fact that for much of the novel, we cannot know if events are dreamed or if they actually occur (Saeta 1994). This important consideration blurs boundaries between the real and the dream, and affects the extent to which the characters are trustworthy or reliable as narrators of their own desires, activities, and lives. Although here I choose to focus on the tourist-exile figure of the hero in my analysis, I am aware that in the text everything is filtered through a series of potentially unreliable narrators, and that to an extent, the reader can never fully know the other characters of the text. Overall, although I do not wish to dismiss a sympathetic reading of Pastora, I read Max as more multidimensional and problematic than most critics have. Elyette Benjamin-Labarthe (1996) gives an interesting psychoanalytic reading of the text, seeing both Max and Pastora as heroic, claiming that they are involved in a sadomasochistic, narcissistic relationship that is only realized through the frustration of hatred. Taking an interesting angle, Benjamin-Labarthe reads the text as divided into "white" and "nonwhite," where both Pastora and Max harbor internalized desires for whiteness, and she particularly cites Pastora and Perla's relationship as one where the former is attracted to the latter's whiteness, even though Pastora adopts the "Chicana" label that allows her to celebrate brownness.

4. Althusser's assessment of the policeman's hailing or interpellation of the subject suggests that the individual hailed almost always turns around at the sound of the "hey, you there," and that this hailing of individuals exemplifies the existence of ideology. In this ideology, the relationship between two individuals is established at the moment of interaction. An authority figure's "you there" interpellates the subject as about to be interrogated and examined. (Althusser, 1994, 131). The fact that the Immigration and Naturalization Service officials wrongly interpellate Max as one of them, as a member of their community, suggests that there are cracks in the ideological system, cracks in which masked, anonymous performers, liars, or exiles reside.

5. Importantly, Max's grandparents are shot inside their own house, thus showing how the civil uprisings of the country enter and disrupt the interior private space of citizens.

6. In a similar vein, Sandra Cisneros writes about a man's regret in loving a woman: "If I knew the words I'd explain / how a man loves a woman before love / and how he loves her after / is never the same. How the two halves split / and can't be put back whole again" (Cisneros 1994, 63).

7. This argument still leaves open the question that some critics ask, that is, who the hero of the text is. Those who view Pastora as the hero do so because she goes against the grain of what is expected of her, demanding sexual freedom and promiscuity. However, some, like Yvonne Yarbro-Bejarano, see Pastora as entirely passive, insisting that she relate to him on his own terms, as a sexual toy (1992, 69). A decision about the hero of the text is not crucial in my analysis, but I would agree that Pastora's subversive impulses move her to separate and connect memories in her quest for community. Max, on the other hand, is preoccupied with a more individualistic quest, but insofar as his quest overlaps with Pastora's, he also undergoes experiences of connection and memory. Calling Pastora the hero of the text, in short, should not eliminate the complexities of Max's relationship with her and with his past. I would go so far as to say that the text even shows the fragility of applying the concept of hero to a borderland place, because the hero narrative normally requires a natural and naturalized context that is missing in a border text.

8. Max's experience of Pastora in dreams is part of the undecidable dream tone of the whole text. The dream intrusion here is symptomatic, for example, of the tourists being haunted by his suppressed home (his Other).

9. It is perhaps significant that Laura's surname, Jefferson, is that of the founding father, Thomas Jefferson, who wrote the Declaration of Independence. The Jefferson that represents the giving of a green card carries echoes of the document that originally created the American state. Thomas Jefferson himself designed and built his own house.

10. "When her adversaries had mutilated Coatlicue—says the myth—her hair turned to grass, to trees, to flowers. Her skin was transformed into fertile soil, her eyes to holes filled with water, wells and springs. Her mouth changed into great caves, which offered shelter to men. Out of her nose were formed hills

and valleys . . ." (Rebolledo 1995, 50). This depiction of Coatlicue as land furthers the interpretation of Pastora as a manifestation of Sapogonia.

11. Rosemary Marangoly George writes "the sentiment accompanying the absence of home—homesickness—can cut two ways: it could be a yearning for the authentic home (situated in the past or in the future) or it could be the recognition of the inauthenticity or the created aura of all homes" (George 1996, 175).

*Works Cited*

Althusser, Louis. 1994. "Ideology and Ideological State Apparatuses (Notes Towards an Investigation)." In *Mapping Ideology,* ed. Slavoj Zizek, 100–140. London: Verso.

Anzaldúa, Gloria. 1987. *Borderlands/La Frontera.* San Francisco: Aunt Lute Books.

Arteaga, Alfred. 1997. *Chicano Poetics: Heterotexts and Hybrídíties.* Cambridge: Cambridge University Press.

Bachelard, Gaston. 1994. *The Poetics of Space.* trans. Maria Jolas. 2nd ed. Boston: Beacon Press. Originally published as *La poétique de l'espace.* Paris: Presses Universitaires de France, 1958.

Benjamin-Labarthe, Elyette. 1996. "L'amour et la haine dans un roman Chicano contemporain: *Sapogonia* d'Ana Castillo." In *États-Unis/Mexique: Fascinations et Répulsions Réciproques.* ed. Serge Ricard, 193–208. Paris: L'Harmattan.

Castillo, Ana. 1994. *Sapogonia.* New York: Anchor Books.

Chambers, Iain. 1990. *Border Dialogues: Journeys in Postmodernism.* London: Routledge.

Cisneros, Sandra. 1987. "Ghosts and Voices: Writing from Obsession" *The Americas Review* 15: 69–79.

———. 1994. "With Lorenzo at the Center of the Universe, el Zócalo, Mexico City." In *Loose Woman,* 60–63. New York: Vintage.

George, Marangoly Rosemary. 1996. *The Politics of Home: Postcolonial Relocations and Twentieth-century Fiction.* Cambridge: Cambridge University Press.

Gómez-Vega, Ibíz. 1994. "Debunking Myths: The Hero's Role in Ana Castillo's *Sapogonia.*" In *The Americas Review: A Review of Hispanic Literature and Arts in the U.S.A.* 22:1–2, 244–58.

Kaplan, Caren. 1996. *Questions of Travel.* Durham, NC: Duke University Press.

Kristeva, Julia. 1991. *Strangers to Ourselves.* New York: Columbia University Press.

McCracken, Ellen. 1989. "The House on Mango Street: Community-Oriented Introspection and the Demystification of Patriarchal Violence." In *Breaking Boundaries: Latina Writing and Critical Readings,* ed. Asunción Horno-Delgado et. al., 62–72. Amherst: University of Massachusetts Press.

Olivares, Julian. 1996. "Sandra Cisneros' *The House on Mango Street* and the Poetics of Space." In *Chicana Creativity and Criticism: New Frontiers in American Literature,* ed. Maña Herrera-Sobek, Helena Maña Viramontes, 233–244. Albuquerque: University of New Mexico Press.

Rebolledo, Tey Diana. 1995. *Women Singing in the Snow.* Tucson: University of Arizona Press.

Rochel, Juan Antonio Perles. 1997. "Social Change in Ana Castillo's Narrative." In *Women: Creators of Culture,* American Studies in Greece: Series 3, 127–132. Thessaloniki: Hellenic Association of American Studies.

Saeta, Elsa. 1994. "Ana Castillo's *Sapogonia*: Narrative Point of View as a Study in Perception." *Confluencia: Revista Hispánica de Cultura y Literatura,* 10:1, 67–72.

Saldívar, José David. 1997. *Border Matters: Remapping American Cultural Studies.* Berkeley: University of California Press.

Rushdie, Salman. 1989. *Shame.* New York: Vintage.

Yarbro-Bejarano, Yvonne. 1992. "The Multiple Subject in the Writing of Ana Castillo." *The Americas Review* 20: 65–72.

**Renee H. Shea (essay date March–April 2000)**

SOURCE: "No Silence for This Dreamer: The Stories of Ana Castillo," in *Poets & Writers,* Vol. 28, No. 2, March–April, 2000, pp. 32–39.

[*In the following essay, Shea discusses Castillo's life, writings on feminism and Xicanisma, and her upcoming works.*]

Ana Castillo was on the ballot. When the *Chicago Sun Times* put together a survey in 1999 to determine the greatest Chicagoans of the century, Castillo, "writer," was featured in an alphabetical list that included a saint—Mother Cabrini—legendary sportscaster Harry Caray, and First Lady Hillary Clinton. Does that inclusion mean that this outspoken, passionate, and determined woman, who has gained an international reputation as one of the strongest voices in contemporary Chicana literature, has gone mainstream? Or has the mainstream, with its growing interest in Latin culture, finally discovered her work and worth? It's probably a little of both for Castillo, who for the past 25 years has been steadily gaining both attention and acclaim for her poetry, essays, fiction, and journalism, and who has now written a children's book, **My Daughter, My Son, the Eagle, the Dove,** forthcoming from Dutton Books this spring.

To survey Castillo's career is to chronicle the growing recognition of Chicana literature in the United States during the last three decades, when many of these writers have moved from small presses to more powerful publishing houses. Her first novel, **The Mixquiahuala Letters,** published by the small Bilingual Press in 1986, won an American Book Award from the Before Columbus Foundation, and *Sapogonia* (1994), her next novel, was published by the same press. Norton published her third novel, *So Far from God* (1993), which won both a Carl Sandburg Award and a Mountains and Plains Booksellers Award. In 1995, Norton republished its edition of her 1988 book *My Father Was a Toltec,* a collection of poems, some written in English, some in Spanish, telling the story of her father as member of the Toltec street gang, and included in the volume a selection of her earlier poems. Along with the publication last September of *Peel My Love like an Onion,* Doubleday reissued her first two novels. By Carolyn Heilbrun's definition of power as "the ability to take one's place in whatever discourse is central to action and the right to have one's part matter" (*Writing a Woman's Life,* 1988), Castillo has become a powerful presence not only in the literature of Chicanas—Mexican-American women—but in the literature of the Americas.

She specifically identifies herself with Chicana authors: the vanguard writers publishing in the early 1970s, such as Lorna Dee Cervantes and Lucha Corpi, and her contemporaries and friends like Sandra Cisneros, Cherrie Moraga, and Denise Chavez. The label *Chicana* is problematic, however, according to Castillo, because it is a matter of perception as well as bloodline. She points out that women of Mexican descent or background—Mexic Amerindians—or Latinas born in the U.S. but closely linked to Mexican culture all might be called Chicana because they are all part of the Chicana/o diaspora in the U.S. In fact, she champions the working-class "brown women," who are joined by their economic position regardless of ethnicity, in a world where the black/white dichotomy prevails.

These are the people who are the subject of her fiction and the people with whom she grew up. Born, raised, and still living in Chicago, Castillo is the daughter of Mexican-American parents Raymond and Raquel Rocha Castillo. She declines discussion of her upbringing—"It wasn't horrible or anything," she says, "but I prefer not to discuss it with the public"—although she will talk about her father. He was born in 1933 in Chicago and "raised in the neighborhood for so many immigrants of that period—Jewish, Italian, black, Mexican. . . . He had an ear for the mambo and learned to beat out rhythms on cardboard suitcases in the factory where he worked as a teenager." Castillo attended public schools, became a political activist in the 1970s, and received a BA degree in liberal arts from Northeastern University and an MA in Latin and Caribbean Studies from the University of Chicago. For years she made her living as a teacher—early on in Chicago at Malcolm X Junior College, later at Sonoma State College, the University of California at Santa Barbara, and the University of New Mexico—but never considered teaching as a primary career. A self-taught writer who is deliberate about her decision not to participate in traditional MFA programs or workshops, she began writing, she says, not out of a desire to become a writer but out of a firm conviction that she had something to say: "My academic background is in the social sciences—philosophy, women's studies, sociology, literature. I figured that would all inform my writing. Twenty-five years after I started writing, I feel I still have a message to share. I don't want to see myself proselytizing but sharing some real concerns, and I will find ways to do that one way or the other."

In her most recent novel, *Peel My Love like an Onion,* the central character is the unlikely heroine Carmen la Coja, a flamenco dancer whose childhood bout with polio left one foot "bald and featherless, a limp dead heron fallen from its nest." Carmen might be a reincarnation of the Mexican painter Frida Kahlo—who also suffered from polio as a child—or at least her spiritual heir, particularly since in her journal she quotes Kahlo: "What do I need feet for when I have wings?" Castillo is quick to play the similarity down, conceding that they're "both passionate artists," but pointing out that Carmen reflects on that quote in her usual irreverent way, saying, "Easy for her to say. She was a painter, not a dancer."

Perhaps more apt is a link between Kahlo and Castillo, because Castillo is known for her hard-hitting political art. In *The Mixquiahuala Letters,* an epistolary novel written when she was 23, and *Sapogonia,* she explores gender relationships in a patriarchal and racist society and the cost of living as a marginalized group. In *So Far from God,* a magical realist narrative, she posits an alternative worldview in a spiritual community created by the main character, Sofi, and her three daughters. Critic Roland Walter, writing in the journal *MELUS—Multi-Ethnic Literature in the United States*—sees all three novels as "an examination of self through both individual and collective history, linking it to a search for place among one's people." These are serious works that challenge the balance of power.

The quirky characters and the love story of Carmen and Manolo and his godson Augustin suggest that *Peel My Love like an Onion* is a departure from the probing political consciousness of the earlier work, but Castillo disagrees: "I think this story is very political. Carmen is not naive or a victim; she understands the consequences of her choices, and she is telling us all the things that concern Ana Castillo as a Chicano, a Latina, a woman of color, and one of them is the abuse of female labor and children's labor. We learn about that not by the narrator beating us over the head with the message, but by virtue of her experience [when Carmen and her mother go to work in a sweatshop]."

While, of course, Castillo would like for her work to be admired and to have a wide readership, what is most important to her is for it to be understood, particularly by the brown women who are so much like her—the audience she imagines when she is writing and an audience she feels has been overlooked and undervalued. She has made these ideas quite explicit in her ground-breaking theoretical work, *Massacre of the Dreamers: Essays on Xicanisma* (University of New Mexico, 1994), in which she defines the "Mestiza/Mexic Amerindian woman's identity" through the concept of "Xicanisma," a term she coined to capture the concept of Chicana feminism. Writing against an Anglocentric perspective and carefully distinguishing her concerns and position from those of white feminists, Castillo's essay collection is a manifesto on racism, machisma, sexuality, mothering, spirituality, and language. The title derives from the legend that the Aztec ruler Montezuma sought out the people who he had heard dreamed of the fall of his empire and had them massacred. No one, after that, dared tell of their dreams. Castillo includes herself in "we, the silenced dreamers" who must reclaim the vision of wholeness—a spiritually grounded self defined apart from "the greed on which patriarchy is based" and living in harmony with the natural world. In this work, she analyzes the forces that have instilled self-contempt in the mestiza and calls for recognition of the vast difference between the reality of the mestiza and that of the dominant cultures. Castillo intends for this collection, as she writes in her introduction, to be a contribution to "the ongoing polemic of our 500-year status as countryless residents on land that is now the United States."

***Massacre of the Dreamers*** made her Dr. Castillo. The University of Bremen in Germany awarded her a Doctorate in American Studies in 1991, accepting this collection in lieu of a conventional doctoral dissertation. Castillo explains that since the 1970s, European academics have taken an interest in Native American and Chicano studies, and by the 1980s had become interested in women within these groups. Dieter Herms, former dean of the American Studies Program at the University of Bremen, had traveled to the U.S., where he met Castillo and invited her to give a keynote address for an annual conference of German Americanists. ***My Father Was a Toltec*** and ***The Mixquiahuala Letters*** were being used in Germany as Chicana feminist theory, and when Castillo told Herms that one day she was going to sit down and write her ideas out in essay form, he told her that when she did, she should submit it as a formal dissertation.

In the tradition of the academic world, the approval process was lengthy and often contentious, but Herms, who became very ill with cancer, remained Castillo's champion and shepherded the book through the necessary channels. Castillo traveled to Germany, where she successfully defended the work a few months before Herms's death. While ***Massacre of the Dreamers*** has the requisite theoretical underpinnings expected of a dissertation in interdisciplinary studies, including references to critical work in social sciences, history, and literature, the stark difference is in approach. Subverting the objective voice of an allegedly impartial researcher, this work, as Castillo announces in her introduction, "directed itself to the subject of this thesis rather than to the academy." This is a dissertation by, for, and about Chicanas. It seeks to raise consciousness of their history and to incite change in their self-awareness and, thus, their future. In the call for inclusion, its message is a revolutionary one calling for change throughout the culture.

Not surprisingly, one of those changes, Castillo argues, will come about through a "re-visioning" of language. Not interested in becoming part of an existing discourse, Castillo looks toward creating a new, more inclusive one. She calls for a critical understanding of the consequences of being marginalized from the language of the dominant society and writes of the need to take on "the re-visioning of our own culture's metaphors"—not only to understand but to act on the bone-and-blood link between language and identity, the topic of an earlier poem, **"A Christmas Gift for the President of the United States, Chicano Poets, and a Marxist or Two I've Known in My Time"**:

> My verses have no legitimacy.
> A white woman inherits
> her father's library,
> her brother's friends, Privilege
> gives language that escapes me.
> Past my Nahua eyes
> and Spanish surname, English syntax
> makes its way to my mouth
> with the grace of a club foot.

Castillo writes and publishes some poetry in Spanish, but she writes mostly in English, a decision, she says, she made over 20 years ago—"not because I was trying to reach a gringo audience. But I was raised in Chicago without the privilege of bilingual education, so the people I thought would read my work would be the Chicanos who read English. I didn't learn to write in Spanish." She has stated in interviews that the English she writes is not "white standard English" and that an essential element of her work is the distinctive language of the narrator, particularly in ***Sapogonia***, where the narrator's pretentiousness is signaled by the second-language English he proudly uses.

When she sits down to write, language is not the only choice Castillo has to make, since she feels equally at home in poetry, fiction, and nonfiction. She claims that the choice is sometimes hers, sometimes not—"Sometimes with poetry, it's like a meteorite"—and that sometimes there is no real need for choice: "I have what people have told me is a quick left brain/right brain switch. I have worked, for example, on ***Massacre of the Dreamers*** with ***So Far from God***, then the short stories, then back to painting, then some poetry—and that was all in one day! At some point, I say, 'Enough is enough,' go back to the easel, and spend the rest of the day painting." Although Castillo originally intended to be a visual artist, she had stopped painting for over 17 years, then resumed around 1990 when she was in New Mexico and a friend gave her a box of paints and brushes, along with the encouragement to take up art again: "I felt confident enough in my writing at that time that it didn't matter what people thought of me as a painter. I paint for myself." And she paints herself: "My son has gotten me to do a couple of him, but very rarely. Usually, I paint myself in whatever is going on at the moment. Then, I don't necessarily put that in my writing."

Castillo is never alone in her creative process. One of the key chapters in ***Massacre of the Dreamers*** is about spirituality. In the doctrine of Xicanisma, spirituality involves acceptance of self in the context of forces that Western thought might consider "supernatural" and requires rejection of the hierarchical thinking characteristic of Western culture. In Chicana culture, spiritualism is embodied in *curanderas* and *brujas*, the latter spiritual healers or psychics, by Castillo's definition, the former "specialized healers, learned in the knowledge of specifically healing the body." Castillo is the granddaughter of a *curandera*, and it is she, Castillo says, "who taught me how to love and care for other living things. We lived in the heart of Chicago in a flat in the back with a kitchen looking out into a nasty, rat-infested alley. Yet she grew her herbs there, in coffee cans." In the introduction to **Toltec**, Castillo tells a moving story of beginning to write at age nine when this grandmother, her *abuelita*, died. "My lines were short, roughly whittled *saetas* [flamenco-style songs] of sorrow spun out of the biting late winter of Chicago," she writes—and so Ana the writer was born out of the death of the woman who was and is her spiritual guide.

Castillo is herself a *curandera*, but explains that she has been reluctant to take on that lifestyle. In 1997, she was crowned "a *curandera* and hail-maker by the Nahua people of Central Mexico, the region of my ancestry." She believes this is work she is destined to do, but chooses not to elaborate on what that means: "I'm not trying to be mysterious, but as I learn and accept my responsibilities and duties, I must humbly keep them private."

Castillo is also a follower of the Virgin of Guadalupe and always wears a large square ring honoring this figure. Her poem **"La Wild Woman"** is dedicated "Para Clarissa" to Clarissa Pinkola Estés, kindred spirit and author of the best-seller *Women Who Run With the Wolves: Myths and Stories of the Wild Woman Archetype* (1992). They met at a convention, and, Castillo explains, "When she got close to give me a hug, I saw she wore a medal of the Virgin of Guadalupe, so I saw we had a connection." In 1996, Castillo published **Goddess of the Americas: Writings on the Virgin of Guadalupe,** a series of pieces she commissioned from Latino artists and writers, including Estés, to explore the meaning of "la Virgencita at the end of the millennium." Authors of these essays refuse to separate spirituality and sexuality, much as Castillo herself refused in **Massacre of the Dreamers,** seeing them as part of the same energy. Reviewing the essays in *Commonweal* magazine, Robert Orsi saw nothing surprising about their "pervasive eroticism," claiming that "the erotic here signals the refusal of the writers to be rendered other by an image of the sacred that excludes or denies them or that would prohibit them, for whatever politically repressive, racist, homophobic reason, from living inside their skins."

The erotic and spiritual coexist in **Peel My Love like an Onion,** which Margot Mifflin, in reviewing it for the *New York Times,* called a "fiery novel; it's all hot chili peppers." At 40 years old, Carmen describes herself as starting "to look like a Picasso forgery," but, as Castillo puts it, "she knows herself to be beautiful inside and out. This novel's about self-love." Unlike the Carmen of Bizet's opera, this one refuses to be a tragic heroine: "Something about a grand final exit doesn't appeal to me as much as the idea of being asked for an encore." She's the one who brings clients in the beauty parlor, where she is the shampoo girl, to tears when she demonstrates the flamenco—in her cross-trainers.

Where did Castillo find this unlikely middle-aged, feisty, working-class Carmen? Carmen found her, Castillo insists, during the hot Chicago summer of 1995. She was staying with her mother, who was not well at the time, in a non-air-conditioned house, working, usually after midnight, on a borrowed laptop in the basement, trying to meet the deadline for **Loverboys** (1997), her short story collection: "I would turn on a fan my parents had nailed to the window about twenty years ago—when you cranked it up, it sounded like a small plane starting—and work every night until about two in the morning. One of those nights, when I turned on the laptop, this narrator begins to speak. She's taking a power walk, and she starts talking about when she was in love, and, co-incidentally, she's also in Chicago. When she bends down to tie one of her new cross-trainers, she says, 'It isn't easy with the leg brace on.' That's when I realized there was a problem here, a condition, and somehow I knew this would not be the voice for a short story."

So Carmen didn't merely waltz into Castillo's imagination, she flamencoed into a novel about the Chicano and gypsy cultures of Chicago. An irresistible metaphor, flamenco is more a way of life than a dance, one that begins not with the feet but with the heart. Although Castillo is not a professional flamenco dancer, she does not deny that she can do some fancy footwork herself: "You don't have to be tall and svelte or have shiny hair or even all your teeth. The other night on the book tour, there was a flamenco dancer as part of the event—and she's about sixty years old, five feet tall, and sort of all-the-way round—and she gave a really great performance! Flamenco is a very passionate dance, like the tango; it comes from the streets, from poor people, and it's like the blues, an expression of loss, oppression, migrations."

In her latest venture Castillo has taken on yet another genre: children's literature. **My Daughter, My Son, the Eagle, the Dove** is a collection of poems based on Aztec rites of passage from the conquest period in Mexico that Castillo discovered during her research for **Massacre of the Dreamers**: "There are chronicles of talking. Imagine that you're coming of age, getting married, going off to war, and you're brought to the elders, who tell you the significance of the event. I took passages of those speeches, which the Spaniards documented from the Aztecs, and turned them into two chants—one for the son, one for the daughter." This lyrical advice is not so different, Castillo says, from what parents say—or should say—to children today when offering counsel about life:

> When you speak, speak
> not too loud

and not soft
but with honest words
always.

Like Castillo's other work, there is an emphasis on ancestry and history as a source of pride:

Understand, my daughter
that you are of noble
and generous blood;
you are precious as an emerald,
precious
as sapphire.
You were sculpted
of relations
cultivated like jade.

Castillo says she is particularly excited about the book, as well as its sequel—for the newborn—because of her own son, Marcel Ramon, who is 16 and the subject of a number of poems in her newest, unpublished collection, *I Ask the Impossible.* One of these, the whimsical "El Chicle," appears in the New York City subway as part of the Poetry in Motion series and recalls a younger Marcel in more innocent times. Castillo says her major concern today is how her son is perceived as a young, brown-skinned male on the streets of Chicago: "I grew up in a world that was racist, and young people were harassed by the police and by kids from other neighborhoods, but we're living now in a much more dangerous time. My biggest worry is not the choices he's going to make, but how the world has become so much more violent and aggressive."

How does Castillo feel about the mainstreaming of Latino culture or about phenomena like the immensely popular Ricky Martin? "No pun intended," she says slyly, "but what does it all have to do with the price of beans? The mass appeal really doesn't affect most people, except the thirteen-year-old girls who spend their money to hear him. It doesn't translate into much of a difference in everyday lives. The idea that we can become homogenized and rendered as sheer entertainment is not a personal victory for me as a Chicana." Still, Castillo never entirely closes off a possibility, and without a doubt, her Carmen la Coja is an appealing character for film. So, she muses, "On the other hand, if he wants to play in the movie . . ." And it hardly seems a stretch to imagine poet, novelist, activist, journalist, teacher, *curandera,* editor, and theorist Ana Castillo adding "screenwriter," or even "director," to her vita.

## Ralph E. Rodriguez (essay date Summer 2000)

SOURCE: "Chicana/o Fiction from Resistance to Contestation: The Role of Creation in Ana Castillo's *So Far from God,*" in *MELUS,* Vol. 25, No. 2, Summer, 2000, pp. 63–82.

[*In the following essay, Rodriguez explores Castillo's contesting of political, social, sexual, and religious standards and beliefs in* So Far from God.]

The past two decades have given us a wealth of Chicana and Chicano literature, both because of the exemplary work of the Recovering the U.S. Hispanic Literary Heritage project in discovering and recovering older texts and because of the sheer boom in Chicana/o publications over the last fifteen years. Even the nonspecialist now recognizes the names of Chicana/o authors such as Sandra Cisneros, Benjamin Alire Saenz, Ana Castillo, Rolando Hinojosa, and Denise Chavez, to name only a few. Their work, as well as that of their contemporaries, complements the publications of the heralded Chicana/o movement, which included Corky Gonzalez's epic poem "Yo Soy Joaquin" (1967), Tomas Rivera's *Y no se lo trago la tierra . . . / And the Earth did not Devour Him . . .* (1971), Rudolfo Anaya's *Bless Me, Ultima* (1972), Oscar Zeta Acosta's *Revolt of the Cockroach People* (1973), and Estela Portillo Trambley's *Rain of Scorpions and Other Writings* (1975). The corpus of Chicana/o writing, in short, has grown exponentially. While many of the contemporary writers share the social and political concerns of the Movement writers, what I find particularly interesting is the strategic shift these writers have made from a resistance literature to what I identify as a contestatory literature. This essay examines the theoretical framework and historical conditions surrounding that shift and illustrates by example how a contestatory literature engages in social critique. After charting the historical and theoretical ground for the shift from resistance to contestation, I examine the role of the creation narrative in Ana Castillo's romance *So Far from God* (1993).[1]

In establishing a framework for my definition of contestatory literature, I would like first to consider resistance literature. Taking her lead from the Palestinian writer and critic Ghassan Kanafani, Barbara Harlow has written the definitive text on resistance literature, a text which carefully examines the relationship between this literature and third world national liberation movements. "Resistance literature," states Harlow, "calls attention to itself, and to literature in general, as a political and politicized activity. The literature of resistance sees itself furthermore as immediately and directly involved in a struggle against ascendant or dominant forms of ideological and cultural production" (28–29). The writers from the various sites (e.g., Palestine, Lebanon, and South Africa) that she discusses, though not necessarily bearing arms, are so intimately tied into the armed struggle, that she is able to demonstrate powerfully the mutually reinforcing relationship between the cultural and paramilitary programs. Indeed, Harlow asserts, "The resistance writer, like the guerrilla of the armed liberation struggle, is actively engaged in an urgent historical confrontation. The questions raised by the resistance leaders are the questions faced by the writers as well" (100).

Consequently, the alliance between the national liberation movements and the literature that Harlow discusses demarcates a sharp boundary for me between resistance literature and contestatory literature. For the term "resistance literature" is used most appropriately when discussing armed liberation movements that have direct links to territorial claims, where there is literally a battle for terrain and governance at stake. In addition while Harlow takes the necessary measures to define the terms of her argument, the term "resistance literature" has become nearly ubiquitous since the publication of her book eleven years ago. Critical omnipresence of a term, though not necessarily bad, typically drains it of its specificity. In short, I believe the term "resistance literature" has been bandied about so much that it has lost its critical impact and function.

Before moving further ahead, I would like to reflect for a moment on the role of resistance literature in the United States, which Harlow has absented from her study,[2] though many scholars, Ramon Saldivar among them, have subsequently adopted her model to talk about Chicana and Chicano literature. How compatible, though, is the resistance model for Chicana/o literature? The corpus of Chicana/o writing which most closely approximates the literature Harlow discusses is the writing that came out of the Chicana and Chicano movement (ca. 1966–1972). Many people at that time were interested in reclaiming Aztlan as the Chicana/o homeland (see Anaya and Lomeli), otherwise known as the Southwest United States. This section of land, stretching from Texas to California, was violently taken from Mexico in the Mexican-U.S. War (1846–1848), a war which saw Mexico lose half of its territory for a paltry fifteen million dollars, not to mention the loss of innumerable lives. As chronicled in Rudolfo Acuna's aptly titled *Occupied America* (1972), the desire to reclaim Aztlan, the territory lost in the war and the site from which the Aztecs initiated their pilgrimage into Mexico, manifested itself most vociferously in the 1960s and 1970s. Witness, for example, Reies Lopez Tijerina's armed efforts to expropriate territories from the U.S. which, according to Spanish land grants and under the Treaty of Guadalupe Hidalgo, rightfully belonged to their Mexican inheritors.[3] Similarly most consider "The Ballad of Gregorio Cortez" (so eloquently retold and assayed by Americo Paredes in his 1958 study *With His Pistol in His Hand*) a strong articulation of Mexican resistance against a racist Anglo power structure. Though the ballad, about a man unjustly accused of theft who single-handedly fought off numerous Texas Rangers and defied a racist legal system, clearly predates the Chicana/o movement, Paredes' critical study gave the heroic image of Gregorio Cortez a new life for many young Chicana/os and generated intellectual inspiration for Chicana and Chicano writers, intellectuals, and activists[4]

In addition to the impact of Paredes' study, consider the assessment of Alurista, who is regarded as one of the celebrated poets of the Chicano/a movement. In a 1973 study, he offered an analysis and a proposed plan of action:

> The Chicano experience is one of internal kolonization which is bound to a dehumanizing degree with economic dependence on the cultural, political, and military paternalism of the Yankee Empire. Internal revolution is inevitable and imperative. But . . . where do we begin? . . . with the rifle or the pen? With the armed revolt for the popular take-over of the Yankee state or with the cultural revolution for the organization of the popular revolutionary conscience of the Chicano peoples north of Mexico. The first alternative is heroic suicide. The second is protracted (long-range) insurrection, the aim of which, must be fourfold: 1) the organization of Chicano peoples, 2) The liberation of land north of Mexico, 3) the unification of the mestizo nations of Amerindia, and 4) The humanization of the socioeconomic order of the earth. This cultural revolution against kolonization combats repression with reflection and dedicated study, combats suppression with the expression and communication of knowledge and social conscience. And, finally, overcomes oppression with the liberation of people and land occupied and dominated by the Yankee Empire in Amerindia.
>
> (Alurista n. pag., ellipsis in original)

Alurista's revolutionary discourse—his invocation of armed insurrection and internal colonization, his orthographic flourishes, and his belief in self-empowerment—is characteristic of much of this period's writing. Moreover his proposed bilateral approach, which includes cultural as well as armed insurrection, resonates harmoniously with Harlow's model of resistance literature. Indeed, it mandates that I recognize a tradition of resistance literature in Chicana/o letters. Consequently, I submit that some of the writing from this period exhibits traces of resistance literature.

However, the corpus of Chicana and Chicano fiction from roughly 1984 to the present, what might perhaps be called a new wave of Chicana/o writing, bears no resemblance to what Harlow describes as resistance literature. The fundamental union in resistance literature between the armed national liberation fronts and the cultural workers is not to be found in this new wave of Chicana/o fiction. Sandra Cisneros' *House on Mango Street* (1984), for instance, tellingly unveils patterns of gender oppression and of class exploitation, but it is not part of a unified national liberation struggle as are resistance texts such as Manlio Argueta's *One Day of Life* (1980), which comes out of revolutionary El Salvador, or Omar Cabezas' autobiographical *Fire from the Mountain* (1985) about the Sandinistas. In contrast, consider Benjamin Alire Saenz's "Cebolleros" (1992), which subtly exposes the problems of commodity fetishism and of alienated labor in the Chicana/o farmworker community. Both Cisneros and Saenz engage in important social critiques, but the quintessential union between armed struggles for national liberation and cultural production is absent from their work and from other examples of this new wave of Chicana/o fiction. Consequently, I find it ineffective to use the resistance model to analyze these texts. Lest I be misunderstood, I am not valorizing one form of cultural production over the other; rather I am noting a paradigmatic shift from resistance to contestation. While not part of territorial or governance battles per se, these new wave texts continue to struggle against antagonistic forces of oppression, such as racism and sexism. Thus, I opt for the terms contestatory literature or a literature of contestation.

A contestatory literature employs varying narrative strategies to critique, resist, and oppose racism, sexism, homophobia, and/or classism. A particular text need not be solely engaged in enumerating the sundry forms of social injustice to be deemed contestatory. Indeed, if it were engaged exclusively in contestation, I imagine it would become laboriously dogmatic and tiringly doctrinaire. Further, a ready-made formula cannot be had that equates x incidents of critique with a contestatory text, for any mathematical attempt to quantify a work's merits sterilizes the function of the text. If a work fundamentally opposes the deprecation of an individual or a group based on race, class, gender, or sexuality, let us consider that text an exemplar of the literature of contestation. Bear in mind, too, that a contestatory literature is not necessarily a revolutionary literature. To contest something, to call something into question at the linguistic level, does not axiomatically translate into material change.

Though tangible manifestations are certainly desired, the positive results of a writer's act of contestation are not easily assessed. For example, the effects of Ana Castillo's trenchant critique of corrupt dictatorial regimes in her anti-romance, *Sapogonia* (1990), are not easily measured. Does this render her critique futile? Does this make *Sapogonia* any less of a contestatory text? To both questions I answer resoundingly no. Though the results of Castillo's efforts may not be easily charted, she has demonstrated a fundamental opposition to the system of social abuse she describes, rendering hers a contestatory text. In other words, one can demonstrate with textual examples the contestatory capacity of a particular utterance, paragraph, text, etc., without necessarily being able to measure the results of that contestation, though those results, of course, remain of interest.

What precipitated the change from a literature of resistance to a literature of contestation in Chicana/o fiction? The answer can be found, I believe, in the consolidation of the forces of late capital and the historical maturation of the postmodern. Late capital follows the two prior stages of capital: market and then monopoly or imperial capital. Although periodization is a sticky affair, theorists generally consider that the onset of late capital followed the second World War, a period which witnessed a dramatic change in the production sector (i.e., a shift from Fordism to flexible accumulation)[5] as well as an unprecedented rise in consumption. While the principal analysis of late capital remains Ernest Mandel's *Late Capital* (1975), Fredric Jameson offers a useful summary of its constituent features:

> Besides the forms of transnational business mentioned above, its features include the new international division of labor, a vertiginous new dynamic in international banking and the stock exchanges (including the enormous Second and Third World debt), new forms of media interrelationship (very much including transportation systems such as containerization), computers and automation, the flight of production to advanced Third World areas, along with all the more familiar social consequences, including the crisis of traditional labor, the emergence of yuppies, and gentrification on a now-global scale.
>
> (xix)

Above all, Jameson demonstrates the sundry ways in which capital has grown exponentially and has become increasingly more savvy in militating against the forces of labor. Capital has, for Jameson, spun a vast web which entraps all and reduces culture to a mere commodity. Postmodernism and its attendant disorders, which include superficiality, the waning of affect, a fragmented subjectivity, schizophrenia, loss of a historical sense, and life in the continuous present, represent the cultural logic of late capital in the same way that realism and modernism represented respectively the cultural logic of market and monopoly capital (Jameson ix–54).

Why then if postmodernism is the cultural logic of late capital and if the mid-forties marked the onset of late capital, did we witness a resistance literature in Chicana/o letters in the 1960s and 1970s? My answer is two-fold. First, I would argue that from the 1940s to the 1970s late capital was in its incipient stages; it had not worked itself out in all the complexities that Jameson was able to enumerate in 1991. Second, we must remember that, as Jameson is careful to note, postmodernism is a cultural dominant. It does not nor cannot constitute all cultural production:

> the totalizing account of the postmodern always included a space for various forms of oppositional culture: those of marginal groups, those of radically distinct residual or emergent cultural languages, their existence being already predicated by the necessarily uneven development of late capitalism, whose First World produces a Third World within itself by its own inner dynamic. In this sense postmodernism is "merely" a cultural dominant. To describe it in terms of cultural hegemony is not to suggest some massive and uniform cultural homogeneity of the social field but very precisely to imply its coexistence with other resistant and heterogeneous forces which it has a vocation to subdue and incorporate.
>
> (159)

The Chicana and Chicano fiction I discuss forms one such group working outside of the cultural dominant of late capital. These writers have developed strategies of contestation able to cope with the machinations of late capital.

I suggested in the first part of my answer that late capital was in an incipient state in the 40s to 70s, but had fully matured by the 1980s and 1990s. Therefore, the 1960s and 70s strategies of resistance were no longer applicable. In "Beyond the Gender Gap," for example, an article which details a five-step program for revitalizing the women's movement, Martha Burk, president of the Center for the Advancement of Public Policy and steering committee member of the Council of Presidents of National Women's Organizations, and Heidi Hartman, president of the Institute for Women's Policy Research and co-chair of the council's Welfare Reform Task Force, note that "While young people may yet be induced to come out to the streets, again, activism in the old sense is increasingly difficult to sustain for the average woman. To become more effective as a movement we must invent new forms of activism" (20; emphasis mine). In short a correlative relationship developed between capital and alternative cultural formations. As the workings of capital and its accompanying economic and social oppression became more subtle, so too did the corresponding forms of opposition, creating what I call a literature of contestation or a contestatory literature.[6] We witness this contestatory turn in Ana Castillo's *So Far from God.*

Let's first think more specifically about Ana Castillo and the cultural, historical, political, aesthetic, and regional contexts within which she wrote *So Far from God,* in order to provide a richer understanding of her contestatory practices. We know from Castillo's **Massacre of the Dreamers: Essays on Xicanisma** (1994) that Sigrid Weigel's essay, "Double Focus: On the History of Women's Writing" influenced Castillo's own writing: "In 1987 I found this article [Weigel's] immensely insightful and helpful in viewing my own works and my life as a woman writer" (236; fn 17). Given that Castillo received her Ph.D. in American Studies in 1991 from the University of Bremen, Germany, it is not odd that someone like Castillo, who identifies so closely with both her indigenous and Mexican heritage, should be influenced by a German feminist. The confluence between Weigel's feminist theory and Castillo's feminist literary practice strikes one immediately. Moreover, the majority, if not the entirety, of Castillo's contestations in *So Far from God* stem from the oppression of women, meriting a closer look at Weigel, whom Castillo identifies as influencing her own feminism.

In contemplating the representation of women in literature and the emergence of the woman author, Weigel traces a history of women's writing. She concerns herself with finding that space in which women can write as an "authentic" not a "second" sex. "The history of a female literary tradition," states Weigel, "can be described as the step-by-step liberation of writing from the male perspective to an authentic women's writing and language" (64). Although the modifier "authentic" confounds precise definitions and though the term "woman" is not a homogenous one (consider issues of race, class, and sexuality), her meaning is clear. She is talking about the writing of women-defined women, female characters as presented by women. The shift away from the male perspective to a liberatory women's writing manifests itself clearly in *So Far from God* in which Castillo recounts the story of "a woman named Sofia and her four fated daughters." For those readers unfamiliar with the text, Castillo's narrator conveys the, at times, supernatural story of Sofia and her four daughters, Fe (Faith), Esperanza (Hope), Caridad (Charity), and La Loca. With the exception of the inclusion of a fourth daughter, La Loca, the story of Sofia and her daughters modernizes the myth of Faith, Hope, and Charity, and their mother Sophia (Wisdom) dating back to perhaps the second century.[7]

*So Far from God* follows the lives of Sofia and her four daughters, as they pass from youth to maturity in the town of Tome. The story opens with the supposed death of La Loca and her resurrection. By the close of the text, we witness the martyrdom of each of the four daughters. As we move through the approximately 250 pages of the text, Ana Castillo, via her female narrator, writes almost exclusively of these women, with men playing, at best, supporting roles. Although Castillo certainly is not the first woman to author a woman-defined text, *So Far from God,* in addition to her other writings, marks the important shift from the male perspective to authentic women's writing.

Furthermore, Weigel goes on to note the efficacy of using fiction as a weapon against oppression. Noting that non-fiction critiques of patriarchy did not begin to surface until the mid-nineteenth-century, Weigel asserts that "Disguise in the form of literature gives protection as well as the chance to overstep the boundaries of the real and to postulate utopias." "Fiction," she continues, "is a space in which to learn to walk, to fantasize, and to experiment in order to open up a creative way out of the tension between the 'limitations of the strategies and the unsuitability of the desires in the real lives of women'" (67). We hear in Weigel a testimony to the power of fiction as a zone of contestation.

In addition to Weigel's more general feminist positioning, Castillo situates herself and is informed by Chicana feminism, or in her terms, Xicanisma. Anglo feminism has come under attack for failing to recognize class and race differences among women. Many of the early Anglo feminists treated "woman" as a stable and homogenous category; however, as texts such as **This Bridge Called My Back: Writings by Radical Women of Color** (1981) attest, the experiences of women are multifarious and need to be dealt with in their fullest complexities. More specifically, the male dominated Chicano movement of the 1960s and 1970s brought many Chicanas to push for Chicana feminism. In "The Development of Chicana Feminist Discourse, 1970–1980," Alma Garcia states that "Chicana feminists began the search for a 'room of their own' by assessing their participation within the Chicano movement. Their feminist consciousness emerged from a struggle for equality with Chicano men and from a reassessment of the role of the family as a means of resistance to oppressive societal conditions" (219, see also Chabram-Dernersesian, Fernandez, Garcia's *Chicana Feminist* Thought, Martinez, and Moraga). In *So Far from God,* Castillo critically refigures the role of the mother in the family, as she raises her daughters by herself. Castillo's romance circulates and participates in the ongoing discourse of Chicana feminism and is intimately linked to the Chicana and Chicano struggle: "This political movement [Chicana feminism] is inseparable from the historical experience of Chicanos in this country since 1848, an experience marked by economic exploitation as a class and systematic racial, social and linguistic discrimination designed to keep Chicanos at the bottom as a reserve pool of cheap labor" (Yarbro-Bejarano 732). *So Far from God,* then, must be situated in a series of interlocking aesthetic, political, and cultural discussions.

In his study of the American Renaissance, *Visionary Compacts,* Donald Pease suggests that in the anxious years preceding the Civil War, the American Renaissance writers looked to the nation's past to find common ground to unite the nation:

> Restoring these [agreed-upon] relations meant reminding Americans of the agreements that made them possible, which meant reminding nineteenth-century Americans of the hopes, ideals, and purposes they shared with their ancestors. It meant restoring their relationship with the nation's past, and involved an acknowledgment of a living tradition of cultural ideals, begun in the past but demanding realization and renewal by subsequent generations. Such a collective memory would remind individuals of the memorable life they shared with everyone else in the community.
>
> (x)

While Pease's writers—Hawthorne, Whitman, Poe, Emerson, and Melville—looked for past cultural agreement and commitment to restore civil order to social relations in nineteenth-century America, Castillo, writing in the romance tradition, likewise looks to the past in *So Far from God* for an originary myth which does not denigrate the role of women. This impulse to create or revive past mythologies is consonant with the historical inclination of the romance, which Nathaniel Hawthorne identifies as an "attempt to connect a by-gone time with the very Present that is flitting away from us. It is a Legend, prolonging itself, from an epoch now gray in the distance" (3). Castillo quests for a myth which will move women away from the role of "second sex" to the stature of "authentic sex."

Indeed, one of the principally contested grounds in *So Far from God* is the subordination and oppression of women, which Castillo traces back to the Bible and the Catholic church. "I argue," states Castillo,

> that we have been forced into believing that we, as women, only existed to serve man under the guise of serving a Father God. Furthermore, our spirituality has been thoroughly subverted by institutionalized religious customs. The key to that spiritual oppression has been the repression of our sexuality, primarily through the control of our reproductive ability and bodies"
>
> (*Massacre* 13).

In the service of a patriarchal religion, women have been made subordinate to their male counterparts; we need think only of Eve and the accountability thrust on her for being cast out of Eden. More directly linked to our generic discussion, we should consider the role women have played in romances dating back to the medieval quest romances. In the Roman de la Rose, the story of Virginius who murdered his daughter to keep her from Appius reappears; Chaucer also recounts this story in his "Physician's Tale." As with Eve, women in romances have traditionally had their fates determined by men. Consequently, Castillo searches for a spirituality devoid of gender oppression.

In *So Far from God,* the quest for this spirituality surfaces most explicitly in the character of Caridad. Like her two older sisters, Esperanza and Fe, Caridad experiences the infidelity of man. While Caridad is pregnant with her husband Memo's child, he carries on an adulterous affair. Subsequently Caridad leaves him and begins to live it up in the bars around Tome. One evening, she is violently raped and mutilated by what is described as a supernatural force (the malogra). The rape leaves her in the hospital for three months, and it is only through the miraculous healing powers of her baby sister, La Loca, that Caridad is saved. After her recovery and a brief display of her nascent clairvoyant powers, Caridad opts to take her mare, Corazon, and move out of her parents' house. Upon vacating her parents' home, Caridad engages most fully with alternative forms of spirituality, not prescribed nor circumscribed by the practices of the Catholic church.

Accompanied by her mare, Caridad finds and rents a trailer from dona Felicia, the local curandera. Dona Felicia teaches Caridad how to be a healer, for which the key to success is invoking faith in God. Consequently, dona Felicia makes an annual pilgrimage to Chimayo during Holy Week, and she brings her new apprentice, Caridad, along with her: "She [dona Felicia] prepared a lonche to last three days, put on a cap with 'Raiders' written across it to protect her head from the sun, and gave another one to Caridad, signaling to her that she was going along and that was that" (72). It appears that dona Felicia and Caridad are simply readying themselves for the journey to Chimayo, yet couched within this description of their preparation lurks an indication of suspicion about this pilgrimage, namely the sartorial expression of donning "Raiders" caps: black caps with a silver and black logo of a modified skull-and-cross-bones' pirate flag. The caps suggest that this holy pilgrimage may be something less than holy; the pilgrims may be seen as raiders, encroachers on holy space. Recall that the Oakland Raiders' dynasty, dating back to the 1970s, was founded on an identity as the National Football League's nasty outsiders. The Raiders established a tradition of excellence, but in a new tenor. While the cap clearly refers to the football team, one also remembers Steven Spielberg's Indiana Jones's movies in which Jones does battle with the dubious efforts of other archaeologists and villains to recover the Holy Grail, the chalice from which Jesus drank at the last supper. The potential exists, then, for understanding the pilgrims en route to Chimayo as religious poachers.

Furthermore, the pilgrimage witnesses the first clash between institutionalized religion and indigenous spiritual practice as the narrator recounts the founding of Chimayo as a holy site:

> In that valley in the Sangre de Cristo foothills nearly two centuries before, a Penitente Brother performing his penances during Holy Week ran toward a bright

light coming out of the ground not far from the river. He dug at the spot where the light emitted and found a statue of Our Lord of Esquipulas.

Now, of course there are a lot of amazing aspects to this legend because Nuestro Senor de Esquipulas was the black Christ of the far-off land of the converted Indians of Esquipulas, Guatemala, and how He got to the land of the Tewa is anybody's guess! But he most certainly had a mission, which was to let people know of the healing powers of the sacred earth of Tsimayo—just like he had done in Esquipulas—so shortly after his appearance, the Catholic Church endorsed as sacred what the Native peoples had known all along since the beginning of time.

(73)

Surrounded by the legendary mist of Chimayo and Nuestro Senor de Esquipulas, the reluctant-to-attend Caridad grows interested in the pilgrimage. One cannot help but think that her growing interest stems from this alternative construction of the Christ-figure as a person of color, a black Christ. In his essay "Comrade Jesus: Postcolonial Literature and the Story of Christ," Norman Carey asserts that this refiguration of Eurocentric Christianity has been a powerful tool of liberation for many postcolonial authors: "they subvert and replace the central figure [Jesus] in the Christian discourse they have received with 'hybridized' figures who are interpreted in terms of the very religions and cultures the Europeans sought to supplant. The postcolonial Jesus becomes an indigenous Jesus" (171). In its attempt to undermine through parody the hegemonic force of the church, the black Christ thus symbolizes a potentially liberatory moment for Caridad.

Further, it should also be noted that the reappearance of Nuestro Senor de Esquipulas in Chimayo marks a trail of Spanish conquest in the Americas which bleeds through in the narrator's flippant assertion that how the black Christ got to the land of the Tewa "is anybody's guess!." The exclamation mark underscores the narrator's sarcastic tone. The Spanish Conquistadors commissioned the carving of the black Christ in 1594 in Esquipulas, Guatemala, and, upon its completion in 1595 it was placed in the local church.[8] Recall that Don Juan de Onate's conquest of New Mexico began in 1595, shortly after the carving of the black Christ. Consequently, one can, without much hesitation, speculate that replicas of the black Christ made their way to North America, with the spread of Spanish colonization. Combined with this narrative of the alternative Christ figure, Castillo critiques the Catholic Church for positioning itself as the arbiter of religious affairs and for arrogantly assuming the authority to deem what counts as sacred and what as profane for the peoples of the world. This air of religious superiority informed their efforts to Christianize the "heathen" Indians.

While the legend of Nuestro Senor de Esquipulas sparks Caridad's interest in the pilgrimage, her enthusiasm wanes when she falls in love for the first time since her relationship with Memo. The narrator even glibly comments that she will focus on the story of Caridad falling in love, for it surpasses the spectacle of the pilgrimage. Ultimately, this romance becomes a narrative strategy for ruminating on creation and offering an alternate genesis myth. Incapable of approaching her new love interest, Woman-on-the-wall, Caridad returns home from the pilgrimage distracted beyond relief. dona Felicia suggests that she go to Ojo Caliente for a mineral bath and a vacation. Caridad subsequently disappears and becomes a hermit for a year, during which time the town members convince themselves that she must have saintly powers, for she was able to resist "with passive yet herculean strength" the efforts of three men to remove her from the cave. Like her sister La Loca she seems to be not of this earth. Caridad does finally make it to Ojo Caliente, where she encounters Woman-on-the-wall (also known as Esmeralda) working as an attendant at the mineral bath. By this juncture, Castillo has created such a mythical aura around Caridad that we expect nothing short of the supernormal. A brief relationship develops between Caridad and Esmeralda which culminates with their jumping off the mesa in Sky City because they hear the spirit god Tsichtintako calling. Esmeralda and Caridad are not (as they would be in a realist novel) shattered by the fall, but, rather, are subsumed by the earth, taken in whole:

> But much to all their [the onlookers] surprise, there were no morbid remains of splintered bodies tossed to the ground, down, down, like bad pottery or glass or old bread. There weren't even whole bodies lying peaceful. There was nothing.
>
> Just the spirit deity Tsichtintako calling loudly with a voice like wind, guiding the two women back, not out toward the sun's rays or up to the clouds but down, deep within the soft, moist dark earth where Esmeralda and Caridad would be safe and live forever.

(211)

One senses not a tragedy in these lines, but a romantic connection to the earth and a rebirth. A deep feeling of spirituality fills the termination of Caridad's and Esmeralda's lives, as they forsake them for a nobler spiritual union. They have returned to what the Acoma myth of creation refers to as the earth's womb (Adams Leeming 3).

The deaths of Esmeralda and Caridad for the sake of Tsichtintako provide the reader with another effort on Castillo's part to refigure the patriarchal constructions of Catholicism. Indeed, many of Castillo's contestations consist of the production of counter-narratives, narratives written against the grain of dominant discourses. The legend of Tsichtintako tells the story of creation not with woman as the second sex or as the guilty partner responsible for the eviction of humans from paradise. Rather the story of Tsichtintako and Castillo's adoption of it give us a genesis myth and romance which venerate women. The Acoma society from which this story springs is a matrilineal society; that is, ownership of property is passed down through the female. In the Acoma story of creation, two sister-spirits—later named Iatiku (Life-Bringer) and Nautsiti (Full

Basket)—are born underground. Tsichtintako, a female spirit, raises them. When the appropriate time comes, the sisters are each given a basket, one contains plant seeds and the other clay sculptures of animals. With the assistance of a badger, a locust, and Tsichtintako, the sister-spirits leave the underground world to populate the world created by Uchtsiti with their plants and animals. The emphasis on women's worldly creational abilities in this narrative dramatically diverges from the dominant creation story of the Book of Genesis.[9] Though the world comes from a blood clot of the male god, Uchtsiti, the sister spirits play a fundamental role in completing the creation of the world. They are, if you will, co-participants in this genesis story, which figures the Earth as a life-bearing mother from whose womb the two sisters, Iatiku and Nautsiti, usher forth.

Castillo connects her 1990s romance to the Acoma creation myth in order to question the pattern of female submission passed down through the Biblical account of creation. Indeed, the importance of this alternative genesis myth for Castillo must not be underestimated. In her essay, "'In the Beginning, There Was Eva,'" she states "As Xicanistas and heiresses of a Christian based culture, the book of Genesis is the document where we may witness the male takeover of woman's autonomy" (**Massacre** 108). The sacrificial deaths of Esmeralda and Caridad to Tsichtintako permit Castillo to draw on the myth-making potential of the romance to reinsert an alternative creation narrative into *So Far from God,* countering what she identifies as the, not a, source of the loss of woman's autonomy.

With the legendary impulse of the romance, Castillo reaches back into an epoch now distant from us to unsettle the foundations of patriarchal dominance. This move to destabilize patriarchal structures exemplifies the writings of a contestatory author, for Castillo finds herself not as part of an armed movement for national liberation, but as a strong voice in an on-going struggle for social justice. Drawing on the legends of the second-century martyrs (Faith, Hope, Charity, and Sophia), of Nuestro Senor de Esquipulas, and of Tsichtintako, Castillo revitalizes and emboldens the representation of women, in the face of the ideological construction of supposed preternatural myths, such as the Christian genesis myth. Indeed, Castillo recuperates the Acoma creation myth to demonstrate the availability of alternative originary narratives and their usefulness in critiquing social domination. This polyphonic structure, the pitting, that is, of what Bakhtin has called centripetal, homogenous voices against centrifugal, heterogeneous ones, wrests control away from the hegemonizing, masculinist, creation narratives which serve to subordinate women. Thus, this act of rewriting creation places Castillo squarely in the realm of a contestatory literature, a literature which uses varying narrative strategies to oppose social domination. In a world in which gross social inequities exist, the cultural and political significance of these contestatory voices cannot be underestimated. The struggle for social justice continues.

*Notes*

1. I use Castillo as an illustrative, not exhaustive, example of the shift from resistance to contestation. I am currently engaged in a book-length study which explores this shift across a much broader range of genres and writers than I am capable of exploring in this brief essay.

2. In the case of the United States, the term resistance literature could be most adequately applied to the writing of Native Americans, especially during the early genocidal phases of US colonization, as well as to many of the slave narratives.

3. Nabokov offers a more extensive treatment of Tijerina and the Alianza Federal de Pueblos Libres.

4. For a more comprehensive treatment of Paredes and "The Ballad of Gregorio Cortez," see Limon's *Mexican Ballads,* especially chapters 2 and 3. Saldivar's discussion of Paredes in chapter 2 of *Chicano Narrative* is also insightful. The interested reader will find an encyclopedic study of Chicano politics in Gomez-Quinones' two volumes.

5. See Harvey for a thorough analysis of the shift from Fordism to flexible accumulation. For now, his brief definition of flexible accumulation will suffice: "Flexible accumulation, as I shall tentatively call it, is marked by a direct confrontation with the rigidities of Fordism. It rests on flexibility with respect to labour processes, labour markets, products and patterns of consumption. It is characterized by the emergence of entirely new sectors of production, new ways of providing financial services, new markets, and, above all, greatly intensified rates of commercial, technological, and organizational innovation. It has entrained rapid shifts in the patterning of uneven development, both between sectors and between geographical regions, giving rise, for example, to a vast surge in so-called 'service-sector' employment as well as to entirely new industrial ensembles in hitherto underdeveloped regions (such as the 'Third Italy,' Flanders, the various silicon valleys and glens, to say nothing of the vast profusion of activities in newly industrializing countries)" (147).

6. For a similar argument about the effects of late capital and postmodernism on the Chicana/o community, an argument from which I have greatly benefited, see Limon's *Dancing With the Devil,* especially chapter five, "Emergent Postmodern Mexicano."

7. Butler offers the following account of the legend of the four martyrs:

> The Roman widow St. Wisdom and her three daughters suffered for the faith under the emperor Hadrian. According to a spurious legend St. Faith, aged twelve, was scourged, thrown into boiling pitch, taken out alive, and beheaded; St. Hope, aged ten, and St. Charity, aged nine, being unhurt in a furnace, were also beheaded; and their mother

suffered while praying over the bodies of her children. Some have maintained that the whole story is a myth, but the universality of their cultus both in the East and the West suggests that there may have been early martyrs of these names. Indeed, there is reference to two groups of them; a family martyred under Hadrian and buried on the Aurelian Way, where their tomb under the church of St. Pancras was afterwards resorted to: their names were Greek Sophia, Pistis, Elpis, and Agape; and another group of martyrs of an unknown date, Sapientia, Fides, Sapes, and Caritas, buried in the cemetery of St. Callistus of the Appian Way.

(8)

See also the brief entries in Meagher, O'Brien, and Aheme.

8. For a more detailed account of Nuestro Senor de Esquipulas, see Branas and Solorzano Pas.

9. For a fuller account of the Acoma creation myth, see Adams Leeming (3–4). Weigle examines the myth in even greater detail.

### Works Cited

Acuna, Rodolfo. *Occupied America: A History of Chicanos.* 1972. 3rd ed. New York: Harper Collins, 1988.

Adams Leeming, David and Margaret. *Encyclopedia of Creation Myths.* Santa Barbara, CA: ABC-CLIO, 1994.

Alurista. *The Chicano Cultural Revolution: Essays of Approach.* Unpublished Manuscript.

Anaya, Rudolfo, and Francisco Lomeli, eds. *Aztlan: Essays on the Chicano Homeland.* 1989. Albuquerque: U of New Mexico P, 1991.

Anzaldua, Gloria, and Cherrie Moraga, eds. *This Bridge Called My Back: Writings by Radical Women of Color.* Watertown, MA: Persephone P, 1981.

Argueta, Manlio. *One Day of Life.* 1980. New York: Vintage, 1983.

Bakhtin, M. M. *The Dialogic Imagination.* Ed. Michael Holquist. Trans. Caryl Emerson and Michael Holquist. 1981. Austin: U of Texas P, 1992.

———. Problems of Dostoevsky's Poetics. Ed. and Trans. Caryl Emerson. Minneapolis: U of Minnesota P, 1985.

Branas, Cesar. *Vision y Ensueno de Esquipulas.* Guatemala, CA: Union Tipografica, 1943.

Burk, Martha, and Heidi Hartman. "Beyond the Gender Gap." *The Nation* 262.23 (June 10, 1996): 18–21.

Butler, Alban. *The Lives of Saints.* Ed and Rev. Herbert Thurston, S. J., and Donald Attwater. Vol. 8 (August). London: Burns Oates and Washbourne Ltd., 1933.

Cabezas, Omar. *Fire from the Mountain: The Making of a Sandanista.* New York: Crown, 1985.

Carey, Norman R. "Comrade Jesus: Postcolonial Literature and the Story of Christ." *Postcolonial Literature and the Biblical Call for Justice.* Ed. Susan VanZanten Gallagher. Jackson: UP of Mississippi, 1994. 169–82.

Castillo, Ana. *So Far from God.* 1993. New York: Plume, 1994.

———. *Massacre of the Dreamers: Essays on Xicanisma.* New York: Plume, 1995.

Chabram-Dernersesian, Angie. "I Throw Punches for My Race, but I Don't Want to Be a Man: Writing Us—Chicanos (Girl, Us)! Chicanas—into the Movement Script." *Cultural Studies.* Ed. Lawrence Grossberg, Cary Nelson, and Paula Treichler. New York: Routledge, 1992: 81–95.

Cisneros, Sandra. *House on Mango Street.* 1984. New York: Vintage, 1991.

Fernandez, Roberta. "Abriendo caminos in the Brotherland: Chicana Writers Respond to the Ideology of Literary Nationalism." *Frontiers* 14.2 (1994): 23–50.

Garcia, Alma. "The Development of Chicana Feminist Discourse, 1970–1980." *Gender and Society* 3.2 (1989): 217–38.

———. ed. *Chicana Feminist Thought: The Basic Historical Writings.* New York: Routledge, 1997.

Gomez-Quinones, Juan. *Chicano Politics: Reality and Promise, 1940–1990.* Albuquerque: U of New Mexico P, 1990.

———. *The Roots of Chicano Politics, 1600–1940.* Albuquerque: U of New Mexico P, 1990.

Harlow, Barbara. *Resistance Literature.* New York: Methuen, 1987.

Harvey, David. *The Condition of Postmodernity: An Enquiry into the Origins of Cultural Change.* 1989. Oxford: Basil Blackwell, 1992.

Hawthorne, Nathaniel. *The House of Seven Gables.* 1851. Rutland, VT: Everyman, 1995.

Jameson, Fredric. *Postmodernism or, The Cultural Logic of Late Capitalism.* 1991. Durham: Duke UP, 1993.

Limon, Jose. *Mexican Ballads, Chicano Poems: History and Influence in Mexican-American Social Poetry.* Berkeley and Los Angeles: U of California P, 1992.

———. *Dancing with the Devil: Society and Cultural Poetics in Mexican-American South Texas.* Madison: U of Wisconsin P, 1994.

Mandel, Ernest, *Late Capitalism.* London: Verson, 1980.

Martinez, Elizabeth. "Chingon Politics Die Hard: Reflections on the First Chicano Activists Reunion." *Z Magazine* Apr. 1990: 46–50.

Meagher, Paul Kevin, Thomas C. O'Brien, and Sister Consuelo Maria Aheme, eds. *The Roman Martyrology and Encyclopedic Dictionary of Religion.* Vol. F-N. Washington, D.C.: Corpus Publications, 1979.

Moraga, Cherrie. *The Last Generation: Prose and Poetry.* Boston: South End Press, 1993.

Nabokov, Peter. *Tijerina and the Courthouse Raid.* 1969. Berkeley: Ramparts Press, 1970.

Paredes, Americo. *With His Pistol in His Hand: A Border Ballad and Its Hero.* 1958. Austin: U of Texas P, 1988.

Pas Solorzano, Juan. *Historia del Santo Cristo de Esquipulas.* 2nd ed. Guatemala de la Asuncion: n.p., 1943.

Pease, Donald. *Visionary Compacts: American Renaissance Writings in Cultural Context.* Madison: U of Wisconsin P, 1987.

Saenz, Benjamin Alire. "Cebolleros." *Flowers for the Broken.* Seattle: Broken Moon P, 1992. 3–16.

Saldivar, Ramon. *Chicano Narrative: The Dialectics of Difference.* Madison: U of Wisconsin P, 1990.

Weigel, Sigrid. "Double Focus: On the History of Women's Writing." *Feminist Aesthetics.* Trans. Harriet Anderson. Ed. Gisela Ecker. Boston: Beacon, 1985. 59–80.

Weigle, Marta. *Creation and Procreation: Feminist Reflections on Mythologies of Cosmogony and Parturition.* Philadelphia: U of Pennsylvania P, 1989.

Yarbro-Bejarano, Yvonne. "Chicana Literature from a Chicana Feminist Perspective." *Feminisms.* Ed. Robyn R. Warhol and Diane Price Herndl. New Brunswick: Rutgers UP, 1993. 732–37.

## Silvio Sirias and Richard McGarry (essay date Summer 2000)

SOURCE: "Rebellion and Tradition in Ana Castillo's *So Far from God* and Sylvia López-Medina's *Cantora*," in *MELUS,* Vol. 25, No. 2, Summer, 2000, p. 83.

[*In the following essay, Sirias and McGarry compare Castillo's* So Far from God *and Sylvia López-Medina's* Cantora, *noting similar characters and situations in both novels, but contrasting the characters' responses and actions.*]

The Chicana "voice" in literature, according to Ramón Saldivar, comprises a discourse that creates "an instructive alternative to the exclusively phallocentric subject of contemporary Chicano narrative" (175). As Cordelia Chávez Candelaria reports, Chicana/Latina and other women writers have struggled for centuries to attain the right "to express and assert the validity of woman-space and the textured zone of women's experience" (26). Over the last two decades, the body of work that Chicana novelists have contributed to the totality of Chicano artistic discourse has managed to expand the formally predominant sociopolitical themes of the text so that it now includes the politics of gender. In the process, the Chicana novel has appropriated topics considered taboo in Latino culture: physical and sexual abuse, and heterosexual and lesbian sexuality (Arias and Gonzales-Berry 649). This new discourse is rebellious and can at times become very subversive. Its exploration of previously censored areas holds up an unforgiving mirror to the patriarchal practices of Chicano/Latino culture. Alvina Quintana asserts, while referring directly to Ana Castillo's writings, that the Chicana feminist is "interested in scrutinizing the assumptions that root her own cultural influences, unpacking so called traditions and political institutions that shape patriarchal ways of seeing" ("The Novelist" 74).

Although most Chicana novelists address similar feminist preoccupations in their writings, they employ vastly different discursive strategies in their narratives. They may tell similar stories, but the form, vision, and tone with which they approach their objective reflect the heterogeneity that exists in the Chicana novel. Evidence of this difference arises when we compare Ana Castillo's *So Far from God* (1994) and Sylvia López-Medina's *Cantora* (1993). Both works tell of the losses and hardships in the lives of the female characters, and of how these women find the strength to survive. Nevertheless, the discourses that Castillo and López-Medina employ reside at opposite ends of the narrative spectrum. *So Far from God* is a novel that incites rebellion against the norms and values of Chicano patriarchal society while *Cantora,* although calling for changes, always does so within a framework that respects centuries' worth of traditions and cultural beliefs. This essay compares the importance that naming, gender relations, and religion play in the development of the female characters. It also examines how the novelistic discourse of Castillo and López-Medina either calls for rebellion or demonstrates a deep respect for tradition.

In *Women Singing in the Snow,* Tey Diana Rebolledo recognizes the importance that naming plays in the "struggle for interpretive power." A central concept in marginalized American cultures, naming describes and therefore expresses the identity of the named. Under patriarchy, naming constitutes a tool of domination through its power to symbolically confine the named within the parameters of an imposed gender identity. Naming, however, can also function as a tool for empowering self-definition, a means by which to redefine women's identity and reject imposed descriptions of the self. Rebolledo states that "Chicanas are very much engaged in an articulation of accurate naming and the acceptance of all the cultural and social premises that lie behind the 'names'" (103). Ana Castillo's *So Far from God* reflects the positive dynamics of naming. The novel has Sofia, the embodiment of "wisdom," at its core, a mother who survives the death of her four daughters: Esperanza, Fe, Caridad, and La Loca. The names of the first three daughters denote the three major Christian ideals. However, in the cruelest of ironies, the destiny of each of these characters is the antithesis of the ideal the name represents.

Esperanza, the most liberated of the sisters, devotes the energy of her college years to the Chicano Movement. She lives her life as a glowing example of La Raza Politics, working to better the lives of her people. But her death as a television reporter covering the Gulf Crisis is utterly meaningless. The reader is left without any hope or, better yet, "Esperanza," of finding redemption in this character's demise.

Fe, the sister who most subscribes to the traditions of her culture, desires nothing more than to participate fully in society's patriarchal mandate for women to marry and serve their husbands.[1] When her first fiancé, Tom, bails out of their engagement, she surrenders to her first crisis of faith and of identity. Her reaction to her disillusionment humorously becomes known to the members of her family as the era of "El Big Grito," which consisted of "one loud continuous scream that would have woken the dead" (30). For months after she is jilted, Fe is unable to produce any discourse other than the scream. As a result of the straining of her vocal cords during her crisis, Fe is left with a speech impediment whereby she cannot vocalize every word in a sentence.[2] Although "El Big Grito" disqualifies Fe from realizing her potential (for instance, she is refused a promotion at work), she does find a man who will fulfill her dream of marrying: her cousin Casimiro. He is completely devoted to her, and together they plan a blissful future. In order to secure this, however, Fe leaves her safe position at the bank for a higher paying job at an arms manufacturing company. She tackles her work with her usual diligence and earns a promotion. Thus, her faith in the American Way of Life is rewarded. This "promotion," however, proves fatal as the company exposes her to a hazardous chemical that causes her death from cancer. In the end, the faith that Fe places in the basic tenets of society and its culture completely fails her. Thus, faith also becomes meaningless.

Caridad, after being abandoned by her husband, became known for "loving anyone she met at the bars who vaguely resembled Memo" (27). Because of her promiscuous life, she is brutally raped and disfigured by a mysterious and misogynist spirit identity known as the "malogra." In this manner, Caridad's charity towards men is severely punished.[3] However, she heals miraculously and from that moment on, she no longer has an interest in men. Caridad becomes an apprentice *curandera,* and during a religious pilgrimage with her mentor, she spots a woman with whom she instantly falls in love. Caridad never reconciles herself with her homosexual feelings until she suddenly and dramatically leaps off of a cliff while holding hands with Esmeralda, the object of her affection, as they are being pursued by Francisco el Penitente, Caridad's obsessed stalker.[4] Those who witness the jump search for the bodies, but they are never found. What the witnesses do hear, however, is:

> the spirit deity Tsichtinako calling loudly with a voice like wind, guiding the two women back, not out toward the sun's rays or up to the clouds but down, deep within the soft moist dark earth where Esmeralda and Caridad would be safe and live forever.
>
> (211)

An ancient Pre-Columbian god emerges at the appropriate moment and wholly embraces the lovers, taking them into mother earth's womb where they can become one and live in peace.[5] There they will dwell far from society's condemnation of their relationship, and be free to plant the seeds of their affection.[6] In spite of her life-affirming end, Caridad constitutes a *pharmakos* for the community of Tome. Her lesbianism is unacceptable, and she is sacrificed in order to purify patriarchal society.

La Loca is without question the most intriguing of the sisters. Dead at age three, she resurrects and is immediately believed to possess miraculous powers. The residents of Tome accept the young girl's return from the dead as being of a divine nature and they dub her "La Loca Santa." Following her return, however, she shuns human contact and only lets her mother touch her. She also rarely speaks, but her resurrection has spoken volumes for her. La Loca is the embodiment of a miracle; she cannot be preoccupied with the mundane task of finding a job, like her sisters. She remains at home, content in her solitude. Her household chores are to tend her animals, keep the house clean, and cook. She does, though, assist in the healing of Fe and Caridad, and she performs abortions for the latter because La Loca instinctively "knew all about a woman's pregnancy cycle" (164). Toward the novel's end, she becomes ill and is diagnosed with the HIV virus, even though she had never participated in any activity commonly associated with its acquisition. La Loca's virtually unexplainable illness becomes one of the novel's most subversive moments in terms of its discourse. It represents a remarkable case of aporia. The gap between the linguistic and the philosophical coherence of the event causes the text to resist interpretation. Such subversion serves not only to reverse interpretation, but also to open the text to a myriad of possibilities, thus making the text undecidable while at the same time challenging the patriarchal quest for systematization.

Ultimately, La Loca's destiny, like those of her sisters, is to die at an early age. On a surreal death pilgrimage to an Albuquerque hospital, the people canonize her and eventually declare her the patron saint of kitchens, new brides, and progressive grooms. La Loca's life, then, is characterized by her first death, resurrection, contraction of AIDS without human contact, and her canonization. After the deaths of hope, faith, and charity, the three theological ideals of the Church, and the death of what can arguably be construed as the female personification of Jesus Christ in the personage of La Loca, all that remains is Sofia's wisdom.

In this tale of the lives and deaths of Sofia's daughters, Castillo destroys several powerful archetypes of patriarchal society in order to build the world anew. A timid character at the novel's onset, Sofia begins to awaken as a character when she declares to her *comadre* that she will run for "La Mayor of Tome." Her discourse from this point on becomes assertive. She organizes several collectives and the women of Tome benefit as a result. Sofia begins to devote herself to the good of the collective. Through her efforts her fellow citizens gain a class consciousness and become acutely aware of the political and material conditions of their existences. She also awakens the women of Tome, and although she suffers the loss of her four daughters, in the end she gains wisdom. When a set of tarot cards is created to commemorate "La Loca Santa," Sofia is "simultaneously represented by the Empress card and by the Queen of Swords, a quick-witted, dance-loving strong woman who was nevertheless powerless to the sorrow she suffered" (250). With her hard-earned wisdom and her newly-discovered talents for social activism, Sofia founds M.O.M.A.S. ("Mothers of Martyrs and Saints"). This organization, by its very nature, excludes men, and its yearly convention becomes more popular than the World Series and the Olympics. By establishing this organization, Sofia has created a social movement that outshines any male-dominated one. With the painful lessons learned throughout her life, she empowers women like herself who have long suffered, and with their help she sets out to redefine society. Her actions represent a call for women to rebel against patriarchal practices, and that call resides at the heart of the novel's practice in naming.[7]

The relationship between the names of the predominant female characters and their actions is also important in Sylvia López-Medina's *Cantora*. The story gravitates around Amparo, the book's narrator, who tells us of her quest to reconstruct her family's history. With regard to this character, Rebolledo writes:

> López-Medina's narrative hero reconstructs a history of her family as well as an identity for herself. Her name, appropriately, is Amparo, from the Spanish *Amparar*, meaning to help, to assist, to shelter. It is through her "translation" of the not-said, of the silence in the stories told to her by her great-grandmother, grandmother, and mother that she comes to understand the family secrets—to identify and name them—thus liberating herself as well as the women who have preceded her in the family clan.
>
> (199)

This pattern of women struggling to liberate themselves, to determine their own futures, repeats itself throughout the novel. Rosario, Amparo's great-grandmother, claims her life for herself. In fact, the familiar usage of the name Rosario means "backbone." Her "backbone" enables her to flee from her father's control. Rosario eventually faces the hardships of a young widow with six children with strength and resolve. It is thanks to her fortitude and bravery that they endure.

The narrative then turns its focus upon Pilar, the "pillar" of the story. Left at an early age in a convent, she grows up in a silent and peaceful environment, completely isolated from the society that exists beyond the walls of the religious institution. Later in the narrative, with Pilar unable to fend for herself, her family enters into a contract with a wealthy store-owner that provides the young girl with enough financial support for the remainder of her life. This includes the purchase of a house that he places in her name. All of this is given in return for allowing Pilar to become his mistress, though eventually they will fall genuinely in love. Several years later, after Gabriel's death, Pilar's inherited wealth allows her to help her family move to Santa Barbara, California. As a young woman with economic means, Pilar flexes her muscles before the traditions of patriarchal society and becomes the decision-maker in her family. Perhaps most importantly, she constitutes the bridge that allows the family's tale to span across four generations.

Amparo, the novel's narrator, grows up in admiration of her "Aunt" Pilar's storytelling abilities:

> There was always a hush when Pilar related the family's history. As a child, I sat quietly while she told me of her memories of the tiny Mexican village where she was born. There are Yaqui Indians in her memories, swooping down into the village, taking food and every young girl they could find. There are villages burned and families moving on to other places to rebuild their lives. There is the love story, the magical love story of my aunt; and there are the brutal deaths of her father and older brother. There is the exodus to western Mexico, a trek by my twenty-three-year-old Grandmother Rosario and her six remaining small children through a mountain range. There is the survival. This is the story of that survival, my Grandmother Rosario's and my Aunt Pilar's.
>
> (2)

As we can see, Amparo's narrative acknowledges that Pilar's tales are the foundation of her work.[8] Motivated by certain gaps, or more appropriately, deliberate silences in her Aunt Pilar's stories, and by ongoing events in her own life, Amparo begins to investigate in earnest her maternal family's history. She discovers that her life parallels many of the tales that she uncovers about her family. Like the women in her family who preceded her, Amparo finds the strength to cope with life's difficulties after the death of her mate, and she states that she will raise her daughter with the same values and traditions as the women before her.[9] Through the strength and caring reflected in their names, the characters protect their legacy throughout the generations. As the narrative voice explicitly states, *Cantora* is a simple tale of survival. Its discourse is not overtly rebellious or subversive. In contrast to **So Far from God**, the meaning of the story rests upon the surface, at the grasp of every reader.

In both novels, the female characters and their stories need to be examined in opposition to their male counterparts. The men represent patriarchy's systematic domination of women as achieved and maintained through male control of cultural, social, and economic institutions. In **So Far from God**, Castillo creates a cast of male characters who are, in essence, emasculated. Sofia's husband, Domingo, an addicted gambler, cannot earn a living or fix a thing. His sole purpose in the household is to watch television and decipher Caridad's cryptic episodes of clairvoyance so he can place winning bets. Eventually, he begins gambling away Sofia's property, and when she discovers her own assertive voice, she serves him with divorce papers, and Domingo meekly disappears from the narrative.

Her daughter, Esperanza, had one love in her life: her college sweetheart Rubén. He holds a formidable spell over Esperanza and controls her until she wises up and leaves him to pursue her career. In the end, after Esperanza's death, Rubén becomes a pathetic figure who, sad and alone, remembers how the days with most meaning in his life were those of his youth spent observing and admiring Esperanza's militancy in the cause of La Raza:

> Back in college, if it wasn't for la Esperanza who led the protest, they never would have had one Chicano Studies class offered on the curriculum. If it wasn't for la Esperanza, who would have known about the struggle of the United Farm Workers on campus? Who would have ever told him about anything at all?
>
> (239)

Without Esperanza to open his eyes, Rubén would have seen very little. Now, without her, he will see nothing and therefore signify even less.[10]

Fe has two men in her life. The first one, Tom, breaks his engagement with Fe, prompting the era of "El Big Grito." When Sofia visits Tom's house in search of an explanation for the breakup, his mother informs her that Tom has become a victim of *susto*, or, simply put, cold feet. In response, Sofia angrily questions Tom's manhood: "*¿Susto? ¿Susto? . . .* You think that cowardly son of yours without pelos on his maracas has *susto*" (30). Tom's destiny following his relationship with Fe is to lead a desperate, lonely life, where he remains forever locked into repairing Big Slurpy machines as the manager of a convenience store. Fe's second love is her cousin, Casimiro, a man totally and hopelessly devoted to her. Although college-educated, or perhaps because he is college-educated, Casimiro is as meek as men come. A soft-spoken man, his gentle discourse includes bleating like a sheep, a trait inherited over seven generations of sheepherding. As Fe becomes increasingly ill, Casimiro is too timid to urge her to seek medical attention, and he waits until Sofia intervenes. By then it is too late.

By far the most intriguing male character in **So Far from God** is Francisco el Penitente. A Vietnam veteran who after the war loses himself in drugs and failed relationships, Francisco finds his calling as a *santero*, a maker of *bultos* (figures of saints carved from wood), whose creations are guided by divine inspiration. It does not take long before Francisco el Penitente becomes a religious fanatic. He deprives himself of all worldly pleasures and lives his entire life in penance. He meets Caridad after she has taken on the identity of "La Armitana," the hermit who lived for a year in seclusion in a cave, and he falls hopelessly and platonically in love with her.[11] He dubs Caridad "The Handmaiden of Christ" and projects qualities of sainthood upon her. He imagines her pure and virginal, a strong confirmation of one of Castillo's beliefs that society forces Chicanas to deny their sexuality: "Most of our female saints, maintained as our models," notes Castillo, "established their beatitude as a result of the repudiation of sex" ("**La Macha**" 33).

Francisco el Penitente, however, is diametrically opposed to his gentle namesake, Saint Francis of Assisi. Obsessed with Caridad, Francisco el Penitente begins stalking her, and while spying on her he discovers her secret passion for Esmeralda. At first, Francisco's distant relationship indicates a simple case of scopophilia. His voyeurism appears to be an intermediary stage along the path to some sort of sexual/religious fulfillment. However, Caridad's lesbianism violates the patriarchal codes to which he strongly subscribes, and he perversely snaps. Castillo implies that his fanatical pursuit and condemnation of their homosexuality force the women to leap from the cliff. Like Judas Iscariot, Francisco el Penitente is incapable of forgiving himself for the extreme act to which he drove Caridad and he hangs himself from a tree. As we can observe, the male characters in **So Far from God** are either powerless beings, completely lacking in fortitude, or zealots, as in the case of Francisco el Penitente, who will go to any length to protect male dominance in our society.[12]

The males in *Cantora,* on the other hand, loom powerful over the female characters. They intimidate and dominate the women, thus behaving fully within the accepted parameters of Chicano/Latino society and culture. In family decisions, the men's desires always supercede those of the women. In spite of this, genuinely caring relationships develop between men and women. Both sets of characters subscribe to the codes of patriarchy. Because of those shared values, deep emotional connections between the genders are allowed to be made. Alejandro, Rosario's husband, tells her after she flees from her father: "It is all right, Rosario. It will be all right. I am going to take care of you now" (37). This leitmotif recurs throughout the successive generations of women.

Following Alejandro's death, Rosario takes responsibility for her family, but she later abdicates this when her eldest son, Victorio, becomes old enough to make the decisions. It is Victorio who negotiates the contract with Don Gabriel so that the wealthy merchant can "take care of Pilar, as if she were (his) wife" (137). It is also Victorio who takes away Pilar and Gabriel's child and invents an elaborate story so that the child may be raised in legitimacy. Victorio is dispassionate and controlling as the substitute father figure. Rosario, adhering to tradition, relinquishes all control of the family to her son. Even as a weakened old man, when Amparo confronts him in search of the truth, Victorio constitutes a terrifying entity: "He looked at Amparo sternly, and she was just as frightened of him then as she was when she was a child. Sitting in his chair, he was still an imposing man, dominating, controlling everyone in his line of vision" (262). His power as head of the family extends far into the clan's horizon. In the end, Amparo liberates him from his fabrication at the same time that she assures him that he did "the right thing" (269). Although his choices afflicted everyone in the family, Amparo forgives him in the name of tradition and honor.

Genuine love and concern for one another characterize Gabriel and Pilar's union. The wealthiest person in Hermosillo, Gabriel literally buys Pilar. Yet he gently wins her affection, his patience being rewarded on the day that he brings her a simple gift of flowers that they plant together in the courtyard. He provides generously for Pilar's wellbeing. His death, although devastating to Pilar, allows her to move along and discover her strong, independent self.

Peter, the man in Amparo's life, is, like the other men in *Cantora,* a dominating figure. Also a wealthy individual, he provides for his mate. Upon Peter's death, Amparo realizes what his loss means to her because "He always took care of everything" (246). Her abbreviated union with John, Peter's friend, permits her to look at her life from a new perspective, and she realizes that she does not need a man in order to grow and be happy. She, like the other women in her family, finds within herself the strength to continue her life independently.

The man who establishes himself as the most dominant male figure in *Cantora* is Amparo's great-grandfather, Don Ramón. A Spanish aristocrat, he adheres fully to Old World traditions of male dominance. He "loved and ruled over Pilar (his wife) for the twenty-one turbulent years that ended in her death at the age of thirty-eight" (60). He arranges a marriage for his daughter and forbids his wife to voice her opinion on the matter. The narrative describes him as being "proud, stern, and forceful" (33) as well as cold and aloof. With his sense of honor violated when Rosario refuses his marriage arrangement and instead runs away from home with a commoner, he cannot find forgiveness in his heart for this transgression. He sends his daughter and grandchildren on a trek across the Sierra Madre that nearly costs them their lives. In what the reader may consider a case of divine retribution, Don Ramón dies alone and senile, hallucinating in a world full of distant ghosts. In spite of their overwhelming dominance, the male figures in *Cantora* are, with the exception of Don Ramón, caring individuals who operate respectably, and forcefully when necessary, within the narrow confines of their social paradigms. They are extremely protective of their mates, and it is upon their premature deaths that the women embark on journeys that lead them to the discovery of their inner strength and independence.

Both novels also explore the most formidable force in the Hispanic patriarchal universe: the Catholic Church. Indeed, the discourse in *So Far from God* constitutes a direct confrontation with Catholicism. In an interview with Marta A. Navarro, Castillo states: "One of the guiding principles in our life is Catholicism. And as much as we try not to subscribe to it, it's completely permeated into our psyche" (119). Indeed, Catholicism and its principles loom significantly and oppressively in Castillo's work.

From the novel's title to the basic tenets that Castillo deconstructs through her archetypal female characters, the church is the focus of an aggressive attack. Father Jerome, the priest of Tome, questions whether La Loca's resurrection is of divine or Satanic origins. Sofia responds to his query by "calling the holy priest a pendejo ["pubic hair"] and hitting him" (24). To counterbalance Francisco el Penitente's fanatical devotion to Catholicism and its patriarchal structure, Sofia creates M.O.M.A.S. (Mothers of Martyrs and Saints). This purely matriarchal response will determine for itself the religious beliefs of the women who join the organization. Castillo's authorial stance makes it evident that the Church's strong patriarchal posture and its binary philosophical system alienates Hispanic American women. Castillo's characters seek inclusion, freedom of action, and freedom of thought within the Catholic Church. Yet, what they find in *So Far from God* is the condemnation of their humanity rather than its exaltation.

*Cantora* also portrays Catholicism as unresponsive to the needs of women. The priests in López-Medina's novel are just as ineffectual as they are in Castillo's work. A village priest is too cowardly to protect the women and children from the Yaqui raids. He later informs them that during the next raid no one is to seek refuge in the church, leaving the villagers to fend for themselves. Another church serves as a refuge for Rosario and her family after they cross the treacherous Sierra Madre. However, this protection is ephemeral. When Rosario seeks the church's help in caring for her children while she establishes herself in Hermosillo, the convent director reluctantly agrees to take care of only one child, obliging Rosario to leave Pilar there alone. But the church fails to protect her as Pilar is raped while in the convent's care. By the time the family arrives in the United States, Catholicism no longer plays an important part in their lives. Amparo recalls her great-grandmother Rosario performing her own worship services, made up of ancient Mayan religious practices with Christian undertones, which the young girl finds much more genuine and meaningful than the empty rituals of the Masses performed at the Catholic school that she attends. As with the female characters of *So Far from God,* the female characters of *Cantora* find that the church has little relevance in their lives. Although they do not venture so far as to show disrespect, they withdraw from this oppressive institution that seeks to negate their independence.

As we have observed up to this point, *So Far from God* revolves around the theme of rebellion. The novel even rebels against the normative use of language for narrative.[13] Traditionalists would accuse Castillo of abusing or ignoring the proper use of English grammar.[14] Castillo's sentences repeatedly employ double negatives, and in at least two cases a triple negative ["The truth of it was that she was just truly a santita from ever since her fatal experience at the age of three and she didn't have to prove nothing to no one" (248); "Nobody and nothing able to know what was going on around them no more" (189)]. Castillo, however, does code-switch with great imagination and agility. The language that Castillo employs clearly coincides with her artistic goal: to write a novel that narrates the story of women who rebel against the norms imposed on them by patriarchal society.

In contrast, the discourse employed in *Cantora* reveals the profound respect that López-Medina has for the traditional narrative. Her language usage is evocative. She strives to place the reader in the midst of a world governed by traditions that must be respected and held dearly, and she succeeds. However, her language, at times, can be excessively formal and, unfortunately, contrived. The author seldom uses contractions, even in the most informal situations of dialogue. Code-switching is non-existent, and she translates terms of endearment from Spanish into English ("My little sky," "My heart," "My little one"). Yet again, this matches perfectly with the novel's macro-discursive strategy of narrating a tale of survival in the midst of the restrictions placed on women by outmoded traditions while in the same instance realizing the need to approach these with respect. López-Medina recognizes that customs, values, beliefs, styles, and other forms of culture are passed down from one generation to the next, as well as the feeling, both encouraged and resented, that this inheritance should be respected for the important influence that is exerts on the present.

In contrast, *So Far from God* constitutes a modern-day allegory that attacks tradition. It is a narrative that has multiple meanings, several of which are partially concealed by the visible or literal meaning. Castillo incorporates abstractions into her novel that are present in society and religion and presents them in the form of the leading female characters. Therefore, Sofia and her daughters represent archetypes. They are models of certain important continuities of Hispanic American life throughout time. The difference lies in that now women have the choice of whether to pass on the traditions or break the hold that these have over them. The narrative of *So Far from God* represents what Quintana labels the "literature of new vision." This literature holds "the possibility for real social change and transformation" (*Home Girls* 89). This is why the reader is not deeply moved by the deaths of Sofia's daughters. The reader remains aware, whether consciously or unconsciously, that Castillo is destroying abstractions and not people. Furthermore, this story extends well beyond its conclusion. Its dianoia, or general meaning, is archetypal. In the end, what matters most upon reading the last page of the book is Sofia's potential to transform society.[15]

*Cantora,* on the other hand, employs a discourse that is soothing, gently embracing the emotions of the reader. Perhaps it is the narrator of the story who describes it best as she invites us during the novel's prologue to become immersed in her tale:

> My name is Amparo. Join me here with my aunt. Sit here beside us. Cover yourself with this quilt. My grandmother Rosario made it. Warm yourself with it. The mystery of our lives is to be found in its varicolored threads. I will share the tears and the triumphs of these lives. I will show you how to survive anything. We will show you how to survive everything.
>
> (2)

What the reader encounters here is a promise of warmth and comfort in this tale. There is also the explicit promise of learning skills vital for us all: the skill to survive and the skill to protect and shelter our own stories. *Cantora* reads like a wonderful lesson, with all the traditions and culture that the art of quilt-making involves. The novel stands for what Quintana terms the "literature of apology." This literature "is liberal in the sense that it develops the argument that traditions and cultural values kept women from developing to their full potential" (*Home Girls* 39).

*So Far from God* is rebellious; *Cantora* seeks comfort in tradition. Still, they tell the same story of women who discover their inner-strength and independence as they confront enormous sorrows. In addition, each text directly challenges what Saldivar refers to as "the ideologies of patriarchal oppression" (173). Both writers admirably represent their communities at the same time that they illustrate the vast heterogeneity that exists in Chicana literary discourse. As Rebolledo states:

> Chicana writers have struggled to become the subjects of their own discourse, . . . they have created not only a discourse of resistance to the dominant culture in multiple subversive ways, but also a dialogue of affirmation that sees the positive sides of self, family, culture and community.
>
> (208)

The success that Ana Castillo's and Sylvia López-Medina's novels have found with major publishing companies is an indication that Chicana discourse is becoming respected and valued by the dominant reading community that has long neglected the Chicana/Latina artistic voice. Both authors fulfill the demand that Trujillo makes of all Chicanas: "Chicanas, both lesbian and heterosexual, have a dual purpose ahead of us. We must fight for our own voices as women, since this will ultimately serve to uplift us a people" (124).[16]

### Notes

1. Trujillo best describes the possible consequences for women who, like Fe, rely on a male to establish their identity: "Women who participate in the privileges of a male sexual alliance may often do so at the cost of their own sense of self, since they must often subvert their needs, voice, intellect, and personal development in these alliances" (119).

2. In the text, morphemes, function words, and a few content words are omitted leaving the reader, the interpreter of the discourse, with the responsibility of filling in the empty spaces.

3. Gonzales-Berry finds suffering similar to that of Caridad to be a common component of feminist literary discourse: "Trials leading to sexual maturity are im-

portant components of the *bildungsroman*. In the female version, however, coming to terms with sexuality is often more difficult and painful than it is for the male protagonists" (42).

4. Caridad's secrecy about her homosexuality reflects Castillo's belief that: "Because of the strict social attitudes towards open sexual expression, most lesbians of our culture have not politicized their desires nor declared them openly as a way of life" (Interview by Navarro 37).

5. The event that Castillo narrates falls well within the parameters of magical realism, which Walter considers an integral part of the Chicano novel: "the Chicano magical realism is a fusion of two conflicting views of reality, the rational mode which is centered upon reasoning . . . and the magical mode which is centered on the unconscious, dreams and imaginations—a mode grounded on the Chicano's Hispanic and Indian Heritage" (136).

6. Chicano/Latino society remains unaccepting of homosexuality. The women's life-affirming plunge reflects Castillo's hope that society can one day accept the validity of homosexual feelings: "if we cannot claim anything for ourselves, let us begin at least the gradual process of integration of the mind, soul and body, however we can, and make our principal struggle one toward which we ultimately experience the beauty of our whole selves—an organic, unified entity rejoicing in our connection with all living things on earth" (Interview by Navarro 47).

7. Castillo, in an interview conducted by Saeta, explains her authorial intent in the following quote: "In the early Christian medieval mythology, they've taken Sofia, who is a Greek goddess, and her daughters and turned them into martyrs. At the very ending of that story of the martyrs, Sofia is on the grave crying for her three martyred daughters. So that's how I originally ended my story. But my agent, who was reading the manuscript commented that 'Well, this is very depressing. You know, you promised Norton a happy ending.' So I thought, 'what would she [Sofia] do to change that, particularly as a religious figure. What would she do?' She takes over, she doesn't submit to that point in history when patriarchy took over her authority" (8).

8. Eysturoy reminds us that there is an inherent danger in Amparo's acceptance of Pilar as a role model: "In a patriarchal context, . . . the relationship between mother and daughter is charged with ambiguities, because accepting the mother as a role model may signify accepting oppressive, socially prescribed norms of womanhood" (116).

9. Amparo's societal stance falls into the following category of feminism defined by Pesquera and Segura: "*Chicana Cultural Nationalism* articulates a feminist vision anchored in the ideology of *la familia*. While advocating feminism this perspective retains allegiance to cultural nationalism which glorifies Chicana culture. *Chicana Cultural Nationalism* overlooks the possibility that these cultural traditions often uphold patriarchy. This speaks to the difficulty of reconciling a critique of gender relations within the Chicano community while calling for the preservation of Chicano culture" (107–108).

10. The dynamic among Esperanza, Rubén, and the La Raza Movement, reveals Castillo's personal frustration when she was a socially committed young woman: "As a political activist from El Movimiento Chicano/Latino, I had come away from it with a great sense of despair as a woman. Inherent to my despair, I felt, was a physiology that was demeaned, misunderstood, objectified, and excluded by the politic of those men with whom I had aligned myself on the basis of our mutual subjugation as Latinos in the United States" (Interview by Navarro, 124).

11. Caridad withdrew from society because of her guilt about homosexuality. Caridad's withdrawal embodies the premise that Trujillo espouses: "A Chicana lesbian must learn to love herself, both as a woman and a sexual being, before she can love another (118).

12. The acts of Francisco el Penitente typify the fears that Chicano society at large have toward lesbians. This is evident in the following statement by Trujillo: "The vast majority of Chicano heterosexuals perceive Chicana lesbians as a threat to the community. Homophobia, that is, irrational fear of gay or lesbian people and behaviors, accounts for part of the heterosexist response to the lesbian community. However, I argue that Chicana lesbians are perceived as a greater threat to the Chicano community because their existence disrupts the established order of male dominance, and raises the consciousness of many Chicano women regarding their own independence and control" (117).

13. In reference precisely to Castillo's subversive discourse, Yarbro-Bejarano states: "Writing the Chicana 'I' questions the authority of dominant discourses, and resists the appropriation of the knowing subject either male or female that 'forgets' race and class oppression. Chicana writers', like Castillo's, struggle to claim the 'I' of literary discourse is inseparable from their struggle for empowerment in the economic, social, and political spheres" (72).

14. The following quote from Saeta's interview reveals Castillo's attitude towards traditionalists who teach both English and Spanish: "I decided that I would never ever take a class with anybody or any university . . . because I was so afraid that I would be discouraged and told that I had no right to be writing poetry, that I didn't write English well enough, that I didn't write Spanish well enough. Now, I don't have the fear as much because I suppose I've learned—after 20 years on my own—to have an eye for what I want to do in my work" (6).

15. Although Castillo, not known for her happy endings, had yet to write *So Far from God*, she foresaw at the time of Navarro's interview the possibility of providing a hopeful ending in her future works: "I have been asked why I don't portray some of my figures in a happy state, and obviously, I don't see us living in a happy state. We're bombarded by so much. But now that we've survived, there's a possibility to introduce that, even if only in terms of a vision" (114).

16. The authors would like to acknowledge their indebtedness to their colleague, Professor Judith Rothschild, for her valuable comments with regard to the content and form of this essay.

### Works Cited

Arias, Santa, and Erlinda Gonzales-Berry. "Latino Writing in the United States." *Handbook of Latin American Literature*. Ed. David William Foster. 2nd ed. New York: Garland, 1987.

Castillo, Ana. Interview with Ana Castillo by Marta A. Navarro. *Chicana Lesbians: The Girls Our Mothers Warned Us About*. Ed. Carla Trujillo. Berkeley: Third Woman P, 1991.113–32.

———. Interview with Ana Castillo by Elsa Sacra. *Baneke: A Latino Arts and Literature Review* 2 (1995): 6–11.

———. "La Macha: Toward a Beautiful Whole Self." *Chicana Lesbians: The Girls Our Mothers Warned Us About*. Ed. Carla Trujillo. Berkeley: Third Woman P, 1991.24–48.

———. *So Far from God*. New York: Plume, 1994.

Chávez Candelaria, Cordelia. "The 'Wild Zone' Thesis as Gloss in Chicana Literary Study." *Chicana Critical Issues*. Ed. Norma Alarcón et al. Berkeley: Third Woman P, 1993.21–31.

Eysturoy, Annie O. *Daughters of Self-Creation: The Contemporary Chicana Novel*. Albuquerque: U of New Mexico P, 1996.

Gonzales-Berry, Erlinda. "Unveiling Athena: Women in the Chicano Novel." *Chicana Critical Issues*. Ed. Norma Alarcón et al. Berkeley: Third Woman P, 1993.33–44.

López-Medina, Sylvia. *Cantora*. New York: Ballantine, 1993.

Pesquera, Beatriz M., and Denise A. Segura. "There Is No Going Back: Chicanas and Feminism." *Chicana Critical Issues*. Ed. Norma Alarcón et al. Berkeley: Third Woman P, 1993.95–115.

Quintana, Alvina E. "Ana Castillo's *The Mixquiahuala Letters*: The Novelist as Ethnographer." *Criticism in the Borderlands: Studies in Chicano Literature, Culture, and Ideology*. Ed. Héctor Calderón and José David Saldívar. Durham: Duke U P, 1991.72–83.

———. *Home Girls: Chicana Literary Voices*. Philadelphia: Temple UP, 1996.

Rebolledo, Tey Diana. *Women Singing in the Snow: A Cultural Analysis of Chicana Literature*. Tucson: U Of Arizona P, 1995.

Saldívar, Ramón. "The Dialetics of Subjectivity: Gender and Difference in Isabella Ríos, Sandra Cisneros, and Cherríe Moraga." *Chicano Narrative: The Dialectics of Difference*. Ed. Ramón Saldívar. Madison: U of Wisconsin P, 1990. 171–99.

Trujillo, Carla. "Chicana Lesbians: Fear and Loathing in the Chicano Community." *Chicana Critical Issues*. Ed. Norma Alarcón et al. Berkeley: Third Woman P, 1993. 117–25.

Walter, Roland. *Magical Realism in Contemporary Chicano Fiction*. Frankfurt am Main: Vervuet Verlag, 1993.

Yarbro-Bejarano, Yvonne. "The Multiple Subject in the Writing of Ana Castillo." *The Americas Review* 20.1 (1992): 65–72.

## FURTHER READING

### Criticism

Binder, Wolfgang. "An Interview with Ana Castillo in Chicago, Illinois, January 18, 1982." *Partial Autobiographies: Interviews with Twenty Chicano Poets*, edited by Wolfgang Binder, pp. 28–38. Verlag Palm & Enke Erlangen, 1985.

    Castillo discusses her formative years and the impact that her personal experiences have on her writing.

Delgadillo, Theresa. "Forms of Chicana Feminist Resistance: Hybrid Spirituality in Ana Castillo's *So Far from God*." *Modern Fiction Studies* 44, No. 4 (Winter 1998): 888–916.

    Delgadillo explores the various forms of social, religious, and gender role resistance addressed in *So Far from God*.

Garza, Melita Marie. "Homecoming." *Chicago Tribune Books* (26 November 1996): 1, 7.

    Garza examines Castillo's childhood, education, feminism, and body of work.

González, Ray. "A Chicano Verano." *Nation* (7 June 1993): 772–74.

    González provides an overview of recent literary offerings from prominent Chicano/a writers, including a negative assessment of Castillo's *So Far from God*.

Hampton, Janet Jones. "Ana Castillo: Painter of Palabras." *Americas* 52, No. 1 (January 2000): 48.

Hampton examines the life experiences and political opinions that shape Castillo's writing.

May, Barbara Dale. Review of *The Mixquiahuala Letters,* by Ana Castillo. *Hispania* 71, No. 2 (May 1988): 313-14.

May praises Castillo's ingenuity in crafting three different versions of *The Mixquiahuala Letters.*

Navarro, Marta. "An Interview with Ana Castillo." *Chicana Lesbians: The Girls Our Mothers Warned Us About,* edited by Carla Trujullo, pp. 113-32. Third Woman Press, 1991.

Castillo and Navarro discuss Castillo's opinions about feminism and sexuality, as well as the roles that these ideas have in the lives of Chicana and Latin-American women.

Orsi, Robert. Review of *Goddess of the Americas: Writings on the Virgin of Guadalupe,* edited by Ana Castillo. *Commonweal* 124, No. 5 (14 March 1997): 24-25.

Orsi explores the deep attachment to—and importance of—the Virgin of Guadalupe as shown by the contributors to *Goddess of the Americas: Writings on the Virgin of Guadalupe.*

Platt, Kamala. "Ecocritical Chicana Literature: Ana Castillo's 'Virtual Realism.'" *Interdisciplinary Studies in Literature and Environment* 3 (Summer 1996): 67-96.

Platt defines the terms "environmental justice" and "environmental racism" and draws parallels between non-fictional injustices and the environmental problems that plague Sofi in *So Far from God.*

Rothschild, Matthew. Review of *Massacre of the Dreamers,* by Ana Castillo. *Progressive* 59, No. 1 (January 1995): 41.

Rothschild expresses admiration for the strong voice Castillo incorporates into *Massacre of the Dreamers: Essays on Xicanisma.*

---

**Additional coverage of Castillo's life and career is contained in the following sources published by the Gale Group:** *Authors and Artists for Young Adults,* **Vol. 42;** *Contemporary Authors,* **Vol. 131;** *Contemporary Authors New Revision Series,* **Vols. 51 and 86;** *Contemporary Women Poets; Dictionary of Literary Biography,* **Vols. 122 and 227;** *Feminist Writers; Hispanic Writers,* **Vol. 1;** *Literature of Developing Nations for Students;* **and** *Literature Resource Center.*

# Atom Egoyan
## 1960-

Canadian screenwriter and director.

The following entry presents an overview of Egoyan's career through 1999.

## INTRODUCTION

Egoyan is a Canadian screenwriter and director known for his innovative, postmodern dramas that focus on the nature of family, assimilation, identity, and alienation. His films typically feature fragmented, nonlinear storylines with characters who are isolated and emotionally paralyzed. A contemporary of Canadian film auteur David Cronenberg, Egoyan often uses video as a metaphor for memory and technology as a social filter through which his characters relate. He is best known for *Exotica* (1994) and *The Sweet Hereafter* (1997), an adaptation of the Russell Banks novel, which received two Academy Award nominations. Several film critics have included Egoyan among the best directors of his generation, applauding his experimental style and his refusal to compromise his personal vision.

## BIOGRAPHICAL INFORMATION

Egoyan was born on July 19, 1960 in Cairo, Egypt, to parents of Armenian descent. His parents were both formally trained artists, and his father owned a successful art gallery. They named their son Atom after atomic energy. In 1962 the family immigrated to Canada, where Egoyan's parents managed a furniture store in British Columbia. Egoyan faced difficulties assimilating into a community with few Armenian families. During this period, he rejected his native culture, refusing to speak Armenian altogether. Egoyan eventually became interested in theatre and began to write experimental plays. He attended the University of Toronto, graduating with a B.A. in international relations from Trinity College in 1982. While he was in college, Egoyan's creative interests expanded into the world of filmmaking. He produced his first short film, *Howard in Particular,* in 1979, and it won a prize at the Canadian National Exhibition's film festival. Through the 1980s Egoyan directed television episodes and made-for-television movies for the Canadian Broadcasting Corporation, as well as American television programs filmed in Toronto. He used his salary from his television work, along with private money and government grants, to produce several independent films that he wrote and directed. His first full-length feature film was *Next of Kin* (1984). As

Egoyan's body of work expanded, his films became increasingly popular with critics and audiences in Canada and Europe, and he won the Moscow Film Festival award for *The Adjuster* (1991). Egoyan used the prize money from the award to fund his next film, *Calendar* (1993). In 1994, he received considerable praise for *Exotica,* which earned the International Film Critics Award at Cannes and numerous Genie awards. His next film, *The Sweet Hereafter,* brought Egoyan both critical and commercial success, including Academy Award nominations and several Cannes Film Festival awards. Egoyan has continued to direct short films—including one starring famed cellist Yo Yo Ma—and has directed and written the scores of several operas. He is married to Armenian actress Arsinee Khanjian with whom he has one son.

## MAJOR WORKS

Throughout a career spanning more than two dozen films, Egoyan has created a highly recognizable visual and narrative style. He often revisits themes of alienation, estrangement, and dysfunctionality, particularly in family relationships. In *Next of Kin,* the main character flees his birth family and pretends to be the lost son of a local Albanian immigrant family in order to receive the emotional support that has been lacking in his life. The father and son in *Family Viewing* (1987) are engaged in a bitter power struggle: the son, Van, wants his father, Stan, to help take care of his grandmother, but Stan is content to leave her in a retirement home. Van's mother left them several years earlier, and Stan is methodically recording over their old family videos with scenes of him having sex with his mistress. Egoyan has consistently used video as a metaphor for memory, exploring the ways in which characters attempt to shape and possess their past. He portrays recorded images as a tool that his characters use to communicate with each other. In *Speaking Parts* (1989), one of the main characters is a screenwriter who "visits" her dead brother through a video mausoleum. The characters in Egoyan's films are often emotionally distant and unable to make personal connections. *The Adjuster* features a couple who live together in the same house, but who are emotionally isolated from each other. The husband, Noah, is an insurance adjuster who experiences a voyeuristic thrill in getting involved in the personal lives of his customers. His wife, Hera, works for the National Film Censor Board and secretly copies the pornographic films that she classifies. *Exotica* focuses on five characters whose lives center around the erotic dancers at a local nightclub. One of the characters, Francis, is a father who cannot find closure after his daughter's death. His daughter's former babysitter, Christina, is a dancer at the club, and Francis becomes emotionally dependent on watching her dance. Even while interpreting the work of others—such as his adaptations of Russell Banks's *The Sweet Hereafter* and William Trevor's *Felicia's Journey*—Egoyan consistently revisits his recurring themes and crafts his plots in a unique style. Egoyan's narratives often recount events in nonlinear order, mixing incidents from various time frames and omitting essential details about characters and plot events until the conclusion of the film.

## CRITICAL RECEPTION

Critics and peers alike consider Egoyan one of the leading independent filmmakers in Canada and have compared his unusual style to those of Cronenberg, David Lynch, and Peter Greenaway. Reviewers have noted that audiences either seem to love or hate Egoyan's works, with little room in-between. His critics have argued that his films are too fragmented and that his characters lack emotional depth or passion. Other reviewers have criticized his adaptations—such as *The Sweet Hereafter*—for being too focused on Egoyan's own agenda and not doing justice to the source material. However, even his harshest critics have complimented Egoyan's films for their complexity and thought-provoking material. Many reviewers have applauded Egoyan for his careful attention to detail, skillful use of editing, and continuing development of his recurring cinematic themes. Egoyan has been commended by critics for his rejection of false sentimentality and his refusal to emotionally manipulate his audiences. While some reviewers judge his characters as cool and detached, others consider them realistic and unexaggerated. Characterized as an "uncompromising" filmmaker, Egoyan and his body of work have developed a strong cult following in Canada and abroad.

## PRINCIPAL WORKS

*Howard in Particular* (screenplay) 1979
*Next of Kin* (screenplay) 1984
*Family Viewing* (screenplay) 1987
*Speaking Parts* (screenplay) 1989
*The Adjuster* (screenplay) 1991
*Calendar* (screenplay) 1993
*Exotica* (screenplay) 1994
*The Sweet Hereafter* [adaptor; from the novel by Russell Banks] (screenplay) 1997
*Felicia's Journey* [adaptor; from the novel by William Trevor] (screenplay) 1999

## CRITICISM

### Suzanne Moore (review date 7 October 1988)

SOURCE: "Unhappy Families," in *New Statesman and Society,* October 7, 1988, p. 46–47.

[*In the following review, Moore praises Egoyan's exploration of the nature of family in* Family Viewing, *but finds fault with his use of prostitution to suggest alienation.*]

All is not well in the heart of that most sacred bastion of society—the family. If you believe what you read you will know that this most fundamental institution is under attack from a multitude of directions. Promiscuous single parents, campaigning homosexuals, morally-irresponsible television programmes and, of course, feminists who claim that the family is the site of woman's oppression par excellence, are all seen to threaten normal family life. You might wonder how something as supposedly natural and institutionalised can feel itself to be so fragile and flimsy.

This week's films may in part provide the answer. For although they are "about" families, they all point to the emptiness of traditional family life.

*Family Viewing* is an extraordinary film from a Canadian director, the wonderfully-named Atom Egoyan. As far as video technology is concerned it would appear that the family that plays together is erased together. At the centre of this blackest of comedies are father and son, Stan and Van. Stan is a semi-catatonic video salesman who can only be turned on when the camera is switched on or by second-hand telephone sex. Sandra, his hapless mistress, is instead preoccupied with 17-year-old Van who is increasingly worried about "not feeling connected."

As his father erases home movies of Van's mother who has "run away" with home-made remote control porn, Van visits his Armenian grandmother who has been put into a seedy nursing home, in an effort to retrieve his past.

Egoyan cleverly mixes different kinds of film—the authentic looking jumpy home-movies providing another texture to the stilted apartment scenes which he shoots on video. Using the inane laughter of sit-coms on the sound-track, he flattens out these traces of family life so that we are always reminded that they are in Godard's famous words "just an image." With ridiculous anti-naturalistic dialogue the film is in turn hilarious and desperately sad.

In the midst of all this alienation Van conspires to construct another kind of family with his grandmother and Aline, the young women who works for the telephone sex service patronised by his father. Pursued by the obsessive Stan, they become once more the objects of surveillance. Throughout the film we are aware of the presence of video cameras—in shops, lifts, hospitals and hotels—and of the way that this everyday surveillance coerces us all into behaving "properly" wherever we are.

*Family Viewing* succeeds in posing all sorts of questions about memory—about a culture that records everything but remembers nothing, in a brilliantly haunting way. But why, oh why, do all these arty directors from Wenders to Godard, and now Egoyan, have to resort to that tired old metaphor of prostitution whenever they want to conjure up a bit of alienation? Why couldn't Aline have worked in a shop instead of selling sex to pay her mother's nursing-home bills? My own suspicion is that while parading as some kind of critique, prostitution is vaguely titillating to male directors and audiences. All those screen whores service the fantasies of thousands of the right-on men who sit there believing that, come the revolution, they could take them away from all this.

What is interesting about *Family Viewing* is that the nuclear family looks so perverse and sinister by comparison with Van's self-created family who actually provide love and care.

Yet we all know where "pretend family relationships" can lead to, don't we? For it is homosexuality that is perceived to undermine the very basis of familial life. As usual, no amount of theorising can express the stupidity of this idea as eloquently as the words of an "ordinary person." In the American documentary about gay rights, *Rights and Reactions,* an elderly gay woman says: "When people say I'm a threat to the family—I think of pay kids, my grandchildren, my son-in-law." In the background protestors who believe that "we should do away with gays if possible" hold banners that say it all: "Tradition, Family, Property."

Which is why a short New Zealand film, *A Death in the Family,* should be compulsory viewing. Andy, dying of AIDS, goes back to New Zealand to be looked after by his friends. Unlike the British television dramas *Intimate Contact* and *Sweet as You Are,* which presented AIDS as essentially a crisis for the heterosexual family, *A Death in the Family* puts Andy's dying and its effect on his gay friends at the core of the film. When his conservative family, who have never accepted his gayness, come to visit, it is once again the *real* family that appears emotionally impoverished.

The film never glosses over the realities of an appalling loss. Andy says himself, "This is one bitch of a death." I, for one, don't subscribe to the idea that learning to die is somehow good for you. When it comes to AIDS, tears are not enough. Many people dying of AIDS will not get a place in a hospice, let alone have a network of friends to care for them. *A Death in the Family* is an elegant and quietly intense film that should be shown on television immediately.

It seems that those who portray the family as under siege from pernicious outside influences have got it (deliberately?) wrong. What is tearing the family apart is the eruption of tensions that have always existed *within* the family. What these films suggest, in quite different ways, is not that we should all go off and live in communes, but that it is possible even in the midst of the fall-out from the nuclear family, to make new kinds of families, new kinds of communities.

In the light of Cleveland and the Clause, "pretend family relationships" have never seemed like such a good idea.

**Amy Taubin (essay date November–December 1989)**

SOURCE: "Memories of Overdevelopment: Up and Atom," in *Film Comment*, Vol. 25, No. 6, November–December, 1989, pp. 27–29.

[*In the following essay, Taubin explores Egoyan's use of technology as a metaphor in* Speaking Parts *and* Family Viewing.]

The very voluble Atom Egoyan is hesitant to say how small the budget was for *Speaking Parts,* his third feature. He has a theory about recent independent films—that by conforming to Hollywood production standards, they've begun to attract a broader audience. Broader, that is, than the audience for grimy, grainy 16mm. With its gracefully arcing camera movement, spookily luminous interiors, and arresting, though totally unknown, actors, *Speaking Parts* looks a lot more expensive than its "well under a million dollar budget," which is as close to specific as Egoyan's willing to get now that the film is making the festival circuit and a U.S. opening is likely around the New Year.

It's questionable whether your average viewer will find attractive visuals and subtle acting a sufficient reward, given *Speaking Parts* evasive, fragmented narrative, shifty-eyed, narcissistic characters and morbidly chill tone. Actually the film's most appealing quality is its gallows humor, to which the New York Film Festival audience made frequent, audible response. In short, *Speaking Parts* is not exactly *sex, lies, and videotape,* although it's hard to imagine a more appropriate title for not only this film, but Egoyan's entire oeuvre. *Speaking Parts* was screened in the Director's Fortnight at the 1989 Cannes Film Festival where *sex, lies, and videotape* won the competition; Egoyan admits that he was so upset by Soderbergh's title (i.e. that he hadn't thought of it himself) that he's yet to see the film.

Egoyan was born in 1960 in Egypt of Armenian parents. His family emigrated to Canada when he was three years old, but he didn't learn English until after his grandmother was placed in an old-age home four years later. "I resented her being sent away but that's when my assimilation began," Egoyan remarks, savoring the contradiction. It's tempting to relate Egoyan's insistence on holding back verbal information at the openings of his films to this childhood experience of alienation. In *Speaking Parts,* eight minutes lapse before the first bit of dialogue occurs, and it's twice that before one begins to grasp the situation. The beginning of *Family Viewing,* Egoyan's previous film, is equally enigmatic and disorienting. Egoyan ascribes his idiosyncratic expositions to his desire to break "the Hollywood rule about needing to grab the audience in the first ten minutes."

While majoring in international affairs at the University of Toronto, Egoyan made several short films, one of which was broadcast on the Canadian Broadcasting Corporation (CBC). He used the TV sale to partially finance *Next of Kin,* his first independent feature, which CBC also televised, leading to his being hired to direct *In This Quarter,* a one-hour TV show about an IRA terrorist who becomes involved with an Irish-Canadian boxer. "The action sequences in *In This Quarter* caught the eye of some commercial producers and I was hired to direct episodes of *Alfred Hitchcock Presents* and *The Twilight Zone,* two American TV series shot in Toronto," Egoyan explains, adding that at this point his career became totally schizophrenic.

"My exposure to Hollywood filmmaking taught me what I was up against and clarified my direction. In mainstream production, what's onscreen is the budget—you know that Hollywood expression, 'The money's all on the screen.' What's on the screen in independent filmmaking is spirit, an idiosyncratic vision. So instead of coming up with a more mainstream script, as most people expected, I wrote *Family Viewing.*"

Budgeted at $160,000, *Family Viewing* was financed with private money and state-funded arts grants. Egoyan stayed away from Canadian film production entities like Telefilm because he wanted to retain complete control. *Family Viewing* was Egoyan's first film to win recognition outside Canada and in a well-publicized incident at the Montreal Film Festival, Wim Wenders asked the jury to turn over his first prize for *Wings of Desire* to Egoyan.

Relentlessly claustrophobic and intentionally ugly, *Family Viewing* is about the oedipal struggle between Stan, a video equipment salesman, and his son, Van. Having driven his wife (Van's mother) away and placed her mother (Van's grandmother) in a nursing home, Stan is dedicatedly taping over treasured home video recordings—replacing idyllic images of young Van and his mother romping in the grass with clinically-depicted sexual encounters between himself and his live-in girlfriend, who not-so-secretly also has the hots for Van. With the help of a young woman who works in a telephone sex establishment (where Stan is one of her clients), Van rescues the tapes from Stan's clutches, his grandmother from the nursing home, and his mother from a homeless shelter. He sets up a new household with the three women, while Stan, in frantic pursuit, collapses of a heart attack.

*Family Viewing* is remarkable, not only for its multiple layering of satire and creepily intimate realism, but for its use of video technology. Stan's bedroom diary and Van's baby pictures were recorded on consumer VHS: the living room scenes involving Stan, Van, and the girlfriend were shot TV sitcom-style with three studio cameras linked by a switcher. Broadcast images from omnipresent TV sets and surveillance camera footage are frequently intercut with the action. Transferred to film, the degraded, degenerated video images function both expressively and metaphorically and depart from the usual 16mm look.

"Video images are suggestive of the images that go on inside people's heads," Egoyan remarks, adding later that, "there's a profound difference in attitude toward the two mediums video and film. In terms of home movies, everyone using film knows in the back of their minds that they are going to have to pay for a roll. That means no matter how obsessive they are about recording, they have to chose. With video, the process can be indiscriminate. You can record an entire day in real time without any form of selection. That experience of time is extremely dangerous. Some people never look at what they record but by recording something, they make it a possession. It has an effect on the process of memory. We give away responsibility for memory to a piece of technology. I don't think film was so insidious."

The phrase "family viewing" evokes both the 6pm-8pm broadcast time slot and a funeral parlor ritual. *Speaking Parts* opens with a video image of a woman wandering through a cemetery. Several shots later, we see the same woman sitting in a mausoleum watching a videotape of her late brother walking toward and away from the camera, home movie style. In both films, video is associated with desire (incestuous and therefore guilty) and loss (abandonment or death).

"In terms of the technology—video mausoleums, videophones—*Speaking Parts* is set about five years in the future," Egoyan explains adding that he's heard that they already have videotape mausoleums in Japan.

His insistence on a medicalized, mediated body and a nightmarishly technological future/present environment connects Egoyan to filmmakers like David Lynch, Peter Greenaway, and his fellow Canadian, David Cronenberg. *Speaking Parts* is, to state the story in the crudest terms, about the making of a movie about organ transplants which takes the form of a TV talk show. "It's preposterous," he shrugs.

The main setting of *Speaking Parts* is a hotel which also functions as a movie production office. Lisa (Arsinee Khanjian) a zealously truthful, mopey chambermaid is in love with Lance (Michael McManus), an aspiring actor and Rob Lowe look-alike who also works in the hotel as a steward-cum-hustler. Every night, Lisa rents videotapes of the films in which Lance has been an extra and watches his scenes on a kind of TV shrine. Lance and Lisa never touch or make eye contact. When they cross paths, they look as furtive and guilty as actors in a Bresson film. Occasionally Lisa begs Lance to let her love him.

Lance discovers that Clara (Gabrielle Rose), one of the hotel guests, has written a film. Clara is obsessed with her brother who died after donating his lung to save her life. Her script is about their relationship. She's struck by Lance's resemblance to her dead brother and angles to get him the part. Clara and Lance begin an affair and when Clara goes out of town, they engage in mutual masturbation via videophone.

Egoyan says that while *Family Viewing* was about the absence of familial love, *Speaking Parts* is about the withholding of romantic love. Which doesn't mean that it's any less an Oedipal story. The Producer (David Hemblin, who also played the father in *Family Viewing*) is *Speaking Parts*' evil genius. His beefy face, with its congealed expression of self-aggrandizement, spreads across the videophone screen, as he supervises the proceedings from some remote location. The Producer has secretly written Clara out of her own story, so that now the film's about two brothers rather than a brother and sister.

Arresting though they are, the characters in *Speaking Parts* are too self-absorbed to invite identification. Nor does Egoyan intend for them to do so. His basic editing design (repeated throughout the film) involves subverting what at first appears to be a point of view shot—the traditional device for creating audience identification—by following it, not with the usual 180 degree reverse angle, but with a moving camera shot, 90 degrees off to the side. The second shot is not identified with any character. Rather it functions as an intrusion in the scene, as if the camera were not only coming between the characters, but going out of its way to make the audience aware of its gaze. This moving camera, in Egoyan's terms, "is a character"—the absent presence of the filmmaker.

While encompassing the Producer's film, *Speaking Parts* is also its dreamlike subtext. "A movie that takes the form of a talk show is very original," the Producer says. "I'd watch it and people have always watched what I like to watch." *Speaking Parts* gleefully satirizes the Producer's (mainstream films') banality and also offers another way of telling a story.

The lynchpin in the film's construction is a sequence toward the end in which the suicidal Clara revisits the mausoleum to, once again, watch the video of her brother. One has, until this point, tacitly assumed that Clara shot the tape—that when the brother smiles at the camera, he is, or rather, was, on that happier occasion, smiling at Clara. But this time, the tape runs past its usual cut-off point, and as the shot widens, we're surprised to see Clara, herself, in the upper right corner of the frame, filming her brother with a super-8 film camera. A cut to a head-on close-up of Clara's camera lens adds to the disorientation. Should the shot be read from the brother's POV or from the POV of the mysterious second camera which has taken over the scene? Then Clara slowly lowers her camera to her side. (Egoyan says that for him, this is the most moving moment in the film.) Sister and brother gaze directly at each other in what, for a split second, we naively believe is unmediated intimacy. Then the presence of the camera reasserts itself, and we understand that, like the characters, we've been set up.

It's telling that when Egoyan discusses technology, he focuses so heavily on its domestic use. In both *Family Viewing* and *Speaking Parts,* the social structure is imploded so that the family becomes the only operative institution. A claustrophobic immigrant culture is displaced onto a technological one. The recording apparatus is the object of a tug of war between the younger generation who need it to preserve childhood memory (incestuous yearnings) and the bad fathers who employ it to display and extend their power, rewriting personal history in the process. The VCR is a sex toy which fuels forbidden fantasies. All the characters in *Family Viewing* are bound by blood or marriage, except the two women who function as concubines for the father (one of whom is rescued and then claimed by the son). Sexuality is either incestuous or venal. In *Speaking Parts,* parental relationships are superimposed on the workplace. The Producer, who's away on business, asserts his authority via a closed circuit TV image, dominating not only production meetings, but the wedding of one of his employees, over whom he also exercises *droit du seigneur.* Similarly the hotel's head housekeeper is also the madame of its prostitution service, in charge of scheduling and regulating the sexual activities of both staff and guests.

The festishized scraps of home video (of Van and his mother/Clara and her brother), inscribed with incestuous longing and the pain of loss are not only "felt" images, they are the springboard for narrative. Interestingly, they also are the place where the son emerges as leading man. In that sense, *Family Viewing* resolves positively—Van saves both the women of the household and the tapes (cultural history.) *Speaking Parts* is a much darker film. Clara's brother, in saving her life, has abandoned her to the whims of the Producer. And Lance, the brother substitute, has no investment in the integrity of Clara's story; he's only too willing to betray it (and her) for the advancement of his own career.

Egoyan comments that, although Van seems like a savior, "he's still his father's son." *Speaking Parts'* ironic hall of mirrors suggests a similar complicity between Egoyan (the absent presence behind the camera) and the Producer (who "phones in" his picture.) Both derive power from the manipulation of images.

"If I have a set of concerns and a set of conflicting attitudes, then I have a film," Egoyan says. "I don't subscribe to a messianic view of filmmaking and I don't disguise the fact that I haven't reached a conclusion. I encourage the audience to be aware that I am photographing people and to be deeply suspicious of my reasons."

### Jonathan Romney (review date June 1992)

SOURCE: A review of *The Adjuster*, in *Sight & Sound*, Vol. 2, No. 2, June, 1992, p. 38.

[*In the following review, Romney praises Egoyan's work in* The Adjuster, *particularly his skillful use of repetition.*]

[In **The Adjuster**,] Noah Render, an insurance loss adjuster, lives in the only occupied house on an uncompleted estate with Hera, her sister Seta and their son Simon. Called out to the scenes of fires, he arranges for clients to be lodged in a motel while they wait for their claims to be sorted. On the subway, Hera witnesses an incident involving Bubba and Mimi, a rich couple who stage elaborate sex charades for Mimi to star in. Hera works as a film censor, classifying acts in pornographic films and videotaping them for Seta to watch at home.

At the motel Noah reassures an anxious client Tim, with whose wife he is having an affair. He also embarks on an affair with his latest client Arianne, who has allowed her house to burn down because "something had to change." Bubba visits the Renders posing as a location scout and persuades them to allow him to use their house for filming.

Hera is caught videotaping by Tyler, a young censor, who reports her to their boss Bert. The latter is delighted to hear that Hera shares their excitement at watching the films, but is disappointed when she explains that she does it so that Seta can learn about her work. Noah suggests that the family move to the motel while the 'film crew' use the house. Bubba and Mimi move into the house to film a sex scene in which she plays a mother at a children's party.

During a private screening arranged by Bert, Hera allows Tyler to fondle her. While Noah is in the bedroom of Matthew, a gay client, Hera, Seta and Simon leave. Driving home to look for them, Noah finds Bubba dousing the house in paraffin before setting it alight. As the house burns down, Noah remembers meeting Hera for the first time, as her house was burning . . .

In the past, Atom Egoyan seemed to have one thing to say and a number of elegantly complex ways to say it. Dispensing with the more mannered aspects of his earlier features, and adopting a more downbeat realism in his visual tone, Egoyan here manages to spread his thematic net considerably wider. His main insight has always been a fairly conventional one—into urban alienation in the video age, and into the aridity of interpersonal relationships entailed by the arrangement of the world into categories and representations.

In *Family Viewing* and *Speaking Parts,* the point was overstressed with a rather too insistent interplay of film and video media. Here he jettisons that device—so much so that, even though film and TV are omnipresent, we only hear their soundtracks, whether the banal jingles of children's TV or the all too eloquent grunts and gobbles of hard porn. Instead of television *per se*, Egoyan shows us TV-style spectacle enacted in the real world, like the sexual performance art staged by Bubba for Mimi's benefit (unless it is the other way round).

Noah's social role is one such spectacle: he could be the friendly insurance man in a TV ad, or at least tries to play the part. He is an adjuster before he is Hera's 'husband,' and their relationship is strained all the more because Hera herself is not satisfied with the constraints of her job description. As a sexual being, she finds that looking is not enough; an exchange of glances on the subway with a dashing chiropodist has to turn into direct physical contact, if only between his fingers and her feet. Noah's sexuality, on the other hand, is subsumed entirely into his role as consoler of fire victims, and if he embarks on affairs with them, we can only suppose that it is as an extension of his good services.

The film's dislocation—very short scenes, implied relations between characters that only become clearer as the film proceeds—traditionally goes hand in hand with themes of alienation. But Egoyan's particular achievement here is to hint at the possibility of some underlying order beneath the fragmentation. Noah, who is at least a semi-benevolent manipulator, is seen by his clients as an angel of infinite goodwill, ensuring them a continuity of life even after disaster has struck. His counterpart among the censors is Bert, who sits in the screening room like an impassible god, guaranteeing the possibility of sexual pleasure by reducing it, classifying by letter the manifestations of its excesses ("No Gs," he says after one film, "surprising").

*The Adjuster* works brilliantly as a layering of repetitions and parallelisms. Egoyan rings his characteristic changes on the theme of voyeurism—Seta watching porn in order to experience Hera's life at one remove; a passing masturbator watching her watching; Hera seeing Mimi's exhibitionistic subway charade; Bubba taking photos of a pornographer's most perverse delight, the spectacle of the 'happy home.' The repetition works, too, at the level of the way people keep a record of their lives, most simply in the photographs which enable Noah to value their life style. The point that the photos establish the life, rather than vice versa, is neatly made when Matthew's naked body on the bed—after he and Noah have presumably slept together—duplicates a pose in the portraits he had shown Noah previously.

Egoyan is often accused of not having real characters, but that is precisely the point. 'Real' life, 'inner' life, is only alluded to here through its absence, which shows as a glaring void behind the characters' neurotic manoeuvres and empty verbal equivocations. In this sense, two touches of performance stand out—the tension between Elias Koteas' twitching, panicked features and the codified banalities he speaks; and the telling scene in which Bubba, explaining the 'film' he is about to make, ends up desperately communicating his own impasse as a character in a film—in this film, in fact. The film's self-reflexivity points towards a rather desperate moral realisation—Egoyan's characters may be just characters in a movie, but they also know with increasing anxiety that they can never be characters in that elusive domain, the real.

### Amy Taubin (review date June 1992)

SOURCE: "Burning Down the House," in *Sight & Sound,* Vol. 2, No. 2, June, 1992, pp. 18–19.

[*In the following review, Taubin explores the recurring themes common in* The Adjuster *and Egoyan's earlier films.*]

The protagonist of *The Adjuster,* Atom Egoyan's discomforting fourth feature, is named Noah Render. "The allusions are so obvious, they're hysterical," says Egoyan during an interview. "What satisfaction could there be in analysing such a name?," he scoffs. "So what if you realise that the motel where Noah boards his clients is like his ark?" Without pausing for breath, he does an about face and gleefully runs through dictionary definitions of the word 'render': "to represent, to break down into simple forms . . . What I like about 'render' is that it has so many contrary meanings."

Or, as he remarked on another occasion: "If I have a set of concerns and a set of conflicting attitudes, then I have a film. I don't subscribe to a Messianic view of film-making and I don't disguise the fact that I haven't reached a conclusion. I encourage the audience to be aware that I am photographing people and to be deeply suspicious of my reasons for doing so."

With its wide-screen format, velvety lighting, and speaker-taxing, low-frequency musical effects, *The Adjuster* (1991) is more sumptuous than Egoyan's earlier features. *Next of Kin* (1984), *Family Viewing* (1987) and *Speaking Parts* (1989). Nevertheless, all four films probe the same dilemma—the relationship between so-called family values and a sexual desire which is defined as either incestuous or promiscuous (in other words, as guilty). Always reflexive, the films are littered with references to home movies and pornography; often they're one and the same. Egoyan is as attracted to hardcore as his fellow-Canadian David Cronenberg is to horror. But unlike Cronenberg's films, which pay off in genre terms, Egoyan's evade the 'money shot.' Here, it's the scene of pornography, rather than the mechanics of the body, that's delivered.

Like their director/writer, whose characteristic nervous gesture is to wrap the five fingers of his right hand around the middle fingers of his left and hang on for dear life, Egoyan's films fling their Oedipal castration anxiety in our faces. It's what makes this otherwise chilly work both touching and terrifying.

"On New Year's Eve, 1989, my parents' house was devastated by a fire," Egoyan explains. "We worked with an insurance adjuster and I was struck by the power he had over the rematerialisation of our lives. He had to assign value to objects and decide what our standard of living was. He was very professional, an ordinary guy, but I began to think what if he was going through a bad period and he didn't know how to evaluate his own life. *The Adjuster* came out of that experience."

*The Adjuster*'s Noah Render (Elias Koteas) is a compassion junkie; he wants to be indispensable to his clients. He arranges temporary motel housing, pays them daily visits, coaxes lists of lost objects from them, pours over family photographs in search of evidence to support a claim. "Is that a purebred?," Noah gently enquires of a gay couple who've just shown him a picture of themselves with their dog. They look at him with disgust, but he's not deterred. "What did you pay for it? $500? What was the approximate value?"

Later one of the men seductively offers Noah a set of porn photographs taken in his former apartment. "You can't see much of the background," comments Noah perplexedly. Then he has sex with the man, as if, by recreating the images in the photograph, he will be able to assign them a value. Noah is also sexually involved with two women clients. He offers his body to alleviate their anxiety and boredom. "You're in a state of shock," he tells each of them, although his monotone voice, robotic gestures and guilt-stricken face suggest that he's really talking about himself.

Noah's domestic life revolves around Hera (Arsinée Khanjian), a film censor who lives with her sister and son in a model home in an otherwise abandoned housing tract.

The film encourages us to assume that Noah and Hera are a couple. Noah is frequently in Hera's bedroom, but never in her bed. She treats him with a familiar contempt bordering on hatred. Hera knows that Noah's solicitousness is both paternalistic and narcissistic; nevertheless, she remains passively under his protection.

At work, Hera functions as errant daughter to the head of the censorship board (played by David Hemblen, the beefy-faced *pater familias* of *Speaking Parts* and *Family Viewing*). We never see the porn films the censors are rating, but we hear their moaning and groaning soundtracks. Hera's face remains inscrutable as cries of "do-me-Daddy" fill the auditorium. Secretly, she's been videotaping the juiciest bits to show to her sister. A recent émigrée from Armenia who speaks no English, the sister becomes addicted to the tapes. They're her primer in the language and customs of North America.

Noah and Hera function as mediators, classifying and assigning value to objects. Unlike Noah, Hera is aware of her alienation. Copying the films is a subversive act; as punishment, the head censor's assistant traps Hera in the screening room, and while his boss watches from the projection booth, he tries to rape her.

*The Adjuster*'s third 'family' unit is a rich couple—Bubba (Maury Chaykin) and Mimi (Gabrielle Rose). "They have the means to have everything they want, but they don't know what they need, so they try different things," Bubba explains to Noah, describing himself and his wife in the third person as if they were characters in the 'home movie' he plans to make using Hera and Noah's model home as the principal location. Among the "things" Bubba and Mimi have tried is a performance in which an entire football team lines up in an empty stadium to watch Mimi cheerlead to the rhythms of 'High School Confidential.' As the team captain prepares to reward Mimi for her efforts, Bubba turns his back on the scene and stares straight into the camera, protecting his wife from our gaze and reminding us of our complicity with his voyeurism.

Bubba's invasion and recreation of other people's lives is a more perverse version of what Noah does. Noah acquiesces to Bubba's desires—he rents the model house to him and moves Hera and the rest of the family to the motel where he keeps his other clients. Bubba's home movie climaxes with him burning down the house. As Talking Heads puts it, "He fights fire with fire." Noah catches Bubba spreading gasoline on the floor. "You've come in just when the person in the film who's supposed to live here decides it's time to stop playing house. So are you in or are you out?," Bubba bellows, shoving his face into Noah's. Noah flees and the house goes up in flames with Bubba and Mimi inside.

By destroying Noah's sham domesticity, Bubba proves that he is the real adjuster. The flashback which closes the film confirms what should have been obvious all along. Noah is not a man who leads a double life, cheating on his wife with his clients. Noah has no wife. Hera is just another client who was burned out of her house and whose claim was never settled. Noah hasn't lost his home because he never had one.

Although Noah is the only leading character not directly involved in film-making, he's the one who acts most like a director. Rushing from motel room to motel room, and from location to location, he desperately tries to keep everything under control. Named after a biblical patriarch, his position is that of a son struggling against his father's power. He resents the authority of the insurance company, which uses him "to clean up their messes," and allows the rapacious Bubba to rewrite his life.

Egoyan edits the film to Noah's rhythms, breaking the operatic flow of the narrative by compulsively shifting the scene just when the action starts to heat up. The editing not only represses the erotic fantasies the film threatens to unleash, it also heightens our awareness of our own voyeurism by refusing to allow us to see. Add to this the interlocking power struggles in which the only allowable positions are parent or child, and the entire film takes on the repulsive allure of the primal scene.

*The Adjuster* is an elaboration of the material Egoyan laid out more brutally in *Family Viewing*. Relentlessly claustrophobic, *Family Viewing* is about the Oedipal struggle between Stan, a video equipment salesman, and his son Van. Having driven his wife (Van's mother) away and placed her mother (Van's grandmother) in a nursing home, Stan is dedicatedly taping over treasured home video recordings—replacing idyllic images of young Van and his mother romping in the grass with clinically depicted sexual encounters between himself and his live-in girlfriend, who not-so-secretly also has the hots for Van. With the help of a young woman who works in a telephone sex establishment (where Stan is one of her clients), Van manages to rescue the tapes from Stan's clutches, his grandmother from the nursing home, and his mother from a homeless shelter. Van establishes a new household with the three women, and Stan, who's been frantically pursing them, is wiped out by a heart attack.

*Family Viewing* is remarkable for its use of video technology. Stan's bedroom diary and Van's baby pictures were actually recorded on consumer VHS; the living-room scenes involving Stan, Van and the girlfriend were produced sitcom-style, using three studio television cameras. Surveillance camera footage and broadcast images were frequently intercut with the action. Transferred for theatrical release to 16mm, the image has a degenerated look which functions both expressively and metaphorically in relation to the narrative.

Egoyan followed *Family Viewing* with *Speaking Parts.* In terms of its technology, the film is set about five years in the future. In one of the more memorable scenes, two characters engage in mutual masturbation via videophone. In another, a sister discovers something she never knew about her beloved dead brother by watching a home movie in a video mausoleum. Roughly described, *Speaking Parts* is about the making of a movie about organ transplants which takes the form of a television talk show. "If *Family Viewing* is about the absence of familial love," says Egoyan, "then *Speaking Parts* is about the withholding of romantic love." (And *The Adjuster* is about the confusion of the two.)

All relationships in both *Family Viewing* and *Speaking Parts* are mediated and transformed by video technology. The home video apparatus is a sex toy which fuels forbidden fantasies. It's the object of a tug of war between the sons or daughters who need it to preserve childhood memories (incestuous yearnings) and the bad fathers who employ it to extend their power, rewriting personal history in the process.

Excepting Godard and Cronenberg, no other film-maker has explored the connection between technology and voyeurism and between home movies and pornography so intensely or intelligently. "It's the difficulty of representing the self in a society completely obsessed with representation that interests me." But if that's the problem Egoyan is addressing, then the 35mm wide-screen format of *The Adjuster* seems a bit of a dinosaur—cumbersome, irrelevant and outdated. Especially since Egoyan isn't using it to make 'gloss' Hollywood films.

If *The Adjuster* leaves Noah no choice but to start his life from scratch, Egoyan is in a similar position with regard to his film-making career. While *The Adjuster* has done well on the festival circuit, it's too unnerving a film to attract a large art house audience. And Egoyan openly admits that he doesn't want to be trapped into making more and more expensive films in order to placate audiences with mainstream production values. On the other hand, his relative fame makes him an unlikely candidate for arts council funding. Given the institutional constraints of film financing, it won't be easy for Egoyan to go back to using low-end technology. But nothing else will do.

**James M. Wall (review date 3 March 1993)**

SOURCE: A review of *Calendar*, in *Christian Century*, Vol. 110, No. 7, March 3, 1993, pp. 227–28.

[*In the following review, Wall discusses the central plot and thematic material in* Calendar.]

Canadian director Atom Egoyan is a quiet man who avoided a press conference after the initial screening of his sixth feature film, *Calendar*. A few of us caught up with him just outside the theater where he willingly chatted about his picture, which deals with a photographer, played by Egoyan, who like the director is from an Armenian family but doesn't speak the language. His wife plays the role of Egoyan's movie wife, but she does speak the language—which sets up the film's drama of failed communication and experiences not shared.

The couple travels to Armenia to take pictures of churches for a calendar. (The film is co-produced by the Armenian government, a German television company and Egoyan's Canadian company.) The film's premise is simple: a local guide drives the photographer and his wife to remote church sites and describes the significance of the architecture and history of the buildings. (In one delightful exchange he refers to a point of "energy" which determined the location of the structure.) The wife translates for her husband, but it soon becomes obvious that she is also developing a rapport with the guide; they share a love for the country and its churches, and they have a common language which the husband lacks. But more than the Armenian language is missing from this marriage. The husband is someone who observes but cannot participate. From the wife's first attempt to translate the deep feelings the guide has for country and church, it is clear that it is only a matter of time before their rapport will translate into love.

Egoyan tells his story of a disintegrating marriage on several levels, cutting from a subjective 8 mm segment, which he shoots as the wife and guide talk, back to the film's regular camera, which captures the increasing tension between husband and wife. The film also alternates between the period in Armenia before the marriage fails and a period in Canada a year later as Egoyan's character "conducts" a series of dates with women he seeks out because they speak different languages and because they will reject him after they finish a bottle of wine together. Tension is created by long sections in which only Armenian is spoken, which neither the photographer not the film's audience can understand. And always there is the countryside of Armenia, and the centuries-old churches, which stand as mute witnesses to the folly of a man who has removed himself from life by recording rather than experiencing what he sees.

When I asked Egoyan if the film was autobiographical, he smiled and said he and his wife are still married. But he acknowledged that as a director he fears falling into the trap of the photographer, an observer who records but understands very little of the inner meaning of what he sees. Unlike the Jost film, Egoyan's picture is humorous—though the laughter is tinged with sadness, as when the wife tries to translate her husband's increasingly aloof mood to the guide, and the guide can't understand a word the man says until he mentions "more money." The musical score also enlivens the picture's good humor, alternating between Armenian folk music and Canadian pop songs. (One college-age German viewer told me later that Egoyan's script contains an amusing reference to a recent popular song about a young woman who can't be Egyptian because she doesn't "walk like an Egyptian.")

**Chris Chang (review date November–December 1993)**

SOURCE: "Ruined," in *Film Comment*, Vol. 29, No. 6, November–December, 1993, p. 73.

[*In the following review, Chang describes the history behind Egoyan's* Calendar *and explores the film's major plot elements.*]

Atom Egoyan won the Moscow Prize for ***The Adjuster*** in 1991. The award took the form of one million rubles in production funding and came with the stipulation that the work be done in the (then) Soviet Union. As location, Egoyan chose Armenia, his ancestral home—then saw his budget devalued, by secession and independence, to some $4,000 U.S. Last-minute assistance from German television allowed him to get on the plane with a limited budget, strict completion timeline, no script, and three ideas: 1) The film would be improvised. 2) A photographer on assignment shoots images of churches for a calendar. 3) A relationship disintegrates. As a friend of mine remarked, "All filmmakers should be forced to work this way."

In ***Calendar,*** Egoyan himself plays the photographer, his onscreen wife is played by his offscreen wife, Arsinée Khanjian, and Ashot Adamian plays their Armenian guide. Landscape photography marks another stage in the Egoyan film canon's continuing fixation on desensitized voyeurs and sentient cameras, and playing the eye that looks through the camera makes a fitting acting début for this director. It also increases the waffled subjectivity that turns ***Calendar***'s pages.

Cutting back and forth between the hard-copy images of the completed calendar and the diaphanous events surrounding their capture, we revisit that old postmodern mechanism of inauthentic experience. The wife translates for the guide: "He wants to know if you want to touch it." "Caress the church? No. . . ." "He wants to know if you'd be here if it weren't for your job." "No." Later, declining an offer for a walk while on location, Egoyan watches the two of them "disappear into a landscape I'm about to photograph." She is becoming rerooted in her past; he will only come as close as the rootless image allows. Back home in Canada, the photographer turns to a sophisticated escort service that provides him with women who, when cued, make erotic phone calls in foreign languages ("Is Macedonian okay?") to provide him with inspirational nostalgia for his estranged wife. What deters the film from falling into self-indulgent existential malaise are, among other things, his contrapuntal camcorder memories of his wife, dancing about a foreign landscape, shot in a way that reflects the true warmth and whimsy of roadtrips in love. She is a Mona Lisa smile in search of lost time, but nonetheless a phantom available only through image fragments of architectural landscape. The medium is the memory.

Memory and loss also dwell in Chantal Akerman's *Moving in* (*Le Déménagement*), a 37-minute crawling zoom in on and into a man (Sami Frey) who has just moved to a new modern apartment. He has left behind a melancholy space of relations, relations dominated by his former neighbors, a trio of female "social science students." He now sits alone, he hasn't unpacked, he is unsure and not quite comfortable. His monologue is delivered to the camera as we move in on him. The mnemonic trinity, Béatrice/Elisabeth/Juliette, form a unified field of identity, a strength in numbers that only Sami truly understands. When the first of the trio encounters the "contamination of marriage," he is puzzled why the groom chooses against tripartite consummation. That hurts. But there are still all the good times, the small moments: Elisabeth coming to his door for salt: "I'm out of salt" . . . "Darn," "The way she said that, 'Darn,' I was *exhilarated.*" (This is very French.) A menu of the commonplace, the insignificant social niceties, the color of a dress, a pat on the head, the moment a photo was taken. "Where is that photo now?" It's the only baggage Sami is unpacking. When the camera achieves its closest point, when the lines of his face fill the screen, he stops talking, the eyes make contact, they are penetrating through, connecting in spite of absurdity, an empty man in an empty room. I think he tries to smile; the screen goes black. Somehow, he's still there.

**Bart Testa (review date Winter 1994)**

SOURCE: A review of *Speaking Parts,* in *University of Toronto Quarterly,* Vol. 64, No. 1, Winter, 1994, pp. 238–41.

[*In the following review, Testa argues that the published script of* Speaking Parts *fails to support Egoyan's reputation as a leading postmodern director.*]

The publication of scripts of English-Canadian films is regrettably a rarity. Coach House's ***Speaking Parts,*** the script of Canadian film director Atom Egoyan's 1989 film, is a model of how a script should be presented. In addition to the script, there is an introductory essay by Professor Ron Burnett of McGill University, an interview with the director conducted by film critic Marc Glassman, a short piece by the director, and a well-prepared filmography.

The appearance of the book raises several issues. The first is the necessity of its elaboration, which is a bit saddening. Since his mid-twenties, Egoyan, now thirty-three, has frequently been declared to be the leading English-Canadian director of his generation. However, no critic has come forward with a cogent account of why he is to be so highly regarded. The writing on Egoyan is little more than press publicity and, for a director of his notable intellectual and artistic ambition, this must be a disappointment. For those of us less impressed by the idea of Atom Egoyan projected by the press—and who have never been able to see that idea realized on the screen—the postponement of some substantiation of all the claims made for him seems inexplicably long. His films, and ***Speaking Parts*** especially, have become classroom fixtures and Egoyan has become today's object of Canadian film culture's desire for an 'art cinema' hero. The least question (though it is also a most polysemous question) we doubters might like to have answered is 'What does Atom Egoyan mean?'

In this respect, appreciation of this volume must be limited to the merely ceremonial. Egoyan's interview with Glassman and Burnett's introductory essay are no help in answering our question. The interview strays away from

*Speaking Parts* into comfortable chatter around the director's familiar media persona. Burnett's article is a little fatuous, the sort of thing academic critics can be depended upon to click on when they are unsure what to say and are grasping for ready-made assertions of aesthetic importance. Today, these are themes of disassociated subjectivity and narrative disjunctiveness. Here are some of Burnett's thesis paragraphs:

> Egoyan is concerned with the relationship between image and identity: his film proposes that images have transformed the personal and public spaces between his characters. It suggests that there is no point of separation between image and identity, no 'ground zero' (as Jean-Luc Godard once called it) where reality and image can be posited as different from each other. As the opening shots of the film reveal, there seems to be a point of departure and no end point where this proliferation of images can be explained with the kind of depth for which Egoyan is searching. In other words, although the film seeks to explore how its characters grapple with the past, history is absent. . . .
>
> This sense of fragmentation, bounded by questions of truth and morality, drives the narrative of the film forward. Although Egoyan remains faithful to the idea that a story must be told, he questions conventional strategies of storytelling through a dispersal of image and narrative.

The problem with such thematic claims is that *Speaking Parts* does not speak to them. In the film itself 'history' is uncovered. The source of the guilt that troubles the female protagonist, Clara, while enigmatic in 'the opening shots,' is revealed to be her past and it is dramatically exhausted by the last scene. Moreover, 'history' is re-presented throughout, for Clara has written it in the form of a television script. The male protagonist, Lance, has read it and grasped it, and it bears the mark of truth for both of them and for the viewer. Clara's true history is betrayed by the villain, the sinister TV producer, and that betrayal confirms its representation by making such an issue of deforming it. Similarly, image and identity are constantly asserted to be different in this film, and the script ensures that the drama of Clara's betrayal hinges on it. Visually, too, Egoyan's rhetoric sharply juxtaposes lower-fidelity video footage with film footage to express this difference.

Even a child, then, could recognize what Clara and Lance recognize, that truth has been written and is being bowdlerized. The confused one is Lisa, the somnambulistic hotel chambermaid in love with Lance. Lisa reveals that she has less savvy than a child and, as played by Arsinée Khanjian (Egoyan's wife and favourite actress) with her patented dazed naïvety, Lisa serves in an idiotic capacity as the slight, ambiguating pressure in *Speaking Parts*. But the accent should definitely fall on *slight*. As for 'fragmentation' and 'dispersal' of images, nowhere does Burnett, or the printed script, tell us why *Speaking Parts* seems so narratively fragmented. The reason is simple: Egoyan has broken up his plotting's straightforward linearity (Burnett's 'a story must be told') through a formal convolution. Stripped of normal transitional markers of ellipsis or simultaneity, or punctuating counterpoints, the film's editing is often arbitrary. The connections between narrative segments (written simply as numbered scenes in the script) seem to have been composed by a sleep-walker, hence the sense of disassociation. Nonetheless, before long, the viewer does catch on to the dramatic fact that the disassociative editing pattern is merely decorative.

Burnett elsewhere opens a door to what Egoyan's mannered decoration of *Speaking Parts* means. The TV set in the mausoleum where Clara conducts her seances probably does, for example, signify incest aping sacrality, as Burnett suggests. But the film's structure is anything but a denial of history, memory, or identity. If anything, Egoyan's films are about the maddening attachment to these things. From the start of his filmmaking, at least since ***Open House*** (1982) and ***Next of Kin*** (1984), he has gone on (and on) about how sentimentally wrenching the discovery of memory and identity within the family can be. Clara possesses them already and it is their enactment—through 'art' (a TV movie!)—that promises her some confessional release from her private guilt.

However, all this hardly validates Burnett's 'transformation' of public and private. This cannot be exactly what 'concerns' Egoyan, for it is a frustrated will to enact such a transformation that grips Clara and drives the plot. Either the director conceives this transformation to be impossible, or he is as foolish as Clara is. In any case, Egoyan denies her the chance to turn her personal history into a speaking part. This is his own wise refusal to allow her to seem foolish, or, one suspects, to seem foolish himself. Expressed simply through plot machinations that contrive to steal Clara's memories and history (actually she sells them), his narrative refusal to test the hypothesis of such transformation permits Egoyan to sustain Clara's slight pathos, and even to moralize it when she becomes the woman betrayed.

Just as he does with Lisa's role and the mannered editing of his film, Egoyan's plotting, then, deliberately veils what he intends and leaves us asking what he means altogether. Whatever the director might have intended, common sense suggests that the obvious significance *Speaking Parts* implies is woefully sentimental, an obviousness Egoyan only complicates with melodramatic betrayals. Moreover, it should be understood, these complications derive from nothing mysterious or theoretical, which is what Burnett's facile essay wants anxiously to claim for *Speaking Parts*. Indeed, much about the film's plotting suggests ways Atom Egoyan continues to reveal himself still to be a somewhat classical man of the theatre (his field of study while a student at University of Toronto) more than he is the postmodern Canadian art-cinema filmmaker proclaimed in the press and in some classrooms.

## Brian D. Johnson (essay date 3 October 1994)

SOURCE: "Exotic Atom: With *Exotica*, Atom Egoyan Has Become the Most Celebrated Canadian Filmmaker of His

Generation," in *Maclean's,* Vol. 107, No. 40, October 3, 1994, pp. 44-47.

[*In the following essay, Johnson explores Egoyan's career, influences, and the filmmaker's concerns about his future.*]

Rolling up to a movie premiere in a limousine is a familiar ritual. But at the recent Toronto International Film Festival, Canadian director Atom Egoyan elected to walk to the North American premiere of his new movie, ***Exotica.*** Egoyan knew that refusing a limo could seem as pretentious as accepting one—but he had taken the luxury route two nights earlier with absurd results. After the festival's opening-night party, he and his partner, actress Arsinee Khanjian, found themselves ushered into a preposterously long stretch limo. "I was ready to jump into a cab," recalls the film-maker, but his handlers at Alliance Releasing "had insisted we ride around in these limos." He directed the chauffeur to Riverdale, on the eastern edge of downtown, where Egoyan, Khanjian and their one-year-old son, Arshile, share a modest semi-detached house on a narrow little street—so narrow that the driver could not get around the corner. "He spent 15 minutes trying to negotiate the turn," Egoyan laughs. "You could see the dismay in the driver's face. He started to think maybe he'd taken the wrong people home."

It was an Egoyanesque moment, the kind of bizarre incident that could be a premise for one of his movies—a limo driver and a moviemaker go through the motions of a ritual neither believes in. One way or the other, Egoyan's films are all about ritual. They are stories of separation and loss, featuring characters with strangely fetishized occupations. In ***Speaking Parts,*** a hotel chambermaid is infatuated with a co-worker who moonlights as an extra in B-movies. In ***The Adjuster,*** a fire-insurance claims investigator provides his dispossessed clients with sexual solace. And in ***Exotica,*** a young stripper does therapeutic table-dancing for a tax auditor mourning his daughter.

Egoyan's movies are dark, disturbing and encoded with mystery. His tautly controlled visions of alienation can seem exquisite or excruciating. But over the course of his 10-year career, after writing and directing six features, Egoyan has created a unique body of work. His films do not look like anyone else's. The 34-year-old director, who was born in Cairo to Armenian parents and raised in Victoria, B.C., is now the most celebrated Canadian filmmaker of his generation. Last May, ***Exotica*** became the first English-Canadian film in 10 years to be accepted for official competition at the Cannes Film Festival, where it won the prestigious International Critics' Award. And at the Toronto festival, Egoyan won the annual prize for best Canadian film for the third time.

A favorite at film festivals around the world, Egoyan has a serious following in Europe—a German TV crew just finished filming a one-hour documentary about him. Now, his appeal is broadening. With each of his movies, he has gradually expanded his budget and his audience. Even before opening commercially, ***Exotica*** has recouped its $2-million cost with sales to distributors. In the United States, it was picked up by the Disney-owned Miramax Films. And Hollywood scripts are regularly showing up in Egoyan's mail. "His star is definitely ascending," says fellow Canadian director David Cronenberg (*The Fly, Naked Lunch*). "He has a world of possibilities opening up to him."

Cronenberg, whom Egoyan considers his mentor, recognizes some parallels in their work. "There's a dry intellectual humor coupled with a mischievous sexuality," says Cronenberg. "I think we both have that, a cerebral approach with some earthiness—the lascivious professor." And, just as Cronenberg has turned down offers to direct the likes of Tom Cruise, Egoyan seems determined to pursue his own vision. Both directors make movies that "get under your skin" says American film-maker Quentin Tarantino (*Pulp Fiction, Reservoir Dogs*). "But while everyone talks about the voyeurism and creepy feeling in Atom's films, they forget that he's a really great storyteller."

Saturday morning. Dressed in a black T-shirt and black jeans, Egoyan serves black coffee in his kitchen, apologizing for the lack of milk. The house is a slim three-storey affair, renovated by the previous owner—its oddest feature being an undulating pine banister that ends in the form of a bird's beak. There are various artworks about the place, including one by each of his parents, and a New Mexican painting bequeathed to him by the late Jay Scott, *The Globe and Mail* film critic who helped put Egoyan on the map.

Sitting down at a patio table in the small, fenced-in yard, Egoyan reflects on his latest dealings with the Miramax publicity machine. "They are telling me there are certain phrases I shouldn't use in interviews," he says. "They don't like me talking about 'ritual.' They would prefer I talk about 'game-playing.'" The director seems more amused than offended by the attempt to doctor his image. "Maybe I should do everything they suggest," he says, only half joking. "I'd be curious to see if it makes a difference."

While Egoyan's films tend to be chilling, hermetic and austere, the director comes across as a warm, genial presence, with an eager sense of humor. For an artist who has achieved such acclaim so soon, he remains gracefully modest and down-to-earth. "I've been very lucky to make my living at what I do," he declares. "Arsinee and I are new Canadians, and we are extraordinarily appreciative of the opportunity to make films in this country that couldn't be made anywhere else."

Arsinee Khanjian has been Egoyan's partner in life and art ever since he cast her in his first feature, ***Next of Kin,*** 10 years ago. And she plays a crucial role in his career. The 36-year-old actress, an Armenian who immigrated from Lebanon at the age of 17 and speaks five languages, has appeared in all of his movies. But she also serves as his artistic foil, questioning his decisions at every turn. Although her screen characters are often eerily restrained, offscreen she is convivial and exuberant. Together, they make a striking couple—their faces forming a symmetry of bold eyebrows and seductive smiles.

The relationship, however, seems fuelled by creative friction. Their closest friend, producer Niv Fichman, says it is "probably the most volatile and tempestuous relationship I've ever experienced, and yet the most true. He knows he has her support, but there are so many eruptions and tests that she puts him through. And that gives him such confidence because he knows that he's had to go through the wringer to make a decision." Egoyan concurs. "It's not a romantic process making movies together, not at all," he says. "It's fraught with tension and anxiety. But that chemistry creates something interesting when it works well."

Egoyan and Khanjian underwent an unusually difficult ordeal in making *Exotica.* By the time they were shooting the film, during a July heat wave in 1993, Khanjian was seven months pregnant with Arshile. Egoyan had written the script before learning he was to be a father. Had he known, he doubts he would have written it.

The story revolves around a father's ritualistic grief over the death of his young daughter. A tax auditor named Francis (Bruce Greenwood) frequents a striptease emporium called Exotica, where Christina (Mia Kirshner), a dancer tricked out like a schoolgirl in a tartan skirt, performs at his table. Francis is a voyeur who just wants to talk. And during his evenings at the club, he hires his niece (Sarah Polley) to "babysit" an empty house. With lambent flashbacks to a search party combing for a body in a sunlit field, layers of mystery are gradually stripped away. "It was such a perverse film for a new parent to have made," acknowledges Egoyan, who now has a babysitter of his own. "But it wasn't conceived that way."

Khanjian's pregnancy was incorporated into the script. She plays Zoe, Exotica's enigmatic owner, who is involved in a tense triangle with its emcee (Elias Koteas) and the schoolgirl stripper. A deadpan Don McKellar plays Thomas, a pet-store owner who smuggles exotic animals and gets investigated by the auditor. Khanjian says that she and Egoyan were first thrilled by the way her pregnancy enriched the story—"We thought it would be a great metaphor, the way you inherit life and pass it on." Zoe and Thomas both inherited establishments from parents. And Egoyan, leaving no symbol unturned, points out that Thomas's act of smuggling eggs by taping them to his stomach is a kind of artificial pregnancy.

But the idea was more fun than the execution. "It was very disturbing," says Khanjian. "I was going through those incredible moments of doubt and need for complete attention. And here was this guy who every day was going on the set to direct what seemed to be a very perverse environment. I realized how much parents can become completely conservative. Suddenly, I was thinking, 'Oh my God, we are both parents for this child. What are we going to pass on to him? Is this the world we are introducing him to?'"

Egoyan's parents, Joseph and Shushan, emigrated from Cairo when he was three. Settling in Victoria, they changed their name from Yeghoyan to the more pronounceable Egoyan. Atom, named in honor of atomic energy, disliked being called that when he was growing up. And it did not help that his younger sister (now a concert pianist in Toronto) was named Eve—Atom and Eve jokes soon wore thin.

As a child, Egoyan worked hard to assimilate, refusing to speak Armenian at home and covering his ears when his parents spoke it. Although they made their living with a small furniture store, both had set out with artistic ambitions. His mother had a painting accepted by the National Gallery of Armenia. His father had attended the Chicago Art Institute as a 16-year-old prodigy. But "he didn't really stick it out," says Egoyan, who was 10 when his father staged his last major show. "They gave him the whole second floor of the provincial museum in Victoria, and his show was just images of dead birds—it did not go over well. The year before, our house was full of dead birds hanging by strings from the walls and ceiling, birds he'd collected on the beach, dead sea gulls and stuff. He would pose them around the house and paint them." Adds the director: "I think I had a very early exposure to a very excessive mentality."

Egoyan says his parents had "a volatile relationship, and I saw the pain they felt in not being able to do what they wanted as artists." He appeared determined not to suffer the same fate. At 12, for a Christmas pageant skit, Egoyan set up a camera onstage and asked the audience to smile. "I remember everyone being stunned," he recalls. "It was a wonderful moment for me, feeling the power to undercut people's expectations."

From the age of 13, Egoyan wrote plays, soaking up influences from such writers as Eugene Ionesco, Samuel Beckett and Harold Pinter. Later, after enrolling as an arts undergraduate at the University of Toronto's Trinity College, he began to make short films. And by the age of 23, he was shooting his first feature, *Next of Kin*—the tale of a bored 23-year-old who abandons his quarrelling WASP parents and masquerades as the long-lost son of an Armenian couple in Toronto. Directed with startling assurance, *Next of Kin* contains all the basic threads that would distinguish his later work: the theme of family loss, the use of videotaped memories as a narrative device and the sense that the camera is conducting surveillance.

The movie also introduced Atom to Arsinee. While casting, he showed up at a rehearsal for an Armenian play in Montreal. Khanjian and her husband of two years, an Armenian dental student, were both performing. "Atom arrived in this beige tweed suit, with a nice tie and rimless glasses," the actress recalls. "The moment I saw him I thought, 'My God, if I had any ideal man in mind, this is it.'" Egoyan says he had a similar response: "I had this shining image of an Armenian princess—I used to joke with my roommate about it—and when I found her I was sure she was that person."

They did not meet until the next night, when Khanjian and her husband saw Egoyan at another play. Khanjian wanted to ignore him, but her husband insisted on going over to introduce himself. He then summoned his wife, who blushed in embarrassment as he persuaded Egoyan to audition her for *Next of Kin*. The director gave her a role, and during the filming they began an affair that would end her marriage. "My parents were mortified," she says. "I had a high-bourgeois life waiting for me, and here I was going off with this guy who had no obvious future."

*Next of Kin* was virtually ignored, which left Egoyan demoralized as he struggled to make ends meet, working for $5 an hour as a porter at the U of T's Massey College. But after gaining some experience as a TV director, he made his second feature, *Family Viewing* (1987). The protagonist is an 18-year-old boy. He discovers that his father (David Hemblen), who is estranged from the boy's Armenian mother, has been taping over the family's home videos with scenes of himself having sex with his mistress.

Egoyan still considers *Family Viewing* the film closest to his heart, and at film festivals around the world it established his reputation. Two years before Steven Soderbergh's *sex, lies and videotape*, *Family Viewing* explored video as a literal metaphor for distressed, disembodied memory. Egoyan stretched the idea even further in *Speaking Parts,* which featured video-linked phone sex and a mausoleum with video images of the deceased. The story takes place in a hotel, with Khanjian playing a chambermaid. (As a teenager, Egoyan himself spent four summers working in a hotel in Victoria.) *Speaking Parts* had a hot debut in Cannes: the third reel burst into flames. But the audience sat through the 40-minute delay, and the movie received warm praise from critics. "For someone just turning 30," wrote Georgia Brown of *The Village Voice,* "Atom Egoyan may be unforgivably sophisticated. His ideas about sex, lies and you-know-what make Steven Soderbergh look like a naive schoolboy."

With its narcotic pacing and deliberately stilted acting style, *Speaking Parts* could also seem unforgivably precious. But in his next movie, *The Adjuster* (1991), Egoyan grafted his otherworldly vision onto strong, naturalistic performances—by Elias Koteas as a fire-insurance adjuster who beds his clients, Khanjian as his film-censor wife and Maury Chaykin as an ex-football player with a demented fantasy life. Once again, Egoyan found the spark for the script close to home—a fire that destroyed his parents' furniture store on New Year's Eve in 1989.

For his fifth feature, the director downshifted to an intimate, low-budget experiment called *Calendar* (1993). Working both sides of the camera, Egoyan played a photographer who travels to Armenia to take calendar pictures of churches, and whose wife (Khanjian) leaves him for their tour guide. A simulated home movie, *Calendar* appealed to a narrow art-house audience. But its witty blend of postmodern formalism and unscripted cinema verite delighted critics.

By contrast, *Exotica* is Egoyan's most stylish, ambitious and broadly appealing work to date. With its haunting Middle Eastern score and aquarium-cool images, it casts a hypnotic spell that is sustained from beginning to end. All the performances seem tuned to the same weird wavelength. "I wonder how that happens," muses McKellar, who acted in both *Exotica* and *The Adjuster,* "because Atom never told me to act in an Atom Egoyan style."

Despite its dangerous premise, which is based on a confusion between the babysitter and the babe-stripper, *Exotica* is so brilliantly controlled that it never seems prurient. Egoyan dissects the paradox of table-dancing—an intimate act in a public place—without exploitation or moralism.

Khanjian, meanwhile, seems remarkably sanguine about her partner's choice of material. "I've never felt uncomfortable with Atom's portrayal of sexuality," she says. "It probably fulfils my own hidden fantasies, God knows." But she does have her criticisms of his work. "I get annoyed sometimes by the fact that he is very suspicious of expressing emotions in an overt way," she says. "It took me a long time to realize that it was not a gimmick, because he's incredibly emotional in real life." But the most contentious issue between them, she adds, is the role of women in his work. "I find his movies very male-psyche. I'm not saying macho or misogynist—he uses a lot of androgyny. But he channels his subtleties through the male characters. The female characters are very condensed."

Still, Khanjian offers her partner wholehearted support. Although she recently took a role as a doctor's wife in CBC-TV's new series *Side Effects,* she suggests that she would put her career on hold for him if necessary. "It sounds tacky," she says, "but I'm going to be there for him if I can be of any use." Then she adds: "I get scared for him sometimes. He's very smart, and he has his head on his shoulders, but this is a profession where people love turning you into a god, then crucifying that god."

In fact, Egoyan seems to be conducting his career with supreme caution. As the senior producer on all his movies, he has a reputation for finishing them on time and under budget. Other film-makers envy the steady support he has received from government funding agencies such as Telefilm Canada. But his skill behind the camera makes a $2-million movie look like $10 million. And Alliance chairman Robert Lantos, who co-financed *Exotica,* says its budget could have been larger if Egoyan had wanted it— "he has a very strong sense of fiscal responsibility."

Now that there is mounting pressure for Egoyan to go mainstream, Lantos says that "making a movie that someone else could make could be damaging to his career."

Egoyan agrees: "The biggest myth in this industry is that you should go out and make your big commercial movie so you can do what you really want. It never works." The one time Egoyan did direct a movie that he did not write—CBC-TV's *Gross Misconduct* (1992), about hockey player Brian Spencer—he seemed to lose his bearings. Although he says he is proud of it and loved making it, *Gross Misconduct* is uncharacteristically lurid and incoherent.

Now, Egoyan's options continue to multiply. He receives a lot of American scripts, typically dysfunctional family dramas and quirky sci-fi thrillers. "I get confused," he says, "because I have the option at any time of just crossing over. The fact that I'm even courting it makes Arsinee unsure." Filming his own material has become "addictive," he adds. "There's a child-like thrill in being able to tell these dark fables that come from the deepest recesses of your imagination and project them in full theatres. It seems unreal. That's what Arsinee gets upset about—that lately I've been taking it for granted."

At the Toronto festival, a full theatre awaits the premiere of *Exotica*. Egoyan, Khanjian and Lantos stand near the stage with the director's father, an elegant man dressed all in black who looks like Leonard Cohen. Joseph Egoyan has made a special request to meet Lantos, the money man. "Art without business, you can forget it," he tells the Alliance president as they are introduced. "Atom is an astute businessman," Lantos replies. "He learned that from me," proclaims Joseph with a grin.

Egoyan is called to the stage. He confesses that he is more nervous than he was at Cannes, thanks everyone he can think of, then sits down to watch his movie one more time. At the closing credits, the audience breaks the movie's spell with generous applause, and Egoyan takes the stage to field questions, working the crowd with wit and charm. The first question is breathtakingly erudite, a mini-thesis about editing and memory. Someone else inquires about the etiquette of clients touching table dancers. Then, a man stands up to say he was reminded of Michelangelo's painting in the Sistine Chapel—"hands touching but not touching." The director does a double take. This is too much, even for him. "Yes, thank you, Michelangelo!" he quips, drawing laughter from the audience. And for a moment, Atom Egoyan seems to have found a place for himself in show business.

## Kristine McKenna (review date 12 March 1995)

SOURCE: "This Director's Got a Brand Noir Bag," in *Los Angeles Times,* March 12, 1995, pp. 21–23.

[*In the following review, McKenna explores the differences between* Exotica *and Egoyan's earlier films.*]

"People often describe my work as cold and clinical, but I just can't see it that way—to me it's about nothing *but* emotion," says Canadian filmmaker Atom Egoyan.

"True, the people in my films often try to deny their emotions and usually have a hard time understanding what they're feeling. Nonetheless, the emotions are always bubbling away in there at an almost operatic level."

The reason critics often describe Egoyan's work as cold could have something to do with the tendency in his films for the "operatic" emotions to implode rather than explode—and the fact that the media are usually positioned as central characters in his narratives.

From his 1984 feature debut, *Next of Kin,* to his recently released sixth film, *Exotica,* Egoyan has looked with a cool eye at our willingness to hand the reigns of our consciousness over to technology and at the barrage of images that have invaded human experience.

Those ideas are percolating away in *Exotica,* but the film is a departure in other ways. Egoyan's works have always been provocative—and *Exotica,* doesn't disappoint on that score—but he has never made such a nakedly emotional film before. The story, revolving around the relationship between a stripper (Mia Kirshner) and one of the patrons of the club where she works (Bruce Greenwood), blossoms into a multilayered tale chronicling various experiences of loss, betrayal and obsession.

More than anything, however, *Exotica* is a meditation on the mysteriousness of the connections between people and how powerful those connections can be.

*Exotica*—which also stars Elias Koteas, Arsinée Khanjian and Don McKellar—marks another change for Egoyan in that his previous works eschewed linear narrative in favor of a highly fragmented approach to storytelling. The new film is loosely structured as a conventional thriller.

"I've been heavily influenced by thrillers, and if I was to associate myself with any genre, that's the one it would be," the 35-year-old director says during a meeting at the Westwood hotel where he is staying with Khanjian, who is his wife and the star of all his films, and their infant son.

"And as with a thriller, *Exotica* comes together like a puzzle and only works if you trust what the filmmaker's up to. If you watch it suspiciously and worry that you're not 'getting it,' it begins to slip into the distance.

"People tend to discuss my films in terms of theory, but I'm not a theorist—my stories are told to communicate emotions," Egoyan says in explaining the change of direction in his work.

"It's true that ideas about media, realities once removed and surrogates have been central to my films, but I never intended to address those themes in purely theoretical terms. I was beginning to feel that my stories were revolving to too large a degree around technology, so the challenge with *Exotica* was to show that the need to behave in certain ways is deep within us, and we act it out with or without technology."

A theme that Egoyan has turned to repeatedly is the relationship between technology, the fantasies it gives rise to and sexuality. In *Exotica,* this idea is central.

"For most people, I think sex resides more in fantasy and in the imagination than in the body," Egoyan says. "Ideally the two should obviously be in sync, but we're surrounded by such a plethora of images that we're almost taught to be as satisfied with images of people.

"Ironically, the central relationship in *Exotica* isn't very sexual at all, even though on a superficial level that appears to be the *only* thing it's about. In fact, this is a story about a man who becomes involved in an odd ritual that began as a healing process but has degenerated into something quite tormenting.

"I had this amazing screening of *Exotica* for the Toronto Psychoanalytic Society, and I learned several fascinating things," says Egoyan, who lives in Toronto. "First, they assured me that the kind of relationship that's central to the film definitely exists in real life.

"They also told me that all my films deal with a process known as 'faulty mourning,' which is a Freudian term referring to the phenomenon of people who are in the process of mourning and think they're dealing with their loss, but the means they've devised to deal with it actually exaggerates the loss and leaves them addicted to the process of mourning. Why would anyone choose to behave in this way? Because it's a project. People look for a project in their lives, and the project of trying to come to terms with unhappiness is quite consuming."

Invariably, the characters in Egoyan's films are struggling to come to terms with unhappiness—a fact that's rather curious considering that Egoyan seems to have led something of a charmed life.

Egoyan, who was named after the atom, was born in Cairo to Armenian parents in 1960 and raised in Victoria, British Columbia.

"There was no Armenian community in Victoria, and one of the major challenges of my life has been learning to honor my own heritage," says Egoyan, whose 1993 film *Calendar* deals specifically with this theme.

"There was an underlying racism there—I can remember a teacher calling me 'little Arab'—and as a child I wanted nothing more than to be like everyone else.

"My parents were both painters, so I was raised in an environment where people made things. My parents had a tumultuous relationship, and from a young age I was always playing therapist and trying to bring them together. I've always found the process of conciliation challenging, and when I went to college I majored in international relations planning to be a diplomat."

Egoyan earned a bachelor's degree in international relations at Trinity College in Toronto in 1982, but his career as a diplomat never took root, probably because he had also been turning out plays at a prodigious rate from the time he was 13.

"I wrote tons of very wordy plays, which an adviser at school pointed out to me were influenced by the theater of the absurd," he recalls. "After he told me that, I tracked down some books by Ionesco, Beckett and Pinter, and I was so excited by their ideas that I was just running around and laughing out loud. The theater of the absurd corresponded with so many things I was trying to understand and was so rich with comic possibility—it introduced me to a dramatic world where anything could happen and had a huge impact on me."

Shortly after graduating from college, Egoyan came to the conclusion, he says, that "I was never going to find my voice in theater."

"From the moment I made my first film, however, I realized that the camera lens can be a metaphor for a missing character—that struck me as such a powerful device!" he says, referring to *Howard in Particular,* a 14-minute short he completed in 1979.

After his first feature, *Next of Kin,* Egoyan directed several programs for Canadian television and four more feature films (*Family Viewing* in 1987, *Speaking Parts* in 1989, *The Adjuster* in 1992 and *Calendar* two years ago) that shared the same basic thematic concerns.

"I'm fascinated by the process of how people hurt each other, and anything that illustrates the fragility of human existence is appealing to me," he says. "The characters I find most dramatically compelling are usually dysfunctional people who think they have control of their lives but have lost themselves in a pattern of behavior that perpetuates their dysfunction. People create rituals in my films, and there's something compulsive about how my characters behave.

"I'm also drawn to stories that have a sense of moral ambiguity, where the characters are lost in a universe where they're trying to put together some sense of moral values."

Long a darling of the art film crowd, Egoyan stands a good chance of reaching a broader audience with *Exotica,* which has already won several prizes on the film festival circuit.

Asked if Hollywood had come courting yet, he shyly confesses, "Well, yes, I have been given lots of scripts, and I've enjoyed reading several of them. I have really eclectic tastes and love some Hollywood films.

"I'm already at work on my next project, though—I've optioned Russell Banks' *The Sweet Hereafter.* I fell in love with it when I read it in 1991 and think it's a perfect novel for me. I'm working on an adaptation, but I don't know if it will in fact be my next film, because I've never worked from someone else's material. It remains to be seen if I'll be as happy with my screenplay as I am with Russell's book."

Although Egoyan concedes that his films are difficult to "get" while they're in production, he stresses that "my films aren't remotely surreal to me—everything that happens in them is within the realm of possibility."

"At the same time," he says, "the strongest moments in cinema for me are the ones when you can't believe you're watching what you're watching. Scenes that extend the viewers' ideas about what they *should* be watching, but at the same time inspire trust and confidence—that's the tricky balance I'm trying to pull off in my work."

**Peter Harcourt (essay date Spring 1995)**

SOURCE: "Imaginary Images: An Examination of Atom Egoyan's Films," in *Film Quarterly,* Vol. 48, No. 3, Spring, 1995, pp. 2–14.

[*In the following essay, Harcourt, who teaches at Carleton University in Ottawa, traces the themes and cinematographic techniques characteristic of Egoyan's films and places the director's work in a Canadian context.*]

> *I'm attracted to people who are lost in a world that I can navigate.*[1]
>
> —Atom Egoyan

There is a sequence in *Exotica,* the latest film by 35-year-old Canadian film-maker Atom Egoyan, that makes me think of Andrew Wyeth. There is a long shot of an extended grassy field. In the distance, a number of people appear on the horizon, walking in unison. They are looking for something. As in Wyeth's "Christina's World," there is a surreal combination of beauty and dread. Are they on a ramble, these people, looking at flora and fauna? Or are they looking for something else? Not until well into the film, as we continually return to this particular sequence, will we receive an answer to these questions.

Like other Egoyan films, *Exotica* (1994) interweaves three narrative elements. Images are established, characters are introduced; but their relationship to one another is unclear. This is Egoyan's form of cinematic suspense. Like other Egoyan films, *Exotica* focuses on the problems of looking—on the desire to spy, the need to see.

During the first scene, at an airport, we watch Thomas, an eccentric character, shuffling through customs. We can also see a customs officer peering at him through a pane of one-way glass. He is exhorting his assistant to also look. He must learn to detect, the officer explains, that something hidden which you have to find. "Look at him!" he exclaims. "Carefully! What do you see?"

This exhortation also applies to us. When we are watching a film by Atom Egoyan, there is always something hidden that we have to find. In *Exotica,* there are the scenes involving Thomas, who runs an "exotic" pet shop and who goes to the ballet in the evenings; there are the search scenes already referred to; and there are scenes involving Francis, a tax auditor, who frequents a strip club called Exotica. These scenes crisscross one another in the contrapuntal fashion that characterizes Egoyan's work, sometimes suggesting parallels, sometimes differences.

> *A person who is "here" but would rather be somewhere else is an exile or a prisoner; a person who is "here" but thinks he is somewhere else is insane.*[2]
>
> —Margaret Atwood

Although it hasn't seen itself in this way, Canadian cinema has often reflected the insecurities of a colonial world. It has also registered inclinations toward a postcolonial escape.

In the early days, À *tout prendre* (1963), *Nobody Waved Goodbye* (1964), *Le chat dans le sac* (1964), and *Paperback Hero* (1973) all constructed cultures of entrapment, as *Termini Station* (1989) and *Léolo* (1992) do today. Furthermore, *Entre la mer et l'eau douce* (1967), *Goin' Down the Road* (1970), *l'Acadie, l'Acadie* (1971), and, more recently, *Highway 61* (1991) are all films of displacement and migration. The classic Canadian dilemma as formulated by Northrop Frye a good many years ago concerns less the existential question, Who am I? than the cultural one, Where is here?[3] Canadian ontology has always been bound up with a dialectics of space, and one of the dominant narrative modes both in literature and film involves the quest.

As if to underline this colonial dependence, many commentators have remarked on the absence of real men in Canadian films, on the absence of father figures or even of elder brothers.[4] During the 1960s and early 1970s, there are no fathers at all in Quebecois films; and when an actual father appears in an Anglophone film like *Nobody Waved Goodbye,* his authority is so flaccid that the filiation is refused.

While the faces and the colors of Canada are changing, metonymically in our films the situation remains the same. In *Sitting in Limbo* (1986), a quasi-fictional study of a group of young English-speaking blacks in Montreal, there is a distinct absence of responsible males. Similarly, in *Welcome to Canada* (1989), *Perfectly Normal* (1990), *Masala* (1991), and *Léolo,* there are few admirable authority figures.

Most consistently contestational, however, about the inadequacy of fathers is the work of Atom Egoyan. As a deliberately self-constructed Canadian of Egyptian birth and Armenian descent, Egoyan devises films that register the personal uncertainties of people who are striving to find a place of rest within a culture not their own. His six theatrical features, together with a number of shorts and television dramas, reflect and analyze the cultural uncertainties of the Canadian situation.

In *Next of Kin* (1984), his first feature, Egoyan both acknowledges the twin cinematic inheritance established 30 years ago by *Nobody Waved Goodbye* and *Le chat dans le sac* and refuses to accept their cultural implications.⁵ Like the protagonist in *Nobody Waved Goodbye*, Egoyan's character is called Peter. He too lives in a suburban split-level home in which there is no privacy. And here too, the parents are always quarreling about their son's future. Peter (Patrick Tierney) wants none of it. He doesn't want to do anything. He wants to pretend. He wants to be someone else.

The film opens with shots of an airport, the site both of flight and of change—a scene, incidentally, that will not be diegetically placed until later in the film. After a shot of Peter in bed, pulling the duvet over his head to block out his parents' quarreling, we see him sitting by a swimming pool. He introduces himself. "My name is Peter," he says. "I'm 23 years old and I've lived at home all my life, watching my parents dislike one another." The film then constructs what Peter is planning to do to escape from his suburban cultural trap.

Recognizing that identity is less a matter of essence than of cultural positioning, less an inheritance than a potential politics, Egoyan's Peter refuses his West Coast Angloceltic filiations in order to ally himself with an Armenian family in Toronto. It is through this deliberate repositioning that Peter is able, so to speak, to come into his own. As he says later in the film:

> I've figured out a long time ago that being alone was easier if you became two people. One part of you would always be the same, like an audience; and the other part would take on different roles, like an actor.

Only by accepting some form of cultural schizophrenia—indeed, a chiasmatic sense of self—can Peter begin to negotiate his way out of the stifling inheritance of the Angloceltic middle classes. By exchanging his wimpy, WASP father for a passionate, if bigoted, Armenian father, he is able to devise a new feeling of identity.

> *Can any representation of a human being . . . be taken at face value? What does "face value" mean when all the faces are so carefully composed and lit to be as dramatically amplified as possible within the frame?*⁶
>
> —Atom Egoyan

**Next of Kin** establishes what will be, for Egoyan, some recurring themes and stylistic strategies. First of all, there is the family. For Egoyan, the family provides a microcosm of the social world. However, its values must always be contested. This leads to the second theme that pervades Egoyan's world: the characters' need to reconstruct their identity, to try on different roles until they find one that might fit. This entails an abrogation of inheritance and an appropriation of the ideas of difference, of alterity, of something other—but less an *external* other than the other which, although inside us, has been denied.

It is through Peter's fictional transformation of himself into Bedros, the family's long-lost Armenian son, and through his intimate conversations with Azah (Arsinée Khanjian, the film-maker's wife), his newfound "sister," that Peter can begin fully to be himself. If at the beginning of the film we see him *pretending* to play the Spanish guitar, at the end we see Bedros *actually* playing it. Meanwhile, Azah is arranging her new photographs in her family album.

This acceptance of the immanent other often entails some kind of exile—the third recurring theme in Egoyan's films. Where Peter chooses his exile, Azah has hers thrust upon her. She is thrown out of her home for dressing "like a whore," as her father says. So Azah, too, must renegotiate her inherited identity. As a woman, she wants some of the freedoms established by Angloceltic culture in North America, while Peter wants some of the commitments of his adopted Armenian household.

If there are three basic themes in Egoyan's work involving family, identity, and the necessity of exile, there are also three stylistic strategies. These strategies relate to acting, dialogue, and narrative structure.

Egoyan instructs his actors to deliver their lines in a flat, deadpan way. He has his Brechtian/Bressonian reasons for this type of direction, as he once suggested:

> Rather than inviting the viewer to lose himself in a screen presence, the actor asks the viewer to question what it is about the character he's *supposed* to identify with. In this way, a more profound relationship can be established.⁷

This style of acting, however, is also appropriate to the characters' uncertain sense of self, to their efforts to relinquish received identities and to renegotiate new ones, as cinematic spectators must negotiate new ones with them.

Allied to this strategy is Egoyan's Pinteresque dialogue. His characters speak in a series of non sequiturs—in staccato, absurdist statements that enact a dimension of alienation but which also serve to abstract the *personae* from any simple notion of psychological realism, from a merely reflective mimesis.

Thirdly, both the flatness of the acting and the deployment of absurdist dialogue facilitate Egoyan's desire to achieve a contrapuntal structure for his films. Skilled in music and theater, he thinks out his films' structures in deliberately musical ways, like three-part inventions as we know them from Bach. Furthermore, the absurdist repetition of situations and scraps of dialogue bestows upon his narratives a serial dimension. We sense the presence of a rational intelligence ordering these experiences and directing our attention to relationships among them. Indeed, we might be profoundly moved by them—especially by the thrill of their intricate orchestration—but the "meaning" is seldom clear.

Finally, if through his treatment of actors, his dialogue, and his contrapuntal structures Egoyan's cinema is a cinema of surfaces, these surfaces are generally troubled in his films by photographic or televisual technologies of reproduction. *Next of Kin, The Adjuster, Calendar,* and *Exotica* all utilize photographs; *Next of Kin, Family Viewing, Speaking Parts,* and *Calendar* all utilize television. Video is everywhere—recording experience, mediating experience, "surveilling" experience, reducing reality to replica.

Egoyan's cinema is an art of images within a culture supersaturated with the overproduction of images. As he has explained:

> I'm somebody who's torn constantly between a deep suspicion of images and a desire and a seduction by the process of making images. That I think is laced through all the work I'm doing. It's a very exciting terrain to be exploring at this point, at the end of the century. It seems to be *the* fundamental issue in a society completely overrun by images.[8]

This intense concern with images is distinctly Canadian. Growing up saturated with images of the United States, we have a special problem in distinguishing between what is imaginary and what is real. This was the situation of Rick Dillon in *Paperback Hero,* and it certainly provides the central theme of David Cronenberg's *Videodrome* (1982). In fact, *Videodrome* is perhaps the *Urtext* for a whole generation of Toronto film-makers. Containing in the figure of Brian O'Blivion a parodic representation of Marshall McLuhan, *Videodrome* charts the central character's growing inability to distinguish between his real life and his video imaginings. "Television is reality: reality is less than television," as O'Blivion declaims. "Your reality is already half video hallucination. . . ."

From this film springs not only *Family Viewing* and *Speaking Parts,* but also Patricia Rozema's *I've Heard the Mermaids Singing* (1987) and David Wellington's *I Love a Man in Uniform* (1993). It is a specifically Canadian dilemma to sort out the differences between images imagined for us by ourselves and images imagined for us by other people—let alone making a distinction between all these imaginary images and what we might still want to call, on occasion, the "real world."

> We're all aware of images that we've seen that chronicle or depict behavioural states that we try to replay. The question of whether or not that renders our actions natural or unnatural lies at the core of my desire to make films.[9]
>
> —Atom Egoyan

In Egoyan's ***Family Viewing*** (1987), his second feature film, video images are everywhere. The film takes as its central theme the desire to make connections—away from false images toward true images, away from pornography toward affection, away from the father toward the mother, and away from the Angloceltic world toward an Armenian world, a large part of which has been lost. Indeed, the central character in this film is called Van—a name that implies links, that requires completion.

Van (Aidan Tierney) lives in a sterile condominium with his father, Stan (David Hemblen), and his father's lover, Sandra (Gabrielle Rose), who appears to be Van's lover as well.[10] Stan likes to videotape all his lovemaking with Sandra although he requires the stimulus of an additional female voice on the telephone to get him started. This voice belongs to Aline (Arsinée Khanjian) who makes her living by offering telephone sex. She is also a friend of Van.

When Van discovers the sexual tapes of Stan and Sandra, he also discovers that his father has been recording over previous tapes of Stan's original family, when the mother and *her* mother were still part of the home and Van was just a child. A section of this childhood tape is returned to again and again in the film, in a kind of Edenic garden, like a prelapsarian dream.

This scene is extraordinarily choreographed. We see Stan at the left of the screen, watching his family in the garden through a window, separated both by glass and by language. Young Van is there, a Mickey Mouse doll clutched to his chest, with his mother and grandmother, talking in Armenian. Stan gives instruction to his son through the window by miming gestures that he wants him to imitate. This moment suggests both continuity between the generations and patriarchal control. Finally, in the fullest version of this scene, the mother brings Van inside to Stan, for whom Van sings "Ba, Ba, Blacksheep" in English. In its recurrence, intensified by ascending string octaves supplied by composer Mychael Danna, this scene haunts the film like a discarded memory of familial affection.

The story of ***Family Viewing*** centers around Van's repeated attempts to find a proper home for Armen, the grandmother, whom Stan had dumped in a home when his wife ran away. He moves her first to Aline's, then into an unused wing of a hotel in which he is now working, where he finally disguises her as a bag lady, just to keep her away from Stan's clutches.

The penultimate scene intercuts images of Van watching Armen being carted off in an ambulance to some unknown destination with shots of Stan racing up the hotel stairs as if to find Armen, but actually to encounter the memory of his wife, appropriately (if alogically) appearing on a television screen.

The film ends with Aline and Van visiting Armen in a women's hostel. Television cameras are in place as part of a surveillance system, but also, for spectators, to trigger a visual echo of the video memories that we have previously seen. Miraculously, (because again alogically), the mother is also there.

But where are they, really, this reconstructed family? Where will they go? And what will they do? What is the meaning, finally, of the concluding moments in this film? Although Egoyan's work resists simple paraphrase, a few things might be said.

First of all, there is Van's quest, his need to make connections. On this level, the film has a "happy ending." He is there in the frame with his mother and *her* mother and with the young woman, Aline, who is also Armenian and might well become his wife. He has made connections both with the feminine and with his past. He seems to have rediscovered his ancient, ethnic soul, to have encountered his "other," the other that he has always felt was within him.

At the same time, on a social level, what has been accomplished? These characters have all endured a series of displacements in their journey toward this family reunion. They end up, moreover, within the confines of a site more restrictive than any other within the imaginative world constructed by this film.

If the film ends with a mystery, it is a deliberate mystery. Although there are no narrative resolutions for this or for any other Egoyan film, by recapitulating all the visual motifs in these final moments, including the prelapsarian dream, the director can bring his film, formally, to an end.

***Speaking Parts*** (1989) further refines the polyphonic structure of the narrative and continues Egoyan's investigation of images, but now the ubiquity of television images is associated with morbidity and death. The first image we see is of Clara (Gabrielle Rose) walking through a graveyard on her way to a video mausoleum. On each gravestone is a photograph; the mausoleum contains a haunting collection of looped video records of lost loved ones. Throughout the film, we repeatedly see Clara in this mausoleum, reviewing the ghostly footage of her brother—ghostly because he died in the attempt to donate one of his lungs to her and because the footage is eerily without sound.

The opening sequence is intercut with one of Lisa (Arsinée Khanjian) watching a video that is equally eerie because, except for Mychael Danna's music, this moment is also without diegetic sound. The subject of the scene is a piano recital, but that is of little interest to Lisa: the camera of her imagination tracks in past the foreground of the image to isolate a young man sitting in the audience, someone whom we will later know as Lance (Michael McManus)—the obscure object of Lisa's desire.

Egoyan again advances three stories simultaneously, while suggesting links among them—a procedure assisted by the continuity of the music. Lisa is drawn by images of Lance; Clara by images of her dead brother; Lance by the desire to move beyond the image into speech—to achieve a speaking part. Through its visual organization, however, *Speaking Parts* might seem to endorse the voodoo belief that televisual reproductions of the self can behave as the extractor of human souls, that reproductions can rob the self of essence. Certainly, in *Speaking Parts*, the televisual representations consistently lead to a death-desiring nostalgia for something that is either not really there (the indifferent Lance) or no longer there (Clara's dead brother).

Throughout the film, all events are mediated through these televisual representations. The telephone sex in ***Family Viewing*** becomes television sex in ***Speaking Parts***. Everything from orgies to weddings requires a video record. During the wedding sequence, the busy producer is also there—but only on a television monitor. If Lance and Clara employ teleconferencing technology to simulate sex with each other, the producer uses it to maintain the distanced authority of his masculine control.

The penultimate sequence, staged as a television talk show, not only brings together the three narrative units in a kind of cinematic stretto but also collapses the real into the imaginary. As the characters in Egoyan's film momentarily trade places with the characters in the film being made by the producer, we cannot distinguish reality from representation.

The film ends in silhouette, with Lance collapsed on the floor of Lisa's room—initially reaching out for her only to be rebuffed. Lisa then reaches out for him. Finally, ever so tentatively, they kiss.

Has Lance been so burned out by his involvement with the televisual imaginary that he is prepared to return to the real? Lisa's face now looks softer, her hair less severely drawn back, her attitude perhaps chastened. After all the media interventions, are both now prepared to accept each other as one another's other, as one another's "real"?

> *The most resonant moments for me as a viewer always come when I don't quite know what it is I'm watching. I'm lost in a wash of emotions and feelings that don't originate from something that I can identify immediately. They're the most exhilarating passages in cinema because they come so close to the dream state.*[11]
>
> —Atom Egoyan

With ***The Adjuster*** (1991), Egoyan expanded both his palette and his budget. His previous films had been made for virtually no money at all. In Canadian dollars, ***Next of Kin*** cost $37,000; ***Family Viewing*** $160,000; ***Speaking Parts*** (the first to be shot on 35mm) $800,000; but ***The Adjuster*** was budgeted at $1,500,000—still a modest sum, even by Canadian standards.

The film opens on a close-up of a hand moving within the darkness. The hand belongs to Noah Render (Elias Koteas), the "adjuster" in this film. He floats through life, dealing with the aftermath of fires, shooting arrows into the darkness at the billboards that mark the extremities of the estate on which he resides.

Noah lives with Hera (Arsinée Khanjian), *apparently* his wife. Reinforced by the silence of her sister, Seta (Rose Sarkisyan), who is constantly "in touch with" Hera's son,

Simon (Armen Kokorian), Hera seeks to be a center. While Seta and Simon are always holding each other, Hera is often in bed, troubled by unrecallable dreams. Actual, physical touch dominates the film, within and across both gender and generation. The less the characters have a settled sense of their own identities, the more they seem "out-of-touch" both with themselves and with one another.

This extended family inhabits a model home built for an urban subdevelopment that has never taken place. Although the billboards display names like "Sherwood Forest Estate," there is scarcely a tree in sight. If this terrain comments on the speculative insanities of late capitalism, it also creates an atmosphere that is increasingly surreal.

Like the motel which provides the other principal site in this film, the pop-art patterns of its balconies color-coordinated with the parked cars below, the model home suggests impermanence. "Something had to change," says one of Noah's clients later in the film, as she observes the spark that sets her house on fire. "So I watched while it did."

In *The Adjuster*, although fire is a source of trauma for many of the characters, it is also an agent of purgation. Fire eliminates the past futility of their lives. It also projects them into the "ark" of this motel that Noah has arranged for them.[12] Noah is their savior. All his clients love him. As the chambermaid exclaims one evening, "They think you're an angel."

Noah's angelic role, however, is largely impersonation. He has no imagination. He endlessly repeats to all his clients the same professional clichés. "You may not feel it, but you're in a state of shock." In order to value anything, he has to quantify it. He takes photographs. He makes lists. He has to put a price on everything. Questioning a client who had everything destroyed by his fire, even his academic diploma, Noah enquires, "What did it cost to frame?"

Although there is no intimacy at all between him and Hera in the film, he beds all his clients, whether male or female, while discussing their claims. Hera, on the other hand, who as a film censor also makes lists, surreptitiously records all the pornographic films she views for her sister, who stays at home all day looking after Simon. Furthermore, both Seta and Simon are locked within the mute Armenian space of their incomprehension of the English language. In the course of the film, "Bubba" is the only word that Simon acknowledges.[13]

The characters in *The Adjuster* are not what they seem. If they are all acting out parts only partially of their own devising, the potential madness of the imaginary life is centered in the character who is actually named Bubba (Maury Chaykin) and in his companion, Mimi (Gabrielle Rose). Uselessly rich and terminally bored, they try on different roles in the effort to flagellate themselves into a meaningful existence. Like Peter in *Next of Kin,* they pretend. They play games. The games they play, however, lead not to the liberation of self-realization but to a maniacal desire for self-immolation.

All the characters in *The Adjuster* are drained of initiative through living less within the real than through mediations of the real. While Noah is reluctant to awaken Hera from her sleep when he is in the bedroom with her, he does so on his cellular phone when he is driving away in his car. Although the speechless Seta is unaffected by the pornographic violence of the pirated videotapes, she screams in terror when a flasher appears at her window.

If the film opens with an extreme close-up of Noah's hand, it ends with a shot of his hand held up within the darkness against the flames, as if trying to touch the reality of watching his own house burn down. The final scene is the culmination of the need for touch in this film and of the sense of fire as a necessary purgation. It is complicated, however, by a sudden cut back in time.

Hera and Seta are there, looking distressed. Hera is carrying a baby in her arms, someone too small to be the Simon we have seen. Noah approaches them, as if he had never seen them before, touching Hera tentatively on the shoulder. "Is this your house? I'm an adjuster." Meanwhile, the Arabic sounds of a *duduk* within the plaintive "emotional minimalism" of Mychael Danna's music[14] reinforce the traumatized silence of this Armenian family to suggest the "otherness" which, in *The Adjuster,* has been denied. As Noah holds out his hand to the fire, moving toward the final image, we are left once again with an uncertain sense of the meaning of this film.

Did Noah acquire his family through adjusting their claim? Is he, in fact, married to Hera? Where did Simon come from? While watching the film, we might have imagined that he was also Noah's son. Where lies the reality in what we have just witnessed? Have we just *imagined* what we have seen in this film?

Egoyan has suggested that the most powerful moments in cinema are analogous to dreams, as if wanting his own work to enter directly into consciousness, bypassing intellectual controls. With its absurd objets trouvés, its barren landscapes, and isolated model home—itself both replica and parody of what a true home might be—with the recurring presence of irrational and bizarre moments, *The Adjuster,* more than any other Egoyan film, achieves a surreal force.

> *For the Armenian people, churches have a strong significance because they suggest timelessness. In the Armenian psyche, they are objects of adoration unto themselves. They are icons.*[15]
>
> —Atom Egoyan

*Calendar* came about by chance; through a prize won at the Moscow Film Festival, Egoyan was given $100,000 to visit Armenia and shoot whatever he wished. The resulting film, shot on 8mm video and 16mm film, is simple in the extreme. Indeed, for spectators who resist the intricate irrationalities of Egoyan's cinema, it is their favorite film. Certainly it is his most accessible.

As money was tight, Egoyan cast himself as the photographer on assignment with his wife (Arsinée Khanjian) and an Armenian driver (Ashot Adamian) to shoot 12 ancient Armenian churches for a photographic calendar. The churches lend to this film not only an enormous beauty but also a spiritual dimension. More deliberately than other Egoyan films, *Calendar* (1993) is about the passing of time and its irretrievable changes. Yet here there is the sense that something will survive the impermanence of relationships and the uncertainty of individual identities.

Because the photographer speaks no Armenian and the driver no English, his wife serves as translator. The photographer is more comfortable with his technology than he is with either his partner or his driver. He likes to point but refuses to touch. When asked to go for a walk with the two of them, the photographer declines. He wants to remain apart. What he really wants, as he explains later in what appears to be a letter to his wife, is to go on standing there, "watching while the two of you leave me and disappear into a landscape that I am about to photograph."

In *Calendar,* we witness the gradual transfer of the wife's affection from her past relationship with the photographer to a future relationship with the driver. At the same time, by choosing the driver, she is also choosing to return to her Armenian roots—an option not available to the photographer, who has been too thoroughly assimilated into North American culture. Furthermore, as we gradually realize, the faded color of the video footage is appropriate for the photographer's fading memory of the Armenian events.

If *Calendar* is concerned with time, it is also concerned with space. Early in the film, referring to the differences between himself and his wife, the increasingly alienated photographer says, "We're both from here; yet being here has made me feel as if I'm from somewhere else."

At the end, when the photographer has returned to Toronto, we can hear his wife on the answering machine—as always with Egoyan, a mediated communication—wanting to explain what has happened to them. She wants to describe the moment when he lost her, when the car was surrounded by sheep and the driver first reached out for her. "He grasped my hand," she explains, "while you grasped your camera. Did you know? Were you there? Are you there?"

> *I have great suspicions about conveying screen emotion. It's my feeling that it can be too easy to just fix the camera on someone going through emotional turmoil. There's something very disturbing about that for me.*[16]
>
> —Atom Egoyan

As he moves toward greater acceptance, anxious at the same time not to alienate his present-day admirers, Egoyan is finding ways to flesh out more engagingly the characters in his films. Although the Pinteresque non sequiturs still abound and a deadpan detachment continues to inform the acting, there is now a richer sense of psychology. In *Exotica,* the characters elicit our compassion. The film still displays, however, a triadic, polyphonic structure. There are three recurring sites and three different men, each of whom relates to the three women in the film.

First of all, there is the exotic pet shop, inherited by Thomas (Don McKellar) from his mother. We have already seen him smuggling exotic eggs for his shop past the customs officers at the airport at the beginning of the film. Because of this illegal activity, his shop is visited by Francis (Bruce Greenwood), an auditor for the federal tax department. (In the evenings, Thomas also attends an opera house, in which we hear—but do not see—Prokofiev's *Romeo and Juliet.* This opera house, however, more European than North American in design and therefore just as "exotic" as the pet shop, is as much a pick-up joint for homosexuals as it is a site for cultural consumption.)

The second major site is that extended grassy field—the "Wyeth" sequence with which I began this essay. In a way structurally similar to the prelapsarian dream in *Family Viewing,* this scene is returned to repeatedly—finally, as a postlapsarian nightmare.

Thirdly, there is Exotica, the strip club presided over by Zoe (Arsinée Khanjian), which she inherited from *her* mother. The club specializes in table dancing, where the men may look but never touch. Eric (Elias Koteas) serves as Master of Ceremonies. From the past, he is also emotionally involved with Christina (Mia Kirshner), the major female character in this film.

Before the opening airport scene, the sequence behind the credits consists of a slow track right along the tropical decor of this club, its exotic nature further emphasized by the eastern strains of Mychael Danna's music, with a *shehnai*, a kind of Indian oboe, sounding unsettlingly unfamiliar to our Western ears.

This exotic club becomes the site of the feminine in this film. It is the center to which all the men are drawn, a place of dreams and desire—even of fertility, since Zoe's pregnancy is very much in evidence. Indeed, if the clients of the club are not allowed to touch the dancers, most visitors to Zoe's womb-like central office are invited to touch her belly—an invitation that is generally accepted with embarrassment.

In *Exotica,* although all of the characters have their grief, it is Francis's story that most securely grips the viewer. It is his pain that spills over to affect the others and to establish the empathetic center of the film.

Francis leads a double life. An auditor by day, he frequents Exotica by night. At the club, he too has developed a special relationship with Christina, largely because she reminds him of the daughter he has lost. Playing upon her youthful appearance, Christina wears a schoolgirl's uniform and displays a sense of great distress during her public performances on stage.

"What gives a schoolgirl her special innocence, gentlemen?" Eric intones into his microphone as Christina dances. "Is it the way that they smell? The sweet perfume of their hair . . . ?" Indeed, as if to *protect* this innocence, Francis mutters private words of concern to Christina when she dances at his table, baring parts of her vulnerable body less for his sensual pleasure than to allay his physical fears. He keeps explaining that he wants to protect her, to save her from harm.

His fears relate to his lost daughter—the object of the search in that extended grassy field. They also relate to Tracey (Sarah Polley), his young niece, who babysits for him as, when she was younger, we eventually learn that "Chrissy" also had done. Yet now, since his daughter is no longer alive, Tracey plays as much a fantasy role in Francis's life at home as Christina does at the club. If the serial structure of the film still involves the repetition of scraps of dialogue and particular events, it also entails an interlinking of these young women, as (at least in Francis's mind) their roles all tend to merge. And if Francis's pain is privileged, it is because he is the most connected with the others. Furthermore, his obsession with the youthful Christina is less pornographic than compassionate; it is an attempt obsessively to recreate moments from his past as if to bring them to a different conclusion—a desire that can never be fulfilled.

Francis pays money to young women to enact his fantasies for him, to create for him an imaginary world; this activity is analogous to the activity that we all indulge in when, as spectators, we go to the movies. In *Exotica,* Egoyan has not relinquished his critique of our obsessive consumption of images.

During the film's final moments, we see a younger Christina, scarcely recognizable—with her braids and braces—as Mia Kirshner, entering the family home. The scene is full of anguish. The assumed security of a family is now felt as a threat.

Why do those Ionic pillars on that four-square home convey such a strong sense of dread? Is it through their implicit assertion of suburban rationality—a rationality inadequate for all the problems in the film? What is Christina's relationship to the later Tracey or, more distressingly, might her destiny one day be the same as Lisa's—the slaughtered child who was finally found, actually by Eric and Christina, in her schoolgirl's uniform in the middle of that extended grassy field?

For Egoyan, has the linear quest of classic Canadian cinema become a circle? Will the characters go on enacting their compulsions over and over again, devising similar imaginary images, only to encounter the very destiny they have been striving to avoid?

*The films that really excite me are those in which it is unclear if the filmmaker is really aware of how disturbing or moving the image is.*[17]

—Atom Egoyan

The enduring theme, the evolving theme in all of Egoyan's work is the need for personal transformation. Whether assuming a fictitious identity to escape an unwanted inheritance or descending into fantasy in the effort to combat feelings of pain or failure, Egoyan's characters never feel sufficient being what they are. They simulate. They impersonate. In this sense, they are all in retreat, not just from culture—as in the early films—but from nature. Nature seems "natural" only in the old world—in Armenia with its enduring presence of sheep and churches and of people belonging to the earth out of which they have grown.

In North America, within a technologized, urbanized, and increasingly migrant culture, a wondrous stretch of meadow can serve to conceal terrors too horrible to imagine. Nature has become unnatural, as has human nature. It is the fear of the depths of human nature, finally, that either silences Egoyan's characters or drives them into madness—that makes them exiles from themselves.

Within the context of Canadian cinema, Egoyan's earlier films seemed a positive repositioning in relation to our Angloceltic inheritance, a desire to escape the postcolonial uncertainties of the Canadian world. Yet even these films were not revolutionary. They all ended by endorsing the ideology of the family.

As his work has progressed, however, if the concept of alterity remains precise and alluring, the concept of self has become uncertain and obscure. It is as if Egoyan's characters, in their imaginings, have irretrievably abandoned their "originary" home.

At the same time, this desire to transform one's inherited reality parallels the activity of the artist. As Egoyan explains:

> What fascinates me are characters who are very creative but don't know who their audiences are or who have become so aware of the isolating qualities of the creative act that they go a bit mad. And yet, the desire to create is completely comprehensible given what their situations are. Given the traumas in their lives that they've had to deal with, given the things that are left hanging, it's the only thing they can do.[18]

Whatever the forces that motivate Egoyan's own desire to create, over the past ten years he has done so with increasing formal authority. As the demographics of the world continue to shift and change, troubling our sense of who we are and where we belong, we can only wonder how these cultural transitions will be reflected and how new images will be imagined in distinguished films by Atom Egoyan still to come.

### Notes

1. "Emotional Logic: Marc Glassman interviews Atom Egoyan," in *Speaking Parts,* by Atom Egoyan (Toronto: Coach House Press, 1993), p. 48.

2. *Survival: A Thematic Guide to Canadian Literature,* by Margaret Atwood (Toronto: Anansi, 1972), p. 18.

3. "Conclusion to a *Literary History of Canada*" (1965), in *The Bush Garden: Essays on the Canadian Imagination,* by Northrop Frye (Toronto: Anansi, 1971), p. 220.

4. "Coward, Bully, or Clown: The Dream-Life of a Younger Brother," by Robert Fothergill, in *Canadian Film Reader,* ed. Seth Feldman and Joyce Nelson (Toronto: Peter Martin Associates, 1977), pp. 234–50.

5. For this cultural inheritance, see "The Beginning of a Beginning," by Peter Harcourt, in *Self-Portrait: Essays on the Canadian and Quebec Cinemas,* ed. Pierre Véronneau and Piers Handling (Ottawa: Canadian Film Institute, 1980), pp. 64–76.

6. "Surface Tension," essay by Atom Egoyan, in *Speaking Parts,* p. 36.

7. Ibid., p. 33.

8. Talking with Shelagh Rogers on "The Arts Tonight," Canadian Broadcasting Corporation, 14 April, 1993.

9. "Emotional Logic," p. 42.

10. The "sterility" of these scenes is visually reinforced by Egoyan's decision to shoot them all in a television studio on one-inch videotape, utilizing video sound.

11. "Emotional Logic," p. 45.

12. For a serious mythological reading, see "The Place of the Spectator," by Danièle Rivière, in *Atom Egoyan,* by Carole Desbarats, Danièle Rivière, Jacinto Lageira, and Paul Virilio, transl. Brian Holmes (Paris: Editions Dis Voir, 1993), pp. 83–101.

13. Ironically, "Bubba" is an Arabic word for father.

14. Mychael Danna's own description of his musical style. Personal interview with Atom Egoyan in Toronto, 8 March, 1994.

15. Atom Egoyan on "The Arts Tonight," CBC, 14 April, 1993.

16. "Emotional Logic," p. 57.

17. Ibid., p. 52.

18. Personal interview, 8 March, 1994.

## Jonathan Romney (review date May 1995)

SOURCE: "Exploitations," in *Sight & Sound,* Vol. 5, No. 5, May, 1995, pp. 6–8.

[*In the following review, Romney offers a negative assessment of* Exotica, *criticizing Egoyan's style of filmmaking as unfulfilling.*]

Atom Egoyan makes bitterly disappointing films. They begin by stirring our curiosity—our desire to play detective or analyst, or simply our prurient longing for a glimpse of the louche, the exotic. And when finally they deliver what we're looking for, they invariably frustrate us—all we discover is that revelation can never be satisfactory. We learn that there are always more layers to the onion, or that it was never really an onion in the first place. As Egoyan's new film *Exotica* makes explicit, this director's work resembles the consummate art of male frustration that is striptease—we await the moment of laying bare only to have it dawn on us that the body is the one thing we *don't* want to see (just yet). His films are structured to exemplify a full-blown erotics of cinema, with all the attendant play of sadism and masochism. In that sense, his is the most profoundly *anti*-erotic cinema imaginable.

Egoyan's first feature *Next of Kin* (1984) began with the image of an unidentified bag going round on an airport carousel. It immediately poses the key questions that underlie his films. Whose baggage is this? Where's it from? What do we find if we unpack it? *Exotica* revisits this image. Its first words, spoken by one customs official to his junior as they scan a suspected smuggler, are: "You have to ask yourself—what brought the person to this point? You have to convince yourself that this person has something hidden that you have to find." This is a pitch to our curiosity, too, and it's not that different from the come-on spiel that strip-club MC Eric (Elias Koteas) gives his customers as he invites them to pay $5 to have a stripper "reveal the mysteries of her world."

But if we pay the price of admission, what guarantees satisfaction? At one point in the film, a younger Eric says he feels he wasn't ever meant to be satisfied. The woman he's talking to replies, "Maybe you want it to slip away—the thing you think you're about to have." And consequently the film itself—a baroque construction of ellipses, flashbacks and repetitions—is angled to provide us with the constant anxiety/satisfaction of deferral.

His most complex essay in the Cinema of Disappointment, Egoyan's *Exotica* is built around the metaphors of striptease as psychological unmasking, narrative unpacking, commerce and contract. Layer after layer of meaning is revealed, although we're never quite sure whose "mysteries" we expect to discover (the film makes it remarkably difficult to identify a 'central' character). In the first 20 minutes, the threads come at us thick and fast. Thomas (Don McKellar), a nervous young pet shop owner who is smuggling goods, makes it through customs and shares a cab with a man who offers him ballet tickets instead of his share of the ride; Thomas will later use the tickets, at the ballet to procure himself a series of male sexual partners. He is meanwhile being audited by Francis (Bruce Greenwood), a tax official and a regular customer of the strip club Exotica, who is obsessed by Christina (Mia Kirshner), who performs, dressed as a schoolgirl. Exotica is presided over by proprietor Zoe (Arsinée Khanjian), who has made a contract with Eric to make her pregnant.

Eric, also obsessed with Christina, presides over the club, spurring his customers to buy across-the-table intimacies with the dancers. The circle of avoidance and negotiation is complete when Francis, banned from his club, does a deal with Thomas—an outsider sexually, but also the outsider in terms of the narrative—and brings him into the world of Exotica as his substitute.

It's only at the end, in a downbeat and extremely simple flashback scene, that Egoyan gives us some sort of 'explanation' of what's on these people's minds, of what's making their lives unworkable. But it's no sort of conclusion—it only makes us want to go back to the beginning and start again. It's a structure Egoyan has used before—notably in *The Adjuster* (1991), whose final moment similarly explains nothing but rather, so to speak, incinerates what's gone before. (Egoyan films tend to come together or fall apart with real or figurative conflagrations).

In his Director's Statement, Egoyan accepts that *Exotica* is structured like a striptease; but points out that this was only his analysis after the event. "The film wasn't meant to support a theory," he says, "it wasn't constructed that way. I do find it fascinating how the ending is very cathartic for some people, and other people find it wasn't what they expected or needed at that point. I liked the ending. All these relationships, where people's emotions are so carefully guarded and so tenuously exchanged . . . *suddenly* you can see that for all the pretence, everything is rooted in this very real relationship between Christina and Francis."

The most film's controversial element is the way it plays with the suggestion of paedophilia, with Christina doing her act dressed in a schoolgirl's tartan skirt, white shirt and tie. Eric repeatedly teases his customers with the riddle, "What gives a schoolgirl her special innocence?" This disguises another question: what makes him, or Francis or us, want to invest in the mystique of innocence, and how does it become sexualised?

What Egoyan's also offering us is a tease which places the film in a particular art-movie niche: the erotic psychological thriller, one that French directors have been exploiting since time immemorial. Of course, there's a perilous borderline between alluding to exploitation. and exploitation period.

"There are two answers—one is what the film itself represents, the other is how it's marketed. I've been very demanding that the image of Christina dressed as a schoolgirl won't be used on any of the posters, because it's an image that only makes sense in the context of the film. It was an image I was very protective of, not in the sense of creating a mystification round it, but I was aware of how it could be abused.

"The film does play with that tension, there's no question about it. There is that use of titillation, sexual manipulation. Because when you get down to it, I don't think it's an erotic film at all. You begin by assuming the relationship between Francis and Christina is perverse, that he has a paedophilic attraction to her. When you realise what is actually going on. it's platonic in the truest sense. He's projecting onto her something that's extremely pure. Though that has its consequences as well.

The environment [of the club] is sexual, so that can't help but imbue what he's seeing in her with a sexual content. And that tortures him, as he's trying to work out some sort of therapeutic relationship with her. He's trying to heal some sense of grief—which becomes infused with guilt, because of where he's chosen to conduct this therapy."

All Egoyan's films could be said to explore therapy in one way or another, with his characters elaborating byzantine rituals of repetition, and constantly displacing their obsessions onto other characters who may or may not fit them. In *Next of Kin* (1984), an isolated young man invents an alternative family for himself; in *Speaking Parts* (1989), a woman tries to 'cast' an actor as her dead brother; the hero of *The Adjuster* obsessively becomes involved with his clients, while his own household is invaded by a couple who live out their own fantasies as meticulously staged performance art. Therapy in Egoyan's films always goes too far, and is invariably compromised by the vehicles people choose for it, usually TV or video technology.

"There's a group of analysts in Toronto who have looked at all my films. They've told me that from their point of view, all my films deal with a process called 'faulty mourning'—when a patient builds a ritual of mourning which only accentuates and exaggerates the sense of loss which they think they're dealing with.

"In all the films there seems to be someone who's in the process of grieving another person's loss. But in the process, they're somehow underlining and distorting what it is that they've lost in the first place. In all of them, people extend this sense of loss through the relationship with an image, and because technology has the ability to preserve a moment, that moment can become fetishised and live way beyond its anticipated life.

"In *Exotica,* I've taken away the insistence on technology—apart from one video moment—but it's replaced by the transposition of someone into an icon. Christina's uniform becomes what video technology was in the other films."

Because the ubiquitous video eye for once recedes into the background, *Exotica* is harder than its predecessors simply to pigeonhole as an 'Egoyan film'—his preoccupations and tropes have been so consistent that he's practically created his own genre. It may not, ultimately, be as tight-knit a film as *The Adjuster,* in which the hermetic anxiety genuinely admits of no relief. It could be argued that *Exotica* has too many thematic and narrative strands for its own good—although it's that very sense of unresolved over-abundance that makes it so suggestive and hard to exhaust. The one notion of exoticism that seems insufficiently assimilated into the film's argument is that which attaches to race; and that's partly because it centres on characters who are less central, or even absent. Francis' wife and daughter are black; another white character, Harold, lives with his daughter in a black neighbourhood almost parodically dangerous. There's a clear mirror image of Francis here; what's not so clear is how it dovetails with the rest—a problem Egoyan admits he hasn't entirely resolved.

"There are two ideas being explored in the film—that which is outside your cultural experience, and that which is outside your own way of perceiving your memory. At what point do our own experiences and feelings become exotic to us? At what point do we transpose people we're attracted to onto the level of metaphor? If I deal with that theme, I have to suggest it through what the viewer is also projecting. So you have Harold in a clearly black atmosphere wearing a Bob Marley T-shirt—he's someone who feels more comfortable in that cultural context but there is something askew about it. He's made a parody of himself.

"I want the film to provoke controversy, but what I find far more controversial than the image of a schoolgirl is the use of colour in the film—the fact that Francis' wife is black, that Harold lives in a black environment, that Thomas purchases men of colour. I wanted these images to be outrageous, to really provoke a level of anger—but somehow that doesn't seem to be as integral to the viewing experience as I thought they would be."

Ethnic identity has been a constant enigma in Egoyan's films—the jigsaw piece that always refuses to fit. Many of his films draw on Egoyan's situation as a film-maker on one hand committed to a post-modern notion of identity constructed through technology, and on the other involved with his own Armenian origins, with all the connotations they carry of a 'pure,' 'natural' identity and unmediated history. It's a situation he analysed in uncomfortably personal terms in his 1993 film *Calendar,* made for German TV. Egoyan himself appears as a photographer obsessed with the wife who left him on a visit to Armenia (played by his own wife, and regular star, Arsinée Khanjian). His hardest film to watch—both formally and for the discomfort it evokes—*Calendar* is still the fullest résumé of Egoyan's therapeutic mechanisms.

"I'm a prisoner of the situation I've been talking about—we do have an inexplicable desire to make a metaphor of our own neuroses. That's what art is about—all the characters in my films are failed or unrecognised artists. Francis is directing his life. The adjuster is a director. They are all involved in a process that I am myself am engaged in. I make a film like *Calendar* to come to terms with that process. You believe that by putting yourself in a context where there's cultural fragmentation and dissociation, you will deal with your own sense of dislocation—you normalise your own worst fears. It becomes perverse when you set into motion the machinery which may define the level of destruction you find in the film itself."

Egoyan's films are undoubtedly as perverse as they might conceivably be therapeutic. They're scarcely a feel-good experience for the viewer; they don't provide catharsis as easy relief. And as a film-maker, he is surely aware that by working through your own anxieties on screen, you're less likely to quell them than you are to reaffirm their centrality. If you pick up Pandora's box, that neat package spinning round on the baggage carousel, then sooner or later, you have to take it through Customs.

Still, the intensely self-referential manner in which Egoyan works does offer some immediate consolations. "The most important thing," he says, "is to be open about the process, at every opportunity to demystify the process of making films—there's nothing romantic about it at all. If my work only serves to illustrate the contradictions and perversities of making images of that, I'll be happy."

### Atom Egoyan with Richard Porton (interview date Spring 1997)

SOURCE: "Family Romances: An Interview with Atom Egoyan," in *Cineaste,* Vol. 23, No. 2, Spring, 1997, pp. 8–16.

[*In the following interview, Egoyan discusses the nature of the film industry, his approach to filmmaking, and the influence of Canadian identity.*]

Widely regarded as Canada's leading independent filmmaker, Atom Egoyan is frequently hailed as brilliantly innovative and occasionally damned as a purveyor of arid cinematic parables. Egoyan's wry self-deprecation, however, allows him to view both acclaim and derision with a jaundiced eye. In fact, the critical response to Egoyan's films often seems several steps behind the director's unsparing assessments of his own work. Egoyan's personal modesty has never interfered with his professional assurance, enabling him to explore a cluster of interrelated themes—the erosion of ethnic identity in the face of modernity, the relationship between technology and alienated sexuality, and the black humor that can be derived from the travails of irrevocably dysfunctional families.

Egoyan's debut feature, *Next of Kin* (1984), typifies the absurdist tenor which suffuses his work. A lighthearted film which provides a glimpse of darker ironies, *Next of Kin* focuses on an elaborate wish-fulfillment fantasy concocted by Peter, a nondescript young WASP who flees his affluent middle-class family to effortlessly become part of a warm but fractious Armenian clan. Never one to offer glib panaceas, Egoyan mercilessly skewers both the puritanical Anglo-Canadians and the feuding Armenians; the Candide-like protagonist's search for ethnic bonhomie proves futile.

A few ludicrous videotaped family therapy sessions in *Next of Kin* foreshadow the all-encompassing preoccupation with video surveillance and voyeurism that comes to the fore in Egoyan's subsequent films. Even if the narcissistic protagonists of *Family Viewing* (1987) and *Speaking Parts* (1989) seem inextricable from the media-saturated landscape—a world which fetishizes the ability to instantaneously record and play back images—Egoyan is not committed to a crude technophobia. He is merely bemused by how new technologies become harbingers of perceptual and cultural upheavals.

The Canadian critic Geoff Pevere remarks that these early works create a world where "identity becomes as erasable as videotape and as ephemeral as battery power." *Family Viewing* deals explicitly with the permeability of one young man's identity, a Toronto WASP named Van. Van's discovery that his authoritarian father has erased an entire archive of video images proves pivotal; amateur pornography featuring the smug dad's sexual romps with his mistress obliterate the son's cherished images of a childhood spent with a now-absent mother and grandmother. Van's unlikely alliance with a phone-sex operator culminates in a strangely upbeat triumph over the enemies of historical memory.

*Speaking Parts,* a less optimistic cinematic fever dream, can be savored as a savage parody of the culture industry's tendency to reduce serious discourse to a series of banalities. Set in an antiseptic Toronto hotel, the narrative plunges us into a vertiginous and often hilarious tale of bumbling solipsists. Clara, a naive young woman, writes a heartfelt but plodding script in an attempt to commemorate her brother's death. But the script is eventually bowdlerized by a wily producer who replaces its earnest platitudes with a talk-show format. Both Clara and Lisa, a pouty chambermaid, are dazzled by the film's leading man, Lance. Nevertheless, they usually cannot enjoy his sexual allure in person, but must resign themselves to gaping at his image on a video monitor. Even grief has become subservient to electronic razzmatazz; in *Speaking Parts*' dystopian universe, video mausoleums convert mourning into a private spectacle. While *Family Viewing* concluded with a qualified optimism, *Speaking Parts* refuses to comfort the audience with even a glimmer of hope.

Equally pessimistic, *The Adjuster* (1991), Egoyan's first wide-screen film, bestows an epic dimension on its protagonists' concerted disengagement from reality. Noah Render, the eponymous insurance adjuster, is an unsavory mixture of therapist and con artist. Superficially empathetic towards his clients, his compassion for the bereaved emanates from a need to control their lives. And Render's arrogance is bizarrely congruent with his wife Hera's job as a film censor—a task that fuses anal-retentive zeal with furtive prurience. By the film's end, the semicatatonic Renders are eventually victimized by the schemes of more diabolical narcissists—a wealthy couple who spend their time staging increasingly violent private fantasies. *The Adjuster* unveils the authoritarian implications of a world where the genuine pursuit of pleasure has been replaced by loss of affect and asocial hedonism.

Casting a wider esthetic and thematic net, *Calendar* (1993) and *Exotica* (1994)—a low-budget experimental film and a lush, relatively high-budget psychodrama—were incrementally less claustrophobic and even flirted with a renewed sense of hope. *Calendar* offered an opaquely personal gloss on the preoccupation with assimilation already evinced in *Next of Kin* and *Family Viewing.* When a Canadian-Armenian photographer and his Armenian-born translator wife (played by Egoyan and his actual wife, Arsinee Khanjian) return to their homeland, the chasm between North American affluence and a culture wounded by war and deprivation becomes glaringly apparent. The failure of Egoyan's alter ego to confront a submerged past leads to the dissolution of his marriage; his moral hibernation is rife with both personal and political reverberations.

While *Exotica* was indisputably Egoyan's commercial breakthrough, it is also his most problematic work. This elaborately mounted puzzle film unfolds like a quasisurreal parody of a psychoanalytic session: a nubile stripper assumes the role of a surrogate shrink while the opulent sex club referred to in the film's title serves as a commodious couch. Audiences were understandably seduced by the film's rapid-fire plot twists and visual panache, but *Exotica*'s soft-core titillation, as well its facile resolution, seemed to pander to an art-house audience.

Fortunately, *The Sweet Hereafter* (1997), Egoyan's most recent film, is one of his most textured and compassionate efforts. Like *Exotica,* this imaginative adaptation of Russell Banks's novel is concerned with personal devastation, the ravages of incest, and the deleterious effects of self-delusion. But the collective anguish of a troubled rural community supplants the urban anomie of the earlier films. *The Sweet Hereafter*'s central cataclysmic event—a school bus accident in which many of the town's children perish—provides the springboard for an open-ended moral inquiry in which a pragmatic litigiousness is pitted against one courageous individual's resistance to bottom-line acquisitiveness. Mitchell Stephens (played with nuanced intensity by veteran British actor Ian Holm) hubristically believes that he can salve the town's wounds with a whopping cash settlement, while Nicole Burnell, a young accident victim, simultaneously resists the lawyer's blandishments and transforms her childhood traumas (the scars wrought by both her father's incestuous advances and the accident itself) into personal triumph.

Egoyan's decision to eschew the predictability of a linear narrative for an intricate skein of flashbacks and flashforwards pays off brilliantly. Avoiding the pitfalls of a tabloidish melodrama focusing on a lurid accident and its outcome, *The Sweet Hereafter*'s insistent splintering of chronology allows us more profound access to a community's dark night of the soul. Egoyan's informal stock company—Khanjian, Maury Chaykin, Gabrielle Rose, Bruce Greenwood, and David Hemblen—display an impressive virtuosity. Usually cast as urban neurotics, these skillful character actors portray small-town bus drivers, motel owners, and mechanics with genuine conviction.

*Cineaste* spoke with Egoyan soon after **The Sweet Hereafter** won the Grand Prix at the 1997 Cannes Film Festival and several months before its American premiere at the 1997 New York Film Festival. In the following interview, he speaks lucidly, and frequently wittily, on topics ranging from cinephilia and the

[*Porton:*] **The Sweet Hereafter** *is your first adaptation of another author's material. Did you feel that it was time to change gears and integrate other perspectives with your own?*

[Egoyan:] After I finished *Exotica,* I felt that I had gone as far as I could, given a certain set of impulses that had formed a lot of my work. I was afraid of parodying myself. It was a very confusing time after *Exotica,* because it was a film that broke through. I wanted to surprise myself, and I think that any filmmaker wants to, more than anything, exceed his own expectations. And, after a certain point, when you become so identified with a style and approach, you want to challenge people's expectations.

When I read *The Sweet Hereafter,* I felt that it was a story that I would never have been able to come up with. Yet I saw similarities to my work and I felt that I could serve the material. It was worth pursuing, since Russell Banks was extraordinarily generous. The book was optioned by another studio, but he was prepared to release it and let me make the film. With his encouragement, and also with this need that I felt to challenge myself, I went into the project. It was a treacherous journey, because I was also involved with a studio film myself at that point with Warner Bros. which I had to leave in order to pursue **The Sweet Hereafter.** As an independent, you have to understand what that all means and wade through it. I think that I was smart in trusting my instincts.

*But weren't you initially fond of this Hollywood project?*

Yeah, because I liked the script and had a fairly good idea of how it could be cast. But, ultimately, it all got bogged down; there were disagreements over casting. There seem to be two reasons to make an independent film. One is as a calling card, so you can enter the more mainstream industry. The other is that it just suits your nature: you can think and do better work when you don't have to respond to a number of other people. I've become so used to having complete control over my own work that entering a studio-driven project will inevitably be fraught with all sorts of difficulties.

*You're also accustomed to working with what could be called your own repertory company. Given your working method, I'd imagine that it would be difficult to have to deal with actors who, at least in your view, weren't appropriate for the material.*

That's so important. There's a certain degree of necessary self-delusion that goes with filmmaking. You have to be ready to shoot. You have to believe that you're the right person to do it. And sometimes you have to believe that someone is the right actor to play in it. Somewhere deep inside you, you know that may not be the case. But once a project assumes a certain momentum, you have to go with it. And that's when it becomes frightening, because then we lose our rational instincts and you surrender to what you need to believe in to get the project done. It happens all the time, and it's then that mistakes can be made.

*What kind of assistance or feedback did you receive from Russell Banks while you were working on the script?*

It was very important to have Russell's approval and support, even though it wasn't contractually necessary or anything I needed to do. But since it was the first time I was doing an adaptation, and I was making some major departures from the book, I wanted to get a sense that he felt that I was keeping its spirit. I should use this opportunity to talk about the collaboration I have with the script editor, Allen Bell, who I've been working with on all my films since *Family Viewing.* When I told Allen what this film was about, he said that it sounded like a modern version of the pied piper. This sent goose pimples up and down my arm, because I realized what an amazing controlling metaphor that could be, and I went out and reread the Browning book. Though this seemed so beautiful and rich, it was important for me to have a response from Russell as well. He loved it and became quite envious of it; he felt that it was something he might have used if he had thought of it. Since I had claimed complete authorship for all of my previous films, I wanted to feel that I was being true to what Russell intended. But he never raised an eyebrow or said that I was moving in a strange direction.

**The Sweet Hereafter** *seems much more determined to offer the audience a sense of emotional catharsis than your early films. Unlike the straightforward trauma of the current film, the earlier films required the characters to engage in some kind of ritual or repetition compulsion.*

Or family romance. Emotional immediacy is exactly the thing that makes the experiment of **The Sweet Hereafter** work so well. Ultimately, all you need to know is that a school-bus accident has occurred and that it's about a community before and after that accident. I wasn't really aware of how simple that fundamental sense of placement would be. Everyone knows how cataclysmic such an accident would be. There is a degree of confusion and timelessness that people will accept because the characters have lost their sense of time as well due to their grief and shock.

*Although* **The Sweet Hereafter** *marks somewhat of a new direction for you, it also continues to explore the obsession with family dynamics emphasized in your other films, doesn't it? You even highlight this in your director's statement, since you explicitly link the current film with the closing scene of* **Exotica.**

Yes. I find cinema is a great medium to explore ideas of loss, because of the nature of how an image affects us and how we relate to our own memory and especially how memory has changed with the advent of motion pictures with their ability to record experience. Our relationship as filmmakers to those issues has changed radically over the past fifteen or twenty years. And people in our society have the instruments available to document and archive their own history. In my earlier films, I was exploring this in quite a literal way. But the ways in which our ability—and our need—to remember have been transmogrified comes very much into the spirit of this film as well.

There's nothing casual about accessing memory or the way experience is evoked. There's something very self-conscious, quite determined about it—the way people manipulate or use their own experience to get things they want from other people. Or the way some people want to relate to their loss in a very immediate and private way and are threatened by having that intruded upon them. But what is great about this material is that, for the first time, the characters are really full-blooded. They're not schematically conceived. In the other films, there was a more figurative approach to the characters, because that's what those films needed. The characters were lost to themselves, so they were really just shells looking for some sort of purpose. But in this film you have some characters who know exactly who they are and what they're doing. It gives a different dimension to the piece.

*Incest seemed like more of a submerged theme in your other films. In* **The Sweet Hereafter,** *it moves to the forefront.*

On reading the book and working on the adaptation, it was one of those situations where something had become a cliche; the entire depiction of incest in films had become very banal and lazy. I felt that there was another experience of incest that many people have experienced, but that has not been depicted in films—instead of it being a coercive act it becomes something where distinctions are blurred. Lines are crossed, and characters find themselves in situations which are just as damaging—or more damaging—than the other kind of incest. It's more confused; guilt and responsibility are not as easy to assign. These are the incestuous relationships that perhaps have a deeper impact on the individuals involved, because they don't quite know how to extricate themselves from the situation. The reality is that if the accident hadn't occurred that relationship would probably have continued until Nicole was in her twenties and she would have been even more messed up.

As it is, I think what happens is not so much that she realizes that she's abused but rather that, seeing her father in such an extreme state of denial, and then seeing him bartering her broken body for a reward, she becomes outraged in a quiet but very determined way. So the effect is quite different than it is in the book. I also wanted to see if I could shoot an incest scene from the point of view of the person who is involved as it is occurring. That scene in the barn is my attempt to show how Nicole would have described that scene at that particular moment. It's challenging for the viewer, because you're not quite sure how to evaluate it. But I think it contributes to the extraordinary power of the ending.

*So the point was to compress the experience in one shot so the event takes on a greater resonance by the end of the film?*

In some ways, it's not dissimilar from the way the accident itself was shot—from Billy's point of view, as Billy would have experienced it at that moment. As opposed to the more expected Hollywood money-shot point of view, which would be to cover that accident from as many angles as possible, and to try to experience the visceral effect of what it would be like to be in that bus. That wasn't where I wanted to position that camera. As an independent filmmaker, I have the privilege of being able to construct this incredible stunt and shoot it with only one camera from quite far away. I don't think a studio would have ever allowed me to do that.

*Jonathan Rosenbaum links your work to films by other Canadian filmmakers like Guy Maddin and David Cronenberg, who treat incest as a symptom of puritanism and repression.*

It's perhaps a cliche to think that we're all bundled up so we play with each other. But, perhaps it's fair to say that one of the residual affects of our colonial experience is a very particular view we have of parents or people who are in positions of responsibility. We are all just now understanding our relationship to both what the explicit British colonial influence in Canada was and what the American cultural colonial experience continues to be. We probably have to define ourselves through that very complex relationship between those two forces.

*Do you view the concept of the 'sweet hereafter' as a utopian antidote to repression?*

Of course, because it is a community that is entirely virtual and that exists entirely on principles that the individuals need to sustain themselves in that community. Certainly, at the end of the film, Nicole has arrived at a point where what she does effectively destroys the community as it existed before but paves the way for a new one. To me, that's what makes it such a crowning moment. It's a complete reappropriation of her own dignity by that decision.

*There's also a connection between what seems to be the father's key line in* **Family Viewing***—"I like to erase." Nicole's struggle is against erasure.*

Yes. It's a struggle against cultural and personal erasure.

*After reading the novel, I was struck by the fact that all of the characters, even the less intelligent ones, were unusually self-conscious. I'm sure that this must have appealed to you, but it's also apparent that you've restructured the* novel so that Mitchell Stephens becomes the central character. Russell Banks seemed to regard him as only one link in the narrative chain.

I guess it was just the way I read the book. When I noticed that character, I became very inspired by him. As a director, I'm always drawn to the characters who are close to conducting themselves in the way that I do. There's an aspect of my job that involves manipulating people, that involves trying to seduce people and gather people and follow me into a project. In a way, I, like any filmmaker, am a pied piper. You try to seduce people in order to get money, you try to seduce a crew, you try to seduce a cast. It's all very much about having other people believe that you have a vision that's worth dedicating themselves to. So when I encountered Mitchell Stephens, with his audacity of going into this town and believing that he had an answer for their grief with his claims of moral responsibility, there was something that made me feel very uneasy, yet quite sympathetic towards him and his projected mission.

*I understand you were quite impressed by Holm's performance in Pinter's* The Homecoming. *How did that influence your decision to cast him in* **The Sweet Hereafter**?

One of the thrills of working with Ian was being in such close contact with someone who had worked with Pinter—one of my gods. One of the best gifts he gave me after the shooting was over was a signed edition of *The Homecoming*. He's a remarkably generous man.

*Of course, with the exception of* **Calendar,** *all of the previous films have been set in Toronto. The more pastoral milieu of* **The Sweet Hereafter** *also transforms your view of the characters. Your earlier films seemed to focus on the erosion of community, as traditional communities were replaced by so-called 'virtual communities' governed by technology.*

They have a sense of community; they know where they're from. They're not lost like urban individuals. This, more than anything else, was the gift Russell Banks gave me. I've never lived in a town like that and I wouldn't have known how to begin telling a story based in a town like that. In making the adaptation, there was a huge challenge, which is that this community is, in some ways, quite virtual and unrealistic. In order for the drama to work, we have to feel that the children of the town completely disappear. If you look at it realistically, there is a school bus picking up kids from the outskirts of town, and there must be a central community, there might be kids who don't need to take the school bus and who just walk to school. So the town is bigger than you feel in the film and yet you never see that.

That's why in doing the adaptation, I couldn't show the crowd scenes, I couldn't show the funeral. If we represented the whole town, we'd diminish the dramatic effect of the story. A writer has the privilege of being able to do that because he's able to emphasize particular people so the background becomes abstract. But the moment you train a camera on a huge fairground and see other children, it takes away the fairy tale-like feeling that I wanted to create.

*And your choice of a wide-screen format gives the film the feel of an intimate epic.*

Yes, and this large canvas that you have gives you a feeling of vastness. There's no question that it transforms scenes to an epic level. And there's also this relationship to other films about strangers coming into town.

*Some of the casting seems to reflect your fondness for narrative ambiguity. For example, was it accidental that the actress who portrayed Alison looked quite a bit like Nicole?*

That was entirely intentional and very much a part of my casting. That's what Stephens is spooked by as well. It's probably why he confesses to her as much as he does.

*Didn't a controversy erupt when you decided to show* **The Sweet Hereafter** *at a benefit for your son's school?*

It only generated controversy among the people who were subjected to it. That was a classic example of complete denial—showing this at a benefit to a group of parents who every morning send their children off to a school bus was a perverse decision. But it was not intended to arouse the degree of shock that it did. Russell told me that he couldn't understand how someone who had just had a child could have made this film. I couldn't understand what I was doing until the film was finished and I had some distance.

*It would seem accurate to term* **The Sweet Hereafter** *your most affirmative film. For example, both Christina in* **Exotica** *and Nicole in the current film have been traumatized by incest. But Christina is unable to transcend her childhood trauma, while Nicole succeeds in breaking through and changes.* **Speaking Parts,** *on the other hand, could be termed your most pessimistic film.*

Absolutely—and **The Adjuster** as well. Although if you look back at the really early films, like **Next of Kin,** there's a bit more optimism. I think that **The Adjuster** went about as far as you could go in rendering the characters almost completely absurd because of their inability to define themselves. There was something quite humorous at some level about the repetitive patterns of behavior that the people were forced to reenact over and over again. Emotionally, the films are obviously quite bleak. There's not really any invitation to identify with any of the characters. As a matter of fact, you're always very aware of the fact that you're watching them, and that becomes what those experiences are about. They're very much about watching, and what happens when a relationship is entirely conducted through a lens, either in a literal or a figurative sense. In a way, the censor's relationship to the images she sees in **The Adjuster** are characteristic of how all of those relationships work. Material is gathered in an archive, and then stored and preserved.

*Were these sequences focusing on censorship in* **The Adjuster** *your critique of the practices of the Ontario censorship board?*

Yes, this also refers to my own experiences of being censored as a journalist. It is not as extreme as it once was. After the film was made, *Tokyo Decadence* was banned. The censorship board is a fascinating organization, because there's this casualness about the way the board defended themselves. They had this idea that they existed because there was a need to defend certain social values. Though Toronto was a very liberal city, they're a provincial board, and they felt they had a wider mandate to defend the interest of a wider cross section, people who wouldn't go to art cinemas in Toronto.

In the early Eighties, when I was a student at the University of Toronto, we were experiencing the most vicious period of censorship. It was around the time that *The Tin Drum* was banned. I wrote an article about that for a student newspaper and met Mary Brown, who at the time was the head censor. She took me to this room and showed me what she called the shock reel. It was literally a reel that had all the scenes that had been cut and were then pasted together. Of course, this was designed to place the viewer in a state of shock. After the lights came on, she came into the theater, and said rather smugly, "And now you know what we do." That experience was so important because it was so absurd. At that moment, I wanted nothing more than to agree with her, because those were images that I would never want to see. But those images were completely out of context, and some of them were culled from films that I later saw in their complete versions.

*It would be absurd, for example, to evaluate* In the Realm of the Senses *only from the vantage point of the castration scene.*

Yes—or you could make similar points about *Salo*. That idea of context, and the way in which you see an image, are issues which are really important to me and they are certainly ideas that become part of the narrative structure. I like to replay scenes, moments, or ideas from different viewpoints that challenge the viewer to question the authenticity, not only of where the material or where the images are sourced from, but why those people need to express those views.

That takes us back to **The Sweet Hereafter,** where we have Mitchell Stephens, a character who is similar to the title character of **The Adjuster** in some ways. While Noah Render was completely numbed by his own lack of self-awareness, and is not particularly a bright man, Mitchell Stephens is a brilliant lawyer who is able to manipulate and to adapt his course, depending on whom he's confronted with. And yet, he's not a wise person. Unlike Nicole, Mitchell is just destined to repeat an immediately satisfying occupation—immersing himself in other people's grief, but without really understanding how to deal with, in the longer term, his profound sense of loss.

*The consistency of your work is remarkable. The deliberate blurring of Nicole and Alison is almost a throwback to the beginning of* **Speaking Parts,** *a film where the viewer has a great deal of difficulty in distinguishing the two female protagonists for about the first ten minutes.*

It's a problem that other filmmakers don't seem to run into as much as I do. But viewers do feel confused by similarities and parallels in my films. Any viewer is very sensitive to the attitudes that a filmmaker has when making an image. And because I'm so aware of the construct, image, and presentation of characters, and because there's something so delicate about that, people approach my characters with a degree of caution. In a film like **Speaking Parts,** which is so aggressively mystifying, you are quite untethered in making those decisions. You don't necessarily have anyone pointing you in one direction or another. That's what the film is about, ultimately, the fact that people resemble each other and have the ability to play certain roles based on their ability to remind someone of someone else.

It's always a matter of finding a form or texture which reflects the underlying psychology of what the film is about. In **Speaking Parts,** it was about substitution, projection, and people living with other people as images and being able to trade or barter those images. The film has to reflect that. So, almost by definition, it couldn't be an easy film to watch. It couldn't be a film where identification was made comfortable or simple. There are films that could deal with those issues so that the viewer might be more immediately entertained. But the residual effect on the viewer's subconscious might not be as strong.

*There's a sense in which reality has caught up with what seemed to be the sci-fi premise of* **Speaking Parts**—*a world of constant surveillance and instantaneously accessible image banks. I recently heard about a college student who voluntarily subjects herself to twenty-four hour video surveillance through the Internet.*

One article I remember reading around that period involved a man whose parents had divorced. He wanted to show his son how happy his parents had been before they became divorced, so he brought his divorced parents together and recreated videotapes of their family life so he could show his son. It probably had an enduring affect on my sensibility.

*Surveillance is usually thought of as Orwellian, but in your early films the characters are quite complicit with their own surveillance.*

This is a way that the characters find out things. In **Family Viewing,** there's a real ambiguity about the role of technology. It's the means by which the father controls the family, but it's also ultimately the way in which the boy recovers his past. It's very easy to take a moralistic position and condemn these technologies, but the fact is that they are with us. It's a question of educating people how to use the technology, instead of demonizing technology or allowing it to become casual. It's important to understand how unusual those things are.

I've been editing this Yo-Yo Ma film, and I'm shocked that all this technology really does, despite the fact that it allows us to do something so much faster than it was ever possible to do with a Steenbeck, is make us more anxious. It's not as though we're using the extra time we're given to allow ourselves to rest or to reduce our stress. It's as though there's this lag between what the technology can provide and our own ability to absorb and understand it.

*At the risk of sounding simplistic, the ambivalence towards technology in theorists like McLuhan or filmmakers like David Cronenberg might lead one to think that this position is typically Canadian.*

As a culture, we are so completely overwhelmed by our access to American identity through technology. All of our major cities are no more than 200 miles from the border. From a very young age, we've all been bombarded with images of a culture that's not ours but seems to mirror certain aspects of our upbringing. But we're fundamentally different in many ways; in order to understand ourselves, we've had to understand our own relationship to these images which have completely crept into our cultural and social makeup.

*And, of course, your early films, particularly* **Next of Kin** *and* **Family Viewing,** *are about both national identity and ethnic identity.*

Right. I'm aware that I'm a person who came to this country from another culture and had to form an identity in order to think of myself as an assimilated Canadian. Even though I am very much a part of the mainstream fabric of English Canada, I'm aware of what I had to go through to become that way. That predisposes one to think of identity in a general sense as a construct. My suspicion about what it means to be natural has been an ongoing concern.

*In his recent memoir,* Black Dog of Fate, *the Armenian-American poet Peter Balakian observes that he was encouraged to become "more American than the Americans." As an Armenian who was encouraged to become totally assimilated, do you see any similarities to your own experience?*

That speaks very directly to me. My strongest experience in childhood probably comes from being settled in a town where we were the only Armenian family there and then having to reconstruct myself as an English boy. And learning all those traits and absorbing them so completely that I was more English than the English or thought I was.

**Calendar** *quite deliberately circled around Armenian history; the viewer has to fill in the blanks. You don't mention the Armenian genocide, for example.*

Yes, that was quite deliberate. It's a fundamental issue which I'm very nervous about treating casually. It's very interesting the response that some Armenians have towards **The Sweet Hereafter,** because they almost see it as being a clear metaphor for the genocide. That never even occurred to me when I considered my own attraction to the story. When I hear that, it seems almost obvious. But I was so thankful that this didn't occur to me while I was making the film or I would have analyzed it excessively.

The Armenian genocide hasn't just been repressed. It's this very curious type of denial where, in the face of so much openness about the nature of holocaust, the Armenians are in a curious position where the perpetrators have never really admitted it. There's a vagueness about the whole event. And, as it recedes more and more into our history, as the century has found other events to deal with, the necessity about determining what happened in Armenia at the turn of the century seems to be diminished. Yet, as an Armenian, its emotional consequences are still overwhelming.

*Your TV film,* **Gross Misconduct,** *has never been released here. The subject, a family's relationship with hockey, would appear to be quintessentially Canadian.*

That is one of the best Gothic stories to emerge from this country. It's an incredible, true story about this young boy from a small town in northern Canada whose father always dreamed that he would be a hockey player and trained him with an incredible degree of violence—the father was quite psychotic. He hammered this obsession with hockey into the boy until he was finally invited to join the NHL. On the night he was playing his first big league game that was supposedly being broadcast across the country, the father in the small town turned on his TV only to find out that it wasn't being broadcast in the western part of the country. He flipped out, took a gun, drove to the local TV station and held it hostage and demanded that they broadcast the game. At the very moment that his son was being interviewed between periods on each network, the RCMP ambushed the station and shot the father dead. It could never really make it to network TV in the U.S. because it's a fractured narrative.

*Although your films often deal with eroticism, you've avoided explicit sexuality.* **Exotica** *is, after all, about striptease. The desire to stimulate the viewer's imagination relates to what has been called the 'interactive' nature of your films.*

It always surprises me that you can conceive of an erotic scene, but the moment you actually shoot it and construct it, it immediately reduces its ability to excite. And yet, what's interesting about **Exotica** is that it's interactive in that you know the film is going to unfold in a certain way and you have to determine what you're feeling in response to what you know is inevitable. The film will continue to give out information and give out scenes and give out glimpses of these characters. That is much more attractive, in a way, than a situation where you are genuinely interactive, when you control the narrative.

That's what a lot of filmmakers had to contend with about ten years ago with the advent of the CD-ROM. It was thought that maybe this whole aspect of storytelling would become redundant now that we just need to think of drama as an interactive video game. It's not anywhere near as compelling as having to determine what your relationship to a predetermined story is. One of the results of having a child is that you realize that little human beings want stories. They want to imagine those stories in relationship to images they have as opposed to some controlling set of images.

*I read that you were quite taken with Cronenberg's* Videodrome. *Do you see any affinities between that film and your own work?*

I didn't think I was influenced by the film when it first came out. In fact, I had some problems with it. Looking back on the film now, I realize that it did have a tremendous influence on me. This notion of how we are encouraged to hallucinate and the idea that there are shadow worlds that exist in tandem with our reality was, for me, the most compelling aspect of *Videodrome*. It seems like a very simple film, but what it proposes is very shocking in a literal way. I think the difference between David's work and mine probably is that he gave up a certain formalism, much to his commercial success. His early films, *Crimes of the Future* and *Stereo,* are very esoteric, and he just turned away from that very early in his career. He realized that, if he was to continue making films at that time, he had to work within the horror genre. That gave him a certain freedom to take the conventions of that genre and, of course, delusion is quite an accepted motif within horror films. *Videodrome* explored that in quite a strident and brilliant way. There were also other films which explored this, such as Godard's *Numero Deux.*

*Your admiration for hallucinatory narratives evokes an observation you made some years ago in which you claimed that "nothing is more artificial than mainstream realism."*

I don't know whether I would still agree with that. Mike Leigh has been one of the filmmakers who has really had an impact on me since I made that statement. I was on the jury at Cannes last year and found his use of realism in *Secrets & Lies* quite a devastating experience. Everyone makes images the way they need to make them. I would be foolish to say that there's nothing more artificial than mainstream realism—it's just artificial to me. I'm completely swayed by the sincerity of many images, which actually allows me to enjoy a film like *Private Parts*. In a perverse way, it's quite sincere. It's very arrogant to be prescriptive about how a film should be made, because one can always be surprised.

*There's an interesting contrast between your films and Leigh's character-driven movies. it's always been possible to offer thumbnail sketches of Leigh's characters, while you've always viewed the characters with a great deal of detachment.*

I've always felt that my own characters were in a place where they didn't quite understand what their own feelings were and what they had to contribute to any relationship.

And, in a way, that's an enduring influence of my early exposure to the theater of the absurd, playwrights like Ionesco, Genet, and Pinter. They assumed that there was an inherent mystery in the meeting of any two people and that there is a whole nest of motivations and reasons that are completely belied by the casualness of that meeting. In my early films, I wallowed in that; that was a very exciting place for me to explore. I am naturally attracted to the grotesque and extremes of human behavior—the extent that people will go to convince themselves that something is normal and the casualness with which people will embark on modes of behavior which, in any other context, would be quite aberrant.

In **Exotica,** for example, there's this man who goes to this sex club every night. There's something quite habitual about that and he doesn't quite understand the damaging affect of this type of behavior merely because he's allowed himself unquestioned access to repetition. We think we've found a way of coping with our sense of grief, but in fact we've only distorted it; we're only reflecting it until we think that we've absorbed it. It doesn't cease to astonish me how I can show a film as intimate as **Calendar** and find that these images, which seem so hermetic and drawn from a seemingly unapproachable personal history, can make themselves public and people can draw from it and find emotional sustenance.

I've always wanted to resist films which have the ability to make people think that what they're seeing is real. Maybe I'm grown out of that at this point. And certainly the challenge in **The Sweet Hereafter** was to create a very vivid sense of what this community was about and who these people were within a very unorthodox structure. It's completely nonlinear, but because you have a strong sense of who the people are and what the community is about and what the central event is, you have tremendous freedom to play with that structure.

*Of course, New Wave directors like Resnais also liked to fracture time. Was this stylistic choice an intuitive decision?*

There's no great design. For me, it's the most natural way of telling a story. I love weaving time, because I want to be surprised by the images I make. When I write in a linear way, it seems to detract from my desire to actually direct the film. There's not a lot left to discover when I feel that the story is unfolding from point A to point B. I don't have a problem watching those movies or reading those scripts. But when I'm asked to write or make that kind of film, I get very impatient. I find it more exciting when I'm not entirely sure what the alchemy of it all will be and I have to shoot those images and put them together and find out. There's an element of surprise, there's also a greater risk of failure. All of that drives me on.

*And the convoluted structure of a film like* **Speaking Parts** *satirizes how talk shows trivialize both historical and personal issues and transform them into entertainment.*

Yes, it's very prescient about what's happened to our culture since 1988. On shows like Jerry Springer's, there's this notion of the confessional, the staged moment where the truth is supposedly uncovered in public on television. All the work we do as dramatists to formulate a story seems to be obliterated by the way this type of communication has taken over our imagination. It bludgeons us into taking sides and seems to be the antithesis of what drama can do.

What's perverse about **Speaking Parts** is that the producer actually has a point. He's taken what is probably a very uninteresting and melodramatic script written by Clara and changes it into what may well be quite an innovative television program. Does that give him the right to take that story? And who has the responsibility to tell the story and at what point does the own person's talent or vision weigh on their right to keep that story and to be the conveyor of it. That is a very provocative issue for me. In **Speaking Parts,** you have a premise which deals with helplessness— our society is divided into people who make images and people who watch images. Authority is granted to people when they have the ability to turn themselves into producers. Nicole succeeds in producing her own history by the end of **The Sweet Hereafter.** She takes the format of a talk show where people are encouraged to tell the truth and then subverts it. I was really inspired by her ability to reconstruct her own sense of experience.

It's more hallucinatory in **Speaking Parts.** When Clara appears at the talk show, we imagine that she shoots herself or Lance imagines that she shoots herself. We're not quite sure whose inhabiting what role. That whole last reel is just a bombardment of various images and projections.

*Did you consciously avoid the shot/reverse shot pattern in your earlier films? You often followed a close-up with a moving camera shot.*

Coming from theater, I was very unsettled by the idea of manipulated time and the ease with which you could distort and break the moment of observation. What was powerful about a camera was the way it looked, and the moment you cut away from its look, you diminished the responsibility of the gaze. I was very consumed with that for the longest time. All of my earlier films continued to deal with characters who felt lost. I thought that the camera was the way to embody the look of that person as they watched the people they left behind. I was very attracted to long unblinking shots where you would really feel the power of observation. I felt that cutting away would corrupt that. It might have been that, on a purely technical level, I didn't understand coverage. I didn't go to film school, no one had really explained it to me. No one ever told me what I was doing was wrong. But I certainly learned from some very obvious mistakes in film grammar that I made during the early shorts.

I feel that cinema syntax is based on images that we project in our own mind when we dream. This is probably the reason why we found a grammar for cinema so quickly, as opposed to the other arts, where it took centuries of evolution to find and determine notions of perspective. Cinema came really quickly, because I think we found an instrument that allowed us to conjure the way we dream. And, perhaps, in our unconscious state, we have an 180-degree line that we don't cross. And maybe we use master shot coverage in our dreams. I guess we'll never really know that for sure. But it seems only natural that cinema, which has remained so unchanged since the beginning of the art form, conforms to something that we've all been watching for eons. And that's why a lot of those experiments of the New Wave, which tried to break those conventions, never really took hold.

*Since you're a cinephile, I suppose there's always a tension between film history and your personal vision. You once mentioned Teorema as a film that impressed you, and there are at least some superficial resemblances between the Pasolini film and* **Next of Kin.**

Yes. I'm taken with this idea of an interloper, somebody who finds their way into an environment where you wouldn't think they would be welcome, but where they find or make their own welcome and insinuate themselves. This theme recurs in **The Sweet Hereafter** as well; this lawyer comes into people's homes and makes himself indispensable. Where this comes from, or why, I'm not quite sure. As a child, I was always aware of going into other people's homes and seeing how friends from different backgrounds lived their lives. I also felt that I was intruding or coming into a situation that wasn't mine.

*Your work seems to have generated a certain amount of critical misunderstanding over the years. Some of your harshest critics, for example, failed to acknowledge the bleak humor of those early films, didn't they?*

If you don't see the humor, you're not going to enjoy the films at all. I noticed this with **Family Viewing** especially. The way I can test an audience is the scene in the nursing home when the father makes a mistake about which grandmother he's giving the flowers to. There are people who take that moment really seriously and I never quite know what they can make of the rest of the film. There's an obliviousness that the characters have to the consequences of their actions which is very funny.

*The early films were considered 'cold' by certain critics and viewers.*

It has continued to an extent with **The Sweet Hereafter,** but less so. I just find it really odd, because, for me, a film like **Speaking Parts** is operatic!

You cannot get warm and cuddly with the films. That's maybe what people are talking about; they can't simply sit back and have a story told to them and identify and lose themselves. They have to be always aware of their position and their relationship to these images. There are people who will even see this new film, and given what the subject matter is, find it distant and not really understand that, if it wasn't distanced, it'd be a TV movie! The more classical way to shoot this is to be right up there, with them, whatever that means. I'm always aware of certain things: Why am I shooting this? What is it about this story that needs to be shown? What am I hoping to achieve by depicting these people? If that means that I'm a formalist, fine. Formalism is a concern with the process of depiction and that informs every gesture I'll ever make in movies.

**Brian Johnson (review date 8 September 1997)**

SOURCE: "How Sweet It Is: His New Film Signals a Change of Direction for Egoyan," in *Maclean's,* Vol. 110, No. 36, September 8, 1997, pp. 60–61.

[*In the following review, Johnson compares* The Sweet Hereafter *with Egoyan's previous works, stating that* Hereafter *features more natural and fully developed characters.*]

Inevitably, directors get tired of their own movies. And after finishing **The Sweet Hereafter,** Atom Egoyan watched it so many times that by the time it premiered at the Cannes Film Festival last May, he no longer knew what to make of it. But last month—rested after vacationing in Italy with his wife, actress Arsinee Khanjian, and their four-year-old son, Arshile—the Canadian film-maker was ready to take a fresh look at **The Sweet Hereafter.** The occasion was a private screening in Toronto for the Directors Guild of Canada. Halfway through, the fire alarm went off. There was no fire, but the theatre was soon filled with firemen. "It was so bizarre," recalls Egoyan. "Usually firemen are all, like, 'Everybody leave the building now!' But they were so casual. They were thrilled because they'd read about the film. So I ended up doing a photo session with all these firemen. They all wanted pictures, and they gave me their cards."

If Atom Egoyan is hot stuff in the fire hall, perhaps it is official that he has finally made his mark in the mainstream. Not too many years ago, despite his popularity in Europe, Egoyan's name in North America was synonymous with cinema's art-house fringe. But *Exotica* (1994), his hermetic drama of school-girl striptease and adult bereavement, was a modest hit, grossing $15 million. Now, **The Sweet Hereafter,** Egoyan's seventh feature, takes his career to a new threshold. To the consternation of many critics, the film fell short of winning the Palme d'or, the top prize at Cannes, but it received more awards than any film in the festival: the second-place Grand Jury Prize, the International Critics Prize and the Ecumenical Jury Prize.

***The Sweet Hereafter*** also marks a departure for Egoyan. Based on the 1991 novel by Russell Banks, it is his first script adapted from another source. And although the film's tone of acute existential paralysis is familiar from his previous work, for once its characters are ostensibly normal people. Filming in the B.C. interior, the 37-year-old director also left behind urban claustrophobia and took his camera into Canada's wilderness for the first time.

But shooting in the mountains "wasn't that shocking," says Egoyan, sipping an espresso in the kitchen of the converted house that serves as his production office in downtown Toronto. "I was raised on the West Coast, so natural beauty is part of me." (Born in Cairo to Armenian parents, he moved to Victoria at the age of 3.) "What makes this film such a huge step forward," he adds, "is that for the first time you can identify with the characters. You're not outside them. In all my other films, the characters have been fragments or aspects of my own personality. They were people looking for their own identity through rituals or gestures. But they were just shells."

Now he tells us.

So does this mean that all those naysayers who felt stymied by his films were right all along? No—Egoyan stands by his original work, but he felt he had reached an impasse. "After *Exotica,* I felt that everything I was writing I had dealt with somehow before," he says. "I was treading water. I have natural attractions to the grotesque and the absurd, and extreme and obsessional behavior, but I can almost predict that. I want to surprise myself, and surprise others." Adds the director: "I think my film-making is going to be split between projects I write myself, which will become smaller and more intimate, and these adaptations, which I really enjoy."

Egoyan's career, a kind of multimedia work in progress, extends beyond film. Giving Robert Lepage a run for his money as a directorial Renaissance man, he is writing a libretto for an opera titled **Elsewhereless.** He will direct **Dr. Ox's Experiment,** a new work by leading British composer Gavin Bryars, for the English National Opera in London next spring. In November, Egoyan is remounting his provocative version of the opera **Salome** with the Vancouver Opera. And he is currently polishing off his contribution to a six-part series of films about cellist Yo Yo Ma—a playful fiction in which Ma's limousine gets stuck in traffic on his way to a concert, and then he has to put up with a coughing fit in the audience.

The next movie project, meanwhile, is another literary adaptation. Backed by Mel Gibson's Icon Productions in Los Angeles, Egoyan is writing and directing a screen version of ***Felicia's Journey,*** based on the 1994 novel by Irish author William Trevor. Icon was involved in Egoyan's last brush with Hollywood—as the producer of *Dead Sleep,* a thriller that he was preparing to direct two years ago. After a quarrel with Warner Bros. over casting the female lead, Egoyan backed out, and *Dead Sleep* was dead in the water.

The director is more optimistic about ***Felicia's Journey.*** It would become his first non-Canadian movie, although he made an unsuccessful bid to transplant the setting to

Canada. Trevor's novel, which won the Whitbread Prize, is about an Irish country girl who travels to England, pregnant and penniless, looking for the lover who left her. Instead, she falls in with a gentle, mild-mannered psychopath who tries to convince her to have an abortion so he can kill her with a clean conscience. The subject matter certainly seems Egoyanesque. But Egoyan suggested turning the woman into a Quebecoise who travels to Victoria-a revision that was vetoed by the author.

Banks, meanwhile, seems delighted with Egoyan's treatment of *The Sweet Hereafter,* although the director shifted the setting from New England to British Columbia, reordered the narrative structure, added a car-wash scene at the opening, stripped the story of its demolition-derby climax, and embellished it with readings from The Pied Piper of Hamelin. "It's a brilliant film," Banks told Maclean's in Cannes. "He's disassembled my novel and reassembled it like a mosaic. And he doesn't judge any of the characters." The Pied Piper motif, Banks added, gives the story the quality of a fable, and he would have used it in the novel if it had occurred to him.

But perhaps Egoyan's boldest invention is his portrayal of the incest between the teenage Nicole (Sarah Polley) and her father, Sam (Tom McCamus). He films it in a candlelit barn as a gauzy romantic reverie, as if seen through the girl's confused eyes. "A lot of people will be quite shocked by it," says the director, "because they won't quite know what they're supposed to feel. But that's exactly what Nicole is experiencing." Then he adds: "I try to show things that haven't been shown before. And what we have never seen is that type of incest from the viewpoint of the person who's going through it."

*The Sweet Hereafter,* meanwhile, offers more natural performances than any of Egoyan's previous work. "These characters were fully formed," he says, "and I knew that the worst thing to do would be to stylize them." British stage veteran Ian Holm stars as the ambulance-chasing lawyer, Mitchell Stephens—replacing Donald Sutherland, who dropped out 10 days before cameras were set to roll last winter. But the cast is dominated by Canadian alumni of other Egoyan films: Bruce Greenwood, Gabrielle Rose, Maury Chaykin, Polley and Khanjian.

The director seems to inspire loyalty in actors. Aside from his affection for misanthropic themes, one of the quintessentially Canadian things about him is that he—like his older colleague David Cronenberg—is a notoriously nice guy. Polley says she has never worked with an easier director. "Even if he was a really bad film-maker," she suggests, "I think I'd still want to work with him."

Egoyan brings a mischievous sense of fun to the set. Actors appreciate his playful, almost childlike fascination with the creative process. But the director combines it with a clinical instinct for control—like the claims man in *The Adjuster,* the auditor in *Exotica* or the lawyer in his current film. There is a scene in *The Sweet Hereafter* where Stephens, the lawyer, tells the driver who crashed the school bus that she must learn to express her suffering for the sake of his lawsuit. When she finally does so, and is overtaken by grief, he rudely cuts her off: "And then what happened?" Egoyan can identify. "That's what a director does," he says. "We go to incredible lengths to seduce an actor to do something, only to disregard it if it doesn't work for us."

Egoyan, meanwhile, is gradually seducing his audience, like a Pied Piper of Canadian cinema. And where he is leading it is anybody's guess.

### Tony Rayns (review date October 1997)

SOURCE: A review of *The Sweet Hereafter,* in *Sight & Sound,* Vol. 7, No. 10, October, 1997, pp. 60–61.

[*In the following review, Rayns argues that Egoyan's failure to sustain a sense of community in* The Sweet Hereafter *detracts from the film's overall impact.*]

In *The Sweet Hereafter,* Lawyer Mitchell Stephens arrives in Sam Dent, a small town in British Columbia, where the community is paralysed by a recent accident: the school bus, driven by Dolores Driscoll and carrying 22 children, went off an icy road and plunged into a lake, causing 14 deaths. Stephens hopes to mobilise the bereaved parents into a class-action lawsuit against the bus company; he will act without a fee, against one-third of any settlement reached. (Stephens himself has deep emotional problems; divorced from his wife Klara, he keeps his drug-addicted, drop-out daughter Zoe at arm's length.)

He turns to the local motel owners Wendell and Risa Walker for advice on which grieving parents to approach. He also meets Dolores (and her husband Abbott, victim of a stroke) and hears her account of the day of the accident. The first to sign up for his class action are the Ottos, Hartley and Wanda, who lost their adopted son Bear. Risa is the next, followed by Sam and Mary Burnell, whose daughter Nicole survived the accident but is now wheelchair-bound. (Stephens provides a computer for Nicole, to sweeten the deal.) But garage-owner Billy Ansell, a widower who lost both his children, threatens Stephens with violence and advises others in the community to have nothing to do with him.

Called to give her legal deposition about her experience of the accident, Nicole (who has previously insisted that she will not tell lies) destroys the law-suit by testifying that Dolores was driving too fast. Stephens is left smarting, but the community regains a sense of solidarity and learns to come to terms with its grief.

This narrative is intercut with flashbacks to the periods before, during and immediately after the accident, centred on the day-to-day lives of the main characters. Billy regularly hires Nicole to babysit his children while he pursues a secret affair with Risa. Nicole is trying to make it as a rock singer, and has an incestuous relationship with her father Sam. Stephens himself recalls an episode from Zoe's infancy, when he and Klara raced against time to get her to a hospital in a medical emergency. There are also glimpses of the future: some time later, Stephens is on an internal flight and finds himself sitting next to Allison, a childhood friend of Zoe's. The encounter forces him to go over the gradual breakdown of his relationship with his daughter and to describe his deeply unresolved feelings for her. On arrival at his destination, he sees Dolores driving a hotel shuttle-bus. In Sam Dent, Nicole feels that the community has entered a new and happier phase which she dubs "the sweet hereafter." But her own thoughts still centre on the days when she used to babysit Billy's children—and dreamed of marrying Billy herself.

Atom Egoyan has been notably frank about his reasons for adapting Russell Banks' novel and making—for the first time—a film not based on an original screenplay of his own. "I felt I had made a number of films inspired by stories that came from the universe that was in my own head, but it was becoming all too familiar for me. I wanted to find something that would challenge me and still provide a framework on which I could impose my own structural concepts, and this was the perfect story for that." He is also eager to cement a direct link between this film and its predecessor: "*Exotica* ends with a shot of Christina walking towards the house. What happens there has had a great deal of influence on her life. She is not protected in the house. And **The Sweet Hereafter** takes us inside the house." (Both quotes are from the Alliance Communications pressbook.)

This is a not uncommon syndrome among writer-directors who base their work on deeply personal preoccupations and use it to confront issues they want to resolve for themselves or to exorcise personal demons: they tend to reach a point (sometimes temporary, sometimes permanent) when the well runs dry. Fassbinder dealt with it by co-opting favourite books (*Effi Briest, Berlin Alexanderplatz*) or by giving a revered classic a good kicking (*Nora Helmer*). Paul Schrader dealt with it by remaking *Cat People*. Egoyan has taken what seems at first sight the Cronenberg route of filming an 'unfilmable' novel. His adaptation of **The Sweet Hereafter** certainly *looks* like an Atom Egoyan film; simply as an exercise in superimposing one sensibility on to another, the film is so ingenious, so skilful and so nuanced that it's easy to forget that it has literary roots at all. All of which makes it hard to explain why the film is ultimately so disappointing.

The core problem seems to be that Egoyan has miscast himself as the adapter of a novel in which a sense of community is paramount. Few directors have *less* sense of community than Egoyan: his work has always centred on obsessives and eccentrics trapped in solipsistic worlds, most of whom have cause to regret their forays into social and sexual intercourse, and the surly bonds that interest him most are those within families. Here he does not even present a plausible topography of the town, which never feels like anything but a patched-together collection of locations, let alone provide any inkling of the ways its citizens interact socially. For the purposes of the film, Sam Dent is a group of five unhappy households, a garage and a civic courthouse. And the only elements which knit the households together prior to the accident are an adulterous affair and the feelings of a young woman trapped in an incestuous affair with her father who dreams of marrying the town's most eligible widower and becoming a 'mother' (rather than just a babysitter) to his kids. In short, Egoyan's Sam Dent is not a million miles from *Peyton Place*.

Banks' novel is divided into four sections, each with its own narrator: the structure helps the author to build a real sense of the community which has been struck by the tragedy. In line with his earlier films, Egoyan appears to replace the idea of plural voices with an omniscient directorial point-of-view. **The Sweet Hereafter** has a fantastically complicated time structure: it has hardly begun before it plunges into free-range cross-cutting between the pasts, presents and futures of its characters, and it feels free throughout to make connections across all bounds of time and space. Egoyan's method of constructing and narrating his films has always had an element of tease: he likes to drop hints, make insinuations, leave room for the viewer to speculate . . . and to surprise with sudden revelations. **The Sweet Hereafter** does all these things, only more so. It's as if what Egoyan responds to most strongly in the novel is simply the range of characters and time-frames it provides as grist to the mill of his structural machinations.

The most surprising (and daring) of the film's countless linkages is that between the bus accident itself and the day when Stephens' then-infant daughter Zoe almost died from the side-effects of an insect bite. Egoyan effects the link simply by presenting one event after the other. The implications are anything but clear-cut: the juxtaposition *could* be suggesting that Stephens' quest to mount the Sam Dent class-action suit is an oblique expression of his unresolved rage at the breakdown of his own marriage and the loss of his own daughter—not to an insect bite and an insufficiently concerned doctor but later, to narcotics. The one thing which *is* clear (and Egoyan underlines it heavily by using the image of the Stephens family asleep moments before the calamity strikes Zoe as the background to his main title at the front of the film) is the directorial sleight-of-hand which equates a community tragedy with a family crisis.

It's revealing that the 'glue' which Egoyan uses to weld the many disparate fragments together is 'The Pied Piper of Hamelin.' The poem is first heard as Nicole's bedtime reading to Billy's children: it subsequently blankets the film, appearing on the soundtrack even when, at some unspecified point in the future, Stephens discusses Zoe's fate with one of her old friends on a plane. (Browning's poem is not in the novel, although Banks now says he wishes it had been.) The prominent use of the poem 'rhymes' Sam Dent with Hamelin and implies that the children who died in the bus-crash were somehow 'culled' as a punishment for the sins of their parents. (It also, of course, identifies Nicole with the "lame child" left behind by the piper.) This is a smart and snazzily post-modern way of connoting 'community,' but Egoyan cannot make it stick when nothing in the rest of the film supports it. Five pained/guilty families do not a community make.

Banks and Egoyan do, however, reach simultaneous climaxes with the crucial scene of Nicole's testimony about the crash, the only genuinely moving moment in the film. For Egoyan, Nicole's rationally inexplicable decision to scuttle the law-suit by lying represents both an act of tremendous courage and a decisive break with "what happens to her inside the house"—her incestuous idylls with her father, which take place in a barn dangerously festooned with candles. His respect for the novel obliges him to show Nicole's action having a community-wide effect, something he attempts in a rather bizarre way with a shot of a ferris wheel over which Nicole's voice enthuses about everything being "strange and new." But he follows this by showing Nicole's retreat into her memories of the days when she was Billy's babysitter, closing the film as he began it: with an image of domestic bliss which we know will very soon be shattered. On the face of it, a classic Egoyan moment. But it doesn't kick either emotionally or intellectually, because the ingenuity of the adaptation has obstructed the real thrust of the film.

**Craig Turner (review date 23 November 1997)**

SOURCE: "The Great White (North) Hope," in *Los Angeles Times,* November 23, 1997, pp. 8, 94–95.

[*In the following review, Turner argues that Egoyan's past works inform* The Sweet Hereafter *and notes ways in which the film deviates from his earlier works.*]

The taxi pulls into a narrow lane in downtown Toronto's western fringes, where artists' lofts share the neighborhood with storefront restaurants and converted warehouses.

On the north side of the street, a red-brick, Victorian-era duplex unmarked by any sign houses the headquarters of Atom Egoyan, at 37 an icon of the Canadian cinema and a writer-director edging toward the center of the Hollywood radar screen.

The interior gives off a dormitory feel, with film posters covering the walls, cardboard file boxes stacked on the floor, old props leaning against walls, and doors flapping with the passage of young and youngish employees. The atmosphere had been described perfectly a few weeks earlier by New York author Russell Banks, whose novel *The Sweet Hereafter,* as filmed by Egoyan, is gaining critical acclaim. Entering Egoyan's office, Banks said in an interview during the New York Film Festival, "I felt like I was visiting a bunch of funky, brilliant graduate students, all deeply serious and very funny at the same time."

This is a long, long way from Hollywood—and we're not just talking about miles and the need for snow tires. But the scene is characteristic of Canada's small but hardy movie industry, dominated as it is by low-budget independents such as Egoyan.

Wiry and owlish, with a penetrating intelligence and a restless artistic drive, Egoyan has a small but loyal following in the United States among critics and film buffs fond of his cool, elliptical stories of men and women skating along the brink of anomie.

That circle of admirers figures to widen with the commercial release of *The Sweet Hereafter,* which opened Friday trailing awards and critical huzzahs from the Cannes, Toronto and New York film festivals. It is the most mainstream and commercial of Egoyan's movies, and Fine Line Features is marketing it with an emphasis on the critical buzz and hope that there may be Oscar nominations in its future.

The film explores the effect of a fatal school bus crash on the residents of a small border community in British Columbia, and on the predatory attorney who arrives from out of town promising justice and restitution. The lawyer is performed with nuance by British actor Ian Holm, who at 66 has his first film starring role. Holm is surrounded by an Egoyan repertory company of Canadian actors, including Bruce Greenwood, 18-year-old Sarah Polley, Alberta Watson and Arsinee Khanjian, Egoyan's wife.

But to say that *The Sweet Hereafter* is about a bus crash is a bit like saying *Citizen Kane* is about a sled. The movie, which shifts about in time and place, gradually peels away layers of mystery in its characters and setting.

"It's about our relationship with fate, really," says Egoyan, perched on a chair in his sunlit office in the back of the Victorian. "To what extent do we want to control our lives, and to what extent do we let things just happen to us?"

"People will hopefully come out of this movie talking and debating," says Holm, who leaped at the role of the lawyer when Donald Sutherland had to bow out at the last minute. "It's asking questions that maybe nobody knows the answer to."

Even before its opening, *The Sweet Hereafter* has lifted Egoyan closer to the Hollywood jet stream. Egoyan jerks a thumb at a foot-high stack of screenplays, novels and manuscripts resting on a chair. They have been sent from Los Angeles by his agent, and "I'm supposed to read them by the weekend," he explains.

And every morning, after dropping off his and Khanjian's 4-year-old son, Arshile, at kindergarten, Egoyan spends three or four hours in front of a computer, tapping out a film script of Irish author William Trevor's psychological thriller *Felicia's Journey.* He is signed to write and direct the movie version for Mel Gibson's Icon Productions.

He also is preparing to direct two new operas, one in London for the English National Opera and one in Toronto that he coauthored. Egoyan is executive producer of two films being developed by his assistants, recently completed a 55-minute short with cellist Yo-Yo Ma for PBS and supervises distribution and television sales of his early features. In January, he is scheduled to become the backup director to Michelangelo Antonioni on a new movie shooting in Los Angeles. The bonding company requires that Egoyan be ready to step in if Antonioni suffers a relapse in his recovery from a stroke.

To hear Egoyan tell it, this upward curve in his career has followed an almost geometric logic.

"I've been working through these skills, starting with micro, micro budgets and increasing from project to project," he says. "It has made me very aware of what the market for my movies is, how it's grown, how it continues to grow, what I can do and still maintain the freedom I need to make the films the way I want."

Nor is he daunted by the prospect that Hollywood has come calling, for he has been down that road before. He spent much of 1995 in a long, ultimately frustrating relationship with Warner Bros. over a script that never was produced. Egoyan walked away when he and the studio could not agree on casting, but today he classifies it as educational exercise.

"Looking back, in a way I would have paid to have had that experience," says Egoyan, who as a college student considered a career in diplomacy. "It allowed me to have a front-row seat in seeing how films were made there without actually going through the process of making what probably would have ended up being a compromised work."

If **The Sweet Hereafter** does score a breakthrough at the U.S. box office or in awards nominations, there will be cheers throughout the Canadian film industry, for it would be seen not just as recognition of the popular Egoyan but as a longed-for American acknowledgment of a neighboring artistic community that often seems like an interesting little boutique operating in the shadow of a giant supermall.

The list of Canadians who have had successful careers in Hollywood is long and impressive; it begins with silent-movie director Mack Sennett, the inventor of screen comedy, and Mary Pickford, the first star, and extends to director James Cameron (*Terminator 2*, the upcoming *Titanic*) and comic Jim Carrey. But those Canadian movie-makers who stay home labor in relative obscurity.

Even Canadians shun most domestically produced movies in favor of American films. Egoyan's biggest gross to date is 1994's **Exotica,** which earned $5 million in the U.S., $1 million in Canada, another $5 million overseas and is classified as a major hit by Canadian standards.

"We want our *Piano* or *Crocodile Dundee* or *Full Monty,* a film that will break out of our domestic market and do a lot of business across North America," acknowledges Wayne Clarkson, executive director of the Canadian Film Center in Toronto, an academy modeled on the American Film Institute.

If Egoyan leads the way, Clarkson adds, it would be especially fitting. Along with David Cronenberg (*The Fly, Crash*), Egoyan is Canada's best-known director, and "he makes his films entirely on his own terms and at his own pace; it's almost the perfect career path for someone in the Canadian cinema," Clarkson says.

"Atom Egoyan is the filmmaker that every film student in Canada wants to become," summarizes Mina Shum, 31, a Vancouver writer-director whose debut feature, *Double Happiness,* a comedy about growing up Chinese Canadian on the West Coast, won plaudits two years ago.

Egoyan was born in Cairo to Armenian parents and raised in Victoria, British Columbia. His parents were trained as artists in Egypt and owned a successful gallery in Cairo. When they tried to transfer that business to Victoria, however, there was no real market for fine art in what was then a provincial and insular town. Instead, Egoyan's father found success running a furniture store.

"I was very aware of the frustration in their lives between this desire to make art and the practical reality of what they needed to do to make a living," says Egoyan, who adds that the experience accounts for his fixation on holding down his film budgets and for his reputation as an astute negotiator with producers and distributors.

As a struggling playwright and aspiring director in Toronto in the early 1980s, Egoyan faced the decision every would-be filmmaker in Canada must make: whether to go south. He enlisted an unusual family connection to get some inside counsel. One of his mother's close friends knew Danny Arnold, the Los Angeles producer of "Barney Miller" and other television series, and she got the young Egoyan an appointment.

"Danny Arnold gave me this amazing bit of information," Egoyan recalls. "He said: 'Nobody comes to L.A. to become a better writer. They come to make a lot of money. So you have to decide what your priority is.' . . . That word of advice has stayed with me."

Back in Toronto, Egoyan's emerging career coincided with one of the periodic bursts of spending on the arts that Canadian governments embark on when they get fretful of American cultural dominance. He quickly mastered the system, forming his own production company, Ego Film Arts, and cobbling together movie funding from a spectrum of government and private sources. Television work paid the bills while he poured his creativity into feature films, in which he served as producer, director, screenwriter and, in one case, co-star.

His early movies got limited distribution, played the film festival circuit and made little or no money, but critics in Canada and Europe took notice.

In 1991, Egoyan formed a crucial partnership with Robert Lantos, the chairman of Alliance Communications, Canada's largest producer of film and television. The deal they struck was this: If Egoyan could stay within a limited budget—usually less than $2 million—Alliance would raise the financing, from government and private sources and by selling the film in advance in Europe. In return, Egoyan could make whatever movie he wanted. Lantos just insisted on veto rights over the title.

The bargain has paid off for both parties.

"He's amazingly fiscally responsible; none of his films for us has ever lost money," says Lantos. "For someone who makes eccentric movies so far away from formula-driven popcorn movies, for someone who lives in that world, that's very unusual."

Unpredictable and often bizarre, Egoyan's films up to *The Sweet Hereafter* usually feature outsiders seeking an identity, often in unconventional ways. Despite elements of voyeurism and what Egoyan calls "the energy of aggressive perversion," the films are surprisingly cool in tone.

Geoff Pevere, a leading Canadian film critic, compares their chilly ambience and searching characters to the work of Sweden's Ingmar Bergman, although he also contends there is something "hopelessly Canadian" about their restraint.

"His films are almost as interested in the intervals between the dramatic high points as in the dramatic high points," Pevere says. "It's a cultural trait we've got. Canadians have grown up incredibly influenced by the United States, but not part of the United States. . . . It's made us . . . accustomed to standing apart, taking it all in and analyzing it."

Indeed the most frequent rap on Egoyan's films is that they are too distant from the audience's experience. That echoes a criticism of Canada's movies generally, in part stemming from film financing, which is heavily dependent on government subsidies and thus is driven more by the concerns of filmmakers and bureaucrats than commercial considerations.

It has made for what Clarkson calls "a cinema of auteurs," but it also helps account for the inability of most English-language Canadian movies to draw big audiences. (Canada's French-language films play mainly in the province of Quebec and are more popular, something usually attributed to the language barrier separating them from most things American.)

Egoyan argues—and critics agree—that he has crossed into much more mainstream territory with *The Sweet Hereafter.*

"It's only gradually that I've been able to reconcile my artistic tendencies and formalist impulses with character-driven stories that people can relate to," he says.

"The other films were not about characters that people could identify with. . . . This film is really asking you as a viewer: What would you do in this situation?"

Still, there is that sense of restraint. In a pivotal sequence in *The Sweet Hereafter,* a school bus filled with children plunges off a road, skids across a frozen lake, comes to a halt and then, after an agonizing pause, crashes through the ice. The scene is shot with one camera from the viewpoint of the father of two of the children, who has been following the bus in his pickup truck.

It's hard to picture a Hollywood director passing on the opportunity to raise the emotional pitch with close-ups of terrified children.

"There *is* something perverse about holding back that far away from the action, but I think it ultimately makes it more powerful," Egoyan contends. "It's horrifying because you have to imagine what's going on as opposed to seeing it."

Because *The Sweet Hereafter* does not lend itself to a one-paragraph summary, even those close to the film are uncertain of its commercial potential, although they certainly are hopeful.

"I think it's going to be a hard picture to sell. . . . It will be very much by word of mouth," says Holm. "This is a modest little film, but modest little films are in now, and I think it's important that Hollywood people see this kind of film. . . . The loose ends are not all tied up, and it's not a package where you come out and say, 'Oh, that's great,' and forget it. It provokes discussion."

**Sharon Waxman (essay date 14 December 1997)**

SOURCE: "Atom Egoyan's Particles of Faith: Director of *The Sweet Hereafter* Believes in Smart Audiences for His Complex Films," in *Washington Post,* December 14, 1997, p. G10.

[*In the following essay, Waxman notes that viewers must work to unravel the plot elements in* The Sweet Hereafter.]

Watching Atom Egoyan's new film *The Sweet Hereafter* can be rather like living through the turbulent events it depicts.

The film tells the story of a school bus accident in a small rural Canadian town and the big-city lawyer—himself a tormented soul—who arrives looking for a lawsuit.

As the film wends its way through the town's heartbreak, it focuses on several families—some hippies who lose an adopted Indian son, a widower who witnesses the crash and loses his twins, a talented teenage girl who survives but is scarred by incest. With no regard to time frame or context, the scenes flow from flashback to present day and back again.

It sounds confusing, but, instead, this approach immerses the viewer in the community's confused anger and grief, denial and, ultimately, a wounded sort of acceptance—which is what Egoyan intended.

"You want things to be loaded, to know that there is more going on than meets the eye," he said after a recent screening of the film. "The characters themselves are drifting, trying to understand what happened. It was important to find a way of telling the story that implicates the viewer in that process. . . . You have to place yourself in relation to what you are seeing."

The director, small and energetic, sips a double espresso as he talks. He wears owlish sunglasses and the European-intellectual look—rumpled-white-shirt-with-dark-jacket—his bouffant hair an incongruous dark halo in the California sunshine.

Placing some of the burden of unraveling the story on the viewer is a tricky business, but Egoyan just shrugs when asked about it. "What I'm trusting is the viewer's desire to explore, their infinite curiosity," he says. "I can't be afraid to do that, to believe in the viewer's being trusting and exploratory and very—" he thinks—"very curious." He smiles. "I have high expectations of the viewer."

The 37-year-old filmmaker must be right somewhere because *The Sweet Hereafter* won no less than three awards at this year's Cannes Film Festival. For Egoyan, who has steadily worked his way to prominence among independent filmmakers, *The Sweet Hereafter* represents a departure from the themes of his earlier films but a continuation of his intense examination of morality and human need, and the creaky balancing act of life.

If the director comes off as intense and somewhat complicated, it isn't unexpected given his background. Start, for example, with the fact that he's named after a particle.

Egoyan was born in Cairo to Armenian parents (themselves the children of refugees from Armenia), who named him Atom as a tribute to Egypt's development of nuclear power (make that would-be development of nuclear power). Troubled by the rise of Arab nationalism, his family moved to Victoria, Canada, when Egoyan was 3, where the dark-haired, olive-skinned boy stood out—and not in a way that made him feel comfortable.

To fit in, he rejected his Armenian background, refusing to speak his native tongue (which he eventually relearned as an adult). He excelled in school. Though interested in film and theater in high school, Egoyan enrolled in the University of Toronto to study international relations, with the thought of becoming a diplomat. He soon realized that diplomacy would be boring, and instead focused on artistic endeavors, writing plays and making short films as a student. His first feature film, *Next of Kin* (1984), is the story of a disaffected WASP named Peter who is adopted by a troubled Armenian family—a kind of Egoyan fantasy in reverse.

His other films, including *Family Viewing, The Adjuster* and the critically acclaimed *Exotica* and *Calendar,* have consistently grappled with the impact of technology and media images on modern life and on the alienation created by a society driven by corporate interests.

Egoyan's work earned the admiration of critics, actors and fellow filmmakers. "I think Atom is a master craftsman, a real genius," says Ian Holm, the only non-Canadian actor in *The Sweet Hereafter.* (Egoyan tends to work with the same group of actors in his films.) "I regard the film rather like a [Harold] Pinter play; he doesn't dot the i's and cross the t's, so that there are questions posed in the film: What do you think that meant?"

Canadian film critic Geoff Pevere writes, "For him, the process of . . . making us question our reason for watching his movies simply re-poses the most essential questions of our cinema. '. . . Who are we anyway? And where is here?'"

Russell Banks, who sold Egoyan the rights to his novel after a project at 20th Century Fox fell through, was initially skeptical about working with the director, having seen his other films. "But then I saw that he shares the same obsessions as me," says Banks. "How people know each other, what they can and can't know about each other, people's sense of disconnectedness and their need to cross over that and connect."

Ultimately, Banks says, Egoyan was more faithful to his novel than any Hollywood filmmaker would have been. "The thing that mattered most to me, finally, was that he held on to the moral center of the novel; that's what is most meaningful to a writer and it's what most filmmakers take away," says Banks. "In Atom's case he was most concerned with those issues, the relationships between parents and children, the role children play in our larger community, how we are robbed of our futures."

Central to *The Sweet Hereafter* is the relationship between a teenage girl, Nicole (played by Sarah Polley), who has a promising career as a singer before the accident, and her too-loving father. Their incest is no more than a brief, almost benign scene in the narrative; only at the end of the film can it be perceived for the perversion that it is. Parallel to that relationship is the one between Stephen Mitchell, played with depth by British actor Holm, and his own drug-addicted daughter, a source of constant anger and torment to the lawyer.

These protagonists are intriguingly ambiguous. Nicole ultimately frees herself from the incest through an act that is at once courageous and cowardly: She lies about the accident, implicating the bus driver, who is not at fault. And then there is Mitchell: Is he a hearse-chasing bloodsucker, playing to the vulnerability of the grieving parents? Or does he sincerely believe, as he tells the parents, that it is his role to help them assign blame and win some compensation—and thus closure? It isn't clear.

Again, intentional. Egoyan, whose natural intensity punctuates his rapid-fire theorizing, almost cackles in savoring these shades of gray. "It is the lawyer's job to create a story that he can get other people to believe in," he says. "Sometimes that story happens to be true, sometimes not. The truth is crucial. But ultimately the story that isn't true may be the better story. So it's not as much about law as it is about who tells a better narrative."

If *Hereafter* is a shift from Egoyan's previous films, it may be because the director himself has moved on from the sort of arch intellectualism that marked them. In 1988, he told an interviewer he thought the family was suspect as a "biological structure" because of the "psychological demands that are placed on an individual. . . . The notion that you surrender yourself to a group purely because they're linked to you biologically is naive, especially if those people have not attempted to make an emotional connection with you," he said.

Nearly a decade later Egoyan is now married to actress Arsinee Khanjian (who plays a hippie in the film) and they have a 4-year-old son, Arshile. The family unit is the touchstone of *The Sweet Hereafter,* symbolized by the hauntingly beautiful tableau that is its signature image, a mother and father asleep in bed with their naked infant curled at the mother's breast.

Is this all too remote for the average moviegoer? Sadly, until now, it has been; the director's work has been limited to small runs in art house theaters while garnering near-fanatic praise at film festivals. More's the pity, for Egoyan doesn't intend to make any compromises from his end. Movies, he says, are "a way of addressing experience, of showing us through the trick of the camera that what we are seeing is real."

He thinks, but only for an instant. Then he says, "Movies should be like that all the time."

### Stephen Hunter (review date 25 December 1997)

SOURCE: "*The Sweet Hereafter*: A Cry of Hope," in *Washington Post,* December 25, 1997, p. C01.

[*In the following review, Hunter suggests that* The Sweet Hereafter's *ambiguity and unusual chronology are among its strengths, but notes that these elements may bother some viewers.*]

Here's one way to look at it: Man is a meaning-seeking creature. Pitiful being, he cannot accept the random cruelty of the universe. That is his biggest failing, the source of his unhappiness and possibly of his nobility as well. He paws through disasters with but one question for God: Why? And God never answers.

He certainly doesn't answer in Atom Egoyan's superb *The Sweet Hereafter,* which watches a mad, vain scrambler seeking to impart his own meaning on someone else's terrifying disaster. As derived from the intense Russell Banks novel, the story follows lawyer Mitchell Stephens (Ian Holm) on his peregrinations through a western Canadian town where a school bus has recently fallen through the ice, drowning 14 children and leaving an enamel of grief as blinding as the snow that blankets the place. This lawyer: greedhead or pilgrim of pain?

This town: victim of horrid coincidence or of God's vengeance?

This story: remembered myth or spontaneous occurrence?

The answer to the questions is: All of the above. And one more thing is certain, and that is uncertainty. The movie is of the mode called postmodernism, which no one understands but everyone recognizes. To borrow from Kurt Vonnegut, its story has come unstuck in time, and though the narrative materials are eventually clarified, we seem to drift for a period between now and then, here and there. Some people can't handle this willed ambiguity and grow restless, if not anxious, in the absence of a clear chronology. But as in *The English Patient,* the chronological looseness is part of the pleasure of the piece, which magically reassembles in the last reel into something strong, lucid and compellingly powerful.

Basically, its "now" appears to be a plane ride in which Stephens returns, in defeat, from his trip. As he tells the story to his seat-mate, a friend of his daughter, the whole story emerges in bright and tragic vignettes, seen from a dozen perspectives, revealing the heart of the observer.

It turns out that in one sense, it's the most old-fashioned of narrative archetypes, the small-town story. Sam Dent, as the place is named, picturesque in the Canadian Rockies, soon reveals itself to be another in the form revealed by Grace Metalious all those years earlier in *Peyton Place,* a caldron of promiscuity, alcoholism, even some terrifying sexual child abuse.

In his recollection, as he bobs about the town in support of his lawsuits against the school board, the county that maintains the road and hires the driver, even the bus manufacturer, in search of a villain, any villain, Stephens encounters instead human weakness and culpability in all its forms. A was sleeping with B, C was molesting his daughter, D was cheating on her husband and on and on.

On top of this, Egoyan adds something that Banks never thought of. That's an overlay of myth, as he impresses Robert Browning's "The Pied Piper of Hamelin Town" on the events as if to ask the question, that eternal question: Who took the children? Who was the piper? Why did the portal in the mountain—an actual portal in the ice at the bottom of the mountain in the movie's most shattering scene—why did the portal open up and why did they disappear? As the saying goes: You've got to pay the piper. Why didn't the townspeople pay the piper? But the final ambiguity is the lawyer himself. As it advances, the film makes clear he's not merely in search of wealth (though he may be), but driven by the need to impose meaning. He wants to inflict punishment on them. Them? Oh, you know: Them, they, the unknown agents of all destruction, workers for Lucifer, corporate, municipal or ecclesiastical, as the case may be. For he is also a parent in mourning: He once loved his daughter, Zoe, so much that he went beyond taboo and attempted to save her life with an emergency tracheotomy, taking upon himself the moral weight of cutting into his own daughter's flesh. Zoe is among the lost, not in this accident, but in another, larger accident called society.

Zoe phones him, wheedles for money, pretends to be his old Zoe, but she is clearly of that subset of living dead, the hopelessly addicted, her soul crippled with lust for heroin, her immune system finally overcome. We realize that the lawyer has gone west seeking meaning in the larger society of a town of lost children in hope of finding meaning in his own lost child.

Of course, it's hopeless. One can, after all, never know the reasons and the meanings. But there's something so human in the attempt that the movie, despite the crushing weight of the pain it contains, ultimately feels hopeful. The sweet hereafter of the title is that zone of wisdom where we ultimately come to accept the unacceptable and in some provisional, broken way, go on living.

### James M. Wall (review date 18 February 1998)

SOURCE: A review of *The Sweet Hereafter,* in *Christian Century,* Vol. 115, No. 5, February 18, 1998, p. 163.

[*In the following review,* Wall *describes* The Sweet Hereafter *as emotionally demanding and calls* Hereafter *one of the best films of 1997.*]

Over the past few months I have led discussions of three films that I count among the top pictures released in 1997. Two of the discussions were in religious settings, the other in a secular setting, but I found the same range of responses: some participants picked up on the religious dimensions of the films while others wondered what had happened to just plain fun at the movies.

What happened to fun at the movies may be found in 1997's biggest financial success, *Men in Black.* Those who want more than fun should find plenty of food for thought in the following ten films. I should point out that the harsh language, violence and sexual content in some of these pictures will sharply limit their audiences.

With this caution, I recommend the following, beginning with the three that were the focus of my presentations: *The Apostle,* Robert Duvall's film about a Pentecostal preacher; *Good Will Hunting,* director Gus Van Sant's sensitive depiction of a young mathematical genius; and Canadian director Atom Egoyan's **The Sweet Hereafter,** based on Russell Bank's haunting novel about a school bus accident that kills 14 children.

Religious themes are obvious in *The Apostle,* more subtle in the other two films. *Good Will Hunting* is about a psychologist, played by Robin Williams, who has to reexamine his own identity as he helps a young man, played by Matt Damon, break through his entombed personality. Their moment of breakthrough is more of a spiritual than a psychological experience.

The most demanding of the films is **The Sweet Hereafter.** It provokes many "hunches" about the director's intentions, which makes the discussion afterwards especially valuable. What I had thought was a subtle allusion to Abraham was regarded by one viewer as "obvious." Another member of the group linked an opening scene, in which a lawyer is trapped in a car wash, to the tragic drowning sequence in which the 14 children are killed. These connections are not thrust on the viewer; they just resonate as part of the experience.

One viewer of **The Sweet Hereafter** came armed with excerpts from Robert Browning's poem "The Pied Piper of Hamelin," which plays a crucial role in the film (though it's not in the novel). The poem is read by a baby-sitter to children involved in the bus crash. This literary addition is important because the film focuses on precisely the problem of the villagers of Hamelin, who fail to fulfill their promise to pay the piper. This broken promise in Browning's poem—and in the German folk tale that inspired it—leads to the disappearance of the children. In Egoyan's film, the loss of the town's children reminds the community of their own broken promises.

Egoyan is not suggesting a cause-and-effect divine intervention; he is lamenting a failure that encompasses the entire community, a condition that the families must confront in their grief.

British exports seem to be limited to two kinds of films: those that celebrate classic English literary texts from Shakespeare to Austen and those that deplore what Margaret Thatcher's conservative government did to the country's working classes. One of the better examples of the latter category is *The Full Monty,* a comedy with a strong dose of pathos. The plot involves a group of unemployed miners who decide to put on an all-male strip show. The film examines the devastating effect of economic change on working-class families. The film has some difficulty surmounting the language barrier; the working-class accents call for subtitles.

A comedy overly full of vulgarities and insulting language is *As Good As It Gets,* featuring Jack Nicholson as a compulsive-obsessive neurotic. It's a film that depicts struggling relationships among individuals who live on the margins. Nicholson is so obnoxious that the only "friend" he has is a waitress, played by Helen Hunt, who tolerates Nicholson's behavior long enough for the two of them to fall into what passes for love.

Another comedy that works better than many may expect is *Deconstructing Harry,* Woody Allen's latest venture into self-exposure. It follows a successful novelist on a journey back to his old school (an homage to Ingmar Bergman's *Wild Strawberries*). Beneath Allen's sharp wit is evidence of considerable personal pain.

When *Wag the Dog* was released it seemed that director Barry Levinson's satire about a president who escapes a sex scandal by starting a phony war might be too heavy-handed. Not so now, with President Clinton embroiled in a sex scandal and considering whether to attack Iraq. *Wag the Dog* deserves attention entirely apart from the real-life parallels, however; its delineation of the influence political spin-doctors have is a needed reminder of the collapse of integrity in public life.

*Amistad,* Steven Spielberg's well-intentioned effort to give the same attention to slavery that he gave to the Holocaust in *Schindler's List,* is inaccurate about some of the religious figures involved in the story and somewhat didactic, but it provides vital information about slave conditions. Of special note is an effective sequence in which two African prisoners discuss the biblical story of Jesus which they cannot read but can grasp from pictures of a man who walks around with a small sun around his head and who is unfairly put to death, only to rise again—a fate they believe will now come to them.

*The Ice Storm,* an adaptation of a novel by Rick Moody, is set in the 1970s, amid suburban couples who think they can find love and happiness in unmitigated sexual freedom, a misguided concept they pass along to their unloved children. Director Ang Lee's use of the ice metaphor effectively conveys the barren landscape of loveless lives.

Rounding out my list is a film from first-time director Kasi Lemmons about a dysfunctional African-American family. *Eve's Bayou* is told through the eyes of a young girl who adores her wayward father, played by Samuel L. Jackson, a doctor who, in his own words, "pushes aspirin to older folks" and who has a weakness for women who need him to be a hero. A story of repeated betrayals and lies, this film covers some of the terrain featured in *The Ice Storm* and *The Sweet Hereafter.* Apparently the loss of "family values" cuts across racial and cultural boundaries.

## Patricia Pearson (essay date April 1998)

SOURCE: "The Sweet Here and Now," in *Saturday Night,* Vol. 113, No. 3, April, 1998, pp. 67–72.

[*In the following essay, Pearson compares the commercial and critical success of* The Sweet Hereafter *to Egoyan's background as an independent screenwriter and director.*]

Atom Egoyan always said he was deeply suspicious of the Oscars. Then he got nominated.

The first time I spied Atom Egoyan, at a Christmas party for Toronto's arts and letters set, the handsome thirty-seven-year-old director was engrossed in conversation with Greg Gatenby, head of the International Festival of Authors. Slightly hunched, with one hand grasping his chin, he seemed unaware that the crowd surrounding them had come alive with whispers and glances. "Is that Atom Egoyan?" someone near me inquired excitedly. "Hey," someone else hissed, "I think that's Egoyan." A hiply clad woman with honey hair approached and stuck out her hand: "Atom, I don't know if you remember, I interviewed you in London."

The buzz about Egoyan was that he had a shot at the Oscars. His seventh independent feature film, **The Sweet Hereafter,** is a gorgeous and poignant adaptation of the Russell Banks novel about a small community shattered by the loss of their children in a school-bus accident. By December, the movie had hit 200 top-ten lists. *Premiere* magazine had just pegged him as a "good bet" for a best-director nod. The National Board of Review in New York had already awarded a best ensemble-acting prize to his largely Canadian cast. In Toronto, a city with one of the highest film production and attendance levels in the world, the prospect of a homegrown, Hollywood-anointed film celebrity was heady stuff.

I ran into Egoyan towards the end of the party, in a corridor, peering at framed pictures through his round, dark glasses. It seemed appropriate to find him there, ever curious about his surroundings, but wary of other people's curiosity about him. Part of the problem with the Oscar hype, as he saw it, was that it set him up as someone whose mission was to score for the flag. "I remember when I won three prizes at Cannes," he pointed out, referring to **The Sweet Hereafter**'s debut on the Riviera last May, "I was thinking, 'Finally! Respect!' Then, I was so appalled when I got home—and a lot of the reporting was 'Oh, it was second place, not quite.' I thought 'Come on! Give me a break!'"

He didn't want to take the same tsk-tsk over Oscar. "My distributor wants me to fly down and spend the whole month of January in L.A.," he added, referring to the increasingly aggressive Academy Award campaigns mounted these days by the studios, "but I can't. I have too much work to do." Egoyan's voice is elegant, the intonation courteous and cultured, but he sounded a touch plaintive on this point. True, he was working on a new film script, and preparing to direct two operas in the spring, but it's fair to say that most men within reach of an Academy Award would hop on a plane.

Egoyan, however, is an unusual bird. He is extremely ambitious, which is what has brought him to this threshold of acclaim, but he is not one to play by the rules. He refuses to live in L.A.; he rejects Hollywood's cinematic style; he ignores the box office; and he spurns big-budget studio pictures in favour of retaining creative control of small, highly personal films. "He's succeeded by being stubbornly anti-Hollywood," his friend, the actor Don McKellar, says. "That's the great irony of this."

Early in the new year, I visited Egoyan at his downtown Toronto office, a narrow Victorian semi with two cluttered rooms on the ground floor and an editing suite upstairs. He graciously offered me the remaining half of his take-out latte—having no coffee pot—and gave me an update on his four-year-old son, Arshile, whose chickenpox had almost capsized his work day.

He was feeling anxious about the Oscar campaign, but he still refused to rearrange his schedule. He had to promote *The Sweet Hereafter* in Europe; the European critics and festivals have been essential to his success. "Everyone has a fantasy of how their work should be situated," he explains, caressing the neck of his worn black T-shirt, "and for me that has always been Cannes and the critical response." So he's struck a compromise. He's agreed to fly to New York to address members of the Directors Guild, and to appear on a talk show. He'll also do a photo shoot for *Vanity Fair,* having been persuaded by his distributor at Fine Line that all these gestures will buy him prestige, which is the only currency he can trade in to secure his independence.

"As suspicious as I am of the Academy Awards," he says, "and I'm deeply suspicious, I cannot dismiss what they would mean. We are all colonized by these benchmarks of status."

Egoyan often proclaims his suspicion of things. At one time or another, he's been suspicious of awards, and of "mainstream acceptance" and of "on-screen emotion," and of "image-making." It's as if it's his shtick to play the doubting professor.

He leapt up and glided around his office while we talked, procuring clippings and phone numbers and the last name "of that guy, what's his name?, who writes so brilliantly about Canadian nationalism?"—finally phoning a friend to find out. "Ah, Bruce Powe!" Clearly, one of the keys to his talent is this ability to focus, to instantly carry a notion through into consequence: he thinks, therefore he directs.

Since high school, in fact, he has been directing prodigiously, with a remarkable constancy of vision. His films are filled with bewildered, faintly absurd characters who engage in perverse occupations and pursuits in an effort to connect with one another. Invariably, their connections are filtered through machines: they watch one another on video tape, or gaze longingly through telephoto lenses, or engage in phone sex; scenes take place from the vantage point of apartment-building security monitors; conversations are held on answering machines.

A scene in *The Sweet Hereafter* is vintage Egoyan: a teenage runaway places a collect call to her father from a pay phone, and he answers on his cell phone, in his car, while trapped in a car wash. The communication between them is that tenuous, their capacity for movement towards one another that impossible, but the yearning so keen you can almost hear it.

Egoyan has built up a huge following in Europe, where film critics and communications theorists fall over each other to praise his critique of technology and modern communication. North American audiences have been more indifferent, preferring, as we do, to hunker down to proven pleasures. His distributor's attempts to promote Egoyan here have verged on the comical, packaging hopelessly cerebral, ambiguous films as if they were thrillers. Egoyan laughed in bafflement when he saw the trailer for his 1994 film *Exotica.* The trailer opened with a shotgun blast, when the only action in the film is people brooding. "Miramax sent me on a huge tour of the States for *Exotica*," he says. But he was too intellectual, "and my interview schedule petered out after the first few appearances."

Egoyan's office walls are tick-tacked with snapshots: his wife, the actress Arsinee Khanjian, his son, and his friends and collaborators, who include Don McKellar (the writer and star of CBC's "Twitch City"), the director Bruce McDonald (*Highway 61* and *Hard Core Logo*), the director and cinematographer Peter Mettier, and his mentor, David Cronenberg. For years, they have been acting in one another's films, coproducing projects and screening each other's rushes, bound by a sense of humour that is dark, acerbic, and deadpan. "I need to say something mean about Atom" Don McKellar told me in a phone interview, with no hint of joking. "He needs to be punished." He couldn't think of anything mean, though. Egoyan is universally liked in the film community, considered to be charming and charismatic, but also diplomatic, so that people don't notice him getting his way.

"The reason people can be so proud and happy for Atom," McKellar says, "is because he's so Atom. There's no point in envying him, because you could never do what he does."

Atom Egoyan was born in Cairo, the eldest child of two Armenian artists. His father's parents had fled their homeland in the aftermath of Turkish genocide. "My parents thought it would be cool to name their son after what was going to be a predominant source of energy for the future," he told *Interview* magazine, "as opposed to calling me television monitor." In 1962, the Egoyans emigrated to Victoria, B.C., and set up a modern furniture shop. They also continued with their art, some of which is on permanent display in the Armenian National Gallery in Yerevan.

"Atom comes from a family that I always imagined an artist should come from," his friend, the novelist Doug Cooper, says. "His parents were warm and encouraging, but they were also exacting and tough-minded. They wanted a son who was a perverse filmmaker and a daughter who was an experimental pianist. How many people have parents like that?"

"There were tensions" Egoyan qualifies, of this idyllic artist-childhood, "but those were interesting too."

While Eve learned the piano, Atom concentrated on classical guitar, which he still plays, and on reading novels and writing plays. One of the defining experiences of his adolescence was his friendship with a girl who was having an incestuous affair with her father. "I remember an absolute confusion on my part as to what was happening," he recalls. "I never talked to her about it, and no-one else did either." Yet, he maintains, everybody knew. In *The Sweet Hereafter,* Egoyan was finally able to get at this memory, casting Canada's sweet Sarah Polley as the consenting lover to her own father. "We go to great lengths to avoid and to obfuscate things that are unbearably obvious," he says. "The need for clarity, but also for mystery, is the defining question in my drama."

At eighteen, he flew east to the University of Toronto and quickly began directing his own plays at the Trinity College Dramatic Society. 'Atom had a much older sensibility than any of us," Cooper recalls. "It was really rare to meet someone straight out of high school who was already serious about Pinter and Beckett."

His plays were not the sentimental favourites of the college-theatre season. "I was trying to prove that I had something to express, but at the same time I never wanted to bend to what was popular," Egoyan explains, echoing a persistent theme in his subsequent career. Cooper's more emotionally engaging play won over the campus audience, and Egoyan remembers "feeling completely marginalized. He got a standing ovation, and I thought: 'I will never enjoy that,' and resigned myself."

If Egoyan was convinced that he wouldn't become popular, he nevertheless remained driven to prove that his take on the world was worth attention. "Atom is very, very wilful," says Cooper. He began to make short films, submitting each effort to festivals—only to feel "devastated and excluded" when they weren't accepted.

Then, with $37,000 in grants from the Canada Council and the Ontario Arts Council, Egoyan produced his first feature. *Next of Kin* is about two families in therapy, one WASP, the other Armenian, whose paths cross when the Anglo son sees the videotaped therapy session of the Armenian family, realizes that they are torn up about a long-lost child, and decides to pose as their grown-up son. *Next of Kin* made it into the Perspectives Canada programme at the Toronto Festival of Festivals, a triumph for Egoyan. From there, it went to the Mannheim film festival in Germany and picked up a prize. Egoyan was also nominated for best director at that years Genies. He was not yet twenty-five.

The erudite young director was quickly adopted by Canada's culture elite as what he calls "multiculturalism's prize pony." Robert Fulford crowed over Egoyan in *Saturday Night,* applauding his "essay on ethnicity in Canada." Peter Harcourt, in *Film Quarterly,* described the filmmaker's themes as expressing "the classic Canadian dilemma as formulated by Northrop Frye. . . . Egoyan devises films that register the personal uncertainties of people who are striving to find a place of rest within a culture not their own."

Egoyan instantly disliked this characterization. "I'm about as assimilated as you can get," he protests. "The idea that I straddle communities is a bit ridiculous" Well, not really. He pointedly reached into Canada's Armenian acting community to cast *Next of Kin,* which is where he found his wife, Arsinee Khanjian, whom he spotted starring in an Armenian-language version of *The Mousetrap* in Montreal. He also shot his 1993 film *Calendar* in Armenia. "I did sublimate my first culture, so the process of retrieval is important to me," he concedes.

What offends him, perhaps, is the attribution of a politics to his work, and in particular an identity politics. "If you're feeling confused about who you are, saying it's because you're from somewhere else becomes very convenient," he says.

If arts mandarins at the Canada Council, Telefilm, and the Ontario Film Development Corporation backed Egoyan because he was addressing politically correct themes, others backed him because he had star quality. "It was really the uniqueness of Atom's vision that attracted me," says the producer Camelia Frieberg, who joined him for *Next of Kin* and has seen Egoyan through to the Oscars. "I just felt he was somebody who was really going to go places."

In 1987, his second grant-funded feature, *Family Viewing,* won an honourable mention at the Festival of New Cinema in Montreal, which placed him on the stage with the legendary German director Wim Wenders, who was accepting an award for *Wings of Desire.* Out of the blue, Wenders handed his cash prize to Egoyan, which instantly won him international attention. "The great myth was that he loved my film so much that he wanted the world to embrace me," Egoyan says, "but actually he hadn't seen the film. What he really wanted to embrace was the notion that a young filmmaker needed money more than he did.

"I couldn't admit that to people for years," he says, laughing. "If you'd asked me, this a few years ago, I would have said 'Yes, he loved the movie.' I wanted to believe that. Eventually I did a performance piece at the Rivoli (a restaurant in Toronto) in which I apologized to the public for this great lie, and explained how I finally had to separate myself from Wenders's approval."

In 1993, Egoyan passed the torch by impulsively offering John Pozer, director of *The Grocer's Wife,* his own $20,000 festival prize. "It was," he reflects, "one of the stupidest things I've ever done in my life. I really needed the money."

Over the next several years, buoyed by growing fame on the festival circuit, Egoyan continued to toil away at what *Entertainment Weekly* described as his "kinky, avant-gardish doodles," writing his scripts around things that popped up in his life. ***The Adjuster*** was prompted by a devastating fire that destroyed his parents' house in 1989 and got him thinking about how strange it would be to suddenly be completely emotionally dependent upon an insurance guy; ***Calendar*** involved him and Arsinee improvising as they toured around Armenia, with Egoyan playing himself—"well, my worst nightmare of myself"—filming his girlfriend as she fell in love with their tour guide. ***Exotica*** was plotted on his being audited. When Arsinee got pregnant, he wrote that into the film, too.

Among his detractors, Egoyan was famous for eliciting stiff, almost monotonous performances from his actors, which impressed the intellectual film set—"the actor asks the viewer to question what it is about the character he's supposed to identify with," one enthused—and kept viewers away in droves.

Arsinee Khanjian publicly chastised her husband for his suspicion of on-screen emotion. "He doesn't feel that we are entitled, it seems, to our emotional explosions," she told Doug Cooper in 1994, for an interview on the *Sundance Film Festival* website. "There is no embarrassment in making public your emotions. You don't always have to hide behind smarts, or wit, or darkness, in order to validate the honest nature of emotions per se."

"There's a certain kind of acting that you do for Atom that follows from the linguistic style of his script," says Don McKellar, who was in ***Exotica*** and ***The Adjuster***. "It asks you to approach your part as subtext-laden. I've never seen him say to an actor: 'more stilted.'"

David Cronenberg passionately defends Egoyan's style. "We both have a horror of the cheap emotional affect of Hollywood movies," Cronenberg says. Both directors deliberately disorient their viewers' emotional expectations by experimenting with structure, acting style, and multiple viewpoints (the character being watched on video by another character who's being watched by you)." It's almost impossible to imagine a film that doesn't do what Hollywood does," Cronenberg argues, "which is to take some very unsubtle point and hammer it in twelve times. If you grow up exposed to the classics, and to great literature, then subtlety and ambiguity should be a part of your expectation for storytelling. That that is no longer the case is a serious, serious problem."

He has a point. We don't hold cinema to the same standards as other art forms. We want movies that lift our spirits or let us weep, and if they make us think, we want to think along pre-drawn lines. "People get mad when the release they're expecting from a movie isn't there," says Cronenberg, "and I'm saying, emotional release is a possibility, but it's not a necessity of cinema. We accept that when we look at a painting or read a book. Why nor in movies? If your private life is so atrophied that you have to go to a movie to find some cathartic emotional experience, then I'd say you're in trouble."

Odd, that the two directors who most consistently reject this Hollywood template live and work within miles of each other. "It's a mystery," says Cronenberg, "and it's suspicious, because we're both Torontonians, both Canadian, and we both come from family backgrounds that are solidly middle-class, very strong, and artistic."

Perhaps their backgrounds make them feel, simultaneously, brave enough and entitled enough to reject the American view of itself as the centre of the universe. "Beneath official Canadian culture," Douglas Cooper argues, "there's always been an extremely coherent subversive streak. I would call it a kind of Northern grotesque. It's a point of view that's very clear-eyed, and nasty. As an educated culture on the margins of empire, we really have something to contribute, because we can gaze at the brutality of empire with a cold eye."

In the case of film, Cooper is referring to the brutality of image-making, to the relentless assault of Walt Disney emotion. John Knechtel, who edits Toronto's *Alphabet City,* argues that Egoyan's films comment on the way our whole world has been altered by "the cinematic paradigm. The structure of perception and the structure of relationships are being retold through Hollywood. People perceive each other with cinematic passion."

Surely, one of the reasons that ***The Sweet Hereafter*** lit up so many critics is that Egoyan played so brilliantly on their cinematic expectations of a tragedy. They expected to sob along with the movie's small-town parents over the loss of little children. They expected to see the bus crash the way they saw James Cameron's *Titanic* sink, in awe-inspiring, heart-in-throat detail. But Egoyan offers no such thing. On the contrary, he makes you realize over the course of the film that that is what you're expecting, and that's your problem, not his: you are the hopeless voyeur.

Unlike Egoyan's earlier films, ***The Sweet Hereafter*** does not simply make that one point. 'In Russell Banks's deeply stirring novel, Egoyan found a rich tale to tell about sorrow and hope and redemption. For the first time, he was able to bring characters to the screen who were fully formed and, dare I say it, readily identifiable to viewers. "Working with someone else's material gave him the courage to open up emotionally," McKellar says.

By the time he had it ready for Cannes, Egoyan knew he'd made his best film. But he was still unprepared for the breadth of the acclaim. Virtually every critic in Europe and North America hailed ***The Sweet Hereafter*** as brilliant. "I think it's safe to say," Don McKellar ventures, "that none of us expected this. We just thought it was another Atom Egoyan film."

On February 12, Egoyan was sound asleep in a New York hotel room, having partied at the Tavern-on-the-Green into the wee hours after the National Board of Review awards dinner. The news broke in a cascade of wake-up calls: he'd been nominated for Oscars as best director, and best writer of an adapted screenplay. He instantly threw his cool Oscar scepticism out the window. "I'm really, really excited about this," he told me a few days later. "I've been watching the Oscars since I was a kid." When I brought up his earlier ambivalence, he said: "Maybe my reticence was a way of protecting myself."

Egoyan is going to continue to need to protect himself, because triumph brings invitations. At the moment, he's working on a script for Mel Gibson's Icon Productions, an adaptation of the spooky William Trevor novel, *Felicia's Journey*. He has already travelled to Ireland to meet Trevor, trying, unsuccessfully, to persuade the author to allow him to transplant the story to Canada. The executives at Icon, he says, were fascinated that a director would actually want to meet a writer.

Now he is trying to persuade Icon to allow him final cut, which he has always taken for granted in Canada. "The big thing now in Hollywood is screenings," he explains. "Short of final cut the producers will give you three screenings, in which the public grades the film. So, nowadays, negotiations with directors are like: 'Okay, we'll let you have a seven, or even a six, but if it gets below a six we get to make changes.' I don't think my films would survive the screening process."

American directors are already used to the process of self-censorship. From the outset, no matter how outre or cutting edge, they must formulate their films with an eye to the sale. "You can go into a meeting with any executive in Hollywood," Egoyan says, "and they are not dumb, bottom-line people. They've all read the same books you've read, they are able to talk about those works in a way that's familiar to you, and yet their survival instinct is different." Money doesn't just talk to these guys. It screams.

Cronenberg agrees. "Contrary, to popular belief," he says, "the people in Hollywood are extremely smart and articulate. What's fascinating is watching the arcane and arabesque systems of rationalization they devise for why they can be so smart and produce such dreck."

A couple of years ago, Egoyan almost got seduced into producing dreck when Warner Bros. signed him to direct a "mediocre thriller." At the eleventh hour, he backed out. "It was so empowering to be able to walk away from that," he says. "To have made *The Sweet Hereafter* instead, outside that system, and brought it in through the back door, is so satisfying."

Icon's picture will not be a back-door enterprise. Egoyan has been getting an earful of cautionary words from his friends. "Atom's wanting to seize the momentum he has built with *Sweet Hereafter* could prevent him from writing another original screenplay," Cronenberg warns, "because it's time-consuming, he'd have to disappear for a year, and he can no longer afford to do that. But your sensibility is not as all-encompassing when you adapt someone else's material. It's one step removed from your own nervous system."

"Atom's on a slippery slope," his longtime producer, Camella Frieberg, says. "And he knows it."

Egoyan is adamant that he can retain his footing. He has no intention of surrendering final cut to Icon, and even less of moving to L.A. "One can be really daunted by the extraordinary persuasion and brilliance of an informed American response," he reflects. "They do it with such an alarming degree of excitement and hype. The only way you can defend yourself is to believe that there should be something more solid and rooted in your own culture to support your sense of self. Why can't we, as Canadians, say that we've earned the right to live here, because we have a responsibility to our own culture?"

In March, Egoyan and Khanjian bought a new house in Toronto, trusting, in part, in a huge increase in his director's fee as a result of U.S. studio backing. On March 3, Egoyan announced to the press that Icon had capitulated, and granted him final cut.

### Atom Egoyan with Richard Porton (interview date Winter 1999)

SOURCE: "The Politics of Denial: An Interview with Atom Egoyan," in *Cineaste*, Vol. 25, No. 1, Winter, 1999, p. 39.

[*In the following interview, Egoyan describes his development of the Hilditch character in* Felicia's Journey, *his relationship with author William Trevor, and the influence of Alfred Hitchcock.*]

Atom Egoyan's *The Sweet Hereafter* (1997) was the Canadian director's breakthrough film. While Egoyan had enjoyed a cult following during the 1980s, *The Sweet Hereafter* appeared on more than 200 'Ten Best' Lists in 1998 and won him a much larger audience. The initial reception for his latest film, *Felicia's Journey,* while respectful, has been considerably less rapturous. This critical ambivalence can probably be attributed to assumptions that Egoyan's talent is not suited to the well-worn thriller genre and a feeling that the new film is less innovative and ambitious than *The Sweet Hereafter.* Cineaste interviewed Egoyan shortly before his new film's American premiere at the 1999 New York Film Festival. He clarifies his decision to adapt William Trevor's novel with his usual lucidity and states his reasons for making a film about a serial killer with an honesty that functions as an implicit reply to his critics.

[*Porton:*] *Do you think that* **Felicia's Journey** *benefits from your status as a foreigner examining Irish and English culture? One thinks of other films about Britain made by outsiders such as Antonioni's* Blowup *and Skolimowski's* Deep End.

[Egoyan:] When you do something from outside, you question your right to take a story and tell it. I did far more research than I really needed to do, since I saw Felicia as the embodiment of every Irish martyr in romance and literature. I went through a number of Irish writers, but inevitably you are looking at it from the outside. There's a distance and that accommodates my style very well, since there's a self-consciousness and a tentativeness to my approach.

I had to deal with my fantasy of both Ireland and the Midlands and then with the reality of what was actually there. With Ireland, there was the shock of realizing that what was in the book is very hard to find now. Ireland is very prosperous and a lot of the towns are all tarted up for the tourist industry. You'd be hard-pressed to find a place which we see in the movie; it's an Ireland from the late Eighties-early Nineties.

The bigger issue was with the Midlands, which we all have engraved in our minds from Blake as the home of "dark, satanic mills." We expect to see faces blackened with soot and chimneys churning out sulphur. It's not like that at all. In fact, I went into a tailspin when we were scouting locations and I realized that there was nothing to distinguish the industrial parks from any in North America. But then you begin to think of how to convey Felicia's initial perception of the industrial park. For example, when Hilditch leaves the car park for the first time, there is a very slow pan around and we see her figure emerge. It's the anonymousness of it that makes it so creepy and the fact that you've decided to train a camera on something which doesn't seem to have any distinguishing features. Then you begin to look at architecture which does look strange from a North American perspective, such as the gasometers, metal Victorian structures which we never had here. And the water cooling towers, which look to us like nuclear silos, appear twice in the film. It becomes heightened and monstrous for us, since we would never have nuclear silos near a major highway!

*Some of the early commentary on* **Felicia's Journey** *compares it to Hitchcock, but your style seems considerably more meditative and less manipulative.*

I see the film as being anti-Hitchcockian, because Hitchcock is all about making the viewer privy to something that the characters aren't aware of. For example, in *Sabotage* we know that a bomb is going to go off and the characters don't. By contrast, my whole filmmaking approach is about trying to enter into the characters' experience about how they would see themselves. The suspense is more about the dislocation between how they see themselves and how they really are, as opposed to traditional Hitchcockian suspense. The only moment that's kind of a homage to Hitchcock (and I'd also say that, from that point on, the film is sort of Hitchcockian) is when Hilditch comes up the stairs and the viewer knows that he wants to kill Felicia. But I'd say that most of it is an attempt to deconstruct Hitchcock.

Hitchcock has had a huge influence on me, so I can't be totally cavalier. Certainly, when it comes to camera movement, composition, and the role of psychology in the movie, there are similarities. But it's kind of misleading for people to go in expecting a kind of Hitchcockian film.

*In a way, this film is more of an essay on the rudiments of the thriller genre than an example of it.*

Directors like Hitchcock seem to know what an audience expects. I can have a fantasy audience in mind, which is infinitely curious and exploratory, and wants nothing more than to be mystified and is very trustful of my intelligence. My audience is not the one that Hitchcock imagined. I assume that the audience might want to be self-conscious and I don't have any fantasies about engendering a collective response. It's antithetical to the way I work, but I imagine that Hitchcock probably found nothing more pleasurable than the monolithic nature of manipulating a large group of people in a dark room. My fantasy is based on quite a subjective journey through my projected imagery.

*Perhaps there's a double edge to the film's style, since it seems that you're trying to create both a creepy ambiance and poeticize the landscape as well.*

Take the conversation that the father has about Irish history within the ruins of a castle. There are two things working here. First, there's the decision that the father makes to take Felicia to that place to tell her that story. He reinforces the impact of that story by putting her in the ruins of a castle that was destroyed by Cromwell and saying that this is the nature of the English monster. Then, there is a point when she's having the abortion and has this dream where the image comes back to her. The castle, which is an edifice used for defending an idea, can be used as a prop for a father telling a story. That's not a conscious decision he made, he just thought it was the right place to take her to tell that story. But there's a latent history there that is being sourced. I find that those sort of things are really fascinating, like the moment when Hilditch takes that little mannequin and says, "Can I keep this?" He's someone who's in complete denial of consciousness, and as soon as he sees this little totem which might represent himself, he uses it to objectify himself. This becomes doubly significant when it comes back later: a shot of him waking up in the morning with this totem is intercut with shots of the castle.

*The poignancy of Felicia's plight is that she's no more at home in Ireland than she is in England.*

What I ultimately found so powerful about her passage is that she comes from a place where oral tradition is very important, where stories are told, where a great-grandmother speaks in an ancient tongue, letters are hand delivered and everything is done by direct contact and transmission. She then enters into this universe where she's lost, but through contact with evil and ultimately through the recitation that Hilditch gives of the names of the women that he's taken away, she uses this oral tradition to reconstruct her own dilemma. That history actually reflects her own experience and she almost has a sacred duty now to commemorate those names. That is very much based on her tradition. Irish culture is all about remembering the names, but the names that her father has given her don't have meaning for her anymore, whereas the names that she's just heard from the mouth of this killer do.

*She therefore gains access to personal history rather than political history.*

Exactly, which is also political history in a different way. Notions of history and retrieval are important in the film. I don't think that Hilditch has any conscious memories, except when he meets her because she's going to be a mother. He finds this disturbing, so when he steals that money from her he goes back, for the first time probably, to an actual organic memory of an original sin when he first stole money. That wallet finds its way back to the end of the film when he's digging her grave. The combination of finding this wallet and the meaning that it has, combined with having to deal with these two female evangelists staring at him, shakes him. It's not what they're saying, but the fact that they're looking at him. He has to return the gaze.

This story seems simple, but the issues are multilayered. After the structural ambitions of **The Sweet Hereafter,** which attempts a portrait of an entire community, I was looking for something more intimate.

*Did the idea of adding the video extracts of Hilditch's victims, as well as the excerpts from his mother's cooking program, come to you early on while writing the script?*

Yes. In the book, he makes reference to his victims as being part of a picture gallery. Trevor envisioned it photographically, but video seemed a natural extension of that. The way it links with the cooking-show videos is related to the fact that he comes to associate the archival evidence as providing access to a control of intimacy. He's been taught to believe that this sort of control is empowering.

*Do these videotapes explain his trauma in an almost psychoanalytic fashion or does his psyche remain opaque?*

I hope it's opaque—in the book it's a bit too literal. That was one of the big problems that I had with the book. The book is beautifully written, but it's actually quite reductive in terms of why Hilditch is who he is. I don't agree with Trevor's psychoanalysis.

Serial killing in our culture has become a job. Films have treated serial killers like lawyers or doctors. It's become so commonplace in our cinema that a shorthand has emerged, and part of that shorthand includes an ignorance of why some of us are genetically encoded to do these kind of things. Studies have demonstrated that if children do very sadistic things, like pulling the wings off flies, that's an indicator. But, as a child, I did certain sadistic things, like burning bugs with a magnifying glass, and I didn't become a serial killer. There are certainly upbringings that can enhance these qualities and others that can hold them in check. I'm cautious about easy explanations and this film isn't about that. All we need to know is that there's a relationship that he has with his own personal history, which is about denial. That's what interests me— the psychology and politics of denial and how that affects both of these characters. She, in a very identifiable and common way, is in the throes of first love and is unable to see how things are. She is incapable of sensing that Johnny has no feelings towards her and that he's a cad. Her denial is very clear, but his is much more submerged and we don't need to reveal it specifically. Trevor felt that he did and I find it a fault in the book.

*Perhaps Trevor is stuck in a literary tradition where he has to tie up the loose ends. On the other hand, earlier in the book, the reader experiences a kind of vertigo as he attempts to figure out what's actually happening.*

That's my favorite part of the book, when you don't actually know what's happening. It's kind of perverse that this was what attracted me to the book. It's sort of like the Russell Banks book where what attracted me was the demolition derby which I didn't even end up filming. In **Felicia's Journey,** I was intrigued with the thirty pages where she escapes and he gradually gains consciousness of the fact that she's left—and once he becomes conscious of that fact he kills himself.

*Appropriately enough, Hilditch's house is both enormous and seemingly claustrophobic.*

The first dolly through the house is taken from the height of a young boy wandering through the house and finally encountering himself in the kitchen. It's the same path he takes at the end as he decides to commit suicide. When you document a house that a person has travelled through many times, there are certain trajectories that are loaded.

It was a great privilege for me to create a set. I had never been able to afford one before. The nature of the films I had done before meant that I had to build rooms in warehouses and wait for trains to stop. You just don't have the control that you do when you're using a huge studio like Shepperton and I took full advantage of that. For instance, when you make a set like that and want to populate it in England, there are prop houses where they've kept everything from every film that's ever been made. I don't know if it's done here. In Canada, we don't have that depth. For instance, I needed a mixer from the 1950s and had five choices of models that had been stored; that seemed really remarkable. When you're making a period film, it's a real treat to be making it in a culture that enshrines the notion of collection.

*It's quite surprising that the British press and public don't take Bob Hoskins seriously as an actor these days.*

He's overexposed in England. He did a whole series of ads for British Telecom and there are a number of films that he makes for that market that we don't see. A lot of people winced when I mentioned that I was planning to use him in the film. It's not like here where he's regarded as a fine actor. He sort of reinvents himself in this film, since we're used to seeing him in very expansive roles. This is very far away from his performance in *Who Framed Roger Rabbit.*

*Did you have as close a relationship with William Trevor on this film as you did with Russell Banks on* **The Sweet Hereafter**?

It was close. I sent him drafts and we met a number of times. The main difference is that Russell loves movies and movie culture. Russell is coming to the opening tomorrow night, but William never would. He's just not into the film scene. Russell was visible and on the set and wanted to be a part of it. William enjoyed reading the drafts, but he is from a different generation and is less interested in the hype and tensions of contemporary film production.

*Although the Hoskins character is the most psychotic of any of your protagonists, you've remarked that, unlike some of your other anti-heroes, he emerges successfully from a pattern of repetition compulsion.*

What I wanted to say is that, unlike some of the male characters, he achieves a kind of ironic breakthrough. Certainly, some of the female characters, like Nicole in **The Sweet Hereafter,** do emerge from their quandaries. Most of the male characters are suspended, and he actually makes a decision to change his life by sentencing himself to death. What I find striking is the that the police will come and find this man hanging in the kitchen and these bodies in the garden. It will be publicized and people will go, "Oh, he got away with it." But, when someone decides to kill himself, he's not getting away with it. By the end of this film, we understand that action even if we don't condone it. That's what makes the film so provocative. I love when people come up to me at the end of the film and ask, "Is it OK to feel sorry for him?"

### Richard Porton (review date Winter 1999)

SOURCE: A review of *Felicia's Journey,* in *Cineaste,* Vol. 25, No. 1, Winter, 1999, p. 42.

[*In the following review, Porton offers a positive assessment of* Felicia's Journey, *noting Egoyan's skill in creating relationships between characters.*]

Neither a straightforward genre film nor a simple portrait of mental aberration, Atom Egoyan's **Felicia's Journey** brilliantly subverts the conventions of the standard Hollywood thriller as well as the cliches of the by-now hackneyed serial killer subgenre. While Egoyan's adaptation of William Trevor's novel possesses superficial affinities to the work of Hitchcock and Chabrol, the Canadian director's more meditative style prevents us—as audience members—from being pawns of an autocratic auteur. The emphasis in this film is less on individual psychosis than on the web of relationships (both social and implicitly political) that engender it.

**Felicia's Journey** promotes a distinctively contemplative form of suspense by recounting the commingled destinies of two mismatched protagonists: Felicia (Elaine Cassidy), an astonishingly naive teenager who yearns for a reconciliation with her unfaithful boyfriend, and Joseph Ambrose Hilditch (Bob Hoskins), a deceptively mild-mannered catering manager from the Birmingham suburbs with a penchant for befriending young women. When the newly pregnant Felicia, in flight from an almost premodern Irish adolescence, travels from her sheltered home to the Midlands' antiseptic industrial landscape (virtually a character in its own right), she has a fateful and near-fatal encounter with Hilditch. And, perhaps most tellingly, both characters are, to varying degrees, suspended in time. Felicia comes from an almost ludicrously verdant Irish village (in sharp contrast to contemporary Ireland's vibrant modernity) where her father treats the Easter 1916 rebellion as an event that might have happened yesterday and her great-grandmother invokes Eamon de Valera's memory in Gaelic. Hilditch, on the other hand, lives in a stodgy, commodious house where he recreates the supposedly more innocent 1950s with mementos from his childhood and syrupy recordings of obscure crooners.

Just as Trevor's novel marked the 'Chekhovian' humanist's newfound interest in the morbid terrain best personified by Patricia Highsmith's novels, Egoyan's film flirts with genre conventions that are, in the final analysis, skillfully deflected. Unlike charismatic killers such as Robert Walker's Bruno in *Strangers on a Train* or diabolically clever madmen like *The Silence of the Lambs*' Hannibal Lecter, Hilditch is an almost laughably banal psychotic. A man with exquisite manners who reveres the memory of his mother, a comically flamboyant TV chef, he fails to conform to the standard movie profile of a homicidal maniac. Despite recourse to violence that appears antithetical to this dullard's placid demeanor (the film itself is resolutely unviolent), his delusional reveries are not much different from the convoluted fantasies of garden variety neurotics in previous Egoyan psychodramas. The perverse alchemy that leads Hilditch to murder the objects of his affection, however, is (quite wisely) never clearly in focus. We only know that this pudgy, incurably lonely man, depicted (in vignettes that are equally farcical and macabre) cooking elaborate dinners for himself that could easily feed a dinner party for fifteen people or more, fancies himself a father figure to young women in need. In a key scene, Hilditch derides a salesman's pitch for an automated catering system, insisting that "food must be served by caring hands." Aptly enough, Hilditch—affable culinary expert—is close to being an automaton himself. Trevor's empathetic but ultimately unsparing portrait of this pathetically frustrated nurturer occasionally resembled a case study that verged on vulgar Freudianism. Egoyan's more detached portrayal of a colorless middle-class Everyman is, paradoxically, more frightening. Hilditch's fondness for kitsch pop music, especially the ultra-derivative ditty, "You Are My Special Angel," drives home the point that sentimentality can often conceal lethal delusions.

The film's boldest departure from its source material involves video interludes chronicling both Hilditch's eclectic gallery of female victims and his mother's zany cooking program. Egoyan once remarked that many of his protagonists were stymied by their "lack of self-awareness." Unable to emerge from a debilitating narcissism, these terminally alienated characters attempt to gain access to an identity that proves elusive by immersing themselves in hyperreal, although ultimately spectral, video images. Even though the source of Hilditch's madness cannot be fully explained, his mistaken belief that this repertoire of images, ritualistically played again and again in his womblike home, provides genuine solace unquestionably promotes his dissociation from reality. His video 'memory lane' only reinforces his mental deterioration: an eclectic assortment of young women (multiracial; innocent runaways as well as prostitutes—he is an equal opportunity killer) appear to him as an undifferentiated mass of wayward girls who have abandoned him. Similarly, his mother Gala's vaudevillian turns as a loopier version of Julia Child (played with brio and a wink to the audience by Arsinee Khanjian) hint at a deep-seated trauma that is never completely revealed. Undoubtedly a mamma's boy, Hilditch's is, nevertheless, far from a Norman Bates clone.

Egoyan's characteristically audacious editing and use of camera movement are also key components of his 'defamiliarization' of the suspense genre. For example, as Hilditch's anxiety reaches its apogee, a few well-chosen images economically pinpoint his festering masochism—a television set displaying a campy moment from Rita Hayworth's performance as Salome is immediately juxtaposed with his memory of Strauss's "Salome," which frightened him as a child. Traveling shots of water towers (adjacent to—but not glimpsed by—Felicia and Hilditch as they travel by car to pay a visit to the murderer's imaginary wife) are much more reminiscent of sequences from Antonioni's *Red Desert* than the shooting style embraced by most thriller directors. These unpeopled glimpses of ordinary industrial appurtenances, both ominous and lyrical, complement the central narrative's oscillation between sinister and poetic moments.

Although Hilditch's growing delirium at times threatens to subsume Felicia's own saga, her painful transition from innocence to hard-won experience constitutes a mini-Bildungsroman. In perhaps the film's cruelest scene, Hilditch accompanies Felicia to a pub where the object of her English quest—caddish boyfriend Johnny—strenuously ignores her. The fact that she is able to survive brutal rejection, as well as the more tangible threat to her life posed by Hilditch, imbues grisly material with cautious optimism. Like Nicole in *The Sweet Hereafter*, Felicia achieves a kind of secular redemption (totally unlike the hokey version of fundamentalist redemption touted by the film's Jamaican evangelist, Miss Calligary) because, against all odds, she is able to leave girlhood behind and become a free woman.

Felicia's self-liberation is far from treacly, but Egoyan is an ironist who eschews the smarminess of what currently passes for social satire in films. Avoiding the cartoonish characters who have become staples in recent facile attempts to unmask suburbia or the nuclear family, he evinces empathy for even his most repellent protagonists. In *Felicia's Journey*, he is greatly aided by the contributions of a gifted cast, particularly the brilliant Bob Hoskins. Known primarily for blustery, exuberant performances, he gives an astonishingly nuanced portrayal of Hilditch—even his tiniest gesture conveys this gentle monster's inner chaos.

**Brian D. Johnson (essay date 13 September 1999)**

SOURCE: "Atom's Journey: Canada's Celebrated Director Reveals the Rite of Passage behind His Cinematic Obsessions," in *Maclean's*, September 13, 1999, p. 54.

[*In the following essay, Johnson considers the unique voice in Egoyan's films and explores the sources of his recurring cinematic themes.*]

Lunch with Atom Egoyan. He arrives late, on the run in a day of interviews. This is Toronto, his home town, but he might as well be on tour. His personal publicist hovers close by; a driver waits at the curb outside the restaurant. Affable and full of energy, Egoyan takes a seat in the corner booth, a dark wood enclosure with a thick curtain that can be drawn for privacy. Should it be open or closed? "Closed," Egoyan suggests. The curtain is drawn and suddenly the booth feels strangely private, like a sleeper compartment on a train. It is the kind of place where secrets could be revealed, with the awkward intimacy that you would expect to find . . . in an Atom Egoyan film. The only question is, how to catch the waiter's eye?

It is the sort of dilemma Egoyan can appreciate. He has built a career out of creating coolly hermetic worlds on film, dramas that are ripe with understated menace and employ none of the usual tricks to catch the eye of the audience. His latest movie, *Felicia's Journey*—which opens the Toronto International Film Festival (Sept. 9 to 18) this week—tells the eerie story of a gentle serial killer (Bob Hoskins) closing in on an Irish girl (Elaine Cassidy) adrift in the industrial barrens of England. There is not a single scene of violence, but there is an overwhelming sense of violation.

Egoyan's films are all about violations of innocence and trust. And, as he eventually reveals over lunch, the theme is rooted in a trauma from his own teenage years that he has been reluctant to discuss until now. "It was a really primal adolescent experience," he says. "The way in which people can camouflage things is absolutely vital to my experience of growing up."

Born in Cairo of Armenian parents, Egoyan immigrated to Victoria with his family at the age of 3. Now 39, he is the most accomplished Canadian director of his generation. With eight features to his credit, he has received two Oscar nominations, five Genies, four prizes from Cannes, five honorary degrees and a French knighthood. He lives in Toronto with his Armenian wife, Beirut-born Arsinee Khanjian, and their five-year-old son, Arshile. Khanjian, who has appeared in all his films, is now a rising star in her own right. And their creative marriage has become the quintessential Canadian immigrant success story, an artful romance of two outsiders working their way from the margins to the heart of the cultural elite.

The name Atom Egoyan, meanwhile, has become synonymous with the peculiar identity of Canadian cinema, which has acquired a reputation for introversion and sexual pathology. But despite his reputation for chilly abstraction, there is a deeply personal sense of compassion that runs through all of Egoyan's films, a fixation on the secrets and lies buried at the core of the nuclear family. From *Family Viewing* (1987) to *The Sweet Hereafter* (1997), Egoyan returns again and again to tales of bereft parents and lost children, stories in which sexuality keeps striking uncomfortably close to home.

Anyone looking at Egoyan's recent movies cannot help but notice a disturbing pattern. In 1994's *Exotica,* a father mourns the violent death of his daughter by ritually doting on a young stripper costumed as a schoolgirl. In *The Sweet Hereafter,* a father carries on an incestuous affair with his adolescent daughter. And now in *Felicia's Journey,* a pregnant teenager slides into the clutches of a paternal predator. Three movies. Three stories of father figures obsessed with teenage girls. It is one thing for a director to keep coming back to the same themes—Catholic redemption for Martin Scorsese, technological mutation for David Cronenberg—but the pattern in Egoyan's work is so specific, so personal and ultimately so creepy, it raises the question: What is at the bottom of it?

The obsession goes back to an experience Egoyan had as a teenager growing up in Victoria, which he has finally agreed to talk about. "There was a young woman," he says, "whom I adored from a very young age, and who was inaccessible to me for the longest time. Later on, it was revealed that there was an abusive relationship with her father. All the clues were there. But it wasn't a society at that point that could read them or respond to them, and I felt kind of helpless about it. So rather than address it, I went into denial over it, like everybody else."

The father's behaviour left Egoyan with a distressing lesson in life and art. "I suppose the thing that confused it more than anything," he says, "is that he himself was an artist, and it was so obvious what was going on, from the work he was doing and presenting publicly and the way he was behaving. But no one could actually talk about it. There was this incredible shroud of secrecy. And I was completely, madly in love with her. From about 13 to 18. And it wasn't until the last year when it became more. . . ." Egoyan pauses. "I feel weird about it, because it's her story," he says. "The pain that she went through was a lot more than mine. I was an observer."

Egoyan never talked to the father about the incest, but ended up in awkward negotiations with him about the terms of his own romantic intentions. "When the father realized I was serious about her," he says, "I had to make promises to him which I ultimately couldn't keep—in terms of keeping my relationship with his daughter platonic. It was a very strange time, because I was living a double life." Complicating things even further is the fact that, for the girl, the incest had an element of romantic delusion. "And that's what *The Sweet Hereafter* explored," explains Egoyan. "What is the experience of incest on the victim when it's not the obvious exercise of violent power, but this blurring of love?"

Egoyan says that he himself had an "ideal upbringing." His parents, Joseph and Shushan, who met at art school in Egypt, are both painters. His mother, now 65, recently mounted her first solo exhibition in Victoria. And when Atom was 10, he remembers going to the provincial museum for a show of his father's work called *Birds*—"which was a very attractive title to the population of Victoria, until they realized these were canvases of dead birds. My father would suspend dead birds around the house. It was a little bit gothic."

His parents, who supported their art by running a small furniture store, "gave me great work models as to what an artist does," adds Egoyan, who worked in the store from a young age. "I became very aware of the mechanics of operating a small business. That gave me a very practical sense of how to manage a production, and how to be modest. And I became very aware of the making of art, and the appreciation of art. I was around it all the time. A lot of my father's friends were artists. And my sister [Eve Egoyan] is a concert pianist doing very unusual music."

But as an Armenian child trying to assimilate, Atom endured a degree of culture shock. He did not speak English when he first went to school. "I remember very clearly episodes where my parents had to explain to the teacher, 'If he says this it means he has to go to the bathroom, and if he says that, it means he's hungry.' I remember saying to a teacher in Armenian, 'I'm hungry,' and then being shown to the bathroom."

Egoyan developed a love for the absurd at an early age, crafting teenage plays in the spirit of Ionesco, Beckett and Pinter, then short films as an undergraduate at the University of Toronto. By the time he made his first feature, *Next of Kin* (1984), at the age of 23, he says he had become "really aware of the fact that identity is possibly a construct."

Much of Egoyan's work dwells on blurred identity, a Canadian "construct" if ever there was one. In *Next of Kin*—which opens with a shot taken from a camera on an airport baggage carousel—a young man joins an Armenian family in Toronto by pretending to be a long-lost son. In *Family Viewing,* a young man learns that his father is erasing the family's home videos by shooting sex scenes with his new wife. A series of shadowy father figures began to emerge in Egoyan's films—the seductive insurance man in *The Adjuster,* the grieving accountant in *Exotica,* the manipulative lawyer in *The Sweet Hereafter.* But none are as dark as Hilditch, the mild-mannered monster played by Hoskins in *Felicia's Journey.*

Based on the 1994 novel by Irish author William Trevor, it is a spare drama that brings two characters together with quiet, claustrophobic intensity. Felicia is a naive 17-year-old from rural Ireland who has come to the English city of Birmingham searching for Johnny, the lover who has left her pregnant. Lost, alone and unable to find him, she is befriended by Hilditch, a quiet catering manager who has made a macabre pastime of collecting and disposing of homeless girls.

Living alone in the gloomy house where he grew up, Hilditch seems locked in a time warp. He spends his nights preparing elaborate meals while watching black-and-white videos of a 1950s cooking show hosted by his dead mother. Played by Khanjian, she is a comically flamboyant character with a French accent who cruelly exploits her son (Hilditch as a chubby boy) on camera. Hilditch's video archive also includes tapes of his victims, recorded with a camera hidden in his Morris Minor. Egoyan has been developing the idea of fetishized video artifacts ever since *Family Viewing.* And by grafting it onto Trevor's novel, along with the burlesque horror of the cooking show, he has placed a surreal signature on an essentially realistic drama.

Repression builds in *Felicia's Journey* with the claustrophobic weight of English weather. Cutting between past and present, Egoyan shifts from Ireland's green fields to Britain's bleak industrial landscape, and from the sharp intolerance of Felicia's Irish-Catholic father to the insidious comfort of her English benefactor. The movie is an underhanded thriller, bereft of catharsis. And as Egoyan slowly tightens the noose of suspense (which turns out to be a slipknot), the stalking, predatory camera seems more sympathetic to the killer than to his prey. "The camera betrays the feelings of the person behind it at all moments," Egoyan explains. "I was far more fascinated in Hilditch than in Felicia. The story of a young woman looking for the father of her child is not as interesting to me, dramatically, as this monster who is responsible for evils beyond description, yet doesn't seem aware of it."

Egoyan's empathy for Hilditch popped into alarming focus during the filming. Hoskins fell sick on the day he was to improvise the videotaped scenes of the victims talking to Hilditch in his car. So Egoyan played the killer's role, which is largely off-camera. "I put on his gloves, I put on his coat, and I had to go through a serial rejection of each of these women in a car," the director recalls. Hilditch's side of the dialogue does not appear in the film, "but when you see him grab one of the women, it's my arm," says Egoyan. "What I realized in the process is that so much of my job is about trying to seduce people. The darkest side of what we do as directors is make people do something they wouldn't do otherwise—and what is Hilditch if not a director?"

So what does the director's wife think of all this, a husband who likens his metier to that of a serial killer? "There is a man of immense contradiction in Atom," says Khanjian. "There is one side of him that is very cynical and obsessed with control. He can be very dark and arrogant. But his vision is humanistic. He is obsessed with the human condition, with how innocence can be abused and how a person is redeemed."

Khanjian is her husband's fiercest supporter and most vigilant critic. "She can be brutal with him," says their friend, actor-director Don McKellar. "She challenges him all the time." Khanjian is especially wary of commercial temptations that come his way. In 1994, when Hollywood was courting him with an offer to make an erotic thriller called *Dead Sleep,* Egoyan says his wife "saw me in the worst kind of delusion." In the end, Egoyan declined to make the film because he wanted to cast Susan Sarandon and the studio insisted he choose from a limited "A-list" of younger, more bankable stars. "We really felt vindicated when Susan went on to win the Oscar for *Dead Man Walking,*" adds the director.

With *Felicia's Journey,* Egoyan explores the thriller genre for the first time, even if he tries his best to subvert it. And the exceptionally sensitive performances that he draws from Hoskins and Cassidy show a huge progression from the archly distanced acting in his early films. *Felicia's Journey* is also the first movie he has not produced himself—he made it for Mel Gibson's company, Icon Entertainment International. And it is the first he has shot entirely outside his own country. (Initially, he hoped to set it in Canada, and make the heroine a francophone girl from Quebec travelling to British Columbia, but Trevor insisted the book's Irish themes were integral to the story.)

*Felicia's Journey* marks a watershed. For 10 years, ever since *Speaking Parts,* Egoyan has launched his movies at the Cannes Film Festival. And with each outing, his international profile has climbed a notch, peaking with *The Sweet Hereafter,* which won three prizes in Cannes and was nominated for two Oscars. Then last May, he showed up with *Felicia's Journey* and came home empty-handed. It was a bit of a shock, given that Egoyan's home-town mentor, David Cronenberg, headed the jury that snubbed the film—especially since it was an open secret that, when Egoyan was on the jury in 1996, he fought to create a special prize for Cronenberg's *Crash.*

According to McKellar, who is friends with both Egoyan and Cronenberg, "Atom took it very personally. It's sad because we have a very close-knit, supportive film community. And Atom has always really admired David." Egoyan hesitates to discuss what he calls "a really loaded issue." But, echoing widespread outrage, he says he was mystified that the Cannes acting prizes all went to non-actors: "There's a dogmatism to the decisions," he says. "The jury was trying to make a statement. And given that there were professional actors on that jury, I don't know what was going through their heads." Khanjian is more vociferous, calling Cronenberg and his jury "stingy" and "self-indulgent."

Cronenberg pleads innocence. "We just reacted to the performances that affected us," he says. "It's happenstance that it looked like a statement." Asked if he and Egoyan are still speaking, he says they have exchanged phone messages. "As far as I'm concerned, there is no rift between me and Atom."

As Canada's leading writer-directors, who both create severely idiosyncratic films, Egoyan and Cronenberg may seem joined at the hip in the public eye. But their visions are radically different. And by now, as a directorial one-man band, Egoyan has marched beyond his mentor's shadow. Working flat-out for the past three years, he has made two features, staged three operas (*Salome, Dr. Ox's Experiment* and his own *Elsewhereless*), and created a delightful short film, *Bach Cello Suite #4: Sarabande,* for a TV series devoted to cellist Yo Yo Ma. Meanwhile, as he explores his passion for music, there is a mounting sense of operatic urgency to his work—in *Felicia's Journey,* Mychael Danna's strident sound track drives the drama with martial force.

Now, Egoyan is ready for a moment of silence. "It's been a real whirlwind," he says, "I'd like to see what happens if I just concentrate on something. I miss the solitude." He will get his chance this fall, with Arshile at school and his wife onstage in Japan and France for three months. After making two movies from novels, he keeps getting asked to do literary adaptations—he just turned down an offer from Icon to adapt D. M. Thomas's *The White Hotel*—and Icon wants to lock him into a multi-picture deal. But the director is keeping his options open. And he has embarked on an original screenplay, which he will only say has "elements of a historical epic."

Egoyan felt a certain romance with the past in making *Felicia's Journey,* which is, after all, an odyssey to the Old World. The movie is set in the present, but as he points out, the characters are trapped in the past, "so it feels like a period film." In a sense, all Egoyan's pictures feel like period films, stories of rituals and artifacts. They also feel like foreign films, in a uniquely Canadian way—portraits from an artist whose journey keeps circling back to the essential strangeness of home.

**Patricia Hluchy (review date 15 November 1999)**

SOURCE: "Starvation of the Soul: Atom Egoyan's Latest Is a Troubling Minor Masterpiece," in *Maclean's,* November 15, 1999, p. 148.

[*In the following review, Hluchy offers a positive assessment of* Felicia's Journey, *arguing that it is less contrived than Egoyan's earlier work.*]

William Trevor's 1994 novel *Felicia's Journey* is a small masterpiece of literary creepiness, a tale of deception told with exhilarating insight. Atom Egoyan's adaptation of the Irish author's book is a small masterpiece of cinematic creepiness, in which the perversion comes with a large measure of humanity. The tale of a guileless 17-year-old Irish girl who leaves home and falls into the hands of a Birmingham psychopath, *Felicia's Journey* shows Canadian film-maker Egoyan, who both directed and wrote the screenplay, to be at the height of his powers. So much about the movie is breathtaking: the acting of Elaine Cassidy as the title character and Bob Hoskins as the man who preys on her, Egoyan's fleet-footed jumps between present and past, Paul Sarossy's cinematography of a landscape blighted by industrial detritus and tangled highways, Mychael Danna's nerve-jangling score. The film is also laden with evocative minor details, right down to the endearingly clunky sandals, made of wood and blue leather, worn by the hapless Felicia.

The story begins with her passage by ferry to England. Felicia is pregnant and hopes to be reunited with the baby's father. But Johnny Lysaght is nowhere to be found. As Felicia walks through the industrial zone of Birmingham looking for the lawn-mower factory where Johnny has told her he works, she meets Joseph Hilditch (Hoskins), a pudgy, middle-aged bachelor who holds the position of catering supervisor in one of the plants Felicia visits on her doomed pilgrimage.

Joseph is a primly aproned, platitude-spouting manifestation of the banality of evil. By day, he is a satisfier of workmen's appetites, a man whose face lights up when the factory kitchen cooks up a tolerable steamed raspberry pudding. He seems as quaint, and as safe, as his vintage forest-green Morris Minor. By night, however, Joseph pursues his sick, probably sexless, fascination with what he calls "lost girls"—mainly prostitutes.

Or he stays at home and makes elaborate meals according to video instructions in an old cooking show featuring his now-deceased mother (Arsinee Khanjian). Embellishing on Trevor's novel, Egoyan has added the detail of the gourmet-TV mom. And it is an ingenious addition. The mother is named Gala, and she is an exotic creature indeed—too exotic, in fact, to be much of a maternal figure. Flashbacks of her taping the show reveal a fabulously turned-out woman with no patience for her morose, overweight son. No wonder Joseph grows up to be obsessed with her, and with food.

With frequent cuts to Gala's program, Egoyan explores the way video can offer a spurious sense of intimacy. And as Joseph methodically prepares a crown roast of lamb or a turkey with all the trimmings, and then dines alone by candlelight, the effect is both pathetic and terrifying. "Food must be served by caring hands," he pronounces, rejecting a pitch from a vending-machine salesman. "It makes us feel loved."

Hoskins is devastating in the role of Joseph, his rough-hewn face shifting from fastidious control to anguish and rage. Cassidy, despite the fact that she has been acting since the age of 5, has the naturalness of a first-time-lucky amateur. Her Felicia is a young woman of transparent emotions and few defences, but with surprising mettle beneath it all.

As in Egoyan's only other adaptation and his most recent movie, *The Sweet Hereafter* (1997), the director's touch here is more emotionally direct, less contrived, than in many of his earlier features. Most astonishing about *Felicia's Journey* is the degree—greater than in the novel—to which it evokes compassion for Joseph. Longtime Egoyan collaborator Danna, meanwhile, has composed a score that is manipulative and obtrusive, but in all the right ways—this is strikingly original, tormented music. *Felicia's Journey* emphatically is not a feel-good experience. But it is an exquisite film.

**Stephen Hunter (review date 19 November 1999)**

SOURCE: "*Felicia's Journey*: Soup to Nut," in *Washington Post,* November 19, 1999, p. C05.

[*In the following review, Hunter focuses on Egoyan's treatment of the serial killer Mr. Hilditch in* Felicia's Journey.]

*Felicia's Journey* offers something new, at least: the figure of the sociopathic killer as lovelorn lonely guy who only needs a nice hug to set him free.

This creepy but compelling image is at the center of the film that director Atom Egoyan chose to make after the sublime *The Sweet Hereafter.* Like *Hereafter,* it is derived from a distinguished text, a prize-winning novel by the highly regarded Irish novelist William Trevor. Its pedigree—including the Whitbread Prize—is unassailably literary, and what distinguishes this serial killer story from many other serial killer stories is what separates serious fiction from pulp fiction: the question of motive. Trevor, unlike, say, Thomas Harris, is at pains to discover what turns a man into a monster and not terribly interested in the flamboyance of that monstrosity.

It is this line that Egoyan follows, and it brings him to the bizarre moral proposition that the slaughterer of at least 10 young girls in England is as much a victim as a villain. You cannot hate Mr. Hilditch. Poor Mr. Hilditch grew up in an unusual milieu. That is, on television. His mother, the domineering, sexy, beautiful Gala (Arsinee Khanjian), was one of the first TV gourmet cooks, back in the old black-and-white days of the '50s. With her dark French charisma and her gigantic maracas, she became a media star, even to the point of endorsing products like a vegetable mulcher. But she also used the son who loved her so desperately, turning him into a little fatty-cakes buffoon. She'd stuff food down his throat, and when he gagged, the camera zoomed in and a nation laughed. See little boy frow up!

Now he's grown up into a fastidious little man who appears to work as the director of food services for a huge factory. He is beloved, if a little weird, as he pads around the plant with little pans of sample food for the hard-hat-wearing forge guys. And how is the bread pudding today, David? Um (gulp), it's fine, Mr. Hilditch.

What nobody knows is that Mr. Hilditch—played with something like Richard Attenborough's smarmy pinkishness by Bob Hoskins—goes home, puts on his apron and vids of his ma's old show, and fixes the meals of the '50s under her guidance with their rich creams and their gleaming breasts of poultry. In his mind, she's somehow still alive, and when he eats, he still occasionally gags. Then he goes out and kills a girl.

The usage of the videotape is interesting, for Mr. Hilditch is a fastidious student of the vid. He has his mother's all arranged by chronology (it's not specified but, yes, these are probably videotapes of kinescopes, since videotape wasn't in wide use in the '50s, so please don't send me any letters), and his experiences with each girl neatly catalogued alphabetically. He may not even know he kills them, at least not in the front part of his brain.

What brings all this to the fore is the arrival of a new girl. This is poor Felicia (Elaine Cassidy), an Irish teenager with her own sad story. Seduced, impregnated and abandoned by a young lout, the poor dear has, even worse, been exiled by her fierce father, because the boy who did her went and, rumor has it, joined the British army, which Dad regards as an act of treason. Now Felicia is over here—the Leeds area—looking for him, though she has no address or phone and, in fact, doesn't even know he's in the service.

At first Felicia is just like the others, easily picked up and manipulated by Hilditch under the guise of his kindness, even as he's veering ever closer to adding her to his tote board. But Felicia is somehow different, more resilient, less pathetic. Mr. Hilditch responds to her more deeply; she stirs something in him he thought long dead; that awakening is the thrust of the movie.

For the record, Egoyan uses the same trick here that he used in *The Sweet Hereafter,* the buried fairy tale. In *Hereafter,* it was the Pied Piper of Hamelin, who drew the children from the village to a hole in the mountain (which was a hole in the ice). Here the ur-story is Bluebeard, the fearsome French nobleman who, it is claimed, murdered his wives in a secret room that he kept locked up. A new wife arrived and was forbidden to open the locked room. But she had to.

There is indeed a locked room in *Felicia's Journey,* which she unlocks, but more to the point, it's his locked heart that she liberates.

# FURTHER READING

## Criticism

Diamond, John. Review of *The Sweet Hereafter*, by Atom Egoyan. *New Statesman* (26 September 1997): 56–57.

    Diamond suggests how a Hollywood version of *The Sweet Hereafter* might have differed from Egoyan's, and argues that the film—unlike Egoyan's earlier works—has a sense of hopefulness beneath the surface.

Egoyan, Atom with Lawrence Chua. "Atom's Id." *Artforum* 33, No. 7 (March 1995): 25–28.

    In this interview, Egoyan discusses his screenwriting process and the importance of colonial power in *Exotica*.

Howe, Desson. "Film Notes: After *The Sweet Hereafter*." *Washington Post* (19 November 1999): N53.

    Howe offers a positive assessment of *Felicia's Journey*, calling it "precise" and "elegant."

Johnson, Brian D. "Bleak Beauty." *Maclean's* (30 September 1991): 68.

    Johnson offers a positive assessment of *The Adjuster*, describing the film as "seductive, subversive and disturbing."

Jones, Kent. "The Cinema of Atom Egoyan." *Film Comment* 34, No. 1 (January 1998): 32.

    Jones discusses Egoyan's body of work and how audiences have reacted to his films.

Kauffmann, Stanley. "Stanley Kauffmann on Films: A Stricken Town." *New Republic* 217, No. 23 (8 December 1997): 30–31.

    Kauffmann offers a positive assessment of *The Sweet Hereafter*, and identifies the film's principal themes.

Klawans, Stuart. Review of *The Sweet Hereafter*, by Atom Egoyan. *Nation* (8 December 1997): 35–36.

    Klawans explores Egoyan's recurring fascination with portraying characters who have recently suffered a loss in their lives.

———. "The Heat in the Kitchen." *Nation* (6 December 1999): 50–52.

    Klawans offers a generally positive assessment of *Felicia's Journey*, noting that the film "is made vivid by Bob Hoskins' endlessly crafty performance."

Merkin, Daphne. "Not Just Child's Play." *New Yorker* 73, No. 36 (24 November 1997): 137–38.

    Merkin offers a positive assessment of *The Sweet Hereafter*, describing the film as an "undidactic study of the survival instinct."

Rayns, Tony. "Everybody Knows." *Sight & Sound* 5, No. 5 (May 1995): 9.

    Rayns compares *Exotica* to Egoyan's earlier films, *The Adjuster* and *Calendar*.

Romney, Jonathan. "This Green Unpleasant Land." *Sight & Sound* 9, No. 10 (October 1999): 34–35, 44.

    Romney offers a positive assessment of *Felicia's Journey*, noting that the film captures the spirit of William Trevor's novel.

Thomas, Kevin. "*Exotica* Offers a Metaphor for Contemporary Sexuality." *Los Angeles Times* (3 March 1995): F10.

    Thomas offers a positive assessment of *Exotica*, calling the film "a haunting fable of loss and desire."

Turan, Kenneth. "Egoyan's Clear Vision Guides Surreal Spin of *Adjuster*." *Los Angeles Times* (5 June 1992): F12.

    Turan contrasts the fragmented structure of *The Adjuster* with the film's elegance and depth.

———. "*Sweet Hereafter* Soars with Silence." *Los Angeles Times* (21 November 1997): F10.

    Turan offers a positive assessment of *The Sweet Hereafter*, describing it as an evocative transformation of the original book.

Wilmington, Michael. "A World of Mixed-Up Media in Egoyan's *Speaking Parts*." *Los Angeles Times* (27 April 1990): F10.

    Wilmington offers a mixed assessment of *Speaking Parts*, arguing that the film is too sentimental and cerebral.

---

**Additional coverage of Egoyan's life and career is contained in the following sources published by the Gale Group: *Contemporary Authors*, Vol. 157; and *Literature Resource Center*.**

# Donald Hall
## 1928-

(Full name Donald Andrew Hall, Jr.) American poet, essayist, memoirist, children's writer, short story writer, editor, playwright, and critic.

The following entry presents an overview of Hall's career through 1999. For further information on his life and works, see *CLC,* Volumes 1, 13, 37, and 59.

## INTRODUCTION

Hall is considered by many to be among America's greatest living poets. He achieved success early in his career, with his poetry collection *Exiles and Marriages* (1955), and his reputation as a poet has steadily increased over time. His later poetry is generally regarded as the best of his career, and some consider it the best of his generation. Critics have compared Hall with such poets as Robert Bly, James Wright, and James Dickey, who favor simple, direct language combined with surrealistic imagery. Hall is also a respected essayist, educator, and editor, and his thoughtful prose—like his carefully crafted poetry—is widely praised for its clarity and integrity.

## BIOGRAPHICAL INFORMATION

Hall was born in Hamden, Connecticut, a middle-class suburb of New Haven, in 1928. He often spent summers at his grandparents' farm in New Hampshire, and his memories of this time and of the rural landscape figure prominently in his poetry and children's literature. Hall attended Phillips Exeter Academy and later attended Harvard University, where he received his bachelor of arts and socialized with fellow poets John Ashbery, Robert Bly, and Adrienne Rich. After receiving a second bachelor's degree from Oxford in 1953, Hall became a member of Harvard's Society of Fellows. It was during this period in which Hall published *Exiles and Marriages.* From 1953 to 1961, Hall served as the poetry editor for *Paris Review.* Hall turned his attention to academia in 1957 and accepted a professorship at the University of Michigan. He eventually left the position in 1975 to begin writing full-time at his family's farm in New Hampshire. He lived at the farm with his second wife, noted poet Jane Kenyon, until her death resulting from leukemia in 1995. An accomplished speaker, Hall was the host of *Poets Talking,* a series of television interviews with poets in 1974, and has given poetry readings at more than 1,500 colleges, universities, schools, libraries, prisons, and community centers. Hall won the Lenore Marshall/*Nation* Prize for his collection *The Happy Man* in 1986 and the National Book Critics Circle Award for Poetry for *The One Day* in 1988.

## MAJOR WORKS

Hall garnered critical acclaim with *Exiles and Marriages,* a landmark in his early career, in which he wrote in a tightly structured style with an extremely formal application of rhyme and meter. The poetry in both *Kicking the Leaves* (1978) and *The Happy Man* reflect on Hall's return to his family's farm in New Hampshire, a place rich with memories and links to his past. Many of the poems explore and celebrate the continuity between generations, as the narrative voice in his poetry often reminisces about the past and anticipates the future. Hall's award-winning *The One Day* is one long poem consisting of 110 stanzas divided into three sections. The poem presents several narrative voices which comment on the meaning of life from the perspective of an individual experiencing the onset of old age. In the first and final segments of the poem, Hall alternates between a male and female narrator, speaking in blank-verse stanzas that expose personal details about their lives. *Old and New Poems* (1990) is divided into nine time periods, collecting revised poems from earlier collections and poems that had not previously been published. The earlier poems are more classical in form, while the later poems mix traditional and modern styles. In *The Museum of Clear Ideas* (1993), Hall examines how individuals cope with change and death. The collection also includes one of Hall's more famous works, "Baseball," which serves as his ode to the American past-time. The poem is structured around the sequence of a baseball game, but instead of innings, it contains nine stanzas with nine lines each. The poems in *Without* (1998) confront Hall's grief over the death of his wife, Jane, and examine the details of his life after her passing. *Without* gives an objective appraisal of Kenyon's illness and relates many of Hall's emotions about being left alone after sharing his life with another. In addition to poetry, Hall has written many prose works. In *Remembering Poets: Reminiscences and Opinions* (1978)—which was revised and expanded as *Their Ancient Glittering Eyes: Remembering Poets and More Poets* (1992)—Hall recounts his conversations with and impressions of poets such as T. S. Eliot, Ezra Pound, Dylan Thomas, and Robert Frost. He has also authored several books on the craft of writing, including *Writing Well* (1974) and *The Weather for Poetry* (1982). In 1993, Hall published *Life Work*, a memoir recounting his life at Eagle Pond Farm and his years working in literature. The book highlights Hall's rigorous daily writing schedule and his bout with liver cancer, which threatened to upset the balance between his life and his work.

## CRITICAL RECEPTION

While *Exiles and Marriages* received a favorable response from reviewers, it is the work from the latter part of Hall's career that has received the most critical acclaim. Lawrence Joseph stated in his review of *Old and New Poems* that Hall's writing "reflects the gifts of a poet whose powers have expanded during his fifties, into his sixties—a rare accomplishment." Reviewers have praised Hall for continuing to be ambitious and challenging in his poetry, while keeping his subject matter firmly rooted in the everyday. They have also complimented the simplicity of his style and the naturalness of his imagery. Many critics were particularly fond of *The One Day,* with Frederick Pollack stating that it "may be the last masterpiece of American Modernism. Any poet who seeks to surpass this genre should study it; any reader who has lost interest in contemporary poetry should read it." In addition to his accomplishments as a poet, Hall is respected by critics as an academic who has made significant contributions to the study and craft of writing. Hall is considered by several of his peers, as Peter Thorpe asserted, to be "one of the few living American examples of an authentic Man of Letters, after the grand old manner of Edmund Wilson and T. S. Eliot."

## PRINCIPAL WORKS

*Fantasy Poets No. 4* (poetry) 1952
*Exiles and Marriages* (poetry) 1955
*Andrew and the Lion Farmer* (juvenilia) 1959
*String Too Short to Be Saved: Recollections of Summers on a New England Farm* (essays) 1961; revised 1979
*A Roof of Tiger Lilies* (poetry) 1964
*An Evening's Frost* (play) 1965
*The Alligator Bride: Poems, New and Selected* (poetry) 1969
*The Yellow Room: Love Poems* (poetry) 1971
*Writing Well* (essays) 1974
*A Blue Wing Tilts at the Edge of the Sea: Selected Poems, 1964–1974* (poetry) 1975
*The Town of Hill* (poetry) 1975
*Kicking the Leaves* (poetry) 1978
*Remembering Poets: Reminiscences and Opinions* (essays) 1978
*The Ox-Cart Man* (juvenilia) 1979
*The Weather for Poetry: Essays, Reviews, and Notes on Poetry, 1977–1981* (essays) 1982
*Fathers Playing Catch with Sons: Essays on Sport (Mostly Baseball)* (essays) 1985
*The Happy Man* (poetry) 1986
*Winter* [with Clifton C. Olds] (essays) 1986
*The One Day* (poetry) 1988
*The Ideal Bakery* (short stories) 1990
*Old and New Poems* (poetry) 1990
*The One Day; and, Poems, 1947–1990* (poetry) 1991
*Here at Eagle Pond* (poetry) 1992
*Life Work* (memoirs) 1993
*The Museum of Clear Ideas* (poetry) 1993
*Death to the Death of Poetry* (essays and interviews) 1994
*Lucy's Christmas* (juvenilia) 1994
*Lucy's Summer* (juvenilia) 1995
*Principal Products of Portugal: Prose Pieces* (essays) 1995
*The Old Life* (poetry) 1996
*The Milkman's Boy* (juvenilia) 1997
*Without* (poetry) 1998
*The Oxford Illustrated Book of American Children's Poems* [editor] (poetry) 1999

*This work was revised and republished under the title *Their Ancient Glittering Eyes: Remembering Poets and More Poets* in 1992.

## CRITICISM

**Donald Hall with Liam Rector (interview date January–February 1989)**

SOURCE: "Donald Hall: An Interview by Liam Rector," in *American Poetry Review*, Vol. 18, No. 1, January–February, 1989, pp. 39–46.

[*In the following interview, Hall discusses his body of work and the state of contemporary poetry and poetry criticism.*]

[*Rector:*] *You've written poignantly about time and generation. Jose Ortega y Gasset had a scheme for generation:*

1–15 Childhood

15–30 Youth

30–45 Initiation

45–60 Dominance

60–75 Old Age, "Outside of Life"

*How have these moments moved in consort with the time of your life, your work, and the scheme of literary generations as you've experienced them?*

[Hall:] Schemes irritate me. Maybe this scheme annoys me because I'm supposed to move "outside of life" in a few months and I'm damned if I'm ready to. Rigidities, separations get my back up. Maybe I left childhood at fourteen and remained adolescent until forty-three. I like the word "dominance"—and I suppose I felt it first at about fifty, though I think I was looking for it from the age of fifteen. So I respond, not by generality on the schemer's level, but autobiographically or egotistically. Chronological skeletons—like somatic or psychological types, like classes, like historical determinism: hell, like the god-damned horoscope!—provide things to talk about, frameworks for discussion. . . . But if you accept them, and not rebel against them, you actively desire the comfort of prison! Everything's done for you; relax: prison . . . or *tenure.*

*In the essay* **"Rusticus,"** *you said you grew up in Hamden, Connecticut, a suburb of New Haven, in a "massclass" neighborhood wherein everyone more or less shared four convictions: "1) I will do better than my father and mother. 2) My children will do better than I do. 3) 'Better' includes 'education,' and education provides the things of this world. 4) The things of this world are good."* **String Too Short to Be Saved** *speaks powerfully for the summer life in New Hampshire you experienced as a boy, but could you say more about the culture and class in which you grew up in Hamden? Have you done better?*

In the suburban neighborhood where I grew up in Connecticut, the houses were like each other; the cars that belonged to the houses resembled each other; the fathers, working at their different jobs, had incomes roughly similar; the mothers weren't supposed to work, and their leisure or volunteer-work decorated the fathers. In school, there were rewards for conformity and punishments for difference. In the culture of the country, where I spent my summers, there was fantastic diversity—in education, aspiration, income, appearance; what you wore, what you ate, what you did for fun: from house to house along the roads and lanes. Eccentricity was a *value*; a major ethical notion was everybody's right to be different. I belonged to the Connecticut culture and longed for the other. I live in the other now—it's not greatly changed—and live by it, observe it, write about it—but of course I will never be truly *of* it. My whole life comes out of the conflict of these cultures—and my choice to love and inhabit the one rather than the other.

*You went to the Phillips Exeter Academy and then to Harvard, Oxford, and Stanford. Did the students at these schools share the cultural and class background you outlined in* **"Rusticus"**? *You then went on to the public, sprawling world of the University of Michigan to teach. What led you to attend these schools as a student, and what went into the decision to teach at Michigan?*

The class structure in England is unlike ours, and I won't try to describe it. Sure, other students at Exeter were mostly from the same suburbs, where people try to resemble each other, but most came from more money than I did. My parents sent me there because they knew it was a good school, I don't think for social reasons at all. They weren't social people. At Exeter the best teachers all came from Harvard; the best students were going there—quickly I knew I wanted to go there. Some Exeter kids came from money that had been around in the family longer. At Harvard I felt less of this: There was more diversity there, at least among the people I knew. Even at that time Harvard was more high school than prep school, trying to get the best high school students from all over the country. They were a bunch of tigers locked in a small cage; I liked that. I tried for a fellowship to Oxford because it was a plum and because it sounded like fun to travel and live in another country. While I was there England was in a bad way economically. I never saw my English friends on the continent during holiday because they were only allowed to take twenty-five pounds out of the country in a year. There were already lots of scholarship boys at Oxford, but I was so separate culturally—older, from another nation. Being an outsider gave me privileges which I enjoyed, privileges to be weird.

One of the reasons I went to the University of Michigan was to get away from the Harvard which I liked so much. After I did the B.A. I spent only three years away at first—Oxford and Stanford—then returned for three more years in the Society of Fellows. There were pathetic sorts around the Square who would take any sort of rotten job in order not to leave Cambridge, or—perish the thought!—go to the *Middle West.* (America's geographical snobbery is repulsive.) I wanted to get away, to try another kind of institution, and Michigan made a good offer. Ironically—probably predictably!—I went to an institution which, within Michigan and nearby states, is considered rather snobbish, rather old school tie. Some students' grandparents and parents had belonged to the same fraternities and sororities—but there were children of lineworkers. I liked that variety, that looseness.

*We both grew up spending our summers with our grandparents on farms, you in New Hampshire and I in Virginia. In* **String** *you wrote of how this shaped your imagination and that residence where imagination and memory com-*

*mingle. Living now on that same farm where you spent summers, what is your memory, your imagination of the large cities?*

I've never lived in a great city. For me, large cities are excitement, energy, vitality, almost mania. When I go to New York I never sleep. Oh, I've lived for a month or two at a time in London, Paris, Rome. Because Cambridge is virtually Boston, and I went to school there, I suppose I *did* live in a big city—but living in a college isn't the same. I contrast the country not to the city but to the suburbs; Ann Arbor is a suburb without an urb. (Technically it's a city.)

This place is no longer a farm but the rural culture remains amazingly intact, although thirty years ago I thought it was vanishing. I love the landscape more deeply all the time; I am content sitting on the porch and gazing at Kearsarge, or walking in the woods. Carol Bly speaks somewhere of writers who are "mindless nature describers." Touché; I guess I'm a mindless nature lover, but I love also the independence and solitude of the country, which is by no means only a matter of population density. I don't suffer from the deference, mostly ironic, that hangs around writers in universities; I'm the "fellow over there who writes books for a living" and that's a freedom.

*Your work has been haunted not only by the grandfather but the father. Did your father encourage your becoming a writer?*

My father was soft and volatile, a businessman who hated being a businessman and daydreamed for himself a life in the academy—probably prep school rather than college—where everybody would be *kind* to everybody else. He read books; mostly he read contemporary historical fiction like Hervey Allen and Kenneth Roberts. He was finicky about good prose and suffered from polysyllabic tendencies, especially if he was depressed: "It is necessary to masticate thoroughly." Politically he was conservative and not very thoughtful. He wept frequently and showed feelings which other men would hold back. He desperately wanted people to like him and many did. He was nervous, continually shaking; quick, alert, sensitive, unintellectual. When he was forty-two he hemorrhaged with a bad bleeding ulcer and remained sickly until he got lung cancer at fifty-one and died at fifty-two. As an adolescent I needed to feel superior to him; when I was about twenty-five, when my son was born, I felt reconciled. I don't think we talked about matters of great substance but we could love each other. He read my things and mostly praised them, but I don't think either of us wanted to talk about them. He tried to encourage me in one direction, constantly, by telling me that my poetry was just fine but my prose was really great. . . . Some of this at least was his desire that I might possibly be able to make a living. When he realized that I was going into teaching, it pleased him because of his imaginary academy.

*Your new book,* **The One Day,** *is in many ways a departure from* **Kicking the Leaves** *and* **The Happy Man,** *both in its elliptical form, its being a book-length shoring of fragments, and its engagement with the very old and the very new, aside from your personal remembered past which sets much of the tone in the two books before. How do you account for this shift? One section of* **The One Day** *was printed in* **The Happy Man.** *What made you decide to foreshadow the long poem by printing* **"Shrubs Burned Away"** *there? Had you yet seen the shape that* **The One Day** *would assume?*

If you look at everything from the beginning in 1955, there is lots of moving about and shifting. Surely you're right that the form of *The One Day* is modernist, with its multiple protagonist—but I guess I don't want to. . . . Really, I don't want to talk about the form of it. It's new; I'm still finding out what I did.

The poem began with an onslaught of language back in 1971. Over a period of weeks I kept receiving messages; I filled page after page of notebooks. If I drove to the supermarket, I had to bring the book and pull over three or four times in a few miles to transcribe what was coming. It was inchoate, sloppy, but full of *material*: verbal, imaginative, recollected. And it was frightening. After a while the barrage ceased, but from time to time over the years more would come—with a little label on it, telling me that it belonged to this *thing*. (In my head for a long time I called it *Building the House of Dying*.) The first part was there in inchoate form, much of the first two of **"Four Classic Texts,"** much of the "one day" theme in the third part. Every now and then, over the years, I would look at these notebooks, and feel excitement and fear. In 1980 I began to *work* on it; to try to do something with these words. First I set it out as a series of twenty-five or thirty linked free verse poems: Nothing marched. I worked on it for a year or two; I remember reading it aloud to Jane one time, and when I finished I was full of *shame*! Shame over what I revealed, shame over bad poetry; after that, I couldn't look at it for a year.

At some point early in the 1980s, Robert Mazzocco suggested casually in a letter that I ought sometime to write a book of linked poems, like Lowell in *Notebook* or Berryman in *Dream Songs*. Thinking of this notion I developed my ten-line stanza, making some into almost-discrete ten-line poems, using others as stanzas. I thought of Keats's *Ode* stanza, developed out of the sonnet and the desire to write the longer ode form. This notion helped me get to work: bricks—cement blocks?—for the house. I worked with these stanzas for a couple of years, then maybe in 1984 developed a three-part idea that *somewhat* resembles the present version, except that the middle part is totally different. I showed a draft to a few people. I remember Bly saying, with his usual diffidence, that the first part was the best thing I had ever done and the second part was the worst thing I had ever done. The second part was a problem until I worked out the notion that turned into **"Four Classic Texts"**; I stole "Eclogue" from Virgil, which always helps. I still thought the third part was my real problem, and sometimes doubted that I would ever finish the whole—because I wouldn't be able to make the third part.

When I put *The Happy Man* together I had **"Shrubs Burned Away"** more or less finished, **"Four Classic Texts"** just beginning, and **"In the One Day"** lying about in pieces. I thought it would be ten years before I would be able to finish the poem as a whole, if I ever did. I had no notion that I might finish it within a couple of years. But I think that printing **"Shrubs"** in *The Happy Man* allowed me to finished the whole poem. Response was encouraging . . . and some reviews helped me understand what I was doing, like David Shapiro's in *Poetry,* with his reference to Freud and the movement from hysterical misery to ordinary unhappiness!

*What about your work in children's books?*

I've worked on children's books for twenty-five years, starting when Andrew was a little boy, and I've written many—but only published four. The first was **Andrew the Lion Farmer,** which I may rewrite and reissue. That one came out of story-telling with Andrew when he was four years old. I made up lots of stories. Then one day he said he had a great, scary idea: He was going to go to the lion store and buy a lion seed and grow a lion from a pot! . . . Wow! I was *off!* Now I don't have four-year-olds around anymore—maybe I'll make up stories for grandchildren one day—but there's a permanent four-year-old in my head, to whom I tell my stories. I've worked on three in the last year, but none is any good. If you have the proper shape, the *fable,* maybe they're not so hard to write—economy, limits of diction, right details. . . . But finding the fable is hard! For each of my juveniles, the publisher's found the illustrator, asking my approval; then the illustrator has asked me questions, maybe shown me samples. I've been fortunate: Barbara Cooney, Mary Azarian.

*Does the war of the anthologies (yours and Pack's and Simpson's versus the Donald Allen anthology) stay with you to this day? (Even though you included the work of Ginsberg, Snyder, and others in a later anthology you edited for Penguin?) What young Turks have you lived to see become old Deacons?*

The war of the anthologies was real enough, back at the end of the fifties. For some nostalgic and sentimental people it still goes on; ah, the barricades! They remind me of people in my parents' generation, who lived out their lives in nostalgia over Prohibition. Bathtub gin! Speakeasies! . . . I speak without disinterest, because I am still loathed here and there as a leader of the Eastern Establishment, Mr. Hallpack Simpson, Enemy, Archbishop of Academic Poetry! . . . People want to relive their youths, when good was good and bad was stanzas.

For the most part good poets want no part of it. Creeley and I, Ginsberg and I, were famous enemies . . . but we stopped twenty-five years ago. In 1961, Denise Levertov, who was poetry editor at *The Nation,* asked me to review Charles Olson's first *The Maximus Poems.* Ecumenism was already there. In 1962 I did my Penguin with Levertov, Creeley, and Snyder, only five years after Hallpack. (Five years is a long time when it starts in your twenties.) By 1961 I was abashed by the rigidity that defended my citadel when I was in my mid-twenties.

I don't think that *particular* war endures except for nostalgic die-hards—but there will always be outs and ins; and the first shall be last: sometimes. I see geographical complacency and enmity now. What is a Los Angeles poem? (I don't think there's a New Hampshire poem.) For the most part, geographical groups are diffident folk trying to build castles to feel safe in. To hell with it. I want to be a poet by myself, not a New England poet or a deep image poet or what have you. In my own generation in America, the poet I admire the most is not considered a member of my gang. Robert Creeley.

*Those anthologies provided a dialectic for their time. Does such a dialectic exist now, or is it a time of synthesis, revision, mannerism, or utter impasse? Was the aesthetic distance between your and Allen's anthology a real one? Are you ever tempted to edit another anthology of younger poets, at your age?*

I've been asked to edit an anthology of the young and I have refused. Let the young edit the young. I could do it—but the passion would not be there, and if I made fewer gross mistakes the whole thing would be a big mistake. I don't like recent anthologies of younger poets because they are too damned big. Out of generosity or whatever, probably whatever, they include too many aspirants and contribute to the confusion of numbers.

I don't really think there's a dialectic now though it seems so to some. Metrical poets against the world. Free-verse plain-talk poets against the world. Language Poets against the world. Narrative poets against the world. There's a comfort in being *out,* and people warm themselves by that cold fire. But conflict *does* make energy. Maybe it's a time of warring tribes, Balkanization, rather than a time of dueling superpowers. Oh, it wasn't really superpowers ever, not even back then. . . . Allen Ginsberg, Frank O'Hara, Robert Duncan, Denise Levertov, and John Ashbery did not resemble each other.

*What's good about growing older?*

What's bad about growing older is the knowledge that you have less *time,* the frustration that you will not live to write the books or the poems; or to read all the books you want to. What is good, paradoxically enough, is patience. With less time I feel or act as if I had more. When I begin a poem of any ambition, I know that I will be working on it five years from now; I *sigh* a little . . . but I get on with it. I feel more energy, need less sleep, feel more excitement about work than I did when I was thirty or forty. I've been lucky in my second marriage, in living where I want to live; these are not inevitable results of aging.

*Simpson says he has scolded you for writing so much about the business of poetry—the number of books sold, number of readings, etc. What do you think about that? (Rexroth also wrote of these matters, yes?)*

Louis and I fight about lots of things. He was outraged when I wrote an article about poetry readings. I write essays in poetic theory, and essays of appreciation, but from time to time I write essays of fact. I am interested, for example, in how writers make their livings: *New Grub Street*, biographies. Think of Emerson making his living by traveling around the country, at first by steamer and stagecoach, lecturing week after week—like Robert Bly. It annoys me that people generalize, as if facts were common knowledge, when they don't know the facts. One constantly hears how poetry sells less than it ever did—even publishers say so—and the numbers are different. The *facts* don't necessarily have anything to do with quality—I grant Louis that—but let's find out the facts before we generalize. If poets typically make a living as teachers, is their workday unrelated to the poetry that they write? I used to be fascinated by all the English poets who lived by their wits free-lancing. A couple of centuries ago a good many were vicars. The poetry reading must explain a great deal—good and bad—about the kind of poetry that is written today. There is also the phenomenon of the creative writing industry.

*What do you think accounts for the dearth of polemics in current writings about poetics? Compared to Pound and Lewis's* Blast, *Bly's* The Fifties, *why do we see so few picking up the cudgel these days? Is it part of an "I'm okay; you're okay" relativism and "Make Nice" culture, or just a period of exhaustion, politeness, or fear?*

Compare the reviews in English magazines! Nastiness is a dumb convention over there as our nambypambyness is a dumb convention here. "Boost Don't Knock," said the Boosters Club. How many poets have you heard say that they don't want to review anything unless they can praise it? Oh, I don't believe in taking a cannon to kill a flea. It's a waste of time to write a savage review of a book that nobody is going to read. But I believe in taking a cannon to kill a flea continually described as an eagle. I've tried to do it once or twice.

*What do you think about creative writing programs being separated from English Departments and being put under the aegis, say, of a Fine Arts Department, along with dancers, musicians, theater people?*

Separating creative writing from the regular English Department is a disaster. "Here are the people who can read; here are the people who can write. People who can write can't read; people who can read can't write." Wonderful. Specialization is a curse, especially for poets. Separate departments divide old poetry from new. Some places have literature departments *within* creative writing departments, where writers teach reading to would-be writers. But the value of writers to English Departments lies not in teaching of creative writing; it's their teaching of literature classes for regular undergraduates or graduates. Of course most Ph.D.s are dopes; so are most poets. Undergraduate English majors—or engineers and nurses taking an elective—suffer because they never get to be taught by a writer. The faculty suffers because separations make for complacency; nobody's challenging you with an alternative; but the teacher of creative writing suffers most. When you teach literature you spend your days with great work—reading it, talking about it, reading papers about it. Great literature rubs off and you *learn* by teaching, by encountering what you don't know well enough, teaching it to people who know it even less. This separation makes for narcissism, complacency, and ignorance: It's the worst thing that has happened with the creative writing industry. People spend whole lives talking about line-breaks and *The New Yorker*!

*The first readers for your poems—Bly, Kinnell, Simpson, Bidart, Orr, and others. . . . How have their readings changed and developed over time?*

Jane Kenyon is my first reader and has been for fifteen years. Robert Bly has read virtually every poem I've written for forty years. Simpson, Snodgrass, Kinnell. . . . These people have helped me enormously through the years. For a while in our twenties Adrienne Rich and I worked on each other's poems. When we lived near each other, Gregory Orr helped me. I haven't known Frank Bidart so long but he has been extremely helpful; Robert Pinsky on occasion; Wendell Berry very often. Bly's reading has changed the most. He used to cut and rewrite; sometimes I took his corrections and put them in print: more often they showed me what was wrong and helped me make my own changes. More recently he has taken to speaking more about the underneath of the poem, touching the text less. Galway is a marvelous editor, a great cutter. Snodgrass is superb at a Johnsonian reading, following syntax and implication, allowing himself to be puzzled.

*You're one of the few writers your age I know who still reads and comments on the work of younger writers, aside from people who formally teach or are busy writing blurbs. Most writers, once they reach fifty or so, confine themselves to reading the work of their own generation and work of the distant past. Why has this been different for you?*

I keep looking. I'm *curious*: What's happening? What's going to happen? I've seen nothing so extraordinary as the increased *numbers* of poets, people with at least some ability; the numbers especially of young women, compared to earlier generations, including mine. Because I was so rigid when I was young, I try to stay open to kinds of poetry alien to my own; of course openness can become a mindless relativism or nambypambyness. You have to worry: Do I just want them to *like* me? One thing I learned ten or twenty years ago: If you read something that upsets you, that violates every canon you ever considered . . . look again, look harder: It might be *poetry*. This notion helped me read Frank Bidart. I read the Language Poets without great success, but some please me more than others: Perelman, Palmer, Hejinian, Silliman.

You can't keep up forever. I look into as many as six hundred new books a year. I'm not telling you that I read every poem; I get tired. Like everybody else I get tired reading the same poem over and over again, but it's not only that. When I was in my twenties Richard Eberhart, who was only fifty, told me that he could no longer tell the young apart. He was not being insulting; he was complaining, not bragging. I suppose it happens to everyone. Maybe it begins to happen to me; but I remain avid to *keep up*. I suppose the feeling is more acquisitive than altruistic, but from time to time I can help someone. On the other hand, I continually get booklength manuscripts by mail from strangers, usually wanting me to find them a publisher. I cannot even read them all. Too much!

*Your work as an editor for* The Harvard Advocate, The Paris Review, *the Wesleyan poetry series, Harper and Row, the University of Michigan series, and* Harvard Magazine—*how has this affected your life? What advice might you have for editors, for a long life spent tending to the work of other poets?*

When you edit you impose your own taste. Especially when I was younger and passionate about the work of my own generation, I wanted to impose my taste on *everybody*. Of course at this point I no longer agree with all my old taste; but I don't disavow the motive. Other editors worked a counter-taste. Conflict makes energy, and I'm all for it. I started the Poets on Poetry series with the University of Michigan Press because I wanted to be able to read the books. I'd read an article here and there by this poet or that, but when I wanted to lay my hands on an essay I couldn't find it. I made the series in order to preserve fugitive and miscellaneous pieces—interviews, book reviews, full dress articles, what have you.

Advice: Never edit by committee! Advocate, disparage, make public what you love and what you hate! When you stop loving and hating, stop editing.

*The Michigan Series, Poets on Poetry—Robert McDowell said in a review of the series that "The Mum Generation Was Always Talking." Which ones are you proudest of? How do the books sell? I have the suspicion, along with McDowell, that if this series were not done we would have precious little record of the poetics of your generation. Did growing up, coming to fruition in the shadow of the New Critics inhibit poets from writing prose about their poetry, from writing any kind of criticism at all? W. S. Merwin once said it had that effect on him. . . .*

Yes, many of us felt the way Merwin speaks. You had a feeling that some older poets would *rather* write an essay than a poem! And we reacted. Now there's a further reaction, parallel to and symptomatic of the separation of the English department from creative writing, which says that if you think about poetry—or utter thoughts about it, or allude to any poet born before 1925—you're a pedant. Bah!

*How long did you write textbooks before you could count on any royalties from them as a basis for your income as a freelance writer?*

When I quit teaching I had no confidence that my income was great enough to support my family, with my children going to college. At that time **Writing Well** made more money for me than any other book, but I couldn't count on it. Really, it hasn't been textbooks that have supported us. My income derives from such a variety of sources—textbooks, juveniles, trade books—many old things bring in a pittance every year: poetry readings, magazine sales. . . . **Writing Well** doesn't sell so well as it used to; other textbooks help but I don't rely on them. The many sources do a couple of things: They provide extraordinary variety in the work I do; and they have the virtues of a multiple conglomerate: if one sort of writing dwindles—if I lose interest or the market crumbles or my ability diminishes within a genre—there's something else to pick it up. Of course these advantages are accidental; I didn't become so various on purpose. I always take pleasure in trying something new.

*Bly looks at the world as a Jungian and you as a Freudian. How has Freud affected your view of things? What have the insights of psychology, and psychoanalysis in particular, meant to you and your generation of poets?*

I started reading Freud in 1953. Ten years later I started psychotherapy with a Freudian analyst, the only analyst in Ann Arbor who would do therapy. Reading Freud was exciting and gave me ideas; I could have found much the same in Heraclitus: Whenever somebody shows you north, suspect south. Later, the experience of therapy was profound. It touches me every day and it goes *with* the poetry rather than against it. You learn to release, to allow the ants—and the butterflies—to come out from under the rock; but first you have to know the rock's there! The names of the things that run out are up to you. Psychotherapy properly is never a matter of the explanations of feelings, nor of "Eureka!" as in Hollywood. It is a transforming thing. It makes your skin alert; it builds a system of sensors. Jung, on the other hand, seems a mildly interesting literary figure, full of fascinating ideas and disgusting ones mixed together with more regard for color than for truth. Freud is as nasty as the world is, as human life is. Jung is decorative. Freud is the streets and Jung is a Fourth of July parade through the streets, a parade of minor deities escaped from the zoo of polytheism. Freud has the relentlessness of monotheism.

*Will you ever write an autobiography of your adult life?*

No.

*You came to Whitman in your middle age? Some came to him early and take his words as scripture (I think of Ginsberg and Kinnell, particularly, here) and others arrived at him later, such as yourself and Richard Howard. What do you think might account for this?*

It was my good fortune that I delayed Whitman, but as so often the provenance of the good fortune was dumb. I grew up reading poems the new critical way, which worked for Donne, and Hart Crane, but didn't work for Whitman. When I tried reading him he looked silly. My inadequacy saved him for me. He was brand new and exciting when I found him in middle age—by which I mean thirty or thirty-two.

*Who, aside from writers, have been your most important teachers?*

Henry Moore. I spent a good deal of time with him, talking with him, watching him work. He had the most wonderful attitude toward work and his art. He was interested only in being better than Michelangelo, and he knew he never achieved it; so he got up the next morning and tried again. He was a gregarious man who learned to forego companionship for the sake of work. He knew what he had to do. He remained decent to others, although it is difficult; people make it difficult for you when you're that damned famous. He knew the difference between putting in time—you can work sixteen hours a day and remain lazy—and really working as an artist, trying to *break through.*

*How would you place your poems among the poems of the past? I'm thinking here of Keats's statement, which you mentioned in* **"Poetry and Ambition,"** *that "I would sooner fail, than not be among the greatest." You've also wisely said that we are bad at judging our own work—we either think too much of it or too little of it? But take a crack at it?*

I can't place my poems among the poems of the past and I doubt the sanity or the intelligence of people who say that they can. When Keats said that he would "sooner fail than not be among the greatest," note that he did not tell us that he *was* among the greatest. He *wishes* to be among the English poets when he is dead; he does not tell us that he already *is.* When I was young I had the illusion that at some point or other you would *know* if you were good. I no longer believe that such knowledge is possible. Some days you feel you're terrific; some days you feel you're crap. So what? Get on with it.

**The One Day** *works with the kind of "multiple protagonist" voice we find in "The Waste Land." Why did you make this choice, rather than staying in the fairly mono-lyrical voice which has before characterized much of your work?*

Picasso said that every human being is a colony. An old friend of mine said that she was not a person but ran a boarding-house. One of the many problems with the "mono-lyrical" is that it pretends that each of us is singular.

*Your work is your church. Have you always been Christian? How does being a Christian enter your work? Isn't the absence of a god (or gods) or an agnosticism an important part of much contemporary poetry? How do you see your work amidst that? If it is something you shy from speaking of, why do you shy from it? Better left unsaid, bad manners, or just refusing to talk about politics and religion and politics at the dinner table?*

I was brought up a Christian, suburban Protestant variety. When I was twelve I converted myself to atheism. During the years I spent in the English village of Thaxted, I used to go to church every Sunday, telling myself that I went because the carving and architecture were so beautiful, because I loved the Vicar (high church and a Communist), because the ceremony was beautiful. . . . Now I think I was kidding myself, in saying that my feelings were aesthetic. Yes, I am shy of speaking about it. The figure of Jesus is incredibly important, the astonishing figure from the Gospels. I used to think that people who went to church were either swallowing everything or pretending to, hypocritically. Now I know that intelligent practicing Christians often feel total spiritual drought and disbelief; still, even in such moments, ancient ritual and story can be entered, practiced, listened to, considered. . . .

*Not too long ago you did a review of small, literary presses for* Iowa Review. *John Hollander has said that when he was first publishing you could count on a few of the elders to let you know what kind of noises your work was making. Very few older writers now review the work of younger writers, or emerging presses, except to write blurbs for them. Why is this? What is your "policy" about writing blurbs, and why?*

Thirty years ago I was asked to write blurbs for a few books. I was flattered to be basked, and wrote the blurbs. When the books came out I looked like an ass. Then I looked at other peoples' blurbs; *they* looked like asses. There are honorable exceptions but almost every blurb is foolish. The formula for a blurb is an adjective, an adverb, and a verb which usually combine opposites. X is both free-swinging and utterly orderly; Y is classic and romantic; Z is high and at the same time, amazingly, low. Many book reviewers review blurbs rather than the poetry. Blurbs are the Good Housekeeping Seal of Approval. I think it's far worse in poetry than it is in fiction or anything else. Although doubtless many poets write blurbs out of generosity, it doesn't look that way; it gives vent to the widespread notion that poets live by taking in each other's laundry. It hurts poetry. It's done because publishers are too lazy to name what they're printing. Almost always, it would be better to print a poem or an excerpt from a poem . . . but, oh, these terrible blurbs. I refuse to do it.

Although I've refused 2,457 times, although I've written essays against the practice, I still receive two hundred and fifty or three hundred requests a year to write blurbs. How could I add three hundred books and three hundred mini-essays to my life every year? This is *not* my reason for refusing to do them but it would be reason enough. When publishers quote from reviews, excerpts from journalistic occasions, nobody can stop them. Blurbs are *pseudo-reviews,* and they appear to be used in lieu of dinner invitations, thank-you letters, and gold stars. They're nacreous.

Reviewing is in terrible shape. There's more poetry than ever—more readings, more books, more *sales* of books—and less reviewing. And worse reviewing. Literary journalists like Malcolm Cowley, Louise Bogan, and Edmund Wilson made their livings, in large part, by writing book reviews. Their descendants have tenure instead and teach Linebreaks 101. *The New Yorker* by appointing Helen Vendler resigned from reviewing poetry. *Atlantic* and *Harper's* and the old *Saturday Review* reviewed poetry regularly; no more. *The New York Review of Books* isn't interested in poetry and it is stupid when it pretends to. *The New York Times* is at its worst on poetry, especially under the current editor. What's left? *The New Republic* and *The Nation* are honorable; there are the quarterlies, each of them read by few people. *APR* reviews little. We suffer from a lack of intelligent *talk* about poetry. I don't know why. Maybe it's the same cultural separatism that splits creative writing and literature in the university, an epidemic of ignorance, willful know-nothingism. Many young poets if they criticize poetry at all adhere to the philosophy of the booster club, Boost Don't Knock. When Vendler is the leading critic of contemporary poetry we're in a bad way. She can write a sentence but she has *no taste*. She's a bobbysoxer for poets she croons over: some good, some bad, she can't tell the difference. I can't imagine why she chose this line of work.

*You went to Harvard with Ashbery, Bly, O'Hara, Koch, Davison, Rich, and others. You said you dated Adrienne Rich. More to say on The Poet's Theatre started there?*

Harvard 1947–51 was a lively place. There was a wonderful independent theater group, down at the Brattle. We started the Poet's Theater out of the coincidence of theatrical and poetic activity, and the momentary ascendency of poor old Christopher Fry; of course Eliot worked at poetic drama. Now, the Poet's Theater never produced anything memorable, but it was another center where energy gathered.

At the *Advocate* we sat around and argued all night. Koch, Ashbery, Bly. Of course O'Hara was around, and Rich. Bly became my best friend. He and I doubledated, with Rich my date. I think Adrienne and I went out twice. At least once I was *awful*: I got pissed and argued with Bly, showing off. Adrienne was *polite*. Much later, when I was married and at Oxford and she was living there as a Guggenheim Fellow, we got to be friends, and we were close for quite a while. I feel gratitude to her, and affection. . . . Bly remains my best friend. O'Hara and I were friends for a while, then we quarreled over something or other. . . . He was wonderfully funny and alert and lively, a nifty spirit. Ashbery was intelligent and quiet and smart and talented. It was a good time. We competed, you might say.

*You've championed the work of poets as different as Robert Creeley and Geoffrey Hill. What accounts for the catholicity of your taste?*

Sometimes I fear that my catholicity is another name for mindlessness . . . but I don't *really* think so. I like to say things like, "If you can't admire both Hill and Creeley, you can't read poetry." (That isn't true either.) Hell, Creeley resembles nobody so much as Henry James. Take a late Henry James sentence and break it into two-or three-word lines and see what you get. Hill makes the tensest language in the universe, with more sparks flying between adjacent words than any other poet since Andrew Marvell. Both are geniuses. Of course they can't read each other. I'm delighted to say that Helen Vendler can't read either of them.

*How do you avoid the whining and the bitterness?*

Well, to start with, I whine bitterly a whole lot. . . . They *are* a waste, and they hurt—reason enough to avoid them. You feel bitter about trivial things: *They* have left you out of the Final Anthology—the last bus to the Immortality Graveyard. Or: Everybody *else* gets this prize.

But . . . there are things I try to remember, which help: All prizes are rubber medals. All grapes are sour as soon as you taste them. I haven't won the Pulitzer; if I ever win it, within five minutes I will recollect all the dopes, idiots, time-servers, and class-presidents of poetry who have won the Pulitzer; I will know that getting the Pulitzer means that I'm no damned good. Needless to say, I still want to undergo this disillusion!

Also, it matters to remember: *You're never going to know whether you're good*. Nothing in the inside world stays secure. Nothing in the outside world—like three Nobels for Literature in a row, retiring the trophy; like the sale of one million copies of your collected poems in two weeks; like effigies of your person selling in K-Marts from coast to coast—will convince you that you're any damned good. So: Give up the notion; what's left? What's left is work.

Of course you'll still feel annoyance and anger when you're abused. When somebody says something nasty, you can't get the tune out of your head. Words burn themselves into your brain the way an electric needle burns a slogan onto pine; you etch-a-sketch the unforgivable words onto your skull. It would be good not to read reviews but it's impossible, because if a critic gets nasty there's someone out there who'll xerox the worst parts and mail them to you. The emperor was right to execute the messenger.

But . . . I know so many aging poets, who ream their brains out with range over mistreatment, neglect, slights both imagined and true. A terrible thing to watch! Because I've seen it so much, I extend energy fending rage off—whining and bitterness—within myself, explaining to myself, over and over again, how the reputation stock-market rises and falls as irrationally as Wall Street does; remembering literary history and all the *famous* poets no one has heard of; reminding myself: *Get back to work*.

## Bill Christopherson (review date Winter 1990)

SOURCE: A review of *The Ideal Bakery*, in *Studies in Short Fiction*, Vol. 27, No. 1, Winter, 1990, pp. 121–22.

[*In the following review, Christopherson offers a positive assessment of* The Ideal Bakery, *calling Hall "one of contemporary literature's gourmet chefs."*]

The characters in Donald Hall's first collection of short stories, *The Ideal Bakery,* are mainstream, and their plights are all too recognizable: a divorced father trying to get back in touch with his bookish nine-year-old during a weekend fishing trip; a middle-aged professor trying to rekindle a relationship with an embittered former lover; a graduate student of literature whose stationery-store-proprietor husband will never be the romantic she dreams of. But that is not to say the stories are common. On the contrary, Hall shows uncommon sensitivity in treating themes like loneliness, loss, and the erosion—or demolition—of innocence by experience.

In the title story, the narrator reminisces about the breakfasts he and his father used to share at a local bakery, where they would chat about the Brooklyn Dodgers' prospects and banter with the shop's proprietors, Gus and Mrs. Gus. This plotless reminiscence ("no story at all," apologizes the narrator: "a boy and his father eat crullers") is followed by a coda cataloguing the deaths, illnesses, tragedies and indignities that have overtaken the narrator's parents, the bakery's owners, and the narrator himself in the decades since he and his father drank coffee at Gus's. So demeaning are their fates that, by comparison, the remembered breakfasts seem like idylls, while adulthood assumes the character of a hell in which childhood must, as it were, be atoned for.

Hall sets up repeatedly for such reversals. "I was happy in my own world of snow, as if I were living inside one of those glass paperweights that snow when you shake them," says the narrator of **"Christmas Snow,"** thinking back to his tenth Christmas Eve, spent at Grandma's house in the New Hampshire woods. The scene couldn't be cozier: a wood-burning stove, piles of presents, Grandma's freshbaked donuts, aunts reminiscing about the oranges and popcorn balls of Christmastimes past—even a timely snowstorm. Then an uncle, under the sway of a painful association, tells the story of a punishment his father administered to him during a snowstorm forty-nine years earlier—a tale of such refined cruelty that we feel as if Hall had, figuratively speaking, dashed the glass paperweight of his story against a wall.

Nor are these endings melodramatic. Rather, they grow out of the circumstances of the stories and are all the more disturbing for their credibility. (One exception is the discovery of the corpse beside the trout pond at the end of **"The Figure of the Woods"**—a climax that, despite its photorealistic presentation, may strike some readers as too fantastic.) What saves such fictions, meanwhile, from disappearing altogether into the black holes their nihilistic endings create is the richness with which Hall details his "before" shots. Those unspoiled, familial tableaux are resurrected as well as razed by the story, and they remain with us all the more because they are destroyed before our eyes.

There simply isn't much to criticize in *The Ideal Bakery,* a collection assembled over the course of twenty-five years. Hall is a professional, from his story conceptions to his spare, but adroit, symbolism, to his sense of irony and nuance, to his characterizations and dialogue. *The Ideal Bakery,* in short, offers both the delight and the nourishment its title conjures. And that is as it should be—for Hall, as readers of his poems and essays will attest, is one of contemporary literature's gourmet chefs.

### Frederick Pollack (review date Winter 1990)

SOURCE: "Donald Hall's *The One Day,*" in *Salmagundi,* Nos. 85–8, Winter, 1990, pp. 344–50.

[*In the following review, Pollack offers a positive assessment of* The One Day *and classifies the poem as a modernist work.*]

Born in Hamden, Conn. in 1928, Donald Hall has lived since 1975 in a New Hampshire farmhouse where his grandmother was born in 1878 and his mother in 1903. The mother seems a supportive figure; when, as a child, the poet cried for her after lights-out, she made much less fuss about it than, say, Proust's mother. Hall (by which I mean both the reigning persona of the poems and the man in the interviews) seems remarkably unalienated. Not "happy"; Freud's remark about replacing "hysterical misery" with "ordinary unhappiness," one of the epigraphs in *The One Day,* is its article of faith. What is true of sense of self also applies to that of history: the speaker in Part I of Hall's poem imagines "an old man hedging and ditching / three hundred years ago in Devon"; someone in Part II announces that "For four hundred years and sixteen generations, I kept / my castle while vassals baked flatbread." Such pasts are easier to bear than the past of pogroms and gas chambers, but not necessarily easier to write about.

The stories Hall has told about himself in essays and interviews, and in **"A Note on this Poem,"** are germane to *The One Day.* In the first stanza the mother tells the speaker a bedtime story about a boy and his sister who build a house in the woods. The actual New Hampshire farmhouse becomes the "house of dying" we must build and the "house" we should build. The poem has been compared to *The Wasteland* and *Four Quartets*; it is distinguished from the first by its refusal to project the self's problems onto culture, from the second by its secularism, and from both by the fact that the narrative, though multiple, is coherent. *The One Day* is a lyric poem about midlife crisis. But it is a lyric vastly expanded in range and subtlety by narrative elements, a plural narrator, speculation about the composite nature of consciousness, and political awareness; its crisis is that of a society as well as of a life.

The seventeen years of work Hall put into the poem have made it a model of modern prosody. The ten-line stanza used throughout is like a fine baby-grand piano, instantly responsive to change of tone. The free-verse lines, ranging from between four and seven stresses in a variety of rhythms, succeed each other inevitably. The lines describe actions: strong verbs, simple but loaded nouns replace overt metaphor. The form transmits dreamlike logic without dreamlike blur. This logic has two interconnected rules. The first is that, as in neurosis, or in the Freudian session that uncovers neurosis, time may be shuffled or reversed. The second stanza warns us of this effect:

> . . . The old man alone in the farmhouse
> makes coffee, whittles, walks, and cuts an onion
> to eat between slices of bread. But the white loaf
> on the kitchen table comes undone:
> Milk leaks, flour and yeast draw apart;
> sugar and water puddle the table's top.

At age 12, the second main speaker of the poem (later a famous sculptress) spends a wonderful summer painting watercolors of her grandmother's farm. But the stanza that describes this summer comes *after* the one that tells how, at 15, she gives up art to take care of her mother. (The father has died in a car crash; the mother descends into alcoholism.) Both stanzas are in the past tense. The effect of this simple inversion is to deny our deep-seated expectations of growth, happy endings, reward for effort. When her son is 15, and her daughter six, the sculptress leaves them, describing their anguish with a terrible detached sympathy. She says nothing about the father or what led to this move. One tells oneself it has something to do with her art but she doesn't say this either. The moment detaches itself from ordinary causality and enters another kind of time: that of a curse, or of fixation.

The logic of the poem merges people as well as moments. Picasso's remark that "Every human being is a colony" is one of the epigraphs, and this is the aspect Hall discusses most in his "Note." In Parts I and III, he says, "two characters speak and each quotes others"; the "male 'I'" is the poet, but there is also "a general consciousness." Only the sculptress's words are italicized. An early stanza describes "other citizens / and colonists": an unemployed gay actor, a suicidal drunk, and a man in Woodbridge:

> . . .—ironic, uxorious, the five
> children grown and gone; he waters his lawn with
> irony;
> he works forty hours of irony a week and lives
> to retire.

But these are all non-speaking roles, and the narrative situation is more complex than Hall suggests. The reader broods over clues and leads. In Part I, Hall mentions the airplanes of youth: "The Bee Gee, huge engine and tiny stub wings, / snapped around pylons in the Nationals; each year / they clipped more wing off." But by Part III, as the sculptress describes the pills, institutions and therapy of her middle life, the airplanes have become hers: "*I crashed like my daredevil pilots; it was what / I wanted.*" She remarries; he does not say that he does, but the wife who, in Part I, waits upstairs at 2 A.M. while he drinks seems different from the wife of Part III. There is also the mystery that begins when Hall's dissatisfied father "[shakes] his fist over my cradle: 'He'll do / what he wants to do!'" Dying at 51, the father cannot deliver a grade-school graduation speech. Hall says, "As I took my father's / place, my head shook like a plucked wire. / I told the fourteen-year-olds: 'Never do anything except what you want to do.'" Later in Part I, a very alienated drinker describes his life around Sunset and Hollywood Boulevards. One thinks this must be the Hall-character during the bad period he has mentioned. Then this speaker says "My father's head shook like a plucked wire" and quotes the talismanic phrase, which by now has choked on its own ironies.

The effect of this treatment of time and character is to put the reader in an unfamiliar space. Neither a narrow chamber of subjectivity, nor a transhistorical infinity like *The Wasteland* or *The Cantos,* it is a realm where social forces can become visible. I am not saying that Hall constructed the poem to reveal these. I suspect he was tracing out certain emotional sequences (such as: loss, grief, greed, betrayal, self-indulgence, self-destruction, renunciation) and realized that these currents neither exist only in individuals, nor generate themselves. In Part II, a shepherd and a milkmaid discuss the sources of joy:

> *Phyllis*: and I carry, my dearest, the supermarket's paperbags
> into my clean kitchen; I align the cans on shelves
> just so. I set the oven for two hours and ten minutes
> while I cross-country. Dryads with slim exact
> hips and hair assemble in my livingroom for bridge.
> I am cheerful in order to be approved of. We forget
> every skill acquired over ten thousand years of labor.
> I practice smiling; I forget how to milk a goat.
> You forget how to construct aqueduct, temple, and cloaca.
> We vote for the candidate who vows to abolish caritas.

> *Marc*: I live in an unfenced compound among swineherds
> and milkmaids identical in age, income, and education.
> I am unacquainted with anyone who lives in a trailer
> or wears a tattoo, except for Joseph who mows my
> grass, whom I fear and despise. O Phyllis, O Elzira,
> You never sat by a cooling stove while the clock struck
> to study the word by candlelight. I never doubted
> that money excused anything done to acquire it . . .

Part II is called **"Four Classic Texts."** What makes them classic is not form but the purpose that animates each form. **"The Prophecy"** is a literal Jeremiad. What at first seems funny and indiscriminate flailing—everything is damned from Ronald McDonald to plutonium waste to Elzira's adulteries—soon makes perfect sense (though the humor remains). A prophet is not a member of a party. Alone, he attacks an evil way of life. A way of life implicates every object in it, even a little styrofoam cup that reappears in glory in Part III. (One reviewer's comparison between this section and Ginsberg's "Howl" is inexact. A prophet, however angry, still hopes that ethical reform will avert doom. Ginsberg's model, St. John the Divine, has no such hope.) Hall's **"Pastoral"** fulfills the same function as

Theocritus': a lament for lost innocence on behalf of compromised urban intellectuals. The effect of progress has been to make the guilt greater and more articulate, but no more easily purged. "You make rules, piper, by which you cannot be fired," Phyllis murmurs to her lover; "You weep, my love, chained to the trireme's oar." The *history* fulfills its classical task of drawing from events a moral that can be phrased in terms of character. When Juvenis cut his thumb, says, Senex,

> . . . Always he imagined for one heartbeat
> that he might undo the error and prevent the upsurge
> of consequent blood . . .

Juvenis is wrong; but so, Senex believes, are John Ball and Spartacus, who "assemble plutonium for love, constructing a device / to reverse history's river." Senex, "president-emperor," who of course is Juvenis, watches impassively, meanwhile continually killing. The Eclogue looks back to Virgil's Fourth Eclogue, which the Middle Ages regarded as a prophecy of Christ. As in the **"Pastoral,"** everything that was originally naive has become sophisticated, what may have been latent is now retrospective—yet no less tremulous and elegiac. It is a section of considerable beauty.

Part III is entitled **"To Build a House."** The movement of the poem required a resolution, yet after everything we have seen no resolution could be completely satisfying. One is glad that, at 90, the sculptress is flown to the White House; one ponders her last remark: "*I felt no pain except when I stood for the medal.*" The main speaker's (second) marriage is properly autumnal, vital, happy. The wife, however, is treated differently from anyone else in the poem. She is neither a speaking role nor a "colonist" but a character, and, as such, rather flat: not speaking, part of a "we," being delightedly observed by Hall as she does the same things he does—reading, picking apples. We realize that she is his Other, and that relationship is part of the "house" we are being urged to build; but sound psychology makes weak poetry, and we are more interested in the "others" he has found in himself. Similarly, an urban sensibility may have to strain to derive a metaphorical "house" (of coherent ego, of responsibility) from Hall's actual farmhouse and orchard; however real these are, they seem as distant as Horace's Sabine farm.

But these are minor objections, which the poem itself anticipates: in Part III Hall separates himself from his "colonists." The latter collectively reappear as (what else?) delegates leaving the Constitutional Convention in Philadelphia. Somehow, none of them quite make it home; they are last seen "descending the cloverleaf together / to engage another Convention at the Hollywood-La Brea Motel— / wearing their nametags, befuddled, unable to argue." There are also several stanzas that rear up suddenly with the form and rhythm of the following:

> There are ways to get rich: Find an old corporation,
> self insured, with capital reserves. Borrow
> to buy: then dehire managers; yellow-slip maintenance;
> pay public relations to explain how winter is summer;
> liquidate reserves and distribute cash in dividends:
> Get out, sell stock for capital gains, reward the usurer,
> and look for new plunder—leaving a milltown devastated,
> workers idle on streetcorners, broken equipment, no cash
> for repair or replacement, no inventory or credit.
> Then vote for the candidate who abolishes foodstamps.

These impersonal instructions, inimical to any hope of fulfillment (and, it is stressed, to any farm), are also a call to wider responsibility.

*The One Day* is one of the greatest American poems of the last few decades; what remains is to ask what kind of poem it is. Fashionable postmodernists could not have imagined it. Rejecting "voice" entirely, they would not have created such interesting voices; reducing history to stylistic pastiche, they could not place personae in so long a perspective. A Modernist poem, then—but modernist in a rather English way. Spender in the '30s wrote of "All those other 'I's,' who long for 'We, dying.'" Hall has been almost unique among American poet-critics in his love for contemporary English poetry. *The One Day* combines the urbane historicism of a Roy Fuller or a Geoffrey Hill with American warmth and scope. Deeper than such influences is an unexpected affinity with Matthew Arnold (who also provides an epigraph). Like Arnold, Hall works in a long Romantic stanza; like Thyrsis and the Scholar-Gypsy, Hall's protagonists act out the most complex concerns of intellectuals in a stylized, often bucolic landscape; like Arnold (and few poets since), Hall seeks to dramatize sanity and wholeness. Paradoxically, it is in this affinity for a sage—more importantly, in his belief that the poet *should* be a sage, rather than shaman, technician, or patient—that Hall most resembles the earlier Modernists: Eliot the cooler Tennyson, Pound the self-proclaimed heir of Browning. *The One Day* may be the last masterpiece of American Modernism. Any poet who seeks to surpass this genre should study it; any reader who has lost interest in contemporary poetry should read it.

### George Looney (review date Spring 1990)

SOURCE: "Keeping the World Going," in *Ohio Review*, No. 46, Spring, 1990, pp. 116–28.

[*In the following excerpt, Looney offers a positive assessment of* The One Day, *complimenting the poem for its sense of wonder and beauty.*]

In "Toward a Changed Poetics," the final chapter of *Praises and Dispraises* (1988), Terrence Des Pres wrote that "Writers must, it seems to me, vote to see the world keep going." About this there can be no sane argument. What is arguable is how writers must go about casting that vote. If the imagination is, as Wallace Stevens suggested, "a violence from within that protects us from a violence without," a "pressing back against the pressure of reality," then Terrence Des Pres' call for a poetry of witness to the horrors, political and personal, of the twentieth century may be self-defeating. If, as Des Pres suggests it is, the horror of this century is primarily the result of the intrusion of the political into our personal lives, then what's needed is a poetry that presses back against any such intrusion and, while certainly not being blind to or denying the forces that would intrude into our lives and into language itself, keeps that intrusion from being complete exactly by the act of not allowing it to intrude into poetry. The poet's vision certainly can, and should, include the intrusiveness of politics, but it must not be another victim of that intrusion. What we need are poets whose sense of the world, and the place of the personal in it, is sound and confident enough to attack the horror by praising that which the horror, and the political machinery that creates and sustains it for its own purposes, would deny.

In his chapters on the poetry of Yeats, Des Pres speaks at length of the bards of ancient Ireland, and the legendary power of their praises and curses, and ends up voting for the curse as the more powerful. This seems short-sighted. The curse's potency is temporal, and intrinsically connected to the thing cursed. The praise, however, lives on by its own merits, by how well it reclaims and redeems that which is praised. Think of those animals on the cave walls in France. Those figures are powerful and haunt us because they are an act of praise, of love. Because, by their existence, they keep alive and redeem a part of the world now lost. It is the courage to be human, and humane, in the face of terror that we need. Des Pres himself provided the evidence of this in *The Survivor*, which moves us not because it curses the terror of the death camps but because it praises the strength of the human spirit not to be denied its humanity and not to be silenced. It is not courageous to give in to the terror, to allow it to claim itself as the nature of the world. In fact, it is precisely that, the nature of the world, that we must offer as a pressing back against the terror. That is how we remain human in inhumane times.

The element of praise as a force against terrors both natural and man-made is found in all three books under consideration here. But one, **The One Day** by Donald Hall, is all about such praise. This book-length poem longs to be whole enough to contain the world and be a keeper of it, to care for it well enough that through it the world is made a little healthier and survives longer as what it is. Donald Hall has long been associated with the call for ambition in contemporary poetry, and this book lives up to that call. It is ambitious. And its ambition is to be strong enough to embrace the world and create, if not sense out of it, at least the chance for sense.

In the epigraph to the second section of the poem, **"Four Classic Texts,"** Hall quotes Nadezhda Mandelstam. "Poetry is preparation for death," Osip's wife wrote. But how can poetry, which is after all merely words, be "preparation for death"? How can we be prepared for death? By life. Life is the only preparation for death. And poetry can prepare us only by reacquainting us more fervently with life, with, as Hall writes, the "single day that presides / over our passage through the thirty thousand days / from highchair past work and love to suffering death." It is this that Hall ambitiously sets out to do in a poem which tests the limits of narrative, using a method sometimes referred to as "fractured narrative" that allows him to weave the substance of a life and incorporate into that fabric the joys and fears and pains and passions of all human life. One of the several voices in the poem, a sculptress, speaks for Hall's ambition when she says,

> I embrace the creation, not for what it signifies,
> but for volume and texture thrusting up
> from the touched places.

**("To Build a House")**

And the textures touched in this book are rich and varied. Hall turns his attention to both our real and imagined lives. Collected here are "the young women's bodies, / their smooth skin intolerably altered by ointments." We also find a middle-aged couple who, "in muscular bodies," "walk to their deaths together." We find scenes which offer quiet and moving praise for life.

> Dreaming of tomorrow only, we sleep in the painted
>   bed while
> the night's frail twisting of woodsmoke assembles
>   overhead from
> the two chimneys, to mingle and disperse as our
>   cells will disperse
>     and mingle when they lapse into graveyard dirt.

**("To Build a House")**

We find the small aches that accompany us, and dreams which rise from us and assume their own reality. We find all this here, though it would be more accurate to say we find all this here noticed in language. And the words are the true praise, the song made of the things that, as Rilke wrote, perish. At least part of the power poetry can lay claim to is the power language well-used evokes, the ability of words to name and to go on naming, over and over with each new reader, each new generation of readers. This is perhaps the most profound aspect of the position we, as creatures of reason, hold in the order of things. When we write of the world, as Hall does in this poem, out of a sense of love and wonder and respect, we make the world that much more human, and ourselves that much more natives of the world. Language can be the conduit for a healthy and reverent relationship between the world noticed and the noticer, but not if those who use it set out only to condemn, to consign the world and all its life and beauty to the emptiness that terror desires to consign us to.

Poets do have a difficult task. They must not only use words to reclaim and redeem the world they are a part of, they must do it in such a way that they also reclaim and redeem the words themselves from the political and mercantile destruction of language that is a constant and ongoing threat to the only conduit we have to the world and to ourselves.

This is not to suggest that all poetry can do is praise. Terrence Des Pres was correct in his contention that anger can be a source of poetic energy, even if that energy may be, like cold fusion, only occasional and unreliable. Donald Hall includes in his poem the anger of a man of common sense living in a world run by those forces which are too often the enemies of sense. **"Prophecy,"** one of the **"Four Classic Texts,"** begins with a chanted litany of things the voice rejects.

> I reject the old house and the new car; I reject
> Tory and Whig together; I reject the argument
> that modesty of ambition is sensible because the bigger
> they are the harder they fall; I reject Waterford;
> I reject the five and dime; I reject Romulus and Remus;
> I reject Martha's Vineyard and the slamdunk contest;
> I reject leaded panes; I reject the appointment made
> at the tennis net or on the seventeenth green; I reject
> the Professional Bowlers Tour; I reject matchboxes;
> I reject purple bathrooms with purple soap in them.

The rejections are followed by prophecies of what will come of those who live for and by these things. And as the poem goes on, we begin to sense that this voice is not the voice of a person speaking in defense of a world wronged by the short-sightedness and callousness of human beings, but the voice of the world itself. A world that will outlast our petulant attempts to conquer it, and whose inevitable victory is hinted at "Where the drive-in church raises a chromium cross," by the fact that "dandelions and milkweed will straggle through blacktop."

Curses, though, are not what this poem is about. This poem is an act of love. This poem is the product of the vision of a human being who has experienced the world and struggled to remake it as best he can. It's been fashionable since Auden's poem on the death of Yeats to use his line about poetry making nothing happen as an excuse not to do the hard work that real love requires, to instead write things that look like poems but are filled by the belief that emptiness is the only possibility and, more than that, a legitimate refuge for battered, self-indulgent souls. Donald Hall has not accepted that fashion. ***The One Day*** does make something happen. It makes the world seem a little more possible for us. Along the way it offers a reverent praise for those acts of creation that make us human, and praises the solace found in any work well done. "Work, love, build a house, and die. But build a house," he writes. Donald Hall has built a house we can feel at home in, a poem which brings us together with the knowledge we were never separate. . . .

Poetry must be such a refuge. Poets must have the courage and the vision, as the three discussed here do, to take on the challenge of countering the terror, the ultimate negation Des Pres speaks of, countering it with affirmation, with praise. Poetry must be allowed to remake the world in words so well that the pressure of the words might help the world keep going.

### Donald Hall with George Myers Jr. (interview date Spring 1991)

SOURCE: "An Interview with Donald Hall about *The One Day*," in *Ploughshares*, Vol. 17, No. 1, Spring, 1991, pp. 71–75.

[*In the following interview, Hall discusses the process he used to write* The One Day *and the events that inspired the poem.*]

[*Myers:*] *Your work on* **The One Day** *lasted more than a decade, I believe. How long exactly?*

[Hall:] It was sixteen years from the time I started the poem—not knowing what I was starting—until I finished it. (I'm always tempted to put quotations around the word, when I say "finished," because, when I have a chance to republish anything, I tinker.) I wasn't working on it all that time. After the initial onslaught of language, I worked on it very little for the next eight or nine years; I looked at it, every now and then, resolved to get back to it . . . and then I quailed, and closed the book. I was frightened of the material; I was also frightened by the magnitude of the task, but the first fear was greater.

*Did you know at the start that you were working on a poem that would run fifty pages?*

No, because I did not know what I was working on. It felt like something big, something long, but I did not know—I did not have any notion—*what* it would turn out to be, *or if it would turn out to be anything.* In my head, I called it *Building the House of Dying,* and this was before I used the phrase when I wrote **"Kicking the Leaves."** As I was drafting that poem, in haste and excitement, that phrase popped into a line—and I knew where it came from. Maybe at the moment of composition, I thought that **"Kicking the Leaves"** might be a part of *Building the House of Dying.*" I'm not sure. At the beginning of anything, I'm not sure of what will happen or where I'm going.

*In the explanatory note you've attached to* **The One Day,** *you say, "The poem began in the fall of 1971" (my emphasis), and referred to having written the poem as though you were taking dictation. Have there been other poems, long poems, that came at you like this?*

A good many poems have started as if I were taking dictation. At some point in my mid-twenties, I demanded that I understand a poem before I write it—a brief aberration. Beginning with **"The Long River"** and possibly earlier, in 1957 or '58, I was willing to write down any language that came heavy-laden, whether I knew what it was about or not.

*So you, personally, haven't needed to know what you've wanted to say?*

Not at the beginning. Generally, by the time I finish a poem—often years after I start it—I have a good idea of what I've *said*. I don't know what I want to say until I say it; and then I cannot be sure that is what I "wanted to say" before the words came.

But, from time to time, I have something like paraphrasable content in my head before I begin to write. Poems begin any way they please. I am more *interested* in poems that begin mysteriously—or possibly in mania—as if they were dictated.

Right now I'm working on a long thing, which is at the moment sixty-six ten-line poems. These ten-line units do not resemble the bricks of **The One Day** in anything but number. The language is different, and unlike anything I have ever written. Certainly these came—over an extended period, however—like dictation. Maybe they are no good but they excite me. A working title is *My Life and Times*—because these poems seem to have absolutely nothing to do with my life and times.

*I want to return to your word "dictation"—a word I believe Jack Spicer used in the same way. What is the source of dictation? From where do these works and poems come?*

I don't know. "Dictation" is a dead metaphor that declares that you feel passive to the flow of words: I've also called it receiving messages from the mother ship—more passive receptivity. When you speak of "the unconscious mind," you've said nothing. Freud's unconscious can't talk, so calling it the source of language says nothing.

But parts of the mind are always asleep, always dreaming; many sorts of mental activity continue, without alert awareness or with infrequent awareness. I observe things come into my brain, whole, and sometimes understand that they are made of parts that have combined somehow and somewhere. Sometimes I feel as if I can encourage a benign receptivity that stimulates combinations. Often when I look later at language that has come "as if dictated" I can identify bits and pieces—sources in experience, in things overheard, in ruminations, in reading. It is like looking at the new baby and saying the forehead comes from Uncle Charlie, the nose from Great-Grandmother Belle . . .

*Did you begin* **"Kicking the Leaves"** *the same way?*

It began almost automatically, or at least rapidly; I was at least partly aware, in that poem, of what I seemed to be talking about. **"Eating the Pig"** came in such a rush that I actually dictated a prose-rush of language onto a tape. Later I labored the paragraphs into lines at my leisure.

*You speak of* **The One Day** *as something of a happy accident, "impulse validated by attention," though we know an imposing talent was behind it. But* **The One Day** *does read as though it was written in the way the long modernists poems were written: by a piecemeal process of composition, and with no deliberate intention. It succeeds, for me, through allowance of subject matter: You've permitted what came into it to stay.*

When I used that phrase, "impulse validated by attention," I was not talking about a happy accident. I'm talking about working over the texture of its language. Impulsively, I set down a word or a phrase or even a series of lines; "impulsively" means I do it rapidly, in excitement, without malice aforethought, intuitively—in a manic state. By inspiration. But I don't just leave it there on the scattery page; I *attend* to it. I look at it every morning for one thousand mornings. After the eight-hundred-and-second morning, I find that I don't like this word, take it out and impulsively put in another. After the nine-hundred-and-sixty-second morning, I remove the new word and restore the old one. On the one-thousandth, two-hundred-and-thirty-second morning, I realize that two words here and two words there link up with seven words eight pages later in the manuscript . . . and I am pleased with myself.

Impulse is creation; attention is critical intelligence.

*Would* **The One Day** *seem, to you, too discontinuous without those uniform units of ten lines?*

Yes . . . finding that brick, after working on the poem steadily, over four or five years, was a major breakthrough. Before that, as I remember, it was a series of thirty-five free verse poems of several pages each. . . . You would recognize patches, in that old version, but it was *no bloody good.*

When I found my unit and my shape, the language improved. Finally everything in a poem has to happen at once, with an effect of joyous or possessed spontaneity. But in composition the lucky strikes accrue separately and bit by bit.

When Keats wrote the Odes, he invented that stanza by reference or maybe by association to the sonnet. I think the stanza sprung him loose. Not to compare myself to the glorious dead, I think that the shape of my stanza, and the sense of what it could contain—how it could live by itself or set a sequence—sprung me loose.

FROM *MY LIFE AND TIMES*

"A HISTORY OF SOLITUDE"

> Before there was anything else, solitude
> filled space in the form of gas—lavender,
> thin, smelling like mouthwash. When solitude
>
> studied itself in school, it turned into
> a sphere the size of a ball bearing,
> unbreakable, yet soft as beans soaked
>
> to make soup. When it grew old, solitude
> sprouted leaves like the winter oak's. Dead,
> its molecules dispersed through space
>
> emitting perfumes of rectitude and prospect.

"A THEORY OF WOE"

Harm soup simmers on each body's woodstove
where gelatin soaks from shinbones
and combines with effluence from cabbages

of loss to build gray froth. Nouns
of perpetual accumulation sip woe
three times a day from a wooden spoon

as machines doze in the separated hayfield.
There are no shadows in this blue country.
Woe's nutriment nourishes. Scum feathers

gather on harm soup in the dolce twilight.

"A HISTORY OF HISTORY"

Gibbon, Tacitus, and Thucydides fished
from a rowboat while it rained
oysters. "Look," said Tacitus, "it's

pouring Rome's grief on my temple." "No,"
said Gibbon: "Phyllis has emigrated."
History takes correction from immaculate

leopards who remain alive—but history
retains *nothing*; it stuffs fact stew
into its face, vomits, and gorges again,

as the guitarist plays "mournful melodies."

**Lawrence Joseph (essay date Fall 1991)**

SOURCE: "Donald Hall's *Old and New Poems*," in *Michigan Quarterly Review,* Vol. 30, No. 4, Fall, 1991, pp. 699–716.

[*In the following essay, Joseph explores how* Old and New Poems *is an example of how Hall's poetry has evolved throughout the years and how the collection relates to the genre of American Modernist poetry.*]

I

In 1978, when he was fifty, Donald Hall published his seventh book of poems, *Kicking the Leaves,* to widespread acclaim. Hall's reputation as a critic, anthologist, editor, literary journalist (and, arguably, one of our leading persons of letters) was by then already established. Almost suddenly Hall was talked about as a poet. The publication of his next book, *The Happy Man,* eight years later, more than enhanced Hall's reputation. At fifty-eight, Hall not only was writing poems as well as he ever had, but was writing, some claimed, as well as anyone in his generation. *The Happy Man* (which received The Lenore Marshall/*Nation* Prize) served as a prelude for *The One Day,* published two years later, on Hall's sixtieth birthday. In *The Washington Post Book World,* David Lehman unequivocally declared the book "major work." Widely, often extravagantly, praised, *The One Day* received the 1988 National Book Critics Circle Award for Poetry.

Last year Ticknor & Fields—in a beautifully-designed edition—published Hall's *Old and New Poems. Old and New Poems* isn't a "new and selected poems." In fact, Hall doesn't present his "old" poems by the books in which they appeared; instead, he divides the poems into nine time periods, the "old" poems beginning "1947–1953" and ending "1979–1986," the twenty-two "new" poems (which have the force of a book) designated "1987–1990." The poems from *The One Day* are excluded. In a Note, Hall acknowledges that he has altered many of the "old" poems; he is among those poets (Yeats, Moore, and Lowell are others) who sometimes (and sometimes extensively) revise earlier published work. Clearly, in *Old and New Poems,* Hall presents the "old" work in the context of the "new," so that the reader sees the poems as part of a work continuously in progress.

*Old and New Poems* is an important book. It not only represents the achievements of one of the best poets of a prodigiously talented generation; its qualities also measure American poetry at the end of the Modernist century. Hall's poetry is aesthetically ambitious—as complex, actually, as the century's aesthetic undercurrents. *Old and New Poems* also reflects the gifts of a poet whose powers have expanded during his fifties, into his sixties—a rare accomplishment.

There are multiple ways Hall's poetry might be valuably critiqued: a textual scrutiny—a variorum—of his revisions, comparing the changes; an analysis of the compelling metamorphoses of certain subjects and emotions; or a look at the relationship of Hall's prose—both literary and journalistic—to his poetry. But, at the very least, Hall's poetry requires an appreciation of its formal and aesthetic dimensions. Hall's ability to embody the aesthetic landscapes of post-World War II America immediately impresses the reader of *Old and New Poems.* Hall is part of a generation that has had to confront the continuous effects of Modernism. His catholic critical tastes (as an anthologist, most recently of *The Best American Poetry* (1989) he has been a tastemaker); his passion for chronicling the art (as the first Poetry Editor of *The Paris Review,* he helped popularize the interview form); his editorial largesse (as an advisor to Wesleyan University Press during the 1960s, he had a say in publishing the early work of James Wright, John Ashbery, Louis Simpson, James Dickey, Robert Bly); his cutting-edge essays and reviews on the state of the art written from outside the creative writing business: Hall keeps in touch with poetic currencies. *Old and New Poems* and *The One Day* reveal that Hall's appreciation of the art of poetry first of all exists in his poems.

II

In a 1981 essay, **"The Poetry Notebook: Two,"** in talking about the avant-garde, Hall accurately observed: "If one notion ties much of the avant-garde together, over the past thirty years, it is concentration on construction rather than feeling or idea. This construction may be aleatory, a concentration on the method of construction rather than on an intended shape." In addition, Hall described the distinction between constructivism and expressionism which focuses, critically, on a poem's aesthetic emphasis on either "form" or "feeling":

> [f]rom time to time people have fiddled with dividing art into two camps called after the names of the two movements: constructivism and expressionism. (I use small letters to indicate a usage more general than the movements named by capitalization.) Expressionist art expresses feeling (by distortion, exaggeration, fantasy); feeling is its end. Constructivism concentrates on form . . .[1]

This commonly-used conceptualization of Modernist art, however—valid as it is—doesn't take into account what actually distinguishes Modernist poetry: the critical role of a poem's language. When language becomes the primary focus, the "form"-"feeling" dichotomy takes on secondary importance; "constructivism" and "expressionism" take on different meanings.

As good a place as any to begin defining Modernist notions of poetic language is Sigurd Burckhardt's little-known but brilliant 1956 essay, "The Poet as Fool and Priest":

> If there were a language pure enough to transmit all human experience without distortion, there would be no need for poetry. But such a language not only does not, it cannot exist. Language can no more do justice to all human truth than law can to all human wishes. In its very nature as a social instrument it must be a convention, must arbitrarily order the chaos of experiences, allowing expression to some, denying it to others. It must provide common denominators, and so it necessarily falsifies, just as the law necessarily inflicts injustice. And these falsifications will be the more dangerous the more "transparent" language seems to become, the more unquestionably it is accepted as an undistorting medium. It is not windowglass but rather a system of lenses which focus and refract the rays of an hypothetical unmediated vision.[2]

Modernist language cannot be "transparent"; language, by its nature, is "social"; language "arbitrarily orders," by expression, "the chaos of experience"; verbal meaning arises out of a language of juxtaposed refraction. In this sense, "expressionism"—as its most astute and eloquent proponent Gottfried Benn argued—is at the heart of Modernism: "the complete parallel in aesthetic terms to modern physics and its abstract interpretations of the world, the expressive parallel to non-euclidian mathematics, which abandoned the classical concept of the last 2,000 years in favor of abstract spatial dimensions. . . . The expressionist [knows] the profound, technical mastery that art demands, its craft ethos, the moral of form."[3] The language of Modernist poetry, as Susanne K. Langer argues, is "abstract": "The relation of poetry to the world of facts is the same as that of painting to the world of objects; actual events, if they enter into its orbit at all, are motifs of poetry, as actual objects are motifs of painting."[4] A modernist poem must be aware of its form.

If the emphasis is on language, a poem's verbal constructions are more important, in the first instance, than an emphasis on either "form" or "feeling." As Burckhardt put it: "The first purpose of poetic language . . . is the very opposite of making language more transparent." Restated, the first purpose of poetic language is verbally to refract or focus, to form meanings which, because of the nature of language, are social. Looked at this way, the aesthetic topography of Modernist poetry is more complex than the "form"-"feeling" dichotomy. On one side of the spectrum is poetry that does nothing creatively to dispel or refract "transparent" language. Over the past fifteen years, many critics have lambasted a certain type of "first-person" "free verse" poem. The type of poem that deserves disdain, however, isn't, necessarily, a "free verse" poem that uses "I" (a patently absurd basis of critique), but, instead, a poem which, by its formal decisions, does nothing to focus or refract the subjective language of the "I"—by meter, rhyme, lineation, diction, rhythm, stanza, syntax, as well as rhetorical devices such as irony and anaphora. In fact, the "new-formalist" poem that apes conventional metrical and rhyming devices is as "transparent" as the earnest "free verse" poem that does nothing formally or structurally to focus or refract meaning. As Burckhardt perceived, the essential problem with a poem that makes its language transparent is that it fundamentally lies: . . . "[S]uch a language not only does not, it cannot exist." It is artifice, not art. Its verbal effects are no more artistically viable than the verbal effects of journalism; nothing in its language—to paraphrase Pound—creates "news that stays news."

Once poems that make language transparent are appropriately dismissed, a reader is, aesthetically, in the realm of poetry—where language is most intensely refracted and focused into meaning and emotion. To understand the intricate aesthetic variations that exist within this realm, I often return to an essay by Roland Barthes, "Is There Any Poetic Writing?" in which Barthes makes the distinction between "classical" and "modern" poetic language. "Classical" language, he says, is full of connections that

> lead the word on, and at once carry it toward a meaning which is an ever-deferred project. . . . Classical language is always reducible to a persuasive continuum, it postulates the possibilities of dialogue, it establishes a universe in which men are not alone, where words never have the terrible weight of things, where speech is always meeting with the other.

On the contrary,

> modern poetry destroyed relationships in language and reduced discourse to words as static things. This implies a reversal in our knowledge of nature. The interrupted flow of the new poetic language initiates a discontinuous nature, which is revealed only piecemeal. . . . Modern poetry is a poetry of object.[5]

Barthes doesn't say it, but it is important to see that a poem written in "classical" language need not be formally "transparent"; a poet can form, through "possibilities of dialogue," language that refracts or focuses "transparent" discourse. Of major twentieth-century poets, Yeats, Rilke, Frost, and Brecht are examples of "classical" poets—all masters, in different ways, of form, but at the same time believers in the communicative and dialogical values of words. What Barthes classifies as "modern" poetic language, on the other hand, defies the very notion of "transparent" language. Among major American poets—to varying, complicated extents—Williams, Moore, Pound, and Stevens could be classified as "modern" under Barthes's distinction. Of course, none of these poets completely denies "classical" dialogue (Stevens especially). But, as different as they are, these "modernists" share, imaginatively, a profound sense of the fragmentation of social and emotional realities, and a strong sense of the poem's form containing, at least at some level of perception, something that can be looked at separately, something "objective," different, and apart, from the poem's more communicative expressions. Not surprisingly, each of these poets, again in different ways, considered him -or herself part of the "avant-garde" (although, today, the avant-garde is identified, for the most part, with poets who completely reject the dictates and fictions of "classical" language). What is clear at the end of the Modernist century is this: critical tensions in American poetry exist between "transparent" poetic language, on the one hand, and "refracted" poetic language on the other, and—among refracted poetries—between poetic languages that are "classical" or "modern."

### III

What is clear from Donald Hall's **Old and New Poems** is his consistent, even aggressive, resistance to "transparent" language. From the very beginning, Hall creates language that refracts unmediated "transparency." Hall's poetic impulse is fundamentally formal. This isn't to say that Hall is a poet without subject matter: he very much is, and always has been. From the beginning, he has articulated, metamorphosed, and combined his themes: an acute awareness of grief and loss grounded in personal experiences with death; a strong sense of family and genealogy; a deeply-felt reaction to the elements, to things of the earth; a moralist's edginess toward power and its manifestations, especially war; identification with children, both on social and personal levels; a compelling sense of the physical universe; an awareness of art, and its making; a strong desire for happiness and love, on personal, religious, and social levels; and a profound historical sense of place (especially the locale of his ancestral farm in New Hampshire, where he now lives). But it is, critically, impossible to think of Hall's subjects without considering the ways in which he consciously forms his language to include them.

The language of the early poems is exclusively "classical." In the first two time designations in **Old and New Poems**, "1947–1953" and "1954–1958," the poems are written mostly according to metrical schemes, in syllabics, with end-rhymes, and in stanzas of consistent linear lengths throughout a poem (in the poems "1954–1958," less imposed, more "open" forms are occasionally used). All of these poems have vitality still—verbal sharpness, emotional sting. Listen, for example, to the edgy, almost colloquial pentameter of the concluding stanza of the lament, **"Exile"**:

> Exiled by years, by death no dream conceals,
> By worlds that must remain unvisited,
> And by the wounds that growing never heals,
> We are as solitary as the dead,
> Wanting to king it in that perfect land
> We make and understand.
> And in this world whose pattern is unmade,
> Phases of splintered light and shapeless sand,
> We shatter through our motions and evade
> Whatever hand might reach and touch our hand.

Or, to the intensely compressed and subtly rhymed syllabic quatrains of **"Je Suis Une Table,"** in which the poem's formalization of language is, itself, a subject to which the poet responds emotionally:

> It has happened suddenly,
> by surprise, in an arbor,
> or while drinking good coffee,
> after speaking, or before,
>
> that I dumbly inhabit
> a density; in language
> there is nothing to stop it,
> for nothing retains an edge.
>
> Simple ignorance presents
> later, words for a function,
> but it is common pretense
> of speech, by a convention,
>
> and there is nothing at all
> but inner silence, nothing
> to relive on principle
> now this intense thickening.

Or listen, for a change of pace, to the opening pentameter lines of **"1934"**—a narrative packed with historical details—quickened by rhymed couplets:

> In nineteen-thirty-four we spent July
> At a small farm, my mother's father's. I
> Was five years old. Father got *White's News Letter,*
> Fridays, which said that things were looking better.
> Bright Model A's kept speeding past each day,
> Fouled by the eagles of the N.R.A.
> And blew their brassy horns at us, the farm
> Where nothing and no one ever came to harm.

Or, for a more flexibly expressed emotional density, the opening quatrain of **"The Kiss"**:

> The backs twist with the kiss
> and the mouth which is the hurt
> and the green depth of it
> holds plainly the hour.

By 1958—at the age of thirty—Hall's formal and substantive range are impressive: his primary sense of a poem already is its language. You can't miss the poet's preoccupation with metrical, linear, and syntactical expressions, his deep imaginative response to the ways words, within formal structures, come to sound in language.

In the poems after 1958, though, something altogether different aesthetically happens: Hall pretty much abandons predictable metrical lineation and end-rhymes, aggressively compressing his language within "open" verbal structures. His focus shifts to visual, musical, and psychological expressions of image. As the aesthetic expands, so do Hall's probings into the relationship between form and emotion. One extremely strong poem, **"Internal and External Forms,"** is directly on point:

> What the birds say
> is colored. Shade
> feels the thickness
> shrubs make in a
> July growth,
>
> heavy brown thorns
> for autumn, curled
> horns in double
> rows. Listening
> the birds fly
>
> down, in shade. Leaves
> of darkness turn
> inward, noises
> curve inward, and
> the seed talks.

Like **"The Kiss," "Internal and External Forms"** is based upon a work of art—**"The Kiss"** after an Edvard Munch painting, **"Internal and External Forms"** after a sculpture by Henry Moore (whom Hall has referred to as his "most important teacher"[6]). By not referencing the poems, Hall gives them an immediate abstract quality. Then, by the juxtaposition of images, the compressed quality of the quatrains, and the lovely shaped sounds accentuated by enjambments, Hall makes the poem primarily an object for aesthetic satisfaction—like a piece of sculpture. The poem's first "meanings" are the ways in which its language forms; the poem's other "meanings"—the inward and outward existences of the physical world—are located within the language. Henry Moore was an avowed Modernist; **"Internal and External Forms"** is primarily a "modern" poem—as are many others written by Hall during this time. One of the most beautiful is **"The Long River"**:

> The musk ox smells
> in his long head
> my boat coming. When
> I feel him there,
> intent, heavy,
>
> the oars make wings
> in the white night,
> and deep woods are close
> on either side
> where trees darken.
>
> I rowed past towns
> in their black sleep
> to come here. I passed
> the northern grass
> and cold mountains.
>
> The musk ox moves
> when the boat stops,
> in hard thickets. Now
> the wood is dark
> with old pleasures.

The poem certainly has a "surreal" quality about it. But surrealism is a form of Modernist expressionism; a "surreal" poem—one that refracts and disassociates expected, conventional images, syntax or grammar—is, at the very least, antithetical to "transparent" language. Read this poem out loud, pausing slightly, as one should, at the end of each line: the pleasures are deeply musical; **"The Long River"** is, in Pound's term, melopoeic. A poem primarily musical is, of course, a poem formed, to some extent, into an "object" of aesthetic appreciation. Through an imagistic expressionism, Hall has entered a realm of "modern" language.

"Internal" and "external" images dominate the poems from "1966–1969," and almost all of the poems from "1970–1974." A number of these are among Hall's best, for example **"The Alligator Bride," "Apples," "Gold,"** and the gorgeous **"The Town of Hill"**:

> Back of the dam, under
> a flat pad
>
> of water, church
> bells ring
>
> in the ears of lilies,
> a child's swing
>
> curls in the current
> of a yard, horned
>
> pout sleep
> in a green
>
> mailbox, and
> a boy walks
>
> from a screened
> porch beneath
>
> the man-shaped
> leaves of an oak
>
> down the street looking
> at the town
>
> of Hill that water
> covered forty
>
> years ago,
> and the screen

> door shuts
> under dream water.

The poem—one sentence—is apparently discursive. But the language, intensely heightened by the line lengths and breaks, the space around the couplets, and the "dream water" ending, is what primarily impresses. Hall, here, reminds me of Zukofsky, another poet who masterfully knows how to empty a poem's meaning into its song. Some critics (many of whom admire Hall's "classical" work) refer to Hall's poems from 1958 to 1974 as "deep image." The notion of "deep image" may apply to poetry less formally inclined than Hall's, but it ridiculously misstates Hall's aesthetic. During these years, Hall imaginatively explored language as a primary poetic activity—emotional effects are achieved, first of all, through verbal formulations. Discourse isn't the primary objective of these poems—although it is often an effect. The poems demonstrate a complicated tension between form as the poem's primary subject, and its other subjects; part of what Hall is doing is inquiring how meanings come through, or don't come through, a poem's language.

Then, during the next three years, in a radical shift, Hall almost completely abandons a "modern" aesthetic. Writing the poems that would be included in **Kicking the Leaves,** Hall returns to discursive "classical" language. But, again, he also expands his formal range. The switches have explosive effects: the expanding language holds expanding subject matter. The poems "open" into language no one had ever quite seen or heard before from Hall. The formal expansion of discursive language continues with equal, if not more, force into the poems from "1979–1986," which include poems from **The Happy Man.**

The variety of the poems from 1975 to 1986 dazzles. On the one hand you have the sensuous, euphonious perceptions of **"Twelve Seasons"**:

> After two weeks of heat pressing on sweetcorn—
> haze dropping on hay, opaque air—this morning wakes
> cool with a bright wind, and the mountain
> clear, Kearsarge blue under transparent
> running air, cold rapid energy sharp as pitchforks.
> It is morning for fires in the stove,
> wood's architecture opening shafts and corridors of
>   fire,
> vacancies, gases. It is a day for clearing
> rocks from the fields, volunteers, elm saplings.
> Tomorrow we eat the body and drink the blood
> in the community of the white church
> where the day's pleasure occupies a pew beside suf-
>   fering.

On the other hand, the dark, troubling narrated discourse of **"My Friend Felix"**:

> "Beginning at five o'clock, just before dawn rises
> in the rearview mirror, I drive at eighty, along,
> all through Texas. I am a pencil extending
> a ruler's line to the unchangeable horizon

> west as I repeat a thousand quarrels with my wives
> . . ."

Or there's the sharp-eyed, memory narration from **"Kicking the Leaves"**:

> This year the poems came back, when the leaves fell.
> Kicking the leaves, I heard the leaves tell stories,
> remembering, and therefore looking ahead, and build-
>   ing
> the house of dying. I looked up into the maples
> and found them, the vowels of bright desire.
> I thought they had gone forever
> while the bird sang I love you, I love you
> and shook its black head
> from side to side, and its red eye with no lid,
> through years of winter, cold
> as the taste of chickenwire, the music of cinderblock.

During the time he was writing the groundbreaking "classical" poems of **The Happy Man,** Hall also began forming together pieces of a poem he'd started in the fall of 1971. The result was Part II of **The Happy Man, "Shrubs Burned Away."** Set in the center of **The Happy Man,** it is a profoundly "modern" poem. Revised and retitled **"Shrubs Burnt Away,"** the poem becomes Part I of Hall's celebrated next book, **The One Day,** "a poem in three parts."

There is really no poem in American poetry quite like it. Taking his "modern" impulse well beyond the "internal" and "external" formal objectification of images, Hall combines multiple voices, rhetorics, and subject matter within ten-line stanzas written in "long-line" variable meters. The poem's narrators are subsumed within competing discourses and subjects. **The One Day** works on multiple levels, a number of which include, as subjects of aesthetic inquiry, the poem's formal expressions: you can't read the poem without being struck by its complexity and interplays, how meanings "objectify" inside the poem's music. For example, consider this stanza from **"Shrubs Burnt Away"**:

> The world is a bed, I announced; my love agreed.
> A hundred or a thousand times our eyes encountered:
> Each time the clothes sloughed off, anatomies
> of slippery flesh connected again on the world's bed
> and the crescent of nerves described itself
> in the ordinary curve of bliss. We were never alone;
> we were always alone. If we were each the same
> on the world's bed, if we were each manikins of the
>   other
> then the multitude was one and one was the multi-
>   tude;
> many and one we performed procedures of comfort.

Or this, the third stanza of **"Prophecy,"** carried over to the fourth:

> Men who lie awake worrying about taxes, vomiting
> at dawn, whose hands shake as they administer Va-
>   lium, -

skin will peel from the meat of their thighs.
Armies that march all day with elephants past pyramids
and roll pulling missiles past generals weary of saluting
and past president-emperors splendid in cloth-of-gold,—
soft rumps of armies will dissipate in rain. Where square
miles of corn waver in Minnesota, where tobacco ripens
in Carolina and apples in New Hampshire, where wheat
turns Kansas green, where pulpmills stink in Oregon,—

dust will blow in the darkness and cactus die
before its flowers . . .

Meanings as overlaid and rich as these simultaneously empty and fill into their own music throughout this masterpiece in which Hall creates an almost infinite depth.

Now, two years after *The One Day,* we have *Old and New Poems.* The new poems—if they had been issued as a separate book—would merit the response *Kicking the Leaves, The Happy Man,* and *The One Day* received. The "new" poems are distinguished by an astonishing imaginative mix between "classical" and "modern" forms. Hall's range continues not only to broaden, it also deepens; the poems sometimes come right off the page with intensity. One, for example, **"Tubes"**—written in five parts, composed in syllabics, and combining first and third person ironic narratives—is especially compelling. This is its concluding Part V:

"Of all illusions,"
said the man with the
tubes up his nostrils,
IVs, catheter,
and feeding nozzle,
"the silliest one
was hardest to lose.
For years I supposed
that after climbing
exhaustedly up
with pitons and ropes,
I would arrive at
last on the plateau
of *Walking-level-
forever-among-
moss-with-red-blossoms,*
or the other one
of *Lolling-in-sun-
looking-down-at-old
valleys-I-started-
from.* Of course, of course:
A continual
climbing is the one
form of arrival
we ever come to—
unless we suppose
that wished-for height
and house of desire
is tubes up the nose."

The book's final poem, **"Praise for Death,"** comprised of thirty-eight sectioned cinquaines, is as "modern" as *The One Day.* By wildly shifting diction and syntax, rhetorical modes, rhythms, multiple meanings and ironies—interspersing personal and historical narratives and textual references to earlier poems—Hall makes the poem sing at an impassioned pitch:

31

. . . in our mouths: pass, pass away, sleep, decease, expire.
Quickly by shocking fire that blackens and vanishes,
turning insides out, or slowly by fires of rust and rot,
the old houses die, the barns and outbuildings die.
Let us praise death that removes nails carpenters hammered

32

during the battle of Shiloh; that solves the beam-shape
an adze gave an oak tree; that collapses finally
the seller's roof into his root cellar, where timber sawn
two centuries ago rots among the weeds and saplings. Let us
praise death before the house erected by skill and oxen.

33

Let us praise death in old age. Wagging our tails,
bowing, whimpering, let us praise sudden crib-death
and death in battle: Dressed in blue the rifleman charges
the granite wall. Let us praise airplane crashes.
We buried thirty-year-old Stephen the photographer

34

in Michigan's November rain. His bony widow, Sarah, pale
in her loose black dress, leaned forward impulsively
as the coffin, suspended from a yellow crane, swayed
over the hole. When she touched the shiny damp maple
of the box, it swung slightly away from her . . .

Multiply this intensity and depth imaginatively at least ten times and you get some idea of the poem's cumulative power.

Then, there is—befitting a poet acutely aware of the tensions between "classical" and "modern" poetries within himself and within the art—**"This Poem."** Its powers resemble Stevens's "The Plain Sense of Things" and "The Planet on the Table." **"This Poem"** not only captures the central imaginative impulse of Hall's old and new poems, but also expresses, as only Donald Hall can, exactly what a Modernist poem at the end of the century is:

1

This poem is why
I lie down at night

to sleep; it is why
I defecate, read,
and eat sandwiches;
it is why I get
up in the morning;
it is why I breathe.

2

You think (and I know
because you told me)
that poems exist
to *say* things, as you
telephone and I
write letters—as if
this poem practiced
communication.

3

One time this poem
compared itself to
new machinery,
and another time
to a Holstein's cud.
Eight times five times eight
counts three hundred and
twenty syllables.

4

When you require it,
this poem consoles—
the way a mountain
comforts by staying
as it was despite
earthquakes, Presidents,
divorces, frosts.
Granite continues.

5

This poem informs
the hurt ear wary
of noises, and sings
to the weepy eye.
When the agony
abates itself, one
may appreciate
arbitrary art.

6

This poem is here.
Could it be someplace
else? Every question
is the wrong question.
The only answer
saunters down the page
in its broken lines
strutting and primping.

7

It styles itself not
for the small mirror

of its own regard—
nor even for yours:
to fix appearance;
to model numbers;
to name charity
"the greatest of these."

8

All night this poem
knocks at the closed door
of sleep. "Let me in."
Suppose all poems
contain this poem,
dreaming one knowledge
shaped by the measure
of the body's word.

## IV

No other poet of Donald Hall's generation has written with Hall's breadth in both "classical" and "modern" poetic languages. Only Hall has imaginatively embodied—only Hall has ambitiously probed—the depths of the borderlines between these languages.

***Old and New Poems*** shows that Hall's imaginative tensions and ambitions evolved over time. He has been—perhaps inevitably—misread. But, with ***Old and New Poems*** and ***The One Day***, the work need not be misread in any reductive way. Imaginatively, Hall, like Yeats and Stevens, discovered the depth of his aesthetic in his fifties. We see this in no other poet of his generation: most (including many who received more acclaim in their thirties and forties) by their fifties, and into their sixties, have confined themselves—often with embarrassing results—to writing out of decades-old formal and substantive modes. Hall has, and continues to have, what the best always have, the imaginative capacity, to paraphrase Montale, to break the language continuously into the art of poetry.

### Notes

1. Donald Hall, *The Weather for Poetry: Essays, Reviews and Notes on Poetry, 1977–1981* (Ann Arbor: The University of Michigan Press, 1982), p. 352.

2. Sigurd Burckhardt, "The Poet as Fool and Priest," *ELH: A Journal of English Literary History,* Vol. 25, No. 4 (December 1956), pp. 279–98.

3. Cited in J. M. Ritchie, *Gottfried Benn: The Unreconstructed Expressionist* (London: Oswald Wolff, 1972), pp. 103–4.

4. Cited in Michael Hamburger, *The Truth of Poetry* (New York: Harcourt, Brace & World, 1969), p. 25.

5. Cited in Rachel Hadas, *Form, Cycle, Infinity: Landscape Imagery in the Poetry of Robert Frost and George Seferis* (Lewisburg: Bucknell University Press, 1985), p. 31.

6. An Interview with Donald Hall," *The Day I Was Older: On the Poetry of Donald Hall,* ed. Liam Rector (Santa Cruz, CA: Storyline Press, 1989), p. 135.

## Publishers Weekly (review date 29 June 1992)

SOURCE: A review of *Their Ancient Glittering Eyes: Remembering Poets and More Poets,* in *Publishers Weekly,* Vol. 239, No. 29, June 29, 1992, pp. 48–49.

[*In the following review, the critic offers a positive assessment of* Their Ancient Glittering Eyes.]

"Curiosity endures, surviving criticism or philosophy," affirms poet and critic Hall (**Here at Eagle Pond**) as he introduces a distinguished gallery of poets [in ***Their Ancient Glittering Eyes: Remembering Poets and More Poets***]—Frost, Thomas, Eliot, Moore, MacLeish, Winters, Pound—with verisimilitude and freshness enough to satisfy readers. An expansion and revision of ***Remembering Poets*** (1978), this records the younger Hall's involvement with the "old ones" even as it adds depth and grace to his designated genre of "literary gossip." His respect for the writers does not preclude frankness or significant revelations: readers learn that the elderly Frost, behind his mask of benign farmer-poet and eventual reputation as a monstrous egotist, was startlingly vulnerable—burdened with sadness, driven by guilt. The most thorough portrait follows Hall's relations with Eliot, disclosing a personality rather than a "monument"—an unusually humorous and surprisingly "American" poet. And his reminiscences of the lonely, disconcerted Pound may be the book's most insightful. Although Hall's voice in these recollections and interviews is quiet, even self-effacing, he writes as a trustworthy and sympathetic witness, one who reveres his subjects: "Their presences have been emblems in my life, and I remember these poets as if I kept them carved in stone."

## Suzanne Keen (review date 24 September 1993)

SOURCE: "A Poke Over the Wall," in *Commonweal,* Vol. 120, No. 16, September 24, 1993, pp. 21–23.

[*In the following positive review, Keen argues that* The Museum of Clear Ideas *is primarily about how humans cope with endings and issues of closure.*]

Donald Hall's new book of poems, ***The Museum of Clear Ideas,*** made me want to run out into the yard and shout. And check the tomatoes, and the box scores. To reread Horace, James Wright, and to undertake a study of the undervalued art of tone. As I write, we have shaken loose the bonds of the basketball season, and turned our full attention to baseball. If you're near a major league stadium, you're probably close to a bookstore that carries poetry. Get ***The Museum of Clear Ideas***; it's perfect for the season, and you can reread it when winter comes and the tyranny of the hoop grips the nation once again.

Clad in Williams-and-Sonoma yuppie green, the book's cover only hints at its organizing conceit with an outline of home plate. The poems in this volume tackle the problem of coming to an ending from a variety of perspectives and forms: elegy, lyric sequence, and Horatian ode. Hall deploys his work in and against these genres in a sequence that invites meditation on their characteristic relations to time and to human means of marking time.

If the shape of the sequence **"Baseball,"** in nine innings, made of nine, nine-line stanzas suggests that the end must occur exactly where it does, when the form actually runs out, the poem leaves the reader in a condition of suspension between games, between actions, between memory of past seasons and appetite for another season:

> 9. No Red Sox tonight, but on Friday
> a doubleheader with the Detroit
> Tigers, my terrible old team, worse
> than the Red Sox who beat the
>    Yankees
> last night while my mother and I
>    watched
> —the way we listened, fifty years
>    back—
> spritely ghosts playing in heavy snow
> on VHS 30 from Hartford,
> and the pitcher stared at the batter.

Though they watch in the hospital, the outcomes of the illnesses that **"Baseball"** has documented go unreported; with a deft hand Hall waves away the symbols and allegories that so often infest literary versions of baseball. No home-run and heaven here. He directs our attention away from the diamond to the natural world:

> By the railroad goldenrod stiffens;
> asters begin a late pennant drive
> in front of the barn; pink hollyhocks
> wilt and sag like teams out of the race.

Good old-fashioned metaphor conjures up two kinds of time in a delightful shimmer of tenor and vehicle. **"Baseball"** inhabits an alternative realm already, a fictional space suspended outside of ordinary time. Addressed to the Dada collagist Kurt Schwitters (1887–1948), the poem attempts an explanation of the theory and practice of baseball, through meditations obliquely related to the 9 x 9 x 9 form. The enjambment, or running over lines, between the stanzas of the **"First Inning"** contrast with the businesslike picked-up pace of the **"Third Inning."** In this fashion the shape of the sequence instructs its imagined reader in the pace(s) of the game. Yet the material contained in this vessel of Hall's invention suggests the reach and amplitude of an imagination at play in the fields of memory, opinion, prophecy, and fresh experience. Hall's ability to use varied sentence-structure, and the cohabitation of sentence and line in stanzas, to emphasize shifts in tone and rhetorical strategy keeps this long poem from dulling in the ear. This interesting communication makes a significant contribution to poetry's conversation about the relations between visual art and literature.

In focusing on **"Baseball,"** I have leapt ahead in the order of the book, which begins, wryly, with **"Another Elegy."** When I heard Hall read this poem, he explained that the fiction of the poem allowed him to write his long-stalled elegy for the poet James Wright, who died in 1980. Bill Trout, the dead poet remembered in **"Another Elegy,"** is a creature of invention, but this has been the case in poets' elegies for fellow poets, from Milton at least. How much does "Lycidas" tell us about dead Edward King, and how much about ambitious John Milton? Even the rhetoric of praise and blame distorts the remembered life. Hall writes a canny critique of the form and its history:

> It is twelve Aprils since we buried
>   him. Now dissertation-
> salt preserves *The Collected Poems
>   of William Trout*
> like Lenin. Here is another elegy in
>   the tradition
> of mourning and envy, love and self-
>   love—as another morning
> delivers rain on the fishbone leaves
>   of the rotted year.

The humor with which Hall delivers and lampoons the conventions of elegy is carried further by the hilarious spoof of the canonizing poet's bio, "from" the imaginary *The Norton Anthology of Contemporary Verse.* Appearing in the "notes" section of ***The Museum of Clear Ideas,*** this further fiction lays bare a convention of contemporary poetry books: the appendix of notes used as an exhibit of the poet's learning and as a key to obscurities the reader will have encountered.

Hall identifies the *persona,* Horace Horsecollar, who speaks the odes of the poem **"The Museum of Clear Ideas,"** in such a note: "Lacking Latin, he follows his master visually—the number and shape of stanzas in Horace's first book of odes." These poems form the volume's second sequence, in which the range of tones and topics widens even further. As in **"Another Elegy"** and **"Baseball,"** the state of contemporary poetry comes under Hall's scrutiny; Horsecollar does not exempt his ventriloquizer when he criticizes: "Praising our places, we / praise ourselves while pretending to look outward." Poets build shrines to themselves,

> in every *Poetry,* by printing
>   reflections, in free verse
>     without noticeable attention to
> line breaks, on snapshots of the
>   poetic mother and father,
>     in their weird clothes, on
>       vacation, before
> the poet was born: How poignant it
>   is, how remarkable
>     that one's parents were older
>       than oneself!
> Then they died. Oh.

This cutting indictment of the bland subject matter and weak form of contemporary poetry does not attempt to disguise Hall's own interest in remembering persons and places, in fixing the details of daily life in verse. In ***The Museum of Clear Ideas*** a reader will find love poems, poems about a sick parent, frightening diagnoses, aging, sex, and the old neighborhood. Hall does not eschew the ordinary; he inhabits it. Books and poems and language belong in this poet's everyday world, so we find poems about old affairs or old friends cheek by jowl with his criticism of contemporary poetry.

Hall's determination to renew language's energetic engagement with the world calls our attention to the rhetoric we use in our daily interactions. Hall deplores the falsity of what he calls "The Jargon of Things," and "The Tongue of High Coy." In a book preoccupied with the problem of making an end, of reacting honestly to the endings that herald our own foregone conclusion, the danger of language's misuse should not be underestimated.

The final poem in the book, **"Extra Innings,"** takes up the fear of death directly. In these extra poems, which surprise the reader with a return to **"Baseball,"** Hall suggests that compassionate actions and the solaces of dailiness can hold fear at bay. Loss is forestalled but not denied in the conclusion to **"Extra Innings,"** which recalls the penultimate game of the 1975 World Series:

> I wear my yellow sweater;
>   we eat scrambled eggs from blue and
>     white dishes; her
> hair's kerchief is yellow. We gather
>     yellow days
> inning by inning with care to appear
>     careless,
> thinking again how Carlton Fisk
>     ended game Six
> in the twelfth inning with a poke over
>     the wall.

Do I need to point out that the Red Sox go on to lose the Series in the seventh game? Anyone who has suffered with a team, or waited for the results of the blood test to come in, knows the condition that Hall describes, "inning by inning with care to appear careless." Hall celebrates the ceremonial calendar of the baseball season in its relation to human lives. In poetry, in patterned language unleashed in time, Hall arrests us in the moment of hope that holds off the end.

### Vincent Sherry (review date Summer 1994)

SOURCE: "The High Pasture," in *Sewanee Review,* Vol. 102, No. 3, Summer, 1994, pp. lxxxix-xc.

[*In the following review, Sherry offers a positive assessment of both* Life Work *and* The Museum of Clear Ideas.]

[***Life Work*** and ***The Museum of Clear Ideas***] are olympian books. They are wise, but are written against every convention of wisdom.

***Life Work*** turns its diary of the quotidian into a treatise in which the duties and pleasures of labor are measured. The mixed attitude of duty and joy suffuses Mr. Hall's prose, its cadences alternately stately and capricious, elegiac and carnivalesque. A mock-classical decorum provides tonal unity for the long title poem of *The Museum of Clear Ideas,* whose shadowy protagonist—Horace Horsecollar—holds the sequence together in a fusion of Horatian gravities and cartoon simplicities.

Such combinations are high artifice, and the hand of a master craftsman shows in his fashioning of sentences into *sententiae*. But, if one moral can be attached to the story told in *Life Work,* the lesson is that it is only through work that ideas come at all: discipline is the one effort we can make at wisdom. It is a writerly wisdom to which Mr. Hall has attained, and if his yoke seems easy, his burden light, this impression is fostered by a success that is primarily stylistic, a success evidenced equally in prose and verse.

What animates the words and message of *Life Work* is a paradox that is no contradiction: the twelve or more hours a day that this author puts into writing and related activities seems a wholly gratuitous enterprise, a revel of dedications. "Technique *is* the test of a man's sincerity," as Ezra Pound counseled those earnest but incompetent versifiers of 1913; and Mr. Hall proves the truth of his enabling paradox in his verbal fabric, in his crafting of a physical body of language that is easy but never boneless, supple but not lax. His is a style of elegant plainness, at once dignified and natural. As such it is remarkably supple in accommodating the range of emotions rushing into this moment in the writer's life: a recurrence of cancer has enforced a sense of imminent endings and has caused an understandable sharpening of the pleasures lived through in the interim. These are *verbal* pleasures; there is always the sensuous and almost erotic rustling of word against word; and this sensuousness is lined by a silence that comes from a more ascetic discipline, and that speaks here of last things.

The poems in *The Museum of Clear Ideas* vary widely in tone and manner, ranging from the condensed and sometimes bitter eloquence of **"Another Elegy,"** written for a poet whose dissipations appear to have been inextricably linked with his distinctions, to the game-playing ingenuity of **"Baseball,"** a sequence composed on the magic number of nine—nine poems (for nine innings), each one consisting of nine stanzas of nine lines with nine counts each. If syllabic verse goes against the natural (accentual) grain of English, it is fair to say that this sequence remains mechanical rather than organic—prosody is not poetry, after all; and the speaker seems (inadvertently) contorted to the rococo-baroque of the rules, which do not of themselves generate a voice.

It is the voice of the title poem that remains the most extraordinary thing about this collection. Its syntax reminds us of neoclassical Latinity; its tonalities are learned and sometimes pedantic; it offers these ample resources up to the counter-rhythm of the heckler: "Or say" opens the second part of two-poem pairings within the sequence, and this antiphonal speaker turns the voice back upon itself, doubling, enriching:

> When I was young and sexual
>   I looked forward to cool Olympian
>     age
> for release from my obsessions.
>   Ho, ho, ho. At sixty the body's
>     one desire
>
> sustains my pulse, not to mention
>   my groin, as much as it ever did,
> if not quite so often.

The syntactic convolutions and inflated diction in this mock-classical piece—

>         As for Horsecollar,
> Decius, he'll take this desk, this blank
>     paper,
> this Bic, and the fragile possibility
> that, with your support, the Muse
>     may favor him

—turn *over* statement into poetic possibility, for the classical hype is a record of human hope no less moving than absurd. It is a sonority rinsed and chastened by its own opposition, and that the opposite possibilities dance so well together is a major achievement in a poetic career that has featured several major achievements in the last decade.

### Joanne Schott (review date May 1995)

SOURCE: A review of *Lucy's Summer,* in *Quill & Quire,* Vol. 61, No. 5, May, 1995, p. 51.

[*In the following positive review, Schott commends Hall's ability to bring the past to life in* Lucy's Summer.]

Lucy is the author's mother and this account of the events of the summer of 1910, Lucy's seventh, come from the stories she told about her childhood. Her mother started a home-based millinery business that summer but still had to can hundreds of jars of peas, beans, tomatoes, and rhubarb. The routine is broken by an itinerant photographer who takes a portrait of Lucy and her little sister, by the Fourth of July parade, and by a trip to Boston, where Mother buys supplies for her hats.

One of the trip's wonders is a visit to the penny toy counter in Woolworth's. Some of those toys, along with the old hat pedestals, still rest in an upstairs room of the house where Hall himself now lives. No wonder he can make the past so real and so immediate. A prize-winning poet, he illuminates the ordinary events of that summer with careful detail and expressive language.

Accurate detail and variety in perspective make these illustrations strongly narrative. The scratchboard technique gives them a richness of texture and an appropriately old-fashioned appearance, and creates almost magical effects of glowing light and dark shadows. [*Lucy's Summer*] is a book to pore over often, with text and pictures giving renewed pleasure with every reading.

## Peter Thorpe (review date July–August 1995)

SOURCE: A review of *Life Work,* in *Bloomsbury Review,* Vol. 15, No. 4, July–August, 1995, p. 29.

[*In the following review, Thorpe offers a mixed assessment of* Life Work, *faulting the work for indulging in too much "name-dropping."*]

There are plenty of definitions of work, including the cynical one by Bertrand Russell—that it's merely moving matter from one location to another. Additional words—or ideas—for work include labor, toil and moil, struggle, swink (archaic), drudge, grub, plod, exert, strain, and goodness knows how many others.

This memoir by Donald Hall [*Life Work*] seeks to put the concept of work into a context of the literary and intellectual life, yet not lose sight of the word's basic denotations of laboring or "swinking." In the full sense of the term, work is as spiritual as it is physical. The idea that "labour" is somehow spiritual too is not new—it goes back at least as far as the "Works and Days" of Hesiod in ancient Greece, and it figures beautifully in the "Georgics" of Virgil in ancient Rome. What Donald Hall seeks is to put his own idiosyncratic stamp on the term and to share it with a large audience of general readers.

*Life Work* is a (salubrious) book for several reasons. The chief of these is that Hall is one of the few living American examples of an authentic Man of Letters, after the grand old manner of Edmund Wilson and T. S. Eliot. We read Hall as an engaging jack-of-all-trades—as the author of literary criticism, poetry, children's books, general essays, and even a fascinating volume on the topic of baseball. Like Eliot and Wilson, he has won a variety of literary prizes and he can write convincingly for all audiences on just about any subject.

If this book has a special power and poignancy to it, it is because Hall discovered, when he was halfway through writing it, that he had metastasized cancer of the liver. He pauses in his writing to undergo surgery in which two-thirds of his liver is removed, and then returns to his task. Needless to say, the latter parts of *Life Work* have about them a new sense of urgency and a new eloquence. Yet the language never descends into alarmism, nor does Hall's calm voice ever lose its measured pace and its ability to keep our interest on every page.

The business at hand, for Hall, is the precise nature of work and the benefits arising therefrom. To buttress his sentiments about it, he likes to refer to other famous "workers" in the arts and humanities, using them not so much as authorities but rather as touchstones in the manner of Matthew Arnold. He likes what Henry Moore (the sculptor) said:

> *The secret of life is to have a task, something you devote your entire life to, something you bring everything to, every minute of the day for your whole life. And the most important thing is—it must be something you cannot possibly do!*

Certainly a theme throughout *Life Work* is that the mental, if not the physical, task must have an impossibly severe challenge to it. Here is the goal which Hall sets for himself in his poetry:

> *My own high road is to make poems better than Dante, Homer, and Virgil, not to mention folks closer to home like Whitman, Dickinson, Frost, Stevens, and Kinnell.*

(Some readers will find the last one rather anticlimactic.)

The colloquialism of "folks closer to home" is symbolic of Hall's versatility. He is a writer with the highest of highbrows, yet he can talk cows with the farmers of New England where he was born. In *Life Work* he descants on doing farm chores with nearly the same solemnity that he uses when talking of poetry. He also puts a strong creative labor into maintaining relationships with colleagues, friends, or relatives, and he is a nearly compulsive letter writer. All of this is merely a part of the general fabric of work, and Hall's dominant message emerges as a belief that work is to be identified with life itself and that life, for all practical purposes, ceases when we no longer have the will to labor on the spiritual or physical level.

If there is anything weak about Hall's memoir, it may have to do with his fairly constant name-dropping: appellations of big-time writers, critics, and artists turn up with distressing frequency, lending an ever-so-slight hint of the pompous to what would otherwise be a totally charming autobiography. On the other hand, Hall has for decades been a member in good standing of the literati, so perhaps we have to expect a certain amount of references to the luminaries. This "shortcoming," however, need not detract from the readability and incisiveness of what Donald Hall has to say, even as he slowly turns to face his own death.

## R. S. Gwynn (review date January 1996)

SOURCE: "Proseurs," in *Sewanee Review,* Vol. 104, No. 1, January, 1996, pp. 142–49.

[*In the following excerpt, Gwynn criticizes Hall's use of publishing sales figures to defend modern poetry in* Death to the Death of Poetry.]

What happens when poets turn their hands to prose? We might expect that they would have an easy go of it, wouldn't we? Prose, after all, is *easier* to forge than poetry. Prose writers are spared having to learn phrases like *medial caesura* or *substitute foot*: all that each of them has to know is how to put a semicolon in its place and make subjects and verbs agree. Poets, on the other hand, go mad worrying about such silly matters as when to end their lines; now that everyone uses a computer, prose writers have even that minimal decision made automatically for them, courtesy of Bill Gates. Any hack can write a sentence like "So much depends upon a red wheelbarrow glazed with rain water beside the white chickens," but it takes a true genius, a *poet,* to break it into eight lines that have kept English majors bemused for the better part of a century. Yes, when poets shed all that nasty baggage of rhyme, meter, and terminology they have been forced to lug across the Landscape from Hell ("All out for Onomatopoeia. Next stop Synecdoche") you'd expect them to soar. For the most part they do, though some soar distinctly higher than others.

The works of critical prose under review here, which represent several years' accumulation, range widely from the lordly (or *ladily,* in this case) work of scholarship to the more informal collections of reviews, occasional pieces, and the interview, that mainstay of the contemporary poet's repertoire. No works of fiction by poets have crossed my desk recently, though at least three of the authors discussed here have produced widely admired specimens; but much that lies in the autobiographies and memoirs that I can mention only briefly here might pass for such (and, yes, the pun was intended). One of the poet-critics under discussion has even produced a genuine best-seller, a spirited *apologia* for homosexuality that takes a tack different from the shrill invective of the gay-rights activists.

One of the monuments of this century's literature is the distinguished body of criticism by American poets. I recently edited an anthology of American poet-critics born between 1888 and 1916, and I was consistently taken with the quality of the writing, beginning with Pound, Eliot, and Ransom and ending with Jarrell, Hayden, and Ciardi; they look even better when their prose is compared with the unreadable mumbling that passes for much contemporary academic criticism. We may have no poet-critics of comparable stature today, but there are many doing distinguished work, most of them as practical critics, a class largely overlooked in this age of theory....

. . . Hall's ill-titled ***Death to the Death of Poetry*** takes its prompt from a widely discussed essay in *Commentary* by Joseph Epstein, "The Death of Poetry." Hall answers Epstein by cleverly resurrecting an essay by Edmund Wilson—"Is Verse a Dying Technique?"—which foretold the same imminent demise sixty years earlier: "Poetry was never Wilson's strong suit. It is worthwhile to remember that Wilson found Edna St. Vincent Millay the great poet of her age—better than Robert Frost, Marianne Moore, T. S. Eliot, Ezra Pound, Wallace Stevens, and William Carlos Williams." Hall is unsparing in his attack on Epstein, who describes a reading by two unnamed but identifiable younger poets as symptomatic of the art's terminable disease: "heavily preening, and not distinguished enough in language or subtlety of thought to be memorable." Hall responds: "Such disparagements are pure blurbtalk. He does not quote a line by either poet he dismisses. As with the aging Edmund Wilson, Epstein saves time by ignoring particulars of the art he disparages."

I might have found Hall's rebuttal more convincing if he had not fallen back on a tired recitation of publishers' sales statistics to prove that poetry is alive and well. The list of poets who have "sold their books by the tens of thousands" provides me with only the coldest of comforts: "Adrienne Rich, Robert Bly, Allen Ginsberg, John Ashbery, Galway Kinnell, Robert Creeley, Gary Snyder, Denise Levertov, Carolyn Forché; doubtless others." He might have added Suzanne Somers, Leonard Nimoy, and Jimmy Stewart to the list if sheer quantities provide any index of good health. Hall's book doesn't have a discernible order, with interviews alternating with reviews and autobiographical essays; but there are so many juicy insider's glances that it seems silly to carp about structure. My favorite moment is a description of a double date from the poet's Harvard years in which the participants were Hall, a "beautiful, bright, blonde" Radcliffe student, Robert Bly, and Adrienne Rich! I will leave it to the curious reader to discover who was with whom.

### Lawrence Goldstein (review date Fall 1996)

SOURCE: "The Harvard Advocate," in *Michigan Quarterly Review,* Vol. 35, No. 4, Fall, 1996, pp. 745–54.

[*In the following review, Goldstein assesses three examples of Hall's nonfiction works—*Principal Products of Portugal, Death to the Death of Poetry, *and* Life Work,*—and explores what these works reveal about his poetry.*]

These days the theory of literature has taken up, again, the infinitely interesting matter of literary production—how writing gets written, revised, edited, published, distributed, reviewed, reprinted, canonized. It is a subject that has fascinated Donald Hall all of his life, the more so after 1975, when he resigned from his tenured position in the English Department at the University of Michigan to return to his ancestral farmhouse in New Hampshire and begin life as a free-lance in the literary marketplace. His principal goal in going it alone, liberated from the routine of teaching, grading, serving on committees and socializing with other academics, was to write the major poetry he felt stirring within him, his equivalent of T. S. Eliot's *Four Quartets* or, in his own generation, Galway Kinnell's *The Book of Nightmares* (1971), John Ashbery's *Three Poems* (1972), or Adrienne Rich's *Diving into the Wreck* (1973). His much-honored volumes, ***Kicking the Leaves*** (1978), ***The Happy Man*** (1986), ***The One Day*** (1988), ***The Museum of Clear Ideas*** (1993), and ***The Old Life*** (1996), are installments of what might be considered a single project best named by the rejected title of one of the volumes, *Building the House* of *Dying*. How these poems have gotten written and published is one subject Hall speaks frequently about in the three nonfiction books under review, but one subject only. The books are compendiums of diverse materials, by-products of his commitment to the making of major poetry.

The title **Principal Products of Portugal** is "code for things miscellaneous, unrelated, boring and probably educational." The phrase reminds us of data we were taught in elementary school because it was good for us to have knowledge of the world's business, no matter how remote from our little patch of experience. The title is disarming, apologetic, a cover for the republication of many commissioned pieces that paid the bills while Hall toiled each morning on his verse. A history of "Casey at the Bat," interviews with Bob Cousy, Carlton Fisk, and Red Auerbach, an appreciation of Henry Adams's historical writing, a survey of Andrew Marvell's poetry, a tribute to Henry Moore, a night-piece on graveyards, a memoir of having been affected viscerally as a child by the movie *Last Train from Madrid*—twenty-five pieces of this kind do have the randomness of olive oil, cork, pulpwood, wine, petroleum, and figs. How many poets in twentieth-century America could have earned a commission by writing an essay entirely about the Detroit Tigers' decision to move Mickey Stanley from centerfield to shortstop in the 1968 World Series? Not T. S. Eliot. Not John Ashbery. And yet, we are not talking about Grub Street. Baseball is as much a part of Hall's imaginative world as the pastoral elegy, and his ability to make the connection between those two subjects, and so many others, defines him as a capacious man of letters, a mediating spirit of our time.

"If we stick to what we already know, we stick to what we already do," Hall writes. He has been able to broaden the range of his poetry by casting his net, of financial necessity, beyond his accustomed sphere of interests. Retirement has abetted this tendency, as Hall has sought to amplify his writing by educating himself further in history, religion, and science. Having read the 2,597 pages of Henry Adams's *History of the United States during the Administrations of Jefferson and Madison,* Hall is outraged that more writers don't read this "major work of American literature," nor Gibbon, Motley, and Parkman. He rightly claims that poets will sooner read very minor poetry of the past and present than the greatest works of history. His reading of Adams et al., which was *not* work for hire, nourished **The One Day** and informs the experimental poems he has written since. Characteristically, Hall turns the facts of Adams's chronicle against the rational act of tracing cause and effect in time. In **The One Day** Hall writes a deadpan stanza about the delegates to the Constitutional Convention in Philadelphia, then follows it with this send-up of history-writing as a mode of understanding how heroes persist in cultural memory:

> Some delegates hitched rides chatting with teamsters;
> some flew stand-by and wandered stoned in O'Hare
> or borrowed from King Alexander's National Bank:
>   None
> returned to plantation, farm, or townhouse.
> They wandered weary until they encountered each
>   other
> again, converging on Hollywood Boulevard bordered
>   with bars
> in their absurd clothing like movie extras, Federalist
> and Republican descending the cloverleaf together
> to engage another Convention at the Hollywood-La
>   Brea Motel—
> wearing their nametags, befuddled, unable to argue.

Even Henry Adams would get a laugh out of this surreal invention at the expense of our founding fathers. Indeed, the stanza reflects Adams's central discovery, as Hall defines it: "People do the opposite of what they say (and think) they do." These delegates thought they were forging a virtuous new nation from the chaos of human appetites; but they created a libertarian society in which citizens were permitted to build cities like Hollywood in order to ceaselessly indulge their appetites. Adams's history enables Hall to articulate his sense of a civilization spinning out of control, toward the kind of terminal confusion that oppressed Adams himself when he wrote his autobiography.

Hall's prose, like his verse, is witty and pungent. It intends to be memorable, to be jotted down in commonplace books, to be quoted in the halls of Congress and in schoolrooms. "Sensible people agree: A day spent without the thought of death is a wasted day." "Art is the source of the compassion by which we prefer funding misery over funding the arts." "Design is nutrition for mind as food for body." "The existence of honest, difficult, human intelligence consoles us. Poetry's thinking consoles us." Epigrammatic and condensed to the point of proverbial economy, such sentences keep the reader alert to the nuances of Hall's prose. When Hall says that he would like to wallpaper his room with Henry Adams's sentences he indicates how important sentences are to a sensibility in need of the richest possible linguistic nourishment. A prose work like **"Trees"** erases the distinction between verse and prose; it is as highly wrought and rhythmically sophisticated as a poem of Marvell's. If it were in French it would be acclaimed by the admirers of Ponge and Bonnefoy as the cutting-edge of the contemporary *parole*.

Part of Hall's powerful style is a certain dogmatism that will arouse occasional resistance; this is a problem only for readers who can't tolerate opinions contrary to their own. Hall quotes William Blake's line, "O Rose, thou art sick," and then asserts, "it is useless to ask, 'What does *Rose* mean? What does *sick* mean?'" I think most readers would respond that it's not useless at all, that Blake especially, one of the most disputatious of all poets, expects us to ask precisely those questions on the way toward a full appreciation of the poem. Hall says of the generation of American writers born in the 1920s that it was "the first generation in American history for whom Europe was not an issue." "Not an issue" is not precise enough to base an argument upon, but surely it would be difficult to speak very long about the likes of Richard Wilbur, Anthony

Hecht, Donald Justice, John Ashbery, and W. S. Merwin, not to mention the more complex cases of Robert Bly, Frank O'Hara, and Adrienne Rich, without describing very powerful European influences on their work. To be fair, the statement occurs in a memoir of James Wright, the best essay in the volume, in which Hall is seeking to define the unique, native voice of this Ohio poet and claim it as the essential voice of his generation.

Hall becomes polemical only when writing of literature, which is why those essays are the most fun. He would never make a statement as preposterous as the following if he were writing about baseball or the Constitution: "Victorian England . . . [was] a literary culture that saw poems as commendable ideas accompanied by sugary noises; a literary culture that never found room in its poetry—except for the unpublished Hopkins—for the powers of ambivalence and conflict." The remark will be red meat in graduate seminars devoted to Browning, Arnold, and the Rossettis. It catches Hall at a critical location too far outside the academy, where the presence of informed colleagues and students, and a library of commentary, would chasten such dogmatism. Fortunately, remarks like these are like the few spoiled grapes that come in succulent bunches from the groves of Portugal.

***Death to the Death of Poetry*** is Hall's fourth volume of essays, reviews, notes, and interviews in the Poets on Poetry series published by the University of Michigan Press. This one is shorter and slighter in content, perhaps because ***Principal Products of Portugal*** siphoned off some material that might have enhanced this collection—the essay on E. A. Robinson, certainly, and the ones on Marvell and James Wright. The interviews with Liam Rector and Peter Stitt that comprise 53 of the book's 157 pages are available in other books. I suspect that Hall sent the book to press a bit sooner than he would have in earlier years (***The Weather for Poetry,*** in 1982, numbered 335 pages) because he was eager to enter the controversy he engages in the title essay. In the last few years a number of books and articles have decried the supposed unpopularity of poetry and predicted possible extinction for verse in the near future. Hall is exasperated with these doomsayings and in the volume's title essay he sets his impressive polemical skills against them.

As he points out, critics are always declaring poetry in a state of crisis. In the early 1930s Edmund Wilson, in his essay "Is Verse a Dying Technique?" claimed that poetry was losing its public, in large part because it had become so difficult to understand. Had Hall wished to move backward historically he could have found voices like Wilson's in every generation. David de Laura has written that "from about 1820, well into the 1850s, the continuous context for the discussion of poetry in England was a fear that it was nearly defunct." Now the Victorian and modernist eras are seen as periods when poetry had both prestige and a large following, just as thirty years from now the same situation deplored by our contemporaries will be proclaimed by critics as a golden age. Hall believes that this *is* a golden age for poetry: "More people write poetry in this country—publish it, hear it, and presumably read it—than ever before." He cites statistics to prove the vitality of contemporary poetry and affirms—there is no way to prove it—that a substantial portion is of sufficiently high quality to stand with the masterpieces of the past. Critics who loudly deplore the writing of their time can never acknowledge the fact of its excellence. As Max Apple said in a recent interview, critics of today complain that there is no Faulkner among us. But when Faulkner was publishing his masterpieces the same kind of critics were complaining that there was no Henry James among them. Such people can never be satisfied—except by the stir of controversy they promote around themselves by their melodramatic pronouncements.

Hall's essay on the subject is important because it is grounded in evidence not easily dismissed, including his long memory of the history of poetry since the early 1940s. Harvard was the crucible in which his expansive tastes took form. He edited the undergraduate literary magazine, the *Harvard Advocate,* and in 1950 published as his first book an anthology of undergraduate writings from the eighty-four years of "Mother *Advocate.*" (His chief editorial coup was prying loose from T. S. Eliot nine tyro poems.) In those giddy years in Cambridge Hall associated with Robert Bly, John Ashbery, Frank O'Hara, Adrienne Rich, John Ciardi, Kenneth Koch, Richard Wilbur, Robert Creeley, Archibald MacLeish, Richard Eberhart. "Quite a bunch!" he exclaims. Thanks in large part to this fostering milieu, Hall enjoys the full range of poetries written in the postwar period, a period whose taste he has helped to shape through his anthologies, textbooks, essays and reviews, teaching, lectures, and readings. If you like only one kind of poetry you can get depressed if you don't see abundant attention being paid to it. (People don't seem to be talking about the poets with whom you feel the most affinity? This must signal the imminent doom of poetry.) Because Hall's taste is capacious and even contradictory, he takes heart from the general enthusiasm for all manner of poetry and song. It comes as a surprise to hear him say that the poet he admires most in his generation is Robert Creeley, in part because he rarely mentions Creeley when he analyzes poems, and in part because Hall tends to favor his personal friends when he glorifies his generation in print: Bly, Kinnell, Wright, Simpson, Geoffrey Hill. The future of poetry is assured so long as the independence and originality of writers like Creeley—who has grounded his innovative practice on a prolonged study of poetics—are rewarded by the respect of commentators like Hall.

"I was a fierce advocate for the contemporary," Hall says of his earlier self, and it's true that, though he is famous for his encouragement of new talent, his principal interest is and will always be his own generation. For poets born before 1920, like Lowell and Berryman, Hall displays very mixed feelings. Berryman, he writes, is a "problem," a poet whose work often incites "disgust" though Hall acknowledges that he is always snatched back into respect for Berryman by some graceful or pungent poem. Hall passionately loved Lowell's early work but grew increasingly unhappy with the late style, which he considers self-indulgent and slack. Hall will not be negative in print about personal friends, a limitation of his criticism, but he does not study them in print either. We shall have to wait for a collection of letters to find his expert discriminations of their work, and theirs of his own. His review of W. D. Snodgrass's *Selected Poems* gives us a peek into his opinions on that poet and friend, but Hall withdraws tactfully from analysis in favor of autobiography. Finally, Hall is concerned to place poets in terms of his own development in the historical era that followed modernism. He will not, he says, act the "bobbysoxer" like Helen Vendler, the current Harvard tastemaker, swooning over Jorie Graham and Brad Leithauser, nor the curmudgeon, like Yvor Winters, dispraising everyone but his own epigone. Hall claims larger sympathies because of the generous New England upbringing that established his temperament.

Hall's parents lived in suburban Connecticut, where, he claims, everyone wanted to be just like everyone else. But he spent his summers on the New Hampshire farm to which he eventually retired, and this rural world nourished his literary sensibility: "In the culture of the country . . . there was fantastic diversity—in education, aspiration, income, appearance; what you wore, what you ate, what you did for fun—from house to house along the roads and lanes. Eccentricity was a *value*; a major ethical notion was everybody's right to be different." For Hall poetry became the living symbol and agent of that diversity. When he praises poets it is for their ability to capture attention by the force of a compelling style. He was "immediately enthralled" when he read Theodore Roethke's *The Lost Son*. "I remember the general flabbergast when Thom Gunn's first poems went public," he writes. In a series of short notices from the *Harvard Review* he praises the "natural speech" of Etheridge Knight and the "dailyness" of Wendell Berry and the "headlong assault" of Gerald Burns. He likes to be caught off guard by both the familiar and the unfamiliar. He lives in a mixed neighborhood of poetry, enjoying the plurality of voices as he would at a community fair or church social.

Hall has guaranteed that we cannot talk about his literary opinions or his verse without recurring to the alpha and omega spot of his personal universe: Eagle Pond, New Hampshire. "I have modeled my late life in this house on my grandparents' as they lived here in work, love, and double-solitude," he writes in *Life Work,* his summing-up of the lessons he learned at his two residences in the old manse. As a boy he first heard poetry recited by his grandfather Wesley Wells, as the old man milked the cows or worked in the field; and he watched with fascination as his grandmother Kate worked incessantly at the multitudinous domestic chores of a mixed farm. Faithful readers of Hall's writing since his first volume of poems, *Exiles and Marriages,* in 1955, have come to know this family intimately. In **"Elegy for Wesley Wells,"** written in the early 1950s after his grandfather's death, Hall wrote, "I number out the virtues that are dead, / Remembering the soft consistent voice / And bone that showed in each deliberate word." He has never stopped remembering or numbering out those virtues, and *Life Work* is the most ambitious memoir thus far of the time he shared with the eldest members of his family. Even readers who feel like they could write a full-length biography of Wesley and Kate Wells out of Hall's already-published writing will be surprised to find a density of new detail and revised judgement in this book as Hall confronts his own mortality in the land of his ancestors.

*Life Work* is written in journal form, a sequence of meditations that begins casually and then is jolted into urgency halfway along by news of the author's cancer and a succession of lab tests, treatments, and operations. Notations about the meaning of work that had seemed rather disinterested and speculative in Part One become tense and dramatic as Time's winged chariot carries the author faster and faster toward the imagined finale of his many literary projects. He is comforted by his wife and friends, and keeps working in defiance of death. (In a ghastly irony, after publication of the book Hall's wife, the poet Jane Kenyon, contracted leukemia and died of it in 1995.) The nature of his work, he comes to understand, is a recapitulation of his grandparents' work; it is joyful and exhausting and interminable, and it binds together past, present and future by its enabling rules and conventions. The grandparents did the work of husbandry Virgil described in his Georgics and Eclogues; Hall writes here and in some of his poems in the manner of Virgil about the timeless and eternally recurring processes of manual labor.

The prose of *Life Work* is not artless exposition but has the charged intensity of verse. Listen to the rhythms of a sample descriptive passage:

> Later in the winter he drove an ox up hill pulling a sledge, loaded up the cordwood and brought it down for sawing, splitting, drying, and stacking in the woodshed next summer for the winter to follow. After woodchopping, probably the next most difficult task of the year was carting ice from Eagle Pond to store in the icehouse behind the tie-up's watering trough. Neighbors worked together taking ice from the pond, often in February, when the ice was two feet thick. First, they scraped snow off, then with horse-drawn cutters scraped long lines onto ice, back and forth, making a checkerboard of ruts, then split the ice into great oblong chunks, then floated ice-slabs to shore, making watery channels for more slabs. Ice-farming hazards were the cold and the wet, slipping into the freezing water, even drowning dragged down by heavy winter clothes.

The sonic architecture makes the sentences a pleasure to read, as the alto vowels are deployed against the plosive consonants: the i of "ice" especially and the heavy t and d sounds crescendoing in the final phrase. But these regional details are not offered for the sake of mere musicality. One hears in passages like this the solemnity of a historian who will not allow significant human activity to pass into oblivion. Most readers of Hall will be as ignorant about the methods of ice-cutting as of making syrup and spreading manure. Hall feels obliged to educate his readers and immortalize his grandfather's way of life at the same time.

Increasingly, Hall has not only modeled his work habits after his grandparents but made persistent use of them as subject matter as well. Compare the prose passage above to his long poem of reminiscence, **"Daylilies on the Hill."** In the following passage Hall describes the efforts of a neighbor to help his grandparents clean out a well clogged with mud after a hurricane:

> Wesley milked his girls in the barn, gave
> Riley some oats and water, shook hay down for the
>   sheep,
> then watered and grained the hens and harvested eggs.
> When he climbed up hill, first thing he saw
> was the forked branch stuck in the ground, its lantern
>
> burning faint in the dawn's light. Then, as he watched,
> Freeman hauled his shape up from the narrow well,
> finished at last, proud and weary, pointing to lucid
> spring water pooling at the bottom, gathering.

Lengthy descriptive passages of this kind dare the reader to declare them boring. The cosmopolitan tone and accelerated speed of modernist poetry supplanted the Romantic, retrospective mode Hall is now trying to reclaim. Though Hall has experimented with the aleatoric and the surreal, his characteristic rhetorical stance is defiance of the neurasthenic T. S. Eliot and all the urban wastelands of modernist verse. When first reading Hall's poetry of pastoral recollection, one thinks of Wordsworth's pleasure in returning during middle-age to the Lake District of his youth after years at Cambridge, London, and elsewhere. But Hall does not, as Wordsworth does, write brief lyrics that enact epiphanies brought on by strange "spots of time." Rather, he writes anecdotally about the minute particulars of work, the "dailyness" of country labor he praises in the prose and verse of Wendell Berry.

It might be going too far to compare the detached paragraphs of *Life Work* to the blocks of ice or clumps of hay to which Hall devotes such attention; but certainly the value given to steady work at determinate and sequential tasks is shared between the generations. "Anyone who loves accomplishment lives by the clock and the list," he writes, and to illustrate the point he makes lists of duties in the book, itemizes a typical day, calculates how long he must write and revise everything from a long poem to a book review before they reach resolution and conclusiveness. To undertake a substantial amount of work, he acknowledges, is to enslave yourself to the dreaded constraints of time. The love of work arouses morbidity, Hall's childhood temperament, just as it arouses joy in achievement and good humor under pressure. Hall asks for a larger range of vocabulary that will distinguish the drudgery of the assembly line from the labor of sustaining a whole existence on a farm, and those kinds of work from the ludic task of writing a poem. And how do we distinguish, likewise, the hours of leisure/recreation/amusement? For his grandfather, listening to a baseball game on radio was pure recreation; for Hall it is a pleasure to observe the work of athletes on television, but it is also primary research for work he may later undertake for *Sports Illustrated* at so much a word, and then for a substantial poem like **"Baseball"** in *The Museum of Clear Ideas.* A writer's work is never done because the best writers bring the totality of their knowledge and experience to bear on each piece of writing. Like the ox-cart man he has written about in different formats, who takes his goods to market and then sells the cart and ox as well and starts all over again when he returns to his village, Hall aspires to transfer all that he has and knows into his late, long works. "Only when you empty the well does water return to the well," he writes in **Death to the Death of Poetry.**

*Life Work,* then, shows Hall moving spiritually well beyond the literary politics fomented by his Harvard experience. He has become a Christian, or rather, recaptured the piety he once felt when visiting the local church with his grandfather (who slipped him candies with a wink). He will continue to comment on poems and reputations, all the more securely for locating himself in a two thousand year old tradition of religious belief. As he describes his own daily experience he senses increasingly the presence of his progenitors at his shoulder: Virgil, Whitman, Pound, Eliot, Moore, Frost, and Williams. And in the devoted tones of the advocate he seeks to reanimate the life before poetry, when as a child he watched his grandmother design her gardens and his grandfather seed his fields. "I speak his name against the beating sea," Hall wrote elegiacally of Wesley Wells almost fifty years ago. In *Life Work* he concludes by saying, "I repeat stories I grew up on, stories that created me." It is territory that no other poet can steal from him, a realm of ever-renewing inspiration, a well that never runs dry. Making it known to readers has been the work of a lifetime, and in the process Hall has made his books of central importance in the national literature.

### Chris Walsh (essay date 1998)

SOURCE: "'Building the House of Dying': Donald Hall's Claim for Poetry," in *Agni*, Vol. 47, 1998, pp. 175–83.

[*In the following essay, Walsh discusses the role of history and modernity in* The One Day.]

> "In my head for a long time I called it *Building the House of Dying.*"
>
> —Hall on the book that became *The One Day*

"Diatribes from our current art-bashers—columnists, senators, fundamentalists—bring nothing new to our culture," says Donald Hall, characteristically blunt in his most recent collection of literary essays, **Death to the Death of Poetry** (1994). "America's eminent know-nothings have always understood: *Artists are sissies providing pastimes for rich folks.*" His italics, his sarcasm. Hall's not here to help pass the time. He's more ambitious than that. He's nothing if not ambitious. "As I like to say," he writes in his paean to vocation, *Life Work,* "I average four books a year—counting revised editions of old books, counting everything I can damned well count. Counting books, book reviews, notes, poems, and essays, I reckon I publish about one item a week, year-in, year-out." But Hall's ambition runs deeper than numbers. He laments the limited aspirations and achievement of contemporary American poetry. "McPoems," he calls the typical product. "Usually brief, they resemble each other, they are anecdotal, they do not extend themselves, they make no great claims, they connect small things to other small things." Hall's written more than a few of these himself. See his **Old and New Poems** for a very enjoyable sample.

*They make no great claims*—but what are rich folks or any folks to make of this, from Hall's 1988 book-length poem **The One Day**?

> Your children will wander looting the shopping malls
> for forty years, suffering your idleness,
> until the last dwarf body rots in a parking lot.

Nothing here to help the digestion between rounds at Kiawah. Even if the children aren't looting, what if they're just shopping the shopping malls (though this would deprive us of the pleasure of *looting's* diminution into our lot—*lot*), is that any consolation? The prophecy holds. This in itself may not be a great claim, but it is the beginning of a great claim—a great question. If virtue and invention come of necessity, then does the lack of necessity in modern life, the luxury we have to idle (granted, the idle is set frenetically high for many) mean the end of virtue and human resourcefulness, the end of what millennia of experience have taught us to think of as distinctly, valuably, essentially human? "We forget / every skill we acquired over ten thousand years of labor," Hall writes. "I practice smiling; I forget how to milk a goat." Does abundance mean atrophy? Does push-button technology render us effete and ineffectual, as in "Of course I couldn't kill a rat with a putter / even if it shuddered in my daughter's crib," so that we have no response to and indeed no ideas better than the looming barbarian solution?

> . . . Tribes wandering
> in the wilderness of their ignorant desolation,
> who suffer from your idleness, will burn your illumi-
>   nated
> missals to warm their rickety bodies.
> Terrorists assemble plutonium because you are idle
>
> and industrious.

What are we to do? **The One Day** asks this question quite clearly, quite emphatically. It also, and this is what makes it a risky, great book, answers the question it poses.

Not that one reads the poem for this big question and answer, the *meaning*; such is, in T. S. Eliot's phrase, "a bit of nice meat for the house-dog" of the mind. Hall teases the appetite in the early going: "Never do anything except what you want to do." But this is more morsel than meal or, to change the metaphor, more alarum than answer. It haunts the rest of the poem—and it is the haunted poem itself that is Hall's answer, or, to use his more appropriate term, his claim.

The prospect of meaning diverts the reader so that the poet-burglar can do his essential work, work that does not admit of simple or even complex paraphrase, such as I have begun to attempt here. The essential work involves delight and mystery—moving, not convincing, the reader.

And **The One Day** delights and moves in myriad ways. Hall's great mastery of sound is the first mover, striking the ears first, naturally, but reminding us that the auditory canal courses deep into the skull. Sound vibrates fluid and air in there under the eyes, behind the nose. It fills mouth and throat and lungs. The flesh and bones of even the silent reader feel all this before the mind figures. The body thrills at the crash and trill of "course," "couldn't kill," "rat," and the mounting rhyme of "putter," "shuddered," and "daughter's" in the lines quoted above, which end with the frustration and resignation of the plosive stop consonant of "b" in "crib." The lower lip protrudes babyishly, you can't help it. And listen to the assonance, the nasals, sibilants, dentives, and liquids (one doesn't know these terms offhand, but exhilaration moves him to explication) of "the young women's bodies, / their smooth skin intolerably altered by ointments." Isn't there something gooily intolerable about the word "ointment"? It tastes funny.

Then the mind has the pleasure of experiencing the great history of poetry that constitutes, in a strict sense, **The One Day,** which is not to say that it is text-bookish in the least. It's not *about* the history of poetry; it *is* history, an embodiment and extension of tradition, of, as Eliot has it, not that which "is dead," but that which is "already living." Maybe it's best to say that Hall used everything he knows of poetry to write the poem, and he knows an awful lot.

There is, for instance, the modernist trick of multiple voices with which Hall enacts his epigraph from Picasso, "Every human being is a colony":

> (Who is it that sets these words on blue-lined paper?
> It is the old man in the room of bumpy wallpaper.
> It is the girl who sits on her drunken mother's lap
> or carries her grandmother's eggs. It is the boy who
>   reads
> the complete works of Edgar Allan Poe. It is the
>   middle-
> aged man motionless in a yellow chair, unable to read,
> daydreaming the house of dying. The colony takes
>   comfort
> in building this house which does not exist, because
> it does not exist—as I stare at the wrist's knuckle,
> idle, without purpose, fixed in a yellow chair.)

Hall prophesies apocalypse à la Revelations, but is more specific and modern, as in the "looting the shopping malls" lines, or more viscerally horrifying: "Fat will boil in the sacs of children's clear skin."

The last lines of the poem fulfill Marianne Moore's request (Hall has published a study of Moore) in "Poetry" for "imaginary gardens with real toads in them":

> . . . Together we walk in the high orchard
> at noon; it is cool, although the sun poises upon us.
> Among old trees the creek breathes slowly,
> bordered by fern. The toad at our feet holds still.

Vying for Whitmanian sweep, Hall puts even the bathroom, if not the kitchen, sink in front of the reader's mind's eye:

> I reject Martha's Vineyard and the slamdunk contest;
> I reject leaded panes; I reject the appointment made
> at the tennis net or on the seventeenth green; I reject
> the Professional Bowlers Tour; I reject matchboxes;
> I reject purple bathrooms with purple soap in them.

Here Hall reveals, even revels in, the Jeremiah in him that Whitman repressed in the later editions of *Leaves of Grass*—a querulousness, a bitter despair not often associated with the Good Gray Poet. See "Respondez" in *The Neglected Walt Whitman*:

> Let the people sprawl with yearning, aimless hands!
>   let their tongues be broken!
> . . . . . . . . . . . . . . . . . . . . . . . . . . . . . . . .
> Let all the men of these States stand aside for a few
>   smouchers! let the few seize on what they choose!
>   let the rest gawk, giggle, starve, obey!

and compare it to Hall's:

> Because professors of law teach ethics in dumbshow,
>   let the colonel become president; because chief executive
> officers and commissars collect down for pillows,
>   let the injustice of cities burn city and suburb;
> let the countryside burn; let the pineforests of Maine
>   explode like a kitchenmatch and the Book of Kells
>   turn
> ash in a microsecond; let oxen and athletes
> flash into grease:—I return to Appalachian rocks;
> I shall eat bread; I shall prophesy through millennia
> of Jehovah's day until the sky reddens over cities. . . .

Yet violent as the imagery is, as much as it rejects, we find that rejections become formations, that prophecy itself is left standing. Destruction constructs, in the words of the author's note that follows the poem, "ten-line bricks which could build the house and remain whole." It is this paradoxical phenomenon of building by wrecking and wreaking that gives **The One Day** its momentum.

This is especially true of the middle of the poem. In the section titled **"Pastoral,"** the poem suffers and parodies mid-life crisis:

> *Phyllis*: My Hermes, you sit with your pipes pocketed
>   at committee
> meetings and eat nonbiodegradable donuts and drink
>   whitened coffee without protest. You play sets of tennis
> with the director you dislike, and laugh shaking your
>   head
> as your baseline shots fall continually past the baseline.
> You make rules, piper, by which you cannot be fired.
> I cheat my employer; I quit and take unemployment
> because I deserve it. You exploit your employees.
> My friend in the city attorney's office reduces the
>   charges.
> You weep, my love, chained to the trireme's oar.
>
> *Marc*: I fly with my family to San Juan for a week
>   attended
> by Moriscos. Drunk after the party, I fumble to embrace
> the babysitter, taking her home, who will not sit
> for my children again. I choose a girl from Records
> instead, who is twenty-three and thinks I am rich.
> Later when I am bored I disengage myself,
> sending her presents. Ingratiating to boss, insulting
> to employees, I endure my days without pleasure
> or purpose, finding distraction in Rodeo Drive, in
> duplicate bridge, in gladiators, and in my pastoral
>   song.

Some pastoral. Hall perverts the form to effect what he calls "dreamlike monstrosity." Monstrosity helps clarify choices, and "never do anything except what you want to do" haunts because it requires incessant choice. Something monstrous is easier to reject, and, because there is so much *not* to do, rejection is the first business of doing what you want to do.

Though not the last: abjuring purple bathrooms may be a start, but where does one go from there? After such irony, what engagement? It takes Hall forty pages to earn earnestness, to muster the wherewithal to overcome irony, but he most unmistakably does:

> Gazing at May's blossoms, imagining bounty of
>   McIntosh,
> I praise old lilacs rising in woods beside cellarholes;
> I praise toads. I predict the telephone call
> that reports the friend from childhood cold on a staircase.
> I praise children, grandchildren, and just baked bread.
> I praise fried Spam and onions on slices of Wonder
>   Bread;
> I praise your skin. I predict the next twenty years,
> days of mourning, long walks growing slow and painful.
> I reject twenty years of mid-life; I reject rejections.
> The one day stands unmoving in sun and shadow.

It takes the entire poem to show that the way to meaning lies not in rejection of all but the self, not in self regard, not even in "each other," but in "a third thing: / a child, a ciderpress, a book." Recognition and acceptance of the necessity of death replace distraction and denial. "From burnt houses and blackened shrubs, green rises / like bread." The house of dying and the house of living, it turns out, are one, and our true lot, Hall proclaims, is to "Work, love, build a house and die. But build a house."

He is as emphatic as Whitman in the preface to the 1855 edition of *Leaves of Grass*: "This is what you shall do: Love the earth and sun and the animals, despise riches, give alms to everyone who asks, stand up for the stupid and the crazy. . . ." Whitman goes on, as you may recall or imagine, while Hall is not as specific or exhaustive (who is?). He lists less. But Hall's example of combining bitter rejection with hopeful proclamation argues better than any critical essay could against Whitman's (and the Modern Library's) decision to elide the darkest shade of the Good Gray Poet, for the extreme negativity of **The One Day** intensifies, even as it qualifies, its eventual affirmation.

Still, one may be impressed with Hall's language, the sweep of his vision, the ingenuity with which he shapes bricks and puts them together, and yet ask, what do you mean, "build a house"? Bravo that you lived through your mid-life crisis, that you have a nice home, with old lilacs and all, but what good does it do homeless me? To put it in the most dreaded way, who cares? This is the 20th century. I don't have time for anything more than a McPoem, if that.

Yet Hall has noted that there are more American poets and poems out there now than ever before, and the phenomenon of the "sensitive poet" is prevalent enough in the U.S. to provoke a cartoon from Matt Groening (best known as the creator of *The Simpsons* television program, but also author of the darkly funny *Life in Hell* books). After offering some useful questions for figuring out "if you are the sensitive poet type"—

> Are you "different"?
> Do you feel "special"?
> Are you "complicated"?
> Do you enjoy "poverty"?

—Groening suggests that beginners equip themselves with "pencil, paper, somber clothing." More advanced sensitive poets will need "pencil, paper, bitterness." The cartoon then offers the following exercise: "Write a poem about a fleeting emotion unique to you," the cartoon instructs, "using a complex and private system of symbols that no one else can possibly understand."

So many poets and poems, so bafflingly little communication. Eliot wrote that "the uses of poetry certainly vary as society alters, as the public to be addressed changes." In the late 20th century, then, does poetry serve to pad solipsism, to aid the escape from modern reality by modern reality's spoiled, somberly clothed, over-sensitive and under-employed children? The poet's greatest pride and achievement is his miraculously intact sensibility, the elaborated beauty of his isolation—therein the preciosity of much of what currently gets called poetry. Recall Hall's recipe for McPoems: "they do not extend themselves . . . they connect small things to other small things." Many poets aren't men speaking to men, but men speaking to themselves, consigning the reader to the dubious pleasure of eavesdropping on a solitary mumbler.

But maybe this is for the best. Maybe modernity has so thrown us back upon ourselves that we have no common ground, only our separate, "complex and private," incommunicable systems. At least one psychologist has suggested that the "sensitive poet" type, detached from the outside and elaborately connected inside, might be the ideal model for contemporary identity. In *Love and Will*, Rollo May writes that such a "schizoid character" is necessary in a "schizoid world . . . in which, amid all the vastly developed means of communication that bombard us on all sides, actual personal communication is exceedingly difficult and rare." Only a schizoid character, focused inwardly on his complex and private system, can "stand against the spiritual emptiness of encroaching technology and . . . not let himself be emptied by it." Only such a character can "live and work with the machine without becoming a machine."

Well, Hall does co-opt modern technology as analog for the structure of his poem. "If I succeed," he writes, "the surface of the poem should look smooth but, like the great console radios of my youth, when you look behind this facade you see a maze of tubes and wires to connect everything with everything else. And there is something faintly smug about the "third things" he esteems in **The One Day**. It is easy to write:

> The one day speaks of July afternoons, of February
> when snow builds shingle in spruce, when the high
>    sugarmaple
> regards the abandoned barn tilted inward, moving
> in storm like Pilgrims crossing the Atlantic under sail.
> The one day recalls us to hills and meadows, to moss,
> roses, dirt, apples, and the breathing of timothy—
> away from the yellow chair, from blue smoke and
>    daydream.
> Leave behind appointments listed on the printout!
> Leave behind manila envelopes! Leave dark suits behind,
> boarding passes, and soufflés at the chancellor's house!

. . . if you live, as Hall does, on an ancestral farm in New Hampshire.[1] Such a landscape makes for Hall a lovely background for "an instressing of his own inscape," to use Gerard Manley Hopkins' phrase for Lucifer's treasonous song, and indeed there is much inscaping in **The One Day**. The devil makes him do it, maybe—or the bombardment of modernity. Colonize yourself, or your self will be colonized for you. Poetry, obviously, helps in this endeavor; and so it can lead to the sensitive poet phenomenon. But the third things Hall esteems counter this tendency. A child, a ciderpress, a book . . . the history of poetry—

these things we hold in common, and in communing over them we find value outside ourselves, beyond the limits of our space and time. The very nature of poetry recalls us to these third things. While in prose, words are means for the message they are deployed to convey, the words of a poem insist that they are ends in themselves, that we feel them with our senses and hearts even as we manipulate them for some purpose. Each brick has heft and texture worth the moment's measure.

Thoreau reminds us that home-building is (if you'll forgive a pun) an edifying occupation:

> Who knows but if men constructed their dwellings with their own hands, and provided food for themselves and families simply and honestly enough, the poetic faculty would be universally developed, as birds universally sing when they are so engaged? But alas! We do like cowbirds and cuckoos, which lay their eggs in nests which other birds have built, and cheer no traveller with their chattering and unmusical notes. Shall we forever resign the pleasure of construction to the carpenter?

Hall has published poetry since **The One Day** and has plans to publish more soon, but this book stands as his central achievement. It is ambitious. It makes a great claim, then backs it up. "Work, love, build a house and die. But build a house." Reading the poem we feel the "pleasure of construction."

Hall has observed that:

> In the act of reading, the reader undergoes a process—largely without awareness, as the author was largely without intention—which resembles, like a slightly fainter copy of the original, the process of discovery or recovery that the poet went through in his madness or his inspiration.

What are we to do when necessity's discipline no longer obtains, when milk magically flows from the plastic udder, when nothing need be done? If Hall's equation of reading to writing is true, and certainly poetry, of all literary forms, inspires and requires the most active engagement on the part of the reader, then in reading **The One Day** we exercise the poetic faculty, we cultivate our capacity for *poiesis*. Reader, in other words, becomes poet, and a poet, to paraphrase Thoreau, is someone who, having nothing to do, finds something to do.

### Note

1. Hall is careful to note elsewhere that he paid hard-earned dollars for his place in New Hampshire, ancestral though it is. He bought the farm himself.

## Donald Hall with Michael Scharf (interview date 23 March 1998)

SOURCE: "Donald Hall: Elegies from Eagle Pond," in *Publishers Weekly*, Vol. 245, No. 12, March 23, 1998, pp. 72–73.

[*In the following interview, Hall discusses the death of his wife (poet Jane Kenyon), his editing of her last collection of poetry, and* Without, *his own poetry collection about their life together.*]

Eagle Pond Farm is familiar to even the casual reader of Donald Hall. The weather-beaten spread, hard by Route 4 at the foot of Ragged Mountain in Wilmot, N.H., has been home to Hall's maternal clan since 1865. It is the subject or setting of many of his poems and essays, providing a consistent reference point for more than 40 years of work. It is the place where Hall spent summers growing up, returning for good in 1975 after remarrying and giving up tenure at the University of Michigan to write full-time. And it is the house where his wife, the poet Jane Kenyon, died in 1995.

In **Without**, due from Houghton Mifflin in April, Hall records the unbearable facts of a present he and Kenyon were powerless to alter. A slow-motion portrait of Kenyon's descent into the horrors of aggressive treatment following her leukemia diagnosis in 1994 at the age of 46, the collection continues without recoil through to her last days, spent choosing the poems for Kenyon's *Otherwise: New & Selected Poems,* and her final minutes. A second section addresses Kenyon directly, after her death. With their deliberate cadences, the poems seem written from a place beyond solace or anguish, a contracted world that leaves Hall bereft, with no relief, but still insisting on trying to say what has happened.

Readers will of course be tempted to draw parallels between Hall's book and Ted Hughes's best-selling *Birthday Letters* whose publication made front-page news: both men were married to poets whose work was often highly personal and who were beset by depression and mania, and both collections address the poet's departed spouse in verse. While the real-life likenesses end there, **Without** is already generating the kind of attention unthinkable for many books of poetry. The book has a first printing of 10,000 copies (perhaps five times the usual); Hall has recently been profiled in *Mirabella* and for National Public Radio; more media attention is sure to follow. While some of the reception is obviously due to a master poet who has written a culminating work, it raises questions about what it takes for a book of poems to penetrate the national consciousness.

In **Without,** Hall is forced to fight it out with a career's worth of demons: death, family, sex and how to proceed in a life that offers no guarantee of value or redemption. The struggle is made still more poignant by the fact that no one expected Hall to be alive to tell of it. Hall had written about his own illness a few short years before in books like **The Museum of Clear Ideas** and **Life Work,** both published in 1993, speaking plainly of his colon cancer and the metastasis that took more than half of his liver. An Emmy Award-winning Bill Moyers special, *A Life Together,* found Hall and Kenyon resolved to make the most of their time together at Eagle Pond, as the threat of recurrence loomed. But with Kenyon's diagnosis, **The Old Life,** as Hall called the book of poems he published the year of her death, was over.

That Hall has remained at Eagle Pond Farm, where Kenyon "led the way back" after their marriage, seems fitting at the very least. On a gray February morning, *PW* is met at the kitchen door by Hall, and by Gus, the long-haired "dear mongrel" who makes appearances in Kenyon's poems and, more frequently now, in Hall's. Almost immediately, Hall ushers us into his study, closing the door to reveal the wall of photos of Kenyon he writes of as "The Gallery" in ***Without.***

"That's the woman I married," Hall says of a young, slightly awkward Kenyon hidden behind thick framed glasses. "And that's the beauty she became," he says, gesturing to Kenyon "foxy / and beautiful at 45," with tresses of dark hair offset with silver framing her strong features and even gaze.

Hall's own appearance has changed dramatically from the man of the Moyers special, reading tours and book jackets. Wisps of thinned red hair reach his shoulders, and a nearly gray beard spreads densely across much of his face. Hall is also rather tall; the net effect is authoritative, if not imposing. As he moves to sit in a chair by a window facing the road, waving *PW* to a couch across the room, it's difficult not to feel a little daunted. But Hall quickly makes one feel at ease, talking with what one recognizes as characteristic frankness about his prolific and esteemed career.

That career now includes 13 books of poems and what Hall calls the work that "supports my poetry habit": essay collections, textbooks, profiles of poets and artists, children's books and short stories. Hall's 1955 poetic debut at age 27, ***Exiles and Marriages*** (having himself married three years earlier), was such a success that he had trouble living it down. Part formalist send-up of bourgeois dalliance and divorce and part grave T. S. Eliot-influenced metaphysical inquiry, the book captured the literary zeitgeist of the period Robert Lowell called "the tranquilized fifties" perhaps too well. A glowing *Time* magazine review—rare even then for poetry—ran along with a photo of Hall as a serious young Harvard graduate (his colleagues on the *Advocate* included John Ashbery, Kenneth Koch and Robert Bly, who remains his best friend), one who would go on to win the Lamont poetry prize for his first outing. Hall, now 69, chuckles over his younger self's precocity. "I remember the man who wrote those poems, and in the immortal words of Richard Nixon, 'I peaked too soon.' I began to do better work later on," such as ***A Roof of Tiger Lilies*** (1964), "that wasn't noticed."

If that initial burst of fame tapered off after a while, it was enough to fuel a transition to a successful academic career. Having picked up a second bachelor's at Oxford and spent time as one of Harvard's Society of Fellows, Hall settled at the University of Michigan at Ann Arbor in 1957. He had two children with his first wife, and went on to publish and edit widely during the ensuing two decades. The marriage ended in 1969, and Hall entered what he has called "a bad patch of mid-life." When he met Kenyon in Ann Arbor, she was 22 and he 42; they married two years later. The impetus to move to Eagle Pond, inhabited by the family ghosts that populate Hall's work, came from Kenyon. The two were to devote themselves to writing, with Hall embarking on a freelance career that continues to this day. Hall's textbook, ***Writing Well*** (now in its ninth edition, with Addison Wesley Longman), was selling briskly, which "made it possible to think about coming here" in 1975.

***Kicking the Leaves*** vaulted Hall back into prominence in 1978, going on to sell nearly 100,000 copies over the years. Many of its poems reappeared in ***Old and New Poems*** (1990). "The standard sentence in the reviews of that book," Hall quips, "is that Hall has been around a long time and published a lot of books, but it wasn't until he quit teaching and moved to the New Hampshire house with his second wife, the poet Jane Kenyon, that he began to get good." Hall begs to differ somewhat but allows the pundits a measure of truth. "I felt a little aggrieved for some of my old poems, but if my work got better while I was here, I think it was partly because I was watching Janie, with tremendous stubbornness and hard work, get better and better."

Kenyon had just published her third book (exclusive of her translations of Anna Akhmatova), *Let Evening Come,* to warm reviews, and the two began to read together more frequently. Hall had already found further critical success with ***The Happy Man*** (1986) and ***The One Day*** (1988). The latter, a long poem in four parts that was 17 years in the making, won the NBCC Award for poetry and was a Pulitzer nominee. The book also, along with a collection of naturalist essays called ***Here at Eagle Pond,*** inaugurated Hall's long relationship with Houghton Mifflin, its (now defunct) imprint Ticknor & Fields and editor Peter Davison.

Hall remembers these times as some of the couple's happiest. "Jane's reputation had finally caught up with her poetry. And we went out and read together, and we lived in this house, and got up early, and worked. We had to make boundaries in order to live together and do the same thing, but we did, and it was just magnificent." Kenyon's *Constance* came out in 1993, along with Hall's ***Museum of Clear Ideas*** and ***Life Work.*** After Hall's illness, the couple went out on a joint book tour and also traveled to India for a second time.

They did their last reading together in January 1994, at Bennington. "We came back here, and she began to have flu symptoms. And I flew down to Charleston to do a reading and a lecture, two nights gone." After missing a connection on the way back, "I called and asked how she was doing. She told me about this terrible nose bleed, and how she had gone to the hospital to have it stopped, and that they were doing blood work. She was more upset, though, about the car's not starting and having to get it towed. This is hard to believe," Hall says, visibly agitated and upset, "but as I stood there, I thought 'Jane has leukemia.'" He pauses again, apologetically: "I can't stop telling this story."

Hall began drafting *Without* during Kenyon's treatment. "I nursed Jane here and at the hospitals, but there was a lot of other time to fill, and the most absorbing thing I could do was write. She often couldn't, but she was glad somebody could." As they had done during Hall's illness, the couple resolved to take things exactly as they came. "Jane and I were not deniers, we were proclaimers. We were not cheerful with one another. Writing about this is what I would have expected from us, and Jane did, too."

After Kenyon's death, Hall stayed at Eagle Pond, drafting and redrafting—often up to 200 times—the poems that would become *Without*. Slowly, he began to send them to friends and to read them in public. "People came up to me and spoke as if I had been brave to read these poems aloud. I don't feel brave. Talking of grief, talking of suffering, is something I seem to need to do. For some people, that's not their way. But to bring it to someone else, I think, relieves me." Seeing *Otherwise* through to press was also a comfort.

Asked if he thinks that the circumstances of Kenyon's death have anything to do with her increased posthumous fame, Hall concurs: "Her fame is infinitely greater since her death, but she was aware that people were talking about her more and more, and reading her more, before she even got sick, so I don't feel too badly about that. She knew that people were beginning to find her." If *Without* gets more people to discover Kenyon's work, Hall will be all the more pleased. "She'd kick my ass if she thought I was promoting her at all before."

The idea of a glimpse into the raw stuff of a writing life shared—and, in different ways, cut tragically short—between two accomplished poets may be the main attraction for readers of both Hughes's *Birthday Letters* and Hall's *Without*. In the latter's case, the book will almost certainly be taken up, as Hall notes, "as a companion to the grief of others." But, he continues, "Art is what gets it from here to there." Just as any work must put up or shut up, it is the poems themselves that will hold readers to *Without*. "I may have failed in what I attempted to do, but a poem is not a poem unless it is a work of art. It may begin with a scream of pain, but you make that into a work of art or you have utterly failed."

Since completing *Without*, Hall has not sent out any new poems to magazines, although he has been writing, and is "not ready to think about" his next collection. He will do a stint "teaching literature to poets" at New York University after a 10-city reading tour, where he will read Kenyon's work as well as his own. "Before, she wouldn't let me, but I'm reading her because I want to be with her. And I think that everything I write for the rest of my life will be affected by Jane, by the loss of her and her poetry. I'm surrounded by her. She's here."

## John Bayley (review date 16 July 1998)

SOURCE: "The Way We Write Now," in *New York Review of Books,* Vol. 45, No. 12, July 16, 1998, p. 41.

[*In the following excerpt, Bayley discusses Hall's exploration of grief in* Without.]

Poets must often write to cheer themselves up, and in so doing the good ones can cheer up their readers as well. Thomas Hardy's passionate love lyrics to his dead wife, the wife to whom when she was alive he had paid very little attention for thirty years and more, are also an acknowledgment of himself as he was, an acceptance of what he had done, or failed to do. So moving are these poems, and in a sense so self-delighting, that the reader too feels calmed and blessed at second-hand, endowed while he reads them with the same sort of self-acceptance.

This is the art that moves Donald Hall's poems to and for his dead wife, the poet Jane Kenyon [in *Without*]. These, too, are poems addressed to the dead which in reality can only have been written for the poet and for his reader. Unlike Hardy's they celebrate a marriage of deep intimacy and great happiness, but all things come to the same in the end. Hardy mourned that his wife had abruptly left him, just as she sometimes did when callers came to the house. She had departed finally "in the same swift style," as if to say "Goodbye is not worthwhile." Like all who have been bereaved, Hall in his poems lives among the same sort of memories.

> I want to sleep like the birds,
> then wake to write you again
> without hope that you read me.
> If a car pulls into the drive
> I want to hide in our bedroom
> the way you hid sometimes
> when people came calling.

So many poets—Virgil, Dante, Chaucer, Tennyson, the one following the other—have pointed out that nothing is worse in a bad time than the memory of good ones. Hall adds his own variant:

> Remembered happiness is agony;
> So is remembered agony.
> I live in a present compelled
> by anniversaries and objects.

But the paradox holds: the poets were incorrect, at least where their poetry is concerned. For the reader, and surely for the poet too, Hall's extraordinarily clear awareness of what is over and gone is more present and more appealing in words now than it could have found room to be in life. The house, the hospital, the course of his wife's leukemia, the dog Gus, the cemetery, the mountain and lake nearby, "Perkins," Jane Kenyon's nickname for her husband, the gothic horror of her complex and meticulous treatments—all these, together with the sense of an unbroken human intimacy, make the poems almost mesmerically readable.

It is as if they were not poems at all but experiences undergone with and by another human being. And yet art remains of course; for

> Art was dependable, something
>  to live for.

And we can only be together in the saving dishonesty of art, the *hypocrite lecteur* and the poet who makes poetry out of what he has suffered, even out of the grotesque medical rituals which can be inflicted on us today to keep us going.

> . . . blood-oxygen numbers
>  dropped towards zero and her
>  face went blue.
> The young nurse slipped oxygen
>  into Jane's nostrils and
>  punched
> a square button. Eight doctors
> burst into the room, someone
> pounded Jane's chest, Dr.
>  McDonald gave orders like
> a submarine captain among depth
>  charges, the nurse fixed
> a nebulizer over Jane's mouth
>  and nose—and she breathed.

The symbolism of technology leaks into the verbal patterns of Hall's poetry like the chemicals from an intravenous drip, seeming native as well as natural to the mode, just as their own state-of-the-art life-handling technology did to Lowell's *Life Studies* and Berryman's *Dream Songs*. As in Hall's last collection, **The Old Life,** the mosaic of a whole period, with all its inner moods and its physical accessories, is masterfully accomplished: a time seen in the sad debris which seems to survive all the changes and chances, as the prayer book calls them (Hall and his wife were both believers), of our fleeting world.

> Yesterday
> I cleaned out your Saab
>  to sell it. The dozen tapes
> I mailed to Caroline.
> I collected hairpins and hair ties.
> In the Hill's Balsam tin
> Where you kept silver for tolls
> I found your collection
>  of clips from fortune cookies:
> YOU ARE A FANTASTIC
>  PERSON!
> YOU ARE ONE OF THOSE
>  PEOPLE
> WHO GOES PLACES IN THEIR
>  LIFE!

The clock given "our first Christmas together" keeps bad time.

> . . . Now it speeds
> sixty-five minutes to the hour, as if
>  it wants to be done with the day.

This poetry is too meticulously aware of itself not to know how much it must itself be comforted by the past and its losses, even luxuriate in them, as Hardy did in "After a Journey," his magic poem for his dead wife, Emma. When Jane Kenyon is in remission and seems on the road to recovery

> He felt shame
>  to understand he would miss
> the months of sickness and taking
>  care.

In such crises it has to be one's own feelings that count. No poem here misses the irony of Jane's cry: "I wish you could feel what I feel."

> It must have been unbearable
> while she suffered her private
>  hurts
>  to see his worried face
> looking above her, always
>  anxious to *do*
>  *something* when there was
> exactly nothing to do.

The truest misery of terminal conditions—cancer, Alzheimer's—is the isolation they enforce on each once non-separate partner, and the concentration the still intact partner can only feel on his or her own feelings. Both in this case were poets, but one poet cannot console another with art, any more than believers can with belief. Both were practicing Christians, but in the poetry that fact emerges only in accounts of happenings, not in affirmations. . . .

## Donald Hall with Jeffrey S. Cramer (interview date Winter 1998–1999)

SOURCE: "With Jane and Without: An Interview with Donald Hall," in *Massachusetts Review,* Vol. 39, No. 4, Winter, 1998–1999, pp. 493–510.

[*In the following interview, Hall discusses his relationship with his late wife and how he has coped emotionally since her death.*]

Anyone acquainted with the story of Donald Hall and Jane Kenyon cannot help but stand in awe of the irony which, if it appeared in fiction, would appall by its tear-jerking manipulation. The reality, as I stand before Jane Kenyon's grave, leaves me saddened and numb.

The lines on their shared stone are from Kenyon's poem, "Afternoon at MacDowell." Although she wrote it with Hall in mind when he, as he has said, was "supposed to die," they now stand in testimony to Kenyon, and look, mistakenly, like words he must have written for her:

> I BELIEVE IN THE MIRACLES OF ART BUT WHAT
> PRODIGY WILL KEEP YOU SAFE BESIDE ME

Four miles North of the Proctor cemetery on Route 4, just past Eagle Pond Road, in the shadow of Ragged Mountain, is Eagle Pond Farm. There is no sign, no name on the mailbox, but the satellite dish overwhelming the North side yard announces the home of a man who cannot live unconnected to his beloved baseball games.

The living room seems truly a living room, a room lived in, informal. It is surrounded, as would be expected, by books; an open book of pictures of sculpture by Henry Moore lays on the coffee table in front of the couch on which I sit. By the window Hall's chair faces the T.V. and VCR which must have received, recorded and replayed thousands of ballgames. The Glenwood stands nearby. On one wall is a gallery of photographs, some already familiar from *String Too Short to Be Saved.* Beyond are rooms I am curious about but will not see.

This is Hall's ancestral home, but it was Kenyon's "absolute love of this place and desire to live here" which enticed him back, turning it from the place of which he once wrote, "I will not rock on this porch / When I am old," to the place, as he would later write, that held "love and work together." Coming back to Eagle Pond was the second smartest thing he and Kenyon had done, he now admits.

> The first smartest thing was getting married. And Jane really brought me here—this is my old family place—but I was sensible: I had tenure and I had children in college. Jane said she would lock herself, chain herself rather, into the root cellar rather than go back to the academic world, and I followed her. I really wanted to do what she was suggesting, and we came here, and she absolutely flowered.
>
> She came from a town where her family lived and she had friends. She didn't want to party very much, but there were people around, and she had a job. She came here and she was alone. She had her garden. She had poetry and she began to read it more thoroughly and more seriously and to write it everyday, to work on it every single day. Well, there were times of depression when she couldn't, but mostly she really threw herself into it.
>
> When I came out a few years ago with *Old and New Poems,* it got a lot of reviews. (I mean, some of my books had *two* reviews.) There was one characteristic sentence in all the reviews that said "Hall had been around for a long time, published for twenty years, but he really started to get good when he and his second wife moved from the academic world to New Hampshire and settled down.
>
> One thing that's tragic about that is that I was forty-seven when we moved here; Jane was forty-seven when she died. She didn't have the chance. She made the most of her years.

For most of us 1969 was the year of Woodstock, Manson, and Chappaquiddick, it was the year we lost both Jack Kerouac and Judy Garland, and it was the year Neil Armstrong walked on the moon, but for Donald Hall it would become a year to be remembered for a different reason. He had hit a low point in his life, a "bad patch of midlife" lasting six years. He had been separated for two years and was now divorced. In the spring, at the University of Michigan, he led a class of more than 100 students in a large lecture hall. Although he didn't know it, Jane Kenyon was among those students, so she got to know him, to observe him, as a poet and teacher, before he was ever aware of her.

> Every Autumn I taught a poetry writing class, ten or twelve kids, and I put a notice on my office door saying, "If you would like to be in this class, by August 1st leave me a selection of . . ."—I don't know what I said, five or ten poems. One of the envelopes that year was from Jane Kenyon. It was the first time I remember seeing her name.
>
> I remember one particular poem in there, which is in *From Room to Room,* and it's in *Otherwise.* It's a poem called "The Needle." Strangely enough there are many things in it that are characteristic of her later work, although she wrote it originally perhaps when she was 19 or 20. In between she wrote a lot of poems, some of which are in *From Room to Room,* and others never got there, which were not characteristic of her later work.
>
> But there was that poem, and there may have been others in that manuscript that I admired a lot, but I don't remember them. I think maybe that poem got her in the class. Thank God.

Hall got to know Kenyon in this class. They would all meet one night a week for a few hours in his living room.

> We were very familiar, the whole class. I became one of the class, not a leader. At the beginning I would lead because they didn't know each other and I would establish vocabulary. Later, I had to put up my hand to be allowed to speak. I exaggerate. It was very good: This class met as a workshop without me for two-and-a-half years after the class was over. They were really good. She was by far the best poet out of it, to date—and probably will be, but there are several others who have published and done books.
>
> Last summer I finally went through Jane's papers and notebooks and in one notebook, college notebook, I found: "When I discovered that I lived not three doors from Donald Hall it was like when I learned that Dublin was a Viking stronghold or when I wanted to take the goldfish out of the bowl but found that the water was too cold to sustain life." That had to be at the very beginning of the class, because this was 1969, everybody called me Don, not Donald Hall . . . That amused me to no end.

At this time Hall's interest was not even remotely romantic.

> I was in between marriages, shortly after my divorce, two years after my separation, shortly after the actual divorce, and I was petrified of marriage or of commit-

ting myself to one person. What I did about that was to have lots of girlfriends, a prophylactic promiscuity. I saw different people all the time, daytime or nighttime.

Jane was twenty-two then. She was not particularly attractive. By the time she turned forty she'd become beautiful. It's extraordinary that she went in that direction, but I wasn't originally that attracted to her. I liked her personally. After that class we saw each other when she'd come to office hours with a poem.

I knew she went to live with a guy, her boyfriend, the following June, and then the following October or November I heard from mutual friends that they weren't getting on and that she was going to move out. She had been skeptical about this relationship anyway. He wanted to get married, and moving in was a compromise, but she felt miserable—there is no contradiction there—about the breakup, felt like a failure. I was told she was depressed afterward. So I called her up, maybe in December of 1970, and said "Come on over and I will cook supper," or "I'll take you out to dinner." She spent the entire time talking about this guy and so I came up with an inventory of disasters of my own and we talked about other people. This went on for awhile. We saw each other about once a week and then I noticed that my other girlfriends were dropping off. They'd move away and I didn't replace them. I had to go out to California that summer and Jane was the last person I saw before I went out and the first person that I saw when I got back.

I began to get worried that this was getting serious. After all, I was 19 years older than Jane and she would be a widow for 25 years, but we kept coming closer and closer together. When we first mentioned marriage we decided the age difference was too great. We dismissed it, but then it came back again, and finally around Christmas or New Year's '71–72 we decided to get married. We got married in April of '72.

Three years later they moved to Eagle Pond. Their first January was the coldest on record in New Hampshire. With no central heating, no insulation and no storm windows, they relied heavily on the heat generated from the single wood-burning Glenwood in the parlor, with a little heat filtering in from the kitchen beyond. Hall would write at the dining room table twenty feet away, feeling the cold, but often both he and Kenyon would be writing or reading in chairs on either side of the woodstove, trying to stay warm.

By the following winter, woodstoves in place in both their studies, as well as new storm windows and insulation, they began to establish the daily routines that would allow them to make a workable life together. It was a house of habit, of pattern. They developed a series of daily routines that set boundaries, and by setting boundaries, created a kind of freedom within.

> We lived by routine. I would get up about five or so, a little before Jane, and start the coffee and go get the *Boston Globe,* come back, and I would take a cup of coffee into Jane. I am the type who leaps out of bed and is wide-awake. Jane was a morning person. She liked to get up early. But she was slower, and to have the odor of coffee beside her was bliss for her. And then I would read the paper, have my breakfast and get to work. Again, Jane was a little slower: she would walk the dog up the hill—she would be gone a half an hour—and then she would be ready to get to her study. She got to her study a little later than I did but we both worked in the morning. We never interrupted each other. Once a year we had to knock on each other's door but we were very polite about it. We would have lunch together and take a nap together perhaps, and in summer Jane did a lot of gardening, and I did a lot of working on children's books or other prose for the rest of the day.

Often the two poets did not meet or talk most of the day as they lived parallel lives. During their working hours they lived separately together. "We were very scrupulous in our separateness," Kenyon said.[1] Hall has called this separateness a "double solitude." In his brief essay, **"Life After Jane,"** Hall writes, "For 20 years we had lived alone together in our big old house, making separate poems in a common enterprise. Our marriage was close, and dread of separation only brought us closer until it seemed that we made a single soul."

> We had studies that were as far apart as possible. Mine was on the ground floor in the northwestern corner; hers was the second floor in the southeastern corner. We were in the same house and we wanted to be, but just as far apart as possible. I'm always talking about the double solitude. We were rather reclusive. We got together and had a wonderful time together, but we spent the day in the same house without a great deal of contact. Sometimes we would meet in the morning, coming in the middle from our two studies far apart, and get a cup of coffee. We wouldn't even speak. I would pat her on the butt, and we'd get back to work.

> We lived together twenty-three years, and we lived together much of the time simply in the same house.

While in Michigan, Kenyon had not been writing very much, nor had she yet established work habits that would enable her to devote the time her writing required. "Of course I've had to establish and learn to honor my own habits of work," Kenyon said, "My own pace, my own areas of interest and struggles. When we married, he had long since established all of these things for himself. My work habits have evolved over time, just as his had." Hall says:

> She wasn't writing so much and, when we were first married, we had the problem of her getting over me having been her teacher. At first when she wrote a poem it was when I was out of the house. I would go off to a poetry reading for a couple of days and I'd come back and she would have a draft. I was obviously inhibiting her and I worried about that. I'm sure that she did, too.

> I worried that I'd be a living reproach because I work so much. Her first book came out the year my sixth book came out, and that could be hard to deal with, but Jane was very stubborn. I think that being isolated with me and doing a lot of reading helped her.

Living in isolation at Eagle Pond, sharing the same work, could be a setting for fierce competition and envy. Add in the egos that writers sometimes carry and it could be a case for pure strife.

> People say, "Were you competitive?" Well, we weren't in any petty way that bothered us and let us get mad at each other, but I think that we were both stimulated by the presence of the other doing work, and there was a point when—well, Jane moved ahead gradually up to a point—and there was a point, I think sometime in the early '80s when she brought me a bunch of poems that just knocked me on my rear, because she made a great move—toward the end of her second book really. I wanted to write poems that were that good. If that's competition, it's great.
>
> You know, nobody was getting mad at anybody, but it happened a few times. On the same day, one of us would get an acceptance from one magazine and the other a rejection, and it just meant that the one who was accepted couldn't be quite so happy as he/she would have been otherwise. But we handled it all right. Nobody quarreled.

One way in which Kenyon was able to keep things in perspective was to be part of a workshop, what she called "The Committee," with two other poets, Joyce Peseroff and Alice Mattison. "My own group of peers," Kenyon said, "has been equally important to my development of skills and nerve." It gave her support different from that she received from Hall, as well as a kind of permission to oppose Hall's opinions.

> I saw her get stronger, and with the help of the women's movement, still stronger. The help of working with two other women was very important: Joyce Peseroff and Alice Mattison. I would accompany them or they would workshop here sometimes and I would be very careful to stay away while they worked. A couple of times we all met down at the Lord Jeffrey Inn in Amherst and I stayed out of their room when they were workshopping.
>
> They gave each other courage. They gave each other courage as women, I think, simply the courage to be ambitious, the courage to take on the work. I think they genuinely helped each other that way, derived partly from the feminist movement.
>
> She'd come to them when I had insisted that some word was wrong and she'd say, "Well, Perkins says . . ." and they would overrule me sometimes. It wasn't automatic. These are my friends, too, Joyce and Alice.

Kenyon gave Hall the name "Perkins" after a trip to Maine.

> We happened to be driving in Perkins Cove and there was Perkins Drug Store, and Lawyer Perkins, and so on, and Janie laughed and said "This Perkins must be quite a fellow" and began to call me Perkins. I think behind it is the fact that I was her teacher and I was kind of an institution at the University of Michigan and "Donald Hall" is not the name of your husband; it was the name of a statue in a park somewhere. I think that's where Perkins came from.

A natural-born promoter, a man generous with his time, often helping young writers, Hall found himself in the position of needing to reign in his liberality.

> She kept an eye on me. Alice Mattison says that if some editor took her poem, Jane would think it was because that editor had had lunch with me once sixteen years before. She talked with her friends about it, that maybe she should discount this success because somebody was just trying to please Don. It was a real burden for her. Living with a poet who is older than you and has had some success may help you some but you have to doubt the help. In a way it is like being rich: "Do they love me or my money?"

Although they ultimately were to become each other's first readers, in the beginning it was difficult. Perhaps because of their initial relation as teacher-student, it took time for Kenyon to feel comfortable in their relationship as peers. They had begun to workshop in Michigan with Gregory Orr and, as long as a third person was present, they were able to talk about each other's poetry.

Hall, however, was comfortable from the beginning. He recognized in Kenyon someone who was neither deferential nor dishonest.

> Well, I never doubted her for a minute, and I felt enormously friendly toward her within the first week or so of knowing her. It was a wonderful class where people were friendly to each other and were frank with each other, but she was particularly funny and sharp all together.
>
> I remember her coming to my office hours one time after the class was over. We were talking about one of her poems, and I suddenly thought of a poem of mine that reminded me of hers. There happened to be a copy of it there. I picked it up and I looked at it and I saw something I could revise, so I began revising my poem in front of her and then trying it on her, and I never felt—oh, she was aware of the disparity between my years and my experience and hers, of course—but she never felt deferential in any icky way at all. There was something stubborn in her, something that needed to defy authority. I think she was a straight and honest person.
>
> By the time we moved here we could help each other. We didn't do this helping everyday, you know. We both kept things close to ourselves until we'd revised them a lot and we were ready to show them to somebody else, and then virtually always the other was the first reader. That might happen every two or three months. I'd say, "I left two or three things on your footstool," and wait for her response.

Often the asked-for response was greeted with a certain amount of skepticism. As Kenyon said:

> I reach the point where I just can't see one more thing to do with a poem. I've poked and poked. Yet I sense that it needs more. Even if I think it is finished, I still want Don to confirm my opinion. We can't either of us finish poems without each other's critical opinion. Once

I have Don's ideas, and the ideas of my workshop, then I can complete the work. Finally, of course, I must please myself, taking some suggestions and rejecting others.

Everything in me resists what Don is saying at the moment he's saying it and when I climb the stairs I'm saying, "He's dead wrong, he just doesn't get this." The next day I sit down, look at his suggestions, and think, "Why don't I just type it up that way to see what it looks like?" Sure enough, he's found something.

Hall confirms:

Oh, sure, I did the same thing, and with other people, too. I can never say, "Yes, you're right." Rarely did I see suddenly that something was right. I could sometimes and so could she. Often I'd say, "I'll write that down," or "I'll give it a try," and then discover, in fact, that I wanted it that way. And so, yes, Jane said that she used to mutter going up the stairs, "Perkins just doesn't get it," and then, she said, "I'd go and do everything he said." Well, I don't think she went and did everything I said, nor I everything she said. Sometimes when I read her poems aloud I see one word that I remember objecting to.

I wanted confirmation all the time from her, and I was always a little dissatisfied. She could never quite tell me what I wanted to hear. She was very tough and not at all given to any holding back of criticism. One night she was reading the manuscript of a whole book of mine, *The Museum of Clear Ideas*. Now, it's a book that a lot of people like, and I like, but Jane didn't like it—and half way through reading it—she had seen parts of it all along, but she was reading right through it, and she was coming almost to the end of it—she was sitting on the sofa over there and I was sitting here and she looked up weeping, and saying, "Perkins, I don't really like it," and I wept and said, "That's all right, that's all right."

Jane would be writing and she would think, "Perkins is not going to like this" but, if she decided to go ahead with it, she had made her decision. I think my trick of repeating words close to each other was something I picked up from Yeats who could do it so gorgeously. I was doing it without a brogue. When I did that I knew Jane wasn't going to like it. Is she going to be right? Would I do better to change? You know the two lines that are on Jane's tombstone are from her poem "Afternoon at MacDowell": "I believe in the miracles of art but what / prodigy will keep you safe beside me?" I might have said miracle twice. Jane used a thesaurus and if you look up miracle the first word is prodigy.

It was a natural, if somewhat arrogant, assumption, given their age difference and Hall's established career, that Kenyon would always remain in the role of apprentice. Kenyon herself said, "Whatever it is that I know about writing poems, I have learned most of it from being with Don, moving to his ancestral farm, keeping my ears open when his peers come to visit. One very important thing I've learned from Don is to be ambitious. Just do it, and take the knocks and praise as they come." Hall has strong feelings about how much he learned from Kenyon.

I think the most important thing for me was watching the progress of Jane, watching her learn to be a poet by such assiduous work. She read in a way different from me. I was an extensive reader. I wanted to add more books to my life list. There was lots of English literature on which she spent little time. She would spend two years reading nothing but Keats, his poems, his letters, biographies, and learn enormously from Keats. I think I did more intensive reading because of her. But it was her daily work that I admired most, that stubborn struggle that came from inside.

Working with Akhmatova, making her translations of Akhmatova, was to her mind the most important thing in her poetic life. She did not have Russian but she worked with a very intelligent, very literary teacher named Vera Sandomirsky Dunham who would talk about individual words in great length until Jane felt she got to know how Akhmatova made her move. That was intensive reading and study even though it was not her language. I watched all this and it made me want to work harder. It made me want to try harder.

When I was an undergraduate, I remember saying a silly thing to John Ashbery. I was a little younger. I said, "Doesn't it make you mad when a friend of yours writes a good poem?" And John said, sensibly, "No. I just want to write a better one." I don't know that I was particularly trying to write a better poem than Jane, but I was trying to keep up with her. People assumed that she would learn more from me than I would from her, for natural reasons of age, and for chauvinistic reasons. I'm 19 years older. I started young. We used to argue about who helped the other more, each naming the other, but now she can't answer me. I think she led me more than I led her.

The assigning of roles to the two poets based upon gender or age, relegating them to some irrelevant rating system, may have prompted the need to establish structure in their public readings as well as in their private lives. Their first reading together was early in their marriage.

I guess it was not until we'd come to New Hampshire. There were several people who knew Jane's poetry who asked us to read together, but then nobody else in the audience knew her. One time someone introduced her as "Joan," and another time some idiot in an English department asked her if she did not feel dwarfed. She got her feelings hurt. She said to me one day, "Perkins, let's not read together any more. We are not going to read together anymore."

Well then, ten years later, when she published two or three books and people were getting to know her, one time we read two days in a row—me one day and her another day—but there was a question period for the two of us in between, and she got three times as many questions as I did. Jane said "Perkins, I think we can read together now."

When we read aloud together the last five years, we read A-B-A-B. When two poets read together, the first one is always the warm up man, and because I was older and male, unthinking people would sometimes ask me to conclude. We had a rule that we would switch each time, that if I was A one week then I would be B the next week and so on. This setting of rules—this sounds rigid—solved a lot of problems.

In their readings together, Hall and Kenyon provided a study in disparate styles. Kenyon's readings were low-keyed and understated. With her the poem was all. Hall is exuberant, enjoying the performance, with vocal intonations that carry the listener on waves of melody and cadence, and hand gestures that help visualize the rhythm. His words are only one part of the total achievement.

> When I read my favorite poems of hers, I sing them in a way that she would never do, dwelling on the vowels. I can't really imitate her way of doing it. Her way was much more understated. When I was a kid I didn't know whether I wanted to be an actor or a poet. My reading style also comes from listening to Dylan Thomas, admiring, requiring a kind of extravagance of performance.
>
> There are poetry readers that I'm very fond of who are low-keyed like Jane. I'm fond of their reading: Galway Kinnell. I know that some people find me too extravagant and that's all right. That's the way that I am. I can't really read like her.

Sharing the same work created comfort and ease. Kenyon said, "I think it is pleasant not to have to explain what I am doing, or trying to do." Hall puts it his way:

> I think that many people presume that a poet should marry someone not connected with poetry. In my own experience, that didn't turn out to be true. With Jane, poetry was part of the intimacy. The problem with poets marrying each other is the difficult problem of being in the same contest and one winning and one losing. This would happen with us with magazines occasionally, but because of the age difference, it seldom bothered us and we handled what we had to handle very well. But in love the lovers cannot spend their whole time looking into each other's eyes. I have written about the doctrine of the third thing. Their eyes join, as it were—in the old notion of vision coming out from the eyes—in the third thing: the baby they have together, which Jane and I didn't do; the dog that we had together; the Boston Red Sox; the South Danbury Church; and poetry, of course, the biggest thing of all. We didn't only talk about poetry. We talked about the weather, we talked about whether our feet hurt, but also we could, driving in the car or in the evening at supper, talk about poetry, not our own poetry but other people's and, of course, well, on occasion each other's poems. Poetry was an enormous third thing between us.

Although not properly diagnosed until she was 38 years old, depression was a constant in Kenyon's life. It was something Hall would also suffer from. Bill Moyers had once suggested to Kenyon that perhaps her depression may have been a gift from which her poems grew. Hall suggested a similar idea when he said of the torturous lives of T. S. and Vivienne Eliot, that if we cherish Eliot's poetry we must be grateful to the marriage and to Vivienne. I asked Hall if he felt now that the poetry ever validated the suffering of an artist or their family.

> That's a question I have been thinking about recently, in fact. I know that many people say "yes" and I would have said "yes" many times, but, a year after Jane died, I became as bipolar as she was. Freud said that this happened 30% of the time in the essay called "Mourning and Melancholy." From some time in June through some time in August, I had agony and depression that were extreme.
>
> We don't have the choice, mind you. We all suffer and we must suffer in this life, and a bipolar person does not have a choice except by seeking chemical help. I seek it as she sought it. She got depressed even with her chemical help, and frequently wrote her best poems while she was coming out of depression. The medication never made her into a flat line like the brain dead line on the monitor. She still had her ups and downs, as I do now. I would say that you don't have a choice in the matter, which invalidates the question—but I'm dodging the question. Therefore my answer is, "I am not sure."

Hall, thinking aloud, steps into the role of interviewer and asks himself, "Why does bipolarity exist? What is the Darwinian explanation of it, if there need be one?"

> Stephen Gould would say there doesn't have to be a Darwinian explanation for everything. Look at this: if mania includes finding the wheel—was it Archimedes in the tub who sang "Eureka?"—if mathematicians, scientists and poets are manic—then mania benefits not only the poet and the writer and his family, but humanity. Depression typically only affects the poet and the poet's family. So that would mean that from the point of view of DNA or the generality of society, of the species, there would be a function to bipolarity or at least to the manic part.
>
> Both Robert Lowell and Theodore Roethke were Bipolar-I, which means that in a manic period you do things that get you locked up. There is a trail of destruction among many, many marriages of the poets. I am not at the moment thinking of many who had only one wife: William Stafford, I know. Robert Frost, I'm sure, was faithful to Eleanor as long as she lived. I'm sure if we go back there would be many more examples. In modern times, I would say, probably the percentage of divorce is even greater than it is in the general population—always miserable. Wendell Berry is an exception, a very happy exception. Dick and Charlee Wilbur stayed together.
>
> When Jane was depressed, extremely depressed, in the absolute pits, I couldn't do anything for her. When she was mildly depressed there were many ways in which I could help. It probably also makes you—there's something to be skeptical about there—it makes you important. But if you can genuinely help, that makes the secondary gain not terribly important.
>
> When Jane went manic, which was rare, she would lose her sensitivity to the feelings of others. That happens when you are hypo-manic or Bipolar-II. When I am manic, I become careless of what I am saying and to whom I am talking. This happened rarely with Jane. For the most part she was tremendously alert, almost over alert, to the feeling temperature of everybody in the room.
>
> My daughter and her husband used to tease Jane because she would come into a room and say, "Are you all right? Your color doesn't look good." She would be

hypochondriacal for the dog and the automobile. She was alert to others, one reason I think she was reclusive. Sometimes people would call on me and she'd go hide in her study or the bedroom. When she was with someone, she related to them so intensely. One phenomenon I've heard again and again after her death: "I only knew her for twenty minutes but I felt as if I knew her forever." Peter Kramer, who wrote *Listening to Prozac,* said that to my editor, Peter Davison. It was exhausting for her and so, if she were mildly depressed, especially, she would avoid company.

I had seven years of Freudian therapy with an analyst. Jane had some time in psychotherapy. Her depression was a chemical event but the intelligence can deal with depression to a degree. The talking cure can provide you ways of looking at things. For instance, I remember that earlier in my life I would be with someone and I'd decide that person was angry with me, grumpy, and I'd think "why?" and I'd get grumpy. I learned the Freudian art of reversing everything. If I thought Jane looked grumpy I would say, "What am I mad about?" Then I would often find it was a letter I had read the night before. It didn't have anything to do with her. The brain can help, with training.

She was often depressed, but she tried not to be.

Out of the maelstrom, poetry is created, and the reader is drawn, enjoyably, toward the sadness.

We all have depression and sadness. It's about us. Poetry, writing about suffering is beautiful because the language is beautiful. If this is a contradiction, I think energy comes from contradiction.

There's a poem by Thomas Hardy that I say all the time, "During Wind and Rain." If you paraphrase it, it's all depressing. I read it and I am exhilarated. I love it. The dance on my tongue, in my mouth, is so happy.

Now when a poem is a happy poem beautifully done, it's perfectly fine, but there's not much energy. The energy comes from the conflict, I say, between the sensual delight of the body of the poem and the facing of sad reality in the paraphraseable content.

And now, in that true facing of sad reality without Kenyon, how does Hall work?

Something strange has happened to me: I can still write poetry—I work on poetry every day—but I cannot do anything good in prose. I have tried to write prose because I want to, I like to, it helps me to. Nothing is so distracting as writing.

I am lonely now. I miss her terribly, and if I could throw myself into work, well, I would be happier. The happiest time of the day for me is when I am working on poems, but you can't do that all day. I have worked on fiction. I have worked on essays. I have worked on a prose book about Jane and her illness. I wrote that book three times long hand but the prose never started to be prose. I know when the rhythm comes and the syntax works and you flow with it. My prose now is just "blah, blah," sentence after sentence. It's not satisfactory. It's curious—Jane died three-and-a-quarter years ago and I have not, with minor exceptions, been able to write prose since. My day is working on poetry, maybe trying to work on some of the prose, going to sleep to rise and work on poems again.

Writing without Kenyon as his first reader, Hall sometimes finds himself asking, "How would Jane do it?"

I don't think *Without* or subsequent poems resemble her closely. I don't think they are plagiarism, but I do think they're a little closer, the later poems—especially the last one in *Without,* **"Weeds and Peonies,"** and the poetry I have been writing since. After all, *Without* was finished two years ago and I have been working on poetry every day. I'm not about to think about another book for a while. I certainly have enough poems for another book but if I keep them around, they will weed out or get better. I hope.

As I get ready to leave, Hall holds his dog, Gus, by the collar. Gus has a habit of keeping visitors from leaving. Honored at first that Gus wants me to stay, I then think that maybe he wants everyone to stay.

Driving toward Boston, I play our conversation over and over in my head, thinking of Donald Hall and Jane Kenyon, and the long white house that held love and work together:

We meshed terribly well. She had a bad relationship with her boyfriend, which had broken up badly, and I had come out of a divorce, and we seemed to discover a secret that practically nobody else has ever discovered because it is so difficult to understand, so profound . . .

Here Donald Hall, the actor, takes over. A smile, subtly small, and a spark in his eye, indicate that he is manipulating me, his audience of one, creating a buildup that hits, not like the crescendo expected, but with the power of a whisper:

We found that we could be kind to each other, virtually all the time.

We had a fight every four years and therefore it was dreadful. We seldom got irritated or said anything snappy and we'd try to make the way easy for each other without, I think, the one deferring to the other.

We were determined to be happy in our relationship. We set out to do it, and when things came up that could hurt the relationship, like somebody saying "Don't you feel dwarfed?" which made her a little person compared to me, we avoided that situation—in order to be happy.

We had a good time together. There were certain things, private things that we did: going down to the pond in the summer by ourselves, playing ping-pong in the cellar by ourselves, me reading aloud to her almost every day. I read her *The Ambassadors* aloud twice from beginning to end. There were just so many pleasures.

We decided that it was permitted to be happy.

*Note*

1. All Jane Kenyon quotations, unless otherwise noted, are from "Two Writers under the Same Roof—A

Conversation with Donald Hall & Jane Kenyon" by Marian Blue (*AWP Chronicle,* May/Summer 1995, Volume 27, Number 6, pp. 1–8).

## Robert McDowell (essay date Winter 1999)

SOURCE: "Expansive Poetry," in *Hudson Review,* Vol. 51, No. 4, Winter, 1999, pp. 792–802.

[*In the following excerpt, McDowell argues that* Without *is an example of expansive poetry and lacks the sentimentality one might expect from the emotional subject matter.*]

More then a decade has passed since the anthologies *Ecstatic Occasions, Expedient Forms,* edited by David Lehman, and *The Direction of Poetry,* edited by Robert Richman, made the first ensemble attempts to recognize a change in our poetry: the renewed interest in form. It has been ten years since the special issue of *Crosscurrents* (1989), edited by Dick Allen, gave the name Expansive poetry to the writing of a number of poets, most of them in their thirties, who argued for more accessible poetries, including the use of form and story, and honest, clear, critical prose that illuminated texts for general readers.

Since then the early Expansive poets, and others of their generation with whom they share common ground, have published more than a hundred books of poetry and criticism, and hundreds of magazine and newspaper essays and reviews. All of this work has served many useful purposes, not the least of which was giving the lie to the claims of some critics (who seldom bothered to read the writers they were criticizing) that Expansive poets could not back up their goals with their own poems. Like it or not, the poems, essays, and reviews by Expansive poets have done much of the work that needed to be done in order to open up the field, making the appreciation of poetry outside writing programs and the academy possible once more. Expansive poets created an atmosphere of greater tolerance for poetry written in traditional meters, for poetry that rhymes, for poetry that tells stories. One need only look at the latest issue of one's favorite literary quarterly to witness more and more established free verse poets suddenly writing in form and narrative.

"Do you get the feeling you've won?" Donald Hall said to me at the Associated Writing Program convention two years ago in Washington, D.C. I was standing outside a room where more than two hundred people had crowded in to hear a panel built around *Rebel Angels: 25 Poets of the New Formalism,* the first anthology to represent the Expansive poets. Of course, Hall knows, as I do, that poets who get caught up in winning as they attempt to revise the canon stride through dangerous brush. Poets who get carried away with winning prizes are equally misguided. In the poetry business, the prize-giving process is usually so tainted by conflicts of interest that only the uninitiated and the naive can possibly be impressed. Winning is not the point. Having something artful and important to say, and having an opportunity to say it, is really all that matters. Like the successful writers before them, Expansive poets have had to fight for the opportunity to be heard, and I suppose that *is* a kind of winning—the right to address an audience at large.

But even as Expansive poets and their concerns have become a significant part of our poetry landscape, strange disappointments shadow them. One is that many of their critics still have not read their work. Another is the odd attitude recently adopted, it seems, by some older, established poets, that Expansive poetry never really happened, that it doesn't mean a thing. In a recent *American Book Review* article, the reviewer claims that Expansive poets can't be taken seriously until they write as well as John Ashbery, Jorie Graham, and Robert Pinsky. One might be puzzled by the list, for Pinsky has himself been linked to Expansive poetry. And one can summon up a growing legion of readers who would argue that many Expansive poets *do* write as well as, or better than, Ashbery and Graham. Such an assertion, in such a review, is confusing, but only until one recognizes the embarrassing attempt at favor-trading, the smack-smack-smack of lips kissing up, kissing up. Still, the *ABR* writer finds an ally in a recent *Parnassus* writer's opinion that Expansive poets are bad because they are Populists. Dozens of urban and ethnic Expansive poets are no doubt grateful to be instructed in their populist roots. Others might ask, with Mark Twain "*Is* Populism bad?"

If this type of shrill name-calling is sad to see, the other development is even worse. At that AWP panel, Henry Taylor surprisingly attacked Expansive poetry. As far as most of us could make out, he was just tired of it all. In the introduction to the latest volume of *Best American Poetry,* editor John Hollander dismisses new formalism, which is to say Expansive poetry, as just silly. These reactions by an older guard remind me of the envy and regret felt by some who loiter on the dock as a ship they would like to be on sails out to sea.

The world of poetry has always had its moments of generosity. Some, no matter how busy, will write jacket comments for new books if they possibly can; some donate money to favorite literary organizations, or to writer-friends in need. But today, it seems that acknowledgement and attribution are in short supply. Some older poets appear to be genuinely surprised, even caught off guard, by the success and growing influence of Expansive poetry. What else but fear can possibly be at work here, fear concerning who or what will have the last word? I have noticed a deer-in-the-headlights look to much of the dismissive protest waged against Expansive poetry. It is the most banal of desperate, historical revisions. Where fifteen years ago the status quo held that free verse was good, formal verse was bad, and Expansive poets hardly existed, today their argument holds that free verse *and* form are good, but Expansive poets are evil.

The practice of criticizing work you have not read, and the attitude that a thing does not exist when in fact it does, are as goofy as the Disney character himself. Through their talent and diligence, Expansive poets are most responsible for the sea change in American poetry. They have opened up more possibilities, more terrain, for all poets. Only the small-minded, the running scared, persist in denying the truth. . . .

The story that drives Donald Hall's thirteenth collection of verse, **Without,** is familiar even to many casual readers who do not pay much attention to poetry.[1] In January 1994, Hall's wife, the poet Jane Kenyon, was diagnosed with leukemia. In April 1995, she died in their bed at Hall's ancestral farm outside Wilmot, New Hampshire. These are only the facts. The poems in this book offer up all of the intense living and dying that filled those last sixteen months. They also help us to understand the extraordinary partnership, based on work, sex, and an abiding mutual respect and kinship, that endured for twenty years. The title poem is really a sequence of poems that mark the progress of Kenyon's illness and the heroic, desperate attempts to save her.

> Daybreak until nightfall,
> he sat by his wife at the hospital
>     while chemotherapy dripped
> through the catheter into her heart.
>     He drank coffee and read
> the *Globe*. He paced; he worked
>     on poems; he rubbed her back
> and read aloud. Overcome with dread,
>     they wept and affirmed
> their love for each other, witlessly,
>     over and over again.

The book concludes with a series of letters Hall wrote to Kenyon in the year after her death. This chronicle of goodbyes, of grief and survival, cannot fail to move readers. Yet despite its universal themes, the artistic success of **Without** was no sure thing. In fact, to publish such a book at all amounts to taking a great chance. I have heard, on occasion, the book dismissed by some who have not read it on grounds that it must be sentimental. They are wrong. There are times, akin to walking out of a dark room into blinding sunlight, when we meet a true fellowship of art and life. I think of van Gogh's paintings, and try to imagine my response to them if I were ignorant of the details of his sorry life. Something essential would, for me (and I am sure for others, too) be lost. Very little art successfully risks sentimentality and self-pity to portray what George Crabbe called "the life itself." **Without** is art stripped of all artifice, which is to say stripped of all opportunities for dishonesty. Perhaps because these poems are so clearly life-in-art, and art-in-life, we cannot put them away, even though we might wish to. . . .

I've implied throughout this chronicle that the detractors of Expansive poetry should read more of the work before wailing, and they could start with [William] Logan's new book, *Vain Empires* or, in fact, with all of the books I've discussed. Like it or not, the fact alone suggests a serious literary movement. The proof is in the written record, which already exists and is growing, and which only need be read.

*Note*

1. *Without,* by Donald Hall. Houghton Mifflin Company.

### Leslie Ullman (review date February 1999)

SOURCE: A review of *Without,* in *Poetry,* Vol. 173, No. 4, February, 1999, p. 312.

[*In the following positive review, Ullman compliments Hall's candor and his ability to put his grief into words in* Without.]

Grief's soundings—their depth and intricacy—arise from Donald Hall's thirteenth poetry collection as naturally as mist over water, even as they also provide the harshness from which the book takes its form. **Without** is described by the publisher as "a companion volume" to Hall's most recent collection, **The Old Life,** which also is autobiographical but covers a greater territory of Hall's life up to the present and offers names, events, and gossipy or literary recollections that might appeal to a reader of biography as well as poetry.

**Without,** in contrast, is more focused and, understandably, more steeped in feeling that is never excessive yet never lets up. It trains a magnifying beam on the fifteen months his wife, the poet Jane Kenyon, battled leukemia, and on the following year of mourning during which Hall shapes his grief, his memories, and his solitary experience of their once-shared home and friends into letter-poems addressed to her.

These poems are marked by candor that is often helpless, always stoic. Many of them display a simplicity, a domesticity, and a willingness—or maybe a need—to hover in the silence of white space, all of which call to mind the grace and restraint of Kenyon's own poems. But their references to routine, the presence of pets, and the nuances of weather and of seasonal change are infused with the approach, and then the fact, of her absence. They are not so much meditations as retrievals: "I drive and talk to you crying / and come back to this house / to talk to your photographs."

Like his wife's eyes which, in the days before her death, she fixes on him "shining, unblinking, / and passionate with love and dread," these poems are luminous with hard fact, especially two long sequences, **"Her Long Illness"** and **"Last Days,"** which chronicle the brutalities of illness, treatment, and relinquishment. Writing of the Total Body Irradiation that precedes a bone marrow transplant, he describes Jane lying on a gurney "alone in a leaden /

room between machines that resembled / pot-bellied stoves. . . . / It was as if she capped / the Chernobyl pile with her body." Sleeping with her the night before the most heroic of her treatments, he refers to their bodies assuming their familiar spoon-like positions, perhaps for the last time: "the spoons clattered / with a sound like the end man's bones."

Even the most habitual aspects of married life are enlarged by the irony of circumstance. Upon hearing Jane's prognosis, they "[rocked] on the bed in their horror, / they wept and held on / against the proliferation of her blasts. . . . / This ardent / merging recollected / old passionate connections at two / in the afternoon: / brief, breathless, ecstatic, then calm."

A particularly poignant passage reports that, having learned the leukemia is back and there is nothing more to be done against it, the couple spends two of Jane's last good days picking funeral hymns, writing her obituary, and working on her final book of poems. It concludes: "Later, as she slid exhausted into sleep, / she said, 'Wasn't that fun? / To work together? Wasn't that fun?'"

Hall's acts of witness, unflinching before the harshest realities, accommodate levity as well. When he visits Jane in the antibiotic cube to which she is confined after intense radiation, he spends fifteen minutes covering himself in hat, mask, booties, surgical gown, and latex gloves: "Jane said he looked like a huge condom." A year after her death, he writes to her, "Every day Gus and I / take a walk in the graveyard. / I'm the one who doesn't / piss on your stone."

Several self-contained poems are placed between, sometimes within, the longer sequences, offering subtle variations in voice, subject and sometimes form or strategy. "**A Beard for a Blue Pantry,**" whose title comes from a friend's dream, weaves associations of "blue" and "beard" into flexible word-and-memory-play, a gymnastic flight of consciousness that circles the fact of illness and impending loss. "**The Porcelain Couple,**" a poem full of furniture and figurines, poignantly enacts Hall's experience of packing up the possessions of his recently deceased mother and then returning home numbed and exhausted to see his and Jane's possessions through the same lens, as artifacts of vanished life. "**Without,**" reprinted from Hall's previous collection, erupts with raw grief, feeling in violent rebellion, through a headlong progression of nouns and sentence fragments: "silence without color sound without smell / without apples without pork to rupture gnash / unpunctuated without churches uninterrupted." An especially powerful poem, "**The Ship Pounding,**" sustains the shockingly apt metaphor of a hospital as a huge ship "that heaves water month / after month, without leaving / port, without moving a knot, / without arrival or destination."

Caught up in facts and feelings vastly beyond his control, Hall has managed in this collection to make them shapely and shareable. His grief, so keenly and elegantly sustained, provides a map for others to follow if they risk, as he has, loving what they may well lose.

## Donald Hall with Cynthia Huntington, Heather McHugh, Paul Muldoon, and Charles Simic (essay date September 1999)

SOURCE: "How to Peel a Poem: Five Poets Dine Out on Verse," in *Harper's Magazine*, Vol. 299, No. 1792, September, 1999, pp. 45–60.

[*In the following roundtable discussion, poets Hall, Cynthia Huntington, Heather McHugh, Paul Muldoon, and Charles Simic discuss their favorite poems and what makes them special.*]

Poetry has been described, in eras past, as "the natural language of all worship," "the hop-grounds of the brain," "devil's wine," and "the bill and coo of sex." Contemporary assessments tend to be less poetic. Poetry today is something that the federal government should fund, that our publishing houses must support, that the public schools ought to permit a larger place on the syllabus, that our creative-writing programs might give more recognition, that we honor each year (as we do "Quality," "Math Awareness," and "Medical Librarians") with a "National Poetry Month." Rarely does the public discourse on poetry speak directly to the value of poems; rarer still is the suggestion that poems simply be read and heard and enjoyed.

Hoping to correct this oversight, and taking a cue from the Chinese proverb "Recite poetry only with a poet," *Harper's Magazine* invited five practitioners of the art to dine together at the Algonquin Hotel in New York City. Each was asked to bring to the table a poem he or she truly loved, and then to tell us why.

Donald Hall is the author of fifteen books of poetry, the latest of which, ***Without***, received the 1999 PEN-Winship Award for the best book of 1998 by a New England writer.

Cynthia Huntington is professor of English at Dartmouth College and the director of the creative writing program. She is the author of two books of poetry and *The Salt House,* a memoir.

Heather McHugh is the Milliman Distinguished Writer in Residence at the University of Washington in Seattle. Her *Hinge & Sign* was a finalist for the National Book Award in 1994. Her latest collection of poetry is *The Father of the Predicaments.*

Paul Muldoon is the Howard G. B. Clark '21 University Professor in Humanities at Princeton University and the newly elected Oxford Professor of Poetry. His most recent collection, his eighth, is *Hay*.

Charles Simic is the author of fourteen collections of poetry, the latest of which is *Jackstraws*. He won the Pulitzer Prize in 1990 for *The World Doesn't End*.

I.

APÉRITIFS

[Charles Simic:] All these poems have one very simple virtue. When you finish reading them, you want to go back to the beginning and start reading them again. Most poems are forgettable. They may strike us as witty and clever, but once we're done we have no particular wish to return to them. To make someone reread something you've written is no small achievement.

[Cynthia Huntington:] You approach a poem, you go through it, you get it, you go away. The poems we've chosen don't allow that. They disappoint, or deflect your expectations, and that's why you go back to them.

[Paul Muldoon:] If the poem has no obvious destination, there's a chance that we'll all be setting off on an interesting ride.

[Heather McHugh:] I think one of poetry's functions is *not* to give us what we want.

[Donald Hall:] In logic no two things can occupy the same point at the same time, and in poetry that happens all the time. This is almost what poetry is for, to be able to embody contrary feelings in the same motion.

[McHugh:] I will misquote Simic here, to the effect that the poet isn't always of use to the tribe. The tribe thrives on the consensual. The tribe is pulling together to face the intruder who threatens it. Meanwhile, the poet is sitting by himself in the graveyard talking to a skull.

[Hall:] I'm surprised that we all picked twentieth-century poems.

[McHugh:] I was tempted to pick an earlier one, and then I thought, "Everybody else is going to be doing that."

[Simic:] I expected that Heather and Paul and Don would pick something with great verbal richness. So I wanted to get something really plain. The kind of poem that cats and dogs could understand.

[Muldoon:] Or write, perhaps.

[Huntington:] All our poems have animals, except for Ezra Pound.

[Muldoon:] There's a "shag" in Ezra Pound.

[McHugh:] There's at least one in everybody.

[Muldoon:] I mean the bird.

[McHugh:] Where there's God there are animals. The shop window, by the way, occurs in each of our choices.

[Muldoon:] Oh, that's interesting. The flaneur.

[Hall:] "During Wind and Rain" has a shop window?

[McHugh:] Well, your poem is the least susceptible to this reading.

[Huntington:] Heather has this urge to bring things together.

[McHugh:] It's a hermit's foible.

[Huntington:] No, it's wonderful.

II.

THE SOUP

"DURING WIND AND RAIN" (1917)

BY THOMAS HARDY

> They sing their dearest songs—
> He, she, all of them—yea,
> Treble and tenor and bass,
>     And one to play;
> With the candles mooning each face. . . .
>     Ah, no; the years O!
> How the sick leaves reel down in throngs!
>
> They clear the creeping moss—
> Elders and juniors—aye,
> Making the pathways neat
>     And the garden gay;
> And they build a shady seat. . . .
>     Ah, no; the years, the years;
> See the white storm-birds wing across!
>
> They are blithely breakfasting all—
> Men and maidens—yea,
> Under the summer tree,
>     With a glimpse of the bay,
> While pet fowl come to the knee. . . .
>     Ah, no; the years O!
> And the rotten rose is ript from the wall.
>
> They change to a high new house,
> He, she, all of them—aye,
> Clocks and carpets and chairs
>     On the lawn all day,
> And brightest things that are theirs. . . .
>     Ah, no; the years, the years;
> Down their carved names the rain-drop ploughs.

[Hall:] I'm happy to say this is the most beautiful poem in the English language. The paraphrase of the poem is, "People have a lot of fun together, especially in families, and then they get old and sick and die." For me the sensuous pleasure of the poem is in conflict with its melancholy paraphrase. And in this poem the conflict between the enormous, beautiful, erotic sounds of the poem and the decay, death, sickness of its—for a lack of a better word—content makes for an explosion. There are only three metaphors in this poem. There's "mooning," which is common, as the candelabrum shines off the faces as the sun shines off the moon; "reel," which can be a number of things—dancing, for instance—but in this context it's the reeling of somebody old and feeble; and then, finally, the last word of the whole poem, "ploughs," which is an extraordinary word, because the rain-drop is to the granite as the plough is to the earth. Time suddenly elongates, and the sound of the word does the elongating. That last line is equal, metrically, to "And the rotten rose is ript from the wall," but it takes forty-seven times longer to say because it has all those long vowels and consonants: the assonance of "names," "rain" and "down," "ploughs"—all dipthongs that you can hold on to forever. And the wonderful hiatus between "drop" and "ploughs." Earlier, with "carved names," to get from one vowel to another you have to climb over the boulders of four consonants—*r, v, d, n.* I think we read poems with our mouths, not with our eyes, not with our ears, not with our intelligences. And this is a poem with enormous mouth-joy. This is like oral sex, this extraordinary pleasure of these words in the mouth. He originally wrote the last line: "On their chiseled name the lichen grows." I don't think that Thomas Hardy sat down and said, "Ah, let me see, I'll have the identical dipthongs first and last, and a different pair of dipthongs in the middle." He fiddled with it until it *felt* right. That's what poets do. And when it felt right, he went on and wrote another poem. I think there's a terrible line here. That's my rule: there has to be something awful. "And the rotten rose is ript from the wall" is pretty bad. He had originally written, "And the wind-whipped creeper lets go the wall." I think I like that better.

[Muldoon:] What did he have first for the last line?

[Hall:] "On their chiseled names the lichen grows."

[McHugh:] Now, that's a better revision.

[Muldoon:] He was concerned about the rhyme with "house," I guess.

[Hall:] And fiddling around to make the rhyme better, he made everything else better. Does anybody hate this poem?

[Simic:] It's a great poem. What I find interesting is how each stanza is a tableau, an idealized family scene cut short by an ominous concluding image.

[Hall:] I think that "While pet fowl come to the knee" is second in sound to the last line. There's that long vowel in the middle, that terribly short one at the beginning, that rather short one afterward. And it seems to me explosive.

[Muldoon:] I wonder if what really makes this poem fly off the page has to do with the imagery in the last stanza—this extraordinary vision of the graveyard furniture. And I wonder if that in a way doesn't really compensate for some of the perhaps less than wonderful moments along the way. Because I think the poem is quite risk-taking, assuming that he's aware of the risks he's taking.

[Hall:] Who knows what Thomas Hardy was aware of? Believe the poem, not the poet.

[Muldoon:] The poem knows but someone has got to be keeping a little eye on how the poem is coming out.

[McHugh:] I love his attempt to luster up the material versions of their lives by furnishing them with the very best in carnal effects: "a high new house." "All of them, . . . Clocks and carpets and chairs / On the lawn all day, / And brightest things that are theirs. . . ." All those alls! All those utmosts! The ultimate in appointments, but still, "Ah, no." They can't avoid *the* ultimate appointment.

[Hall:] I have a different reading of the last stanza. I think it's parallel to the singing and the breakfasting. I think they are simply moving house.

[Simic:] They're getting richer, but time is passing.

[Muldoon:] You know, Don, you're absolutely right. Literally, of course, they are moving to a new house. I always read "high" as "on a higher plane." I've never read it literally, if such a thing is possible.

[Hall:] I'm very literal. But I allow that there are different possible readings. "Reel," for instance.

[McHugh:] And the great thing about readings is they needn't be ranked.

[Hall:] Each present tense, which we discover by the end of the first stanza, is the memory of someone who looks back and laments. Scenes of singing together around the piano, gardening, men and maidens together, and what has happened? The years have intervened. "The rotten rose is ript from the wall." "How the sick leaves reel down in throngs!" Images of frailty and debility, and then, finally, images of the long dead.

[Huntington:] What's so rich here is that all the positive images are very time-bound too. Music is measured in time. Clearing the moss, breakfasting—movement through the day, movement through their lives. Time the killer is also the time in which songs are sung. Time the killer is also the time in which the moss grows, in which you breakfast, in which you move house.

[McHugh:] I love the degree to which the first and last stanzas' provisions against time employ the superlative—"their dearest songs," "And brightest things." Yet at each turn some equally embodied *small* thing—the leaves, the birds, the rose, and then a single raindrop—becomes the incarnation of all time. That's what does them in: one raindrop down their names. That's what's so excruciating. You think that some particular will save you, but it's the particular that effaces you.

[Hall:] The first line rhymes with the last line, every time. And then in between we have the interlocking rhymes of B C B C and the refrain line of "years" and "O's."

[Muldoon:] "The years O" is such a powerful refrain that he wants to resist using "yea" each time. He's got "yea" and then he's got "years O." Then he's changed it to "aye," which where I come from we would pronounce "eye," though I gather here it's pronounced "ay." If he had Y-E-A at the end of the line and Y-E-A-R-S at the end of the line further down, some subliminal little danger signal would be sent to the reader.

[Hall:] If it is pronounced "eye," he is doing what Emily Dickinson did all the time, which is to take two dipthongs and rhyme on the second part. He rhymes the long "e" in each case, as it goes "eyeee . . . dayeee." So that's a rhyme, too. It's the kind of off-rhyme I don't associate with Hardy, but the possibility is there.

[McHugh:] It also permits the subliminal other of the words rhymed with "aye"—"ply," "guy," "by/buy," and "die." These are unsaid perhaps but pocketed in the understudy of the poem.

[Huntington:] And the punctuation—every line is controlled by punctuation, given a precise timing.

[Hall:] Punctuation and syntax are the last things anybody thinks about these days. Maybe they're the last things I think about, but I think about them a long time. I've been talking about the mouth part of the poem, but the rest of the body of the poem is the hands moving, the legs moving, the dance. And the dance is determined by punctuation and line breaks.

[Muldoon:] I once knew a woman who broke off a relationship because the man used ellipses and three exclamation marks after every sentence. Yet the gap the ellipses imply in this poem, the sense of time having passed, and the shift in each of those stanzas—if those ellipses weren't there it wouldn't work.

[McHugh:] And if you look at the words that precede them, three out of four are body parts. There is this momentum of the living toward itself, which Hardy then cuts off, or contains.

[Hall:] Richard Wilbur once said that the genie gets his strength from being enclosed in the bottle. The passion here of letting flow, the impossibility of acceptance, and the absolute tightness and closure—these are the qualities that we tend not to have in contemporary free verse.

[Muldoon:] I wonder here if, in preparation for "Down their carved names the rain-drop ploughs," Hardy isn't wittingly presenting a line that is less than stellar: "How the sick leaves reel down in throngs!" "See the white storm-birds wing across!" "And the rotten rose is ript from the wall." Don pointed out that this last line was worse than the one he originally had. I'm pretty sure Hardy would've known that.

[Huntington:] You think he's holding back for the big moment.

[Simic:] The hopelessness of a poetic gesture in the face of the inevitable.

[Hall:] It could be simply that he fiddled with it until it felt better.

III.

THE FISH

"THE TAXIS" (1963)

BY LOUIS MACNEICE

In the first taxi he was alone tra-la,
No extras on the clock. He tipped ninepence
But the cabby, while he thanked him, looked askance
As though to suggest someone had bummed a ride.

In the second taxi he was alone tra-la
But the clock showed sixpence extra; he tipped according
And the cabby from out his muffler said: "Make sure
You have left nothing behind tra-la between you."

In the third taxi he was alone tra-la
But the tip-up seats were down and there was an extra
Charge of one-and-sixpence and an odd
Scent that reminded him of a trip to Cannes.

As for the fourth taxi, he was alone
Tra-la when he hailed it but the cabby looked
Through him and said: "I can't tra-la well take
So many people, not to speak of the dog."

[Simic:] What are the extra charges? Other people's baggage?

[Muldoon:] Or his own. In each instance some further version of the self is coming into play. Donald, in particular, was talking about the poem beginning with the mouth, and I think in that sense the poem teaches you how to read it. My reading of "The Taxis" comes out of "I can't tra-la well." It's a version of "I can't bloody well," or "I can't fucking well," or something along those lines. "I can't tra-la well take / So many people, not to speak of the dog." I am always tempted to read this poem from end to beginning, despite the fact that its shape has got to do with building on the notion of multiple personalities and the accrual and accretion of personae on a journey or throughout a life. In a certain sense, he carries the reader's bags also, to get back to Charlie's point. The reader becomes invested in some way in the poem and recognizes something about the situation while hoping for a revelation.

[Hall:] When we talked about the Hardy, I talked mostly about its mouth sounds, the last line especially. This poem is more the dance than the mouth, the pulse and thrust of limbs, with the "tra-la" making a tricky step. It becomes a movable refrain. The dance surprises us in its flourishes, then concludes with a turn-and-hold that resolves itself. It's *sound* again, but dance or muscle pleasure more than mouth pleasure. It's all iambic in a very disguised way—iambic pentameter. I have looked at it, in a general way, as the accrual of experience but also in particular as the accrual of the erotic life.

[McHugh:] Eventually the cabby knows there's somebody else.

[Hall:] He probably sees all these women.

[McHugh:] Yes. Freud tells a terrible old Austrian teaser in *Jokes and the Unconscious*: A wife is like an umbrella. Sooner or later one takes a cab.

[Muldoon:] MacNeice was one of those writers who in Ireland were perceived as being English. In England he was perceived as being Irish. I think he fell between the cracks.

[Hall:] I have two other MacNeice lines going through my head:

> It's no go the Yogi-Man, it's no go Blavatsky;
> All we want is a bank balance and a bit of skirt in a taxi.

[Muldoon:] "Bagpipe Music" is a great poem. I think there were probably numerous bits of skirts in taxis.

[Simic:] Let's not forget the dog.

[Huntington:] I think the primary meaning of this poem is very much as we've put it, but it's interesting to entertain the idea that he's wrong. Everyone but him seems to know there are six people in the taxi. Perhaps he only *thinks* he's alone.

[Hall:] That magnificent conflict between "alone" and the many is what makes energy in this poem. I also think the dog is enormously funny. "Not to speak of the dog."

[Simic:] You have the sense it's a large dog, right?

[Muldoon:] The dog is Cerberus too, and for the first time it strikes me that a rough anagram of *canis,* "dog," occurs in MacNeice's very name. And he would be conscious of this.

[Hall:] We bet on him being conscious.

[McHugh:] Even of the unspeakable, the music of opportunity, the "tra-la."

[Huntington:] When he's alone "tra-la" sounds kind of simple, but by the time we get to "I can't tra-la well take / So many people" it's darkened itself quite a lot.

[McHugh:] By the last stanza the "tra-la" has deserted him and has fled from the first line to the second, into the cabby's territory. By *his* "tra-la" the cabby means something entirely less dreamy than does his passenger. The cabby is some sort of supervisory tollkeeper, the protonotary of sins. There's not only a dog in this poem but a god as well.

[Hall:] The "tra-la" is a musical, nonsensical interjection that confirms the poetry of poetry.

[McHugh:] I kept thinking of *taxis* and *logos* in their old Greek senses, as in *taxis de pasa logos,* which is roughly paraphrased as "form is in the very nature of things." In poems in general, the tra-la always half resists the poetic forms. In this poem, the forms it resists are social forms too. But however much the "tra-la" may hope to be free, nevertheless there's the *taxis*—with its meter running.

[Hall:] A poem is not an essay, and the music and the body of it are there as counter-sense; they are countering sense.

[Muldoon:] Yeats wrote, "You can refute Hegel but you cannot refute 'A Song of Sixpence.'"

[Simic:] I was particularly spooked by those "tip-up seats" in the third stanza.

[Hall:] That's one of the clues to the gender of these extra people.

[McHugh:] Ah, the gender doesn't matter. Only the sex.

[Huntington:] The dog's a bitch.

[McHugh:] Seeing as we are at the Algonquin, did you know that Dorothy Parker never house-trained her dogs?

[Muldoon:] And why would she? Then she'd have to bring them inside.

IV.

THE MEAT

"MUSIC" (1954)

*BY FRANK O'HARA*

> If I rest for a moment near The Equestrian
> pausing for a liver sausage sandwich in the Mayflower
>   Shoppe,
> that angel seems to be leading the horse into Berg-
>   dorf's
> and I am naked as a table cloth, my nerves humming.
> Close to the fear of war and the stars which have dis-
>   appeared.
> I have in my hands only 35 cents, it's so meaningless
>   to eat!
> and gusts of water spray over the basins of leaves
> like the hammers of a glass pianoforte. If I seem to
>   you
> to have lavender lips under the leaves of the world,
>   I must tighten my belt.
> It's like a locomotive on the march, the season
>     of distress and clarity
> and my door is open to the evenings of midwinter's
> lightly falling snow over the newspapers.
> Clasp me in your handkerchief like a tear, trumpet
> of early afternoon! in the foggy autumn.

As they're putting up the Christmas trees on Park Avenue
I shall see my daydreams walking by with dogs in blankets,
put to some use before all those coloured lights come on!
But no more fountains and no more rain,
and the stores stay open terribly late.

[Huntington:] I love Frank O'Hara. He's so funny, and not in a throwaway sense but by tripping you up every time you think you know where you're going. The disordered syntax, the images that seem to promise a depth and yet stop you before you can go further with them. The false connectives. The most mysterious line to me is "If I seem to you / to have lavender lips under the leaves of the world, / I must tighten my belt." That makes complete grammatical sense, but what the hell does it mean? It has a lot of possible meanings within the context of the poem, but when you take it out of context it has strands going in different directions. This could be a reworking of a Wordsworth poem, with a lot of subversive intent. Everything is conditional. It all follows from "If I rest for a moment . . . that angel seems to be leading the horse into Bergdorf's"—if you can accept that, you can accept the rest of the poem. There's an opportunity for fantasy and imagination to enter this very ordinary lunchtime scene and change everything. I also love the way there's such a personal voice in here but no person. It's a deliberate pose, and we know we're invited to play along with it. I think O'Hara loves New York the way people who aren't from New York love New York. It never stops being exotic to him.

[Hall:] His nerves are always humming. He surprises me every time he makes a turn: "and I am naked as a table cloth."

[McHugh:] The trail from the stony equestrian to the liver sausage to the angel and nakedness and those disappeared celestial bodies seems to me a trail from materialism to spirit. There's an urge toward exhaustions of the flesh. If his lips seem lavender, then they aren't purple enough; he cinches his belt a little tighter. He's aiming for some end, and that's dysfunctional in a society of means—a consumer society.

[Huntington:] This poem's definitely about consuming: shopping, Bergdorf's, sandwiches, women with dogs in blankets.

[Simic:] Whitman has poems like this, and so do early twentieth-century French poets, in which the speaker moves through the city like a camera. O'Hara mentions places like Bergdorf's and the Mayflower Shoppe the way Apollinaire would name neighborhoods and streets in Paris to give the poem the feel of verisimilitude. Different realities collide in a city. "I could live so many lives here," one says to oneself. O'Hara's poem is a little ode to the transformative powers of the imagination.

[Huntington:] In O'Hara there's always that undercurrent of melancholy, and in the poems it comes and it goes. It's not dismissed, it's not solved, and it's not denied, but it doesn't take control. It never takes a dramatic leap into the abyss. It's skating between emotional levels.

[Muldoon:] That's partly because the beginning, the middle, and the end are not necessarily in that order in the conventional sense, because the first three, four lines would conventionally be the end of the poem, where there is some kind of resolution and a rocket goes up and "The End" comes up on the screen. And somehow the lack of resolution at the end is, I suppose, what's really of interest to him. "If I rest for a moment": if we did think of that as the end of the poem, the poem is about a momentary stay against confusion, except it's much more interested in the confusion than in the stay. "If I rest for a moment" is basically what any poem is about from line to line—it rests at the end of the line, and it might rest even in a world where no rest is possible, perhaps, where maybe lunch isn't even going to happen.

[Huntington:] I think resting is slightly dangerous in this poem. "If I rest," all of these things are going to happen, but if you keep going, then you can stay on the surface of things and you're okay.

[Simic:] Just as you think he's going to take off and make great claims about What I've Seen and What I Understood, he undercuts himself and ends quietly.

[Hall:] I feel that if I rest I'll sink under the lack of sensation. It's as if there's an absolute necessity to keep moving in order not to sink. He has to keep the ball in the air all the time, and I find it always attractive, that restlessness, nerves humming, that spinning it out of the gun.

[McHugh:] And also what makes for that underlying basso continuo that you love, it seems to me, has to do in this poem—and again I really think it's a poem about the consumer and the consumed—with indentation. I do think that the indented lines, the lines with teeth, are the low-lying lines. Semantically, those indented lines are all lines of fatality. And that helps give this poem the register that saves it from mere restlessness, high jinks.

[Simic:] "No more fountains and no more rain, / and the stores stay open terribly late." To use an old jazz term, he's "cooking" now. He can say anything that pops into his head and it'll sound great.

[Muldoon:] Is it a particularly American phenomenon, this Mayflower Shoppe?

[Simic:] The Mayflower Shoppe was on Park near Fifty-ninth Street. I used to go there. It was just a cheap place to eat. I knew Frank O'Hara in those days. If you had thirty-five cents for lunch your options were limited and you sat over at the fountain—near the Plaza Hotel. And the lavender business, I think, has to do with the trees, the way the sunlight would come down and the way people would look around. I mean this is, to me as a New Yorker, an ex—New Yorker, what is impressive here. There's a real city scene here, a hard-core realism.

[Huntington:] The Mayflower Shoppe does not take you to the Mayflower.

[Hall:] The poem becomes less particular as it goes toward the end, and it seems to me that ten years later or five years later, however long Frank had lived, he would not have gone into "early afternoon! in the foggy autumn . . . no more fountains and no more rain." There is the kind of yearning and melancholy at the end, as opposed to the Mayflower Shoppe and Bergdorf's, that changes the direction of the poem.

[Simic:] There's a wealth of possible meanings. When he mentions the Mayflower Shoppe and Christmas, he knows these words will give rise to certain associations in the reader, but he leaves it at that. This is not a poem with an elaborate subtext of ideas.

[Huntington:] The idea that the stores stay open late should be a very nice thing, but it's not.

[Hall:] It's one of the great surprises in the poem, that "terribly." Such a dumb word, but it comes alive here, and actually a kind of terror comes through.

[Simic:] Well, it's urban solitude. A lone speaker who is going to be alone as the stores stay open terribly late.

[Huntington:] The other use of the word "open" in this poem is "my door is open to the evenings of midwinter's / lightly falling snow," and again there's the sense not that things are open and welcoming but that they haven't closed down as they should. There's a feeling of danger.

[Hall:] I don't understand the connection between "locomotive" and "march." I mean "march" is walking, for God's sake.

[McHugh:] That's a misfortune—everybody is allowed one.

[Hall:] I say there's no wonderful poem without at least one crummy word in it.

[McHugh:] Then he had to redeem "march" by putting in "season."

[Huntington:] When I find these things in O'Hara, I think I'm way too susceptible to them, because I think, "Oh well, he knew that was a terrible line, and it's hilarious." That's not necessarily a good way to read people.

[McHugh:] Well, he redeems it in other ways. That is, if you look, as I can't help doing always, at the first and last lines, it's also a poem about time, which is another way of saying consumability. The relation between "for a moment" and "terribly late" is potent. You would think that the urban was the place of the very fast, but in fact in this poem what O'Hara articulates is the possibility of the urban as a kind of perpetuity, with resting for a moment as the poetic occasion, which is a fleeting occasion.

[Hall:] I love that line of abstraction—"distress and clarity." If things are clear they are melancholy—"distress and clarity." The essence of lyric poetry is oxymoron.

[Muldoon:] I'm just thinking about the "lavender lips under the leaves of the world," "tighten my belt."

[Huntington:] I'm thinking of O'Hara's comment on form in poetry: you want your pants to be tight enough so everyone will want to go to bed with you.

[Muldoon:] The "tighten my belt" thing has to do with, "If I'm hungry, if I tighten my belt, I won't feel it." But I agree that there is a sexual aspect running throughout the poem: "the lavender lips," wherever they might be; "under the leaves of the world, / I must tighten my belt"; the locomotive—it sounds like a bad film. And I think that's why he recovers himself insofar as he can on "march."

[Hall:] Frank O'Hara could not use the word "lavender" without thinking of being gay.

[Muldoon:] That's the undertow of this, isn't it?

[Simic:] All lyric poems are narcissistic. They are the earliest form of personal ad. They've been saying for more than a thousand years, "I'm a sensitive, vulnerable, misunderstood, barely solvent, lovable little fellow who would like to meet a person of exquisite taste who is not averse to an occasional roll in the hay."

[Huntington:] I think it's defended at the same time. He shows some vulnerability like a tease. Perhaps this will get the crowd—I'll show my vulnerable side. But at the same time he's being overt and open and dramatic, he's also mocking that whole movement that seems to lead, at that point in the poem, to the great Romantic statement. And in the syntax of a great Romantic statement, he speaks nonsense: "Clasp me in your handkerchief like a tear, trumpet / of early afternoon!"

[Simic:] Roman poets sometimes do this kind of stuff: you evoke all the clichés of the tradition, all the self-pity, but you're playing off all these things and having a great old time doing it. These are usually poems written by incredibly sophisticated, clever individuals who know the traditions, and every time they look at something, they think of something else, like the trumpet business. Allusions, allusions, allusions.

[McHugh:] The voice of continence!

[Simic:] It's that wonderful play between the poet and the tradition. What is amazing is that the end product sounds genuine. He's making it all up, and yet I find myself deeply moved. Great french fries.

[McHugh:] Be it noted that all the poets picked red meat.

[Hall:] Does anyone know a good poet who's a vegetarian?

V.

SALAD AND CHEESES

"TRAVELING THROUGH THE DARK" (1962)

BY WILLIAM STAFFORD

Traveling through the dark I found a deer
dead on the edge of the Wilson River road.
It is usually best to roll them into the canyon:
that road is narrow; to swerve might make more dead.

By glow of the tail-light I stumbled back of the car
and stood by the heap, a doe, a recent killing;
she had stiffened already, almost cold.
I dragged her off; she was large in the belly.

My fingers touching her side brought me the reason—
her side was warm; her fawn lay there waiting,
alive, still, never to be born.
Beside that mountain road I hesitated.

The car aimed ahead its lowered parking lights;
under the hood purred the steady engine.
I stood in the glare of the warm exhaust turning red;
around our group I could hear the wilderness listen.

I thought hard for us all—my only swerving—,
then pushed her over the edge into the river.

[Simic:] This is a poem I've known for about thirty years, and as I was re-reading it I was struck by the speed and matter-of-factness of the narrative. Plain language, no striving to be poetic, a commonplace American experience retold. "Traveling through the dark" has a kind of literary echo—Dantesque, dark night of the soul—but the specificity of what he finds makes you forget the opening phrase. Then it's plain details, but Dante's still there: the narrator finds himself in a kind of hell; he has to make a very difficult decision. Where his art comes in—and I've never thought of Stafford as a very artful poet—is how quickly I'm implicated in this hell, this difficult moral decision. When he's standing over her after he says, after this police report, "she had stiffened already, almost cold. / I dragged her off; she was large in the belly. / My fingers touching her side brought me the reason," and then I, too, as a reader, am stuck. This is a poem of huge solitude, because every time we make moral decisions we're alone, if we're really honest. And the car turns into a partner there: "lowered parking lights," as if embarrassed. Stafford doesn't say what his emotions are, but his car is becoming emotional, and then we get this very strange line: "around our group I could hear the wilderness listen." Group? What group? The car? The fog? The dead deer? This is a kind of cop-out—it's not just me, we're all in this together. We always assume that we must save *all* the innocent, but in truth choices must be made. Stafford was a conscientious objector, so the issue of sacrificing the innocent in order to save others would have been very big for him. And if you know anything about country roads, there are curves, and there could be teenagers coming back from . . .

[Muldoon:] Prom?

[Simic:] Yes—driving fast, coming around the curve. Or maybe Heather is driving.

[McHugh:] I'm the world's best driver.

[Huntington:] What's his difficult moral choice?

[Simic:] The other innocent—the prom kids, say—are ideas, but this is the immediate life. I have to kill the one who is here before me, to save the abstract others.

[Hall:] Is he thinking of performing a cesarean?

[Huntington:] I think Don's point is that he really sets up a false idea that there is a choice to be made. Is he going to take this little fawn fetus home in his car?

[McHugh:] And there's an anterior problem. As soon as you say "to swerve might make more dead"—which is actually one of the moments I love most, because there are four stresses in a row—then to *stop* might make more dead also. And he stops. He could have killed somebody then.

[Huntington:] He's got his lights on.

[Hall:] I do think that the moral dilemma is, in a sense, trivial. But I agree that it's a hard thing to do, as to kill your own cat is a hard thing to do.

[Huntington:] You've killed a cat?

[Hall:] I haven't done it, actually.

[Simic:] We happen to have a cat here tonight.

[McHugh:] And we've just eaten it.

[Muldoon:] The fact that the "swerve" is repeated there in the "swerving" might easily be problematic, because the "swerving," by the end of the poem, more significantly has to do with the moral dilemma. The moment I make that argument I see the contrary argument, which is that there is a terrifically throwaway aspect to the poem. When one reads "dead on the edge," one has a little swerving, because it's not absolutely certain whether it means that the narrator is on the edge or that the deer is on the edge.

[Hall:] It's that wonderful repetition of the vowel sounds there: "dead," "edge."

[Simic:] What we need to understand is that you don't have much time to make this decision, because, as Heather pointed out, if you stop the car, someone can come around the curve and kill you, too.

[Muldoon:] You either push it over the side or what? You shoot it?

[Hall:] Perform the cesarean?

[Huntington:] It's not really a choice. I distrust this poem on a certain level. I have a distrust for "I could hear the wilderness listen," for the certainty of the speaker that Nature, History, Culture, Morality are all overseeing his choice.

[Simic:] I think it's ironic. I don't think he really means it.

[Huntington:] "I could hear the wilderness listen." You think that's ironic?

[Simic:] I think it's a description of the great silence that surrounds you in that moment.

[Huntington:] But that's not what he said.

[Muldoon:] There's an awkwardness throughout that stanza. "Under the hood purred the steady engine" is not exactly a line that's changing the state of poetry. In another context one would say it's absolutely clichéd. "I stood in the glare of the warm exhaust turning red." Hold on, is the exhaust turning red or am I turning red? But what I would say in favor of this knowing awkwardness is that it's constantly forcing one to ask, "What is my reading here of this situation, of this poem, from word to word?" And maybe we've done it a little bit of an injustice by suggesting that there's a choice involved. He doesn't really present it as a choice.

[Hall:] I think "aimed" is a wonderful word, because it's threatening. What do you aim? You aim a gun, an arrow. A commonplace, yes, but it's the perfect word. It's subtle, the way Stafford is. I talked a moment ago about killing a cat. There's one cat in this poem I'd damn well like to kill. "Purred." Disgusting word. Every good poem has one disgusting word in it. It's a damned dead metaphor.

[Muldoon:] Except, of course, that there is an argument to be made for Stafford's witting use of the metaphor, being conscious of it as a cliché. I said it myself that in another context it'd be dreadful. But it's possible that this clichéd way of discussing things was simply an attempt to record the event as it happened, which is basically, I think, what he's trying to do. It's a hand-held poem.

[Huntington:] Perhaps it's not a poem about making a moral choice but a poem about having to endure the moment.

[McHugh:] That word "still" keeps being drawn both to "still alive" and to "stillborn," which are opposites. There is a sense in which this poem stays in that static moment—the undecidability of things. There is the unmoving thing dead on the edge, and then there is the edge of the river, which is eternally moving and also dividing. Then there's the thing that splits one thing from another, the thing that makes the canyon that it's "best to roll them into."

[Muldoon:] The poem has gone over the edge, and he's conscious of its having gone over the edge.

[McHugh:] It's a self-criticism in a way.

[Muldoon:] The arguments for keeping both the "swerving" and the "swerve" is that he has "dead on the edge" in the second line and he comes back to it.

[Hall:] The comma with "still" bothers me, because if the fetus is still how do you know it's alive? Alive still? How does he know it's alive? I read once from the speech of a Language poet who ridiculed this poem because it was William Stafford saying, "I'm a nice guy. What a nice guy I am."

[Muldoon:] I don't think that's what he's saying.

[Simic:] Oh, no, no, no, no, no.

[Huntington:] That's reductive.

[Simic:] The strength of this poem is that we find ourselves in his shoes. I ask myself, what would I have done in the circumstances? I would have done the same thing, and it would have been very difficult. To me the strength of the poem is that it draws me in. I don't feel any separation.

[McHugh:] The one word you object to, Don, is "purred," and from my point of view what that word calls up is the poetic intention to make another animal worth as much as the doe.

[Hall:] There's no cat in the word "purred."

[McHugh:] But I don't mean the particular cat any more than he means the particular "purred." What I do mean is that there's another animal claim on the moment.

[Simic:] I think it's an unfortunate choice.

[McHugh:] It's a cutesifying choice in a certain way, but to my mind that's the reason that the indecisiveness is the greater power of the poem.

[Muldoon:] I think it's infelicitous, but an argument can be made for its infelicity.

[Hall:] I know, but I think it's a bad argument.

[Muldoon:] To be devil's advocate, what would be wrong with the poet, the speaker in the poem, coming out and appearing to be a good guy?

[McHugh:] It's rarely loved. I've never liked this poem myself, but one of the perks of this evening's convocation is that I find myself beginning to understand why the poem might so appeal to Charlie.

[Simic:] Why?

[McHugh:] There is a moment of necessary decisiveness not necessarily rooted in the evidences of the world. There are all kinds of evidences there, but decisions must be made. For me, there's this kind of haplessness about happenstance.

[Simic:] What is very true to me about this poem is that it seems like a great moral decision, and that gives you a kind of heroic sense, of making a decision between life and death. But then there's a kind of a horror when you realize it's not a moral decision, that you're just doing the inevitable, which is much worse. If you have a moral decision you can walk away feeling moral.

[Hall:] I love the quiet cadence of this poem, way behind its iambic pentameter. I find it assuring.

[McHugh:] That's part of Stafford's charm.

[Hall:] When he's good, which is often. Somebody once asked, "Mr. Stafford, what happens when your poem is not up to your standards?" And he said, "I lower my standards."

VI.

DESSERT

"THE LAKE ISLE" (1916)

BY EZRA POUND

O God, O Venus, O Mercury, patron of thieves,
  Give me in due time, I beseech you, a little
    tobacco-shop.
With the little bright boxes
    piled up neatly upon the shelves
  And the loose fragrant cavendish
    and the shag,
  And the bright Virginia
    loose under the bright glass cases,
  And a pair of scales not too greasy,
And the whores dropping in for a word or two in
  passing,
For a flip word, and to tidy their hair a bit.

O God, O Venus, O Mercury, patron of thieves,
Lend me a little tobacco-shop,
    or install me in any profession
Save this damn'd profession of writing,
    where one needs one's brains all the time.

[McHugh:] This is the poem of a pedant who dreams of hanging out with the pedestrians, who appear here quite literally as streetwalkers. The brightness he inveighs against in brains is present as a glow in the carnal display cases. The poem he parodies here—Yeats's "The Lake Isle of Innisfree"—is very young Yeats and deserves parody in the sense that a whole genre of Romantic pastoral in English poetry deserved parody at just that moment. But although I chose to bring Pound's poem to dinner, by nature I'm much more given to the poem it makes fun of. Yeats writes:

> I will arise and go now, and go to Innisfree,
> And a small cabin build there, of clay and wattles
>   made:
> Nine bean-rows will I have there, a hive for the
>   honey-bee,
> And live alone in the bee-loud glade.

To "live alone in the bee-loud glade" sounds great to me. Pound writes his poem just after Yeats has declared Romanticism dead. Pound has even stayed at Yeats's place for a while. The parodic impulse is thus rooted partly in affection. But affection is more Yeats's métier than it is Pound's. I am thinking of the last line of Yeats's poem: "I hear it in the deep heart's core." You sense that the "heart" is only an anagrammatical twist away from the "earth," and you can't help feeling a landed love—not just a love of nation but some kind of geophilia. I see Pound's failings written into the triumph of his poem—his raving and pounding away at usury and fools. The "neatly" and the "loose" can't help fighting each other here, and there's a sense in which the neatness of all of that pounding can't help seeking its release in the "loose" and the "shag."

[Hall:] Pounding, eh?

[McHugh:] Yes, yes. I have a secret theory that most poets, at one time or another, write into their poems their own self-criticism. Ezra Pound's anagram is "A proud zen"—his zen is his great stuff, but his pride does him in. He pounds his humor away over time with tendentiousness.

[Huntington:] I think what's fond and appreciative about the parody is that there's a sense of personal power in Pound here—he's not contending with Yeats. Pound is great when he's contentious and constrained, but in this poem there's an assuredness that makes him more likable.

[McHugh:] You're right. There's a way in which he's Yeats's friend at the moment, and I love that redemption. He's humbling himself, doffing his hat: "O God, O Venus,

O Mercury, patron of thieves." The whole poem is about restraint: all I want is "a little tobacco-shop." Even at the end: "Save this damn'd profession of writing, / where one needs one's brains all the time." Brains were the thing Pound thought made poetry. Yeats knows, and says all the time, that the heart is the thing that makes poetry. For me it's a very interesting convocation, that of these two souls.

[Hall:] I don't think it's parody, though. Maybe I'm just quibbling, but I think it's friendly comic allusion to the Yeats poem. I once asked a young poet, "What do you write?" And she said, "I write God-gimmes. God gimme a house by the side of the road, and so on." This is a God-gimme. It's not parody. Parody is an antithesis within style, using the same style and making it ridiculous, and this does not do that at all. There are a zillion Pounds, and this is one of them. It's the ironic, prosey Pound, where one needs one's brains all the time. Think of all the Pounds there are: the Provençal Pound, the Cathay Pound—which leads to this sarcastic, prosey Pound—and then the Mauberley Pound, which is quite contentious. No one has bequeathed so many styles to twentieth-century poetry as Ezra Pound did. It's extraordinary.

[McHugh:] Well, you love the lovely Pounds, and I love the ugly Pounds.

[Hall:] No, I love this because—well, it is rather beautiful in its little descriptions.

[Simic:] It's a very literary poem. It echoes so many smart-ass Roman poets who found poetry in being anti-poetic. The poet pretends that he'd rather be a mule driver or a toll collector than waste his days writing love poems to some snotty heartless floozy. I've had that thought myself—a nice little pastry shop next to a Catholic girls' school wouldn't be so bad.

[McHugh:] "Innisfree" is that same small wish. In that sense, too, the Pound is not so much a parody.

[Muldoon:] It's a reversal. It's a reversal of thought.

[Hall:] So it's an homage. He works with point of view: "For a flip word, and to tidy their hair a bit." Who's saying "a bit"? It's the whores who are saying it.

[McHugh:] That's right. The power of this poem is that it invests itself in investment, in the teaspoonfuls or the inches—the bits. The formal strategy of the poem is to get more and more mincing about its loves and then burst out in "this damn'd profession of writing, / where one needs one's brains all the time," that grandeur of the thing it claims not to want.

[Hall:] It's a small poem by Pound, but the pacing of it is just so precise and accurate. It's a poem I keep coming back to.

[Muldoon:] This must be one of the earliest uses of "flip" in that sense: "flippant."

[Hall:] Did anybody bring an *OED*?

[Muldoon:] "Flip" is what this poem's about.

[McHugh:] And it's wonderful that it works the way the "bright" does—it looks toward the brains at the end and refuses them. From the first line you can see this trajectory: "O God" to "patron of thieves," that diminuendo. It's a rejoicing in the diminuendo, but it knows that at the end it's going to burst out in the thing it really wished for.

[Simic:] The poem also relates to Frank O'Hara. Forget about nature, he seems to be saying. Urban life is so much more interesting.

[Hall:] He has perfect pitch for diction: "in due time, I beseech you, . . ."

[McHugh:] Yes, and it comes to "all the time" at the end. It starts with "in due time" and it comes to "all the time."

[Hall:] "Give me," "Lend me," "install me."

[McHugh:] Yes—he starts with "give me," and then he goes to "Lend me," and then he says, "At least *install* me in a profession, at least make me work." American poems go in the opposite direction generally. They start from thieves and brains and aim for God and Venus, the Romantic grandeurs.

[Hall:] I do love the clever, young, funny fellow who wrote this poem. There are so many Pounds to love and so many Pounds to hate.

[McHugh:] A ton of Pounds.

[Simic:] I love the poem except for those last two lines. "Save this damn'd profession of writing, / where one needs one's brains all the time." I don't believe it for a minute. Ordinarily, Pound is a genius at recycling literary clichés, but not in these final lines.

[McHugh:] But he discovers himself in those last two lines. High reference and low irreverence are the great conjunction in Pound.

[Hall:] What saves the last two lines for me is the contradiction to the earlier style. There's a fake elevation all the way through—the wonderful description of things, the poetical thing, and then the sarcastic drop in tone. It's a young man's poem.

[McHugh:] As is Yeats's. I mean, "Nine bean-rows will I have there, a hive for the honey-bee / And live alone in the bee-loud glade"—that's beautiful writing, but the poem's pastoralism smacks of the errors of the contemplative ideal, as surely as Pound's refutation of the pastoral smacks of the errors of commerce.

### VII.
### Digestifs

[Muldoon:] Here's a question that's come up throughout the course of the evening: How conscious is the writer?

[McHugh:] In poets, there is no such thing as poetic intention. Only in scholars.

[Hall:] It's dangerous. When we talk about Hardy's bracketing of vowels and so on, we are not saying that he went to the blackboard and decided he would write his poem by formula. People can think we are talking about the poet as a crossword-puzzle maker, and that's why I tend to deny it.

[McHugh:] I love the argument, Don, which I very much take to heart and have always repeated, that the poet *feels* his way toward the finished-ness of the poem.

[Muldoon:] But surely the poet must know.

[McHugh:] There is a kind of protoknowing.

[Huntington:] You say: "This is a really good line, even if I don't know what it means." And then when you finally figure it out, everybody else knew all along.

[McHugh:] And it's always nice if someone *says* you knew.

[Hall:] I want to rewrite a little bit of almost every poem I read. There are many times that I think I have such high notions of what poetry should be that no poem is ever good enough. Henry Moore said that every time he began a sculpture he wanted to be better than Donatello or Michelangelo, and every time he finished he knew he hadn't been. But he had the temperament to say, "Well, maybe the next one."

[McHugh:] Oscar Wilde said of tobacco that it's exquisite and it never leaves one satisfied—what more could one want? For me no destination is adequate. What I'm interested in about faith is the requirement that there be no comprehensible end.

[Huntington:] It's not that I fiddled until I came across the Final Truth but that I fiddled until I got something I didn't know I was going to get—something surprising and satisfactory.

[McHugh:] And beyond one's self, beyond one's ken.

[Huntington:] And you leave it alone when you understand that it might not be perfect but there is some serendipity and some grace. Something unexpected has entered in, and you don't know quite what it is, but you know well enough to leave it alone.

[Muldoon:] Because you've recognized something.

[Hall:] There always comes a time when I can't see any more to do, and believe me, I do not mean that what I leave alone is necessarily a good poem. I hope to hell it is, but what might ultimately be good about a poem is something that I was not consciously aware of. Still, I did it. Something in me did it. One writes in a largely intuitive and sensual manner and then leaves it alone until perhaps one's friend points out a bloody stupid line.

[Muldoon:] That's either the very simple or the very complex element—that one's own capacity for self-delusion is major. Everything looks great, somehow, at the time.

[Hall:] In the act of plunging one's self into writing at the desk, one leaves one's identity behind. And in that sense it's without ego. But of course the attempt to make great art is not an act of humility.

[Muldoon:] No, but to try to make it involves humility, selflessness before the idea of it being made.

[Hall:] I'm not sure.

[McHugh:] Well, the it is not just an id.

[Huntington:] Moses has the ego to go up the mountain and talk to God, but when he goes up there he gets his socks knocked off.

[McHugh:] Only God has the ego to mark those words in stone.

[Hall:] I intend a poem, a line, only insofar as I do not cross it out.

[Muldoon:] I'm not interested in what the poet intends, I'm only interested in what the poem intends.

[Simic:] I agree. God, in his infinite mercy, made poems far smarter than poets.

[McHugh:] We tend the poem. The intending is something else.

# FURTHER READING

### Criticism

Burke, Kathleen. "Smithsonian's Notable Books for Children, 1996." *Smithsonian* 27, No. 8 (November 1996): 161–64.

    Burke discusses Hall's skillful evocation of farm life in his children's fiction.

Gavin, Tim. Review of *The Old Life,* by Donald Hall. *Library Journal* 121, No. 10 (1 June 1996): 112.

> Gavin discusses the intimate relationships described in the poems of *The Old Life*.

Lane, J. B. "Disengaged." *Canadian Literature,* No. 133 (Summer 1992): 152–54.

> Lane offers a negative assessment of *Here at Eagle Pond,* criticizing the essays as superficial.

Skow, John. "Misty about Baseball." *Time* 141, No. 12 (22 March 1993): 70, 72–73.

> Skow explores Hall's use of a baseball game as the framing device for his poem "Baseball" in *The Museum of Clear Ideas.*

---

**Additional coverage of Hall's life and career is contained in the following sources published by the Gale Group:** *Contemporary Authors,* Vols. 5–8R; *Contemporary Authors Autobiography Series,* Vol. 7; *Contemporary Authors New Revision Series,* Vols. 2, 44, and 64; *Contemporary Poets; Dictionary of Literary Biography,* Vol. 5; *DISCovering Authors Modules: Poets; Literature Resource Center; Major 20th-Century Writers,* Edition 1; *Reference Guide to American Literature;* and *Something About the Author,* Vols. 23 and 97.

# Kathryn Harrison
## 1961-

American novelist and memoirist.

The following entry presents an overview of Harrison's work through 2000. For further information on her life and works, see *CLC,* Volume 70.

## INTRODUCTION

Harrison received a measure of critical praise for her first three novels, *Thicker Than Water* (1991), *Exposure* (1993), and *Poison* (1995). However, her fourth book, a memoir entitled *The Kiss* (1997), in which Harrison details a lengthy incestuous relationship she had with her father, met with widespread criticism that was largely sparked by its controversial subject matter. Harrison had previously fictionalized this relationship in her novel *Thicker Than Water.* While *The Kiss* has been faulted by many commentators for its titillating confessions and for what they see as a rehashing of an earlier work, other critics have lauded the memoir's stark intensity and lyrical prose.

## BIOGRAPHICAL INFORMATION

Harrison was born in 1961 to Edward and Carole Lang, in Los Angeles, California. Her parents separated when Harrison was young, and shortly after, her father remarried. Harrison attended Stanford University and later the University of Iowa Writers' Workshop. When Harrison was twenty years old, she entered into a consensual incestuous relationship with her father, an affair that began with a single kiss, which served as the inspiration for the title of Harrison's memoir. For four years, Harrison and her once-estranged father maintained a sexual relationship, always meeting far away from Harrison's college and her father's community where he had a family and worked as a preacher. The affair ended when Harrison's mother passed away. Harrison has worked as an editor at Viking Publishers in New York. She was awarded a James Michener Fellowship in 1989 and a New York Foundation for the Arts' artist fellowship in 1994.

## MAJOR WORKS

In *Thicker Than Water,* Harrison depicts the dark side of what seems to be a glamorous Los Angeles lifestyle. Isabel, the story's narrator, is part of a wealthy yet highly dysfunctional family. She endures a childhood fraught with neglect and abuse, an adolescence encumbered by psychological problems, and a young adulthood marked by her mother's death and an incestuous relationship with

her father. *Exposure* centers around a woman struggling with issues from her childhood and her relationship with Edgar, her father. Edgar is a successful photographer who uses his young daughter as a model for sexually suggestive and morbid photographs. In *Poison,* Harrison chose to set her novel in seventeenth-century Spain and again addresses themes of illicit eroticism and the mistreatment of women. By intertwining the tales of two very different women, Maria Luisa and Francisca, Harrison underscores her recurrent themes by contrasting a strong, assertive character with a meeker, repressed character who is forced to live under bleak circumstances. Harrison's most well-known and controversial work, *The Kiss,* is a memoir that recounts her four-year consensual affair with her father while she was in her early twenties. Harrison returned to historical fiction with *The Binding Chair* (2000), which focuses on two women, May Cohen and Alice Benjamin. May is Shanghai prostitute who has fled the confines of her stifling first marriage after being wed to a wealthy Jewish client from her brothel. Alice, May's niece by marriage, is an independent and rebellious youngster who defies her family's attempts at a traditional upbringing. The novel follows the two women through their struggles and concludes with Alice travelling to the French Riviera to become a ward of her aunt.

## CRITICAL RECEPTION

Critical response to Harrison's first three novels was generally favorable. Reviewing *Exposure,* Wendy Smith wrote, "Harrison, who even in her first book displayed exceptional artistic assurance and control, has crafted a multilayered text. . . . the delineation, in superbly modulated prose, of a woman's painful, tentative journey toward self-knowledge." Critical assessment of *The Kiss* has varied widely. Many reviewers panned the memoir as a publicity stunt or as Harrison's attempt to exact revenge on her mother. Jonathan Yardley referred to the book as "trash. . . . not an artful word in it." Tobias Wolff entered into a spirited public debate with Yardley concerning the work and the merits of the memoir genre as a whole. Wolff complimented the courage it took Harrison to write *The Kiss* and commented that "[t]he truth is that they are using her as a target of convenience for their animus against the genre she's working in—the memoir." Looking beyond the initial controversy, Joanne Kaufman hoped that "[p]erhaps *The Kiss* will serve as the means by which Harrison can finally exorcise her demons and begin to broaden the terrain of her fiction." Reviewers were again divided in their response to *The Binding Chair.* Several critics remarked that Harrison's prose was scintillating, while others found the events depicted to be too gruesome and reminiscent of her previous works. Some commentators noted in their reviews of *The Binding Chair* that perhaps the mixed critical reactions to *The Kiss* caused Harrison to lose sight of what her readers expect from her, and thus lose faith in her own abilities as a novelist.

## PRINCIPAL WORKS

*Thicker Than Water* (novel) 1991
*Exposure* (novel) 1993
*Poison* (novel) 1995; published in England as *A Thousand Orange Trees*
*The Kiss: A Memoir* (memoir) 1997
*The Binding Chair: or, A Visit from the Foot Emancipation Society* (novel) 2000

## CRITICISM

### Vince Passaro (review date 14 February 1993)

SOURCE: "Private Eye," in *Los Angeles Times Book Review,* February 14, 1993, pp. 3, 7.

[*In the following positive review of* Exposure, *Passaro praises Harrison's prose, comparing it to the works of novelist and journalist Joan Didion.*]

Kathryn Harrison, on the heels of her disturbing and elegiac first novel, **Thicker Than Water** has written a second, **Exposure** that plays off a newsworthy subject and creates an intense portrait of an artist's (and a father's) capacity for exploitation and betrayal.

The novel's damaged and unraveling heroine is Ann Rogers, daughter of a renowned photographer, Edgar Rogers, who made his fame with morbid, suggestive and visually stunning black and white pictures taken of her when she was a child and a blossoming teen. The similarities of Ann's situation to that of the children of the increasingly notorious photographer Sally Mann instantly suggest themselves: Mann takes beautiful and rather unnerving photos of her children—many of them, like Edgar's of Ann, elaborately posed recreations of actual domestic moments, often involving death-like postures and various bruises and wounds. Childhood sexuality recurs also as a motif. A great deal of controversy has arisen about these photos; Harrison's novel, aside from its considerable literary merits, contributes to that ongoing debate in tangential, dreamlike ways.

That Ann has been severely damaged by her father remains the emotional fulcrum on which the novel propels itself, although Harrison leaves room for an interpretation in which it was the man's joyless distance and brutal disregard, rather than his art, that did his daughter in. Most likely it was both. The story takes place when Ann is an adult, marginally coping with her father's suicide, which occurred when she was 19, her marriage and her career—she too is a photographer, and a partner in a successful videotaping outfit hired for weddings and such. She is also a diabetic, addicted to speed, a compulsive and very high-end shoplifter; her eyesight is going, a particular frightening side-effect of her condition, given what she does for a living, but this is not enough to get her off drugs or make her take minimal care of her health. She is falling apart at her job and letting her marriage slide into a chasm of secrecy and alienation. We observe her, through a series of third-person fragments, during the weeks leading to a major showing of her father's work in the Museum of Modern Art, a show which will mark the first time many long-suppressed photographs—the most sexually explicit ones, of Ann as a teen-ager, masturbating, making out with her boyfriend, et cetera—will be seen. The show sends her into a frantic period of dramatic self-destruction, culminating, just after the opening night party, in a grand larceny that is sure to get her caught and does.

Harrison weaves into this story a number of other narrative voices, first-person memories of Ann's childhood, court documents, letters and medical diagnoses, all of which point to Ann's profoundly unhappy childhood. The over-all effect of this cutting back and forth is appropriately disjointed and emotionally relentless, a narrative montage that mimics Edgar Rogers' photographs, obsessive and unsettling. Harrison's achievement resides in her coercion of her readers into seeing more—far more—of a painful life than we think we wish to see, a conviction that is itself belied by our fascination, our inability to stop looking, our refusal to turn away.

One of the bedrock strengths of *Exposure* is its corporal reality—Harrison mires Ann's psychic dilemma in a tangle of physical details; each of her crises relates in one way or another to her body. For her diabetes Ann must twice daily measure her blood sugar and continually modulate her diet against the insulin she takes by injection in her thighs. She often fails to do this, and her history is one of using her disease, when she's under severe emotional strain, as an instrument of near suicide. At the same time, being accustomed to dosing herself, it feels natural for her to treat her emotional incapacities in the same way she deals with her diabetes—fitfully, with speed, a quarter hit for low stress management, a half or full for anxieties higher on the scale. Her compulsive thievery too has a physical aspect; the clothes she steals become a kind of armor against a world she rightly sees as obsessed with looking at her; she makes herself a master of the quick change, often slipping off one outfit and putting on another in a moving taxi. She leaves the discards in the cab marking her trail.

And her central problem, her father, and his coldblooded use of her as an aesthetic object, denying her his love or even his basic friendliness as an equal human being, has an ultimate corporeal result his photographs, gigantic prints of Ann and her mother (who died, hemorrhaging, in childbirth), close-ups of a wrist or a breast or a slashed and blood-dripping leg. The show at the Modern, which has so spun Ann out of control, is a landscape of bodily obsessions, the viewers' eyes filled with Ann's limbs and grimaces.

Harrison also makes you feel the chemical ebb and flow of Ann's life, the almost hourly adjustments necessary to keep her functional. It is noteworthy, though, that she pays scant attention to Ann's monthly shiftings, her menstrual cycle and its hormonal hit squads. This absence matches up with a kind of sexual freeze in the book: everything Ann does, the snoutsfull of crystal math, the secreting of stolen objects, even the penetration of her body with hypodermics full of insulin, Harrison has charged with an underlying sexual tension and suggestiveness; but actual sex, desire itself, remains for Ann distant and strange. This, presumably, is Harrison's conscious method, accurate in terms of the abuse Ann has suffered. The body obsession of *Exposure* even taken to these extremes, or especially so (for that is its achievement), feels overpoweringly familiar and shameful.

In its frightening, fragmentary and almost hallucinogenic visions, Harrison's writing reminds you of a kind of 1970s sensibility, in which personal loss is devastating and unnameable, and the major routes of self-destruction are chemical and illegal. *Exposure* in turns recalled for me Joan Didion's *Play It As It Lays* and Kate Braverman's astonishing first novel, *Lithium for Medea* both books of the mid-to-late 1970s. The clipped and ironic understatement also remind one of Didion, a sharp intelligence taking the measure, hopelessly, of an absurd and sinister universe. This personal universe, like the larger one, inexorably expands. It catches you in it and sends you bounding out into a limitless darkness, a fearsome void. That Harrison has accomplished this, twice now in as many tries, marks her as one of the most promising new writers of her generation.

### Kathryn Harrison with Patricia A. O'Connell (interview date 1 March 1993)

SOURCE: "Kathryn Harrison: Her Harrowing Psychological Novels Are Fiction, but Seem Vividly Real," in *Publishers Weekly,* Vol. 240, No. 9, March 1, 1993, pp. 33–34.

[*In the following interview, O'Connell offers a positive assessment of* Exposure, *and Harrison states that the events dramatized in her first novel,* Thicker Than Water, *are entirely fictional.*]

Kathryn Harrison's critically acclaimed first novel, ***Thicker Than Water***, was a gripping story of incest, fatal illness and emotional deprivation. Her second novel, *Exposure* was called "harrowing but spellbinding" in a *PW* boxed review ("Fiction Forecasts," Nov. 30); the plot features methedrine abuse, compulsive shoplifting and parental neglect. When a former colleague from her days as an associate editor at Viking learned that Harrison's third novel would invoke the Spanish Inquisition and its aftermath, he wailed, "Oh, fine, another happy little book from Kathryn!"

In person Harrison, 32, is anything but bleak. Her favorite color and most of her attire may be black, but vivid purple socks break up the slender dark line of clothing from shoulder to foot. She laughs easily and talks with her hands. When she meets with *PW* in Brooklyn at her Park Slope brownstone, three-year-old daughter Sarah and eight-month-old son Walker contentedly share their mother's limelight.

Her husband, Colin Harrison, is a senior editor at *Harper's* magazine; they met at the Iowa Writers' Workshop in 1986. He is also a novelist: his first book was *Break and Enter* and his second, a corporate thriller called *Bodies Electric,* earned a star in *PW*'s Feb. 22 issue. Kathryn says of their relationship: "People often ask, leaning forward with a look to invite confession, 'So, what's it like to have two writers in the household?' They imagine, I guess, that we're two fragile, bloated egos, each shredding the other's manuscript pages and sabotaging the rival's word processor. Actually, we're very supportive of each other. It helps that our talents and the sorts of books we write are quite different."

In *Exposure* (a BOMC selection), she has written a very different book indeed. The novel alternates between Ann Roger's current life as a Manhattan videographer and flashbacks to her childhood as the subject of her famous father Edgar's photography, sometimes in sexually suggestive or morbid poses. Introduced with a rueful epigraph quoting Diane Arbus, the story is told stunningly through a variety of literary forms: straight narrative, interior monologue, photo legends, newspaper articles, court transcripts, correspondence, even the precise schedule of a private eye hired by Ann's husband to tail her when he suspects she's shoplifting and doing speed (a habit especially dangerous to her because she's an insulin-dependent diabetic).

The decision to portray Ann and her disintegration in this manner was a deliberate one: "I had a character who was going through crisis and change; although intelligent, she was not self-aware. I needed a number of mechanisms by which we could see into her, new angles for viewing her, because she's not good at telling us about herself."

In the acknowledgements, Harrison thanks various people who helped her research material for this book—physicians, legal authorities, a photographer, people who are diabetics. She herself made numerous information-gathering trips to high-priced New York clothing stores in order to learn the mechanics of shoplifting and of outwitting security systems (human and otherwise). She also spent time in a darkroom.

The work of contemporary (and controversial) photographer Sally Mann is sure to be mentioned in reviews of *Exposure,* and Harrison is philosophical about the likely comparison of Edgar's photos to those that real-life Mann takes of her children: 'The big *New York Times Magazine* piece about Mann came out when *Exposure* was in galleys; her work was not the catalyst for my book. I've always been interested in photography." As, apparently, is daughter Sarah, who, upon arriving home from playschool, mistakes the *PW* tape recorder for a camera and shouts gleefully, "Take my picture!"

Her mother continues: "If I thought of any specific artist's work while writing *Exposure* it was Robert Mapplethorpe's. He photographed actions involving, for example, bullwhips, that the rest of us would consider quite intimate. I wrote about a photographer because I wanted a relationship between a parent and a child in which the former stole something from the latter, and the thing taken was somewhat slippery. What was it? Light recorded on photographic paper, when you get right down to it. And the story evolved from there, from Edgar's being a parent taking pictures of his child to his compromising her health in overextended studio sessions, then further to the point where he did steal photographs, those that resulted from his spying on her.

"Consequently, as an adult, Ann walks the fine line between being someone who is practically unlovable because she's such a fuck-up and someone whom you really want to throw your arms around. That's what human beings are, whether you're shoplifting expensive jewelry in Manhattan or stealing something minor from Kmart in the Midwest. She escaped her upbringing, but the issues for her as an adult are still the same.

She's impoverished on a spiritual level and is taking things to cover herself. Bergdorf's and New York City are just props, but the location and the stuff she steals do up the ante on the risk factor. She could get into real trouble with the law."

Another midtown Manhattan institution that figures prominently in *Exposure* is the Museum of Modern Art, where a retrospective of Edgar's photography takes place, with Ann's approval. Feminist protesters wearing T-shirts bearing Ann's name picket the exhibit; they denounce the show as misogynist pornography. Harrison comments, "I'm not indicting all feminists, though I'm always suspicious of people who are very sure only they know what's really going on. Here these picketers are not a positive or generous force, they're just more people trying to exploit and appropriate Ann for their own selfish purposes."

Her first novel, ***Thicker Than Water,*** has also been appropriated, in an oddly complimentary manner, by some reviewers. A number of critics were so struck with the immediacy and force of her work that they wanted to categorize it as memoir, not fiction. The author says the incestuous relationship forced upon the main character, Isabel, in that novel is completely a product of her imagination, although creator and protagonist do share some common history: childhood in L.A. with grandparents, nursing a mother afflicted with terminal cancer, British ancestors in the Orient (in fact, gracing her living room wall is a kimono Harrison inherited from her grandmother).

The dreams described in her books are likewise so real that one wonders if they spring from her own experience. When *PW* comments that some readers do not enjoy dream passages in fiction, she laughs. "I do many things in my books that seem inadvisable! Some of the dreams I dream on purpose for the character," she says, admitting that she deliberately thinks about the character before she falls asleep, to encourage the dreaming process. "And sometimes I fall into a fugue state while I'm at my desk, and produce them. To work, they have to have a fey, surprising quality. Otherwise, it's almost as if the author planted a neon sign in the text that says: 'Message! Key to Ann's character!' which is incredibly irritating."

Harrison writes her first drafts in longhand; the word processor comes later. "I never compose on the screen because, like a doubting Thomas, I can't deal with the sense of limbo that happens when the words roll up into nowhere. I also never edit on the computer, always on hard copy."

Because her plots proceed in a nonlinear fashion, Harrison takes a similarly low-tech approach to structuring her fiction—laying out the pages on the floor of her study to arrive at temporary arrangements of chapters. She admits that it's "an agonizing task. I would love to sit down in a Dickensian fashion and just write chapter one, and so on. Some passages of my writing are obviously juxtaposed, so the power they gain from one another—that following this—adds up to more than the two pieces held apart. A lot is trial and error."

Her husband begins reading her work when she's about six months into it. "Colin will tell me exactly what he thinks. And, because he has a much more organized, analytical mind than I do, he more readily catches the sorts of mistakes I miss. He'll say, 'Oh, who's this guy? We've never met this person before and suddenly he's pivotal.' He's like a trainer who watches my serve and says, 'No, no, you'll never get the ball over the net with that approach.'"

Harrison also acknowledges the valuable advice she receives from editor Kate Medina: "She's good with pacing and suspense. For *Exposure,* she said, 'By the time we readers get to page 50, you have to bump up the stakes.' She makes specific comments and suggestions, too— 'Wouldn't Ann be someone who . . . ?' or 'What about . . . ?' She's a good counterweight to my own tendency, which is dark, probably more oppressive than is really marketable. Although I do write toward some sort of redemption or hope, my first draft of *Exposure* was pretty grim, and Kate said, 'I can't take much more of this, and I don't think other readers will be able to, either.'"

Medina bought her work from ICM agent Binky Urban, who decided to represent Harrison while she was still at Viking. Harrison had already won a Michener Fellowship on the basis of a partial manuscript for *Thicker Than Water,* but still had no sense of her writing as publishable. Michael Pollan, a colleague of her husband's at Harper's (and also one of Urban's clients), and her Viking boss, Nan Graham, encouraged her to submit the manuscript to the high-profile agent. When Urban invited Harrison to come to her office, "I said to myself, she can't really want to insult me to my face, can she? I was eight months pregnant, so I felt like a ship arriving at ICM for that meeting, which was on a Thursday. The following Monday Binky phoned and said, 'I've got this offer from Random House to preempt.' I recall asking, 'What do you think I should do?' And Binky sort of barked at me, 'I think you should take it.'"

Harrison's in-house publishing career ended not long after she returned to work from maternity leave. With too little sleep and too many responsibilities, she realized that one of her roles had to go. Full-time writing and family won. But she is grateful for her experience as a publishing insider, not only for the editorial skills she gained there and now applies to her own writing, but also for the broader "demystifying" knowledge of the industry she acquired: "I didn't go into my first publication with unrealistic expectations."

If you're not aware of the sheer volume of books coming out, you have no idea beforehand that it's not even 15 minutes of fame, it's more like 15 nanoseconds of attention that your work will get in the marketplace."

Having been profiled for such periodicals as *Harper's Bazaar* and *New York,* Harrison will no doubt spend more than nanoseconds in the public eye. She has a national reading tour planned for *Exposure,* but otherwise she ignores most of the trappings of her chosen career. Of the vaunted writing program she attended, she says, "I liked it at the time, but I have a horror of the 'Continuing Iowa' syndrome." Nor is she a joiner of writing groups. "I show my writing to as few people as possible," she says. "It's basically a solitary career I've chosen, and by myself I have to construct an area of psychic energy, including internal feedback, in which to pursue my creative goals. I don't know how anyone gets any work done in a place like the Writer's Room. You really have to trust your own vision, enforce your own discipline."

The effort is most rewarding when she gets letters from readers indicating that her writing has touched them. She does not regret that her life as a writer-wife-mother is far from the career she originally planned as a premed major at Stanford. Speaking fervently about the relationship between body and spirit, she says, "I'm not a doctor, so clinical diagnosis is not my realm. But both physical and mental illnesses are factors in my work. I hope that my imagination in some way illuminates the human condition."

### Wendy Smith (review date 7 March 1993)

SOURCE: "Shooting His Daughter," in *Washington Post Book World,* Vol. 23, No. 10, March 7, 1993, p. 7.

[*In the following review, Smith offers a positive assessment of* Exposure, *but notes that the novel misses the chance to explore the larger social issues raised by its troubled heroine's life.*]

Although it opens with Ann Rogers slipping on her shoplifted green suede skirt in the back seat of a Manhattan taxi, then shows her scoring three grams of crystal methedrine from the receptionist at her successful video business, *Exposure* is not—thank God—a simple tale of overprivileged angst. As in her first novel, *Thicker Than Water,* Kathryn Harrison sets the personal story of a daughter's struggle to deal with the psychic consequences of a disturbed family life against a sharply sketched social landscape that enriches the individual drama.

A short flashback sandwiched between her taxi ride and her arrival at Visage Video shows 16-year-old Ann, for more than a decade the subject of her father's photographs, rejected as a model because her adolescent body too clearly displays the signs of adult sexuality. Edgar Roger's work (which inevitably brings to mind real-life photographer Sally Mann's controversial pictures of her children) has depicted his daughter naked, seemingly dead, scarred by marks of self-mutilation. His photographs of Ann remain so incendiary that in the summer of 1992 a woman sets herself on fire in the Museum of Modern Art's sculpture garden to protest its forthcoming Edgar Rogers retrospective.

Ann dreads the retrospective, although she has agreed to it as executor of her father's estate, and her behavior becomes increasingly erratic and self-destructive as the opening approaches. She is careless about her insulin shots, continues taking speed although it worsens her diabetes-related health problems, shoplifts so blatantly that she is arrested. Her husband, Carl, who restores historic buildings, can't tear down the wall of denial Ann has built around herself. "I am not a . . . renovation!" she screams when he tries to convince her that they must uncover the foundations of her pain and fear.

In counterpoint to the narrative of Ann's unraveling, Harrison unfolds the complex fabric of her relationship with her father. We see her as a child desperately trying to learn more about her mother, whose death while giving birth to Ann left Edgar incapable of happiness or love for anyone else. The photographic sessions bring no real father-daughter intimacy; instead they create a stifling, claustrophobic atmosphere in which the aloof, mysterious artist manipulates a subject so alienated that she welcomes slipping into insulin shock, "the strange but increasingly familiar territory of her semiconsciousness [in which] the recording figure of her father became almost irrelevant."

Ann thinks she can escape her father's frightening demands by submitting passively to his camera but never sharing her thoughts and feelings with him. But after Edgar's suicide in 1979—he gave himself a lethal injection in the director's chair on which she had stenciled "Papi," taking six Polaroids of his death—Ann learns of the grotesque lengths to which he had gone to invade the areas of her life she tried to keep to herself. In the novel's most shocking moment, Edgar's dealer shows Ann an assortment of photographs her father had taken without her knowledge, images that violate the most basic notions of privacy and respect for individual dignity. This discovery sends the 19-year-old into an emotional and physical tailspin that foreshadows her 1992 crackup.

Harrison, who even in her first book displayed exceptional artistic assurance and control, has crafted a multilayered text that explores Ann's ordeal from a variety of perspectives. She takes us inside her protagonist's head for a first-person revelation of the emotional havoc wrought by a bizarre childhood, but she also creates judicial records, private detectives' reports, business correspondence, newspaper articles and psychiatric evaluations to delineate other people's responses to Ann's actions. These serve a dual function: They add a cooler, more objective tone to the intense narrative; and, through the clever use of minor factual inconsistencies and occasional comments that reveal an observer's ignorance, they remind us that the mysteries of creativity and the human heart can never be fully understood.

Unsettling questions about the limits of artistic freedom, parents' power over their children and men's attitudes towards women resonate beneath the surface of the text but are never explicitly explored, which is a shame. To my mind, Harrison's work would have gained intellectual depth and excitement if she had openly confronted the larger issues raised by Ann's life. It could be argued, however, that by concentrating on her attractive, intelligent heroine's personal dilemma she has written a more accessible novel, and it is certainly true that any regrets about what Harrison chose *not* to do are more than compensated for by the reader's pleasure in what she *has* accomplished: the delineation, in superbly modulated prose, of a woman's painful, tentative journey toward self-knowledge.

### Jeffrey Ann Goudie (review date July 1993)

SOURCE: "When Fiction Meets Fact," in *Women's Review of Books,* Vol. 10, No. 10–11, July, 1993, p. 34.

[*In the following excerpt, Goudie argues that narratives of childhood sexual abuse—such as* Exposure—*have social significance even when they do not succeed artistically.*]

I mentioned to a colleague that I was reviewing two novels revolving around the sexual abuse of children. "Novels?" he responded, with surprise. To render this social issue in fiction would seem the ultimate challenge; Susan Palwick's first novel, *Flying in Place* and Kathryn Harrison's second, *Exposure* both illustrate its difficulty. Both suffer from being too driven by plot and pat psychology: reading the novels in tandem leaves one with the leaden sense that life is only too knowable—that it has all the mystery of a social services pamphlet.

Still, I feel uncomfortable when I criticize these two books, the first earnest but clumsy, the second a bit slick: both overexplained. I recall how I felt when I taught college composition and received themes on incest or rape in response to requests for personal narratives. In the face of such material, discussion of comma splices seemed trite, the assignment of a grade tactless. But if *Flying in Place* and *Exposure* do not quite succeed as art, they serve as evidence that women are writing and speaking of what was previously unspeakable. And that's important. . . .

Kathryn Harrison's *Exposure* is about a different kind of sexual abuse: voyeurism. Photographer Edgar Rogers has made his artistic reputation with pictures of his daughter Ann that stirred debate about whether art should know or respect boundaries of privacy. As the novel opens, Ann, 33, has become a videographer, creating tidy films of weddings and christenings out of messy real-life material. As a major museum retrospective of her father's work approaches, Ann has fallen back onto an old addiction, crystal meth—or speed—and an old compulsion, shoplifting.

The passages describing Ann's substance abuse and her stealing are convincing and gripping. The shoplifting sequences in designer corners of major department stores ring with authoritative detail, from the padlocks at the end of the plastic-sheathed cables that hold these expensive garments to the "imported tungsten shears" Ann uses to liberate the objects of her desire.

The texture of these sections, however, is overwhelmed by Harrison's heavy-handed treatment of the root of Ann's criminal behavior. Ann's beautiful mother died in their kitchen giving birth to her; Ann's father never transcends his grief. A photographer on a small West Texas newspaper, he is vaulted into fame and prestige with a chance photo of his five-year-old daughter asleep under some football bleachers, looking almost dead, or like a discarded piece of trash. The rest of Ann's childhood is squandered as her father's photographic model, always gaunt and lifeless. He poses her, mostly nude, until her developing breasts put a halt to her use as a model. As he coldly writes to his dealer: "Puberty meant that Ann lost what she had and became frankly rather than implicitly sexual, which is not interesting, and so I cannot take any more good pictures."

As the retrospective nears, various feminist activist groups stage demonstrations at the art museum, in particular one group Harrison unfortunately names "'Crusaders for a United Terrorist Sisterhood,' or, more informally, CUNTS." It is jarring when feminists make cameo appearances as objects of satirical derision in a novel that deals with an issue feminists have worked hard to bring to light. A young woman wearing only underpants and a T-shirt bearing Ann's name even sets her hair on fire to protest the upcoming exhibit. The pressure of this public outcry—feminists expressing for Ann what she can't express for herself—intensifies her self-destructive bingeing. A diabetic careless about her health, she becomes more reckless with her diet, her insulin injections and her substance abuse.

*Exposure* sags beneath too much explanation, which, in the end, amounts to fiction by mathematical or psychological formula. Harrison even includes a full psychological profile of Ann made by a psychiatrist, following a showy attempted theft of a big diamond ring from Tiffany's.

At novel's close, Ann is hospitalized, but her doctors allow her to continue the weekly volunteer work she's done for years—holding abandoned babies in the pediatric ward of Bellevue. The connection between this particular volunteer and the neglected babies is only too apparent.

As I read these novels I kept thinking that neither author had enough emotional distance from her material to produce the nuance of rich fiction. Perhaps as a culture we are not yet ready to make art out of such painful, newly exposed subject matter. On the other hand, maybe the sexual exploitation of children can never be transformed into art. For the power of fiction derives from its allusiveness and mystery, its ability to suggest what's unknowable; whereas the impulse when handling such disturbing material is to search for, and even labor, a definitive explanation.

**Judith Dunford (review date 4 June 1995)**

SOURCE: "Love and Death, High and Low," in *Chicago Tribune Books,* June 4, 1995, p. 3.

[*In the following review, Dunford offers a generally positive assessment of* Poison, *noting that Harrison's prose is often too stylized.*]

Fans of Kathryn Harrison's last novel, *Exposure,* a psychological study as up-to-date as the chilling Metropolitan section of the daily paper, may be surprised by *Poison.* Harrison has moved backward in time, some 300 years.

*Poison* takes place in late 17th Century Spain. Long past its Golden Age, the country is in economic and political decline; the Venetian ambassador writes home in 1690 that Spain is "a series of unending calamities." On the throne sits Charles II, the infantile, physically and mentally damaged consequence of constant Hapsburg intermarriage. He would die childless at 35, the last of the Spanish Hapsburgs.

Relentless ethnic cleansing is taking place, 300 years since the first Grand Inquisitor, Tomas de Torquemada, persuaded their Majesties, Fernando and Isabella, that state security demanded the expulsion or conversion of Spain's Jews. The Inquisition, which had faded in other parts of Europe, was still rooting out lapsed Murranos, Moriscos, Moors, witches. Denounced people disappeared into the Inquisition's prisons, their shoes left behind as a sign.

Harrison is fascinated by doubles, by mirror images. In *Exposure* she probed the space between a woman's public and private histories. Here she gives us two women, one high, one low. One has a rapturous, forbidden love affair with a priest, the other lives in a world parched of human sympathy. Both are crushed by the anxiety, corruption and religious fanaticism that hang like a miasma over the country.

Francisca de Luarca is the daughter of a Castilian family of silk-worm farmers. Having little to begin with, they lose it all when Felix, the father, gambles on a new type of mulberry tree. When the leaves mature they are inedible; his silkworms starve. His wife, who pregnant or not overflows with milk, becomes a wet nurse. Eventually she attracts the attention of the palace, is brought there to suckle the sickly 7-year-old king whose lifelong diet will be bread sopped in breast milk. When she finally comes home it is to die, depleted and exhausted, of tuberculosis. At her deathbed is Alvaro, the thoughtful village priest. He fascinates Francisca, agrees after a time to teach her to read, as her mother learned to at court. Liberating her soul this way has dire consequences. He becomes the Paolo to her Francesca (Harrison is careful with names), and as in Dante, the day comes when they read no more.

Once at the Morgan Library in New York I saw a display of private love letters of some of the world's greatest writers. For the most part they were as flat and trite as any declaration of the inarticulate Christian de Neuvillette in the play *Cyrano de Bergerac.* Love, always a bright surprise to lovers, can be as interesting as a retreaded tire to readers. So Harrison's take is all the more remarkable—crystalline prose perfumed (but not too much; she knows just when to stop) with musky eroticism, bigger enough than life to carry you away. In a book full of memorable passages the love scenes of Alvaro and Francisca stand out.

Inevitably the pair grows careless. They are denounced, swept up by the Inquisition. Alvaro is put to death, Francisca made to wear the Sanbenito, Spain's scarlet letter, a yellow overgarment. Embroidered on the front in scarlet stitches are a quill and scroll representing Letters and a breasted serpent representing Lust; on the back an image of the devil pitchforking a woman into the Eternal Flames. Eventually the Inquisitors come for her, intending to torture out of her a confession that she and her dead mother are witches responsible for the fact that, in the palace, the queen is barren.

The unhappy queen is Maria Luisa, once Marie Louise of France, the niece of *le Roi Soleil,* Louis XIV. Raised in the splendors of Versailles, she is married at 18 to the adolescent king. The alliance is political; her only purpose is to breed another Spanish king. Although her husband is as impotent as he is repulsive, it is the queen who is called barren. The court tries everything—holy relics, the most modern medical attention—but it all fails. In her panic she feigns pregnancies and miscarriages with the help of accomplices and a few liters of pig's blood. Like Francisca, she is found out; poisoned, she is dead at 28, a sacrifice to the exigencies of the Crown.

If Harrison writes meltingly about sexual love, she does even better at sexual loathing of the hold-your-nose, close-your-eyes variety, and the mixture of disgust, longing, pity and duty in the couplings of Charles and Maria Luisa.

Where *Poison* is weakest is, appropriately enough, the mirror image of where it is strongest. The writing is not so much written as embroidered on the page (fittingly, since it is silk that threads the book together). As a result the characters sometimes freeze into figures in a tapestry, vivid in their way but often seeming posed, overly stylized. Perhaps this is what Harrison intended, to reproduce the unreal, nearly hallucinatory quality of the period. Yet it can distance the reader from a continuing sense that the characters are solid and alive.

Texture and realism in *Poison* come in the warp and woof of information generously included and wholly fascinating. The daily grind of silk-worm farming. How cocoons are unrolled, cleaned, dyed. How silkworms are killed without spoiling the silk. Silkworm eggs hatching in a little leather bag in the warmth between Concepcion's breasts. The silk house where you can hear the whir of the silkworms' jaws as they ceaselessly feed on mulberry leaves. Seventeenth Century medicine, as brutal and absurd in its bleedings and analyses of fluids as 20th Century medicine will seem 300 years from now. The excesses of the Inquisition—the cut-out tongues and tongue locks to prevent the further spread of heresy. The purple and white hoods of the Inquisitors through which only their eyes glitter. Most of all, the queen's slow death by poisoning:

> Dr. Severo's touch is cool and dry. He kneels before Maria's feet, and he takes the left one in his hands. He runs his thumb along the top of that arch where one promising vessel protrudes stark and blue against her pale skin. The assistant lays a square of linen on the floor beside the basin. On it he places a fleam and a lancet kit containing four delicate, bright blades. . . . The prick of the lancet is expert, relatively painless, and on . . . the fourth try, her blood spurts out. Each beat of her heart sends a feeble jet that runs down her foot and drips warm as bathwater from her big toe and its neighbor.

Flaubert once marveled at how long it took him to shake off the smell of arsenic after writing Madame Bovary's death scene. Readers of *Poison* may feel the same.

## Ron Hansen (review date 18 June 1995)

SOURCE: "The Faithless Priest and the Obsessed Harlot," in *Los Angeles Times Book Review,* June 18, 1995, p. 8.

[*In the following positive review, Hansen argues that* Poison *is an elegant example of well-written historical fiction—a genre that typically portrays the contrasts and similarities between a past era and the current one.*]

In 1679 Marie Louise de Bourbon, the niece of Louis XIV, the Sun King, married Carlos II, the last of the Spanish Hapsburgs, in the village of Quintanapalla, Spain. She and Carlos were both 18. The princess was tall, beautiful and vivacious, fond of frolics and horseback riding; the king was short, ugly and gloomy, given to paranoia and superstitions and so many everlasting illnesses that he confined his food to bowls of breast milk supplied by a platoon of healthy wet nurses.

With Carlos infirmities and probable impotence or sexual ineptitude, it is not surprising that the regents were childless during the 10 years of their marriage, but the fault was laid on the foreign wife who became hugely disliked by a people who regularly fought wars with France. In the afterword to her novel, Kathryn Harrison notes that on Feb. 8, 1689, Maria Luisa as she was called in Spain, fell from a horse and was put to bed. "At five o'clock on the morning of February 10, she awoke feeling suffocated and suffering a severe gastrointestinal upset. Her condition deteriorated rapidly throughout that day and the next, and she died on the morning of February 12. While it was never proved that the queen was poisoned, most historians assume that she was."

*Poison* is a fantasy on the Queen's life and death told by the fictional Francisca Luarca, the daughter of a failed Castilian silk grower, as she is held in an underground prison during the Inquisition. King Carlos had made an official statement from the royal balcony in the Plaza Mayor: "'The failure of Queen Maria Luisa to get with child,' he said, 'is due to sorcery.'" Within a day 17 witches were found in the royal residence, and all persons who'd been employed in the palace from the year of Carlos's birth until the present were investigated. Since Francisca's gracious and bountiful mother had been one of the child king's wet nurses and was now dead, the Luarca family fell under great suspicion and the Inquisition found out that Francisca often wandered far afield, which was at best unseemly, that she'd been taught to read for some possibly nefarious purpose and that her teacher was a faithless priest, Alvaro Gajardo, by whom she was pregnant and with whom she was obsessively in love. Either she was a witch, then, or a fool.

> Alvaro's fate was certain: he would be tortured; whatever confession he made would be recorded. For the sake of his soul, he would be pressed to implicate whatever other sinners he could. But he would not betray me, he would do what he could to save me and our child. After they had as much as they needed, or as much as they could get, the Holy Office would excommunicate him, and the Church would then abandon Alvaro to secular justice. The Church sheds no blood, not even that of denounced heretics and seducers. Spain, however, would take her due.

Francisca's fate is less furious but no less painful. She could not be hanged or tortured while she was carrying a child, and she was thought to have been abused and led astray by a priest "so the Church could hardly punish me as it might any other harlot." She is let free, then, to mother her son, to be feared and hated by townspeople, to grieve for Alvaro, to seek healing miracles at shrines and to live as a prostitute in the old silk house where "every swain and his father knew. I was there for the taking."

But through it all she imagines Queen Maria Luisa; because she was born at the exact time Francisca was and was precipitously married in the Luarca family's hometown, Francisca thinks of her as a kind of twin and soulmate, a female companion in misery. She fantasizes herself in the sorrowful palace, watching Queen Maria fight with her fierce mother-in-law, befriend the famous dwarfs of the Spanish court, avoid "the hour of wifely obligation" by playing late night games of trocero and piquet. "Was she stupid?" Francisca thinks. "Was the new queen entirely, even willfully naive? Without betraying any worry, Maria began to misbehave. She did things for which she would not be forgiven. She made the wrong enemies. Some people do."

Kathryn Harrison's *Thicker Than Water* (1991) and *Exposure* (1993) were harrowing contemporary novels, so it's gratifying to find that in this book she's handled the forbidding obligations of historical fiction so well. Harrison acknowledges guidance in her research from such institutions as the Hispanic Society of America, the National Health Museum, the Prado and the Textile Museum Library, and none of that good learning has gone to waste. She gives elegant lessons in how silk is made, how human anatomy was fleetingly taught in the age of chirurgeons, how the aristocracy so sought loftiness that they often stood on stilts, how stinging blister beetles are ground into cantharidian powder, a poison whose tincture is known as Spanish fly.

*Poison* is a fascinating, feminist princess-and-pauper story, gorgeously written and hauntingly told. It is a tale of passion, hopelessness and thwarted ambitions in a harsh and hate-filled century that was, as in all fine historical fiction, quite different than and disturbingly like our own.

### Nicola Humble (review date 23 June 1995)

SOURCE: "Endless Torments," in *Times Literary Supplement*, No. 4812, June 23, 1995, p. 26.

[*In the following positive review of* A Thousand Orange Trees (*the British title for* Poison), *Humble notes that the novel focuses on the connection between beauty and cruelty.*]

Set in seventeeth-century Spain, ***A Thousand Orange Trees*** twists together the stories of two women born on the same day, whose lives are devoured by the bloodthirsty Spanish state. Francisca de Luarca, the daughter of a Castilian silk-grower, is arrested by the Inquisition after a love affair with a priest and is tortured as a witch. Marie Louise de Bourbon, the niece of Louis XIV, is transported from her beloved Versailles to marry the childish and impotent Spanish king, and is tormented by his court when she fails to provide an heir.

The stories of both women's lives are narrated by Francisca, who has been taught to read and write—another sign of her witchcraft—by her priest-lover. In between bouts of Inquisitional torture, she waits in her prison cell, one of thousands in the "other city" hidden beneath Madrid, conjuring up memories of her past and dreams of the Queen's life. The narrative is patterned through similarities and near-connections between the two women. Francisca's mother was one of the wet-nurses who had suckled the sickly adolescent king Marie was to marry. The Spanish girl watches the secret wedding of the king and queen; Marie witnesses the trial where Francisca is condemned with many others as a witch. While Francisca endures the attentions of the Inquisitors beneath the palace, Marie is dying, poisoned, in the state apartments above.

Harrison blends fact, fantasy and speculation, fleshing out the bones of the past and clothing them in a net of images as finely woven as Francisca's father's silk: the thousand orange trees of the title, each planted in its silver tub, adorning the galleries of Versailles in the Queen's memories of home; the orange-blossom-scented blood continually pouring from the feet of the freak Estrellita, one of the Spanish court's many living miracles; the stinking pig's blood the Queen pours over herself to fake a miscarriage; and the fires which roast heretics.

Fragile emotions such as Francisca's joy in her short-lived passion, her detailed evocation of the beauty of silk, and the love both she and Marie feel for their lost mothers stand for the potential for happiness in a world dominated by violence, betrayal and despair. The Queen's favourite horse is put to death after she has a riding accident, her pets are destroyed on her mother-in-law's orders and her medical treatment as she lies on her deathbed is to be wrapped in the bleeding skin flayed from a living goat. Finally, she is murdered by the only person she trusts.

In her first venture into historical fiction, the New York writer Kathryn Harrison has avoided the traps of costume romance and dryasdust factual accuracy; revivifying her history with audacious feats of imagination, she triumphantly justifies her ambitious narrative project. In its unrelenting piling up of images of horror, this rich and complex novel is both harrowing and compelling, but it disturbs most of all in its insistence that cruelty is intimately related to beauty. The silkworms are killed in their thousands; the enchanting smell of the dead queen is the perfume pumped into her eviscerated body; and the ladies of the French court release their cherished birds of paradise in their dozens to dash themselves to death against the glittering mirrors of the Palace of Versailles.

**Roz Kaveney (review date 28 July 1995)**

SOURCE: "Fate in Frocks," in *New Statesman and Society,* Vol. 8, No. 363, July 28, 1995, pp. 40–41.

[*In the following excerpt, Kaveney offers a generally positive assessment of* A Thousand Orange Trees.]

Kathryn Harrison's last novel dealt with kleptomania and photography in uptown New York. In ***A Thousand Orange Trees,*** her new heroines have neurosis in common with the earlier one, but are unlike her in being doomed without reprieve. Francisca bears a priest's child and ends on the racks of the Spanish Inquisition as a witch; Marie, the queen fails to produce a child and is poisoned by mother-in-law. Some centuries, women just can't win.

This may sound like Mary Daly, but is actually more like Ronald Firbank. Harrison is interested in 17th-century Spain for the frocks as much as anything—Francisca's family are failed silk growers and even the Inquisition rustle round in silk. This is a highly decorative novel, not to its disadvantage, of a society of passion, decadent luxury and colourful poverty in which the depraved, pathetic Carlos II, the Bewitched, lies curled like a worm in an apple. Francisca and Maria share a sort of flippant gaiety that makes them grand.

**Taki (review date 29 March 1997)**

SOURCE: "Incest Chic," in *Spectator,* Vol. 278, No. 8800, March 29, 1997, p. 53.

[*In the following review, Taki offers a negative assessment of* The Kiss, *and states that he doubts the truth behind the events recounted in the memoir.*]

There are very few taboos left in the world—especially here in the Home of the Depraved—incest being one of them. No longer. Random House editor, Harry Evans—yes, our very own little Harry, hubby of Tina—has extolled ***The Kiss: A Memoir*** as a masterpiece, while one Phillip Lopate in *Vanity Fair* calls it lyrical and dry. Other slimebags have gone even further. Words such as uncanny, heartbreaking, fearless, amazing abound.

Mind you, it was bound to happen. After same-sex marriage taboos were removed by those nice guys, who think they know what's good for us small-timers, incest chic was next in line. 'Boy, did I have a wild one last night, I've never seen Jocasta so randy. Ma and I woke up all of Thebes.' ***The Kiss: A Memoir,*** in which the author Kathryn Harrison writes about the four-year affair she had with her father, has Big Bagel literati in a tizzy. *Newsweek* has called Harrison brave. I imagine in the sick mind of the *Newsweek* critic that the fact Harrison has a four-year-old son and a six-year-old daughter makes her even braver. We are, after all, living in the age of Clinton.

The bad news is that culture today is presided over by non-talented leftists who constantly push the limits of perversity and promiscuity. The good news is that, although the book has been publicized in one of the most successfully orchestrated campaigns, it is only the degenerate phonies posing as literati that are swinging 20 greenbacks for it. Needless to say, our very own Tina Brown in her very own weekly, *The Big Bagelite,* is excerpting parts of the Oedipal yarn her hubby published. It is, after all, a family magazine.

The horror of publishing such rot is not in the act itself—there are worse things happening daily, although I cannot think of some right now—but in what I suspect is an effort to normalize incest. Harrison voluntarily entered into an affair with her old man when she was 20, one she kept up for four years. Worse, she is revelling in it. She and her husband have become ubiquitous: *Vogue, Vanity Fair, the Washington Post.* She will obviously do all the talk-shows next, perhaps cry a little on Oprah, and then get invited to the White House.

I may be going out on a limb here—and I will defend my own case in a British court in case the slimebag sues—but I wonder whether she's really telling the whole truth and nothing but the truth. Now this is not as foolhardy as it seems, nor am I anxious to give *la* Harrison some of my drachmas. She already has her eyes firmly on the bank. Here is why I don't find her sleaze completely convincing.

***The Kiss*** is presented as a memoir without a single date, location, or names other than the two slimy ones ever being mentioned. All the other principals of the story—like her step-mother, in whose house the affair began—are now conveniently dead. Better yet, many scenes in ***The Kiss***—written in somnambulant tones and absurd victim-speak—have already appeared in Harrison's first and unsuccessful novel, ***Thicker Than Water.*** This was 1991. She told Pub-

*lisher's Weekly* that she had made the whole thing up. Six years later she is telling us that it really happened. Which story should we believe?

'It is my conviction that secrets are more costly in the long run than honesty,' says *la* Harrison. Especially as Harry Evans doesn't pay for keeping things secret. I say secrecy (once known as privacy) should have been a plus where her own children are concerned. ('Mommy, was grandad a good f—?') And there is something else she forgot. Decency. Have you absolutely no decency, Mrs. Harrison?

**Rhonda Lieberman (essay date 1 April 1997)**

SOURCE: "Double Exposure," in *Voice Literary Supplement,* Vol. 42, No. 13, April 1, 1997, pp. 10–11.

[*In the following excerpt, Lieberman offers a negative assessment of* The Kiss, *finding Harrison's effort an unworthy contribution to the memoir genre.*]

In this era of "realness" and recovery—when our two favorite national pastimes are voyeurism and shopping for an identity—who should be surprised that the memoir has emerged as the literary genre of the '90s? While the self-exposé of the famous person is a beloved genre, what is new is the legion of "normal" people sounding their lives for a marketable hook, like guys with metal detectors scouring the beach for change.

Like indie rock, the memoir offers potential validation and exposure to a wider range of voices. But that doesn't mean there's no filter in place to weed the hypable hit from the dud; the most Oprah-friendly memoirs reveal how this "democracy" is possible in a cutthroat marketplace. At a moment when the so-called grand narratives of family, faith, and nation—the myths that supposedly made sense out of experience—are disintegrating, the memoir proposes an "aesthetic" solution to the problem of living without a tribe, which automatically gives shape and/or meaning to the events in one's life.

As with any genre in an exciting state of mutation, the memoir form has been revitalized as it levels the difference between star and schlepp by broadening the range of lives deemed worthy of representation. And as such, it promises to restore something like the sacred to real lives. While the big goal for the noncelebrity writer had been, up to the '60s, the Great American Novel, the current ambition is less artistic and more identity-based. Indeed, while authors used to claim that characters based on reality were wholly "fictitious," the new trend is to be out and proud with one's "nonfictional" status.

The recent trend toward memoir makes sense in the age of the Web, in which authority is "decentered," the means of literary production are dispersed, and everyone is a potential publisher of his or her own life story (cf. the trickle of exhibitionists posting their diaries on the Web). The aesthetics of this new inclusiveness are familiar to anyone who has been following the art world, where "formal" issues have been eclipsed by questions of "identity" and the quest for the Masterpiece has been replaced by an acceptance of pieces with less grandiose agendas.

When writing his "nonfiction novel" *In Cold Blood,* Truman Capote predicted that fiction and nonfiction would eventually merge, "coming into a conjunction like two great rivers." The recent enthusiasm for the memoir has proven him right, with a '90s twist that reflects our talkshow culture's taste for the confessional. The New Journalists of the '60s (Tom Wolfe, Gail Sheehy, Gay Talese, and Capote himself) used the dramatic, subjective techniques of fiction to give reporting the immediacy of the first-person point of view, and to reflect a moment when the "objective" authority of the news was put in question. Having questioned their own "authority" for years, both journalism and are helped sow the seeds for our current acceptance of anybody's point of view as equally valid, as long as it has an audience. While the "nonfiction novel" is the legitimate spawn of real evolution in both reporting and High Art, Kathryn Harrison's *The Kiss* reflects the worst possible conjunction: the lund talk-show confessional mounts the high horse of "serious" prose—a truly yucky spectacle—like a naked Sally Jesse scurrying to wrap herself in the demure robes of literature.

The much hyped *The Kiss* is a J. Crew version of Marguerite Duras in which the author tells of her consensual love affair with her dad, conducted over four years when she was in her early twenties. The action seems to take place against a background as generic as a shopping mall, upon which the oedipal freak show is projected. The obscene story surges on with admirably constructed momentum as the rest of the world seems to fall away, and Daddy/Mommy/Me act out the emotional truth of a world as solipsistic and as out of context as the cases we see each night on *Jenny Jones*.

*The Kiss* opens up with a whopper, an inappropriate tongue in the mouth from Dad, a minister, when he picks up his estranged college-age daughter for one of their creepy family visits. If you're the type who stops to look at a car wreck you will inevitably read on, with the same sense of queasy complicity. Lest one confuse the sensational content of *The Kiss* with anything vulgar, the tone of the writing is affectedly spare, as if to reassure you that you're not reading trash. "'God gave you to me,' he says. When the preacher in my father speaks, I lose what's left of my power to defend myself."

This reader, too, felt violated as Harrison set out her oedipal soft-porn-fest with the craftsmanship and virtuosic lack of irony of Martha Stéwart arranging a casual country brunch that just happens to be ready when her TV guests drop by.

The family romance is conducted on road trips, in motels, by letter, by phone, and tape-recorded greetings. Father takes daughter to see his parents, each separately remarried. Remembered by his son as "sexually magnetic in his youth," and now dying of prostate cancer, Grandpa nevertheless makes a pass at the author: "My father betrays neither surprise nor disapproval. Maybe it's genetic." Dad even seduces Harrison when he takes her to Grandma's house: "His mother's house! I think the words over and over aware that such a setting for his advance cannot be insignificant, but not understanding its meaning." Eventually, when "my father offered to support me for a year while I [wrote]," Harrison moves in with him and his second wife, and uses an office at his church.

The author struggles with her longing for and anger toward her "selfish" mother, who had her when she was very young, left her with her grandparents, and moved into an apartment nearby; the mother had an unlisted phone number but visited frequently. And Harrison's also ambivalent about her manipulative father who, if this stuff is true, is such a mess that any child of his deserves kudos for mastering even minimal coping skills, and could certainly be indulged for the relatively minor sin of histrionic writing. Going one better than the most overachieving therapy patient, as she explores the mesmeric hold that immature parents wield so well, she seeks to locate and disentangle herself in a prose poem of martyrdom.

> In years to come, I'll think of the kiss as a kind of transforming sting, like that of a scorpion. . . . The kiss is the point at which I begin, slowly, inexorably, to fall asleep, to surrender volition, to become paralyzed. It's the drug my father administers in order that he might consume me. That I might desire to be consumed.

By the end of the saga, you feel like you've been trapped in an elevator with a narcissist confident that the mere display of her naked emotional wares is a big turn-on. In a timely move that merits a Literary No-Shame Award, *The Kiss* has Harrison repackaging material that in her 1991 novel *Thicker Than Water* was said to be "a work of fiction." When the same characters turn up in *The Kiss* they are "openly autobiographical." With much of the descriptive flesh melted away, the latter book is pared down to fully foreground the trauma: the emotional mechanics of literal incest. Incest functions in this newer, improved version as sugarcoating for the medicine of literature.

A few years back, in his film *Spanking the Monkey,* David Russell dealt with incest between mother and son with wit and depth, and expressed the suffocation of the nuclear family, trapped and folded in upon itself in the suburbs. *The Kiss* reads more like a symptom of the problem than a fully worked-through treatment, like the Oprah guest who has survived, "forgiven," but is still bereft. The author's considerable craft has the effect of merely gentrifying her prurient subject, serving up the horror with the technical panache of those Joel-Peter Witkin photos of anatomically unusual persons in artistic mise-en-scènes. While some admire this aesthetic, others will think *The Kiss* is an upper-middle-brow freak show.

**Kathryn Harrison with Nicci Gerrard (interview date 13 April 1997)**

SOURCE: "Father, We Have Sinned," in *Observer,* April 13, 1997, p. 17.

[*In the following interview, Harrison reacts to the critical controversy and personal attacks prompted by the publication of* The Kiss.]

When Kathryn Harrison was 20, her father kissed her. He pushed his tongue inside her mouth, "wet, insistent and exploring." And with that kiss, she says to me, she "crossed a line, like a line of fire." She became unspeakable. Now 35, she has written an appalling memoir: "a bridge of words back to the place to which I can never return. But I didn't know that people would hate me so much for it."

For several years, Harrison had an affair with her father (she never calls it abuse, instead she calls both father and daughter "dishonourable," "treacherous"). He was a preacher who had been absent since she was six months old, was still desired by her mother (who also abandoned her when she was five) but was snipped out of family photographs by her grandmother, so becoming the black hole into which all her longing for love could be sucked. When they finally met, he put his tongue in her mouth and she did not resist him; several weeks later, in a dim and unbecoming room, he put his tongue between her legs while she lay as in a dream, helpless and compelled. Finally, he penetrated his daughter; she lay beneath his substantial flesh (he, the preacher, is "word made flesh"), inert, obliterated, willing. He literally possessed her: every time he took her, she was depleted until there was almost nothing of her left to save.

She left college and rented a basement room. They met in places where no one would recognise them, places Lolita might have gone to with her father-lover. They both felt rage toward her mother, his wife, by whom both felt abandoned: she became the shadowy third in their hellish triangle, the real object of desire. When the mother died, the daughter could leave the father and start to reclaim the remains of her life. "I poured gasoline on the house of my childhood," says Harrison, "and set a match to it. I wanted to destroy it all; me too." *The Kiss,* which has created a furore in America ("witch-hunt," Harrison corrects me wryly), is written in the present tense so that, like a novel, it invites the reader to collude with what is happening, though we devoutly do not wish for the sexual consummation. It is stark, with a dream-like quality that has led critics to suggest that, in writing it, Harrison has simply re-experienced the unmetabolised, dissociated despair of that past ("Yeah, well, that was mild compared to the abuse that came after"). It is also unequivocally, almost oppressively, literary, folding together episodes of deprived early childhood and terrifying early adulthood in eerily beautiful prose, making exposure and self-viscerating confession into an art form. Harrison has been accused of extreme cynicism, of queasy bad taste, of jumping on the bandwagon of the confession-fest, of treating the world as her shrink, of being a bad wife, bad mother bad woman, of even, she says, "almost having the affair so I could write about it—now that's cynicism." Even her looks have been turned against her: when I meet her, she is slim in blue jeans, ash blonde hair falling onto her blonde suede jacket; with a narrow head and wide, wrap-around lips. Her gaze is grey and level; her hands graceful. "This Kathryn Harrison of the media," she says, "well, I know I'm quite polished, but it's not me; I don't recognise her." Harrison is less bruised than she had expected by the hostility: "The level of hysteria is strangely useful," she says. "It enables me to think it says more about them than about me." But she understands the deep ambivalence any reader will have on reading *The Kiss*. "It is antagonistic; it had to be. I was writing about something very bad, dangerous." Just as the affair was not something she chose, though she takes responsibility for it, incest is not a subject she chose: "It chose me; it was a book I had to write. I had been writing about it in concealed ways always, and I've gradually been drawing closer to its heart. My first novel (*Thicker Than Water*) was about an incestuous relationship between a father and daughter, though it was cloaked and warped by fiction. I felt squeamish about it afterwards, as if I'd betrayed myself, my history, which was so much more complicated and complicit. Yet it was the only thing I could write at the time; I wasn't ready." In the next two novels (*Exposure,* about a damaging father-daughter relationship, and *A Thousand Orange Trees,* a historical novel about a forbidden love affair between a young woman and a priest during the Spanish Inquisition), the engine of her fiction is yet again the terrible, obsessive secret of her life. Reading them, especially in hindsight, one feels the disastrous throb of personal experience.

She was working on her fourth novel: "It wasn't working. I found myself saying, to my horror, that I didn't want to write this book; that I had to write about my father." She describes "a sudden window of clarity, honesty. I was able to admit I was really culpable; that I wasn't just manipulated but manipulating. I knew that if I walked away from that clarity, there would be a spiritual cost. Also, I had the feeling that while I didn't write about it, it remained our secret. That meant he was still present. Writing would be getting rid of him at last. My father is no longer in my house." This is close to writing as therapy; the addictive, self-propelling self-exposure that has made confession into a new and troubling genre. But Harrison says: "I never write just for myself. I write for a reader. Writing is my only way of knowing myself. I take pride in *The Kiss.* It is a good book, though I know it's hard. Although I've exposed myself walked naked before the firing squad I stand behind it. As art, it shields me even as it makes me vulnerable. "Also . . ." she continues, holding up a hand to ward off my but, "I know how terribly complicated motivation is. I like to be visible. My mother would never look at me as a child." Her mother never saw her and her father consumed her with his gaze; her mother made her feel as if she did not exist and her father told her she only existed when he saw her "and I like to be seen. I have a terror of being invisible; I look in mirrors to make sure I'm still there. This book makes me visible." She laughs ruefully. "Very visible." Words have saved her: she is writing for her life.

In many ways, the memoir feels like a long letter to the mother who betrayed her and whom she betrayed; whose death released her, but whom she did not forgive until many years after. In a bizarre episode in *The Kiss,* Harrison recounts how her mother insisted, before she went to college, that she, a virgin, be fitted for a diaphragm. The doctor inserted plastic green penises into her vagina as the mother watched, until the hymen broke and blood flowed. The daughter was in effect deflowered by the mother before she was penetrated by the father: f–ed up by both.

Yet the book's love story is that between mother and daughter. The only really erotic moments occur between them when Kathryn cuts off her waist-length hair and gives it to her; when they meet in the kitchen in their nightdresses and brush against each other, girlish after all those years of treachery; above all, with uncanny neatness, when the mother is lying dead and Harrison caresses the soles of her feet, breathes in the smell of embalming fluid, kisses her face and fingertips touches her as she was never allowed to in life. Harrison still misses her; is still "in love. She is the creature who continues to seduce me."

The father is alive and Harrison will not disclose where he is. She has not seen him for a decade and never wants to again. She has a "compassion" for him, his wrecked and twisted life, but does not forgive him. "I can't, perhaps I never will." She cannot remember the sex in their affair ("Oh, I know the facts, but I can't remember what it felt like. I'm anaesthetised; I think I'm not ready to face that"), and thinks that, anyway, sex was just a mechanism for a far greater betrayal. "He seduced me into betraying the people I loved; he so easily cultivated my anger against my mother. He returned intending to possess me completely, and he believed that I was his." Harrison has a husband now, Colin (writer, support, confessor, analyser, mate), and two children. Many critics think it unacceptable that she has exposed them as well as herself. She does not think she will always be "that woman" for the world, or for her son and daughter. She knows her revelations will be hard for them to bear when they grow older (they are seven and four), but believes it is preferable to keeping the secret fenced in, a no-go area for intimacy. She has, as she says, survived.

"Am I irretrievably damaged? Perhaps. I feel set apart. I feel a great deal of remorse and pain, and yet I also feel, finally, that that is connected with my humanity. I behaved with great dishonour, but I am not a monster. I know who I am now. I think I'm a good mother. I've learnt to" she hesitates, grimaces "like myself." Images of hunger collect in *The Kiss* (Harrison says she is the "most ravenous person I know, so hungry for love"), and of starvation (young Kathryn is starving, anorexic, bulimic; these are her only means of flight). Also the death of feeling. When a shark tears someone's leg off, she says, they often feel nothing.

"The pain is so great you can't feel it life is just leaking out of you and the shock is so huge it feels like nothing. My father was that shark, and I was in the water and I was dying." The shark's gone, but with *The Kiss* so fine, nauseating and troubling that even now I can't decide what I thought about the act of publishing it, she is still in the deep dark waters he left in his wake.

**Selina Hastings (review date 19 April 1997)**

SOURCE: "The Sins of the Father," in *Spectator*, Vol. 278, No. 8803, April 19, 1997, pp. 38–39.

[*In the following negative review of* The Kiss, *Hastings applauds Harrison's courage in publishing her controversial memoir, but argues that the work is stilted and poorly written.*]

The story Kathryn Harrison tells in *The Kiss* is so terrible that I felt guilty at being bored by it. The experience of her miserable childhood and her incestuous relationship with her father is appalling in every detail, and yet she recounts it with such portentous solemnity, in such a laboriously elevated style that I entirely failed to be moved.

When Kathryn Harrison was six months old, her parents divorced, she and her mother moving in with her grandparents. Her mother, a cold, discontented woman, was incapable of showing affection and coped with her chronic depression by spending much of the day asleep under a satin eye-mask. A little more than five years later, she leaves to live on her own in a nearby apartment, calling round regularly to see her daughter but refusing to reveal her address, unwilling to be troubled by childish illness or anxieties.

Emotionally neglected, Kathryn does badly at school, starves herself, drops out of college. Then when she is 20, her father, seen only twice during her childhood, arrives on a visit. A pastor of German extraction, he is a commanding presence, tall, and with a disconcerting sense of familiarity towards his now beautiful daughter, with whom he quickly becomes obsessed. For her part, she falls painfully and precipitously in love, both longing for and dreading the sexual element fast developing in his overwhelming attentions towards her. When he is due to fly home, she drives him to the airport, and it is there that he kisses her, not as a father but as a lover:

> My father pushes his tongue deep into my mouth: wet, insistent, exploring, then withdrawn.

From that moment there is no going back. Her father pursues her, telephoning daily, jealous, selfish, demanding, eventually insisting that she allows him to make love to her to prove that she is completely his. Bewitched and helpless to reject him, Kathryn capitulates, but subconsciously resisting, she, like her mother, uses sleep as a drug, becoming comatose as soon as her father touches her, falling into a narcoleptic trance when she hears his voice on the telephone.

The reader has to accept the reality of the power of this horrible man, who eventually exercises such control over his pathetic victim that she is made to move into his house, living like a poor relation with his second wife and young family. Her descriptions of him, however, are rarely such as to make it easy to understand the fascination. His flesh is waxy white, his eyes behind spectacles forever brimming with self-pitying tears, and he is corpulent, his stomach bulging over his belt, his breasts as big and soft as a woman's.

The few actual glimpses we are given of this monster are vivid and shocking, and in startling contrast to the rest of the book. Written in a contrived and monotonous present tense, it is largely drained of life by a deadening feeling of self-consciousness, by an effortful attempt at fine writing that fails to come off. Kathryn's mother's eyes, for instance, are 'unplumbed pools of sorrow into which I can tumble and drown'; a bedroom is decorated in 'understated fugues of beige.' Places are described as vague visual impressions, people as two-dimensional archetypes. No doubt the author needed to distance herself from the anguish of the actual, but for the reader the results are disappointing.

In spite of this, however, Kathryn Harrison deserves our admiration. *The Kiss* must have taken enormous courage to write, and I was relieved to discover that the author, now a promising novelist, lives in New York with a husband and children of her own—safely out of reach, I fervently hope, of her brute of a father.

**Joanne Kaufman (review date 20 April 1997)**

SOURCE: "Novelist Kathryn Harrison's Memoir of Her Affair with Her Father," in *Chicago Tribune Books*, April 20, 1997, p. 3.

[*In the following negative review of* The Kiss, *Kaufman states that the distance and vagueness of Harrison's narrative voice weaken the memoir's hold on its readers.*]

There are lots of really swell ways for authors to market their works these days: Concoct an elaborately clumsy piece of fiction but swear on a stack of *Publishers Weeklys* that it's non-fiction (check out *Sleepers* by Lorenzo Carcaterra). Slap between covers what is essentially non-fiction, call it fiction and credit it to Anonymous (Joe Klein's *Primary Colors*). Give potential customers something extra for their money by outfitting the book with a CD—it's got a good beat and you can read to it (a la Joyce Maynard and Laura Esquivel)! Or (with, perhaps, a certain amount of cynicism) put forward a memoir that traffics in the salacious and/or sensational, and become the subject of magazine and TV feature stories, in the manner of critically acclaimed novelist Kathryn Harrison.

*The Kiss* chronicles the affair, 16 years ago, between Harrison, then a college student, and her minister father. The product of a perfervid romance between two 17-year-olds who married in shotgun-wedding haste and divorced with dispatch, Harrison was raised mostly by her grandparents, Mom having decamped to live her own life, Dad, whom Harrison saw only twice during her childhood, having been summarily forced out of the picture.

> It was in the garden . . . that my grandfather told my father that it was over between him and my mother. . . . My grandparents thought they could end it, erase my mother's unfortunate mistake. There was the baby, of course, the life that sprang from my mother's rebellion . . . there was me to consider, but I was a cost they'd accept. He, however, had to go.

Unsurprisingly, perhaps, Harrison had a troubled childhood and adolescence—nightmares, anorexia, bulimia. It was a landscape bordered by her narcissistic grandmother, her self-centered, withholding mother, a sometimes-endearing grandfather who became increasingly uncomfortable with Kathryn as she passed through puberty, and by her shadowy, letter-writing father. When she sees him at 20 for the first time in 10 years, "my once-bobbed hair long, and my flat chest filled out, my father's eyes are fixed on me; he tears his gaze away with reluctance. This kind of besotted focus is intoxicating, especially for a girl schooled in self-effacement and taught that virtue believes more in its ugliness than in its beauty. . . . I don't know it yet, not consciously, but I feel it: my father, holding himself so still and staring at me, has somehow begun to *see* me into being."

He has bloodshot eyes, he's overweight, he sleeps with Harrison's mother the first time all three of them are together (despite, the fact that he is remarried with children), then talks about it in most ungallant terms with Harrison. "'I didn't do it because I wanted to,' he says. Humiliated on behalf of my mother, and shocked that he would betray her this way, I look not at him but at my plate."

That indiscretion doesn't begin to prepare Harrison for the indiscretion at the airport as her father prepares to return to his other family. He "pushes his tongue deep into my mouth: wet, insistent. . . . In years to come, I'll think of the kiss as a kind of transforming sting, like that of a scorpion: a narcotic that spreads from my mouth to my brain. The kiss is the point at which I begin, slowly, inexorably, to fall asleep, to surrender volition, to become paralyzed. It's the drug my father administers in order that he might consume me. That I might desire to be consumed."

What draws the two of them together in this unholy alliance is "her," Harrison's distant mother, her father's elusive former wife; they are united in their love for a woman who can't, won't love them back. The affair, which is preceded by countless fulminations by Harrison's father that "God gave you to me," is played out at scenic points of interest and truck-stop motels across the Southwest, and it ends only with the death of Harrison's mother due to bone cancer.

Unfortunately, *The Kiss* which reads rather like a fever dream, doesn't probe as deeply or as far as Father's tongue. While the story is set forth in the present tense, accruing to it an unsettling immediacy, Harrison has (understandably) so distanced herself from the events she recounts that the book's impact is greatly blunted. The reader wants, needs, what feels spontaneous; the reader gets something studied, carefully literary.

More problematic, *The Kiss* is told as though through a scrim; innuendo rather than specifics is the coin of the realm here. In so saying, one feels like a greedy voyeur (of course, one feels like a voyeur by the very act of opening the book), but the fact is, if you're going to commit to telling the story Harrison has chosen to tell, either tell it and tell it in detail or don't publish it.

What this memoir confronts as fact has utterly informed Harrison's three novels. *Thicker Than Water* which at the time the author insisted was purely a product of her imagination, covers precisely the same ground as *The Kiss* if in more textured, graphic fashion. The potent *Exposure* deals with a woman haunted and almost undone by the erotic pictures taken of her in childhood by her celebrated photographer father. *Poison* is about a woman who has an affair with a priest (a different sort of father). Perhaps *The Kiss* will serve as the means by which Harrison can finally exorcise her demons and begin to broaden the terrain of her fiction. If so, it will have been worth it for the reader, certainly for Harrison.

### Brooke Allen (review date May 1997)

SOURCE: "Devouring Love," in *New Criterion,* Vol. 15, No. 9, May, 1997, pp. 64–69.

[*In the following excerpt, Allen offers a negative assessment of* The Kiss, *suggesting that Harrison's real motive behind writing the book was the author's hatred of her mother.*]

Just what does it say about the New York literati that the book that has made the single biggest splash this season is a thin, poorly written volume, chockablock with bathos and cheap melodrama, dealing with the author's incestuous affair with her father? Magazine editors and media pundits have fallen over one another in their rush to book Kathryn Harrison and either tout or fulminate against her new memoir, *The Kiss.*[1] A single issue of *The New York Observer* contained three pieces on it, including a parody; the ever-topical *New Yorker* made a bid to publish an excerpt in its pages. (*New Yorker* readers were deprived of this treat when Random House pushed *The Kiss*'s publication inconveniently forward.) Kathryn Harrison and her husband, Colin, a writer and editor, have eagerly encouraged the feeding frenzy, Kathryn by giving soulful interviews and striking sexy poses in the mags, Colin by writing a ludicrously solemn exclusive for that serious, sensitive publication *Vogue* on his relationship with his wife and how her sordid past has affected—no, enriched—their marriage.

In recent years, so many people have claimed some sort of victim status, whether in print or on "Oprah," that a slight backlash has occurred, and poor-little-me authors have taken note and changed their tune. Even Fergie, the Duchess of York, has in her recent memoir taken care to place the blame for her disgrace (at least overtly) on no one but herself: "I pinned on my scarlet letter—mine would be a T, for toe-sucking," she writes, not without grim humor. Ms. Harrison tries to play the same game. She is aware that the fact that she was twenty years old at the time she began sleeping with her father deprives her of victim status in the eyes of many, and she is careful not to shirk her share of responsibility in the matter. "There are no heroes and no villains in this story," she says righteously.

Wrong. In the narrative as Harrison presents it, there are only villains—or rather, irresponsible, self-obsessed people. The central figure of this particular family drama is Kathryn's mother, whom the child loves obsessively but who eludes her until the very end. She gave birth to Kathryn while still a teenager, and split up with her husband not long afterwards; soon, finding motherhood demanding and exhausting, she abdicated much of the responsibility for child-rearing to her own mother, a neurotic woman whom Harrison describes as screaming uncontrollably whenever her sexy daughter went out on a date.

At one time during Kathryn's early childhood the mother lived alone in one apartment while the child and her grandparents lived in another. As time went on, however, the family appears to have grown closer, perhaps because the mother herself began to grow up. At any rate, mother and daughter were close enough to act out the traditional mother-daughter power struggle, a universal, even banal scenario which Ms. Harrison seems to see as unique to her own situation. "Even at the age of seven I understand . . . that my mother's love for me (like her mother's for her) depends on my capitulation." So what else is new? Mothers have always been like that, and will be to the end of time.

It is not too surprising to discover that once Kathryn hit adolescence, she struck out at her mother through anorexia. "*You want thin? I remember thinking, I'll give you thin. I'll define thin, not you.*" She has reclaimed her sexuality from her mother, and her mother, she claims, is furious. "The one thing she can't stand about my being so thin is that I don't menstruate: I lose my capacity to get pregnant, to be in a danger of the kind that precipitated the abrupt fall from grace she endured. . . . she takes me to doctor after doctor, accompanying me into the consulting room and even the examining room." Perhaps—just perhaps—Harrison is right to interpret her mother's feelings as rage, but it seems to me that a mother who watches her child waste away might be genuinely, and desperately, worried.

The mother's next iniquity is to insist that her daughter be fitted for a diaphragm. The doctor says that it can't be done without breaking the girl's hymen; the mother insists; the doctor proceeds to insert a graduated series of plastic dildos into Kathryn's vagina, until one comes out smeared with blood. Symbolic rape by the mother seems to be a popular theme these days; the young Haitian writer Edwidge Danticat featured it in her pretentious, overrated (but highly praised) book *Breath, Eyes, Memory*. In Harrison's case, it is likely that her mother meant, however misguidedly, to protect her. But Harrison treats the incident with narcissistic melodrama: "What was murdered that day: girlhood, hope, any notion of being safe anywhere, with anyone."

When Kathryn's lecherous father reenters her life after a gap of ten years, Kathryn, now twenty, is more than ready for him. Their mutual rage against the rejecting mother has focused their attention on one another; without actually discussing it, they realize that a sexual alliance between father and daughter is the most efficient way of hurting her. At the airport, upon his departure, he gives Kathryn the by now famous kiss: "My father pushes his tongue deep into my mouth; wet, insistent, exploring, then withdrawn."

Oooh, grody to the max! Kathryn is (no kidding) disturbed by the incident; when she asks her boyfriend back in college whether he thinks it was weird, he yells "Yes, it's weird! Of course it's weird! It's wrong!" Wise words indeed, but after such a display of horse sense the boyfriend, inevitably, is history, and the mesmerized Kathryn embraces her destiny. Her wish to possess, devour, and destroy her mother, however, is not quelled. When her mother lies dying of cancer, Kathryn never quits her side: "You're always there, aren't you?" the mother asks, a little nervously it seems; "'Yes,' I say," writes Harrison. "Even when I'm with him, I'm standing by your bed. Especially then." All this comes to a final climax in a nasty necrophilic scene at the funeral home where the mother's corpse is reposing. Kathryn asks to be left alone with the body, and when the undertaker leaves she lets loose. "I reach under the bottom half of the lid for the catch to unlock it but find none. I slip my hand down as far as I can, past her knees, past the hem of her white dress. I want to touch and know all of her, want her feet in my palms." It almost makes you feel sorry for poor Mom.

In an interview sent out with the review copies of **The Kiss** Kathryn Harrison is quoted as saying, "**The Kiss** was a book I couldn't avoid, rather than one I set out to write," and refers to "the implicit dishonesty of keeping a secret such as this." The concept of honesty, and Harrison's courage in being so very honest, is also stressed in the quotes that Random House has chosen to adorn the book jacket. Philip Lopate writes of the author's "consummate artistry and honesty"; Tobias Wolff marvels at "the courage it took to write this book"; Mary Karr, the author of a more intelligent family memoir, lauds Ms. Harrison's "bravery," while Mary Gordon, the perpetrator of an execrable one (of which more later), asserts that she is "fearless." Robert Coles (who since he endorsed the book has recanted on his puff, claiming that he didn't know Ms. Harrison had children) called the book "a moral victory."

These statements would seem to imply that honesty is always, under every circumstance, a good thing. "The truth shall make you free," as the Gospel of John tells us. Yet we would all do well to leaven this thought with Oscar Wilde's extremely sensible remark that "the truth is rarely pure, and never simple." All the people who have been bowled over by Harrison's incredible honesty—including Christopher Lehmann-Haupt in the daily *New York Times* and Susan Cheever in the *Times Book Review*—really ought to remind themselves that there is honesty, and then there is indiscretion, and they are not the same thing at all. Incest is hot, as Harrison surely knew, and such a very, very honest book about such a very hot subject was sure to find a place among the literary crowd equivalent to that which the Jon Benet Ramsey murder investigation has assumed for readers of *The National Enquirer*.

For Harrison's own sanity, she may well have felt that the book was one that demanded to be written. But as James Wolcott pointed out in his review of *The Kiss* in *The New Republic*, there is a difference between needing to write the book and needing to publish it. What greater good is Harrison serving by making many thousands of people privy to an intimate and shameful story that should really be between herself, her husband, her analyst, and, if she has one, her God? The public does *not* need to know, and neither, assuredly, do the Harrisons' children. If Harrison were really courageous, as her supporters assert, she would have fought her demons in private and protected her children at any cost.

Aside from that issue, which has been well worked-over in the press, there is an even deeper hypocrisy at work in *The Kiss,* a pretense that to write such a book is not an act of hostility but one of love, in particular love for her mother. Harrison dedicates the book to her mother ("Beloved: 1942–1985") and ends the narrative with a smarmy postscript in which she dreams that her dead mother appears and the two finally express the love they had never expressed in life. But the reality is that the daughter's hatred still rages, exorcised neither by the affair with the father nor by the mother's early, painful death. If Kathryn Harrison felt real love for her mother, and had come to terms with their relationship, she would have resisted the temptation to expose the beloved's coldness, her withdrawal, and her husband and daughter's betrayal of her. *The Kiss* is an act of hate, superficially against a predatory father, but in fact against a mother who, for all her myriad faults, seems to have done as well as she was able.

*Note*

1. *The Kiss,* by Kathryn Harrison; Random House, 224, $20.

### Lisa Alther (essay date July 1997)

SOURCE: "Blaming the Victim," in *Women's Review of Books*, Vol. 14, No. 10–11, July, 1997, pp. 33–34.

[*In the following essay, Alther discusses the critical reaction to* The Kiss *and how it has changed the perception of the memoir genre, particularly as practiced by women.*]

*The Kiss* is a disturbing and moving memoir about Kathryn Harrison's four-year love affair with her father, which began when she was twenty. In spare, flat prose that mirrors her numb state of mind at the time, Harrison documents the dynamics of the deadly triangle consisting of herself, her remote mother and her frantic father, who was ejected from the household by his domineering parents-in-law when Kathryn was six months old.

Harrison's mother moved out when she was six, leaving the child in the care of these grandparents. Harrison saw her father only twice before she was twenty. She grew up harboring like a fatal virus a hunger for parental acceptance and a rage at having been abandoned. These emotions play themselves out in her tortured entanglement with her father, who had by then remarried and become a minister in a distant town.

As a child, Harrison stood over her mother by the hour, watching her sleep: "I make any noise I can that might rouse my mother but that can't be judged as a direct and purposeful assault on the fortress of her sleeping. Because for as long as my mother refuses consciousness of me: I do not exist." In contrast, when the twenty-year-old Harrison encounters her father, his eyes "burn like a prophet's, a mad-man's, a lover's. Always shining, always bloodshot, always turned on me with absolute attention." Clearly, in *his* eyes she exists at last. So much so that when he bids her farewell, he pushes his tongue into her mouth, "wet, insistent, exploring, then withdrawn." The kiss, the kiss of the title, Harrison will eventually come to think of as "a kind of transforming sting, like that of a scorpion: a narcotic that spreads from my mouth to my brain. . . . It's the drug my father administers in order that he might consume me. That I might desire to be consumed."

Almost as interesting as *The Kiss* itself is the way in which it has been reviewed. Reading a dozen of the most "important" reviews and interviews, I noticed that only three were written by women. Yet had I been a book review editor, I would have assumed that few men could accurately assess the damage done to a daughter by a mother's rejection and a father's inappropriate form of acceptance. In fact, the most perceptive piece I have seen is by Cathleen Medwick, writing in *Mirabella*. Medwick identifies the mother as Harrison's primary object of desire; of the father, she says he "hardly exists for her." Harrison and her father use their affair as a desperate bid for the mother's attention and as a way to punish her for her seeming rejection of them both. Once the mother dies, the affair ends.

Meanwhile, the male reviewers have been staging a food fight. Jonathan Yardley in the *Washington Post* maintains that the book is "trash. . . . not an artful word in it." Michael Shnayerson in *Vanity Fair* accuses Harrison of writing the book simply to garner publicity and fortune (as though other writers are pure and shining creatures who at all times concern themselves solely with Art). James Wolcott, who calls Harrison and her writer husband "the Sonny and Cher of dysfunction," maintains in *The New Republic* that Harrison is a wicked mother for publishing the book, thereby visiting upon her own children the misery she herself experienced as a child. Robert Coles, who gave a glowing jacket blurb, recanted it in *The Observer* upon learning that Harrison has children of her own.

Christopher Lehmann-Haupt in *The New York Times*, at the end of a perceptive and generally favorable review that calls the book "appalling but beautifully written," does a judo throw, claiming that "the mystery of her [Harrison's] healthy survival remains a flaw." His assumption seems to be that if someone actually undergoes such an experience, she will be left too traumatized to tell the tale. Yet every fourth woman one meets has been raped or beaten or has experienced incest, and most survive with at least the semblance of health. Telling the truth about what one has undergone—whether in therapy, to a friend, on the written page, or in the confessional—is one way people struggle to recover from trauma, and *The Kiss* bears the hallmarks of just such an attempted exorcism.

Lehmann-Haupt also insinuates that Harrison is a spin doctor for her own life, wondering "if a memoir can ring too artistic for the truth." But the boundaries between fiction and memoir have always been blurred. Everything a novelist writes can be considered autobiographical, in the sense that a writer must know about what he or she portrays, whether through direct, fantasized, or researched experience. And everything a memoirist writes is, to some extent, fiction. When someone makes the decision to tell this story rather than that one, from this point of view rather than that, a lived situation sheds some of its complexity and begins to take on a false coherence. The difference between memoir and fiction lies primarily in the contract with the reader. The novelist says, "What I'm about to tell you may or may not have really happened." The memoirist says, "What I'm about to tell you really did happen—and to me."

Frank McCourt, who himself wrote the best-selling memoir *Angela's Ashes*, about his impoverished Irish Catholic childhood, complains in *The New York Times* that Harrison "should have waited until he [her father] was dead. . . . In some ways, there's a feeling of subconscious vendetta and it makes me queasy." But why shouldn't Harrison enjoy some retaliation against a father whose irresponsible behavior has damaged her, perhaps irreparably? (Consider the disordered sensibility she displays in a recent *New Yorker* piece about torturing a tick she finds in her daughter's hair.) And why is it that whenever women describe their experience of life in a public forum, they are automatically accused of being bad wives, mothers, or daughters, while if they nurse their wounds in silence, they are accused of being hypocrites and martyrs?

In fact, one of the virtues of *The Kiss* is that there are no true villains. Each person in the triangle is presented as acting out of overwhelming need, pain and narcissism. Surely the real issue is not whether Harrison should have published this book, but rather how such a destructive situation could have evolved in the presence of so many alleged adults. Harrison's story poignantly reminds us of how vulnerable children are—even at twenty—and of how much they crave parental acceptance and protection. It also reminds us that adults who are themselves still children, emotionally speaking, have no business undertaking parenthood.

So why do these male reviewers seem so outraged by this book that they need to throw hissy fits all over the printed page? Tobias Wolff, one of the few to defend Harrison (if only because he initially gave her a rave jacket blurb and because he himself has written a powerful memoir about his abusive stepfather), claims on the op-ed page of *The New York Times* that these fits aren't about Harrison's book per se: "The truth is that they are using her as a target of convenience for their animus against the genre she's working in—the memoir. All of them preface their attacks on her with expressions of suspicion or downright contempt for the personal writings that have recently found favor with readers." In other words, it may be the phenomenon that a prominent New York editor predicted to me several months ago—Memoir Backlash.

Apart from Wolff's and McCourt's memoirs, the most successful ones in recent years have been written by women—the Delany sisters' *Having Our Say* Mary Karr's *The Liars' Club,* Caroline Knapp's *Drinking: A Love Story,* among many others. Historically, with few exceptions, women writers have gravitated towards some variety of realism. Through fiction or memoir they have attempted to understand life and its injustices and to communicate their findings to others, rather than to distract attention from these injustices via stylistic pyrotechnics. Systematically excluded from the *garde,* most women have felt little need to protest its conventions by joining an *avant-garde.*

The recent popular success of memoirs is a surprise, no doubt an unpleasant one for the guardians of high culture. But the venom generated by Harrison's book signals more than just a backlash against the memoir as a genre, or against women as its primary practitioners. It is a well-known psychological phenomenon that those who react most fiercely against something are those who are unconsciously drawn to it, homophobia being one bratant example. Could those so intent on suppressing and demolishing *The Kiss* be titillated by its incest? If not, why the overkill? Why not just the normal hatchet job visited upon women writers who are daring and gifted?

### Suzanne Moore (review date 15 August 1997)

SOURCE: "How Was It for Me?" in *New Statesman,* Vol. 126, No. 4347, August 15, 1997, pp. 44–45.

[*In the following review, Moore offers a mixed assessment of* The Kiss, *arguing that a memoir can only be effective if the reader is persuaded to feel a connection with the author.*]

The subject that obsesses us at the end of this long century is subjectivity itself. "How was it for me?" we continually ask ourselves. Such navel-gazing could be attributed to the fragmentation of modern life, the end of ideology, the collapse of the grand narratives or any postmodern, premillennial panic that you care to theorise. We cannot know or be certain of anything outside ourselves; it is all just too confusing. As the grand narratives shatter into millions of smaller ones, all crying "me, me, me," myriad voices whisper: "I may not be a novelist but I know what I'm like."

This belief in the subject as the only viable subject, the self as both author and authored, is not a purely literary phenomenon. Television likes authored documentaries in which quirky presenters give their entirely personal views. The art world likes self-revelatory bad girls such as Tracy Emin and Sam Taylor Wood; newspapers are brimming with the "new solipsists" who write of nothing but themselves, or just of nothing; music loves its self-made stars such as Liam Gallagher, who acted like a pop star long before he ever was one. We are in thrall to "attitude," whatever that means.

It is possible to read all this as incredibly liberating, allowing a plurality of voices that have not been heard before. Or it is possible to see it as the symptom of a supreme crisis of confidence in which no one can speak for anyone outside themselves, in which everyone emotes but no one thinks any more.

The memoir is hardly a new form, but at the moment it seems as though everyone who has had any experience of anything from cutting their toenails to giving birth feels compelled to write one. There is an element of undergoing therapy in public in much of what is published. These are the true self-help books. In the age of Oprah we know that speaking up, spitting it out, will help us "come to terms" with our pasts. But there is also the voyeuristic thrill of watching others who not only wash their dirty linen in public but also point out filthy stains of particular interest. A psyche-babbling culture, combined with media intrusion, has made a mockery of the old divide between private and public.

Despite the excesses, I still feel that this has been a good thing, because those who resent it most are usually the most powerful—and power rests, as we know, on a ruthless separation of the personal from the political. Whether this always makes for good writing is another issue. I have read too many dire feminist novels involving incest or eating disorders in my time and I think that much of this stuff would be better left unpublished. Writing it down may well do the author good but inflicting it upon others is an act of sadism by committed masochists. Anyway, these days the people making money out of rewriting their pasts are the boys, who just seem so much jollier than we do, perhaps because they get a round of applause for merely admitting that they have emotions at all. . . . The thing about the laying bare of personal pain is that you have to like or want to connect with the person displaying their life before you.

This was part of my difficulty with Kathryn Harrison's book *The Kiss,* which is an easier book to admire than to like. It is the beautifully written tale of the affair Harrison had with her father when she was 20. Never feeling good enough for her narcissistic mother, she ends up seduced by her monstrous father. With chilling intensity she describes how the destruction of his internal barriers destroyed hers, and how the affair was a way of trying to penetrate her mother by using her father. In the jargon Harrison is the victim, yet there is something about this memoir that suggests a need to exonerate herself. Is she not culpable? Does an unhappy childhood or even the obvious psychoanalytic interpretation excuse what she has done? Does the quality of her writing cover up the narcissism she has inherited from both parents?

**Sue Halpern (review date 25 September 1997)**

SOURCE: "The Awful Truth," in *New York Review of Books,* Vol. 44, No. 14, September 25, 1997, pp. 13–15.

[*In the following excerpt, Halpern compares specific passages from* Thicker Than Water *and* The Kiss, *noting the similarities in the subject material.*]

The response to Kathryn Harrison's memoir, *The Kiss* . . . illustrates how one's expectation defines one's reception—how what a book is called determines how the reader reads it. *The Kiss,* as everyone knows by now, is about Harrison's four-year affair with her father, a pastor, which began when the author was twenty. The book is written in a cool, hypnotic monotone, as if the writer were unattached to the events she records (and therefore not culpable). "We spend our nights in motels not so much sordid as depressing. Sordid has a style and swagger these places lack, rooms with curtains cut from the same orange fabric as the bedspread, ceilings of plaster textured like cottage cheese," she writes. And, in the book's most sexually explicit passage:

> . . . He lifts the hem of my nightgown. He doesn't speak, and neither do I. Nor do I make any attempt to stay his hands. Beneath the nightgown I am wearing no underpants, and he opens my legs and puts his tongue between them. . . . What he does feels neither good nor bad.

The writing is so painstakingly flat and uninflected, so *reported,* that it seems to detach the writer from her own willfulness. It is, deliberately, amoral.

When *The Kiss* came out this spring, critics complained that it was both meretricious and poorly written, and in a rare moment of collective outrage castigated both author and publisher for the opportunism in bringing the book to market. Other critics, citing a number of recent books by male authors revealing their defiance of sexual taboos that did not meet such opprobrium, accused these critics of sexism, among other sins. Meanwhile, the author's husband—perhaps opportunistically, perhaps not—took to the pages of *Vogue* to defend his wife. His main argument: *The Kiss* was a book Kathryn Harrison said she *had to* write, and who was he to deny her? What is interesting about this justification is that it suggests a compulsion: not only could Colin Harrison not stop his wife, she could not stop herself.

And the manifestation of a compulsion may be exactly what *The Kiss* is, for it is not the first book she's written that chronicles the affair and other family pathologies. Harrison's first novel, *Thicker Than Water,* tread that fertile ground six years ago. But writing about it once, apparently, was not enough. Harrison came back to the affair, though not to portray it differently. Indeed, the two books share a lot: images, conversations, paragraphs. (One critic, in fact, accused Ms. Harrison of "self-plagiarism.") What is different, though, is that one book is a novel, the other a memoir. One is supposed to be fiction, the other fact.

From the novel, *Thicker Than Water*:

> When I was fifteen, my mother made me get my first diaphragm. . . . My mother was in the examining room when the doctor broke my hymen so he could fit me properly for the device. He used a series of graduated green plastic phalli. First a tiny little boy sized one, then a larger and larger one, until he withdrew one whose shaft had been discolored by a smear of blood. My mother leaned against the wall, watching.

From the memoir, *The Kiss*:

> He uses a series of graduated green plastic penises. . . . One after another he inserts them, starting with the smallest—no bigger than his little finger—until the second to last one comes out smeared with blood. This doctor deflowers me in front of my mother.

From the novel, *Thicker Than Water*:

> In line at the salad bar he pulled my plate out of my hand and let it fall to the floor and shatter, cherry tomatoes rolling between my feet. When he thus had the attention of all the diners he said loudly, "You're a slut, just like your mother." One entire family turned around in their seats and looked to see who I was.

From the memoir, *The Kiss*:

> My father leans across the table. His face is the same shape but much larger than mine, seemingly larger than other men's. At close range, it seems planetary. "You," he says, too loudly for a restaurant, "are a slut just like your mother." Everyone who hears turns to see who the big man is talking to with such righteous conviction.

When it was published, *Thicker Than Water* received many favorable reviews. The writer, who was thirty years old, was praised for her use of language, which was at once direct and distilled, and for her command of the material. But one review in particular, by Scott Spencer, writing in *The New York Times Book Review,* is especially prescient: "The first two words of *Thicker Than Water* are 'In truth,' and as the novel plunges into a woman's painfully frank and unsparing revelations about her miserable childhood, and her struggle to awaken from its dank, hypnotic spell, this reader felt, at times, that he was reading a harrowing, fully imagined work of nonfiction." And so, it turned out, he was.

What is interesting about this comment in retrospect is that neither Mr. Spencer nor any of the other reviewers who suspected that *Thicker Than Water* detailed real events chastised Ms. Harrison for writing about the affair. No one argued that it was exploitative or potentially damaging to her children or that her rendering was meretricious. No one suggested that she should not have written it or, at least, if she had to write it, that she should not have published it. No one said anything of the sort because the story was told behind the veil of fiction. As long as there was the slightest possibility that the story was not true, veracity could be the object of speculation, not the subject of criticism. As long as the story was just a story, no one needed to consider its impact on the family or the author's motive in publishing the book. As fiction, both the writer, and the reader, were protected.

Call it something else, though—nonfiction, true crime, autobiography, or the murkier "memoir"—and the reader cracks the binding with certain (and different) assumptions. Knowing that the events are really "real" raises questions of culpability, intent, and motivation. Not only is the writing—the telling of the story—under scrutiny, the writer's life is, too. The outrage people have expressed about Ms. Harrison "outing" herself has as much, and maybe more, to do with her real-life behavior vis-à-vis her father (and mother) as they do with the content or style of her book. Calling the book a memoir afforded them this liberty: the life as well as the work are fair game. One suspects that Ms. Harrison knew this and that this, in fact, was one of the reasons she chose to tell the story again, in this form. In the vitriolic controversy that occurred after *The Kiss* came out, greed, notoriety, and revenge were each suggested to be the author's motivation for writing and then publishing the book. If so, it would not be the first time a book was drawn from any of these wells. But more likely, *The Kiss* first came from a deeper place—the need to lay bare—that only a book that has no pretense can get at.

Still, in a curious way, the impulse works to Ms. Harrison's disadvantage. *The Kiss* is a stronger book than its predecessor precisely because it gets at its subject more directly. Forget subplot, forget ancillary action—this book has one subject, one narrative line, and it clings to it almost desperately. There is no relief from the story, no diversions, no humor, nothing to keep the reader from getting sucked into Ms. Harrison's reality. And that is the problem. It is another seduction—this one of the reader. In the beginning this feels all right—it is, in fact, what good books do—but some time later the author's confession begins to seem manipulative. The somnolent, distant voice through which she makes that confession, and which at first contributes to its authenticity by suggesting how truly damaged Ms. Harrison has been by the affair, is so self-consciously "written" as to be suspect. In another context its mesmerizing quality would be an achievement. In this one though it cannot help but raise questions of trust. And trust is essential to the enterprise of nonfiction, even to memoir.

**Ruth Scurr (review date 12 May 2000)**

SOURCE: "Shoeless in Shanghai," in *Times Literary Review,* No. 5067, May 12, 2000, p. 21.

[*In the following review, Scurr offers a negative assessment of* The Binding Chair *and suggests that* The Kiss *was an unfortunate turning point for the worse in Harrison's career.*]

Kathryn Harrison had published three novels before *The Kiss* (1997), a memoir about her incestuous affair with her father, brought her notoriety. She was admired for breaking "the last taboo." But she was also suspected of attempting to catapult a decent but unremarkable novelistic career into a more glamorous stratosphere. Grounds for this suspicion could have been located in the fact that Harrison's first novel, *Thicker Than Water* (1991), had a plot strikingly similar to her later memoir. The uncharitable interpretation of *The Kiss* is much more interesting retrospectively than it was in 1997, when it seemed mean-minded and cynical. Harrison's new novel, *The Binding Chair,* recounts the life of a victim of Chinese foot-binding, a Shanghai prostitute who marries an Australian client in 1899 and ends up on the French Riviera in time for the Jazz Age. It compares unfavourably with Harrison's earlier historically inspired novel *Poison* (1995, published in the UK as *A Thousand Orange Trees,*) and suggests not only that she is an irritatingly sensationalist writer, but that *The Kiss* may also have damaged her perception of herself as a novelist.

*Poison* was set at the time of the Spanish Inquisition, and the Marquis de Sade was coyly included in Harrison's acknowledgements. It lacked the literary grace of Jenny Diski's *Nothing Natural,* but the torture and transgressive sex were at least woven into an interesting story. In contrast, they protrude obscenely from *The Binding Chair,* where the narrative is more eccentric than the kind that commonly links the scenes in a pornographic video or novel, but no less insubstantial. One explanation for this arises from the frequency with which sex and sexual imagery appear in the novel. In Chapter Three, for example, five-year-old May appeals to her father to release her from the binding chair. He refuses and reflects that "after all, he himself enjoyed marriage to a nimble and delicate woman—a woman whose whole foot he could take into his rectum, even as her left hand cupped his testicles, her right squeezed the shaft of his penis, and her mouth wet his glans. There was a price for luxury. . . ." I find it hard to believe that this account details a historical motivation for foot-binding, and harder still to imagine how evidence for it could be collated. At the end of *Poison,* Harrison very carefully explained which parts of her novel were directly borrowed from history and which had been imaginatively elaborated. *The Binding Chair* includes no such explanations and the presence of two further scenes centred on anal sex tips the balance towards imaginative licence.

But imaginative licence counts for little in this novel. Harrison is audibly impatient with her own story, always hurrying on to the next sensational scene and brusquely dismissing the finer details. May runs away from an abusive marriage, carried on the back of a servant to whom she promises her jewelry. This has the compelling, if limited, logic of a fairy story. However, it closely follows a scene in which an older May and her niece witness a young girl being slowly and publicly cut in half as a punishment for running away from marriage and bringing disgrace to her family. Why wasn't May pursued and punished? Harrison dismisses these questions: "Probably [her husband] was grateful for the peace that returned once May had gone." She is more interested in describing how May, despite running for her life, took the time to stop at her parental home and urinate over her grandmother's tiny silk shoes.

Still more ludicrous is the scene in which May's future husband starts to unbind her feet expecting to find a perfect miniature foot inside the wrappings, instead of the broken, rotting (allegedly erotic) reality. In some characters this ignorance could be credible. Arthur Cohen, however, is a member of the Foot Emancipation Society. Harrison quickly explains the surprising lacuna in his knowledge: he missed the society's indoctrination meeting and the lecture from the surgeon who explained the crippling fractures of the binding process. He missed both events, did not bother to question his fellow missionaries and still made it to Shanghai? The tendency to slovenliness culminates in a ridiculous scene in Fortnum and Mason's where May, carried in a makeshift sedan chair, improbably deputed by her family to visit her nieces who were only sent to boarding school in the first place because of her own corrupting influence, inadvertently causes a riot, rather in the mode of *Paddington Goes to the Sales.* Bad novels are rarely interesting. But the trajectory of Harrison's literary career is. Her promising start was overshadowed by a harrowing memoir in which she displayed her own sexual disturbance. Now she writes as though her public wanted and expected nothing but sex from her. It's not true.

# FURTHER READING

### Criticism

Argiri, Laura. "Mass Historia." *Village Voice* 40, No. 20 (16 May 1995): 82, 84.

    Argiri offers a positive assessment of *Poison,* praising Harrison's sensuous prose and historical accuracy.

Bush, Trudy. "Putting a Life in Order." *Christian Century* 114, No. 17 (21 May 1997): 519–23.

    Bush offers a negative assessment of *The Kiss.*

Chisholm, Anne. "Honey under the Silk." *Observer* (25 June 1995): 16.

> Chisholm offers a negative assessment of *A Thousand Orange Trees*, arguing that the novel lacks emotional impact.

Crossen, Cynthia. "Know Thy Father." *Wall Street Journal* CCXXIX, No. 43 (4 March 1997): A16.

> Crossen offers a negative assessment of *The Kiss*.

Dickstein, Mindi. "A Woman Trapped in Her Father's Photos." *Chicago Tribune Books* (21 February 1993): 5, 11.

> Dickstein commends Harrison's use of multiple narrative forms—first and third person passages, court transcripts, and letters—to tell the story in *Exposure*.

Emerson, Sally. "Sins of the Fathers." *Washington Post Book World* 21, No. 23 (9 June 1991): 11.

> Emerson offers a positive assessment of *Thicker Than Water*, praising Harrison's attention to lyrical dialogue.

Fields, Suzanne. Review of *The Kiss*, by Kathryn Harrison. *Insight on the News* 13, No. 17 (12 May 1997): 48.

> Field offers a negative assessment of *The Kiss* and states that the memoir is an example of how modern culture has lost its moral compass.

Hall-Balduf, Susan. "Women Bound at the Feet and by Expectations." *Detroit Free Press* (4 June 2000): 4E.

> Hall-Balduf offers a positive assessment of *The Binding Chair*, praising Harrison's ability to hold readers' attention with her prose.

Harrison, Kathryn with Mary Gordon. "Sex with Daddy." *Harper's Bazaar*, No. 3425 (April 1997): 136–37.

> Gordon interviews Harrison about the difficult personal situations portrayed in *The Kiss* and offers her own assessment of the memoir.

Hodo, David W. Review of *The Kiss*, by Kathryn Harrison. *Journal of the American Medical Association* 278, No. 8 (27 August 1997): 688.

> Hodo offers a positive assessment of *The Kiss* and recommends the memoir to physicians as a study in taboo and normality.

Linfield, Susie. "Les Liasons Dangereuses." *Los Angeles Times Book Review* (11 May 1997): 8.

> Linfield offers a positive assessment of *The Kiss*.

Medwick, Cathleen. "Shattered." *Mirabella* 82 (March 1997): 38–42.

> Medwick interviews Harrison about the events that inspired *The Kiss* and the notoriety caused by her memoir.

Mendelson, Daniel. "Hideous Kinky." *New York* 33, No. 19 (15 May 2000): 70–71.

> Mendelson offers a negative assessment of *The Binding Chair* and notes that Harrison has the makings of a fine novelist, but her limited range of themes "continues to cripple her work."

Powers, Elizabeth. "Doing Daddy Down." *Commentary* 103, No. 6 (June 1997): 38–41.

> Powers offers a negative assessment of *The Kiss*, arguing that the memoir fails to move readers emotionally with its employment of nonchronological and other unconventional narrative techniques.

Press, Joy. "Bound, not Gagged." *Village Voice* 45, No. 20 (23 May 2000): 73–74.

> Press interviews Harrison about the reactions of critics and readers to *The Kiss*.

Scott, R. C. Review of *Poison*, by Kathryn Harrison. *Insight on the News* 11, No. 25 (26 June 1995): 24–25.

> Scott offers a positive assessment of *Poison*.

Udovitch, Mim. "The Evil Dads." *New York* 30, No. 10 (17 March 1997): 57–58.

> Udovitch compares and contrasts *The Kiss* with Mia Farrow's autobiography, *What Falls Away*.

Wolcott, James. Review of *The Kiss*, by Kathryn Harrison. *New Republic* 216, No. 13 (31 March 1997): 32–36.

> Wolcott offers a negative assessment of *The Kiss* and also discusses Harrison's short story "The Tick."

---

**Additional coverage of Harrison's life and career is contained in the following sources published by the Gale Group:** *Contemporary Authors*, **Vol. 144;** *Contemporary Authors New Revision Series*, **Vol. 68; and** *Literature Resource Center.*

# Maureen Howard
## 1930-

American novelist, memoirist, editor, and short story writer.

The following entry presents an overview of Howard's career through 1998. For further information on her life and works, see *CLC,* Volumes 5, 14, and 46.

## INTRODUCTION

Howard has garnered widespread critical acclaim for her novels about women searching for identity amid their career aspirations and within their socially prescribed roles. The female characters in her novels are frequently conflicted and struggle to assert their individuality, often by breaking from their families—particularly from mother figures. Howard celebrates the assertion of the human will to affect change, yet, in her works, such action does not always insure a happy or conclusive ending. Critics have commended Howard's precise use of language, her double-edged humor, and the loose structure of many of her novels, which allows readers to draw their own conclusions about characters and incidents. Howard is best known for her critically acclaimed memoir, *Facts of Life* (1978), which received the National Book Critics Circle Award for general nonfiction.

## BIOGRAPHICAL INFORMATION

Howard was born on June 28, 1930, in Bridgeport, Connecticut. The city of Bridgeport played a large role in Howard's formative years, and she would later use the town as the setting for several of her novels. Howard was raised in Bridgeport's Irish neighborhoods, and her Irish-immigrant father, William, was the county detective for Fairfield County. Howard attended Smith College and earned a bachelor's degree in 1952. After college, she worked for several publishing and advertising firms. In 1961, Howard published her first novel, *Not a Word about Nightingales.* From 1967 to 1968, she worked at the New School for Social Research, in New York City, as a lecturer in English and creative writing. Howard has continued to teach and lecture on such subjects as drama, English, and creative writing, holding positions at the University of California, Santa Barbara, Columbia University, Yale University, Amherst College, and Brooklyn College. She was awarded a Guggenheim fellowship in 1967 and the National Book Critics Circle Award in 1980. She has also been nominated several times for the American Book Award for autobiography/biography and the PEN/Faulkner Award for nonfiction.

## MAJOR WORKS

*Not a Word about Nightingales* focuses on the disruptions within a family when the father decides to leave his wife and children to pursue a life of "feeling" during a vacation in Peruvia. After eighteen months, his wife sends their daughter to bring him back; by this time, her father has become disenchanted with his hedonistic lifestyle and returns without much resistance. In *Bridgeport Bus* (1966), Mary Agnes Keeley, an aspiring middle-aged writer, leaves her hometown of Bridgeport on the bus to begin a new life in New York City. Mary Agnes has difficulty adjusting to life in the city and finds herself surrounded by a neurotic roommate and a suicidal cousin. She eventually returns to Bridgeport, unmarried and pregnant, to take care of her widowed mother. The award-winning memoir *Facts of Life* directly addresses Howard's affinity for rewriting and reinterpreting personal narratives, this time using her own life story. The work vividly portrays her parents' conflicting personalities and the consequences of her strict Catholic upbringing. Howard uses the memoir genre to call the "facts" of her life into question, demonstrating the differences and discrepancies between perception and memory. In *Expensive Habits* (1986), Margaret Flood, a famous American writer, undergoes bypass heart surgery and is given a new lease on life. During her recovery, she discovers that her life and career are filled with lies and untruths, some of which have hurt others. As she heals physically, she also attempts to heal the mistakes she has made in the past. *Natural History* (1992) is both a narrative and an anthropological assortment of facts about Bridgeport, Connecticut. The novel's loose plot focuses on Billy Bray, a county detective and the patriarch of a large family. Set in 1943, the story focuses on Bray's investigation of the murder of a soldier by an officer's wife. Bray quickly closes the investigation, but his family is plagued for years by the murdered man's brother, who seeks revenge for what he feels was Bray's inability to bring his brother's killer to justice. The novel is filled with details concerning the people, history, and culture of Bridgeport. A section titled "Double Entry" juxtaposes the narrative events with arcane Bridgeport trivia. *A Lover's Almanac* (1998) is stylistically similar to *Natural History* in that each includes both pages of straight narration and alternative bits of history, weather forecasts, folk wisdom, and trivia. The novel opens with the ending of a romantic relationship between two characters, Louise Moffett and Artie Freeman, who are splitting apart on the eve of the millennium. After the break-up, Louise and Artie attempt to impose order and criteria on their love lives, much as an almanac provides an order for natural events by presenting predictions based on facts. In 2001, Howard published *Big As Life: Three Tales for Spring*, a mixture of short stories and memoirs, focusing on renewal and the season of Spring.

## CRITICAL RECEPTION

Howard has been referred to by some critics as a "woman's writer" due to her recurring focus on female characters searching for self-awareness. Reviewers have consistently praised her prose and her well-drawn characters, both central and minor. Critics have compared her narrative style to that of Virginia Woolf, Henry James, and Toni Morrison. Howard has been noted for her skill at presenting differing points of view and her ability to seamlessly handle transitions between the past, present, and future. Many critics have applauded how Howard appropriates different literary genres for use in her fiction. For example, *Natural History* makes use of the screenplay, encyclopedia, diary, and history book genres within the central narrative. However, several critics have objected to Howard's tendency toward digression and loose plot structures. Some reviewers have argued that these tangential details make her novels—most notably *Natural History* and *A Lover's Almanac*—self-conscious and difficult to read. Some critics have panned the innovative and experimental narrative techniques used in these two works, such as the use of parallel texts on the right- and left-hand pages in *Natural History*, which Noel Perrin called "a semi-psychedelic melange." Critical reaction to Howard's seemingly endless fascination with the city of Bridgeport has also been mixed. Some reviewers have derided her continual use of the city as a focus in her novels as repetitive and uninteresting. However, other commentators have praised Howard's utilization of the city as a major character. Many agreed with Pearl K. Bell, who stated that the depiction of Bridgeport in Howard's works ultimately seeks "to defy the evanescence of memory, . . . . [and] lament the irrevocable dissolution of vanished experience."

## PRINCIPAL WORKS

*Not a Word about Nightingales* (novel) 1961
*Bridgeport Bus* (novel) 1966
*Before My Time* (novel) 1975
*Seven American Women Writers of the Twentieth Century* [editor] (nonfiction) 1977
*Facts of Life* (memoirs) 1978
*Grace Abounding* (novel) 1982
*The Penguin Book of Contemporary American Essays* [editor] (nonfiction) 1984
*Expensive Habits* (novel) 1986
*Natural History* (novel) 1992
*A Lover's Almanac* (novel) 1998
*Big As Life: Three Tales for Spring* (short stories and memoirs) 2001

## CRITICISM

**Noel Perrin (review date 27 May 1984)**

SOURCE: "The Lure of the Bright Lights," in *Washington Post Book World,* May 27, 1984, p. 11.

[*In the following review, Perrin offers a positive assessment of* Bridgeport Bus, *praising Howard's treatment of the theme of personal transformation.*]

Mary Agnes Keeley, 35 years old, 5 feet 11 inches tall, thin as a pencil, lives with her widowed mother in Bridgeport, Connecticut. Her father, a Bridgeport fireman, died when she was 15. Right after high school she went to work to help put her brother through Fordham. He is now an FBI agent, assigned to the Buffalo, New York, office, with a wife and three children. Mary Agnes is secretary to the president of Standard Zipper in Bridgeport. She is a virgin. She is also on the edge of martyrdom to her mother, a natural genius at using guilt feelings and ill health to control her children.

That martyrdom does not occur. Instead this novel does. Mary Agnes takes the Bridgeport bus. That is, she quits her job, leaves home, and goes to New York. Mary Agnes—only let's call her Ag, as most people do—has always been bright. Her one defiance of her mother over the years has been the taking of a whole series of night courses in literature. She reads voraciously, has ambitions to write.

In fairly short order she is writing: not glamorously, to be sure, only advertising copy for a manufacturer of Velcro fasteners. But she's living in an apartment on Ninth Street, meeting artists, putting on weight. By Chapter 5 she has both lost her virginity and begun to write fiction.

This basic plot is a familiar one, because it expresses one of the very commonest of human fantasies. Ugly duckling becomes a swan. Man or woman trapped in a boring routine breaks loose, makes a new start, achieves the glamorous life. Seemingly ordinary person proves exceptional. All of us are exceptional, at least to ourselves, only the world fails to treat us so. It is deeply gratifying to read about someone who gets a grip on himself or herself, and makes the world respond properly.

Maureen Howard's treatment of this theme is something else. In the usual book of this kind—and I am talking about genuine novels, not easy romances—the Ag character has center stage all to herself, while we, entranced, watch her transformation. And in the usual book of this kind, swanhood turns out to be a really nice thing. Some of the other swans may prove vicious; some of the glitter of the great world may prove to be tinsel; the transformed life may even end in tragedy. But that it is a glorious thing to become a swan, and that the great world is truly great, these assumptions are not questioned.

*Bridgeport Bus* is not like that. It has three heroines. Ag is certainly the main one—and most of the time the narrator—but there are two other young women whose stories are told and whose presence makes the value of swanhood much more dubious.

One is Lydia Savaard. Ag meets her when she first arrives in New York, and stays briefly at a hotel for women, a genteel place on Fifth Avenue. Lydia is 25, rather mousy, as WASPly Protestant as Ag is Irish Catholic. She grew up in a nice upper-middle-class family in Cleveland, went to Vassar, and then married a young aristocrat just out of Princeton. The Savaards, though they have now lost most of their money, have been high society for two centuries. What Lydia didn't realize, marrying Henry Savaard, was that his upper-classness is a burden he can't handle. He simply can't live up to his concept of what a Savaard should be. He married Lydia principally because he thought Miss Mouse wouldn't see through him, and would join him in worship of the Savaard past. But he sees through himself, and the knowledge breaks him. At 26 he is in a mental institution, which is why Lydia is at the women's hotel. She's trying with the aid of pills to sleep 20 hours a day, and in the other four making feeble attempts to get an annulment. (Her lawyer is one of the many superbly drawn minor characters.) Ag partially rouses poor Lydia from this lethargy, and the two of them take the little apartment on Ninth Street together. It is hard to envy the aristocratic WASP life once you've got to know Lydia and Henry.

The third heroine is Ag's first cousin, Sherry Henderson. Sherry, born Mary Elizabeth Hurley, grew up in Bridgeport even more drably than Ag herself. But she was redheaded, very pretty, irresistibly attractive to men. She took the Bridgeport bus long before Ag. She left at 16. First she became a chorus girl, later a budding starlet. Alas, she didn't have quite enough talent or quite enough sense. There is no blossom-time. Though she stays in the world of luxury and privilege—she eventually marries a wealthy older man—she is as unable as Henry Savaard to sustain the role of swan. Sherry is a suicide at 33.

And Ag herself? Ag is a survivor. At the end of the book Ag is about to have a baby. Ag has become a very good writer. One of the marvelous things in *Bridgeport Bus* is the interpolated play that occupies about a quarter of the book. Ag wrote it. She herself is one of the main characters; the other seven are her parents, her brother, the two Savaards, Sherry, and Stanley Sarnicki, her principal lover in New York. The play is tragic, symbolic, surrealistic—and wildly funny. It is a tremendous tour de force. If only it could stand alone (it can't), I would love to see it on Broadway.

But Ag, tough, perceptive and witty as she is, suffers from the same malady that Sherry and Lydia and Henry do. It is a malady I know well myself. It is the incapacity to forgive life for being so mundane. My first fully conscious experience of it occurred when I was a young man, in love with a slightly older woman, a divorcée with a small daughter. The three of us were in a supermarket on a Friday night, buying food for the weekend.

The store was packed with other shoppers, mostly harassed. Martha, the little daughter, was crying. I longed to be gone. But Lois, the mother, kept thinking of more grubby things we needed: paper towels, detergent, Wesson oil. In the end it all seemed so unutterably beneath what I wanted life to be like that I began drifting further and further back from the shopping cart (a squalid enough object itself). I didn't want to be associated. Lois, a clever woman, divined at once what was in my mind, and we later had a sharp scene about it.

Ag—and, of course, Maureen Howard behind her—sees almost everywhere that failure of life to be what it should be. If you escape the shopping carts, as on the Savaard estate on Long Island, then you merely have a high-class setting in which the actors mostly fail to sustain their parts. It is the special brilliance of *Bridgeport Bus* that it turns this rueful awareness into gallant and high comedy.

**Jonathan Yardley (review date 11 May 1986)**

SOURCE: "Maureen Howard: Satire and Sympathy," in *Washington Post Book World,* May 11, 1986, p. 3.

[*In the following review, Yardley offers a positive assessment of* Expensive Habits, *commenting on the ways that the novel breaks from Howard's earlier work.*]

By contrast with Maureen Howard's four previous novels, **Expensive Habits** is long and, in the conventional sense, ambitious: the other books are delicate miniatures, elegantly crafted and somewhat elliptical in narrative method, but **Expensive Habits** attempts to paint a relatively large canvas and does so in a rather straightforward manner. The novel appears—the impression is fortified by the attendant publicity campaign—to be Howard's attempt to reach for a larger readership than she has thus far enjoyed; it is an honorable effort, and in no way does Howard compromise her exceptionally high standards in the process, but **Expensive Habits** is an odd book that is more likely to provoke curiosity and respect than affection and admiration.

Readers familiar with Howard's earlier fiction and her fine autobiography, *Facts of Life,* will find much here that is agreeably familiar. She writes equally well about two strikingly different milieus, both of which are present in *Expensive Habits*: the domestic life of genteel but threadbare Roman Catholic families, and the bitchy, narcissistic world of the New York illuminati. Her prose has a distinct and refreshing individuality; she moves with ease between high and low styles, changing gears so smoothly that the reader rarely feels she is calling attention to herself. The sense of irony that permeates all of her work is uncommonly acute, yet it becomes merely judgmental; she recognizes all the weaknesses and self-indulgences of the people she describes and the fashionable ideas they embrace, but her satire is tempered by sympathy, even when silliness is endemic.

There is a good deal of silliness in **Expensive Habits,** much of it committed by the central character, Margaret Flood. She is a 46-year-old writer who has just been told that she suffers from a heart condition that will kill her in a matter of months: "A mechanical malfunction of the body, the doctors with their machines, Providence, if you will, has taken over. What a swindle—she has paid her dues, but that's not it. At last she comes to the hard little core of her misery, small and painful as a pebble in the shoe: for years that now seem always, she has controlled the plot." Even now, she cannot resist trying, and indeed it seems she may succeed; she drags herself from New York down to Baltimore, undergoes bypass surgery, and emerges from it with an opportunity to live a new life.

But the brush with "death's bright angel" has had a traumatic effect on this difficult, demanding, temperamental, arrogant woman: it has forced her to examine her past and its many errors, to attempt a rewriting of that past. Before leaving for the hospital "she had worked with a frenzy to set the record straight, as though she were ripping out the seams of her life." After the surgery she does not abandon this effort but continues it with new determination, possessed as she is by the conviction that her books, which are the story of her life, have told that story wrong—that they are riddled with self-serving falsehoods that have damaged others.

Chief among these, she believes, is her first husband, Jack Flood, whom she married while he was in medical training; they divorced following her discovery that he was having an affair with a nurse. This became the subject of her first novel, in which she portrayed him as altering the results of his medical research in order to obtain an MH grant; all of these years she has known that "I contracted with myself to write a revenge tragedy, to make an unsupportable thesis of my marriage to Jack Flood." Now it is to him, a distinguished surgeon, that she turns not merely for medical help, but also for forgiveness for "bitter words and fancies, my only consolation, having lost the game."

It is one of many she has lost, thinking she has won: thinking that by reordering life, by faking it in fiction, she can recoup her losses and heal her wounds. But then she is made victim of an irreplaceable loss, one that shakes her house of fiction down to its foundation, and she confronts life's inescapable truth: "For twenty years she has ordered the world, made it accessible, trimmed and fit her stories. More recently, under the trumped-up threat of extinction, she has revised, confessed, approached—well, her version of the truth. . . . Now she counts herself defenseless, the victim of others' stories—inaccurate, vicious, consoling. Motives beside the point. . . . Mute, diminished, she is no one in the vast audience. Squinting, on the wrong side of the arena she cannot pick herself out, she cannot heckle."

This discovery of her mere humanity is arrived at by more routes than those provided by Jack Flood and a terrible personal calamity. Others with whom she must contend include her present husband, Pinkham Strong, a spineless patrician from whom she is separated; their son, Bayard, a 16-year-old of exceptional character and maturity; her first editor, Philo Pierce, a cynical fellow traveler in literary and political circles; Sol Negaly, a Hollywood producer with whom she once made a movie—it sounds for all the world like *Nashville*—that "so easily reviled our country and patronized the lower, lower-middle, middle classes"; a Hispanic maid, named (with an excess of irony) Lourdes, whose idle chatter has dreadful consequences; and a small band of ancient radicals—"grand men and women—flawed, perhaps fallen, but gods in their day"—about whom she is attempting to write a book.

It is, on the whole, a larger cast of characters (and the themes they bring along as baggage) than the novel can comfortably contain. Although it is clear what Howard means to do with each particular person, these schemes don't always seem necessary to the central concerns of the book; even when their connection to the major themes—

fate, history, nostalgia, illusion—is clear, their presence can seem gratuitous. Pinkham Strong rummaging around in the history books, the old women conjuring up memories of their glorious past—Howard can't let sleeping themes lie, but pokes away at them with a didacticism that is most uncharacteristic. Neither does it help matters that Margaret Flood is never really brought to life, never really takes control of her own story; we are meant to feel a sympathy for her that she never manages to earn.

But if *Expensive Habits* is a disappointment, it is principally so by comparison with Howard's earlier work: those terse, elusive books that are so much larger than the sum of their parts. By comparison with most contemporary American fiction, on the other hand, it is a serious and accomplished piece of work. Here as in her other work Howard writes about the fads and fashions of the day, about a society eager to cash in on any passing joy or sorrow, but she is having none of that herself; she stands apart, observing "the dumb glory of it all" with an eye that is sharp but kind. If *Expensive Habits* is not the major work her publisher believes it to be, it is certainly a book rich in integrity and elegance, by a writer who matters.

**Nora Johnson (review date 18 May 1986)**

SOURCE: A review of *Expensive Habits*, in *Los Angeles Times Book Review*, May 18, 1986, p. 1.

[*In the following mixed review, Johnson argues that* Expensive Habits *is a well-written work, but argues that there are several unclear plot elements and character motivations.*]

Maureen Howard's fine fifth novel attempts more, and accomplishes more, than all the others, marking her steady progress toward the highest rank of American fiction writers. The prose of *Expensive Habits* is dense, complex, disturbing, authoritative. Its several voices suit her story and vividly demonstrate her literary intelligence. It's dazzling to see how deftly she wields her author's tools. Point of view, constricting for some writers, becomes in her ken a group of handy launching pads for better views of the territory; and as for the knotty business of time, she slides gracefully from now to then to tomorrow without a sign of discomfort.

The story, set in Manhattan, is—I believe—about death; how Margaret Flood, a famous American writer who has usually managed to be around the action of the decades, avoids a medical death sentence by a successful bypass operation, only to be "faked out by death: It found her" in a shocking climax I won't reveal.

To "set the record straight," she tells of her first husband, Jack Flood, who deceived her with a nurse, and her real love—I think—Pinky Strong, frail tag end of an old WASP family. Pinky, deeply involved, like Margaret, in '60s causes, is the presumed father of her son, Bayard. There's Sol Negaly, her Hollywood director, and her "fashionable and fussy" editor, Fred Peach, who signs her up for a sizzling expose of the Old Left. There was the early novel about her family she rewrote to suit her fascinating first editor, Philo Pierce, and the one written to avenge herself on Jack Flood, now a prominent New York cardiologist, in which she claimed he'd cooked the evidence in the crucial paper that got him his first grant.

Now divorced—Margaret an invalid, Pinky an alcoholic, running a thrift shop winningly called "Golden Oldies"—the couple are brought back together by a remarkably drawn maid named Lourdes and the 17-year-old Bayard, parent of his two helpless parents, in a curious set of circumstances that ends in tragedy.

I've tripped over some of this because, after one careful reading, I'm not sure of some of the events and motivations in this novel. Though the story is carefully crafted and well-paced, Howard has a way of setting down a brilliant dab of description—"Margaret Flood's editor—very neat, sewn out of mousy flannel; like a toy, muzzle and whiskers atremble, adorable soft belly . . ." and then leaving it, an unexamined treasure, to sit alone. The characters are tantalizingly presented but often in shadow, rarely emerging into the light where we can watch them engage in real action. Important motivations are sometimes hard to find; I kept going back rather fretfully, wondering if I'd missed something. Was there more significance than I thought to Jack Flood's Chinese pen pal, or to the shopping trip of Tina (Sol Negaly's outrageous wife) to Golden Oldies? Howard ducks and runs at important dramatic junctures—a tendency she's had in her other books too. She'll line up, flex her muscles, salute . . . and then walk off the field.

Margaret is tough and feisty, but puzzling. Is she the cruel caricature of a writer, putting everybody but herself under her camera eye, or is she a loving and lovable female? I didn't know why she so resented her son's sexuality, or why, in the last section, she and Pinky returned to clean out and sell the Vermont house where they lived in the '60s. And did the author intend the fascinating but veiled suggestion that Margaret's work was molded, distorted, even battered by the opinions of men until the moment when she gave Peach back his check and resolved to write her book the way she wanted? Is *that* what the novel is really about? I wish I knew.

These are hard times for fiction. Serious novelists strive to avoid the shopworn—which by now includes just about everything—by angling in on their material, barely touching those pressure points where lesser writers would land with a thud. Better to circle, to infer, to let the explosion take place underground, going for the greater wallop the reader gets from making his own discovery. Then style, having a heavier role, becomes visible. The brilliant Byzantine curlicues of a William H. Gass or a Maureen Howard are always a pleasure to read, but sometimes too ripely self-conscious; the packaging tends to outshine the contents.

Howard is so good, so talented, I want her to be perfect.

**Thomas R. Edwards (review date 3 September 1992)**

SOURCE: "Design for Living," in *New York Review of Books,* December 3, 1992, pp. 30–32.

[*In the following review, Edwards argues* Natural History*'s unconventional narrative structure complements the novel's thematic material.*]

Anyone who loves natural history museums knows that the first moment we enter one, particularly as children, we understand that the collections are not the main point; they are for soberer minds. The point is the dioramas, those magical windows opening on times and places we will never actually visit. And the best dioramas, for our purposes, include not just simulacra of animals and plants but also the human forms posed among them, as if delicately alluding to the human artifice that puts dioramas in natural history museums. We are looking to see not so much nature and its history as ourselves in nature and history, and the nearer the figures come to "life size" the better they please.

*Natural History,* which includes Maureen Howard's reflections on dioramas and the American past, first shows us particular human figures in a particular time and place: Bridgeport, Connecticut, in the 1980s, though this "present" is deeply shaded by the past. Bridgeport is where Howard's main characters, a brother and sister named James and Catherine Bray, happened to grow up. Much of the novel consists of their memories, of themselves when young and of their often difficult and now dead parents. But as it proceeds, the city itself moves more and more to the foreground, while the Brays, though still very much in the picture, seem less conspicuous individually.

The known history of James and Catherine begins during World War II. Their father, Billy Bray, short and balding, like Jiggs in the comic strip, is the "one and only" detective in the local state's attorney's office. A strict, moralistic Irish Catholic, Billy is puzzled and angered by his bright and rebellious son's devotion not to "normal" pleasures like sports but to magic tricks and movies. Nell, their mother, the daughter of a prosperous cement manufacturer who built the fine house she and her family now live in, worries obsessively about James's physical safety, takes Catherine less seriously, and admires but also fears her husband's competence in his dangerous job. Catherine, the younger child, is devout, hard-working, not pretty, a Girl Scout soberly intent on acquiring merit badges.

In 1943 something happens that will deeply affect James and Catherine's adult lives. Their father is called to investigate a death in North Stamford, where a young war bride from Texas, whose husband, an army major, is serving in Italy, has shot and killed a soldier in the kitchen of her mock-Tudor house. The circumstances are suspicious: Mrs. Poole claims that Private Litwak followed her home uninvited from a local tavern, prowled through the shrubbery, and abused her verbally and physically; yet she evidently had the time to fetch her husband's gun from upstairs and shoot Litwak four times at close range. From her speech and manner, Billy Bray judges her to be a floozie, but there are no witnesses or evidence and her husband is from a socially prominent family. The press makes much of her case; and on Billy's recommendation she is indicted for second-degree murder. But her trial is a fiasco and she goes free.

The book moves on to the subsequent lives of the Bray children. We gradually learn that James, a charming boy, dropped out of Yale to become an actor in New York, and finally went to Hollywood, where in the antiheroic 1960s his offbeat handsomeness won him moderate celebrity. The less favored Catherine, after leaving Marymount, worked in New York as a fact-checker for *Time,* had affairs with men who treated her like the "second lead, the tough comedienne" in a musical, and occasionally flirted with suicide. She has returned to Bridgeport, where in 1984, helped by a modest inheritance from her mother, she shares a suburban ranch house with an attractive former nun turned social worker, spinning and dyeing fine wool to sell to the "crafties," as she calls the home weavers of New England. At fifty, she makes out of order and work a monastic kind of life, though not a cheerless one.

But Howard is less interested in the details of these lives than in the continuous self-imagining that any life entails. The Brays are treated as historical "objects" only in the book's first and last sections; between lie eight sections called "Museum Pieces," which, from various points of view, suggest the ways in which an imagination may offer not the external "truth" about a life but some idea of the inner self that enables it to continue and to change.

In "Closet Drama" and "Screenplays," we observe James recalling and fantasizing about the events of his life. Now fifty-two, he lives comfortably at his California ranch with his second wife, Lilah, and their teen-age daughter, Jen. His film career is at a stand-still, and his agent is urging him to accept the lead in a new TV series. But James, who would never call movies "art" yet takes them seriously, wants to direct his own black-and-white picture on the Poole-Litwak case, with himself playing Billy Bray. In cinematic episodes reminiscent of the Nighttown section of *Ulysses,* James raptly watches old *film noir* classics in his private screening room and mixes into them memories and fantasy reconstructions of events in his and others' lives: his first meeting with the beautiful but rather inscrutable Lilah while acting in a low-budget movie; the New Jersey boyhood of Morty Ziff, the coarse and brutal studio money man with whom his career has long been involved; Lilah's own impoverished beginnings in rural California, her brief career as a rodeo queen and then anthropology major, her fascination with horses and Indian artifacts, her determination "to be natural, to remove herself from human accommodations," even those offered by her husband and daughter. In all of this re-creation James is at once the director, an actor "doing" the various characters, and the audience of the show within his mind.

The "Museum Pieces" show a character or an authorial voice revising stories as new material becomes available. Some of the revisions are peripheral to the Brays themselves. For example, the life of Private Litwak's inarticulate brother, who intends to kill Billy Bray for letting Mrs. Poole go free, is unexpectedly diverted when he meets at a baseball game a Puerto Rican girl whom he marries; he becomes the owner of a prosperous tool-and-die company. Other figures in Howard's museum stand closer to the story of the Brays. Mary Boyle, with whom Catherine shares her house, has exchanged convent life for social work in a rough housing project, where she looks after Peaches, the abandoned black child of a hooker. The lonely child uses found materials to make astonishing effigies of her mother and her mother's clients, and has surrounded herself with photographs of her kid brothers, now wards of the state, taped to the TV screen so as to lend them an aura of life and glamour.

Peaches is a natural artist whose work is "an ongoing narrative" she can freely revise as momentary needs or whims dictate. She inspires a kind of creative passion in Mary herself—to rescue Peaches from the welfare system, to delouse and feed and clothe and love her, and make her part of the dream of performing sanctified works that, in another form, directs Catherine's dedication to her craft.

But Mary Boyle is "a good girl not fulfilled by goodness." When James returns to Bridgeport in 1984 to plan his movie, he meets her and, in a scene the aspiring director has not pre-imagined, she impulsively seduces him in his hotel room. This lapse, as much James's fault as Mary's, estranges her from Catherine and Peaches; it also causes James to decide that his picture about lust and crime is not worth making.

Catherine has opposed the movie project since first hearing about it. After the Litwak killing, when she was nine years old, she accidentally came upon evidence that Billy, the uncorruptible investigator, had allowed himself to be seduced by Mrs. Poole, and that he helped her to beat a murder conviction. Now, in 1984, hoping to discourage James from making the movie, Catherine is on the brink of telling him of their father's secret "fall from grace." But after learning of James's own fall with Mary Boyle and hearing him declare his own change of heart about the movie ("Too straight," he calls it, "the fancy woman and the soldier"), she decides to tell him that no one really knows what happened forty years earlier. She is then astonished to recognize that this is true. The case against her father, which she has believed for so long and which has helped to turn her against men, was flimsy from the start, something she had wanted to believe because "it was after all my story, the story of a foolish life."

But all survive their painful experience. James and Lilah have a new baby, and James is a hit in the TV series he has accepted after all, in which he plays a cop with something like Billy's gravel voice and swagger. Mary Boyle watches the show approvingly in Pittsburgh, where she is looking after her failing parents while contemplating good works yet to be done in Central America or Asia. Jen, James's rebellious daughter, enters Yale as her rebellious father did; she has genuine intellectual possibilities, and enjoys being near her Aunt Catherine, who is now well known in the crafts world. Even Peaches at least gets her mother back.

With the serenity of the novel's close, Howard preserves its mood of high romance. Yet the characters themselves, interesting and unexpected as they are, are not the book's primary concern. In "Double Entry," the longest and most demanding of the "Museum Pieces," Howard reveals ambitions that go well beyond the realistic and personal. "Double Entry" is something like a split-screen movie in print, almost eighty pages in which two separate narratives proceed side by side on facing pages. On the right we read the story of James Bray searching through his native city for the "essence of old Bridgeport" in order to flavor his picture; he encounters Mary Boyle and abandons his project. Meanwhile, on the left side, a voice we can call the author's, someone who knows what's happening across the book's center fold but takes no part in it, assembles a full account, with pictures, of what Bridgeport and other places used to be, the "essence" that James had vainly hoped to capture and exploit.

We can't of course read two texts at once, and the voice on the left-hand page gives this advice:

> In the beautiful concept of double entry bookkeeping, the debit and credit must always agree; no inaccuracies or altered circumstances are admitted, no rambling daybook or mere journal will stand the check of the other side of the ledger. Dip in, flip back or simply read on. Read on—you are free to follow the story.

Readers who try to balance the account will notice some bridges between the texts. For example, P. T. Barnum, Bridgeport's most famous resident and benefactor, appears on the right hand side in James's Don Giovanni-like dream of being visited by Barnum's statue, who compares James's kind of show business unfavorably with his own. And the pseudonym James uses in Bridgeport, "Felix Young," is, as the narrator explains to anyone needing help, the name of the cheerful youth in Henry James's *The Europeans,* who brings presentiments of artistic and emotional freedom to a staid New England community. But the historical verso text is mostly intended to look past the dreadful urban blight James discovers in Bridgeport to a time when industrial America was productive, culturally vigorous, a fit scene for human effort.

This half of "Double Entry" reflects an impressive knowledge of local history and Americana, and it is full of striking details: that Bridgeport led the nation in corset-making around 1905; that it was governed between 1929 and 1952 by an Irish Socialist mayor who hated to expend public money; that Seaside Park, Barnum's gift to his city, was one of Frederick Law Olmsted's failures in urban design. But such historical details are meant as something much more than "background" to set off a "human" story. The background merges with the story and is central to it.

In a short section in "Double Entry," "The Arcade," the historian's voice takes notice of Bridgeport's only shopping arcade, a glass and steel forerunner of our shopping malls. "Half block of wonders," Howard remarks, speaking for the young Catherine,

> which, as a girl, she did not notice, short cut to the bus that's all, no one to see you though in the eerie light Cath could see herself swimming through handbags and fedoras, wedding china, empty eye-glass frames; herself among the goods. The shop windows displaying, reflecting her. . . .

The mixing of transparency and reflection in seeing oneself "among the goods" is an effective analogy for historical self-consciousness, identifying our forebears and ourselves as makers and users of objects that are not natural, as figures in particular cultures.

The analogy, in various mutated forms, is I think what impressively holds together a novel whose tendencies are often digressive and episodic. The arcade is at once an emporium, a museum, and a theater of dreams like the movies that would follow. Though its origins are European, it seems especially congenial to America, with its excited uncertainties about the difference between "high" and "popular" forms of culture and about what each may be worth. Starting from the arcade, with references to Lewis Mumford, Walter Benjamin, and others, Howard traces the changes in the way in which city culture meets people's dreams. It is a fairly short step from arcades to "promenades," those window-lined shopping streets, like New York's Broadway or Bridgeport's (and Disneyland's) Main Street, which in industrial cities (Mumford suggested) serve as both Agora and Acropolis. From there we move to the movies or TV or the malls, to the fabulous boxes of Joseph Cornell or the dioramas of the natural history museum itself, while aware from the rest of the book, and particularly from the right hand pages, of the sad, depressed places that Bridgeport and cities like it have become.

The scenes and changes in public life Howard evokes usually offer us something of value—something salable or beautiful or interesting—though the values they reflect are decidedly mixed. When Howard juxtaposes Walter Benjamin and his Paris *Arcades Project*—with its suggestion that acquiring modern culture may be something like shopping or collecting—with Walt Disney and Walt Kelly (another Bridgeport native), one has a disturbing sense of our own unstable cultural values. For all its appearance of rational completeness, double-entry accounting, whose figures may or may not be accurate, is quite as susceptible to error and fraud as any other form of bookkeeping is. In fact, Howard's "Double Entry" itself doesn't balance—the verso text is longer than the recto narrative, which amusingly requires the inclusion of several blank pages to make up the difference, in the manner of *Tristram Shandy*.

But if at any given moment the true balance between past and present is undeterminable, since anything can be added or subtracted at any time, historical accounts can at least tell us something about the conditions of their composition. Contrary to legend, for example, the invention of double-entry bookkeeping was not almost simultaneous with Columbus's first voyage, but was only first described in print then; yet Howard sees that the legend is true in another way, clarifying something about the "new world" mood of the Renaissance that associated geographical discovery with balance sheets and profits. Or we can follow Howard to the Museum of Natural History in New York, where Carl Akeley's great gorilla diorama, for all its magnificence, tells us less about West African wildlife than about America when the diorama was made in the 1920s:

> It's not Africa the visitors to the museum look upon, but an American landscape of bright mornings, of time stopped at the innocent moment of discovery before guiltless acquisition, before the gorillas looked back at us in furious recognition.

Though not a particularly long novel, **Natural History** is in other senses a big one, big enough to have room for a remarkable variety of images of Americans, then and now, "an ongoing narrative" whose ending is unknowable and not really the point anyway. This immensely impressive book treats its people as creatures of the history of a place, but not of a past that is forever dead and gone, whatever the devastations of present-day Bridgeport may suggest. Maureen Howard's kind of "natural history" is about ourselves imagining a past that, for better or worse, remains in our own lives.

### Carol Anshaw (review date 25 October 1992)

SOURCE: "Circling Back to Bridgeport: Maureen Howard's Unconventional Saga of a Family and a City," in *Chicago Tribune Books*, October 25, 1992, p. 1.

[*In the following positive review of* Natural History, *Anshaw commends the novel's "subtle and subjective notion of story."*]

Stories can't always be held within conventional forms. Although novels most often put one page after the other in a forward progression, most narratives in life are not composed of a neatly chronological sequence of events, or even of just the events themselves. In truth, stories jump forward then back again, head off in several directions at once and include the imaginings of the participants as well as their behavior. It is this subtle and subjective notion of story that Maureen Howard plies in her latest novel.

*Natural History* is the story of both a family, the Brays, and a city, Bridgeport, Conn., (Howard's own home town). The first section of the book covers just a single March Saturday during World War II, following each of the Brays—parents Billy and Nell, children James and Cath—through small, quotidian events that nonetheless demonstrate the characters that will determine their fates.

Billy, a county detective, begins investigating the shooting death of a young soldier by the "Double Indemnity"-ish, 23-year-old wife of an absent Army major. Cath is humiliated when her project—Cotton, Queen of the South—does not win at the Girl Scout jamboree. James takes a clarinet lesson, buys some new magic tricks, and ducks the afternoon in the continuous night of a movie theater. While Nell worries obsessively about James coming to harm on his boyish way through his day, picturing the aftermath of a bicycle accident, "his fair head come to rest on a granite curb," Cath is in fact running toward her father's passing car, out into the street with her failed project, "where she is hit—gently, unimportantly—by an oncoming car."

From this one-city, one-day, Irish-American saga of swirling points of view, Howard jumps into an even more Joycean sequence of obliquely narrated pieces, tracking Cath and James into their very different adulthoods—his start as an aspiring actor in New York, hers as a low-rung editor in the Luce empire, a bad-luck girl with men who don't love her, then leave her to battle "the terrors of Saturday night" with enough Miltown to stop the pain that accompanies consciousness.

The novel's form then becomes eerily cinematic, with stage directions and props set out for James' ghostly narrator to tell the story of his rise to the middle rungs of fame.

"*James steady almost inaudible*: EX-ERCISE. You are permitted one direction, bare-assed in bare room. Let it be this: 'Actors should be like martyrs but alive, still signalling to us from the stake.' Anto-neen Artaud.

"*The woman's laugh again then an intimate whisper*: Later . . . yes, later, I gave my self to one cowboy, then another, beer breath, Westerns on TV. . . ."

The woman is a rodeo queen James meets on location, Lilah, who improbably becomes his devoted wife, throwing in her lot with him for the long run. Which has surprising turns. An unexpected last shot at parenthood. A late-in-life burst onto the mainstage of fame as the star of a detective show. In the end, James becomes loved by millions for impersonating the father who thought his acting a waste of lawyerly talents.

Meanwhile Cath has settled outside Bridgeport with her "particular friend," Mary Boyle, a nun turned social worker who takes on the horrors of the projects every day while Cath sits at her loom, becoming a cult celebrity, a weaver in the ancient traditions, a curator of forgotten patterns.

Events do occur in the book, sometimes even in rough sequence. James, for instance, comes back to Bridgeport in hopes of making a movie based on his father's infamous case—the one with the 23-year-old wife and the dead soldier in her kitchen. While he's in town doing research, he meets Mary Boyle and, for an afternoon, they become lovers:

"James Bray doesn't know Mary Boyle from Minnie Mouse, from some cute extra, day hire on a film. Their intimacy crisscrossing time is the wily trick of an old Hitchcock thriller; or maybe his coming home, call it that, casts him back to lovesick boy, a role he never had much time for."

But it is the reverberation of events—of Billy Bray's infamous case, of James' interlude with Mary Boyle, of Lilah's breeding her prize mare—that form the center of the novel, for it is really, Howard seems to be saying, the vibrations between us that add up to life, more than our individual actions.

The author is also drawn to the importance of place. Bridgeport, a city in decline through the whole of the Bray children's lives, looms as a character in their story. To give this background its full due, Howard lays out a long middle section of the book—"Double Entry"—with the narrative progressing along the righthand pages while the left-hand ones are cluttered with an old Sears catalog hodgepodge of lore on "The Park City," on P. T. Barnum, who headquartered there (the commissioning in 1945 by Barnum & Bailey's Circus of George Balanchine to choreograph "The Elephants' Polka" to the music of Igor Stravinsky is my personal favorite), portraits of Tom Thumb and Jumbo the elephant, quotes from Louis Aragon, Sigmund Freud, Walter Benjamin, along with scattered diagrams ranging from a scrap of crossword puzzle to one of Buckminster Fuller's Dymaxion car.

"Dip in, flip back or simply read on," Howard instructs the reader, confronted with this peculiar format, and later she quotes Emerson: "All the facts of natural history, taken by themselves, have no value, but are barren like a single sex. But marry it to human history, and it is full of life." Which would seem to be arguing for an amplification of the sort of story that can be told from a single point of view, with an ordinary narrator, leaving out all the bytes of public culture that inform our private affairs. Still, it's sometimes hard to see what Howard hopes to gain by this fragmentation.

Although readers may sometimes get lost in the maze of this book, those who persevere will be amply rewarded. *Natural History* is more than a story; it is an exponential explosion of all our complacent ideas of what a story is, how big it can be, how deep it can run, and how strong the currents are that pass through its wires of connection.

**Richard Eder (review date 25 October 1992)**

SOURCE: "The Fragmentation of Reality," in *Los Angeles Times Book Review,* October 25, 1992, p. 3.

[*In the following review, Eder offers a mixed assessment of* Natural History, *noting that Howard's narrative technique is too unfocused and self-conscious.*]

**Natural History** is a novel about the dissolution of American immigrant values in the second half of the 20th Century, and of our industrial cities where those values once flourished. This, though, is like saying that Magritte's famous painting is about a curved wooden pipe. What the painting really is about is a displacement of reality achieved by the words at the bottom: "This is not a pipe."

Maureen Howard has tunneled beneath her story of what happens over the last 40 years to Billy and Nell Bray of Bridgeport, Conn., and their children, James and Catherine. She lays a train of metafictional gun powder that explodes and scatters the story. She is a powerful writer, and the unexploded bits are shards of a richly mordant family novel.

But Howard senses that such a thing, like Newtonian physics, is not adequate to our times, and that the reality it encapsulates accounts for too little. Unless it is disrupted, her fragmented method suggests, realism cannot convey the simultaneously horrific and trivial quality of Bridgeport's collapse into crack houses, jobless ghettos, welfare deserts and a gutted central city over which the elevated Interstate runs, "draining life like a rubber tube." And the lives of James and Catherine, now in their 50s—he a so-so Hollywood and television actor, she a burned-out magazine researcher who becomes a weaver—cannot be conveyed in linear novelistic terms.

For close to a century, modernists and postmodernists have taken the narrative and bent it, scrambled it, interrupted it, drugged it, argued with it or floated it away altogether: Joyce and Kafka, Pirandello and Unamuno, Georges Perec, Thomas Pynchon and Robert Coover, to take the smallest and most random of samples. Realistic fiction goes on nevertheless, occasionally producing a masterpiece.

Howard's method is to run chunks of straight narration and chunks of undermined narration alternately or side by side, rather chunkily. It is a hybrid and there is a justification for trying it. The result, though, is as fragmented as the method—sometimes effective and frequently laborious.

The first section of **Natural History** is a set of cameos of James' and Catherine's childhood. Billy, their father, is a colorful public figure, the chief detective of the county. Nell, daughter of a wealthy contractor, alternates grandiloquent dreaminess—she goes about in a sealskin coat—and hyperconscientious domesticity. She cooks prodigiously and worries about James, high-spirited and artistic, being run over as he bops around on his bicycle. It is Catherine, formidably serious, who gets hit by a car, though the injury is slight.

The deflected expectation is a key. That tight, high-powered family unit of the 1950s has all kinds of invisible breaches through which a shapeless outside world shows itself. James takes music lessons in a dark, cold house smelling of furniture wax and his Italian music teacher's frustrations. The neighborhood fruit seller suddenly strokes Nell's cheek. The fatherly Greek proprietor of the neighborhood store where James buys his magician's paraphernalia is tied to the mob. And Billy has a corrupt secret.

These childhood scenes are written with a somber magic of recall. They are individually luminous. But in their perfection, there is something deliberately smothering and stagnant. It can't be sustained; and that is Howard's point as, in the following sections, she breaks out into a variety of styles and techniques.

They do much more than tell us a story. At times, as we shall see, they un-tell it. First, there is James at 50, living near Santa Barbara with a prosperous but unfulfilling career in second-rate films. He is married to a former rodeo star who now raises horses. His daughter, whose notebooks are quoted, is a studious adolescent who is forging a suggestive but still undefined artistic voice for the year 2000.

James spars with his wolfish producer. He is offered a lucrative television series playing an old detective. It taps the memory of his father too cheaply; instead, he returns to Bridgeport to scout out a noir-style film about a celebrated murder scandal that Billy once investigated. The producer sees box office; James sees art, the evocation of a lost place and time, and the redemption of his past.

None of this is narrated. Howard writes it as a filmed interview, with cuts, splices, a profusion of camera directions and continual shifts among levels of reality and tone. It is immensely elaborate. The purpose is to replace the richly grounded narrative of childhood with a nervous blurring of the line between what life does and what a camera does. By turns, it is glitzy cliché, wry anecdote and modest reflection.

It is immensely worked; it is hard work to follow, and the effect is to work into the ground the modestly interesting story of James' adult life. Howard's point is that when the world is run by hype and camera angles, these are more real than any story. Real; perhaps so, but also curiously monotonous.

The most distinctive technique comes in a central section. Howard writes her story on the right-hand pages. It tells of James' return to Bridgeport; his encounter with Catherine, who is initially nervous that his film will uncover their father's corruption; his brief love affair with Catherine's house-mate, Mary, and his conclusion, after touring Bridgeport, that the past is too far gone to evoke.

Each left-hand page is a dizzying miscellany. Ranging from snippets to brief essays, there are reports on Bridgeport's statues and bits on such natives as Robert Mitchum and Walt Kelly, Pogo's creator. There are guidebook excerpts, a quotation from Raymond Chandler, and Lincoln praising Bridgeport's fried oysters. There are extended passages on P. T. Barnum, the 19th-Century Bridgeport promoter and hypester who stands for both the city's real glory and the expansive hyper-reality that would make its gritty factories die. There are engravings, doodles and diagrams.

Sometimes, James or Catherine wander briefly over from the right-hand pages, and Barnum makes sorties rightward into James' dreams. Throughout, there is the author's voice, standing up for her miscellanea and grumbling at the novel across the way. By double-entry-accounting principles, she insists, both sides are equal: shivaree and artistic ordering.

Maybe so, but there is a problem. Howard cites Walter Benjamin, the pre-World War II German-Jewish writer and critic, on his proposal for literature as an assortment from which readers can make their own selections and patterns. "In his Arcades project . . . Benjamin expected no less than to alter our relation to the page, to let us *shop,* that's the whimsy, through his chosen topics and cultural totems."

We can shop for oranges; we want them for themselves. Words and images have no value alone; they exist in a context of attention, the author's. We may contest the intention, or the intention may include *renouncing* intention, and that, too, provides a context. It is one that fades, though, and is not susceptible to being used more than once or twice. With Benjamin, it was a scintillating exploration. In Howard's massive application—we lurch back and forth from right-hand to left-hand pages and our attention becomes fixed mainly on when to switch—it is sheer swiveling neck work. It is too self-conscious to succeed.

The most wonderful section in the book is a relatively straightforward narrative. It tells of Catherine's floating and tormented life in New York, and of her hard-won, triumphant stability as a spinner and weaver. After years of promiscuity and a breakdown, she is stumpy, shabby and free; a creator of beauty.

"Straightforward narrative," of course, is a misnomer; the writing pulses around its confines like heat lightning. And it suggests the wild and floating nature of modern life more disturbingly than the more obviously experimental sections do. This is not to deny the power that breaking the narrative can have, but to venture that Howard, stumpy and fierce as her Catherine, is not particularly suited to it. Her most formidable talent, seems to lie in stretching.

**Marc Robinson (review date 9 November 1992)**

SOURCE: A review of *Natural History,* in *New Republic,* November 9, 1992, pp. 46–49.

[*In the following review, Robinson praises the experimental narrative techniques used by Howard in* Natural History.]

Maureen Howard writes about her abiding subject, the family, with fierce rigor, as though she were at the same time writing in defense of the family novel itself. Not for her the cozy domestic zones where passions are labeled and personal histories are smugly untangled into "relationships." In the seven books she has published since 1960, Howard's humor and ready sympathy are buttressed by a stubborn refusal to slim down her people and their stories. She insists on taking her time, conferring on her novels such seriousness that reading them takes time, too. The narratives are bumpy, full of abrupt turns, disconcerting stops and starts. Readers keep busy putting together all the pieces she lays before them. "Come now," she seems to say, "You didn't expect me to do all the work for you."

Howard deliberately makes it impossible to generalize about her families, fending off the sociologists with a barrage of complicating information. "I may have a fatal resistance to abstractions," she wrote in her deft 1978 memoir, **Facts of Life.** Indeed there are few "key" passages in Howard's books where significances are at last spelled out, for she knows that a bald statement, untempered by self-deprecation, risks toppling her entire narrative. Instead Howard works by accumulation of more portable details—totemic objects, deceptively offhand utterances, telling gestures. It's by such small observations—a woman's "frayed Keds sliced for the bunions"; a man unwittingly acquiring his father's favorite conversation starter, "tell me"—that Howard's characters are best measured. They show off new aspects of their personalities with such frequency that we are challenged to keep making acts of recognition, to hold off reaching conclusions. At the very moment someone seems finally to have selected a permanent mask, Howard proposes a contradictory way of looking at him, one that is just as convincing. The "facts of life," the character's life, are constantly in dispute.

In **Bridgeport Bus** (1965), for instance, the character Mary Agnes Keely is ever more inventive at self-renovation, but also determined at times to tarnish her new luster and retreat to familiar ground. Pinkham Strong in **Expensive Habits,** from 1986, renounces his aristocratic breeding and opens an East Village used-clothing store, but also obsessively investigates his family's labelled past. Still another character, Margaret Flood in the same novel, wants to lock into her relationships with friends, offspring, spouses current and ex, yet at the same time longs to get out from under the suffocating attention. She relies on routine—familiar wisecracks, well-rehearsed fumblings in love and enmity—but nonetheless thrills to those times when routine breaks down in a moment of flirtation or blasphemy.

Such mercurial characters occupy a rigid institution like the family only tentatively, and rarely for long. Howard's families are never more vivid than when they dissolve; never more poignant than when they try, and usually fail, to regroup.

Howard's refreshing distrust of psychological consistency and ultimate "meaning" informs her new novel, *Natural History,* making its emotional appeal indirect, unassuming, yet all the more satisfying once found. Again the central figures form a family, and again the family imperfectly coheres, demands to be seen in fragments. But now Howard reaches further, beyond domestic history into histories of places, beliefs, longings, and vices.

In *Natural History* Howard returns to her native Bridgeport, Connecticut, the city fled in **Bridgeport Bus** and later retrieved in **Facts of Life.** This time she comes upon Bridgeport just as it slides from World War II prosperity, when its industries profited handsomely from military contracts, to the gray beleaguerment and dog-eared homeliness it still retains. As the war winds down, Billy Bray is comfortably settled in his tiny fiefdom as county detective, on easy terms with both the district attorney and the local mob, an expert at making his indifference seem charming and masking his bewilderment with banter.

Billy's family doesn't know much more about him than his colleagues do. Nell, his wife, no longer presses him for intimacy and instead tries to obscure her disappointment with elaborate facades. Her efforts only make the sadness more obvious: the woman reared to expect dignity and order in the domestic sphere has never quite given up hoping for a reprieve. She's always tidying shelves of majolica plates and Toby jugs, tearing down cobwebs, patching frayed elbows, or sewing loose buttons tighter—all the while worrying that others will notice the seam, the flaw, the dust.

Nell's daughter, Catherine, inherits some of the same intense self-abnegation. Even at age 11, she's anxious about her salvation, pursued by visions of mortal sin, desperate to learn how to transcend the everyday and give herself over to a redeeming mission. Catherine's brother, James, the fourth corner in the family, also wants a way out of household claustrophobia, but can't imagine what might follow such a violent severance. He is cocky and secretive, in love with movies and magic tricks, able to turn his family into rapt spectators at his performance as son and brother.

"Four faces . . . each dealt a small portion of wrong and pain," Howard writes. But even at its most acute, the pain never quite breaks through the surface of their well-practiced stoicism—even when Billy's detective work takes him into the middle of a tabloid-tailored murder case and he suffers public humiliation from the acquittal of the sulky socialite who shot the soldier on leave. Not for another forty years, with Billy and Nell long dead, would their children, now in their 50s—Catherine a professional weaver, James a Hollywood actor looking for a way to regain his bankable allure—return to Bridgeport and try to identify what, if anything, held the Brays together.

Just as her characters spend most of their lives trying to dodge destined identities and elude the consequences of their past, Howard achieves her own amazing formal sleight of hand, assuming numerous guises in which to tell her story. *Natural History* is a novel always in the midst of breaking free of itself, its pages filled with brilliant variations on the screenplay, the encyclopedia, the diary, and, of course, the history book. In a prefatory note, Howard refers to the novel's "entries," as if *Natural History* were a captain's log.

Acknowledging its affinities with the distinguished tradition of narrative restlessness and genre-trespassing headed by Sterne and Joyce, *Natural History* is part mystery story, part domestic etude, part epic saga. Chapters of telegraphic reflection presented in a clipped first person vie with aloof, majestic narration in other chapters; points of view swerve violently. Often the book jumps literary boundaries altogether and reaches toward the greater tangibility of the collage. A middle section called "Double Entry" presents one story on its right-hand pages and, on the opposite pages, an assortment of drawings, photographs, diagrams, doodles, essays (including a particularly apt homage to Joseph Cornell), and scavenged images and quotations from brochures, calling cards, menus, advertisements, and newspapers—all of which speckle another written version of the Bray chronicle.

With welcome leniency, Howard announces at the start of "Double Entry" that readers should feel free to "dip in, flip back, or simply read on." She learned of the pleasures of multiplicity and distraction, she says, from Walter Benjamin, whose shade hovers over the entire novel as a sort of ideal reader. But Howard doesn't adopt the flaneur's wide-ranging curiosity simply for the amusements available. Such resourcefulness is necessary if she (and her characters) are ever going to understand their relationship to what is remembered. A subtle current of desperation runs beneath the novel—fear at the consequences of not retrieving the past, perhaps, or worry about what might happen if the search is successful—and that tension seems to impel Howard toward greater and greater acts of narrative ingenuity.

Perhaps the atmosphere in *Natural History* is so pressed because, having exerted its attractions in book after book, the city of Bridgeport has assumed an almost mystical awesomeness. Here Howard writes as if she wants to compass and contain its force once and for all. Thus *Natural History* periodically returns to cool descriptions of Bridgeport's layout: at the start Howard explicitly maps the territory, chanting its streets and avenues—North, Parrott, Main, Iranistan, Golden Hill—as if thereby to elicit their secrets one by one. But real information about this town and its citizens isn't so tractable. A long chapter called "Closet Drama," in which the prose is rigged with stage directions and notes about lighting, allows more of one character, James, to come into view. His monologue provides details of his failed marriages, show-biz rivalries and debacles, and a sudden resolution to change his fate, but most of all it allows us to hear his voice. His uneasy blend of chutzpah and self-disgust—his "you bet!" and "babe!" giving way to long silences, stammerings, and blustery impersonations—reveals the soured man hoping to act his way out of himself.

Catherine's lingering, exploratory rhythm is a marked change from her brother's. And still different voices come from Catherine's feisty roommate Mary Boyle, a social worker; Mr. De Martino, an old clarinet teacher; and James's wife, the rodeo-smitten Lilah. Having netted these lives in her imagination, Howard pulls them apart with ever-steady fastidiousness, acquiring their varied languages, dictions, ways of carrying themselves.

If Walter Benjamin is one inspiration for the novel's style, Bridgeport's favorite son, P. T. Barnum, is surely the other. He is a constant presence, captivating in his unabashed love of performance, his tireless search for the extraordinary specimen and dazzling event designed to guarantee enchantment. James is his most obvious emulator, but Barnumism in one form or another overtakes most of the characters. Whenever he's most pinched by a sense of his own weakness, Billy plays up the hardboiled detective role, tossing salty quotables to the adoring reporters. Peaches, a neglected girl under Mary Boyle's care, creates macabre tableaux in her housing project living room, spectacular visions of her mother's many lives and lovers—her way to regain a family. Others in *Natural History* are always self-consciously fretting about how convincing they are as seductress, mover-and-shaker, martyr, or madwoman, as though they still believe that a sharp style can cover up a troubled and troubling substance.

Linguistically acrobatic, imaginatively daring, Howard herself is the most debonair performer in *Natural History*. Her attraction to theater animates many of her previous books; here, however, she gives herself full rein to ponder the form explicitly—in screenplay fragments, in monologues, in musings on the daily circuses at and away from home. This constant experimenting may offer her a way to transcend the sometimes exhausting inwardness of her fiction. With earlier books she reached a challenging impasse, having brought a program of character dissection to its apparent limit and running the risk of ending up in an airless world. Rather than back away from her sensibility and retrench, however, Howard chooses to barrel onward, extending her method of snaring experience to its extreme. Only occasionally does her writing idle ("Closet Drama" has its intermittent longueurs), but in general Howard widens her emotional reach, moving closest to the psychological complexity envisioned in her earliest works.

When *Natural History* does pause in its progress through styles and forms, it is usually to show that Howard has not embraced her narrative strategy uncritically. Her love of spectacle prevails, yet to a degree never reached by her characters she also understands the sham of performance—the actor's flight from sustained scrutiny, the razzmatazz that blinds real insight. A performed self, she cautions, can often become a simplified self. The distrust she brought to family fiction always remains ready to turn on herself: in the increasing flamboyance of her forms, she shows how often she has questioned the rightness of showing off all the tricks, wondered if she shouldn't have been more discreet with her characters and herself.

That mixture of fascination and aversion lends Howard's writing its unusually charged energy. A passage in which she expresses genuine wonder at one aspect of a personality will be followed by a section grounded in "been-there, done-that" tones. Throughout *Natural History*, she sounds jaded, but not yet resigned, disillusionment having made her tougher on the people that catch her attention. She's cosmopolitan company, but also fed-up with the fashionable and weirdly thrilled by Bridgeport's boarded-up buildings in smelly alleys and its aluminum-sided houses with lawn gnomes. Howard negotiates a persona for herself in which the self-mockery doesn't wilt into self-effacement, and in which the confident pace doesn't smooth over the ripples of insecurity, the spasms of self-doubt. A lived life—its disappointments, hard work, minor elations—shows in her prose, her survivor's patter, its don't-waste-my-time jauntiness:

> It's the insupportable present goads me to project on the defenseless past, brings me back like James to better times. He's primed for his movie, his art, which gives us the sensation of living without direct experience of life. Please, forgive me that last if I enter a slight adjustment to the books: I do not talk to any intellect in nature, but am presuming an infinite heart somewhere into which I play—Henry David Thoreau, Dec. 24, 1840. Play—as an actor? Instrument? On a Christmas Eve play into, as to an audience or congregation, surely. Lord, it's good to come up with the answers, but abandon all thought that I am second sight, able to predict from my side that Cath won't on her life, that James will for the hell of it.

Howard's deep skepticism explains why *Natural History* isn't a history at all, and never could be. After rummaging in her characters' lives and roaming the byways of her city, she accepts the deviousness of her prey: the past, she writes, is "unrecoverable." It can't be seen whole, she realizes; its unities are illusory; one looks in vain for its beginning, middle, and end. On its own, the conclusion isn't anything special—what novelist hasn't had to acquire such wisdom?—but what makes it unusual here is Howard's tone: she's elated.

A palpable relief buoys the final chapters of *Natural History*, as the Bray children leave their histories undisturbed. Having come to Bridgeport to scout locations for a movie he's planning about the socialite-and-soldier murder case, James had hoped to unravel the confusion surrounding his father's involvement—but Catherine successfully thwarts him. We know she's right to do so, not just because there is a sordid secret better left unrevealed, but because, once it appears to be understood, the past will be reduced and shelved. It will no longer have the anchoring weight or the cautionary force of mystery.

This novel glows only subtly with a warmth that, for want of a better word, can be called spiritual—yet such is the quality of Howard's faith in the power of description and inquiry. Character and author alike stand before their lives, remembered conversations, emptied rooms, and once-treasured hand-me downs—and persist in contemplation, asking question after question, hoping to articulate these things back into circulation. It is the writer's (and characters') ignorance and the inevitable frustration of their effort at knowledge that keeps them alive. If fiction can ever be said to be "moral," it achieves such stature not in legislating "the moral of the story," but rather in resisting easy catharsis, fixing the reader's attention on the ambiguous and the unanswerable.

**Noel Perrin (review date 22 November 1992)**

SOURCE: "Lost in Bridgeport," in *Washington Post Book World,* November 22, 1992, p. 6.

[*In the following review, Perrin offers a negative assessment of* Natural History, *calling the novel "almost unreadable."*]

In 1965, Maureen Howard published a stunningly good novel called **Bridgeport Bus.** It's about a 35-year-old virgin named Mary Agnes Keeley. She lives in Bridgeport, Conn., with her suffocating Irish mother (her fireman father is dead) and works as secretary to the president of a zipper company. Then she breaks loose and goes to New York. She finds men, adventures, a somewhat better job; she writes one part of the book herself in a surrealistic mode.

Thirteen years later, Maureen Howard published an exceptionally well-written memoir called **Facts of Life.** The central character is another M. K., only this time it is Howard herself. Maiden name: Maureen Kearns. The book tells of her childhood in an Irish section of Bridgeport, Conn., where her father was a policeman. Not a cop on the beat, but a detective—in fact, the County Detective for Fairfield County.

Now Maureen Howard has published an almost unreadable novel called **Natural History.** It's about an Irish family in Bridgeport, Conn., named Bray. Billy Bray, the father, is the County Detective for Fairfield County. Like the Keeleys and the Kearnses, he has two children, a daughter and a son, and they are the principal human characters in the book. Only this time the son gets more space than the daughter.

Lots of artists work a narrow vein. It has been said of Vivaldi that he wrote the same concerto 400 times. Jane Austen's novels could be described as six variations on the theme of upper-middle-class courtship in England around the year 1800. There is no sin in Howard's going back to Bridgeport and to an Irish family of four. The sin is the unreadability of the latest version.

The plot, if you can call it that, runs thus. In 1945, Billy Bray, County Detective, investigates a murder. The slightly sluttish wife of an army major shoots and kills an army private in her bedroom. Detective Bray fails to get her convicted, and the dead soldier's brother stalks the Bray family for a time, planning revenge. He doesn't go through with it.

Meanwhile, the two Bray kids, aged 11 and 13 at the time of the shooting, grow up and leave Bridgeport. You learn their adult histories in bits and snatches, in stream of consciousness, in an interminable imaginary stage-show. Cath, the daughter, goes to a New York, becomes a researcher with *Time*. At some point she turns suicidal, but doesn't go through with it. Instead she moves back to Bridgeport, and now leads a reclusive and mostly unhappy life as a weaver. James, the son, becomes a movie star, has a mostly miserable life, and eventually returns to Bridgeport to make a movie about the shooting. He doesn't go through with it. The book dribbles to an end. It has about as much suspense as a phone book.

But then, Maureen Howard clearly did not intend it to have suspense—or to tell any conventional sort of story. She clearly no longer believes in stories. What does she believe in? Disillusionment. Loss. Human folly.

As far as I can tell, the real character in this book is the city of Bridgeport itself, and the author's purpose is to say goodbye to Bridgeport in two different ways. Goodbye first to the city a child would know—that city so much more perfect than it could possibly ever appear to adult eyes. Goodbye, that is, to the illusion of wise parents, happy neighborhood, secure life.

But second, goodbye to the historical Bridgeport of 1945 (and also the earlier Bridgeport of P. T. Barnum). That city has turned to slums and depression and homeless people in parks, and the book is a kind of wake.

There is much daring in how the wake is presented. One 80-page section, for example, has the "narrative" on right-hand pages only, while on the left-hand pages there is a semi-psychedelic melange. It includes bits of history: a letter from P. T. Barnum to Mark Twain, the entry for Bridgeport in the 1911 *Encyclopedia Britannica*. It also includes poems, quotes from Abraham Lincoln (he liked Bridgeport oysters) and much tightrope dancing by Maureen Howard herself. At one point (right-hand pages) a statue of Barnum comes alive and visits James in his bedroom.

But I have to say: daring, yes; successful, no. Some individual passages are wonderful—Maureen Howard is, after all, a very good writer—but it is hard to imagine the person who would read the whole book for pleasure.

What one can hope is that Howard now truly has Bridgeport out of her system, and is free to apply her great talent to other and perhaps more readily tellable matters.

### Gail Pool (review date December 1992)

SOURCE: "Tales of Two Cities," in *Women's Review of Books,* Vol. 10, No. 3, December, 1992, p. 20.

[*In the following review, Pool argues that the series of "natural, social, and personal histories" portrayed in* Natural History *do not add up to a compelling whole.*]

Anyone seeking to pinpoint the nature of the contemporary novel will have a rough time of it. Wearing old-fashioned stays, postmodern garb, or singular outfits with no designer labels at all, our novels march their many ways, fulfilling the possibilities or landing in the pitfalls of their chosen modes.

Both of these novels, for example, revolve around an American city and family, American lives and life. But from Maureen Howard's Bridgeport, Connecticut, to Marilyn Dorn Staats' Atlanta, Georgia, lies an enormous fictional plain. Staats in her modest first novel invites a traditional suspension of disbelief. Howard in her extravagant sixth does a tango with the very concept of "once upon a time," which she refers to in *Natural History* as the "contract between teller and all children, by which I mean us kids, lead-in to magic remodeling of reality."

In *Looking for Atlanta,* Staats tells a familiar tale, and she tells it in a familiar mode, even if her narrator is unusually situated on her best friend's roof, accompanied by her yardman, Harold, and armed with a bottle of booze. The date of this rooftop vigil is April 17, 1981. The place is an upward-reaching Atlanta suburb. And the narrator is Margaret Hunter Bridges, a "43-year-old lapsed Southern Belle," a former debutante (known in the local parlance as a "Buckhead Pink"), who on her rooftop perch is writing her journal: the story of a life that has veered painfully off its expected course, the story which, at its conclusion, will mark what she calls "the end of my past."

What is it that has brought Margaret to expose herself so shockingly on a rooftop? This is certainly not the behavior prescribed by her mother, whose "favorite credo," found in her well-worn copy of *Mrs. Dull's Guide to Southern Etiquette,* reads: "If something unpleasant is happening, pretend not to notice. To do otherwise would embarrass your guests and family."

At first, the main reason for her transgression appears to be her husband Peter's desertion for a younger woman. I confess I was less than eager to read about yet another fickle male's midlife crisis, however humorously described—and Staats can be very funny, whether describing Margaret's husband or other macho males, her narrow-minded and often mean-spirited friends, or her own comically misdirected efforts. But gradually we come to see that the reason is more complex: it is really the recent death of Margaret's seventeen-year-old daughter Meg that has torn this family apart.

That death was accidental: "'No crime,' the police assured me . . .' Margaret tells us. "'No crime has been committed here.'" But the effects of grief and guilt have been devastating. In one moving sequence, Staats follows Margaret's train of thought from a love scene in *From Here to Eternity* to the various things that can interfere with lovemaking when you've been married a long time. Such as cystitis. Or a bad back. Or perhaps grief. "And when you are grieving," she says,

> one of you may not feel the same way at the same time as the other one of you who is grieving. One of you may just want to lie quietly on her back under the father of her first-born child who died and do nothing at all. And the other one of you may want to do everything in a hurry. He may need to get back at his daughter's death by proving to himself, with angry, pain-inflicting thrusts, that he, at least, is still alive.
>
> (p. 101)

The novel's central issue, then, is not an unfaithful husband, nor is its central question whether he will come home. In fact, Staats treats the marital rift as comedy, even farce, which balances the grimmer issue of grief.

Is Margaret really planning to jump off the roof, as her grandmother did? At no point did I believe that. Hers is a voice too filled with energy and life to be seriously contemplating death. That voice with its frank intelligence, its canny humor, its Southern lilt, carries the novel, lifting it above its weaknesses. This is not to say that Margaret is altogether admirable. For all her silent apologies to Harold, the devoted black yardman who is with her—for her inherited privilege, for the fact of her whiteness—Margaret remains a Southern white woman to the end, much as Harold remains in his old age as subservient as he was in his youth. "We're two anachronisms," Margaret reflects. "Two products of the same dying culture."

With its old-fashioned storytelling and characters, *Looking for Atlanta* may itself strike some readers as an anachronism. It is not a book John Barth would call "technically up-to-date." Maureen Howard's *Natural History* is a different affair. An ambitious, sprawling novel, it draws on an array of artistic techniques to tell its story of the Brays, an Irish family of Bridgeport; to tell the story of Bridgeport; and to tell a story of America itself. Appropriately, the novel includes some violence, celebrity and glitz: it has a murder, a movie-star protagonist and a location that was the operating base of P. T. Barnum, the master of hype.

*Natural History* starts straightforwardly enough, introducing us to the Brays and to Bridgeport, Howard's own birthplace (and the setting of her autobiography *Facts of Life* which received the National Book Critics Circle Award for Nonfiction in 1978). In prose that is sweeping but precise, deftly changing perspectives as she did in her earlier work, Howard focuses on a Saturday in the 1940s. We see Nell Bray, the mother, concentrating on family and home, obsessively concerned for her son; we see her son James, at thirteen already a musician, a magician, a charmer, off to his clarinet lesson; we see his sister Catherine, at eleven already compulsive, determined to win a Girl Scout competition; and we see William Aloysius Bray, a swaggering county detective, investigating the shooting of a soldier by the seductive Isabelle Poole.

In subsequent chapters, Howard turns to other styles as she follows the lives of James and Catherine, "the one child who will always know what he wants and the one who will never get what she wants." Two large sections seem to dominate the book. The first is the long "Closet Drama," a performance piece complete with script directions, in which James, now 52, tells us about his life, his movie career, his second marriage to a beautiful rodeo star, his daughter, and his decision to direct his own film in which he will play his father, a detective investigating the soldier's murder in Bridgeport.

The second large section is titled "Double Entry" and is arranged as a double entry, "the beautiful concept . . . of bookkeeping," the text explains, in which "the debit and credit must always agree." On the right-hand side of the page, the author follows the story of James in Bridgeport, where he has come to make his film and where he meets up with Catherine, who knows a terrible secret about the murder. On the left-hand side of the page, Howard gives us a compendium of excerpts, letters, cartoons, facts relating to Bridgeport, to P. T. Barnum and his show, but also fictions relating to her characters. Here, for example, we have the story of Jumbo, the "best-loved pachyderm," killed by a Canadian freight train in 1885; here we have data on Bridgeport's Arcade and a letter from Barnum to Samuel Clemens.

"If yearning for the outcome," says Howard.

> you may depart this side of the page, read on in the story—the will he? the won't she? whatever will become of? It's your right, the pleasure you take in how they will meet once more—those threads; . . . Read on, flip back, dip in.
>
> (p. 224)

It may be that in this compendium, Howard not only wants to give us Bridgeport but also, like Walter Benjamin, whose Arcades Project she discusses—"a collection of aphorisms, quotes, contemplations accruing to the industrial culture"—she intends "no less than to alter our relation to the page, to let us *shop*, that's the whimsy, through . . . chosen topics and cultural totems . . ." And it may be that in offering this history-album beside her invented story, she is having fun, creating an entertainment.

I only wish that I had found all of this more entertaining. "Closet Drama" struck me as tedious. "Double Entry" seemed to offer on the one hand a less than compelling story of Catherine, now a spinner and weaver, and of James, now making love to Catherine's friend, an ex-nun turned social worker; and on the other hand, an elaborate gimmick. Nor was I especially eager to finish the story, even with Catherine's secret yet to be revealed—the only bit in the novel which, though introduced late, offers some needed momentum.

Maureen Howard is a wonderful writer, and I have enjoyed her earlier works immensely. But this one strikes me as something of a stew. Though she juxtaposes strands of natural, social and personal history, patterns of American hopes and familial ties, she fails to weave these threads together into an enlightening or moving whole. Let me say straight out that I may be in the minority in this opinion. But try as I did to appreciate this work by a very fine writer, I couldn't feel its force.

### Hope Hale Davis (review date 14 December 1992)

SOURCE: "Around and over and about Bridgeport," in *New Leader*, December 14, 1992, pp. 24–25.

[*In the following review, Davis compares Howard's novels to the works of novelist Toni Morrison.*]

Matched in her spectacular range perhaps only by Toni Morrison, Maureen Howard can write in any style she chooses. Almost defiantly she follows her fancy wherever it leads, gathering unlikely personalities along the way. **Natural History** might be called, as one of its characters, P. T. Barnum, in a letter to Mark Twain, called his own most famous production, "a colossal traveling exhibition never before equaled." The novel's multimedia form (well over a hundred pages are screenplay) gives easy passage from coast to coast and across the ocean. Well, not quite easy; multimedia productions on the printed page make their demands. But trust Howard; she always finds her way back to Bridgeport, Connecticut.

As with earlier works, Howard tells her story in separately complete segments. In the first of eight "Museum Pieces," whose title suggests the Barnum Museum in Bridgeport, she describes an imaginary wall map: "The county entire, Fairfield County is shown as fabulously simple, the shallow blue waters of Long Island Sound, the pale green of its slight elevations in Redding and Trumbull, the heavy pink populace of the industrial centers—your city and others, Danbury, Stamford, Norwalk. Less than you imagined; unstoried, general issue, yet you dare not snap it back into oblivion as though . . . as though it is not your jurisdiction."

In that last line Howard may be addressing James Bray, a popular actor who is planning throughout much of the novel to make a serious movie about the life of his father, a Bridgeport police detective until he died relatively young. The film will explore the mystery of his suspicious failure to send to prison a seductive young woman who murdered a World War II soldier.

Or the jurisdiction could rightfully belong to James' neglected younger sister, "Catherine, archivist from age 12, hooked early on queer secrets of the past. . . . Collecting dates, names, inventions, acts of God or man—truth of it all. . . ." By this time middle-aged and a genuine spinster (as craftswoman, she spins the wool she weaves), Catherine has gone to the public library to get out the old newspapers James will need to create the background for the film she desperately wants him not to make.

Or the author may be addressing herself, conceding her own need to keep searching among the detritus turned up from her continuing Bridgeport dig. Passionate about possible secrets, she is ambivalent about revealing them.

The characterization of Catherine as archivist occurs in a section called "Double Entry," laid out in facing pages set in contrasting type. The left-hand pages, devoted to Bridgeport history, mostly from contemporary sources, are in boldface and inventively illustrated. Tom Thumb, the Siamese twins and Jenny Lind appear among hundreds of charming old linecuts. This section also uses lists, statistics, descriptions of gifts to the Barnum Museum from celebrities, poems (apparently the author's own), and scores of quotations, ranging from Sherlock Holmes to Oliver Wendell Holmes, all relating to Bridgeport legends. But Howard frees herself from rules: On a historical page she doesn't hesitate to speak directly to the reader or her characters and even add to their stories, which we expect to find on the facing pages.

*Natural History* might cause her fans to wonder if Maureen Howard had made a New Year's resolution to abstain from straightforward sentences. Here Lilah Lee, James' rodeo star third wife, gives a hint of her life before she became an anthropology student: "Sold myself to the horses, but inevitable as my tumble in the dust, I fell for one of those cowboys . . . another and another, bare-assed in bare rooms. Fairly innocent men, not always nice, mostly timid fellas who switched channels to find Westerns on TV. Crossing fully into their world, because the motel rooms were too empty or when the satin shirt and boots were off for the night, riding for the crowd was being no one."

Howard attracted a following with her first two novels, *Not a Word about Nightingales* and *Bridgeport Bus*. But in 1976, with the publication of the third, her unwillingness to pander to those looking for an easy read brought a warning from the Library Journal that *Before My Time* was only "for discriminating readers." Three years later, with the appearance of her memoir *Facts of Life*, described by one reviewer as a "caustic, sarcastic, unaffectionate memoir," the Journal sounded another alarm: "Recommended only for libraries where her novels are popular." Yet in 1986 critics called her novel *Expensive Habits* the work of "a brilliant comic writer." And *Grace Abounding* (1982) begins with a delightfully bawdy scene in which a middle-aged heroine driving home from a grim visit to her aged mother enlivens the trip with fantasies about the variously succoring males who might rescue her after the blowout of a tire she purposely keeps in a perilous condition.

Here we have an author who has fun using her talents. Too much, perhaps, if you think of fun as self-indulgence. She seems to write around and over and about Bridgeport to assuage the urgencies of her own obsessions, her compulsion to go back and keep touching the personal wounds that never heal.

Therein, I think, lies the difference between Maureen Howard and Toni Morrison. Though Morrison writes about individuals, their lives connect with great concerns. Big things have happened in Bridgeport, too; far bigger than Barnum's Museum with all its campy fascination. Howard tells of Elias Howe and the invention of sewing machines, but nothing of the life of the people who made them. Early in the century the Bridgeport factory workers never saw winter daylight from one week's end to the next. Wasn't it there that the women, desperate, placed their bodies on the pavement, blocking the rinks coming to break their strike? In the whole section devoted to Bridgeport history we find no mention of such crucial moments.

Phone calls between James Bray and Hollywood types take up much of *Natural History.* From these, for all the dialogue's acuteness, we learn nothing new. But the reader will surely remember and respond to the brief passages telling of Catherine's social worker roommate visiting a Bridgeport housing project. There she develops an almost demented yearning to adopt and give a future to the spunky, talented seven-year-old daughter of a drug-pushing prostitute. Howard employs all her offhand, unsentimental mastery of specifics to make us suffer through these scenes.

Good writers, even remarkable writers, can limit themselves to their own families. But the great writers, while telling about people they know, somehow by illuminating those lives manage to shine light beyond them, on the world outside. I hope her glimpse of that beguiling child of the project, with vermin in her curls, has caught Howard's imagination and opened her eyes to great new vistas, even in Bridgeport.

### Merle Rubin (review date 14 December 1992)

SOURCE: "Novel Strains for Effect," in *Christian Science Monitor,* December 14, 1992, p. 12.

[*In the following review, Rubin offers a negative assessment of* Natural History, *criticizing the novel's format and structure.*]

Maureen Howard's much-heralded novel *Natural History,* is a penitential, quasi-Joycean chronicle/collage that purports to do for Bridgeport, Conn., what James Joyce did for Dublin. Winner of a National Book Critics Circle prize for her memoir *Facts of Life,* and the author of five previous novels, Howard is a sincere and serious writer. Her intentions are doubtless worthy, but this novel never gets off the ground.

The central characters are an American family of Irish descent, the Brays, whom we first encounter during the later years of World War II. Jovial Billy Bray, the father, is a crackerjack police detective. His wife Nell is a gentle, extremely overanxious woman who can scarcely stand hearing her husband mention, let alone divulge any details of, cases he is working on. Murder, rape, arson—even graft and petty corruption—distress her deeply.

The Brays have two children. James is a musically talented lad who loves practicing magic tricks. Catherine is a stolid, bright, hardworking, rather humorless girl. The glimpses of their childhood we are shown are singularly ungalvanizing: James going to his clarinet lesson, Catherine putting together a painstaking cardboard display about the history of cotton for a Girl Scout competition. The next thing we know, they're adults: James has become a reasonably successful film star, on his second marriage (to an ex-rodeo queen). Catherine, following a brief stint as a wise-cracking New York career gal all too popular with opportunistic married men who love her and leave her, has retreated to Bridgeport, making her living as a spinster/weaver. (Her work is prized on the artsy-craftsy circuit.)

James has taken it into his head to make a movie about an old murder case his father was involved in: the story of a rich, brassy woman who shot a soldier and got away with it. He plans to play the part of his father, the investigating detective. Catherine, however, is afraid of raking up the past. James's agent, a standard-issue tough cookie, is not very keen on the idea either—for commercial reasons. The same holds true for James's crony Morty Ziff, a predictably crass and foul-mouthed Hollywood producer. The space devoted to reproducing the unbelievably trite conversations between James and his showbiz buddies is in itself reason to wish that an editor had taken things in hand.

Eschewing straightforward chronological narration, Howard has divided her novel into 10 sections, wildly varying in style and format. Everything she tries, from a screenplay-style depiction of the actorish James to a postmodern, Jacques Derridan escapade involving parallel texts on the right- and left-hand pages (called "Double Entry"), has been done before and done much better. Having to wade through leaden pages of this hand-me-down, avantgarde style is like watching someone shuffle endlessly though a worn deck of playing cards.

Even in the first, most promising section, which introduces the Brays and Bridgeport, the characters are fuzzily drawn and their lives made to seem less interesting than any life has a right to be. Here, for instance, is the mother, Nell:

> "She heads downhill, down home, still hoping to see the flash of her boy's red head and a bike. Sad fact, the garbage men are at her drive, and James, whose job it is, has not put the trash cans to the curb. She hefts them against her, twice stumbling down the back path, thank God in time."

Alas, we seldom get to see Nell when she is *not* worrying about James on his bike or about the trash cans. Or occasionally, worrying about her husband.

Never using one word in place of six or seven, never missing an opportunity to incorporate a cliché or echo a dull phrase from her own previous paragraph, Howard proceeds to drain any vestige of life from her characters and their story.

In place of storytelling and character development, Howard offers a pseudo-anthropological assortment of facts and artifacts.

In "Double Entry," James meets the spirit of Bridgeport-based showman P. T. Barnum on the right-hand pages, while the left-hand pages feature a collage of pictures, miscellaneous facts, authorial asides, and pretentious references to everyone from Emily Dickinson to the ever-so-chic Walter Benjamin. The reader is invited to build his or her own narrative by picking and choosing among the offerings.

But the offerings in this section and throughout the book are not very tempting. A dash of family saga, a soupcon of film-noir murder mystery, a clumsy swipe at Hollywood, and a straining for postmodern special effects: This hodgepodge of prefabricated odds and ends does justice neither to the fictitious Bray family nor the real-life city of Bridgeport.

**Pearl K. Bell (review date 1993)**

SOURCE: A review of *Natural History,* in *Partisan Review,* Vol. LX, No. 1, 1993, pp. 68–70.

[*In the following review, Bell argues that* Natural History's *"uncontainable ingenuity" overshadows the novel's plot.*]

The hero of Maureen Howard's *Natural History* is Bridgeport, Connecticut, where she was born and bred in an Irish Catholic family. A once-thriving manufacturing center on Long Island Sound, Bridgeport, like many such industrial towns of New England, fell victim to blight and decay after the Second World War. In several of her novels and the memoir *Facts of Life,* Bridgeport has been Howard's Dublin, the native ground that has possessed her imagination with the ferocious tenacity of a demon—the demon of memory—that will never let her go. In this new, enormously ambitious and eccentric novel, Howard concentrates on yet another Irish Catholic family, the Brays, whom we first meet toward the end of the War.

Billy Bray, the father, is a swaggering county detective; his wife Nell, who "married down," is chronically worried about her teenage children, James and Catherine, and tries to exorcise her amorphous anxieties in fanatical housekeeping. James is obsessed with magic tricks and movies; Catherine is an earnest Girl Scout, miserably unsure of herself and dreamily pious. Suddenly the family romance is thrust aside by a murder (*again!*) that Billy is assigned to investigate in a nearby town. An aggressively sexy woman, whose husband is a major in the Army in Italy, has shot a young soldier. She claims the soldier followed her home from a local tavern and was plainly up to no good. Years after the murder, which relentlessly haunts the Bray children, Catherine suspects that Billy had treated himself to the sexual favors of the accused woman and made sure she was acquitted. It is never explained, however, why her father's supposed transgression plagues Catherine well into middle age.

But any attempt to convey what passes for plot in **Natural History** is doomed, for Howard has a great deal more than straightforward narrative in mind. As it develops—or rather, flits hither and yon with antic restlessness—the novel becomes a pinwheel of history: by turns an assemblage, a jigsaw puzzle, a scrapbook, a hodgepodge, a three-ring circus (the exploits of the great showman P. T. Barnum, a luminary of Bridgeport, play a prominent part in the book), a recycling bin, a screenplay, and much more. Within bits of murky suggestion and fragments of fact, we learn that James becomes a Hollywood actor. When he realizes his film career isn't going anywhere, he decides to return to Bridgeport to make a movie about the wartime murder, in which he will play the father-detective. Thus the long chapter called "Closet Drama" takes the form of a screenplay, complete with lighting and stage directions, that wanders erratically through James's movie career, marriages and children, his unrealistic expectations about the film, and his sister's opposition to the whole idea because it might expose the unsavory truth about their father.

But the display of Howard's uncontainable ingenuity in "Closet Drama" is only one segue. Midway through **Natural History,** she embarks on the most arduously daring of extravagant improvisations, an eighty-page section called "Double Entry" (as in bookkeeping, presumably because the author is totting up the debits and credits of the Bray family and of Bridgeport). Splitting the text literally, Howard offers, in the right-hand pages, the story of James's ill-fated movie, which he eventually abandons; his affair with a former nun turned social worker; and Catherine's return, after some catastrophic years in New York, to Bridgeport, where she becomes a famous spinner and weaver. In the left-hand pages, Howard jumbles memory and history, collective and personal, in a mad anthologist's mishmash of quotations (from Sir Thomas Browne to Walt Disney); Bridgeport lore, including the fact that the city was once the leading American manufacturer of corsets; a rummage sale of miscellaneous pop-culture Americana, old engravings, photos, and greeting cards; a tribute to crusty Jasper McLevy, the Irish Socialist roofer who was mayor of Bridgeport for many years; movies and movie houses; the collage boxes of Joseph Cornell; a lengthy detour into Walter Benjamin's thoughts about the arcades of Paris (because Bridgeport once boasted a beautiful arcade of its own); and ending with the world-shaking revelation that Robert Mitchum, no less, was born in Maureen Howard's beloved hometown.

Once we stop to catch our breath—or nudge ourselves awake—after this breakneck roller-coaster ride, we begin to guess what Howard is attempting: to defy the evanescence of memory, to confront the irrecoverability of the past in its living wholeness, to lament the irrevocable dissolution of vanished experience, yet clinging to whatever connections we can impose on the bits and pieces that have endured. Yet all these free associations remain ambiguous, irresolute, and exhausting, in part because the very shapelessness of her "evidence" is self-defeating, in larger part because of her style. Fussy and overburdened, the sentences are so clotted or fidgety that we can't find our way out of the maze. With all the brio and wit that Howard has lavished on her pursuit of lost time, she has not illuminated the past but buried it under the clutter.

### Irving Malin (review date 12 February 1993)

SOURCE: "On the Other Hand . . . ," in *Commonweal*, February 12, 1993, p. 23.

[*In the following review, Malin offers a positive assessment of* Natural History, *complimenting the novel's complexity and depth.*]

***Natural History*** deserves more than a brief review. It moves on at least three levels: it is, first, a study of the Bray family—Billy and Nell, the parents, and James and Catherine their children; it is also a study of "history," a meditation, if you will, on what the word means not only to the Bray children but to all who want to recapture the "past" and discover that it never existed as implacable fact; it is, finally about the "mix" of art and reality, of "word" and "world." These three levels, in effect, do not move in any linear manner; thus any page of the novel combines the various levels and, indeed, makes them into a maze of meaning, an epistemological labyrinth.

If, for example, we simply read the story of Billy Bray, we discover that his life is dominated by one event—the investigation of the murder of a soldier by a woman who pleads self-defense. I underline investigation because we eventually learn that in the investigation, any exploration of motives is unclear. Bray, who works as a detective for the state government, offers one version of the murder. But this version is a perversion; it is his story; it does not account for the full complexity of the event.

And Bray's investigation is viewed in different ways. Catherine, a spinster at age fifty, recognizes that her childhood and adulthood have, in a mysterious way, been shaped by Bray's testimony. She lives alone because she cannot ever be sure about the motives of men, including those of her brother James. An actor (of limited ability),

James has been influenced by his father; he has refused to accept "ordinary" happenings. He tries to rewrite—or, better yet—to recreate Billy in a movie he wants to sell to his agent.

The second level of the novel has as its setting more than the "private" Bridgeport or Bray family. It is a bold "double entry" into the way "history" is an odd, mysterious fiction. Perhaps the centerpiece of the novel is the section called "Double Entry." We are told that in "the beautiful concept of double-entry bookkeeping the debt and credit must agree; no inaccuracies or altered circumstances are admitted. . . ." This section of the novel can be read in several ways; we can read the fascinating references to Bridgeport in the life of P. T. Barnum, Lincoln, and other famous historical figures. (Barnum is, perhaps, the secret hero of the novel because he was not only a citizen of Bridgeport but a genius who recognized the need to carry history into the unreality of life. Indeed, he saw history—whatever it is—as a kind of duplicity, a hoax, a stage show.) On the right-hand side of this section of Double Entry we can continue to read about the Brays. Howard is, in a sense, questioning the relation of private and public history, of those uncanny associations which can never be correctly explained. She writes: "Double entry, designed to place equivalencies . . . when something is missing . . . when something is lost, you simply set down a number on the other side of the page to compensate, reconcile . . . as if to balance, naturally . . . as if to insist that the beautiful system must hold."

The "beautiful system" in effect, leads us to the third level of the novel. What exactly is the relationship of language to life? Can words ever capture life? Is it possible to describe those longings which lie at the heart of "simple" Billy or James? It is interesting to note that Howard ends her "double entry"—now notice the dark pun!—with a series of speculations on vowels. She is aware that "a" or "e" or "o" are symbols; they exist because they began as "pictures": "In the beginning was the picture. It was the initial A, peak and crossbar simpler than drawing of horse upon the wall of cave."

The three levels intersect in our minds. We recognize that we can never understand "nature" or "history" in any completely rational way. We crosscut events and motives in an unconscious way. We manipulate them—or are manipulated by them?—so that our constructions are in continual flow, refusing finality.

Perhaps the invisible message of the entire novel is that humanity is flawed, that it can never know unearthly designs.

### George O'Brien (essay date Spring 1993)

SOURCE: "Assimilation Blues: Maureen Howard's *Facts of Life*," in *MELUS*, Vol. 18, No. 1, Spring, 1993, pp. 95–102.

[*In the following essay, O'Brien explores the themes of assimilation and ethnic identity in* Facts of Life.]

Narratives of exile and immigration arguably bring into sharper focus than other autobiographical modes the concept identified by Philippe Lejuene as "the autobiographical pact."[1] One reason why this may be the case is that there is an implicit struggle in autobiography, an application to the self of the sense of confrontation and critique that is applied to the objective world in Realist fiction. The experience typified and challenged in both Realist fiction and autobiography can, very generally, be called change. And in the age of capitalism, which also happens to be the age when change has become the structural principle of both social reality and the models of identity to which that reality gives rise, no change is more comprehensive than that articulated by the immigrant experience. Its comprehensiveness may be appreciated not only with regard to the actual immigrant generation itself, but also in view of its lingering effects on subsequent generations.

Quite apart, therefore, from its numerous artistic excellences and from the fact that its combination of detail and insight make it a unique record of the Irish-American experience of embourgeoisement,[2] Maureen Howard's *Facts of Life*[3] functions as a meditation on the mercuriality of an identity trained in, but not conditioned by, a strong awareness of ethnicity. The roots of the tension between training and self-awareness that pervades Howard's novels are explored in a way that reveals the limitations of identity conceived of solely in terms of its ethnic origins and the problematic shapelessness of identity conceived of without an adequate negotiation of those origins.

The vehement panache of Maureen Howard's *Facts of Life* is not just a matter of style, a matter of applying the cosmetics purchased through a Smith education and life in academia (if "life" is what institutions offer academic wives). The ability to put on the makeup is certainly there:

> I wish someone had noted for art's sake—it is pure Chekhov—my grandfather's feelings when he bought the property on which he was to build his grandiose house from Mr. and Mrs. William Abbott Parrott, the faded Yankee gentility for whom his mother had served as the Irish maid.
>
> (97)

More often than not, though, "art's sake" is beside the point. A sardonic, satirical, self-mocking tone announces its impatience with high gloss and finishing school and the assumption that one of the objects of experience is syntactical etiquette.

> Time and again the social surface doesn't hold good. My lace mantilla lay gently folded in a puff of tissue paper: it was finer than the veils the parish girls would wear (always, always finer, the single tedious note of our supposed distinction). My white gloves buttoned at the wrists with pearls. These clothes would never be worn. I picked up a grapefruit knife and tried to commit suicide.
>
> (34)

This, from later life, of a literary luncheon: "There was something pure in the utter filth of the experience" (117). Writing, here, is not an apology for order. Its force and conviction derive from its resistance to conferred codes, a resistance all the more winning for the attempts to identify with those codes—whether they are the attitudes (posture, deportment and declamation as the budding daughters of middle-class Bridgeport should embody them) or as a faculty spouse: "My education and career were sham intentions, smart mid-century substitutes for the embroidery work and social graces of an earlier time" (73).

Is there an alternative to belonging? Not on your life. But it seems that there is also no alternative to the pressures that ostensibly belonging brings. The question forever naggingly remains, belonging to what?

Maureen Howard organizes her "life" and its "facts" in three categories—culture, money and sex—one of the effects of which is to remind the reader of race, class and gender. And an obvious case might well be made for the synonymity of class and money, gender and sex. Maureen Howard doesn't make it, possibly because of its banality, though possibly also because issues of empowerment and disenfranchisement arise more predictably in the context of these two categories. They've entered our awareness. They're easier to assimilate, seem prominent in public discourse. They may even be related: sex is a kind of money, gender a sub-set of class. Or at least to say something like this tends to be less provocative than to speak about the possibly denaturing effects culture—the normality of manners, the quotidien participation in "civilized society"—can have on race, a category which, like many others, culture believes it can control by erasing.

Whatever inherent interest culture and race possess, intersections between them are of interest if only because of the interminable dialogue of the deaf that the two categories seem to carry on in America. Perhaps the dialogue only seems that way because of the difficulty the immigrant has in getting a hearing, or because a hearing only seems plausible when mimicry is the mode of articulation. Chico Marx says, "wadsa madda for you?" We laugh, being given to believe we know what he means. The black butler is by definition happy in his work, we accept him (he's presented as acceptable) because he's always smiling, according to the popular image, according to an image the very transmission of which defines the power of cultural institutions. The image validates that power, not the subject upon which it feels free to draw. Notre Dame sports teams are nicknamed "The Fighting Irish"—but that's different (we're different), that's good, clean fun: no harm meant, no harm done, don't be so sensitive, all it means is that we Irish have made it. . . .

Maureen Howard is not an immigrant, though. She comes to us by way of a Seven Sisters education, university teaching, publications with the brightest and best in toney journals. So why is so much of her story taken up by contests against images of conformity, with distinguishing oneself in terms but against the grain of institutional standards and expectations, with a persistent sense of breaking off, breaking out, breaking away? Partly—the understandable part?—because of admissions like these:

> I said yes to the academic poetry of that time which had grown out of stale criticism [the scene is Kenyon College] and yes to the limp refined productions of Shakespeare that had begun to seep out of our new repertory theaters over the fetid landscapes of high culture and yes to the staggering simplifications of all the Abstract Expressionists, because—ever aiming to please I had let myself be told.
>
> (78)

But partly too, perhaps, because her origins were Irish. This part is more obscure, less easy to find a language for, rooted in a landscape whose character, whose difference, seems to exist because it was the site of those first, formative rejections and resistances. If life at Kenyon was "a colonial existence which seemed unreal even as I lived it," (79) that may have been because it was all too reminiscent of the limbo of designated culture that was the author's girlhood. "Colonial" seems to mean here vulnerable, adrift, frontier in the depressing sense, marginal—terms which are usually associated with the colonized.

The point here is not so much an uncharacteristic verbal lapse as an expression of the difficulty in establishing a place to be, a difficulty which culture is supposed to render recognizable and then sublimate (green thoughts in green shades). A more complicated example of the same bifocal state of mind may be elicited from the following. Northrop Frye, on a visit to Kenyon, gives "the impression of a generous man, so committed to his work that he could not fathom my triviality" (78). Compare the man of culture's impact with that of Jasper McLevy, "the famed Socialist mayor of Bridgeport" (3). He is presented only to be satirically dismissed by the author's mother with the help of "Ah, did you once see Shelley plain" (3). The dismissal is replicated by "famed"—the very thing McLevy is not.

What is of interest here is not drawing attention to those occasions on which the author's language seems to say the opposite of what it means, or to note the empty irony of the dismisser dismissed, much less to accuse the author of snobbery, or even to make a case for the rehabilitation of McLevy on the grounds that one more anecdote about Northrop Frye is of much less interest than a word or two, however cursory, on what "socialist" meant in Bridgeport long ago.[4] Rather—as in the case of the dual applicability of "colonial" and "colonized"—what emerges most convincingly is the writer's position between high and low, between the preacher and the converted, between local and international, between home and world. The position could be that of a person undergoing both the inevitability of assimilation and the failure of assimilation to be completely successful or credible. The position could be that of the writer negotiating between the various versions of being declasse and marginal, between origin and apotheosis, between facts and the life that they betoken.

What her mother experienced as contradictory, the author takes fully conscious responsibility for by making it problematic.

> I sensed that my mother was a misfit from the first days when, dressed in a linen hat and pearls, she walked me out around the block. She was too fine for the working-class neighborhood that surrounded us. (4) At Smith College she was homesick but stuck it out. She dare not disappoint her father. One of the social clubs was called the AOH, mocking the Ancient Order of Hibernians, and the members took shanty Irish names— Mudeater O'Climint and Annie Rooney Terhune. She made tea dates and went on happy walks with a few friends. In the name of the Burns family she read Heine and Schiller, Faust and more Faust. The answers to mathematical problems that no one could solve in class came to her in her dreams.
>
> (100)

Mother is a misfit because she has espoused culture, dragging the young Maureen and her brother to concerts, citing and reciting fragments from years of spare time immersed in minor and not so minor poetry, establishing standards, suggesting roles, indicating paths onward and upward, *per ardua ad astra,* the *ne plus ultra* of the immigrant's dream of education (not that she is an immigrant either: she is faithful to her immigrant father's educational designs for her, however, not daring to disappoint). Mother's father, Grandpa Burns the asphalt magnate, is a "provincial patriarch" (102). He designs and builds a car, "the supreme American machine" (103)—Maureen Howard quotes from a book produced to commemorate this automotive phenomenon. The book contains a story of pleasurable escapism in the form of a world tour. At the end, the lucky lady tourist in question, widow of an industrialist,

> stands midst her souvenirs looking out the window of the anvil works on the flourishing cornfield by the Delaware River where she hopes, magnificently, to build homes for all her men and their families. There are no trade unions, no anarchists, nor is there any child labor in the land. It is the willed romance of the early twentieth century.
>
> (102)

Culture is a vehicle to the promised land, en route to which Mickishness and its squalid struggles are jettisoned. To be cultured is the assimilationist dream. To be cultured is to be as empowered as one's masters, to speak their language. Culture is a replica of wealth, internalized, edifying, sanitary, harmlessly acquired, beneficiary retained. Grandpa Burns's car was a flop, but the "willed romance" of its fetishism persists. And, in Maureen Howard, persists with such completeness that only interrogation, challenge and repudiation will preserve it, will preserve its true nature: "what the past will yield if we are truthful" (51). True nature is a tendentious, not to mention arrogant phrase. A nature that is more satisfying to behold because rendered more complexly, rather than as a rationale, rather than as the kind of response to cultural experience articulated by the author's father.

> I'm circling back to the problem of Joseph McCarthy. I have refused to understand my father's admiration for that twirp who manipulated two Presidents. I have tried to justify his allegiance on the grounds that my father wanted revenge, along with the Senator from Wisconsin, on a society that had treated the Irish like guttersnipes and cartoon drunks when he was a kid.
>
> (67–8)

Such a scenario seems just as far-fetched as the existence of a socialist mayor of Bridgeport. But it might well be just as true. And it is a scenario that is difficult to come to grips with, speaking as it does of bitternesses, resentments and frustrations that are hardly convincing watchwords of assimilation. The escapism of culture and its mythology of assimilation (the best things in life are free) are more understandable than a politics of vengeance, articulated by the patriotic Senator in terms of purity and danger, terms that delimit the immigrant's hope and his voyage towards it, his ghetto (sorry, neighborhood) and the world beyond it. Better culture than race. Better Faust, a thousand times, read in a chilly dorm, late into the night, alone, in the cause of self-improvement and rising in the world and belonging.

Part of the conviction of *Facts of Life* is Maureen Howard's awareness that she is saying something that has not been said before. This awareness underlies much autobiography, understandably, with its interest in recuperation, rehabilitation, naming of unfamiliar parts, coloring in a landscape where a cultural desert was thought to have existed. Chicago or Boston may be thought worthy of the quality of attention she brings to her story—but Bridgeport? Chicago and Boston would have furnished different books, however, less intimate, a little more predictable perhaps, whereas the very unlikelihood of Bridgeport seems to make for piquancy: its anonymity is given its alter ego in the notoriety and daring of Maureen Howard's view of it. She makes it complex, the way real places are supposed to be. In her hands it both is and is not "a vaudeville joke of a town" (11). And all the details are in place, the way they tend to be in autobiography, presented as an inventory of personal and family appurtenances, but utterly familiar as soon as they're mentioned. Whoever writes his or her life turns out to have written the lives of many.

And, being autobiography, tension between a self that longs and a world that lures is only to be expected, with routines and rituals of assimilation as temporary reliefs from the tension. Race and roots are what you belong to; culture what you grow into. Everybody who might read this book has been somewhere within its orbit. We are all educated, we all leave, we are melted down, recast. We can't go home again. Here again, strictly from the point of view of genre and without belittling the qualities or diminishing the pleasures of *Facts of Life,* Maureen Howard has not done anything exceptional by reminding us of a generation's uncertain but distinctive trajectory from home to world. It's the same old story, the one about identity as a venture capitalist's prospectus, a tale of virginity and how to lose it, all too familiar, yet ever fresh in each retelling, with Listerine-breathing nuns and boyfriends from rough neighborhoods, "Catholics in good standing, pure potato-famine Irish, gone fine with our cut glass and linens from McCutcheon's" (13).

What gives *Facts of Life* its urgency and its pointed, rather flaying, style is that it also speaks of something unmeltable, irreducible: At the shaded, turreted Academy of Our Lady of Mercy the nuns all but insisted that my body was on loan like a library book or a company car. My arms and legs but above all my womanly appurtenances, mons veneris, the very curve and tilt of my womb existed for a higher purpose. How many years has it taken to claim myself—big ass, caesarean scar, broad hands good for scooping potatoes out of the dirt of Killarney . . . the mockery, will I ever leave off. (172)

Probably not, if we're lucky (in answer to those last words). And it's not that the earthy coalescence of the feminine and the Irish should be noted in order to clinch some kind of case. There isn't a case to be made, because the making of cases is part of the process of assimilation, tending to standardize in terms of a prefabricated good what should be allowed its own particularity and distinction. Maureen Howard is nowhere more convincing than when she shows how she could not be institutionalized. Besides, that's not a particularly well-written sentence, its fragmentariness seemingly enacting a resistance to what it seeks to order. (And in any case, Killarney dirt . . . ?! Or is that a joke at the expense of Emerald Islers?)

What seems new is the celebration—mordant, ironic, merciless, restless, as is often the condition of the autobiographing "I"—of certain energies that have resisted virtually everything to which they've been attracted. There's something here that is a continual going on from, as *Facts of Life*'s closing paragraph (to cite the most obvious instance) winningly attests:

> I am walking up lower Madison Avenue in an old straw hat, circa 1918. Yes, always the heightening. The last golden hour of the day. Everything is clear: the rose marble of the Morgan Library, mahogany bushes, tulips on the verge. Soon to marry, I am twenty-three years old in a blue suit, size eight. Natural time. I hardly touch ground the last blocks to Grand Central, but come triumphantly to rest alone on Forty-second Street, on the edge of evening. I am beginning. My life is beginning which cannot be true.
>
> (182)

There's something here that, by being a continuum of uncertainty, is true to life. And it isn't even that that in itself is new, particularly (there's no intention, much less need, to Molly-Bloomify the author)—though one respects and is glad for "always the heightening," which is undoubtedly one way to characterize unassimilable energy. More than that, it seems that what *Facts of Life* most powerfully and poignantly reminds us of is how few books there are like it, how little known they are (beyond *Memories of a Catholic Girlhood* and *Harp*), how prone we seem to be to representing ourselves in the cultural graffiti of Greenery—proofs, perhaps, of assimilation and its discontents.

*Notes*

1. Philippe Lejeune, *Le Pacte Autobiographique* (Paris: Editions de Seuil, 1975). The theoretical essay on which this volume is based appears in translation in Philippe Lejeune, *On Autobiography,* translated by Katherine Leary (Minneapolis: U of Minnesota P, 1989): 3–30. In his foreword to this volume, Paul John Eakin summarizes the concepts as follows: "In effect, the autobiographical pact is a form of contract between author and reader in which the autobiographer explicitly commits himself or herself not to some impossible historical exactitude but rather to the sincere effort to come to terms with and to understand his or her own life."

2. Unique as to quality of recall and formal complexity, as comparisons with Mary McCarthy's *Memories of a Catholic Girlhood* (New York: Harcourt, Brace, 1957) and John Gregory Dunne's *Harp* (New York: Simon and Schuster, 1989) readily reveal.

3. Maureen Howard, *Facts of Life* (Boston: Little, Brown: 1978; New York: Penguin, 1980). Subsequent citations to Penguin edition.

4. A treatment of the life and times of Jasper McLevy may be found in Maureen Howard, *Natural History* (New York: Norton: 1992) at the conclusion of the "Double Entry" section, facing pp. 295–97.

## Paula Friedman (review date 25 January 1998)

SOURCE: "Millennium Light," in *Los Angeles Times Book Review,* January 25, 1998, p. 6.

[*In the following review, Friedman offers a positive assessment of* A Lover's Almanac.]

"Lightness is his affliction," Louise Moffett says of her lover Artie in Maureen Howard's comic tour de force, *A Lover's Almanac,* a novel about love, art and life precariously poised at the edge of the third millennium. Patching into the narrative excerpts from works dating as far back as the Greek and Roman classics and as contemporary as the lyrics of a Joni Mitchell song, Howard extends the boundaries of her love story into a broader meditation on Western thought. The story begins on New Year's Eve 2000 with Artie and Louise frenetically celebrating at a party somewhere near Central Park in New York City. The evening's disaster and the central breach in the relationship between Louise and Artie occur when, having drunk too much champagne, he playfully spills his drink down the front of Louise's blue retro silk dress, an act that pushes her to the end of her patience with him: ". . . for can it be that one night can unravel their years, one rotten night of Artie's misdemeanors? The answer is yes. Her Artie will never give up on his lightness. And the years that stretch ahead offer a diminishing view in which he will never change."

This "lightness" and the "hedging ironies," reflected both by the couple and by the age itself, prove limiting, Howard suggests, making it difficult for her characters to spontaneously express themselves. Louise, an artist—who had become "somewhat famous" for her Botanicals, paintings of trees in which the foreground is made background and the background is blown up, intricately detailed, creating a "simple reversal of scale"—finds herself limited to ironic mockery in most of her work. Having been raised on a dairy farm in a manner she found stifling, Louise makes the family operation—brimming with cows, silos and barns—the subject of much of her work. Artie, a New Age computer whiz, works for his friend Boyce "designing plausible graphics . . . stylish bar charts and pies, seductive pictograms out of mightily inferential statistics." Artie's work is big on flash and low on purpose.

With well-aimed but playful pokes, Howard hints that her confused characters have plenty of talent but find themselves lacking any solid perspective. This problem is not peculiar to Louise and Artie, Howard implies, but one that has characterized the frantically uncertain atmosphere of an age cowering before the looming millennium.

Nostalgia, even ironic, becomes the guide for stance and style. Louise isn't the only one of the pair given to retro clothing. After Artie's disgrace at the New Year's party, he finds his "sodden garments on the floor. . . . The coat is an Eisenhower jacket with military emblems and campaign ribbons now stained." While Louise is working on a new series of photographs titled "Postcards," her art dealer drops by to survey the work, commenting on how she and her generation are "so adept at appropriation" or even "counterfeit." The dealer's comments address the idea that Postmodern work specifically interests itself in imitation, a phenomenon arising from the belief, on the one hand, that everything has already been thought and done and, on the other hand, that all art is appropriation: Postmodern work simply makes the process more explicit. Howard's own use of historical excerpts within the narrative—whether she draws from the Iliad or the Bible—supports this view, demonstrating her own dependence on historical texts for the shape and substance of her novel.

Howard uses a quote from the American historian Henry Adams to comment on the writer's task: "The secret of education still hid itself somewhere behind ignorance, and one fumbled over it as feebly as ever. In such labyrinths, the staff is a force almost more necessary than the legs; the pen becomes a sort of blind-man's dog, to keep him from falling into the gutter. The pen works for itself, and acts like a hand, modeling the plastic material over and over again to the form that suits it best." Howard joins such eminent precursors as Laurence Sterne in taking a book-within-a-book approach to her novel, yet there are moments when the reader might wish Howard would simply get on with her tale. But this sort of impatience occurs whenever narrative is interrupted by other forms of extended commentary and, in fact, *A Lover's Almanac* relies on this impatience for bringing a sense of suspense into the otherwise familiar territory of contemporary love.

In exploring the relationship between her central characters, Howard wittily suggests the mechanistic use of genuinely valuable knowledge, in this instance targeting Freudian psychology and its offshoots. As Artie attempts to sift through his feelings for Louise, trying to understand why he seems to himself so incapable of sustaining deep feelings, he ponders his early loss of his mother. Howard evokes cyberspeak as she describes this process: "Artie, sensing that his heart is adulterated, gives up on love, on Louise. Click AVOIDANCE DISORDER to find your way out, your way back to the old attraction, the mysteries of his mother's past. . . . Click REENACTMENT OF LOSS, which images love on the simu-scape, which tests pain beyond endurance." Believing themselves "free of conventional family tales," Louise and Artie are, on the contrary, as bound as we all are to history and specifically to our own personal pasts: "They will not make it out of the happenstance of birth and are headed for yet another shopworn romance. . . ."

Yet Howard does not leave her characters hopelessly stranded. Artie's hostility toward a woman artist who has the year 2000 tattooed on her arm, Auschwitz style, hints at the limits of what he will swallow. However familiar and incremental their steps, Artie and Louise do move—at least somewhat—outside the trap of Postmodern limitations. For it is within the acceptance of their very ordinariness that they begin to grapple with their difficulties, shedding superficial impulses toward individuality as they attempt to nourish themselves on ordinary, if uncommon, human love.

### Diane Simon (review date 26 January 1998)

SOURCE: "Seasoning Love," in *Nation,* January 26, 1998, pp. 29–32.

[*In the following review, Simon offers a positive assessment of* A Lover's Almanac, *noting its stylistic similarities to* Natural History.]

> About your arcade. You do see the pathos and pretension of the great Parisian arcades popping up in Bridgeport—your little glassed-over alley!
>
> —Maureen Howard, ***Natural History***

Once celebrated as a hallmark of America's cheery future, its robust inner health, the suburb has fallen from grace. No longer do aluminum siding, pink shutters and identically plotted lawns signal comfort and ease. These are the trappings of the Doll House (as in "Welcome to . . ."), the setting for key parties and other signs of marital decadence and cultural malaise. The Bradys are not a happy memory of family blending, before race, gender and Reaganomics got in the way; they are a symbol of our collective delusion. What we thought was success was really melanoma—a sunspot that's rotten underneath.

But with crime on the wane and the squeegee people in jail, the city is picking up where the suburbs left off. Even television, arguably our most accommodating cultural medium, has ventured forth with gusto into the urban jungle. The Friends frolic in Central Park, Susan has suddenly become herself in San Francisco and loads of sexy, eligible Chicago doctors kiss each other under the el and jog along Lake Michigan; only once in a blue moon do they get mugged or caught in the crossfire of drug-infested neighborhoods. More often, television cities—like movie cities and the cities of political campaigns—are stimulating, hopeful places where white people have black friends and sometimes you meet someone who teaches you something. Even cop shows seem to flaunt the benignity of the city's ills: Unlike angst, alienation and anomie, murders and robberies can be solved, their perpetrators punished.

Maureen Howard has long been a champion of the glorious city—even when the cities she was writing about seemed, on the surface at least, rather unlovely. A native of Bridgeport, Howard often sets her stories in the crucible of urban Connecticut, where, if they linger long enough, every Pilgrim meets a millhand, a machine Boss and a mallrat. The peculiar economy of Connecticut—some of the nation's richest suburbs pitted with some of its poorest cities—has become for Howard a stage on which to set grand, sweeping novels, novels where the past is the only weapon available to fight the future. *Bridgeport Bus,* reissued recently by Penguin, is the byword for her particular brand of urban irony, for the ways splendor fades into decay. For those who lived in the milltowns along the Housatonic, the bus to Bridgeport was once a transport of hope; now, its alliterative promise is a joke, a fare to Nowhere.

Howard's *Natural History,* which appeared in 1992, is both a paean to Bridgeport and a meditation on the accretions of urban life. Ostensibly the story of a Fairfield County detective, Billy Bray, and his family, *Natural History* swings from the starved fields of Ireland to the Hollywood hills as Bray's descendants—his daughter, Catherine, his son, James, and his granddaughter, Jen—puzzle with the pieces of Bray's life. As in Faulkner's *Absalom, Absalom!,* Bray's offspring draw us into the web of their own fallible truths. We get a remarkably tactile vision of Bridgeport in the forties—Billy in a brown fedora; a sexy murder suspect with silk stockings and a war-hero husband; an old Irish neighborhood where the Brays, their big house inherited from Nell Bray's made-good parents, are both too much and not enough. And we get a remarkably stark portrait of contemporary Bridgeport, which Catherine Bray can neither leave nor embrace (she lives in the suburbs, not yet stained by the muddy excavations of Hollywood), and to which James Bray returns in an aborted effort to make a movie of his father's life. Along the way, Howard treats us to excursions: visits with P. T. Barnum, the ghost of Bridgeport's prosperous past, the guiding spirit of industrial hokum; the musings of Aaron Burr, Samuel Clemens and the Roman alphabet, in which Y is the final letter that matters.

What we do not get is the facts about Billy Bray—what he thought, where he went on those evenings when he was investigating the murder of a young soldier by a woman whose husband was overseas. Howard's bricolage takes on a logic of its own, a compendium of family memory and urban folklore. Toward the end of the book, we meet Walter Benjamin in small print, and in Howard's introduction to his "Arcades" project, we find some of the wisdom of her ways. "Benjamin," she writes, "expected no less than to alter our relation to the page, to let us *shop,* that's the whimsy, through his chosen topics and cultural totems; to rifle the bins of 'Dream City,' 'Museum.'"

And so, in a celebration of the possibilities of modern life, we shop through *Natural History* (nature's story)—for the Bridgeport story that makes sense to us, for the bits we'd like to keep. We know only the barest facts absolutely—Billy, Nell, their names, occupations, paternity. Everything else carries with it the surreal aura of movieland props: a hovering urban smog, the fixed smile of a shop-window mannequin. Howard's Bridgeport, like Barnum's, is subtle, gallant pastiche.

> It is a question for the ages whether people who live in cities envy country people as much as they say they do.
>
> —*The Old Farmer's Almanac,* 1998

Despite its urban busyness, *Natural History* has a strong connection to a rural world. Its title gestures toward the enterprise of historical study—the "natural" layering of events—but it also gestures toward a primal moment, a time before the city became itself and lost its agricultural memory. Indeed, like the suburbs that are the uncanny spawn of rural expanse and urban industry, *Natural History* occupies a space between worlds. Between literary genres as well: If *Natural History* owes a debt to Benjamin's "Arcades," it owes one too to Jefferson's *Notes on the State of Virginia,* another project of observation and classification created for the casual perusal of acquisitive customers.

Howard's latest novel, *A Lover's Almanac,* owes similar debts. It too is the product of a rural genre—*The Farmer's Almanac*—claimed for the telling of a quintessentially urban tale, the loft-based love of a New York City couple, Louise Moffett, a painter, and Artie Freeman, a conflicted designer of market messages. The romantic chronicle of Lou and Artie, who when we meet them are separating after five years, is punctuated by zodiac dials, homey proverbs, charts detailing the "Remarkable Days" had by January, February, March. Howard has magnified the tiny historical markers found in *The Farmer's Almanac,* so that Louise, Artie, their friends and families share narrative space with Alexander Graham Bell, Henry Adams and Ann Lee, celibate mother of the Shakers. As in *Natural History,* Howard has amplified the micro-story of her characters, placed them in the shadows of the world stage, where the lighting is good and the sets spectacular. Sandwiched between "The Flintstones" and "The Celebrated Soup," William James explains the magnetic pull of the *Almanac*'s narrative, its effect as novel, history and exercise in humanity. "The world is full of partial stories that run parallel to one another," he tells us, "but we cannot unify them completely in our minds. In following your life-history, I must temporarily turn my attention from my own."

This is exactly what Louise Moffett and Artie Freeman are doing when we first meet them, at a New Year's Eve party they have thrown to greet the millennium: December 31, 1999. In grasping for a theme, Louise and Artie have settled upon the early fifties. Their party is part millennial frenzy, part domestic fantasy: guests in satin thrift-store party dresses doing the cha-cha and nibbling on Ritz crackers spread with spread; Artie in his grandfather's Korean War uniform, his hair freshly buzzed. Drunk, he botches his marriage proposal to Lou and is ejected from the party, exiled from her life. The story that follows is both reunion journey and zodiac-managed time travel, for before Lou and Artie can join the march into the twenty-first century, they must first make peace with the twentieth. Nostalgia is one thing, history another.

Hobbled by yearning for another decade—a decade when the trajectory of their love would have been obvious, marriage and babies following professional establishment for him and renunciation for her—Artie and Lou are displaced people. Lou has left behind the Wisconsin farm of her youth, where her ambitious father lavishes attention on his cloned cow, Dossie. And Artie is equally estranged from his origins, for though he cares deeply for the grandfather who raised him, he has never met the father who sired him. His mother, out of defiance, named her son "Freeman," distancing him from both his own origins and herself. Louise's art dealer cynically praises her generation—"so adept at appropriation"—but we know from the start that he's wrong. True appropriation might satisfy, but used clothing does not.

Alternatively, Howard solicits our sympathy: "Born into Generation X 1/2 or Y, into the willed innocence at the end of a century, they have lived without a war . . . without poverty to give them just cause." Artie and Lou, for the moment, are living on borrowed traumas, the unnutritious aspirations of another place and time.

It is appropriate, then, that their story is told through the medium of a displaced genre, the homiletic tone of the *Almanac* overlaying both the byzantine twists of Howard's prose and the urban chaos of Lou's and Artie's lives. What saves Lou and Artie is a combination of theatrical emotion—*Love! Valour! Compassion!*—and simple cosmography: Like the grateful Shakers who danced for Ann Lee, Artie and Lou come down where they ought to be. Ultimately, it is the persistence of the *Almanac* that comes to their rescue—its conviction that order can be imposed on the whims of nature, that prediction and understanding are not, despite the warnings of theorists, zealots and random cynics, completely outside our grasp. Following the natural wisdom of Poor Richard, Louise and Artie learn that love can be alternately fertile and barren. Love, like history, has seasons.

**Susan Dooley (review date 8 February 1998)**

SOURCE: "Stormy Weather," in *Washington Post Book World,* February 8, 1998, p. 5.

[*In the following review, Dooley offers a negative assessment of* A Lover's Almanac, *criticizing the novel's lack of focus and cohesion.*]

For more than 600 years, almanacs have been counting us through the calendar, helping us to calculate the position of the sun, moon and planets, entertaining us with feeble jokes, providing us with reminders of famous birthdays, cautioning that on such and such a day people in such and such an area will rise to find their world buried under snow. Once the almanac may have filled a need, but now it is a magpie collection of bright and shiny lore, a compendium of disparate information where everything stands alone and, wherever you chance to poke in your thumb, you'll pull out a plum.

And that is what Maureen Howard offers us in her new novel, *A Lover's Almanac,* with its collection of quotes, birthdays, astrological plotting, and stray bits of information patching together a love story firmly anchored to the end of the 20th century. There are so many voices, so many shiny bits of inessential information, so many things going on that the book never gets a firm hold on itself, never totally draws the reader in. The characters can't overcome the idea behind the book, can't climb over all the extraneous information that surrounds them and present themselves as real people.

Howard is a wonderful writer with a mind full of fabulous facts, and she lays them out for us to show the ways in which people slide by each other, bumping but never connecting. But to this end she spins out not one love story but two, three, four, until she has a book with so many hearts that ultimately it takes an entire art gallery to hold them. These hearts, symbols of all the loving and losing life has to offer, are placed in the gallery by Louise Moffett, whose latest conceptual art project is making a statement about marriage. With devastating concentration, she paints and piles thousands of shiny red hearts in a see-through vat, where gallery goers can grasp at them with a mechanical hand but can't remove them from their container. Like the lovers in Howard's novel, they can get hold of these alien hearts, but no one is able to keep them.

*A Lover's Almanac* is a paradigm for New York at the millennium, where the more pressing the crowds, the more precious the privacy—and the more people seek to seal themselves safely away. If even one person should break through the boundary, would we find ourselves overtaken by all?

Louise's lover, her dilemma, is Artie Freeman, a cybergoof who uses computers to hack out a paycheck and jokes to fend off the world. Born out of wedlock, he bears the burdensome name Freeman because his mother, refusing to tell him who his father was, had stripped him of the problems of a past. Naturally, Artie has devoted his life to finding the ties that will bind him in place.

Louise Moffett knows exactly what life she is fleeing, the rural world of Wisconsin where she was the farmer's daughter. Not just any farmer but a "global milkman, breeder of lactatious good will," who has genetically created and then cloned "Dossie . . . Engineered for the new century, grazing arid land, she will produce 20,000 pounds of Product within the year." With her art, Louise has attempted to dominate her past by first painting it in miniature and then creating pictures that dissect that rural world. Louise and Artie are a very modern pair, carefully casual about love, but they enter the millennium with the same problems lovers bore a thousand years ago.

There are many other voices in Howard's book: an old couple who met and parted many years ago, an aunt who briefly exchanges science for love and finds herself betrayed, a homeless child fantasizing affection, an assortment of steadfast wives, who stay on course out of habit rather than passion. There are even voices that float in out of nowhere, telling stories which seem to have no connection to anything that's gone before.

Among the many quotes Howard places throughout her almanac is this, from the philosopher William James: "The world is full of partial stories that run parallel to one another, beginning and ending at odd times. They mutually interlace and interfere at points, but we can not unify them completely in our minds . . ."

Well, actually, we can when a novelist pulls them together for us, but Howard has chosen to follow James and let disunity define her tale. Even in the hands of a writer as gifted as she is, the material is overwhelming and the characters never entirely get free of it. Occasionally one story bumps into another, but no one is changed by the encounter or even aware that fate may have offered a footnote on the past or a different future. In *A Lover's Almanac,* Howard has written a book that is less about how people come together than about the many ways in which they stay apart.

### Jack Schwartz (review date 27 March 1998)

SOURCE: "Far from Home," in *Commonweal,* March 27, 1998, p. 24.

[*In the following review, Schwartz offers a mixed assessment of* A Lover's Almanac, *arguing that the novel's minor characters are more compelling than the protagonist.*]

In *A Lover's Almanac,* Maureen Howard moves far afield from the literary precincts of spirited Irish-Catholic women where she has made her mark. In this more youthful, futuristic venue, Howard's protagonists are a star-tossed couple, Louise (Lou, Lou-Lou) Moffett, an aspiring artist on the cusp of Downtown success, and her boyfriend Arthur (Artie) Freeman, a computer-graphics adept for a cyberspace ad agency. The opening scene is a fifties-style New Year's costume party, replete with tuna and taffeta, to greet the year 2000. Artie, who has sampled too many martinis, assaults two of the guests, including Louise's art dealer, and is unceremoniously hauled out of the apartment and hurled from Lou's life. The next two-thirds of the book is devoted to Artie's efforts to get himself back into Lou's good graces. The outcome is never in doubt. What we have here, as Howard readily acknowledges, is an extended lover's quarrel, hardly the stuff of millennial reckoning. So what is the author doing? Surely a novelist of Howard's heft (**Grace Abounding, Expensive Habits, Natural History**) has something more up her sleeve than providing love-tipped arrows for Generation Y.

It turns out that the book's most captivating character is Arthur's grandfather, Cyril, who has brought up the fatherless boy from age eleven when his mercurial mother, Fiona, died in a boating accident. With Cyril, the son of a boozy Irish cop, himself a scholarship lad who married up and did well on Wall Street, we are back on Howard's home turf. It is Cyril's story, a life of accommodation to a loveless marriage and a meaningless career, with which the novelist seems most comfortable. We are beguiled when Sylvie, the widowed Cyril's bygone lover, appears after fifty years to rekindle the fires of a brief but memorable encounter. The other characters are interesting acquaintances; Cyril is an old friend who confides in the author more easily than the rest. It is his failures of nerve, their consequences, and Arthur's own efforts to break loose from their quiescent legacy that inform this parable on the downward pull of generations.

The plot reverberates between flashbacks to Cyril's could-have-beens and fastforwards to the young lovers' still-might-be's, all of it wound on the metaphorical spool of the *Almanac.* If our faults lie in ourselves, our stars certainly give us a nudge and the almanac provides a handy device for Howard to comment on our struggle to give free will room to maneuver within destiny. Interspersed throughout the novel are homilies, folk wisdom, weather forecasts, zodiac signs, auguries, factoids, advice, biographical sketches (Benjamin Franklin, Isaac Newton) and other commonplaces that have graced the genre from Poor Richard's debut (1733) to the perennial *Farmer's Almanac* which will serve as inspiration for Louise to turn the demons of her rustic past to artistic purpose. The design is clever but the results are mixed. After a while the adages and advisories become intrusive; whatever their symbolic quotient they are distracting and finally wearying.

More disquieting is the author's reversion to stereotype in evoking her minor characters. Arthur's false friend Bud Boyce is lampooned as an exploitative cyber hustler, a Bill Gates wannabee, and a lecher. Louise's dairy-farmer father, who conducts Strangelovian experiments in cow-cloning and who is variously referred to as the Mighty Milkman and The Big Cheese, is an ogre: insensitive, oppressive, malevolent; he does everything but intone fee, fi, fo, fum. A lapsed priest who writes popular spiritual tomes is a bopbag Deepak Gantry.

Also annoying is the use of overheated language. For whatever reason, Howard has chosen to use the conventions of Harlequin Romance to project modern angst. She announces her intentions early with Lou's anguish after the disastrous New Year's party: "And, having sworn off the man, she's into it again, choking back saltwater sorrow, for can it be that one night can unravel their years, one rotten night of Artie's misdemeanors. The answer is yes." And later, pining away: ". . . for she has neglected all her friends, imprisoned herself with the legend of her sorrow, her abandonment . . . and shame. . . ." For someone with Howard's usually unerring ear, this time out she can't seem to resist a cliché: "Every day tells Louise Moffett this is the winter of her discontent"; or a bad pun—the cynical art dealer's "schlock of recognition."

But the real problem with the novel is that the key to its mystery—Artie's mother Fiona—is a wraith. The novel follows Arthur's quest to find the identity of his father. The trails leads to a failed Jesuit, Father Joe Murphy, now a harmless math teacher at a Catholic high school in Connecticut but once tapped for higher calling before he had an era. Fiona was no mere ripe and randy flower-child but a charismatic presence with a deep moral dimension that stirred everyone she met. But we never learn why "they had all been in love with that redhead." In the novel it is simply a given, but we want more. Still, Fiona and Father Murphy, briefly sketched, are far more intriguing than Lou-Lou and Artie wholly rendered. Interestingly, the writing here is strong and spare, dispensing with the coy affectations that too often mar the novel.

Howard is too skillful an author to write a bad book, but she has not written a good one. What could have been a movable feast of the century is little more than a confection, a harmless enough soufflé lightened by the occasional divertissement, but lacking the grit and grace of hard-earned lives that represent the author's best work.

## Michael Wood (review date 16 July 1998)

SOURCE: "On the Love Boat," in *New York Review of Books,* July 16, 1998, pp. 31–35.

[*In the following review, Wood explores the literary technique of utilizing correspondence to narrate a story, citing* A Lover's Almanac *as a prime example.*]

1.

Milan Kundera's new novel, *Identity,* written in French and marked at its end as "completed in France, Autumn 1996," reads like a modest commentary on a famous page in Proust's *Remembrance of Things Past.* Charles Swann's love for Odette de Crécy, entering its unhappiest phase, is described as an illness, in which physical desire, and even Odette's person, play only a small part. Swann can scarcely recognize her in a photograph, can't connect her face with his pain—"as though suddenly we were to be shown a detached, externalized portrait of one of our own maladies, and we found it bore no resemblance to what we are suffering." The switch from Swann to us is striking; our identification with his condition is swiftly taken for granted. Proust's narrator then, even more strikingly, relates love and death, not, he says, because of any of the "so vague" resemblances which are "always" discussed, but because both make us interrogate further, *interroger plus avant,* "the mystery of personality." Who is it we love, and who are we, in love or out of it?

There are really only two characters in *Identity,* although to call them "characters" is pushing it a bit. Chantal and Jean-Marc are lovers, have been for years. They are happy, have no thought of separating, but then certain thoughts disturb their relationship, as if thoughts were worse than infidelity, more dangerous than distance or violence. These thoughts are what matter in Chantal and Jean-Marc, so that everything else about them, their jobs, their bodies, their past lives, their friends, their apartment, their styles of speech or dress, is merely sketched in, or not even sketched in.

The first words of the book are: "A hotel in a small town on the Normandy coast, which they found in a guidebook." No name except that of the region, no evocation; not so much as a main verb to take the sentence beyond the effect of notation. Chantal has been married, and has had a child, who died, but that's all the boy is: a child who died, his death merely the premise for her current freedom. "Child," Kundera writes: "an existence without a biography," but that wouldn't distinguish a child from anyone else in this book. Chantal's dead child is what allows her to despise the world, because "it's impossible to have a child and despise the world as it is, because that's the world we've put the child into." Translation: the novelist has given her this child and taken it away again in order to make this point about the world.

It would be absurd to ask for documentary realism of Kundera, who specializes in erratic and edgy mentalities; but the people in this novel do seem to be very skimpily and casually imagined, unlike the characters in most of his earlier works, who are solidly and quirkily alive among abstractions, and whose very ideas become flesh. Here the flesh itself is an idea, if that. The novel's abrupt dips into Chantal's mental idiom—"Ah, how she hated that, eating alone!"—seem blandly conventional, and Kundera wheels out clichés as if they were a form of worldly (masculine) wisdom: "Suddenly it is the immemorial situation of a woman being chased down by a man," "this immemorial action of women hiding a letter among their undergarments." The imagery, too, comes from well-worn general stock: "I was cold as an ice cube"; She is icy with honor." Is this the effect of Kundera's no longer writing in Czech? His previous, similarly very thin novel, *Slowness,* was also written directly in French. The language may be one answer, and the French isn't any fresher than the English translation, but I think rather that Kundera is deliberately looking for bareness and the plain style and has gone too far; or that he overestimates the interest of what's left.

Chantal's disturbing thought occurs on the beach in that Normandy town. All the men she sees are carrying children or pushing strollers, and she decides that "men have daddified themselves. They aren't fathers, they're just daddies, which means; fathers without a father's authority." She wonders what would happen if she made a pass at one of these daddies. Would the man even be able to turn around? Then she thinks, "I live in a world where men will never turn to look at me again." She is amused by this idea at first, but when she tells Jean-Marc about it she can't get the tone right. "She tried to say it as lightly as possible, but to her surprise, her voice was bitter and melancholy."

Jean-Marc hears the melancholy and feels excluded—why does she need other men to turn to look at her?—but he also has had his own disturbing thought. Arriving in the town after Chantal and looking for her on the beach after she has returned to the hotel, he momentarily mistakes another woman for her. This other person is "old, ugly, pathetically other." How could this happen? "How is it possible that he cannot distinguish the form of the being he loves most, the being he considers to be beyond compare?" At this point the Proustian echoes, intended or not, seem particularly clamorous, and Kundera executes a number of variations on this theme. When Jean-Marc catches up with Chantal at the hotel, she doesn't look like herself any more: "Her face is old, her glance strangely harsh. As if the woman he had been waving at on the beach must, now and forevermore, replace the one he loves. As if he must be punished for his inability to recognize her." Chantal is changed twice, so to speak: once by her own experience on the beach, and once by Jean-Marc's.

A few pages later Jean-Marc has a dream in which Chantal appears with "an alien and disagreeable face. Yet it is not someone different, it is Chantal, his Chantal, he has no doubt of that, but his Chantal with a stranger's face, and this is horrifying, this is unbearably horrifying." Even awake, Jean-Marc finds Chantal's social self different from the person he loves, and his terror, in his bad moments, is not that he will lose Chantal but that he will no longer be able to distinguish her from other women, "that she would come to mean as little to him as everybody else." The self-directed phrasing is important. Just as Chantal is free to despise the world as soon as her child is gone, Jean-Marc despises everything and everyone except Chantal. A lovely couple. Chantal is Jean-Marc's "sole emotional link to the world. . . . She and she alone releases him from his apathy. Only through her can he feel compassion." His love for her is his love of his ability to love her, a fragile form of self-congratulation.

Neither of the lovers is very secure in the self they prefer to the world. Troubled by Chantal's need to feel looked at, Jean-Marc starts to write her anonymous admiring letters. She is touched and aroused by them, keeps them and hides them. When she realizes, by a few careful acts of deduction, that Jean-Marc is writing them, she thinks he is trying to trick her and get rid of her. He can't understand why she is so upset by what he meant as a gesture of kindness, and their mutual misunderstanding sends Chantal off to London, with Jean-Marc trailing miserably after her. Certain sudden shifts of scenery and oddly recurring characters now suggest we have entered a realm of fantasy or hallucination, where Chantal gets trapped in an orgy and thinks she may be dead, and where Jean-Marc can trace her but can't reach her. The end of the novel finds the lovers back together again, anxiously reassuring each other about their presence.

Just before this Kundera has teased us with speculations: "And I ask myself, who was dreaming? Who dreamed this story? Who imagined it? She? He? Both of them? Each one for the other? And starting when did their real life change into this treacherous fantasy?" These questions are less interesting than the one they seem to have displaced: Why would love, even happy love, be so prone to doubt and anxiety; what mysteries of personality have come unraveled here?

Letters and separation also figure significantly in *The Notebooks of Don Rigoberto* and **A Lover's Almanac**; and John Bayley's *The Red Hat* is, among many other things, a delicate meditation on the rewriting of love. The letters are anonymous and at the heart of Vargas Llosa's novel; signed but not immediately opened in Maureen Howard's book. In *The Red Hat* a timid and languid Englishman almost falls in love on reading a young woman's letter to a friend and writes his own modest, bewildered companion piece. With all four of these novels in mind we might want to add a line to Proust's parallel, and say that not only love and death but also love and writing keep turning up questions about personality. In writing as in love we see, if not our maladies, at least what may be a piece of ourselves externalized and independent, living a life of its own in the world. This other self is ours, but not recognized. Or it is recognized, but not our self. You don't have to be a graphologist to get caught up in this riddle; and of course in writing about love the whole spectacle is dizzily doubled.

*The Notebooks of Don Rigoberto* picks up precisely where Vargas Llosa's *In Praise of the Stepmother* (1988) left off, although the new work is much more densely elaborated. In the earlier novel the angelic stepson, Fonchito, all golden ringlets and blue eyes, short trousers and school uniform—we are told he has recently taken his first Communion—seduces or is seduced by his beautiful stepmother Doña Lucrecia. He is young enough to be repeatedly called a child and to present a perfect picture of sexual innocence; old enough to enjoy sleeping with his stepmother and, with seeming calculation, to let his father know of the (recurring) event. The boy's father, Don Rigoberto, throws the wife out, which may be what the boy wanted all along.

In the new novel the boy is living with his father but secretly visits his stepmother after school each day. There are no further sexual misdemeanors on these occasions, but there is much suggestive talk, often focused on the drawings and paintings and life of Egon Schiele, who has become a passion with the boy. When the married couple are finally reunited, after a year of living apart, Lucrecia confesses that her abstinence had nothing to do with virtue. "I didn't go to bed with him, but wait. Not because of any virtue in me, but because of him. If he had asked, if he had made the slightest suggestion, I would have done it. With the greatest of pleasure, Rigoberto." These are hard words for a husband to hear, but perhaps not as hard for Don Rigoberto as for some, since he has made a nightly career out of mental voyeurism.

Don Rigoberto is an insurance lawyer, director of a company, a rich, conservative citizen of Lima, a man with huge ears and a corkscrew nose, poor equipment, we might think, for a would-be libertine. But then he is a very special kind of libertine, a connoisseur of lingering fleshly pleasure, but only with his own wife, in person before their break-up, and in the shape of her imagined, lovingly evoked phantom when she is away. Don Rigoberto has other interests too. He has a collection of "four thousand volumes and one hundred prints," a number he maintains exactly by burning a book or a picture every time he acquires a new one, on the grounds that "it was stupid to inflict on other eyes a work I had come to consider unworthy of mine."

He worries about these acts of destruction at first, but comes to think he is "engaging in literary and artistic criticism as it should be practiced: radically, irreversibly, and flammably." Don Rigoberto writes elaborate, polemical letters (which he does not send) to an ecologist, a feminist, a sports enthusiast, a Rotarian, a patriot, a bureaucrat. He writes a fan letter to a voyeur. His tune is always the same, although the rhetoric is different each time. He will not and cannot join in what he calls "municipal" pleasures and projects. His only religion is his faith in "the rule of the free and sovereign individual"—accompanied where possible by his wife.

Don Rigoberto sees himself as "an intractable and unclassifiable spirit." What about his job at the insurance company, we may ask, and his impeccably conformist upper-class life, the complete absence from the Peruvian social or political scene of the slightest trace of his libertarian dissent? Well, that's the trick. Don Rigoberto is not saying he's a hero, or even a philanderer. He is just a "modest epicurean and anarchist concealed in the civil body of a man who insures property." He needs the job and the money to protect not only the privacy of his hedonist separatism, but its very possibility: "The world of fantasy, pleasure, and liberated desire, my only homeland, would not have survived unscathed subjected to the rigors of need, deprivation, economic worries, the stifling weight of debts and poverty."

Don Rigoberto is eloquent rather than appealing, and I kept wondering whether he and Chantal and Jean-Marc might want to get together in a little society of scorn. But he is also one of Vargas Llosa's finest and most self-renewing comic figures, caught up in all the social contradictions he keeps denying, and there is considerable pathos and bravery in his cantankerousness, since it is mainly a side effect of his attempt to get fantasy to do more than it ever can.

For all but the last few pages of this novel, Don Rigoberto is desperately dreaming of the presence of his absent wife, putting her through all kinds of erotic paces (sex amid a pile of Angora cats, a trip to Paris and Venice with a former suitor, a partner-switching night with his brother and his spouse, a couple of lesbian moments with a maid and a visiting diplomat's wife, an incident *à trois* in a seedy club in Mexico), but only in his mind. He thinks of Calderón's famous play *La Vida es Sueño*—"Life Is Dream"—and Vargas Llosa, in a chapter subtitle, amiably inverts the phrase to read *El Sueño es Vida*, but Don Rigoberto's sorry discovery is that the proposition is untrue both ways. "Life was not a dream, dreams were a feeble lie, a fleeting deception that provided only temporary escape from frustration and solitude. . . ."

There is an interesting, perhaps insuperable difficulty of translation here, since the famous Spanish phrase lacks an article, and the usual version, sensibly followed by Edith Grossman, tells us only that *Life Is a Dream* (or *Dream Is a Life*), not that life is (inescapably, completely) indistinguishable from the state of dreaming. The whole of life is dream, Calderón says, and dreams are dreams too: *que toda la vida es sueño, / y los sueños, sueños son.* Don Rigoberto, I should add, understands the Spanish as if it were idiomatic English; and writes, in the passage I have just quoted, exactly as the translation says, *"La vida no era un sueño."*

What brings Don Rigoberto and Doña Lucrecia happily if nervously back together is a sequence of anonymous letters each has received, and which each thinks comes from the other. They all turn out to be the work of the angelic Fonchito, who has rifled his father's notebooks to get a sense of his taste and manner, and has made up his stepmother's style by borrowing freely from the works of the sentimental writer Corín Tellado. Fonchito no doubt wants to repair the damage he has done in the earlier novel, but he is such a wonderfully ambiguous figure that there is really no knowing what he is up to. What is called the "savage little light" in his eyes is ultimately unreadable. He is clearly smarter and more mature (and more devious) than anyone else in the book, so perhaps he means to prepare both a happy ending and the possibilities of intricate and perverse disaster in the future. The ominous last words of the novel, after Don Rigoberto and Doña Lucrecia have failed to decide what to do about Fonchito—they can't keep him with them and they can't send him away—are: "In spite of everything we're a happy family, aren't we, Lucrecia?" Cue for a sequel to the sequel.

2.

Time, appearing as a chorus in Shakespeare's *The Winter's Tale*, says it pleases some and tries all of us. It's a cheerful thought, since most writers, ancient and modern, find time merely trying, possibly redeemable but hardly ever a source of pleasure. "A Winter's Tale," a subtitle, are the first words before the story starts in Maureen Howard's acute and haunting new novel, and the play itself is quoted later, to signal a narrative elision, a time beyond what seems to be the end of the tale:

> *I turn my glasse, and give my Scene such growing As you had slept between*

**A Lover's Almanac** tells the story of three months in the lives of various lovers, lost and found, young and old, past and present—chiefly those of two thirtysomethings, Louise Moffett, a New York painter, and Artie Freeman, a sporadically employed computer whiz. The months are January, February, and March of the year 2000—Howard has reserved the other months, perhaps of different years and almost certainly inhabited by different characters, for two future volumes to make up a trilogy.

The millennium, barely over in the opening pages of the book, seems at first to be just a missed chance. "Louise Moffett cries in the ruins," we read at the start of the story. The ruins are those of Louise's party, held for New Year's Eve, the last moments of the old century and the first of the new, and she has had a row with Artie, whom she loves and wants to marry but who is too shaky in his sense of himself to contemplate such a drastic descent into stability. The party, to complicate our sense of time, was in 1950s fancy dress. It takes Louise and Artie most of the three months of the novel to get back together again, but that's quick compared with Don Rigoberto's and Doña Lucrecia's twelve-month estrangement. Artie sends letters, calls Louise; she doesn't answer. He visits his grandfather, thinks about looking for a real job. Louise pulls herself out of her gloom and gets back to work. She leaves the door of her loft open for Artie's return, a forlorn hope until one night he is there when she gets back from an art show. The reunion is ecstatic but the future uncertain. The millennium, though, or at least the next quarter-century, now looks like an opportunity.

Louise has all but cut herself off from her farm childhood in Wisconsin, and from her aggressive, all-modern-methods farming dad and her mild, submissive mother. Her family is too much, while Artie's is too little. His mother died in a boating accident when he was eleven, and, raised by her parents, he has never known who his father is. Louise's moment of illumination, and paradoxically the renewal of her faith in the possibility of marriage, comes about when she realizes that her mother can be separated from her father and be happy, that even the most conventional of persons may know how to rebel, and Artie's moment comes when he finds and meets two men, old admirers of his free-loving mother, one of whom may be his father. In fact, one of them is, although Artie can't see his idea of "father" in the defeated priest that this man has become. But Artie's freedom resides in his finally knowing how to give up his quest for his father, not in defeat but in a turning from an imaginary then to an actual now.

Not all is splendor or cheer, though, which is why the illumination makes so much sense. "He quits the believing . . . if ever it was belief in the phantom father . . . yet his sorrow is immense, real as the knowledge that he can't subtract loss from what he never gained." You can't lose the sense of loss, and you shouldn't try. One of the strongest connections between Artie and Louise is his feeling for the unkinder meanings of the word "home." "I see," he says when he first looks at her little paintings of the family farm, recreated not as it was but as it felt to a child. "Home. The crippled viewer, the crippling view."

Times and places crisscross through memories and flashbacks in the novel: New York and Wisconsin and elsewhere in the 1950s and 1960s and the year 2000. We learn about the other lovers, whose lives have been affected by the century's horrors in ways that the young people find it hard to imagine: Louise's independent-minded Aunt Bea and her refugee intellectual; Artie's grandfather, Cyril, and his once abandoned and now reencountered lover, Sylvie. Sylvie is an Austrian escapee from the *Anschluss,* raped as a little girl by a German soldier and unable, even in old age, to forget the sour smell of that violence. Her mother, Inge, is a more versatile survivor, hanging out with émigré intellectuals in California and then marrying the rich Billy Ray Boots, of River Oaks, Texas. Still, Sylvie finds something like peace in her reunion with Cyril, whose wife of many years is now dead, and whose only family tie is Artie. What is said of Cyril could also be said of Sylvie: "old and strangely in love or in love strangely, go figure." This too is a way of talking about the mystery of personality.

All of this is evoked in rich, crowded, metaphor-making prose. Sometimes we wonder who is speaking, whose consciousness this is which runs so fast, and then we realize it is the writer's, in and out of her characters' heads. Artie buys a steak and a soup bone for his grandfather, for instance, and takes a bus across Central Park. The butcher's bag in the following quotation is his. The eyes and thoughts, however, except for the thought about the destination of the Pope's blessing, seem to be his and everyone's.

> The passengers . . . observe the iced rocks shimmering black in the sun, toppled trees and torn branches, a shutter flapping at the barracks where patrol cars snort, ready to drive their routes where no dog or jogger or criminal element yet roams. A still, colorless world: ebony limbs, white hillocks severed sharp as canyons by the wind, lamp posts crowned with turbans of snow. Grand, the close-up as well as the panoramic view. As the bus skids toward the Museum, a woman in a leather hat, slick black hide pulled tight to her skull, follows the rivulet of blood which drips from the butcher's bag across the face of her *New York Times,* miraculously published this day, across the face of the Pope in his white robes blessing Artie's beef bone.

It's almost too much, too busy; or seems so, until we remember the work this restless notation of details and associations is doing, and the model it has drawn on.

*The Old Farmer's Almanac* (established 1792), glanced at in Howard's title, is a compendium of dates and facts and sagacity, confident in its predictions, a little garrulous, in the manner of Shakespeare's talking Time. For June 1998, for instance, after telling us about the conjunction of the stars and the phases of the moon, times of sunrise and sunset and of high tide at Boston, it gives us three amiable paragraphs on June butterflies, a quotation from Einstein ("gravitation cannot be held responsible for people falling in love"), a couple of bits of anonymous wisdom ("Nature does nothing in vain," "A trusting heart is an easy mark for the cunning scoundrel"), and lists a series of feasts and events for particular days of the month: St. Boniface (5th), first drive-in movie, Camden, N.J., 1933 (6th), Magna Carta sealed, 1215 (15th), Amelia Earhart flies across the Atlantic, 1928 (17th), Willie Mays graduates from high school, 1950 (20th). Information seems endlessly available, recyclable, but also eccentric and random. What logic produces these snippets and not others? Could there be such a logic?

*A Lover's Almanac* reads entirely like a (very good) novel in which the lives and sensibilities of such characters as Louise and Artie become memorable; but it borrows an effect from the *Farmer's Almanac* by inserting into the story brief, casual-seeming almanac entries. We learn, for the first months of the year 2000, of the Feast of the Circumcision and the Eve of St. Agnes, the birthdays of William James and FDR (all January); of the birthdays of Gertrude Stein, Edison, and Ann Lee, founder of the celibate Shakers, the death of John von Neumann in 1957, the burning of Jefferson's library in 1770, Hitler's threat to annex Austria in 1938, the conversion of Saul of Tarsus on the road to Damascus (February), the birthdays of Alexander Graham Bell, Edgar Rice Burroughs, and Haydn, and the founding of the New York Stock Exchange in 1817 (March).

The result of these brief and lively lessons, often but not always associated with events in the lives of Howard's fictional characters, is that all these historical persons and occurrences, in spite of their different centuries, seem to belong to one circling year, as if they are bound to keep coming back, cropping up again and again but also each time for the first time. And more important still, these quirky acts of cultural memory, through the eager, grasshopping curiosity which animates them, and through their very failure to add up to anything more than fragments, suggest something of the immensity of what we might know but don't. *The Farmer's Almanac* was born in the century of the great French *Encyclopedia*, but it looks like an encyclopedia in reverse: a demonstration that only pieces of knowledge can be represented, or even that knowledge is just a matter of pieces. This is of course a late-twentieth-century reading of the almanac's achievement, but that, Howard would say, is where we are.

Time for Howard is always then and now, but the really difficult time, the one we need to love and have such trouble with, is now. We need to learn, as in *The Winter's Tale*, that time can be on our side as well as against us, and this is where the details, even random details, may help—since their scattering and incoherence, combined with their unmistakable concreteness, may defend us against the coercion of large stories, either oppressively upbeat or irredeemably glum. Howard is moved by the thought of Haydn in London, jotting down the price of a roasting chicken, of a measure of coal, interested to know how many baskets of gooseberries were served at Lord Barrymore's ball. We may be skeptical, Howard suggests, about Haydn's self-proclaimed "cheerful heart," perhaps even about the untormented perfection of his music, but his attention to detail brings him closer to us, just as Howard's own prose catches us up and won't let us go.

> No, in honesty we cannot, in these hellish, postindustrialist days, sell you the elixir, the tonic of Haydn.... We must cut Franz Joseph down to fit the page of our Almanac, as we have trimmed Franklin, Edison, Bell, von Neumann, noting their failures and amusing foibles....

We have to do this, Howard's narrator is suggesting, although we are "poorer" for it. Honest but poor, that's us. But the Haydn who was interested in the price of a chicken was also "in love with a charming widow." We can care about this couple and their attachment to "domestic details"—as we can also care about Howard's modern characters—without selling any elixirs or cutting anyone down to our idea of size.

All three of the novels discussed in detail so far are explicitly dated on their last page. France, autumn 1996 (Kundera). London, June 28, 1997 (Howard). October 19, 1996 (Vargas Llosa, in the Spanish edition). Howard even tells us, about a quarter of the way through her book, what the time is now, as she writes, calling it a "blessed moment": "9½ minutes before 2 p.m. of this 23rd day of August, A.D. 1996." The symmetry among the three texts is even neater if you think, as I do, that *A Lover's Almanac* is eloquently and unmistakably a New York novel, so that the name of the city scarcely needs writing with the date.

The suggestion of these discreet but insistent traces of the hand of the actual author is that love is not timeless, but local, a matter of particular places and times, identifiable countries and cities and years. Howard explicitly compares Louise Moffett's artwork *The Progress of Love* with a work of the same title by Fragonard, "a series of wall panels in which lovers are restored to the garden where they play erotic games under a china-blue sky." Louise's show, by contrast, has two plexiglass bins full of plasticine hearts and cheap charms and favors, old bridal photographs, a kitsch image of the Sacred Heart.

"We see how diminished our time," the narrator comments, "how black-and-white earnest the libidinal nature of consumerism," but the narrator is getting carried away by anti-presentism. What the contrast between the two artworks suggests, in the context of the novel, is not simple diminishment but a ratcheting up of the difficulty of love, which now has to find its way not among courtly subterfuges but among self-consuming ironies, among the endless ambushes of late-modern mockery and despair. "It seems," Louise thinks, "you must reinvent yourself to meet love's impossible demands." This is probably true of most times and places, but the language of invention must change, and perhaps the very notion of impossibility changes too. It almost certainly couldn't be the same in the eighteenth century and the early days of the twenty-first. This is not to say that love's impossible demands cannot be met, in any time or place, if you are lucky, and if your self-invention is up to scratch.

3.

John Bayley doesn't date *The Red Hat,* doesn't appear, in this sense, on his own pages at all. The author stays tactfully dead and leaves all the talking (all the writing) to his characters. But this also is a novel about self-invention, and about love as an interrogation of personality. The first half of the book takes the form of a letter written from Nancy Deverell to her friend Cloe Winterbotham—the names seem to place as somewhere between P. G. Wodehouse and Anthony Powell. "Friend" is not quite the right word, as Nancy is quick to tell us. "Cloe is supposed to be what we once used to call my best friend."

> Cloe is my best friend, yes: but actually I hate the idea of best friends. Or friends of any sort, come to think of it. What's the point of them?—why such a big idea? There are people you know, and a great many more whom you don't, and that's about it.

This sounds like cynicism, and similar remarks in Kundera's *Identity* are cynical, weary dismissals of the very notion of friendship, but Nancy is too breezy and lighthearted for cynicism. She just thinks friendship is a tie, a restriction, and she wants to be on the move: Nancy is in The Hague with Cloe and Cloe's fiancé Charles, "about as queer as they come," according to Nancy, but "trying pretty doggedly to be in love with Cloe."

They are there to see a Vermeer show, and to have a good time. Cloe and Charles take themselves and Vermeer very seriously, and bicker a lot; Nancy's not too serious about herself or the art, but she identifies strongly with the person in the picture called *Girl with a Red Hat.* Is this person a girl? "She's a girl," Nancy says, determined to be sophisticated about gender matters, "and yet she's not a girl. She's a boy. That's obvious. At least it's obvious if you really start to think about it." Nancy also thinks this figure bears a startling resemblance to herself, although no one else comments on it, so perhaps she's projecting a little. What Nancy likes about the person in the painting is that he/she seems not only to have been lively once but to be lively now, ready to skip the frame:

> It's the picture of Vermeer, perhaps the only one, which has a future, if you see what I mean. That girl or boy is going somewhere, though he or she doesn't know where. None of the others are: they have become their pictures. That red hat person is getting out—is on the way out as she looks at you.

Nancy takes the red hat as the sign of adventure, a disguise which is also a permission. "It was a real red hat situation," she says, and wonders, "What would the girl in the red hat have done?" She has plenty of occasions for asking, since she meets a dark, mysterious man in the hotel elevator, who later comes and makes love to her in the night, and later still tells her he is a Mossad agent and threatens to kill her. Nancy wears an improvised red hat to a fancy-dress ball, loses it in the drunken aftermath of the festivities, and closes her account of these Dutch doings with a report of her reconciliation with the putative secret agent, who's got over wanting to kill her, it seems. He has bought her a splendid red hat to replace the one she has lost.

> It's black velvet lined with white silk, under the red plumes. I put it on every evening . . . and look at myself in the mirror. I'd thought of sending it to you, Cloe, before I go, as a sort of consolation prize. But now I think not. No, I shall take it with me on my journey back to him.

The second half of the book presents a memoir by Roland, a diffident chap with a private income who is a friend and admirer of Cloe's. Roland has read Nancy's letter, and agrees, at Cloe's suggestion, to go to France and see if he can find Nancy, where she has apparently gone to live with her Israeli, if that's what he is. "I was struck by her tale of events," Roland says, sounding like Bertie Wooster when he is concentrating hard, "to the point of wishing with what for me is quite remarkable intensity to get to know this peculiar girl."

The narrative voices are beautifully done and are among the great pleasures of this book. Roland is as elegantly stuffy as Nancy is casual and scatty. Nancy is fond of words like "rackety," for example, and mildly says, "What has to be called my mind was still divided between the two possibilities." Roland uses phrases like "the fishiest part of the whole business," and his high point of romance comes when he almost lets himself go. Nancy is strolling across the top of the great viaduct of the Pont du Gard, Roland is watching from down below, by the river. She waves, and "her gesture . . . seemed to carry an immense significance. I felt suddenly and at once that I loved her: needed her, wanted to protect her. She was so far away, and in the last few days we seemed to have come so close." This is so unlike him that he is glad to get it over with. "All an impulse of the moment of course," he says in the next sentence. "By the time she was back beside me at the car I felt quite normal again. . . ."

Quite normal. Roland has fallen in love with Nancy's story, and is half in love with Nancy, because he thinks the whole tale is a fabrication, a harmless alternative to a cozy life. He is perfectly sure that there is no swarthy Mossad agent whom Nancy is hooked on, and who may return at any moment to beat her up—until someone remarkably like this fellow turns up and threatens them both. Carrying a red hat. The chances are that Nancy has been telling the unlikely truth all along, but her truthfulness is not the main preoccupation of this very engaging novel. What Bayley is asking us to think about is our sense of what's odd and what's not. What is out of the range of our experience is not necessarily implausible. What seems probable is not necessarily what's happening. "And was she so incomprehensible?" Roland asks about Nancy. "Perhaps she was no odder than anyone else?" She is more fun than anyone else Roland knows, and when he learns that her Dutch/French affair is over and that she is returning to England, he is overwhelmed by "a really ghastly depression." Can it be that she is "just like everybody else"? Can one give up wearing the red hat? Perhaps one has to.

*Identity* is the only unalluring book among these four novels about love. Its air is too thin, and its ideas, interesting as they are, are just dangled rather than worked on. *The Notebooks of Don Rigoberto* is immensely accomplished, the book of a craftsman, only a little dogged in pursuit of the formal scheme it has set itself, each section repeating the shape of the last. *A Lover's Almanac* is the richest, most substantial book of the four, the one to return to, because it is crowded with detail and associations, not always easy to gather at first go. *The Red Hat* is the lightest and most surprising of the books, driven by the purest sense of mischief.

> So had Nancy become odd, or strange or peculiar or whatever one called it, because of what she had written down about herself? Rather in the same way that people in portraits become strange and unique to our eyes just by being painted. If the painting's good enough, that is . . .

Becoming peculiar or whatever we call it may be a way of becoming ourselves: not eccentric but clarified. One of the lessons of love and writing, and above all of the writing of love.

# FURTHER READING

### Criticism

Coulter, Moureen. "Bridgeport Revisited." *Belles Lettres* 9, No. 1 (Fall 1993): 15.

> Coulter discusses the recurring characters in Howard's works and the cinematic prose style of *Natural History*.

Flower, Dean. "Politics and the Novel." *Hudson Review* 46 (Summer 1993): 395–402.

> Flower explores political issues in the writings of Maureen Howard, Julian Barnes, Imre Kertész, Ian McEwan, Rita Dove, and Wendell Berry.

Leonard, John. "Up from Bridgeport." *New York Times Book Review* (1 July 2001): E10.

> Leonard offers a positive assessment of *Big As Life: Three Tales for Spring,* calling it an "amazing novel."

---

**Additional coverage of Howard's life and career is contained in the following sources published by the Gale Group:** *Contemporary Authors,* **Vols. 53–56;** *Contemporary Authors New Revision Series,* **Vols. 31 and 75;** *Contemporary Novelists*; *Dictionary of Literary Biography,* **Vol. 83;** *Literature Resource Center;* **and** *Major 20th-Century Writers,* **Editions 1 and 2.**

# The Joy Luck Club

## Amy Tan

(Full name Amy Ruth Tan) American novelist, screenwriter, and children's writer.

The following entry presents criticism on Tan's *The Joy Luck Club* (1989). For further information on her life and works, see *CLC,* Volumes 59 and 120.

## INTRODUCTION

*The Joy Luck Club* (1989) is Tan's most successful and widely acclaimed novel. It is regarded as a significant achievement in documenting the hardships and struggles of immigrants in America and in portraying the complexities of modern Chinese-American life.

## PLOT AND MAJOR CHARACTERS

*The Joy Luck Club* is a collection of sixteen interrelated stories, centered around the diverse emotional relationships of four different mother/daughter pairs. To escape war and poverty, the four mothers emigrate from China to America. In the United States, they struggle to raise their American-born daughters in a vastly different culture. The novel opens with the death of Suyuan Woo, the matriarch of the Joy Luck Club, a social group of women who play the Chinese tile game mah-jongg and rely on each other for support. Suyuan founded the club in China and later reformed it in San Francisco. Suyuan's daughter, Jing-mei, takes her mother's place at the east side of the club's mah-jongg table. Jing-mei's interactions at the table with her older "aunties" symbolize the generational conflicts that play a major role in all of the stories. Each of the mother/daughter pairs has their own personal and cultural conflicts that are unique to their situation. In each relationship, events in the mother's past deeply affect how she identifies with and relates to her daughter. Because Suyuan lost a husband and was forced to abandon her twin daughters during the Japanese invasion of China, she consistently pushed Jing-mei to succeed and make a better life for herself. But her mother's high expectations paralyze Jing-mei, who begins to doubt her own talents and abilities. "Auntie" Lindo managed to escape her disastrous arranged marriage by manipulating her husband's family. In America, Lindo's daughter Waverly becomes a junior chess champion whose achievements give Lindo a great sense of pride. Waverly feels that Lindo takes too much credit for her success and, eventually, she accuses her mother of living vicariously through her. This confrontation causes each of them to question their own personal identity and the respect they have for each other. "Auntie" Ying-Ying grew up in a wealthy family. After her husband leaves her, Ying-Ying is forced to move in with some of her poorer relatives. She emigrates with her second husband, Clifford, to America, where she is forced to change her name to "Betty" and adjust to an even lower standard of living. Ying-Ying's daughter, Lena, is a successful architect, but her husband doesn't value her. Furthermore, Lena's lifestyle and materialism clash with Ying-Ying's traditional Chinese ways, which she fears will be forgotten. "Auntie" An-mei Hsu's mother served as a wealthy gentleman's concubine. Because of her mother's occupation, young An-mei was raised surrounded by riches, but was not allowed to share in any of the luxuries. Her mother eventually commits suicide, giving An-mei a way to escape the life of a concubine. Rose Hsu Jordan, An-mei's daughter, struggles with filing divorce papers after her husband leaves her. Rose's indecisiveness comes from recurring nightmares, inspired by her mother's stories and her mother's assertion that she can read Rose's mind. The novel concludes with Jing-mei, who decides to discover the end of her mother's life story by finding and meeting her abandoned twin half-sisters. Her aunties give Jing-mei the money she needs to travel to China, affirming the healing effect of storytelling and the very real—if elusive—bond between generations.

## MAJOR THEMES

The major theme of *The Joy Luck Club* concerns the nature of mother-daughter relationships, which are complicated not only by age difference, but by vastly different upbringings. The daughters—who have grown up embracing the American emphasis on individuality—feel that their mothers are "Old World fossils." They rebel against the Chinese tradition of heeding their elders and pleasing parents above all else. The mothers are appalled at their daughters' insolence. They fear that their daughters' desire to achieve the American Dream will prevent them from ever learning about or understanding their Chinese heritage. Despite these fears, all four of the mothers attempt to give their children the best of both worlds. As Lindo states, "American circumstances but Chinese character. . . . How could I know these two things do not mix?" The painful events in the mothers' pasts and their "Chinese character" have a definite impact on their daughters' present lives. The power and importance of storytelling is another significant theme in the novel. One reason the mother-daughter relationships suffer is that neither generation speaks the language of the other—literally and metaphorically. The mothers try to compensate for this difficulty in communication by relating information through stories. However, most of the stories only frustrate their daughters, who are at a loss to interpret what they really mean. When the daughters—particularly Jing-mei—are finally able to see the true meaning behind their mothers' tales, they find that the stories are an important form of instruction and comfort. Issues of self-worth and identity are also central to *The Joy Luck Club*. All of the women (both mothers and daughters) wrestle with their past, their present, their ethnicity, their gender, and how they view themselves, as they struggle to construct their own life story and find a place for themselves in the world.

## CRITICAL RECEPTION

Many critics have asserted that although the characters in *The Joy Luck Club* are Chinese-American, their struggles have a strong resonance for all people, especially women raised in America. Reviewers have studied the novel from a variety of angles and have generally agreed that the book presents a poignant, insightful examination of not only the generation gap between mothers and daughters, but of the gaps between different cultures as well. Critics have argued that the book works as an exploration of the issues that are vital to all immigrants in America—including ethnicity, gender, and personal identity. Some reviewers have identified the mother-daughter relationships in the book as part of a growing tradition of matrilineal discourse that is becoming ever more popular in America. Others have lauded the multiple perspectives presented in the novel, citing the work's multiple viewpoints as a unique strength that invites analysis on several levels. One critic has even analyzed the fable-like qualities of *The Joy Luck Club*, interpreting it as a modern-day fairy tale. Although several reviewers have argued that the novel presents stereotypical portrayals of China and of Chinese people, many critics feel that it addresses important universal issues and themes—common to all, despite their age, race, or nationality.

# PRINCIPAL WORKS

*The Joy Luck Club* (novel) 1989
*The Kitchen God's Wife* (novel) 1991
*The Moon Lady* (juvenilia) 1992
*The Joy Luck Club* [with Ronald Bass] (screenplay) 1993
*The Chinese Siamese Cat* (juvenilia) 1994
*The Hundred Secret Senses* (novel) 1995
*The Bonesetter's Daughter* (novel) 2001

# CRITICISM

**Malini Johar Schueller (essay date Winter 1992)**

SOURCE: "Theorizing Ethnicity and Subjectivity: Maxine Hong Kingston's *Tripmaster Monkey* and Amy Tan's *The Joy Luck Club*," in *Genders*, No. 15, Winter, 1992, pp. 72–85.

[*In the following comparative essay on Maxine Hong Kingston's* Tripmaster Monkey *and Tan's* The Joy Luck Club, *Schueller writes that Kingston uses a subversive male protagonist to illustrate how ethnicity is socially constructed, while Tan uses four separate mother-daughter relationships to simultaneously embrace and thwart conceptions of ethnicity and gender.*]

When women of color began to voice their estrangement from the theories and concerns of white feminists, they dramatized the fact that they had for too long been the objects of representation.[1] The task of these women was twofold: that of deconstructing the male/female binary opposition of white feminism by interjecting concerns of race, colonialism, and imperialism; and that of constructing theories of "identity" (and I use the term deliberately with caution) for women of color. Understandably, it was the deconstructive project that was (and is being) first undertaken with great energy. To mention only a few critics, there were those like Gayatri Spivak who deconstructed liberal feminist literary criticism and revealed its investment in the emancipation of white women alone[2] women like bell hooks revealed the concerns of Euro-American feminism to be restricted to those of middle-class white women;[3] critics such as Valerie Amos and Pratibha Parmar questioned the politics of feminists who viewed imperialism as having been historically progressive for Third World women[4] However, the task of construction has been much more complicated and fraught with ambivalences. On the one hand, women of color have had to emphasize their particular concerns, their differences from ideologies of universal womanhood—whether Anglo-American or French—while on the other hand they have been concerned about the problems of espousing a racial/ethnic essence. The concern with essentialism in feminist debates today, in other words, is also a major concern in theoretical discussions of ethnicity as well as in fictional works of women of color[5] Here, I wish to examine the task of construction in discussions of ethnicity and show how a focus on representation and the discursivity of identity offers possible alternatives to the notion of a racial/ethnic essence.[6] I argue that such a focus is not restricted to theory but is, in fact, a major concern in two recent texts by Chinese-American women writers: *Tripmaster Monkey* by Maxine Hong Kingston and *The Joy Luck Club* by Amy Tan.

Some of the difficulties associated with constructing ethnicity in the context of a posthumanistic consciousness are evident in Lisa Lowe's insightful essay on the Asian-American subject. Lowe stresses the heterogeneity of Asian-American culture in order ultimately to "disrupt the current hegemonic relationship between 'dominant' and 'minority' positions."[7] Yet it is necessary, Lowe further acknowledges, to keep the concept of ethnic identity "for the purpose of contesting and disrupting the discourses that exclude Asian American(s)."[8] To completely give up the model of oppression in formulations of ethnicity is to give up too much. Indeed the most problematic use to which ethnicity has been put has been the one that depoliticizes the term, dissociates it from marginalization and oppression, and opposes it to a supposedly fixed concept of race. To this camp belong Anglo-American critics who invoke the ideology of the melting pot and, without any sensitivity to relations of power and dominance, see a similarity among all "ethnic" groups—Irish-American, Italian-American, African-American.[9] Of course one only has to glance at the centuries of hysteria about racial miscegenation in the United States to see the problems in invoking such; similarities.[10] Such a concept of ethnicity is of little use to women of color and must, indeed, be regarded with suspicion. The question seems to be the use to which ethnic definitions are put. There needs to be a healthy suspicion of definitions because it is precisely by using the strategy of restrictive definition and hierarchical binary opposition that the dominant culture has oppressed marginal groups. But this also does not mean that there is no political importance in appropriating the second term in the hierarchy and empowering it in slogans such as "black is beautiful." However, such slogans are empowering precisely because they question the hierarchy; what is empowering is the act of appropriation "Black is beautiful" expresses a political solidarity but does not suggest that there is an essential "blackness" to be empowered. The difficult task for women of color, then, is to articulate a politics of resistance and difference without resorting to purely definitional conceptions of ethnic identity.

The first step toward such a construction is to think of ethnicity not simply as essence but as representation, as something linguistically constructed. (After all, it is representations such as the black rapist, the duplicitous Asian, or the passive Asian woman that are used to dominate and suppress minorities) While constructions of subjectivity by liberal white feminists have typically relied on notions of the singular, autonomous self, women of color have typically relied on collective and social subjectivities.[11] Marxist theorists of language and subjectivity have similarly rejected the isolated, autonomous psyche of Freudian psychology for a conception of the psyche as a social and discursive entity. The psyche, according to Bakhtin, "enjoys extraterritorial status . . . [as] a social entity."[12] Experience is available to this psyche not in some immediate fashion but through a network of signs, most importantly, language. "Not only can experience be outwardly expressed through the agency of the sign . . . but also aside from this outward expression (for others), experience exists even for the person undergoing it only in the material of signs. Outside that material there is no experience as such."[13] The importance of a discursive notion of self in thinking about ethnicity is that it provides a powerful indictment of the idea of an essential, abstract biological self beyond language and society. It is a way of retaining the concept of identity, but as a social construct, constantly reformulated and reformulating itself through language. It is also a way of resisting essentialist definitions of ethnicity.

In *Tripmaster Monkey* and ***The Joy Luck Club***, Kingston and Tan affirm a politics of resistance and difference and thematize the construction of a Chinese-American identity. Interestingly, representation plays a key role in the formation of ethnic identity in both works. Both works also emphasize the socially constructed, discursive nature of gender and ethnic identity. Kingston uses the discursivity of ethnic identity to completely subvert the idea of cultural origins while Tan uses discursivity to show how cultural origins are multiple and complex. In very different ways, the two works raise questions about ethnicity, identity, and difference which are crucial to the concerns of women of color.

*Tripmaster Monkey* is about the hopes, anxieties, fears, and angers of Wittman Ah Sing—first-generation Chinese-American, Berkeley graduate, fired retail employee, cynical lover, long-haired peacenik, passionate playwright—as he walks the streets of San Francisco reflecting on his place in American society and reading Rilke aloud to passengers on a Bay Area bus. It ends with Wittman staging a play for his Chinese-American audience and using the theater as a public forum to comment on the pathologizing of Chinese as exotic. In *The Woman Warrior* Kingston wrote polemically as a Chinese-American woman battling an oppressive white male culture and also deconstructed hierarchical oppositions between Chinese and American, male and female.[14] In *Tripmaster Monkey* Kingston further problematizes and subverts restrictive ethnic definitions by emphasizing the complex processes of representation and interpretation involved in the formulation of any such definition.

In a sense, the entire novel is an extended meditation on representation. Kingston emphasizes the marginalization of people of color by rewriting the "classic" texts of white American writers. Her hero, named Wittman by his actor father, is the latter-day incarnation of the poet of democracy and diversity, the supremely American poet who embraces the high and the low, the bleeding slave and the Indian. But Kingston, by presenting her novel as a modern "Song of Myself," compellingly confronts us with the fact that the prerogative to speak to and embody all America has always been a white male one: "'Call me Ishmael.' See? You pictured a white guy, didn't you? If Ishmael were described—ochery ecru amber umber skin—you picture a *tan* white guy. Wittman wanted to spoil all those stories coming out of and set in New England Back East—to blacken and to yellow Bill, Brooke, and Annie. A new rule for the imagination: The common man has Chinese looks. From now on, whenever you read about those people with no surnames, color them with black skin or yellow skin."[15]

Kingston's appropriation of *Moby Dick,* the classic American epic, is an act of empowerment through which the Chinese Other can have a voice in America. And just as Kingston examines the hegemony of white American culture through its literary representation, thus emphasizing the discursivity of American identity, she similarly emphasizes the constructed nature of Chinese ethnic identity. Although Wittman despises the "Oriental Tea Garden" variety of exoticism, his own perceptions of Chinese people are influenced by the representations of Chinese in American popular culture. Walking the streets of San Francisco, Wittman sees "a Chinese dude from China, hands clasped behind, bow-legged, loose-seated, out on a stroll—that walk they do in kung fu movies when they are full of contentment on a sunny day" (*TM* 4–5). Interestingly, this is a description of a "Fresh Off the Boats" immigrant Chinese, one who should logically be the repository of an "original" culture. Kingston, however, suggests that the very idea of what an ethnic essence is comes out of popular representations. What Wittman is presented with, through the narrating voice, is both the nominal "original" and the second-hand represented simultaneously. Representation and reality, the socially constructed stereotypical and the experiential are inseparably mixed in Wittman's perceptions of ethnic difference.

It is, therefore, extremely significant that Kingston chooses the profession of playwright for her hero.[16] Wittman is agonizingly conscious of the different social roles he plays and keeps a running narrative of the play he is currently writing. He constantly undermines and subverts the narrow roles assigned to Chinese people in American culture. Instead of conforming to the demure and decorous look of Ivy League Chinese, Wittman flaunts his long-haired hippie look. To the officer at the unemployment office who attempts to classify him as a potential retail manager, as his last job indicates, he insists he be listed as a playwright. As his friend Nanci, the aspiring actress, constantly finds, being accepted in America means playing certain ethnic roles. At her auditions, Nanci is told to "act more Oriental." "You don't sound the way you look. You don't look the way you talk" (*TM* 24). Angered by the straitjacketing Chinese are faced with, Wittman vows to wrest the theater back for the Chinese.

Wittman's stage production literally becomes an arena for alternative enactments of ethnicity. The cast of characters, which includes nearly all the characters in the book, participate in Wittman's play based on the epic Chinese *Romance of the Three Kingdoms*. But these Chinese-Americans, despite the mediation of the play and Wittman's attempts to subvert narrow racial definitions, are still subject to essentialist racial interpretation. Reviews of the play praise it as "East meets West," "sweet and sour," and "singing rice," much in the same manner as many of the reviews of Kingston's own works.[17] Kingston does not suggest that the Chinese are simply the passive objects of Western definition. Like the natives who, in a colonial situation, internalize the norms and values of colonizers, the Chinese, too, see themselves through the eyes of their American viewers and enthusiastically applaud the reviews. Angered by the inability of the Chinese to perceive their own pathologizing, Wittman uses the stage to harangue his audience: "We're about as exotic as shit. Nobody so special here. No sweet-and-sour shit. No exotic chop suey shit. So this variety show had too much motley; they didn't have to call it 'chop suey vaudeville' . . . Do I have to explain why 'exotic' pisses me off, and 'not exotic' pisses me off? They've got us in a bag, which we aren't punching our way out of" (*TM* 308). Giving voice to the culturally marginalized is thus not a question of proclaiming the primacy of certain ethnic values over others—indeed, Kingston has her protagonist constantly scoff at what are perceived as particularly "Chinese" traits—but rather that of adopting a conscious political position of resistance to the oppressive definitions of the dominant culture. Indeed, Kingston makes her protagonist challenge these definitions by taking them seriously at the literal level and thus revealing the racial ideologies such definitions seek to hide. As Wittman shouts to his audience: "I'm common ordinary. Plain black sweater. Blue jeans. Tennis shoes ordinaire. Clean soo mun shaven. What's so exotic?" (*TM* 308).

It is also important to emphasize that this resistance to definition is part of a politics of difference and not a coded longing to be part of a common "American" humanity.

Kingston's works have too often been misread as exactly that. *The Woman Warrior*, for example, has been read as an attempt of the narrator to escape from Chinese restriction to American freedom. Similarly Wittman's politics in *Tripmaster Monkey* have been seen as "his identification with the ideals of the melting pot."[18] But the ideology of the melting pot is a stance of pluralism and traditional liberal humanism. Humanism argues that at the end of all theorizing we are left with an essential humanity, a metaphysical identity which it is the purpose of activism to affirm and defend. The assumption is that although there are different social groups, these groups are positioned in relations of democratic equality and any consensual ideology emerges from an equal participation by all groups. Such an assumption denies the existence of class structure and the very real inequalities of power and position that all marginalized groups, particularly women of color, are subject to. Kingston, too, is conscious of the disempowerment of Chinese-Americans and is determined not to subsume their interests under the hegemony of a unified melting pot ideology. When Wittman rails about having "failed . . . to burst through their Kipling" and argues that in his play "there is no East. . . . West is meeting West," he ruptures the hierarchical division which views the East as aberrance and challenges his American viewers to nurture a society of radical differences (*TM* 308). Instead of accepting the definitions of the dominant culture, Wittman argues for a strategic and political group identity. Knowing full well that the term "American" is used "interchangeably with 'white,'" Wittman suggests that the Chinese politicize their identity. "It's our fault they call us gook and chinky chinaman," says Wittman. "We've been here all this time, before Columbus, and haven't named ourselves. Look at the Blacks beautifully defining themselves" (*TM* 326).

Kingston's conception of social difference and her view of ethnicity as a represented, social construct are both intimately related to her rejection of the stable and unified subject on which both humanist and essentialist racial visions depend.[19] The loquacious and energetic hero of *Tripmaster Monkey*, unlike the sage after whom he is named, is not the transcendent poet who can rise above the social-material world into visions of spiritual unity but the person of this world whose identity is constituted by Otherness and is always changing. *Tripmaster Monkey* begins with a vision of Wittman's body scattered into fragments as he laconically contemplates suicide much in the manner of Hart Crane's speaker in *The Bridge*. Throughout the novel, Wittman enacts changes of character and identity. Accosted on the bus by a Chinese woman who stereotypes him as the quiet Asian science whiz, Wittman plays the role to fit the part:

> "I don't know what you say," says Wittman. Know like no, like brain. "I major in engineer."
>
> "Where do you study engineering?"
>
> "Ha-ah." He made a noise like a samurai doing a me-ay, or an old Chinese guy who smokes too much.
>
> (*TM* 75)

At other times, Wittman talks rap, wishes the Chinese had their own jazz and blues, and tries to appropriate the demeanor of the "heroic Black man" when he hears people at a restaurant cracking "chink joke[s]" (*TM* 214). Wittman thrives on being multifaceted, on driving his car like "an international student from a developing country" or like an "Oakie" (*TM* 208). At Coit Tower he plays at getting married to a white girl, Tana, by a man who is possibly a minister, while the production of his play turns into a marriage celebration as the Chinese actor-audience shower rice on the couple. Life and art, play and reality, Kingston suggests, are not easily demarcated.

Just as Kingston sees ethnicity and subjectivity as constituted by representation and social construction, she also views gender as a social construct and a site of difference. In *The Woman Warrior* Kingston had emphasized the variability of femininity and deconstructed oppositions between male and female, American and Chinese. Kingston "violate[d] the law of opposition making gender dichotomies proliferate into unresolved gender differences."[20] In *Tripmaster Monkey* she deliberately undermines any notion of an essential, singular female identity by making Wittman her central character and thus challenging easy experiential identification. At the same time, Kingston makes clear that gender boundaries are always constructed. It is significant that PoPo, the grandmother who has partly raised Wittman and to whom he is emotionally attached, calls him "honey girl" and "Wit Man." And the guise in which Wittman most frequently appears subverts traditional gender and ethnic dichotomies. Wittman is the modern-day reincarnation of Monkey King, the mythological trickster figure from Wu Cheng-en's sixteenth-century novel *The Pilgrimage to the West*. As a figure of Chinese mythology the monkey is firmly anchored within the culture, yet subject to change. The monkey breaks taboos, is punished by the gods, but manages to escape difficult situations through trickery. He goes along with the monk on a pilgrimage to get Buddhist scriptures, but he demonstrates the real impracticality of Buddhist pacifism in fighting with devils. The monk is spiritual, devout, and unquestioning: the monkey is earthly, appetitive, sensual, and changing. Unlike the monk, the monkey can change into different forms and can see through the various guises taken on by devils.

Kingston's use of the monkey as the figure for the ethnic subject is an affirmation of difference and resistance. Like the Afro-American signifying monkey who dwells in the margins of discourse and who challenges the dominant culture by multiple voicings. Kingston's Chinese-American Monkey King speaks for the people of Chinatown but refuses a singular ethnic discourse.[21] As a feminist of color it is important for Kingston to reject ethnic discourses which celebrate a singular Chinese identity. Such discourses belong to the language of patriarchal absolutism that women of color need to cast off. Kingston's decision to use a male protagonist instead of dealing directly with the experiences of women (as she did in *The Woman Warrior*) also suggests her determination to dissociate the concerns of women from simple biodeterminism alone. Kingston herself has suggested that the "omniscient narrator in *Tripmaster Monkey* is a Chinese American woman; she's Kwan Yin (the Goddess of Mercy) and she's me."²² It is not as if Kingston associates her male protagonist with more "universal" values. Instead, she uses him to suggest the problems with gender dichotomies that equate maleness with singularity and universality and thus uses the occasion of the male protagonist to subvert gender oppositions much like she did in *The Woman Warrior*. The same is the case with ethnicity. If there is no "real" China or Chinese-American culture to valorize, there is no "real" Americanism that immigrants need espouse. Indeed, the striking feature of the book is that although it is so concerned with immigrant experience and the politics of assimilation, there is no Oedipal quest structure, the end of which is the attainment of a certain kind of ethnicity. There is, instead, a celebration of multiple enactments of ethnicity. Through Wittman, Kingston shows how ethnic identity as a shifting, constantly reformulated concept, related to an "origin" only through linguistic representations and fictions, is, in fact, empowering.

In contrast to *Tripmaster Monkey*, Amy Tan's **The Joy Luck Club** deals explicitly with the experiences of Chinese-American women and their acculturation in a new environment. The narrative centers around the lives of four Mandarin-speaking Chinese immigrant mothers in San Francisco who have formed a mahjongg group called the Joy Luck Club and the American-born daughters of these mothers. The narrative unfolds through the four different mother-daughter narrators telling the stories of their lives. Tan places a decided emphasis on mother-daughter relationships, and much of the work can be seen as a celebration of values such as nurturance and connectedness that have been seen by many feminists to characterize women as opposed to male values such as separation and autonomy.²³ But Tan ensures that her work cannot simply be recuperated as an ahistorical feminism without attention to the particular status of women of color within universalist feminism. Like Kingston who presents ethnicity as a construct, Tan presents Chinese-American women's identity as resistance by appropriating (and thus questioning) the rhetoric of universalist feminism.

In order to appreciate Tan's appropriation, we need to consider the representations of women of color when they are the objects of feminist analysis. Aihwa Ong explains the dynamics of these representations as follows: "By portraying women in non-Western societies as identical and interchangeable, and more exploited than women in dominant capitalist societies, liberal and socialist feminists alike encode a belief in their own cultural superiority. . . . Studies on women in post-1949 China inevitably discuss how they are doubly exploited by the peasant family and by the socialist patriarchy."²⁴ Within white American culture the dichotomies between Western and Asian women are clearly seen as those between activity and passivity, freedom and restraint, independence and submission. Tan is aware of these dichotomies and attempts to undermine the imperialism within universalist feminism. In **The Joy Luck Club** Tan polemically records the marginalization and disempowerment of all women within patriarchal institutions—whether in China or America. While wives within the traditional Chinese family are taught to find satisfaction in waiting on their husbands and their families, in America the mass media insidiously reinforces the same subservience. As Lindo Jong, one of the Chinese mothers, reflects. "I hurt so much I didn't feel any difference. What was happier than seeing everybody gobble down the shiny mushrooms and bamboo shoots I had helped prepare that day? . . . How much happier could I be after seeing Tyan-yu eat a whole bowl of noodles without complaining about its taste or my looks? It's like those ladies you see on American TV these days, the ones who are so happy they have washed out a stain so the clothes look better than new."²⁵ Tan's subversion of the distinction between the progressive (Euro-American) woman and the traditional Asian woman is radical here. Lindo Jong, the woman who was married at the age of eight and sent to live with her husband's family at the age of twelve, is not only equated with the (ostensibly) free American woman but is also given the power to interpret her Western counterpart. Similarly, Tan uses another Chinese immigrant mother to voice the idea of the disempowerment of women across cultures and generations. Reflecting on the despair of her American-born daughter over an impending divorce, An-Mei Hsu concludes: "If she doesn't speak, she is making a choice. . . . I know this, because I was raised the Chinese way: I was taught to desire nothing. . . . And even though I taught my daughter the opposite, she still came out the same way! Maybe it was because she was born to me and she was born a girl. And I was born to my mother and I was born to be a girl. All of us are like stairs, one step after another, going up and down, but all going the same way" (*JL* 215). Tan's formulation of a common oppression shared by what is traditionally perceived as Chinese-raised and American-raised women again subverts East-West cultural dichotomies. Tan carefully relies upon and upsets these hierarchical cultural expectations. "Because I was raised the Chinese way" in the above passage, for example, strategically reveals the imperialist racial context within which such casual formulations are taken as completely explanatory. In another instance Tan deconstructs the myth of American freedom. Male polygamy in China sanctions the mistreatment of women and their relegation to concubine status, the humiliation of which An-Mei Hsu's mother escapes only through suicide. However, in America, the ethnic woman is subject to dual disempowerment of ethnicity and gender. The seemingly lovable Irish husband of Ying-Ying St. Clair proudly imagines himself having "saved" his Chinese wife from some hideous, unimaginable life and passes this myth on to his daughter. In reality, as Ying Ying reflects, she was "raised with riches he could not even imagine" and he had to wait for four years "like a dog in a butcher shop" before she consented to marry him (*JL* 250). Once in America, St. Clair, in a sense, enslaves Ying-Ying. He crosses out Ying-Ying's Chinese name on her passport papers, names her Betty St. Clair, gives her a new birthdate, and insists she speak English. "So with him, she spoke in moods and gestures, looks and silences. . . . Words cannot come out. So my father put words in her mouth" (*JL* 106). The result: madness.

Just as Tan depicts a common oppression of women, she also depicts a resistance through maternal bonding and nurturing. The novel begins with the death of Suyan Woo, mother of Jing-Mei Woo and founder of the Joy Luck Club. A woman of incredible strength and moral courage, Suyan Woo started the Joy Luck Club, a mah-jongg group, during the Japanese invasion of China. Amidst the destruction and poverty caused by the invasion, the women decided to create an oasis of good cheer in which they pretended to be rich and carefree. The novel ends with Jing-Mei Woo going to China to meet her half-sisters, the two daughters Suyan Woo was forced to abandon during the invasion but which she never gave up trying to locate. Jing-Mei Woo's journey to China is thus a journey back to her mother, a retrieval of her memory into the present. "Together we look like our mother. Her same eyes, her same mouth, open in surprise to see, at last, her long-cherished wish" (*JL* 288). Throughout the book we see the intensity and power of mother-daughter bonds. An-Mei Hsu's mother literally tears off her flesh and offers it in sacrifice in an attempt to revive her dying mother; Rose-Hsu Jordan is able to demand her divorce rights by imaginative identification with her mother; and Jing-Mei Woo looks for the memory of her mother to help her understand the present.

And this female identity as defined through the mother-daughter bond is integrally linked to ethnic identity. As Amy Ling suggests, the lost mother is a trope for lost motherland.[26] The return to the mother is also the return to cultural roots; separation from the mother is a separation from one's own cultural origins. Ying-Ying St. Clair's determination to bridge the separation between her daughter and herself is a synecdoche of the narratives of separation and togetherness that inform the text. "There is a part of her mind that is part of mine. . . . All her life I have watched her as though from another shore. And now I must tell her everything about my past. It is the only way to penetrate her skin and pull her to where she can be saved" (*JL* 242).

But Tan builds up the romantic concept of cultural origins and lost ethnic essence only in order to radically undermine and reconfigure the notion of an ethnic essence. The narrative of separation and return—symbolized by Jing-Mei Woo's return to China/mother—on the plot level is questioned by the rhetorical structure of the text which undercuts any notions of simple identification of origins or of a cultural "reality" easily available for access. The experiences of Chinese immigrants in America and their past lives in China are not documented by a seemingly objective narrator but by a series of participants narrating their extremely subjective experiences. Tan's decision to have several mothers and daughters telling their different stories reflects her awareness of ethnicity as a constantly shifting social construct and her commitment to community. The mothers and daughters tell their stories within the framework of the Joy Luck Club, the purpose of which is to keep alive a memory of the past and create a community. Each section of the novel actually creates a different version of femininity and ethnicity. While the first section of the novel emphasizes the loss of separation from mothers, the second emphasizes the competitiveness of the relationship. Thus we have An-Mei Hsu's mother, who determinedly, despite the curses of her family, takes her daughter to live with her even though she only has the status of concubine; we also have Jing-Mei Woo, the Chinese-American daughter who wishes to understand and unite with the memories of her dead mother.[27] On the other hand, we have immigrant Chinese mothers who project their cultural anxieties on their daughters. Waverly Jong's mother, for instance, parades her daughter's chess trophies and lectures to her about winning tournaments while Suyan Woo tries unsuccessfully to create a musical child prodigy out of her unmusical daughter Jing-Mei Woo.

Further, Tan's construction of ethnic identity is not based on a vision of a stable and unchanging China that can be recalled at will. Although the theme of estrangement from, and unification with, cultural origins is integral to the work, these origins are multiple and discursive. Part of Tan's purpose in having four different Chinese-born mothers is to introduce different versions of China, neither of which is prioritized over the other. At the most obvious level, there are clear class differences among the mothers' experiences of China. Auntie Lin's family in China revels in consumerism, surrounding itself with color TV sets and remote controls; An-Mei Hsu's family, on the other hand, is awed at having a relative in the land of consumer goods. More importantly, for the American-born daughters, the Chinese past exists discursively, in language, through the stories told about it by their mothers. Ethnic origins, in other words, are always already complicated by representation. For An-Mei Hsu, a Chinese mother, for example, "China" is a mixture of memories of her mother's suicide and of peasant uprisings that she reads of in magazines from China, all of which have to be sorted out by her psychiatrist (*JL* 241). The most interesting example of ethnic origins being based on multiple and changing representations is the history of the Joy Luck Club itself. Suyan Woo tells her daughter the history of the Joy Luck Club which she started in Kweilin, but the history changes with each retelling. Her daughter, who has heard the story many times, never thinks her mother's Kweilin story about the origins of the Joy Luck Club is "anything but a Chinese fairy tale. The endings always changed. Sometimes she said she used that worthless thousand-yuan note to buy a half-cup of rice. She turned that rice into a pot of porridge. . . . The story always grew and grew" (*JL* 25). In many ways, the club itself deconstructs traditionally perceived oppositions between history and fiction, the experiential and the discursive. The club is formed as a make-believe celebration of plenty during the devastation of Japanese occupation and thus has a fictive function. Yet the club survives as Suyan Woo's most "real" memory of the war period. The club is based on stories, "stories spilling out all over the place" (*JL* 24). The women tell each other stories about "good times in the past and good times yet to come," pretending each week is a new year, and this self-consciously fictive club becomes the basis for creating an immigrant community in California.

Similarly, Tan's mode of narration questions the very idea of historical context as something that can be retrieved through a recording of facts. Tan uses a dialogic mixture of myth, fantasy, reverie, and historical facts without demarcating any as more true than the other and thus questions the truth status of a national history. Within "true" stories of the Chinese past of immigrant mothers, stories of arranged marriages and Japanese occupation, there are affective images of mythical women like the Moon Lady and grotesque images of destructive mothers dismembering their daughters. The concept of a Chinese woman's identity, Tan suggests, is a discursive one. Similarly, the last section of the book, which includes four narratives of mothers and daughters coming to an understanding, is titled "Queen Mother of the Western Skies" and obviously involves the figure of Queen Mother, the feminization of Buddha who appears (in White Lotus Buddhism) as the creator of mankind and the controller of time. The blend of myth and traditional historical storytelling that informs the narratives about China suggests that ethnic origins are always created and recreated in the complex process of social representation. To think of ethnicity as an essence is to fall prey to the fortune cookie syndrome, to create monologic definitions in order to manage differences. As An-Mei Hsu tells Lindo Jong about fortune cookies, "American people think Chinese people write these sayings." "But we never say such things!" I said. "These things don't make sense" (*JL* 262).

Tan's simultaneous use of the motif of the return to origins and her complication of these origins raises a matter of unquestionable importance for women of color. Is it desirable for a radical feminist politics to view femininity and ethnicity as ever-changing social constructs? Is it possible to demand and affect social change without the construction of a whole and unified subject? The answer to both those questions has to be a yes if only because the alternatives are so dangerous. As an example of the problems inherent in momentarily positing a singular ethnicity and femininity we can look, for a moment, at Tan's text. The last chapter of **The Joy Luck Club** presents an idealized moment of ethnic identity, set deliberately against the multiplicities of the rest of the novel. The chapter concerns Jing-Mei Woo's trip to China to meet her two half-sisters whom her mother was forced to abandon and who have been miraculously located by the members of the Joy Luck Club. The trope of the lost motherland and the lost mother become one here. Jing-Mei Woo feels herself "becoming" Chinese as the train crosses the border from Hong Kong. "Once you are born Chinese, you cannot help but feel and think Chinese. . . . It is in your blood" (*JL* 267). The entire chapter enacts a rhapsody of ethnic identity as Jing-Mei and her father meet old relatives and finally the two lost sisters. Here Jing-Mei Woo understands an ethnic identity that is beyond language: "And now I also see what part of me is Chinese. It is so obvious. It is my family. It is in our blood. After all these years, it can finally be let go" (*JL* 288). But while Tan celebrates this moment of ethnic wholeness, she is also aware of the problems that such essentialist concepts pose. Moments such as these deny the class differences between the tourist gazer and the ethnic subject and suggest an ethnic oneness that the text thus far has questioned. Tan therefore chooses to end her narrative not with this moment but with a commentary on it. The text ends with Jing-Mei and her sisters looking at a Polaroid photo of themselves that Jing-Mei's father has just taken, and with Jing-Mei recognizing her mother in the composite of the three sisters. Jing-Mei recognizes an ethnic identification but only through her active interpretation and by deliberately framing ethnic "subjects" in a momentary stasis beyond language.

Kingston and Tan succeed in creating a space for women of color to articulate themselves because they refuse to use definitional modes of locating gender and ethnic identity. Kingston presents a constructed and discursive ethnic identity by having her protagonist take on multiple roles and constantly enact versions of ethnicity, while Tan does so by presenting multiple representations of ethnic origins. The emphasis on the discursivity and contextuality of ethnic identity does not mean that Kingston and Tan are attempting to write from beyond ethnicity or that they are denying the importance of racial divisions in society. On the contrary, it attests to the determination of these women to use ethnicity as resistance, to articulate it in such a manner that it cannot be reduced to definitional criteria which have always been used to marginalize people of color.

*Notes*

1. I use the term *women of color* deliberately in order to stress a political rather than biological category and also to maintain the insistence of many women of color (Alice Walker's use of "womanist" comes to mind) who have refused to use the label "feminist" because of its association with white feminism alone. See Chandra Talpade Mohanty's explanation of the term in the "Introduction" in *Third World Women and the Politics of Feminism* (Bloomington: Indiana University Press, 1991), 7.

2. Spivak's critique of feminists who touted Jane Eyre as a feminist text and ignored the relationship of dominance between Jane and the West Indian, Bertha, is exemplary here. See Spivak's "Three Women's Texts and a Critique of Imperialism," *Critical Inquiry* 12 (1985): 243–261.

3. bell hooks begins her discussion of the difference of women of color by pointing out how Betty Friedan's position in *The Feminine Mystique* assumed that all women were middle-class housewives with leisure. Constructions of womanhood under slavery, as hooks points out, clearly show the very different concerns

of white versus African-American women. See bell hooks, *Feminist Theory: From Margin to Center* (Boston: South End Press, 1984).

4. See Valerie Amos and Pratibha Parmar's questioning of Maxine Molyneux's endorsement of imperialism. Such thinking, Amos and Parmar write, implies that "it is only when Third World women enter into capitalistic relations will they have any hope of liberation." Valerie Amos and Pratibha Parmar, "Challenging Imperial Feminism," *Feminist Review* 17 (Autumn 1984): 6.

5. The first issue of *Differences* (1989) was devoted to discussions of essentialism with feminist theory.

6. The terms *ethnicity* and *race* have themselves been the objects of much discussion. Ethnicity has sometimes been seen as synonymous with culture, as opposed to the biological concept of race, or has been seen as a broader concept that, in fact, includes race. Some feminists have objected to the use of the term *race* because of its biological and definitional associations. Floya Anthias and Nira Yuval-Davis, for example, object to the essentialism they see inherent in the concept of race and favor using the concept of ethnicity instead. Ethnicity, they believe, can address the complex and historically specific conjunctures of ethnicity, gender, and class better than the concept of race. See Floya Anthias and Nira Yuval-Davis, "Contextualizing Feminism—Gender, Ethnic and Class Divisions," *Feminist Review* 15 (1983): 63. Michelle Barrett and Mary McIntosh, on the other hand, argue in favor of retaining the concept of race because of its politically charged associations: "To reject the black/white distinction in favor of a concept of ethnic division is to reject the political, social and ideological force of racism in our society" (27). But while seeming to favor the concept of race in a somewhat purist manner, Barrett and McIntosh go on to use the term *black* in their analysis to "people of Asian, African and West Indian origin," in other words, all marginalized people of color in England (28). We can clearly see that whether we use the category of ethnicity or race, the important point is to maintain the linkage of these terms to the politics of oppression and domination. See Michele Barrett and Mary McIntosh, "Ethnocentrism and Socialist Feminist Theory," *Feminist Review* 20 (Summer 1985): 23–47.

7. See Lisa Lowe, "Heterogeneity, Hybridity, Multiplicity: Marking Asian American Differences," *Diaspora* (Spring 1991): 28.

8. Ibid., 39.

9. Werner Sollors' collection of essays, *The Invention of Ethnicity*, is designed to accomplish this purpose. Sollors rightly criticizes essentialist ethnic definitions but completely misrepresents the debates about ethnicity and race by insisting that critics who want to retain the concept of ethnicity want to do so in rigid, definitional form (xiii). According to Sollors' argument, the only alternative to essentialist ethnicity is a belief in the reality of the American melting pot (xiv). It is perhaps a revealing absence in Sollors' collection that there are no essays by the most well known but radical theorists of race who have never espoused racial essentialism—Gayatri Spivak, Edward Said, Homi Bhabha, Barbara Johnson. Henry Louis Gates, etc. See Werner Sollors, ed., *The Invention of Ethnicity* (New York: Oxford University Press, 1989).

10. In the United States it is clear that ethnicity as a concept of marginalization and demarcation is used only with reference to people of color. Ishmael Reed cites the instructive example of a David Brinkley show in which three "ethnic" writers appeared: William Kennedy (Irish-American), E. L. Doctorow (Jewish-American), and Toni Morrison (African-American). Of the three, only Toni Morrison's ethnicity was cited. Thus, Ishmael Reed cynically concludes. "In the United States ethnicity is interchangeable with being black" (Ishmael Reed, in "Is Ethnicity Obsolete?" in *The Invention of Ethnicity*, 226).

11. See Lourdes Torres, "The Construction of Self in U.S. Latina Autobiographies," in *Third World Women*, pp. 274–275.

12. M. M. Bakhtin and V. N. Volosinov, *Marxism and the Philosophy of Language*, trans. Ladislav Matejka and I. R. Titunik (Cambridge, Mass.: Harvard University Press, 1973), 39.

13. Ibid., 28.

14. I have made this argument in my essay "Questioning Race and Gender Definitions: Dialogic Subversions in *The Woman Warrior*," *Criticism* 31 (1989): 421–438.

15. Maxine Hong Kingston, *Tripmaster Monkey: His Fake Book* (New York: Vintage International, 1989), 34. All subsequent references will be made parenthetically as *TM*.

16. Based on a personal conversation with Kingston, Amy Ling has suggested that Wittman might be modeled after the playwright Frank Chin. However, Ling does not analyze the ramifications of Kingston choosing as a protagonist a playwright who has been extremely critical of her work. *Between Worlds: Women Writers of Chinese Ancestry* (New York: Pergamon Press, 1990).

17. Reviewers of *The Woman Warrior* praised the book for its "myths rich and varied as Chinese brocade" and prose that "achiev[ed] the delicacy and precision of porcelain" (Elaine H. Kim, *Asian American Literature: An Introduction to the Writings and Their Social Context* [Philadelphia: Temple Press, 1982], xvi).

18. Tom Wilhelmus, "Various Pairs," *Hudson Review* 43 (Spring 1990): 150.

19. Some critics have seen Kingston's attempts as exactly the opposite. Linda Morante, for instance, reads *The Woman Warrior* as a text in which the act of

writing "preserves the identity of the creator." Linda Morante, "From Silence to Song: The Triumph of Maxine Hong Kingston," *Signs* 12 (1987): 78.

20. Leslie W. Rabine, "No Lost Paradise: Social and Symbolic Gender in the Writings of Maxine Hong Kingston," *Signs* 12 (1987): 474.

21. Henry Louis Gates uses the figure of the signifying monkey to explain the double voicing of African-American writing. See "'The Blackness of Blackness': A Critique of the Sign and Signifying Monkey," *Critical Inquiry* (1983): 685–723.

22. Ling, *Between Worlds*, 150.

23. Feminist theorists have often identified maternal bonding as constitutive of the experience and morality of women. Nancy Chodorow, for example, identifies relationships among women as means that women evolve to maintain the feminine sense of self which, unlike the masculine, thrives on connectedness to others. See Nancy Chodorow, *The Reproduction of Mothering: Psychoanalysis and the Sociology of Gender* (Berkeley: University of California Press, 1978), 169. Others see the productivity of thinking based on maternal practice or the importance of sustaining friendships between women. Sara Ruddick, for instance, finds in women a particular kind of maternal thinking that is holistic and open-ended (Sara Ruddick, "Maternal Thinking," *Feminist Studies* 6, no. 2 [1980]: 342–367).

24. Aihwa Ong, "Colonialism and Modernity: Feminist Re-presentations of Women in Non-Western Societies," *Inscriptions* 3, no. 4 (1988): 85. Chandra Talpade Mohanty similarly writes how Third World women as a group are "automatically and necessarily defined as religious (read 'not progressive'), family-oriented (read 'traditional'), legal minors (read 'they-are-still-not-conscious-of-their-rights'), illiterate (read 'ignorant'), domestic (read 'backward')" ("Under Western Eyes," in *Third World Women*, 72).

25. Amy Tan, *The Joy Luck Club* (New York: Putnam's, 1989), 56. All subsequent references will be cited parenthetically as *JL*.

26. Ling, *Between Worlds*, 132.

27. Lisa Lowe points out that "by contrasting different examples of mother-daughter discord and concord, *Joy Luck* allegorizes the heterogenous culture in which the desire for identity and sameness (represented by Jing-Mei's story) is inscribed within the context of Asian-American differences" (Lowe, "Heterogeneity," 36).

## Marina Heung (essay date Fall 1993)

SOURCE: "Daughter-Text/Mother Text: Matrilineage in Amy Tan's *Joy Luck Club*," in *Feminist Studies*, Vol. 19, No. 3, Fall, 1993, pp. 597–616.

[*In the following essay, Heung addresses how* The Joy Luck Club *portrays mothers and daughters struggling to maintain female-centered relationships—through language and storytelling—in the face of cultural and social pressures.*]

The critical literature on matrilineage in women's writings has already achieved the status of a rich and evolving canon.[1] At the same time, in recognizing race, class, and gender as crucial determinants in writings by women of color, some critics have indicated the need to develop a distinct framework for understanding these works. For example, Dianne F. Sadoff has examined the literature by African American women to note that "race and class oppression intensify the black woman writer's need to discover an untroubled matrilineal heritage." Referring to Alice Walker's adoption of Zora Neale Hurston as a literary foremother, Sadoff shows how "in celebrating her literary foremothers . . . the contemporary black woman writer covers over more profoundly than does the white writer her ambivalence about matrilineage, her own misreadings of precursors, and her link to an oral as well as written tradition."[2] Readers like Sadoff[3] suggest that, although matrilineage remains a consistent and powerful concern in the female literary tradition, the recognition of culturally and historically specific conditions in women's lives requires that we appropriately contextualize, and thereby refine, our readings of individual texts.

In the realm of writings by Asian Americans, this work has begun. Although it does not focus explicitly on the idea of matrilineage, Amy Ling's *Between Worlds: Women Writers of Chinese Ancestry* is the first book to outline the literary tradition of one group of Asian American women. Her effort, Ling says, is inspired by Walker's "search for our mothers' gardens."[4] Similarly, in a recent essay, Shirley Geok-lin Lim identifies Monica Sone's *Nisei Daughter* as a "mother text" for Joyce Kogawa's *Obasan*. In discussing these authors, Lim enumerates literary characteristics shared by Asian American and Asian Canadian women writers, such as "multiple presences, ambivalent stories, and circular and fluid narratives."[5] Lim's analysis points toward a commonality between Sone and Kogawa and two other writers, Maxine Hong Kingston and Chuang Hua.[6] In Kingston's *Woman Warrior* and Hua's *Crossings*, antirealistic narrative strategies and a provisional authorial stance correlate with experiences of cultural dislocation and of destabilized and fluid identities.[7] Thus, the works of Sone, Kogawa, Kingston, and Hua collectively define an emerging canon cohering around concerns with racial, gender, and familial identity and the concomitant rejection of monolithic literary techniques.

In *Nisei Daughter, Obasan, The Woman Warrior,* and *Crossings,* the theme of matrilineage revolves around the figure of the daughter. With the exception of *Crossings* (which focuses on a daughter-father relationship), each of these works depicts how a daughter struggles toward self-definition by working through the mother-daughter dyad. The daughter's centrality thus places these writings firmly in the tradition delineated by Marianne Hirsch in *The Mother/Daughter Plot: Narrative, Psychoanalysis, Feminism. Examining women's fiction from the eighteenth century through postmodernism, Hirsch notes the predominance of the daughter's voice and the silencing of the mother. This inscription of the "romance of the daughter" forms part of the feminist revision of the Freudian family plot.

> It is the woman as *daughter* who occupies the center of the global reconstruction of subjectivity and subject-object relation. The woman as *mother* remains in the position of other, and the emergence of feminine-daughterly subjectivity rests and depends on that continued and repressed process of *othering* the mother. . . . Daughter and mother are separated and forever trapped by the institution, the function of motherhood. They are forever kept apart by the text's daughterly perspective and signature: the mother is excluded from the discourse by the daughter who owns it.

Interestingly, Hirsch's few examples of departures from this pattern are drawn only from the writings of African American women. As she suggests, the scantiness of this sampling of "corrective" family romances, incorporating rather than repressing maternal discourse, reinforces the argument that feminist writers need to construct a new family romance to move the mother "from object to subject."[8]

Published in 1989, Amy Tan's novel, *The Joy Luck Club*, is about four Chinese American daughters and their mothers.[9] Like *The Woman Warrior* and *Crossings,* the novel contains autobiographical elements. In an interview, Tan describes how she was moved to establish a dialogue with her mother: "When I was writing, it was so much for my mother and myself . . . I wanted her to know what I thought about China and what I thought about growing up in this country. And I wanted those words to almost fall off the page so that she could just see the story, that the language would be simple enough, almost like a little curtain that would fall away."[10] But despite Tan's explicit embrace of a daughter's perspective, *The Joy Luck Club* is remarkable for foregrounding the voices of mothers as well as of daughters. In the opening chapter of the novel, Jing-Mei Woo (also known as June) stands in for her recently deceased mother at an evening of mah-jong held by the Joy Luck Club, a group of elderly aunts and uncles. On this evening, three of her "Joy Luck aunties" give her money to fly to China to meet two half-sisters, twins who were abandoned by her mother during the war. In the last chapter of the novel, June makes this trip with her father. Her story (taking up four chapters) is told in her voice. The rest of the chapters are similarly narrated in the first person by three of June's coevals (Waverly Jong, Rose Jordan Hsu, and Lena St. Clair) and their mothers (Lindo Jong, An-Mei Hsu, and Ying-Ying St. Clair). Thus, totaling sixteen chapters in all, the novel interweaves seven voices, four of daughters, and three of mothers. In the way that it foregrounds maternal discourse, *The Joy Luck Club* materializes Marianne Hirsch's vision of a mother/daughter plot "written in the voice of mothers, as well as those of daughters . . . [and] in combining both voices [finds] a double voice that would yield a multiple female consciousness.[11] But because the maternal voices in the novel bespeak differences derived from the mothers' unique positioning in culture and history, the subjectivities they inscribe, in counterpointing those of the daughters, also radically realign the mother/daughter plot itself.

In the chapter, "Double Face," in *The Joy Luck Club,* a scene implicitly illustrates the incompleteness of a model of the mother/daughter dyad defined only from the daughter's perspective. Here, the central motif is a mirror reflecting a mother and a daughter. Interweaving the themes of vision, recognition, and reflection, this scene shows the limits of viewing identification as an issue problematic for the daughter alone. The scene is set after Waverly has persuaded her mother to get her hair cut. Lindo is seated before a mirror as Waverly and Mr. Rory (the hairdresser) scrutinize her hairstyle. Sitting silently, Lindo listens to the two discuss her "as if [she] were not there." Her daughter translates Mr. Rory's questions for her, even though Lindo can understand English perfectly well. When Waverly speaks directly to her, she does so loudly, "as if [Lindo has] lost [her] hearing." But because this scene is narrated from Lindo's perspective, her vision and subjectivity are in fact in control. Even as her daughter seems determined to nullify her presence, Lindo sees the superficial social ease between Waverly and Mr. Rory as typical of how "Americans don't really look at one another when talking." Despite her silence and apparent acquiescence, she interposes herself nonverbally through her smiles and her alternation between her "Chinese face" and her "American face" ("the face Americans think is Chinese, the one they cannot understand") (p. 255).

The scene turns on Mr. Rory's sudden exclamation at seeing the uncanny resemblance between mother and daughter reflected in the mirror. Lindo notes Waverly's discomfiture: "'The same cheeks.' [Waverly] says. She points to mine and then pokes her cheeks. She sucks them outside in to look like a starved person" (p. 256). Waverly's response exhibits her "matrophobia," defined by Adrienne Rich as the daughter's fear of "becoming one's mother."[12] Feminists have analyzed the daughter's ambivalence toward identification with the mother,[13] but Lindo's response in this scene allows us to consider identification from a maternal perspective. Much as Lindo possesses a "double face," she also has access to a "double vision." Seeing herself mirrored in her daughter, she recalls her own mother in China.

> And now I have to fight back my feelings. These two faces, I think, so much the same! The same happiness, the same sadness, the same good fortune, the same faults.
>
> I am seeing myself and my mother, back in China, when I was a young girl.
>
> (P. 256)

With her "double vision," Lindo is not threatened by her daughter's attempted erasure of her; in fact, she is moved by her daughter's resemblance to her, even as she registers

Waverly's response. Lindo's perspective is informed by her personal history and by her ability to bridge time and cultures. At the same time, Lindo's knowledge of family history provides one key to her sense of ethnic identity. As critics have noted, in writings by Asian American women, issues of matrilineage are closely bound with those of acculturation and race. Thus, Shirley Lim writes: "The essential thematics of maternality is also the story of race . . . [The mother] is the figure not only of maternality but also of racial consciousness."[14] But in presenting the mother as the potent symbol of ethnic identity, Lim implicitly adopts the perspective of the daughter. In her scheme, the mother's primary role is to set into motion the daughter's working through toward a separate selfhood and a new racial identity. Yet this elevation of the daughter as the figure around whom the "dangers of rupture and displaced selves" converge[15] marginalizes maternal subjectivity and voicing. But surely the issues of identification, differentiation, and ethnic identity have meaning for mothers as well, and this meaning must to a significant degree devolve from their relationships with their own mothers. As exemplified in this episode in "Double Face," *The Joy Luck Club* moves maternality to the center. It locates subjectivity in the maternal and uses it as a pivot between the past and the present. In so doing, it reclaims maternal difference and reframes our understanding of daughterly difference as well.

Recent feminist revisions of the Freudian Oedipal family romance assume a culturally and historically specific model of the nuclear family. In her influential book, *The Reproduction of Mothering: Psychoanalysis and the Sociology of Gender,* Nancy Chodorow shows how the institution of motherhood based on childcare provided by women sustains the central problematics of separation and differentiation for daughters.[16] Using a paradigm that is white, middle-class, and Western, Chodorow's analysis is not universally applicable. In this vein, Dianne E Sadoff and Ruth Perry and Martine Watson Brownley show how the Black family, distorted through the history of slavery in particular, needs to be understood through alternative models.[17] Such a culturally specific critique needs to be applied to the traditional Chinese family as well. Because of their historical devaluation, women in the Chinese family are regarded as disposable property or detachable appendages despite their crucial role in maintaining the family line through childbearing. Regarded as expendable "objects to be invested in or bartered," the marginal status of Chinese women shows itself in their forced transfer from natal families to other families through the practice of arranged marriage, concubinage, adoption, and pawning.[18] The position of women—as daughters, wives, and mothers—in Chinese society is therefore markedly provisional, with their status and expendability fluctuating according to their families' economic circumstances, their ability to bear male heirs, and the proclivities of authority figures in their lives.

This pattern of radical rupture within families is illustrated by the family histories of An-Mei, Lindo, and Ying-Ying in *The Joy Luck Club.* As a child, An-Mei is raised by her grandmother; she has only confused memories of her mother. One day, when her grandmother is dying, her mother appears and removes her to Shanghai; An-Mei is then adopted into a new family where her mother is the fourth concubine of a wealthy merchant.

In contrast to An-Mei, Lindo is removed from her natal family through marriage, not adoption. At age two, Lindo is engaged to a young boy who is a stranger to her. A bride in an arranged marriage at sixteen, Lindo finally succeeds in freeing herself through a ruse by which she convinces her husband's family to find a concubine for him.

Like Lindo, Ying-Ying is chosen as a bride by a stranger, a man who associates deflowering her with the act of *kai gwa* ("open the watermelon"). A "wild and stubborn" girl in her youth, Ying-Ying's spirit is destroyed in this brutal marriage. Later, when she is pregnant, her husband leaves her for another woman; she decides to get an abortion.

In *The Joy Luck Club,* family allegiances are complicated and disrupted within a kinship system in which blood ties are replaced by a network of alternate affiliations. When Lindo is engaged to the son of the Huang family, for instance, her family relationships are immediately reconfigurated. Her mother starts treating her "as if [she] belonged to someone else," and she begins to be referred to as her future mother-in-law's daughter.

For An-Mei, the breakage and realignment of relationships involving parents and siblings are even more radical and arbitrary. When her mother removes her from her grandmother's household, her brother—her mother's first son—is left behind because patrilineal claims on male children cannot be challenged. After her adoption into her new family, An-Mei is introduced to three other wives in the family—each a potential surrogate mother. For instance, her mother tells her to call the Second Wife "Big Mother." She also acquires a new brother, Syaudi, who now becomes her "littlest brother" (p. 230). But An-Mei has to undergo one final upheaval when she finds out that Syaudi is truly her brother by blood and not adoption. This happens when her mother's attendant tells her how An-Mei's mother was forced into concubinage and bore a son; this son was then adopted by the Second Wife as her own. In this way, An-Mei makes a shocking discovery: "That was how I learned that the baby Syaudi was really my mother's son, my littlest brother" (p. 237).

Unlike Lindo and An-Mei, Suyuan Woo (June's mother) sees her family dispersed as a result of cataclysmic historical events. During the Japanese bombardment of Kweilin during the war, she is forced to flee south without her husband; discarding her possessions along the way and desperate for food, she finally abandons her twin daughters on the road. Later in America, her new daughter, June, grows up with the knowledge of a truncated family, haunted by her mother's words: "Your father is not my first husband. You are not those babies" (p. 26).

These stories of disrupted family connections, of divided, multiplied, and constantly realigned perceptions of kinship, constitute a pattern clearly diverging from the monolithic paradigm of the nuclear family. In *The Joy Luck Club,* their experiences of broken and fluctuating family bonds inspire Lindo, An-Mei, and Ying-Ying to construct stories of bonding with the mother precisely in answer to their memories of profound rupture and abandonment. Speaking from their experiences of mother loss, these immigrant mothers offer altered versions of the "romance of the daughter." Whereas typical versions of this romance highlight generational conflict and the repression of the mother, An-Mei, Lindo, and Ying-Ying construct consoling tales enacting a fantasy of symbiosis with the maternal. Recalling her first sight of her mother after a long separation, An-Mei describes how their exchange of gazes locks them into instant identification: "[My mother] looked up. And when she did, I saw my own face looking back at me" (p. 45). An-Mei also privileges her mother's story about two turtles joined through suffering; from this parable of shared grief, An-Mei derives a message connecting her to her mother: "That was our fate, to live like two turtles seeing the watery world together from the bottom of the little pond" (p. 217). In this way, An-Mei transforms common experiences of pain and victimization into testimonials of mother/daughter bonding. Similarly, instead of feeling outrage at her mother's collaboration in her arranged betrothal and marriage, Lindo actually chooses collusion with her mother, behaving as the proper daughter-in-law so that her mother will not lose face (p. 55).

However, years later, in America, Lindo's assertion of instinctive bonding with her mother is contested by new realities. She comes to regret how her mother "did not see how [her] face changed over the years. How [her] mouth began to droop. How [she] began to worry but still did not lose [her] hair . . ." (p. 257). Acknowledging these inevitable changes in herself, Lindo implicitly admits the loss of symbiosis. Her transplantation into American culture and her advancing age have made her face no longer a perfect match of her mother's. Quite simply, her new "double face" reflects her changed cultural identity: "I think about our two faces. I think about my intentions. Which one is American? Which one is Chinese? Which one is better? If you show one, you must also sacrifice the other" (p. 266).

At the same time, Lindo's recognition of her own doubled identity has implications for how she understands her relationship with her daughter. Like her, Waverly is the product of two cultures, but Lindo sees that Waverly's experience of cultural mixing is different from her own: "Only her skin and hair are Chinese. Inside—she is all American-made" (p. 254). The otherness of her daughter's hybridized self for Lindo makes it unlikely that mother and daughter can achieve perfect identification: the burden of differences in personal history and cultural conditioning is too great. Yet, in *The Joy Luck Club,* the mothers' ability to accept their own loss of the maternal image also enables them to separate from their daughters. As Ying-Ying says: "I think this to myself even though I love my daughter. She and I have shared the same body. There is part of her mind that is part of mine. But when she was born, she sprang from me like a slippery fish, and has been swimming away from me since" (p. 242). Thus, in Tan's novel, the maternal experience of generational conflict and differentiation takes into account the realities of cultural difference; through this awareness, the Joy Luck mothers can negotiate their ambivalences about their daughters' desires for cultural assimilation and autonomous selfhood.

As the essential medium of subjectivity, language is the ground for playing out cultural differences. Gloria Anzaldúa has written about her language use as an insignia of her "borderlands" identity situated between Mexico and America: "Ethnic identity is twin skin to linguistic identity—I am my language. Until I can accept as legitimate Chicano Texas Spanish, Tex Mex and all the other languages I speak, I cannot accept the legitimacy of myself." The speaker of this "language of Borderlands," Anzaldúa suggests, has the freedom to "switch codes" at will; it is a "bastard" language located at the "juncture of culture [where] languages cross-pollinate and are revitalized."[19] In *The Joy Luck Club,* the language of the mothers—their border language—marks their positioning between two cultures. However, in exposing linguistic limits, the novel also argues for reclaiming language as an instrument of intersubjectivity and dialogue, and as a medium of transmission from mothers to daughters.

In the novel, the daughters understand Chinese, but they speak English exclusively. The mothers, in contrast, speak a version of Anzaldúa's "language of the Borderlands," a *patois* of Chinese and English that often confuses their daughters. Observing her aunties, June thinks: "The Joy Luck aunties begin to make small talk, not really listening to each other. They speak in their special language, half in broken English, half in their own Chinese dialect" (p. 34). Embarrassing at times to the daughters, this language is a form of self-inscription in an alien culture, a way of preserving significance in the new reality of America. For one, the nuggets of foreign words incorporated into this speech duplicate aspects of self-identity that have no equivalent in another language. Words like *lihai, chuming* and *nengkan* must remain in their original Chinese in order to retain their power and meaning. For Ying-Ying, the essence of her youthful character before she became a lost soul, a "ghost," is contained in the word *lihai*: "When I was a young girl in Wushi, I was *lihai*. Wild and stubborn. I wore a smirk on my face. Too good to listen" (p. 243). Her confidence in her special knowledge is expressed by *chuming,* referring to her "inside knowledge of things" (p. 248). For Rose, *nengkan* expresses her mother's ability to act on pure will and determination, as shown in An-Mei's summoning of her son's spirit after he has drowned at the beach (pp. 121–31). On another occasion, An-Mei's command of this hybrid language enables her to articulate, on her daughter's behalf, Rose's disorientation during her divorce. When An-Mei complains that Rose's psychiatrist is making her *hulihudu* and *heimongmong,* Rose ponders: "It was true. And everything around me seemed to be *heimongmong*. These were words I have never thought about in

English terms. I suppose the closest in meaning would be 'confused' and 'dark fog'" (p. 188).

In discussing the use of "multilanguedness" in women's writings, Patricia Yaeger suggests that the "incorporation of a second language can function . . . as a subversive gesture representing an alternative form of speech which can both disrupt the repressions of authoritative discourse and still welcome or shelter themes that have not yet found a voice in the . . . primary language."[20] Although Yaeger is concerned with specific narrative strategies used in women's texts, her analysis has resonance for the significance of maternal speech in **The Joy Luck Club.** Without being overtly political or subversive, the mothers' bilingualism in the novel is nonetheless strategic. Switching from English to Chinese can express rejection and anger, as when June's mother berates her for not trying hard enough at her piano playing: "'So ungrateful,' I heard her mutter in Chinese. 'If she had as much talent as she has temper, she would be famous now'" (p. 136). Or, the switching of codes may initiate a shift into a different register of intimacy, as when the same mother speaks in Chinese when making her daughter a gift of a jade pendant (p. 208). To express her resentment against an American husband who persistently puts English words in her mouth, Ying-Ying uses Chinese exclusively with her daughter (p. 106). Deliberate deformations of language, too, are used to convey veiled criticisms, as when Ying-Ying snidely refers to her daughter's profession as an architect as "arty-tecky" (p. 242), and An-Mei dismisses Rose's psychiatrist as "psyche-tricks" (p. 188). Finally, the use of Chinese is a form of resistance to a hegemonic culture. In the following exchange, initiated when Waverly slyly asks about the difference between Jewish and Chinese mah-jong, Lindo's use of Chinese is self-reflexive; her switch from English to Chinese in itself expresses her sense of cultural difference and superiority.

> "Entirely different kind of playing," she said in her English explanation voice. "Jewish mah jong, they watch only for their own tile, play only with their eyes."
>
> Then she switched to Chinese: "Chinese mah jong, you must play using your head, very tricky. You must watch what everybody else throws away and keep that in your head as well. And if nobody plays well, then the game becomes like Jewish mah jong. Why play? There's no strategy. You're just watching people make mistakes."
>
> (P. 33)

In **The Joy Luck Club,** "multilanguedness" bears the imprint of their speakers' unique cultural positioning, but this assertion of difference is also vexed by its potential to confuse and exclude. For the daughters, the special meaning of maternal language requires translation. After her mother's death, June thinks: "My mother and I never really understood each other. We translated each other's meanings and I seemed to hear less than what was said, while my mother heard more" (p. 37). Another question is how effectively maternal language functions as a medium of transmission between generations. The mothers in the novel worry that the family history and knowledge preserved in their hybrid language will be elided after their deaths. At one point, June comes to understand how important it is for her aunties to preserve the meaning of "joy luck": "They see that joy and luck do not mean the same to their daughters, that to these closed American-born minds 'joy luck' is not a word, it does not exist. They see daughters who will bear grandchildren born without any connecting hope from generation to generation" (pp. 40–41).

Hybrid in its origins, maternal language in **The Joy Luck Club** possesses multiple, even contradictory, meanings. As an assertion of cultural identity, it both communicates and obfuscates. At the same time, it stands in counterpoint to maternal silence. To the daughters, maternal silence hints at "unspeakable tragedies" (p. 20), and the maternal injunction to "bite back your tongue" (p. 89) binds daughters and mothers in a cycle of self-perpetuating denial. Yet both daughters and mothers resist this bind. The Joy Luck aunties, after all, plead frantically with June to tell her mother's—and, by implication, their own—history ("Tell them, tell them"). Similarly, Lena is aware of the power of the unspoken: "I always thought it mattered, to know what is the worst possible thing that can happen to you, to know how you can avoid it, to not be drawn by the magic of the unspeakable" (p. 103). Finally, it is the incomprehension enforced by silence that keeps mothers "othered" in the eyes of their daughters. An-Mei, for instance, is dismissed by Suyuan as a woman with "no spine" who "never thought about what she was doing" (p. 30), and Ying-Ying is seen by June as the "weird aunt, someone lost in her own world" (p. 35). As for Lindo, her special insight allows her to understand why her daughter and her friends see her as a "backward Chinese woman" (p. 255).

In the tradition of breaking silence that has become one of the shaping myths in the writings of women of color,[21] maternal silence in the novel is transformed from a medium of self-inscription and subjectivity into an instrument of intersubjectivity and dialogue. For the mothers, storytelling heals past experiences of loss and separation; it is also a medium for rewriting stories of oppression and victimization into parables of self-affirmation and individual empowerment. For the Joy Luck mothers, the construction of a self in identification with a maternal figure thus parallels, finally, a revisioning of the self through a reinterpretation of the past.

In Lindo's case, the brutality of a forced marriage is transformed, through its retelling, into a celebration of courage and resistance. She recalls looking into a mirror on the day of her wedding and being surprised at seeing her own purity and strength: "Underneath the scarf I still knew who I was. I made a promise to myself: I would always remember my parents' wishes, but I would never forget myself" (p. 58). Through a clever scheme, Lindo escapes from her marriage. After arriving in America, she chooses her second husband, getting him to propose by inserting a message inside a fortune cookie. Because all her jewelry was taken from her during her first marriage, she makes sure that she receives genuine gold jewelry from her husband and as gifts that she buys for herself: "And every few years, when I have a little extra money, I buy another bracelet. I know what I'm worth. They're always twenty-four carats, all genuine" (p. 66).

For An-Mei and Ying-Ying, self-articulation remedies early teachings in silence and self-denial. Both begin to recall painful memories when they see how their speech can save their daughters. Ying-Ying is stirred to speak directly to Lena when she sees her daughter's unhappy marriage. At one time a "tiger girl" who gave up her *chi* ("breath" or "lifeforce") in an unhappy marriage, Ying-Ying now recognizes that her daughter has "become like a ghost, disappear" (p. 163). The emptiness of Lena's life—with her fancy swimming pool, her Sony Walkman, and cordless phone—is apparent to her. Watching Rose go through a difficult divorce, An-Mei recalls her own mother's dying words, that "she would rather kill her own weak spirit so she could give me a stronger one" (p. 240). In the end, An-Mei and Ying-Ying find their voices: Ying-Ying to "wake up" Rose (p. 240) and Lena to "penetrate her skin and pull her to where she can be saved" (p. 242).

The stories of their lives are the mothers' gifts to their daughters in the spirit with which the Joy Luck Club was originally founded. Years ago, June's mother formed the club in Kweilin in order to transmute the painful history of women like herself into a communal expression of defiance and hope, so that "each week [they] could forget past wrongs done to us . . . hope to be lucky" (p. 25). In breaking silence, these mothers reproduce the past as tales of "joy" and "luck." Like the scar on An-Mei's neck that her mother rubs in order to bring back a painful memory (p. 48), these narrations effect a passage from pain to catharsis, moving their tellers from inward knowledge to intersubjective dialogue. Significantly, each of the mother's stories suspends its mode of address between "I" and "you."[22] Thus, the closing sentence in Lindo's story is: "I will ask my daughter what she thinks" (p. 266). In inviting the daughters' interjections, the shift from interior monologue to dialogue enables the mothers to discover how they will mediate between the past and the present for their daughters. Their choices take them on the path, described by Kim Chernin, by which mothers can become "co-conspirator[s]" with their daughters to stand "outside the oppressive system, united in some common effort." Chernin suggests that a mother must ally herself with her daughter's struggle by first acknowledging that she too has passed "knowingly through a similar time of urgency and [has] been able to develop beyond it." She concludes that a mother's entry into collaboration with her daughter involves a commitment to speech. She must be willing to "admit her conflict and ambivalence, acknowledge the nearness or actuality of breakdown, become fully conscious of her discontent, the hushed, unspoken sense of her life's failure."[23] After all, as Adrienne Rich proposes, "the quality of the mother's life—however embattled and unprotected—is her primary bequest to her daughter." Thus, the determination to provide models of "courageous mothering," as envisioned by Rich,[24] is finally the subtext of the stories told by stories in *The Joy Luck Club.* Not the least of this maternal courage is the mothers' reclaiming of storytelling as an act of self-creation, one by which they enact, with a full complement of ambivalence and doubt, their passage from loss and dispossession to hope and affirmation.

In the opening story of the novel, June represents her recently deceased mother at a meeting of the Joy Luck Club. Feeling out of place, she imagines that the three Joy Luck aunties "must wonder now how someone like me can take my mother's place" (p. 27). The three aunties give her $1,200 to travel to China to meet her twin half-sisters, saying, "You must see your sisters and tell them about your mother's death. . . . But most important, you must tell them about her life" (p. 40). But until the moment of the meeting, June asks herself: "How can I describe to them in Chinese about our mother's life?" (p. 287).

The four stories told from June's point of view constitute pure family romance, in which family members are separated, lost, and reunited. The guiding spirit of this myth is June's mother, Suyuan. However, as told by June, the story is unmistakably the daughter's version of the family romance, in which a mother's death opens up the space for a daughter's recuperation of a lost maternal image.[25] Even while protesting that she doesn't know enough to tell her mother's story, June nevertheless proves correct her aunties' insistence: "Your mother is in your bones! . . . her mind . . . has become your mind" (p. 40). She starts cooking the same dishes for her father as her mother did; one evening she finds herself standing at the kitchen window, in imitation of her mother, rapping at a neighborhood cat (p. 209). Arriving in Shenzhen, China, just over the border from Hong Kong, she starts to feel different: "I can feel the skin on my forehead tingling, my blood rushing through a new course, my bones aching with a familiar old pain. And I think, My mother was right. I am becoming Chinese" (p. 267). Earlier she imagines that by dying her mother has left her, "gone back to China to get these babies" (p. 39). But as it turns out, it is she who is returning to China as her mother's emissary. Arriving in China with her father, she hears the final episode of her mother's story: how her mother was forced to abandon her twin babies and continued her search for them through the years. Turning to her father for this history, June urges him to tell it in Chinese: "No, tell me in Chinese. . . . Really, I can understand" (p. 281).

During the scene of June's reunion with her sisters, the rebounding of mirror images enacts a climactic moment, binding mother to daughter and sister to sister.

> Somebody shouts, "She's arrived!" And then I see her. Her short hair. Her small body. And that same look on her face. She has the back of her hand pressed hard against her mouth. She is crying as though she had gone through a terrible ordeal and were happy it is over.

And I know it's not my mother, yet it is the same look she had when I was five and had disappeared all afternoon, for such a long time, that she was convinced that I was dead. And when I miraculously appeared, sleepy-eyed, crawling from underneath my bed, she wept and laughed, biting the back of her hand to make sure it was true.

And now I see her again, two of her, waving, and in one hand is a photo, the Polaroid I sent them. As soon as I get beyond the gate, we run toward each other, all three of us embracing, all hesitations and expectations gone.

(P. 287)

In this encounter, sisterly and maternal identities are blurred, and through the recovery of lost sisters, the foundling myth is conflated with the romance of the daughter. Looking into her sisters' faces, June also sees mirrored in them part of her own ethnic identity: "And now I also see what part of me is Chinese. It is so obvious. It is my family. It is in our blood. After all these years, it can finally be let go" (p. 288).

At the beginning of the novel, while representing her mother at the Joy Luck Club, June muses: "And I am sitting at my mother's place at the mah jong table, on the East, where things begin" (p. 41). June's story ends with her further east still in China, where there is yet another beginning. The meeting of the three sisters makes their generation whole again; resembling their mother as well as each other, the sisters' mutual identification recuperates maternal loss. Now June remembers her mother's remark to her: "Our whole family is gone. It is just you and I" (p. 272). With June's reunion with her sisters, however, the continuity of the family—but through the female line of descent—is reestablished. And finally, since the word the sisters speak upon recognizing each other—"Mama, Mama"—has common currency across cultures, matrilineage here signifies not only the possibility of a nurturing sisterhood but also the melding of cross-cultural linkages.

Although June's story matches the pattern of the idealized family romance, the overall structure of the novel offers such closure as a provisional possibility only. As we have seen, although maternal speech in the novel turns in the direction of intersubjectivity, this movement is tentative and incomplete. The narratives by Lindo, An-Mei, and Waverly shift from "I" to "you," but the absence of a reciprocal progression in their daughters' stories (from a daughterly "I" to the maternal "you") suggests the truncation of a truly dialogic process. Further, the novel's overall structure consciously resists any attempt to shape it definitively. As Valerie Miner has noted, the novel is "narrated horizontally as well as vertically"[26] Thus, June's symbolically complete and symmetrical story is contained within an overarching framework wrapping around a grouping of other stories whose arrangement is neither causal nor linear. Thus, although June's story offers closure in its progression from loss to recuperation, the other narratives are grouped in loose juxtaposition with each other. The mothers' stories are included in the first and last of the four main units in the novel and recount incidents in China; the daughters' stories appear in the middle two sections and are set in the immediate past or proximate present.

On closer reading, even the autonomy of each story as a clear-cut unit begins to dissolve, giving way to a subterranean pattern of resonances and motifs erasing the definite boundaries between individual narratives. Under this scrutiny, actions and motifs mirror each other from story to story, undermining absolute distinctions of character and voice. Thus, the formative moment of Lindo's story, when she looks into the mirror on her wedding day and pledges "never to forget" herself, is duplicated by June's standing in front of a mirror as a teenager, contemplating her self-worth under the assault of her mother's expectations: "The girl staring back at me was angry, powerful. This girl and I were the same. I had new thoughts, willful thoughts, or rather thoughts filled with lots of won'ts. I won't let her change me, I promised myself. I won't be what I'm not" (p. 134). Similarly, Ying-Ying learns from the Moon Lady that the woman is "yin [from] the darkness within" and the man is "yang, bright with lighting our minds" (p. 81). Ying-Ying's lesson about the yin and the yang is echoed in Rose's description of her marriage: "We became inseparable, two halves creating the whole: yin and yang. I was victim to his hero. I was always in danger and he was always rescuing me." Or, to cite a final example of how the novel converges particular motifs: just before Rose's divorce, An-Mei tells her daughter that her husband is probably "doing monkey business with someone else" (p. 188); Rose scoffs at her mother's intuition, but a later discovery proves her mother right. Elsewhere, Lena similarly remarks on her own mother's "mysterious ability to see things before they happen"; in her case, Ying-Ying's uncanny foresight, like An-Mei's, predicts the collapse of Lena's marriage.

Signaling the author's intent to undermine the independence of individual narrative units, even the chapter titles, by connecting motifs between disparate stories, seem interchangeable. The title of Rose's story, "Half and Half," is echoed at the end of a story narrated by June when, turning to the piano she has abandoned for many years, she plays two old tunes and realizes that they are "two halves of the same song" (p. 144). The theme of "half and half" is continued in the story told by Waverly, in which her mother tells her that she has inherited half of her character traits from each parent: "half of everything inside you is from me, your mother's side, from the Sun clan in Taiyuan" (p. 182). In another illustration of how thematic echoes proliferate in the novel, this same story, entitled "Four Directions," encourages us to trace its various motifs elsewhere. Waverly's "good stuff" that she has inherited from her mother reiterates the theme of "best quality" that is continued in another story told by June: in "Best Quality," June's mother chides her for not wanting the best for herself. Meanwhile, the theme of "Four Directions" takes us back to the first story in the novel, where we find June and her aunties seated at the mah-jong table, each occupying one of its four directions.

Obviously, the notion of "four directions" is emblematic of the novel's centrifugal structure. At one point, Lena asks: "How can the world in all its chaos come up with so many coincidences, so many similarities and exact opposites?" (p. 154). Or, as June intones, in a more complaining mood, "It's the same old thing, everyone talking in circles" (p. 21). With its mirrored motifs and interchangeable characterizations, *The Joy Luck Club* demands a reading that is simultaneously diachronic and synchronic. Aligning itself with the modernist tradition of spatial form in narrative,[27] the novel defeats any effort to read it according to linear chronology alone. Instead, the reader's construction of interconnections between motif, character, and incident finally dissolves individualized character and plot and instead collectivizes them into an aggregate meaning existing outside the individual stories themselves.

The multivalent structure of *The Joy Luck Club* resists reduction to simple geometric designs; nevertheless, two figures—the rectangle and the circle—help to chart Tan's play on the theme of maternality. As the novel begins, June takes her place with three Joy Luck aunties around the mahjong table. Her position at one of the table's cardinal points determines the direction of her journey east which ends in China. At the end point of June's story, the trope of the rectangle merges with that of the circle: June's arrival in China brings her full circle to the place where her mother's story began, and her meeting with her half-sisters sets into motion a circulation of mirrored relationships blurring identities, generations, and languages. Because it repudiates linearity and symmetry, the circle is a privileged motif in feminist writings, one that suggests the possibility of reconfiguring traditional familial dynamics and dismantling the hierarchical arrangements of the Oedipal triangle and the patriarchal family. For instance, in her book on the reclamation of the pre-Oedipal in women's novels, Jean Wyatt envisions "the possibility . . . of imagining alternative family relations based on preoedipal patterns—family circles whose fluidity of interchange challenges the rigid gender and generational hierarchies of the patriarchal family." In Wyatt's analysis, there persists, in women's writings, the fantasy of a nurturant family where "family members come forward to share the work of fostering others' development [so that] the responsibility for nurturing [is extended] to a whole circle of 'mothering' people."[28]

In *The Joy Luck Club,* the discrete identities of familial members are woven into a collectivized interchangeability through the novel's parataxis its use of contiguous juxtapositions of voices, narratives, and motifs.[29] Through the novel's interweaving of time frames and voices, three generations of women are included within a relational network linking grandmothers, mothers, daughters, aunts, and sisters. For these women, however, mutual nurturance does not arise from biological or generational connections alone; rather, it is an act affirming consciously chosen allegiances. As Wyatt suggests, mothering as a "reciprocal activity" generally presupposes "a strong mother figure who has a central position in the family," but even "when the mother is not there, the circle remains, its diffuse bonds extends to a circle of equals who take turns nurturing each other."[30] In *The Joy Luck Club,* the death of June's mother, Suyuan, invites the Joy Luck aunties to step into the circle of "mothering reciprocity"; indeed, it is Suyuan's absence that inaugurates the meeting between June and her half-sisters, when they confirm their mutual identification as each other's sisters *and* mothers.

As we have seen, the maternal voices in *The Joy Luck Club* begin to shift from "I" to "you" to engage the discrete subjectivities of mother and daughter in a tentative exchange of recognitions and identifications. In the same way, the novel's resonant structure and its use of parataxis effectively write the reader into the text as a crucial participant in the making of meaning.[31] The reader of *The Joy Luck Club* is a weaver of intricate interconnections who must, like Suyuan's unraveling of an old sweater, randomly "pull out a kinky thread of yarn, anchoring it to a piece of cardboard, [roll] with a sweeping rhythm, [and] start [a] story" (p. 21). This way of engaging the reader as an active constructor of meaning allows the feminist novel to project a community of sisterly readers.[32] In tracing a family history that blurs the demarcations between the roles of mothers, daughters, and sisters, *The Joy Luck Club* breaks down the boundary between text and reader in order to proffer the notions of sisterhood as a literary construction and as a community constituted through the act of reading. At once disintegrative and constructive in its operations, the novel holds its dual impulses in unresolved suspension and fulfills its fundamentally transformative project—a mutation from daughter-text to mother-text to sister-text.

*Notes*

1. See Sandra M. Gilbert and Susan Gubar, eds., *The Norton Anthology of Literature by Women: The Tradition in English* (New York: W. W. Norton, 1985). For a useful survey of the critical literature on this subject, see Marianne Hirsch, "Mothers and Daughters," *Signs* 7 (Autumn 1981): 200–222.

2. Dianne F. Sadoff, "Black Matrilineage: The Case of Alice Walker and Zora Neale Hurston," in *Black Women in America: Social Science Perspectives,* ed. Micheline R. Malson, Elisabeth Mudimbe-Boyi, Jean O'Barr, and Mary Wyer (Chicago: University of Chicago Press, 1988), 198.

3. Marianne Hirsch reminds us of the need for "Western" frameworks to be "modified, reconstructed, and transformed" in considering the works of African American women writers. See Marianne Hirsch, *The Mother/Daughter Plot: Narrative, Psychoanalysis, Feminism* (Bloomington: Indiana University Press, 1989). See also Ruth Perry and Martine Watson Brownley, *Mothering the Mind: Twelve Studies of Writers and Their Silent Partners* (New York: Holmes Meier, 1984), 144–63; Natalie M. Rosinsky, "Mothers and Daughters: Another Minority Group," in *The Lost Tradition: Mothers and Daughters in Lit-*

*erature*, ed. Cathy N. Davidson and E. M. Broner (New York: Frederick Ungar, 1980), 280–90.

4. Amy Ling, *Between Worlds: Women Writers of Chinese Ancestry* (New York: Pergamon Press, 1990), xi. See also Elizabeth J. Ordoñez, "Narrative Texts by Ethnic Women: Rereading the Past, Reshaping the Future," *MELUS* 9 (Winter 1982): 19–28.

5. Shirley Geok-lin Lim, "Japanese American Women's Life Stories: Maternality in Monica Sone's *Nisei Daughter* and Joy Kogawa's *Obasan*," *Feminist Studies* 16 (Summer 1990): 290–91.

6. Maxine Hong Kingston, *The Woman Warrior: Memoirs of a Girlhood among Ghosts* (New York: Alfred A. Knopf, 1977), originally published in 1975; Chuang Hua, *Crossings* (Boston: Northeastern University Press, 1986), originally published in 1968.

7. See Malini Schueller, "Questioning Race and Gender Definitions: Dialogic Subversions in *The Woman Warrior*," *Criticism* 31 (Fall 1989): 421–37; Amy Ling, "A Rumble in the Silence: *Crossings* by Hua," *MELUS* 9 (Winter 1982): 29–36.

8. Hirsch, 136–37, 6–8, 11, 178–91 (Hirsch's examples are *Sula* and *Beloved* by Toni Morrison and Alice Walker's "Everyday Use"), 12. The emphasis on daughters' narratives in writings by Asian American women is reflected in Helen M. Bannan's essay, "Warrior Women: Immigrant Mothers in the Works of Their Daughters," *Women's Studies* 6 (1979): 165–77.

9. Amy Tan, *The Joy Luck Club* (New York: G. P. Putnam's Sons, 1989). All references are to this edition; subsequent citations appear in parentheses in the text.

10. Amy Tan, "How Stories Written for Mother Became Amy Tan's Best Seller," interview by Julie Lew, *New York Times*, 4 July 1989, 19(N).

11. Hirsch, 161.

12. Adrienne Rich, *Of Woman Born: Motherhood as Experience and Institution* (New York: Bantam Books, 1977), 237.

13. See Nancy Chodorow, *The Reproduction of Mothering: Psychoanalysis and the Sociology of Gender* (Berkeley: University of California Press, 1978); Jane Flax, "The Conflict between Nurturance and Autonomy in Mother-Daughter Relationships and within Feminism," *Feminist Studies* 4 (June 1978): 171–89; Christine Olivier, *Jocasta's Children: The Imprint of the Mother*, trans. George Craig (New York: Routledge, 1989); Rich, 218–58.

14. Lim, 293. Rosinsky (p. 280) writes: "Members of racial, ethnic, sexual, and economic minority groups, in particular, have delineated their apprehension of the social forces which intervene between mother and daughter. Perhaps because the added oppression of minority group membership exacerbates this often painful relationship, these writers seem particularly aware of its tragic destructiveness." Mary Dearborn has also written about how generational conflict is felt by many historians of ethnicity to be the most striking feature of ethnic American identity. See Mary V. Dearborn, *Pocahontas's Daughters: Gender and Ethnicity in American Culture* (New York: Oxford University Press, 1986), 72–73.

15. Elise Miller, "Kingston's *The Woman Warrior*: The Object of Autobiographical Relations," in *Compromise Formations: Current Directions in Psychoanalytic Criticism*, ed. Vera J. Camden (Kent: Kent State University Press, 1989), 148.

16. See Chodorow.

17. See Sadoff, 203; Perry and Brownley, 160. Hirsch similarly warns (p. 10) against the "androcentric and ethnocentric" biases inherent in the Freudian model of the family. For two critiques of Chodorow's analysis, see Elizabeth V. Spelman, *Inessential Woman: Problems of Exclusion in Feminist Thought* (Boston: Beacon Press, 1988), 83–113; Elizabeth Abel, "Race, Class, and Psychoanalysis? Opening Questions," in *Conflicts in Feminism*, ed. Marianne Hirsch and Evelyn Fox Keller (New York: Routledge, 1990), 185–204.

18. Sue Grunewold, *Beautiful Merchandise: Prostitution in China, 1860–1936* (New York: Harrington Park Press, 1985), 38, 37–45. See also Maria Jaschok, *Concubines and Bondservants: The Social History of a Chinese Custom* (London: Zed Books, 1988); Julia Kristeva, *About Chinese Women*, trans. Anita Barrows (New York: Marion Boyars, 1986), 66–99.

19. Gloria Anzaldúa, *Borderlands/"La Frontera": The New Mestiza* (San Francisco: Spinsters/Aunt Lute Book Co., 1987), 59; Preface, unpaginated.

20. Patricia Yaeger, *Honey-Mad Women: Emancipatory Strategies in Women's Writing* (New York: Columbia University Press, 1988), 40, 44. For a discussion of a second language as an alternate form of self-inscription, see David Leiwei Li, "The Naming of a Chinese American To Cross-Cultural Sign/ifications in *The Woman Warrior*," *Criticism* 30 (Fall 1988): 515; Shirley K. Rose, "Metaphors and Myths of Cross-Cultural Literacy: Autobiographical Narratives by Maxine Hong Kingston, Richard Rodriguez, and Malcolm X," *MELUS* 14 (Spring 1987): 3–15. Michael M. J. Fischer has discussed the use of bilingualism and "interlinguistic play" in relation to ethnic autobiography; see "Ethnicity and the Arts of Memory," *Writing Culture: The Politics and Poetics of Ethnography*," ed. James Clifford and George E. Marcus (Berkeley: University of California Press, 1986), 218.

21. Roberta Rubenstein states, "If women are typically muted within their own culture even when they constitute a demographic majority, then women of ethnic

22. Lindo's narratives interweave first-person discourse with second-person address throughout. Her first story, "The Red Candle," begins with her addressing Waverly directly, beginning: "I once sacrificed my life to keep my parents' promise. This means nothing to you, because to you promises mean nothing" (p. 49). In her second story, "Double Face," she addresses Waverly by referring to "My mother—your grandmother . . ." (p. 256) and asking "Why do you always tell your friends that I arrived in the United States on a slow boat from China? . . . Why do you always tell people that I met your father in the Cathay House . . . This is not true! Your father was not a waiter, I never ate in that restaurant" (p. 259). Ying-Ying begins her story, "The Moon Lady," in the third person; she ends her second story, "Waiting between the Trees," with the declaration that "now I must tell my daughter everything" (p. 252). An-Mei's story, "Magpies," is the most distinctive in its clear shift from first-person narration to second-person address. When the story begins, she describes her daughter Rose's psychiatric treatment: "She lies down on a psychiatrist couch, squeezing tears out about this shame" (p. 215). At the end of the same story, she addresses Rose directly: "You do not need a psychiatrist to do this. A psychiatrist does not want you to wake up" (p. 241).

23. Kim Chernin, *The Hungry Self: Women, Eating, and Identity* (New York: Harper & Row, 1985), 82, 51, 86.

24. Rich, 250.

25. The process by which a mother's death inspires women writers to begin to explore the meaning of the maternal has been written about by a number of scholars. In discussing women's writings in the 1920s, Hirsch has noted (p. 97) a pattern by which works by women artists "are not composed by the daughters until the mothers are dead. Only then can memory and desire play their roles as instruments of connection, reconstruction, and reparation." Similarly, Bell Gale Chevigny has examines how Margaret Fuller imagined her mother's death in her fiction in order to be able to "contemplate her mother's life much more freely than before." See her "Daughters Writing: Toward a Theory of Women's Biography," *Feminist Studies* 9 (Spring 1983): 86. See also Judith Kegan Gardiner, "A Wake for Mother: The Maternal Deathbed in Women's Fiction," *Feminist Studies* 4 (June 1978): 146–65.

26. Valerie Miner, "The Daughters' Journeys," *The Nation,* 24 Apr. 1989, 66.

27. See Joseph Frank, "Spatial Form in Modern Literature," in *Criticism: The Foundations of Modern Literary Judgment,* ed. Mark Schorer, Josephine Miles, and Gordon McKenzie (New York: Harcourt, Brace, World, 1958), 379–92; and Jeffrey R. Smitten and Ann Daghistory, eds. *Spatial Form in Narrative* (Ithaca: Cornell University Press, 1981).

28. Jean Wyatt, *Reconstructing Desire: The Role of the Unconscious in Women's Reading and Writing* (Chapel Hill: University of North Carolina Press, 1990), 3, 201 (I am indebted to an anonymous reader of the manuscript of this essay for referring me to this book).

29. Eric S. Rabkin, "Spatial Form and Plot," in *Spatial Form in Narrative,* 96–97.

30. Wyatt, 201.

31. As Eric S. Rabkin notes (p. 99), the "notion of spatial form directs our attention most specifically to works . . . in which the ultimate point of view must be foisted on the reader by the parataxis of the text."

32. This strategy has emerged as a signature of some recent fiction by women of color. See Deborah E. McDowell's discussion of Alice Walker's construction of a sisterhood of readers in *The Color Purple* in "'The Changing Same': Generational Connections and Black Women Novelists," *New Literary History* 18 (Winter 1987): 297; Gayle Greene's analysis of the participatory reading elicited by Toni Morrison's *Beloved* in "Feminist Fiction and the Uses of Memory," *Signs* 16 (1991): 318; and Wendy Ho's characterization of *The Woman Warrior* as a "self-talking story" that insists on writing as "something to be decoded and reconstructed through the reader's or listener's collaborative efforts" in her essay, "Mother/Daughter Writing and the Politics of Race and Sex in Maxine Hong Kingston's *The Woman Warrior,*" in *Asian Americans: Comparative and Global Perspectives,* ed. Shirley Hune, Hyung-chan Kim, Stephen S. Fugita, and Amy Ling (Pullman: Washington State University Press, 1991), 236. See also Fischer, "Ethnicity and the Arts of Memory," 232.

**Ben Xu (essay date Spring 1994)**

SOURCE: "Memory and the Ethnic Self: Reading Amy Tan's *The Joy Luck Club,*" in *MELUS,* Vol. 19, No. 1, Spring, 1994, pp. 3–18.

[*In the following essay, Xu argues that the way that Tan constructed the story of* The Joy Luck Club *is similar to how an individual pieces together his or her past through memory.*]

The Chinese-American milieu in a San Francisco neighborhood furnishes the main contingent of characters in Amy Tan's *The Joy Luck Club.* What the four families in that book, the Woos, Jongs, Hsus, and St. Clairs, have in common is mother-daughter relations. The mothers are all first generation immigrants from mainland China, speaking very little English and remaining cultural aliens in their new world. The daughters are all born and educated in America, some even married to "foreigners." Within the microcultural structure of family, the only means available for mothers to ensure ethnic continuity is to recollect the past and to tell tales of what is remembered. Lamenting the failing marriage of Lena, her daughter, and Lena's unfamiliarity with the "Chinese ways of thinking," Ying-ying St. Clair voices the anxiety and helplessness shared by all the mothers in the book:

> All her life, I have watched her as though from another shore. And now I must tell her everything about my past. It is the only way to penetrate her skin and pull her to where she can be saved.
>
> (274)

In her mother's eyes, because Lena, without a memory of the past, allows herself to be borne by the bustle of life, she doesn't know who she is, and cannot hold herself together. It may be true that through her mother's memory, Lena will learn to share a belief in certain rules, roles, behaviors and values which provide, within the family and the overseas Chinese community, a functional ethos and a medium of communication. But will she, even if she unexpectedly finds herself confronted by an hour which has a special connection with her mother's past, have access to her mother's deeply buried anxiety, psychic need, specific mental habits, and life-world perception? Can she really share her mother's unrepeatable life-experience? Can she ever learn how to overstep her own existential limits through her mother's story? What if she has to take cognizance of a barrier in her present existence that will eternally be a barrier between her and her mother? These questions can be asked not only about Lena, but also about all the other daughters in *The Joy Luck Club.* I will take a close look here at the conflict between the two generations of the book and the existential unrepeatability that separates them. Through examining the complexity of the operations of memory, I will also explore how the recollection and narration of the past are related to a present sense of ethnic identity.

"Memory" is an intellectually seductive concept, capable of drawing on diverse literatures, from the cognitive concerns of speculative philosophy to experimental psychological probes of the processing-storage-retrieval function of mind.[1] Yet because the intellectual roots are so diffuse, and the connotations quite varied, I should clarify the two basic assumptions that I make when I use this term in my discussion of ethnic identity in *The Joy Luck Club*: first, a premise of the narrative construction of memory, and second, an emphasis on its social-psychological mechanism.

Most of the philosophical thinking on memory lapses almost inadvertently into the idiom of the static picture by conceiving of memory as a particular content of the mind, as an "image," a "presentation," an "impression," and so on.[2] However, it is not just that we have "images," "pictures," and "views" of ourselves in memory, but that we also have "stories" and "narratives" to tell about the past which both shape and convey our sense of self. Our sense of what has happened to us is entailed not in actual happenings but in *meaningful* happenings, and the meanings of our past experience, as I will explore and defend in my reading of *The Joy Luck Club,* are constructs produced in much the same way that narrative is produced. Identity, as well as the implicated self-definition and self-narrative, almost certainly will be activated from memory. Recent social-psychological studies have shown that self-images bring forth a host of intricately related self-knowledge and self-identity, whose information, values, and related beliefs are socially situated as well as psychologically useful.[3] Such understanding of the social-psychological mechanism of memory narrative is also implied in recent studies of narrative. Hayden White suggests that, in the narrative of individual life as well as in the narrative of history, the meaning of a given set of events, which he recognizes as taking the form of recurring tropical enfigurations, is not the same as the story they consist of (White 111). Using, as a guideline, his differentiation of two kinds of narrative meanings without committing to his tropological explanation of them, we may, in memory narrative, distinguish its *life-story* from the *existential perception* it entails. If the life-story is marked by a seeming actuality, the existential perception is what transforms the casual daily events into a functioning mentality or an existential concern that is not self evident.

This bifurcate view of memory narrative permits us to consider a specific life-story as imagery of existential themes or problems about which the story is told, and the existential perception as a comprehensive context in which meaningful questions can be asked about the factual events of that life-story (what, how, and especially why). A functioning mentality, such as the survival mentality which characterizes all the mother characters in *The Joy Luck Club,* hardly enters into view with factual occurrences. It manifests itself only in the distribution of existential themes of the memory narrative. Memory narrative does not represent a perfect equivalent of the events it purports to describe. It goes beyond the actuality of events to the determination of their coherency as an existential situation, and this general picture of life in turn assigns exemplary values to the events which are awakened in memory by a functioning mentality.[4]

This awakening of memory by a person's present mentality is illustrated by Ying-ying St. Clair's story of her childhood. When Ying-ying was four years old, she got separated from her parents on a Moon Festival trip to a scenic lake, and while watching a performance of Moon Lady, she made a wish which she could not remember for many decades. It is only after her first broken marriage, and a second one to a kind but alien Irishman, and many "years washing away my pain, the same way carvings on stone are worn down by water," when she was "moving every year closer to the end of my life," that she remembers that, on that night, as a child of four, she "wished to be found" (64, 83).

Of the four mother characters in *The Joy Luck Club,* Ying-ying had the happiest childhood. Her family was very wealthy and took good care of her. Her getting lost from her family on a festival trip was no more than a small accident with no harmful consequences. However, this insignificant incident in her early childhood is remembered as an emblem of her unfortunate life. This is the memory of a survivor of bad times, who has lost her capacity to remember a different life even though she did once experience it. The memory itself has become a psychic defense, which helps to justify her social disengagement, her fatalistic perception of the world as a system of total control, and her fascination with extreme situations and with the possibility of applying their lessons to everyday life.

Ying-ying's survival mentality is typical of all the woman characters who belong to the Joy Luck Club. All the Club Aunties have experienced two kinds of extreme situations: one kind is famine, war, forced marriage, and broken family in China, and the other is cultural alienation, disintegration of old family structure, and conflict between mother and daughter in America. In order to survive the drastic changes in their lives, these women need to maintain a psychological continuity, a coherent picture of lifeworld, and a continuity of self. Such a need requires the assuring structure of memory narrative: life-story narrative, with the genre's nominal continuity of aims and intentions, and hopes and fears. Memory is for them a socializing, ego-forming expression of anxieties, hopes, and survival instinct.

Indeed, the Joy Luck Club itself, with a magnificent mah jong table at its center, is an expression and embodiment of that survival mentality and its strategies of psychic defense. Suyuan Woo, mother of the book's first narrator, started the first Joy Luck Club in wartime Kweilin as a refugee running away from the triumphantly advancing Japanese troops. In times of trouble, everyday life became an exercise in survival, both physical and mental. If "hero" means someone who takes decisive action during a time of crisis, then for Suyuan Woo, whose life was in crisis, survival itself became a decisive action—a heroic action, albeit a pathetic and disenchanted one. In order to hang on to living, the club members in Kweilin tried to "feast," to "celebrate [their] good fortune, and play with seriousness and think of nothing else but adding to [their] happiness through winning" (11). As Suyuan herself explains:

> It's not that we had no heart or eyes for pain. We were all afraid. We all had our miseries. But to despair was to wish back for something already lost. Or to prolong what was already unbearable.
>
> (11–12)

Suyuan starts the second Joy Luck Club in San Francisco in 1949. This time she is a refugee fleeing from the triumphant Communists in China. This second club is both a memory of the first club and a renewed means of survival. For those new club members newly immigrated to America, "who had unspeakable tragedies they had left behind in China and hopes they couldn't begin to express in their fragile English," the happy moments of playing mah jong are the only time they can "hope to be lucky"—"That hope was our only joy" (6, 12).

If the mah jong club reflects and is part of the Club Aunties's survival endeavor, it is not just a common sense survival that describes the difficulty of making ends meet or alludes to the fear of poverty. It expresses the perception that they are all survivors in the sense that they have lived through dark times and have emerged in the new world. It indicates the urgency to hold one's life together in the face of mounting pressures, which are seen in the dire light reflected from their memories of specific events that once victimized them in earlier times. Understanding is made necessary when one encounters the unfamiliar, the unknown, the uncanny. The process of understanding ordinarily begins with the displacement of the thing unknown toward something that is known, apprehended, and familiar. The process of understanding thus begins with an experiential shift. The domain of the unknown is shifted, by renewing the old strategy of survival, toward a domain or field presumably already mastered. All the stories included in the first section of the book are about mother-narrators's experiences of victimization. These old memories help shift the narrators, especially in an unfamiliar environment, to a growing belief that people are all victimized, in one way or another, by events beyond their control.

However, memories are not one-way tracks, as some early philosophers would like to suggest.[5] If the past casts a shadow on the present through memory, the present also pre-imposes on the past by means of memory. It is worth noting that John Perry, a philosopher who has written widely on the relationship between memory and personal identity, believes that "a sufficient and necessary condition of my having participated in a past event is that I am able to remember it" (69). The one-way track memory is what Nietzsche calls the "inability to forget," a symptom of a sick person who has given in to past failures and discomforts, making the present unbearable and the future hopeless. What we find with the Joy Luck Club mothers is what Nietzsche calls "memory of the will," an active memory that is sustained by the will to survive (Nietzsche "Second Essay"). Suyuan told her refugee story in so many varied ways that her daughter does not know how to relate them to reality and can only take them as "a Chinese fairy tale" (12). These stories, in the form of memory, test Suyuan's ability to forget. These stories are her symptomatic records of a traumatized soul making a desperate effort to push back the memory of the tragic loss of a husband and two baby daughters during the war. The real memory was suppressed but did not go away; and Suyuan, as her second husband feels intuitively, "was killed by her own thoughts," which she could not even articulate to her husband and daughter (5).

Not only does Suyuan's early experience of extreme situations result in a defensive contraction of self, but also it transforms her relationship with her daughter into one of survival: a fear that she will lose her connection with her daughter, and that her experiences, thoughts, beliefs, and desires will have no future successors. The daughter may look like the mother, or even identify with her; and yet, the two are still worlds apart from each other. Perry makes a very important differentiation between "identification" and "identity," and points out, "Identity is not a necessary condition of identification. I can identify with the participant in events I did not do, and would not do, even if they were to be done" (76). Georges Rey, in his study of the existential unrepeatability of personal experience and identity, emphasizes the impossibility of passing on identity through the narrative of memory:

> There are . . . an alarmingly diverse number of ways in which one person might come to share the seeming memories of another: vivid stories, hallucinations. . . . All my and my grandfather's hopes to the contrary, he does not survive as me, no matter how much I seem to recollect (and even take as my own) the experiences of his life from having heard of them at his knees. This is partly because we were both alive when I heard and identified with them; and, for all our not inconsiderable mutual concern, none of it was (strictly) personal. I didn't thereafter enjoy any privileged access to his feelings and thoughts.
>
> (Rey 41)

Memory is not just a narrative, even though it does have to take a narrative form; it is more importantly an experiential relation between the past and the present, projecting a future as well. It is the difference of experiential networks between Suyuan Woo and her daughter that accounts for the daughter's resistance to the mother's nagging about hard work and persistence, as well as for her confusion about the mother's constant sense of crisis.

Hard work and persistence are with the mother—and most "diligent" Chinese immigrants—less self-sufficient virtues than means and conditions of survival. These qualities are desirable to her just because she learnt from her previous experiences that they are attributes of a "winner" in life, and she is going to treat them only as such. It is only on the usefulness of these qualities that she will base her self-approval for exercising them. Even though she knows pretty well that her daughter will never get a Ph.D., she keeps telling her friends and neighbors that Jing-mei Woo is working on it. This is less a lie or wishful thinking than an expression of her survival instinct: what the mother seeks from her friends and neighbors is not the kind of approval that applauds her daughter's personal qualities, but the conviction for herself that her daughter possesses the attributes of a survivor. It is too easy to advance diligence, frugality, or whatever as Chinese ethnic qualities. What is wrong in such a view is an essentialist interpretation of these qualities as *inherent* "Chinese" attributes, and a blindness to their special relations with a particular kind of ethnic memory.

The disposition for many first generation Chinese immigrants in America to see life as a constant test of survival, to the extent that it almost becomes ethnic symbolism, is a complex mentality. It is deeply rooted in China's past of hardship and numerous famines and wars. The word in Chinese that denotes "making a living in the world" is *qiusheng*—seeking survival, or *mousheng*—managing survival. The Chinese classics are full of wisdom on how to survive, whether it be Taoist escapism, Confucian doctrine of the mean, or Legalist political trickery. The lack of religion and of a systematic belief in an after-life in Chinese culture indicates the preoccupation with the urgency of surviving in the present world. The simultaneous contempt for business (and "the rich")[6] and love of money (in the form of thriftiness) support the view of money not as a measure of success but as a means of survival.

However, survival mentality in China has never become a symbol of nationality and ethnicity. It is part of the living conditions which have remained intact with little change throughout centuries; but it has never been mobilized and turned into what Werner Sollors, in his *The Invention of Ethnicity,* calls "kinship symbolism." Only when a Chinese person is uprooted from his or her own culture and transplanted into an alien one does he or she become aware of the fluidity, proteanness, and insecurity of his or her self. It is not until then that he or she feels the need to define himself or herself by a reference group, or even deliberately manages a certain image or presentation of self using the symbolism of survival. "Ethnicity," as Sollors aptly observes, "is not so much an ancient and deep-seated force surviving from the historical past. . . . It marks an acquired . . . sense of belonging that replaces visible, concrete communities whose kinship symbolism ethnicity may yet mobilize in order to appear more natural" (xiv). The newly acquired ethnic awareness of being Chinese in America and the sense of urgency about the individual's and the group's preservation and survival register the waning of the old sense of a durable public world, reassuring in its definiteness, continuity, and long-tested survival strategies.

Once the imagery of confinement, insecurity, alienation, and extreme situations takes hold of the imagination of an ethnic group, the temptation to extend this imagery to lesser forms of stress and hardship and to reinterpret every kind of adversity or difference in the light of survival proves almost irresistible. Things as trifling as the Chinese way of playing mah jong, which, according to the mothers in *The Joy Luck Club,* is different from and far superior to the Jewish mah jong, is jealously guarded as a matter of immense significance. The excessive concern with being "genuinely Chinese" announces the abandonment of efforts to adapt to a mixed and heterogeneous society in favor of mere ethnic survival.

Even at the mah jong table people have to face the agony of how to survive. "We used to play mah jong," explains Auntie An-mei to Jing-mei, "winner take all. But the same people were always winning, the same people always losing." This is what life has always been: there has to be someone who is a loser and a victim. But the San Francisco Joy Luck Club Aunties reformulate their mah jong game so that it becomes, symbolically at least, a game with no losers:

> We got smart. Now we can all win and lose equally. We can have stock market luck. And we can play mah jong for fun, just for a few dollars, winner take all. Losers take home leftovers!
>
> (18)

The change in the mah jong game may appear insignificant. But it reflects the Club Aunties's view of the loser as a victim who fails to survive, and their belief that one should make every effort to defend oneself against the bruising experience of being a loser, even at a mah jong table. Such a view can alter the way competition and rivalry are experienced. Competition, whether it be in a chess game, in a piano performance, or for a college degree, now centers not so much on the desire to excel as on the struggle to avoid a crushing defeat. A willingness to risk everything in the pursuit of victory gives way to a cautious hoarding of the reserves necessary to sustain life over the long haul. For Lindo Jong, her daughter's chess championship is not just proof of her talent. It is more essentially her attribute of being "lucky" and being a winner. Worldly success has always carried with it a certain poignancy, an awareness that "you can't take it with you"; but among the Chinese, glory is more fleeting than ever, and those who win a game worry incessantly about losing it.

Lindo Jong gives her daughter Waverly her own talisman of luck—"a small tablet of red jade which held the sun's fire" (98)—in order to add to the latter's "invisible strength." Her daughter's chess battle becomes her own battle. But the worry and concern of her subtle survivalism is not appreciated by her daughter, who accuses her mother of using her to show off and trying to take all the credit. Lindo Jong's "all American made" daughter has a hard time understanding why her mother believes that "luck" and "tricks" are more valuable and more important than "skill" and "smartness." "You don't have to be so smart to win chess," Lindo Jong tells her daughter. "It is just tricks" (187).

Waverly Jong feels immobilized by her mother's "sneak attack" (191), and at first completely misses the disenchanted heroic style that underlies the "sneakiness" of her mother's attack. What she fails to see is that her mother's "sneakiness" is meant to prepare her for dealing with the unpredictable, in which she will constantly find herself faced with unstructured situations and the need to survive on her own. In contrast to the American strategies of survival that Waverly has been introduced to (such as upward mobility, security in legal protection, and active individual choice), Lindo Jong's survivalist strategy of "sneakiness" or "trickiness" is miserably nonheroic and shamefully "Chinese." Waverly fears and despises her mother, and resists her mother's teaching. Puzzled by her daughter's reaction, Lindo Jong confesses:

> I couldn't teach her about the Chinese character. How to obey parents and listen to your mother's mind. How not to show your own thoughts, to put your feelings behind your face so you can take advantage of hidden opportunities. Why easy things are not worth pursuing. How to know your own worth and polish it, never flashing it around like a cheap ring. Why Chinese thinking is best.
>
> (289)

The wearing of a mask is to Lindo Jong an heroic act—an act necessary for the survival of poor immigrants like herself, who feel "it's hard to keep your Chinese face in America" (294). Wearing a mask means the ability to suppress one's true feelings and emotions—even to deceive—in order to be allowed to live. She is not unaware of the debt that the mask wearer has to pay to human guile; but in her understanding there is no rage that rips the heart, no passion of combat which stresses the heroic deeds of ethnic rebellion. With many Chinese-Americans like Lindo Jong, survivalism has led to a cynical devaluation of heroism, and to a resignation that is tinged with a bitter sense of humor.

When they first arrived in America, Lindo Jong and An-mei Hsu worked in a fortune cookie factory, making Chinese sayings of fortune for American consumption. Lindo Jong was wondering what all this nonsense of Chinese fortunes was about. An-mei explained to her.

> "American people think Chinese people write these sayings."
>
> "But we never say such things!" [Lindo Jong] said. "These things don't make sense. These are not fortunes, they are bad instructions."
>
> "No, miss," [An-mei] said, laughing, "it is our bad fortune to be here making these and somebody else's bad fortune to pay to get them."
>
> (299–300)

Lindo Jong knows that the Chinese wearing of the mask, just like those Chinese fortunes, can convince many Americans that they know and understand Chinese people. She also has an unusual insight into the risk that the mask wearer can become psychologically dependent upon the mask, even when the mask is not needed. Continued wearing of the mask makes it difficult for the wearer of the mask to be her real self. Maskedness has almost become the ethnic symbolism for Chinese-Americans like Lindo Jong, who thinks like a person of "two faces," being neither American nor Chinese (304).

In a self-consciously two-faced person like Lindo Jong we find a detached, bemused, ironic observer, who is almost fascinated by the fact that she has not a self that she can claim as "me." The sense of being an observer of one's own situation and that all things are not happening to "me" helps to protect "me" against pain and also to control expressions of outrage or rebellion.[7] Survivors have to learn to see themselves not as free subjects, but rather as the victims of circumstances, be they the current situation or prefixed fate or disposition.

Chinese Taoist culture helps to maintain this kind of victim mentality because it reinforces a passive if not fatalist attitude toward life. The influence of Taoism, in its popularized form, is obvious in how *ying-yang-wu-hsing* is used by the mothers in **The Joy Luck Club** as a physiotherapy that helps explain why the life of the unlucky people is what it is. In this popularized form of Taoism, human life is a constant struggle for a precarious balance between *ying* and *yang*, affected even by the placing of your bedroom mirror or the location of your condominium apartment. *Wu-hsing* (the five elements: water, fire, wood, metal, and earth), which were conceived by the Taoist masters as five fundamental phases of any process in space-time, become the mystical ingredients that determine every person's character flaw according to one's birth hour. "Too much fire and you had a bad temper.... Too much water and you flowed in too many directions" (19).

Rose Hsu Jordan, like her mother, An-mei, has too little wood, and as a consequence, she bends to other people's ideas. Her marriage with Ted breaks down because he is annoyed by her lack of decision. Measured by the *Wu-hsing* system, none of us has all the five character elements perfectly balanced, and therefore, every one of us is by nature flawed. This view of human imperfection may appear like the Greek idea of tragic flaw. But the Chinese view of character flaw has no interest in any unyielding defiance to fate. The wily Chinese wisdom and belief that heroes do not survive informs the disenchantment with conventional codes of defiance and heroism. While the Greek tragic heroes face their inevitable destruction with dignity and grace, the believers in *Wu-hsing* want to survive by amending the flaw through non-heroic small acts such as taking special names—the "rose" in Rose Hsu Jordan's name, for example, is supposed to add wood to her character.

Both Rose Hsu Jordan and her mother regard themselves as victims of circumstances, but, belonging to two different generations, they resort to different strategies in order to alleviate their fear of disaster. An-mei Hsu copes with everyday mishaps by preparing for the worst and by keeping faith in hope. Her faith in God, which she held for many years before her youngest boy was drowned, was less a religious belief for which she was ready to sacrifice herself than a survival strategy of keeping herself in hope. Although An-mei keeps telling her daughter to make her choice, or even to indulge in a fantasy revenge for the wrongs suffered by women, she is prepared to accept the worst thing that can happen to a woman: the fate of being a woman, "to desire nothing, to swallow other people's misery, to eat my own bitterness" (241).

An-mei's faith in God, or, after the death of her boy, in hope, is to her American-made daughter only a fatalist's self-created illusion. "[My mother] said it was faith that kept all these good things coming our way," Rose Hsu Jordan tells us with her tongue in cheek, "only I thought she said 'fate,' because she couldn't pronounce that 'th' sound in 'faith.'" Rose has to be tempered by her own suffering before she will discover that "maybe it was fate all along, that faith was just an illusion that somehow you're in control" (128).

Instead of relying completely on her mother's advice, Rose, devastated by her broken marriage, goes to her psychiatrist. Psychiatry, for Rose the young Chinese-American, has played the role of modern successor to religion. In psychiatry, the religious relief for souls has given way to "mental hygiene," and the search for salvation to the search for peace of mind. Rose tells her psychiatrist about her fantasy revenge against Ted, and feels like having "raced to the top of a big turning point in my life, a new me after just two weeks of psychotherapy." She expects an illuminating response from her psychiatrist. However, just like her mother was forsaken by God, Rose is let down by her mundane saver: "my psychiatrist just looked bored" (211). It is only after her frustrating experience with her psychiatrist that Rose feels an accidental connection of a shared fate between herself and her mother. The mother and daughter are co-victims of a common threatening force over which they have no control. It is when Rose, in her dream, sees her mother planting trees and bushes in the planter boxes, adding wood to both of them, that she lets us get a close view of a mother-daughter relation that is defined neither by blood tie nor by material service, a relation that is neither Chinese nor American, but Chinese-American.

This mother-daughter relationship with a unique ethnic character is what we discern not only in the Hsu family, but also in the families of Woos, Jongs, and St. Clairs. The family tie between the mother and daughter in each of these Chinese-American families is no longer what determines the Chinese daughter's obligation or the Chinese mother's authority. Family features shared by mother and daughter in those Chinese-American families are not something to be proud of, but rather something that causes embarrassment on one side or the other, and often on both sides. However, neither does this mother-daughter relationship rest, as is common in the American family, on material service. The cross-generation relationship rests on a special service the mother renders to the daughter: the mother prepares the daughter for the extreme situations of life, gives her psychic protection whenever possible, and introduces her to resources she needs to survive on her own. The mother does all this not in the capacity of a self-righteous mother, but as a co-victim who has managed to survive. The traditional role of a Chinese mother has been greatly curtailed in America. If formerly she represented an automatic authority, now she is unsure of herself, defensive, hesitant to impose her own standards on the young. With the mother's role changed, the daughter no longer identifies with her mother or internalizes her authority in the same way as in China, if indeed she recognizes her authority at all.

The loosened family tie and shaky continuity between the two generations represented in *The Joy Luck Club* account for the particular narrative form in which their life acts and events are told. These stories share no apparently recognizable pattern or fully integrated narrative structure. The character relations are suggested but never sufficiently interwoven or acted out as a coherent drama. Our attention is constantly called to the characteristics of fiction that are missing from the book. It is neither a novel nor a group of short stories. It consists of isolated acts and events, which remain scattered and disbanded. It has neither a major plot around which to drape the separate stories, nor a unitary exciting climax which guides the book to a final outcome.

Yet all these customary habitual ingredients have a place in *The Joy Luck Club*. The successions of events are fully timed and narrators of these events are carefully grouped in terms of theme as well as generation distribution (mothers and daughters). The book's sixteen stories are grouped into four sections: the two outer sections are stories by three mother-narrators, and Jing-mei Woo, who takes the place of her recently deceased mother; and the two inner sections are stories by four daughter-narrators. The stories in the first two sections are followed by successive denouements in the next two sections, leading to a series of revelations. All the energies set in motion in the first story of the book, which is told by the book's "framework" narrator, come to fruitful release in the book's last story told by the same narrator, Jing-mei Woo.

Just as the mah jong table is a linkage between the past and present for the Club Aunties, Jing-mei Woo, taking her mother's seat at the table, becomes the frame narrator linking the two generations of American Chinese, who are separated by age and cultural gaps and yet bound together by family ties and a continuity of ethnic heritage. It is Jing-mei Woo who tells the book's two frame stories, the first and the last. These two frame stories, ending with a family reunion in China, suggest strongly a journey of maturity, ethnic awakening, and return-to-home, not just for Jing-mei Woo, but metaphorically for all the daughters in the book. This experience is like a revelation—a sudden unveiling of the authentic meaning of being "Chinese." The ecstatic character of this experience is well expressed by Jing-mei Woo:

> The minute our train leaves the Hong Kong border and enters Shenzhen, China, I feel different. I can feel the skin on my forehead tingling, my blood rushing through a new course. My mother was right. I am becoming Chinese.
>
> (306)

At this moment, she seems to come to a sudden realization that to be "Chinese" is a lofty realm of being that transcends all the experiential attributes she once associated with being a Chinese, when she was unable to understand why her mother said that a person born Chinese cannot help but feel and think Chinese.

> And when she said this, I saw myself transforming like a werewolf, a mutant tag of DNA suddenly triggered, replicating itself insidiously into a syndrome, a cluster of telltale Chinese behaviors, all those things my mother did to embarrass me—haggling with store owners, pecking her mouth with a toothpick in public, being color-blind to the fact that lemon yellow and pale pink are not good combinations for winter clothes.
>
> But today I realize I've never really known what it means to be Chinese. I am thirty-six years old. My mother is dead and I am on a train, carrying with me her dreams of coming home. I am going to China.
>
> (306–7)

The book has, for other daughters, other moments of revelation like this one experienced by Jing-mei Woo, though they are of a more subtle nature and of less intensity. It is at these moments of revelation, often after their own sufferings in life, that the daughters come to realize the value and reason of their mothers's survival mentality and the disenchanted heroism of mask and endurance, and begin to hear the rich and multiple meanings in their mothers's stories instead of mere dead echoes of past acts and events. They become less resistant to identifying with their mothers and more receptive to the humble wisdom of the previous generations. The change from resistance to acquiescence signifies simultaneously the growth of a mature self and the ethnicization of experience.

The need to ethnicize their experience and to establish an identity is more real and more perplexing to the daughters than to the mothers, who, after all, are intimate with and secure in their Chinese cultural identity in an experiential sense, in a way their American-born daughters can never be. The daughters, unlike their mothers, are American not by choice, but by birth. Neither the Chinese nor the American culture is equipped to define them except in rather superficial terms. They can identify themselves for sure neither as Chinese nor American. Even when they feel their identity of "Americanness" is an estrangement from their mothers's past, there is no means of recovering the Chinese innocence, of returning to a state which their experiential existence has never allowed them. They are Chinese-Americans whose Chineseness is more meaningful in their relationship to white Americans than in their relationship to the Chinese culture they know little about. The return to their ethnic identity on the part of the daughters is represented in *The Joy Luck Club* as realizable on a level where a real split between the existential self and the ethnic self is alluded to by a narrative rivalry between "tale of the past" and "tale of the present." Not only are the contrast and discontinuity between the two types of tales metaphorical of the split of self, but also their organizing narrator, Jing-mei, is symbolic of the split self of the daughters's generation.

The ethnicization of experience does not automatically mean an ethnic identity. The ethnicized and mature self acquiesces to the ethnic affiliation that fixes its patterns and meanings, but at the very point of acquiescence, registers discomfort with such constraints. Indeed the strange blending of acquiescence and resistance accounts for the fact that the return to the motherland in *The Joy Luck*

*Club* is temporary and disillusioning, no more than a "visit." Such a visit is at once an assertion of "going home" and a painful realization of "going home as a stranger."

Therefore, the significance of the book's frame device of return-to-home and its satisfaction of the reader's formal expectations should not disarm our critical query as to whether the ethnic self really represents a higher form of self or self-awareness. The book's frame device suggests the split between the true but unrecognized self and the false outer being whose sense of self and identity is determined by the need to adjust to the demands of a fundamentally alien society. Such a dualist view of self offers the reassuring but problematic concept of ethnic reality as that which is familiar and recuperated, and which, in the homeland, loyally awaits our return even though we turn from it. It assumes that the "inner" or "true" self is occupied in maintaining its identity by being transcendent, unembodied, and thus never to be discovered until the moment of epiphany. Not only does this cozy view of return to the authentic self suggest a split between the existential self and the ethnic self, but also a fixed hierarchy of them, with the changing and trapped existential self at the bottom, and the essential and free ethnic identity at the top. However, this hierarchy is unstable: the ethnic self, just like the existential self, is neither free nor self-sufficient, and therefore, never an authentic or genuine self. Our ethnic experience, no less than our existential experience, depends on the mediation of others. We become aware of our ethnicity only when we are placed in juxtaposition with others, and when the priority of our other identities, such as individual, class, gender, and religious, give place to that of ethnicity. Like other kinds of identities, ethnic identity is not a fixed nature, or an autonomous, unified, self-generating quality. It is a self-awareness based on differentiation and contextualization. The self is not a given, but a creation; there is no transcendent self, ethnic or whatever else. Ethnic awareness is not a mysteriously inherited quality; it is a measurable facet of our existence, whose conditions and correlates are the only context in which we can understand how we reconstitute feelings and inner knowledge of our own ethnic being.

*Notes*

1. Philosophers dealing with memory are typically concerned with its representative function, as capable of bringing to our mind "images" (St. Augustine and others), "presentation" (Aristotle), "impressions" (Aristotle and others), "ideas" (Locke and Hume), and the "immediate" or "present" objects in memory (A. D. Woozley and others). See, for example, Aristotle, "On Memory and Reminiscence," in R. McKeon, ed., *The Basic Works of Aristotle* (New York, 1941). Augustine, *Confessions.* Many translations and editions. Book X, 8–19; John Locke, *An Essay Concerning Human Understanding,* 2 vols., ed. A. C. Fraser (Oxford, 1894), Book II, Ch. 10; David Hume, *A Treatise of Human Nature,* ed. L. A. Selby-Bigge (Oxford, 1888), Book I, Pt. I, Sec. 3 and Pt. III, Sec. 5; A. D. Woozley, *Theory of Knowledge* (London, 1949), Chs. 2–3. The psychological study of memory owes a substantial debt to Hermann Ebbinghaus, who singlehandedly moved memory from the domain of the speculative philosopher to the province of the experimental scientist. In the two-volume *Practical Aspects of Memory: Current Research and Issues* (Chichester, England: John Wiley and Sons, 1988), M. M. Gruneberg, P. E. Morris, and R. N. Sykes put together a whole variety of approaches and methods that are used today in experimental psychological studies of memory, such as eyewitnessing, autobiographical memory, maintenance of knowledge, etc.

2. Aristotle, St. Augustine, John Locke, David Hume, etc., op. cit.

3. See for example, H. Markus, "Self-schemata and Processing Information about the Self," *Journal of Personality and Social Psychology* 35 (1977): 63–78; S. T. Fiske and S. E. Taylor, *Social Cognition* (Reading, MA: Addison-Wesley, 1984); B. R. Schlenker, "Self-Identification: Toward an Integration of the Private and Public Self," in R. F. Baumeister, ed., *Public Self and Private Self* (New York: Springer-Verlag, 1986), 21–62.

4. John Perry refers to this cognitive hermeneutic circle of memory, and the reciprocal reality between a person who remembers and the things that he remembers. He writes, "That my present apparent memory of a past event stands at the end of a causal chain of a certain kind leading from that event is not something I can directly perceive, but something believed because it fits into the simplest theory of the world as a whole which is available to me" (69).

5. This view was most representatively voiced by the nineteenth-century British philosopher Sir William Hamilton, who regarded memory as one of the undeniable conditions of consciousness. See, for instance, *Lectures on Metaphysics and Logic,* ed. H. L. Mansel and John Weitch (Edinburgh: W. Blackwood and Sons, 1859–1860), "Lecture XI," 205. Identity is explained as constituting in the assurance that our thinking ego, notwithstanding the ceaseless changes of state, is essentially the same thing. What such a view fails to see is that in remembering, a person not only records what has happened to him but also strives toward a restitution of his own ego—a construction of a continuous, integrated sense of his real existence in relation to time, nature and society, cause and effect.

6. The Chinese proverb *weifu buren* suggests the incompatibility between "being rich" and "being benevolent."

7. In today's mainland China, the wearing of a political mask is still practiced as a gesture of self-preservation, and hopefully, of potential resistance.

### Works Cited

Nietzsche, Friedrich. *On the Genealogy of Morals.* Trans. Walter Kaufman and R. J. Hollingdale. New York: Vintage, 1967.

Perry, John. "The Importance of Being Identical," in Amelie Oksenberg Rorty, ed., *The Identities of Persons.* Berkeley: U of California P, 1976. 67–90.

Rey, Georges Rey. "Survival," in Amelie Oksenberg Rorty, ed., *The Identities of Persons.* Berkeley: U of California P, 1976.

Sollors, Werner, ed. *The Invention of Ethnicity.* New York: Oxford U P, 1989.

Tan, Amy. *The Joy Luck Club.* New York: Ivy, 1989.

White, Hayden. *Tropics of Discourse: Essays in Cultural Criticism.* Baltimore: Johns Hopkins U P, 1978.

**Esther Mikyung Ghymn (essay date 1995)**

SOURCE: "Mothers and Daughters," in *Images of Asian American Women by Asian American Women Writers,* Peter Lang, 1995, pp. 11–36.

[*In the following comparative essay on Maxine Hong Kingston's* The Woman Warrior *and Tan's* The Joy Luck Club, *Ghymn discusses the fable-like quality of* The Joy Luck Club *and studies how cultural expectations affect the mother-daughter relationships portrayed in the novel.*]

The images of Asian American mothers and daughters as drawn by Kingston and Tan are so similar that it seems they have created a new set of stereotypes. Strikingly different from the familiar Madame Butterflies and Suzy Wongs, the new images of dragons, tigers, swans, shadows, bones, and stairs are the newly created metaphors for Asian American mothers and daughters. As Tan remarks to Emory Davis, "It's the images that are so important to me. That's where the mystery of the writing and the beauty of the story is" (Davis, Vol 1. No. 1. p. 9). These new images define the Asian American woman as seen by the major Asian American women writers.

For Kingston and Tan the right image is not necessarily a realistic one, but one which fits into the moral of their stories and provides the right perspective. The right balance in form and message is achieved when the daughters realize that they are not alone in the universe; that the ties to their mothers and grandmothers will always keep them in balance; that life does not change from generation to generation despite shifts in space and time; that, in a sense, all characters are stereotypes in a universe where "each and all are the same." As in the last line of Emerson's "Each and All" ("I yielded myself to the perfect whole"), the mothers and daughters in *The Woman Warrior* and ***The Joy Luck Club*** finally realize that they are all part of each other.

### I

*The Woman Warrior* is a complex narrative of varied voices, songs, and images. It is a book about Anju's quest for self-identity. Born in Stockton, California, to an old Chinese couple, Anju finds it difficult to communicate at home and at school. Although born in the year of the dragon like her mother, she is at first characterized as quiet and fearful. These traits are not usually associated with those born with the most favorable zodiac sign. In China the dragon symbolizes strength and wisdom, and such traits are transformed into images and words such as "dragon," "brave," and "warrior" throughout the book. Thus, Anju's weaker qualities are inevitably replaced by images of inherent strength when she realizes true selfhood at the end of the novel.

Anju hates herself at school because she hates to talk. Her low self-image makes her hate the sound of her own voice: "It spoils my day with self-disgust when I hear my broken voice coming skittering out into the open. It makes people wince to hear it" (*The Woman Warrior,* p. 191). Her low self-esteem is heightened by her assumption that her mother thinks her ugly. Her mother does not give her the recognition that she craves. When Anju tells her mother, "I got straight A's, Mama," her mother replies, "let me tell you a true story about a girl who saved her village" (*The Woman Warrior,* p. 54). Communication between mother and daughter is at best difficult. When Anju tries to tell her mother about "three hundred things," her mother says, "Senseless babblings every night. I wish you would stop. Go away and work. Whispering, whispering, making no sense. Madness, I don't feel like hearing your craziness" (*The Woman Warrior,* p. 233). Her mother wants Anju to go to a typing school: "learn to type if you want to be an American girl." Anju refuses because she wants to do something better. She shouts to her parents, "I'm smart. I can do all kinds of things. I know how to get A's, and they say I could be a scientist or a mathematician if I want. I can make a living and take care of myself" (*The Woman Warrior,* p. 234).

Anju retreats and fantasizes about becoming a woman warrior. She wants to know how she can storm across the States and fight her own battles. She wonders how she can use this ancient warrior example in her contemporary life. But Anju is afraid to act. Kingston characterizes this fear by using ghostly images. Anju and her family see real people as ghosts. To them there are white ghosts, black ghosts, and Mexican ghosts. Feelings of fear are conceptualized into images of ghosts and shadows. Kingston typically uses contrasting images as the images of fear balance images of strength mentioned earlier. These images are parallel and interrelated, creating contrasting rhythms in this surrealistic novel form.

All Anju knows about China is what she has seen in the movies and what she has heard from her mother. What she has heard from her mother is the tale of the legendary Fa Mu Lan and the tale of the forgotten No Name Woman. Fa

Mu Lan is a woman warrior who takes the place of her father in battle. As such, she is the metaphorical center of this novel and an extended metaphor of a sense of continuity in Asian women's lives. On the other hand, the No Name Woman is a disgrace, for an unmarried pregnant woman is considered very shameful in China. She commits suicide by drowning herself in the family well when the villagers come to punish her. Kingston's strategy is to create such contrasting characters clothed in different images.

These tales, however, make it difficult for the confused daughter to find her own identity. In frustration, Anju addresses the reader: "Chinese-Americans, when you try to understand what things in you are Chinese, how do you separate what is peculiar to childhood, to poverty, insanities, one family, your mother who marked your growing with stories from what is Chinese? What is Chinese tradition and what is the movies?" (*The Woman Warrior*, p. 6). Anju analyzes herself as she compares herself to Fa Mu Lan and the No Name Aunt. The shifting back and forth from her imagination to reality enables the narrative to sublimate the distinction between them. In real life her mother, Brave Orchid, and Aunt Moon Orchid also serve as models. Brave Orchid is a strong woman who earned a medical degree in China but who struggles in the States with her husband at the steaming laundry day after day to feed their six children. Moon Orchid, on the other hand, is weak. She eventually ends up in a mental asylum as she is unable to cope with her disappointments in life which culminate in being rejected by her husband. Should Anju become strong like Fa Mu Lan and Brave Orchid, or should she become weak like the No Name Aunt and Moon Orchid? At the end Anju chooses the stronger models.

When mother and daughter cannot speak the same language to explain adequately the reasons and feelings behind the words, frustration is inevitable. The first words of the book are, "'You must not tell anyone,' my mother said, 'what I am about to tell you'" (*The Woman Warrior*, p. 3). Anju thinks her mother wants to silence her so much that (in her fantasy) she cuts out her own tongue. The daughter, not understanding the real meaning behind her mother's broken English, screams, "And I don't want to listen to any more of your stories; they have no logic. They scramble me up . . . You can't stop me from talking. You tried to cut off my tongue, but it didn't work" (*The Woman Warrior*, p. 235). Here Anju does not understand her mother's desire or her reply when she says, "I cut it to make you talk more, not less, you dummy!" (*The Woman Warrior*, p. 235). Although this remark is confusing, it reveals that the mother has a plan to motivate her daughter. Anju, in the meantime, struggles toward self-understanding.

The use of words is a major unifying thread that sews the novel together. "You must not tell anyone . . . what I am about to tell you" (*The Woman Warrior*, p. 3). The mother's admonition reflects her determination to control Anju. Anju resents and resists such control. She blames her mother for her own quietness, saying that her mother cut out her tongue. Although she hates quietness, Anju is unable to break out of it. Thus, going to school becomes a dreadful burden. In the first years of school she colors everything black to symbolize her dread. She notices that other Chinese girls also do not talk very much at school, so she associates being Chinese with silence. In particular there is one girl whom she hates for her quietness. This hatred erupts into violence when Anju beats her up one day.

On the other hand, Kingston wants to make it clear to the reader that speaking is properly associated with strength. For example, when the woman warrior prepares for battle, her father carves words of revenge on her back. Such pain is endured because it is only through such carving that the warrior becomes empowered to act. Each Chinese character etched in blood is worthy of a fighting warrior. The warrior says, "When I could sit up again, my mother brought two mirrors, and I saw my back covered entirely with words in red and black files, like an army, like my army" (*The Woman Warrior*, p. 42). It is as if the words empower her to act. Thus, words signify empowerment.

The mother/daughter relationship evolves through various stages until it reaches a reconciliation. As a child Anju follows her mother around the house singing the song of the woman warrior. The chanting makes her believe that she will also grow up to be a warrior. It seems that the singing is a source of inspiration and communication. Night after night the mother tells stories of the woman warrior. Perhaps the reason for telling the stories is that they give the mother a feeling of hope and power. As Nancy Walker points out, "Fantasy of the 'woman warrior' in Kingston's book, are (sic) at least empowering because they allow the characters to escape imaginatively the boundaries of their lives as 'young women'—they permit images of freedom and power denied by the characters' immediate social context" (Walker, p. 115). Perhaps as a mother working in a laundry after earning a medical degree she needs to have a dream to instill in her daughter. Thus Brave Orchid inspires her daughter through songs and words.

It is also through words and singing that mother and daughter reconcile. As a child, Anju remembers how she followed her mother around the house singing about Fa Mu Lan and her victories in battle. At the end she joins her mother in singing about Poetess T'sai. "She brought her songs back from the savage lands, and one of the three that has passed down to us is 'Eighteen Stanzas for a Barbarian Reed Pipe,' a song that Chinese sing to their own instruments. It translated well" (*The Woman Warrior*, p. 243). This episode parallels Brave Orchid's situation, for like the poetess, Brave Orchid is in a foreign land. Her story is translated by Anju who becomes the narrator of these stories.

Reconciliation occurs at the end when Anju and her mother tell a story together. "Here is a story my mother told me, not when I was young, but recently, when I told her I also talk story. The beginning is hers, the ending mine" (*The

*Woman Warrior,* p. 240). It seems that as the narrator grows older she also comes to "talk story." The book begins with the mother talking and ends with the daughter speaking. Suzanne Juhasz points out that "at the core of the relationship between daughter and mother is identification" (Juhasz, p. 176). As Kingston says, "[critics] read the beginning and can't understand that things are resolved by the end. There is a lot of resolution—the mother and daughter come out okay, you know. But it's the price of a lifetime of struggle" (Yalom, *Women Writers of the West Coast* p. 14). Temporal displacement is replaced by generational continuity. By joining their voices they find their place in the community and continuity of women's spirits.

In Kingston's novel the cycle of mother and daughter conflict and recovery plays itself out poignantly. At the end Anju achieves a balanced and peaceful state of mind as she reconciles herself to her mother. For an Asian American girl who has grown up ashamed of herself and her Chinese heritage, this is a very positive conclusion, for many second generation Chinese Americans reject their parents and their culture for the white majority culture and values. By selecting old Chinese legendary heroines as her role models and joining her mother in the singing, Anju clearly values herself as a Chinese American woman. *The Woman Warrior* is therefore a triumph not only for the individual woman but also for the Chinese heritage. This line from grandmother to granddaughter can be linear but also circular. Understanding of self produces understanding of mother, family, and society. Layer after layer of confusion is peeled off to arrive at the core of understanding.

These layers of confusion are structurally and aesthetically powerful as they underscore the struggles between mother and daughter. Although the novel seems disjointed at first glance, as I mentioned earlier, there is a definite pattern to Kingston's artistry. Marilyn Yalom argues that *The Woman Warrior* is an example of "modern aesthetics" with its various stylistic techniques (Yalom, "Postmodern Autobiography" p. 112). Like music, variation upon variation makes the work more exquisite. Joan Lidoff also comments on the complexity of Kingston's work: "In Kingston we don't get a single account of an incident; we are given alternative conjectures about the same 'fact.' . . . Memory and conjecture bracket all tellings of the past: fantasy is as real as incident, and any event has multiple interpretations" (Lidoff, p. 119). Indeed, to peel the outer layers of meanings is like untying a very complicated knot. However, if one looks closely there is a definite pattern or backbone to the novel, as parallel characters contrast with or complement each other. As mentioned earlier, for example, Fa Mu Lan and Brave Orchid are both depicted as strong characters. On the other hand, the No Name Woman and Moon Orchid are portrayed as similarly weak. The parallels between warrior and mother and the two aunts especially unify the book.

There are also decisive chapter endings which often point to the theme of mothers and daughters. The last paragraph in each of the five chapters helps the reader to arrive at each chapter's meaning. For example, at the end of chapter one, "No Name Woman," Anju writes, "My aunt haunts me—her ghost drawn to me because now, after fifty years of neglect, I alone devote pages of paper to her, though not origamied into houses and clothes" (*The Woman Warrior,* p. 19). Again, at the end of chapter two, "White Tigers," Anju remarks, "The reporting is the vengeance—not the beheading, not the gutting, but the words" (*The Woman Warrior,* p. 63). And again at the end of chapter three, "Shaman," Anju reflects, "I am really a Dragon, as she is a Dragon. Both of us born in dragon years" (*The Woman Warrior,* p. 127). This identification with her mother moves the novel towards final reconciliation between mother and daughter.

Mother and daughter both battle with real and imagined ghosts. Ghosts exist in old China as they do in Stockton, California. The use of ghosts also helps to unify the novel, for ghostly images are embedded throughout. The No Name Woman has become a ghost who has to fight other ghosts for food. As the dead aunt has no one to remember her on her memorial day, she must steal from other ghosts' tables. This allusion refers to the Asian tradition of preparing a special meal for one's dead relatives. As everyone is ashamed of the No Name Woman, no one would honor her on her memorial day by serving a special meal. Ghosts also represent fear. Like background music, the use of ghosts makes the reader understand the sense of fear which drives Anju to quiet and drives her aunt to insanity. The subtitle of the book is "Memoirs of a Girlhood among Ghosts." Thus, images of ghosts—black ghosts, Mexican ghosts, and white ghosts—exist everywhere for Anju and her mother. The weaving of such images reinforces fear of the unknown throughout the novel.

For the Chinese American daughter, one must understand and accept one's own mother to find out about oneself. Barker Nunn points out that in China individuals are insignificant by themselves. Only in the context of their families do the women find significance. And it is not only the immediate family but the long line of women that goes back even to ancestors. To reinforce this point, Kingston repeats circular images. "The round moon cakes and round doorways, the round tables of graduated size that fit one roundness inside another, round windows and rice bowls—these talismans had lost their power to warn this family of the law: a family must be whole, faithfully keeping the descent line by having sons to feed the old and the dead, who in turn look after the family" (*The Woman Warrior,* p. 15). The repeated use of the word "round" and its synonyms underlines the concept of continuity. For the Chinese lineage triumphs over individualism, unity defeats isolation. Anju realizes this point at the end and stops struggling. As a Chinese American she finally accepts the harmonious Chinese view of the universe and joins her mother in singing ancient tales. The emphasis is on collectivity as the voices of mother and daughter form a duet echoing the multiple voices of mothers, aunts, and sisters in the past. Kingston's telling reasserts the spirit of the women and their need to be articulate and to be heard. Matrilineal ancestry becomes life giving.

The title *The Woman Warrior* is therefore the central image of the book, an image which represents strong women like Brave Orchid. Kingston's work is not only about Fa Mu Lan but the concept of the woman warrior. The archetype of the woman warrior is an extended metaphor of a cultural ancestor. Anju realizes that she herself can be a word warrior; indeed, it is only by speaking and writing that she can become such a warrior. Anju's singing is an affirmation of her understanding. As one unravels all the threads in this novel it is clear that the moral fable is a call to action. One should use the power of the spoken or written word to overcome her own weaknesses. As Kingston says to Yalom, "The daughter becomes the inheritor of the mother's oral tradition, which subsequently becomes a written tradition. . . . I went through a time when I did not talk to people. It's still happening to me but not so severely. I'm all right now but I do know people who never came out of it" (Yalom, *Women Writers of the West Coast*, p. 17). As I note in *The Shapes and Styles of Asian American Prose Fiction*, "Kingston's moral fable is existentialist in the most basic sense. Her call is for the reader to pick up his or her sword of knowledge" (Ghymn, p. 113). By carrying on the oral tradition, one is linked to the community of women and ancestral spirits. Community triumphs over individuality. This is an appropriate conclusion as it fits the Chinese philosophy of life.[1]

## II

In *The Joy Luck Club,* the relationship between mothers and daughters starts with imbalance and finally ends with a definite balance. In this book, as in *The Woman Warrior,* the structure is the key through which the messages are to be deciphered. The daughters searching for their mothers' real pasts finally arrive at their own identities. The confusion or anger that they feel towards their mothers while growing up is dissolved. Tan explains that the key to the structure of her novel is finding the right balance: "The basic one in the book is a question about balance. Where is the part of balance that we're searching for in our lives? What throws our lives off balance and how can one restore balance?" (Davis, Vol. 1 No. 2, p. 7). As with Anju, the daughters in *The Joy Luck Club* have to find their own understanding through all the conflicts they have with their mothers. Tan says in an interview, "Part of my writing the book was to help me discover what I knew about my mother and what I knew about myself" (Henderson, p. 22). This understanding is achieved when, like Anju, the daughters in *The Joy Luck Club* realize the sameness in themselves and their mothers. Together mothers and daughters create a satisfying wholeness from generation to generation.

The first page of *The Joy Luck Club* lists the characters. Interestingly, the names of the mothers and daughters are set opposite each other as if the book were a chess game. Indeed, chess is an appropriate analogy for Tan's strategy. In a chess game when a pawn reaches the other side of the board she becomes a queen; likewise, daughters have to travel through many conflicts to achieve independence and self-understanding. Like such canonical figures as Ishmael and Huckleberry Finn, daughters have to journey into the unknown to find their own identities. To these second generation Chinese American women Emerson's "Know Thyself" is the motivating energy.

Images of doubles, ghosts, and shadows misdirect the daughters' journeys. The use of the double is an especially prominent structural device. The word "two" and its synonyms are used several times in chapter titles: "Half and Half," "Two Kinds," "Double Face," "A Pair of Tickets," and "American Translations." Like Humbert and Quilty in *Lolita,* the characters serve as doubles for other characters. Images of ghosts and shadows fit that purpose as well. The total image pattern is that of a fable, which is typically defined as "a brief tale, either in prose or verse, told to point a moral. The characters are most frequently animals, but people and inanimate objects are sometimes the central figures" (Holman and Harmon, p. 197). Tan admits that she wanted to write such a fable. "In fairy tales and fables there's often a moral attached. I didn't want to have something that was exactly the moral but I wanted to have something that was equivalent because I see an ending as a release of some type, and for me releases are always emotional" (Davis, Vol 1. No 1. p. 8). The "equivalent" in *The Joy Luck Club* is a growing up lesson and fairytale elements can be found throughout Kingston's and Tan's works.

In a comic book the violence seems amusing rather than frightening. Likewise the overall comic tone of *The Joy Luck Club* subdues the violent details of some of the scenes. Just as we can laugh rather than shudder when we watch Mickey Mouse or Donald Duck smash each other, so can we read Tan's novel. The flat characters are surrounded by mysterious forces, filled with fairytale elements of ghosts, animals, and magical objects. I believe that Tan deliberately used flat characters because she was writing a fable. Tan says, "When she [my mother] read the stories, the ones set in China, she laughed. She didn't see that they were anything like herself. There was one story in particular, 'The Moon Lady' that has nothing to do with her life. She did not live in that area, she never went out on a boat during the moon festival, she never fell into the water, and she never saw a shadow play" (Davis, Vol 1. No 2. p. 6). Thus we cannot really believe the stories that the mothers tell about themselves in *The Joy Luck Club.* Real people do not cut their mothers' flesh and cook it. Why then does Tan create such scenes? I think that she does so to make the stories more mysterious and entertaining. At one point Davis asks, "So the struggle in the writing process is to find the right image. The one that works for that story?" Tan replies, "The one that is the most mysterious" (Davis, Vol 1. No 1. p. 9). The mysterious images make Tan's story a modern fairytale. In the last section, the queen mother of "The Queen Mother of the Western Skies" is a fairy. Like Cinderella's fairy godmother, the queen mother provides essential wisdom. In the book's first section, "Feathers from a Thousand Li Away," Tan presents the stories of Jing-mei Woo and three mothers,

Anmei Hsu, Lindo Jong, and Ying Ying St. Clair. Jing-mei Woo's mother has already died, so Jing Mei speaks in her place. Jing Mei remembers that her mother's story is like that of a fairytale. "I never thought my mother's Kweilin story was anything but a Chinese fairytale" (*The Joy Luck Club*, p. 25). This statement seems to apply not only to Jing Mei's story but to all the mothers' stories.

The American-born daughter dismisses China as puzzling, Chinese customs and clothes as mysterious. Jing Mei Woo says, "These clothes were too fancy for real Chinese people, I thought, and too strange for American parties" (*The Joy Luck Club*, p. 28). To the daughters, the mothers are part of an unknown world, a world complicated by their own imaginations. "I imagined Joy Luck was a shameful Chinese custom, like the secret gathering of the Ku Klux Klan or the tom-tom dances of TV Indians preparing for war" (*The Joy Luck Club*, p. 28). Indeed, the mothers' worlds as seen by the daughters are unreal. "I used to dismiss her criticisms as just more of her Chinese superstitions, beliefs that conveniently fit the circumstances" (*The Joy Luck Club*, p. 31), Jing Mei reflects. "These kinds of explanations made me feel my mother and I spoke two different languages, which we did" (*The Joy Luck Club*, p. 33). Limited in American perception, language, and customs, the mothers can't understand that their daughters don't understand them. They say in unison, "Imagine, a daughter not knowing her own mother!" (*The Joy Luck Club*, p. 40). This is an ironical statement because it reveals the lack of understanding the mothers have towards their daughters in presuming that the daughters should understand them despite cultural and generational differences. Jing Mei starts to see things a little differently when she says, "And then it occurs to me. They are frightened. In me, they see their own daughters, just as ignorant, just as unmindful of all the truths and hopes they have brought to America. They see daughters who grow impatient when their mothers talk in Chinese, who think they are stupid when they explain things in fractured English" (*The Joy Luck Club*, pp. 40–41). Interestingly, the mothers see their daughters as "ignorant" and the daughters think their mothers are "stupid." As Marie Wunsch points out, "When conflicts arise the mothers and daughters seem only players in a world so personal, so foreign to the other, that any understanding of the other is impossible" (Wunsch, p. 139). To the daughters, the mothers are embarrassing, confusing, and humiliating; to the mothers, the daughters are rebellious, unyielding, and stubborn.

The four short prologues that introduce the four main chapters advance Tan's moral intentions by clarifying this generational conflict. The prologues suggest that Tan was deeply influenced by her father, a Baptist minister. "He would tell these stories and I realize one of the things that was so amazing was that he could keep them simple so that they would reach everybody. He had an absolute belief in what these stories had to mean" (Davis, Vol 1. No 1. p. 6). Tan follows in her father's footsteps in using the form of the fable. The first prologue's fable is that of a mother bringing a swan to the States. Unlike Hans Christian Andersen's ugly duckling who becomes a beautiful swan, this Chinese swan is already grown. "She cooed to the swan: 'In America I will have a daughter just like me . . . Over there nobody will look down on her, because I will make her speak only perfect American English. And over there she will always be too full to swallow any sorrow!'" (*The Joy Luck Club*, p. 17). The swan is taken away by the customs' officials. In this section the irony of the mothers' lack of American customs is revealed in a humorous way as Tan sets out to convey in English Chinese rhythms and idiomatic intonations.

In the second prologue, "26 Maligant Gates," the mother warns her daughter by quoting from an old Chinese book: "Do not ride your bicycle around the corner." The daughter replies, "You can't tell me because you don't know! You don't know anything!" (*The Joy Luck Club*, p. 87). The girl runs outside, jumps on her bicycle, and falls before she reaches the corner. The message of this section is that the mother is always right. This juxtaposition of old Chinese proverbs with American reality, continued throughout the book, is without question purposeful. In this section the four daughters tell their own childhood stories. Waverly Jong becomes a national chess player by her ninth birthday, much to the delight of her proud mother. Waverly does not, however, feel equally proud of her mother. When Waverly talks back to her mother, her mother shouts, "'Embarrass you be my daughter?' Her voice was cracking with anger. 'That's not what I meant. That's not what I said'" (*The Joy Luck Club*, p. 99). Waverly's conversation with her mother reveals her growing resentment and also demonstrates the crucial misunderstandings between mothers and daughters.

As portrayed in this prologue the other daughters are no less anxious. Lena St. Clair is confused by what is real and what is unreal. She fantasizes about her neighbors, a mother and daughter whose loud voices often come through the thin walls. She sees the girl pull out a sharp sword and tell her mother, "Then you must die the death of a thousand cuts. It is the only way to save you." After this ordeal the mother says that she has "perfect understanding" (*The Joy Luck Club*, p. 115). The neighbor and her daughter act as doubles for Lena and her mother. Fighting voices, echoing through the walls, make Lena fantasize.

Rose Hsu Jordan's childhood is darkened by the death of her younger brother, Bing, for which she feels responsible: "I knew it was my fault. I hadn't watched him closely enough" (*The Joy Luck Club*, pp. 126–127). Jing Mei Woo also feels that she is to blame for her mother's disappointment. Her mother wants her to be a concert pianist, but Jing Mei feels that she will never make it: "It was not the only disappointment my mother felt in me. In the years that followed, I failed her so many times, each time asserting my own will, my right to fall short of expectations. I didn't get straight A's. I didn't become class president. I didn't get into Stanford. I dropped out of college" (*The Joy Luck Club*, p. 142). Her feelings of guilt, rejection, and doubt haunt Jing Mei.

In the third prologue, "The American Translation," the daughters are all grown up. Two have married Caucasian husbands despite their mothers' protests. However, their marriages do not go well. Lena and Harold are constantly battling about different budgets and thinking of divorce. Rose Hsu and Ted are in the process of getting a divorce. Rose says, "Over the years, I learned to choose from the best opinions. Chinese people had Chinese opinions. American people had American opinions. And in almost every case, the American version was much better. It was only later that I discovered there was a serious flaw with the American version. There were too many choices, so it was easy to get confused and pick the wrong thing" (*The Joy Luck Club*, p. 191). Waverly Jong is not as unfortunate. She is dating Rich, a Caucasian, and although Rich and her mother have their misunderstandings, all three plan to visit China together. Jing Mei, still single, even achieves self-understanding. She thinks of her mother who has died: "And she's the only person I could have asked, to tell me about life's importance, to help me understand my grief" (*The Joy Luck Club*, p. 197).

How does the third prologue correlate with the stories in this section? In the prologue, a daughter asks, "What is peach blossom luck?" "The mother smiled, mischief in her eyes. 'It is in here,' she said, pointing to the mirror. 'Look inside. Tell me, am I not right? In this mirror is my future grandchild, already sitting on my lap next spring.' And the daughter looked and haule! There it was: her own reflection looking back at her" (*The Joy Luck Club*, p. 147). The use of the mirror is like that in "Cinderella" when the stepmother asks the mirror, "who is the fairest of them all?" The reflections of mother, daughter, and grandchild appear much the same and the daughters are revealed as the "American translations" of the mothers.

In the last prologue, "Queen Mother of the Western Skies," the grandmother tells the baby, "Thank you, Little Queen. Then you must teach my daughter this same lesson. How to lose your innocence but not your hope. How to laugh forever" (*The Joy Luck Club*, p. 213). The word "lesson" reinforces the fable elements while the word "laugh" adds a comic touch. The mother talks to the baby who has lived forever. The grandmother and baby seem to be one, just as the mother and daughter seem to be identical. The idea of wholeness again reminds us of "Each and All," in which Emerson writes about the transcendent unity of the many and the one.

In this section the mothers unveil their pasts in China, but they are unreliable narrators. Their stories are unrealistic and exaggerated, mixed with the supernatural. As Janet Burroway notes, the unreliable narrator has become one of the most popular characters in modern fiction but "is far from a newcomer to literature and in fact predates fiction. Every drama contains characters who speak for themselves and present their own cases and from whom we are partly or wholly distanced in one area of value or another" (Burroway, p. 274). Tan chooses to make this section the most unrealistic, perhaps because the material is the most unfamiliar to her. For example, An-Mei Hsu tells her daughter, "This is how a daughter honors her mother. It is *shou* so deep it is in your bones. The pain of the flesh is nothing. The pain you must forget. Because sometimes that is the only way to remember what is in your bones. You must peel off your skin, and that of your mother, and her mother before her. Until there is nothing. No scar, no skin, no flesh" (*The Joy Luck Club*, p. 48). The idea of peeling her mother's flesh and cooking it is unrealistic, of course. This violent scene is like Kingston's in *The Woman Warrior* when Fa Mu Lan's mother cuts the warrior's back with a knife engraving the list of wrongs to be avenged. Yet unlike apparently comparable scenes in *The Silence of the Lambs*, say, these scenes are not gruesome, but magical.

Limited by their cultural experiences, the mothers think and speak alike. One mother can easily substitute for another and seem to be characterized as mere Chinese-American abstractions. Ying Ying St. Clair says, "I think this to myself even though I love my daughter. She and I have shared the same body. There is a part of her mind that is part of mine. But when she was born, she sprang from me like a slippery fish" (*The Joy Luck Club*, p. 242). Lindo Jong says, "And now I have to fight back my feelings. These two faces, I think, so much the same! The same happiness, the same sadness, the same good fortune, the same faults" (*The Joy Luck Club*, p. 256). An-Mei Hsu says, "And even though I taught my daughter the opposite, still she came out the same way! Maybe it is because when she was born to me and she was born a girl. And I was born to my mother and I was born a girl. All of us are like stairs, one step after another, going up and down, but all going the same way" (*The Joy Luck Club*, p. 215). Likewise, Anju in *The Woman Warrior* describes her mother looking out of her Chinese medical school graduation photo: "She stares straight as if she could see me and past me to her grandchildren and grandchildren's grandchildren" (*The Woman Warrior*, p. 68). The identification that the mothers feel with their daughters is not based on common interests or thoughts but on biological factors. Jing Mei Woo, a seeming spokeswoman for the daughters' side, also admits, "And now I also see what part of me is Chinese. It is so obvious. It is my family. It is in our blood. . . . Together we look like our mother. Her same eyes, her same mouth, open in surprise to see, at last, her long-cherished wish" (*The Joy Luck Club*, p. 288). Reconciliation occurs when mothers and daughters realize the unbreakable bonds between them.

Indeed, the sameness of the daughters and mothers is the novel's central image. Thus the images of the mothers are conventionalized. The mothers do not appear as real women and some of their traits are especially exaggerated. It is true that there are moments of realistic portrayal, but these moments are intertwined with fantasies such as the women carrying swans and a woman cooking a mother's flesh. While the daughters are characterized realistically, the mothers are depicted as unreal. Despite this difference, the mothers and daughters are described as physically alike as the central image takes precedence over realistic portrayal.

Although the activities described are gruesome, the audience does not feel disgust but a mild, amused shudder, because the treatment of these scenes seems to be in the tradition of the comic novel. As Booth points out, "In much of the great comic fiction, for example, our amusement depends on the author's telling us in advance that the characters' troubles are temporary and their concern ridiculously exaggerated" (Booth, *The Rhetoric of Fiction,* p. 175). Tan herself notes, "So with the stories in ***The Joy Luck Club,*** I often began with a frame, which was 'the reason' for telling the story" (Davis, p. 10). Thus, it would be inaccurate for anyone to see these images as those of real mothers struggling in the United States, though we do get glimpses of reality. In a way there is an element of "faking," as Frank Chin points out in *The Big Aiiieeeee*: "Kingston, Hwang, and Tan are the first writers of any race, and certainly the first writers of Asian ancestry, to so boldly fake the best-known works from the most universally known body of Asian literature and lore in history" (Chin, *The Big Aiiieeee,* p. 3). However, the fairytale elements in the stories make the serious and sad relationships interesting and light. Creating a light touch to handle heavy materials, the authors are able to amuse and entertain the reader even as they write about confusion and painful relationships.

In ***The Joy Luck Club*** four separate mother/daughter relationships are explored, but the struggles are really variations of each other. The mothers tell from their own points of view their stories in China while the daughters recount their stories of growing up. The four mothers seem to speak in similar voices, making it difficult for the reader to distinguish among them. Likewise, although the episodes are different, the daughters also seem to speak in similar tones. The daughters resist their mothers but somehow always seem vulnerable to their mothers' opinions. As Waverly says, "In her hands I always became the pawn. I could only run away. And she was the queen, able to move in all directions, relentless in her pursuit, always able to find my weakest spots" (***The Joy Luck Club,*** p. 180). As in a chess game the daughter runs away until she reaches the far end of the board and then becomes a queen herself by being able to identify with her mother.

Realistically speaking, there is a wide gap between first generation mothers and second generation daughters. As Patrica Lin suggests, "The polarity between traditional Chinese and American values is felt with particular keenness by American-born Chinese women. Unlike their mothers, such women face conflicting demands from two opposing cultures. While American-born daughters are familiar with the cultural nuances of Chinese life, their dilemmas frequently stem from having to vacillate between 'Chinese-ness' and 'American-ness.' Their Chinese-born mothers, in contrast, are less plagued by the complexities of being Chinese, American, and woman" (Lin, p. 41). Jing Mei makes much the same point: "These kinds of explanations made me feel my mother and I spoke two different languages, which we did" (***The Joy Luck Club,*** pp. 33–34). Despite their differences, however, the mothers and daughters are portrayed as equals. In fact, in *The Woman Warrior* both the mother and daughter are said to be dragons. In ***The Joy Luck Club*** Lena St. Clair as well as her mother, Ying Ying St. Clair, are born in the year of the tiger. Ying Ying St. Clair states, "I was born in the year of the Tiger. It was a very bad year to be born, a very good year to be a Tiger. . . . The bad spirit stayed in the world for four years. But I came from a spirit even stronger, and I lived. This is what my mother told me when I was old enough to know why I was so heartstrong in my ways. Then she told me why a tiger is gold and black. It has two ways. The gold side leaps with its fierce heart. The black side stands still with cunning, hiding its gold between trees, seeing and not being seen, waiting patiently for things to come" (***The Joy Luck Club,*** p. 248). "Two ways" again underlines the idea of the double. The mother like a tiger is strong and shrewd. Her survival and character are attributed to being born in the year of a tiger. Literally, these animals are part of the Chinese zodiac; metaphorically, the image contributes to the work's fairytale atmosphere.

In China, women born in the year of the tiger or a dragon are considered too strong to be desirable mates. Women born in the year of the rabbit or pig are said to have gentler personalities, so they are selected before women born in the year of the tiger or dragon. It is interesting that Kingston and Tan have reversed the culture-bound stereotypes of femininity. But then they are looking through American eyes. To them, strength, fierceness, and power are positive signs.

As depicted by Tan, the battle between mother and daughter is especially fierce because both possess equal strength. Both mother and daughter are depicted as tigers. The mother uses her experience to control the daughter but the daughter resists such control even if it is from her own mother. The daughters continue to resist until they realize the truth about the universe. The universe is one and harmonious. Thus both mothers and daughters are winners and losers. The opposing sides of nature complement and balance each other. Both yin and yang enforce the recurring pattern of life. Their combat does not end in a victor or victim; the daughters are not better or worse than their mothers. Holbrook explains this relationship in psychological terms: "The problem of woman is thus the problem of life and its secret. Woman can create us—by reflecting us—and enable us to seek meaning in existence, or, she can leave us without a created identity and in a condition of meaninglessness. No wonder she is feared and hated, as well as respected and loved" (Holbrook, p. 62). This explanation clarifies Waverly's reaction when she sees her mother lying quietly on the sofa. "And then I was seized with a fear that she looked like this because she was dead. I had wished her out of my life, and she had acquiesced, floating out of her body to escape my terrible hatred" (***The Joy Luck Club,*** p. 180). Waverly is relieved to find her mother just sleeping. When Lindo Jong awakens and calls her daughter by a childhood name, "Meimei-ah," Waverly's anger dissolves and she feels "as if someone had unplugged me and the current running through me had stopped" (***The Joy Luck Club,*** p. 181). Likewise, Anju feels as if a "weight lifted from me" when her mother calls her "Little Dog," an endearing term from childhood (***The Woman Warrior,*** p. 127). And as in all fairy tales the stories end on a positive note when the daughters realize the truth about their world.

Motivated by ambition and fear, the mothers try to control their daughters. As Helen Bannan says,

> "immigrant women fought to survive, to preserve what they considered to be the essence of their cultural origins, and to pass on both survival skills and cultural traditions to their daughters. When the women of the second generation chose American survival over ethnic tradition, they sometimes brought the war home, but they were often following battle strategies for which their mothers had, perhaps unwillingly, performed the reconnaissance."
>
> (Bannan, p. 165)

Therefore, as Barker-Nunn notes,

> These painful episodes are a result of the difficulty mother and daughter have separating from one another; this is the darker side of connection. The daughters' resentment springs from what they see as a lack of willingness on their mothers' part to see them as they are, to accept them as having lives both different and separate from those of their own.
>
> (Barker-Nunn, p. 59)

The degree to which the daughters' growing identities depend upon their unquestioning acceptance of their mothers is central to the novel's conclusion.

Tan invokes truly widespread, if not universal, patterns. According to Simone de Beauvoir, "real conflicts arise when the girl grows older; as we have seen, she wishes to establish her independence from her mother. This seems to the mother a mark of hateful ingratitude; she tries obstinately to checkmate the girl's will to escape; she cannot bear to have her double become an other . . . Whether a loving or a hostile mother, the independence of her child dashes her hopes. She is doubly jealous: of the world, which takes her daughter from her, and of her daughter, who in conquering a part of the world robs her of it" (Beauvoir, pp. 489–490). Perhaps this is the reason why Tan's mothers attempt to control their daughters' lives.

Tan's mothers are very ambitious for their daughters. Jing Mei remembers her mother wanting her to be like Shirley Temple and starting her on a series of piano lessons despite Jing Mei's protests. At a talent show, she "played this strange jumble through two repeats, the sour notes staying with me all the way to the end" (***The Joy Luck Club,*** p. 139). But it is the expression on her mother's face that truly affects her. "But my mother's expression was what devastated me: a quiet, blank look that said she had lost everything" (***The Joy Luck Club,*** p. 140). Jing Mei does care deeply what her mother thinks of her. She feels that her mother has indeed lost everything and is haunted by a sense of failure. She explains, "And for all those years, we never talked about the disaster at the recital or my terrible accusations afterward at the piano bench. All that remained unchecked, like a betrayal that was now unspeakable. So I never found a way to ask her why she had hoped for something so large that failure was inevitable" (***The Joy Luck Club,*** p. 142). In exasperation she shouts at her mother, "You want me to be someone that I'm not!. . . . I'll never be the kind of daughter you want me to be." The insensitive mother retorts, "Only two kinds of daughters. . . . Those who are obedient and those who follow their own mind!" "Then I wish I wasn't your daughter. I wish you weren't my mother," Jing Mei replies (***The Joy Luck Club,*** p. 142). Real communication is blocked by language problems. The mother's inability to speak English well denies her the opportunity to explain her true thoughts and feelings to her daughter. In broken English the mother tries to teach her daughter by using her knowledge of old Chinese proverbs and chants. Frustration breaks out on both sides and the scene ends with shouting and ultimatums.

The ambition of Waverly Jong's mother is to make her daughter a champion chess player. "And my mother loved to show me off, like one of my many trophies she polished. She used to discuss my games as if she had devised the strategies" (***The Joy Luck Club,*** p. 170). However, one day Waverly must respond, "I hated the way she tried to take all the credit. And one day I told her so, shouting at her on Stockton Street, in the middle of a crowd of people. I told her she didn't know anything, so she shouldn't show off. She should shut up" (***The Joy Luck Club,*** p. 170). Her mother's loud Chinese voice cracking with broken English words is embarrassing. The mother doesn't behave the way a white mother behaves, not knowing any better, so she is a source of humiliation for the daughter. Likewise, a daughter telling her mother "to shut up" is a disgrace for the mother. And yet the mothers have a strong hold over the daughters. Waverly feels that "in her hands, I always became the pawn. I could only run away. And she was the queen, able to move in all directions, relentless in her pursuit, always able to find my weakest spots" (***The Joy Luck Club,*** p. 180). Entrapped in her sensitivities, the daughter struggles and rebels.

Despite the daughters' rebellions, their sense of guilt, need for approval, and desire for reassurance tie them to their mothers' judgments. Yet their fears of being rejected make them hesitate. An Hsu hesitates about explaining her divorce to her mother. Waverly Jong wants desperately for her mother to approve her white boyfriend, Rich. She tells him, however, that her mother doesn't think anyone is good enough for her. When Waverly shows her mother her present from Rich, a mink coat, her mother replies, "This is not so good." "It is just leftover strips. And the fur is too short, no long hairs'" (*The Joy Luck Club*, p. 169). Waverly observes, "My mother knows how to hit a nerve. And the pain I feel is worse than any other kind of misery. Because what she does always comes as a shock, exactly like an electric jolt, that grounds itself permanently in my memory. I still remember the first time I felt it" (*The Joy Luck Club*, p. 170).

Just as the daughters hesitate, so too the mothers wait to reveal their pasts. Ying Ying St. Clair states, "My daughter does not know that I was married to this man so long ago, twenty years before she was even born" (*The Joy Luck Club*, p. 246). Jing Woo's mother dies before revealing her whole past to her. Jing Woo goes on a quest to find out more about her dead mother and to find her lost sisters. This lack of communication and honesty between daughter and mother is one of the major sources of conflict and misunderstanding. Only when the mothers start to reveal their true natures do the daughters begin to understand their mothers and themselves. Ying Ying St. Clair says, "All these years I kept my true nature hidden, running along like a small shadow so nobody could catch me. And because I moved so secretly now my daughter does not see me. She sees a list of things to buy, her checkbook out of balance, her ashtray sitting crooked on a straight table. And I want to tell her this: We are lost, she and I, unseen and not seeing, unheard and not hearing, unknown by others" (*The Joy Luck Club*, p. 67). The longer the mothers wait, the deeper become the misunderstandings.

Reconciliation occurs after a series of reversals and recognitions. The daughters realize that the mothers are just as sensitive as they are, that their mothers can be hurt just as they themselves are hurt. Waverly feels torn: "Oh, her strength! Her weakness!—both pulling me apart. My mind was flying one way, my heart another. I sat down on the sofa next to her, the two of us stricken by the other" (*The Joy Luck Club*, p. 181). At one point Lindo Jong says to her daughter, "Yes, but you said it just to be mean, to hurt me, to. . . ." And when her daughter responds with more abuse, she is horrified. "So you think your mother is this bad. You think I have a secret meaning. But it is you who has this meaning. Ai-ya! She thinks I am this bad!" (*The Joy Luck Club*, p. 181). And just as Waverly feels acutely her mother's remarks, so any rude remarks that Waverly makes give Lindo sharp pain. As Ling points out, "Tan's implication is clear: we all take our mothers (and motherlands) for granted. They are just there, like air or water, impossible really to know or understand because we are so intimate, and more often than not they have seemed a force to struggle against" (Ling, *Between Worlds*, p. 136).

Ying Ying believes that by revealing the secrets of her past she can help her daughter. "Now I must tell my daughter everything. . . . I will gather together my past and look. I will see a thing that has already happened. The pain that cut my spirit loose. I will hold that pain in my hand until it becomes hard and shiny, more clear. And then my fierceness can come back, my golden side, my black side. I will use this sharp pain to penetrate my daughter's tough skin and cut her tiger spirit loose. She will fight me, because this is the nature of two tigers. But I will win and give her my spirit because this is the way a mother loves her daughter" (*The Joy Luck Club*, p. 252). And when Lindo and Waverly Jong are at the beauty parlor, the mother thinks, "And now I have to fight back my feelings. These two faces, I think, so much the same! The same happiness, the same sadness, the same good fortune, the same faults" (*The Joy Luck Club*, p. 256). Likewise the daughter sees her mother as so weak and frail that she comes to a new understanding. "I saw what I had been fighting for: It was for me, a scared child, who had run away a long time ago to what I had imagined was a safer place. And hiding in this place, behind my invisible barriers, I knew what lay on the other side: Her side attacks. Her secret weapons. Her uncanny ability to find my weakest spots. But in the brief instant that I had peered over the barriers I could finally see what was really there: an old woman, a wok for her armor, a knitting needle for her sword, getting a little crabby as she waited patiently for her daughter to invite her in" (*The Joy Luck Club*, pp. 183–84). The clash of these wills is finally stilled in a moment's revelation.

At the end, when Jing Mei goes to China to find her two lost sisters, she is all but overcome: "And now I see [my mother] again, two of her, waving, and in one hand there is a photo, the Polaroid I sent them. As soon as I get beyond the gate, we run toward each other, all three of us embracing, all hesitations and expectations forgotten. 'Mama, Mama,' we all murmur, as if she is among us" (*The Joy Luck Club*, p. 287). Eager yet hesitant, happy but somewhat shy, Jing Mei embraces her lost sisters. When Jing Mei looks at the polaroid picture of herself and her two Chinese sisters, she realizes their perfect likeness: "The gray-green surface changes to the bright colors of our three images, sharpening and deepening all at one . . . Together we look like our mother. Her same eyes, her same mouth, open in surprise to see, at last, her long-cherished wish" (*The Joy Luck Club*, p. 288). The dim shadowy images give way to the sharply focused features underlined by the similar bone structures. These images of likeness break down the walls of resistance. As Holbrook notes, "The symbolic use of faces and eyes is found in fairy tales, as well as in the fantasies of C. S. Lewis, George MacDonald, Lewis Carroll, and others. Symbolism of the mother's body, of birth, and of play may also be found—associated with existence and development" (Holbrook, p. 64). This development is achieved when Jing Mei's search for the mother ends by finding her sisters.

Jing Mei's need to find her own identity is realized when she meets her sisters. Pearson notes that "women writers in particular emphasize the female hero's need, following her liberation from male definition, for reconciliation with the mother. They also emphasize how inextricably bound together are the search for the mother and the search for the self" (Pearson and Pope, p. 197). The image of the mother superimposed on the sisters' reflections brings about this revelation. As Lazarre says, "It is the process of quiet, loving, insistent identification, the repeated testifying of one to the other that says, I am the same as you, that unlocks the doors and unravels the tangles" (Pearson and Pope, p. 203). Mirror images reflect the unbreakable bonds between mother and daughter.

Jing Mei's journey correlates with Holbrook's explanation of how fantasies work in stories by writers like C. S. Lewis and George MacDonald. "There is a journey, and during the journey something crucial has to be sought in the bleak world and brought back to restore meaning. This often is something shiny, magical, fruitful or potent. This quest is symbolic of the need of the individual who cannot complete mourning to find the dead mother—in the world of death—and to obtain from her the completion of reflection, thus restoring meaning to life. The loss has left the individual aware of the lack of meaning in his existence, consequent upon the insufficiency of the mother's creative reflection. Therefore, the individual must find her . . . or her magic attributes . . . to complete the existential process" (Holbrook, p. 65). When Jing Mei sees herself in the photo which serves as a magical mirror, she is restored. And the restoration she achieves is mirrored in the fates of her sisters, both Chinese and American.

Kingston's and Tan's images are more figurative and original than those of other, more conventional writers who tend to offer traditional images of the loving mother and dutiful daughter. Kingston's and Tan's images are more memorable and revealing of the problems of first generation Asian American mothers and their daughters. In *The Woman Warrior* and **The Joy Luck Club,** however, real separation never occurs, although the mother-daughter bond is problematic. Although at various times there is a tug of war, the bond between mothers and daughters is never broken. This concept fits in perfectly with the Chinese view of the universe. In the end the American-born daughters accept and affirm their Chinese heritage. In both *The Woman Warrior* and **The Joy Luck Club** resolution occurs when the daughters accept their mothers. They realize that despite differences of environment and culture they share a deep and unchanging bond with their mothers. Kingston's and Tan's philosophies truly fit Emerson's in "Each and All." Like the speaker in the last line of this poem, the mothers and daughters in *The Woman Warrior* and **The Joy Luck Club** finally yield themselves to the perfect whole.

*Note*

1. For a more detailed discussion of these unifying devices, see my book *The Shapes and Styles of Asian American Prose Fiction,* pp. 91–115.

## Wendy Ho (essay date 1996)

SOURCE: "Swan-Feather Mothers and Coca-Cola Daughters: Teaching Amy Tan's *The Joy Luck Club,*" in *Teaching American Ethnic Literatures,* University of New Mexico Press, 1996, pp. 327–45.

[*In the following essay, Ho argues that Tan accurately and realistically portrays the complicated lives of immigrant Chinese mothers and their American-born daughters and that these fictional portrayals are instructive, especially when placed in the context of the oppression of women in China.*]

A. ANALYSIS OF THEMES AND FORMS

Amy Tan's **The Joy Luck Club** is not a book in praise of "Oriental exotics" or passive victims. Nonetheless a number of critics and readers think that Amy Tan writes stories about a tantalizing, mysterious, and romanticized Old China or an exoticized Other. Some reviewers comment more about Tan than about the book, referring to her as "the flavor of the month, the hot young thing, the exotic new voice" (Streitfeld, F8); others invoke stereotypes in their review of the book: "Snappy as a fortune cookie and much more nutritious, **The Joy Luck Club** is a jolly treatment of familiar conflicts" (Koenig, 82). Another critic asserts that the Joy Luck mothers' memories of China are not anchored in "actual memory," but overtaken by "revery" for the China of their childhood past. He disappoints in encouraging readers to "dream" through the Old China sequences in Tan's book (Schell, 28). In *The Big Aiiieeeee!,* a groundbreaking anthology of Asian American literature, the writer-editors are highly critical of what they perceive as Tan's exoticization of China and the Chinese for a white mainstream audience. For them, her book simply resurrects racist images of an inscrutably corrupt East; of heartless, sexist (if not invisible) Chinese men; and of fragile, lotus-blossom women who appear to be too good for the decadent, ignorant society and culture from which they come (Chan et al.). Such one-dimensional Western representations are indeed destructive to the Asian American community. They are derived from the Orientalist school that Edward Said has so eloquently critiqued in his two books *Orientalism* and *Culture and Imperialism.*

But contrary to what the above critics may say or think, Amy Tan is not out to resurrect shallow stereotypes or Chinese exotica in **The Joy Luck Club.** As teachers, we need to seek out new and empowering interpretive strategies for reading Tan's texts rather than appropriating to ourselves—consciously or unconsciously—ways of reading our emerging writers that are based on racist, sexist perspectives. In this regard, I think it is important for readers to do the hard work of carefully processing the new literary, talk-story texts as intimately anchored not only in the psychodynamic tensions between Chinese immigrant mothers and their Americanized daughters within different familial situations, but also in the concrete socioeconomic, cultural, and historical realities of a hybrid diaspora culture in the United States.

The Joy Luck mothers' imaginations are not so overtaken by "revery" that they cannot comprehend the intersecting struggles of their lives in China or America, or the sexism and racism that they and their families must deal with in their lives. Tan resurrects women's untold personal stories of daily survival and resistance as a form of counter-memory: Their multiple stories counter, rather than support, the monolithic imperialist, patriarchal gaze and narratives that have denied them agency, complexity, and visibility in not only their own ethnic communities but also in the dominant Western culture in the U.S. Through her semiautobiographical fiction, Amy Tan advocates the value of reclaiming and understanding these Chinese women's neglected stories in China and America and of preserving and reimagining their Chinese heritage even as they tell of their bewildering new dilemmas as Chinese women in the United States. (For the semiautobiographical nature of her book, consult personal interviews by Seaman; Somogyi and Stanton; Tan, 1990.) Her book is dedicated to her mother, Daisy Tan: "To my mother and the memory of her mother. You asked me once what I would remember. This and much more." From these mother roots, daughter-writers such as Tan draw strength to survive, adapt, and create new stories and myths, new definitions of self-in-community, new strategies for cultural/historical survival that will honor their mothers and communities as well as their Chinese pasts. (See Friedman on the importance of group identity in the discussion of self in the writings of women, minorities, and many non-Western peoples.) Such links of the self in new and old communities will sustain them in the dangerous minefields of Anglo American life and culture.

Tan's *The Joy Luck Club* is structured around four central mirroring pairs of mothers and daughters: Suyuan Woo and Jing-mei "June" Woo; An-mei Hsu and Rose Hsu Jordan; Lindo Jong and Waverly Jong; and Ying-ying St. Clair and Lena St. Clair.[1] In *The Joy Luck Club,* the stories of these four pairs are interwoven in four major segments, with the mothers and daughters telling their stories of how it is they came to be where they are in life. Each of the four major segments of the book opens up with a vignette, which is followed by four chapters. The first and last segments involve the Joy Luck mothers' individual stories ("Feathers from a Thousand Li" and "Queen Mother of the Western Skies"). These two mother segments figuratively embrace the two middle segments ("The Twenty-Six Malignant Gates" and "American Translation") in which their daughters speak as second-generation Chinese women in America. In an interesting twist, Jing-mei, the daughter who has reluctantly assumed the place of her deceased mother Suyuan at the mah jong table at the beginning of the book, tells her mother's story in the final chapter, "A Pair of Tickets." She fulfills her mother's dream of returning to China to see her twin daughters—Jing-mei's lost sisters. She finally begins the process of re-identifying with a mother whom she had long neglected—whom she had often dismissed as an exotic Other. The daughter's recognition and reclamation of the intimate bonds with her mother is in counterpoint to the cultural and institutional images and definitions of women as mirrored in patriarchal/imperialist discourse. There is an impending change of guard at the end of the book which suggests the potential for continuity and transformation of mother-and-daughter bonding among a new generation of Chinese American women.

Tan's multiple pairings of mother-daughter stories mirror the strong links between the individual mothers and daughters as well as among all the women of the Joy Luck Club. Rather than focusing on a single primary mother-daughter relationship, Tan gives the reader a sense of the diversity of mother-daughter bonds within Chinese American families. As Tan says, "And when you talk to 100 different people to get their stories on a situation, that's what the truth is. So it's really a multiple story" (Seaman, 256). The links between these mothers and daughters in America are further complicated by the bonds between the Joy Luck mothers and their mothers (and foremothers) in China. Tan enriches the reader's understanding of a single woman's history and of these Chinese American mother-daughter pairs by extending the resonances to the past and to the spidery links to mother-daughter bonds embedded in Chinese culture and society. For example, we witness Lindo Jong's sad separation from her beloved mother and the development of her feisty and clever private self in an arranged marriage—a self that is reflected in a complicated relationship with her own strong-willed daughter. In An-mei Hsu's story, we explore the roots of her frustrations and anger as a woman in the telling of her mother's oppressive life and death as a concubine in feudal China. We begin to understand the links between her personal liberation and the revolutionary changes in China—of a woman and a nation finding a new voice. Tan links Hsu's personal-political struggles with a sociohistorical awareness and participation in her people's struggle for justice and equality. Through the book's intersecting storylines, the reader is exposed to the rich variations and interconnections in the relationships and communications between Chinese mothers and daughters in China and/or in America as they attempt to talk out the silences and distances and to process what is really being described and felt by each other as women.

In *The Joy Luck Club,* the mothers and daughters continually struggle not only to reclaim and speak their stories, but also to "talk back" as complex subjects. But in order to speak up in the larger community and to transform women's lives in a sexist, racist society, Tan's mothers and daughters have to learn to be friends and allies to each other. For women, one important place to begin this primary, necessary work is in the problematic relationships and communications between mothers and daughters. (For an introduction to mother-daughter writing, see, for example, Hirsch.) In *The Joy Luck Club,* mothers and daughters find a compelling need to set the record straight on the specific actualities of their lives in China and America; but they find it difficult to articulate their honest intentions, emotions, and experiences to each other. Jing-mei Woo's mother gives her an heirloom jade pendant—her life's importance—by which she will know her mother's meaning. But as Jing-mei notes, it seemed that she and other jade-pendant wearers were "all sworn to the same secret covenant, so secret we don't even know what we belong to" (198). Much miscommunication takes place between the mothers and daughters. It is a tricky and risky task for them to dredge up and decipher each other's personal stories—these palimpsests that are shrouded in layers of silence, secrecy, pain, ambiguity, collusion, and prohibition within the varied discourses, institutions, and power relations in a society.

However, this is precisely the work that Tan takes up. Each woman has her story of hopes and ambitions, of failure, of survival and resistance. The mothers, for example, must confront the personal archive of tragedy, alienation, suffering, and loss in their own lives; they must negotiate the shame and guilt of leaving country, family, home, and mother. Each woman must wrestle with what to tell the other amid the false images and narratives that obscure or silence their personal stories as Chinese American women. They must overcome the sense that their daughters often look upon them as outcasts, as Other, in America. Jingmei thinks of her mother's mah jong gatherings as "a shameful Chinese custom, like the secret gathering of the Ku Klux Klan or the tom-tom dances of TV Indians preparing for war" (28). In this less than hospitable context, Suyuan Woo struggles continually to translate her tragic war stories to a resisting daughter. Tan does not neglect to portray the serious dilemmas and ironies that these mothers confront in creating and maintaining a protective environment, a material, cultural and psycho-political bastion, for themselves or their families in America.

Nevertheless, the Joy Luck mothers work painfully to decipher and speak the buried, bittersweet pain of their lives in order to reclaim their own stories and to protect their bewildered daughters from similar pain and oppression as women in America. Through their personal recall, they begin to recognize the insidious links between their pasts and present struggles in America and between their pasts and their daughters' present lives. It is important to read these women's stories as the complicated physical, psychological, cultural, and sociohistorical positionings for personal and communal survival and resistance in the Chinese diaspora communities of the United States. In this light, these stories record not detached reveries or myths about China but, rather, daily heroic actions of many of the Joy Luck mothers, who struggle to raise children under stressful political and sociohistorical conditions.

Like their mothers, daughters must overcome their personal anger, resentment, guilt, and fear toward their mothers. Tan demonstrates how the daughters tend to stereotype their mothers—to freeze them in time as old-fashioned ladies; they do not often give their mothers the space to particularize themselves or to cross over into their lives. They are second-generation, English-speaking Chinese American women, who are located or positioned in an Anglo American homeland that has a long history of oppressing Asian Americans. In living in America, the daughters assimilate certain stereo-typical and racist views of the Chinese that alienate them from their own mothers and heritage. They find it distasteful to be identified with their mothers or their stories; with speaking the Chinese language, or with keeping the old ways and customs. Joy Luck daughters often fail to recognize the difficult but vital work and nurture of their working-class, immigrant Chinese mothers. Yuppie Waverly Jong, for example, makes up jokes to tell her friends about her mother's arrival in America and about her parents meeting and marriage. She trivializes their stories of struggle and joy. Waverly does not know the true story about the difficulties of her feisty immigrant mother; the poignant story of how her parents courted by surmounting ethnic and linguistic difficulties; or the story of how her name was chosen to express her mother's love and hopes for her.

Within this problematic framework, the Joy Luck women struggle to maintain vital communication with each other and to piece together the fragmented memories and talk-story of their actual lives. In *The Joy Luck Club,* it is a struggle, with varying successes and failures, for the mother-daughter pairs to know and love each other for their own strengths, weaknesses, and contexts. As we see in the individual stories, it is easy for mothers and daughters to get lost in the intense psychodynamic love—hate struggles within themselves and with each other. Both can be nurturing and suffocating, protective and negligent, trusting and distrustful, arrogant and humble, powerful and weak, affiliative and competitive toward each other. Each Joy Luck mother-daughter pair attempts to articulate positions that are rooted in their intertwined needs for individuation, mutual respect, and attachment to each other and their communities.

In addition, these psychodynamic tensions are embedded in particular socioeconomic and historical circumstances in China and in America that further complicate their relationship and communications with each other; that is, internal tensions between mothers and daughters are exacerbated and even generated by external factors. In *The Joy Luck Club,* mothers and daughters often have a difficult times smoothly negotiating the great sociohistorical expanses of their specific *weltanschaung*. For example, mothers and daughters are separated by historical time, cataclysmic natural disasters and wars, generations, classes, sociocultural systems and values, and languages. The traumatic translation of devalued and ambitious Chinese-speaking immigrant mothers from their motherland to an unfriendly and alien country and the assimilation of their second-generation, English-speaking Chinese daughters into mainstream America cause serious fractures in their relationship and communication with each other.

For the Joy Luck women to communicate with each other and to speak up as women against the invisibility—the distorted images and stereotypes of women in China and America—is to begin to imagine the histories that have been left out. (For instance, see Kim, especially 3–22, on stereotypes of Asian American people in literature, media, and society.) As some of their own mothers struggled to teach them, Joy Luck mothers want to teach their daughters how to acknowledge and deal with pain; how to know true friends; how to trust that their mothers know them inside and out; how to be free of confusion; how to survive under tricky and marginal circumstances with grace and joy luck. Some of the mothers especially desire to pass on to their daughters a sense of *shou,* a respect and honor for their mothers; *nengkan,* an ability to accomplish anything they put their mind to; and *chuming,* an inner knowing of each other as women. Most desire to reclaim their daughters by fighting for their hearts and minds and by responsibly educating them to survive and to subvert the oppressive systems in which they live. Joy Luck mothers teach their daughters that personal and cultural identity need to be maintained not only through the preservation of Chinese heritage but also through a continually active, fluid, multidimensional agency that can negotiate the fluctuations of oppressive social, cultural, and historical processes.

On the one hand, Asian American women have suffered under imperialist and patriarchal power structures. To deny these oppressive factors in any culture—whether in China or America—is, as Frank Chin likes to say, to live in the "fake world," not the "real world." The Asian American mothers and daughters in ***The Joy Luck Club*** are struggling subjects and agents encountering a not very perfect world in China and in America. Sometimes they lose their battles in the oppressive systems in which they live and position themselves; they comply, negotiate, and/or betray themselves and others in their search for sheer survival or status within systems of power. Tan shows us the complicity and compromise that can mire her female characters as they struggle to come to consciousness and voice about their lives and circumstances. For example, women are complicit in destroying Anmei's mother through the patriarchal power arrangements of family and society. Wu Tsing's childless Second Wife arranges to entrap An-mei's mother as a concubine for her husband. As a rich woman, Second Wife uses the borrowed class, wealth, and power of her husband to oppress and manipulate other women. This oppression of the other wives is her attempt to guarantee her own tenuous position and status in Wu Tsing's competitive female household. Tan is not out to valorize or privilege all women's language and actions. She paints a painfully problematic picture of women's complicity not only in another woman's oppression, but in their own continuing oppression in and maintenance of male-dominated culture.

On the other hand, Asian women are not always or simply powerless, passive, exploited dupes and sexual objects, domestic drudges, illiterates, and/or traditional women in patriarchal or imperialist systems (see Mohanty). In teaching this book, one must not neglect to take into account that Tan shows us how ordinary women, located in the specific context of their own times and personal circumstances, have challenged and subverted the socioeconomic and political systems under which they have lived and are living in many different ways. At the same time that their lives bespeak oppression and tragedy, the Joy Luck mothers do not neglect to pass on empowering interventions to their daughters. These resistances counter the patriarchal and imperialist systems that they are exposed to in China and America, which have forced them to speak, see, think, and act often in disempowering terms.

Such communication provides vital entry into the past, present, and future. The mothers' life-stories are the valuable maps not only of the powerlessness, servility, frustration, defeat, and compromise, but also of the powerful strategies of intervention and subversion that help women survive with a certain amount of grace, anger, strength, connectedness, and love. Mothers and daughters come to realize their fierce love and respect for each other as friends and survivors. They come to realize that there are rich challenges and meanings embodied even in the silences, fragments, tensions, and differences.

Doing the work of talk-story as a way to resist oppressive, monolithic patriarchal and imperialist institutions and metanarratives can lead to the inscription of new and fluid woman-centered spaces for women. In ***The Joy Luck Club,*** we learn just how vital it is for mothers and daughters to continually talk-story—not to wait, for instance, to speak only until spoken to or given authority to do so or till one can speak perfect American English. It can be personally and politically empowering and heroic for women to tell their stories and attend to each other—not to be decentered objects whose stories are continually co-opted or translated for them or to them by those in power. In this way, women can be empowered to challenge society. During the Chinese Revolution, Chinese women learned to stand up and speak against not only their landlords but also their husbands and fathers. The slogan for this emancipation of people was *fanshen,* which meant "to stand up and overturn the oppressing classes." Women learned to speak the bitterness in their daily lives. Within their consciousness-raising women's groups in the countryside and cities, women learned, first of all, to speak up about the poverty, the hunger, the physical and psychological abuse and fear, the socioeconomic and political inequities. (See description of *suku,* or the "indictments of bitterness," in Ono, 170–75.) Women had access to each other's true feelings and contexts in an affiliative, nurturing environment. In this way, they learned they were not alone, separate from other women or other oppressed groups. Many Chinese women were empowered to speak and act together in transforming their lives and society. Likewise, Tan's mothers want to teach their daughters how to read situations clearly and how to stand up and fight for themselves. They want their daughters to be bolder, more self-assured women; to be independent from their husbands; to have status and voice on their own merit. As the critic bell hooks has powerfully stated, talking back is a way of speaking up for one-self as a woman, boldly and defiantly. It is "not solely an expression of creative power; it is an act of resistance, a political gesture that challenges politics of domination that would render us nameless and voiceless. As such it is a courageous act—as such, it represents a threat. To those who wield oppressive power, that which is threatening must necessarily be wiped out, annihilated, silenced" (8).

Like Maxine Hong Kingston, Amy Tan is a daughter-writer, who has come to realize that locating, defining, and reporting women's stories and the crimes against women and community are part of the constructive, articulated anger and revenge against the narratives and institutions that oppress them. To recover multiple histories and to talk back as women united is to do real battle against oppression in their personal and communal lives. In reading Tan, one becomes acutely aware that this is serious, painful, complicated excavatory work; it is also subversive, creative, freeing, and responsible work for mothers and daughters who wish to connect as women-allies.

### B. Teaching *The Joy Luck Club*

An understanding of the Joy Luck mothers' (and their foremothers') Chinese past can help make the problematic interactions with their second-generation Americanized daughters—how they perceive and treat them and why—more accessible to readers. Teachers can assign introductory background readings on women in Chinese and Chinese American history.[2] The mother-and-daughter relationships cannot be fully understood as simply personal, internal problems to be worked out between Chinese mothers and their daughters. The bonds are problematized or complicated, in part, by their embeddedness in the particular psychological, socioeconomic, cultural, and historical realities of a traditional Confucian society that socialized and oppressed women in China.

As Julia Kristeva notes, Confucianists saw women as small human beings (*hsiao ren*) to be categorized with babies and slaves (Ling, 3). Women were not suited by nature for the intellectual life of a scholar or a statesman. Women's lives were to revolve around the Three Obediences and Four Virtues:

> The Three Obediences enjoined a woman to obey her father before marriage, her husband after marriage, and her eldest son after her husband's death. The Four Virtues decreed that she be chaste; her conversation courteous and not gossipy; her deportment graceful but not extravagant; her leisure spent in perfecting needlework and tapestry for beautifying the home.
>
> (Ling, 3)

These delimiting societal prescriptions for women's gender roles and for a "true" Chinese womanhood can permit the physical and psychological abuse of women. The Joy Luck mothers experience their mothers' as well as their own difficult compromises and failures in a restrictive patriarchal culture and society. For example, An-mei Hsu learns the lessons that attempt to strain and destroy her relationship with her mother. Both An-mei and her mother live in traditional familial and societal structures, which often deny their personal needs, sufferings, and struggles and ask them to conform to a male-dominated culture against their own individual and common interests as women. An-mei grows up with stories, which attempt to break the spirit of strong-willed girls, the disobedient types—like her hidden self. These patriarchal stories are powerful forms of socialization into her proper and public roles in traditional Chinese society as a daughter, wife, mother, woman. The film version of Tan's ***The Joy Luck Club*** (Wayne Wang) dramatically depicts the tragic experiences of the mothers in China and its parallels and consequences in the lives of their daughters in the United States. A viewing of the film—a real tearjerker—could provide another way to access the psychodynamic tensions between the mother-daughter pairs in the book. For a view of women's lives in prerevolutionary China, students can read the Chinese novel *The Family* by Pa Chin. The film *Small Happiness* (Carma Hinton and Richard Gordon) can provide a sense of women's lives in a specific Chinese context. In exploring the impact of a Chinese Confucian system on women's socialization into gender roles and identity, students can better understand the relationships of the Joy Luck mothers to their own mothers in China. In addition, this information can help students to understand the complex interactions between the Joy Luck mothers and their own daughters in America.

The historical events and natural disasters in China also play a role in shaping the Joy Luck mothers. They and their mothers before them, in one way or another, experience a range of horrific wars and chaos, evacuations, deaths, economic turmoil, revolutionary changes, poverty, floods, and famines that seriously impinge on their personal relationships and communications with their daughters. In the 1800s to middle 1900s, there were horrendous wars for colonial dominance over China waged by imperialist powers such as England, the United States, and Japan. There was bloody civil war between the Chinese Communist Party (Mao Zedong) and the Guomindang (Chiang Kai-shek) rumbling through China (see Ono). Chinese women suffered the terrible consequences of these chaotic events, especially the toll they took on the socioeconomic and political situations in their daily lives. For instance, Suyuan Woo's life, fears, and ambitions are clearly influenced by the chaos and brutalities of war, separation from family, death of a husband, and loss of her baby daughters. Suyuan's abandonment of her twin daughters during her escape from the invading Japanese is vividly portrayed in the film version of ***The Joy Luck Club.*** Young Lindo Jong remembers the painful, lonely separation from her beloved mother: she is sent to her boy-husband's household after disastrous floods, famine, and poverty make it difficult for the family to keep a "useless" daughter. Ying-ying St. Clair's concerns for her daughter's safety and her own fears at being sexually harassed on an Oakland street by a stranger could be rooted in her own bitter experiences as a lone married woman migrating from the poor countryside to Shanghai, a city notorious for its foreign decadence and the murder, rape, kidnapping, and prostitution of Chinese women in the early to middle 1900s. However, it was also a significant revolutionary period of change, not only in terms of women's rights but also for the Chinese nation. Students need to keep in mind that the Joy Luck mothers are the products of these revolutionary times. They are women of old and new China.

Besides an understanding of the Joy Luck mothers' Chinese roots, it is important to consider their traumatic translation to the United States. The mothers are excited by the potential opportunities in America for themselves and their families. But they are also socialized into silence by American racism and haunted by the history of immigration policies that have excluded Asians from entry into America. Before the arrival of the Joy Luck mothers in 1949, America already had a long and ugly record of discriminatory attitudes and policies aimed not only against successive groups of Asians, but also specifically against the Chinese (see S. Chan, Daniels, and Wong). Besides numerous Chinese immigration exclusionary laws enacted between 1882 and 1904, there were also a number of immigration policies that specifically deterred the immigration of Chinese women to America (such as the 1875 Page Law and the 1924 Immigration Act). These restrictive forms of social and legal legislation affected the numbers of Asian women entering the country and the subsequent formation of Asian families in America. Racist/sexist stereotypes portrayed Chinese women as lewd and immoral women, who were unfit to enter the country. Sensational news-media coverage on the evils of Chinese prostitution created the long-standing stereotype of Chinese women as prostitutes. As audiovisual resources, films such as *Slaying the Dragon* (Deborah Gee) and *New Year* (Valerie Soe) can provide a visual introduction to the many stereotypes of Asian American women/people. With this long history of racism and sexism in the United States, Tan shows us why it is not difficult to understand the Chinese immigrant mothers' fear of the police, deportation, and backlash from white Americans based on their race and gender.

Despite all her years in America, An-mei Hsu lives with fears of deportation. An-mei's fears are well grounded, especially if one remembers America's severe anticommunist paranoia of the 1950s. Likewise, Ying-ying St. Clair is forced to invent a fictive self that is oriented to her present and future life in America, but which does not account for her frightening past life. In this foreign and suffocating space, she feels numb, off balance, and lost, living in small houses, doing servant's work, wearing American clothes, learning Western ways and English, accepting American ways without care or comment, and raising a distant daughter. Upon her arrival in America, Ying-ying is processed at Angel Island Immigration Station, where agents try to figure out her classification: war bride, displaced person, student, or wife. She is renamed Betty St. Clair; she loses her Chinese name and identity as Gu Ying-ying and gains a new birthdate. In the Chinese lunar calendar, she is no longer a tiger but a dragon. It takes her a long time to recover and pass on her tiger spirit to her daughter Lena.

In contrast to the mothers, the daughters, born and raised in contemporary America, have assimilated more easily into the dominant society. But Tan portrays the great cost of assimilation in the miscommunications between the Joy Luck mothers and daughters. Under such circumstances, how can mothers tell their stories to their insider/outsider daughters? How can the Joy Luck mothers articulate their stories fully if they feel they must hide or deny their past? their language in America? How can Americanized Chinese daughters begin to understand the fractured narratives that surface, made up, as they are, of so many lies and truths, so many protective layers set up against the outsiders' *chuming*, an inner knowing, of them? What are the advantages and disadvantages of assimilation for these mothers and daughters? How can these women learn to be friends and allies to each other? How are language and strategies for survival and resistance passed from mothers to daughters? She demonstrates how many intertwined dilemmas can impede or frustrate clear access by daughters to their mothers and to the full stories of their mother's and family's life and history in China and America. Nevertheless, Tan's text emphasizes that this difficult work of recovery is vital to women's well-being and solidarity with each other.

Another way of accessing Tan's book is to analyze her use of traditional Chinese legends (for example, the Moon Lady story) and images to articulate the concerns of Chinese American women. For instance, the Joy Luck mothers want their daughters to turn into beautiful swans—perfect, happy, successful, and independent women. In traditional Chinese stories, swans symbolize married, heterosexual love. Tan subverts and re-interprets the traditional image of swans by applying it to the silenced and intimate pairings between women. In this case, a mother and her daughter. The traditional symbols and narratives are being appropriated, reconstructed, or ruptured by writers like Tan (and Maxine Hong Kingston) who do not wish to focus on the master narratives of patriarchy, but to focus instead on the powerful stories of love and struggle between mothers and daughters, between women in China and in America. The stories in **The Joy Luck Club** give voice to the desires and experiences of female characters who have not had the advantage to write or tell their stories as men have had. It is their neglected stories that they tell and attempt to transmit to their daughters in the oral traditions of talk-story. These hybrid talk-story narratives challenge those who would deny or lessen the power, beauty, value, and pain in these women's lives. This is what Maxine Hong Kingston spent a lot of time learning in her memoir *The Woman Warrior*: "The reporting is the vengeance—not the beheading, not the gutting, but the words" (63). The personal stories of the Joy Luck mothers do battle through gossip, circular talking, cryptic messages/caveats, dream images, bilingual language, and talk-story traditions—not in the linear, logical, or publicly authorized discourse in patriarchal or imperialist narratives. This is talk that challenges the denial of Asian American women's voices and identities—denials not only by a male-dominated Chinese society and a Eurocentric American society but also by their very own daughters who have become so Americanized that they can barely talk-story with their mothers. In many ways, Tan's book can be fruitfully compared with *The Woman Warrior*. As heroic paper daughters in quest of their mothers' stories, Tan and Kingston empower not only their mothers but also themselves and their racial/ethnic communities through a psychic and oral/literary birthing that keeps alive the intimate, ever-changing record of tragedies, resistances, and joy luck for all people.

In the following section, I have included a number of additional discussion and paper topic questions that would be useful in teaching Tan's **The Joy Luck Club**.

1. What are the experiences most remembered by the mothers? Where is "home" for them? How do the experiences of the mothers resonate in the lives of their daughters? Can one see parallels in the daughters' lives? What expectations do individual mothers have for their daughters? and vice versa? What are the obstacles—social, economic, psychological, cultural, historical—that impact on the communications between the mothers and daughters? How does assimilation into dominant Anglo American culture affect their relationship? Is it important for daughters and mothers to communicate with each other? Why? How do mothers and daughters specifically find ways to survive and resist their multiple oppressions as Chinese American women?

2. Discuss how Tan portrays the acquisition of gender identity and roles in the early childhood of the Joy Luck mothers in stories such as "The Moon Lady," "The Scar," or "The Red Candle." How does Tan convey through the language and images the particular conflicts and tensions within the different women? Do they simply adjust to the repression of their own private desires and dreams? How do they negotiate or resist patriarchal/imperialist oppression? Do they succeed and/or fail in their attempts?

3. Discuss the style or structure of Tan's text—for example, her use of a first-person point of view in the text. Or why and how does Tan use and/or transform the Chinese talk-story tradition or the images and legends in her own Chinese American stories? In regard to these topics, students could expand the discussion by comparing and contrasting two other Chinese American mother-daughter literary texts—Jade Snow Wong's *Fifth Chinese Daughter* (1945) and Maxine Hong Kingston's *The Woman Warrior* (1977).

4. (a) For a broader analysis of Asian American mother-daughter interactions, compare/contrast **The Joy Luck Club** with Tan's second novel **The Kitchen God's Wife**, which focuses on the difficult relationship and revelations between the immigrant mother Jiang Weili and her Chinese American daughter Pearl. **The Joy Luck Club** can also be used with Faye Myenne Ng's first novel *Bone*, which reveals the trauma and grief of a San Francisco Chinatown family attempting to deal with the suicide of one of their three daughters. Tan's book also works well with Joy Kogawa's *Obasan* or Hisaye Yamamoto's *Seventeen Syllables and Other Stories*. Both writers deal with the multiple tensions between immigrant mothers and their second-generation daughters in the Japanese American community before, during, and after World War II. There are also a good selection of essays, short stories, and poems by other Asian American writers on this topic in Asian American anthologies listed in section C, "Related Works," below.

(b) Other mother-daughter writing that can be used with Tan's book include Kim Chernin's *In My Mother's House: A Daughter's Story*, Edwidge Danticat's *Breath, Eyes, Memory*, Audre Lorde's *Zami: A New Spelling of My Name*, and Paule Marshall's *Brown Girl, Brownstones*. For example, Paule Marshall's novel, set in Brooklyn during the period of the Depression and World War II, depicts the struggles of a Barbadian immigrant family as it confronts poverty and racism in the United States. In the story, Selina Boyce, a young daughter searching for identity, must confront and resolve the contradictory feelings she has toward her hardworking, ambitious mother. Possible questions to help promote discussion around these novels include the following: What personal, cultural, and sociohistorical struggles do women encounter in their families and mixed cultures in the United States? In what ways do they attempt to construct multiple selves, subjectivities, or positionings that have value against the meaninglessness, oppression, and violence (psychic and physical) that they encounter in their lives? Do they succeed and/or fail in their attempts? How do women empower or destroy other women? How do these diverse writers find innovative ways to rupture racist/sexist language and institutions through their creative use of language and/or narrative strategies? Are there similarities and/or differences in their writing strategies/tactics, stories, experiences? What type of identification and valorization of a women's culture is portrayed in the texts?

5. To provide for more inclusive and personal participation in the discussion of the book, students can compare their own relationships with their mothers and families and how they are situated and constructed in specific and diverse racial/ethnic, social, cultural, and historical contexts. This can be done in small group discussions, journal entries, and/or an oral history project.

6. (a) Students might wish to see the film version of **The Joy Luck Club** and discuss how the film might significantly differ from the book. What stories were left out? which ones kept? and why? Were there any modifications in the stories portrayed in the film? Why? How are men depicted in the book and film? Are the issues of racism and sexism in the United States discussed or left invisible in the film? Why and/or why not?

(b) Compare/contrast the portrayals of the mother-daughter relationship in **The Joy Luck Club** with another film directed by Wayne Wang, entitled *Dim Sum*, which also portrays the daily interactions between an immigrant Chinese mother and her daughter. What are the similarities and/or differences in the representations of Chinese Americans and their experiences in these two films? What were the production contexts (such as funding, decision-making process, studio, writing, and directing) for these two films by Wayne Wang? How do these institutional contexts impact on the final aesthetic product that is produced? Who are the audiences for these two films?

*Notes*

1. Note that mirror imagery is pervasive in Tan's book. For instance, Lindo Jong looks into the mirror and discovers a private self. Waverly also looks into the hairdresser's mirror. Jing-mei looks into the mirror to discover her secret "prodigy" self. There are many references to mothers as mirrors and to the placement of mirrors in rooms. Tan attempts to break down the binary polarizations that patriarchy demands and the separation between one woman and another. Before the freeing bonds between mother and daughters can be re-membered, the miming/doubling in the false mirror of patriarchy and imperialism must be ruptured.

2. On the important roles played by Chinese women in peasant strikes, silk-factory communities, labor movements, and uprisings in pre-and post-revolutionary China, consult Ono and Wolf and Witke. For Chinese American women's history, consult S. Chan, Wong, and Yung.

### C. BIBLIOGRAPHIES

*1. RELATED WORKS*

Chernin, Kim. *In My Mother's House: A Daughter's Story.* New York: Harper and Row, 1983.

Danticat, Edwidge. *Breath, Eyes, Memory.* New York: Soho Press, 1994.

Kingston, Maxine Hong. *The Woman Warrior: Memoirs of a Girlhood among Ghosts.* New York: Vintage, 1977.

Kogawa, Joy. *Obasan.* Boston: David Godine, 1981.

Lorde, Audre. *Zami: A New Spelling of My Name.* Freedom, Calif.: Crossing Press, 1982.

Marshall, Paule. *Brown Girl, Brownstones.* 1959. Reprint, New York: Feminist Press, 1981.

Moraga, Cherríe, and Gloria Anzaldúa, eds. *This Bridge Called My Back: Writings by Radical Women of Color.* New York: Kitchen Table/Women of Color Press, 1981. There are a number of excellent texts on how the issues of race, class, gender, and sexuality impact on the lives of immigrant mothers and second-generation daughters-writers: Cherríe Moraga's "La Güera," Merle Woo's "Letter to Ma," and Gloria Anzaldúa's "La Prieta."

Ng, Fae Myenne. *Bone.* New York: Hyperion, 1993.

Tan, Amy. *The Kitchen God's Wife.* New York: G. P. Putnam's Sons, 1991.

Watanabe, Sylvia, and Carol Bruchac, eds. *Home to Stay: Asian American Women's Fiction.* New York: Greenfield Review Press, 1990. A diverse selection of writing that may be helpful in situating Tan's work with other contemporary Asian American women writers.

Wong, Jade Snow. *Fifth Chinese Daughter.* 1945. Reprint, Seattle: University of Washington Press, 1989.

Yamamoto, Hisaye. *Seventeen Syllables and Other Stories.* Latham, N.Y.: Kitchen Table/Women of Color Press, 1988.

*2. BEST CRITICISM*

Cheung, King-Kok. *Articulate Silences: Hisaye Yamamoto, Maxine Hong Kingston, Joy Kogawa.* Ithaca, N.Y.: Cornell University Press, 1993. Though she does not discuss Tan's work, Cheung provides a useful study of the thematic and rhetorical uses of silences in the articulation of the unspeakable and in defiance of the hegemonic culture that denies the voices/experiences of Asian American women.

Ho, Wendy. "Mother-and-Daughter Writing and the Politics of Location in Maxine Hong Kingston's *The Woman Warrior* and Amy Tan's *The Joy Luck Club*." Ph.D.diss., University of Wisconsin, Madison, 1993. Reprint, Ann Arbor: UMI, 1993. I examine (1) the complex negotiations that Chinese American immigrant mothers and their second-generation daughters perform daily in dealing with diverse, and often conflicting, socioeconomic, cultural, historical, and political frameworks and (2) how Kingston and Tan invent alternative literary-political strategies and positionings to tell their mothers' stories and their own.

Kim, Elaine. *Asian American Literature: An Introduction to the Writings and Their Social Context.* Philadelphia: Temple University Press, 1982. This early classic in the study of Asian American literature provides a sociohistorical introduction to the literary works by Americans of Chinese, Japanese, Korean, and Filipino descent from the nineteenth century to the early 1980s.

Ling, Amy. "Focus on America: Seeking a Self and a Place." *Between Worlds: Women Writers of Chinese Ancestry.* The Athene Series. New York: Pergamon Press, 1990. Ling examines the mother-daughter theme and its links to the notions of the motherland and to the "between-worlds" tensions in the work of Chinese American women writers such as Kingston and Tan.

Lowe, Lisa. "Homogeneity, Hybridity, Multiplicity: Marking Asian American Differences." *Diaspora* 1, no. 1 (Spring 1991): 24–44. By using *The Joy Luck Club* as one of her examples, Lowe explores the concept of hybridity and heterogeneity in Asian American experiences and the importance of considering the complex intersections of race, class, and gender in the mother-daughter trope.

Schueller, Malini Johar. "Theorizing Ethnicity and Subjectivity: Maxine Hong Kingston's *Tripmaster Monkey* and Amy Tan's *The Joy Luck Club*." *Genders* 15 (Winter 1992): 72–85. Using a poststructuralist framework, Schueller examines the socially constructed discursive nature of ethnic and gender identity in Kingston and Tan. She argues that these writers provide alternative ways of resisting authoritarian and essentialist definitions of ethnicity and gender identity that have been used to marginalize oppressed peoples.

Wong, Sau-ling Cynthia. *Reading Asian American Literature: From Necessity to Extravagance.* Princeton, N.J.: Princeton University Press, 1993. In a stimulating critical study, Wong argues for an intertextual framework for reading Asian American texts, which she demonstrates through the study of four motifs. In the food and eating motif, there are brief references to *The Joy Luck Club.*

*3. OTHER SOURCES*

Chan, Jeffrey Paul, Frank Chin, Lawson Fusao Inada, and Shawn Wong, eds. *The Big Aiiieeeee!: An Anthology of Chinese American and Japanese Literature.* New York: Meridian, 1991.

Chan, Sucheng. *Asian Americans: An Interpretive History.* Twayne's Immigrant Heritage of America Series. Boston: Twayne Publishers, 1991.

Daniels, Roger. *Asian America: Chinese and Japanese in the United States since 1850.* Seattle: University of Washington Press, 1988.

Friedman, Susan Stanford. "Women's Autobiographical Selves: Theory and Practice." In *The Private Self: Theory and Practice of Women's Autobiographical Writings,* ed. Shari Benstock, 34–62. Chapel Hill and London: University of North Carolina Press, 1988.

Hirsch, Marianne. "Mothers and Daughters." *Signs: Journal of Women in Culture and Society* 7, no. 1 (Fall 1981): 200–222.

hooks, bell. *Talking Back.* Boston: South End Press, 1989.

Koenig, Rhonda. "Heirloom China." *New York Magazine,* March 20, 1989, 82–83.

Mohanty, Chandra Talpade. "Cartographies of Struggle: Third World Women and the Politics of Feminism." In *Third World Women and the Politics of Feminism,* ed. Chandra Mohanty, Ann Russo, and Lourdes Torres. Bloomington and Indianapolis: Indiana University Press, 1991.

Ono, Kazuko. *Chinese Women in a Century of Revolution*: 1850–1950, ed. Joshua Fogel. Stanford, Calif.: Stanford University Press, 1989.

Schell, Orville. "'Your Mother Is in Your Bones.'" Review of *The Joy Luck Club* by Amy Tan. *New York Times Book Review,* March 19, 1989, 3+.

Seaman, Donna. "The Booklist Interview: Amy Tan." *Booklist* (Oct. 1, 1990): 256–57.

Somogyi, Barbara, and David Stanton. "Amy Tan: An Interview." *Poets and Writers* 19, no. 5 (September/October 1991): 24–32.

Streitfeld, David. "The 'Luck' of Amy Tan." Review of *The Joy Luck Club* by Amy Tan. *Washington Post,* Oct. 8, 1989, sec. F1+.

Tan, Amy. *The Joy Luck Club.* New York: G. P. Putnam's Sons, 1989.

———. "Amy Tan on Amy Tan and *The Joy Luck Club.*" *California State Library Foundation Bulletin* 31 (April 1990): 1–10.

Wolf, Margery, and Roxane Witke, eds. *Women in Chinese Society.* Stanford, Calif.: Stanford University Press, 1975.

Wong, Diane Yen-Mai, and Asian Women United of California, eds. *Making Waves: An Anthology of Writings by and about Asian American Women.* Boston: Beacon Press, 1989.

Yung, Judy. *Chinese Women of America: A Pictorial History.* Seattle: University of Washington, 1986.

## Michael Delucchi (essay date June 1998)

SOURCE: "Self and Identity among Aging Immigrants in *The Joy Luck Club,*" in *Journal of Aging and Identity,* Vol. 3, No. 2, June, 1998, pp. 59–66.

[*In the following essay, Delucchi seeks to demonstrate how literature's "fictionalized life histories" contribute to social science by reading* The Joy Luck Club *as an account of aging and identity formation.*]

This article uses George Herbert Mead's theory of symbolic interaction to examine self and identity among aging immigrants in Amy Tan's novel **The Joy Luck Club** (1989). Social scientists have largely bypassed analysis of fictional accounts of the Asian diaspora. My motivation for employing Mead's theory is to extend social scientific analysis to novels on aging and ethnicity. By examining self-narratives in fictional representations of the aging immigrant experience, I assess how identity develops out of particular social conditions and is achieved through social, psychological processes. Despite some limitations, symbolic interaction offers insights into the process whereby the present brings reinterpretation of the past and individuals are compelled to assign meaning to their life histories.

This essay examines aging and identity in Amy Tan's novel **The Joy Luck Club** (1989) as it develops out of particular social conditions and is achieved through social psychological processes. Specifically, I explore the contribution of George Herbert Mead's symbolic interactionist perspective to the analysis of aging and self among older immigrants. I address how immigrant identity formation is socially negotiated and how the self extends to encompass events from the past. To accomplish this, I seek textual evidence of the sociological processes underlying the narrative of aging.

### BACKGROUND

The autobiography and the novel are similar in that both invite the reader to experience vicariously the life and culture of the characters. Novels are different from autobiographies in that they attempt by definition, to present to the reader the connection between biography and history—that is, the link between the characters' lives and their historic times and places (Fitzgerald 1992). Although many autobiographies provide similar insight, they are not bound to do so. Therefore, the novel, in telling a story, presents the culture and the way its members define reality.

Although the idea of using literature in the social sciences is not new, researchers have largely resisted analysis of literary accounts of aging and ethnicity for two reasons. First, the use of novels is constrained by the relative absence of a theoretical framework that can be used for interpretation of fictionalized life histories. Second, novels are recognized as "metaphors of self" and this inhibits their use as objective sources of data. Nevertheless, recent scholarship has identified literary works on aging as an important component of gerontological research (Combe and Schmader 1996; Deats 1996; Holstein 1994). Moreover, social psychologists now recognize the value of autobiographical literature for purposes of analyzing self-narratives and identity formation (Bielby and Kully 1988). However, few studies combine social psychological research on identity with fictionalized accounts of the aging immigrant experience. By examining the process of self-narrative construction, the novel, can be explored for insights into how individuals are compelled to assign meaning to their lives in old age.

### Theoretical Framework

A central argument of George Herbert Mead's (1932) symbolic interactionist perspective is that although the present implies a past and a future, individuals always experience the past and future through the present. The process by which life material is reviewed by the individual is interpreted within a (present) social context. Consequently, the meanings attached to events, and thus the significance of events, is subject to much variation, depending upon the circumstances of the present. While Mead recognizes the existence of unalterable historical facts, he argues that their subjective interpretation may vary, depending upon the existing present.

This essay explores the utility of Mead's conceptual framework to an analysis of Amy Tan's (1989) *The Joy Luck Club* in particular and novels in general. Mead (1932) describes a process whereby the present is used to reconstruct the past, as one through which individuals assign meaning to their lives. Personal continuity is maintained through an interaction of present events with selected meaningful past events.

I employ two dimensions of Mead's theory of the past as identified by Maines, Sugrue, and Katovich (1983). The first, the social structural past, is that which objectively influences the past and "thus structures and conditions the experiences found in the present" (Maines et al. 1983, p. 163). The second, the symbolically reconstructed past, is central to Mead's analysis of the past. This dimension clarifies the process by which individuals in the present selectively draw from past events so the present may be understood and the future anticipated.

### Textual Analysis

Amy Tan's novel, *The Joy Luck Club,* details the lives of four Chinese women immigrants in San Francisco. It chronicles their bewilderment at American culture and their struggles to instill in their daughters remnants of their Chinese heritage. The novel is presented as sixteen interlocking stories that form two generations of mothers and daughters. For purposes of illustration, I limit my analysis to a single character, Lindo Jong, mother of Waverly Jong. I examine her life by focusing upon two components of the social construction of self-narratives, i.e., the social structural past and the symbolically reconstructed past.

In the analysis presented below, I explore Lindo Jong's life for elements of discontinuity and analyze how she assigns meaning to these experiences. I examine several aspects of her self-narrative, including: 1) social origins; 2) personal tragedies and triumphs; 3) unfulfilled ideals or goals; and 4) unresolved conflict. While not inclusive of all sources of disruption in Lindo's life, they encompass both societal and individual level elements.

### The Social Structural Past

According to Maines et al. (1983), the social structural past establishes micro-level probabilities for experience in the present, which in turn affects perceptions about the past and expectations about the future. While influential, this past is not completely deterministic, but merely predisposing. Lindo Jong begins her narrative with this awareness as indicated by her vivid observations of the structural elements of her childhood. We see a childhood devoid of choices for women. Reflecting on her arranged marriage she notes, "But even if I had known I was getting such a bad husband, I had no choice, now or later. That was how backward families in the country were. We were always the last to give up stupid old-fashioned customs" (pp. 44–45).

After her family promises Lindo to the Huangs's son for marriage, she gives particular attention to family dynamics. ". . . my own family began treating me as if I belonged to somebody else. My mother would say to me when the rice bowl went up to my face too many times, 'Look how much Huang Taitai's daughter can eat'" (p. 45). Separated from her family at the age of twelve to live with the Huangs, Lindo begins a self-directed quest for her freedom. "It was really quite simple. I made the Huangs think it was their idea to get rid of me, that they would be the ones to say the marriage contract was not valid" (p. 59).

Lindo's observations illustrate that many familial elements of her social structural past resonate throughout her perceptions of two fundamental issues in her life, worth and autonomy. "And every few years . . . I buy another bracelet. I know what I'm worth" (p. 63). "I remember the day when I finally knew a genuine thought and could follow it where it went. That was the day I was a young girl with my face under a red marriage scarf. I promised not to forget myself" (p. 63). Thus, her past was never fully resolved in the present, and as a result, the present was continuously resonating throughout the past, seeking resolution for the future.

### Symbolic Reconstruction of the Past

Making the most of one's opportunities was a recurring passion in Lindo Jong's life. Indeed, she was drawn to the belief in unrestricted upward mobility in the United States. "If you are born poor here, it's no lasting shame. You are first in line for a scholarship. In America, nobody says you have to keep the circumstances somebody else gives you" (p. 289). She is disappointed, however, to discover that the values associated with upward mobility in the United States undermine her Chinese identity. "It's hard to keep your Chinese face in America. At the beginning, before I even arrived, I had to hide my true self" (p. 294).

While she does not reject the American Dream, Lindo does adjust her conviction in what it represents, based upon her present situation. Indeed, Lindo attributes her struggles with her daughter to the opportunities and sacrifices demanded by American culture. The impetus of this shift is that as a parent, her mission appeared to be unsuccessful. "It is my fault she is this way. I wanted my children to have the best combination: American circumstances and Chinese character. How could I know these two things do not mix?" (p. 289).

Through Lindo's relationship with her daughter, we are able to uncover discontinuities that hasten Lindo's reassessment of American culture. She comments:

> I taught her how American circumstances work. She learned these things, but I couldn't teach her about Chinese character. No, this kind of thinking didn't stick to her. She was too busy chewing gum, blowing bubbles . . . Only that kind of thinking stuck.
>
> (pp. 289–90)

Clearly, Lindo sought from her daughter commitment to family, characteristic of Chinese culture, while simultaneously she encouraged Waverly to take advantage of America's opportunities for upward mobility. Due to family circumstances, in interacting with the demands of American culture, Lindo was unable to achieve an easy integration of the two. "So now I think, What did I lose? What did I get back in return? I will ask my daughter what she thinks" (p. 305).

Continuities are dependent upon tacit agreement with one's social interactants (Gergen and Gergen 1983). Situational meanings must be negotiated and accepted by significant others. Moreover, significant others must willingly participate in the social interaction; if withdrawn, there is nothing to negotiate. Lindo's realization that her daughter did not share her desire for Chinese character led Lindo to retreat into her Chinese beliefs:

> I wanted you to have the best circumstances, the best character. I didn't want you to regret anything. And that's why I named you Waverly. It was the name of the street we lived on. And I wanted you to think, this is where I belong. But I also knew if I named you after this street, soon you would grow up, leave this place, and take a piece of me with you.
>
> (p. 302)

Here, we clearly see the symbolic reconstruction of the past. Lindo does not go as far as to deny past faith in America, but she does announce and accept a shift in her belief in what she can accomplish as a parent based upon her present relationship with her daughter. Once discontinuity emerged, Lindo's quest for solutions came to rest on the ideology of her past—Chinese culture and beliefs. According to Mead (1932), when experience yields perceptible discontinuity in the chain of events, the past must be reinterpreted considering the present, so that progress to the present can be understood and intention for the future discerned.

### Discussion

I have sought evidence for the sociological processes underlying the social construction of identity among aging immigrants, with particular attention to its manifestation in fictional accounts of individual lives. My primary interest in employing Mead's theory of symbolic interaction is to extend social scientific thinking about narrative accounts (i.e., the effect of the present on the remembered past) to literature on aging and the immigrant experience. I explored the utility of two dimensions of Mead's theory through the fictionalized life narrative of Lindo Jong. By comparing her public behavior with her private thoughts, I have uncovered evidence in support of Mead's social structural past and the symbolically reconstructed past.

The theory of symbolic interaction illustrates how identity is socially negotiated and how identity extends to encompass events from the past. Since behavior in our culture is expected to be consistent across time, as well as purposive, we seek explanations of past behavior that in some cases involve reconstruction, and sometimes reinterpretation of the past (Bielby and Kully 1988). The more public our identity, the more consistency is expected from individuals we interact with, and in response, the more continuity we seek. Even individuals leading ordinary lives have audiences to whom they are accountable, even if it is only one's daughter. Whatever the size or importance of one's audience, the self-narrative still has to be negotiated. The challenge to social scientists is uncovering the event being reconstructed and the occasion that precipitated the renegotiation of the past (Bielby and Kully 1988).

Mead's theory also clarifies the origin and purpose of meaning to an individual's life account. All self-narratives, and especially protagonists in novels, seek links across previous events to establish continuity in lines of conduct. Meaning lies between what actually happened in the past and what continuity the author is compelled to assert, given that it is the protagonist's "present" that needs explanation (Bielby and Kully 1988). For example, Lindo's perception of her relative success as a parent required that she publicly portray faith in the American Dream, even when it was not so obvious to herself.

Mead provides an insightful explanation of the process whereby the present brings reinterpretation of the past, but under what conditions does this happen? Mead (1932) suggests that a break in continuity in the succession of events to the present precipitates reinterpretation or reconstruction of the past. Without novelty itself, continuity could not be discernable, particularly in establishing one's identity (Bielby and Kully 1988). Lindo's narrative portrays this juxtaposition. On several occasions, she realized that her expectations were going unfulfilled: her faith in America, her relationship with her daughter. "I think about our two faces. I think about my intentions. Which one is American? Which one is Chinese? Which one is better? If you show one, you must always sacrifice the other" (p. 304). In each situation, we see an emerging awareness, often in the form of dissatisfaction, with the trajectory of her life. The break in continuity brought with it the realization that the events she had experienced were not progressively moving her toward the goal to which she aspired.

Self-narratives that reconstruct the past in light of the present require acquiescence among interactants for them to be successful. Self-narratives are public accounts of identity, and their construction requires social negotiation. If interactants are unwilling participants, as is true of unresolved conflict where interactants are at an impasse, then one's identity is not accepted as established across time, at least with that individual. That is, in an ongoing relationship, significant others must agree to one's interpretation (Bielby and Kully 1988).

## Conclusion

Mead (1932) offers a sophisticated elaboration of a process in which identity is achieved through use of the past in the present. Through my application of his theory, using Lindo Jong as a case study, I find limitations in its use that center around the social construction of self-narrative, notably of the aging immigrant experience. I offer the following suggestions to address these limitations.

First, there is need for systematic examination of the kinds of events around which the process of modification of the past occurs and an investigation as to whether there are distinct patterns for immigrants. I suggest that one should be able to observe integration and reinterpretation through scrutiny of the same life event reflected upon by the same individual at different times. I believe a comparative approach across personal documents will help account for intrapersonal distinctiveness. Second, there is need for systematic examination of how the process of integrating the past with the present varies depending upon the culture from which the individual has emigrated. While I believe that one ought to be able to observe degrees of candor over time regarding a specific event, interpretations also may vary as a function of culture.

Analyses such as the one presented here have implications for Mead's theory of symbolic interaction. While my analysis of Amy Tan's novel produces constructive results, I recognize the limitations of its use when evaluated against positivist concerns regarding evidence. In conclusion, however, by recognizing how meaning is achieved in self-narratives, I have begun a systematic search for the sociological processes underlying the construction of self-narratives of the aging immigrant experience.

*References*

Bielby, Denise D., & Kully, Hannah S. (1988). *Social Construction of the Past: Autobiography and the Theory of G. H. Mead.* Paper presented at the Annual Meetings of the Gerontological Society of America, San Francisco, California.

Combe, Kirk, & Schmader, Kenneth. (1996). Shakespeare Teaching Geriatrics: Case Studies in Aged Heterogeneity. *Journal of Aging and Identity* 1, 99–116.

Deats, Sara Munson. (1996). The Problem of Aging in *King Lear* and *The Tempest*. *Journal of Aging and Identity* 1, 87–98.

Fitzgerald, Charlotte D. (1992). Exploring Race in the Classroom: Guidelines for Selecting the 'Right' Novel. *Teaching Sociology* 20, 244–247.

Gergen, Kenneth J., & Gergen, Mary. (1983). Narratives of the Self. In T. Sarbin & K. Scheibe (Eds.), *Studies in Social Identity* (pp. 254–389). New York: Praeger.

Hegtvedt, Karen A. (1991). Teaching Sociology of Literature through Literature. *Teaching Sociology* 19, 1–12.

Hendershott, Anne, & Wright, Sheila. (1993). Bringing the Sociology Perspective into the Interdisciplinary Classroom Through Literature. *Teaching Sociology* 21, 325–331.

Holstein, Martha. (1994). Taking Next Steps: Gerontological Education, Research, and the Literary Imagination. *The Gerontologist* 34, 822–827.

Maines, David R., Sugrue, Noreen, & Katovich, Michael. (1983). The Sociological Import of G. H. Mead's Theory of the Past. *American Sociological Review* 48, 161–173.

Mead, George Herbert. (1932). *The Philosophy of the Present.* Chicago: Open Court Publishing Company.

Sullivan, Teresa A. (1982). Introductory Sociology Through Literature. *Teaching Sociology* 10, 109–116.

Tan, Amy. (1989). *The Joy Luck Club.* New York: Ivy Books.

## David Leiwei Li (essay date 1998)

SOURCE: "Genes, Generation, and Geospiritual (Be)longings," in *Imagining the Nation: Asian American Literature and Cultural Consent*, Stanford University Press, 1998, pp. 111–17.

[*In the following essay, Li discusses the emphasis in Tan's works, including* The Joy Luck Club, *on female familial relationships.*]

*Tripmaster Monkey* and *Jasmine*'s narrative claiming of America is almost entirely overshadowed by the meteoric success of Amy Tan's ***Joy Luck Club*** (1989).[1] A book about mother-daughter relationships and cultural displacement and recuperation, ***The Joy Luck Club*** harks back to the familial rifts and reconciliations of *The Woman Warrior* and departs from Kingston and Mukherjee's preoccupation with Asian American integration. If her fellow writers choose to substantiate the individual in terms of the national, situating their protagonists in the reimagined community of the United States, Tan manages to limit the trials and tribulations of her characters to the genealogical family, apparently independent from the larger society.

The focus on the filiality of the "club" rather than the consent of the "country" is an amazing act of narrative "privatization." In identifying family breakdown as the source of all forms of social disarray, and family unity as the floating signifier "for all manner of social ties," ***The Joy Luck Club***'s treatment of female familial experiences exemplifies Tan's active participation in the dominant privatization of social problems (Stacey 1994: 67, 54). Once the biological family is privatized as the essential unit of social coherence and the exclusive locus of her narrative, Tan also finds a common affective denominator that can effectively appeal to her targeted audience of white female "baby boomers," who may not otherwise identify with her Asian characters (Somogyi and Stanton 1991: 29). Although the privileging of the family serves to appropriate both the dominant neoconservative discourse and the white reading community, Amy Tan will have to address the questions that the specific ethnic content of her book raises: whether the Asian values of her book are exemplary of American values, and whether her Asian American families are a metaphor for the national community at large. In approaching these issues of cultural intelligibility and membership, ***The Joy Luck Club*** both implicitly engages Kingston and Mukherjee's nationalist claiming of America and anticipates Frank Chin and David Mura's diasporic revision in "Whither Asia."

### I

The structure of ***The Joy Luck Club*** reflects Amy Tan's conceptions of the family. The novel's sixteen chapters of first-person female narrative are divided into four sections with four stories each. Except for the first and last stories, in which Jing-mei Woo substitutes her own voice for her mother Suyuan Woo's, the American daughters' stories are neatly sandwiched by the autobiographical tales of the novel's Chinese mothers. This maternal enclosure of the daughters' stories is strengthened with local framing by a vignette at the beginning of each section. There, in a quasi-language of myth and fable, the mothers would impart their life lessons to the daughters, whose American ears, for the moment, seem deaf to Chinese accents. At a practical level, the symmetry of Tan's narrative scheme seems intended to fit a cluster of short stories into the novel form, but it also serves thematically to anchor the foundational categories of Tan's family. If its diachronic "mother-daughter plot" echoes *The Woman Warrior* and invokes the feminist fictional alternative to Freud's Oedipal "family romance" (Hirsch 1989), ***The Joy Luck Club***'s woman-centered family trope is also juxtaposed with the synchronic movements of the East and the West, China to America and vice versa. Gender, generation, and geography are thus interwoven and transcoded to exemplify Amy Tan's ideation of an Asian American family amid the familial relations of ethnicity and nation at large.

The novel's opening vignette, "Feathers from a Thousand *Li* Away" illustrates Tan's method. Elaborating on a classic Chinese idiom, which literally translates, "Sending a goose feather from a thousand *li* [about 0.5 km] afar, the gift is light while the affection is heavy," Tan writes:

> The woman and the swan sailed across an ocean many thousands of *li* wide, stretching their necks toward America. On her journey she cooed to the swan: "In America I will have a daughter just like me. But over there nobody will say her worth is measured by the loudness of her husband's belch. Over there nobody will look down on her, because I will make her speak only perfect American English. And over there she will always be too full to swallow any sorrow. . . . Now the woman was old. And she had a daughter who grew up speaking only English and swallowing more Coca-Cola than Sorrow. For a long time now the woman wanted to give her daughter the single swan feather and tell her, "This feather may look worthless, but it comes from afar and carries with it all my good intentions." And she waited, year after year, for the day she could tell her daughter this in perfect American English.
>
> (Tan 1989: 17)[2]

The vignette is both deeply moving and troubling. Tan speaks effectively of the pain of familial incomprehension, the loss of the "mother-tongue," and the unarticulated desire for generational understanding. But the geocultural gap between China and America creates such a division of social spaces that it immediately revives the figment of orientalist imagination with an apparent Chinese authenticity. In an extraordinary demonstration of Tan's artistic ingenuity, the mother in the vignette concocts a "familiar" saying about the worth of a Chinese woman that is found nowhere in Chinese idiom.[3] China, the readers are led to believe, is replete with male chauvinist pigs whose pot bellies rest on their wives' empty stomachs, while in bountiful America those who speak English are automatically well fed and respected. The invention of the authentic-seeming idiom not only effortlessly implies that the Chinese culture has consecrated its sexism in language, it has also erased, through the Coca-Cola and Sorrow contrast, gender inequality from the civilized liberties of America. It is small wonder that the barbarous and backward East should stretch its neck toward the progressive and blissful West.

Helena Michie has concisely argued that "dominant metaphors of feminist critiques of society are familial in origin; the word 'patriarchy' itself . . . locates power in literal and metaphorical fatherhood and defines the family as the scene, if not the source, of women's oppression. . . . The struggle of *many* sisters with a *single* father. . . . disrupt[s] the Oedipal triangle . . . by the introduction of politics and community as they enter onto the familial stage embodied severally as 'sisters'" (1991: 58). Although Michie's analysis suffers from a universal conception of both patriarchy and its feminist alternative, it is precisely to this conception that *The Joy Luck Club* appeals. The narrative's explicit attempt at mother-daughter communication is an implicit attempt to enter the community of white women readers. To this end, the gallery of Asian and Asian American women in the novel must provide points of identification for white female generational anxieties, while the group of Asian and Asian American male characters must function as textual "pawns," not only "for bringing up the conflicts between the mothers and daughters," as Tan puts it, but to so particularize patriarchy as well (Somogyi and Stanton 1991: 29).[4]

Since the majority of the men in the novel are Chinese and its baby-boomer audience is largely white, the racial and geocultural specificity of Amy Tan's gender references are unambiguous. As the oppressor of women, the Asian male begins to epitomize the Eastern origin of patriarchy, which is of course genetically transmittable only to Asian American men. The move has both racialized gender oppression to read exclusively Asian and deflected attention from the practice of domestic sexism. It significantly downplays the important contribution of Asian American feminism, which recognizes the dominant cultural differentiation of Asian American gender roles within the racial hierarchies of the United States (E. Kim 1990: 68–75). What appears to be a frontal assault on the patriarchal system finds a figurehead father either in the remote Orient or the distant ethnic ghetto, leaving the white American patriarch unscratched and unscathed.

Tan's racialization of Asian sexism helps figuratively invoke white women's experience with patriarchy but ultimately precludes any geopolitical solution to it. Likewise, the novel's characterization of Asian American mother-daughter experience helps foster affective bonds among women of different backgrounds while deferring the question of transracial female solidarity. This effect is achieved through a double maneuver. As is evident in the novel's structural arrangement of mother-daughter conflict as a China-America split, generational difference is diagnosed first and foremost as a geocultural chasm. But just as sexism is biologized, both generation gap and geocultural fissure can be miraculously synchronized with genes. The novel masterfully executes this maneuver by elaborating the maternal fables of oriental wisdom and oriental suffering in the vignettes and extending these generational lessons into the main chapters.

Rose Hsu Jordan's doomed marriage, for example, is traced not just to her neglect of her brother but also to the fate and failure of her grandmother's widowhood and concubinage (130, 215). "Even though I taught my daughter the opposite," An-mei Hsu reflects, "still she came out the same way! All of us [mothers and daughters] are like stairs, one step after another, going up and down, but all going the same way" (215). Similarly, daughter Lena St. Clair's marital woes are attributed to her mother Ying-Ying's abuse in her first marriage and the loss of her tiger spirit in the second. Until Ying-Ying recovers her "fierceness," Lena will "ha[ve] no *chi*," the spirit to stand on her own. "I will gather together my past . . . and hold [my] pain . . . to penetrate my daughter's tough skin and cut her tiger spirit loose," Ying-Ying decides; "I will win and give her my spirit, because this is the way a mother loves her daughter" (165, 252). As Lena becomes the beneficiary of Ying-Ying's spirit, daughter Waverly Jong absorbed her mother Lindo's "invisible strength" but rejected "[her] Chinese ways" when she started school (89, 253). It was in the mirror of a beauty parlor, right before Waverly's second marriage, that mother and daughter chanced to "look at each other," both awed by the moment of mutual recognition. "These two faces," Lindo Jong concludes, "[are] so much the same! The same happiness, the same sadness, the same good fortune, the same faults" (256).

Using the mixed language of blood and kinship, superstition and tradition, these chapters attractively express the pedagogical authority of the mother and transform the daughterly articulation of maternal silence into a powerful maternal determination of daughterly identity (Hirsch 1989: 15–16).[5] But strikingly, the maternal lessons are all derived from a pre-immigration and pre-American era. As faithful daughters of China, the mothers may mature and age in America, but their minds and memories are forever mummified in their ancestral land. Unlike *The Woman Warrior*, which engages in an uneasy negotiation between a mother and daughter who share a U.S. history, *The Joy Luck Club* is the narrative of a one-way passage of irrefutable generational destiny. It is predictable that the artificial conflict between generations will find its natural resolution in the genetic fusion of geocultural gaps and historical discrepancies.

In the final chapter, Amy Tan indeed reverses the novel's opening image of the swan stretching its neck toward America by sending Jing-mei, its narrator, back to China. Although the body of *The Joy Luck Club* repeatedly emphasizes Jing-mei's ignorance about her mother's past, an entirely different scenario unfolds some two hundred pages later. The repressed maternal murmur surfaces to reclaim Jing-mei's body and soul: "The minute our train leaves the

Hong Kong border and enters Shenzhen, China, I feel different. I can feel the skin on my forehead tingling, my blood rushing through a new course, my bones aching with a familiar old pain. . . . I am becoming Chinese" (267). What might be her mother's longing for her birthplace is now Jing-mei's natural emotional inheritance, and where this psychological transfer occurs is also of great importance. Jing-mei's becoming Chinese happens within minutes of departing Hong Kong for mainland China. Faithful to the geopolitical borders of the sovereign and colonial China, and more so to the conceptual and symbolic boundaries of East and West, Tan does not consider the then British colony of Hong Kong to be the true China. The miracle island of capitalistic and technological savvy is a principally Western conservatory of Chinese impurity, while the People's Republic is the real good earth of ancient tradition and magical wisdom. It is in the authentic China that Jing-mei is finally home: "'Some day you will see,' said my mother. 'It [Chinese-ness] is in your blood, waiting to be let go.' And when she said this, I saw myself transforming like a werewolf, a mutant tag of DNA suddenly triggered, replicating itself insidiously into a *syndrome*, a cluster of telltale Chinese behaviors" (267).

By the time Jing-mei reaches Shanghai and embraces her newfound half-sisters, her mother's prophecy has come true. "And now I also see what part of me is Chinese," she enthuses, sounding like her mother (267). And later, "It is my family. It is in our blood. After all these years, it can finally be let go" (288). As the Polaroid picture of the three sisters develops, as their image sharpens and deepens, Jing-mei sums up the feeling for all: "Although we don't speak, I know we all see it. Together we look like our mother. Her same eyes, her same mouth, open in surprise to see, at last, her long-cherished wish" (288). With identical visage, identical feelings, and identical attachment to the land of origin, the mother-daughter discord eventually evaporates without a trace of historical justification. China is not only the origin of Suyuan's immigration; it is also, by Amy Tan's reckoning, both the genetic locus of Jing-mei's affective ease and the narrative climax of her symbolic repatriation. The return of the Asian American native to her Asian geopolitical origin is complete.[6]

This chromosomal cohesion of generations, though hinting at the repression of ethnicity, naturalizes both the voluntary removal of Asian Americans from the United States and the essential purity of its European American construction. The genetic integration of the mother and daughter promulgates the filiality of the family and the descent base of the nation, leaving troubling implications for both feminist and multiculturalist reconstructions. Since a plot based on genes is a plot of irreversible lineage, the native-born Asian American women cannot but inherit the inclinations of their immigrant progenitors. Since a plot based on genes is also about ancestral origin, it demands a geocultural allegiance unaffected by personal experience, political history, or place of residence. And since Asian American women are differentiated by both their genetic heritage and their geocultural immutability, the struggle of many sisters against a single father on the familial stage, to echo Michie, is not viable, as the Asian American place in the family of U.S. women itself becomes questionable. Although Asian American women exemplify the kind of mother-daughter tension all women share, Tan appears to say, they actually prefer a separate womanhood. The kind of Asian-American-turned-obedient-Asian-female subjectivity in the course of ***The Joy Luck Club*** thus proves felicitous in dissolving the contradiction between the universal and the particular. A transracial American gender solidarity is finally accomplished upon the withdrawal of Asian American women and their displacement onto an Other nation.

Such voluntary national leave-taking is, not paradoxically, Amy Tan's simultaneous partaking of historical Anglo-American nationalism and orientalism wherein the legitimacy of Asian American membership is always suspect. Her genealogical construction of kinship is also attuned to the 1980s discourse of family values, a neoconservative legacy that the center too has come to embrace (Stacey 1994: 55). In her reading of Eric Hobsbawm, Angelika Bammer has tried to convince us that in the era of the "'post' . . . , the nation . . . is no longer the guarantor of social coherence or cultural authority, [as] ethnicity steps into the breach to provide a new identificatory locus." The "family, in the more literal (domestic) or community/clan sense," should, in her view, become the nation's alternative (94). Amy Tan's affirmation of the private nature of Asian Americans as both filial and parochial is synchronous with this premature definition of a nation's obsolescence. By accentuating the natural and perpetual forms of allegiance and feelings of affinity, ***The Joy Luck Club*** miraculously merges the neoconservative rhetoric of "tribalism" (M. Baker 1981) with poststructural and multicultural celebrations of diasporic subjectivity that overlook the interconnection of race and nation. Moreover, it has revived the Asian American literary desire to return to Asia.

*Notes*

1. The book's commercial and critical success—275,000 hardcover copies sold, $1.2 million paid for paperback rights, and finalist for both the National Book Award and the National Book Critics Circle award (Holt 1989:2; Simpson 1991:66)—was unprecedented for a first-time author. The book is reported to have sold 4.5 million copies by 1996 (Nguyen 1997: 49).

2. This and all further quotations from *The Joy Luck Club* are taken from the edition listed in the bibliography.

3. Cultural invention or misrepresentation that passes for truth is central to Tan's narrative deployment (Sau-ling Wong 1995).

Since much of *The Joy Luck Club*'s aesthetic appeal lies in "the legendary quality" of "the stories from China" (Seaman 1990: 256), the "*recherches* to old

China" that sweep the audience off its feet to be "borne along as if in a dream" (Schell 1989: 28), the relation between its representational mode and its intended audience must be duly noted. Tan's style of narration is akin to the whole genre of explorer accounts whose main motif, according to Marcus and Fischer, is "the romantic discovery by the writer of people and places unknown to the reader" (1986: 129). The concoction of the Chinese idiomatic milieu, the conflation of Chinese festivals, and the calculated use of a vacation topography roughly based on the "scenic wonders of China" all seem to satisfy the voyeuristic inclinations of the armchair reader/traveler. This becomes Tan's trademark, as her later books demonstrate.

4. When the question of her relation to the Asian American community comes up, Tan repeatedly disavows any deliberate connection and emphasizes either the haphazard nature of her character choice ("happening to be Chinese") or their universal significance ("human nature") (see Morris 1994: 219). This universalizing impulse must be appreciated with two facts in mind, however. First, as a former business writer for AT&T, IBM, and other Fortune 500 companies, Tan prides herself on "a real strong batting average on proposals . . . geared to . . . CEOs of major corporations" (Somogyi and Stanton 1991: 27). Second, as Zill and Winglee point out, today's consumers of literature are overwhelmingly white and female.

5. The mother-daughter plot as a model of feminist bonding tends to ignore lesbian desire and identification and accept heterosexual forms of family as the norm. See Eve Sedgwick's call for "disarticulating . . . the bonds of blood, of law, of habitation, of privacy, of companionship and succor—from the lockstep of their unanimity in the system called 'family'" (1993: 6).

6. The remarks of Tan's characters may reveal the relationship between the author's choice of geography and the configuration of her audience. As Lindo Jong comments in *The Joy Luck Club*, "But now she [Waverly] wants to be Chinese, it is so fashionable" (253), Helen of *The Kitchen God's Wife*, Tan's second novel, will point out, "Hard life in China, that's very popular now" (Tan 1991: 80). Given these self-referential statements, it is not difficult to see Tan's dual accommodation of orientalism, first in her affirmation of China as the natural homeland of Chinese Americans, and second in her inflation of the China stock on the orientalist marketplace.

**Patricia L. Hamilton (essay date Summer 1999)**

SOURCE: "Feng Shui, Astrology, and the Five Elements: Traditional Chinese Belief in Amy Tan's *The Joy Luck Club*," in *MELUS*, Summer, 1999, pp. 125–45.

[*In the following essay, Hamilton demonstrates how Tan uses the concepts of feng shui, astrology, and the Five Elements to enhance the characters in* The Joy Luck Club.]

A persistent thematic concern in Amy Tan's *The Joy Luck Club* is the quest for identity. Tan represents the discovery process as arduous and fraught with peril. Each of the eight main characters faces the task of defining herself in the midst of great personal loss or interpersonal conflict. Lindo Jong recalls in "The Red Candle" that her early marriage into a family that did not want her shaped her character and caused her to vow never to forget who she was. Ying-ying St. Clair's story "Waiting between the Trees" chronicles how betrayal, loss, and displacement caused her to become a "ghost." Rose Hsu Jordan recounts her effort to regain a sense of self and assert it against her philandering husband in "Without Wood." Framing all the other stories are a pair of linked narratives by Jing-mei Woo that describe her trip to China at the behest of her Joy Luck Club "aunties." The journey encompasses Jing-mei's attempts not only to understand her mother's tragic personal history but also to come to terms with her own familial and ethnic identity. In all the stories, whether narrated by the Chinese-born mothers or their American-born daughters, assertions of self are shaped by the cultural context surrounding them. However, there is a fundamental asymmetry in the mothers' and daughters' understanding of each other's native cultures. The mothers draw on a broad experiential base for their knowledge of American patterns of thought and behavior, but the daughters have only fragmentary, second-hand knowledge of China derived from their mothers' oral histories and from proverbs, traditions, and folktales.[1] Incomplete cultural knowledge impedes understanding on both sides, but it particularly inhibits the daughters from appreciating the delicate negotiations their mothers have performed to sustain their identities across two cultures.

Language takes on a metonymic relation to culture in Tan's portrayal of the gap between the mothers and daughters in *The Joy Luck Club*. Jing-mei, recalling that she talked to her mother Suyuan in English and that her mother answered back in Chinese, concludes that they "never really understood one another": "We translated each other's meanings and I seemed to hear less than what was said, while my mother heard more" (37). What is needed for any accurate translation of meanings is not only receptiveness and language proficiency but also the ability to supply implied or missing context. The daughters' inability to understand the cultural referents behind their mothers' words is nowhere more apparent than when the mothers are trying to inculcate traditional Chinese values and beliefs in their children. The mothers inherited from their families a centuries-old spiritual framework, which, combined with rigid social constraints regarding class and gender, made the world into an ordered place for them. Personal misfortune and the effects of war have tested the women's allegiance to traditional ideas, at times challenging them to violate convention in order to survive. But the very fact of their survival is in large measure attributable to their belief that people can affect their own destinies. In the face of crisis the mothers adhere to ancient Chinese practices by which they try to manipulate fate to their advantage. Their beliefs and values are unexpectedly reinforced by the democratic social fabric and capitalist economy they encounter in their adopted country. Having immigrated from a land where women were allowed almost no personal freedom, all the Joy Luck mothers share the belief along with Suyuan Woo that "you could be anything you wanted to be in America" (132).

Ironically, the same spirit of individualism that seems so liberating to the older women makes their daughters resistant to maternal advice and criticism. Born into a culture in which a multiplicity of religious beliefs flourishes and the individual is permitted, even encouraged, to challenge tradition and authority, the younger women are reluctant to accept their mothers' values without question. Jing-mei confesses that she used to dismiss her mother's criticisms as "just more of her Chinese superstitions, beliefs that conveniently fit the circumstances" (31). Furthermore, the daughters experience themselves socially as a recognizable ethnic minority and want to eradicate the sense of "difference" they feel among their peers. They endeavor to dissociate themselves from their mothers' broken English and Chinese mannerisms[2] and they reject as nonsense the fragments of traditional lore their mothers try to pass along to them. However, cut adrift from any spiritual moorings, the younger women are overwhelmed by the number of choices that their materialistic culture offers and are insecure about their ability to perform satisfactorily in multiple roles ranging from dutiful Chinese daughter to successful American career woman. When it dawns on Jing-mei that the aunties see that "joy and luck do not mean the same to their daughters, that to these closed American-born minds 'joy luck' is not a word, it does not exist," she realizes that there is a profound difference in how the two generations understand fate, hope, and personal responsibility. Devoid of a worldview that endows reality with unified meaning, the daughters "will bear grandchildren born without any connecting hope passed from generation to generation" (41).

Tan uses the contrast between the mothers' and daughters' beliefs and values to show the difficulties first-generation immigrants face in transmitting their native culture to their offspring. Ultimately, Tan endorses the mothers' traditional Chinese worldview because it offers the possibility of choice and action in a world where paralysis is frequently a threat. However, readers who are not specialists in Chinese cosmology share the same problematic relation to the text as the daughters do to their mothers' native culture: they cannot always accurately translate meanings where the context is implied but not stated. Bits of traditional lore crop up in nearly every story, but divorced from a broader cultural context, they are likely to be seen as mere brushstrokes of local color or authentic detail. Readers may be tempted to accept at face value the daughters' pronouncements that their mothers' beliefs are no more than superstitious nonsense. To ensure that readers do not hear less than what Tan is actually saying about the mothers' belief systems and their identities, references to Chinese cosmology in the text require explication and elaboration.

Astrology is probably the element of traditional Chinese belief that is most familiar to Westerners. According to the Chinese astrological system, a person's character is determined by the year of his or her birth. Personality traits are categorized according to a twelve-year calendrical cycle based on the Chinese zodiac. Each year of the cycle is associated with a different animal, as in "the year of the dog." According to one legend, in the sixth century B.C. Buddha invited all the animals in creation to come to him, but only twelve showed up: the Rat, Ox, Tiger, Rabbit, Dragon, Snake, Horse, Ram, Monkey, Cock, Dog, and Pig. Buddha rewarded each animal with a year bearing its personality traits (Scott). In addition to animals, years are associated with one of the Five Elements: Wood, Fire, Earth, Metal, and Water. Metal years end in zero or one on the lunar calendar; Water years end in two or three; Wood years end in four or five; Fire years end in six or seven; and Earth years end in eight or nine. Thus, depending on the year in which one is born, one might be a Fire Dragon, a Water Dragon, and so on. The entire animal-and-element cycle takes sixty years to complete.

Tan draws on astrology in *The Joy Luck Club* in order to shape character and conflict. Lindo Jong, born in 1918, is a Horse, "destined to be obstinate and frank to the point of tactlessness," according to her daughter Waverly (167). Other adjectives that describe the Horse include diligent, poised, quick, eloquent, ambitious, powerful, and ruthless (Rossbach 168). At one point or another in the four Jong narratives, Lindo manifests all of these qualities, confirming her identity as a Horse. In accordance with tradition, Lindo's first husband is selected by his birth year as being a compatible partner for her. The matchmaker in "The Red Candle" tells Lindo's mother and mother-in-law: "An earth horse for an earth sheep. This is the best marriage combination" (50). At Lindo's wedding ceremony the matchmaker reinforces her point by speaking about "birthdates and harmony and fertility" (59). In addition to determining compatibility, birth years can be used to predict personality clashes. Waverly notes of her mother Lindo, "She and I make a bad combination, because I'm a Rabbit, born in 1951, supposedly sensitive, with tendencies toward being thin-skinned and skittery at the first sign of criticism" (167). Lindo's friend Suyuan Woo, born in 1915, is also a Rabbit. No doubt the Joy Luck aunties have this in mind when they note that Suyuan "died just like a rabbit: quickly and with unfinished business left behind" (19). The friction between Horse and Rabbit mentioned by Waverly suggests why Lindo and Suyuan were not only best friends but also "arch enemies who spent a lifetime comparing their children" (37)[3]

Adherents of Chinese astrology contend that auspicious dates for important events can be calculated according to predictable fluctuations of *ch'i*, the positive life force, which is believed to vary according to the time of day, the season, and the lunar calendar. Thus, the matchmaker chooses "a lucky day, the fifteenth day of the eighth moon," for Lindo's wedding (57). Later, Lindo picks "an auspicious day, the third day of the third month," to stage her scheme to free herself from her marriage. Unlucky dates can be calculated as well. Rose Hsu Jordan recalls that her mother An-mei had a "superstition" that "children were predisposed to certain dangers on certain days, all depending on their Chinese birthdate. It was explained in a little Chinese book called *The Twenty-Six Malignant Gates*" (124). The problem for An-mei is how to translate the Chinese dates into American ones. Since the lunar calendar traditionally used in China is based on moon cycles, the number of days in a year varies. Lindo similarly faces the problem of translating dates when she wants to immigrate to San Francisco, but her Peking friend assures her that May 11, 1918 is the equivalent of her birthdate, "three months after the Chinese lunar new year" (258). Accuracy on this point would allow Lindo to calculate auspicious dates according to the Gregorian calendar used in the West. In a broader sense, Lindo's desire for exactness is a strategy for preserving her identity in a new culture.

Tan uses astrology to greatest effect in the life history of Ying-ying St. Clair, who does not fare at all well in the matter of translated dates or preserved identity. Ying-ying is a Tiger, born in 1914, "a very bad year to be born, a very good year to be a Tiger" (248). Tigers are typically passionate, courageous, charismatic, independent, and active, but they can also be undisciplined, vain, rash, and disrespectful (Jackson; Rossbach 167). Tiger traits are central to Ying-ying's character. As a teenager she is wild, stubborn, and vain. As a four-year-old in "The Moon Lady," she loves to run and shout, and she possesses a "restless nature" (72). According to Ruth Youngblood, "As youngsters [Tigers] are difficult to control, and if unchecked, can dominate their parents completely." Ying-ying's Amah tries to tame her into conformity to traditional Chinese gender roles: "Haven't I taught you—that it is wrong to think of your own needs? A girl can never ask, only listen" (70). Ying-ying's mother, too, admonishes her to curb her natural tendencies: "A boy can run and chase dragonflies, because that is his nature. But a girl should stand still" (72). By yielding to the social constraints placed on her gender and "standing perfectly still," Ying-ying discovers her shadow, the dark side of her nature that she learns to wield after her first husband leaves her.

Long before adulthood, however, Ying-ying experiences a trauma regarding her identity. Stripped of her bloodied Tiger outfit at the Moon Festival, she tumbles into Tai Lake and is separated from her family for several hours. Ying-ying's physical experience of being lost parallels her family's suppression of her active nature and curtailment of her freedom. Whenever she wears her hair loose, for example, her mother warns her that she will become like "the lady ghosts at the bottom of the lake" whose undone hair shows "their everlasting despair" (243). After Ying-ying falls into the lake, her braid becomes "unfurled," and as she drifts along in the fishing boat that picks her up, she fears that she is "lost forever" (79). When one of the fishermen surmises that she is a beggar girl, she thinks: "Maybe this was true. I had turned into a beggar girl, lost without my family" (80). Later she watches the Moon Lady telling her tragic story in a shadow play staged for the festival: "I understood her grief. In one small moment, we had both lost the world, and there was no way to get it back" (81). Even though Ying-ying is eventually rescued, she is afraid that her being found by her family is an illusion, "a wish granted that could not be trusted" (82). The temporary loss of her sense of security and belonging is so disturbing that her perception of her identity is forever altered. She is never able to believe her family has found "the same girl" (82).

Ying-ying's traumatic childhood experience prefigures the profound emotional loss and identity confusion she experiences as an adult. Looking back on her experience at the Moon Festival, she reflects that "it has happened many times in my life. The same innocence, trust, and restlessness, the wonder, fear, and loneliness. How I lost myself" (83). As an adult she is stripped of her Tiger nature once again when she immigrates to America. Since there is no immigration category for "the Chinese wife of a Caucasian citizen," Ying-ying is declared a "Displaced Person" (104). Then her husband proudly renames her "Betty St. Clair" without seeming to realize he is effacing her Chinese identity in doing so. The final stroke is his mistakenly writing the wrong year of birth on her immigration papers. As Ying-ying's daughter Lena puts it, "With the sweep of a pen, my mother lost her name and became a Dragon instead of a Tiger" (104). Unwittingly, Clifford St. Clair erases all signs of Ying-ying's former identity and, more importantly, symbolically denies her Tiger nature.

The belief that personality and character are determined by zodiacal influences imposes predictable and regular patterns onto what might otherwise seem random and arbitrary, thereby minimizing uncertainty and anxiety. In this light, the anchor for identity that astrology offers Ying-ying is beneficial. Over the years she comes to understand what her mother once explained about her Tiger nature: "She told me why a tiger is gold and black. It has two ways. The gold side leaps with its fierce heart. The black side stands still with cunning, hiding its gold between trees, seeing and not being seen, waiting patiently for things to come" (248). The certainty that these qualities are her birthright eventually guides Ying-ying into renouncing her habitual passivity. The catalyst for this decision is her perception that her daughter Lena needs to have her own "tiger spirit" cut loose. She wants Lena to develop fierceness and cunning so that she will not become a "ghost" like her mother or remain trapped in a marriage to a selfish man who undermines her worth. Ying-ying expects resistance from Lena, but because of the strength of her belief system, she is confident about the outcome: "She will fight me, because this is the nature of two tigers. But I will win and give her my spirit, because this the way a mother loves her daughter" (252). Tan uses the Chinese zodiacal Tiger as a potent emblem of the way culturally determined beliefs and expectations shape personal identity.

Another element of Chinese cosmology that Tan employs in *The Joy Luck Club* is *wu-hsing*, or the Five Elements, mentioned above in conjunction with astrology.[4] The theory of the Five Elements was developed by Tsou Yen about 325 B.C. As Holmes Welch notes, Tsou Yen "believed that the physical processes of the universe were due to the interaction of the five elements of earth, wood, metal, fire, and water" (96). According to eminent French sinologist Henri Maspero, theories such as the Five Elements, the Three Powers, and *yin* and *yang* all sought to "explain how the world proceeded all by itself through the play of transcendental, impersonal forces alone, without any intervention by one or more conscious wills" (55). Derek Walters specifies how the Five Elements are considered to "stimulate and shape all natural and human activity":

> The Wood Element symbolizes all life, femininity, creativity, and organic material; Fire is the Element of energy and intelligence; Earth, the Element of stability, endurance and the earth itself; Metal, in addition to its material sense, also encompasses competitiveness, business acumen, and masculinity; while Water is the Element of all that flows—oil and alcohol as well as water itself, consequently also symbolizing transport and communication.
>
> (29)

The Elements correspond to certain organs of the body and physical ailments as well as to particular geometric shapes. An extended array of correspondences includes seasons, directions, numbers, colors, tastes, and smells (Lam 32). In the physical landscape the Elements can be placed in a productive order, in which each Element will generate and stimulate the one succeeding it, or a destructive order, in which Elements in close proximity are considered harmful. To avoid negative effects, a "controlling" Element can mediate between two elements positioned in their destructive order.

Suyuan Woo subscribes to a traditional application of the theory of the Five Elements in what Jing-mei calls her mother's "own version of organic chemistry" (31). As Ben Xu has observed, the Five Elements are "the mystical ingredients that determine every person's character flaw according to one's birth hour." *Wu-hsing* theory posits that "none of us has all the five character elements perfectly balanced, and therefore, every one of us is by nature flawed" (Xu 12). Accordingly; Suyuan believes that too much Fire causes a bad temper while too much Water makes someone flow in too many directions. Too little Wood results in one bending "too quickly to listen to other people's ideas, unable to stand on [one's] own" (31). Jing-mei, who does not understand how Suyuan's pronouncements tie to a larger belief system, associates her mother's theories with displeasure and criticism: "Something was always missing. Something always needed improving. Something was not in balance. This one or that had too much of one element, not enough of another."

According to *wu-hsing* theory, flaws can be amended and balance attained by symbolically adding the element a person lacks. Xu points out that "the 'rose' in Rose Hsu Jordan's name, for example, is supposed to add wood to her character" (12). Conversely, elements can be removed to create an imbalance. When Lindo Jong does not become pregnant in her first marriage, the matchmaker tells her mother-in-law: "A woman can have sons only if she is deficient in one of the elements. Your daughter-in-law was born with enough wood, fire, water, and earth, and she was deficient in metal, which was a good sign. But when she was married, you loaded her down with gold bracelets and decorations and now she has all the elements, including metal. She's too balanced to have babies" (63). Although Lindo knows that the direct cause of her failure to become pregnant is not her having too much metal but rather her husband's refusal to sleep with her, she accepts the matchmaker's reasoning about the Five Elements. Years later Lindo comments: "See the gold metal I can now wear. I gave birth to your brothers and then your father gave me these two bracelets. Then I had you [Waverly]" (66). The implication here is that the gender of Lindo's male children corresponds to her natural deficiency in Metal. Adding Metal back into her composition through the bracelets causes her next child to be female.

More significantly, Lindo, like Suyuan, believes that the Elements affect character traits: "After the gold was removed from my body, I felt lighter, more free. They say this is what happens if you lack metal. You begin to think as an independent person" (63). Tan suggests that Lindo's natural "imbalance" is key to her true identity, the self that she promises never to forget. As a girl she had determined to honor the marriage contract made by her parents, even if it meant sacrificing her sense of identity. But on her wedding day she wonders "why [her] destiny had been decided, why [she] should have an unhappy life so someone else could have a happy one" (58). Once Lindo's gold and jewelry are repossessed by her mother-in-law to help her become fertile, Lindo begins to plot her escape from the marriage. Her feeling lighter and more free without Metal corresponds to her assertion of her true identity. Destiny is not so narrowly determined that she cannot use her natural qualities as a Horse—quickness, eloquence, ruthlessness—to free herself from her false position in the marriage. Because Lindo has secretly blown out the matchmaker's red candle on her wedding night, she has in effect rewritten her fate without breaking her parents' promise. Rather than restricting her identity, her belief in astrology and *wu-hsing* gives her a secure base from which to express it.

As with astrology, Tan uses the theory of the Five Elements not only for characterization but also for the development of conflict in ***The Joy Luck Club.*** "Without Wood" deals with the disastrous effects of Rose Hsu Jordan's not having enough Wood in her personality, at least according to her mother An-mei's diagnosis. An-mei herself has inspired "a lifelong stream of criticism" from Suyuan Woo, apparently for bending too easily to other's ideas, the flaw of those who lack Wood (30–31). An-mei admits to having listened to too many people when she was young. She almost succumbed to her family's urgings to forget her mother, and later she was nearly seduced by the pearl necklace offered to her by her mother's rival. Experience has shown An-mei that people try to influence others for selfish reasons. To protect her daughter from opportunists, An-mei tells Rose that she must listen to her mother if she wants to grow "strong and straight." If she listens to others she will grow "crooked and weak." But Rose comments, "By the time she told me this, it was too late. I had already begun to bend" (191).

Rose attributes her compliant nature to the strict disciplinary measures of an elementary school teacher and to the influences of American culture: "Chinese people had Chinese opinions. American people had American opinions. And in almost every case, the American version was much better" (191). Not until much later does she realize that in the "American version" there are "too many choices," so that it is "easy to get confused and pick the wrong thing." Rose, emotionally paralyzed at fourteen by a sense that she is responsible for the death of her four-year-old brother, grows into an adult who not only listens to others but lets them take responsibility for her so that she may avoid committing another fatal error. Her husband, Ted, makes all the decisions in their marriage until a mistake of his own brings on a malpractice suit and shakes his self-confidence. When Ted abruptly demands a divorce, Rose's lack of Wood manifests itself: "I had been talking to too many people, my friends, everybody it seems, except Ted" (188). She tells a "different story" about the situation to Waverly, Lena, and her psychiatrist, each of whom offers a different response. An-mei chides Rose for not wanting to discuss Ted with her, but Rose is reluctant to do so because she fears that An-mei will tell her she must preserve her marriage, even though there is "absolutely nothing left to save" (117).

Contrary to Rose's expectations, her mother is less concerned that she stay married than that she deal with her inability to make decisions. An-mei wants her daughter to address the personality deficiencies that are the cause of her circumstances. Believing that Rose needs to assert her identity by acting on her own behalf, An-mei admonishes: "You must think for yourself, what you must do. If someone tells you, then you are not trying" (130). An-mei's advice is embedded in the broader context of her Chinese world-view. When Rose complains that she has no hope, and thus no reason to keep trying to save her marriage, An-mei responds: "This is not hope. Not reason. This is your fate. This is your life, what you must do" (130). An-mei believes life is determined by fate, by immutable celestial forces. But like Lindo Jong, she sees fate as having a participatory element. Earthly matters admit the influence of human agency. Consequently, her admonition to Rose is focused on what Rose must "do."

As a child Rose observes that both her parents believe in their *nengkan,* the ability to do anything they put their minds to. This belief has not only brought them to America but has "enabled them to have seven children and buy a house in the Sunset district with very little money" (121). Rose notes that by taking into account all the dangers described in *The Twenty-Six Malignant Gates,* An-mei has "absolute faith she could prevent every one of them" (124).

However, An-mei's optimism about her ability to manipulate fate is challenged when her youngest child, Bing, drowns. An-mei does everything she can to recover her son, but she realizes she cannot "use faith to change fate" (130). Tragedy teaches her that forethought is not the same thing as control. Still, she wedges a white Bible—one in which Bing's name is only lightly penciled in under "Deaths"—beneath a short table leg as a symbolic act, "a way for her to correct the imbalances of life" (116). Although An-mei accepts that her power over fate is limited, she continues to believe that she can positively influence her circumstances. The idea of balance she is enacting is a fundamental element of *yin-yang* philosophy; according to which two complementary forces "govern the universe and make up all aspects of life and matter" (Rossbach 21). As Johndennis Govert notes, "to remove an obstruction to your happiness, regain a state of health, or create a more harmonious household, *yin* and *yang* must be in balance." (7). An-mei may use a Bible to balance the kitchen table, but she rejects the Christian beliefs it represents. Rose notes that her mother loses "her faith in God" after Bing's death (116). The belief system that governs An-mei's actions is Chinese, an amalgam of luck, house gods, ancestors, and all the elements in balance, "the right amount of wind and water" (122).

In contrast to her mother, Rose lacks a means by which she can delineate or systematize her notions of causality and responsibility. Moreover, she eschews any real sense that people can have control over their circumstances. As a teenager Rose is appalled to discover she is powerless to prevent little Bing from falling into the ocean as she watches. Later Rose thinks "that maybe it was fate all along, that faith was just an illusion that somehow you're in control. I found out the most *I* could have was hope, and with that I was not denying any possibility, good or bad" (121). When her husband Ted wants a divorce, Rose compares the shock she receives to having the wind knocked out of her: "And after you pick yourself up, you realize you can't trust anybody to save you—not your husband, not your mother, not God. So what can you do to stop yourself from tilting and falling all over again?" (121). Added to her sense of helplessness is the suspicion that whenever she is forced into making a decision, she is walking through a minefield: "I never believed there was ever any one right answer, yet there were many wrong ones" (120). Rose's lack of any sort of a belief system fosters a crippling passivity characterized by a fear that whatever she chooses will turn out badly. Her inability to make even the smallest decisions becomes the equivalent, in Ted's mind at least, of her having no identity.

Ironically, once Rose realizes that Ted has taken away all her choices, she begins to fight back. She seizes on the metaphor An-mei has used to explain the lack of Wood in her personality: "If you bend to listen to other people, you will grow crooked and weak. You will fall to the ground with the first strong wind. And then you will be like a weed, growing wild in any direction, running along the ground until someone pulls you out and throws you away" (191). Inspired by the weeds in her own neglected garden that cannot be dislodged from the masonry without "pulling the whole building down" (195), Rose demands that Ted let her keep their house. She explains, "You can't just pull me out of your life and throw me away" (196). For the first time in her life she stands up for what she wants without soliciting the advice of others. After her assertion of selfhood, Rose dreams that her "beaming" mother has planted weeds that are "running wild in every direction" in her planter boxes (196). This image, which suggests that An-mei has finally accepted Rose's nature instead of trying to change her, is consistent with the desires the Joy Luck daughters share regarding their mothers. Each one struggles to feel loved for who she is. In part the younger women's insecurity stems from having a different set of cultural values than their mothers. The older women try to encourage their daughters but do not always know how to cope with the cultural gap that separates them. As Lindo states: "I wanted my children to have the best combination: American circumstances and Chinese character. How could I know these two things do not mix?" (254). But Rose's dream-image submerges the fact that Rose has finally acted on her mother's admonition to speak up for herself. An-mei has guessed that Ted is engaged in "monkey business" with another woman, and it is at the moment when Rose realizes her mother is right that she begins to move intuitively toward standing up for her own needs and desires. As it turns out, An-mei is correct in wanting Rose to listen to her mother rather than to her bored and sleepy-eyed psychiatrist in order to be "strong and straight." Ultimately, An-mei's belief that one's fate involves making choices instead of being paralyzed as a victim is validated by Rose's assertion of her identity.

A third element of traditional belief in **The Joy Luck Club** is *feng shui,* or geomancy. The most opaque yet potentially the most important aspect of Chinese cosmology to Tan's exploration of identity, *feng shui* plays a pivotal role in Lena St. Clair's story "The Voice from the Wall," which chronicles her mother Ying-ying's gradual psychological breakdown and withdrawal from life. Ten-year-old Lena, having no knowledge of her mother's past, becomes convinced that her mother is crazy as she listens to Ying-ying rave after the death of her infant son. Even before Ying-ying loses her baby, however, her behavior appears to be erratic and compulsive. When the family moves to a new apartment, Ying-ying arranges and rearranges the furniture in an effort to put things in balance. Although Lena senses her mother is disturbed, she dismisses Ying-ying's explanations as "Chinese nonsense" (108). What Lena does not understand is that her mother is practicing the ancient Chinese art of *feng shui* (pronounced "fung shway"). Translated literally as "wind" and "water," *feng shui* is alluded to only once in the book as An-mei Hsu's balance of "the right amount of wind and water" (122). Although the term "*feng shui*" is never used overtly in conjunction with Ying-ying St. Clair, its tenets are fundamental to her worldview.

Stephen Skinner defines *feng shui* as "the art of living in harmony with the land, and deriving the greatest benefit, peace and prosperity from being in the right place at the right time" (4). The precepts of *feng shui* were systematized by two different schools in China over a thousand years ago. The Form School, or intuitive approach, was developed by Yang Yun-Sung (c. 840–888 A.D.) and flourished in Kiangsi and Anhui provinces. Practitioners focus on the visible form of the landscape, especially the shapes of mountains and the direction of watercourses. The Compass School, or analytical approach, was developed by Wang Chih in the Sung dynasty (960 A.D.) and spread throughout Fukien and Chekiang provinces as well as Hong Kong and Taiwan (Skinner 26). The analytic approach is concerned with directional orientation in conjunction with Chinese astrology. As Walters notes, Compass School scholars have traditionally "placed greater emphasis on the importance of precise mathematical calculations, and compiled elaborate formulae and schematic diagrams" (10). Geomancers using this approach employ an elaborate compass called the *lo p'an,* astrological charts and horoscopes, numerological data, and special rulers.

According to Susan Hornik, the beliefs encompassed by *feng shui* date back 3,000 years to the first practice of selecting auspicious sites for burial tombs in order to "bring good fortune to heirs" (73). As Skinner explains, "Ancestors are linked with the site of their tombs. As they also have a direct effect on the lives of their descendants, it follows logically that if their tombs are located favourably on the site of a strong concentration of earth energy or *ch'i,* not only will they be happy but they will also derive the power to aid their descendants, from the accumulated *ch'i* of the site" (11). By the Han dynasty (206 B.C.), the use of *feng shui* was extended to the selection of dwellings for the living (Hornik 73). The basic idea is to attract and channel *ch'i,* or beneficial energy, and "accumulate it without allowing it to go stagnant" (Skinner 21). Since *ch'i* encourages growth and prosperity, a wise person will consider how to manipulate it to best effect through *feng shui,* the study of placement with respect to both natural and man-made environments. As a form of geomancy *feng shui* is "the exact complement of astrology, which is divination by signs in the Heavens" (Walters 12), but it is based on a different presupposition. Whereas the course of the stars and planets is fixed, the earthly environment can be altered by human intervention through *feng shui.* The practice of *feng shui* offers yet another variation of the belief that people have the power to affect their destiny.

Thus Ying-ying St. Clair's seemingly idiosyncratic actions and their nonsensical explanations in "The Voice from the Wall" are grounded in a coherent system of beliefs and practices concerned with balancing the environment. Since Ying-ying feels her surroundings are out of balance, she does everything she can to correct them. For instance, she moves "a large round mirror from the wall facing the front door to a wall by the sofa" (108). *Ch'i* is believed to enter a dwelling through the front door, but a mirror hung opposite the entrance may deflect it back outside again. Mirrors require careful placement so as to encourage the flow of *ch'i* around a room. Furniture, too, must be positioned according to guidelines that allow beneficial currents of *ch'i* to circulate without stagnating. Through properly placed furniture "every opportunity can be taken to correct whatever defects may exist, and to enhance whatever positive qualities there are" (Walters 46). Hence, Ying-ying rearranges the sofa, chairs, and end tables, seeking the best possible grouping. Even a "Chinese scroll of goldfish" is moved. When large-scale changes are impossible, *feng shui* practitioners frequently turn to symbolic solutions. Strategically placed aquariums containing goldfish are often prescribed for structural problems that cannot be altered, in part because aquariums symbolically bring all Five Elements together into balance (Collins 21). In Ying-ying's case, a picture is substituted for live goldfish, which represent life and growth.

Ying-ying's attempt to balance the living room follows a *feng shui* tradition: "If beneficial *ch'i* are lacking from the heart of the house, the family will soon drift apart" (Walters 42). But Ying-ying is also compensating for negative environmental and structural features that she cannot modify. The apartment in the new neighborhood is built on a steep hill, a poor site, she explains, because "a bad wind from the top blows all your strength back down the hill. So you can never get ahead. You are always rolling backward" (109). In ancient China the ideal location for a building was in the shelter of hills that would protect it from bitter northerly winds. However, a house at the very base of a sloping road would be vulnerable to torrential rains, mudslides, and crashes caused by runaway carts. Ying-ying's concern with psychic rather than physical danger is consistent with modern applications of *feng shui*, but her notion of an ill wind sweeping downhill is based on traditional lore. In addition to the unfortunate location of the apartment building, its lobby is musty, a sign that it does not favor the circulation of *ch'i*. The door to the St. Clairs' apartment is narrow, "like a neck that has been strangled" (109), further restricting the entrance of beneficial energy. Moreover, as Ying-ying tells Lena, the kitchen faces the toilet room, "so all your worth is flushed away." According to the Bagua map derived from the *I Ching,* the ancient Chinese book of divination, every building and every room has eight positions that correspond to various aspects of life: wealth and prosperity; fame and reputation; love and marriage; creativity and children; helpful people and travel; career; knowledge and self-cultivation; and health and family (Collins 61–62). Heidi Swillinger explains the problem of a dwelling where the bathroom is located in the wealth area: "Because the bathroom is a place where water enters and leaves, and because water is a symbol of wealth, residents in such a home might find that money tends to symbolically go down the drain or be flushed away."[5] Even if the St. Clairs' bathroom is not actually in the wealth area, *feng shui* guidelines dictate that it should not be placed next to the kitchen in order to avoid a clash between two of the symbolic Elements, Fire and Water.

In light of the bad *feng shui* of the apartment, Ying-ying's unhappiness with it is logical. Once she finishes altering the living room, she rearranges Lena's bedroom. The immediate effect of the new configuration is that "the nighttime life" of Lena's imagination changes (109). With her bed against the wall, she begins to listen to the private world of the family next door and to use what she hears as a basis for comparison with her own family. It is not clear whether Lena's bed has been moved to the "children" area of the room, which would enhance her *ch'i*, but certainly the new position is more in keeping with the principles of good *feng shui*, which indicate a bed should be placed against a wall, not a window (Walters 53). From this standpoint, Ying-ying's inauspicious positioning of the crib against the window appears to be inconsistent with her other efforts. Lena notes, "My mother began to bump into things, into table edges as if she forgot her stomach contained a baby, as if she were headed for trouble instead" (109). Since according to *feng shui* theory protruding corners are threatening (Collins 47), Ying-ying's peculiar neglect toward sharp table edges along with her placement of the crib suggest that her efforts at generating good *feng shui* are suspended with regard to her unborn baby.

When the baby dies at birth, apparently from a severe case of hydrocephalus and spina bifida, Ying-ying blames herself: "My fault, my fault. I knew this before it happened. I did nothing to prevent it" (111). To Western ears her self-accusation sounds odd, for birth defects such as spina bifida are congenital, and nothing Ying-ying could have done would have prevented the inevitable. However, her Eastern world-view dictates that fate can be manipulated in order to bring about good effects and to ward off bad ones. Ying-ying believes that her violation of good *feng shui* principles constitutes negligence, causing the baby to die. She is accusing herself not merely of passivity but of deliberate complicity with a malignant fate.

The burden of guilt Ying-ying carries over an abortion from her first marriage is the root of her disturbed mental state during her pregnancy. Her bumping into table edges may even be a form of self-punishment. In any case, whether she has subconsciously tried to harm the fetus or has merely failed to fend off disaster through the use of *feng shui*, in blaming herself for the baby's death Ying-ying is clearly wrestling with her responsibility for the death of her first son. In her mind the two events are connected: "I knew he [the baby] could see everything inside me. How I had given no thought to killing my other son! How I had given no thought to having this baby" (112). Instead of finding any resolution after the baby dies, Ying-ying becomes increasingly withdrawn. She cries unaccountably in the middle of cooking dinner and frequently retreats to her bed to "rest."

The presence of *feng shui* in the story suggests that however displaced, demoralized, and severely depressed Ying-ying may be, she is not "crazy," as Lena fears. Ying-ying's compulsion to rearrange furniture does not presage a psychotic break with reality but rather signals that, transplanted to a foreign country where she must function according to new rules and expectations, Ying-ying relies on familiar practices such as *feng shui* and astrology to interpret and order the world around her, especially when that world is in crisis. Lena, of course, is locked into a ten-year-old's perspective and an American frame of reference. She shares Jing-mei Woo's problem of being able to understand her mother's Chinese words but not their meanings. Whereas Clifford St. Clair's usual practice of "putting words" in his wife's mouth stems from his knowing "only a few canned Chinese expressions" (106), Lena's faulty translation of her mother's distracted speech after the baby dies reflects a lack of sufficient personal and cultural knowledge to make sense of Ying-ying's references to guilt.

Ying-ying's story, "Waiting between the Trees," traces the origins of her decline to a much earlier time. At sixteen Ying-ying is married to a man who impregnates her, then abandons her for an opera singer. Out of grief and anger, she induces an abortion. However, after this defiant act she loses her strength, becoming "like the ladies of the lake" her mother had warned her about, floating like "a dead leaf on the water" (248-49). Unfortunately, Ying-ying's Tiger characteristic of "waiting patiently for things to come" (248) turns from easy acceptance of whatever is offered into listlessness and acquiescence over a period of fourteen years: "I became pale, ill, and more thin. I let myself become a wounded animal" (251). She confesses, "I willingly gave up my *chi,* the spirit that caused me so much pain" (251). Giving up her vital energy is tantamount to giving up her identity. By the time Clifford St. Clair takes her to America, she has already become "an unseen spirit," with no trace of her former passion and energy. Nevertheless, she retains her ability to see things before they happen. Her prescience stems from her trust in portents, which constitutes another facet of her belief system. When she is young, a flower that falls from its stalk tells her she will marry her first husband. Later on, Clifford St. Clair's appearance in her life is a sign that her "black side" will soon go away. Her husband's death signals that she can marry St. Clair.

Years later, Ying-ying can still see portents of the future. She knows Lena's is "a house that will break into pieces" (243). Ying-ying also continues to think in terms of *feng shui.* She complains that the guest room in Lena's house has sloping walls, a fact which implies the presence of sharp angles that can harbor *sha,* malignant energy signifying death and decay. With walls that close in like a coffin, the room is no place to put a baby, Ying-ying observes. But it is not until Ying-ying sees her daughter's unhappy marriage that she accepts responsibility for the fact that Lena has no *ch'i* and determines to regain her own fierce spirit in order to pass it on to her daughter. Ying-ying knows she must face the pain of her past and communicate it to her daughter so as to supply Lena with the personal and cultural knowledge of her mother's life that she has always lacked. By recounting her life's pain, Ying-ying will in essence reconstruct her lost identity. To set things in motion, she decides to topple the spindly-legged marble table in the guest room so that Lena will come to see what is wrong. In this instance Ying-ying manipulates her environment in a literal as well as a symbolic sense, drawing on her traditional Chinese worldview once more in order to effect the best outcome for her daughter's life.

Unlike her mother, Lena has no consistent belief system of her own. She inherits Ying-ying's ability to see bad things before they happen but does not possess the power to anticipate good things, which suggests that Lena has merely internalized "the unspoken terrors" that plague Ying-ying (103). According to Philip Langdon, "second-or third-generation Chinese-Americans are much less likely to embrace *feng shui* than are those who were born in Asia" (148). Not only is Lena a second-generation Chinese-American, she is half Caucasian, which makes her Chinese heritage even more remote. Nonetheless, Lena is profoundly affected by Ying-ying's way of perceiving the world. As a child Lena is obsessed with knowing the worst possible thing that can happen, but unlike her mother, she has no sense of being able to manipulate fate. Thus, she is terrified when she cannot stop what she supposes to be the nightly "killing" of the girl next door, which she hears through her bedroom wall. Only after Lena realizes that she has been wrong about the neighbor family does she find ways to change the "bad things" in her mind.

Lena's muddled notions of causality and responsibility persist into adulthood. In "Rice Husband," she still views herself as guilty for the death of Arnold Reisman, a former neighbor boy, because she "let one thing result from another" (152). She believes there is a relation between her not having cleaned her plate at meals when she was young and Arnold's development of a rare and fatal complication of measles. She wants to dismiss the link as ridiculous, but she is plagued by doubt because she has no philosophical or religious scheme by which to interpret events and establish parameters for her personal responsibility: "The thought that I could have caused Arnold's death is not so ridiculous. Perhaps he was destined to be my husband. Because I think to myself, even today, how can the world in all its chaos come up with so many coincidences, so many similarities and exact opposites?" (154). Whereas Ying-ying's belief system affords her a sense of certainty about how the world operates, Lena's lack of such a system leaves her in confusion.

It is Lena's uncertainty about causality together with her failure to take purposive action that leads Ying-ying to believe her daughter has no *ch'i.* Lena tells herself, "When I want something to happen—or not happen—I begin to look at all events and all things as relevant, an opportunity to take or avoid" (152). But Ying-ying challenges her, asking why, if Lena knew the marble table was going to fall down, she did not stop it. By analogy she is asking Lena why she does not resolve to save her marriage. Lena muses, "And it's such a simple question" (165). It is unclear whether Lena has already decided not to rescue the marriage or whether she is simply confused about her capacity to act on her own behalf. But the fact that Lena cannot answer her mother's question quietly privileges Ying-ying's perspective on the situation, much as An-mei's viewpoint of Rose's predicament is validated in "Without Wood."

Marina Heung has pointed out that among works which focus on mother-daughter relations, *The Joy Luck Club* is "remarkable for foregrounding the voices of mothers as well as of daughters" (599). However, Tan goes further than "foregrounding" the mothers; she subtly endorses their world-view at strategic points in the text. Whereas Rose, Lena, and Jing-mei are paralyzed and unable to move forward in their relationships and careers and Waverly is haunted by a lingering fear of her mother's disapproval, Suyuan, Lindo, An-mei, and even Ying-ying demonstrate a resilient belief in their power to act despite having suffered the ravages of war and the painful loss of parents, spouses, and children. Out of the vast range of Chinese religious, philosophical, and folkloric beliefs, many of which stress self-effacement and passivity, Tan focuses on practices that allow her characters to make adjustments to their destinies and thereby preserve and perpetuate their identities. Suyuan Woo is most striking in this regard. She goes outside of conventional Chinese beliefs to make up her own means of dealing with fate. Suyuan invents "Joy Luck," whereby she and her friends in Kweilin "choose [their] own happiness" at their weekly mah jong parties instead of passively waiting for their own deaths (25). Joy Luck for them consists of forgetting past wrongs, avoiding bad thoughts, feasting, laughing, playing games, telling stories, and most importantly, hoping to be lucky. The ritualistic set of attitudes and actions that Suyuan and her friends observe keep them from succumbing to despair. When the war is over, Suyuan holds on to the main tenet of her belief system—that "hope was our only joy"—by refusing to assume a passive role in the aftermath of tragedy. She never gives up hope that by persistence she may be able to locate the infant daughters she left in China. When Suyuan says to Jing-mei, "You don't even know little percent of me!" (27), she is referring to the complex interplay among the events of her life, her native culture and language, and her exercise of her mind and will. These things constitute an identity that Jing-mei has only an elusive and fragmentary knowledge of.

The references in *The Joy Luck Club* to traditional beliefs and practices such as astrology, *wu-hsing,* and *feng shui* emphasize the distance between the Chinese mothers and their American-born daughters. Tan hints through the stories of Lindo and Waverly Jong that a degree of reconciliation and understanding is attainable between mothers and daughters, and she indicates through Jing-mei Woo's journey that cultural gaps can be narrowed. In fact, Jing-mei Woo starts "becoming Chinese" as soon as she crosses the border into China (267). But overall, Tan's portrayal of first-generation immigrants attempting to transmit their native culture to their offspring is full of situations where "meanings" are untranslatable. The breakdown in communication between mothers and daughters is poignantly encapsulated in "American Translation," the vignette that introduces the third group of stories in the book. A mother tells her daughter not to put a mirror at the foot of her bed: "'All your marriage happiness will bounce back and turn the opposite way'" (147). Walters notes that mirrors are "regarded as symbols of a long and happy marriage" but also that "care has to be taken that they are not so placed that they are likely to alarm the soul of a sleeper when it rises for nocturnal wanderings" (55). According to *feng shui* principles, a mirror "acts as a constant energy reflector and will be sending [a] stream of intensified power into the space over and around [the] bed, day and night. It will be a perpetual cause of disturbance" during sleep (Lam 105). The daughter in the vignette is "irritated that her mother s[ees] bad omens in everything. She had heard these warnings all her life." Lacking an understanding of the cosmological system to which her mother's omens belong, the daughter simply views them as evidence that her mother has a negative outlook on life.

When the woman offers a second mirror to hang above the headboard of the bed in order to remedy the problem, she is seeking to properly channel the flow of *ch'i* around the room. The mother comments, "this mirror see that mirror—*haule!*—multiply your peach-blossom luck." The daughter, however, does not understand her mother's allusion to peach-blossom luck, which "refers to those who are particularly attractive to the opposite sex" (Rossbach 48). By way of explanation, the mother, "mischief in her eyes," has her daughter look in the mirror to see her future grandchild. She is acting in accordance to the ancient Chinese belief that the "mysterious power of reflection" of mirrors, which reveal "a parallel world beyond the surface," is magical (Walters 55). The daughter, unfortunately, can only grasp literal meanings: "The daughter looked—and *haule!* There it was: her own reflection looking back at her." The mother is incapable of translating her world-view into "perfect American English," so the daughter's comprehension remains flawed, partial, incomplete. Whether or not she apprehends, from her literal reflection, that she herself is the symbol of her mother's own peach-blossom luck is ambiguous. In the same way, the uneasy relations between the older and younger women in *The Joy Luck Club* suggest that the daughters understand only dimly, if at all, that they are the long-cherished expression of their mothers' Joy Luck.

*Notes*

1. For a discussion of existential unrepeatability and the role of memory in *The Joy Luck Club,* see Ben Xu, "Memory and the Ethnic Self: Reading Amy Tan's *The Joy Luck Club,*" MELUS 19.1 (1994): 3–18. An interesting treatment of language, storytelling, and maternal subjectivity in Tan's novel can be found in Marina Heung, "Daughter-Text/Mother-Text: Matrilineage in Amy Tan's *Joy Luck Club,*" *Feminist Studies* 19.3 (1993): 597–616.

2. Jing-mei Woo thinks her mother's "telltale Chinese behaviors" are expressly intended to embarrass her,

including Suyuan's predilection for yellow, pink, and bright orange (143, 267). When Jing-mei arrives in China, she notices "little children wearing pink and yellow, red and peach," the only spots of bright color amidst drab grays and olive greens (271). Tan seems to suggest through this detail that Suyuan's color preferences reflect not only her personal taste but Chinese patterns and traditions. According to Sarah Rossbach, yellow stands for power, pink represents "love and pure feelings," and orange suggests "happiness and power" (46–47). In this light, Lindo Jong's criticism of Suyuan's red sweater in "Best Quality" is ironic since it is Lindo who provides evidence that red is regarded by the Chinese as an auspicious color connoting "happiness, warmth or fire, strength, and fame" (Rossbach 45). In "The Red Candle" Lindo mentions not only her mother's jade necklace and her mother-in-law's pillars, tables, and chairs but also her own wedding banners, palanquin, dress, scarf, special eggs, and marriage candle as being red.

3. Jing-mei Woo, born in the same year as Waverly (37), is a Metal Rabbit, and like Waverly, she exhibits a "Rabbit-like" sensitivity to criticism, especially when it comes from her mother.

4. The Chinese system of astrology has Buddhist origins, while the theory of the Five Elements derives from Taoist thought. Holmes Welch observes that "there was little distinction—and the most intimate connections—between early Buddhism and Taoism" (119).

5. Similar reasoning obtains in "Rice Husband" when Ying-ying tells Lena that a bank will have all its money drained away after a plumbing and bathroom fixtures store opens across the street from it (149). Lena comments that "one month later, an officer of the bank was arrested for embezzlement."

*Works Cited*

Collins, Terah Kathryn. *The Western Guide to Feng Shui.* Carlsbad, CA: Hay House, 1996.

Govert, Johndennis. *Feng Shui: Art and Harmony of Place.* Phoenix: Daikakuji, 1993.

Heung, Marina. "Daughter-Text/Mother-Text: Matrilineage in Amy Tan's *Joy Luck Club.*" *Feminist Studies* 19.3 (1993): 597–616.

Hornik, Susan. "How to Get that Extra Edge on Health and Wealth." *Smithsonian* Aug. 1993: 70–75.

Jackson, Dallas. "Chinese Astrology." *Los Angeles Times* 20 Feb. 1991, Orange County ed.: E2. *News.* Online. Lexis-Nexis. 15 Mar. 1997.

Lam, Kam Chuen. *Feng Shui Handbook.* New York: Henry Holt, 1996.

Langdon, Philip. "Lucky Houses." *Atlantic* Nov. 1991: 146+.

Maspero, Henri. *Taoism and Chinese Religion.* Trans. Frank A. Kierman, Jr. Amherst: U of Massachusetts P, 1981.

Rossbach, Sarah. *Living Color: Master Lin Yun's Guide to Feng Shui and the Art of Color.* New York: Kodansha, 1994.

Scott, Ann. "Chinese New Year: The Year of the Tiger." *United Press International* 5 Feb. 1986, International sec. *News.* Online. Lexis-Nexis. 15 Mar. 1997.

Skinner, Stephen. *The Living Earth Manual of Feng-Shui.* London: Routledge, 1982.

Swillinger, Heidi. "Feng Shui: A Blueprint for Balance." *San Francisco Chronicle* 8 Sept. 1993: Z1. *News.* Online. Lexis-Nexis. 15 Mar. 1997.

Tan, Amy. *The Joy Luck Club.* New York: G. P. Putnam, 1989.

Walters, Derek. *Feng Shui: The Chinese Art of Designing a Harmonious Environment.* New York: Simon & Schuster, 1988.

Welch, Holmes. *Taoism: The Parting of the Way.* Revised ed. Boston: Beacon, 1966.

Xu, Ben. "Memory and the Ethnic Self: Reading Amy Tan's *The Joy Luck Club.*" *MELUS* 19.1 (1994): 3–18.

Youngblood, Ruth. "Baby-Poor Singapore Looks to Dragon for Help." *Los Angeles Times* 29 Nov. 1987, sec. 1: 41. *News.* Online. Lexis-Nexis. 15 Mar. 1997.

# FURTHER READING

### Criticism

Feldman, Gayle. "*The Joy Luck Club*: Chinese Magic, American Blessings and a Publishing Fairy Tale." *Publishers Weekly* (7 July 1989): 24–27.

> Feldman discusses the methods Tan used to write and publish *The Joy Luck Club.*

Harrison, Patricia Marby. "Genocide or Redemption? Asian American autobiography and the portrayal of Christianity in Amy Tan's *The Joy Luck Club* and Joy Kogawa's *Obasan.*" *Christianity and Literature* 46, No. 2 (Winter 1997): 145–69.

> Harrison explores the differing portrayals of Christianity in *The Joy Luck Club* and Joy Kogawa's *Obasan,* noting that Tan seems to view the religion as being culturally destructive.

Houston, Marsha. "Women and the Language of Race and Ethnicity." *Women and Language* XVII, No. 1 (Spring 1995): 1–7.

Houston traces the importance of multiple languages in *The Joy Luck Club* and Maxine Hong Kingston's *The Woman Warrior*.

Huntley, E. D. "*The Joy Luck Club*." In *Amy Tan: A Critical Companion,* pp. 41–77. Westport: Greenwood Press, 1998.

Huntley examines the literary elements that compose *The Joy Luck Club*.

Souris, Stephen. "'Only Two Kinds of Daughters': Intermonologue Dialogicity in *The Joy Luck Club*." *MELUS* 19, No. 2 (Summer 1994): 99–124.

Souris uses dynamic reader models to illustrate how readers are challenged to find the interconnections in *The Joy Luck Club*.

---

**Additional coverage of Tan's life and career is contained in the following sources published by the Gale Group:** *Asian American Literature; Authors and Artists for Young Adults,* Vol. 9; *Bestsellers,* Vol. 89:3; *Concise Dictionary of American Literary Biography Supplement; Contemporary Authors,* Vol. 136; *Contemporary Authors New Revision Series,* Vol. 54; *Contemporary Novelists; Contemporary Popular Writers,* Vol. 1; *Dictionary of Literary Biography,* Vol. 173; *DISCovering Authors 3.0; DISCovering Authors Modules: Multicultural, Novelists,* **and** *Popular Fiction and Genre Authors Modules; Feminist Writers; Literature Resource Center; Major 20th-Century Writers,* Edition 2; *Novels for Students,* Vol. 9; *Reference Guide to American Literature; Short Stories for Students,* Vol. 9; *Something About the Author,* Vol. 75; **and** *St. James Guide to Young Adult Writers.*

# How to Use This Index

### The main references

> **Calvino, Italo**
> 1923-1985 ....... CLC 5, 8, 11, 22, 33, 39, 73; SSC 3

**list all author entries in the following Gale Literary Criticism series:**

- **BLC** = *Black Literature Criticism*
- **CLC** = *Contemporary Literary Criticism*
- **CLR** = *Children's Literature Review*
- **CMLC** = *Classical and Medieval Literature Criticism*
- **DA** = *DISCovering Authors*
- **DAB** = *DISCovering Authors: British*
- **DAC** = *DISCovering Authors: Canadian*
- **DAM** = *DISCovering Authors: Modules*
  - **DRAM:** *Dramatists Module;* **MST:** *Most-Studied Authors Module;*
  - **MULT:** *Multicultural Authors Module;* **NOV:** *Novelists Module;*
  - **POET:** *Poets Module;* **POP:** *Popular Fiction and Genre Authors Module*
- **DC** = *Drama Criticism*
- **HLC** = *Hispanic Literature Criticism*
- **LC** = *Literature Criticism from 1400 to 1800*
- **NCLC** = *Nineteenth-Century Literature Criticism*
- **NNAL** = *Native North American Literature*
- **PC** = *Poetry Criticism*
- **SSC** = *Short Story Criticism*
- **TCLC** = *Twentieth-Century Literary Criticism*
- **WLC** = *World Literature Criticism, 1500 to the Present*

### The cross-references

> See also CANR 23; CA 85-88;
> obituary CA116

**list all author entries in the following Gale biographical and literary sources:**

- **AAYA** = *Authors & Artists for Young Adults*
- **AITN** = *Authors in the News*
- **BEST** = *Bestsellers*
- **BW** = *Black Writers*
- **CA** = *Contemporary Authors*
- **CAAS** = *Contemporary Authors Autobiography Series*
- **CABS** = *Contemporary Authors Bibliographical Series*
- **CANR** = *Contemporary Authors New Revision Series*
- **CAP** = *Contemporary Authors Permanent Series*
- **CDALB** = *Concise Dictionary of American Literary Biography*
- **CDBLB** = *Concise Dictionary of British Literary Biography*
- **DLB** = *Dictionary of Literary Biography*
- **DLBD** = *Dictionary of Literary Biography Documentary Series*
- **DLBY** = *Dictionary of Literary Biography Yearbook*
- **HW** = *Hispanic Writers*
- **JRDA** = *Junior DISCovering Authors*
- **MAICYA** = *Major Authors and Illustrators for Children and Young Adults*
- **MTCW** = *Major 20th-Century Writers*
- **SAAS** = *Something about the Author Autobiography Series*
- **SATA** = *Something about the Author*
- **YABC** = *Yesterday's Authors of Books for Children*

# Literary Criticism Series
# Cumulative Author Index

**20/1631**
   See Upward, Allen
**A/C Cross**
   See Lawrence, T(homas) E(dward)
**Abasiyanik, Sait Faik** 1906-1954
   See Sait Faik
   See also CA 123
**Abbey, Edward** 1927-1989 .......... **CLC 36, 59**
   See also ANW; CA 45-48; 128; CANR 2, 41; DA3; MTCW 2; TCWW 2
**Abbott, Lee K(ittredge)** 1947- .......... **CLC 48**
   See also CA 124; CANR 51, 101; DLB 130
**Abe, Kobo** 1924-1993 ...... **CLC 8, 22, 53, 81; DAM NOV**
   See also CA 65-68; 140; CANR 24, 60; DLB 182; MJW; MTCW 1, 2; SFW
**Abelard, Peter** c. 1079-c. 1142 ...... **CMLC 11**
   See also DLB 115, 208
**Abell, Kjeld** 1901-1961 ...................... **CLC 15**
   See also CA 191; 111; DLB 214
**Abish, Walter** 1931- ............ **CLC 22; SSC 44**
   See also CA 101; CANR 37; CN; DLB 130, 227
**Abrahams, Peter (Henry)** 1919- .......... **CLC 4**
   See also AFW; BW 1; CA 57-60; CANR 26; CN; DLB 117, 225; MTCW 1, 2; RGEL; WLIT 2
**Abrams, M(eyer) H(oward)** 1912- ... **CLC 24**
   See also CA 57-60; CANR 13, 33; DLB 67
**Abse, Dannie** 1923- ............ **CLC 7, 29; DAB; DAM POET**
   See also CA 53-56; CAAS 1; CANR 4, 46, 74; CBD; CP; DLB 27, 245; MTCW 1
**Abutsu** 1222(?)-1283 ....................... **CMLC 46**
   See also DLB 203
**Achebe, (Albert) Chinua(lumogu)** 1930- ...... **CLC 1, 3, 5, 7, 11, 26, 51, 75, 127; BLC 1; DA; DAB; DAC; DAM MST, MULT, NOV; WLC**
   See also AAYA 15; AFW; BPFB 1; BW 2, 3; CA 1-4R; CANR 6, 26, 47; CLR 20; CN; CP; CWRI; DA3; DLB 117; DNFS; EXPN; EXPS; LAIT 2; MAICYA; MTCW 1, 2; NFS 2; RGEL; RGSF; SATA 38, 40; SATA-Brief 38; SSFS 3, 13; WLIT 2
**Acker, Kathy** 1948-1997 .............. **CLC 45, 111**
   See also CA 117; 122; 162; CANR 55; CN
**Ackroyd, Peter** 1949- .......... **CLC 34, 52, 140**
   See also BRWS 6; CA 123; 127; CANR 51, 74, 99; CN; DLB 155, 231; HGG; INT 127; MTCW 1; RHW
**Acorn, Milton** 1923-1986 ........ **CLC 15; DAC**
   See also CA 103; CCA 1; DLB 53; INT 103
**Adamov, Arthur** 1908-1970 .......... **CLC 4, 25; DAM DRAM**
   See also CA 17-18; 25-28R; CAP 2; GFL 1789 to the Present; MTCW 1; RGWL

**Adams, Alice (Boyd)** 1926-1999 .. **CLC 6, 13, 46; SSC 24**
   See also CA 81-84; 179; CANR 26, 53, 75, 88; CN; CSW; DLB 234; DLBY 86; INT CANR-26; MTCW 1, 2
**Adams, Andy** 1859-1935 ................. **TCLC 56**
   See also TCWW 2; YABC 1
**Adams, Brooks** 1848-1927 .............. **TCLC 80**
   See also CA 123; DLB 47
**Adams, Douglas (Noel)** 1952-2001 .. **CLC 27, 60; DAM POP**
   See also AAYA 4, 33; BEST 89:3; CA 106; CANR 34, 64; CPW; DA3; DLBY 83; JRDA; MTCW 1; NFS 7; SATA 116; SFW
**Adams, Francis** 1862-1893 ............. **NCLC 33**
**Adams, Henry (Brooks)** 1838-1918 ........ **TCLC 4, 52; DA; DAB; DAC; DAM MST**
   See also AMW; CA 104; 133; CANR 77; DLB 12, 47, 189; MTCW 1; NCFS 1
**Adams, John** 1735-1826 ............... **NCLC 106**
   See also DLB 31
**Adams, Richard (George)** 1920- ... **CLC 4, 5, 18; DAM NOV**
   See also AAYA 16; AITN 1, 2; BPFB 1; BYA 5; CA 49-52; CANR 3, 35; CLR 20; CN; FANT; JRDA; LAIT 5; MAICYA; MTCW 1, 2; NFS 11; SATA 7, 69; YAW
**Adamson, Joy(-Friederike Victoria)** 1910-1980 .................................. **CLC 17**
   See also CA 69-72; 93-96; CANR 22; MTCW 1; SATA 11; SATA-Obit 22
**Adcock, Fleur** 1934- ........................ **CLC 41**
   See also CA 25-28R, 182; CAAE 182; CAAS 23; CANR 11, 34, 69, 101; CP; CWP; DLB 40; FW
**Addams, Charles (Samuel)** 1912-1988 ................................ **CLC 30**
   See also CA 61-64; 126; CANR 12, 79
**Addams, Jane** 1860-1945 ................ **TCLC 76**
   See also AMWS 1; FW
**Addison, Joseph** 1672-1719 ................. **LC 18**
   See also BRW 3; CDBLB 1660-1789; DLB 101; RGEL; WLIT 3
**Adler, Alfred (F.)** 1870-1937 ........... **TCLC 61**
   See also CA 119; 159
**Adler, C(arole) S(chwerdtfeger)** 1932- ...................................... **CLC 35**
   See also AAYA 4, 41; CA 89-92; CANR 19, 40, 101; JRDA; MAICYA; SAAS 15; SATA 26, 63, 102; YAW
**Adler, Renata** 1938- ..................... **CLC 8, 31**
   See also CA 49-52; CANR 95; CN; MTCW 1
**Adorno, Theodor W(iesengrund)** 1903-1969 ............................... **TCLC 111**
   See also CA 89-92; 25-28R; CANR 89; DLB 242

**Ady, Endre** 1877-1919 ................... **TCLC 11**
   See also CA 107; EW
**A.E.** .............................................. **TCLC 3, 10**
   See also Russell, George William
**Aelfric** c. 955-c. 1010 .................... **CMLC 46**
   See also DLB 146
**Aeschines** c. 390B.C.-c. 320B.C. ..... **CMLC 47**
   See also DLB 176
**Aeschylus** 525(?)B.C.-456(?)B.C. .. **CMLC 11; DA; DAB; DAC; DAM DRAM, MST; DC 8; WLCS**
   See also AW 1; DFS 5, 10; DLB 176; RGWL
**Aesop** 620(?)B.C.-560(?)B.C. ......... **CMLC 24**
   See also CLR 14; MAICYA; SATA 64
**Affable Hawk**
   See MacCarthy, Sir (Charles Otto) Desmond
**Africa, Ben**
   See Bosman, Herman Charles
**Afton, Effie**
   See Harper, Frances Ellen Watkins
**Agapida, Fray Antonio**
   See Irving, Washington
**Agee, James (Rufus)** 1909-1955 ...... **TCLC 1, 19; DAM NOV**
   See also AITN 1; AMW; CA 108; 148; CDALB 1941-1968; DLB 2, 26, 152; DLBY 89; LAIT 3; MTCW 1; RGAL
**Aghill, Gordon**
   See Silverberg, Robert
**Agnon, S(hmuel) Y(osef Halevi)** 1888-1970 ........... **CLC 4, 8, 14; SSC 30**
   See also CA 17-18; 25-28R; CANR 60, 102; CAP 2; MTCW 1, 2; RGSF; RGWL
**Agrippa von Nettesheim, Henry Cornelius** 1486-1535 ...................................... **LC 27**
**Aguilera Malta, Demetrio** 1909-1981
   See also CA 111; 124; CANR 87; DAM MULT, NOV; DLB 145; HLCS 1; HW 1
**Agustini, Delmira** 1886-1914
   See also CA 166; HLCS 1; HW 1, 2; LAW
**Aherne, Owen**
   See Cassill, R(onald) V(erlin)
**Ai** 1947- ...................................... **CLC 4, 14, 69**
   See also CA 85-88; CAAS 13; CANR 70; DLB 120
**Aickman, Robert (Fordyce)** 1914-1981 ................................. **CLC 57**
   See also CA 5-8R; CANR 3, 72, 100; HGG; SUFW
**Aiken, Conrad (Potter)** 1889-1973 .... **CLC 1, 3, 5, 10, 52; DAM NOV, POET; PC 26; SSC 9**
   See also AMW; CA 5-8R; 45-48; CANR 4, 60; CDALB 1929-1941; DLB 9, 45, 102; EXPS; HGG; MTCW 1, 2; RGAL; RGSF; SATA 3, 30; SSFS 8

**Aiken, Joan (Delano)** 1924- ............... **CLC 35**
See also AAYA 1, 25; CA 9-12R, 182; CAAE 182; CANR 4, 23, 34, 64; CLR 1, 19; DLB 161; FANT; HGG; JRDA; MAICYA; MTCW 1; RHW; SAAS 1; SATA 2, 30, 73; SATA-Essay 109; WYA; YAW

**Ainsworth, William Harrison** 1805-1882 ............... **NCLC 13**
See also DLB 21; HGG; RGEL; SATA 24

**Aitmatov, Chingiz (Torekulovich)** 1928- ............... **CLC 71**
See also CA 103; CANR 38; MTCW 1; RGSF; SATA 56

**Akers, Floyd**
See Baum, L(yman) Frank

**Akhmadulina, Bella Akhatovna** 1937- ............... **CLC 53; DAM POET**
See also CA 65-68; CWP; CWW 2

**Akhmatova, Anna** 1888-1966 ..... **CLC 11, 25, 64, 126; DAM POET; PC 2**
See also CA 19-20; 25-28R; CANR 35; CAP 1; DA3; EW; MTCW 1, 2; RGWL

**Aksakov, Sergei Timofeyvich** 1791-1859 ............... **NCLC 2**
See also DLB 198

**Aksenov, Vassily**
See Aksyonov, Vassily (Pavlovich)

**Akst, Daniel** 1956- ............... **CLC 109**
See also CA 161

**Aksyonov, Vassily (Pavlovich)** 1932- ............... **CLC 22, 37, 101**
See also CA 53-56; CANR 12, 48, 77; CWW 2

**Akutagawa Ryunosuke** 1892-1927 ............... **TCLC 16; SSC 44**
See also CA 117; 154; DLB 180; MJW; RGSF; RGWL

**Alain** 1868-1951 ............... **TCLC 41**
See also CA 163; GFL 1789 to the Present

**Alain-Fournier** ............... **TCLC 6**
See also Fournier, Henri Alban
See also DLB 65; GFL 1789 to the Present; RGWL

**Alarcon, Pedro Antonio de** 1833-1891 ............... **NCLC 1**

**Alas (y Urena), Leopoldo (Enrique Garcia)** 1852-1901 ............... **TCLC 29**
See also CA 113; 131; HW 1; RGSF

**Albee, Edward (Franklin III)** 1928- . **CLC 1, 2, 3, 5, 9, 11, 13, 25, 53, 86, 113; DA; DAB; DAC; DAM DRAM, MST; DC 11; WLC**
See also AITN 1; AMW; CA 5-8R; CABS 3; CAD; CANR 8, 54, 74; CD; CDALB 1941-1968; DA3; DFS 2, 3, 8, 10, 13; DLB 7; INT CANR-8; LAIT 4; MTCW 1, 2; RGAL; TUS

**Alberti, Rafael** 1902-1999 ............... **CLC 7**
See also CA 85-88; 185; CANR 81; DLB 108; HW 2; RGWL

**Albert the Great** 1193(?)-1280 ....... **CMLC 16**
See also DLB 115

**Alcala-Galiano, Juan Valera y**
See Valera y Alcala-Galiano, Juan

**Alcayaga, Lucila Godoy**
See Godoy Alcayaga, Lucila

**Alcott, Amos Bronson** 1799-1888 .... **NCLC 1**
See also DLB 1, 223

**Alcott, Louisa May** 1832-1888 . **NCLC 6, 58, 83; DA; DAB; DAC; DAM MST, NOV; SSC 27; WLC**
See also AAYA 20; AMWS 1; BPFB 1; BYA 2; CDALB 1865-1917; CLR 1, 38; DA3; DLB 1, 42, 79, 223, 239, 242; DLBD 14; FW; JRDA; LAIT 2; MAICYA; NFS 12; RGAL; SATA 100; YABC 1; YAW

**Aldanov, M. A.**
See Aldanov, Mark (Alexandrovich)

**Aldanov, Mark (Alexandrovich)** 1886(?)-1957 ............... **TCLC 23**
See also CA 118; 181

**Aldington, Richard** 1892-1962 ......... **CLC 49**
See also CA 85-88; CANR 45; DLB 20, 36, 100, 149; RGEL

**Aldiss, Brian W(ilson)** 1925- . **CLC 5, 14, 40; DAM NOV; SSC 36**
See also AAYA 42; CA 5-8R; CAAE 190; CAAS 2; CANR 5, 28, 64; CN; DLB 14; MTCW 1, 2; SATA 34; SFW

**Alegria, Claribel** 1924- ........... **CLC 75; DAM MULT; HLCS 1; PC 26**
See also CA 131; CAAS 15; CANR 66, 94; CWW 2; DLB 145; HW 1; MTCW 1

**Alegria, Fernando** 1918- ................ **CLC 57**
See also CA 9-12R; CANR 5, 32, 72; HW 1, 2

**Aleichem, Sholom** ....... **TCLC 1, 35; SSC 33**
See also Rabinovitch, Sholem

**Aleixandre, Vicente** 1898-1984 ... **TCLC 113; HLCS 1**
See also CANR 81; HW 2; RGWL

**Alepoudelis, Odysseus**
See Elytis, Odysseus
See also CWW 2

**Aleshkovsky, Joseph** 1929-
See Aleshkovsky, Yuz
See also CA 121; 128

**Aleshkovsky, Yuz** ............... **CLC 44**
See also Aleshkovsky, Joseph

**Alexander, Lloyd (Chudley)** 1924- ... **CLC 35**
See also AAYA 1, 27; BPFB 1; BYA 5, 6, 7, 9, 10, 11; CA 1-4R; CANR 1, 24, 38, 55; CLR 1, 5, 48; CWRI; DLB 52; FANT; JRDA; MAICYA; MAICYAS; MTCW 1; SAAS 19; SATA 3, 49, 81; SUFW; WYA; YAW

**Alexander, Meena** 1951- ................ **CLC 121**
See also CA 115; CANR 38, 70; CP; CWP; FW

**Alexander, Samuel** 1859-1938 ........ **TCLC 77**

**Alexie, Sherman (Joseph, Jr.)** 1966- ................ **CLC 96; DAM MULT**
See also AAYA 28; CA 138; CANR 95; DA3; DLB 175, 206; MTCW 1; NNAL

**Alfau, Felipe** 1902-1999 .................... **CLC 66**
See also CA 137

**Alfieri, Vittorio** 1749-1803 ............ **NCLC 101**
See also EW; RGWL

**Alfred, Jean Gaston**
See Ponge, Francis

**Alger, Horatio, Jr.** 1832-1899 .... **NCLC 8, 83**
See also DLB 42; LAIT 2; RGAL; SATA 16; TUS

**Algren, Nelson** 1909-1981 ..... **CLC 4, 10, 33; SSC 33**
See also AMWS 9; BPFB 1; CA 13-16R; 103; CANR 20, 61; CDALB 1941-1968; DLB 9; DLBY 81, 82, 00; MTCW 1, 2; RGAL; RGSF

**Ali, Ahmed** 1908-1998 ...................... **CLC 69**
See also CA 25-28R; CANR 15, 34

**Alighieri, Dante**
See Dante

**Allan, John B.**
See Westlake, Donald E(dwin)

**Allan, Sidney**
See Hartmann, Sadakichi

**Allan, Sydney**
See Hartmann, Sadakichi

**Allard, Janet** ............... **CLC 59**

**Allen, Edward** 1948- ........................ **CLC 59**

**Allen, Fred** 1894-1956 .................... **TCLC 87**

**Allen, Paula Gunn** 1939- ....... **CLC 84; DAM MULT**
See also AMWS 4; CA 112; 143; CANR 63; CWP; DA3; DLB 175; FW; MTCW 1; NNAL; RGAL

**Allen, Roland**
See Ayckbourn, Alan

**Allen, Sarah A.**
See Hopkins, Pauline Elizabeth

**Allen, Sidney H.**
See Hartmann, Sadakichi

**Allen, Woody** 1935- ......... **CLC 16, 52; DAM POP**
See also AAYA 10; CA 33-36R; CANR 27, 38, 63; DLB 44; MTCW 1

**Allende, Isabel** 1942- . **CLC 39, 57, 97; DAM MULT, NOV; HLC 1; WLCS**
See also AAYA 18; CA 125; 130; CANR 51, 74; CWW 2; DA3; DLB 145; DNFS; FW; HW 1, 2; INT 130; LAIT 5; MTCW 1, 2; NCFS 1; NFS 6; RGSF; SSFS 11; WLIT 1

**Alleyn, Ellen**
See Rossetti, Christina (Georgina)

**Alleyne, Carla D.** ............... **CLC 65**

**Allingham, Margery (Louise)** 1904-1966 ............... **CLC 19**
See also CA 5-8R; 25-28R; CANR 4, 58; CMW; DLB 77; MSW; MTCW 1, 2

**Allingham, William** 1824-1889 ...... **NCLC 25**
See also DLB 35; RGEL

**Allison, Dorothy E.** 1949- ................. **CLC 78**
See also CA 140; CANR 66; CSW; DA3; FW; MTCW 1; NFS 11; RGAL

**Alloula, Malek** ............... **CLC 65**

**Allston, Washington** 1779-1843 ....... **NCLC 2**
See also DLB 1, 235

**Almedingen, E. M.** ............... **CLC 12**
See also Almedingen, Martha Edith von
See also SATA 3

**Almedingen, Martha Edith von** 1898-1971
See Almedingen, E. M.
See also CA 1-4R; CANR 1

**Almodovar, Pedro** 1949(?)- ............ **CLC 114; HLCS 1**
See also CA 133; CANR 72; HW 2

**Almqvist, Carl Jonas Love** 1793-1866 ............... **NCLC 42**

**Alonso, Damaso** 1898-1990 ............... **CLC 14**
See also CA 110; 131; 130; CANR 72; DLB 108; HW 1, 2

**Alov**
See Gogol, Nikolai (Vasilyevich)

**Alta** 1942- ............... **CLC 19**
See also CA 57-60

**Alter, Robert B(ernard)** 1935- .......... **CLC 34**
See also CA 49-52; CANR 1, 47, 100

**Alther, Lisa** 1944- ............... **CLC 7, 41**
See also BPFB 1; CA 65-68; CAAS 30; CANR 12, 30, 51; CN; CSW; GLL 2; MTCW 1

**Althusser, L.**
See Althusser, Louis

**Althusser, Louis** 1918-1990 ............... **CLC 106**
See also CA 131; 132; CANR 102; DLB 242

**Altman, Robert** 1925- ................. **CLC 16, 116**
See also CA 73-76; CANR 43

**Alurista**
See Urista, Alberto H.
See also DLB 82; HLCS 1

**Alvarez, A(lfred)** 1929- ................. **CLC 5, 13**
See also CA 1-4R; CANR 3, 33, 63, 101; CN; CP; DLB 14, 40

**Alvarez, Alejandro Rodriguez** 1903-1965
See Casona, Alejandro
See also CA 131; 93-96; HW 1

**Alvarez, Julia** 1950- .......... **CLC 93; HLCS 1**
See also AAYA 25; AMWS 7; CA 147; CANR 69, 101; DA3; MTCW 1; NFS 5, 9; WLIT 1

**Alvaro, Corrado** 1896-1956 ............ **TCLC 60**
See also CA 163

**Amado, Jorge** 1912-2001 ... **CLC 13, 40, 106; DAM MULT, NOV; HLC 1**
See also CA 77-80; CANR 35, 74; DLB 113; HW 2; LAW; MTCW 1, 2; RGWL; WLIT 1

**Ambler, Eric** 1909-1998 ............. **CLC 4, 6, 9**
See also BRWS 4; CA 9-12R; 171; CANR 7, 38, 74; CMW; CN; DLB 77; MSW; MTCW 1, 2

**Ambrose, Stephen E(dward)** 1936- ........................................ **CLC 145**
See also CA 1-4R; CANR 3, 43, 57, 83; NCFS 2; SATA 40

**Amichai, Yehuda** 1924-2000 .. **CLC 9, 22, 57, 116**
See also CA 85-88; 189; CANR 46, 60, 99; CWW 2; MTCW 1

**Amichai, Yehudah**
See Amichai, Yehuda

**Amiel, Henri Frederic** 1821-1881 .... **NCLC 4**

**Amis, Kingsley (William)** 1922-1995 ...... **CLC 1, 2, 3, 5, 8, 13, 40, 44, 129; DA; DAB; DAC; DAM MST, NOV**
See also AITN 2; BPFB 1; BRWS 2; CA 9-12R; 150; CANR 8, 28, 54; CDBLB 1945-1960; CN; CP; DA3; DLB 15, 27, 100, 139; DLBY 96; HGG; INT CANR-8; MTCW 1, 2; RGEL; RGSF; SFW

**Amis, Martin (Louis)** 1949- .... **CLC 4, 9, 38, 62, 101**
See also BEST 90:3; BRWS 4; CA 65-68; CANR 8, 27, 54, 73, 95; CN; DA3; DLB 14, 194; INT CANR-27; MTCW 1

**Ammons, A(rchie) R(andolph)** 1926-2001 ...... **CLC 2, 3, 5, 8, 9, 25, 57, 108; DAM POET; PC 16**
See also AITN 1; AMWS 7; CA 9-12R; 193; CANR 6, 36, 51, 73; CP; CSW; DLB 5, 165; MTCW 1, 2; RGAL

**Amo, Tauraatua i**
See Adams, Henry (Brooks)

**Amory, Thomas** 1691(?)-1788 ............. **LC 48**

**Anand, Mulk Raj** 1905- .. **CLC 23, 93; DAM NOV**
See also CA 65-68; CANR 32, 64; CN; MTCW 1, 2; RGSF

**Anatol**
See Schnitzler, Arthur

**Anaximander** c. 611B.C.-c. 546B.C. ..................................... **CMLC 22**

**Anaya, Rudolfo A(lfonso)** 1937- ...... **CLC 23, 148; DAM MULT, NOV; HLC 1**
See also AAYA 20; BYA 13; CA 45-48; CAAS 4; CANR 1, 32, 51; CN; DLB 82, 206; HW 1; LAIT 4; MTCW 1, 2; NFS 12; RGAL; RGSF; WLIT 1

**Andersen, Hans Christian** 1805-1875 ....... **NCLC 7, 79; DA; DAB; DAC; DAM MST, POP; SSC 6; WLC**
See also CLR 6; DA3; EW; MAICYA; RGSF; RGWL; SATA 100; YABC 1

**Anderson, C. Farley**
See Mencken, H(enry) L(ouis); Nathan, George Jean

**Anderson, Jessica (Margaret) Queale** 1916- .................................... **CLC 37**
See also CA 9-12R; CANR 4, 62; CN

**Anderson, Jon (Victor)** 1940- . **CLC 9; DAM POET**
See also CA 25-28R; CANR 20

**Anderson, Lindsay (Gordon)** 1923-1994 ................................ **CLC 20**
See also CA 125; 128; 146; CANR 77

**Anderson, Maxwell** 1888-1959 ...... **TCLC 2; DAM DRAM**
See also CA 105; 152; DLB 7, 228; MTCW 2; RGAL

**Anderson, Poul (William)** 1926-2001 ..................... **CLC 15**
See also AAYA 5, 34; BPFB 1; BYA 6, 8, 9; CA 1-4R, 181; CAAE 181; CAAS 2; CANR 2, 15, 34, 64; CLR 58; DLB 8; FANT; INT CANR-15; MTCW 1, 2; SATA 90; SATA-Brief 39; SATA-Essay 106; SCFW 2; SFW; SUFW

**Anderson, Robert (Woodruff)** 1917- .................. **CLC 23; DAM DRAM**
See also AITN 1; CA 21-24R; CANR 32; DLB 7; LAIT 5

**Anderson, Roberta Joan**
See Mitchell, Joni

**Anderson, Sherwood** 1876-1941 ...... **TCLC 1, 10, 24; DA; DAB; DAC; DAM MST, NOV; SSC 1, 46; WLC**
See also AAYA 30; AMW; BPFB 1; CA 104; 121; CANR 61; CDALB 1917-1929; DA3; DLB 4, 9, 86; DLBD 1; EXPS; GLL 2; MTCW 1, 2; NFS 4; RGAL; RGSF; SSFS 4, 10, 11

**Andier, Pierre**
See Desnos, Robert

**Andouard**
See Giraudoux, Jean(-Hippolyte)

**Andrade, Carlos Drummond de** ..... **CLC 18**
See also Drummond de Andrade, Carlos
See also RGWL

**Andrade, Mario de** ........................ **TCLC 43**
See also de Andrade, Mario
See also LAW; RGWL; WLIT 1

**Andreae, Johann V(alentin)** 1586-1654 ........................ **LC 32**
See also DLB 164

**Andreas Capellanus** fl. c. 1185- .... **CMLC 45**
See also DLB 208

**Andreas-Salome, Lou** 1861-1937 ... **TCLC 56**
See also CA 178; DLB 66

**Andress, Lesley**
See Sanders, Lawrence

**Andrewes, Lancelot** 1555-1626 .............. **LC 5**
See also DLB 151, 172

**Andrews, Cicily Fairfield**
See West, Rebecca

**Andrews, Elton V.**
See Pohl, Frederik

**Andreyev, Leonid (Nikolaevich)** 1871-1919 ................................ **TCLC 3**
See also CA 104; 185

**Andric, Ivo** 1892-1975 .......... **CLC 8; SSC 36**
See also CA 81-84; 57-60; CANR 43, 60; DLB 147; EW; MTCW 1; RGSF; RGWL

**Androvar**
See Prado (Calvo), Pedro

**Angelique, Pierre**
See Bataille, Georges

**Angell, Roger** 1920- ........................... **CLC 26**
See also CA 57-60; CANR 13, 44, 70; DLB 171, 185

**Angelou, Maya** 1928- .... **CLC 12, 35, 64, 77; BLC 1; DA; DAB; DAC; DAM MST, MULT, POET, POP; PC 32; WLCS**
See also AAYA 7, 20; AMWS 4; BPFB 1; BW 2, 3; BYA 2; CA 65-68; CANR 19, 42, 65; CDALBS; CLR 53; CP; CPW; CSW; CWP; DA3; DLB 38; EXPN; EXPP; LAIT 4; MAWW; MTCW 1, 2; NCFS 2; NFS 2; PFS 2, 3; RGAL; SATA 49; YAW

**Anna Comnena** 1083-1153 ............ **CMLC 25**

**Annensky, Innokenty (Fyodorovich)** 1856-1909 ................................ **TCLC 14**
See also CA 110; 155

**Annunzio, Gabriele d'**
See D'Annunzio, Gabriele

**Anodos**
See Coleridge, Mary E(lizabeth)

**Anon, Charles Robert**
See Pessoa, Fernando (Antonio Nogueira)

**Anouilh, Jean (Marie Lucien Pierre)** 1910-1987 ........ **CLC 1, 3, 8, 13, 40, 50; DAM DRAM; DC 8**
See also CA 17-20R; 123; CANR 32; DFS 9, 10; EW; GFL 1789 to the Present; MTCW 1, 2; RGWL

**Anthony, Florence**
See Ai

**Anthony, John**
See Ciardi, John (Anthony)

**Anthony, Peter**
See Shaffer, Anthony (Joshua); Shaffer, Peter (Levin)

**Anthony, Piers** 1934- .... **CLC 35; DAM POP**
See also AAYA 11; BYA 7; CA 21-24R; CANR 28, 56, 73, 102; CPW; DLB 8; FANT; MTCW 1, 2; SAAS 22; SATA 84; SFW; YAW

**Anthony, Susan B(rownell)** 1820-1906 ............................... **TCLC 84**
See also FW

**Antoine, Marc**
See Proust, (Valentin-Louis-George-Eugene-)Marcel

**Antoninus, Brother**
See Everson, William (Oliver)

**Antonioni, Michelangelo** 1912- ........ **CLC 20, 144**
See also CA 73-76; CANR 45, 77

**Antschel, Paul** 1920-1970
See Celan, Paul
See also CA 85-88; CANR 33, 61; MTCW 1

**Anwar, Chairil** 1922-1949 ............. **TCLC 22**
See also CA 121

**Anzaldua, Gloria (Evanjelina)** 1942-
See also CA 175; CSW; CWP; DLB 122; FW; HLCS 1; RGAL

**Apess, William** 1798-1839(?) ........ **NCLC 73; DAM MULT**
See also DLB 175, 243; NNAL

**Apollinaire, Guillaume** 1880-1918 .. **TCLC 3, 8, 51; DAM POET; PC 7**
See also CA 152; EW; GFL 1789 to the Present; MTCW 1; RGWL; WP

**Apollonius of Rhodes**
See Apollonius Rhodius
See also AW 1; RGWL

**Apollonius Rhodius** c. 300B.C.-c. 220B.C. ..................................... **CMLC 28**
See also Apollonius of Rhodes
See also DLB 176

**Appelfeld, Aharon** 1932- ... **CLC 23, 47; SSC 42**
See also CA 112; 133; CANR 86; CWW 2; RGSF

**Apple, Max (Isaac)** 1941- .............. **CLC 9, 33**
See also CA 81-84; CANR 19, 54; DLB 130

**Appleman, Philip (Dean)** 1926- ........ **CLC 51**
See also CA 13-16R; CAAS 18; CANR 6, 29, 56

**Appleton, Lawrence**
See Lovecraft, H(oward) P(hillips)

**Apteryx**
See Eliot, T(homas) S(tearns)

**Apuleius, (Lucius Madaurensis)** 125(?)-175(?) ............................ **CMLC 1**
See also AW 2; DLB 211; RGWL; SUFW

**Aquin, Hubert** 1929-1977 .................. **CLC 15**
See also CA 105; DLB 53

**Aquinas, Thomas** 1224(?)-1274 ..... **CMLC 33**
See also DLB 115; EW

**Aragon, Louis** 1897-1982 .. **CLC 3, 22; DAM NOV, POET**
See also CA 69-72; 108; CANR 28, 71; DLB 72; EW; GFL 1789 to the Present; GLL 2; MTCW 1, 2; RGWL

**Arany, Janos** 1817-1882 ................. **NCLC 34**

**Aranyos, Kakay** 1847-1910
See Mikszath, Kalman

**Arbuthnot, John** 1667-1735 ................. **LC 1**
See also DLB 101

**Archer, Herbert Winslow**
See Mencken, H(enry) L(ouis)

**Archer, Jeffrey (Howard)** 1940- ...... **CLC 28; DAM POP**
See also AAYA 16; BEST 89:3; BPFB 1; CA 77-80; CANR 22, 52, 95; CPW; DA3; INT CANR-22

**Archer, Jules** 1915- ............................. **CLC 12**
See also CA 9-12R; CANR 6, 69; SAAS 5; SATA 4, 85

**Archer, Lee**
See Ellison, Harlan (Jay)

**Archilochus** c. 7th cent. B.C.- ........ **CMLC 44**
See also DLB 176

**Arden, John** 1930- ....... **CLC 6, 13, 15; DAM DRAM**
See also BRWS 2; CA 13-16R; CAAS 4; CANR 31, 65, 67; CBD; CD; DFS 9; DLB 13, 245; MTCW 1

**Arenas, Reinaldo** 1943-1990 . **CLC 41; DAM MULT; HLC 1**
See also CA 124; 128; 133; CANR 73; DLB 145; GLL 2; HW 1; LAW; MTCW 1; RGSF; WLIT 1

**Arendt, Hannah** 1906-1975 ........ **CLC 66, 98**
See also CA 17-20R; 61-64; CANR 26, 60; DLB 242; MTCW 1, 2

**Aretino, Pietro** 1492-1556 .................... **LC 12**
See also RGWL

**Arghezi, Tudor** ................................. **CLC 80**
See also Theodorescu, Ion N.
See also CA 167; DLB 220

**Arguedas, Jose Maria** 1911-1969 .... **CLC 10, 18; HLCS 1**
See also CA 89-92; CANR 73; DLB 113; HW 1; LAW; RGWL; WLIT 1

**Argueta, Manlio** 1936- ....................... **CLC 31**
See also CA 131; CANR 73; CWW 2; DLB 145; HW 1

**Arias, Ron(ald Francis)** 1941-
See also CA 131; CANR 81; DAM MULT; DLB 82; HLC 1; HW 1, 2; MTCW 2

**Ariosto, Ludovico** 1474-1533 ................ **LC 6**
See also EW; RGWL

**Aristides**
See Epstein, Joseph

**Aristophanes** 450B.C.-385B.C. ........ **CMLC 4; DA; DAB; DAC; DAM DRAM, MST; DC 2; WLCS**
See also AW 1; DA3; DFS 10; DLB 176; RGWL

**Aristotle** 384B.C.-322B.C. ..... **CMLC 31; DA; DAB; DAC; DAM MST; WLCS**
See also AW 1; DA3; DLB 176; RGEL

**Arlt, Roberto (Godofredo Christophersen)** 1900-1942 ....... **TCLC 29; DAM MULT; HLC 1**
See also CA 123; 131; CANR 67; HW 1, 2; LAW

**Armah, Ayi Kwei** 1939- ....... **CLC 5, 33, 136; BLC 1; DAM MULT, POET**
See also AFW; BW 1; CA 61-64; CANR 21, 64; CN; DLB 117; MTCW 1; WLIT 2

**Armatrading, Joan** 1950- .................. **CLC 17**
See also CA 114; 186

**Arnette, Robert**
See Silverberg, Robert

**Arnim, Achim von (Ludwig Joachim von Arnim)** 1781-1831 ..... **NCLC 5; SSC 29**
See also DLB 90

**Arnim, Bettina von** 1785-1859 ....... **NCLC 38**
See also DLB 90; RGWL

**Arnold, Matthew** 1822-1888 ..... **NCLC 6, 29, 89; DA; DAB; DAC; DAM MST, POET; PC 5; WLC**
See also BRW 5; CDBLB 1832-1890; DLB 32, 57; EXPP; PAB; PFS 2; WP

**Arnold, Thomas** 1795-1842 ............ **NCLC 18**
See also DLB 55

**Arnow, Harriette (Louisa) Simpson** 1908-1986 ......................... **CLC 2, 7, 18**
See also BPFB 1; CA 9-12R; 118; CANR 14; DLB 6; FW; MTCW 1, 2; RHW; SATA 42; SATA-Obit 47

**Arouet, Francois-Marie**
See Voltaire

**Arp, Hans**
See Arp, Jean

**Arp, Jean** 1887-1966 ........................... **CLC 5**
See also CA 81-84; 25-28R; CANR 42, 77; EW

**Arrabal**
See Arrabal, Fernando

**Arrabal, Fernando** 1932- ... **CLC 2, 9, 18, 58**
See also CA 9-12R; CANR 15

**Arreola, Juan Jose** 1918- .... **CLC 147; DAM MULT; HLC 1; SSC 38**
See also CA 113; 131; CANR 81; DLB 113; DNFS; HW 1, 2; LAW; RGSF

**Arrian** c. 89(?)-c. 155(?) ................ **CMLC 43**
See also DLB 176

**Arrick, Fran** ..................................... **CLC 30**
See also Gaberman, Judie Angell
See also BYA 6

**Artaud, Antonin (Marie Joseph)** 1896-1948 . **TCLC 3, 36; DAM DRAM; DC 14**
See also CA 104; 149; DA3; EW; GFL 1789 to the Present; MTCW 1; RGWL

**Arthur, Ruth M(abel)** 1905-1979 ..... **CLC 12**
See also CA 9-12R; 85-88; CANR 4; CWRI; SATA 7, 26

**Artsybashev, Mikhail (Petrovich)** 1878-1927 ................................. **TCLC 31**
See also CA 170

**Arundel, Honor (Morfydd)** 1919-1973 ................................. **CLC 17**
See also CA 21-22; 41-44R; CAP 2; CLR 35; CWRI; SATA 4; SATA-Obit 24

**Arzner, Dorothy** 1900-1979 ............... **CLC 98**

**Asch, Sholem** 1880-1957 ................... **TCLC 3**
See also CA 105; GLL 2

**Ash, Shalom**
See Asch, Sholem

**Ashbery, John (Lawrence)** 1927- .. **CLC 2, 3, 4, 6, 9, 13, 15, 25, 41, 77, 125; DAM POET; PC 26**
See also Berry, Jonas
See also AMWS 3; CA 5-8R; CANR 9, 37, 66, 102; CP; DA3; DLB 5, 165; DLBY 81; INT CANR-9; MTCW 1, 2; PAB; PFS 11; RGAL; WP

**Ashdown, Clifford**
See Freeman, R(ichard) Austin

**Ashe, Gordon**
See Creasey, John

**Ashton-Warner, Sylvia (Constance)** 1908-1984 ................................. **CLC 19**
See also CA 69-72; 112; CANR 29; MTCW 1, 2

**Asimov, Isaac** 1920-1992 ..... **CLC 1, 3, 9, 19, 26, 76, 92; DAM POP**
See also AAYA 13; BEST 90:2; BPFB 1; BYA 4, 6, 7, 9; CA 1-4R; 137; CANR 2, 19, 36, 60; CLR 12; CMW; CPW; DA3; DLB 8; DLBY 92; INT CANR-19; JRDA; LAIT 5; MAICYA; MTCW 1, 2; RGAL; SATA 1, 26, 74; SCFW 2; SFW; YAW

**Assis, Joaquim Maria Machado de**
See Machado de Assis, Joaquim Maria

**Astell, Mary** 1666-1731 ....................... **LC 68**
See also FW

**Astley, Thea (Beatrice May)** 1925- .. **CLC 41**
See also CA 65-68; CANR 11, 43, 78; CN

**Aston, James**
See White, T(erence) H(anbury)

**Asturias, Miguel Angel** 1899-1974 .... **CLC 3, 8, 13; DAM MULT, NOV; HLC 1**
See also CA 25-28; 49-52; CANR 32; CAP 2; DA3; DLB 113; HW 1; LAW; MTCW 1, 2; RGWL; WLIT 1

**Atares, Carlos Saura**
See Saura (Atares), Carlos

**Athanasius** c. 295-c. 373 ................ **CMLC 48**

**Atheling, William**
See Pound, Ezra (Weston Loomis)

**Atheling, William, Jr.**
See Blish, James (Benjamin)

**Atherton, Gertrude (Franklin Horn)** 1857-1948 ................................. **TCLC 2**
See also CA 104; 155; DLB 9, 78, 186; HGG; RGAL; SUFW; TCWW 2

**Atherton, Lucius**
See Masters, Edgar Lee

**Atkins, Jack**
See Harris, Mark

**Atkinson, Kate** ............................. **CLC 99**
See also CA 166; CANR 101

**Attaway, William (Alexander)** 1911-1986 ......... **CLC 92; BLC 1; DAM MULT**
See also BW 2, 3; CA 143; CANR 82; DLB 76

**Atticus**
See Fleming, Ian (Lancaster); Wilson, (Thomas) Woodrow

**Atwood, Margaret (Eleanor)** 1939- ... **CLC 2, 3, 4, 8, 13, 15, 25, 44, 84, 135; DA; DAB; DAC; DAM MST, NOV, POET; PC 8; SSC 2, 46; WLC**
See also AAYA 12; BEST 89:2; BPFB 1; CA 49-52; CANR 3, 24, 33, 59, 95; CN; CP; CPW; CWP; DA3; DLB 53; EXPN; FW; INT CANR-24; LAIT 5; MTCW 1, 2; NFS 4, 12; PFS 7; RGSF; SATA 50; SSFS 3, 13; YAW

**Aubigny, Pierre d'**
See Mencken, H(enry) L(ouis)

**Aubin, Penelope** 1685-1731(?) .............. **LC 9**
See also DLB 39

**Auden, W(ystan) H(ugh)** 1907-1973 . **CLC 1, 2, 3, 4, 6, 9, 11, 14, 43, 123; DA; DAB; DAC; DAM DRAM, MST, POET; PC 1; WLC**
See also AAYA 18; AMWS 2; BRW 7; CA 9-12R; 45-48; CANR 5, 61; CDBLB 1914-1945; DA3; DLB 10, 20; EXPP; MTCW 1, 2; PAB; PFS 1, 3, 4, 10; WP

**Audiberti, Jacques** 1900-1965 ......... **CLC 38; DAM DRAM**
See also CA 25-28R

**Audubon, John James** 1785-1851 . **NCLC 47**
See also ANW

**Auel, Jean M(arie)** 1936- ......... **CLC 31, 107; DAM POP**
See also AAYA 7; BEST 90:4; BPFB 1; CA 103; CANR 21, 64; CPW; DA3; INT CANR-21; NFS 11; RHW; SATA 91

**Auerbach, Erich** 1892-1957 ............ **TCLC 43**
See also CA 118; 155

**Augier, Emile** 1820-1889 ................ **NCLC 31**
See also DLB 192; GFL 1789 to the Present

**August, John**
See De Voto, Bernard (Augustine)

**Augustine, St.** 354-430 .......... **CMLC 6; DA; DAB; DAC; DAM MST; WLCS**
See also DA3; DLB 115; EW; RGWL

**Aunt Belinda**
See Braddon, Mary Elizabeth

**Aurelius**
See Bourne, Randolph S(illiman)

**Aurelius, Marcus** 121-180 ............. **CMLC 45**
See also Marcus Aurelius
See also RGWL

**Aurobindo, Sri**
See Ghose, Aurabinda

**Austen, Jane** 1775-1817 ...... **NCLC 1, 13, 19, 33, 51, 81, 95; DA; DAB; DAC; DAM MST, NOV; WLC**
See also AAYA 19; BRW 4; BYA 3; CDBLB 1789-1832; DA3; DLB 116; EXPN; LAIT 2; NFS 1; WLIT 3; WYAS 1

**Auster, Paul** 1947- ...................... **CLC 47, 131**
See also CA 69-72; CANR 23, 52, 75; CMW; CN; DA3; DLB 227; MTCW 1

**Austin, Frank**
See Faust, Frederick (Schiller)
See also TCWW 2

**Austin, Mary (Hunter)** 1868-1934 . **TCLC 25**
See also Stairs, Gordon
See also ANW; CA 109; 178; DLB 9, 78, 206, 221; FW; TCWW 2

**Averroes** 1126-1198 .......................... **CMLC 7**
See also DLB 115

**Avicenna** 980-1037 ............................ **CMLC 16**
See also DLB 115

**Avison, Margaret** 1918- ........... **CLC 2, 4, 97; DAC; DAM POET**
See also CA 17-20R; CP; DLB 53; MTCW 1

**Axton, David**
See Koontz, Dean R(ay)

**Ayckbourn, Alan** 1939- ...... **CLC 5, 8, 18, 33, 74; DAB; DAM DRAM; DC 13**
See also BRWS 5; CA 21-24R; CANR 31, 59; CBD; CD; DFS 7; DLB 13, 245; MTCW 1, 2

**Aydy, Catherine**
See Tennant, Emma (Christina)

**Ayme, Marcel (Andre)** 1902-1967 ... **CLC 11; SSC 41**
See also CA 89-92; CANR 67; CLR 25; DLB 72; EW; GFL 1789 to the Present; RGSF; RGWL; SATA 91

**Ayrton, Michael** 1921-1975 ................. **CLC 7**
See also CA 5-8R; 61-64; CANR 9, 21

**Azorin** ................................................. **CLC 11**
See also Martinez Ruiz, Jose
See also EW

**Azuela, Mariano** 1873-1952 . **TCLC 3; DAM MULT; HLC 1**
See also CA 104; 131; CANR 81; HW 1, 2; LAW; MTCW 1, 2

**Baastad, Babbis Friis**
See Friis-Baastad, Babbis Ellinor

**Bab**
See Gilbert, W(illiam) S(chwenck)

**Babbis, Eleanor**
See Friis-Baastad, Babbis Ellinor

**Babel, Isaac**
See Babel, Isaak (Emmanuilovich)
See also EW; SSFS 10

**Babel, Isaak (Emmanuilovich)** 1894-1941(?) ......... **TCLC 2, 13; SSC 16**
See also Babel, Isaac
See also CA 104; 155; MTCW 1; RGSF; RGWL

**Babits, Mihaly** 1883-1941 ............... **TCLC 14**
See also CA 114

**Babur** 1483-1530 ...................... **LC 18**

**Babylas** 1898-1962
See Ghelderode, Michel de

**Baca, Jimmy Santiago** 1952-
See also CA 131; CANR 81, 90; CP; DAM MULT; DLB 122; HLC 1; HW 1, 2

**Bacchelli, Riccardo** 1891-1985 .......... **CLC 19**
See also CA 29-32R; 117

**Bach, Richard (David)** 1936- ............ **CLC 14; DAM NOV, POP**
See also AITN 1; BEST 89:2; BPFB 1; BYA 5; CA 9-12R; CANR 18, 93; CPW; FANT; MTCW 1; SATA 13

**Bachman, Richard**
See King, Stephen (Edwin)

**Bachmann, Ingeborg** 1926-1973 ....... **CLC 69**
See also CA 93-96; 45-48; CANR 69; DLB 85; RGWL

**Bacon, Francis** 1561-1626 ............... **LC 18, 32**
See also BRW 1; CDBLB Before 1660; DLB 151, 236; RGEL

**Bacon, Roger** 1214(?)-1294 ............... **CMLC 14**
See also DLB 115

**Bacovia, George** 1881-1957 ............ **TCLC 24**
See also Vasiliu, Gheorghe
See also DLB 220

**Badanes, Jerome** 1937- ...................... **CLC 59**

**Bagehot, Walter** 1826-1877 ............ **NCLC 10**
See also DLB 55

**Bagnold, Enid** 1889-1981 ...... **CLC 25; DAM DRAM**
See also BYA 2; CA 5-8R; 103; CANR 5, 40; CBD; CWD; CWRI; DLB 13, 160, 191, 245; FW; MAICYA; RGEL; SATA 1, 25

**Bagritsky, Eduard** 1895-1934 ......... **TCLC 60**

**Bagrjana, Elisaveta**
See Belcheva, Elisaveta

**Bagryana, Elisaveta** ........................ **CLC 10**
See also Belcheva, Elisaveta
See also CA 178; DLB 147

**Bailey, Paul** 1937- ............................... **CLC 45**
See also CA 21-24R; CANR 16, 62; CN; DLB 14; GLL 2

**Baillie, Joanna** 1762-1851 ................. **NCLC 71**
See also DLB 93; RGEL

**Bainbridge, Beryl (Margaret)** 1934- . **CLC 4, 5, 8, 10, 14, 18, 22, 62, 130; DAM NOV**
See also BRWS 6; CA 21-24R; CANR 24, 55, 75, 88; CN; DLB 14, 231; MTCW 1, 2

**Baker, Elliott** 1922- ............................ **CLC 8**
See also CA 45-48; CANR 2, 63; CN

**Baker, Jean H.** ................................ **TCLC 3, 10**
See also Russell, George William

**Baker, Nicholson** 1957- .......... **CLC 61; DAM POP**
See also CA 135; CANR 63; CN; CPW; DA3; DLB 227

**Baker, Ray Stannard** 1870-1946 .... **TCLC 47**
See also CA 118

**Baker, Russell (Wayne)** 1925- ........... **CLC 31**
See also BEST 89:4; CA 57-60; CANR 11, 41, 59; MTCW 1, 2

**Bakhtin, M.**
See Bakhtin, Mikhail Mikhailovich

**Bakhtin, M. M.**
See Bakhtin, Mikhail Mikhailovich

**Bakhtin, Mikhail**
See Bakhtin, Mikhail Mikhailovich

**Bakhtin, Mikhail Mikhailovich** 1895-1975 ...................... **CLC 83**
See also CA 128; 113; DLB 242

**Bakshi, Ralph** 1938(?)- ...................... **CLC 26**
See also CA 112; 138; IDFW 3

**Bakunin, Mikhail (Alexandrovich)** 1814-1876 ...................... **NCLC 25, 58**

**Baldwin, James (Arthur)** 1924-1987 . **CLC 1, 2, 3, 4, 5, 8, 13, 15, 17, 42, 50, 67, 90, 127; BLC 1; DA; DAB; DAC; DAM MST, MULT, NOV, POP; DC 1; SSC 10, 33; WLC**
See also AAYA 4, 34; AFAW 1, 2; AMWS 1; BW 1; CA 1-4R; 124; CABS 1; CAD; CANR 3, 24; CDALB 1941-1968; CPW; DA3; DFS 11; DLB 2, 7, 33; DLBY 87; EXPS; LAIT 5; MTCW 1, 2; NFS 4; RGAL; RGSF; SATA 9; SATA-Obit 54; SSFS 2

**Bale, John** 1495-1563 .......................... **LC 62**
See also DLB 132; RGEL

**Ball, Hugo** 1886-1927 .................... **TCLC 104**

**Ballard, J(ames) G(raham)** 1930- . **CLC 3, 6, 14, 36, 137; DAM NOV, POP; SSC 1**
See also AAYA 3; BRWS 5; CA 5-8R; CANR 15, 39, 65; CN; DA3; DLB 14, 207; HGG; MTCW 1, 2; NFS 8; RGEL; RGSF; SATA 93; SFW

**Balmont, Konstantin (Dmitriyevich)** 1867-1943 .......................... **TCLC 11**
See also CA 109; 155

**Baltausis, Vincas** 1847-1910
See Mikszath, Kalman

**Balzac, Honore de** 1799-1850 ... **NCLC 5, 35, 53; DA; DAB; DAC; DAM MST, NOV; SSC 5; WLC**
See also DA3; DLB 119; EW; GFL 1789 to the Present; RGSF; RGWL; SSFS 10

**Bambara, Toni Cade** 1939-1995 ...... **CLC 19, 88; BLC 1; DA; DAC; DAM MST, MULT; SSC 35; WLCS**
See also AAYA 5; AFAW 2; BW 2, 3; BYA 12; CA 29-32R; 150; CANR 24, 49, 81; CDALBS; DA3; DLB 38; EXPS; MTCW 1, 2; RGAL; RGSF; SATA 112; SSFS 4, 7, 12

**Bamdad, A.**
See Shamlu, Ahmad

**Banat, D. R.**
See Bradbury, Ray (Douglas)

**Bancroft, Laura**
See Baum, L(yman) Frank

**Banim, John** 1798-1842 ................... **NCLC 13**
See also DLB 116, 158, 159; RGEL

**Banim, Michael** 1796-1874 ............. **NCLC 13**
See also DLB 158, 159

**Banjo, The**
See Paterson, A(ndrew) B(arton)

**Banks, Iain**
See Banks, Iain M(enzies)

**Banks, Iain M(enzies)** 1954- ............. **CLC 34**
See also CA 123; 128; CANR 61; DLB 194; HGG; INT 128; SFW

**Banks, Lynne Reid** ........................... **CLC 23**
See also Reid Banks, Lynne
See also AAYA 6; BYA 7

**Banks, Russell** 1940- .... **CLC 37, 72; SSC 42**
See also AMWS 5; CA 65-68; CAAS 15; CANR 19, 52, 73; CN; DLB 130

**Banville, John** 1945- .................. **CLC 46, 118**
See also CA 117; 128; CN; DLB 14; INT 128

**Banville, Theodore (Faullain) de** 1832-1891 ................... **NCLC 9**
See also GFL 1789 to the Present

**Baraka, Amiri** 1934- . **CLC 1, 2, 3, 5, 10, 14, 33, 115; BLC 1; DA; DAC; DAM MST, MULT, POET, POP; DC 6; PC 4; WLCS**
See also Jones, LeRoi
See also AFAW 1, 2; AMWS 2; BW 2, 3; CA 21-24R; CAD; CANR 27, 38, 61; CD; CDALB 1941-1968; CP; CPW; DA3; DFS 3, 11; DLB 5, 7, 16, 38; DLBD 8; MTCW 1, 2; PFS 9; RGAL; WP

**Baratynsky, Evgenii Abramovich**
1800-1844 .................... **NCLC 103**
See also DLB 205

**Barbauld, Anna Laetitia**
1743-1825 .................... **NCLC 50**
See also DLB 107, 109, 142, 158; RGEL

**Barbellion, W. N. P.** .......... **TCLC 24**
See also Cummings, Bruce F(rederick)

**Barber, Benjamin R.** 1939- ........ **CLC 141**
See also CA 29-32R; CANR 12, 32, 64

**Barbera, Jack (Vincent)** 1945- ........ **CLC 44**
See also CA 110; CANR 45

**Barbey d'Aurevilly, Jules-Amedee**
1808-1889 ............ **NCLC 1; SSC 17**
See also DLB 119; GFL 1789 to the Present

**Barbour, John** c. 1316-1395 ........ **CMLC 33**
See also DLB 146

**Barbusse, Henri** 1873-1935 ........ **TCLC 5**
See also CA 105; 154; DLB 65; RGWL

**Barclay, Bill**
See Moorcock, Michael (John)

**Barclay, William Ewert**
See Moorcock, Michael (John)

**Barea, Arturo** 1897-1957 ........ **TCLC 14**
See also CA 111

**Barfoot, Joan** 1946- .................... **CLC 18**
See also CA 105

**Barham, Richard Harris**
1788-1845 .................... **NCLC 77**
See also DLB 159

**Baring, Maurice** 1874-1945 ........ **TCLC 8**
See also CA 105; 168; DLB 34; HGG

**Baring-Gould, Sabine** 1834-1924 ... **TCLC 88**
See also DLB 156, 190

**Barker, Clive** 1952- ...... **CLC 52; DAM POP**
See also AAYA 10; BEST 90:3; BPFB 1; CA 121; 129; CANR 71; CPW; DA3; HGG; INT 129; MTCW 1, 2

**Barker, George Granville**
1913-1991 ........ **CLC 8, 48; DAM POET**
See also CA 9-12R; 135; CANR 7, 38; DLB 20; MTCW 1

**Barker, Harley Granville**
See Granville-Barker, Harley
See also DLB 10

**Barker, Howard** 1946- .................... **CLC 37**
See also CA 102; CBD; CD; DLB 13, 233

**Barker, Jane** 1652-1732 .................... **LC 42**

**Barker, Pat(ricia)** 1943- ...... **CLC 32, 94, 146**
See also BRWS 4; CA 117; 122; CANR 50, 101; CN; INT 122

**Barlach, Ernst (Heinrich)**
1870-1938 .................... **TCLC 84**
See also CA 178; DLB 56, 118

**Barlow, Joel** 1754-1812 .................... **NCLC 23**
See also AMWS 2; DLB 37; RGAL

**Barnard, Mary (Ethel)** 1909- ........ **CLC 48**
See also CA 21-22; CAP 2

**Barnes, Djuna** 1892-1982 .... **CLC 3, 4, 8, 11, 29, 127; SSC 3**
See also Steptoe, Lydia
See also AMWS 3; CA 9-12R; 107; CAD; CANR 16, 55; CWD; DLB 4, 9, 45; GLL 1; MTCW 1, 2; RGAL

**Barnes, Julian (Patrick)** 1946- ........ **CLC 42, 141; DAB**
See also BRWS 4; CA 102; CANR 19, 54; CN; DLB 194; DLBY 93; MTCW 1

**Barnes, Peter** 1931- .................... **CLC 5, 56**
See also CA 65-68; CAAS 12; CANR 33, 34, 64; CBD; CD; DFS 6; DLB 13, 233; MTCW 1

**Barnes, William** 1801-1886 ........ **NCLC 75**
See also DLB 32

**Baroja (y Nessi), Pio** 1872-1956 ..... **TCLC 8; HLC 1**
See also CA 104; EW

**Baron, David**
See Pinter, Harold

**Baron Corvo**
See Rolfe, Frederick (William Serafino Austin Lewis Mary)

**Barondess, Sue K(aufman)**
1926-1977 .................... **CLC 8**
See also Kaufman, Sue
See also CA 1-4R; 69-72; CANR 1

**Baron de Teive**
See Pessoa, Fernando (Antonio Nogueira)

**Baroness Von S.**
See Zangwill, Israel

**Barres, (Auguste-)Maurice**
1862-1923 .................... **TCLC 47**
See also CA 164; DLB 123; GFL 1789 to the Present

**Barreto, Afonso Henrique de Lima**
See Lima Barreto, Afonso Henrique de

**Barrett, Andrea** 1965- .................... **CLC 150**
See also CA 156; CANR 92

**Barrett, Michele** .................... **CLC 65**

**Barrett, (Roger) Syd** 1946- .................... **CLC 35**

**Barrett, William (Christopher)**
1913-1992 .................... **CLC 27**
See also CA 13-16R; 139; CANR 11, 67; INT CANR-11

**Barrie, J(ames) M(atthew)**
1860-1937 ........ **TCLC 2; DAB; DAM DRAM**
See also BRWS 3; BYA 4, 5; CA 104; 136; CANR 77; CDBLB 1890-1914; CLR 16; CWRI; DA3; DFS 7; DLB 10, 141, 156; FANT; MAICYA; MTCW 1, 2; SATA 100; SUFW; WCH; WLIT 4; YABC 1

**Barrington, Michael**
See Moorcock, Michael (John)

**Barrol, Grady**
See Bograd, Larry

**Barry, Mike**
See Malzberg, Barry N(athaniel)

**Barry, Philip** 1896-1949 .................... **TCLC 11**
See also CA 109; DFS 9; DLB 7, 228; RGAL

**Bart, Andre Schwarz**
See Schwarz-Bart, Andre

**Barth, John (Simmons)** 1930- ... **CLC 1, 2, 3, 5, 7, 9, 10, 14, 27, 51, 89; DAM NOV; SSC 10**
See also AITN 1, 2; AMW; BPFB 1; CA 1-4R; CABS 1; CANR 5, 23, 49, 64; CN; DLB 2, 227; FANT; MTCW 1; RGAL; RGSF; RHW; SSFS 6

**Barthelme, Donald** 1931-1989 ... **CLC 1, 2, 3, 5, 6, 8, 13, 23, 46, 59, 115; DAM NOV; SSC 2**
See also AMWS 4; BPFB 1; CA 21-24R; 129; CANR 20, 58; DA3; DLB 2, 234; DLBY 80, 89; FANT; MTCW 1, 2; RGAL; RGSF; SATA 7; SATA-Obit 62; SSFS 3

**Barthelme, Frederick** 1943- ...... **CLC 36, 117**
See also CA 114; 122; CANR 77; CN; CSW; DLB 244; DLBY 85; INT CA-122

**Barthes, Roland (Gerard)**
1915-1980 .................... **CLC 24, 83**
See also CA 130; 97-100; CANR 66; EW; GFL 1789 to the Present; MTCW 1, 2

**Barzun, Jacques (Martin)** 1907- ..... **CLC 51, 145**
See also CA 61-64; CANR 22, 95

**Bashevis, Isaac**
See Singer, Isaac Bashevis

**Bashkirtseff, Marie** 1859-1884 ....... **NCLC 27**

**Basho, Matsuo**
See Matsuo Basho
See also RGWL; WP

**Basil of Caesaria** c. 330-379 ......... **CMLC 35**

**Bass, Kingsley B., Jr.**
See Bullins, Ed

**Bass, Rick** 1958- ........... **CLC 79, 143**
See also ANW; CA 126; CANR 53, 93; CSW; DLB 212

**Bassani, Giorgio** 1916-2000 .................... **CLC 9**
See also CA 65-68; 190; CANR 33; CWW 2; DLB 128, 177; MTCW 1; RGWL

**Bastian, Ann** .................... **CLC 70**

**Bastos, Augusto (Antonio) Roa**
See Roa Bastos, Augusto (Antonio)

**Bataille, Georges** 1897-1962 .................... **CLC 29**
See also CA 101; 89-92

**Bates, H(erbert) E(rnest)**
1905-1974 . **CLC 46; DAB; DAM POP; SSC 10**
See also CA 93-96; 45-48; CANR 34; DA3; DLB 162, 191; EXPS; MTCW 1, 2; RGSF; SSFS 7

**Bauchart**
See Camus, Albert

**Baudelaire, Charles** 1821-1867 . **NCLC 6, 29, 55; DA; DAB; DAC; DAM MST, POET; PC 1; SSC 18; WLC**
See also DA3; EW; GFL 1789 to the Present; RGWL

**Baudouin, Marcel**
See Peguy, Charles (Pierre)

**Baudouin, Pierre**
See Peguy, Charles (Pierre)

**Baudrillard, Jean** 1929- .................... **CLC 60**

**Baum, L(yman) Frank** 1856-1919 ... **TCLC 7**
See also CA 108; 133; CLR 15; DLB 22; JRDA; MAICYA; MTCW 1, 2; SATA 18, 100

**Baum, Louis F.**
See Baum, L(yman) Frank

**Baumbach, Jonathan** 1933- .................... **CLC 6, 23**
See also CA 13-16R; CAAS 5; CANR 12, 66; CN; DLBY 80; INT CANR-12; MTCW 1

**Bausch, Richard (Carl)** 1945- .................... **CLC 51**
See also AMWS 7; CA 101; CAAS 14; CANR 43, 61, 87; CSW; DLB 130

**Baxter, Charles (Morley)** 1947- ....... **CLC 45, 78; DAM POP**
See also CA 57-60; CANR 40, 64; CPW; DLB 130; MTCW 2

**Baxter, George Owen**
See Faust, Frederick (Schiller)

**Baxter, James K(eir)** 1926-1972 ....... **CLC 14**
See also CA 77-80

**Baxter, John**
See Hunt, E(verette) Howard, (Jr.)

**Bayer, Sylvia**
See Glassco, John

**Baynton, Barbara** 1857-1929 ......... **TCLC 57**
See also DLB 230; RGSF

**Beagle, Peter S(oyer)** 1939- ........ **CLC 7, 104**
See also BPFB 1; BYA 9, 10; CA 9-12R; CANR 4, 51, 73; DA3; DLBY 80; FANT; INT CANR-4; MTCW 1; SATA 60; SUFW; YAW

**Bean, Normal**
See Burroughs, Edgar Rice

**Beard, Charles A(ustin)**
1874-1948 .................... **TCLC 15**
See also CA 115; 189; DLB 17; SATA 18

**Beardsley, Aubrey** 1872-1898 .......... **NCLC 6**

**Beattie, Ann** 1947- ..... **CLC 8, 13, 18, 40, 63, 146; DAM NOV, POP; SSC 11**
See also AMWS 5; BEST 90:2; BPFB 1; CA 81-84; CANR 53, 73; CN; CPW; DA3; DLBY 82; MTCW 1, 2; RGAL; RGSF; SSFS 9

**Beattie, James** 1735-1803 ............... **NCLC 25**
See also DLB 109

**Beauchamp, Kathleen Mansfield** 1888-1923
See Mansfield, Katherine
See also CA 104; 134; DA; DA3; DAC; DAM MST; MTCW 2

**Beaumarchais, Pierre-Augustin Caron de** 1732-1799 . **LC 61; DAM DRAM; DC 4**
See also EW; GFL Beginnings to 1789; RGWL

**Beaumont, Francis** 1584(?)-1616 ....... **LC 33; DC 6**
See also BRW 2; CDBLB Before 1660; DLB 58, 121

**Beauvoir, Simone (Lucie Ernestine Marie Bertrand) de** 1908-1986 .... **CLC 1, 2, 4, 8, 14, 31, 44, 50, 71, 124; DA; DAB; DAC; DAM MST, NOV; SSC 35; WLC**
See also BPFB 1; CA 9-12R; 118; CANR 28, 61; DA3; DLB 72; DLBY 86; EW; FW; GFL 1789 to the Present; MTCW 1, 2; RGSF; RGWL

**Becker, Carl (Lotus)** 1873-1945 ..... **TCLC 63**
See also CA 157; DLB 17

**Becker, Jurek** 1937-1997 ............... **CLC 7, 19**
See also CA 85-88; 157; CANR 60; CWW 2; DLB 75

**Becker, Walter** 1950- ........................ **CLC 26**

**Beckett, Samuel (Barclay)** 1906-1989 .. **CLC 1, 2, 3, 4, 6, 9, 10, 11, 14, 18, 29, 57, 59, 83; DA; DAB; DAC; DAM DRAM, MST, NOV; SSC 16; WLC**
See also BRWS 1; CA 5-8R; 130; CANR 33, 61; CBD; CDBLB 1945-1960; DA3; DFS 2, 7; DLB 13, 15, 233; DLBY 90; GFL 1789 to the Present; MTCW 1, 2; RGSF; RGWL; WLIT 4

**Beckford, William** 1760-1844 ........ **NCLC 16**
See also BRW 3; DLB 39, 213; HGG; SUFW

**Beckman, Gunnel** 1910- ..................... **CLC 26**
See also CA 33-36R; CANR 15; CLR 25; MAICYA; SAAS 9; SATA 6

**Becque, Henri** 1837-1899 ................. **NCLC 3**
See also DLB 192; GFL 1789 to the Present

**Becquer, Gustavo Adolfo** 1836-1870 .... **NCLC 106; DAM MULT; HLCS 1**

**Beddoes, Thomas Lovell** 1803-1849 ..................... **NCLC 3; DC 15**
See also DLB 96

**Bede** c. 673-735 .............................. **CMLC 20**
See also DLB 146

**Bedford, Donald F.**
See Fearing, Kenneth (Flexner)

**Beecher, Catharine Esther** 1800-1878 ................. **NCLC 30**
See also DLB 1, 243

**Beecher, John** 1904-1980 .................... **CLC 6**
See also AITN 1; CA 5-8R; 105; CANR 8

**Beer, Johann** 1655-1700 .................... **LC 5**
See also DLB 168

**Beer, Patricia** 1924- ........................... **CLC 58**
See also CA 61-64; 183; CANR 13, 46; CP; CWP; DLB 40; FW

**Beerbohm, Max**
See Beerbohm, (Henry) Max(imilian)

**Beerbohm, (Henry) Max(imilian)** 1872-1956 ............................ **TCLC 1, 24**
See also BRWS 2; CA 104; 154; CANR 79; DLB 34, 100; FANT

**Beer-Hofmann, Richard** 1866-1945 ................................ **TCLC 60**
See also CA 160; DLB 81

**Beg, Shemus**
See Stephens, James

**Begiebing, Robert J(ohn)** 1946- ....... **CLC 70**
See also CA 122; CANR 40, 88

**Behan, Brendan** 1923-1964 ...... **CLC 1, 8, 11, 15, 79; DAM DRAM**
See also BRWS 2; CA 73-76; CANR 33; CBD; CDBLB 1945-1960; DFS 7; DLB 13, 233; MTCW 1, 2

**Behn, Aphra** 1640(?)-1689 ....... **LC 1, 30, 42; DA; DAB; DAC; DAM DRAM, MST, NOV, POET; DC 4; PC 13; WLC**
See also BRWS 3; DA3; DLB 39, 80, 131; FW; WLIT 3

**Behrman, S(amuel) N(athaniel)** 1893-1973 ................... **CLC 40**
See also CA 13-16; 45-48; CAD; CAP 1; DLB 7, 44; IDFW 3; RGAL

**Belasco, David** 1853-1931 ................ **TCLC 3**
See also CA 104; 168; DLB 7; RGAL

**Belcheva, Elisaveta** 1893-1991 .......... **CLC 10**
See also Bagryana, Elisaveta

**Beldone, Phil ''Cheech''**
See Ellison, Harlan (Jay)

**Beleno**
See Azuela, Mariano

**Belinski, Vissarion Grigoryevich** 1811-1848 ................. **NCLC 5**
See also DLB 198

**Belitt, Ben** 1911- ............................... **CLC 22**
See also CA 13-16R; CAAS 4; CANR 7, 77; CP; DLB 5

**Bell, Gertrude (Margaret Lowthian)** 1868-1926 ................................ **TCLC 67**
See also CA 167; DLB 174

**Bell, J. Freeman**
See Zangwill, Israel

**Bell, James Madison** 1826-1902 ... **TCLC 43; BLC 1; DAM MULT**
See also BW 1; CA 122; 124; DLB 50

**Bell, Madison Smartt** 1957- ....... **CLC 41, 102**
See also BPFB 1; CA 111, 183; CAAE 183; CANR 28, 54, 73; CN; CSW; MTCW 1

**Bell, Marvin (Hartley)** 1937- ....... **CLC 8, 31; DAM POET**
See also CA 21-24R; CAAS 14; CANR 59, 102; CP; DLB 5; MTCW 1

**Bell, W. L. D.**
See Mencken, H(enry) L(ouis)

**Bellamy, Atwood C.**
See Mencken, H(enry) L(ouis)

**Bellamy, Edward** 1850-1898 ...... **NCLC 4, 86**
See also DLB 12; RGAL; SFW

**Belli, Gioconda** 1949-
See also CA 152; CWW 2; HLCS 1

**Bellin, Edward J.**
See Kuttner, Henry

**Belloc, (Joseph) Hilaire (Pierre Sebastien Rene Swanton)** 1870-1953 ...... **TCLC 7, 18; DAM POET; PC 24**
See also CA 106; 152; CWRI; DLB 19, 100, 141, 174; MTCW 1; SATA 112; WCH; YABC 1

**Belloc, Joseph Peter Rene Hilaire**
See Belloc, (Joseph) Hilaire (Pierre Sebastien Rene Swanton)

**Belloc, Joseph Pierre Hilaire**
See Belloc, (Joseph) Hilaire (Pierre Sebastien Rene Swanton)

**Belloc, M. A.**
See Lowndes, Marie Adelaide (Belloc)

**Bellow, Saul** 1915- . **CLC 1, 2, 3, 6, 8, 10, 13, 15, 25, 33, 34, 63, 79; DA; DAB; DAC; DAM MST, NOV, POP; SSC 14; WLC**
See also AITN 2; AMW; BEST 89:3; BPFB 1; CA 5-8R; CABS 1; CANR 29, 53, 95; CDALB 1941-1968; CN; DA3; DLB 2, 28; DLBD 3; DLBY 82; MTCW 1, 2; NFS 4; RGAL; RGSF; SSFS 12

**Belser, Reimond Karel Maria de** 1929-
See Ruyslinck, Ward
See also CA 152

**Bely, Andrey** ........................ **TCLC 7; PC 11**
See also Bugayev, Boris Nikolayevich
See also EW; MTCW 1

**Belyi, Andrei**
See Bugayev, Boris Nikolayevich
See also RGWL

**Benary, Margot**
See Benary-Isbert, Margot

**Benary-Isbert, Margot** 1889-1979 .... **CLC 12**
See also CA 5-8R; 89-92; CANR 4, 72; CLR 12; MAICYA; SATA 2; SATA-Obit 21

**Benavente (y Martinez), Jacinto** 1866-1954 ........ **TCLC 3; DAM DRAM, MULT; HLCS 1**
See also CA 106; 131; CANR 81; GLL 2; HW 1, 2; MTCW 1, 2

**Benchley, Peter (Bradford)** 1940- . **CLC 4, 8; DAM NOV, POP**
See also AAYA 14; AITN 2; BPFB 1; CA 17-20R; CANR 12, 35, 66; CPW; HGG; MTCW 1, 2; SATA 3, 89

**Benchley, Robert (Charles)** 1889-1945 ............................ **TCLC 1, 55**
See also CA 105; 153; DLB 11; RGAL

**Benda, Julien** 1867-1956 ................. **TCLC 60**
See also CA 120; 154; GFL 1789 to the Present

**Benedict, Saint** c. 480-c. 547 ......... **CMLC 29**

**Benedict, Ruth (Fulton)** 1887-1948 ................................ **TCLC 60**
See also CA 158; DLB 246

**Benedikt, Michael** 1935- ................ **CLC 4, 14**
See also CA 13-16R; CANR 7; CP; DLB 5

**Benet, Juan** 1927-1993 ...................... **CLC 28**
See also CA 143

**Benet, Stephen Vincent** 1898-1943 . **TCLC 7; DAM POET; SSC 10**
See also CA 104; 152; DA3; DLB 4, 48, 102; DLBY 97; HGG; MTCW 1; RGAL; RGSF; WP; YABC 1

**Benet, William Rose** 1886-1950 .... **TCLC 28; DAM POET**
See also CA 118; 152; DLB 45; RGAL

**Benford, Gregory (Albert)** 1941- ...... **CLC 52**
See also BPFB 1; CA 69-72, 175; CAAE 175; CAAS 27; CANR 12, 24, 49, 95; CSW; DLBY 82; SCFW 2; SFW

**Bengtsson, Frans (Gunnar)** 1894-1954 ......................... **TCLC 48**
See also CA 170

**Benjamin, David**
See Slavitt, David R(ytman)

**Benjamin, Lois**
See Gould, Lois

**Benjamin, Walter** 1892-1940 .......... **TCLC 39**
See also CA 164; DLB 242; EW

**Benn, Gottfried** 1886-1956 .. **TCLC 3; PC 35**
See also CA 106; 153; DLB 56; RGWL

**Bennett, Alan** 1934- ......... **CLC 45, 77; DAB; DAM MST**
See also CA 103; CANR 35, 55; CBD; CD; MTCW 1, 2

**Bennett, (Enoch) Arnold** 1867-1931 ............................ **TCLC 5, 20**
See also BRW 6; CA 106; 155; CDBLB 1890-1914; DLB 10, 34, 98, 135; MTCW 2

**Bennett, Elizabeth**
See Mitchell, Margaret (Munnerlyn)

**Bennett, George Harold** 1930-
See Bennett, Hal
See also BW 1; CA 97-100; CANR 87

**Bennett, Hal** .................................. **CLC 5**
See also Bennett, George Harold
See also DLB 33

**Bennett, Jay** 1912- .................... **CLC 35**
See also AAYA 10; CA 69-72; CANR 11, 42, 79; JRDA; SAAS 4; SATA 41, 87; SATA-Brief 27; YAW

**Bennett, Louise (Simone)** 1919- ...... **CLC 28; BLC 1; DAM MULT**
See also BW 2, 3; CA 151; DLB 117

**Benson, E(dward) F(rederic)**
1867-1940 ................... **TCLC 27**
See also CA 114; 157; DLB 135, 153; HGG; SUFW

**Benson, Jackson J.** 1930- ................. **CLC 34**
See also CA 25-28R; DLB 111

**Benson, Sally** 1900-1972 .................... **CLC 17**
See also CA 19-20; 37-40R; CAP 1; SATA 1, 35; SATA-Obit 27

**Benson, Stella** 1892-1933 ............... **TCLC 17**
See also CA 117; 155; DLB 36, 162; FANT

**Bentham, Jeremy** 1748-1832 ........ **NCLC 38**
See also DLB 107, 158

**Bentley, E(dmund) C(lerihew)**
1875-1956 ..................... **TCLC 12**
See also CA 108; DLB 70; MSW

**Bentley, Eric (Russell)** 1916- ............. **CLC 24**
See also CA 5-8R; CAD; CANR 6, 67; CBD; CD; INT CANR-6

**Beranger, Pierre Jean de**
1780-1857 ..................... **NCLC 34**

**Berdyaev, Nicolas**
See Berdyaev, Nikolai (Aleksandrovich)

**Berdyaev, Nikolai (Aleksandrovich)**
1874-1948 ..................... **TCLC 67**
See also CA 120; 157

**Berdyayev, Nikolai (Aleksandrovich)**
See Berdyaev, Nikolai (Aleksandrovich)

**Berendt, John (Lawrence)** 1939- ...... **CLC 86**
See also CA 146; CANR 75, 93; DA3; MTCW 1

**Beresford, J(ohn) D(avys)**
1873-1947 ..................... **TCLC 81**
See also CA 112; 155; DLB 162, 178, 197; SFW; SUFW

**Bergelson, David** 1884-1952 ........... **TCLC 81**

**Berger, Colonel**
See Malraux, (Georges-)Andre

**Berger, John (Peter)** 1926- ............ **CLC 2, 19**
See also BRWS 4; CA 81-84; CANR 51, 78; CN; DLB 14, 207

**Berger, Melvin H.** 1927- .................. **CLC 12**
See also CA 5-8R; CANR 4; CLR 32; SAAS 2; SATA 5, 88; SATA-Essay 124

**Berger, Thomas (Louis)** 1924- .. **CLC 3, 5, 8, 11, 18, 38; DAM NOV**
See also BPFB 1; CA 1-4R; CANR 5, 28, 51; CN; DLB 2; DLBY 80; FANT; INT CANR-28; MTCW 1, 2; RHW; TCWW 2

**Bergman, (Ernst) Ingmar**
1918-1997 ..................... **CLC 16, 72**
See also CA 81-84; CANR 33, 70; MTCW 2

**Bergson, Henri(-Louis)** 1859-1941 . **TCLC 32**
See also CA 164; EW; GFL 1789 to the Present

**Bergstein, Eleanor** 1938- ..................... **CLC 4**
See also CA 53-56; CANR 5

**Berkeley, George** 1685-1753 ............... **LC 65**
See also DLB 101

**Berkoff, Steven** 1937- ........................ **CLC 56**
See also CA 104; CANR 72; CBD; CD

**Berlin, Isaiah** 1909-1997 ............... **TCLC 105**
See also CA 85-88; 162

**Bermant, Chaim (Icyk)** 1929-1998 ... **CLC 40**
See also CA 57-60; CANR 6, 31, 57; CN

**Bern, Victoria**
See Fisher, M(ary) F(rances) K(ennedy)

**Bernanos, (Paul Louis) Georges**
1888-1948 ..................... **TCLC 3**
See also CA 104; 130; CANR 94; DLB 72; GFL 1789 to the Present; RGWL

**Bernard, April** 1956- ........................ **CLC 59**
See also CA 131

**Berne, Victoria**
See Fisher, M(ary) F(rances) K(ennedy)

**Bernhard, Thomas** 1931-1989 ..... **CLC 3, 32, 61; DC 14**
See also CA 85-88; 127; CANR 32, 57; DLB 85, 124; MTCW 1; RGWL

**Bernhardt, Sarah (Henriette Rosine)**
1844-1923 ..................... **TCLC 75**
See also CA 157

**Bernstein, Charles** 1950- ................. **CLC 142**
See also CA 129; CAAS 24; CANR 90; CP; DLB 169

**Berriault, Gina** 1926-1999 ....... **CLC 54, 109; SSC 30**
See also CA 116; 129; 185; CANR 66; DLB 130; SSFS 7,11

**Berrigan, Daniel** 1921- ........................ **CLC 4**
See also CA 33-36R; CAAE 187; CAAS 1; CANR 11, 43, 78; CP; DLB 5

**Berrigan, Edmund Joseph Michael, Jr.**
1934-1983
See Berrigan, Ted
See also CA 61-64; 110; CANR 14, 102

**Berrigan, Ted** ...................... **CLC 37**
See also Berrigan, Edmund Joseph Michael, Jr.
See also DLB 5, 169; WP

**Berry, Charles Edward Anderson** 1931-
See Berry, Chuck
See also CA 115

**Berry, Chuck** ..................... **CLC 17**
See also Berry, Charles Edward Anderson

**Berry, Jonas**
See Ashbery, John (Lawrence)
See also GLL 1

**Berry, Wendell (Erdman)** 1934- ... **CLC 4, 6, 8, 27, 46; DAM POET; PC 28**
See also AITN 1; ANW; CA 73-76; CANR 50, 73, 101; CP; CSW; DLB 5, 6, 234; MTCW 1

**Berryman, John** 1914-1972 ... **CLC 1, 2, 3, 4, 6, 8, 10, 13, 25, 62; DAM POET**
See also AMW; CA 13-16; 33-36R; CABS 2; CANR 35; CAP 1; CDALB 1941-1968; DLB 48; MTCW 1, 2; PAB; RGAL; WP

**Bertolucci, Bernardo** 1940- ............... **CLC 16**
See also CA 106

**Berton, Pierre (Francis Demarigny)**
1920- .............................. **CLC 104**
See also CA 1-4R; CANR 2, 56; CPW; DLB 68; SATA 99

**Bertrand, Aloysius** 1807-1841 ........ **NCLC 31**

**Bertran de Born** c. 1140-1215 ........ **CMLC 5**

**Besant, Annie (Wood)** 1847-1933 ..... **TCLC 9**
See also CA 105; 185

**Bessie, Alvah** 1904-1985 .................... **CLC 23**
See also CA 5-8R; 116; CANR 2, 80; DLB 26

**Bethlen, T. D.**
See Silverberg, Robert

**Beti, Mongo** ............ **CLC 27; BLC 1; DAM MULT**
See also Biyidi, Alexandre
See also AFW; CANR 79; WLIT 2

**Betjeman, John** 1906-1984 ...... **CLC 2, 6, 10, 34, 43; DAB; DAM MST, POET**
See also BRW 7; CA 9-12R; 112; CANR 33, 56; CDBLB 1945-1960; DA3; DLB 20; DLBY 84; MTCW 1, 2

**Bettelheim, Bruno** 1903-1990 ........... **CLC 79**
See also CA 81-84; 131; CANR 23, 61; DA3; MTCW 1, 2

**Betti, Ugo** 1892-1953 ........................ **TCLC 5**
See also CA 104; 155; RGWL

**Betts, Doris (Waugh)** 1932- ..... **CLC 3, 6, 28; SSC 45**
See also CA 13-16R; CANR 9, 66, 77; CN; CSW; DLBY 82; INT CANR-9; RGAL

**Bevan, Alistair**
See Roberts, Keith (John Kingston)

**Bey, Pilaff**
See Douglas, (George) Norman

**Bialik, Chaim Nachman**
1873-1934 ..................... **TCLC 25**
See also CA 170

**Bickerstaff, Isaac**
See Swift, Jonathan

**Bidart, Frank** 1939- ........................ **CLC 33**
See also CA 140; CP

**Bienek, Horst** 1930- ..................... **CLC 7, 11**
See also CA 73-76; DLB 75

**Bierce, Ambrose (Gwinett)**
1842-1914(?) .......... **TCLC 1, 7, 44; DA; DAC; DAM MST; SSC 9; WLC**
See also AMW; BYA 11; CA 104; 139; CANR 78; CDALB 1865-1917; DA3; DLB 11, 12, 23, 71, 74, 186; EXPS; HGG; LAIT 2; RGAL; RGSF; SSFS 9; SUFW

**Biggers, Earl Derr** 1884-1933 ........ **TCLC 65**
See also CA 108; 153

**Billings, Josh**
See Shaw, Henry Wheeler

**Billington, (Lady) Rachel (Mary)**
1942- ........................ **CLC 43**
See also AITN 2; CA 33-36R; CANR 44; CN

**Binyon, T(imothy) J(ohn)** 1936- ....... **CLC 34**
See also CA 111; CANR 28

**Bion** 335B.C.-245B.C. ..................... **CMLC 39**

**Bioy Casares, Adolfo** 1914-1999 ... **CLC 4, 8, 13, 88; DAM MULT; HLC 1; SSC 17**
See also Casares, Adolfo Bioy; Miranda, Javier; Sacastru, Martin
See also CA 29-32R; 177; CANR 19, 43, 66; DLB 113; HW 1, 2; LAW; MTCW 1, 2

**Birch, Allison** ..................... **CLC 65**

**Bird, Cordwainer**
See Ellison, Harlan (Jay)

**Bird, Robert Montgomery**
1806-1854 ..................... **NCLC 1**
See also DLB 202; RGAL

**Birkerts, Sven** 1951- ..................... **CLC 116**
See also CA 128; 133; 176; CAAE 176; CAAS 29; INT 133

**Birney, (Alfred) Earle** 1904-1995 .. **CLC 1, 4, 6, 11; DAC; DAM MST, POET**
See also CA 1-4R; CANR 5, 20; CP; DLB 88; MTCW 1; PFS 8; RGEL

**Biruni, al** 973-1048(?) ..................... **CMLC 28**

**Bishop, Elizabeth** 1911-1979 ...... **CLC 1, 4, 9, 13, 15, 32; DA; DAC; DAM MST, POET; PC 3, 34**
See also AMWS 1; CA 5-8R; 89-92; CABS 2; CANR 26, 61; CDALB 1968-1988; DA3; DLB 5, 169; GLL 2; MAWW; MTCW 1, 2; PAB; PFS 6, 12; RGAL; SATA-Obit 24; WP

**Bishop, John** 1935- ........................ **CLC 10**
See also CA 105

**Bishop, John Peale** 1892-1944 ..... **TCLC 103**
See also CA 107; 155; DLB 4, 9, 45; RGAL

**Bissett, Bill** 1939- ..................... **CLC 18; PC 14**
See also CA 69-72; CAAS 19; CANR 15; CCA 1; CP; DLB 53; MTCW 1

**Bissoondath, Neil (Devindra)**
1955- .............................. **CLC 120; DAC**
See also CA 136; CN

**Bitov, Andrei (Georgievich)** 1937- ... **CLC 57**
See also CA 142

**Biyidi, Alexandre** 1932-
See Beti, Mongo
See also BW 1, 3; CA 114; 124; CANR 81; DA3; MTCW 1, 2

**Bjarme, Brynjolf**
See Ibsen, Henrik (Johan)

**Bjoernson, Bjoernstjerne (Martinius)**
1832-1910 ............................. **TCLC 7, 37**
See also CA 104

**Black, Robert**
See Holdstock, Robert P.

**Blackburn, Paul** 1926-1971 .......... **CLC 9, 43**
See also CA 81-84; 33-36R; CANR 34; DLB 16; DLBY 81

**Black Elk** 1863-1950 ........... **TCLC 33; DAM MULT**
See also CA 144; MTCW 1; NNAL; WP

**Black Hobart**
See Sanders, (James) Ed(ward)

**Blacklin, Malcolm**
See Chambers, Aidan

**Blackmore, R(ichard) D(oddridge)**
1825-1900 ................................ **TCLC 27**
See also CA 120; DLB 18; RGEL

**Blackmur, R(ichard) P(almer)**
1904-1965 ............................. **CLC 2, 24**
See also AMWS 2; CA 11-12; 25-28R; CANR 71; CAP 1; DLB 63

**Black Tarantula**
See Acker, Kathy

**Blackwood, Algernon (Henry)**
1869-1951 ................................ **TCLC 5**
See also CA 105; 150; DLB 153, 156, 178; HGG; SUFW

**Blackwood, Caroline** 1931-1996 .... **CLC 6, 9, 100**
See also CA 85-88; 151; CANR 32, 61, 65; CN; DLB 14, 207; HGG; MTCW 1

**Blade, Alexander**
See Hamilton, Edmond; Silverberg, Robert

**Blaga, Lucian** 1895-1961 ................... **CLC 75**
See also CA 157; DLB 220

**Blair, Eric (Arthur)** 1903-1950
See Orwell, George
See also CA 104; 132; DA; DA3; DAB; DAC; DAM MST, NOV; MTCW 1, 2; SATA 29

**Blair, Hugh** 1718-1800 .................... **NCLC 75**

**Blais, Marie-Claire** 1939- .... **CLC 2, 4, 6, 13, 22; DAC; DAM MST**
See also CA 21-24R; CAAS 4; CANR 38, 75, 93; DLB 53; FW; MTCW 1, 2

**Blaise, Clark** 1940- ............................ **CLC 29**
See also AITN 2; CA 53-56; CAAS 3; CANR 5, 66; CN; DLB 53; RGSF

**Blake, Fairley**
See De Voto, Bernard (Augustine)

**Blake, Nicholas**
See Day Lewis, C(ecil)
See also DLB 77; MSW

**Blake, William** 1757-1827 ....... **NCLC 13, 37, 57; DA; DAB; DAC; DAM MST, POET; PC 12; WLC**
See also BRW 3; CDBLB 1789-1832; CLR 52; DA3; DLB 93, 163; EXPP; MAICYA; PAB; PFS 2; 12; SATA 30; WLIT 3; WP

**Blanchot, Maurice** 1907- .................. **CLC 135**
See also CA 117; 144; DLB 72

**Blasco Ibanez, Vicente**
1867-1928 .......... **TCLC 12; DAM NOV**
See also BPFB 1; CA 110; 131; CANR 81; DA3; EW; HW 1, 2; MTCW 1

**Blatty, William Peter** 1928- .... **CLC 2; DAM POP**
See also CA 5-8R; CANR 9; HGG

**Bleeck, Oliver**
See Thomas, Ross (Elmore)

**Blessing, Lee** 1949- ............................ **CLC 54**
See also CAD; CD

**Blight, Rose**
See Greer, Germaine

**Blish, James (Benjamin)** 1921-1975 . **CLC 14**
See also BPFB 1; CA 1-4R; 57-60; CANR 3; DLB 8; MTCW 1; SATA 66; SCFW 2; SFW

**Bliss, Reginald**
See Wells, H(erbert) G(eorge)

**Blixen, Karen (Christentze Dinesen)**
1885-1962
See Dinesen, Isak
See also CA 25-28; CANR 22, 50; CAP 2; DA3; MTCW 1, 2; NCFS 2; SATA 44; SSFS 13

**Bloch, Robert (Albert)** 1917-1994 .... **CLC 33**
See also AAYA 29; CA 5-8R, 179; 146; CAAE 179; CAAS 20; CANR 5, 78; DA3; DLB 44; HGG; INT CANR-5; MTCW 1; SATA 12; SATA-Obit 82; SFW; SUFW

**Blok, Alexander (Alexandrovich)**
1880-1921 ..................... **TCLC 5; PC 21**
See also CA 104; 183; EW; RGWL

**Blom, Jan**
See Breytenbach, Breyten

**Bloom, Harold** 1930- ................. **CLC 24, 103**
See also CA 13-16R; CANR 39, 75, 92; DLB 67; MTCW 1; RGAL

**Bloomfield, Aurelius**
See Bourne, Randolph S(illiman)

**Blount, Roy (Alton), Jr.** 1941- ........... **CLC 38**
See also CA 53-56; CANR 10, 28, 61; CSW; INT CANR-28; MTCW 1, 2

**Bloy, Leon** 1846-1917 ..................... **TCLC 22**
See also CA 121; 183; DLB 123; GFL 1789 to the Present

**Blume, Judy (Sussman)** 1938- .. **CLC 12, 30; DAM NOV, POP**
See also AAYA 3, 26; BYA 1, 8, 12; CA 29-32R; CANR 13, 37, 66; CLR 2, 15, 69; CPW; DA3; DLB 52; JRDA; MAICYA; MAICYAS; MTCW 1, 2; SATA 2, 31, 79; WYA; YAW

**Blunden, Edmund (Charles)**
1896-1974 ............................... **CLC 2, 56**
See also BRW 6; CA 17-18; 45-48; CANR 54; CAP 2; DLB 20, 100, 155; MTCW 1; PAB

**Bly, Robert (Elwood)** 1926- ....... **CLC 1, 2, 5, 10, 15, 38, 128; DAM POET**
See also AMWS 4; CA 5-8R; CANR 41, 73; CP; DA3; DLB 5; MTCW 1, 2; RGAL

**Boas, Franz** 1858-1942 ..................... **TCLC 56**
See also CA 115; 181

**Bobette**
See Simenon, Georges (Jacques Christian)

**Boccaccio, Giovanni** 1313-1375 ... **CMLC 13; SSC 10**
See also EW; RGSF; RGWL

**Bochco, Steven** 1943- ......................... **CLC 35**
See also AAYA 11; CA 124; 138

**Bodel, Jean** 1167(?)-1210 ................... **CMLC 28**

**Bodenheim, Maxwell** 1892-1954 .... **TCLC 44**
See also CA 110; 187; DLB 9, 45; RGAL

**Bodker, Cecil** 1927- ........................... **CLC 21**
See also CA 73-76; CANR 13, 44; CLR 23; MAICYA; SATA 14

**Boell, Heinrich (Theodor)**
1917-1985 ..... **CLC 2, 3, 6, 9, 11, 15, 27, 32, 72; DA; DAB; DAC; DAM MST, NOV; SSC 23; WLC**
See also Boll, Heinrich
See also CA 21-24R; 116; CANR 24; DA3; DLB 69; DLBY 85; EW; MTCW 1, 2

**Boerne, Alfred**
See Doeblin, Alfred

**Boethius** c. 480-c. 524 ..................... **CMLC 15**
See also DLB 115; RGWL

**Boff, Leonardo (Genezio Darci)**
1938- .... **CLC 70; DAM MULT; HLC 1**
See also CA 150; HW 2

**Bogan, Louise** 1897-1970 ....... **CLC 4, 39, 46, 93; DAM POET; PC 12**
See also AMWS 3; CA 73-76; 25-28R; CANR 33, 82; DLB 45, 169; MAWW; MTCW 1, 2; RGAL

**Bogarde, Dirk**
See Van Den Bogarde, Derek Jules Gaspard Ulric Niven

**Bogosian, Eric** 1953- ................... **CLC 45, 141**
See also CA 138; CAD; CANR 102; CD

**Bograd, Larry** 1953- ........................... **CLC 35**
See also CA 93-96; CANR 57; SAAS 21; SATA 33, 89

**Boiardo, Matteo Maria** 1441-1494 ........ **LC 6**

**Boileau-Despreaux, Nicolas** 1636-1711 . **LC 3**
See also EW; GFL Beginnings to 1789; RGWL

**Bojer, Johan** 1872-1959 .................... **TCLC 64**
See also CA 189

**Bok, Edward W.** 1863-1930 .......... **TCLC 101**
See also DLB 91; DLBD 16

**Boland, Eavan (Aisling)** 1944- .. **CLC 40, 67, 113; DAM POET**
See also BRWS 5; CA 143; CANR 61; CP; CWP; DLB 40; FW; MTCW 2; PFS 12

**Boll, Heinrich**
See Boell, Heinrich (Theodor)
See also BPFB 1; RGSF; RGWL

**Bolt, Lee**
See Faust, Frederick (Schiller)

**Bolt, Robert (Oxton)** 1924-1995 ...... **CLC 14; DAM DRAM**
See also CA 17-20R; 147; CANR 35, 67; CBD; DFS 2; DLB 13, 233; LAIT 1; MTCW 1

**Bombal, Maria Luisa** 1910-1980 ....... **SSC 37; HLCS 1**
See also CA 127; CANR 72; HW 1; LAW; RGSF

**Bombet, Louis-Alexandre-Cesar**
See Stendhal

**Bomkauf**
See Kaufman, Bob (Garnell)

**Bonaventura** ................................ **NCLC 35**
See also DLB 90

**Bond, Edward** 1934- .......... **CLC 4, 6, 13, 23; DAM DRAM**
See also BRWS 1; CA 25-28R; CANR 38, 67; CBD; CD; DFS 3,8; DLB 13; MTCW 1

**Bonham, Frank** 1914-1989 ................ **CLC 12**
See also AAYA 1; BYA 1, 3; CA 9-12R; CANR 4, 36; JRDA; MAICYA; SAAS 3; SATA 1, 49; SATA-Obit 62; TCWW 2; YAW

**Bonnefoy, Yves** 1923- .. **CLC 9, 15, 58; DAM MST, POET**
See also CA 85-88; CANR 33, 75, 97; CWW 2; GFL 1789 to the Present; MTCW 1, 2

**Bontemps, Arna(ud Wendell)**
1902-1973 ...... **CLC 1, 18; BLC 1; DAM MULT, NOV, POET**
See also BW 1; CA 1-4R; 41-44R; CANR 4, 35; CLR 6; CWRI; DA3; DLB 48, 51; JRDA; MAICYA; MTCW 1, 2; SATA 2, 44; SATA-Obit 24; WCH; WP

**Booth, Martin** 1944- ........................... **CLC 13**
See also CA 93-96; CAAE 188; CAAS 2; CANR 92

**Booth, Philip** 1925- ............................ **CLC 23**
See also CA 5-8R; CANR 5, 88; CP; DLBY 82

**Booth, Wayne C(layson)** 1921- ......... **CLC 24**
See also CA 1-4R; CAAS 5; CANR 3, 43; DLB 67

**Borchert, Wolfgang** 1921-1947 ........ **TCLC 5**
See also CA 104; 188; DLB 69, 124

**Borel, Petrus** 1809-1859 ................. **NCLC 41**
See also GFL 1789 to the Present

**Borges, Jorge Luis** 1899-1986 ... **CLC 1, 2, 3, 4, 6, 8, 9, 10, 13, 19, 44, 48, 83; DA; DAB; DAC; DAM MST, MULT; HLC 1; PC 22, 32; SSC 4, 41; WLC**
See also AAYA 26; BPFB 1; CA 21-24R; CANR 19, 33, 75; DA3; DLB 113; DLBY 86; DNFS; HW 1, 2; LAW; MSW; MTCW 1, 2; RGSF; RGWL; SFW; SSFS 4, 9; TCLC 109; WLIT 1

**Borowski, Tadeusz** 1922-1951 ......... **TCLC 9; SSC 48**
See also CA 106; 154; RGSF; SSFS 13

**Borrow, George (Henry)** 1803-1881 ............................. **NCLC 9**
See also DLB 21, 55, 166

**Bosch (Gaviño), Juan** 1909-2001
See also CA 151; DAM MST, MULT; DLB 145; HLCS 1; HW 1, 2

**Bosman, Herman Charles** 1905-1951 .............................. **TCLC 49**
See also Malan, Herman
See also CA 160; DLB 225; RGSF

**Bosschère, Jean de** 1878(?)-1953 ... **TCLC 19**
See also CA 115; 186

**Boswell, James** 1740-1795 ...... **LC 4, 50; DA; DAB; DAC; DAM MST; WLC**
See also BRW 3; CDBLB 1660-1789; DLB 104, 142; WLIT 3

**Bottomley, Gordon** 1874-1948 ..... **TCLC 107**
See also CA 120; 192; DLB 10

**Bottoms, David** 1949- ......................... **CLC 53**
See also CA 105; CANR 22; CSW; DLB 120; DLBY 83

**Boucicault, Dion** 1820-1890 ........... **NCLC 41**

**Boucolon, Maryse**
See Condé, Maryse

**Bourget, Paul (Charles Joseph)** 1852-1935 ..................... **TCLC 12**
See also CA 107; DLB 123; GFL 1789 to the Present

**Bourjaily, Vance (Nye)** 1922- ........ **CLC 8, 62**
See also CA 1-4R; CAAS 1; CANR 2, 72; CN; DLB 2, 143

**Bourne, Randolph S(illiman)** 1886-1918 ................. **TCLC 16**
See also AMW; CA 117; 155; DLB 63

**Bova, Ben(jamin William)** 1932- ...... **CLC 45**
See also AAYA 16; CA 5-8R; CAAS 18; CANR 11, 56, 94; CLR 3; DLBY 81; INT CANR-11; MAICYA; MTCW 1; SATA 6, 68; SFW

**Bowen, Elizabeth (Dorothea Cole)** 1899-1973 . **CLC 1, 3, 6, 11, 15, 22, 118; DAM NOV; SSC 3, 28**
See also BRWS 2; CA 17-18; 41-44R; CANR 35; CAP 2; CDBLB 1945-1960; DA3; DLB 15, 162; EXPS; FW; HGG; MTCW 1, 2; RGSF; SSFS 5; SUFW; WLIT 4

**Bowering, George** 1935- ............... **CLC 15, 47**
See also CA 21-24R; CAAS 16; CANR 10; DLB 53

**Bowering, Marilyn R(uthe)** 1949- .... **CLC 32**
See also CA 101; CANR 49; CP; CWP

**Bowers, Edgar** 1924-2000 ................... **CLC 9**
See also CA 5-8R; 188; CANR 24; CP; CSW; DLB 5

**Bowie, David** ................................... **CLC 17**
See also Jones, David Robert

**Bowles, Jane (Sydney)** 1917-1973 ..... **CLC 3, 68**
See also CA 19-20; 41-44R; CAP 2

**Bowles, Paul (Frederick)** 1910-1999 . **CLC 1, 2, 19, 53; SSC 3**
See also AMWS 4; CA 1-4R; 186; CAAS 1; CANR 1, 19, 50, 75; CN; DA3; DLB 5, 6; MTCW 1, 2; RGAL

**Bowles, William Lisle** 1762-1850 . **NCLC 103**
See also DLB 93

**Box, Edgar**
See Vidal, Gore
See also GLL 1

**Boyd, Nancy**
See Millay, Edna St. Vincent
See also GLL 1

**Boyd, Thomas (Alexander)** 1898-1935 ............................. **TCLC 111**
See also CA 111; 183; DLB 9; DLBD 16

**Boyd, William** 1952- ............... **CLC 28, 53, 70**
See also CA 114; 120; CANR 51, 71; CN; DLB 231

**Boyle, Kay** 1902-1992 ........ **CLC 1, 5, 19, 58, 121; SSC 5**
See also CA 13-16R; 140; CAAS 1; CANR 29, 61; DLB 4, 9, 48, 86; DLBY 93; MTCW 1, 2; RGAL; RGSF; SSFS 10, 13

**Boyle, Mark**
See Kienzle, William X(avier)

**Boyle, Patrick** 1905-1982 ................... **CLC 19**
See also CA 127

**Boyle, T. C.**
See Boyle, T(homas) Coraghessan
See also AMWS 8

**Boyle, T(homas) Coraghessan** 1948- ........ **CLC 36, 55, 90; DAM POP; SSC 16**
See also Boyle, T. C.
See also BEST 90:4; BPFB 1; CA 120; CANR 44, 76, 89; CN; CPW; DA3; DLBY 86; MTCW 2; SSFS 13

**Boz**
See Dickens, Charles (John Huffam)

**Brackenridge, Hugh Henry** 1748-1816 ................. **NCLC 7**
See also DLB 11, 37; RGAL

**Bradbury, Edward P.**
See Moorcock, Michael (John)
See also MTCW 2

**Bradbury, Malcolm (Stanley)** 1932-2000 ....... **CLC 32, 61; DAM NOV**
See also CA 1-4R; CANR 1, 33, 91, 98; CN; DA3; DLB 14, 207; MTCW 1, 2

**Bradbury, Ray (Douglas)** 1920- ... **CLC 1, 3, 10, 15, 42, 98; DA; DAB; DAC; DAM MST, NOV, POP; SSC 29; WLC**
See also AAYA 15; AITN 1, 2; AMWS 4; BPFB 1; BYA 4, 5, 11; CA 1-4R; CANR 2, 30, 75; CDALB 1968-1988; CN; CPW; DA3; DLB 2, 8; EXPN; EXPS; HGG; LAIT 3, 5; MTCW 1, 2; NFS 1; RGAL; RGSF; SATA 11, 64, 123; SCFW 2; SFW; SSFS 1; SUFW; YAW

**Braddon, Mary Elizabeth** 1837-1915 ............................. **TCLC 111**
See also Aunt Belinda; White, Babington
See also CA 108; 179; CMW; DLB 18, 70, 156; HGG

**Bradford, Gamaliel** 1863-1932 ....... **TCLC 36**
See also CA 160; DLB 17

**Bradford, William** 1590-1657 ............. **LC 64**
See also DLB 24, 30; RGAL

**Bradley, David (Henry), Jr.** 1950- ... **CLC 23, 118; BLC 1; DAM MULT**
See also BW 1, 3; CA 104; CANR 26, 81; CN; DLB 33

**Bradley, John Ed(mund, Jr.)** 1958- . **CLC 55**
See also CA 139; CANR 99; CN; CSW

**Bradley, Marion Zimmer** 1930-1999 ............... **CLC 30; DAM POP**
See also Chapman, Lee; Dexter, John; Gardner, Miriam; Ives, Morgan; Rivers, Elfrida
See also AAYA 40; BPFB 1; CA 57-60; 185; CAAS 10; CANR 7, 31, 51, 75; CPW; DA3; DLB 8; FANT; FW; MTCW 1, 2; SATA 90; SATA-Obit 116; SFW; YAW

**Bradshaw, John** 1933- ..................... **CLC 70**
See also CA 138; CANR 61

**Bradstreet, Anne** 1612(?)-1672 ...... **LC 4, 30; DA; DAC; DAM MST, POET; PC 10**
See also AMWS 1; CDALB 1640-1865; DA3; DLB 24; EXPP; FW; PFS 6; RGAL; WP

**Brady, Joan** 1939- ............................. **CLC 86**
See also CA 141

**Bragg, Melvyn** 1939- ......................... **CLC 10**
See also BEST 89:3; CA 57-60; CANR 10, 48, 89; CN; DLB 14; RHW

**Brahe, Tycho** 1546-1601 ..................... **LC 45**

**Braine, John (Gerard)** 1922-1986 . **CLC 1, 3, 41**
See also CA 1-4R; 120; CANR 1, 33; CDBLB 1945-1960; DLB 15; DLBY 86; MTCW 1

**Bramah, Ernest** 1868-1942 ............. **TCLC 72**
See also CA 156; CMW; DLB 70; FANT

**Brammer, William** 1930(?)-1978 ...... **CLC 31**
See also CA 77-80

**Brancati, Vitaliano** 1907-1954 ........ **TCLC 12**
See also CA 109

**Brancato, Robin F(idler)** 1936- ........ **CLC 35**
See also AAYA 9; BYA 6; CA 69-72; CANR 11, 45; CLR 32; JRDA; MAICYAS; SAAS 9; SATA 97; WYA; YAW

**Brand, Max**
See Faust, Frederick (Schiller)
See also BPFB 1; TCWW 2

**Brand, Millen** 1906-1980 ..................... **CLC 7**
See also CA 21-24R; 97-100; CANR 72

**Branden, Barbara** ............................. **CLC 44**
See also CA 148

**Brandes, Georg (Morris Cohen)** 1842-1927 ..................... **TCLC 10**
See also CA 105; 189

**Brandys, Kazimierz** 1916-2000 ......... **CLC 62**

**Branley, Franklyn M(ansfield)** 1915- ............................... **CLC 21**
See also CA 33-36R; CANR 14, 39; CLR 13; MAICYA; SAAS 16; SATA 4, 68

**Brathwaite, Edward (Kamau)** 1930- ...... **CLC 11; BLCS; DAM POET**
See also BW 2, 3; CA 25-28R; CANR 11, 26, 47; CP; DLB 125

**Brautigan, Richard (Gary)** 1935-1984 .... **CLC 1, 3, 5, 9, 12, 34, 42; DAM NOV**
See also BPFB 1; CA 53-56; 113; CANR 34; DA3; DLB 2, 5, 206; DLBY 80, 84; FANT; MTCW 1; RGAL; SATA 56

**Brave Bird, Mary**
See Crow Dog, Mary (Ellen)
See also NNAL

**Braverman, Kate** 1950- .................... **CLC 67**
See also CA 89-92

**Brecht, (Eugen) Bertolt (Friedrich)** 1898-1956 ........ **TCLC 1, 6, 13, 35; DA; DAB; DAC; DAM DRAM, MST; DC 3; WLC**
See also CA 104; 133; CANR 62; DA3; DFS 4, 5, 9; DLB 56, 124; EW; IDTP; MTCW 1, 2; RGWL

**Brecht, Eugen Berthold Friedrich**
See Brecht, (Eugen) Bertolt (Friedrich)

**Bremer, Fredrika** 1801-1865 .......... **NCLC 11**

**Brennan, Christopher John** 1870-1932 ................. **TCLC 17**
See also CA 117; 188; DLB 230

**Brennan, Maeve** 1917-1993 ................. **CLC 5**
See also CA 81-84; CANR 72, 100

**Brent, Linda**
See Jacobs, Harriet A(nn)

**Brentano, Clemens (Maria)**
1778-1842 ...................................... **NCLC 1**
See also DLB 90; RGWL

**Brent of Bin Bin**
See Franklin, (Stella Maria Sarah) Miles (Lampe)

**Brenton, Howard** 1942- ...................... **CLC 31**
See also CA 69-72; CANR 33, 67; CBD; CD; DLB 13; MTCW 1

**Breslin, James** 1935-1996
See Breslin, Jimmy
See also CA 73-76; CANR 31, 75; DAM NOV; MTCW 1, 2

**Breslin, Jimmy** ............................. **CLC 4, 43**
See also Breslin, James
See also AITN 1; DLB 185; MTCW 2

**Bresson, Robert** 1901(?)-1999 ........... **CLC 16**
See also CA 110; 187; CANR 49

**Breton, Andre** 1896-1966 .. **CLC 2, 9, 15, 54; PC 15**
See also CA 19-20; 25-28R; CANR 40, 60; CAP 2; DLB 65; EW; GFL 1789 to the Present; MTCW 1, 2; RGWL; WP

**Breytenbach, Breyten** 1939(?)- .. **CLC 23, 37, 126; DAM POET**
See also CA 113; 129; CANR 61; CWW 2; DLB 225

**Bridgers, Sue Ellen** 1942- ................. **CLC 26**
See also AAYA 8; BYA 7, 8; CA 65-68; CANR 11, 36; CLR 18; DLB 52; JRDA; MAICYA; SAAS 1; SATA 22, 90; SATA-Essay 109; YAW

**Bridges, Robert (Seymour)**
1844-1930 ... **TCLC 1; DAM POET; PC 28**
See also BRW 6; CA 104; 152; CDBLB 1890-1914; DLB 19, 98

**Bridie, James** ..................................... **TCLC 3**
See also Mavor, Osborne Henry
See also DLB 10

**Brin, David** 1950- ............................... **CLC 34**
See also AAYA 21; CA 102; CANR 24, 70; INT CANR-24; SATA 65; SCFW 2; SFW

**Brink, Andre (Philippus)** 1935- . **CLC 18, 36, 106**
See also AFW; BRWS 6; CA 104; CANR 39, 62; CN; DLB 225; INT CA-103; MTCW 1, 2; WLIT 2

**Brinsmead, H(esba) F(ay)** 1922- ...... **CLC 21**
See also CA 21-24R; CANR 10; CLR 47; CWRI; MAICYA; SAAS 5; SATA 18, 78

**Brittain, Vera (Mary)** 1893(?)-1970 . **CLC 23**
See also CA 13-16; 25-28R; CANR 58; CAP 1; DLB 191; FW; MTCW 1, 2

**Broch, Hermann** 1886-1951 ........... **TCLC 20**
See also CA 117; DLB 85, 124; EW; RGWL

**Brock, Rose**
See Hansen, Joseph
See also GLL 1

**Brodkey, Harold (Roy)** 1930-1996 ... **CLC 56**
See also CA 111; 151; CANR 71; CN; DLB 130

**Brodsky, Iosif Alexandrovich** 1940-1996
See Brodsky, Joseph
See also AITN 1; CA 41-44R; 151; CANR 37; DA3; DAM POET; MTCW 1, 2

**Brodsky, Joseph** . **CLC 4, 6, 13, 36, 100; PC 9**
See also Brodsky, Iosif Alexandrovich
See also AMWS 8; CWW 2; MTCW 1

**Brodsky, Michael (Mark)** 1948- ....... **CLC 19**
See also CA 102; CANR 18, 41, 58; DLB 244

**Brodzki, Bella ed.** ............................ **CLC 65**

**Brome, Richard** 1590(?)-1652 ............... **LC 61**
See also DLB 58

**Bromell, Henry** 1947- ........................ **CLC 5**
See also CA 53-56; CANR 9

**Bromfield, Louis (Brucker)**
1896-1956 ...................................... **TCLC 11**
See also CA 107; 155; DLB 4, 9, 86; RGAL; RHW

**Broner, E(sther) M(asserman)**
1930- .............................................. **CLC 19**
See also CA 17-20R; CANR 8, 25, 72; CN; DLB 28

**Bronk, William (M.)** 1918-1999 ........ **CLC 10**
See also CA 89-92; 177; CANR 23; CP; DLB 165

**Bronstein, Lev Davidovich**
See Trotsky, Leon

**Bronte, Anne** 1820-1849 ..... **NCLC 4, 71, 102**
See also BRW 5; DA3; DLB 21, 199

**Bronte, Charlotte** 1816-1855 ...... **NCLC 3, 8, 33, 58, 105; DA; DAB; DAC; DAM MST, NOV; WLC**
See also AAYA 17; BRW 5; BYA 2; CD-BLB 1832-1890; DA3; DLB 21, 159, 199; EXPN; LAIT 2; NFS 4; WLIT 4

**Bronte, Emily (Jane)** 1818-1848 ... **NCLC 16, 35; DA; DAB; DAC; DAM MST, NOV, POET; PC 8; WLC**
See also AAYA 17; BPFB 1; BRW 5; BYA 3; CDBLB 1832-1890; DA3; DLB 21, 32, 199; EXPN; LAIT 1; WLIT 3

**Brontes**
See Bronte, Anne; Bronte, Charlotte; Bronte, Emily (Jane)

**Brooke, Frances** 1724-1789 ............. **LC 6, 48**
See also DLB 39, 99

**Brooke, Henry** 1703(?)-1783 .................. **LC 1**
See also DLB 39

**Brooke, Rupert (Chawner)**
1887-1915 .......... **TCLC 2, 7; DA; DAB; DAC; DAM MST, POET; PC 24; WLC**
See also BRWS 3; CA 104; 132; CANR 61; CDBLB 1914-1945; DLB 19; EXPP; GLL 2; MTCW 1, 2; PFS 7

**Brooke-Haven, P.**
See Wodehouse, P(elham) G(renville)

**Brooke-Rose, Christine** 1926(?)- ....... **CLC 40**
See also BRWS 4; CA 13-16R; CANR 58; CN; DLB 14, 231; SFW

**Brookner, Anita** 1928- . **CLC 32, 34, 51, 136; DAB; DAM POP**
See also BRWS 4; CA 114; 120; CANR 37, 56, 87; CN; CPW; DA3; DLB 194; DLBY 87; MTCW 1, 2

**Brooks, Cleanth** 1906-1994 . **CLC 24, 86, 110**
See also CA 17-20R; 145; CANR 33, 35; CSW; DLB 63; DLBY 94; INT CANR-35; MTCW 1, 2

**Brooks, George**
See Baum, L(yman) Frank

**Brooks, Gwendolyn (Elizabeth)**
1917-2000 .. **CLC 1, 2, 4, 5, 15, 49, 125; BLC 1; DA; DAC; DAM MST, MULT, POET; PC 7; WLC**
See also AAYA 20; AFAW 1, 2; AITN 1; AMWS 3; BW 2, 3; CA 1-4R; 190; CANR 1, 27, 52, 75; CDALB 1941-1968; CLR 27; CP; CWP; DA3; DLB 5, 76, 165; EXPP; MAWW; MTCW 1, 2; PFS 1, 2, 4, 6; RGAL; SATA 6; SATA-Obit 123; WP

**Brooks, Mel** ........................................ **CLC 12**
See also Kaminsky, Melvin
See also AAYA 13; DLB 26

**Brooks, Peter** 1938- ........................... **CLC 34**
See also CA 45-48; CANR 1

**Brooks, Van Wyck** 1886-1963 ........... **CLC 29**
See also AMW; CA 1-4R; CANR 6; DLB 45, 63, 103

**Brophy, Brigid (Antonia)**
1929-1995 ................. **CLC 6, 11, 29, 105**
See also CA 5-8R; 149; CAAS 4; CANR 25, 53; CBD; CN; CWD; DA3; DLB 14; MTCW 1, 2

**Brosman, Catharine Savage** 1934- ..... **CLC 9**
See also CA 61-64; CANR 21, 46

**Brossard, Nicole** 1943- ..................... **CLC 115**
See also CA 122; CAAS 16; CCA 1; CWP; CWW 2; DLB 53; FW; GLL 2

**Brother Antoninus**
See Everson, William (Oliver)

**The Brothers Quay**
See Quay, Stephen; Quay, Timothy

**Broughton, T(homas) Alan** 1936- ...... **CLC 19**
See also CA 45-48; CANR 2, 23, 48

**Broumas, Olga** 1949- .................... **CLC 10, 73**
See also CA 85-88; CANR 20, 69; CP; CWP; GLL 2

**Broun, Heywood** 1888-1939 ......... **TCLC 104**
See also DLB 29, 171

**Brown, Alan** 1950- ............................ **CLC 99**
See also CA 156

**Brown, Charles Brockden**
1771-1810 ......................... **NCLC 22, 74**
See also AMWS 1; CDALB 1640-1865; DLB 37, 59, 73; FW; HGG; RGAL

**Brown, Christy** 1932-1981 .................. **CLC 63**
See also BYA 13; CA 105; 104; CANR 72; DLB 14

**Brown, Claude** 1937- ......... **CLC 30; BLC 1; DAM MULT**
See also AAYA 7; BW 1, 3; CA 73-76; CANR 81

**Brown, Dee (Alexander)** 1908- . **CLC 18, 47; DAM POP**
See also AAYA 30; CA 13-16R; CAAS 6; CANR 11, 45, 60; CPW; CSW; DA3; DLBY 80; LAIT 2; MTCW 1, 2; SATA 5, 110; TCWW 2

**Brown, George**
See Wertmueller, Lina

**Brown, George Douglas**
1869-1902 ...................................... **TCLC 28**
See also Douglas, George
See also CA 162

**Brown, George Mackay** 1921-1996 ... **CLC 5, 48, 100**
See also BRWS 6; CA 21-24R; 151; CAAS 6; CANR 12, 37, 67; CN; CP; DLB 14, 27, 139; MTCW 1; RGSF; SATA 35

**Brown, (William) Larry** 1951- ......... **CLC 73**
See also CA 130; 134; CSW; INT 133

**Brown, Moses**
See Barrett, William (Christopher)

**Brown, Rita Mae** 1944- ........ **CLC 18, 43, 79; DAM NOV, POP**
See also BPFB 1; CA 45-48; CANR 2, 11, 35, 62, 95; CN; CPW; CSW; DA3; FW; INT CANR-11; MTCW 1, 2; NFS 9; RGAL

**Brown, Roderick (Langmere) Haig-**
See Haig-Brown, Roderick (Langmere)

**Brown, Rosellen** 1939- ....................... **CLC 32**
See also CA 77-80; CAAS 10; CANR 14, 44, 98; CN

**Brown, Sterling Allen** 1901-1989 ....... **CLC 1, 23, 59; BLC 1; DAM MULT, POET**
See also AFAW 1, 2; BW 1, 3; CA 85-88; 127; CANR 26; DA3; DLB 48, 51, 63; MTCW 1, 2; RGAL; WP

**Brown, Will**
See Ainsworth, William Harrison

**Brown, William Wells** 1815-1884 ... **NCLC 2, 89; BLC 1; DAM MULT; DC 1**
See also DLB 3, 50; RGAL

**Browne, (Clyde) Jackson** 1948(?)- ... **CLC 21**
See also CA 120

**Browning, Elizabeth Barrett**
1806-1861 ...... **NCLC 1, 16, 61, 66; DA; DAB; DAC; DAM MST, POET; PC 6; WLC**
See also BRW 4; CDBLB 1832-1890; DA3; DLB 32, 199; EXPP; PAB; PFS 2; WLIT 4; WP

**Browning, Robert** 1812-1889 . **NCLC 19, 79; DA; DAB; DAC; DAM MST, POET; PC 2; WLCS**
See also BRW 4; CDBLB 1832-1890; DA3; DLB 32, 163; EXPP; PAB; PFS 1; RGEL; TEA; WLIT 4; WP; YABC 1

**Browning, Tod** 1882-1962 .................. **CLC 16**
See also CA 141; 117

**Brownson, Orestes Augustus**
1803-1876 ..................... **NCLC 50**
See also DLB 1, 59, 73, 243

**Bruccoli, Matthew J(oseph)** 1931- ... **CLC 34**
See also CA 9-12R; CANR 7, 87; DLB 103

**Bruce, Lenny** ........................ **CLC 21**
See also Schneider, Leonard Alfred

**Bruin, John**
See Brutus, Dennis

**Brulard, Henri**
See Stendhal

**Brulls, Christian**
See Simenon, Georges (Jacques Christian)

**Brunner, John (Kilian Houston)**
1934-1995 .......... **CLC 8, 10; DAM POP**
See also CA 1-4R; 149; CANR 2, 37; CPW; MTCW 1, 2; SCFW 2; SFW

**Bruno, Giordano** 1548-1600 .................. **LC 27**
See also RGWL

**Brutus, Dennis** 1924- .......... **CLC 43; BLC 1; DAM MULT, POET; PC 24**
See also AFW; BW 2, 3; CA 49-52; CAAS 14; CANR 2, 27, 42, 81; CP; DLB 117, 225

**Bryan, C(ourtlandt) D(ixon) B(arnes)**
1936- ............................. **CLC 29**
See also CA 73-76; CANR 13, 68; DLB 185; INT CANR-13

**Bryan, Michael**
See Moore, Brian
See also CCA 1

**Bryan, William Jennings**
1860-1925 ..................... **TCLC 99**

**Bryant, William Cullen** 1794-1878 . **NCLC 6, 46; DA; DAB; DAC; DAM MST, POET; PC 20**
See also AMWS 1; CDALB 1640-1865; DLB 3, 43, 59, 189; EXPP; PAB; RGAL

**Bryusov, Valery Yakovlevich**
1873-1924 ..................... **TCLC 10**
See also CA 107; 155; SFW

**Buchan, John** 1875-1940 .... **TCLC 41; DAB; DAM POP**
See also CA 108; 145; CMW; DLB 34, 70, 156; HGG; MSW; MTCW 1; RGEL; RHW; YABC 2

**Buchanan, George** 1506-1582 .................. **LC 4**
See also DLB 152

**Buchanan, Robert** 1841-1901 ....... **TCLC 107**
See also CA 179; DLB 18, 35

**Buchheim, Lothar-Guenther** 1918- .... **CLC 6**
See also CA 85-88

**Buchner, (Karl) Georg** 1813-1837 . **NCLC 26**
See also EW; RGSF; RGWL

**Buchwald, Art(hur)** 1925- ................. **CLC 33**
See also AITN 1; CA 5-8R; CANR 21, 67; MTCW 1, 2; SATA 10

**Buck, Pearl S(ydenstricker)**
1892-1973 ....... **CLC 7, 11, 18, 127; DA; DAB; DAC; DAM MST, NOV**
See also AAYA 42; AITN 1; AMWS 2; BPFB 1; CA 1-4R; 41-44R; CANR 1, 34; CDALBS; DA3; DLB 9, 102; LAIT 3; MTCW 1, 2; RGAL; RHW; SATA 1, 25

**Buckler, Ernest** 1908-1984 .... **CLC 13; DAC; DAM MST**
See also CA 11-12; 114; CAP 1; CCA 1; DLB 68; SATA 47

**Buckley, Vincent (Thomas)**
1925-1988 .................. **CLC 57**
See also CA 101

**Buckley, William F(rank), Jr.** 1925- . **CLC 7, 18, 37; DAM POP**
See also AITN 1; BPFB 1; CA 1-4R; CANR 1, 24, 53, 93; CMW; CPW; DA3; DLB 137; DLBY 80; INT CANR-24; MTCW 1, 2; TUS

**Buechner, (Carl) Frederick** 1926- . **CLC 2, 4, 6, 9; DAM NOV**
See also BPFB 1; CA 13-16R; CANR 11, 39, 64; CN; DLBY 80; INT CANR-11; MTCW 1, 2

**Buell, John (Edward)** 1927- .............. **CLC 10**
See also CA 1-4R; CANR 71; DLB 53

**Buero Vallejo, Antonio** 1916-2000 ... **CLC 15, 46, 139**
See also CA 106; 189; CANR 24, 49, 75; DFS 11; HW 1; MTCW 1, 2

**Bufalino, Gesualdo** 1920(?)-1990 ...... **CLC 74**
See also CWW 2; DLB 196

**Bugayev, Boris Nikolayevich**
1880-1934 ..................... **TCLC 7; PC 11**
See also Bely, Andrey; Belyi, Andrei
See also CA 104; 165; MTCW 1

**Bukowski, Charles** 1920-1994 ... **CLC 2, 5, 9, 41, 82, 108; DAM NOV, POET; PC 18; SSC 45**
See also CA 17-20R; 144; CANR 40, 62; CPW; DA3; DLB 5, 130, 169; MTCW 1, 2

**Bulgakov, Mikhail (Afanas'evich)**
1891-1940 . **TCLC 2, 16; DAM DRAM, NOV; SSC 18**
See also BPFB 1; CA 105; 152; NFS 8; RGSF; RGWL; SFW

**Bulgya, Alexander Alexandrovich**
1901-1956 ..................... **TCLC 53**
See also Fadeyev, Alexander
See also CA 117; 181

**Bullins, Ed** 1935- .......... **CLC 1, 5, 7; BLC 1; DAM DRAM, MULT; DC 6**
See also BW 2, 3; CA 49-52; CAAS 16; CAD; CANR 24, 46, 73; CD; DLB 7, 38; MTCW 1, 2; RGAL

**Bulwer-Lytton, Edward (George Earle Lytton)** 1803-1873 .............. **NCLC 1, 45**
See also DLB 21; RGEL; SFW; SUFW

**Bunin, Ivan Alexeyevich**
1870-1953 ..................... **TCLC 6; SSC 5**
See also CA 104; RGSF; RGWL

**Bunting, Basil** 1900-1985 ..... **CLC 10, 39, 47; DAM POET**
See also BRWS 7; CA 53-56; 115; CANR 7; DLB 20; RGEL

**Bunuel, Luis** 1900-1983 .. **CLC 16, 80; DAM MULT; HLC 1**
See also CA 101; 110; CANR 32, 77; HW 1

**Bunyan, John** 1628-1688 ........ **LC 4, 69; DA; DAB; DAC; DAM MST; WLC**
See also BRW 2; BYA 5; CDBLB 1660-1789; DLB 39; RGEL; WLIT 3

**Buravsky, Alexandr** ......................... **CLC 59**

**Burckhardt, Jacob (Christoph)**
1818-1897 ..................... **NCLC 49**
See also EW

**Burford, Eleanor**
See Hibbert, Eleanor Alice Burford

**Burgess, Anthony** . **CLC 1, 2, 4, 5, 8, 10, 13, 15, 22, 40, 62, 81, 94; DAB**
See also Wilson, John (Anthony) Burgess
See also AAYA 25; AITN 1; BRWS 1; CDBLB 1960 to Present; DLB 14, 194; DLBY 98; MTCW 1; RGEL; RHW; SFW; YAW

**Burke, Edmund** 1729(?)-1797 ........ **LC 7, 36; DA; DAB; DAC; DAM MST; WLC**
See also BRW 3; DA3; DLB 104; RGEL

**Burke, Kenneth (Duva)** 1897-1993 ... **CLC 2, 24**
See also AMW; CA 5-8R; 143; CANR 39, 74; DLB 45, 63; MTCW 1, 2; RGAL

**Burke, Leda**
See Garnett, David

**Burke, Ralph**
See Silverberg, Robert

**Burke, Thomas** 1886-1945 ............. **TCLC 63**
See also CA 113; 155; CMW; DLB 197

**Burney, Fanny** 1752-1840 ........ **NCLC 12, 54**
See also BRWS 3; DLB 39; RGEL

**Burney, Frances**
See Burney, Fanny

**Burns, Robert** 1759-1796 . **LC 3, 29, 40; DA; DAB; DAC; DAM MST, POET; PC 6; WLC**
See also BRW 3; CDBLB 1789-1832; DA3; DLB 109; EXPP; PAB; RGEL; WP

**Burns, Tex**
See L'Amour, Louis (Dearborn)
See also TCWW 2

**Burnshaw, Stanley** 1906- ........ **CLC 3, 13, 44**
See also CA 9-12R; CP; DLB 48; DLBY 97

**Burr, Anne** 1937- ............................ **CLC 6**
See also CA 25-28R

**Burroughs, Edgar Rice** 1875-1950 . **TCLC 2, 32; DAM NOV**
See also AAYA 11; BPFB 1; BYA 4, 9; CA 104; 132; DA3; DLB 8; FANT; MTCW 1, 2; RGAL; SATA 41; SFW; YAW

**Burroughs, William S(eward)**
1914-1997 .. **CLC 1, 2, 5, 15, 22, 42, 75, 109; DA; DAB; DAC; DAM MST, NOV, POP; WLC**
See also Lee, William; Lee, Willy
See also AITN 2; AMWS 3; BPFB 1; CA 9-12R; 160; CANR 20, 52; CN; CPW; DA3; DLB 2, 8, 16, 152, 237; DLBY 81, 97; HGG; MTCW 1, 2; RGAL; SFW

**Burton, Sir Richard F(rancis)**
1821-1890 ..................... **NCLC 42**
See also DLB 55, 166, 184

**Busch, Frederick** 1941- .... **CLC 7, 10, 18, 47**
See also CA 33-36R; CAAS 1; CANR 45, 73, 92; CN; DLB 6

**Bush, Ronald** 1946- ........................... **CLC 34**
See also CA 136

**Bustos, F(rancisco)**
See Borges, Jorge Luis

**Bustos Domecq, H(onorio)**
See Bioy Casares, Adolfo; Borges, Jorge Luis

**Butler, Octavia E(stelle)** 1947- ......... **CLC 38, 121; BLCS; DAM MULT, POP**
See also AAYA 18; AFAW 2; BPFB 1; BW 2, 3; CA 73-76; CANR 12, 24, 38, 73; CLR 65; CPW; DA3; DLB 33; MTCW 1, 2; NFS 8; SATA 84; SFW; SSFS 6; YAW

**Butler, Robert Olen, (Jr.)** 1945- ...... **CLC 81; DAM POP**
See also BPFB 1; CA 112; CANR 66; CSW; DLB 173; INT CA-112; MTCW 1; SSFS 11

**Butler, Samuel** 1612-1680 ............. **LC 16, 43**
See also DLB 101, 126; RGEL

**Butler, Samuel** 1835-1902 . **TCLC 1, 33; DA; DAB; DAC; DAM MST, NOV; WLC**
See also BRWS 2; CA 143; CDBLB 1890-1914; DA3; DLB 18, 57, 174; RGEL; SFW; TEA

**Butler, Walter C.**
See Faust, Frederick (Schiller)

**Butor, Michel (Marie Francois)** 1926- ............ **CLC 1, 3, 8, 11, 15**
See also CA 9-12R; CANR 33, 66; DLB 83; EW; GFL 1789 to the Present; MTCW 1, 2

**Butts, Mary** 1890(?)-1937 ............... **TCLC 77**
See also CA 148; DLB 240

**Buxton, Ralph**
See Silverstein, Alvin; Silverstein, Virginia B(arbara Opshelor)

**Buzo, Alexander (John)** 1944- ........... **CLC 61**
See also CA 97-100; CANR 17, 39, 69; CD

**Buzzati, Dino** 1906-1972 .................... **CLC 36**
See also CA 160; 33-36R; DLB 177; RGWL; SFW

**Byars, Betsy (Cromer)** 1928- ............ **CLC 35**
See also AAYA 19; BYA 3; CA 33-36R, 183; CAAE 183; CANR 18, 36, 57, 102; CLR 1, 16, 72; DLB 52; INT CANR-18; JRDA; MAICYA; MAICYAS; MTCW 1; SAAS 1; SATA 4, 46, 80; SATA-Essay 108; WYA; YAW

**Byatt, A(ntonia) S(usan Drabble)** 1936- ...... **CLC 19, 65, 136; DAM NOV, POP**
See also BPFB 1; BRWS 4; CA 13-16R; CANR 13, 33, 50, 75, 96; DA3; DLB 14, 194; MTCW 1, 2; RGSF; RHW

**Byrne, David** 1952- ............................. **CLC 26**
See also CA 127

**Byrne, John Keyes** 1926-
See Leonard, Hugh
See also CA 102; CANR 78; CD; DFS 13; INT 102

**Byron, George Gordon (Noel)** 1788-1824 ....... **NCLC 2, 12; DA; DAB; DAC; DAM MST, POET; PC 16; WLC**
See also Lord Byron
See also BRW 4; CDBLB 1789-1832; DA3; DLB 96, 110; EXPP; PFS 1; RGEL; WLIT 3

**Byron, Robert** 1905-1941 ............... **TCLC 67**
See also CA 160; DLB 195

**C. 3. 3.**
See Wilde, Oscar (Fingal O'Flahertie Wills)

**Caballero, Fernan** 1796-1877 ......... **NCLC 10**

**Cabell, Branch**
See Cabell, James Branch

**Cabell, James Branch** 1879-1958 .... **TCLC 6**
See also CA 105; 152; DLB 9, 78; FANT; MTCW 1; RGAL

**Cabeza de Vaca, Alvar Nunez** 1490-1557(?) ................................. **LC 61**

**Cable, George Washington** 1844-1925 ................ **TCLC 4; SSC 4**
See also CA 104; 155; DLB 12, 74; DLBD 13; RGAL

**Cabral de Melo Neto, Joao** 1920-1999 ......... **CLC 76; DAM MULT**
See also CA 151; LAW

**Cabrera Infante, G(uillermo)** 1929- . **CLC 5, 25, 45, 120; DAM MULT; HLC 1; SSC 39**
See also CA 85-88; CANR 29, 65; DA3; DLB 113; HW 1, 2; LAW; MTCW 1, 2; RGSF; WLIT 1

**Cade, Toni**
See Bambara, Toni Cade

**Cadmus and Harmonia**
See Buchan, John

**Caedmon** fl. 658-680 ...................... **CMLC 7**
See also DLB 146

**Caeiro, Alberto**
See Pessoa, Fernando (Antonio Nogueira)

**Caesar, Julius** ............................... **CMLC 47**
See also Julius Caesar
See also AW 1; RGWL

**Cage, John (Milton, Jr.)** 1912-1992 . **CLC 41**
See also CA 13-16R; 169; CANR 9, 78; DLB 193; INT CANR-9

**Cahan, Abraham** 1860-1951 ........... **TCLC 71**
See also CA 108; 154; DLB 9, 25, 28; RGAL

**Cain, G.**
See Cabrera Infante, G(uillermo)

**Cain, Guillermo**
See Cabrera Infante, G(uillermo)

**Cain, James M(allahan)** 1892-1977 .. **CLC 3, 11, 28**
See also AITN 1; BPFB 1; CA 17-20R; 73-76; CANR 8, 34, 61; CMW; DLB 226; MSW; MTCW 1; RGAL

**Caine, Hall** 1853-1931 ..................... **TCLC 97**
See also RHW

**Caine, Mark**
See Raphael, Frederic (Michael)

**Calasso, Roberto** 1941- .................... **CLC 81**
See also CA 143; CANR 89

**Calderon de la Barca, Pedro** 1600-1681 .......... **LC 23; DC 3; HLCS 1**
See also EW; RGWL

**Caldwell, Erskine (Preston)** 1903-1987 .. **CLC 1, 8, 14, 50, 60; DAM NOV; SSC 19**
See also AITN 1; AMW; BPFB 1; CA 1-4R; 121; CAAS 1; CANR 2, 33; DLB 9, 86; MTCW 1, 2; RGAL; RGSF

**Caldwell, (Janet Miriam) Taylor (Holland)** 1900-1985 .. **CLC 2, 28, 39; DAM NOV, POP**
See also BPFB 1; CA 5-8R; 116; CANR 5; DA3; DLBD 17; RHW

**Calhoun, John Caldwell** 1782-1850 ................. **NCLC 15**
See also DLB 3

**Calisher, Hortense** 1911- ...... **CLC 2, 4, 8, 38, 134; DAM NOV; SSC 15**
See also CA 1-4R; CANR 1, 22, 67; CN; DA3; DLB 2; INT CANR-22; MTCW 1, 2; RGAL; RGSF

**Callaghan, Morley Edward** 1903-1990 ....... **CLC 3, 14, 41, 65; DAC; DAM MST**
See also CA 9-12R; 132; CANR 33, 73; DLB 68; MTCW 1, 2; RGEL; RGSF

**Callimachus** c. 305B.C.-c. 240B.C. ................. **CMLC 18**
See also AW 1; DLB 176; RGWL

**Calvin, Jean**
See Calvin, John
See also GFL Beginnings to 1789

**Calvin, John** 1509-1564 ....................... **LC 37**
See also Calvin, Jean

**Calvino, Italo** 1923-1985 .... **CLC 5, 8, 11, 22, 33, 39, 73; DAM NOV; SSC 3, 48**
See also CA 85-88; 116; CANR 23, 61; DLB 196; EW; MTCW 1, 2; RGSF; RGWL; SFW; SSFS 12

**Cameron, Carey** 1952- ....................... **CLC 59**
See also CA 135

**Cameron, Peter** 1959- ........................ **CLC 44**
See also CA 125; CANR 50; DLB 234; GLL 2

**Camoens, Luis Vaz de** 1524(?)-1580
See also EW; HLCS 1

**Camoes, Luis de** 1524(?)-1580 ........... **LC 62; HLCS 1; PC 31**
See also RGWL

**Campana, Dino** 1885-1932 ............. **TCLC 20**
See also CA 117; DLB 114

**Campanella, Tommaso** 1568-1639 ....... **LC 32**
See also RGWL

**Campbell, John W(ood, Jr.)** 1910-1971 ..................... **CLC 32**
See also CA 21-22; 29-32R; CANR 34; CAP 2; DLB 8; MTCW 1; SFW

**Campbell, Joseph** 1904-1987 ............. **CLC 69**
See also AAYA 3; BEST 89:2; CA 1-4R; 124; CANR 3, 28, 61; DA3; MTCW 1, 2

**Campbell, Maria** 1940- ......... **CLC 85; DAC**
See also CA 102; CANR 54; CCA 1; NNAL

**Campbell, (John) Ramsey** 1946- ..... **CLC 42; SSC 19**
See also CA 57-60; CANR 7, 102; HGG; INT CANR-7; SUFW

**Campbell, (Ignatius) Roy (Dunnachie)** 1901-1957 ..................... **TCLC 5**
See also AFW; CA 104; 155; DLB 20, 225; MTCW 2; RGEL

**Campbell, Thomas** 1777-1844 ........ **NCLC 19**
See also DLB 93; 144; RGEL

**Campbell, Wilfred** ......................... **TCLC 9**
See also Campbell, William

**Campbell, William** 1858(?)-1918
See Campbell, Wilfred
See also CA 106; DLB 92

**Campion, Jane** ................................. **CLC 95**
See also AAYA 33; CA 138; CANR 87

**Camus, Albert** 1913-1960 ....... **CLC 1, 2, 4, 9, 11, 14, 32, 63, 69, 124; DA; DAB; DAC; DAM DRAM, MST, NOV; DC 2; SSC 9; WLC**
See also AAYA 36; AFW; BPFB 1; CA 89-92; DA3; DLB 72; EW; EXPN; EXPS; GFL 1789 to the Present; MTCW 1, 2; NFS 6; RGSF; RGWL; SSFS 4

**Canby, Vincent** 1924-2000 ................. **CLC 13**
See also CA 81-84; 191

**Cancale**
See Desnos, Robert

**Canetti, Elias** 1905-1994 .. **CLC 3, 14, 25, 75, 86**
See also CA 21-24R; 146; CANR 23, 61, 79; CWW 2; DA3; DLB 85, 124; EW; MTCW 1, 2; RGWL

**Canfield, Dorothea F.**
See Fisher, Dorothy (Frances) Canfield

**Canfield, Dorothea Frances**
See Fisher, Dorothy (Frances) Canfield

**Canfield, Dorothy**
See Fisher, Dorothy (Frances) Canfield

**Canin, Ethan** 1960- ........................... **CLC 55**
See also CA 131; 135

**Cankar, Ivan** 1876-1918 ................ **TCLC 105**
See also DLB 147

**Cannon, Curt**
See Hunter, Evan

**Cao, Lan** 1961- ................................. **CLC 109**
See also CA 165

**Cape, Judith**
See Page, P(atricia) K(athleen)
See also CCA 1

**Capek, Karel** 1890-1938 ... **TCLC 6, 37; DA; DAB; DAC; DAM DRAM, MST, NOV; DC 1; SSC 36; WLC**
See also CA 104; 140; DA3; DFS 7, 11 !**; EW; MTCW 1; RGSF; RGWL; SCFW 2; SFW

**Capote, Truman** 1924-1984 . **CLC 1, 3, 8, 13, 19, 34, 38, 58; DA; DAB; DAC; DAM MST, NOV, POP; SSC 2, 47; WLC**
See also AMWS 3; BPFB 1; CA 5-8R; 113; CANR 18, 62; CDALB 1941-1968; CPW; DA3; DLB 2, 185, 227; DLBY 80, 84; EXPS; GLL 1; LAIT 3; MTCW 1, 2; NCFS 2; RGAL; RGSF; SATA 91; SSFS 2

**Capra, Frank** 1897-1991 .................... **CLC 16**
See also CA 61-64; 135

**Caputo, Philip** 1941- .......................... **CLC 32**
See also CA 73-76; CANR 40; YAW

**Caragiale, Ion Luca** 1852-1912 ...... **TCLC 76**
See also CA 157

**Card, Orson Scott** 1951- ..... **CLC 44, 47, 50; DAM POP**
See also AAYA 11, 42; BPFB 1; BYA 5, 8; CA 102; CANR 27, 47, 73, 102; CPW; DA3; FANT; INT CANR-27; MTCW 1, 2; NFS 5; SATA 83; SFW; YAW

**Cardenal, Ernesto** 1925- ....... **CLC 31; DAM MULT, POET; HLC 1; PC 22**
See also CA 49-52; CANR 2, 32, 66; CWW 2; HW 1, 2; MTCW 1, 2; RGWL

**Cardozo, Benjamin N(athan)** 1870-1938 ................. **TCLC 65**
See also CA 117; 164

**Carducci, Giosue (Alessandro Giuseppe)** 1835-1907 ............................ **TCLC 32**
See also CA 163; EW; RGWL

**Carew, Thomas** 1595(?)-1640 . **LC 13; PC 29**
See also BRW 2; DLB 126; PAB; RGEL

**Carey, Ernestine Gilbreth** 1908- ...... **CLC 17**
See also CA 5-8R; CANR 71; SATA 2

**Carey, Peter** 1943- .................. **CLC 40, 55, 96**
See also CA 123; 127; CANR 53, 76; CN; INT CA-127; MTCW 1, 2; RGSF; SATA 94

**Carleton, William** 1794-1869 ........... **NCLC 3**
See also DLB 159; RGEL; RGSF

**Carlisle, Henry (Coffin)** 1926- ........... **CLC 33**
See also CA 13-16R; CANR 15, 85

**Carlsen, Chris**
See Holdstock, Robert P.

**Carlson, Ron(ald F.)** 1947- ................. **CLC 54**
See also CA 105; CAAE 189; CANR 27; DLB 244

**Carlyle, Thomas** 1795-1881 .... **NCLC 22, 70; DA; DAB; DAC; DAM MST**
See also BRW 4; CDBLB 1789-1832; DLB 55; 144; RGEL

**Carman, (William) Bliss** 1861-1929 .......... **TCLC 7; DAC; PC 34**
See also CA 104; 152; DLB 92; RGEL

**Carnegie, Dale** 1888-1955 ............... **TCLC 53**

**Carossa, Hans** 1878-1956 ............... **TCLC 48**
See also CA 170; DLB 66

**Carpenter, Don(ald Richard)** 1931-1995 ................................. **CLC 41**
See also CA 45-48; 149; CANR 1, 71

**Carpenter, Edward** 1844-1929 ....... **TCLC 88**
See also CA 163; GLL 1

**Carpentier (y Valmont), Alejo** 1904-1980 ..... **CLC 8, 11, 38, 110; DAM MULT; HLC 1; SSC 35**
See also CA 65-68; 97-100; CANR 11, 70; DLB 113; HW 1, 2; LAW; RGSF; RGWL; WLIT 1

**Carr, Caleb** 1955(?)- ............................. **CLC 86**
See also CA 147; CANR 73; DA3

**Carr, Emily** 1871-1945 .................... **TCLC 32**
See also CA 159; DLB 68; FW; GLL 2

**Carr, John Dickson** 1906-1977 .......... **CLC 3**
See also Fairbairn, Roger
See also CA 49-52; 69-72; CANR 3, 33, 60; CMW; MSW; MTCW 1, 2

**Carr, Philippa**
See Hibbert, Eleanor Alice Burford

**Carr, Virginia Spencer** 1929- ............ **CLC 34**
See also CA 61-64; DLB 111

**Carrere, Emmanuel** 1957- ................ **CLC 89**

**Carrier, Roch** 1937- ........ **CLC 13, 78; DAC; DAM MST**
See also CA 130; CANR 61; CCA 1; DLB 53; SATA 105

**Carroll, James P.** 1943(?)- ................. **CLC 38**
See also CA 81-84; CANR 73; MTCW 1

**Carroll, Jim** 1951- ..................... **CLC 35, 143**
See also AAYA 17; CA 45-48; CANR 42

**Carroll, Lewis** ... **NCLC 2, 53; PC 18; WLC**
See also Dodgson, Charles Lutwidge
See also AAYA 39; BRW 5; BYA 5, 13; CDBLB 1832-1890; CLR 2, 18; DLB 18, 163, 178; DLBY 98; EXPN; EXPP; FANT; JRDA; LAIT 1; NFS 7; PFS 11; RGEL

**Carroll, Paul Vincent** 1900-1968 ...... **CLC 10**
See also CA 9-12R; 25-28R; DLB 10; RGEL

**Carruth, Hayden** 1921- ..... **CLC 4, 7, 10, 18, 84; PC 10**
See also CA 9-12R; CANR 4, 38, 59; CP; DLB 5, 165; INT CANR-4; MTCW 1, 2; SATA 47

**Carson, Rachel Louise** 1907-1964 ... **CLC 71; DAM POP**
See also AMWS 9; ANW; CA 77-80; CANR 35; DA3; FW; LAIT 4; MTCW 1, 2; NCFS 1; SATA 23

**Carter, Angela (Olive)** 1940-1992 ...... **CLC 5, 41, 76; SSC 13**
See also BRWS 3; CA 53-56; 136; CANR 12, 36, 61; DA3; DLB 14, 207; EXPS; FANT; FW; MTCW 1, 2; RGSF; SATA 66; SATA-Obit 70; SFW; SSFS 4, 12; WLIT 4

**Carter, Nick**
See Smith, Martin Cruz

**Carver, Raymond** 1938-1988 ..... **CLC 22, 36, 53, 55, 126; DAM NOV; SSC 8**
See also AMWS 3; BPFB 1; CA 33-36R; 126; CANR 17, 34, 61, 103; CPW; DA3; DLB 130; DLBY 84, 88; MTCW 1, 2; RGAL; RGSF; SSFS 3, 6, 12, 13; TCWW 2

**Cary, Elizabeth, Lady Falkland** 1585-1639 ...................................... **LC 30**

**Cary, (Arthur) Joyce (Lunel)** 1888-1957 ............................. **TCLC 1, 29**
See also BRW 7; CA 104; 164; CDBLB 1914-1945; DLB 15, 100; MTCW 2; RGEL

**Casanova de Seingalt, Giovanni Jacopo** 1725-1798 ..................................... **LC 13**

**Casares, Adolfo Bioy**
See Bioy Casares, Adolfo
See also RGSF

**Casas, Bartolome de las** 1474-1566
See Las Casas, Bartolome de
See also WLIT 1

**Casely-Hayford, J(oseph) E(phraim)** 1866-1903 ....... **TCLC 24; BLC 1; DAM MULT**
See also BW 2; CA 123; 152

**Casey, John (Dudley)** 1939- ............... **CLC 59**
See also BEST 90:2; CA 69-72; CANR 23, 100

**Casey, Michael** 1947- .......................... **CLC 2**
See also CA 65-68; DLB 5

**Casey, Patrick**
See Thurman, Wallace (Henry)

**Casey, Warren (Peter)** 1935-1988 .... **CLC 12**
See also CA 101; 127; INT 101

**Casona, Alejandro** ............................. **CLC 49**
See also Alvarez, Alejandro Rodriguez

**Cassavetes, John** 1929-1989 .............. **CLC 20**
See also CA 85-88; 127; CANR 82

**Cassian, Nina** 1924- ............................ **PC 17**
See also CWP; CWW 2

**Cassill, R(onald) V(erlin)** 1919- ... **CLC 4, 23**
See also CA 9-12R; CAAS 1; CANR 7, 45; CN; DLB 6

**Cassiodorus, Flavius Magnus** c. 490(?)-c. 583(?) ..................................... **CMLC 43**

**Cassirer, Ernst** 1874-1945 ............... **TCLC 61**
See also CA 157

**Cassity, (Allen) Turner** 1929- ....... **CLC 6, 42**
See also CA 17-20R; CAAS 8; CANR 11; CSW; DLB 105

**Castaneda, Carlos (Cesar Aranha)** 1931(?)-1998 ....................... **CLC 12, 119**
See also CA 25-28R; CANR 32, 66; HW 1; MTCW 1

**Castedo, Elena** 1937- ........................ **CLC 65**
See also CA 132

**Castedo-Ellerman, Elena**
See Castedo, Elena

**Castellanos, Rosario** 1925-1974 ........ **CLC 66; DAM MULT; HLC 1; SSC 39**
See also CA 131; 53-56; CANR 58; DLB 113; FW; HW 1; LAW; MTCW 1; RGSF; RGWL

**Castelvetro, Lodovico** 1505-1571 ........ **LC 12**

**Castiglione, Baldassare** 1478-1529 ...... **LC 12**
See also EW; RGWL

**Castiglione, Baldesar**
See Castiglione, Baldassare

**Castillo, Ana (Hernandez Del)** 1953- .................................... **CLC 151**
See also AAYA 42; CA 131; CANR 51, 86; CWP; DLB 122, 227; DNFS; FW; HW 1

**Castle, Robert**
See Hamilton, Edmond

**Castro (Ruz), Fidel** 1926(?)-
See also CA 110; 129; CANR 81; DAM MULT; HLC 1; HW 2

**Castro, Guillen de** 1569-1631 ............... **LC 19**

**Castro, Rosalia de** 1837-1885 ... **NCLC 3, 78; DAM MULT**

**Cather, Willa**
See Cather, Willa Sibert
See also AMW; AMWR 1; BPFB 1; MAWW; NFS 2; RGAL; RGSF; RHW; TCWW 2

**Cather, Willa Sibert** 1873-1947 ....... **TCLC 1, 11, 31, 99; DA; DAB; DAC; DAM MST, NOV; SSC 2; WLC**
See also Cather, Willa
See also AAYA 24; CA 104; 128; CDALB 1865-1917; DA3; DLB 9, 54, 78; DLBD 1; EXPN; EXPS; LAIT 3; MTCW 1, 2; SATA 30; SSFS 2, 7

**Catherine, Saint** 1347-1380 ........... **CMLC 27**

**Catherine the Great** 1729-1796 ........... **LC 69**

**Cato, Marcus Porcius** 234B.C.-149B.C. ..................... **CMLC 21**
See also DLB 211

**Catton, (Charles) Bruce** 1899-1978 . **CLC 35**
See also AITN 1; CA 5-8R; 81-84; CANR 7, 74; DLB 17; SATA 2; SATA-Obit 24

**Catullus** c. 84B.C.-54B.C. ............... **CMLC 18**
See also AW 2; DLB 211; RGWL

**Cauldwell, Frank**
See King, Francis (Henry)

**Caunitz, William J.** 1933-1996 ......... **CLC 34**
See also BEST 89:3; CA 125; 130; 152; CANR 73; INT 130

**Causley, Charles (Stanley)** 1917- ....... **CLC 7**
See also CA 9-12R; CANR 5, 35, 94; CLR 30; CWRI; DLB 27; MTCW 1; SATA 3, 66

**Caute, (John) David** 1936- .... **CLC 29; DAM NOV**
See also CA 1-4R; CAAS 4; CANR 1, 33, 64; CBD; CD; CN; DLB 14, 231

**Cavafy, C(onstantine) P(eter)** ... **TCLC 2, 7; DAM POET; PC 36**
See also Kavafis, Konstantinos Petrou
See also CA 148; DA3; EW; MTCW 1; RGWL; WP

**Cavallo, Evelyn**
See Spark, Muriel (Sarah)

**Cavanna, Betty** .................. CLC 12
See also Harrison, Elizabeth Cavanna
See also JRDA; MAICYA; SAAS 4; SATA 1, 30

**Cavendish, Margaret Lucas**
1623-1673 ...................... LC 30
See also DLB 131; RGEL

**Caxton, William** 1421(?)-1491(?) ......... LC 17
See also DLB 170

**Cayer, D. M.**
See Duffy, Maureen

**Cayrol, Jean** 1911- .................. CLC 11
See also CA 89-92; DLB 83

**Cela, Camilo Jose** 1916- ....... CLC 4, 13, 59, 122; DAM MULT; HLC 1
See also BEST 90:2; CA 21-24R; CAAS 10; CANR 21, 32, 76; DLBY 89; EW; HW 1; MTCW 1, 2; RGSF; RGWL

**Celan, Paul** ........ CLC 10, 19, 53, 82; PC 10
See also Antschel, Paul
See also DLB 69; RGWL

**Celine, Louis-Ferdinand** .. CLC 1, 3, 4, 7, 9, 15, 47, 124
See also Destouches, Louis-Ferdinand
See also DLB 72; EW; GFL 1789 to the Present; RGWL

**Cellini, Benvenuto** 1500-1571 ............... LC 7

**Cendrars, Blaise** .................. CLC 18, 106
See also Sauser-Hall, Frederic
See also GFL 1789 to the Present; RGWL; WP

**Centlivre, Susanna** 1669(?)-1723 ......... LC 65
See also DLB 84; RGEL

**Cernuda (y Bidon), Luis**
1902-1963 .......... CLC 54; DAM POET
See also CA 131; 89-92; DLB 134; GLL 1; HW 1; RGWL

**Cervantes, Lorna Dee** 1954- ................ PC 35
See also CA 131; CANR 80; CWP; DLB 82; EXPP; HLCS 1; HW 1

**Cervantes (Saavedra), Miguel de**
1547-1616 .. LC 6, 23; DA; DAB; DAC; DAM MST, NOV; HLCS; SSC 12; WLC
See also BYA 1; EW; LAIT 1; NFS 8; RGSF; RGWL

**Cesaire, Aime (Fernand)** 1913- . CLC 19, 32, 112; BLC 1; DAM MULT, POET; PC 25
See also BW 2, 3; CA 65-68; CANR 24, 43, 81; DA3; GFL 1789 to the Present; MTCW 1, 2; WP

**Chabon, Michael** 1963- ............ CLC 55, 149
See also CA 139; CANR 57, 96

**Chabrol, Claude** 1930- .................... CLC 16
See also CA 110

**Challans, Mary** 1905-1983
See Renault, Mary
See also CA 81-84; 111; CANR 74; DA3; MTCW 2; SATA 23; SATA-Obit 36

**Challis, George**
See Faust, Frederick (Schiller)
See also TCWW 2

**Chambers, Aidan** 1934- .................... CLC 35
See also AAYA 27; CA 25-28R; CANR 12, 31, 58; JRDA; MAICYA; SAAS 12; SATA 1, 69, 108; YAW

**Chambers, James** 1948-
See Cliff, Jimmy
See also CA 124

**Chambers, Jessie**
See Lawrence, D(avid) H(erbert Richards)
See also GLL 1

**Chambers, Robert W(illiam)**
1865-1933 ....................... TCLC 41
See also CA 165; DLB 202; HGG; SATA 107; SUFW

**Chamisso, Adelbert von**
1781-1838 ..................... NCLC 82
See also DLB 90; RGWL

**Chandler, Raymond (Thornton)**
1888-1959 ............... TCLC 1, 7; SSC 23
See also AAYA 25; AMWS 4; BPFB 1; CA 104; 129; CANR 60; CDALB 1929-1941; CMW; DA3; DLB 226; DLBD 6; MSW; MTCW 1, 2; RGAL

**Chang, Eileen** 1921-1995 ................... SSC 28
See also CA 166; CWW 2

**Chang, Jung** 1952- ............................ CLC 71
See also CA 142

**Chang Ai-Ling**
See Chang, Eileen

**Channing, William Ellery**
1780-1842 ..................... NCLC 17
See also DLB 1, 59, 235; RGAL

**Chao, Patricia** 1955- ......................... CLC 119
See also CA 163

**Chaplin, Charles Spencer**
1889-1977 ................... CLC 16
See also Chaplin, Charlie
See also CA 81-84; 73-76

**Chaplin, Charlie**
See Chaplin, Charles Spencer
See also DLB 44

**Chapman, George** 1559(?)-1634 ......... LC 22; DAM DRAM
See also BRW 1; DLB 62, 121; RGEL

**Chapman, Graham** 1941-1989 ......... CLC 21
See also Monty Python
See also CA 116; 129; CANR 35, 95

**Chapman, John Jay** 1862-1933 ....... TCLC 7
See also CA 104; 191

**Chapman, Lee**
See Bradley, Marion Zimmer
See also GLL 1

**Chapman, Walker**
See Silverberg, Robert

**Chappell, Fred (Davis)** 1936- ..... CLC 40, 78
See also CA 5-8R; CAAS 4; CANR 8, 33, 67; CN; CP; CSW; DLB 6, 105; HGG

**Char, Rene(-Emile)** 1907-1988 .... CLC 9, 11, 14, 55; DAM POET
See also CA 13-16R; 124; CANR 32; GFL 1789 to the Present; MTCW 1, 2; RGWL

**Charby, Jay**
See Ellison, Harlan (Jay)

**Chardin, Pierre Teilhard de**
See Teilhard de Chardin, (Marie Joseph) Pierre

**Charlemagne** 742-814 ..................... CMLC 37

**Charles I** 1600-1649 ......................... LC 13

**Charriere, Isabelle de** 1740-1805 .. NCLC 66

**Chartier, Emile-Auguste**
See Alain

**Charyn, Jerome** 1937- ............. CLC 5, 8, 18
See also CA 5-8R; CAAS 1; CANR 7, 61, 101; CMW; CN; DLBY 83; MTCW 1

**Chase, Adam**
See Marlowe, Stephen

**Chase, Mary (Coyle)** 1907-1981 ........... DC 1
See also CA 77-80; 105; CAD; CWD; DFS 11; DLB 228; SATA 17; SATA-Obit 29

**Chase, Mary Ellen** 1887-1973 ............ CLC 2
See also CA 13-16; 41-44R; CAP 1; SATA 10

**Chase, Nicholas**
See Hyde, Anthony
See also CCA 1

**Chateaubriand, Francois Rene de**
1768-1848 ..................... NCLC 3
See also DLB 119; EW; GFL 1789 to the Present; RGWL

**Chatterje, Sarat Chandra** 1876-1936(?)
See Chatterji, Saratchandra
See also CA 109

**Chatterji, Bankim Chandra**
1838-1894 ..................... NCLC 19

**Chatterji, Saratchandra** ................. TCLC 13
See also Chatterje, Sarat Chandra
See also CA 186

**Chatterton, Thomas** 1752-1770 ..... LC 3, 54; DAM POET
See also DLB 109; RGEL

**Chatwin, (Charles) Bruce**
1940-1989 . CLC 28, 57, 59; DAM POP
See also AAYA 4; BEST 90:1; BRWS 4; CA 85-88; 127; CPW; DLB 194, 204

**Chaucer, Daniel**
See Ford, Ford Madox
See also RHW

**Chaucer, Geoffrey** 1340(?)-1400 .. LC 17, 56; DA; DAB; DAC; DAM MST, POET; PC 19; WLCS
See also BRW 1; CDBLB Before 1660; DA3; DLB 146; LAIT 1; PAB; RGEL; WLIT 3; WP

**Chavez, Denise (Elia)** 1948-
See also CA 131; CANR 56, 81; DAM MULT; DLB 122; FW; HLC 1; HW 1, 2; MTCW 2

**Chaviaras, Strates** 1935-
See Haviaras, Stratis
See also CA 105

**Chayefsky, Paddy** ........................ CLC 23
See also Chayefsky, Sidney
See also CAD; DLB 7, 44; DLBY 81; RGAL

**Chayefsky, Sidney** 1923-1981
See Chayefsky, Paddy
See also CA 9-12R; 104; CANR 18; DAM DRAM

**Chedid, Andree** 1920- ........................ CLC 47
See also CA 145; CANR 95

**Cheever, John** 1912-1982 ..... CLC 3, 7, 8, 11, 15, 25, 64; DA; DAB; DAC; DAM MST, NOV, POP; SSC 1, 38; WLC
See also AMWS 1; BPFB 1; CA 5-8R; 106; CABS 1; CANR 5, 27, 76; CDALB 1941-1968; CPW; DA3; DLB 2, 102, 227; DLBY 80, 82; EXPS; INT CANR-5; MTCW 1, 2; RGAL; RGSF; SSFS 2

**Cheever, Susan** 1943- ................. CLC 18, 48
See also CA 103; CANR 27, 51, 92; DLBY 82; INT CANR-27

**Chekhonte, Antosha**
See Chekhov, Anton (Pavlovich)

**Chekhov, Anton (Pavlovich)**
1860-1904 ........ TCLC 3, 10, 31, 55, 96; DA; DAB; DAC; DAM DRAM, MST; DC 9; SSC 2, 28, 41; WLC
See also CA 104; 124; DA3; DFS 1, 5, 10, 12; EW; EXPS; LAIT 3; RGSF; RGWL; SATA 90; SSFS 5, 13

**Cheney, Lynne V.** 1941- ..................... CLC 70
See also CA 89-92; CANR 58

**Chernyshevsky, Nikolai Gavrilovich**
See Chernyshevsky, Nikolay Gavrilovich

**Chernyshevsky, Nikolay Gavrilovich**
1828-1889 ................... NCLC 1
See also DLB 238

**Cherry, Carolyn Janice** 1942-
See Cherryh, C. J.
See also CA 65-68; CANR 10; FANT; SFW; YAW

**Cherryh, C. J.** .................................. CLC 35
See also Cherry, Carolyn Janice
See also AAYA 24; BPFB 1; DLBY 80; SATA 93

**Chesnutt, Charles W(addell)**
1858-1932 .. TCLC 5, 39; BLC 1; DAM MULT; SSC 7
See also AFAW 1, 2; BW 1, 3; CA 106; 125; CANR 76; DLB 12, 50, 78; MTCW 1, 2; RGAL; RGSF; SSFS 11

**Chester, Alfred** 1929(?)-1971 ............. **CLC 49**
See also CA 33-36R; DLB 130

**Chesterton, G(ilbert) K(eith)**
1874-1936 . **TCLC 1, 6, 64; DAM NOV, POET; PC 28; SSC 1, 46**
See also BRW 6; CA 104; 132; CANR 73; CDBLB 1914-1945; CMW; DLB 10, 19, 34, 70, 98, 149, 178; FANT; MSW; MTCW 1, 2; RGEL; RGSF; SATA 27; SUFW

**Chiang, Pin-chin** 1904-1986
See Ding Ling
See also CA 118

**Ch'ien Chung-shu** 1910- ................... **CLC 22**
See also CA 130; CANR 73; MTCW 1, 2

**Chikamatsu Monzaemon** 1653-1724 ... **LC 66**
See also RGWL

**Child, L. Maria**
See Child, Lydia Maria

**Child, Lydia Maria** 1802-1880 .. **NCLC 6, 73**
See also DLB 1, 74, 243; RGAL; SATA 67

**Child, Mrs.**
See Child, Lydia Maria

**Child, Philip** 1898-1978 ............... **CLC 19, 68**
See also CA 13-14; CAP 1; RHW; SATA 47

**Childers, (Robert) Erskine**
1870-1922 ................................ **TCLC 65**
See also CA 113; 153; DLB 70

**Childress, Alice** 1920-1994 .. **CLC 12, 15, 86, 96; BLC 1; DAM DRAM, MULT, NOV; DC 4**
See also AAYA 8; BW 2, 3; BYA 2; CA 45-48; 146; CAD; CANR 3, 27, 50, 74; CLR 14; CWD; DA3; DFS 2,8; DLB 7, 38; JRDA; LAIT 5; MAICYA; MTCW 1, 2; RGAL; SATA 7, 48, 81; YAW

**Chin, Frank (Chew, Jr.)** 1940- **CLC 135; DAM MULT; DC 7**
See also CA 33-36R; CANR 71; CD; DLB 206; LAIT 5; RGAL

**Chislett, (Margaret) Anne** 1943- ...... **CLC 34**
See also CA 151

**Chitty, Thomas Willes** 1926- ............. **CLC 11**
See also Hinde, Thomas
See also CA 5-8R; CN

**Chivers, Thomas Holley**
1809-1858 ................................ **NCLC 49**
See also DLB 3; RGAL

**Choi, Susan** ....................................... **CLC 119**

**Chomette, Rene Lucien** 1898-1981
See Clair, Rene
See also CA 103

**Chomsky, (Avram) Noam** 1928- ..... **CLC 132**
See also CA 17-20R; CANR 28, 62; DA3; DLB 246; MTCW 1, 2

**Chopin, Kate** . **TCLC 5, 14; DA; DAB; SSC 8; WLCS**
See also Chopin, Katherine
See also AAYA 33; AMWS 1; CDALB 1865-1917; DLB 12, 78; EXPN; EXPS; LAIT 3; MAWW; NFS 3; RGAL; RGSF; SSFS 2

**Chopin, Katherine** 1851-1904
See Chopin, Kate
See also CA 104; 122; DA3; DAC; DAM MST, NOV; FW; SSFS 13

**Chretien de Troyes** c. 12th cent. - . **CMLC 10**
See also DLB 208; EW; RGWL

**Christie**
See Ichikawa, Kon

**Christie, Agatha (Mary Clarissa)**
1890-1976 ......... **CLC 1, 6, 8, 12, 39, 48, 110; DAB; DAC; DAM NOV**
See also AAYA 9; AITN 1, 2; BPFB 1; BRWS 2; CA 17-20R; 61-64; CANR 10, 37; CBD; CDBLB 1914-1945; CMW; CPW; CWD; DA3; DFS 2; DLB 13, 77; MSW; MTCW 1, 2; NFS 8; RGEL; RHW; SATA 36; YAW

**Christie, (Ann) Philippa**
See Pearce, Philippa
See also CA 5-8R; CANR 4; CWRI; FANT

**Christine de Pizan** 1365(?)-1431(?) ....... **LC 9**
See also DLB 208; RGWL

**Chubb, Elmer**
See Masters, Edgar Lee

**Chulkov, Mikhail Dmitrievich**
1743-1792 ................................. **LC 2**
See also DLB 150

**Churchill, Caryl** 1938- .... **CLC 31, 55; DC 5**
See also BRWS 4; CA 102; CANR 22, 46; CBD; CWD; DFS 12; DLB 13; FW; MTCW 1; RGEL

**Churchill, Charles** 1731-1764 ................ **LC 3**
See also DLB 109; RGEL

**Churchill, Sir Winston (Leonard Spencer)**
1874-1965 ................................ **TCLC 113**
See also BRW 6; CA 97-100; CDBLB 1890-1914; DA3; DLB 100; DLBD 16; LAIT 4; MTCW 1, 2

**Chute, Carolyn** 1947- ........................ **CLC 39**
See also CA 123

**Ciardi, John (Anthony)** 1916-1986 . **CLC 10, 40, 44, 129; DAM POET**
See also CA 5-8R; 118; CAAS 2; CANR 5, 33; CLR 19; CWRI; DLB 5; DLBY 86; INT CANR-5; MAICYA; MTCW 1, 2; RGAL; SAAS 26; SATA 1, 65; SATA-Obit 46

**Cibber, Colley** 1671-1757 ...................... **LC 66**
See also DLB 84; RGEL

**Cicero, Marcus Tullius**
106B.C.-43B.C. .......................... **CMLC 3**
See also AW 1; DLB 211; RGWL

**Cimino, Michael** 1943- ....................... **CLC 16**
See also CA 105

**Cioran, E(mil) M.** 1911-1995 ............ **CLC 64**
See also CA 25-28R; 149; CANR 91; DLB 220

**Cisneros, Sandra** 1954- . **CLC 69, 118; DAM MULT; HLC 1; SSC 32**
See also AAYA 9; AMWS 7; CA 131; CANR 64; CWP; DA3; DLB 122, 152; EXPN; FW; HW 1, 2; LAIT 5; MTCW 2; NFS 2; RGAL; RGSF; SSFS 3, 13; WLIT 1; YAW

**Cixous, Helene** 1937- ........................ **CLC 92**
See also CA 126; CANR 55; CWW 2; DLB 83, 242; FW; MTCW 1, 2

**Clair, Rene** ....................................... **CLC 20**
See also Chomette, Rene Lucien

**Clampitt, Amy** 1920-1994 .... **CLC 32; PC 19**
See also AMWS 9; CA 110; 146; CANR 29, 79; DLB 105

**Clancy, Thomas L., Jr.** 1947-
See Clancy, Tom
See also CA 125; 131; CANR 62; CPW; DA3; DLB 227; INT 131; MTCW 1, 2

**Clancy, Tom** ........ **CLC 45, 112; DAM NOV, POP**
See also Clancy, Thomas L., Jr.
See also AAYA 9; BEST 89:1, 90:1; BPFB 1; BYA 10, 11; CMW; MTCW 2

**Clare, John** 1793-1864 ... **NCLC 9, 86; DAB; DAM POET; PC 23**
See also DLB 55, 96; RGEL

**Clarin**
See Alas (y Urena), Leopoldo (Enrique Garcia)

**Clark, Al C.**
See Goines, Donald

**Clark, (Robert) Brian** 1932- ............. **CLC 29**
See also CA 41-44R; CANR 67; CBD; CD

**Clark, Curt**
See Westlake, Donald E(dwin)

**Clark, Eleanor** 1913-1996 ............. **CLC 5, 19**
See also CA 9-12R; 151; CANR 41; CN; DLB 6

**Clark, J. P.**
See Clark Bekedermo, J(ohnson) P(epper)
See also DLB 117

**Clark, John Pepper**
See Clark Bekedermo, J(ohnson) P(epper)
See also AFW; CD; CP; RGEL

**Clark, M. R.**
See Clark, Mavis Thorpe

**Clark, Mavis Thorpe** 1909- .............. **CLC 12**
See also CA 57-60; CANR 8, 37; CLR 30; CWRI; MAICYA; SAAS 5; SATA 8, 74

**Clark, Walter Van Tilburg**
1909-1971 ................................. **CLC 28**
See also CA 9-12R; 33-36R; CANR 63; DLB 9, 206; LAIT 2; RGAL; SATA 8

**Clark Bekedermo, J(ohnson) P(epper)**
1935- .. **CLC 38; BLC 1; DAM DRAM, MULT; DC 5**
See also Clark, J. P.; Clark, John Pepper
See also BW 1; CA 65-68; CANR 16, 72; DFS 13; MTCW 1

**Clarke, Arthur C(harles)** 1917- .... **CLC 1, 4, 13, 18, 35, 136; DAM POP; SSC 3**
See also AAYA 4, 33; BPFB 1; BYA 13; CA 1-4R; CANR 2, 28, 55, 74; CN; CPW; DA3; JRDA; LAIT 5; MAICYA; MTCW 1, 2; SATA 13, 70, 115; SCFW; SFW; SSFS 4; YAW

**Clarke, Austin** 1896-1974 ... **CLC 6, 9; DAM POET**
See also CA 29-32; 49-52; CAP 2; DLB 10, 20; RGEL

**Clarke, Austin C(hesterfield)** 1934- .. **CLC 8, 53; BLC 1; DAC; DAM MULT; SSC 45**
See also BW 1; CA 25-28R; CAAS 16; CANR 14, 32, 68; CN; DLB 53, 125; DNFS; RGSF

**Clarke, Gillian** 1937- ........................ **CLC 61**
See also CA 106; CP; CWP; DLB 40

**Clarke, Marcus (Andrew Hislop)**
1846-1881 ................................ **NCLC 19**
See also DLB 230; RGEL; RGSF

**Clarke, Shirley** 1925-1997 ................ **CLC 16**
See also CA 189

**Clash, The**
See Headon, (Nicky) Topper; Jones, Mick; Simonon, Paul; Strummer, Joe

**Claudel, Paul (Louis Charles Marie)**
1868-1955 .......................... **TCLC 2, 10**
See also CA 104; 165; DLB 192; EW; GFL 1789 to the Present; RGWL

**Claudian** 370(?)-404(?) .................. **CMLC 46**
See also RGWL

**Claudius, Matthias** 1740-1815 ....... **NCLC 75**
See also DLB 97

**Clavell, James (duMaresq)**
1925-1994 .. **CLC 6, 25, 87; DAM NOV, POP**
See also BPFB 1; CA 25-28R; 146; CANR 26, 48; CPW; DA3; MTCW 1, 2; NFS 10; RHW

**Clayman, Gregory** ........................... **CLC 65**

**Cleaver, (Leroy) Eldridge**
1935-1998 . **CLC 30, 119; BLC 1; DAM MULT**
See also BW 1, 3; CA 21-24R; 167; CANR 16, 75; DA3; MTCW 2; YAW

**Cleese, John (Marwood)** 1939- ......... **CLC 21**
See also Monty Python
See also CA 112; 116; CANR 35; MTCW 1

**Cleishbotham, Jebediah**
See Scott, Sir Walter

**Cleland, John** 1710-1789 ................. **LC 2, 48**
See also DLB 39; RGEL

**Clemens, Samuel Langhorne** 1835-1910
See Twain, Mark
See also CA 104; 135; CDALB 1865-1917; DA; DA3; DAB; DAC; DAM MST, NOV; DLB 11, 12, 23, 64, 74, 186, 189; JRDA; MAICYA; SATA 100; YABC 2

**Clement of Alexandria** 150(?)-215(?) ............................ **CMLC 41**

**Cleophil**
See Congreve, William

**Clerihew, E.**
See Bentley, E(dmund) C(lerihew)

**Clerk, N. W.**
See Lewis, C(live) S(taples)

**Cliff, Jimmy** ........................................ **CLC 21**
See also Chambers, James
See also CA 193

**Cliff, Michelle** 1946- .......... **CLC 120; BLCS**
See also BW 2; CA 116; CANR 39, 72; DLB 157; FW; GLL 2

**Clifton, (Thelma) Lucille** 1936- ....... **CLC 19, 66; BLC 1; DAM MULT, POET; PC 17**
See also AFAW 2; BW 2, 3; CA 49-52; CANR 2, 24, 42, 76, 97; CLR 5; CP; CSW; CWP; CWRI; DA3; DLB 5, 41; EXPP; MAICYA; MTCW 1, 2; PFS 1; SATA 20, 69; WP

**Clinton, Dirk**
See Silverberg, Robert

**Clough, Arthur Hugh** 1819-1861 ... **NCLC 27**
See also BRW 5; DLB 32; RGEL

**Clutha, Janet Paterson Frame** 1924-
See Frame, Janet
See also CA 1-4R; CANR 2, 36, 76; MTCW 1, 2; SATA 119

**Clyne, Terence**
See Blatty, William Peter

**Cobalt, Martin**
See Mayne, William (James Carter)

**Cobb, Irvin S(hrewsbury)** 1876-1944 ................................ **TCLC 77**
See also CA 175; DLB 11, 25, 86

**Cobbett, William** 1763-1835 .......... **NCLC 49**
See also DLB 43, 107, 158; RGEL

**Coburn, D(onald) L(ee)** 1938- .......... **CLC 10**
See also CA 89-92

**Cocteau, Jean (Maurice Eugene Clement)** 1889-1963 .... **CLC 1, 8, 15, 16, 43; DA; DAB; DAC; DAM DRAM, MST, NOV; WLC**
See also CA 25-28; CANR 40; CAP 2; DA3; DLB 65; EW; GFL 1789 to the Present; MTCW 1, 2; RGWL

**Codrescu, Andrei** 1946- ........ **CLC 46, 121; DAM POET**
See also CA 33-36R; CAAS 19; CANR 13, 34, 53, 76; DA3; MTCW 2

**Coe, Max**
See Bourne, Randolph S(illiman)

**Coe, Tucker**
See Westlake, Donald E(dwin)

**Coen, Ethan** 1958- .......................... **CLC 108**
See also CA 126; CANR 85

**Coen, Joel** 1955- ............................. **CLC 108**
See also CA 126

**The Coen Brothers**
See Coen, Ethan; Coen, Joel

**Coetzee, J(ohn) M(ichael)** 1940- ...... **CLC 23, 33, 66, 117; DAM NOV**
See also AAYA 37; AFW; BRWS 6; CA 77-80; CANR 41, 54, 74; CN; DA3; DLB 225; MTCW 1, 2; WLIT 2

**Coffey, Brian**
See Koontz, Dean R(ay)

**Coffin, Robert P(eter) Tristram** 1892-1955 ............................. **TCLC 95**
See also CA 123; 169; DLB 45

**Cohan, George M(ichael)** 1878-1942 ............................. **TCLC 60**
See also CA 157; RGAL

**Cohen, Arthur A(llen)** 1928-1986 ...... **CLC 7, 31**
See also CA 1-4R; 120; CANR 1, 17, 42; DLB 28

**Cohen, Leonard (Norman)** 1934- ...... **CLC 3, 38; DAC; DAM MST**
See also CA 21-24R; CANR 14, 69; CN; CP; DLB 53; MTCW 1

**Cohen, Matt(hew)** 1942-1999 .......... **CLC 19; DAC**
See also CA 61-64; 187; CAAS 18; CANR 40; CN; DLB 53

**Cohen-Solal, Annie** 19(?)- ................. **CLC 50**

**Colegate, Isabel** 1931- ....................... **CLC 36**
See also CA 17-20R; CANR 8, 22, 74; CN; DLB 14, 231; INT CANR-22; MTCW 1

**Coleman, Emmett**
See Reed, Ishmael

**Coleridge, Hartley** 1796-1849 ........ **NCLC 90**
See also DLB 96

**Coleridge, M. E.**
See Coleridge, Mary E(lizabeth)

**Coleridge, Mary E(lizabeth)** 1861-1907 ............................. **TCLC 73**
See also CA 116; 166; DLB 19, 98

**Coleridge, Samuel Taylor** 1772-1834 . **NCLC 9, 54, 99; DA; DAB; DAC; DAM MST, POET; PC 11; WLC**
See also BRW 4; BYA 4; CDBLB 1789-1832; DA3; DLB 93, 107; EXPP; PAB; PFS 4, 5; RGEL; WLIT 3; WP

**Coleridge, Sara** 1802-1852 .............. **NCLC 31**
See also DLB 199

**Coles, Don** 1928- ............................. **CLC 46**
See also CA 115; CANR 38; CP

**Coles, Robert (Martin)** 1929- .......... **CLC 108**
See also CA 45-48; CANR 3, 32, 66, 70; INT CANR-32; SATA 23

**Colette, (Sidonie-Gabrielle)** 1873-1954 . **TCLC 1, 5, 16; DAM NOV; SSC 10**
See also Willy, Colette
See also CA 104; 131; DA3; DLB 65; EW; GFL 1789 to the Present; MTCW 1, 2; RGWL

**Collett, (Jacobine) Camilla (Wergeland)** 1813-1895 ................................ **NCLC 22**

**Collier, Christopher** 1930- ................. **CLC 30**
See also AAYA 13; BYA 2; CA 33-36R; CANR 13, 33, 102; JRDA; MAICYA; SATA 16, 70; WYA; YAW 1

**Collier, James Lincoln** 1928- ........... **CLC 30; DAM POP**
See also AAYA 13; BYA 2; CA 9-12R; CANR 4, 33, 60, 102; CLR 3; JRDA; MAICYA; SAAS 21; SATA 8, 70; WYA; YAW 1

**Collier, Jeremy** 1650-1726 ..................... **LC 6**

**Collier, John** 1901-1980 ..................... **SSC 19**
See also CA 65-68; 97-100; CANR 10; DLB 77; FANT

**Collingwood, R(obin) G(eorge)** 1889(?)-1943 ........................... **TCLC 67**
See also CA 117; 155

**Collins, Hunt**
See Hunter, Evan

**Collins, Linda** 1931- ........................... **CLC 44**
See also CA 125

**Collins, (William) Wilkie** 1824-1889 ..................... **NCLC 1, 18, 93**
See also BRWS 6; CDBLB 1832-1890; CMW; DLB 18, 70, 159; MSW; RGEL; RGSF; SUFW; WLIT 4

**Collins, William** 1721-1759 . **LC 4, 40; DAM POET**
See also BRW 3; DLB 109; RGEL

**Collodi, Carlo** ................................. **NCLC 54**
See also Lorenzini, Carlo
See also CLR 5; WCH

**Colman, George**
See Glassco, John

**Colonna, Vittoria** 1492-1547 ................. **LC 71**
See also RGWL

**Colt, Winchester Remington**
See Hubbard, L(afayette) Ron(ald)

**Colter, Cyrus** 1910- ........................... **CLC 58**
See also BW 1; CA 65-68; CANR 10, 66; CN; DLB 33

**Colton, James**
See Hansen, Joseph
See also GLL 1

**Colum, Padraic** 1881-1972 ................. **CLC 28**
See also BYA 4; CA 73-76; 33-36R; CANR 35; CLR 36; CWRI; MAICYA; MTCW 1; RGEL; SATA 15

**Colvin, James**
See Moorcock, Michael (John)

**Colwin, Laurie (E.)** 1944-1992 .... **CLC 5, 13, 23, 84**
See also CA 89-92; 139; CANR 20, 46; DLBY 80; MTCW 1

**Comfort, Alex(ander)** 1920-2000 ....... **CLC 7; DAM POP**
See also CA 1-4R; 190; CANR 1, 45; CP; MTCW 1

**Comfort, Montgomery**
See Campbell, (John) Ramsey

**Compton-Burnett, I(vy)** 1892(?)-1969 ......... **CLC 1, 3, 10, 15, 34; DAM NOV**
See also BRW 7; CA 1-4R; 25-28R; CANR 4; DLB 36; MTCW 1; RGEL

**Comstock, Anthony** 1844-1915 ...... **TCLC 13**
See also CA 110; 169

**Comte, Auguste** 1798-1857 ............. **NCLC 54**

**Conan Doyle, Arthur**
See Doyle, Sir Arthur Conan
See also BPFB 1; BYA 4, 5, 11

**Conde (Abellan), Carmen** 1901-1996
See also CA 177; DLB 108; HLCS 1; HW 2

**Conde, Maryse** 1937- .... **CLC 52, 92; BLCS; DAM MULT**
See also BW 2, 3; CA 110; CAAE 190; CANR 30, 53, 76; CWW 2; MTCW 1

**Condillac, Etienne Bonnot de** 1714-1780 ................................. **LC 26**

**Condon, Richard (Thomas)** 1915-1996 ....... **CLC 4, 6, 8, 10, 45, 100; DAM NOV**
See also BEST 90:3; BPFB 1; CA 1-4R; 151; CAAS 1; CANR 2, 23; CMW; CN; INT CANR-23; MTCW 1, 2

**Confucius** 551B.C.-479B.C. .. **CMLC 19; DA; DAB; DAC; DAM MST; WLCS**
See also DA3

**Congreve, William** 1670-1729 ........ **LC 5, 21; DA; DAB; DAC; DAM DRAM, MST, POET; DC 2; WLC**
See also BRW 2; CDBLB 1660-1789; DLB 39, 84; RGEL; WLIT 3

**Connell, Evan S(helby), Jr.** 1924- . **CLC 4, 6, 45; DAM NOV**
See also AAYA 7; CA 1-4R; CAAS 2; CANR 2, 39, 76, 97; CN; DLB 2; DLBY 81; MTCW 1, 2

**Connelly, Marc(us Cook)** 1890-1980 . **CLC 7**
See also CA 85-88; 102; CANR 30; DFS 12; DLB 7; DLBY 80; RGAL; SATA-Obit 25

**Connor, Ralph** ................................ **TCLC 31**
See also Gordon, Charles William
See also DLB 92; TCWW 2

**Conrad, Joseph** 1857-1924 .... **TCLC 1, 6, 13, 25, 43, 57; DA; DAB; DAC; DAM MST, NOV; SSC 9; WLC**
See also AAYA 26; BPFB 1; BRW 6; BYA 2; CA 104; 131; CANR 60; CDBLB 1890-1914; DA3; DLB 10, 34, 98, 156; EXPN; EXPS; LAIT 2; MTCW 1, 2; NFS 2; RGEL; RGSF; SATA 27; SSFS 1, 12; WLIT 4

**Conrad, Robert Arnold**
See Hart, Moss

**Conroy, Pat**
See Conroy, (Donald) Pat(rick)
See also BPFB 1; LAIT 5; MTCW 2

**Conroy, (Donald) Pat(rick)** 1945- ... **CLC 30, 74; DAM NOV, POP**
See also Conroy, Pat
See also AAYA 8; AITN 1; CA 85-88; CANR 24, 53; CPW; CSW; DA3; DLB 6; MTCW 1

**Constant (de Rebecque), (Henri) Benjamin** 1767-1830 ................ **NCLC 6**
See also DLB 119; EW; GFL 1789 to the Present

**Conybeare, Charles Augustus**
See Eliot, T(homas) S(tearns)

**Cook, Michael** 1933-1994 ................ **CLC 58**
See also CA 93-96; CANR 68; DLB 53

**Cook, Robin** 1940- ........ **CLC 14; DAM POP**
See also AAYA 32; BEST 90:2; BPFB 1; CA 108; 111; CANR 41, 90; CPW; DA3; HGG; INT CA-111

**Cook, Roy**
See Silverberg, Robert

**Cooke, Elizabeth** 1948- ................ **CLC 55**
See also CA 129

**Cooke, John Esten** 1830-1886 .......... **NCLC 5**
See also DLB 3; RGAL

**Cooke, John Estes**
See Baum, L(yman) Frank

**Cooke, M. E.**
See Creasey, John

**Cooke, Margaret**
See Creasey, John

**Cook-Lynn, Elizabeth** 1930- . **CLC 93; DAM MULT**
See also CA 133; DLB 175; NNAL

**Cooney, Ray** ........................ **CLC 62**
See also CBD

**Cooper, Douglas** 1960- ................ **CLC 86**

**Cooper, Henry St. John**
See Creasey, John

**Cooper, J(oan) California** (?)- ......... **CLC 56; DAM MULT**
See also AAYA 12; BW 1; CA 125; CANR 55; DLB 212

**Cooper, James Fenimore** 1789-1851 ................ **NCLC 1, 27, 54**
See also AAYA 22; AMW; BPFB 1; CDALB 1640-1865; DA3; DLB 3; LAIT 1; NFS 9; RGAL; SATA 19

**Coover, Robert (Lowell)** 1932- ...... **CLC 3, 7, 15, 32, 46, 87; DAM NOV; SSC 15**
See also AMWS 5; BPFB 1; CA 45-48; CANR 3, 37, 58; CN; DLB 2, 227; DLBY 81; MTCW 1, 2; RGAL; RGSF

**Copeland, Stewart (Armstrong)** 1952- .................................... **CLC 26**

**Copernicus, Nicolaus** 1473-1543 ......... **LC 45**

**Coppard, A(lfred) E(dgar)** 1878-1957 .................. **TCLC 5; SSC 21**
See also CA 114; 167; DLB 162; HGG; RGEL; RGSF; SUFW; YABC 1

**Coppee, Francois** 1842-1908 .......... **TCLC 25**
See also CA 170

**Coppola, Francis Ford** 1939- ... **CLC 16, 126**
See also AAYA 39; CA 77-80; CANR 40, 78; DLB 44

**Corbiere, Tristan** 1845-1875 .......... **NCLC 43**
See also GFL 1789 to the Present

**Corcoran, Barbara (Asenath)** 1911- ............................... **CLC 17**
See also AAYA 14; CA 21-24R; CAAE 191; CAAS 2; CANR 11, 28, 48; CLR 50; DLB 52; JRDA; RHW; SAAS 20; SATA 3, 77, 125

**Cordelier, Maurice**
See Giraudoux, Jean(-Hippolyte)

**Corelli, Marie** ............................... **TCLC 51**
See also Mackay, Mary
See also DLB 34, 156; RGEL

**Corman, Cid** .............................. **CLC 9**
See also Corman, Sidney
See also CAAS 2; DLB 5, 193

**Corman, Sidney** 1924-
See Corman, Cid
See also CA 85-88; CANR 44; CP; DAM POET

**Cormier, Robert (Edmund)** 1925-2000 ........ **CLC 12, 30; DA; DAB; DAC; DAM MST, NOV**
See also AAYA 3, 19; BYA 1, 2, 6, 8, 9; CA 1-4R; CANR 5, 23, 76, 93; CDALB 1968-1988; CLR 12, 55; DLB 52; EXPN; INT CANR-23; JRDA; LAIT 5; MAICYA; MTCW 1, 2; NFS 2; SATA 10, 45, 83; SATA-Obit 122; WYA; YAW

**Corn, Alfred (DeWitt III)** 1943- ........ **CLC 33**
See also CA 179; CAAE 179; CAAS 25; CANR 44; CP; CSW; DLB 120; DLBY 80

**Corneille, Pierre** 1606-1684 ..... **LC 28; DAB; DAM MST**
See also EW; GFL Beginnings to 1789; RGWL

**Cornwell, David (John Moore)** 1931- .................. **CLC 9, 15; DAM POP**
See also le Carre, John
See also CA 5-8R; CANR 13, 33, 59; DA3; MTCW 1, 2

**Corso, (Nunzio) Gregory** 1930-2001 . **CLC 1, 11; PC 33**
See also CA 5-8R; 193; CANR 41, 76; CP; DA3; DLB 5, 16, 237; MTCW 1, 2; WP

**Cortazar, Julio** 1914-1984 ... **CLC 2, 3, 5, 10, 13, 15, 33, 34, 92; DAM MULT, NOV; HLC 1; SSC 7**
See also BPFB 1; CA 21-24R; CANR 12, 32, 81; DA3; DLB 113; EXPS; HW 1, 2; LAW; MTCW 1, 2; RGSF; RGWL; SSFS 3; WLIT 1

**Cortes, Hernan** 1485-1547 .................... **LC 31**

**Corvinus, Jakob**
See Raabe, Wilhelm (Karl)

**Corvo, Baron**
See Rolfe, Frederick (William Serafino Austin Lewis Mary)
See also GLL 1; RGEL

**Corwin, Cecil**
See Kornbluth, C(yril) M.

**Cosic, Dobrica** 1921- ........................ **CLC 14**
See also CA 122; 138; CWW 2; DLB 181

**Costain, Thomas B(ertram)** 1885-1965 ............................... **CLC 30**
See also BYA 3; CA 5-8R; 25-28R; DLB 9; RHW

**Costantini, Humberto** 1924(?)-1987 . **CLC 49**
See also CA 131; 122; HW 1

**Costello, Elvis** 1955- ........................ **CLC 21**

**Costenoble, Philostene** 1898-1962
See Ghelderode, Michel de

**Costenoble, Philostene** 1898-1962
See Ghelderode, Michel de

**Cotes, Cecil V.**
See Duncan, Sara Jeannette

**Cotter, Joseph Seamon Sr.** 1861-1949 ...... **TCLC 28; BLC 1; DAM MULT**
See also BW 1; CA 124; DLB 50

**Couch, Arthur Thomas Quiller**
See Quiller-Couch, Sir Arthur (Thomas)

**Coulton, James**
See Hansen, Joseph

**Couperus, Louis (Marie Anne)** 1863-1923 ............................... **TCLC 15**
See also CA 115; RGWL

**Coupland, Douglas** 1961- ........ **CLC 85, 133; DAC; DAM POP**
See also AAYA 34; CA 142; CANR 57, 90; CCA 1; CPW

**Court, Wesli**
See Turco, Lewis (Putnam)

**Courtenay, Bryce** 1933- ..................... **CLC 59**
See also CA 138; CPW

**Courtney, Robert**
See Ellison, Harlan (Jay)

**Cousteau, Jacques-Yves** 1910-1997 .. **CLC 30**
See also CA 65-68; 159; CANR 15, 67; MTCW 1; SATA 38, 98

**Coventry, Francis** 1725-1754 ............... **LC 46**

**Cowan, Peter (Walkinshaw)** 1914- .... **SSC 28**
See also CA 21-24R; CANR 9, 25, 50, 83; CN; RGSF

**Coward, Noel (Peirce)** 1899-1973 . **CLC 1, 9, 29, 51; DAM DRAM**
See also AITN 1; BRWS 2; CA 17-18; 41-44R; CANR 35; CAP 2; CDBLB 1914-1945; DA3; DFS 3, 6; DLB 10, 245; IDFW 3, 4; MTCW 1, 2; RGEL

**Cowley, Abraham** 1618-1667 ............... **LC 43**
See also BRW 2; DLB 131, 151; PAB; RGEL

**Cowley, Malcolm** 1898-1989 ............. **CLC 39**
See also AMWS 2; CA 5-8R; 128; CANR 3, 55; DLB 4, 48; DLBY 81, 89; MTCW 1, 2

**Cowper, William** 1731-1800 ..... **NCLC 8, 94; DAM POET**
See also BRW 3; DA3; DLB 104, 109; RGEL

**Cox, William Trevor** 1928- ... **CLC 9, 14, 71; DAM NOV**
See also Trevor, William
See also CA 9-12R; CANR 4, 37, 55, 76, 102; CD; CN; DLB 14; INT CANR-37; MTCW 1, 2

**Coyne, P. J.**
See Masters, Hilary

**Cozzens, James Gould** 1903-1978 . **CLC 1, 4, 11, 92**
See also AMW; BPFB 1; CA 9-12R; 81-84; CANR 19; CDALB 1941-1968; DLB 9; DLBD 2; DLBY 84, 97; MTCW 1, 2; RGAL

**Crabbe, George** 1754-1832 ............. **NCLC 26**
See also BRW 3; DLB 93; RGEL

**Craddock, Charles Egbert**
See Murfree, Mary Noailles

**Craig, A. A.**
See Anderson, Poul (William)

**Craik, Mrs.**
See Craik, Dinah Maria (Mulock)
See also RGEL

**Craik, Dinah Maria (Mulock)** 1826-1887 ............................... **NCLC 38**
See also Craik, Mrs.; Mulock, Dinah Maria
See also DLB 35, 163; MAICYA; SATA 34

**Cram, Ralph Adams** 1863-1942 ..... **TCLC 45**
See also CA 160

**Crane, (Harold) Hart** 1899-1932 .... **TCLC 2, 5, 80; DA; DAB; DAC; DAM MST, POET; PC 3; WLC**
See also AMW; CA 104; 127; CDALB 1917-1929; DA3; DLB 4, 48; MTCW 1, 2; RGAL

**Crane, R(onald) S(almon)** 1886-1967 .................. **CLC 27**
See also CA 85-88; DLB 63

**Crane, Stephen (Townley)** 1871-1900 ........... **TCLC 11, 17, 32; DA; DAB; DAC; DAM MST, NOV, POET; SSC 7; WLC**
See also AAYA 21; AMW; BPFB 1; BYA 3; CA 109; 140; CANR 84; CDALB 1865-1917; DA3; DLB 12, 54, 78; EXPN; EXPS; LAIT 2; NFS 4; PFS 9; RGAL; RGSF 2; SSFS 4; WYA; YABC 2

**Cranshaw, Stanley**
See Fisher, Dorothy (Frances) Canfield

**Crase, Douglas** 1944- ........................ **CLC 58**
See also CA 106

**Crashaw, Richard** 1612(?)-1649 .......... **LC 24**
See also BRW 2; DLB 126; PAB; RGEL

**Craven, Margaret** 1901-1980 .......... **CLC 17; DAC**
See also BYA 2; CA 103; CCA 1; LAIT 5

**Crawford, F(rancis) Marion** 1854-1909 ........................ **TCLC 10**
See also CA 107; 168; DLB 71; HGG; RGAL; SUFW

**Crawford, Isabella Valancy** 1850-1887 ........................ **NCLC 12**
See also DLB 92; RGEL

**Crayon, Geoffrey**
See Irving, Washington

**Creasey, John** 1908-1973 ................. **CLC 11**
See also Marric, J. J.
See also CA 5-8R; 41-44R; CANR 8, 59; CMW; DLB 77; MTCW 1

**Crebillon, Claude Prosper Jolyot de (fils)** 1707-1777 ............................... **LC 1, 28**
See also GFL Beginnings to 1789

**Credo**
See Creasey, John

**Credo, Alvaro J. de**
See Prado (Calvo), Pedro

**Creeley, Robert (White)** 1926- .. **CLC 1, 2, 4, 8, 11, 15, 36, 78; DAM POET**
See also AMWS 4; CA 1-4R; CAAS 10; CANR 23, 43, 89; CP; DA3; DLB 5, 16, 169; DLBD 17; MTCW 1, 2; RGAL; WP

**Crevecoeur, Hector St. John de**
See Crevecoeur, Michel Guillaume Jean de
See also ANW

**Crevecoeur, Michel Guillaume Jean de** 1735-1813 ............................... **NCLC 105**
See also Crevecoeur, Hector St. John de
See also AMWS 1; DLB 37

**Crevel, Rene** 1900-1935 ................ **TCLC 112**
See also GLL 2

**Crews, Harry (Eugene)** 1935- ..... **CLC 6, 23, 49**
See also AITN 1; BPFB 1; CA 25-28R; CANR 20, 57; CN; CSW; DA3; DLB 6, 143, 185; MTCW 1, 2; RGAL

**Crichton, (John) Michael** 1942- .... **CLC 2, 6, 54, 90; DAM NOV, POP**
See also AAYA 10; AITN 2; BPFB 1; CA 25-28R; CANR 13, 40, 54, 76; CMW; CN; CPW; DA3; DLBY 81; INT CANR-13; JRDA; MTCW 1, 2; SATA 9, 88; SFW; YAW

**Crispin, Edmund** ............................. **CLC 22**
See also Montgomery, (Robert) Bruce
See also DLB 87; MSW

**Cristofer, Michael** 1945(?)- ... **CLC 28; DAM DRAM**
See also CA 110; 152; CAD; CD; DLB 7

**Croce, Benedetto** 1866-1952 ........... **TCLC 37**
See also CA 120; 155; EW

**Crockett, David** 1786-1836 ............... **NCLC 8**
See also DLB 3, 11

**Crockett, Davy**
See Crockett, David

**Crofts, Freeman Wills** 1879-1957 .. **TCLC 55**
See also CA 115; 195; CMW; DLB 77; MSW

**Croker, John Wilson** 1780-1857 .... **NCLC 10**
See also DLB 110

**Crommelynck, Fernand** 1885-1970 .. **CLC 75**
See also CA 189; 89-92

**Cromwell, Oliver** 1599-1658 ................ **LC 43**

**Cronenberg, David** 1943- .................. **CLC 143**
See also CA 138; CCA 1

**Cronin, A(rchibald) J(oseph)** 1896-1981 ................................ **CLC 32**
See also BPFB 1; CA 1-4R; 102; CANR 5; DLB 191; SATA 47; SATA-Obit 25

**Cross, Amanda**
See Heilbrun, Carolyn G(old)
See also BPFB 1; MSW

**Crothers, Rachel** 1878-1958 ........... **TCLC 19**
See also CA 113; 194; CAD; CWD; DLB 7; RGAL

**Croves, Hal**
See Traven, B.

**Crow Dog, Mary (Ellen)** (?)- ............. **CLC 93**
See also Brave Bird, Mary
See also CA 154

**Crowfield, Christopher**
See Stowe, Harriet (Elizabeth) Beecher

**Crowley, Aleister** ............................. **TCLC 7**
See also Crowley, Edward Alexander
See also GLL 1

**Crowley, Edward Alexander** 1875-1947
See Crowley, Aleister
See also CA 104; HGG

**Crowley, John** 1942- ........................ **CLC 57**
See also BPFB 1; CA 61-64; CANR 43, 98; DLBY 82; SATA 65; SFW

**Crud**
See Crumb, R(obert)

**Crumarums**
See Crumb, R(obert)

**Crumb, R(obert)** 1943- ..................... **CLC 17**
See also CA 106

**Crumbum**
See Crumb, R(obert)

**Crumski**
See Crumb, R(obert)

**Crum the Bum**
See Crumb, R(obert)

**Crunk**
See Crumb, R(obert)

**Crustt**
See Crumb, R(obert)

**Crutchfield, Les**
See Trumbo, Dalton

**Cruz, Victor Hernandez** 1949- ............. **PC 37**
See also BW 2; CA 65-68; CAAS 17; CANR 14, 32, 74; CP; DAM MULT, POET; DLB 41; DNFS; EXPP; HLC 1; HW 1, 2; MTCW 1; WP

**Cryer, Gretchen (Kiger)** 1935- ............ **CLC 21**
See also CA 114; 123

**Csath, Geza** 1887-1919 ..................... **TCLC 13**
See also CA 111

**Cudlip, David R(ockwell)** 1933- ........ **CLC 34**
See also CA 177

**Cullen, Countee** 1903-1946 ......... **TCLC 4, 37; BLC 1; DA; DAC; DAM MST, MULT, POET; PC 20; WLCS**
See also AFAW 2; AMWS 4; BW 1; CA 108; 124; CDALB 1917-1929; DA3; DLB 4, 48, 51; EXPP; MTCW 1, 2; PFS 3; RGAL; SATA 18; WP

**Cum, R.**
See Crumb, R(obert)

**Cummings, Bruce F(rederick)** 1889-1919
See Barbellion, W. N. P.
See also CA 123

**Cummings, E(dward) E(stlin)** 1894-1962 ........ **CLC 1, 3, 8, 12, 15, 68; DA; DAB; DAC; DAM MST, POET; PC 5; WLC**
See also AAYA 41; AMW; CA 73-76; CANR 31; CDALB 1929-1941; DA3; DLB 4, 48; EXPP; MTCW 1, 2; PAB; PFS 1, 3, 12, 13; RGAL; WP

**Cunha, Euclides (Rodrigues Pimenta) da** 1866-1909 ............................... **TCLC 24**
See also CA 123; LAW; WLIT 1

**Cunningham, E. V.**
See Fast, Howard (Melvin)

**Cunningham, J(ames) V(incent)** 1911-1985 ................. **CLC 3, 31**
See also CA 1-4R; 115; CANR 1, 72; DLB 5

**Cunningham, Julia (Woolfolk)** 1916- ........................................... **CLC 12**
See also CA 9-12R; CANR 4, 19, 36; CWRI; JRDA; MAICYA; SAAS 2; SATA 1, 26

**Cunningham, Michael** 1952- ............. **CLC 34**
See also CA 136; CANR 96; GLL 2

**Cunninghame Graham, R. B.**
See Cunninghame Graham, Robert (Gallnigad) Bontine

**Cunninghame Graham, Robert (Gallnigad) Bontine** 1852-1936 .................. **TCLC 19**
See also Graham, R(obert) B(ontine) Cunninghame
See also CA 119; 184; DLB 98

**Currie, Ellen** 19(?)- ........................... **CLC 44**

**Curtin, Philip**
See Lowndes, Marie Adelaide (Belloc)

**Curtis, Price**
See Ellison, Harlan (Jay)

**Cutrate, Joe**
See Spiegelman, Art

**Cynewulf** c. 770- .......................... **CMLC 23**
See also RGEL

**Cyrano de Bergerac, Savinien de** 1619-1655 ................................. **LC 65**
See also GFL Beginnings to 1789; RGWL

**Czaczkes, Shmuel Yosef Halevi**
See Agnon, S(hmuel) Y(osef Halevi)

**Dabrowska, Maria (Szumska)** 1889-1965 ................................. **CLC 15**
See also CA 106

**Dabydeen, David** 1955- ..................... **CLC 34**
See also BW 1; CA 125; CANR 56, 92; CN; CP

**Dacey, Philip** 1939- ............................ **CLC 51**
See also CA 37-40R; CAAS 17; CANR 14, 32, 64; CP; DLB 105

**Dagerman, Stig (Halvard)** 1923-1954 ................................ **TCLC 17**
See also CA 117; 155

**D'Aguiar, Fred** 1960- ........................ **CLC 145**
See also CA 148; CANR 83, 101; CP; DLB 157

**Dahl, Roald** 1916-1990 ....... **CLC 1, 6, 18, 79; DAB; DAC; DAM MST, NOV, POP**
See also AAYA 15; BPFB 1; BRWS 4; BYA 5; CA 1-4R; 133; CANR 6, 32, 37, 62; CLR 1, 7, 41; CPW; DA3; DLB 139; HGG; JRDA; MAICYA; MTCW 1, 2; RGSF; SATA 1, 26, 73; SATA-Obit 65; SSFS 4; YAW

**Dahlberg, Edward** 1900-1977 .. **CLC 1, 7, 14**
See also CA 9-12R; 69-72; CANR 31, 62; DLB 48; MTCW 1; RGAL

**Daitch, Susan** 1954- ........................ **CLC 103**
See also CA 161

**Dale, Colin** .................................. **TCLC 18**
See also Lawrence, T(homas) E(dward)
**Dale, George E.**
See Asimov, Isaac
**Dalton, Roque** 1935-1975(?) ............. **PC 36**
See also CA 176; HLCS 1; HW 2
**Daly, Elizabeth** 1878-1967 ............. **CLC 52**
See also CA 23-24; 25-28R; CANR 60; CAP 2; CMW
**Daly, Maureen** 1921- ...................... **CLC 17**
See also AAYA 5; BYA 6; CANR 37, 83; JRDA; MAICYA; SAAS 1; SATA 2; YAW
**Damas, Leon-Gontran** 1912-1978 .... **CLC 84**
See also BW 1; CA 125; 73-76
**Dana, Richard Henry Sr.**
1787-1879 ................................. **NCLC 53**
**Daniel, Samuel** 1562(?)-1619 ............... **LC 24**
See also DLB 62; RGEL
**Daniels, Brett**
See Adler, Renata
**Dannay, Frederic** 1905-1982 . **CLC 11; DAM POP**
See also Queen, Ellery
See also CA 1-4R; 107; CANR 1, 39; CMW; DLB 137; MTCW 1
**D'Annunzio, Gabriele** 1863-1938 ... **TCLC 6, 40**
See also CA 104; 155; EW; RGWL
**Danois, N. le**
See Gourmont, Remy(-Marie-Charles) de
**Dante** 1265-1321 ......... **CMLC 3, 18, 39; DA; DAB; DAC; DAM MST, POET; PC 21; WLCS**
See also DA3; EFS 1; EW; LAIT 1; RGWL; WP
**d'Antibes, Germain**
See Simenon, Georges (Jacques Christian)
**Danticat, Edwidge** 1969- ............ **CLC 94, 139**
See also AAYA 29; CA 152; CAAE 192; CANR 73; DNFS; EXPS; MTCW 1; SSFS 1; YAW
**Danvers, Dennis** 1947- ...................... **CLC 70**
**Danziger, Paula** 1944- ..................... **CLC 21**
See also AAYA 4, 36; BYA 6, 7; CA 112; 115; CANR 37; CLR 20; JRDA; MAICYA; SATA 36, 63, 102; SATA-Brief 30; YAW
**Da Ponte, Lorenzo** 1749-1838 ........ **NCLC 50**
**Dario, Ruben** 1867-1916 ....... **TCLC 4; DAM MULT; HLC 1; PC 15**
See also CA 131; CANR 81; HW 1, 2; LAW; MTCW 1, 2; RGWL
**Darley, George** 1795-1846 ................ **NCLC 2**
See also DLB 96; RGEL
**Darrow, Clarence (Seward)**
1857-1938 ................................. **TCLC 81**
See also CA 164
**Darwin, Charles** 1809-1882 ............. **NCLC 57**
See also BRWS 7; DLB 57, 166; RGEL; WLIT 4
**Darwin, Erasmus** 1731-1802 ........ **NCLC 106**
See also DLB 93; RGEL
**Daryush, Elizabeth** 1887-1977 ...... **CLC 6, 19**
See also CA 49-52; CANR 3, 81; DLB 20
**Dasgupta, Surendranath**
1887-1952 ................................. **TCLC 81**
See also CA 157
**Dashwood, Edmee Elizabeth Monica de la Pasture** 1890-1943
See Delafield, E. M.
See also CA 119; 154
**Daudet, (Louis Marie) Alphonse**
1840-1897 ................................... **NCLC 1**
See also DLB 123; GFL 1789 to the Present; RGSF
**Daumal, Rene** 1908-1944 ................ **TCLC 14**
See also CA 114
**Davenant, William** 1606-1668 ............ **LC 13**
See also DLB 58, 126; RGEL

**Davenport, Guy (Mattison, Jr.)**
1927- .................. **CLC 6, 14, 38; SSC 16**
See also CA 33-36R; CANR 23, 73; CN; CSW; DLB 130
**Davidson, Avram (James)** 1923-1993
See Queen, Ellery
See also CA 101; 171; CANR 26; DLB 8; FANT; SFW; SUFW
**Davidson, Donald (Grady)**
1893-1968 ......................... **CLC 2, 13, 19**
See also CA 5-8R; 25-28R; CANR 4, 84; DLB 45
**Davidson, Hugh**
See Hamilton, Edmond
**Davidson, John** 1857-1909 .............. **TCLC 24**
See also CA 118; DLB 19; RGEL
**Davidson, Sara** 1943- ......................... **CLC 9**
See also CA 81-84; CANR 44, 68; DLB 185
**Davie, Donald (Alfred)** 1922-1995 .... **CLC 5, 8, 10, 31; PC 29**
See also BRWS 6; CA 1-4R; 149; CAAS 3; CANR 1, 44; CP; DLB 27; MTCW 1; RGEL
**Davies, Ray(mond Douglas)** 1944- ... **CLC 21**
See also CA 116; 146; CANR 92
**Davies, Rhys** 1901-1978 ..................... **CLC 23**
See also CA 9-12R; 81-84; CANR 4; DLB 139, 191
**Davies, (William) Robertson**
1913-1995 ....... **CLC 2, 7, 13, 25, 42, 75, 91; DA; DAB; DAC; DAM MST, NOV, POP; WLC**
See also Marchbanks, Samuel
See also BEST 89:2; BPFB 1; CA 33-36R; 150; CANR 17, 42, 103; CN; CPW; DA3; DLB 68; HGG; INT CANR-17; MTCW 1, 2; RGEL
**Davies, Walter C.**
See Kornbluth, C(yril) M.
**Davies, William Henry** 1871-1940 ... **TCLC 5**
See also CA 104; 179; DLB 19, 174; RGEL
**Da Vinci, Leonardo** 1452-1519 ..... **LC 12, 57, 60**
See also AAYA 40
**Davis, Angela (Yvonne)** 1944- ......... **CLC 77; DAM MULT**
See also BW 2, 3; CA 57-60; CANR 10, 81; CSW; DA3; FW
**Davis, B. Lynch**
See Bioy Casares, Adolfo; Borges, Jorge Luis
**Davis, B. Lynch**
See Bioy Casares, Adolfo
**Davis, Gordon**
See Hunt, E(verette) Howard, (Jr.)
**Davis, H(arold) L(enoir)** 1896-1960 . **CLC 49**
See also ANW; CA 178; 89-92; DLB 9, 206; SATA 114
**Davis, Rebecca (Blaine) Harding**
1831-1910 .................... **TCLC 6; SSC 38**
See also CA 104; 179; DLB 74, 239; FW; RGAL
**Davis, Richard Harding**
1864-1916 ................................. **TCLC 24**
See also CA 114; 179; DLB 12, 23, 78, 79, 189; DLBD 13; RGAL
**Davison, Frank Dalby** 1893-1970 ..... **CLC 15**
See also CA 116
**Davison, Lawrence H.**
See Lawrence, D(avid) H(erbert Richards)
**Davison, Peter (Hubert)** 1928- ......... **CLC 28**
See also CA 9-12R; CAAS 4; CANR 3, 43, 84; CP; DLB 5
**Davys, Mary** 1674-1732 ................. **LC 1, 46**
See also DLB 39
**Dawson, Fielding** 1930- ....................... **CLC 6**
See also CA 85-88; DLB 130

**Dawson, Peter**
See Faust, Frederick (Schiller)
See also TCWW 2, 2
**Day, Clarence (Shepard, Jr.)**
1874-1935 ................................. **TCLC 25**
See also CA 108; DLB 11
**Day, John** 1574(?)-1640(?) ................. **LC 70**
See also DLB 62, 170; RGEL
**Day, Thomas** 1748-1789 ..................... **LC 1**
See also DLB 39; YABC 1
**Day Lewis, C(ecil)** 1904-1972 . **CLC 1, 6, 10; DAM POET; PC 11**
See also Blake, Nicholas
See also BRWS 3; CA 13-16; 33-36R; CANR 34; CAP 1; CWRI; DLB 15, 20; MTCW 1, 2; RGEL
**Dazai Osamu** .................. **TCLC 11; SSC 41**
See also Tsushima, Shuji
See also CA 164; DLB 182; MJW; RGSF; RGWL
**de Andrade, Carlos Drummond**
See Drummond de Andrade, Carlos
**de Andrade, Mario** 1892-1945
See Andrade, Mario de
See also CA 178; HW 2
**Deane, Norman**
See Creasey, John
**Deane, Seamus (Francis)** 1940- ....... **CLC 122**
See also CA 118; CANR 42
**de Beauvoir, Simone (Lucie Ernestine Marie Bertrand)**
See Beauvoir, Simone (Lucie Ernestine Marie Bertrand) de
**de Beer, P.**
See Bosman, Herman Charles
**de Brissac, Malcolm**
See Dickinson, Peter (Malcolm)
**de Campos, Alvaro**
See Pessoa, Fernando (Antonio Nogueira)
**de Chardin, Pierre Teilhard**
See Teilhard de Chardin, (Marie Joseph) Pierre
**Dee, John** 1527-1608 ............................ **LC 20**
**Deer, Sandra** 1940- ............................ **CLC 45**
See also CA 186
**De Ferrari, Gabriella** 1941- ............... **CLC 65**
See also CA 146
**Defoe, Daniel** 1660(?)-1731 .... **LC 1, 42; DA; DAB; DAC; DAM MST, NOV; WLC**
See also AAYA 27; BRW 3; BYA 4; CDBLB 1660-1789; CLR 61; DA3; DLB 39, 95, 101; JRDA; LAIT 1; MAICYA; NFS 9; RGEL; SATA 22; WLIT 3
**de Gourmont, Remy(-Marie-Charles)**
See Gourmont, Remy(-Marie-Charles) de
**de Hartog, Jan** 1914- ......................... **CLC 19**
See also CA 1-4R; CANR 1; DFS 12
**de Hostos, E. M.**
See Hostos (y Bonilla), Eugenio Maria de
**de Hostos, Eugenio M.**
See Hostos (y Bonilla), Eugenio Maria de
**Deighton, Len** ..................... **CLC 4, 7, 22, 46**
See also Deighton, Leonard Cyril
See also AAYA 6; BEST 89:2; BPFB 1; CDBLB 1960 to Present; CMW; CN; CPW; DLB 87
**Deighton, Leonard Cyril** 1929-
See Deighton, Len
See also CA 9-12R; CANR 19, 33, 68; DA3; DAM NOV, POP; MTCW 1, 2
**Dekker, Thomas** 1572(?)-1632 . **LC 22; DAM DRAM; DC 12**
See also CDBLB Before 1660; DLB 62, 172; RGEL
**Delafield, E. M.** ............................ **TCLC 61**
See also Dashwood, Edmee Elizabeth Monica de la Pasture
See also DLB 34; RHW

**de la Mare, Walter (John)**
1873-1956 ..... **TCLC 4, 53; DAB; DAC; DAM MST, POET; SSC 14; WLC**
See also CA 163; CDBLB 1914-1945; CLR 23; CWRI; DA3; DLB 162; EXPP; HGG; MTCW 1; RGEL; RGSF; SATA 16; SUFW; WCH

**Delaney, Franey**
See O'Hara, John (Henry)

**Delaney, Shelagh** 1939- ......... **CLC 29; DAM DRAM**
See also CA 17-20R; CANR 30, 67; CBD; CD; CDBLB 1960 to Present; CWD; DFS 7; DLB 13; MTCW 1

**Delany, Martin Robinson**
1812-1885 ............... **NCLC 93**
See also DLB 50; RGAL

**Delany, Mary (Granville Pendarves)**
1700-1788 ............................ **LC 12**

**Delany, Samuel R(ay), Jr.** 1942- . **CLC 8, 14, 38, 141; BLC 1; DAM MULT**
See also AAYA 24; AFAW 2; BPFB 1; BW 2, 3; CA 81-84; CANR 27, 43; DLB 8, 33; MTCW 1, 2; RGAL; SCFW

**De La Ramee, (Marie) Louise** 1839-1908
See Ouida
See also SATA 20

**de la Roche, Mazo** 1879-1961 ........... **CLC 14**
See also CA 85-88; CANR 30; DLB 68; RGEL; RHW; SATA 64

**De La Salle, Innocent**
See Hartmann, Sadakichi

**Delbanco, Nicholas (Franklin)**
1942- ........................................ **CLC 6, 13**
See also CA 17-20R; CAAE 189; CAAS 2; CANR 29, 55; DLB 6, 234

**del Castillo, Michel** 1933- ............... **CLC 38**
See also CA 109; CANR 77

**Deledda, Grazia (Cosima)**
1875(?)-1936 ............................ **TCLC 23**
See also CA 123; RGWL

**Delgado, Abelardo (Lalo) B(arrientos)** 1930-
See also CA 131; CAAS 15; CANR 90; DAM MST, MULT; DLB 82; HLC 1; HW 1, 2

**Delibes, Miguel** ............... **CLC 8, 18**
See also Delibes Setien, Miguel

**Delibes Setien, Miguel** 1920-
See Delibes, Miguel
See also CA 45-48; CANR 1, 32; HW 1; MTCW 1

**DeLillo, Don** 1936- ...... **CLC 8, 10, 13, 27, 39, 54, 76, 143; DAM NOV, POP**
See also AMWS 6; BEST 89:1; BPFB 1; CA 81-84; CANR 21, 76, 92; CN; CPW; DA3; DLB 6, 173; MTCW 1, 2; RGAL

**de Lisser, H. G.**
See De Lisser, H(erbert) G(eorge)
See also DLB 117

**De Lisser, H(erbert) G(eorge)**
1878-1944 ........................ **TCLC 12**
See also de Lisser, H. G.
See also BW 2; CA 109; 152

**Deloire, Pierre**
See Peguy, Charles (Pierre)

**Deloney, Thomas** 1543(?)-1600 ............ **LC 41**
See also DLB 167; RGEL

**Deloria, Vine (Victor), Jr.** 1933- ...... **CLC 21, 122; DAM MULT**
See also CA 53-56; CANR 5, 20, 48, 98; DLB 175; MTCW 1; NNAL; SATA 21

**Del Vecchio, John M(ichael)** 1947- .. **CLC 29**
See also CA 110; DLBD 9

**de Man, Paul (Adolph Michel)**
1919-1983 ........................ **CLC 55**
See also CA 128; 111; CANR 61; DLB 67; MTCW 1, 2

**DeMarinis, Rick** 1934- ...................... **CLC 54**
See also CA 57-60, 184; CAAE 184; CAAS 24; CANR 9, 25, 50

**Dembry, R. Emmet**
See Murfree, Mary Noailles

**Demby, William** 1922- ......... **CLC 53; BLC 1; DAM MULT**
See also BW 1, 3; CA 81-84; CANR 81; DLB 33

**de Menton, Francisco**
See Chin, Frank (Chew, Jr.)

**Demetrius of Phalerum** c.
307B.C.- ................... **CMLC 34**

**Demijohn, Thom**
See Disch, Thomas M(ichael)

**Deming, Richard** 1915-1983
See Queen, Ellery
See also CA 9-12R; CANR 3, 94; SATA 24

**Democritus** c. 460B.C.-c. 370B.C. . **CMLC 47**

**de Montherlant, Henry (Milon)**
See Montherlant, Henry (Milon) de

**Demosthenes** 384B.C.-322B.C. ...... **CMLC 13**
See also AW 1; DLB 176; RGWL

**de Natale, Francine**
See Malzberg, Barry N(athaniel)

**de Navarre, Marguerite** 1492-1549 ..... **LC 61**
See also Marguerite de Navarre

**Denby, Edwin (Orr)** 1903-1983 ........ **CLC 48**
See also CA 138; 110

**Denis, Julio**
See Cortazar, Julio

**Denmark, Harrison**
See Zelazny, Roger (Joseph)

**Dennis, John** 1658-1734 ........................ **LC 11**
See also DLB 101; RGEL

**Dennis, Nigel (Forbes)** 1912-1989 ...... **CLC 8**
See also CA 25-28R; 129; DLB 13, 15, 233; MTCW 1

**Dent, Lester** 1904(?)-1959 ............... **TCLC 72**
See also CA 112; 161; DLB; SFW

**De Palma, Brian (Russell)** 1940- ....... **CLC 20**
See also CA 109

**De Quincey, Thomas** 1785-1859 ..... **NCLC 4, 87**
See also BRW 4; CDBLB 1789-1832; DLB 110, 144; RGEL

**Deren, Eleanora** 1908(?)-1961
See Deren, Maya
See also CA 192; 111

**Deren, Maya** ............................. **CLC 16, 102**
See also Deren, Eleanora

**Derleth, August (William)**
1909-1971 ............................ **CLC 31**
See also BPFB 1; BYA 9, 10; CA 1-4R; 29-32R; CANR 4; CMW; DLB 9; DLBD 17; HGG; SATA 5; SUFW

**Der Nister** 1884-1950 ...................... **TCLC 56**

**de Routisie, Albert**
See Aragon, Louis

**Derrida, Jacques** 1930- ............... **CLC 24, 87**
See also CA 124; 127; CANR 76, 98; DLB 242; MTCW 1

**Derry Down Derry**
See Lear, Edward

**Dersonnes, Jacques**
See Simenon, Georges (Jacques Christian)

**Desai, Anita** 1937- ..... **CLC 19, 37, 97; DAB; DAM NOV**
See also BRWS 5; CA 81-84; CANR 33, 53, 95; CN; CWRI; DA3; DNFS; FW; MTCW 1, 2; SATA 63

**Desai, Kiran** 1971- ......................... **CLC 119**
See also CA 171

**de Saint-Luc, Jean**
See Glassco, John

**de Saint Roman, Arnaud**
See Aragon, Louis

**Desbordes-Valmore, Marceline**
1786-1859 ............................ **NCLC 97**
See also DLB 217

**Descartes, Rene** 1596-1650 ............ **LC 20, 35**
See also EW; GFL Beginnings to 1789

**De Sica, Vittorio** 1901(?)-1974 .......... **CLC 20**
See also CA 117

**Desnos, Robert** 1900-1945 .............. **TCLC 22**
See also CA 121; 151

**Destouches, Louis-Ferdinand**
1894-1961 ......................... **CLC 9, 15**
See also Celine, Louis-Ferdinand
See also CA 85-88; CANR 28; MTCW 1

**de Tolignac, Gaston**
See Griffith, D(avid Lewelyn) W(ark)

**Deutsch, Babette** 1895-1982 ............. **CLC 18**
See also BYA 3; CA 1-4R; 108; CANR 4, 79; DLB 45; SATA 1; SATA-Obit 33

**Devenant, William** 1606-1649 .............. **LC 13**

**Devkota, Laxmiprasad** 1909-1959 . **TCLC 23**
See also CA 123

**De Voto, Bernard (Augustine)**
1897-1955 ............................ **TCLC 29**
See also CA 113; 160; DLB 9

**De Vries, Peter** 1910-1993 ..... **CLC 1, 2, 3, 7, 10, 28, 46; DAM NOV**
See also CA 17-20R; 142; CANR 41; DLB 6; DLBY 82; MTCW 1, 2

**Dewey, John** 1859-1952 .................. **TCLC 95**
See also CA 114; 170; DLB 246; RGAL

**Dexter, John**
See Bradley, Marion Zimmer
See also GLL 1

**Dexter, Martin**
See Faust, Frederick (Schiller)
See also TCWW 2

**Dexter, Pete** 1943- .. **CLC 34, 55; DAM POP**
See also BEST 89:2; CA 127; 131; CPW; INT 131; MTCW 1

**Diamano, Silmang**
See Senghor, Leopold Sedar

**Diamond, Neil** 1941- ......................... **CLC 30**
See also CA 108

**Diaz del Castillo, Bernal** 1496-1584 .. **LC 31; HLCS 1**
See also LAW

**di Bassetto, Corno**
See Shaw, George Bernard

**Dick, Philip K(indred)** 1928-1982 ... **CLC 10, 30, 72; DAM NOV, POP**
See also AAYA 24; BPFB 1; BYA 11; CA 49-52; 106; CANR 2, 16; CPW; DA3; DLB 8; MTCW 1, 2; NFS 5; SCFW; SFW

**Dickens, Charles (John Huffam)**
1812-1870 .... **NCLC 3, 8, 18, 26, 37, 50, 86, 105; DA; DAB; DAC; DAM MST, NOV; SSC 17; WLC**
See also AAYA 23; BRW 5; BYA 1, 2, 3, 13; CDBLB 1832-1890; CMW; DA3; DLB 21, 55, 70, 159, 166; EXPN; HGG; JRDA; LAIT 1, 2; MAICYA; NFS 4, 5, 10; RGEL; RGSF; SATA 15; SUFW; WCH; WLIT 4; WYA

**Dickey, James (Lafayette)**
1923-1997 .... **CLC 1, 2, 4, 7, 10, 15, 47, 109; DAM NOV, POET, POP**
See also AITN 1, 2; AMWS 4; BPFB 1; CA 9-12R; 156; CABS 2; CANR 10, 48, 61; CDALB 1968-1988; CP; CPW; CSW; DA3; DLB 5, 193; DLBD 7; DLBY 82, 93, 96, 97, 98; INT CANR-10; MTCW 1, 2; NFS 9; PFS 6, 11; RGAL

**Dickey, William** 1928-1994 ........... **CLC 3, 28**
See also CA 9-12R; 145; CANR 24, 79; DLB 5

**Dickinson, Charles** 1951- .................. **CLC 49**
See also CA 128

**Dickinson, Emily (Elizabeth)**
1830-1886 ..... **NCLC 21, 77; DA; DAB; DAC; DAM MST, POET; PC 1; WLC**
See also AAYA 22; AMW; AMWR 1; CDALB 1865-1917; DA3; DLB 1, 243; EXPP; MAWW; PAB; PFS 1, 2, 3, 4, 5, 6, 8, 10, 11, 13; RGAL; SATA 29; WP; WYA

**Dickinson, Mrs. Herbert Ward**
See Phelps, Elizabeth Stuart

**Dickinson, Peter (Malcolm)** 1927- .. **CLC 12, 35**
See also AAYA 9; BYA 5; CA 41-44R; CANR 31, 58, 88; CLR 29; CMW; DLB 87, 161; JRDA; MAICYA; SATA 5, 62, 95; SFW; WYA; YAW

**Dickson, Carr**
See Carr, John Dickson

**Dickson, Carter**
See Carr, John Dickson

**Diderot, Denis** 1713-1784 ..................... **LC 26**
See also EW; GFL Beginnings to 1789; RGWL

**Didion, Joan** 1934- ......... **CLC 1, 3, 8, 14, 32, 129; DAM NOV**
See also AITN 1; AMWS 4; CA 5-8R; CANR 14, 52, 76; CDALB 1968-1988; CN; DA3; DLB 2, 173, 185; DLBY 81, 86; MAWW; MTCW 1, 2; NFS 3; RGAL; TCWW 2

**Dietrich, Robert**
See Hunt, E(verette) Howard, (Jr.)

**Difusa, Pati**
See Almodovar, Pedro

**Dillard, Annie** 1945- .. **CLC 9, 60, 115; DAM NOV**
See also AAYA 6; AMWS 6; ANW; CA 49-52; CANR 3, 43, 62, 90; DA3; DLBY 80; LAIT 4, 5; MTCW 1, 2; NCFS 1; RGAL; SATA 10

**Dillard, R(ichard) H(enry) W(ilde)**
1937- ............................................. **CLC 5**
See also CA 21-24R; CAAS 7; CANR 10; CP; CSW; DLB 5, 244

**Dillon, Eilis** 1920-1994 ...................... **CLC 17**
See also CA 9-12R, 182; 147; CAAE 182; CAAS 3; CANR 4, 38, 78; CLR 26; MAICYA; SATA 2, 74; SATA-Essay 105; SATA-Obit 83; YAW

**Dimont, Penelope**
See Mortimer, Penelope (Ruth)

**Dinesen, Isak** ........... **CLC 10, 29, 95; SSC 7**
See also Blixen, Karen (Christentze Dinesen)
See also EW; EXPS; FW; HGG; LAIT 3; MTCW 1; NFS 9; RGSF; RGWL; SSFS 6; WLIT 2

**Ding Ling** ......................................... **CLC 68**
See also Chiang, Pin-chin

**Diphusa, Patty**
See Almodovar, Pedro

**Disch, Thomas M(ichael)** 1940- ... **CLC 7, 36**
See also AAYA 17; BPFB 1; CA 21-24R; CAAS 4; CANR 17, 36, 54, 89; CLR 18; CP; DA3; DLB 8; HGG; MAICYA; MTCW 1, 2; SAAS 15; SATA 92; SCFW; SFW

**Disch, Tom**
See Disch, Thomas M(ichael)

**d'Isly, Georges**
See Simenon, Georges (Jacques Christian)

**Disraeli, Benjamin** 1804-1881 ... **NCLC 2, 39, 79**
See also BRW 4; DLB 21, 55; RGEL

**Ditcum, Steve**
See Crumb, R(obert)

**Dixon, Paige**
See Corcoran, Barbara (Asenath)

**Dixon, Stephen** 1936- .......... **CLC 52; SSC 16**
See also CA 89-92; CANR 17, 40, 54, 91; CN; DLB 130

**Doak, Annie**
See Dillard, Annie

**Dobell, Sydney Thompson**
1824-1874 ................................... **NCLC 43**
See also DLB 32; RGEL

**Doblin, Alfred** ................................. **TCLC 13**
See also Doeblin, Alfred
See also RGWL

**Dobrolyubov, Nikolai Alexandrovich**
1836-1861 ..................................... **NCLC 5**

**Dobson, Austin** 1840-1921 ............ **TCLC 79**
See also DLB 35; 144

**Dobyns, Stephen** 1941- ..................... **CLC 37**
See also CA 45-48; CANR 2, 18, 99; CMW; CP

**Doctorow, E(dgar) L(aurence)**
1931- ........ **CLC 6, 11, 15, 18, 37, 44, 65, 113; DAM NOV, POP**
See also AAYA 22; AITN 2; AMWS 4; BEST 89:3; BPFB 1; CA 45-48; CANR 2, 33, 51, 76, 97; CDALB 1968-1988; CN; CPW; DA3; DLB 2, 28, 173; DLBY 80; LAIT 3; MTCW 1, 2; NFS 6; RGAL; RHW

**Dodgson, Charles Lutwidge** 1832-1898
See Carroll, Lewis
See also CLR 2; DA; DA3; DAB; DAC; DAM MST, NOV, POET; MAICYA; SATA 100; YABC 2

**Dodson, Owen (Vincent)**
1914-1983 ......... **CLC 79; BLC 1; DAM MULT**
See also BW 1; CA 65-68; 110; CANR 24; DLB 76

**Doeblin, Alfred** 1878-1957 .............. **TCLC 13**
See also Doblin, Alfred
See also CA 110; 141; DLB 66

**Doerr, Harriet** 1910- .......................... **CLC 34**
See also CA 117; 122; CANR 47; INT 122

**Domecq, H(onorio Bustos)**
See Bioy Casares, Adolfo

**Domecq, H(onorio) Bustos**
See Bioy Casares, Adolfo; Borges, Jorge Luis

**Domini, Rey**
See Lorde, Audre (Geraldine)
See also GLL 1

**Dominique**
See Proust, (Valentin-Louis-George-Eugene-)Marcel

**Don, A**
See Stephen, Sir Leslie

**Donaldson, Stephen R(eeder)**
1947- ............... **CLC 46, 138; DAM POP**
See also AAYA 36; BPFB 1; CA 89-92; CANR 13, 55, 99; CPW; FANT; INT CANR-13; SATA 121; SFW

**Donleavy, J(ames) P(atrick)** 1926- .... **CLC 1, 4, 6, 10, 45**
See also AITN 2; BPFB 1; CA 9-12R; CANR 24, 49, 62, 80; CBD; CD; CN; DLB 6, 173; INT CANR-24; MTCW 1, 2; RGAL

**Donne, John** 1572-1631 ........ **LC 10, 24; DA; DAB; DAC; DAM MST, POET; PC 1; WLC**
See also BRW 1; CDBLB Before 1660; DLB 121, 151; EXPP; PAB; PFS 2, 11; RGEL; WLIT 3; WP

**Donnell, David** 1939(?)- ..................... **CLC 34**

**Donoghue, P. S.**
See Hunt, E(verette) Howard, (Jr.)

**Donoso (Yanez), Jose** 1924-1996 ... **CLC 4, 8, 11, 32, 99; DAM MULT; HLC 1; SSC 34**
See also CA 81-84; 155; CANR 32, 73; DLB 113; HW 1, 2; LAW; MTCW 1, 2; RGSF; WLIT 1

**Donovan, John** 1928-1992 ................. **CLC 35**
See also AAYA 20; CA 97-100; 137; CLR 3; MAICYA; SATA 72; SATA-Brief 29; YAW

**Don Roberto**
See Cunninghame Graham, Robert (Gallnigad) Bontine

**Doolittle, Hilda** 1886-1961 . **CLC 3, 8, 14, 31, 34, 73; DA; DAC; DAM MST, POET; PC 5; WLC**
See also H. D.
See also AMWS 1; CA 97-100; CANR 35; DLB 4, 45; FW; GLL 1; MAWW; MTCW 1, 2; PFS 6; RGAL

**Dorfman, Ariel** 1942- ...... **CLC 48, 77; DAM MULT; HLC 1**
See also CA 124; 130; CANR 67, 70; CWW 2; DFS 4; HW 1, 2; INT 130; WLIT 1

**Dorn, Edward (Merton)**
1929-1999 ............................. **CLC 10, 18**
See also CA 93-96; 187; CANR 42, 79; CP; DLB 5; INT 93-96; WP

**Dor-Ner, Zvi** ....................................... **CLC 70**

**Dorris, Michael (Anthony)**
1945-1997 ........ **CLC 109; DAM MULT, NOV**
See also AAYA 20; BEST 90:1; BYA 12; CA 102; 157; CANR 19, 46, 75; CLR 58; DA3; DLB 175; LAIT 5; MTCW 2; NFS 3; NNAL; RGAL; SATA 75; SATA-Obit 94; TCWW 2; YAW

**Dorris, Michael A.**
See Dorris, Michael (Anthony)

**Dorsan, Luc**
See Simenon, Georges (Jacques Christian)

**Dorsange, Jean**
See Simenon, Georges (Jacques Christian)

**Dos Passos, John (Roderigo)**
1896-1970 ... **CLC 1, 4, 8, 11, 15, 25, 34, 82; DA; DAB; DAC; DAM MST, NOV; WLC**
See also AMW; BPFB 1; CA 1-4R; 29-32R; CANR 3; CDALB 1929-1941; DA3; DLB 4, 9; DLBD 1, 15; DLBY 96; MTCW 1, 2; RGAL

**Dossage, Jean**
See Simenon, Georges (Jacques Christian)

**Dostoevsky, Fedor Mikhailovich**
1821-1881 . **NCLC 2, 7, 21, 33, 43; DA; DAB; DAC; DAM MST, NOV; SSC 2, 33, 44; WLC**
See also AAYA 40; DA3; DLB 238; EW; EXPN; NFS 3, 8; RGSF; RGWL; SSFS 8

**Dostoevsky, Fyodor**
See Dostoevsky, Fedor Mikhailovich

**Doughty, Charles M(ontagu)**
1843-1926 ................................... **TCLC 27**
See also CA 115; 178; DLB 19, 57, 174

**Douglas, Ellen** ............................... **CLC 73**
See also Haxton, Josephine Ayres; Williamson, Ellen Douglas
See also CN; CSW

**Douglas, Gavin** 1475(?)-1522 ............... **LC 20**
See also DLB 132; RGEL

**Douglas, George**
See Brown, George Douglas
See also RGEL

**Douglas, Keith (Castellain)**
1920-1944 ................................. **TCLC 40**
See also BRW 7; CA 160; DLB 27; PAB; RGEL

**Douglas, Leonard**
See Bradbury, Ray (Douglas)

**Douglas, Michael**
See Crichton, (John) Michael

**Douglas, (George) Norman**
1868-1952 ................................ TCLC 68
See also BRW 6; CA 119; 157; DLB 34, 195; RGEL

**Douglas, William**
See Brown, George Douglas

**Douglass, Frederick** 1817(?)-1895 .. NCLC 7, 55; BLC 1; DA; DAC; DAM MST, MULT; WLC
See also AFAW 1, 2; AMWS 3; CDALB 1640-1865; DA3; DLB 1, 43, 50, 79, 243; FW; LAIT 2; NCFS 2; RGAL; SATA 29

**Dourado, (Waldomiro Freitas) Autran**
1926- .......................... CLC 23, 60
See also CA 25-28R, 179; CANR 34, 81; DLB 145; HW 2

**Dourado, Waldomiro Autran**
See Dourado, (Waldomiro Freitas) Autran
See also CA 179

**Dove, Rita (Frances)** 1952- ........ CLC 50, 81; BLCS; DAM MULT, POET; PC 6
See also AMWS 4; BW 2; CA 109; CAAS 19; CANR 27, 42, 68, 76, 97; CDALBS; CP; CSW; CWP; DA3; DLB 120; EXPP; MTCW 1; PFS 1; RGAL

**Doveglion**
See Villa, Jose Garcia

**Dowell, Coleman** 1925-1985 .............. CLC 60
See also CA 25-28R; 117; CANR 10; DLB 130; GLL 2

**Dowson, Ernest (Christopher)**
1867-1900 .............................. TCLC 4
See also CA 105; 150; DLB 19, 135; RGEL

**Doyle, A. Conan**
See Doyle, Sir Arthur Conan

**Doyle, Sir Arthur Conan**
1859-1930 ... TCLC 7; DA; DAB; DAC; DAM MST, NOV; SSC 12; WLC
See also Conan Doyle, Arthur
See also AAYA 14; BRWS 2; CA 104; 122; CDBLB 1890-1914; CMW; DA3; DLB 18, 70, 156, 178; EXPS; HGG; LAIT 2; MSW; MTCW 1, 2; RGEL; RGSF; RHW; SATA 24; SFW; SSFS 2; WLIT 4; YAW

**Doyle, Conan**
See Doyle, Sir Arthur Conan

**Doyle, John**
See Graves, Robert (von Ranke)

**Doyle, Roddy** 1958(?)- ........................ CLC 81
See also AAYA 14; BRWS 5; CA 143; CANR 73; CN; DA3; DLB 194

**Doyle, Sir A. Conan**
See Doyle, Sir Arthur Conan

**Doyle, Sir Arthur Conan**
See Doyle, Sir Arthur Conan

**Dr. A**
See Asimov, Isaac; Silverstein, Alvin; Silverstein, Virginia B(arbara Opshelor)

**Drabble, Margaret** 1939- ...... CLC 2, 3, 5, 8, 10, 22, 53, 129; DAB; DAC; DAM MST, NOV, POP
See also BRWS 4; CA 13-16R; CANR 18, 35, 63; CDBLB 1960 to Present; CN; CPW; DA3; DLB 14, 155, 231; FW; MTCW 1, 2; RGEL; SATA 48

**Drapier, M. B.**
See Swift, Jonathan

**Drayham, James**
See Mencken, H(enry) L(ouis)

**Drayton, Michael** 1563-1631 ..... LC 8; DAM POET
See also DLB 121; RGEL

**Dreadstone, Carl**
See Campbell, (John) Ramsey

**Dreiser, Theodore (Herman Albert)**
1871-1945 .... TCLC 10, 18, 35, 83; DA; DAC; DAM MST, NOV; SSC 30; WLC
See also AMW; CA 106; 132; CDALB 1865-1917; DA3; DLB 9, 12, 102, 137; DLBD 1; LAIT 2; MTCW 1, 2; NFS 8; RGAL

**Drexler, Rosalyn** 1926- ...................... CLC 2, 6
See also CA 81-84; CAD; CANR 68; CD; CWD

**Dreyer, Carl Theodor** 1889-1968 ...... CLC 16
See also CA 116

**Drieu la Rochelle, Pierre(-Eugene)**
1893-1945 .............................. TCLC 21
See also CA 117; DLB 72; GFL 1789 to the Present

**Drinkwater, John** 1882-1937 .......... TCLC 57
See also CA 109; 149; DLB 10, 19, 149; RGEL

**Drop Shot**
See Cable, George Washington

**Droste-Hulshoff, Annette Freiin von**
1797-1848 ................................ NCLC 3
See also DLB 133; RGSF; RGWL

**Drummond, Walter**
See Silverberg, Robert

**Drummond, William Henry**
1854-1907 .............................. TCLC 25
See also CA 160; DLB 92

**Drummond de Andrade, Carlos**
1902-1987 ................................ CLC 18
See also Andrade, Carlos Drummond de
See also CA 132; 123; LAW

**Drury, Allen (Stuart)** 1918-1998 ....... CLC 37
See also CA 57-60; 170; CANR 18, 52; CN; INT CANR-18

**Dryden, John** 1631-1700 ........ LC 3, 21; DA; DAB; DAC; DAM DRAM, MST, POET; DC 3; PC 25; WLC
See also BRW 2; CDBLB 1660-1789; DLB 80, 101, 131; EXPP; IDTP; RGEL; TEA; WLIT 3

**Duberman, Martin (Bauml)** 1930- ..... CLC 8
See also CA 1-4R; CAD; CANR 2, 63; CD

**Dubie, Norman (Evans)** 1945- .......... CLC 36
See also CA 69-72; CANR 12; CP; DLB 120; PFS 12

**Du Bois, W(illiam) E(dward) B(urghardt)**
1868-1963 ... CLC 1, 2, 13, 64, 96; BLC 1; DA; DAC; DAM MST, MULT, NOV; WLC
See also AAYA 40; AFAW 1, 2; AMWS 2; BW 1, 3; CA 85-88; CANR 34, 82; CDALB 1865-1917; DA3; DLB 47, 50, 91, 246; EXPP; LAIT 2; MTCW 1, 2; NCFS 1; PFS 13; RGAL; SATA 42

**Dubus, Andre** 1936-1999 ..... CLC 13, 36, 97; SSC 15
See also AMWS 7; CA 21-24R; 177; CANR 17; CN; CSW; DLB 130; INT CANR-17; RGAL; SSFS 10

**Duca Minimo**
See D'Annunzio, Gabriele

**Ducharme, Rejean** 1941- ...................... CLC 74
See also CA 165; DLB 60

**Duchen, Claire** ................................ CLC 65

**Duclos, Charles Pinot-** 1704-1772 ......... LC 1
See also GFL Beginnings to 1789

**Dudek, Louis** 1918- ....................... CLC 11, 19
See also CA 45-48; CAAS 14; CANR 1; CP; DLB 88

**Duerrenmatt, Friedrich** 1921-1990 ... CLC 1, 4, 8, 11, 15, 43, 102; DAM DRAM
See also Durrenmatt, Friedrich
See also CA 17-20R; CANR 33; DLB 69, 124; EW; MTCW 1, 2

**Duffy, Bruce** 1953(?)- ........................ CLC 50
See also CA 172

**Duffy, Maureen** 1933- ........................ CLC 37
See also CA 25-28R; CANR 33, 68; CBD; CN; CP; CWD; CWP; DLB 14; FW; MTCW 1

**Du Fu**
See Tu Fu
See also RGWL

**Dugan, Alan** 1923- ............................ CLC 2, 6
See also CA 81-84; CP; DLB 5; PFS 10

**du Gard, Roger Martin**
See Martin du Gard, Roger

**Duhamel, Georges** 1884-1966 ............. CLC 8
See also CA 81-84; 25-28R; CANR 35; DLB 65; GFL 1789 to the Present; MTCW 1

**Dujardin, Edouard (Emile Louis)**
1861-1949 .............................. TCLC 13
See also CA 109; DLB 123

**Dulles, John Foster** 1888-1959 ....... TCLC 72
See also CA 115; 149

**Dumas, Alexandre (pere)**
1802-1870 ...... NCLC 11, 71; DA; DAB; DAC; DAM MST, NOV; WLC
See also AAYA 22; BYA 3; DA3; DLB 119, 192; EW; GFL 1789 to the Present; LAIT 1, 2; RGWL; SATA 18; WCH

**Dumas, Alexandre (fils)**
1824-1895 ...................... NCLC 9; DC 1
See also DLB 192; GFL 1789 to the Present; RGWL

**Dumas, Claudine**
See Malzberg, Barry N(athaniel)

**Dumas, Henry L.** 1934-1968 ......... CLC 6, 62
See also BW 1; CA 85-88; DLB 41; RGAL

**du Maurier, Daphne** 1907-1989 .. CLC 6, 11, 59; DAB; DAC; DAM MST, POP; SSC 18
See also AAYA 37; BPFB 1; BRWS 3; CA 5-8R; 128; CANR 6, 55; CMW; CPW; DA3; DLB 191; HGG; LAIT 3; MSW; MTCW 1, 2; NFS 12; RGEL; RGSF; RHW; SATA 27; SATA-Obit 60

**Du Maurier, George** 1834-1896 ...... NCLC 86
See also DLB 153, 178; RGEL

**Dunbar, Paul Laurence** 1872-1906 . TCLC 2, 12; BLC 1; DA; DAC; DAM MST, MULT, POET; PC 5; SSC 8; WLC
See also AFAW 1, 2; AMWS 2; BW 1, 3; CA 104; 124; CANR 79; CDALB 1865-1917; DA3; DLB 50, 54, 78; EXPP; RGAL; SATA 34

**Dunbar, William** 1460(?)-1520(?) ........ LC 20
See also DLB 132, 146; RGEL

**Duncan, Dora Angela**
See Duncan, Isadora

**Duncan, Isadora** 1877(?)-1927 ....... TCLC 68
See also CA 118; 149

**Duncan, Lois** 1934- ........................... CLC 26
See also AAYA 4, 34; BYA 6, 8; CA 1-4R; CANR 2, 23, 36; CLR 29; JRDA; MAICYA; MAICYAS; SAAS 2; SATA 1, 36, 75; YAW

**Duncan, Robert (Edward)**
1919-1988 .... CLC 1, 2, 4, 7, 15, 41, 55; DAM POET; PC 2
See also CA 9-12R; 124; CANR 28, 62; DLB 5, 16, 193; MTCW 1, 2; PFS 13; RGAL; WP

**Duncan, Sara Jeannette**
1861-1922 .............................. TCLC 60
See also CA 157; DLB 92

**Dunlap, William** 1766-1839 ............. NCLC 2
See also DLB 30, 37, 59; RGAL

**Dunn, Douglas (Eaglesham)** 1942- .... CLC 6, 40
See also CA 45-48; CANR 2, 33; CP; DLB 40; MTCW 1

**Dunn, Katherine (Karen)** 1945- ....... **CLC 71**
See also CA 33-36R; CANR 72; HGG; MTCW 1
**Dunn, Stephen** 1939- ......................... **CLC 36**
See also CA 33-36R; CANR 12, 48, 53; CP; DLB 105
**Dunne, Finley Peter** 1867-1936 ...... **TCLC 28**
See also CA 108; 178; DLB 11, 23; RGAL
**Dunne, John Gregory** 1932- ............. **CLC 28**
See also CA 25-28R; CANR 14, 50; CN; DLBY 80
**Dunsany, Edward John Moreton Drax Plunkett** 1878-1957
See Dunsany, Lord
See also CA 104; 148; DLB 10; MTCW 1; SFW
**Dunsany, Lord** ........................... **TCLC 2, 59**
See also Dunsany, Edward John Moreton Drax Plunkett
See also DLB 77, 153, 156; FANT; RGEL
**du Perry, Jean**
See Simenon, Georges (Jacques Christian)
**Durang, Christopher (Ferdinand)** 1949- ........................................... **CLC 27, 38**
See also CA 105; CAD; CANR 50, 76; CD; MTCW 1
**Duras, Marguerite** 1914-1996 . **CLC 3, 6, 11, 20, 34, 40, 68, 100; SSC 40**
See also BPFB 1; CA 25-28R; 151; CANR 50; CWW 2; DLB 83; GFL 1789 to the Present; IDFW 4; MTCW 1, 2; RGWL
**Durban, (Rosa) Pam** 1947- ................ **CLC 39**
See also CA 123; CANR 98; CSW
**Durcan, Paul** 1944- ......... **CLC 43, 70; DAM POET**
See also CA 134; CP
**Durkheim, Emile** 1858-1917 ............. **TCLC 55**
**Durrell, Lawrence (George)** 1912-1990 .... **CLC 1, 4, 6, 8, 13, 27, 41; DAM NOV**
See also BPFB 1; BRWS 1; CA 9-12R; 132; CANR 40, 77; CDBLB 1945-1960; DLB 15, 27, 204; DLBY 90; MTCW 1, 2; RGEL; SFW
**Durrenmatt, Friedrich**
See Duerrenmatt, Friedrich
See also RGWL
**Dutt, Toru** 1856-1877 ...................... **NCLC 29**
See also DLB 240
**Dwight, Timothy** 1752-1817 ........... **NCLC 13**
See also DLB 37; RGAL
**Dworkin, Andrea** 1946- ............. **CLC 43, 123**
See also CA 77-80; CAAS 21; CANR 16, 39, 76, 96; FW; GLL 1; INT CANR-16; MTCW 1, 2
**Dwyer, Deanna**
See Koontz, Dean R(ay)
**Dwyer, K. R.**
See Koontz, Dean R(ay)
**Dwyer, Thomas A.** 1923- ................. **CLC 114**
See also CA 115
**Dybek, Stuart** 1942- ......................... **CLC 114**
See also CA 97-100; CANR 39; DLB 130
**Dye, Richard**
See De Voto, Bernard (Augustine)
**Dyer, Geoff** 1958- ............................. **CLC 149**
See also CA 125; CANR 88
**Dylan, Bob** 1941- .... **CLC 3, 4, 6, 12, 77; PC 37**
See also CA 41-44R; CP; DLB 16
**Dyson, John** 1943- ............................. **CLC 70**
See also CA 144
**E. V. L.**
See Lucas, E(dward) V(errall)
**Eagleton, Terence (Francis)** 1943- .... **CLC 63, 132**
See also CA 57-60; CANR 7, 23, 68; DLB 242; MTCW 1, 2

**Eagleton, Terry**
See Eagleton, Terence (Francis)
**Early, Jack**
See Scoppettone, Sandra
See also GLL 1
**East, Michael**
See West, Morris L(anglo)
**Eastaway, Edward**
See Thomas, (Philip) Edward
**Eastlake, William (Derry)** 1917-1997 ................................ **CLC 8**
See also CA 5-8R; 158; CAAS 1; CANR 5, 63; CN; DLB 6, 206; INT CANR-5; TCWW 2
**Eastman, Charles A(lexander)** 1858-1939 ........ **TCLC 55; DAM MULT**
See also CA 179; CANR 91; DLB 175; NNAL; YABC 1
**Eberhart, Richard (Ghormley)** 1904- .. **CLC 3, 11, 19, 56; DAM POET**
See also AMW; CA 1-4R; CANR 2; CDALB 1941-1968; CP; DLB 48; MTCW 1; RGAL
**Eberstadt, Fernanda** 1960- ................ **CLC 39**
See also CA 136; CANR 69
**Echegaray (y Eizaguirre), Jose (Maria Waldo)** 1832-1916 .... **TCLC 4; HLCS 1**
See also CA 104; CANR 32; HW 1; MTCW 1
**Echeverria, (Jose) Esteban (Antonino)** 1805-1851 ................................ **NCLC 18**
See also LAW
**Echo**
See Proust, (Valentin-Louis-George-Eugene-)Marcel
**Eckert, Allan W.** 1931- ...................... **CLC 17**
See also AAYA 18; BYA 2; CA 13-16R; CANR 14, 45; INT CANR-14; SAAS 21; SATA 29, 91; SATA-Brief 27
**Eckhart, Meister** 1260(?)-1327(?) ... **CMLC 9**
See also DLB 115
**Eckmar, F. R.**
See de Hartog, Jan
**Eco, Umberto** 1932- ........... **CLC 28, 60, 142; DAM NOV, POP**
See also BEST 90:1; BPFB 1; CA 77-80; CANR 12, 33, 55; CPW; CWW 2; DA3; DLB 196, 242; MSW; MTCW 1, 2
**Eddison, E(ric) R(ucker)** 1882-1945 ............................ **TCLC 15**
See also CA 109; 156; FANT; SFW; SUFW
**Eddy, Mary (Ann Morse) Baker** 1821-1910 ............................ **TCLC 71**
See also CA 113; 174
**Edel, (Joseph) Leon** 1907-1997 .. **CLC 29, 34**
See also CA 1-4R; 161; CANR 1, 22; DLB 103; INT CANR-22
**Eden, Emily** 1797-1869 .................... **NCLC 10**
**Edgar, David** 1948- .. **CLC 42; DAM DRAM**
See also CA 57-60; CANR 12, 61; CBD; CD; DLB 13, 233; MTCW 1
**Edgerton, Clyde (Carlyle)** 1944- ...... **CLC 39**
See also AAYA 17; CA 118; 134; CANR 64; CSW; INT 134; YAW
**Edgeworth, Maria** 1768-1849 .... **NCLC 1, 51**
See also BRWS 3; DLB 116, 159, 163; FW; RGEL; SATA 21; WLIT 3
**Edmonds, Paul**
See Kuttner, Henry
**Edmonds, Walter D(umaux)** 1903-1998 ............................... **CLC 35**
See also BYA 2; CA 5-8R; CANR 2; CWRI; DLB 9; LAIT 1; MAICYA; RHW; SAAS 4; SATA 1, 27; SATA-Obit 99
**Edmondson, Wallace**
See Ellison, Harlan (Jay)
**Edson, Russell** 1935- ........................ **CLC 13**
See also CA 33-36R; DLB 244; WP

**Edwards, Bronwen Elizabeth**
See Rose, Wendy
**Edwards, G(erald) B(asil)** 1899-1976 .................................. **CLC 25**
See also CA 110
**Edwards, Gus** 1939- ............................ **CLC 43**
See also CA 108; INT 108
**Edwards, Jonathan** 1703-1758 ....... **LC 7, 54; DA; DAC; DAM MST**
See also AMW; DLB 24; RGAL
**Efron, Marina Ivanovna Tsvetaeva**
See Tsvetaeva (Efron), Marina (Ivanovna)
**Egoyan, Atom** 1960- ......................... **CLC 151**
See also CA 157
**Ehle, John (Marsden, Jr.)** 1925- ...... **CLC 27**
See also CA 9-12R; CSW
**Ehrenbourg, Ilya (Grigoryevich)**
See Ehrenburg, Ilya (Grigoryevich)
**Ehrenburg, Ilya (Grigoryevich)** 1891-1967 ........................ **CLC 18, 34, 62**
See also CA 102; 25-28R
**Ehrenburg, Ilyo (Grigoryevich)**
See Ehrenburg, Ilya (Grigoryevich)
**Ehrenreich, Barbara** 1941- ............... **CLC 110**
See also BEST 90:4; CA 73-76; CANR 16, 37, 62; DLB 246; FW; MTCW 1, 2
**Eich, Guenter** 1907-1972 ................... **CLC 15**
See also Eich, Gunter
See also CA 111; 93-96; DLB 69, 124
**Eich, Gunter**
See Eich, Guenter
See also RGWL
**Eichendorff, Joseph** 1788-1857 ........ **NCLC 8**
See also DLB 90; RGWL
**Eigner, Larry** ......................................... **CLC 9**
See also Eigner, Laurence (Joel)
See also CAAS 23; DLB 5; WP
**Eigner, Laurence (Joel)** 1927-1996
See Eigner, Larry
See also CA 9-12R; 151; CANR 6, 84; CP; DLB 193
**Einstein, Albert** 1879-1955 ............. **TCLC 65**
See also CA 121; 133; MTCW 1, 2
**Eiseley, Loren Corey** 1907-1977 ......... **CLC 7**
See also AAYA 5; ANW; CA 1-4R; 73-76; CANR 6; DLBD 17
**Eisenstadt, Jill** 1963- ......................... **CLC 50**
See also CA 140
**Eisenstein, Sergei (Mikhailovich)** 1898-1948 .................................. **TCLC 57**
See also CA 114; 149
**Eisner, Simon**
See Kornbluth, C(yril) M.
**Ekeloef, (Bengt) Gunnar** 1907-1968 ... **CLC 27; DAM POET; PC 23**
See also CA 123; 25-28R; EW
**Ekelof, (Bengt) Gunnar**
See Ekeloef, (Bengt) Gunnar
**Ekelund, Vilhelm** 1880-1949 ............ **TCLC 75**
See also CA 189
**Ekwensi, C. O. D.**
See Ekwensi, Cyprian (Odiatu Duaka)
**Ekwensi, Cyprian (Odiatu Duaka)** 1921- ......... **CLC 4; BLC 1; DAM MULT**
See also AFW; BW 2, 3; CA 29-32R; CANR 18, 42, 74; CN; CWRI; DLB 117; MTCW 1, 2; RGEL; SATA 66; WLIT 2
**Elaine** ................................................. **TCLC 18**
See also Leverson, Ada
**El Crummo**
See Crumb, R(obert)
**Elder, Lonne III** 1931-1996 ................... **DC 8**
See also BLC 1; BW 1, 3; CA 81-84; 152; CAD; CANR 25; DAM MULT; DLB 7, 38, 44

**Eleanor of Aquitaine** 1122-1204 ... **CMLC 39**

**Elia**
See Lamb, Charles

**Eliade, Mircea** 1907-1986 .................. **CLC 19**
See also CA 65-68; 119; CANR 30, 62; DLB 220; MTCW 1; SFW

**Eliot, A. D.**
See Jewett, (Theodora) Sarah Orne

**Eliot, Alice**
See Jewett, (Theodora) Sarah Orne

**Eliot, Dan**
See Silverberg, Robert

**Eliot, George** 1819-1880 ...... **NCLC 4, 13, 23, 41, 49, 89; DA; DAB; DAC; DAM MST, NOV; PC 20; WLC**
See also BRW 5; CDBLB 1832-1890; CN; CPW; DA3; DLB 21, 35, 55; RGEL; RGSF; SSFS 8; WLIT 3

**Eliot, John** 1604-1690 ............................. **LC 5**
See also DLB 24

**Eliot, T(homas) S(tearns)** 1888-1965 ...... **CLC 1, 2, 3, 6, 9, 10, 13, 15, 24, 34, 41, 55, 57, 113; DA; DAB; DAC; DAM DRAM, MST, POET; PC 5, 31; WLC**
See also AAYA 28; AMW; AMWR 1; BRW 7; CA 5-8R; 25-28R; CANR 41; CDALB 1929-1941; DA3; DFS 4, 13; DLB 7, 10, 45, 63, 245; DLBY 88; EXPP; LAIT 3; MTCW 1, 2; PAB; PFS 1, 7; RGAL; RGEL; WLIT 4; WP

**Elizabeth** 1866-1941 ........................ **TCLC 41**

**Elkin, Stanley L(awrence)** 1930-1995 .. **CLC 4, 6, 9, 14, 27, 51, 91; DAM NOV, POP; SSC 12**
See also AMWS 6; BPFB 1; CA 9-12R; 148; CANR 8, 46; CN; CPW; DLB 2, 28; DLBY 80; INT CANR-8; MTCW 1, 2; RGAL

**Elledge, Scott** ...................................... **CLC 34**

**Elliot, Don**
See Silverberg, Robert

**Elliott, Don**
See Silverberg, Robert

**Elliott, George P(aul)** 1918-1980 ........ **CLC 2**
See also CA 1-4R; 97-100; CANR 2; DLB 244

**Elliott, Janice** 1931-1995 ................... **CLC 47**
See also CA 13-16R; CANR 8, 29, 84; CN; DLB 14; SATA 119

**Elliott, Sumner Locke** 1917-1991 ..... **CLC 38**
See also CA 5-8R; 134; CANR 2, 21

**Elliott, William**
See Bradbury, Ray (Douglas)

**Ellis, A. E.** ............................................... **CLC 7**

**Ellis, Alice Thomas** ........................... **CLC 40**
See also Haycraft, Anna (Margaret)
See also DLB 194; MTCW 1

**Ellis, Bret Easton** 1964- ..... **CLC 39, 71, 117; DAM POP**
See also AAYA 2; CA 118; 123; CANR 51, 74; CN; CPW; DA3; HGG; INT 123; MTCW 1; NFS 11

**Ellis, (Henry) Havelock** 1859-1939 ................................ **TCLC 14**
See also CA 109; 169; DLB 190

**Ellis, Landon**
See Ellison, Harlan (Jay)

**Ellis, Trey** 1962- ................................. **CLC 55**
See also CA 146; CANR 92

**Ellison, Harlan (Jay)** 1934- ... **CLC 1, 13, 42, 139; DAM POP; SSC 14**
See also AAYA 29; BPFB 1; CA 5-8R; CANR 5, 46; CPW; DLB 8; HGG; INT CANR-5; MTCW 1, 2; SCFW 2; SFW; SSFS 13; SUFW

**Ellison, Ralph (Waldo)** 1914-1994 .... **CLC 1, 3, 11, 54, 86, 114; BLC 1; DA; DAB; DAC; DAM MST, MULT, NOV; SSC 26; WLC**
See also AAYA 19; AFAW 1, 2; AMWS 2; BPFB 1; BW 1, 3; BYA 2; CA 9-12R; 145; CANR 24, 53; CDALB 1941-1968; CSW; DA3; DLB 2, 76, 227; DLBY 94; EXPN; EXPS; LAIT 4; MTCW 1, 2; NFS 2; RGAL; RGSF; SSFS 1, 11; YAW

**Ellmann, Lucy (Elizabeth)** 1956- ..... **CLC 61**
See also CA 128

**Ellmann, Richard (David)** 1918-1987 ................................ **CLC 50**
See also BEST 89:2; CA 1-4R; 122; CANR 2, 28, 61; DLB 103; DLBY 87; MTCW 1, 2

**Elman, Richard (Martin)** 1934-1997 ................................ **CLC 19**
See also CA 17-20R; 163; CAAS 3; CANR 47

**Elron**
See Hubbard, L(afayette) Ron(ald)

**Eluard, Paul** ................................. **TCLC 7, 41**
See also Grindel, Eugene
See also GFL 1789 to the Present; RGWL

**Elyot, Thomas** 1490(?)-1546 ................. **LC 11**
See also RGEL

**Elytis, Odysseus** 1911-1996 ........ **CLC 15, 49, 100; DAM POET; PC 21**
See also Alepoudelis, Odysseus
See also CA 102; 151; CANR 94; CWW 2; EW; MTCW 1, 2; RGWL

**Emecheta, (Florence Onye) Buchi** 1944- .. **CLC 14, 48, 128; BLC 2; DAM MULT**
See also AFW; BW 2, 3; CA 81-84; CANR 27, 81; CN; CWRI; DA3; DLB 117; FW; MTCW 1, 2; NFS 12; SATA 66; WLIT 2

**Emerson, Mary Moody** 1774-1863 ........................... **NCLC 66**

**Emerson, Ralph Waldo** 1803-1882 . **NCLC 1, 38, 98; DA; DAB; DAC; DAM MST, POET; PC 18; WLC**
See also AMW; ANW; CDALB 1640-1865; DA3; DLB 1, 59, 73, 223; EXPP; LAIT 2; PFS 4; RGAL; WP

**Eminescu, Mihail** 1850-1889 .......... **NCLC 33**

**Empson, William** 1906-1984 ... **CLC 3, 8, 19, 33, 34**
See also BRWS 2; CA 17-20R; 112; CANR 31, 61; DLB 20; MTCW 1, 2; RGEL

**Enchi, Fumiko (Ueda)** 1905-1986 ..... **CLC 31**
See also CA 129; 121; DLB 182; FW; MJW

**Ende, Michael (Andreas Helmuth)** 1929-1995 ................................ **CLC 31**
See also BYA 5; CA 118; 124; 149; CANR 36; CLR 14; DLB 75; MAICYA; MAICYAS; SATA 61; SATA-Brief 42; SATA-Obit 86

**Endo, Shusaku** 1923-1996 ..... **CLC 7, 14, 19, 54, 99; DAM NOV; SSC 48**
See also CA 29-32R; 153; CANR 21, 54; DA3; DLB 182; MTCW 1, 2; RGSF; RGWL

**Engel, Marian** 1933-1985 ................... **CLC 36**
See also CA 25-28R; CANR 12; DLB 53; FW; INT CANR-12

**Engelhardt, Frederick**
See Hubbard, L(afayette) Ron(ald)

**Engels, Friedrich** 1820-1895 .......... **NCLC 85**
See also DLB 129

**Enright, D(ennis) J(oseph)** 1920- .. **CLC 4, 8, 31**
See also CA 1-4R; CANR 1, 42, 83; CP; DLB 27; SATA 25

**Enzensberger, Hans Magnus** 1929- ............................... **CLC 43; PC 28**
See also CA 116; 119; CANR 103

**Ephron, Nora** 1941- ..................... **CLC 17, 31**
See also AAYA 35; AITN 2; CA 65-68; CANR 12, 39, 83

**Epicurus** 341B.C.-270B.C. ............ **CMLC 21**
See also DLB 176

**Epsilon**
See Betjeman, John

**Epstein, Daniel Mark** 1948- ................ **CLC 7**
See also CA 49-52; CANR 2, 53, 90

**Epstein, Jacob** 1956- ........................ **CLC 19**
See also CA 114

**Epstein, Jean** 1897-1953 ................. **TCLC 92**

**Epstein, Joseph** 1937- ....................... **CLC 39**
See also CA 112; 119; CANR 50, 65

**Epstein, Leslie** 1938- ........................ **CLC 27**
See also CA 73-76; CAAS 12; CANR 23, 69

**Equiano, Olaudah** 1745(?)-1797 ......... **LC 16; BLC 2; DAM MULT**
See also AFAW 1, 2; DLB 37, 50; WLIT 2

**Erasmus, Desiderius** 1469(?)-1536 ....... **LC 16**
See also EW; RGWL

**Erdman, Paul E(mil)** 1932- ................ **CLC 25**
See also AITN 1; CA 61-64; CANR 13, 43, 84

**Erdrich, Louise** 1954- ........ **CLC 39, 54, 120; DAM MULT, NOV, POP**
See also AAYA 10; AMWS 4; BEST 89:1; BPFB 1; CA 114; CANR 41, 62; CDALBS; CN; CP; CPW; CWP; DA3; DLB 152, 175, 206; EXPP; LAIT 5; MTCW 1, 2; NFS 5; NNAL; RGAL; SATA 94; TCWW 2

**Erenburg, Ilya (Grigoryevich)**
See Ehrenburg, Ilya (Grigoryevich)

**Erickson, Stephen Michael** 1950-
See Erickson, Steve
See also CA 129; SFW

**Erickson, Steve** ................................. **CLC 64**
See also Erickson, Stephen Michael
See also CANR 60, 68

**Ericson, Walter**
See Fast, Howard (Melvin)

**Eriksson, Buntel**
See Bergman, (Ernst) Ingmar

**Ernaux, Annie** 1940- ......................... **CLC 88**
See also CA 147; CANR 93

**Erskine, John** 1879-1951 ................. **TCLC 84**
See also CA 112; 159; DLB 9, 102; FANT

**Eschenbach, Wolfram von**
See Wolfram von Eschenbach

**Eseki, Bruno**
See Mphahlele, Ezekiel

**Esenin, Sergei (Alexandrovich)** 1895-1925 ................................. **TCLC 4**
See also CA 104; RGWL

**Eshleman, Clayton** 1935- ..................... **CLC 7**
See also CA 33-36R; CAAS 6; CANR 93; CP; DLB 5

**Espriella, Don Manuel Alvarez**
See Southey, Robert

**Espriu, Salvador** 1913-1985 .................. **CLC 9**
See also CA 154; 115; DLB 134

**Espronceda, Jose de** 1808-1842 ...... **NCLC 39**

**Esquivel, Laura** 1951(?)- ... **CLC 141; HLCS 1**
See also AAYA 29; CA 143; CANR 68; DA3; DNFS; LAIT 3; MTCW 1; NFS 5; WLIT 1

**Esse, James**
See Stephens, James

**Esterbrook, Tom**
See Hubbard, L(afayette) Ron(ald)

**Estleman, Loren D.** 1952- ..... **CLC 48; DAM NOV, POP**
See also AAYA 27; CA 85-88; CANR 27, 74; CMW; CPW; DA3; DLB 226; INT CANR-27; MTCW 1, 2

**Euclid** 306B.C.-283B.C. .................. **CMLC 25**

**Eugenides, Jeffrey** 1960(?)- ............... **CLC 81**
See also CA 144

**Euripides** c. 484B.C.-406B.C. ....... **CMLC 23; DA; DAB; DAC; DAM DRAM, MST; DC 4; WLCS**
See also AW 1; DA3; DFS 1, 4, 6; DLB 176; LAIT 1; RGWL

**Evan, Evin**
See Faust, Frederick (Schiller)

**Evans, Caradoc** 1878-1945 ... **TCLC 85; SSC 43**

**Evans, Evan**
See Faust, Frederick (Schiller)
See also TCWW 2

**Evans, Marian**
See Eliot, George

**Evans, Mary Ann**
See Eliot, George

**Evarts, Esther**
See Benson, Sally

**Everett, Percival**
See Everett, Percival L.
See also CSW

**Everett, Percival L.** 1956- ................. **CLC 57**
See also Everett, Percival
See also BW 2; CA 129; CANR 94

**Everson, R(onald) G(ilmour)** 1903-1992 ........................... **CLC 27**
See also CA 17-20R; DLB 88

**Everson, William (Oliver)** 1912-1994 .......................... **CLC 1, 5, 14**
See also CA 9-12R; 145; CANR 20; DLB 212; MTCW 1

**Evtushenko, Evgenii Aleksandrovich**
See Yevtushenko, Yevgeny (Alexandrovich)
See also RGWL

**Ewart, Gavin (Buchanan)** 1916-1995 ............................. **CLC 13, 46**
See also BRWS 7; CA 89-92; 150; CANR 17, 46; CP; DLB 40; MTCW 1

**Ewers, Hanns Heinz** 1871-1943 ..... **TCLC 12**
See also CA 109; 149

**Ewing, Frederick R.**
See Sturgeon, Theodore (Hamilton)

**Exley, Frederick (Earl)** 1929-1992 .... **CLC 6, 11**
See also AITN 2; BPFB 1; CA 81-84; 138; DLB 143; DLBY 81

**Eynhardt, Guillermo**
See Quiroga, Horacio (Sylvestre)

**Ezekiel, Nissim** 1924- ......................... **CLC 61**
See also CA 61-64; CP

**Ezekiel, Tish O'Dowd** 1943- .............. **CLC 34**
See also CA 129

**Fadeyev, A.**
See Bulgya, Alexander Alexandrovich

**Fadeyev, Alexander** ........................ **TCLC 53**
See also Bulgya, Alexander Alexandrovich

**Fagen, Donald** 1948- ........................ **CLC 26**

**Fainzilberg, Ilya Arnoldovich** 1897-1937
See Ilf, Ilya
See also CA 120; 165

**Fair, Ronald L.** 1932- ........................ **CLC 18**
See also BW 1; CA 69-72; CANR 25; DLB 33

**Fairbairn, Roger**
See Carr, John Dickson

**Fairbairns, Zoe (Ann)** 1948- .............. **CLC 32**
See also CA 103; CANR 21, 85; CN

**Fairman, Paul W.** 1916-1977
See Queen, Ellery
See also CA 114; SFW

**Falco, Gian**
See Papini, Giovanni

**Falconer, James**
See Kirkup, James

**Falconer, Kenneth**
See Kornbluth, C(yril) M.

**Falkland, Samuel**
See Heijermans, Herman

**Fallaci, Oriana** 1930- ................. **CLC 11, 110**
See also CA 77-80; CANR 15, 58; FW; MTCW 1

**Faludi, Susan** 1959- ........................ **CLC 140**
See also CA 138; FW; MTCW 1

**Faludy, George** 1913- ....................... **CLC 42**
See also CA 21-24R

**Faludy, Gyoergy**
See Faludy, George

**Fanon, Frantz** 1925-1961 ... **CLC 74; BLC 2; DAM MULT**
See also BW 1; CA 116; 89-92; WLIT 2

**Fanshawe, Ann** 1625-1680 .................... **LC 11**

**Fante, John (Thomas)** 1911-1983 ..... **CLC 60**
See also CA 69-72; 109; CANR 23; DLB 130; DLBY 83

**Farah, Nuruddin** 1945- .. **CLC 53, 137; BLC 2; DAM MULT**
See also AFW; BW 2, 3; CA 106; CANR 81; CN; DLB 125; WLIT 2

**Fargue, Leon-Paul** 1876(?)-1947 .... **TCLC 11**
See also CA 109

**Farigoule, Louis**
See Romains, Jules

**Farina, Richard** 1936(?)-1966 .............. **CLC 9**
See also CA 81-84; 25-28R

**Farley, Walter (Lorimer)** 1915-1989 ................................... **CLC 17**
See also CA 17-20R; CANR 8, 29, 84; DLB 22; JRDA; MAICYA; SATA 2, 43; YAW

**Farmer, Philip Jose** 1918- ............ **CLC 1, 19**
See also AAYA 28; BPFB 1; CA 1-4R; CANR 4, 35; DLB 8; MTCW 1; SATA 93; SFW

**Farquhar, George** 1677-1707 ... **LC 21; DAM DRAM**
See also BRW 2; DLB 84; RGEL

**Farrell, J(ames) G(ordon)** 1935-1979 .................................... **CLC 6**
See also CA 73-76; 89-92; CANR 36; DLB 14; MTCW 1; RGEL; RHW; WLIT 4

**Farrell, James T(homas)** 1904-1979 . **CLC 1, 4, 8, 11, 66; SSC 28**
See also AMW; BPFB 1; CA 5-8R; 89-92; CANR 9, 61; DLB 4, 9, 86; DLBD 2; MTCW 1, 2; RGAL

**Farrell, Warren (Thomas)** 1943- ...... **CLC 70**
See also CA 146

**Farren, Richard J.**
See Betjeman, John

**Farren, Richard M.**
See Betjeman, John

**Fassbinder, Rainer Werner** 1946-1982 ................................... **CLC 20**
See also CA 93-96; 106; CANR 31

**Fast, Howard (Melvin)** 1914- .. **CLC 23, 131; DAM NOV**
See also AAYA 16; BPFB 1; CA 1-4R, 181; CAAE 181; CAAS 18; CANR 1, 33, 54, 75, 98; CMW; CN; CPW; DLB 9; INT CANR-33; MTCW 1; RHW; SATA 7; SATA-Essay 107; TCWW 2; YAW

**Faulcon, Robert**
See Holdstock, Robert P.

**Faulkner, William (Cuthbert)** 1897-1962 ....... **CLC 1, 3, 6, 8, 9, 11, 14, 18, 28, 52, 68; DA; DAB; DAC; DAM MST, NOV; SSC 1, 35, 42; WLC**
See also AAYA 7; AMW; AMWR 1; BPFB 1; BYA 5; CA 81-84; CANR 33; CDALB 1929-1941; DA3; DLB 9, 11, 44, 102; DLBD 2; DLBY 86, 97; EXPN; EXPS; LAIT 2; MTCW 1, 2; NFS 4, 8; RGAL; RGSF; SSFS 2, 5, 6, 12

**Fauset, Jessie Redmon** 1882(?)-1961 ......... **CLC 19, 54; BLC 2; DAM MULT**
See also AFAW 2; BW 1; CA 109; CANR 83; DLB 51; FW; MAWW

**Faust, Frederick (Schiller)** 1892-1944(?) ....... **TCLC 49; DAM POP**
See also Austin, Frank; Brand, Max; Challis, George; Dawson, Peter; Dexter, Martin; Evans, Evan; Frederick, John; Frost, Frederick; Manning, David; Silver, Nicholas
See also CA 108; 152

**Faust, Irvin** 1924- ................................. **CLC 8**
See also CA 33-36R; CANR 28, 67; CN; DLB 2, 28; DLBY 80

**Fawkes, Guy**
See Benchley, Robert (Charles)

**Fearing, Kenneth (Flexner)** 1902-1961 ............................... **CLC 51**
See also CA 93-96; CANR 59; CMW; DLB 9; RGAL

**Fecamps, Elise**
See Creasey, John

**Federman, Raymond** 1928- .......... **CLC 6, 47**
See also CA 17-20R; CAAS 8; CANR 10, 43, 83; CN; DLBY 80

**Federspiel, J(uerg) F.** 1931- ............... **CLC 42**
See also CA 146

**Feiffer, Jules (Ralph)** 1929- ..... **CLC 2, 8, 64; DAM DRAM**
See also AAYA 3; CA 17-20R; CAD; CANR 30, 59; CD; DLB 7, 44; INT CANR-30; MTCW 1; SATA 8, 61, 111

**Feige, Hermann Albert Otto Maximilian**
See Traven, B.

**Feinberg, David B.** 1956-1994 .......... **CLC 59**
See also CA 135; 147

**Feinstein, Elaine** 1930- ...................... **CLC 36**
See also CA 69-72; CAAS 1; CANR 31, 68; CN; CP; CWP; DLB 14, 40; MTCW 1

**Feke, Gilbert David** ......................... **CLC 65**

**Feldman, Irving (Mordecai)** 1928- ..... **CLC 7**
See also CA 1-4R; CANR 1; CP; DLB 169

**Felix-Tchicaya, Gerald**
See Tchicaya, Gerald Felix

**Fellini, Federico** 1920-1993 ......... **CLC 16, 85**
See also CA 65-68; 143; CANR 33

**Felsen, Henry Gregor** 1916-1995 ...... **CLC 17**
See also CA 1-4R; 180; CANR 1; SAAS 2; SATA 1

**Felski, Rita** ........................................ **CLC 65**

**Fenno, Jack**
See Calisher, Hortense

**Fenollosa, Ernest (Francisco)** 1853-1908 ................................ **TCLC 91**

**Fenton, James Martin** 1949- ............. **CLC 32**
See also CA 102; CP; DLB 40; PFS 11

**Ferber, Edna** 1887-1968 ............. **CLC 18, 93**
See also AITN 1; CA 5-8R; 25-28R; CANR 68; DLB 9, 28, 86; MTCW 1, 2; RGAL; RHW; SATA 7; TCWW 2

**Ferdowsi, Abu'l Qasem** 940-1020 . **CMLC 43**
See also RGWL

**Ferguson, Helen**
See Kavan, Anna

**Ferguson, Niall** 1964- ....................... **CLC 134**
See also CA 190

**Ferguson, Samuel** 1810-1886 ......... **NCLC 33**
See also DLB 32; RGEL

**Fergusson, Robert** 1750-1774 ............. **LC 29**
See also DLB 109; RGEL

**Ferling, Lawrence**
See Ferlinghetti, Lawrence (Monsanto)

**Ferlinghetti, Lawrence** (Monsanto)
1919(?)- .... **CLC 2, 6, 10, 27, 111; DAM POET; PC 1**
See also CA 5-8R; CANR 3, 41, 73; CDALB 1941-1968; CP; DA3; DLB 5, 16; MTCW 1, 2; RGAL; WP

**Fern, Fanny**
See Parton, Sara Payson Willis

**Fernandez, Vicente Garcia Huidobro**
See Huidobro Fernandez, Vicente Garcia

**Fernandez-Armesto, Felipe** ............. **CLC 70**

**Fernandez de Lizardi, Jose Joaquin**
See Lizardi, Jose Joaquin Fernandez de

**Ferre, Rosario** 1942- ...... **CLC 139; HLCS 1; SSC 36**
See also CA 131; CANR 55, 81; CWW 2; DLB 145; HW 1, 2; MTCW 1; WLIT 1

**Ferrer, Gabriel** (Francisco Victor) Miro
See Miro (Ferrer), Gabriel (Francisco Victor)

**Ferrier, Susan** (Edmonstone)
1782-1854 ................... **NCLC 8**
See also DLB 116; RGEL

**Ferrigno, Robert** 1948(?)- .................. **CLC 65**
See also CA 140

**Ferron, Jacques** 1921-1985 .... **CLC 94; DAC**
See also CA 117; 129; CCA 1; DLB 60

**Feuchtwanger, Lion** 1884-1958 ........ **TCLC 3**
See also CA 104; 187; DLB 66

**Feuillet, Octave** 1821-1890 ............. **NCLC 45**
See also DLB 192

**Feydeau, Georges** (Leon Jules Marie)
1862-1921 ........ **TCLC 22; DAM DRAM**
See also CA 113; 152; CANR 84; DLB 192; GFL 1789 to the Present; RGWL

**Fichte, Johann Gottlieb**
1762-1814 .................... **NCLC 62**
See also DLB 90

**Ficino, Marsilio** 1433-1499 .................... **LC 12**

**Fiedeler, Hans**
See Doeblin, Alfred

**Fiedler, Leslie A**(aron) 1917- .. **CLC 4, 13, 24**
See also CA 9-12R; CANR 7, 63; CN; DLB 28, 67; MTCW 1, 2; RGAL

**Field, Andrew** 1938- .......................... **CLC 44**
See also CA 97-100; CANR 25

**Field, Eugene** 1850-1895 .................... **NCLC 3**
See also DLB 23, 42, 140; DLBD 13; MAICYA; RGAL; SATA 16

**Field, Gans T.**
See Wellman, Manly Wade

**Field, Michael** 1915-1971 ................. **TCLC 43**
See also CA 29-32R

**Field, Peter**
See Hobson, Laura Z(ametkin)
See also TCWW 2

**Fielding, Helen** 1959(?)- .................. **CLC 146**
See also CA 172; DLB 231

**Fielding, Henry** 1707-1754 ..... **LC 1, 46; DA; DAB; DAC; DAM DRAM, MST, NOV; WLC**
See also BRW 3; CDBLB 1660-1789; DA3; DLB 39, 84, 101; RGEL; WLIT 3

**Fielding, Sarah** 1710-1768 ............... **LC 1, 44**
See also DLB 39; RGEL

**Fields, W. C.** 1880-1946 ................... **TCLC 80**
See also DLB 44

**Fierstein, Harvey** (Forbes) 1954- .... **CLC 33; DAM DRAM, POP**
See also CA 123; 129; CAD; CD; CPW; DA3; DFS 6; GLL

**Figes, Eva** 1932- ............................. **CLC 31**
See also CA 53-56; CANR 4, 44, 83; CN; DLB 14; FW

**Finch, Anne** 1661-1720 .............. **LC 3; PC 21**
See also DLB 95

**Finch, Robert** (Duer Claydon)
1900-1995 ........................... **CLC 18**
See also CA 57-60; CANR 9, 24, 49; CP; DLB 88

**Findley, Timothy** 1930- . **CLC 27, 102; DAC; DAM MST**
See also CA 25-28R; CANR 12, 42, 69; CCA 1; CN; DLB 53; FANT; RHW

**Fink, William**
See Mencken, H(enry) L(ouis)

**Firbank, Louis** 1942-
See Reed, Lou
See also CA 117

**Firbank, (Arthur Annesley) Ronald**
1886-1926 ........................... **TCLC 1**
See also BRWS 2; CA 104; 177; DLB 36; RGEL

**Fish, Stanley**
See Fish, Stanley Eugene

**Fish, Stanley E.**
See Fish, Stanley Eugene

**Fish, Stanley Eugene** 1938- ............. **CLC 142**
See also CA 112; 132; CANR 90; DLB 67

**Fisher, Dorothy** (Frances) Canfield
1879-1958 ........................... **TCLC 87**
See also CA 114; 136; CANR 80; CLR 71,; CWRI; DLB 9, 102; MAICYA; YABC 1

**Fisher, M**(ary) F(rances) K(ennedy)
1908-1992 ........................... **CLC 76, 87**
See also CA 77-80; 138; CANR 44; MTCW 1

**Fisher, Roy** 1930- ........................... **CLC 25**
See also CA 81-84; CAAS 10; CANR 16; CP; DLB 40

**Fisher, Rudolph** 1897-1934 .. **TCLC 11; BLC 2; DAM MULT; SSC 25**
See also BW 1, 3; CA 107; 124; CANR 80; DLB 51, 102

**Fisher, Vardis** (Alvero) 1895-1968 ...... **CLC 7**
See also CA 5-8R; 25-28R; CANR 68; DLB 9, 206; RGAL; TCWW 2

**Fiske, Tarleton**
See Bloch, Robert (Albert)

**Fitch, Clarke**
See Sinclair, Upton (Beall)

**Fitch, John IV**
See Cormier, Robert (Edmund)

**Fitzgerald, Captain Hugh**
See Baum, L(yman) Frank

**FitzGerald, Edward** 1809-1883 ....... **NCLC 9**
See also BRW 4; DLB 32; RGEL

**Fitzgerald, F**(rancis) Scott (Key)
1896-1940 .. **TCLC 1, 6, 14, 28, 55; DA; DAB; DAC; DAM MST, NOV; SSC 6, 31; WLC**
See also AAYA 24; AITN 1; AMW; AMWR 1; BPFB 1; CA 110; 123; CDALB 1917-1929; DA3; DLB 4, 9, 86; DLBD 1, 15, 16; DLBY 81, 96; EXPN; EXPS; LAIT 3; MTCW 1, 2; NFS 2; RGAL; RGSF; SSFS 4

**Fitzgerald, Penelope** 1916-2000 . **CLC 19, 51, 61, 143**
See also BRWS 5; CA 85-88; 190; CAAS 10; CANR 56, 86; CN; DLB 14, 194; MTCW 2

**Fitzgerald, Robert** (Stuart)
1910-1985 ........................... **CLC 39**
See also CA 1-4R; 114; CANR 1; DLBY 80

**FitzGerald, Robert D**(avid)
1902-1987 ........................... **CLC 19**
See also CA 17-20R; RGEL

**Fitzgerald, Zelda** (Sayre)
1900-1948 ........................... **TCLC 52**
See also AMWS 9; CA 117; 126; DLBY 84

**Flanagan, Thomas** (James Bonner)
1923- ................................. **CLC 25, 52**
See also CA 108; CANR 55; CN; DLBY 80; INT 108; MTCW 1; RHW

**Flaubert, Gustave** 1821-1880 .... **NCLC 2, 10, 19, 62, 66; DA; DAB; DAC; DAM MST, NOV; SSC 11; WLC**
See also DA3; DLB 119; EW; EXPS; GFL 1789 to the Present; LAIT 2; RGSF; RGWL; SSFS 6

**Flavius Josephus**
See Josephus, Flavius

**Flecker, Herman Elroy**
See Flecker, (Herman) James Elroy

**Flecker, (Herman) James Elroy**
1884-1915 ........................... **TCLC 43**
See also CA 109; 150; DLB 10, 19; RGEL

**Fleming, Ian** (Lancaster) 1908-1964 . **CLC 3, 30; DAM POP**
See also AAYA 26; BPFB 1; CA 5-8R; CANR 59; CDBLB 1945-1960; CMW; CPW; DA3; DLB 87, 201; MSW; MTCW 1, 2; RGEL; SATA 9; YAW

**Fleming, Thomas** (James) 1927- ....... **CLC 37**
See also CA 5-8R; CANR 10, 102; INT CANR-10; SATA 8

**Fletcher, John** 1579-1625 .......... **LC 33; DC 6**
See also BRW 2; CDBLB Before 1660; DLB 58; RGEL

**Fletcher, John Gould** 1886-1950 .... **TCLC 35**
See also CA 107; 167; DLB 4, 45; RGAL

**Fleur, Paul**
See Pohl, Frederik

**Flooglebuckle, Al**
See Spiegelman, Art

**Flora, Fletcher** 1914-1969
See Queen, Ellery
See also CA 1-4R; CANR 3, 85

**Flying Officer X**
See Bates, H(erbert) E(rnest)

**Fo, Dario** 1926- .............. **CLC 32, 109; DAM DRAM; DC 10**
See also CA 116; 128; CANR 68; CWW 2; DA3; DLBY 97; MTCW 1, 2

**Fogarty, Jonathan Titulescu Esq.**
See Farrell, James T(homas)

**Follett, Ken**(neth Martin) 1949- ...... **CLC 18; DAM NOV, POP**
See also AAYA 6; BEST 89:4; BPFB 1; CA 81-84; CANR 13, 33, 54, 102; CMW; CPW; DA3; DLB 87; DLBY 81; INT CANR-33; MTCW 1

**Fontane, Theodor** 1819-1898 ......... **NCLC 26**
See also DLB 129; EW; RGWL

**Fontenot, Chester** ............................ **CLC 65**

**Foote, Horton** 1916- ......... **CLC 51, 91; DAM DRAM**
See also CA 73-76; CAD; CANR 34, 51; CD; CSW; DA3; DLB 26; INT CANR-34

**Foote, Mary Hallock** 1847-1938 .. **TCLC 108**
See also DLB 186, 188, 202, 221

**Foote, Shelby** 1916- ...... **CLC 75; DAM NOV, POP**
See also AAYA 40; CA 5-8R; CANR 3, 45, 74; CN; CPW; CSW; DA3; DLB 2, 17; MTCW 2; RHW

**Forbes, Esther** 1891-1967 .................. **CLC 12**
See also AAYA 17; BYA 2; CA 13-14; 25-28R; CAP 1; CLR 27; DLB 22; JRDA; MAICYA; RHW; SATA 2, 100; YAW

**Forche, Carolyn** (Louise) 1950- ....... **CLC 25, 83, 86; DAM POET; PC 10**
See also CA 109; 117; CANR 50, 74; CP; CWP; DA3; DLB 5, 193; INT CA-117; MTCW 1; RGAL

**Ford, Elbur**
See Hibbert, Eleanor Alice Burford

**Ford, Ford Madox** 1873-1939 ... **TCLC 1, 15, 39, 57; DAM NOV**
See Chaucer, Daniel
See also BRW 6; CA 104; 132; CANR 74; CDBLB 1914-1945; DA3; DLB 162; MTCW 1, 2; RGEL

**Ford, Henry** 1863-1947 .................. **TCLC 73**
See also CA 115; 148

**Ford, John** 1586-1639 ............... **LC 68; DAM DRAM; DC 8**
See also BRW 2; CDBLB Before 1660; DA3; DFS 7; DLB 58; IDTP; RGEL

**Ford, John** 1895-1973 ...................... **CLC 16**
See also CA 187; 45-48

**Ford, Richard** 1944- ................... **CLC 46, 99**
See also AMWS 5; CA 69-72; CANR 11, 47, 86; CN; CSW; DLB 227; MTCW 1; RGAL; RGSF

**Ford, Webster**
See Masters, Edgar Lee

**Foreman, Richard** 1937- ................... **CLC 50**
See also CA 65-68; CAD; CANR 32, 63; CD

**Forester, C(ecil) S(cott)** 1899-1966 ... **CLC 35**
See also CA 73-76; 25-28R; CANR 83; DLB 191; RGEL; RHW; SATA 13

**Forez**
See Mauriac, Francois (Charles)

**Forman, James Douglas** 1932- ......... **CLC 21**
See also AAYA 17; CA 9-12R; CANR 4, 19, 42; JRDA; MAICYA; SATA 8, 70; YAW

**Fornes, Maria Irene** 1930- . **CLC 39, 61; DC 10; HLCS 1**
See also CA 25-28R; CAD; CANR 28, 81; CD; CWD; DLB 7; HW 1, 2; INT CANR-28; MTCW 1; RGAL

**Forrest, Leon (Richard)** 1937-1997 .. **CLC 4; BLCS**
See also AFAW 2; BW 2; CA 89-92; 162; CAAS 7; CANR 25, 52, 87; CN; DLB 33

**Forster, E(dward) M(organ)** 1879-1970 ...... **CLC 1, 2, 3, 4, 9, 10, 13, 15, 22, 45, 77; DA; DAB; DAC; DAM MST, NOV; SSC 27; WLC**
See also AAYA 2, 37; BRW 6; CA 13-14; 25-28R; CANR 45; CAP 1; CDBLB 1914-1945; DA3; DLB 34, 98, 162, 178, 195; DLBD 10; EXPN; LAIT 3; MTCW 1, 2; NCFS 1; NFS 3, 10, 11; RGEL; RGSF; SATA 57; SUFW; WLIT 4

**Forster, John** 1812-1876 ................. **NCLC 11**
See also DLB 144, 184

**Forster, Margaret** 1938- .................. **CLC 149**
See also CA 133; CANR 62; CN; DLB 155

**Forsyth, Frederick** 1938- ........ **CLC 2, 5, 36; DAM NOV, POP**
See also BEST 89:4; CA 85-88; CANR 38, 62; CMW; CN; CPW; DLB 87; MTCW 1, 2

**Forten, Charlotte L.** 1837-1914 .... **TCLC 16; BLC 2**
See also Grimke, Charlotte L(ottie) Forten
See also DLB 50, 239

**Foscolo, Ugo** 1778-1827 ............... **NCLC 8, 97**
See also EW

**Fosse, Bob** .................................. **CLC 20**
See also Fosse, Robert Louis

**Fosse, Robert Louis** 1927-1987
See Fosse, Bob
See also CA 110; 123

**Foster, Hannah Webster** 1758-1840 ............................... **NCLC 99**
See also DLB 37, 200; RGAL

**Foster, Stephen Collins** 1826-1864 ................................ **NCLC 26**
See also RGAL

**Foucault, Michel** 1926-1984 . **CLC 31, 34, 69**
See also CA 105; 113; CANR 34; DLB 242; EW; GFL 1789 to the Present; GLL 1; MTCW 1, 2

**Fouque, Friedrich (Heinrich Karl) de la Motte** 1777-1843 ...................... **NCLC 2**
See also DLB 90; RGWL; SUFW

**Fourier, Charles** 1772-1837 ............ **NCLC 51**

**Fournier, Henri Alban** 1886-1914
See Alain-Fournier
See also CA 104; 179

**Fournier, Pierre** 1916- ...................... **CLC 11**
See Gascar, Pierre
See also CA 89-92; CANR 16, 40

**Fowles, John (Robert)** 1926- . **CLC 1, 2, 3, 4, 6, 9, 10, 15, 33, 87; DAB; DAC; DAM MST; SSC 33**
See also BPFB 1; BRWS 1; CA 5-8R; CANR 25, 71, 103; CDBLB 1960 to Present; CN; DA3; DLB 14, 139, 207; HGG; MTCW 1, 2; RGEL; RHW; SATA 22; WLIT 4

**Fox, Paula** 1923- ................... **CLC 2, 8, 121**
See also AAYA 3, 37; BYA 3, 8; CA 73-76; CANR 20, 36, 62; CLR 1, 44; DLB 52; JRDA; MAICYA; MTCW 1; NFS 12; SATA 17, 60, 120; YAW

**Fox, William Price (Jr.)** 1926- ........... **CLC 22**
See also CA 17-20R; CAAS 19; CANR 11; CSW; DLB 2; DLBY 81

**Foxe, John** 1517(?)-1587 ...................... **LC 14**
See also DLB 132

**Frame, Janet** .. **CLC 2, 3, 6, 22, 66, 96; SSC 29**
See also Clutha, Janet Paterson Frame
See also CN; CWP; RGEL; RGSF

**France, Anatole** ................................ **TCLC 9**
See also Thibault, Jacques Anatole Francois
See also DLB 123; GFL 1789 to the Present; MTCW 1; RGWL

**Francis, Claude** .................................. **CLC 50**
See also CA 192

**Francis, Dick** 1920- ......... **CLC 2, 22, 42, 102; DAM POP**
See also AAYA 5, 21; BEST 89:3; BPFB 1; CA 5-8R; CANR 9, 42, 68, 100; CDBLB 1960 to Present; CMW; CN; DA3; DLB 87; INT CANR-9; MSW; MTCW 1, 2

**Francis, Robert (Churchill)** 1901-1987 ......................... **CLC 15; PC 34**
See also AMWS 9; CA 1-4R; 123; CANR 1; EXPP; PFS 12

**Frank, Anne(lies Marie)** 1929-1945 . **TCLC 17; DA; DAB; DAC; DAM MST; WLC**
See also AAYA 12; BYA 1; CA 113; 133; CANR 68; DA3; LAIT 4; MAICYAS; MTCW 1, 2; NCFS 2; SATA 87; SATA-Brief 42; WYA; YAW

**Frank, Bruno** 1887-1945 .................. **TCLC 81**
See also CA 189; DLB 118

**Frank, Elizabeth** 1945- ...................... **CLC 39**
See also CA 121; 126; CANR 78; INT 126

**Frankl, Viktor E(mil)** 1905-1997 ....... **CLC 93**
See also CA 65-68; 161

**Franklin, Benjamin**
See Hasek, Jaroslav (Matej Frantisek)

**Franklin, Benjamin** 1706-1790 .. **LC 25; DA; DAB; DAC; DAM MST; WLCS**
See also AMW; CDALB 1640-1865; DA3; DLB 24, 43, 73; LAIT 1; RGAL; TUS

**Franklin, (Stella Maria Sarah) Miles (Lampe)** 1879-1954 .................. **TCLC 7**
See also CA 104; 164; DLB 230; FW; MTCW 2; RGEL; TWA

**Fraser, (Lady) Antonia (Pakenham)** 1932- ................................ **CLC 32, 107**
See also CA 85-88; CANR 44, 65; CMW; MTCW 1, 2; SATA-Brief 32

**Fraser, George MacDonald** 1925- ...... **CLC 7**
See also CA 45-48, 180; CAAE 180; CANR 2, 48, 74; MTCW 1; RHW

**Fraser, Sylvia** 1935- .......................... **CLC 64**
See also CA 45-48; CANR 1, 16, 60; CCA 1

**Frayn, Michael** 1933- ........ **CLC 3, 7, 31, 47; DAM DRAM, NOV**
See also BRWS 7; CA 5-8R; CANR 30, 69; CBD; CD; CN; DLB 13, 14, 194; FANT; MTCW 1, 2; SFW

**Fraze, Candida (Merrill)** 1945- ........ **CLC 50**
See also CA 126

**Frazer, Andrew**
See Marlowe, Stephen

**Frazer, J(ames) G(eorge)** 1854-1941 ................ **TCLC 32**
See also BRWS 3; CA 118

**Frazer, Robert Caine**
See Creasey, John

**Frazer, Sir James George**
See Frazer, J(ames) G(eorge)

**Frazier, Charles** 1950- ...................... **CLC 109**
See also AAYA 34; CA 161; CSW

**Frazier, Ian** 1951- ............................ **CLC 46**
See also CA 130; CANR 54, 93

**Frederic, Harold** 1856-1898 ........... **NCLC 10**
See also AMW; DLB 12, 23; DLBD 13; RGAL

**Frederick, John**
See Faust, Frederick (Schiller)
See also TCWW 2

**Frederick the Great** 1712-1786 ........... **LC 14**

**Fredro, Aleksander** 1793-1876 ......... **NCLC 8**

**Freeling, Nicolas** 1927- ...................... **CLC 38**
See also CA 49-52; CAAS 12; CANR 1, 17, 50, 84; CMW; CN; DLB 87

**Freeman, Douglas Southall** 1886-1953 ................................ **TCLC 11**
See also CA 109; 195; DLB 17; DLBD 17

**Freeman, Judith** 1946- ...................... **CLC 55**
See also CA 148

**Freeman, Mary E(leanor) Wilkins** 1852-1930 ................ **TCLC 9; SSC 1, 47**
See also CA 106; 177; DLB 12, 78, 221; EXPS; FW; HGG; MAWW; RGAL; RGSF; SSFS 4, 8; SUFW; TUS

**Freeman, R(ichard) Austin** 1862-1943 ................................ **TCLC 21**
See also CA 113; CANR 84; CMW; DLB 70

**French, Albert** 1943- .......................... **CLC 86**
See also BW 3; CA 167

**French, Marilyn** 1929- .......... **CLC 10, 18, 60; DAM DRAM, NOV, POP**
See also BPFB 1; CA 69-72; CANR 3, 31; CN; CPW; FW; INT CANR-31; MTCW 1, 2

**French, Paul**
See Asimov, Isaac

**Freneau, Philip Morin** 1752-1832 ... **NCLC 1**
See also AMWS 2; DLB 37, 43; RGAL

**Freud, Sigmund** 1856-1939 ............ **TCLC 52**
See also CA 115; 133; CANR 69; EW; MTCW 1, 2

**Friedan, Betty (Naomi)** 1921- ........... **CLC 74**
See also CA 65-68; CANR 18, 45, 74; DLB 246; FW; MTCW 1, 2

**Friedlander, Saul** 1932- ...................... **CLC 90**
See also CA 117; 130; CANR 72

**Friedman, B(ernard) H(arper)** 1926- ................................ **CLC 7**
See also CA 1-4R; CANR 3, 48

**Friedman, Bruce Jay** 1930- ...... **CLC 3, 5, 56**
See also CA 9-12R; CAD; CANR 25, 52, 101; CD; CN; DLB 2, 28, 244; INT CANR-25

**Friel, Brian** 1929- .... **CLC 5, 42, 59, 115; DC 8**
See also BRWS 5; CA 21-24R; CANR 33, 69; CBD; CD; DFS 11; DLB 13; MTCW 1; RGEL

**Friis-Baastad, Babbis Ellinor** 1921-1970 .................................. **CLC 12**
See also CA 17-20R; 134; SATA 7

**Frisch, Max (Rudolf)** 1911-1991 ... **CLC 3, 9, 14, 18, 32, 44; DAM DRAM, NOV**
See also CA 85-88; 134; CANR 32, 74; DLB 69, 124; EW; MTCW 1, 2; RGWL

**Fromentin, Eugene (Samuel Auguste)** 1820-1876 ................................ **NCLC 10**
See also DLB 123; GFL 1789 to the Present

**Frost, Frederick**
See Faust, Frederick (Schiller)
See also TCWW 2

**Frost, Robert (Lee)** 1874-1963 .. **CLC 1, 3, 4, 9, 10, 13, 15, 26, 34, 44; DA; DAB; DAC; DAM MST, POET; PC 1; WLC**
See also AAYA 21; AMW; AMWR 1; CA 89-92; CANR 33; CDALB 1917-1929; CLR 67; DA3; DLB 54; DLBD 7; EXPP; MTCW 1, 2; PAB; PFS 1, 2, 3, 4, 5, 6, 7, 10, 13; RGAL; SATA 14; WP; WYA

**Froude, James Anthony** 1818-1894 ................................. **NCLC 43**
See also DLB 18, 57, 144

**Froy, Herald**
See Waterhouse, Keith (Spencer)

**Fry, Christopher** 1907- .......... **CLC 2, 10, 14; DAM DRAM**
See also BRWS 3; CA 17-20R; CAAS 23; CANR 9, 30, 74; CBD; CD; CP; DLB 13; MTCW 1, 2; RGEL; SATA 66

**Frye, (Herman) Northrop** 1912-1991 ............................. **CLC 24, 70**
See also CA 5-8R; 133; CANR 8, 37; DLB 67, 68, 246; MTCW 1, 2; RGAL

**Fuchs, Daniel** 1909-1993 ............... **CLC 8, 22**
See also CA 81-84; 142; CAAS 5; CANR 40; DLB 9, 26, 28; DLBY 93

**Fuchs, Daniel** 1934- ........................ **CLC 34**
See also CA 37-40R; CANR 14, 48

**Fuentes, Carlos** 1928- .. **CLC 3, 8, 10, 13, 22, 41, 60, 113; DA; DAB; DAC; DAM MST, MULT, NOV; HLC 1; SSC 24; WLC**
See also AAYA 4; AITN 2; BPFB 1; CA 69-72; CANR 10, 32, 68; CWW 2; DA3; DLB 113; DNFS; HW 1, 2; LAIT 3; LAW; MTCW 1, 2; NFS 8; RGSF; RGWL; WLIT 1

**Fuentes, Gregorio Lopez y**
See Lopez y Fuentes, Gregorio

**Fuertes, Gloria** 1918-1998 ..................... **PC 27**
See also CA 178, 180; DLB 108; HW 2; SATA 115

**Fugard, (Harold) Athol** 1932- . **CLC 5, 9, 14, 25, 40, 80; DAM DRAM; DC 3**
See also AAYA 17; AFW; CA 85-88; CANR 32, 54; CD; DFS 3, 6, 10; DLB 225; DNFS; MTCW 1; RGEL; WLIT 2

**Fugard, Sheila** 1932- .......................... **CLC 48**
See also CA 125

**Fukuyama, Francis** 1952- ................. **CLC 131**
See also CA 140; CANR 72

**Fuller, Charles (H., Jr.)** 1939- ......... **CLC 25; BLC 2; DAM DRAM, MULT; DC 1**
See also BW 2; CA 108; 112; CAD; CANR 87; CD; DFS 8; DLB 38; INT CA-112; MTCW 1

**Fuller, Henry Blake** 1857-1929 .... **TCLC 103**
See also CA 108; 177; DLB 12; RGAL

**Fuller, John (Leopold)** 1937- ........... **CLC 62**
See also CA 21-24R; CANR 9, 44; CP; DLB 40

**Fuller, Margaret** 1810-1850
See Ossoli, Sarah Margaret (Fuller)
See also AMWS 2; DLB 239

**Fuller, Roy (Broadbent)** 1912-1991 ... **CLC 4, 28**
See also BRWS 7; CA 5-8R; 135; CAAS 10; CANR 53, 83; CWRI; DLB 15, 20; RGEL; SATA 87

**Fuller, Sarah Margaret**
See Ossoli, Sarah Margaret (Fuller)

**Fulton, Alice** 1952- ............................. **CLC 52**
See also CA 116; CANR 57, 88; CP; CWP; DLB 193

**Furphy, Joseph** 1843-1912 ............. **TCLC 25**
See also CA 163; DLB 230; RGEL

**Fuson, Robert H(enderson)** 1927- .... **CLC 70**
See also CA 89-92; CANR 103

**Fussell, Paul** 1924- ........................... **CLC 74**
See also BEST 90:1; CA 17-20R; CANR 8, 21, 35, 69; INT CANR-21; MTCW 1, 2

**Futabatei, Shimei** 1864-1909 .......... **TCLC 44**
See also CA 162; DLB 180; MJW

**Futrelle, Jacques** 1875-1912 ............ **TCLC 19**
See also CA 113; 155; CMW

**Gaboriau, Emile** 1835-1873 ............ **NCLC 14**
See also CMW; MSW

**Gadda, Carlo Emilio** 1893-1973 ....... **CLC 11**
See also CA 89-92; DLB 177

**Gaddis, William** 1922-1998 ... **CLC 1, 3, 6, 8, 10, 19, 43, 86**
See also AMWS 4; BPFB 1; CA 17-20R; 172; CANR 21, 48; CN; DLB 2; MTCW 1, 2; RGAL

**Gaelique, Moruen le**
See Jacob, (Cyprien-)Max

**Gage, Walter**
See Inge, William (Motter)

**Gaines, Ernest J(ames)** 1933- ....... **CLC 3, 11, 18, 86; BLC 2; DAM MULT**
See also AAYA 18; AFAW 1, 2; AITN 1; BPFB 2; BW 2, 3; BYA 6; CA 9-12R; CANR 6, 24, 42, 75; CDALB 1968-1988; CLR 62; CN; CSW; DA3; DLB 2, 33, 152; DLBY 80; EXPN; LAIT 5; MTCW 1, 2; NFS 5, 7; RGAL; RGSF; RHW; SATA 86; SSFS 5; YAW

**Gaitskill, Mary** 1954- ........................ **CLC 69**
See also CA 128; CANR 61; DLB 244

**Galdos, Benito Perez**
See Perez Galdos, Benito

**Gale, Zona** 1874-1938 ........... **TCLC 7; DAM DRAM**
See also CA 105; 153; CANR 84; DLB 9, 78, 228; RGAL

**Galeano, Eduardo (Hughes)** 1940- . **CLC 72; HLCS 1**
See also CA 29-32R; CANR 13, 32, 100; HW 1

**Galiano, Juan Valera y Alcala**
See Valera y Alcala-Galiano, Juan

**Galilei, Galileo** 1564-1642 ................... **LC 45**

**Gallagher, Tess** 1943- ....... **CLC 18, 63; DAM POET; PC 9**
See also CA 106; CP; CWP; DLB 212

**Gallant, Mavis** 1922- .. **CLC 7, 18, 38; DAC; DAM MST; SSC 5**
See also CA 69-72; CANR 29, 69; CCA 1; CN; DLB 53; MTCW 1, 2; RGEL; RGSF

**Gallant, Roy A(rthur)** 1924- ............. **CLC 17**
See also CA 5-8R; CANR 4, 29, 54; CLR 30; MAICYA; SATA 4, 68, 110

**Gallico, Paul (William)** 1897-1976 ...... **CLC 2**
See also AITN 1; CA 5-8R; 69-72; CANR 23; DLB 9, 171; FANT; MAICYA; SATA 13

**Gallo, Max Louis** 1932- ..................... **CLC 95**
See also CA 85-88

**Gallois, Lucien**
See Desnos, Robert

**Gallup, Ralph**
See Whitemore, Hugh (John)

**Galsworthy, John** 1867-1933 .... **TCLC 1, 45; DA; DAB; DAC; DAM DRAM, MST, NOV; SSC 22; WLC**
See also BRW 6; CA 104; 141; CANR 75; CDBLB 1890-1914; DA3; DLB 10, 34, 98, 162; DLBD 16; MTCW 1; RGEL; SSFS 3

**Galt, John** 1779-1839 ........................ **NCLC 1**
See also DLB 99, 116, 159; RGEL; RGSF

**Galvin, James** 1951- ............................ **CLC 38**
See also CA 108; CANR 26

**Gamboa, Federico** 1864-1939 ......... **TCLC 36**
See also CA 167; HW 2; LAW

**Gandhi, M. K.**
See Gandhi, Mohandas Karamchand

**Gandhi, Mahatma**
See Gandhi, Mohandas Karamchand

**Gandhi, Mohandas Karamchand** 1869-1948 ........ **TCLC 59; DAM MULT**
See also CA 121; 132; DA3; MTCW 1, 2

**Gann, Ernest Kellogg** 1910-1991 ..... **CLC 23**
See also AITN 1; BPFB 2; CA 1-4R; 136; CANR 1, 83; RHW

**Garber, Eric** 1943(?)-
See Holleran, Andrew
See also CANR 89

**Garcia, Cristina** 1958- ....................... **CLC 76**
See also CA 141; CANR 73; DNFS; HW 2

**Garcia Lorca, Federico** 1898-1936 . **TCLC 1, 7, 49; DA; DAB; DAC; DAM DRAM, MST, MULT, POET; DC 2; HLC 2; PC 3; WLC**
See also Lorca, Federico Garcia
See also CA 104; 131; CANR 81; DA3; DFS 10; DLB 108; EW; HW 1, 2; MTCW 1, 2

**Garcia Marquez, Gabriel (Jose)** 1928- .... **CLC 2, 3, 8, 10, 15, 27, 47, 55, 68; DA; DAB; DAC; DAM MST, MULT, NOV, POP; HLC 1; SSC 8; WLC**
See also AAYA 3, 33; BEST 89:1, 90:4; BPFB 2; BYA 12; CA 33-36R; CANR 10, 28, 50, 75, 82; CPW; DA3; DLB 113; DNFS; EXPN; EXPS; HW 1, 2; LAIT 2; LAW; MTCW 1, 2; NFS 1, 5, 10; RGSF; RGWL; SSFS 1, 6; WLIT 1

**Garcilaso de la Vega, El Inca** 1503-1536
See also HLCS 1; LAW

**Gard, Janice**
See Latham, Jean Lee

**Gard, Roger Martin du**
See Martin du Gard, Roger

**Gardam, Jane** 1928- ........................... **CLC 43**
See also CA 49-52; CANR 2, 18, 33, 54; CLR 12; DLB 14, 161, 231; MAICYA; MTCW 1; SAAS 9; SATA 39, 76; SATA-Brief 28; YAW

**Gardner, Herb(ert)** 1934- .................. **CLC 44**
See also CA 149; CAD; CD

**Gardner, John (Champlin), Jr.** 1933-1982 ...... **CLC 2, 3, 5, 7, 8, 10, 18, 28, 34; DAM NOV, POP; SSC 7**
See also AITN 1; AMWS 6; BPFB 2; CA 65-68; 107; CANR 33, 73; CDALBS; CPW; DA3; DLB 2; DLBY 82; FANT; MTCW 1; NFS 3; RGAL; RGSF; SATA 40; SATA-Obit 31; SSFS 8

**Gardner, John (Edmund)** 1926- ...... **CLC 30; DAM POP**
See also CA 103; CANR 15, 69; CMW; CPW; MTCW 1

**Gardner, Miriam**
See Bradley, Marion Zimmer
See also GLL 1

**Gardner, Noel**
See Kuttner, Henry

**Gardons, S. S.**
See Snodgrass, W(illiam) D(e Witt)
**Garfield, Leon** 1921-1996 .................. **CLC 12**
See also AAYA 8; BYA 1, 3; CA 17-20R; 152; CANR 38, 41, 78; CLR 21; DLB 161; JRDA; MAICYA; MAICYAS; SATA 1, 32, 76; SATA-Obit 90; YAW
**Garland, (Hannibal) Hamlin**
1860-1940 ................... **TCLC 3; SSC 18**
See also CA 104; DLB 12, 71, 78, 186; RGAL; RGSF; TCWW 2
**Garneau, (Hector de) Saint-Denys**
1912-1943 ................................. **TCLC 13**
See also CA 111; DLB 88
**Garner, Alan** 1934- ..... **CLC 17; DAB; DAM POP**
See also AAYA 18; BYA 3, 5; CA 73-76, 178; CAAE 178; CANR 15, 64; CLR 20; CPW; DLB 161; FANT; MAICYA; MTCW 1, 2; SATA 18, 69; SATA-Essay 108; YAW
**Garner, Hugh** 1913-1979 ................... **CLC 13**
See also Warwick, Jarvis
See also CA 69-72; CANR 31; CCA 1; DLB 68
**Garnett, David** 1892-1981 ................... **CLC 3**
See also CA 5-8R; 103; CANR 17, 79; DLB 34; FANT; MTCW 2; RGEL; SFW
**Garos, Stephanie**
See Katz, Steve
**Garrett, George (Palmer)** 1929- .. **CLC 3, 11, 51; SSC 30**
See also AMWS 7; BPFB 2; CA 1-4R; CAAS 5; CANR 1, 42, 67; CN; CP; CSW; DLB 2, 5, 130, 152; DLBY 83
**Garrick, David** 1717-1779 ....... **LC 15; DAM DRAM**
See also DLB 84; RGEL
**Garrigue, Jean** 1914-1972 ............... **CLC 2, 8**
See also CA 5-8R; 37-40R; CANR 20
**Garrison, Frederick**
See Sinclair, Upton (Beall)
**Garro, Elena** 1920(?)-1998
See also CA 131; 169; CWW 2; DLB 145; HLCS 1; HW 1; WLIT 1
**Garth, Will**
See Hamilton, Edmond; Kuttner, Henry
**Garvey, Marcus (Moziah, Jr.)**
1887-1940 ...... **TCLC 41; BLC 2; DAM MULT**
See also BW 1; CA 120; 124; CANR 79
**Gary, Romain** ................... **CLC 25**
See also Kacew, Romain
See also DLB 83
**Gascar, Pierre** ................... **CLC 11**
See also Fournier, Pierre
**Gascoyne, David (Emery)** 1916- ....... **CLC 45**
See also CA 65-68; CANR 10, 28, 54; CP; DLB 20; MTCW 1; RGEL
**Gaskell, Elizabeth Cleghorn**
1810-1865 ......... **NCLC 5, 70, 97; DAB; DAM MST; SSC 25**
See also BRW 5; CDBLB 1832-1890; DLB 21, 144, 159; RGEL; RGSF
**Gass, William H(oward)** 1924- . **CLC 1, 2, 8, 11, 15, 39, 132; SSC 12**
See also AMWS 6; CA 17-20R; CANR 30, 71, 100; CN; DLB 2, 227; MTCW 1, 2; RGAL
**Gassendi, Pierre** 1592-1655 ................... **LC 54**
See also GFL Beginnings to 1789
**Gasset, Jose Ortega y**
See Ortega y Gasset, Jose
**Gates, Henry Louis, Jr.** 1950- ......... **CLC 65; BLCS; DAM MULT**
See also BW 2, 3; CA 109; CANR 25, 53, 75; CSW; DA3; DLB 67; MTCW 1; RGAL

**Gautier, Theophile** 1811-1872 .. **NCLC 1, 59; DAM POET; PC 18; SSC 20**
See also DLB 119; EW; GFL 1789 to the Present; RGWL
**Gawsworth, John**
See Bates, H(erbert) E(rnest)
**Gay, John** 1685-1732 .. **LC 49; DAM DRAM**
See also BRW 3; DLB 84, 95; RGEL; WLIT 3
**Gay, Oliver**
See Gogarty, Oliver St. John
**Gaye, Marvin (Pentz, Jr.)**
1939-1984 ............................. **CLC 26**
See also CA 195; 112
**Gebler, Carlo (Ernest)** 1954- ............. **CLC 39**
See also CA 119; 133; CANR 96
**Gee, Maggie (Mary)** 1948- ................ **CLC 57**
See also CA 130; CN; DLB 207
**Gee, Maurice (Gough)** 1931- ................ **CLC 29**
See also AAYA 42; CA 97-100; CANR 67; CLR 56; CN; CWRI; RGSF; SATA 46, 101
**Gelbart, Larry (Simon)** 1928- .... **CLC 21, 61**
See also Gelbart, Larry
See also CA 73-76; CANR 45, 94
**Gelbart, Larry** 1928-
See Gelbart, Larry (Simon)
See also CAD; CD
**Gelber, Jack** 1932- ............... **CLC 1, 6, 14, 79**
See also CA 1-4R; CAD; CANR 2; DLB 7, 228
**Gellhorn, Martha (Ellis)**
1908-1998 ........................... **CLC 14, 60**
See also CA 77-80; 164; CANR 44; CN; DLBY 82, 98
**Genet, Jean** 1910-1986 .. **CLC 1, 2, 5, 10, 14, 44, 46; DAM DRAM**
See also CA 13-16R; CANR 18; DA3; DFS 10; DLB 72; DLBY 86; EW; GFL 1789 to the Present; GLL 1; MTCW 1, 2; RGWL
**Gent, Peter** 1942- ............................. **CLC 29**
See also AITN 1; CA 89-92; DLBY 82
**Gentile, Giovanni** 1875-1944 .......... **TCLC 96**
See also CA 119
**Gentlewoman in New England, A**
See Bradstreet, Anne
**Gentlewoman in Those Parts, A**
See Bradstreet, Anne
**Geoffrey of Monmouth** c.
1100-1155 ............................. **CMLC 44**
See also DLB 146
**George, Jean**
See George, Jean Craighead
**George, Jean Craighead** 1919- ......... **CLC 35**
See also AAYA 8; BYA 2, 4; CA 5-8R; CANR 25; CLR 1; DLB 52; JRDA; MAICYA; SATA 2, 68, 124; YAW
**George, Stefan (Anton)** 1868-1933 . **TCLC 2, 14**
See also CA 104; 193; EW
**Georges, Georges Martin**
See Simenon, Georges (Jacques Christian)
**Gerhardi, William Alexander**
See Gerhardie, William Alexander
**Gerhardie, William Alexander**
1895-1977 ............................. **CLC 5**
See also CA 25-28R; 73-76; CANR 18; DLB 36; RGEL
**Gerstler, Amy** 1956- ............................. **CLC 70**
See also CA 146; CANR 99
**Gertler, T.** ............................. **CLC 134**
See also CA 116; 121
**Ghalib** ............................. **NCLC 39, 78**
See also Ghalib, Asadullah Khan
**Ghalib, Asadullah Khan** 1797-1869
See Ghalib
See also DAM POET; RGWL

**Ghelderode, Michel de** 1898-1962 ..... **CLC 6, 11; DAM DRAM; DC 15**
See also CA 85-88; CANR 40, 77; EW
**Ghiselin, Brewster** 1903-2001 ........... **CLC 23**
See also CA 13-16R; CAAS 10; CANR 13; CP
**Ghose, Aurabinda** 1872-1950 ......... **TCLC 63**
See also CA 163
**Ghose, Zulfikar** 1935- ....................... **CLC 42**
See also CA 65-68; CANR 67; CN; CP
**Ghosh, Amitav** 1956- ....................... **CLC 44**
See also CA 147; CANR 80; CN
**Giacosa, Giuseppe** 1847-1906 ........... **TCLC 7**
See also CA 104
**Gibb, Lee**
See Waterhouse, Keith (Spencer)
**Gibbon, Lewis Grassic** ................... **TCLC 4**
See also Mitchell, James Leslie
See also RGEL
**Gibbons, Kaye** 1960- ......... **CLC 50, 88, 145; DAM POP**
See also AAYA 34; CA 151; CANR 75; CSW; DA3; MTCW 1; NFS 3; RGAL; SATA 117
**Gibran, Kahlil** 1883-1931 ........... **TCLC 1, 9; DAM POET, POP; PC 9**
See also CA 104; 150; DA3; MTCW 2
**Gibran, Khalil**
See Gibran, Kahlil
**Gibson, William** 1914- .. **CLC 23; DA; DAB; DAC; DAM DRAM, MST**
See also CA 9-12R; CAD 2; CANR 9, 42, 75; CD; DFS 2; DLB 7; LAIT 2; MTCW 2; SATA 66; YAW
**Gibson, William (Ford)** 1948- ... **CLC 39, 63; DAM POP**
See also AAYA 12; BPFB 2; CA 126; 133; CANR 52, 90; CN; CPW; DA3; MTCW 2; SCFW 2; SFW
**Gide, Andre (Paul Guillaume)**
1869-1951 . **TCLC 5, 12, 36; DA; DAB; DAC; DAM MST, NOV; SSC 13; WLC**
See also CA 104; 124; DA3; DLB 65; EW; GFL 1789 to the Present; MTCW 1, 2; RGSF; RGWL
**Gifford, Barry (Colby)** 1946- ........... **CLC 34**
See also CA 65-68; CANR 9, 30, 40, 90
**Gilbert, Frank**
See De Voto, Bernard (Augustine)
**Gilbert, W(illiam) S(chwenck)**
1836-1911 ........ **TCLC 3; DAM DRAM, POET**
See also CA 104; 173; RGEL; SATA 36
**Gilbreth, Frank B(unker), Jr.**
1911-2001 ............................. **CLC 17**
See also CA 9-12R; SATA 2
**Gilchrist, Ellen (Louise)** 1935- .. **CLC 34, 48, 143; DAM POP; SSC 14**
See also BPFB 2; CA 113; 116; CANR 41, 61; CN; CPW; CSW; DLB 130; EXPS; MTCW 1, 2; RGAL; RGSF; SSFS 9
**Giles, Molly** 1942- ............................. **CLC 39**
See also CA 126; CANR 98
**Gill, Eric** 1882-1940 ....................... **TCLC 85**
**Gill, Patrick**
See Creasey, John
**Gillette, Douglas** ............................. **CLC 70**
**Gilliam, Terry (Vance)** 1940- .... **CLC 21, 141**
See also Monty Python
See also AAYA 19; CA 108; 113; CANR 35; INT 113
**Gillian, Jerry**
See Gilliam, Terry (Vance)
**Gilliatt, Penelope (Ann Douglass)**
1932-1993 ................... **CLC 2, 10, 13, 53**
See also AITN 2; CA 13-16R; 141; CANR 49; DLB 14

**Gilman, Charlotte (Anna) Perkins (Stetson)**
1860-1935 ............ **TCLC 9, 37; SSC 13**
See also BYA 11; CA 106; 150; DLB 221;
EXPS; FW; HGG; LAIT 2; MAWW;
MTCW 1; RGAL; RGSF; SFW; SSFS 1

**Gilmour, David** 1949- ........................ **CLC 35**
See also CA 138, 147

**Gilpin, William** 1724-1804 ............. **NCLC 30**

**Gilray, J. D.**
See Mencken, H(enry) L(ouis)

**Gilroy, Frank D(aniel)** 1925- ............... **CLC 2**
See also CA 81-84; CAD; CANR 32, 64, 86; CD; DLB 7

**Gilstrap, John** 1957(?)- ..................... **CLC 99**
See also CA 160; CANR 101

**Ginsberg, Allen** 1926-1997 .... **CLC 1, 2, 3, 4, 6, 13, 36, 69, 109; DA; DAB; DAC; DAM MST, POET; PC 4; WLC**
See also AAYA 33; AITN 1; AMWS 2; CA 1-4R; 157; CANR 2, 41, 63, 95; CDALB 1941-1968; CP; DA3; DLB 5, 16, 169, 237; GLL 1; MTCW 1, 2; PAB; PFS 5; RGAL; WP

**Ginzburg, Eugenia** ........................... **CLC 59**

**Ginzburg, Natalia** 1916-1991 ....... **CLC 5, 11, 54, 70**
See also CA 85-88; 135; CANR 33; DLB 177; EW; MTCW 1, 2; RGWL

**Giono, Jean** 1895-1970 ................... **CLC 4, 11**
See also CA 45-48; 29-32R; CANR 2, 35; DLB 72; GFL 1789 to the Present; MTCW 1; RGWL

**Giovanni, Nikki** 1943- ........ **CLC 2, 4, 19, 64, 117; BLC 2; DA; DAB; DAC; DAM MST, MULT, POET; PC 19; WLCS**
See also AAYA 22; AITN 1; BW 2, 3; CA 29-32R; CAAS 6; CANR 18, 41, 60, 91; CDALBS; CLR 6, 73; CP; CSW; CWP; CWRI; DA3; DLB 5, 41; EXPP; INT CANR-18; MAICYA; MTCW 1, 2; RGAL; SATA 24, 107; YAW

**Giovene, Andrea** 1904-1998 ................. **CLC 7**
See also CA 85-88

**Gippius, Zinaida (Nikolayevna)** 1869-1945
See Hippius, Zinaida
See also CA 106

**Giraudoux, Jean(-Hippolyte)**
1882-1944 .... **TCLC 2, 7; DAM DRAM**
See also CA 104; DLB 65; EW; GFL 1789 to the Present; RGWL

**Gironella, Jose Maria** 1917-1991 ..... **CLC 11**
See also CA 101; RGWL

**Gissing, George (Robert)**
1857-1903 ....... **TCLC 3, 24, 47; SSC 37**
See also BRW 5; CA 105; 167; DLB 18, 135, 184; RGEL

**Giurlani, Aldo**
See Palazzeschi, Aldo

**Gladkov, Fyodor (Vasilyevich)**
1883-1958 ................. **TCLC 27**
See also CA 170

**Glanville, Brian (Lester)** 1931- ........... **CLC 6**
See also CA 5-8R; CAAS 9; CANR 3, 70; CN; DLB 15, 139; SATA 42

**Glasgow, Ellen (Anderson Gholson)**
1873-1945 ............... **TCLC 2, 7; SSC 34**
See also AMW; CA 104; 164; DLB 9, 12; MAWW; MTCW 2; RGAL; RHW; SSFS 9

**Glaspell, Susan** 1882(?)-1948 . **TCLC 55; DC 10; SSC 41**
See also AMWS 3; CA 110; 154; DFS 8; DLB 7, 9, 78, 228; MAWW; RGAL; SSFS 3; TCWW 2; YABC 2

**Glassco, John** 1909-1981 ..................... **CLC 9**
See also CA 13-16R; 102; CANR 15; DLB 68

**Glasscock, Amnesia**
See Steinbeck, John (Ernst)

**Glasser, Ronald J.** 1940(?)- ............... **CLC 37**

**Glassman, Joyce**
See Johnson, Joyce

**Gleick, James (W.)** 1954- ................ **CLC 147**
See also CA 131; 137; CANR 97; INT CA-137

**Glendinning, Victoria** 1937- .............. **CLC 50**
See also CA 120; 127; CANR 59, 89; DLB 155

**Glissant, Edouard** 1928- . **CLC 10, 68; DAM MULT**
See also CA 153; CWW 2

**Gloag, Julian** 1930- ............................. **CLC 40**
See also AITN 1; CA 65-68; CANR 10, 70; CN

**Glowacki, Aleksander**
See Prus, Boleslaw

**Gluck, Louise (Elisabeth)** 1943- .. **CLC 7, 22, 44, 81; DAM POET; PC 16**
See also AMWS 5; CA 33-36R; CANR 40, 69; CP; CWP; DA3; DLB 5; MTCW 2; PFS 5; RGAL

**Glyn, Elinor** 1864-1943 ................... **TCLC 72**
See also DLB 153; RHW

**Gobineau, Joseph-Arthur**
1816-1882 ................................ **NCLC 17**
See also DLB 123; GFL 1789 to the Present

**Godard, Jean-Luc** 1930- ................... **CLC 20**
See also CA 93-96

**Godden, (Margaret) Rumer**
1907-1998 ................................ **CLC 53**
See also AAYA 6; BPFB 2; BYA 2, 5; CA 5-8R; 172; CANR 4, 27, 36, 55, 80; CLR 20; CN; CWRI; DLB 161; MAICYA; RHW; SAAS 12; SATA 3, 36; SATA-Obit 109

**Godoy Alcayaga, Lucila**
1899-1957 ......... **TCLC 2; DAM MULT; HLC 2; PC 32**
See also Mistral, Gabriela
See also BW 2; CA 104; 131; CANR 81; DNFS; HW 1, 2; MTCW 1, 2

**Godwin, Gail (Kathleen)** 1937- ...... **CLC 5, 8, 22, 31, 69, 125; DAM POP**
See also BPFB 2; CA 29-32R; CANR 15, 43, 69; CN; CPW; CSW; DA3; DLB 6, 234; INT CANR-15; MTCW 1, 2

**Godwin, William** 1756-1836 ........... **NCLC 14**
See also CDBLB 1789-1832; CMW; DLB 39, 104, 142, 158, 163; HGG; RGEL

**Goebbels, Josef**
See Goebbels, (Paul) Joseph

**Goebbels, (Paul) Joseph**
1897-1945 ................................ **TCLC 68**
See also CA 115; 148

**Goebbels, Joseph Paul**
See Goebbels, (Paul) Joseph

**Goethe, Johann Wolfgang von**
1749-1832 ....... **NCLC 4, 22, 34, 90; DA; DAB; DAC; DAM DRAM, MST, POET; PC 5; SSC 38; WLC**
See also DA3; DLB 94; EW; RGWL

**Gogarty, Oliver St. John**
1878-1957 ................ **TCLC 15**
See also CA 109; 150; DLB 15, 19; RGEL

**Gogol, Nikolai (Vasilyevich)**
1809-1852 . **NCLC 5, 15, 31; DA; DAB; DAC; DAM DRAM, MST; DC 1; SSC 4, 29; WLC**
See also DFS 12; DLB 198; EW; EXPS; RGSF; RGWL; SSFS 7

**Goines, Donald** 1937(?)-1974 . **CLC 80; BLC 2; DAM MULT, POP**
See also AITN 1; BW 1, 3; CA 124; 114; CANR 82; CMW; DA3; DLB 33

**Gold, Herbert** 1924- ............. **CLC 4, 7, 14, 42**
See also CA 9-12R; CANR 17, 45; CN; DLB 2; DLBY 81

**Goldbarth, Albert** 1948- .................. **CLC 5, 38**
See also CA 53-56; CANR 6, 40; CP; DLB 120

**Goldberg, Anatol** 1910-1982 ............ **CLC 34**
See also CA 131; 117

**Goldemberg, Isaac** 1945- ................... **CLC 52**
See also CA 69-72; CAAS 12; CANR 11, 32; HW 1; WLIT 1

**Golding, William (Gerald)**
1911-1993 ..... **CLC 1, 2, 3, 8, 10, 17, 27, 58, 81; DA; DAB; DAC; DAM MST, NOV; WLC**
See also AAYA 5; BPFB 2; BRWS 1; BYA 2; CA 5-8R; 141; CANR 13, 33, 54; CDBLB 1945-1960; DA3; DLB 15, 100; EXPN; HGG; LAIT 4; MTCW 1, 2; NFS 2; RGEL; RHW; SFW; WLIT 4; YAW

**Goldman, Emma** 1869-1940 ........... **TCLC 13**
See also CA 110; 150; DLB 221; FW; RGAL

**Goldman, Francisco** 1954- ................ **CLC 76**
See also CA 162

**Goldman, William (W.)** 1931- ...... **CLC 1, 48**
See also BPFB 2; CA 9-12R; CANR 29, 69; CN; DLB 44; FANT; IDFW 3, 4

**Goldmann, Lucien** 1913-1970 ........... **CLC 24**
See also CA 25-28; CAP 2

**Goldoni, Carlo** 1707-1793 .......... **LC 4; DAM DRAM**
See also EW; RGWL

**Goldsberry, Steven** 1949- ................. **CLC 34**
See also CA 131

**Goldsmith, Oliver** 1730-1774 . **LC 2, 48; DA; DAB; DAC; DAM DRAM, MST, NOV, POET; DC 8; WLC**
See also BRW 3; CDBLB 1660-1789; DFS 1; DLB 39, 89, 104, 109, 142; IDTP; RGEL; SATA 26; TEA; WLIT 3

**Goldsmith, Peter**
See Priestley, J(ohn) B(oynton)

**Gombrowicz, Witold** 1904-1969 .... **CLC 4, 7, 11, 49; DAM DRAM**
See also CA 19-20; 25-28R; CAP 2; EW; RGWL

**Gomez de la Serna, Ramon**
1888-1963 ..................................... **CLC 9**
See also CA 153; 116; CANR 79; HW 1, 2

**Goncharov, Ivan Alexandrovich**
1812-1891 ............................... **NCLC 1, 63**
See also DLB 238; EW; RGWL

**Goncourt, Edmond (Louis Antoine Huot) de**
1822-1896 ................................... **NCLC 7**
See also DLB 123; EW; GFL 1789 to the Present; RGWL

**Goncourt, Jules (Alfred Huot) de**
1830-1870 ................................... **NCLC 7**
See also DLB 123; EW; GFL 1789 to the Present; RGWL

**Gontier, Fernande** 19(?)- .................. **CLC 50**

**Gonzalez Martinez, Enrique**
1871-1952 ................................ **TCLC 72**
See also CA 166; CANR 81; HW 1, 2

**Goodison, Lorna** 1947- ....................... **PC 36**
See also CA 142; CANR 88; CP; CWP; DLB 157

**Goodman, Paul** 1911-1972 ..... **CLC 1, 2, 4, 7**
See also CA 19-20; 37-40R; CAD; CANR 34; CAP 2; DLB 130, 246; MTCW 1; RGAL

**Gordimer, Nadine** 1923- ...... **CLC 3, 5, 7, 10, 18, 33, 51, 70, 123; DA; DAB; DAC; DAM MST, NOV; SSC 17; WLCS**
See also AAYA 39; AFW; BRWS 2; CA 5-8R; CANR 3, 28, 56, 88; CN; DA3; DLB 225; EXPS; INT CANR-28; MTCW 1, 2; NFS 4; RGEL; RGSF; SSFS 2; WLIT 2; YAW

**Gordon, Adam Lindsay**
1833-1870 .................. **NCLC 21**
See also DLB 230

**Gordon, Caroline** 1895-1981 . **CLC 6, 13, 29, 83; SSC 15**
See also AMW; CA 11-12; 103; CANR 36; CAP 1; DLB 4, 9, 102; DLBD 17; DLBY 81; MTCW 1, 2; RGAL; RGSF

**Gordon, Charles William** 1860-1937
See Connor, Ralph
See also CA 109

**Gordon, Mary (Catherine)** 1949- .... **CLC 13, 22, 128**
See also AMWS 4; BPFB 2; CA 102; CANR 44, 92; CN; DLB 6; DLBY 81; FW; INT CA-102; MTCW 1

**Gordon, N. J.**
See Bosman, Herman Charles

**Gordon, Sol** 1923- .................. **CLC 26**
See also CA 53-56; CANR 4; SATA 11

**Gordone, Charles** 1925-1995 ........ **CLC 1, 4; DAM DRAM; DC 8**
See also BW 1, 3; CA 93-96, 180; 150; CAAE 180; CAD; CANR 55; DLB 7; INT 93-96; MTCW 1

**Gore, Catherine** 1800-1861 ........... **NCLC 65**
See also DLB 116; RGEL

**Gorenko, Anna Andreevna**
See Akhmatova, Anna

**Gorky, Maxim** ....... **TCLC 8; DAB; SSC 28; WLC**
See also Peshkov, Alexei Maximovich
See also DFS 9; EW; MTCW 2

**Goryan, Sirak**
See Saroyan, William

**Gosse, Edmund (William)**
1849-1928 ................. **TCLC 28**
See also CA 117; DLB 57, 144, 184; RGEL

**Gotlieb, Phyllis Fay (Bloom)** 1926- .. **CLC 18**
See also CA 13-16R; CANR 7; DLB 88; SFW

**Gottesman, S. D.**
See Kornbluth, C(yril) M.; Pohl, Frederik

**Gottfried von Strassburg** fl. c. 1170-1215 .................. **CMLC 10**
See also DLB 138; EW; RGWL

**Gould, Lois** .................... **CLC 4, 10**
See also CA 77-80; CANR 29; MTCW 1

**Gourmont, Remy(-Marie-Charles) de** 1858-1915 ................. **TCLC 17**
See also CA 109; 150; GFL 1789 to the Present; MTCW 2

**Govier, Katherine** 1948- .................... **CLC 51**
See also CA 101; CANR 18, 40; CCA 1

**Goyen, (Charles) William**
1915-1983 .................... **CLC 5, 8, 14, 40**
See also AITN 2; CA 5-8R; 110; CANR 6, 71; DLB 2; DLBY 83; INT CANR-6

**Goytisolo, Juan** 1931- .... **CLC 5, 10, 23, 133; DAM MULT; HLC 1**
See also CA 85-88; CANR 32, 61; CWW 2; GLL 2; HW 1, 2; MTCW 1, 2

**Gozzano, Guido** 1883-1916 .................. **PC 10**
See also CA 154; DLB 114

**Gozzi, (Conte) Carlo** 1720-1806 .... **NCLC 23**

**Grabbe, Christian Dietrich**
1801-1836 .................. **NCLC 2**
See also DLB 133; RGWL

**Grace, Patricia Frances** 1937- .......... **CLC 56**
See also CA 176; CN; RGSF

**Gracian y Morales, Baltasar**
1601-1658 .................. **LC 15**

**Gracq, Julien** ................... **CLC 11, 48**
See also Poirier, Louis
See also CWW 2; DLB 83; GFL 1789 to the Present

**Grade, Chaim** 1910-1982 ................. **CLC 10**
See also CA 93-96; 107

**Graduate of Oxford, A**
See Ruskin, John

**Grafton, Garth**
See Duncan, Sara Jeannette

**Graham, John**
See Phillips, David Graham

**Graham, Jorie** 1951- .................. **CLC 48, 118**
See also CA 111; CANR 63; CP; CWP; DLB 120; PFS 10

**Graham, R(obert) B(ontine) Cunninghame**
See Cunninghame Graham, Robert (Gallnigad) Bontine
See also DLB 98, 135, 174; RGEL; RGSF

**Graham, Robert**
See Haldeman, Joe (William)

**Graham, Tom**
See Lewis, (Harry) Sinclair

**Graham, W(illiam) S(idney)**
1918-1986 .................. **CLC 29**
See also BRWS 7; CA 73-76; 118; DLB 20; RGEL

**Graham, Winston (Mawdsley)**
1910- .................. **CLC 23**
See also CA 49-52; CANR 2, 22, 45, 66; CMW; CN; DLB 77; RHW

**Grahame, Kenneth** 1859-1932 ...... **TCLC 64; DAB**
See also BYA 5; CA 108; 136; CANR 80; CLR 5; CWRI; DA3; DLB 34, 141, 178; FANT; MAICYA; MTCW 2; RGEL; SATA 100; YABC 1

**Granger, Darius John**
See Marlowe, Stephen

**Granin, Daniil** .................. **CLC 59**

**Granovsky, Timofei Nikolaevich**
1813-1855 .................. **NCLC 75**
See also DLB 198

**Grant, Skeeter**
See Spiegelman, Art

**Granville-Barker, Harley**
1877-1946 ......... **TCLC 2; DAM DRAM**
See also Barker, Harley Granville
See also CA 104; RGEL

**Granzotto, Gianni**
See Granzotto, Giovanni Battista

**Granzotto, Giovanni Battista**
1914-1985 .................. **CLC 70**
See also CA 166

**Grass, Guenter (Wilhelm)** 1927- ... **CLC 1, 2, 4, 6, 11, 15, 22, 32, 49, 88; DA; DAB; DAC; DAM MST, NOV; WLC**
See also BPFB 2; CA 13-16R; CANR 20, 75, 93; DA3; DLB 75, 124; EW; MTCW 1, 2; RGWL

**Gratton, Thomas**
See Hulme, T(homas) E(rnest)

**Grau, Shirley Ann** 1929- ....... **CLC 4, 9, 146; SSC 15**
See also CA 89-92; CANR 22, 69; CN; CSW; DLB 2; INT CANR-22; MTCW 1

**Gravel, Fern**
See Hall, James Norman

**Graver, Elizabeth** 1964- .................... **CLC 70**
See also CA 135; CANR 71

**Graves, Richard Perceval**
1895-1985 .................. **CLC 44**
See also CA 65-68; CANR 9, 26, 51

**Graves, Robert (von Ranke)**
1895-1985 .. **CLC 1, 2, 6, 11, 39, 44, 45; DAB; DAC; DAM MST, POET; PC 6**
See also BPFB 2; BRW 7; BYA 4; CA 5-8R; 117; CANR 5, 36; CDBLB 1914-1945; DA3; DLB 20, 100, 191; DLBD 18; DLBY 85; MTCW 1, 2; NCFS 2; RGEL; RHW; SATA 45

**Graves, Valerie**
See Bradley, Marion Zimmer

**Gray, Alasdair (James)** 1934- .......... **CLC 41**
See also CA 126; CANR 47, 69; CN; DLB 194; HGG; INT CA-126; MTCW 1, 2; RGSF

**Gray, Amlin** 1946- .................. **CLC 29**
See also CA 138

**Gray, Francine du Plessix** 1930- ..... **CLC 22; DAM NOV**
See also BEST 90:3; CA 61-64; CAAS 2; CANR 11, 33, 75, 81; INT CANR-11; MTCW 1, 2

**Gray, John (Henry)** 1866-1934 ...... **TCLC 19**
See also CA 119; 162; RGEL

**Gray, Simon (James Holliday)**
1936- .................. **CLC 9, 14, 36**
See also AITN 1; CA 21-24R; CAAS 3; CANR 32, 69; CD; DLB 13; MTCW 1; RGEL

**Gray, Spalding** 1941- ..... **CLC 49, 112; DAM POP; DC 7**
See also CA 128; CAD; CANR 74; CD; CPW; MTCW 2

**Gray, Thomas** 1716-1771 ........ **LC 4, 40; DA; DAB; DAC; DAM MST; PC 2; WLC**
See also BRW 3; CDBLB 1660-1789; DA3; DLB 109; EXPP; PAB; PFS 9; RGEL; WP

**Grayson, David**
See Baker, Ray Stannard

**Grayson, Richard (A.)** 1951- ............ **CLC 38**
See also CA 85-88; CANR 14, 31, 57; DLB 234

**Greeley, Andrew M(oran)** 1928- ..... **CLC 28; DAM POP**
See also BPFB 2; CA 5-8R; CAAS 7; CANR 7, 43, 69; CMW; CPW; DA3; MTCW 1, 2

**Green, Anna Katharine**
1846-1935 .................. **TCLC 63**
See also CA 112; 159; CMW; DLB 202, 221; MSW

**Green, Brian**
See Card, Orson Scott

**Green, Hannah**
See Greenberg, Joanne (Goldenberg)

**Green, Hannah** 1927(?)-1996 .............. **CLC 3**
See also CA 73-76; CANR 59, 93; NFS 10

**Green, Henry** .................. **CLC 2, 13, 97**
See also Yorke, Henry Vincent
See also BRWS 2; CA 175; DLB 15; RGEL

**Green, Julian (Hartridge)** 1900-1998
See Green, Julien
See also CA 21-24R; 169; CANR 33, 87; DLB 4, 72; MTCW 1

**Green, Julien** .................. **CLC 3, 11, 77**
See Green, Julian (Hartridge)
See also GFL 1789 to the Present; MTCW 2

**Green, Paul (Eliot)** 1894-1981 ......... **CLC 25; DAM DRAM**
See also AITN 1; CA 5-8R; 103; CANR 3; DLB 7, 9; DLBY 81; RGAL

**Greenberg, Ivan** 1908-1973
See Rahv, Philip
See also CA 85-88

**Greenberg, Joanne (Goldenberg)**
1932- .................. **CLC 7, 30**
See also AAYA 12; CA 5-8R; CANR 14, 32, 69; CN; SATA 25; YAW

**Greenberg, Richard** 1959(?)- ............ **CLC 57**
See also CA 138; CAD; CD

**Greenblatt, Stephen J(ay)** 1943- ...... **CLC 70**
See also CA 49-52

**Greene, Bette** 1934- .................. **CLC 30**
See also AAYA 7; BYA 3; CA 53-56; CANR 4; CLR 2; CWRI; JRDA; LAIT 4; MAICYA; NFS 10; SAAS 16; SATA 8, 102; YAW

**Greene, Gael** ............................................ **CLC 8**
See also CA 13-16R; CANR 10

**Greene, Graham (Henry)**
1904-1991 .... **CLC 1, 3, 6, 9, 14, 18, 27, 37, 70, 72, 125; DA; DAB; DAC; DAM MST, NOV; SSC 29; WLC**
See also AITN 2; BPFB 2; BRWS 1; BYA 3; CA 13-16R; 133; CANR 35, 61; CBD; CDBLB 1945-1960; CMW; DA3; DLB 13, 15, 77, 100, 162, 201, 204; DLBY 91; MSW; MTCW 1, 2; RGEL; SATA 20; WLIT 4

**Greene, Robert** 1558-1592 ................... **LC 41**
See also DLB 62, 167; IDTP; RGEL; TEA

**Greer, Germaine** 1939- ................ **CLC 131**
See also AITN 1; CA 81-84; CANR 33, 70; FW; MTCW 1, 2

**Greer, Richard**
See Silverberg, Robert

**Gregor, Arthur** 1923- ........................... **CLC 9**
See also CA 25-28R; CAAS 10; CANR 11; CP; SATA 36

**Gregor, Lee**
See Pohl, Frederik

**Gregory, Lady Isabella Augusta (Persse)**
1852-1932 ................................. **TCLC 1**
See also BRW 6; CA 104; 184; DLB 10; IDTP; RGEL

**Gregory, J. Dennis**
See Williams, John A(lfred)

**Grekova, I.** ................................................ **CLC 59**

**Grendon, Stephen**
See Derleth, August (William)

**Grenville, Kate** 1950- .......................... **CLC 61**
See also CA 118; CANR 53, 93

**Grenville, Pelham**
See Wodehouse, P(elham) G(renville)

**Greve, Felix Paul (Berthold Friedrich)**
1879-1948
See Grove, Frederick Philip
See also CA 104; 141, 175; CANR 79; DAC; DAM MST

**Grey, Zane** 1872-1939 ....... **TCLC 6; DAM POP**
See also BPFB 2; CA 104; 132; DA3; DLB 212; MTCW 1, 2; RGAL; TCWW 2

**Grieg, (Johan) Nordahl (Brun)**
1902-1943 ................................... **TCLC 10**
See also CA 107; 189

**Grieve, C(hristopher) M(urray)**
1892-1978 ..... **CLC 11, 19; DAM POET**
See also MacDiarmid, Hugh; Pteleon
See also CA 5-8R; 85-88; CANR 33; MTCW 1; RGEL

**Griffin, Gerald** 1803-1840 ................ **NCLC 7**
See also DLB 159; RGEL

**Griffin, John Howard** 1920-1980 ..... **CLC 68**
See also AITN 1; CA 1-4R; 101; CANR 2

**Griffin, Peter** 1942- ............................. **CLC 39**
See also CA 136

**Griffith, D(avid) L(ewelyn) W(ark)**
1875(?)-1948 ............................. **TCLC 68**
See also CA 119; 150; CANR 80

**Griffith, Lawrence**
See Griffith, D(avid) L(ewelyn) W(ark)

**Griffiths, Trevor** 1935- ................. **CLC 13, 52**
See also CA 97-100; CANR 45; CBD; CD; DLB 13, 245

**Griggs, Sutton (Elbert)**
1872-1930 ................................... **TCLC 77**
See also CA 123; 186; DLB 50

**Grigson, Geoffrey (Edward Harvey)**
1905-1985 ............................... **CLC 7, 39**
See also CA 25-28R; 118; CANR 20, 33; DLB 27; MTCW 1, 2

**Grillparzer, Franz** 1791-1872 .. **NCLC 1, 102; DC 14; SSC 37**
See also DLB 133; EW; RGWL

**Grimble, Reverend Charles James**
See Eliot, T(homas) S(tearns)

**Grimke, Charlotte L(ottie) Forten**
1837(?)-1914
See Forten, Charlotte L.
See also BW 1; CA 117; 124; DAM MULT, POET; DLB 239

**Grimm, Jacob Ludwig Karl**
1785-1863 ............... **NCLC 3, 77; SSC 36**
See also Grimm and Grimm
See also DLB 90; MAICYA; RGSF; RGWL; SATA 22; WCH

**Grimm, Wilhelm Karl** 1786-1859 .. **NCLC 3, 77; SSC 36**
See also Grimm and Grimm
See also DLB 90; MAICYA; RGSF; RGWL; SATA 22; WCH

**Grimmelshausen, Hans Jakob Christoffel von**
See Grimmelshausen, Johann Jakob Christoffel von
See also RGWL

**Grimmelshausen, Johann Jakob Christoffel von** 1621-1676 ............................ **LC 6**
See also Grimmelshausen, Hans Jakob Christoffel von
See also DLB 168

**Grindel, Eugene** 1895-1952
See Eluard, Paul
See also CA 104; 193

**Grisham, John** 1955- .... **CLC 84; DAM POP**
See also AAYA 14; BPFB 2; CA 138; CANR 47, 69; CMW; CN; CPW; CSW; DA3; MSW; MTCW 2

**Grossman, David** 1954- ...................... **CLC 67**
See also CA 138; CWW 2

**Grossman, Vasily (Semenovich)**
1905-1964 ................................... **CLC 41**
See also CA 124; 130; MTCW 1

**Grove, Frederick Philip** ................ **TCLC 4**
See also Greve, Felix Paul (Berthold Friedrich)
See also DLB 92; RGEL

**Grubb**
See Crumb, R(obert)

**Grumbach, Doris (Isaac)** 1918- . **CLC 13, 22, 64**
See also CA 5-8R; CAAS 2; CANR 9, 42, 70; CN; INT CANR-9; MTCW 2

**Grundtvig, Nicolai Frederik Severin**
1783-1872 ......................................... **NCLC 1**

**Grunge**
See Crumb, R(obert)

**Grunwald, Lisa** 1959- ......................... **CLC 44**
See also CA 120

**Guare, John** 1938- ........... **CLC 8, 14, 29, 67; DAM DRAM**
See also CA 73-76; CAD; CANR 21, 69; CD; DFS 8, 13; DLB 7; MTCW 1, 2; RGAL

**Gubar, Susan (David)** 1944- .......... **CLC 145**
See also CA 108; CANR 45, 70; FW; MTCW 1; RGAL

**Gudjonsson, Halldor Kiljan** 1902-1998
See Laxness, Halldor
See also CA 103; 164; CWW 2

**Guenter, Erich**
See Eich, Guenter

**Guest, Barbara** 1920- ......................... **CLC 34**
See also CA 25-28R; CANR 11, 44, 84; CP; CWP; DLB 5, 193

**Guest, Edgar A(lbert)** 1881-1959 ... **TCLC 95**
See also CA 112; 168

**Guest, Judith (Ann)** 1936- ........... **CLC 8, 30; DAM NOV, POP**
See also AAYA 7; CA 77-80; CANR 15, 75; DA3; EXPN; INT CANR-15; LAIT 5; MTCW 1, 2; NFS 1

**Guevara, Che** ................. **CLC 87; HLC 1**
See also Guevara (Serna), Ernesto

**Guevara (Serna), Ernesto**
1928-1967 ......... **CLC 87; DAM MULT; HLC 1**
See also Guevara, Che
See also CA 127; 111; CANR 56; HW 1

**Guicciardini, Francesco** 1483-1540 ..... **LC 49**

**Guild, Nicholas M.** 1944- ................... **CLC 33**
See also CA 93-96

**Guillemin, Jacques**
See Sartre, Jean-Paul

**Guillen, Jorge** 1893-1984 ........ **CLC 11; DAM MULT, POET; HLCS 1; PC 35**
See also CA 89-92; 112; DLB 108; HW 1; RGWL

**Guillen, Nicolas (Cristobal)**
1902-1989 ... **CLC 48, 79; BLC 2; DAM MST, MULT, POET; HLC 1; PC 23**
See also BW 2; CA 116; 125; 129; CANR 84; HW 1; LAW; RGWL; WP

**Guillevic, (Eugene)** 1907-1997 .......... **CLC 33**
See also CA 93-96; CWW 2

**Guillois**
See Desnos, Robert

**Guillois, Valentin**
See Desnos, Robert

**Guimaraes Rosa, Joao**
See Rosa, Joao Guimaraes
See also LAW

**Guimaraes Rosa, Joao** 1908-1967
See also CA 175; HLCS 2; LAW; RGSF; RGWL

**Guiney, Louise Imogen**
1861-1920 ................................. **TCLC 41**
See also CA 160; DLB 54; RGAL

**Guiraldes, Ricardo (Guillermo)**
1886-1927 ................................. **TCLC 39**
See also CA 131; HW 1; LAW; MTCW 1

**Gumilev, Nikolai (Stepanovich)**
1886-1921 ................................. **TCLC 60**
See also CA 165

**Gunesekera, Romesh** 1954- ............... **CLC 91**
See also CA 159; CN

**Gunn, Bill** ............................................... **CLC 5**
See also Gunn, William Harrison
See also DLB 38

**Gunn, Thom(son William)** 1929- .. **CLC 3, 6, 18, 32, 81; DAM POET; PC 26**
See also BRWS 4; CA 17-20R; CANR 9, 33; CDBLB 1960 to Present; CP; DLB 27; INT CANR-33; MTCW 1; PFS 9; RGEL

**Gunn, William Harrison** 1934(?)-1989
See Gunn, Bill
See also AITN 1; BW 1, 3; CA 13-16R; 128; CANR 12, 25, 76

**Gunn Allen, Paula**
See Allen, Paula Gunn

**Gunnars, Kristjana** 1948- ................... **CLC 69**
See also CA 113; CCA 1; CP; CWP; DLB 60

**Gurdjieff, G(eorgei) I(vanovich)**
1877(?)-1949 ............................. **TCLC 71**
See also CA 157

**Gurganus, Allan** 1947- . **CLC 70; DAM POP**
See also BEST 90:1; CA 135; CN; CPW; CSW; GLL 1

**Gurney, A(lbert) R(amsdell), Jr.**
1930- ..... **CLC 32, 50, 54; DAM DRAM**
See also AMWS 5; CA 77-80; CAD; CANR 32, 64; CD

**Gurney, Ivor (Bertie)** 1890-1937 ... **TCLC 33**
See also BRW 6; CA 167; PAB; RGEL

**Gurney, Peter**
See Gurney, A(lbert) R(amsdell), Jr.

**Guro, Elena** 1877-1913 ................... **TCLC 56**

**Gustafson, James M(oody)** 1925- ... **CLC 100**
See also CA 25-28R; CANR 37

**Gustafson, Ralph (Barker)**
1909-1995 .................... **CLC 36**
See also CA 21-24R; CANR 8, 45, 84; CP;
DLB 88; RGEL

**Gut, Gom**
See Simenon, Georges (Jacques Christian)

**Guterson, David** 1956- ..................... **CLC 91**
See also CA 132; CANR 73; MTCW 2

**Guthrie, A(lfred) B(ertram), Jr.**
1901-1991 ............................... **CLC 23**
See also CA 57-60; 134; CANR 24; DLB
212; SATA 62; SATA-Obit 67

**Guthrie, Isobel**
See Grieve, C(hristopher) M(urray)

**Guthrie, Woodrow Wilson** 1912-1967
See Guthrie, Woody
See also CA 113; 93-96

**Guthrie, Woody** ...................... **CLC 35**
See also Guthrie, Woodrow Wilson
See also LAIT 3

**Gutierrez Najera, Manuel** 1859-1895
See also HLCS 2; LAW

**Guy, Rosa (Cuthbert)** 1928- ............ **CLC 26**
See also AAYA 4, 37; BW 2; CA 17-20R;
CANR 14, 34, 83; CLR 13; DLB 33;
JRDA; MAICYA; SATA 14, 62, 122;
YAW

**Gwendolyn**
See Bennett, (Enoch) Arnold

**H. D.** ............ **CLC 3, 8, 14, 31, 34, 73; PC 5**
See also Doolittle, Hilda

**H. de V.**
See Buchan, John

**Haavikko, Paavo Juhani** 1931- .. **CLC 18, 34**
See also CA 106

**Habbema, Koos**
See Heijermans, Herman

**Habermas, Juergen** 1929- ............... **CLC 104**
See also CA 109; CANR 85; DLB 242

**Habermas, Jurgen**
See Habermas, Juergen

**Hacker, Marilyn** 1942- ...... **CLC 5, 9, 23, 72, 91; DAM POET**
See also CA 77-80; CANR 68; CP; CWP;
DLB 120; FW; GLL 2

**Haeckel, Ernst Heinrich (Philipp August)**
1834-1919 ............................... **TCLC 83**
See also CA 157

**Hafiz** c. 1326-1389(?) ...................... **CMLC 34**
See also RGWL

**Haggard, H(enry) Rider**
1856-1925 ............................... **TCLC 11**
See also BRWS 3; BYA 4, 5; CA 108; 148;
DLB 70, 156, 174, 178; FANT; MTCW
2; RGEL; RHW; SATA 16; SCFW; SFW;
SUFW; WLIT 4

**Hagiosy, L.**
See Larbaud, Valery (Nicolas)

**Hagiwara, Sakutaro** 1886-1942 .... **TCLC 60; PC 18**
See also CA 154

**Haig, Fenil**
See Ford, Ford Madox

**Haig-Brown, Roderick (Langmere)**
1908-1976 ............................... **CLC 21**
See also CA 5-8R; 69-72; CANR 4, 38, 83;
CLR 31; CWRI; DLB 88; MAICYA;
SATA 12

**Hailey, Arthur** 1920- ...... **CLC 5; DAM NOV, POP**
See also AITN 2; BEST 90:3; BPFB 2; CA
1-4R; CANR 2, 36, 75; CCA 1; CN;
CPW; DLB 88; DLBY 82; MTCW 1, 2

**Hailey, Elizabeth Forsythe** 1938- ...... **CLC 40**
See also CA 93-96; CAAE 188; CAAS 1;
CANR 15, 48; INT CANR-15

**Haines, John (Meade)** 1924- ............... **CLC 58**
See also CA 17-20R; CANR 13, 34; CSW;
DLB 212

**Hakluyt, Richard** 1552-1616 ................. **LC 31**
See also RGEL

**Haldeman, Joe (William)** 1943- ....... **CLC 61**
See also Graham, Robert
See also AAYA 38; CA 53-56, 179; CAAE
179; CAAS 25; CANR 6, 70, 72; DLB 8;
INT CANR-6; SCFW 2; SFW

**Hale, Sarah Josepha (Buell)**
1788-1879 ............................... **NCLC 75**
See also DLB 1, 42, 73, 243

**Halevy, Elie** 1870-1937 ................... **TCLC 104**

**Haley, Alex(ander Murray Palmer)**
1921-1992 . **CLC 8, 12, 76; BLC 2; DA; DAB; DAC; DAM MST, MULT, POP**
See also AAYA 26; BPFB 2; BW 2, 3; CA
77-80; 136; CANR 61; CDALBS; CPW;
CSW; DA3; DLB 38; LAIT 5; MTCW 1,
2; NFS 9

**Haliburton, Thomas Chandler**
1796-1865 ............................... **NCLC 15**
See also DLB 11, 99; RGEL; RGSF

**Hall, Donald (Andrew, Jr.)** 1928- ....... **CLC 1, 13, 37, 59, 151; DAM POET**
See also CA 5-8R; CAAS 7; CANR 2, 44,
64; CP; DLB 5; MTCW 1; RGAL; SATA
23, 97

**Hall, Frederic Sauser**
See Sauser-Hall, Frederic

**Hall, James**
See Kuttner, Henry

**Hall, James Norman** 1887-1951 ..... **TCLC 23**
See also CA 123; 173; LAIT 1; RHW 1;
SATA 21

**Hall, (Marguerite) Radclyffe**
1880-1943 ............................... **TCLC 12**
See also BRWS 6; CA 110; 150; CANR 83;
DLB 191; MTCW 2; RGEL; RHW

**Hall, Rodney** 1935- ............................. **CLC 51**
See also CA 109; CANR 69; CN; CP

**Halleck, Fitz-Greene** 1790-1867 .... **NCLC 47**
See also DLB 3; RGAL

**Halliday, Michael**
See Creasey, John

**Halpern, Daniel** 1945- ...................... **CLC 14**
See also CA 33-36R; CANR 93; CP

**Hamburger, Michael (Peter Leopold)**
1924- ................................. **CLC 5, 14**
See also CA 5-8R; CAAS 4; CANR 2, 47;
CP; DLB 27

**Hamill, Pete** 1935- ............................. **CLC 10**
See also CA 25-28R; CANR 18, 71

**Hamilton, Alexander**
1755(?)-1804 ........................... **NCLC 49**
See also DLB 37

**Hamilton, Clive**
See Lewis, C(live) S(taples)

**Hamilton, Edmond** 1904-1977 ............ **CLC 1**
See also CA 1-4R; CANR 3, 84; DLB 8;
SATA 118; SFW

**Hamilton, Eugene (Jacob) Lee**
See Lee-Hamilton, Eugene (Jacob)

**Hamilton, Franklin**
See Silverberg, Robert

**Hamilton, Gail**
See Corcoran, Barbara (Asenath)

**Hamilton, Mollie**
See Kaye, M(ary) M(argaret)

**Hamilton, (Anthony Walter) Patrick**
1904-1962 ............................... **CLC 51**
See also CA 176; 113; DLB 191

**Hamilton, Virginia (Esther)** 1936- .. **CLC 26; DAM MULT**
See also AAYA 2, 21; BW 2, 3; BYA 1, 2,
8; CA 25-28R; CANR 20, 37, 73; CLR 1,
11, 40; DLB 33, 52; INT CANR-20;
JRDA; LAIT 5; MAICYA; MAICYAS;
MTCW 1, 2; SATA 4, 56, 79, 123; YAW

**Hammett, (Samuel) Dashiell**
1894-1961 .... **CLC 3, 5, 10, 19, 47; SSC 17**
See also AITN 1; AMWS 4; BPFB 2; CA
81-84; CANR 42; CDALB 1929-1941;
CMW; DA3; DLB 226; DLBD 6; DLBY
96; LAIT 3; MSW; MTCW 1, 2; RGAL;
RGSF

**Hammon, Jupiter** 1720(?)-1800(?) . **NCLC 5; BLC 2; DAM MULT, POET; PC 16**
See also DLB 31, 50

**Hammond, Keith**
See Kuttner, Henry

**Hamner, Earl (Henry), Jr.** 1923- ...... **CLC 12**
See also AITN 2; CA 73-76; DLB 6

**Hampton, Christopher (James)**
1946- ............................................. **CLC 4**
See also CA 25-28R; CD; DLB 13; MTCW
1

**Hamsun, Knut** ...................... **TCLC 2, 14, 49**
See also Pedersen, Knut
See also EW; RGWL

**Handke, Peter** 1942- .... **CLC 5, 8, 10, 15, 38, 134; DAM DRAM, NOV**
See also CA 77-80; CANR 33, 75; CWW
2; DLB 85, 124; MTCW 1, 2

**Handy, W(illiam) C(hristopher)**
1873-1958 ............................... **TCLC 97**
See also BW 3; CA 121; 167

**Hanley, James** 1901-1985 ........... **CLC 3, 5, 8, 13**
See also CA 73-76; 117; CANR 36; CBD;
DLB 191; MTCW 1; RGEL

**Hannah, Barry** 1942- ............ **CLC 23, 38, 90**
See also BPFB 2; CA 108; 110; CANR 43,
68; CN; CSW; DLB 6, 234; INT CA-110;
MTCW 1; RGSF

**Hannon, Ezra**
See Hunter, Evan

**Hansberry, Lorraine (Vivian)**
1930-1965 ...... **CLC 17, 62; BLC 2; DA; DAB; DAC; DAM DRAM, MST, MULT; DC 2**
See also AAYA 25; AFAW 1, 2; AMWS 4;
BW 1, 3; CA 109; 25-28R; CABS 3;
CANR 58; CDALB 1941-1968; DA3;
DFS 2; DLB 7, 38; FW; LAIT 4; MTCW
1, 2; RGAL

**Hansen, Joseph** 1923- ....................... **CLC 38**
See also Brock, Rose; Colton, James
See also BPFB 2; CA 29-32R; CAAS 17;
CANR 16, 44, 66; CMW; DLB 226; GLL
1; INT CANR-16

**Hansen, Martin A(lfred)**
1909-1955 ............................... **TCLC 32**
See also CA 167; DLB 214

**Hansen and Philipson eds.** ............. **CLC 65**

**Hanson, Kenneth O(stlin)** 1922- ....... **CLC 13**
See also CA 53-56; CANR 7

**Hardwick, Elizabeth (Bruce)**
1916- ..................... **CLC 13; DAM NOV**
See also AMWS 3; CA 5-8R; CANR 3, 32,
70, 100; CN; CSW; DA3; DLB 6;
MAWW; MTCW 1, 2

**Hardy, Thomas** 1840-1928 .. **TCLC 4, 10, 18, 32, 48, 53, 72; DA; DAB; DAC; DAM MST, NOV, POET; PC 8; SSC 2; WLC**
See also BRW 6; CA 104; CDBLB
1890-1914; DA3; DLB 18, 19, 135;
EXPN; EXPP; LAIT 2; MTCW 1, 2; NFS
3, 11; PFS 3, 4; RGEL; RGSF; WLIT 4

**Hare, David** 1947- ............... **CLC 29, 58, 136**
See also BRWS 4; CA 97-100; CANR 39,
91; CBD; CD; DFS 4, 7; DLB 13; MTCW
1

**Harewood, John**
See Van Druten, John (William)

**Harford, Henry**
See Hudson, W(illiam) H(enry)

**Hargrave, Leonie**
See Disch, Thomas M(ichael)

**Harjo, Joy** 1951- ...... **CLC 83; DAM MULT; PC 27**
See also CA 114; CANR 35, 67, 91; CP; CWP; DLB 120, 175; MTCW 2; NNAL; RGAL

**Harlan, Louis R(udolph)** 1922- ........ **CLC 34**
See also CA 21-24R; CANR 25, 55, 80

**Harling, Robert** 1951(?)- ................... **CLC 53**
See also CA 147

**Harmon, William (Ruth)** 1938- ........ **CLC 38**
See also CA 33-36R; CANR 14, 32, 35; SATA 65

**Harper, F. E. W.**
See Harper, Frances Ellen Watkins

**Harper, Frances E. W.**
See Harper, Frances Ellen Watkins

**Harper, Frances E. Watkins**
See Harper, Frances Ellen Watkins

**Harper, Frances Ellen**
See Harper, Frances Ellen Watkins

**Harper, Frances Ellen Watkins**
1825-1911 ...... **TCLC 14; BLC 2; DAM MULT, POET; PC 21**
See also AFAW 1, 2; BW 1, 3; CA 111; 125; CANR 79; DLB 50, 221; MAWW; RGAL

**Harper, Michael S(teven)** 1938- ... **CLC 7, 22**
See also AFAW 2; BW 1; CA 33-36R; CANR 24; CP; DLB 41; RGAL

**Harper, Mrs. F. E. W.**
See Harper, Frances Ellen Watkins

**Harris, Christie (Lucy) Irwin**
1907- ............................... **CLC 12**
See also CA 5-8R; CANR 6, 83; CLR 47; DLB 88; JRDA; MAICYA; SAAS 10; SATA 6, 74; SATA-Essay 116

**Harris, Frank** 1856-1931 ................ **TCLC 24**
See also CA 109; 150; CANR 80; DLB 156, 197; RGEL

**Harris, George Washington**
1814-1869 ................................ **NCLC 23**
See also DLB 3, 11; RGAL

**Harris, Joel Chandler** 1848-1908 ... **TCLC 2; SSC 19**
See also CA 104; 137; CANR 80; CLR 49; DLB 11, 23, 42, 78, 91; LAIT 2; MAICYA; RGAL; SATA 100; YABC 1

**Harris, John (Wyndham Parkes Lucas) Beynon** 1903-1969
See Wyndham, John
See also CA 102; 89-92; CANR 84; SATA 118; SFW

**Harris, MacDonald** ........................... **CLC 9**
See Heiney, Donald (William)

**Harris, Mark** 1922- ............................. **CLC 19**
See also CA 5-8R; CAAS 3; CANR 2, 55, 83; CN; DLB 2; DLBY 80

**Harris, Norman** .................................. **CLC 65**
**Harris, (Theodore) Wilson** 1921- ...... **CLC 25**
See also BRWS 5; BW 2, 3; CA 65-68; CAAS 16; CANR 11, 27, 69; CN; CP; DLB 117; MTCW 1; RGEL

**Harrison, Barbara Grizzuti** 1934- . **CLC 144**
See also CA 77-80; CANR 15, 48; INT CANR-15

**Harrison, Elizabeth Cavanna** 1909-2001
See Cavanna, Betty
See also CA 9-12R; CANR 6, 27, 85; YAW

**Harrison, Harry (Max)** 1925- ........... **CLC 42**
See also CA 1-4R; CANR 5, 21, 84; DLB 8; SATA 4; SCFW 2; SFW

**Harrison, James (Thomas)** 1937- ...... **CLC 6, 14, 33, 66, 143; SSC 19**
See also Harrison, Jim
See also CA 13-16R; CANR 8, 51, 79; CN; CP; DLBY 82; INT CANR-8

**Harrison, Jim**
See Harrison, James (Thomas)
See also AMWS 8; RGAL; TCWW 2

**Harrison, Kathryn** 1961- ........... **CLC 70, 151**
See also CA 144; CANR 68

**Harrison, Tony** 1937- ................. **CLC 43, 129**
See also BRWS 5; CA 65-68; CANR 44, 98; CBD; CD; CP; DLB 40, 245; MTCW 1; RGEL

**Harriss, Will(ard Irvin)** 1922- .......... **CLC 34**
See also CA 111

**Harson, Sley**
See Ellison, Harlan (Jay)

**Hart, Ellis**
See Ellison, Harlan (Jay)

**Hart, Josephine** 1942(?)- ....... **CLC 70; DAM POP**
See also CA 138; CANR 70; CPW

**Hart, Moss** 1904-1961 ........... **CLC 66; DAM DRAM**
See also CA 109; 89-92; CANR 84; DFS 1; DLB 7; RGAL

**Harte, (Francis) Bret(t)**
1836(?)-1902 ... **TCLC 1, 25; DA; DAC; DAM MST; SSC 8; WLC**
See also AMWS 2; CA 104; 140; CANR 80; CDALB 1865-1917; DA3; DLB 12, 64, 74, 79, 186; EXPS; LAIT 2; RGAL; RGSF; SATA 26; SSFS 3

**Hartley, L(eslie) P(oles)** 1895-1972 ... **CLC 2, 22**
See also BRWS 7; CA 45-48; 37-40R; CANR 33; DLB 15, 139; HGG; MTCW 1, 2; RGEL; RGSF; SUFW

**Hartman, Geoffrey H.** 1929- ............. **CLC 27**
See also CA 117; 125; CANR 79; DLB 67

**Hartmann, Sadakichi** 1869-1944 ... **TCLC 73**
See also CA 157; DLB 54

**Hartmann von Aue** c. 1170-c. 1210 ......................................... **CMLC 15**
See also DLB 138; RGWL

**Haruf, Kent** 1943- ............................... **CLC 34**
See also CA 149; CANR 91

**Harwood, Ronald** 1934- ......... **CLC 32; DAM DRAM, MST**
See also CA 1-4R; CANR 4, 55; CBD; CD; DLB 13

**Hasegawa Tatsunosuke**
See Futabatei, Shimei

**Hasek, Jaroslav (Matej Frantisek)**
1883-1923 .................................. **TCLC 4**
See also CA 104; 129; EW; MTCW 1, 2; RGSF; RGWL

**Hass, Robert** 1941- ... **CLC 18, 39, 99; PC 16**
See also AMWS 6; CA 111; CANR 30, 50, 71; CP; DLB 105, 206; RGAL; SATA 94

**Hastings, Hudson**
See Kuttner, Henry

**Hastings, Selina** ................................ **CLC 44**
**Hathorne, John** 1641-1717 ................... **LC 38**
**Hatteras, Amelia**
See Mencken, H(enry) L(ouis)

**Hatteras, Owen** ............................ **TCLC 18**
See also Mencken, H(enry) L(ouis); Nathan, George Jean

**Hauptmann, Gerhart (Johann Robert)**
1862-1946 ....... **TCLC 4; DAM DRAM; SSC 37**
See also CA 104; 153; DLB 66, 118; EW; RGSF; RGWL

**Havel, Vaclav** 1936- ..... **CLC 25, 58, 65, 123; DAM DRAM; DC 6**
See also CA 104; CANR 36, 63; CWW 2; DA3; DFS 10; DLB 232; MTCW 1, 2

**Haviaras, Stratis** ............................... **CLC 33**
See also Chaviaras, Strates

**Hawes, Stephen** 1475(?)-1529(?) .......... **LC 17**
See also DLB 132; RGEL

**Hawkes, John (Clendennin Burne, Jr.)**
1925-1998 .. **CLC 1, 2, 3, 4, 7, 9, 14, 15, 27, 49**
See also BPFB 2; CA 1-4R; 167; CANR 2, 47, 64; CN; DLB 2, 7, 227; DLBY 80, 98; MTCW 1, 2; RGAL

**Hawking, S. W.**
See Hawking, Stephen W(illiam)

**Hawking, Stephen W(illiam)** 1942- . **CLC 63, 105**
See also AAYA 13; BEST 89:1; CA 126; 129; CANR 48; CPW; DA3; MTCW 2

**Hawkins, Anthony Hope**
See Hope, Anthony

**Hawthorne, Julian** 1846-1934 ........ **TCLC 25**
See also CA 165; HGG

**Hawthorne, Nathaniel** 1804-1864 ... **NCLC 2, 10, 17, 23, 39, 79, 95; DA; DAB; DAC; DAM MST, NOV; SSC 3, 29, 39; WLC**
See also AAYA 18; AMW; AMWR 1; BPFB 2; BYA 3; CDALB 1640-1865; DA3; DLB 1, 74, 223; EXPN; EXPS; HGG; LAIT 1; NFS 1; RGAL; RGSF; SSFS 1, 7, 11; YABC 2

**Haxton, Josephine Ayres** 1921-
See Douglas, Ellen
See also CA 115; CANR 41, 83

**Hayaseca y Eizaguirre, Jorge**
See Echegaray (y Eizaguirre), Jose (Maria Waldo)

**Hayashi, Fumiko** 1904-1951 ........... **TCLC 27**
See also CA 161; DLB 180

**Haycraft, Anna (Margaret)** 1932-
See Ellis, Alice Thomas
See also CA 122; CANR 85, 90; MTCW 2

**Hayden, Robert E(arl)** 1913-1980 . **CLC 5, 9, 14, 37; BLC 2; DA; DAC; DAM MST, MULT, POET; PC 6**
See also AFAW 1, 2; AMWS 2; BW 1, 3; CA 69-72; 97-100; CABS 2; CANR 24, 75, 82; CDALB 1941-1968; DLB 5, 76; EXPP; MTCW 1, 2; PFS 1; RGAL; SATA 19; SATA-Obit 26; WP

**Hayek, F(riedrich) A(ugust von)**
1899-1992 ................................ **TCLC 109**
See also CA 93-96; 137; CANR 20; MTCW 1, 2

**Hayford, J(oseph) E(phraim) Casely**
See Casely-Hayford, J(oseph) E(phraim)

**Hayman, Ronald** 1932- ..................... **CLC 44**
See also CA 25-28R; CANR 18, 50, 88; CD; DLB 155

**Hayne, Paul Hamilton** 1830-1886 . **NCLC 94**
See also DLB 3, 64, 79; RGAL

**Haywood, Eliza (Fowler)**
1693(?)-1756 .............................. **LC 1, 44**
See also DLB 39; RGEL

**Hazlitt, William** 1778-1830 ....... **NCLC 29, 82**
See also BRW 4; DLB 110, 158; RGEL

**Hazzard, Shirley** 1931- ...................... **CLC 18**
See also CA 9-12R; CANR 4, 70; CN; DLBY 82; MTCW 1

**Head, Bessie** 1937-1986 .... **CLC 25, 67; BLC 2; DAM MULT**
See also AFW; BW 2, 3; CA 29-32R; 119; CANR 25, 82; DA3; DLB 117, 225; EXPS; FW; MTCW 1, 2; RGSF; SSFS 5, 13; WLIT 2

**Headon, (Nicky) Topper** 1956(?)- ..... **CLC 30**

**Heaney, Seamus (Justin)** 1939- ..... **CLC 5, 7, 14, 25, 37, 74, 91; DAB; DAM POET; PC 18; WLCS**
See also BRWS 2; CA 85-88; CANR 25, 48, 75, 91; CDBLB 1960 to Present; CP; DA3; DLB 40; DLBY 95; EXPP; MTCW 1, 2; PAB; PFS 2, 5, 8; RGEL; WLIT 4

**Hearn, (Patricio) Lafcadio (Tessima Carlos)**
1850-1904 .................... **TCLC 9**
See also CA 105; 166; DLB 12, 78, 189; HGG; RGAL

**Hearne, Vicki** 1946- ................. **CLC 56**
See also CA 139

**Hearon, Shelby** 1931- ............... **CLC 63**
See also AITN 2; AMWS 8; CA 25-28R; CANR 18, 48, 103; CSW

**Heat-Moon, William Least** .......... **CLC 29**
See also Trogdon, William (Lewis)
See also AAYA 9

**Hebbel, Friedrich** 1813-1863 ........ **NCLC 43; DAM DRAM**
See also DLB 129; EW; RGWL

**Hebert, Anne** 1916-2000 ......... **CLC 4, 13, 29; DAC; DAM MST, POET**
See also CA 85-88; 187; CANR 69; CCA 1; CWP; CWW 2; DA3; DLB 68; GFL 1789 to the Present; MTCW 1, 2

**Hecht, Anthony (Evan)** 1923- ..... **CLC 8, 13, 19; DAM POET**
See also CA 9-12R; CANR 6; CP; DLB 5, 169; PFS 6; WP

**Hecht, Ben** 1894-1964 .................. **CLC 8**
See also CA 85-88; DFS 9; DLB 7, 9, 25, 26, 28, 86; FANT; IDFW 3, 4; RGAL; TCLC 101

**Hedayat, Sadeq** 1903-1951 ............ **TCLC 21**
See also CA 120; RGSF

**Hegel, Georg Wilhelm Friedrich**
1770-1831 ........................ **NCLC 46**
See also DLB 90

**Heidegger, Martin** 1889-1976 .......... **CLC 24**
See also CA 81-84; 65-68; CANR 34; MTCW 1, 2

**Heidenstam, (Carl Gustaf) Verner von**
1859-1940 ........................ **TCLC 5**
See also CA 104

**Heifner, Jack** 1946- .................. **CLC 11**
See also CA 105; CANR 47

**Heijermans, Herman** 1864-1924 .... **TCLC 24**
See also CA 123

**Heilbrun, Carolyn G(old)** 1926- ....... **CLC 25**
See also Cross, Amanda
See also CA 45-48; CANR 1, 28, 58, 94; CMW; CPW; FW

**Heine, Heinrich** 1797-1856 ....... **NCLC 4, 54; PC 25**
See also DLB 90; EW; RGWL

**Heinemann, Larry (Curtiss)** 1944- ... **CLC 50**
See also CA 110; CAAS 21; CANR 31, 81; DLBD 9; INT CANR-31

**Heiney, Donald (William)** 1921-1993
See Harris, MacDonald
See also CA 1-4R; 142; CANR 3, 58; FANT

**Heinlein, Robert A(nson)** 1907-1988 . **CLC 1, 3, 8, 14, 26, 55; DAM POP**
See also AAYA 17; BPFB 2; BYA 4, 13; CA 1-4R; 125; CANR 1, 20, 53; CLR 75; CPW; DA3; DLB 8; EXPS; JRDA; LAIT 5; MAICYA; MTCW 1, 2; RGAL; SATA 9, 69; SATA-Obit 56; SCFW; SFW; SSFS 7; YAW

**Helforth, John**
See Doolittle, Hilda

**Hellenhofferu, Vojtech Kapristian z**
See Hasek, Jaroslav (Matej Frantisek)

**Heller, Joseph** 1923-1999 . **CLC 1, 3, 5, 8, 11, 36, 63; DA; DAB; DAC; DAM MST, NOV, POP; WLC**
See also AAYA 24; AITN 1; AMWS 4; BPFB 2; BYA 1; CA 5-8R; 187; CABS 1; CANR 8, 42, 66; CN; CPW; DA3; DLB 2, 28, 227; DLBY 80; EXPN; INT CANR-8; LAIT 4; MTCW 1, 2; NFS 1; RGAL; YAW

**Hellman, Lillian (Florence)**
1906-1984 .. **CLC 2, 4, 8, 14, 18, 34, 44, 52; DAM DRAM; DC 1**
See also AITN 1, 2; AMWS 1; CA 13-16R; 112; CAD; CANR 33; CWD; DA3; DFS 1, 3; DLB 7, 228; DLBY 84; FW; LAIT 3; MAWW; MTCW 1, 2; RGAL

**Helprin, Mark** 1947- ....... **CLC 7, 10, 22, 32; DAM NOV, POP**
See also CA 81-84; CANR 47, 64; CDALBS; CPW; DA3; DLBY 85; FANT; MTCW 1, 2

**Helvetius, Claude-Adrien** 1715-1771 .. **LC 26**

**Helyar, Jane Penelope Josephine** 1933-
See Poole, Josephine
See also CA 21-24R; CANR 10, 26; SATA 82

**Hemans, Felicia** 1793-1835 ...... **NCLC 29, 71**
See also DLB 96; RGEL

**Hemingway, Ernest (Miller)**
1899-1961 .... **CLC 1, 3, 6, 8, 10, 13, 19, 30, 34, 39, 41, 44, 50, 61, 80; DA; DAB; DAC; DAM MST, NOV; SSC 1, 25, 36, 40; WLC**
See also AAYA 19; AMW; AMWR 1; BPFB 2; BYA 2, 3, 13; CA 77-80; CANR 34; CDALB 1917-1929; DA3; DLB 4, 9, 102, 210; DLBD 1, 15, 16; DLBY 81, 87, 96, 98; EXPN; EXPS; LAIT 3, 4; MTCW 1, 2; NFS 1, 5, 6; RGAL; RGSF; SSFS 1, 6, 8, 9, 11; WYA

**Hempel, Amy** 1951- ........................ **CLC 39**
See also CA 118; 137; CANR 70; DA3; EXPS; MTCW 2; SSFS 2

**Henderson, F. C.**
See Mencken, H(enry) L(ouis)

**Henderson, Sylvia**
See Ashton-Warner, Sylvia (Constance)

**Henderson, Zenna (Chlarson)**
1917-1983 .................... **SSC 29**
See also CA 1-4R; 133; CANR 1, 84; DLB 8; SATA 5; SFW

**Henkin, Joshua** ........................ **CLC 119**
See also CA 161

**Henley, Beth** .................. **CLC 23; DC 6, 14**
See also Henley, Elizabeth Becker
See also CABS 3; CAD; CWD; DFS 2; DLBY 86

**Henley, Elizabeth Becker** 1952-
See Henley, Beth
See also CA 107; CANR 32, 73; CD; CSW; DA3; DAM DRAM, MST; FW; MTCW 1, 2

**Henley, William Ernest** 1849-1903 .. **TCLC 8**
See also CA 105; DLB 19; RGEL

**Hennissart, Martha**
See Lathen, Emma
See also CA 85-88; CANR 64

**Henry VIII** 1491-1547 ...................... **LC 10**
See also DLB 132

**Henry, O.** .......... **TCLC 1, 19; SSC 5; WLC**
See also Porter, William Sydney
See also AAYA 41; AMWS 2; EXPS; RGAL; RGSF; SSFS 2

**Henry, Patrick** 1736-1799 .................. **LC 25**
See also LAIT 1

**Henryson, Robert** 1430(?)-1506(?) ...... **LC 20**
See also BRWS 7; DLB 146; RGEL

**Henschke, Alfred**
See Klabund

**Hentoff, Nat(han Irving)** 1925- .......... **CLC 26**
See also AAYA 4, 42; BYA 6; CA 1-4R; CAAS 27; CANR 5, 25, 77; CLR 1, 52; INT CANR-25; JRDA; MAICYA; SATA 42, 69; SATA-Brief 27; WYA; YAW

**Heppenstall, (John) Rayner**
1911-1981 ................... **CLC 10**
See also CA 1-4R; 103; CANR 29

**Heraclitus** c. 540B.C.-c. 450B.C. ... **CMLC 22**
See also DLB 176

**Herbert, Frank (Patrick)**
1920-1986 ......... **CLC 12, 23, 35, 44, 85; DAM POP**
See also AAYA 21; BPFB 2; BYA 4; CA 53-56; 118; CANR 5, 43; CDALBS; CPW; DLB 8; INT CANR-5; LAIT 5; MTCW 1, 2; SATA 9, 37; SATA-Obit 47; SCFW 2; SFW; YAW

**Herbert, George** 1593-1633 ..... **LC 24; DAB; DAM POET; PC 4**
See also BRW 2; CDBLB Before 1660; DLB 126; EXPP; RGEL; WP

**Herbert, Zbigniew** 1924-1998 ..... **CLC 9, 43; DAM POET**
See also CA 89-92; 169; CANR 36, 74; CWW 2; DLB 232; MTCW 1

**Herbst, Josephine (Frey)**
1897-1969 ................... **CLC 34**
See also CA 5-8R; 25-28R; DLB 9

**Herder, Johann Gottfried von**
1744-1803 .................... **NCLC 8**
See also DLB 97; EW

**Heredia, Jose Maria** 1803-1839
See also HLCS 2; LAW

**Hergesheimer, Joseph** 1880-1954 ... **TCLC 11**
See also CA 109; 194; DLB 102, 9; RGAL

**Herlihy, James Leo** 1927-1993 .......... **CLC 6**
See also CA 1-4R; 143; CAD; CANR 2

**Hermogenes** fl. c. 175- ................. **CMLC 6**

**Hernandez, Jose** 1834-1886 ............ **NCLC 17**
See also LAW; RGWL; WLIT 1

**Herodotus** c. 484B.C.-c. 420B.C. .. **CMLC 17**
See also AW 1; DLB 176; RGWL

**Herrick, Robert** 1591-1674 ........ **LC 13; DA; DAB; DAC; DAM MST, POET; PC 9**
See also BRW 2; DLB 126; EXPP; PFS 13; RGAL; RGEL; WP

**Herring, Guilles**
See Somerville, Edith

**Herriot, James** ............ **CLC 12; DAM POP**
See also Wight, James Alfred
See also AAYA 1; BPFB 2; CA 148; CANR 40; LAIT 3; MAICYAS; MTCW 2; SATA 86

**Herris, Violet**
See Hunt, Violet

**Herrmann, Dorothy** 1941- ................. **CLC 44**
See also CA 107

**Herrmann, Taffy**
See Herrmann, Dorothy

**Hersey, John (Richard)** 1914-1993 .... **CLC 1, 2, 7, 9, 40, 81, 97; DAM POP**
See also AAYA 29; BPFB 2; CA 17-20R; 140; CANR 33; CDALBS; CPW; DLB 6, 185; MTCW 1, 2; SATA 25; SATA-Obit 76

**Herzen, Aleksandr Ivanovich**
1812-1870 ........................ **NCLC 10, 61**

**Herzl, Theodor** 1860-1904 ............. **TCLC 36**
See also CA 168

**Herzog, Werner** 1942- ..................... **CLC 16**
See also CA 89-92

**Hesiod** c. 8th cent. B.C.- ................. **CMLC 5**
See also AW 1; DLB 176; RGWL

**Hesse, Hermann** 1877-1962 ... **CLC 1, 2, 3, 6, 11, 17, 25, 69; DA; DAB; DAC; DAM MST, NOV; SSC 9; WLC**
See also BPFB 2; CA 17-18; CAP 2; DA3; DLB 66; EW; EXPN; LAIT 1; MTCW 1, 2; NFS 6; RGWL; SATA 50

**Hewes, Cady**
See De Voto, Bernard (Augustine)

**Heyen, William** 1940- ................. **CLC 13, 18**
See also CA 33-36R; CAAS 9; CANR 98; CP; DLB 5

**Heyerdahl, Thor** 1914- .................... **CLC 26**
See also CA 5-8R; CANR 5, 22, 66, 73; LAIT 4; MTCW 1, 2; SATA 2, 52

**Heym, Georg (Theodor Franz Arthur)** 1887-1912 ..................... **TCLC 9**
See also CA 106; 181

**Heym, Stefan** 1913- ..................... **CLC 41**
See also CA 9-12R; CANR 4; CWW 2; DLB 69

**Heyse, Paul (Johann Ludwig von)** 1830-1914 ..................... **TCLC 8**
See also CA 104; DLB 129

**Heyward, (Edwin) DuBose** 1885-1940 ..................... **TCLC 59**
See also CA 108; 157; DLB 7, 9, 45; SATA 21

**Heywood, John** 1497-1580 ................... **LC 65**
See also RGEL

**Hibbert, Eleanor Alice Burford** 1906-1993 ............... **CLC 7; DAM POP**
See also Holt, Victoria
See also BEST 90:4; CA 17-20R; 140; CANR 9, 28, 59; CMW; CPW; MTCW 2; RHW; SATA 2; SATA-Obit 74

**Hichens, Robert (Smythe)** 1864-1950 ..................... **TCLC 64**
See also CA 162; DLB 153; HGG; RHW; SUFW

**Higgins, George V(incent)** 1939-1999 ..................... **CLC 4, 7, 10, 18**
See also BPFB 2; CA 77-80; 186; CAAS 5; CANR 17, 51, 89, 96; CMW; CN; DLB 2; DLBY 81, 98; INT CANR-17; MSW; MTCW 1

**Higginson, Thomas Wentworth** 1823-1911 ..................... **TCLC 36**
See also CA 162; DLB 1, 64, 243

**Higgonet, Margaret** ed. .................... **CLC 65**

**Highet, Helen**
See MacInnes, Helen (Clark)

**Highsmith, (Mary) Patricia** 1921-1995 ........... **CLC 2, 4, 14, 42, 102; DAM NOV, POP**
See also Morgan, Claire
See also BRWS 5; CA 1-4R; 147; CANR 1, 20, 48, 62; CMW; CPW; DA3; MSW; MTCW 1, 2

**Highwater, Jamake (Mamake)** 1942(?)-2001 ..................... **CLC 12**
See also AAYA 7; BPFB 2; BYA 4; CA 65-68; CAAS 7; CANR 10, 34, 84; CLR 17; CWRI; DLB 52; DLBY 85; JRDA; MAICYA; SATA 32, 69; SATA-Brief 30

**Highway, Tomson** 1951- ......... **CLC 92; DAC; DAM MULT**
See also CA 151; CANR 75; CCA 1; CD; DFS 2; MTCW 2; NNAL

**Hijuelos, Oscar** 1951- ........... **CLC 65; DAM MULT, POP; HLC 1**
See also AAYA 25; AMWS 8; BEST 90:1; CA 123; CANR 50, 75; CPW; DA3; DLB 145; HW 1, 2; MTCW 2; RGAL; WLIT 1

**Hikmet, Nazim** 1902(?)-1963 ............ **CLC 40**
See also CA 141; 93-96

**Hildegard von Bingen** 1098-1179 . **CMLC 20**
See also DLB 148

**Hildesheimer, Wolfgang** 1916-1991 .. **CLC 49**
See also CA 101; 135; DLB 69, 124

**Hill, Geoffrey (William)** 1932- ...... **CLC 5, 8, 18, 45; DAM POET**
See also BRWS 5; CA 81-84; CANR 21, 89; CDBLB 1960 to Present; CP; DLB 40; MTCW 1; RGEL

**Hill, George Roy** 1921- ..................... **CLC 26**
See also CA 110; 122

**Hill, John**
See Koontz, Dean R(ay)

**Hill, Susan (Elizabeth)** 1942- .... **CLC 4, 113; DAB; DAM MST, NOV**
See also CA 33-36R; CANR 29, 69; CN; DLB 14, 139; HGG; MTCW 1; RHW

**Hillard, Asa G. III** ......................... **CLC 70**

**Hillerman, Tony** 1925- .. **CLC 62; DAM POP**
See also AAYA 40; BEST 89:1; BPFB 2; CA 29-32R; CANR 21, 42, 65, 97; CMW; CPW; DA3; DLB 206; MSW; RGAL; SATA 6; TCWW 2; YAW

**Hillesum, Etty** 1914-1943 ............... **TCLC 49**
See also CA 137

**Hilliard, Noel (Harvey)** 1929-1996 ... **CLC 15**
See also CA 9-12R; CANR 7, 69; CN

**Hillis, Rick** 1956- ............................. **CLC 66**
See also CA 134

**Hilton, James** 1900-1954 ................ **TCLC 21**
See also CA 108; 169; DLB 34, 77; FANT; SATA 34

**Himes, Chester (Bomar)** 1909-1984 .. **CLC 2, 4, 7, 18, 58, 108; BLC 2; DAM MULT**
See also AFAW 2; BPFB 2; BW 2; CA 25-28R; 114; CANR 22, 89; CMW; DLB 2, 76, 143, 226; MSW; MTCW 1, 2; RGAL

**Hinde, Thomas** ..................... **CLC 6, 11**
See also Chitty, Thomas Willes

**Hine, (William) Daryl** 1936- ............ **CLC 15**
See also CA 1-4R; CAAS 15; CANR 1, 20; CP; DLB 60

**Hinkson, Katharine Tynan**
See Tynan, Katharine

**Hinojosa(-Smith), Rolando (R.)** 1929-
See also CA 131; CAAS 16; CANR 62; DAM MULT; DLB 82; HLC 1; HW 1, 2; MTCW 2; RGAL

**Hinton, S(usan) E(loise)** 1950- ......... **CLC 30, 111; DA; DAB; DAC; DAM MST, NOV**
See also AAYA 2, 33; BPFB 2; BYA 2, 3; CA 81-84; CANR 32, 62, 92; CDALBS; CLR 3, 23; CPW; DA3; JRDA; LAIT 5; MAICYA; MTCW 1, 2; NFS 5, 9; SATA 19, 58, 115; WYA; YAW

**Hippius, Zinaida** ......................... **TCLC 9**
See also Gippius, Zinaida (Nikolayevna)

**Hiraoka, Kimitake** 1925-1970
See Mishima, Yukio
See also CA 97-100; 29-32R; DA3; DAM DRAM; MTCW 1, 2; SSFS 12

**Hirsch, E(ric) D(onald), Jr.** 1928- .... **CLC 79**
See also CA 25-28R; CANR 27, 51; DLB 67; INT CANR-27; MTCW 1

**Hirsch, Edward** 1950- ................. **CLC 31, 50**
See also CA 104; CANR 20, 42, 102; CP; DLB 120

**Hitchcock, Alfred (Joseph)** 1899-1980 ..................... **CLC 16**
See also AAYA 22; CA 159; 97-100; SATA 27; SATA-Obit 24

**Hitler, Adolf** 1889-1945 ................. **TCLC 53**
See also CA 117; 147

**Hoagland, Edward** 1932- ............... **CLC 28**
See also ANW; CA 1-4R; CANR 2, 31, 57; CN; DLB 6; SATA 51; TCWW 2

**Hoban, Russell (Conwell)** 1925- . **CLC 7, 25; DAM NOV**
See also BPFB 2; CA 5-8R; CANR 23, 37, 66; CLR 3, 69; CN; CWRI; DLB 52; FANT; MAICYA; MTCW 1, 2; SATA 1, 40, 78; SFW

**Hobbes, Thomas** 1588-1679 ................. **LC 36**
See also DLB 151; RGEL

**Hobbs, Perry**
See Blackmur, R(ichard) P(almer)

**Hobson, Laura Z(ametkin)** 1900-1986 ..................... **CLC 7, 25**
See also Field, Peter
See also BPFB 2; CA 17-20R; 118; CANR 55; DLB 28; SATA 52

**Hoch, Edward D(entinger)** 1930-
See Queen, Ellery
See also CA 29-32R; CANR 11, 27, 51, 97; CMW; SFW

**Hochhuth, Rolf** 1931- .. **CLC 4, 11, 18; DAM DRAM**
See also CA 5-8R; CANR 33, 75; CWW 2; DLB 124; MTCW 1, 2

**Hochman, Sandra** 1936- ................. **CLC 3, 8**
See also CA 5-8R; DLB 5

**Hochwaelder, Fritz** 1911-1986 ......... **CLC 36; DAM DRAM**
See also Hochwalder, Fritz
See also CA 29-32R; 120; CANR 42; MTCW 1

**Hochwalder, Fritz**
See Hochwaelder, Fritz
See also RGWL

**Hocking, Mary (Eunice)** 1921- ......... **CLC 13**
See also CA 101; CANR 18, 40

**Hodgins, Jack** 1938- ..................... **CLC 23**
See also CA 93-96; CN; DLB 60

**Hodgson, William Hope** 1877(?)-1918 ............................. **TCLC 13**
See also CA 111; 164; CMW; DLB 70, 153, 156, 178; HGG; MTCW 2; SFW

**Hoeg, Peter** 1957- ........................ **CLC 95**
See also CA 151; CANR 75; CMW; DA3; MTCW 2

**Hoffman, Alice** 1952- .. **CLC 51; DAM NOV**
See also AAYA 37; CA 77-80; CANR 34, 66, 100; CN; CPW; MTCW 1, 2

**Hoffman, Daniel (Gerard)** 1923- . **CLC 6, 13, 23**
See also CA 1-4R; CANR 4; CP; DLB 5

**Hoffman, Stanley** 1944- ..................... **CLC 5**
See also CA 77-80

**Hoffman, William** 1925- ................. **CLC 141**
See also CA 21-24R; CANR 9, 103; CSW; DLB 234

**Hoffman, William M(oses)** 1939- ...... **CLC 40**
See also CA 57-60; CANR 11, 71

**Hoffmann, E(rnst) T(heodor) A(madeus)** 1776-1822 ............... **NCLC 2; SSC 13**
See also DLB 90; EW; RGSF; RGWL; SATA 27; SUFW; WCH

**Hofmann, Gert** 1931- ........................ **CLC 54**
See also CA 128

**Hofmannsthal, Hugo von** 1874-1929 ...... **TCLC 11; DAM DRAM; DC 4**
See also CA 106; 153; DFS 12; DLB 81, 118; EW; RGWL

**Hogan, Linda** 1947- . **CLC 73; DAM MULT; PC 35**
See also AMWS 4; ANW; BYA 12; CA 120; CANR 45, 73; CWP; DLB 175; NNAL; TCWW 2

**Hogarth, Charles**
See Creasey, John

**Hogarth, Emmett**
See Polonsky, Abraham (Lincoln)

**Hogg, James** 1770-1835 ................... **NCLC 4**
See also DLB 93, 116, 159; HGG; RGEL

**Holbach, Paul Henri Thiry Baron** 1723-1789 ..................... **LC 14**

**Holberg, Ludvig** 1684-1754 ................... **LC 6**
See also RGWL

**Holcroft, Thomas** 1745-1809 ........... **NCLC 85**
See also DLB 39, 89, 158; RGEL

**Holden, Ursula** 1921- ......................... **CLC 18**
See also CA 101; CAAS 8; CANR 22

**Holderlin, (Johann Christian) Friedrich** 1770-1843 ..................... **NCLC 16; PC 4**
See also EW; RGWL

**Holdstock, Robert**
See Holdstock, Robert P.

**Holdstock, Robert P.** 1948- ............... **CLC 39**
 See also CA 131; CANR 81; FANT; HGG; SFW
**Holinshed, Raphael** fl. 1580- ............... **LC 69**
 See also DLB 167; RGEL
**Holland, Isabelle** 1920- .................... **CLC 21**
 See also AAYA 11; CA 21-24R, 181; CAAE 181; CANR 10, 25, 47; CLR 57; CWRI; JRDA; LAIT 4; MAICYA; SATA 8, 70; SATA-Essay 103
**Holland, Marcus**
 See Caldwell, (Janet Miriam) Taylor (Holland)
**Hollander, John** 1929- ......... **CLC 2, 5, 8, 14**
 See also CA 1-4R; CANR 1, 52; CP; DLB 5; SATA 13
**Hollander, Paul**
 See Silverberg, Robert
**Holleran, Andrew** 1943(?)- ................ **CLC 38**
 See also Garber, Eric
 See also CA 144; GLL 1
**Holley, Marietta** 1836(?)-1926 ........ **TCLC 99**
 See also CA 118; DLB 11
**Hollinghurst, Alan** 1954- ............ **CLC 55, 91**
 See also CA 114; CN; DLB 207; GLL 1
**Hollis, Jim**
 See Summers, Hollis (Spurgeon, Jr.)
**Holly, Buddy** 1936-1959 ................ **TCLC 65**
**Holmes, Gordon**
 See Shiel, M(atthew) P(hipps)
**Holmes, John**
 See Souster, (Holmes) Raymond
**Holmes, John Clellon** 1926-1988 ...... **CLC 56**
 See also CA 9-12R; 125; CANR 4; DLB 16, 237
**Holmes, Oliver Wendell, Jr.**
 1841-1935 ..................... **TCLC 77**
 See also CA 114; 186
**Holmes, Oliver Wendell**
 1809-1894 .......................... **NCLC 14, 81**
 See also AMWS 1; CDALB 1640-1865; DLB 1, 189, 235; EXPP; RGAL; SATA 34
**Holmes, Raymond**
 See Souster, (Holmes) Raymond
**Holt, Victoria**
 See Hibbert, Eleanor Alice Burford
 See also BPFB 2
**Holub, Miroslav** 1923-1998 ................. **CLC 4**
 See also CA 21-24R; 169; CANR 10; CWW 2; DLB 232
**Homer** c. 8th cent. B.C.- .. **CMLC 1, 16; DA; DAB; DAC; DAM MST, POET; PC 23; WLCS**
 See also AW 1; DA3; DLB 176; EFS 1; LAIT 1; RGWL; WP
**Hongo, Garrett Kaoru** 1951- ................ **PC 23**
 See also CA 133; CAAS 22; CP; DLB 120; EXPP; RGAL
**Honig, Edwin** 1919- ........................ **CLC 33**
 See also CA 5-8R; CAAS 8; CANR 4, 45; CP; DLB 5
**Hood, Hugh (John Blagdon)** 1928- . **CLC 15, 28; SSC 42**
 See also CA 49-52; CAAS 17; CANR 1, 33, 87; CN; DLB 53; RGSF
**Hood, Thomas** 1799-1845 ............... **NCLC 16**
 See also BRW 4; DLB 96; RGEL
**Hooker, (Peter) Jeremy** 1941- ........... **CLC 43**
 See also CA 77-80; CANR 22; CP; DLB 40
**Hope, A(lec) D(erwent)** 1907-2000 .... **CLC 3, 51**
 See also BRWS 7; CA 21-24R; 188; CANR 33, 74; MTCW 1, 2; PFS 8; RGEL
**Hope, Anthony** 1863-1933 ............... **TCLC 83**
 See also CA 157; DLB 153, 156; RGEL; RHW
**Hope, Brian**
 See Creasey, John

**Hope, Christopher (David Tully)**
 1944- ............................................. **CLC 52**
 See also AFW; CA 106; CANR 47, 101; CN; DLB 225; SATA 62
**Hopkins, Gerard Manley**
 1844-1889 ............ **NCLC 17; DA; DAB; DAC; DAM MST, POET; PC 15; WLC**
 See also BRW 5; CDBLB 1890-1914; DA3; DLB 35, 57; EXPP; PAB; RGEL; WP
**Hopkins, John (Richard)** 1931-1998 .. **CLC 4**
 See also CA 85-88; 169; CBD; CD
**Hopkins, Pauline Elizabeth**
 1859-1930 ...... **TCLC 28; BLC 2; DAM MULT**
 See also AFAW 2; BW 2, 3; CA 141; CANR 82; DLB 50
**Hopkinson, Francis** 1737-1791 ............ **LC 25**
 See also DLB 31; RGAL
**Hopley-Woolrich, Cornell George** 1903-1968
 See Woolrich, Cornell
 See also CA 13-14; CANR 58; CAP 1; CMW; DLB 226; MTCW 2
**Horace** 65B.C.-8B.C. ...................... **CMLC 39**
 See also AW 2; DLB 211; RGWL
**Horatio**
 See Proust, (Valentin-Louis-George-Eugene-)Marcel
**Horgan, Paul (George Vincent O'Shaughnessy)** 1903-1995 . **CLC 9, 53; DAM NOV**
 See also BPFB 2; CA 13-16R; 147; CANR 9, 35; DLB 212; DLBY 85; INT CANR-9; MTCW 1, 2; SATA 13; SATA-Obit 84; TCWW 2
**Horn, Peter**
 See Kuttner, Henry
**Hornem, Horace Esq.**
 See Byron, George Gordon (Noel)
**Horney, Karen (Clementine Theodore Danielsen)** 1885-1952 ............. **TCLC 71**
 See also CA 114; 165; DLB 246; FW
**Hornung, E(rnest) W(illiam)**
 1866-1921 ................................. **TCLC 59**
 See also CA 108; 160; CMW; DLB 70
**Horovitz, Israel (Arthur)** 1939- ....... **CLC 56; DAM DRAM**
 See also CA 33-36R; CAD; CANR 46, 59; CD; DLB 7
**Horton, George Moses**
 1797(?)-1883(?) ........................ **NCLC 87**
 See also DLB 50
**Horvath, Odon von** 1901-1938 ....... **TCLC 45**
 See von Horvath, Oedoen
 See also CA 118; 194; DLB 85, 124; RGWL
**Horvath, Oedoen von** -1938
 See Horvath, Odon von
**Horwitz, Julius** 1920-1986 ................ **CLC 14**
 See also CA 9-12R; 119; CANR 12
**Hospital, Janette Turner** 1942- ........ **CLC 42, 145**
 See also CA 108; CANR 48; CN; RGSF
**Hostos, E. M. de**
 See Hostos (y Bonilla), Eugenio Maria de
**Hostos, Eugenio M. de**
 See Hostos (y Bonilla), Eugenio Maria de
**Hostos, Eugenio Maria**
 See Hostos (y Bonilla), Eugenio Maria de
**Hostos (y Bonilla), Eugenio Maria de**
 1839-1903 ................ **TCLC 24**
 See also CA 123; 131; HW 1
**Houdini**
 See Lovecraft, H(oward) P(hillips)
**Hougan, Carolyn** 1943- ..................... **CLC 34**
 See also CA 139
**Household, Geoffrey (Edward West)**
 1900-1988 ................................. **CLC 11**
 See also CA 77-80; 126; CANR 58; CMW; DLB 87; SATA 14; SATA-Obit 59

**Housman, A(lfred) E(dward)**
 1859-1936 ........ **TCLC 1, 10; DA; DAB; DAC; DAM MST, POET; PC 2; WLCS**
 See also BRW 6; CA 104; 125; DA3; DLB 19; EXPP; MTCW 1, 2; PAB; PFS 4, 7; RGEL; WP
**Housman, Laurence** 1865-1959 ........ **TCLC 7**
 See also CA 106; 155; DLB 10; FANT; RGEL; SATA 25
**Howard, Elizabeth Jane** 1923- ..... **CLC 7, 29**
 See also CA 5-8R; CANR 8, 62; CN
**Howard, Maureen** 1930- ........ **CLC 5, 14, 46, 151**
 See also CA 53-56; CANR 31, 75; CN; DLBY 83; INT CANR-31; MTCW 1, 2
**Howard, Richard** 1929- .......... **CLC 7, 10, 47**
 See also AITN 1; CA 85-88; CANR 25, 80; CP; DLB 5; INT CANR-25
**Howard, Robert E(rvin)**
 1906-1936 ......................... **TCLC 8**
 See also BPFB 2; BYA 5; CA 105; 157; FANT; SUFW
**Howard, Warren F.**
 See Pohl, Frederik
**Howe, Fanny (Quincy)** 1940- ............. **CLC 47**
 See also CA 117; CAAE 187; CAAS 27; CANR 70; CP; CWP; SATA-Brief 52
**Howe, Irving** 1920-1993 ..................... **CLC 85**
 See also AMWS 6; CA 9-12R; 141; CANR 21, 50; DLB 67; MTCW 1, 2
**Howe, Julia Ward** 1819-1910 ......... **TCLC 21**
 See also CA 117; 191; DLB 1, 189, 235; FW
**Howe, Susan** 1937- ................................ **CLC 72**
 See also AMWS 4; CA 160; CP; CWP; DLB 120; FW; RGAL
**Howe, Tina** 1937- ............................... **CLC 48**
 See also CA 109; CAD; CD; CWD
**Howell, James** 1594(?)-1666 ................ **LC 13**
 See also DLB 151
**Howells, W. D.**
 See Howells, William Dean
**Howells, William D.**
 See Howells, William Dean
**Howells, William Dean** 1837-1920 .. **TCLC 7, 17, 41; SSC 36**
 See also AMW; CA 104; 134; CDALB 1865-1917; DLB 12, 64, 74, 79, 189; MTCW 2; RGAL
**Howes, Barbara** 1914-1996 ............... **CLC 15**
 See also CA 9-12R; 151; CAAS 3; CANR 53; CP; SATA 5
**Hrabal, Bohumil** 1914-1997 ........ **CLC 13, 67**
 See also CA 106; 156; CAAS 12; CANR 57; CWW 2; DLB 232; RGSF
**Hrostwitha of Gandersheim** c. 935-c. 1000 ........................................ **CMLC 29**
 See also DLB 148
**Hsi, Chu** 1130-1200 ........................ **CMLC 42**
**Hsun, Lu**
 See Lu Hsun
**Hubbard, L(afayette) Ron(ald)**
 1911-1986 ............... **CLC 43; DAM POP**
 See also CA 77-80; 118; CANR 52; CPW; DA3; FANT; MTCW 2; SFW
**Huch, Ricarda (Octavia)**
 1864-1947 ................................. **TCLC 13**
 See also CA 111; 189; DLB 66
**Huddle, David** 1942- ......................... **CLC 49**
 See also CA 57-60; CAAS 20; CANR 89; DLB 130
**Hudson, Jeffrey**
 See Crichton, (John) Michael
**Hudson, W(illiam) H(enry)**
 1841-1922 ................................. **TCLC 29**
 See also CA 115; 190; DLB 98, 153, 174; RGEL; SATA 35

**Hueffer, Ford Madox**
See Ford, Ford Madox

**Hughart, Barry** 1934- ............... **CLC 39**
See also CA 137; FANT; SFW

**Hughes, Colin**
See Creasey, John

**Hughes, David (John)** 1930- ........... **CLC 48**
See also CA 116; 129; CN; DLB 14

**Hughes, Edward James**
See Hughes, Ted
See also DA3; DAM MST, POET

**Hughes, (James) Langston**
1902-1967 ....... **CLC 1, 5, 10, 15, 35, 44, 108; BLC 2; DA; DAB; DAC; DAM DRAM, MST, MULT, POET; DC 3; PC 1; SSC 6; WLC**
See also AAYA 12; AFAW 1, 2; AMWR 1; AMWS 1; BW 1, 3; CA 1-4R; 25-28R; CANR 1, 34, 82; CDALB 1929-1941; CLR 17; DA3; DLB 4, 7, 48, 51, 86, 228; EXPP 1, X; EXPS; JRDA; LAIT 3; MAICYA; MTCW 1, 2; PAB; PFS 1, 3, 6, 10; RGAL; RGSF; SATA 4, 33; SSFS 4, 7; WCH; WP; YAW

**Hughes, Richard (Arthur Warren)**
1900-1976 ......... **CLC 1, 11; DAM NOV**
See also CA 5-8R; 65-68; CANR 4; DLB 15, 161; MTCW 1; RGEL; SATA 8; SATA-Obit 25

**Hughes, Ted** 1930-1998 . **CLC 2, 4, 9, 14, 37, 119; DAB; DAC; PC 7**
See also Hughes, Edward James
See also BRWS 1; CA 1-4R; 171; CANR 1, 33, 66; CLR 3; CP; DLB 40, 161; EXPP; MAICYA; MTCW 1, 2; PAB; PFS 4; RGEL; SATA 49; SATA-Brief 27; SATA-Obit 107; YAW

**Hugo, Richard**
See Huch, Ricarda (Octavia)

**Hugo, Richard F(ranklin)**
1923-1982 ............. **CLC 6, 18, 32; DAM POET**
See also AMWS 6; CA 49-52; 108; CANR 3; DLB 5, 206; RGAL

**Hugo, Victor (Marie)** 1802-1885 .... **NCLC 3, 10, 21; DA; DAB; DAC; DAM DRAM, MST, NOV, POET; PC 17; WLC**
See also AAYA 28; DA3; DLB 119, 192; EFS 2; EW; EXPN; GFL 1789 to the Present; LAIT 1, 2; NFS 5; RGWL; SATA 47

**Huidobro, Vicente**
See Huidobro Fernandez, Vicente Garcia
See also LAW

**Huidobro Fernandez, Vicente Garcia**
1893-1948 ....................... **TCLC 31**
See also Huidobro, Vicente
See also CA 131; HW 1

**Hulme, Keri** 1947- ..................... **CLC 39, 130**
See also CA 125; CANR 69; CN; CP; CWP; FW; INT 125

**Hulme, T(homas) E(rnest)**
1883-1917 ................. **TCLC 21**
See also BRWS 6; CA 117; DLB 19

**Hume, David** 1711-1776 ................... **LC 7, 56**
See also BRWS 3; DLB 104

**Humphrey, William** 1924-1997 ......... **CLC 45**
See also AMWS 9; CA 77-80; 160; CANR 68; CN; CSW; DLB 212; TCWW 2

**Humphreys, Emyr Owen** 1919- ........ **CLC 47**
See also CA 5-8R; CANR 3, 24; CN; DLB 15

**Humphreys, Josephine** 1945- ..... **CLC 34, 57**
See also CA 121; 127; CANR 97; CSW; INT 127

**Huneker, James Gibbons**
1860-1921 ....................... **TCLC 65**
See also CA 193; DLB 71; RGAL

**Hungerford, Pixie**
See Brinsmead, H(esba) F(ay)

**Hunt, E(verette) Howard, (Jr.)**
1918- ............................... **CLC 3**
See also AITN 1; CA 45-48; CANR 2, 47, 103; CMW

**Hunt, Francesca**
See Holland, Isabelle

**Hunt, Howard**
See Hunt, E(verette) Howard, (Jr.)

**Hunt, Kyle**
See Creasey, John

**Hunt, (James Henry) Leigh**
1784-1859 .... **NCLC 1, 70; DAM POET**
See also DLB 96, 110, 144; RGEL; TEA

**Hunt, Marsha** 1946- ........................ **CLC 70**
See also BW 2, 3; CA 143; CANR 79

**Hunt, Violet** 1866(?)-1942 .............. **TCLC 53**
See also CA 184; DLB 162, 197

**Hunter, E. Waldo**
See Sturgeon, Theodore (Hamilton)

**Hunter, Evan** 1926- ......... **CLC 11, 31; DAM POP**
See also McBain, Ed
See also AAYA 39; BPFB 2; CA 5-8R; CANR 5, 38, 62, 97; CMW; CN; CPW; DLBY 82; INT CANR-5; MSW; MTCW 1; SATA 25; SFW

**Hunter, Kristin (Eggleston)** 1931- .... **CLC 35**
See also AITN 1; BW 1; BYA 3; CA 13-16R; CANR 13; CLR 3; CN; DLB 33; INT CANR-13; MAICYA; SAAS 10; SATA 12; YAW

**Hunter, Mary**
See Austin, Mary (Hunter)

**Hunter, Mollie** 1922- ........................ **CLC 21**
See also McIlwraith, Maureen Mollie Hunter
See also AAYA 13; BYA 6; CANR 37, 78; CLR 25; DLB 161; JRDA; MAICYA; SAAS 7; SATA 54, 106; YAW

**Hunter, Robert** (?)-1734 ...................... **LC 7**

**Hurston, Zora Neale** 1891-1960 .. **CLC 7, 30, 61; BLC 2; DA; DAC; DAM MST, MULT, NOV; DC 12; SSC 4; WLCS**
See also AAYA 15; AFAW 1, 2; AMWS 6; BW 1, 3; BYA 12; CA 85-88; CANR 61; CDALBS; DA3; DFS 6; DLB 51, 86; EXPN; EXPS; FW; LAIT 3; MAWW; MTCW 1, 2; NFS 3; RGAL; RGSF; SSFS 1, 6, 11; YAW

**Husserl, E. G.**
See Husserl, Edmund (Gustav Albrecht)

**Husserl, Edmund (Gustav Albrecht)**
1859-1938 ........................ **TCLC 100**
See also CA 116; 133

**Huston, John (Marcellus)**
1906-1987 ...................... **CLC 20**
See also CA 73-76; 123; CANR 34; DLB 26

**Hustvedt, Siri** 1955- ........................ **CLC 76**
See also CA 137

**Hutten, Ulrich von** 1488-1523 .......... **LC 16**
See also DLB 179

**Huxley, Aldous (Leonard)**
1894-1963 ....... **CLC 1, 3, 4, 5, 8, 11, 18, 35, 79; DA; DAB; DAC; DAM MST, NOV; SSC 39; WLC**
See also AAYA 11; BPFB 2; BRW 7; CA 85-88; CANR 44, 99; CDBLB 1914-1945; DA3; DLB 36, 100, 162, 195; EXPN; LAIT 5; MTCW 1, 2; NFS 6; RGEL; SATA 63; SCFW 2; SFW; YAW

**Huxley, T(homas) H(enry)**
1825-1895 ....................... **NCLC 67**
See also DLB 57

**Huysmans, Joris-Karl** 1848-1907 ... **TCLC 7, 69**
See also CA 104; 165; DLB 123; EW; GFL 1789 to the Present; RGWL

**Hwang, David Henry** 1957- .. **CLC 55; DAM DRAM; DC 4**
See also CA 127; 132; CAD; CANR 76; CD; DA3; DFS 11; DLB 212; INT 132; MTCW 2; RGAL

**Hyde, Anthony** 1946- ..................... **CLC 42**
See also Chase, Nicholas
See also CA 136; CCA 1

**Hyde, Margaret O(ldroyd)** 1917- ..... **CLC 21**
See also CA 1-4R; CANR 1, 36; CLR 23; JRDA; MAICYA; SAAS 8; SATA 1, 42, 76

**Hynes, James** 1956(?)- ..................... **CLC 65**
See also CA 164

**Hypatia** c. 370-415 ........................ **CMLC 35**

**Ian, Janis** 1951- ............................. **CLC 21**
See also CA 105; 187

**Ibanez, Vicente Blasco**
See Blasco Ibanez, Vicente

**Ibarbourou, Juana de** 1895-1979
See also HLCS 2; HW 1; LAW

**Ibarguengoitia, Jorge** 1928-1983 ...... **CLC 37**
See also CA 124; 113; HW 1

**Ibsen, Henrik (Johan)** 1828-1906 ... **TCLC 2, 8, 16, 37, 52; DA; DAB; DAC; DAM DRAM, MST; DC 2; WLC**
See also CA 104; 141; DA3; DFS 1, 6, 8, 10, 11; EW; LAIT 2; RGWL

**Ibuse, Masuji** 1898-1993 ................... **CLC 22**
See also CA 127; 141; DLB 180; MJW

**Ichikawa, Kon** 1915- ....................... **CLC 20**
See also CA 121

**Ichiyo, Higuchi** 1872-1896 .............. **NCLC 49**
See also MJW

**Idle, Eric** 1943-2000 ........................ **CLC 21**
See also Monty Python
See also CA 116; CANR 35, 91

**Ignatow, David** 1914-1997 ....... **CLC 4, 7, 14, 40; PC 34**
See also CA 9-12R; 162; CAAS 3; CANR 31, 57, 96; CP; DLB 5

**Ignotus**
See Strachey, (Giles) Lytton

**Ihimaera, Witi** 1944- ...................... **CLC 46**
See also CA 77-80; CN; RGSF

**Ilf, Ilya** ................................ **TCLC 21**
See also Fainzilberg, Ilya Arnoldovich

**Illyes, Gyula** 1902-1983 ...................... **PC 16**
See also CA 114; 109; DLB 215; RGWL

**Immermann, Karl (Lebrecht)**
1796-1840 .................... **NCLC 4, 49**
See also DLB 133

**Ince, Thomas H.** 1882-1924 ............ **TCLC 89**
See also IDFW 3, 4

**Inchbald, Elizabeth** 1753-1821 ....... **NCLC 62**
See also DLB 39, 89; RGEL

**Inclan, Ramon (Maria) del Valle**
See Valle-Inclan, Ramon (Maria) del

**Infante, G(uillermo) Cabrera**
See Cabrera Infante, G(uillermo)

**Ingalls, Rachel (Holmes)** 1940- ......... **CLC 42**
See also CA 123; 127

**Ingamells, Reginald Charles**
See Ingamells, Rex

**Ingamells, Rex** 1913-1955 ............... **TCLC 35**
See also CA 167

**Inge, William (Motter)** 1913-1973 .... **CLC 1, 8, 19; DAM DRAM**
See also CA 9-12R; CDALB 1941-1968; DA3; DFS 1, 5, 8; DLB 7; MTCW 1, 2; RGAL

**Ingelow, Jean** 1820-1897 ................ **NCLC 39**
See also DLB 35, 163; FANT; SATA 33

**Ingram, Willis J.**
See Harris, Mark

**Innaurato, Albert (F.)** 1948(?)- ... **CLC 21, 60**
See also CA 115; 122; CAD; CANR 78; CD; INT CA-122

**Innes, Michael**
See Stewart, J(ohn) I(nnes) M(ackintosh)
See also MSW

**Innis, Harold Adams** 1894-1952 .... **TCLC 77**
See also CA 181; DLB 88

**Ionesco, Eugene** 1912-1994 ... **CLC 1, 4, 6, 9, 11, 15, 41, 86; DA; DAB; DAC; DAM DRAM, MST; DC 12; WLC**
See also CA 9-12R; 144; CANR 55; CWW 2; DA3; DFS 4, 9; EW; GFL 1789 to the Present; MTCW 1, 2; RGWL; SATA 7; SATA-Obit 79

**Iqbal, Muhammad** 1877-1938 ........ **TCLC 28**

**Ireland, Patrick**
See O'Doherty, Brian

**Irenaeus St.** 130- .............................. **CMLC 42**

**Iron, Ralph**
See Schreiner, Olive (Emilie Albertina)

**Irving, John (Winslow)** 1942- ... **CLC 13, 23, 38, 112; DAM NOV, POP**
See also AAYA 8; AMWS 6; BEST 89:3; BPFB 2; CA 25-28R; CANR 28, 73; CN; CPW; DA3; DLB 6; DLBY 82; MTCW 1, 2; NFS 12; RGAL

**Irving, Washington** 1783-1859 . **NCLC 2, 19, 95; DA; DAB; DAC; DAM MST; SSC 2, 37; WLC**
See also AMW; CDALB 1640-1865; DA3; DLB 3, 11, 30, 59, 73, 74, 186; EXPS; LAIT 1; RGAL; RGSF; SSFS 1, 8; YABC 2

**Irwin, P. K.**
See Page, P(atricia) K(athleen)

**Isaacs, Jorge Ricardo** 1837-1895 ... **NCLC 70**
See also LAW

**Isaacs, Susan** 1943- ....... **CLC 32; DAM POP**
See also BEST 89:1; BPFB 2; CA 89-92; CANR 20, 41, 65; CPW; DA3; INT CANR-20; MTCW 1, 2

**Isherwood, Christopher (William Bradshaw)** 1904-1986 .. **CLC 1, 9, 11, 14, 44; DAM DRAM, NOV**
See also BRW 7; CA 13-16R; 117; CANR 35, 97; DA3; DLB 15, 195; DLBY 86; IDTP; MTCW 1, 2; RGAL; RGEL; WLIT 4

**Ishiguro, Kazuo** 1954- . **CLC 27, 56, 59, 110; DAM NOV**
See also BEST 90:2; BPFB 2; BRWS 4; CA 120; CANR 49, 95; CN; DA3; DLB 194; MTCW 1, 2; WLIT 4

**Ishikawa, Hakuhin**
See Ishikawa, Takuboku

**Ishikawa, Takuboku** 1886(?)-1912 ... **TCLC 15; DAM POET; PC 10**
See also CA 113; 153

**Iskander, Fazil** 1929- ........................ **CLC 47**
See also CA 102

**Isler, Alan (David)** 1934- .................... **CLC 91**
See also CA 156

**Ivan IV** 1530-1584 ............................... **LC 17**

**Ivanov, Vyacheslav Ivanovich** 1866-1949 .................. **TCLC 33**
See also CA 122

**Ivask, Ivar Vidrik** 1927-1992 ............ **CLC 14**
See also CA 37-40R; 139; CANR 24

**Ives, Morgan**
See Bradley, Marion Zimmer
See also GLL 1

**Izumi Shikibu** c. 973-c. 1034 ........ **CMLC 33**

**Auchincloss, Louis (Stanton)** 1917- .. **CLC 4, 6, 9, 18, 45; DAM NOV; SSC 22**
See also AMWS 4; CA 1-4R; CANR 6, 29, 55, 87; CN; DLB 2, 244; DLBY 80; INT CANR-29; MTCW 1; RGAL

**J. R. S.**
See Gogarty, Oliver St. John

**Jabran, Kahlil**
See Gibran, Kahlil

**Jabran, Khalil**
See Gibran, Kahlil

**Jackson, Daniel**
See Wingrove, David (John)

**Jackson, Helen Hunt** 1830-1885 .... **NCLC 90**
See also DLB 42, 47, 186, 189; RGAL

**Jackson, Jesse** 1908-1983 .................. **CLC 12**
See also BW 1; CA 25-28R; 109; CANR 27; CLR 28; CWRI; MAICYA; SATA 2, 29; SATA-Obit 48

**Jackson, Laura (Riding)** 1901-1991
See Riding, Laura
See also CA 65-68; 135; CANR 28, 89; DLB 48

**Jackson, Sam**
See Trumbo, Dalton

**Jackson, Sara**
See Wingrove, David (John)

**Jackson, Shirley** 1919-1965 . **CLC 11, 60, 87; DA; DAC; DAM MST; SSC 9, 39; WLC**
See also AAYA 9; AMWS 9; BPFB 2; CA 1-4R; 25-28R; CANR 4, 52; CDALB 1941-1968; DA3; DLB 6, 234; EXPS; HGG; LAIT 4; MTCW 2; RGAL; RGSF; SATA 2; SSFS 1

**Jacob, (Cyprien-)Max** 1876-1944 .... **TCLC 6**
See also CA 104; 193; GFL 1789 to the Present; GLL 2; RGWL

**Jacobs, Harriet A(nn)** 1813(?)-1897 ............................ **NCLC 67**
See also AFAW 1, 2; DLB 239; FW; LAIT 2; RGAL

**Jacobs, Jim** 1942- ................................ **CLC 12**
See also CA 97-100; INT 97-100

**Jacobs, W(illiam) W(ymark)** 1863-1943 ............................ **TCLC 22**
See also CA 121; 167; DLB 135; EXPS; HGG; RGEL; RGSF; SSFS 2; SUFW

**Jacobsen, Jens Peter** 1847-1885 ... **NCLC 34**

**Jacobsen, Josephine** 1908- ........ **CLC 48, 102**
See also CA 33-36R; CAAS 18; CANR 23, 48; CCA 1; CP; DLB 244

**Jacobson, Dan** 1929- ..................... **CLC 4, 14**
See also AFW; CA 1-4R; CANR 2, 25, 66; CN; DLB 14, 207, 225; MTCW 1; RGSF

**Jacqueline**
See Carpentier (y Valmont), Alejo

**Jagger, Mick** 1944- ............................. **CLC 17**

**Jahiz, al-** c. 780-c. 869 ................ **CMLC 25**

**Jakes, John (William)** 1932- . **CLC 29; DAM NOV, POP**
See also AAYA 32; BEST 89:4; BPFB 2; CA 57-60; CANR 10, 43, 66; CPW; CSW; DA3; DLBY 83; FANT; INT CANR-10; MTCW 1, 2; RHW; SATA 62; SFW; TCWW 2

**James I** 1394-1437 ............................... **LC 20**
See also RGEL

**James, Andrew**
See Kirkup, James

**James, C(yril) L(ionel) R(obert)** 1901-1989 ...................... **CLC 33; BLCS**
See also BW 2; CA 117; 125; 128; CANR 62; DLB 125; MTCW 1

**James, Daniel (Lewis)** 1911-1988
See Santiago, Danny
See also CA 174; 125

**James, Dynely**
See Mayne, William (James Carter)

**James, Henry Sr.** 1811-1882 ............ **NCLC 53**

**James, Henry** 1843-1916 ..... **TCLC 2, 11, 24, 40, 47, 64; DA; DAB; DAC; DAM MST, NOV; SSC 8, 32, 47; WLC**
See also AMW; AMWR 1; BPFB 2; BRW 6; CA 104; 132; CDALB 1865-1917; DA3; DLB 12, 71, 74, 189; DLBD 13; EXPS; HGG; LAIT 2; MTCW 1, 2; NFS 12; RGAL; RGEL; RGSF; SSFS 9

**James, M. R.**
See James, Montague (Rhodes)
See also DLB 156

**James, Montague (Rhodes)** 1862-1936 ................ **TCLC 6; SSC 16**
See also CA 104; DLB 201; HGG; RGEL; RGSF; SUFW

**James, P. D.** ..................... **CLC 18, 46, 122**
See also White, Phyllis Dorothy James
See also BEST 90:2; BPFB 2; BRWS 4; CDBLB 1960 to Present; DLB 87; DLBD 17; MSW

**James, Philip**
See Moorcock, Michael (John)

**James, Samuel**
See Stephens, James

**James, Seumas**
See Stephens, James

**James, Stephen**
See Stephens, James

**James, William** 1842-1910 ....... **TCLC 15, 32**
See also AMW; CA 109; 193; RGAL

**Jameson, Anna** 1794-1860 ............. **NCLC 43**
See also DLB 99, 166

**Jameson, Fredric** 1934- ................... **CLC 142**
See also DLB 67

**Jami, Nur al-Din 'Abd al-Rahman** 1414-1492 ...................... **LC 9**

**Jammes, Francis** 1868-1938 .......... **TCLC 75**
See also GFL 1789 to the Present

**Jandl, Ernst** 1925-2000 ..................... **CLC 34**

**Janowitz, Tama** 1957- ... **CLC 43, 145; DAM POP**
See also CA 106; CANR 52, 89; CN; CPW

**Japrisot, Sebastien** 1931- ................... **CLC 90**
See also CMW

**Jarrell, Randall** 1914-1965 .... **CLC 1, 2, 6, 9, 13, 49; DAM POET**
See also AMW; BYA 5; CA 5-8R; 25-28R; CABS 2; CANR 6, 34; CDALB 1941-1968; CLR 6; CWRI; DLB 48, 52; EXPP; MAICYA; MTCW 1, 2; PAB; PFS 2; RGAL; SATA 7

**Jarry, Alfred** 1873-1907 . **TCLC 2, 14; DAM DRAM; SSC 20**
See also CA 104; 153; DA3; DFS 8; DLB 192; EW; GFL 1789 to the Present; RGWL

**Jawien, Andrzej**
See John Paul II, Pope

**Jaynes, Roderick**
See Coen, Ethan

**Jeake, Samuel, Jr.**
See Aiken, Conrad (Potter)

**Jean Paul** 1763-1825 ......................... **NCLC 7**

**Jefferies, (John) Richard** 1848-1887 ............................ **NCLC 47**
See also DLB 98, 141; RGEL; SATA 16; SFW

**Jeffers, (John) Robinson** 1887-1962 .. **CLC 2, 3, 11, 15, 54; DA; DAC; DAM MST, POET; PC 17; WLC**
See also AMWS 2; CA 85-88; CANR 35; CDALB 1917-1929; DLB 45, 212; MTCW 1, 2; PAB; PFS 3, 4; RGAL

**Jefferson, Janet**
See Mencken, H(enry) L(ouis)

**Jefferson, Thomas** 1743-1826 . **NCLC 11, 103**
See also ANW; CDALB 1640-1865; DA3; DLB 31; LAIT 1; RGAL

**Jeffrey, Francis** 1773-1850 .............. **NCLC 33**
See also DLB 107

**Jelakowitch, Ivan**
See Heijermans, Herman

**Jellicoe, (Patricia) Ann** 1927- ........... **CLC 27**
See also CA 85-88; CBD; CD; CWD; CWRI; DLB 13, 233; FW

**Jemyma**
See Holley, Marietta

**Jen, Gish** .................................................. **CLC 70**
See also Jen, Lillian
**Jen, Lillian** 1956(?)-
See Jen, Gish
See also CA 135; CANR 89
**Jenkins, (John) Robin** 1912- ............. **CLC 52**
See also CA 1-4R; CANR 1; CN; DLB 14
**Jennings, Elizabeth (Joan)** 1926- ...... **CLC 5, 14, 131**
See also BRWS 5; CA 61-64; CAAS 5; CANR 8, 39, 66; CP; CWP; DLB 27; MTCW 1; SATA 66
**Jennings, Waylon** 1937- ..................... **CLC 21**
**Jensen, Johannes V.** 1873-1950 ...... **TCLC 41**
See also CA 170; DLB 214
**Jensen, Laura (Linnea)** 1948- ........... **CLC 37**
See also CA 103
**Jerome, Saint** 345-420 ................. **CMLC 30**
See also RGWL
**Jerome, Jerome K(lapka)**
1859-1927 .............................. **TCLC 23**
See also CA 119; 177; DLB 10, 34, 135; RGEL
**Jerrold, Douglas William**
1803-1857 .................................. **NCLC 2**
See also DLB 158, 159; RGEL
**Jewett, (Theodora) Sarah Orne**
1849-1909 ......... **TCLC 1, 22; SSC 6, 44**
See also AMW; CA 108; 127; CANR 71; DLB 12, 74, 221; EXPS; FW; MAWW; RGAL; RGSF; SATA 15; SSFS 4
**Jewsbury, Geraldine (Endsor)**
1812-1880 ................................ **NCLC 22**
See also DLB 21
**Jhabvala, Ruth Prawer** 1927- . **CLC 4, 8, 29, 94, 138; DAB; DAM NOV**
See also BRWS 5; CA 1-4R; CANR 2, 29, 51, 74, 91; CN; DLB 139, 194; IDFW 3, 4; INT CANR-29; MTCW 1, 2; RGSF; RGWL; RHW
**Jibran, Kahlil**
See Gibran, Kahlil
**Jibran, Khalil**
See Gibran, Kahlil
**Jiles, Paulette** 1943- ..................... **CLC 13, 58**
See also CA 101; CANR 70; CWP
**Jimenez (Mantecon), Juan Ramon**
1881-1958 ......... **TCLC 4; DAM MULT, POET; HLC 1; PC 7**
See also CA 104; 131; CANR 74; DLB 134; EW; HW 1; MTCW 1, 2; RGWL
**Jimenez, Ramon**
See Jimenez (Mantecon), Juan Ramon
**Jimenez Mantecon, Juan**
See Jimenez (Mantecon), Juan Ramon
**Jin, Ha**
See Jin, Xuefei
**Jin, Xuefei** 1956- ................................ **CLC 109**
See also CA 152; CANR 91; DLB 244
**Joel, Billy** ............................................. **CLC 26**
See also Joel, William Martin
**Joel, William Martin** 1949-
See Joel, Billy
See also CA 108
**John, Saint** 107th cent. -100 .......... **CMLC 27**
**John of the Cross, St.** 1542-1591 ........ **LC 18**
See also RGWL
**John Paul II, Pope** 1920- ................. **CLC 128**
See also CA 106; 133
**Johnson, B(ryan) S(tanley William)**
1933-1973 ................................. **CLC 6, 9**
See also CA 9-12R; 53-56; CANR 9; DLB 14, 40; RGEL
**Johnson, Benj. F. of Boo**
See Riley, James Whitcomb
**Johnson, Benjamin F. of Boo**
See Riley, James Whitcomb

**Johnson, Charles (Richard)** 1948- .... **CLC 7, 51, 65; BLC 2; DAM MULT**
See also AFAW 2; AMWS 6; BW 2, 3; CA 116; CAAS 18; CANR 42, 66, 82; CN 7; DLB 33; MTCW 2; RGAL
**Johnson, Denis** 1949- ........................ **CLC 52**
See also CA 117; 121; CANR 71, 99; CN; DLB 120
**Johnson, Diane** 1934- .............. **CLC 5, 13, 48**
See also BPFB 2; CA 41-44R; CANR 17, 40, 62, 95; CN; DLBY 80; INT CANR-17; MTCW 1
**Johnson, Eyvind (Olof Verner)**
1900-1976 ................................. **CLC 14**
See also CA 73-76; 69-72; CANR 34, 101; EW
**Johnson, J. R.**
See James, C(yril) L(ionel) R(obert)
**Johnson, James Weldon**
1871-1938 .. **TCLC 3, 19; BLC 2; DAM MULT, POET; PC 24**
See also AFAW 1, 2; BW 1, 3; CA 104; 125; CANR 82; CDALB 1917-1929; CLR 32; DA3; DLB 51; EXPP; MTCW 1, 2; PFS 1; RGAL; SATA 31
**Johnson, Joyce** 1935- ......................... **CLC 58**
See also CA 125; 129; CANR 102
**Johnson, Judith (Emlyn)** 1936- .... **CLC 7, 15**
See also Sherwin, Judith Johnson
See also CA 25-28R, 153; CANR 34
**Johnson, Lionel (Pigot)**
1867-1902 .................................. **TCLC 19**
See also CA 117; DLB 19; RGEL
**Johnson, Marguerite (Annie)**
See Angelou, Maya
**Johnson, Mel**
See Malzberg, Barry N(athaniel)
**Johnson, Pamela Hansford**
1912-1981 ..................... **CLC 1, 7, 27**
See also CA 1-4R; 104; CANR 2, 28; DLB 15; MTCW 1, 2; RGEL
**Johnson, Paul (Bede)** 1928- ............. **CLC 147**
See also BEST 89:4; CA 17-20R; CANR 34, 62, 100
**Johnson, Robert** ................................ **CLC 70**
**Johnson, Robert** 1911(?)-1938 ........ **TCLC 69**
See also BW 3; CA 174
**Johnson, Samuel** 1709-1784 . **LC 15, 52; DA; DAB; DAC; DAM MST; WLC**
See also BRW 3; CDBLB 1660-1789; DLB 39, 95, 104, 142; RGEL; TEA
**Johnson, Uwe** 1934-1984 .. **CLC 5, 10, 15, 40**
See also CA 1-4R; 112; CANR 1, 39; DLB 75; MTCW 1; RGWL
**Johnston, George (Benson)** 1913- .... **CLC 51**
See also CA 1-4R; CANR 5, 20; CP; DLB 88
**Johnston, Jennifer (Prudence)**
1930- ...................................... **CLC 7, 150**
See also CA 85-88; CANR 92; CN; DLB 14
**Joinville, Jean de** 1224(?)-1317 ..... **CMLC 38**
**Jolley, (Monica) Elizabeth** 1923- ..... **CLC 46; SSC 19**
See also CA 127; CAAS 13; CANR 59; CN; RGSF
**Jones, Arthur Llewellyn** 1863-1947
See Machen, Arthur
See also CA 104; 179; HGG
**Jones, D(ouglas) G(ordon)** 1929- ..... **CLC 10**
See also CA 29-32R; CANR 13, 90; CP; DLB 53
**Jones, David (Michael)** 1895-1974 .... **CLC 2, 4, 7, 13, 42**
See also BRW 6; BRWS 7; CA 9-12R; 53-56; CANR 28; CDBLB 1945-1960; DLB 20, 100; MTCW 1; PAB; RGEL

**Jones, David Robert** 1947-
See Bowie, David
See also CA 103
**Jones, Diana Wynne** 1934- ................ **CLC 26**
See also AAYA 12; BYA 6, 7, 9, 11, 13; CA 49-52; CANR 4, 26, 56; CLR 23; DLB 161; FANT; JRDA; MAICYA; SAAS 7; SATA 9, 70, 108; SFW; YAW
**Jones, Edward P.** 1950- ...................... **CLC 76**
See also BW 2, 3; CA 142; CANR 79; CSW
**Jones, Gayl** 1949- ...... **CLC 6, 9, 131; BLC 2; DAM MULT**
See also AFAW 1, 2; BW 2, 3; CA 77-80; CANR 27, 66; CN; CSW; DA3; DLB 33; MTCW 1, 2; RGAL
**Jones, James** 1931-1978 ...... **CLC 1, 3, 10, 39**
See also AITN 1, 2; BPFB 2; CA 1-4R; 69-72; CANR 6; DLB 2, 143; DLBD 17; DLBY 98; MTCW 1; RGAL
**Jones, John J.**
See Lovecraft, H(oward) P(hillips)
**Jones, LeRoi** ............. **CLC 1, 2, 3, 5, 10, 14**
See also Baraka, Amiri
See also MTCW 2
**Jones, Louis B.** 1953- ........................ **CLC 65**
See also CA 141; CANR 73
**Jones, Madison (Percy, Jr.)** 1925- ....... **CLC 4**
See also CA 13-16R; CAAS 11; CANR 7, 54, 83; CN; CSW; DLB 152
**Jones, Mervyn** 1922- ..................... **CLC 10, 52**
See also CA 45-48; CAAS 5; CANR 1, 91; CN; MTCW 1
**Jones, Mick** 1956(?)- ........................... **CLC 30**
**Jones, Nettie (Pearl)** 1941- ................ **CLC 34**
See also BW 2; CA 137; CAAS 20; CANR 88
**Jones, Preston** 1936-1979 .................. **CLC 10**
See also CA 73-76; 89-92; DLB 7
**Jones, Robert F(rancis)** 1934- ............. **CLC 7**
See also CA 49-52; CANR 2, 61
**Jones, Rod** 1953- ................................ **CLC 50**
See also CA 128
**Jones, Terence Graham Parry**
1942- ......................................... **CLC 21**
See also Jones, Terry; Monty Python
See also CA 112; 116; CANR 35, 93; INT 116
**Jones, Terry**
See Jones, Terence Graham Parry
See also SATA 67; SATA-Brief 51
**Jones, Thom (Douglas)** 1945(?)- ........ **CLC 81**
See also CA 157; CANR 88; DLB 244
**Jong, Erica** 1942- ........... **CLC 4, 6, 8, 18, 83; DAM NOV, POP**
See also AITN 1; AMWS 5; BEST 90:2; BPFB 2; CA 73-76; CANR 26, 52, 75; CN; CP; CPW; DA3; DLB 2, 5, 28, 152; FW; INT CANR-26; MTCW 1, 2
**Jonson, Ben(jamin)** 1572(?)-1637 ... **LC 6, 33; DA; DAB; DAC; DAM DRAM, MST, POET; DC 4; PC 17; WLC**
See also BRW 1; CDBLB Before 1660; DFS 4, 10; DLB 62, 121; RGEL; WLIT 3
**Jordan, June** 1936- ............ **CLC 5, 11, 23, 114; BLCS; DAM MULT, POET**
See also Meyer, June
See also AAYA 2; AFAW 1, 2; BW 2, 3; CA 33-36R; CANR 25, 70; CLR 10; CP; CWP; DLB 38; GLL 2; LAIT 5; MAICYA; MTCW 1; SATA 4; YAW
**Jordan, Neil (Patrick)** 1950- ............ **CLC 110**
See also CA 124; 130; CANR 54; CN; GLL 2; INT 130
**Jordan, Pat(rick M.)** 1941- ................. **CLC 37**
See also CA 33-36R
**Jorgensen, Ivar**
See Ellison, Harlan (Jay)
**Jorgenson, Ivar**
See Silverberg, Robert

**Joseph, George Ghevarughese** ........ **CLC 70**

**Josephus, Flavius** c. 37-100 ........... **CMLC 13**
See also AW 2; DLB 176

**Josiah Allen's Wife**
See Holley, Marietta

**Josipovici, Gabriel (David)** 1940- ...... **CLC 6, 43**
See also CA 37-40R; CAAS 8; CANR 47, 84; CN; DLB 14

**Joubert, Joseph** 1754-1824 ............... **NCLC 9**

**Jouve, Pierre Jean** 1887-1976 ........... **CLC 47**
See also CA 65-68

**Jovine, Francesco** 1902-1950 .......... **TCLC 79**

**Joyce, James (Augustine Aloysius)** 1882-1941 .. **TCLC 3, 8, 16, 35, 52; DA; DAB; DAC; DAM MST, NOV, POET; PC 22; SSC 3, 26, 44; WLC**
See also AAYA 42; BRW 7; BYA 11, 13; CA 104; 126; CDBLB 1914-1945; DA3; DLB 10, 19, 36, 162; EXPN; EXPS; LAIT 3; MTCW 1, 2; NFS 7; RGSF; SSFS 1; WLIT 4

**Jozsef, Attila** 1905-1937 .................. **TCLC 22**
See also CA 116

**Juana Ines de la Cruz, Sor** 1651(?)-1695 ...... **LC 5; HLCS 1; PC 24**
See also FW; LAW; RGWL; WLIT 1

**Juana Inez de La Cruz, Sor**
See Juana Ines de la Cruz, Sor

**Judd, Cyril**
See Kornbluth, C(yril) M.; Pohl, Frederik

**Juenger, Ernst** 1895-1998 ................ **CLC 125**
See also Junger, Ernst
See also CA 101; 167; CANR 21, 47; DLB 56

**Julian of Norwich** 1342(?)-1416(?) . **LC 6, 52**
See also DLB 146

**Julius Caesar** 100B.C.-44B.C.
See Caesar, Julius
See also DLB 211

**Junger, Ernst**
See Juenger, Ernst
See also RGWL

**Junger, Sebastian** 1962- .................... **CLC 109**
See also AAYA 28; CA 165

**Juniper, Alex**
See Hospital, Janette Turner

**Junius**
See Luxemburg, Rosa

**Just, Ward (Swift)** 1935- ................. **CLC 4, 27**
See also CA 25-28R; CANR 32, 87; CN; INT CANR-32

**Justice, Donald (Rodney)** 1925- .. **CLC 6, 19, 102; DAM POET**
See also AMWS 7; CA 5-8R; CANR 26, 54, 74; CP; CSW; DLBY 83; INT CANR-26; MTCW 2

**Juvenal** c. 60-c. 130 ......................... **CMLC 8**
See also AW 2; DLB 211; RGWL

**Juvenis**
See Bourne, Randolph S(illiman)

**Kabakov, Sasha** .................................. **CLC 59**

**Kacew, Romain** 1914-1980
See Gary, Romain
See also CA 108; 102

**Kadare, Ismail** 1936- .......................... **CLC 52**
See also CA 161

**Kadohata, Cynthia** ................... **CLC 59, 122**
See also CA 140

**Kafka, Franz** 1883-1924 . **TCLC 2, 6, 13, 29, 47, 53, 112; DA; DAB; DAC; DAM MST, NOV; SSC 5, 29, 35; WLC**
See also AAYA 31; BPFB 2; CA 105; 126; DA3; DLB 81; EW; EXPS; MTCW 1, 2; NFS 7; RGSF; RGWL; SFW; SSFS 3, 7, 12

**Kahanovitsch, Pinkhes**
See Der Nister

**Kahn, Roger** 1927- ............................. **CLC 30**
See also CA 25-28R; CANR 44, 69; DLB 171; SATA 37

**Kain, Saul**
See Sassoon, Siegfried (Lorraine)

**Kaiser, Georg** 1878-1945 ................... **TCLC 9**
See also CA 106; 190; DLB 124; RGWL

**Kaledin, Sergei** ................................... **CLC 59**

**Kaletski, Alexander** 1946- ................ **CLC 39**
See also CA 118; 143

**Kalidasa** fl. c. 400-455 ........ **CMLC 9; PC 22**
See also RGWL

**Kallman, Chester (Simon)** 1921-1975 ............................... **CLC 2**
See also CA 45-48; 53-56; CANR 3

**Kaminsky, Melvin** 1926-
See Brooks, Mel
See also CA 65-68; CANR 16

**Kaminsky, Stuart M(elvin)** 1934- .... **CLC 59**
See also CA 73-76; CANR 29, 53, 89; CMW

**Kandinsky, Wassily** 1866-1944 ....... **TCLC 92**
See also CA 118; 155

**Kane, Francis**
See Robbins, Harold

**Kane, Henry** 1918-
See Queen, Ellery
See also CA 156; CMW

**Kane, Paul**
See Simon, Paul (Frederick)

**Kanin, Garson** 1912-1999 ................. **CLC 22**
See also AITN 1; CA 5-8R; 177; CAD; CANR 7, 78; DLB 7; IDFW 3, 4

**Kaniuk, Yoram** 1930- ........................ **CLC 19**
See also CA 134

**Kant, Immanuel** 1724-1804 ..... **NCLC 27, 67**
See also DLB 94

**Kantor, MacKinlay** 1904-1977 ........... **CLC 7**
See also CA 61-64; 73-76; CANR 60, 63; DLB 9, 102; MTCW 2; RHW; TCWW 2

**Kaplan, David Michael** 1946- .......... **CLC 50**
See also CA 187

**Kaplan, James** 1951- ......................... **CLC 59**
See also CA 135

**Karageorge, Michael**
See Anderson, Poul (William)

**Karamzin, Nikolai Mikhailovich** 1766-1826 ................... **NCLC 3**
See also DLB 150; RGSF

**Karapanou, Margarita** 1946- ........... **CLC 13**
See also CA 101

**Karinthy, Frigyes** 1887-1938 .......... **TCLC 47**
See also CA 170

**Karl, Frederick R(obert)** 1927- ........ **CLC 34**
See also CA 5-8R; CANR 3, 44

**Kastel, Warren**
See Silverberg, Robert

**Kataev, Evgeny Petrovich** 1903-1942
See Petrov, Evgeny
See also CA 120

**Kataphusin**
See Ruskin, John

**Katz, Steve** 1935- ............................... **CLC 47**
See also CA 25-28R; CAAS 14, 64; CANR 12; CN; DLBY 83

**Kauffman, Janet** 1945- ..................... **CLC 42**
See also CA 117; CANR 43, 84; DLBY 86

**Kaufman, Bob (Garnell)** 1925-1986 . **CLC 49**
See also BW 1; CA 41-44R; 118; CANR 22; DLB 16, 41

**Kaufman, George S.** 1889-1961 ...... **CLC 38; DAM DRAM**
See also CA 108; 93-96; DFS 1, 10; DLB 7; INT 108; MTCW 2; RGAL

**Kaufman, Sue** ................................ **CLC 3, 8**
See also Barondess, Sue K(aufman)

**Kavafis, Konstantinos Petrou** 1863-1933
See Cavafy, C(onstantine) P(eter)
See also CA 104

**Kavan, Anna** 1901-1968 .......... **CLC 5, 13, 82**
See also BRWS 7; CA 5-8R; CANR 6, 57; MTCW 1; RGEL; SFW

**Kavanagh, Dan**
See Barnes, Julian (Patrick)

**Kavanagh, Julie** 1952- ..................... **CLC 119**
See also CA 163

**Kavanagh, Patrick (Joseph)** 1904-1967 ....................... **CLC 22; PC 33**
See also BRWS 7; CA 123; 25-28R; DLB 15, 20; MTCW 1; RGEL

**Kawabata, Yasunari** 1899-1972 ...... **CLC 2, 5, 9, 18, 107; DAM MULT; SSC 17**
See also CA 93-96; 33-36R; CANR 88; DLB 180; MJW; MTCW 2; RGSF; RGWL

**Kaye, M(ary) M(argaret)** 1909- ....... **CLC 28**
See also CA 89-92; CANR 24, 60, 102; MTCW 1, 2; RHW; SATA 62

**Kaye, Mollie**
See Kaye, M(ary) M(argaret)

**Kaye-Smith, Sheila** 1887-1956 ........ **TCLC 20**
See also CA 118; DLB 36

**Kaymor, Patrice Maguilene**
See Senghor, Leopold Sedar

**Kazakov, Yuri Pavlovich** 1927-1982 . **SSC 43**
See also CA 5-8R; CANR 36; MTCW 1; RGSF

**Kazan, Elia** 1909- ..................... **CLC 6, 16, 63**
See also CA 21-24R; CANR 32, 78

**Kazantzakis, Nikos** 1883(?)-1957 .... **TCLC 2, 5, 33**
See also BPFB 2; CA 105; 132; DA3; EW; MTCW 1, 2; RGWL

**Kazin, Alfred** 1915-1998 ...... **CLC 34, 38, 119**
See also AMWS 8; CA 1-4R; CAAS 7; CANR 1, 45, 79; DLB 67

**Keane, Mary Nesta (Skrine)** 1904-1996
See Keane, Molly
See also CA 108; 114; 151; CN; RHW

**Keane, Molly** ..................................... **CLC 31**
See also Keane, Mary Nesta (Skrine)
See also INT 114

**Keates, Jonathan** 1946(?)- ................ **CLC 34**
See also CA 163

**Keaton, Buster** 1895-1966 ................ **CLC 20**
See also CA 194

**Keats, John** 1795-1821 ...... **NCLC 8, 73; DA; DAB; DAC; DAM MST, POET; PC 1; WLC**
See also BRW 4; CDBLB 1789-1832; DA3; DLB 96, 110; EXPP; PAB; PFS 1, 2, 3, 9; RGEL; WLIT 3; WP

**Keble, John** 1792-1866 ................... **NCLC 87**
See also DLB 32, 55; RGEL

**Keene, Donald** 1922- ......................... **CLC 34**
See also CA 1-4R; CANR 5

**Keillor, Garrison** ....................... **CLC 40, 115**
See also Keillor, Gary (Edward)
See also AAYA 2; BEST 89:3; BPFB 2; DLBY 87; SATA 58

**Keillor, Gary (Edward)** 1942-
See Keillor, Garrison
See also CA 111; 117; CANR 36, 59; CPW; DA3; DAM POP; MTCW 1, 2

**Keith, Michael**
See Hubbard, L(afayette) Ron(ald)

**Keller, Gottfried** 1819-1890 .... **NCLC 2; SSC 26**
See also DLB 129; EW; RGSF; RGWL

**Keller, Nora Okja** 1965- ................. **CLC 109**
See also CA 187

**Kellerman, Jonathan** 1949- .. **CLC 44; DAM POP**
See also AAYA 35; BEST 90:1; CA 106; CANR 29, 51; CMW; CPW; DA3; INT CANR-29

**Kelley, William Melvin** 1937- ............ **CLC 22**
See also BW 1; CA 77-80; CANR 27, 83; CN; DLB 33

**Kellogg, Marjorie** 1922- ..................... **CLC 2**
See also CA 81-84

**Kellow, Kathleen**
See Hibbert, Eleanor Alice Burford

**Kelly, M(ilton) T(errence)** 1947- ...... **CLC 55**
See also CA 97-100; CAAS 22; CANR 19, 43, 84; CN

**Kelman, James** 1946- ................. **CLC 58, 86**
See also BRWS 5; CA 148; CANR 85; CN; DLB 194; RGSF; WLIT 4

**Kemal, Yashar** 1923- ................. **CLC 14, 29**
See also CA 89-92; CANR 44; CWW 2

**Kemble, Fanny** 1809-1893 ............. **NCLC 18**
See also DLB 32

**Kemelman, Harry** 1908-1996 ............. **CLC 2**
See also AITN 1; BPFB 2; CA 9-12R; 155; CANR 6, 71; CMW; DLB 28

**Kempe, Margery** 1373(?)-1440(?) ... **LC 6, 56**
See also DLB 146; RGEL

**Kempis, Thomas a** 1380-1471 ............. **LC 11**

**Kendall, Henry** 1839-1882 ............. **NCLC 12**
See also DLB 230

**Keneally, Thomas (Michael)** 1935- ... **CLC 5, 8, 10, 14, 19, 27, 43, 117; DAM NOV**
See also BRWS 4; CA 85-88; CANR 10, 50, 74; CN; CPW; DA3; MTCW 1, 2; RGEL; RHW

**Kennedy, Adrienne (Lita)** 1931- ...... **CLC 66; BLC 2; DAM MULT; DC 5**
See also AFAW 2; BW 2, 3; CA 103; CAAS 20; CABS 3; CANR 26, 53, 82; CD; DFS 9; DLB 38; FW

**Kennedy, John Pendleton** 1795-1870 ..................... **NCLC 2**
See also DLB 3; RGAL

**Kennedy, Joseph Charles** 1929-
See Kennedy, X. J.
See also CA 1-4R; CANR 4, 30, 40; CP; CWRI; SATA 14, 86

**Kennedy, William** 1928- .. **CLC 6, 28, 34, 53; DAM NOV**
See also AAYA 1; AMWS 7; BPFB 2; CA 85-88; CANR 14, 31, 76; CN; DA3; DLB 143; DLBY 85; INT CANR-31; MTCW 1, 2; SATA 57

**Kennedy, X. J.** ..................... **CLC 8, 42**
See also Kennedy, Joseph Charles
See also CAAS 9; CLR 27; DLB 5; SAAS 22

**Kenny, Maurice (Francis)** 1929- ...... **CLC 87; DAM MULT**
See also CA 144; CAAS 22; DLB 175; NNAL

**Kent, Kelvin**
See Kuttner, Henry

**Kenton, Maxwell**
See Southern, Terry

**Kenyon, Robert O.**
See Kuttner, Henry

**Kepler, Johannes** 1571-1630 ................. **LC 45**

**Kerouac, Jack** 1922-1969 ...... **CLC 1, 2, 3, 5, 14, 29, 61**
See also Kerouac, Jean-Louis Lebris de
See also AAYA 25; AMWS 3; BPFB 2; CDALB 1941-1968; DLB 2, 16, 237; DLBD 3; DLBY 95; GLL 1; MTCW 2; NFS 8; RGAL; WP

**Kerouac, Jean-Louis Lebris de** 1922-1969
See Kerouac, Jack
See also AITN 1; CA 5-8R; 25-28R; CANR 26, 54, 95; CPW; DA; DA3; DAB; DAC; DAM MST, NOV, POET, POP; MTCW 1, 2; WLC

**Kerr, Jean** 1923- ................................. **CLC 22**
See also CA 5-8R; CANR 7; INT CANR-7

**Kerr, M. E.** ........................... **CLC 12, 35**
See also Meaker, Marijane (Agnes)
See also AAYA 2, 23; BYA 1, 7, 8; CLR 29; SAAS 1

**Kerr, Robert** ............................. **CLC 55**

**Kerrigan, (Thomas) Anthony** 1918- .. **CLC 4, 6**
See also CA 49-52; CAAS 11; CANR 4

**Kerry, Lois**
See Duncan, Lois

**Kesey, Ken (Elton)** 1935-2001 ... **CLC 1, 3, 6, 11, 46, 64; DA; DAB; DAC; DAM MST, NOV, POP; WLC**
See also AAYA 25; BPFB 2; CA 1-4R; CANR 22, 38, 66; CDALB 1968-1988; CN; CPW; DA3; DLB 2, 16, 206; EXPN; LAIT 4; MTCW 1, 2; NFS 2; RGAL; SATA 66; YAW

**Kesselring, Joseph (Otto)** 1902-1967 ........ **CLC 45; DAM DRAM, MST**
See also CA 150

**Kessler, Jascha (Frederick)** 1929- ...... **CLC 4**
See also CA 17-20R; CANR 8, 48

**Kettelkamp, Larry (Dale)** 1933- ....... **CLC 12**
See also CA 29-32R; CANR 16; SAAS 3; SATA 2

**Key, Ellen (Karolina Sofia)** 1849-1926 ................................. **TCLC 65**

**Keyber, Conny**
See Fielding, Henry

**Keyes, Daniel** 1927- ...... **CLC 80; DA; DAC; DAM MST, NOV**
See also AAYA 23; BYA 11; CA 17-20R, 181; CAAE 181; CANR 10, 26, 54, 74; DA3; EXPN; LAIT 4; MTCW 2; NFS 2; SATA 37; SFW

**Keynes, John Maynard** 1883-1946 ..................... **TCLC 64**
See also CA 114; 162, 163; DLBD 10; MTCW 2

**Khanshendel, Chiron**
See Rose, Wendy

**Khayyam, Omar** 1048-1131 ......... **CMLC 11; DAM POET; PC 8**
See also Omar Khayyam
See also DA3

**Kherdian, David** 1931- ..................... **CLC 6, 9**
See also AAYA 42; CA 21-24R; CAAE 192; CAAS 2; CANR 39, 78; CLR 24; JRDA; LAIT 3; MAICYA; SATA 16, 74; SATA-Essay 125

**Khlebnikov, Velimir** ..................... **TCLC 20**
See also Khlebnikov, Viktor Vladimirovich
See also EW; RGWL

**Khlebnikov, Viktor Vladimirovich** 1885-1922
See Khlebnikov, Velimir
See also CA 117

**Khodasevich, Vladislav (Felitsianovich)** 1886-1939 ................................. **TCLC 15**
See also CA 115

**Kielland, Alexander Lange** 1849-1906 ................................. **TCLC 5**
See also CA 104

**Kiely, Benedict** 1919- ..................... **CLC 23, 43**
See also CA 1-4R; CANR 2, 84; CN; DLB 15

**Kienzle, William X(avier)** 1928- ..... **CLC 25; DAM POP**
See also CA 93-96; CAAS 1; CANR 9, 31, 59; CMW; DA3; INT CANR-31; MSW; MTCW 1, 2

**Kierkegaard, Soren** 1813-1855 ..... **NCLC 34, 78**
See also EW

**Kieslowski, Krzysztof** 1941-1996 .... **CLC 120**
See also CA 147; 151

**Killens, John Oliver** 1916-1987 ........ **CLC 10**
See also BW 2; CA 77-80; 123; CAAS 2; CANR 26; DLB 33

**Killigrew, Anne** 1660-1685 ..................... **LC 4**
See also DLB 131

**Killigrew, Thomas** 1612-1683 ............... **LC 57**
See also DLB 58; RGEL

**Kim**
See Simenon, Georges (Jacques Christian)

**Kincaid, Jamaica** 1949- ..... **CLC 43, 68, 137; BLC 2; DAM MULT, NOV**
See also AAYA 13; AFAW 2; AMWS 7; BRWS 7; BW 2, 3; CA 125; CANR 47, 59, 95; CDALBS; CLR 63; DA3; DLB 157, 227; DNFS; EXPS; FW; MTCW 2; NCFS 1; NFS 3; SSFS 5, 7; YAW

**King, Francis (Henry)** 1923- ....... **CLC 8, 53, 145; DAM NOV**
See also CA 1-4R; CANR 1, 33, 86; CN; DLB 15, 139; MTCW 1

**King, Kennedy**
See Brown, George Douglas

**King, Martin Luther, Jr.** 1929-1968 ............ **CLC 83; BLC 2; DA; DAB; DAC; DAM MST, MULT; WLCS**
See also BW 2, 3; CA 25-28; CANR 27, 44; CAP 2; DA3; LAIT 5; MTCW 1, 2; SATA 14

**King, Stephen (Edwin)** 1947- .... **CLC 12, 26, 37, 61, 113; DAM NOV, POP; SSC 17**
See also AAYA 1, 17; AMWS 5; BEST 90:1; BPFB 2; CA 61-64; CANR 1, 30, 52, 76; CPW; DA3; DLB 143; DLBY 80; HGG; JRDA; LAIT 5; MTCW 1, 2; RGAL; SATA 9, 55; SUFW; WYAS 1; YAW

**King, Steve**
See King, Stephen (Edwin)

**King, Thomas** 1943- ... **CLC 89; DAC; DAM MULT**
See also CA 144; CANR 95; CCA 1; CN; DLB 175; NNAL; SATA 96

**Kingman, Lee** ..................... **CLC 17**
See also Natti, (Mary) Lee
See also SAAS 3; SATA 1, 67

**Kingsley, Charles** 1819-1875 ........... **NCLC 35**
See also CLR 75; DLB 21, 32, 163, 190; FANT; RGEL; YABC 2

**Kingsley, Sidney** 1906-1995 ............... **CLC 44**
See also CA 85-88; 147; CAD; DLB 7; RGAL

**Kingsolver, Barbara** 1955- ......... **CLC 55, 81, 130; DAM POP**
See also AAYA 15; AMWS 7; CA 129; 134; CANR 60, 96; CDALBS; CPW; CSW; DA3; DLB 206; INT CA-134; LAIT 5; MTCW 2; NFS 5, 10, 12; RGAL

**Kingston, Maxine (Ting Ting) Hong** 1940- ......... **CLC 12, 19, 58, 121; AAL; DAM MULT, NOV; WLCS**
See also AAYA 8; AMWS 5; BPFB 2; CA 69-72; CANR 13, 38, 74, 87; CDALBS; CN; DA3; DLB 173, 212; DLBY 80; FW; INT CANR-13; LAIT 5; MAWW; MTCW 1, 2; NFS 6; RGAL; SATA 53; SSFS 3

**Kinnell, Galway** 1927- ..... **CLC 1, 2, 3, 5, 13, 29, 129; PC 26**
See also AMWS 3; CA 9-12R; CANR 10, 34, 66; CP; DLB 5; DLBY 87; INT CANR-34; MTCW 1, 2; PAB; PFS 9; RGAL; WP

**Kinsella, Thomas** 1928- ........ **CLC 4, 19, 138**
See also BRWS 5; CA 17-20R; CANR 15; CP; DLB 27; MTCW 1, 2; RGEL

**Kinsella, W(illiam) P(atrick)** 1935- . **CLC 27, 43; DAC; DAM NOV, POP**
See also AAYA 7; BPFB 2; CA 97-100; CAAS 7; CANR 21, 35, 66, 75; CN; CPW; FANT; INT CANR-21; LAIT 5; MTCW 1, 2; RGSF

**Kinsey, Alfred C(harles)** 1894-1956 ................ **TCLC 91**
See also CA 115; 170; MTCW 2

**Kipling, (Joseph) Rudyard** 1865-1936 ........ **TCLC 8, 17; DA; DAB; DAC; DAM MST, POET; PC 3; SSC 5; WLC**
See also AAYA 32; BRW 6; BYA 4; CA 105; 120; CANR 33; CDBLB 1890-1914; CLR 39, 65; CWRI; DA3; DLB 19, 34, 141, 156; EXPS; FANT; LAIT 3; MAI-CYA; MTCW 1, 2; RGEL; RGSF; SATA 100; SFW; SSFS 8; SUFW; WCH; WLIT 4; YABC 2

**Kirkland, Caroline M.** 1801-1864 . **NCLC 85**
See also DLB 3, 73, 74; DLBD 13

**Kirkup, James** 1918- ........................ **CLC 1**
See also CA 1-4R; CAAS 4; CANR 2; DLB 27; SATA 12

**Kirkwood, James** 1930(?)-1989 .......... **CLC 9**
See also AITN 2; CA 1-4R; 128; CANR 6, 40; GLL 2

**Kirshner, Sidney**
See Kingsley, Sidney

**Kis, Danilo** 1935-1989 ........................ **CLC 57**
See also CA 109; 118; 129; CANR 61; DLB 181; MTCW 1; RGSF; RGWL

**Kissinger, Henry A(lfred)** 1923- ...... **CLC 137**
See also CA 1-4R; CANR 2, 33, 66; MTCW 1

**Kivi, Aleksis** 1834-1872 .................... **NCLC 30**

**Kizer, Carolyn (Ashley)** 1925- ... **CLC 15, 39, 80; DAM POET**
See also CA 65-68; CAAS 5; CANR 24, 70; CP; CWP; DLB 5, 169; MTCW 2

**Klabund** 1890-1928 ........................... **TCLC 44**
See also CA 162; DLB 66

**Klappert, Peter** 1942- ....................... **CLC 57**
See also CA 33-36R; CSW; DLB 5

**Klein, A(braham) M(oses)** 1909-1972 . **CLC 19; DAB; DAC; DAM MST**
See also CA 101; 37-40R; DLB 68; RGEL

**Klein, Norma** 1938-1989 .................... **CLC 30**
See also AAYA 2, 35; BPFB 2; BYA 6, 7, 8; CA 41-44R; 128; CANR 15, 37; CLR 2, 19; INT CANR-15; JRDA; MAICYA; SAAS 1; SATA 7, 57; YAW

**Klein, T(heodore) E(ibon) D(onald)** 1947- ........................................ **CLC 34**
See also CA 119; CANR 44, 75; HGG

**Kleist, Heinrich von** 1777-1811 ...... **NCLC 2, 37; DAM DRAM; SSC 22**
See also DLB 90; EW; RGSF; RGWL

**Klima, Ivan** 1931- ........ **CLC 56; DAM NOV**
See also CA 25-28R; CANR 17, 50, 91; CWW 2; DLB 232

**Klimentov, Andrei Platonovich** 1899-1951 ................... **TCLC 14; SSC 42**
See also CA 108

**Klinger, Friedrich Maximilian von** 1752-1831 ................... **NCLC 1**
See also DLB 94

**Klingsor the Magician**
See Hartmann, Sadakichi

**Klopstock, Friedrich Gottlieb** 1724-1803 ................ **NCLC 11**
See also DLB 97; EW; RGWL

**Knapp, Caroline** 1959- ....................... **CLC 99**
See also CA 154

**Knebel, Fletcher** 1911-1993 ............... **CLC 14**
See also AITN 1; CA 1-4R; 140; CAAS 3; CANR 1, 36; SATA 36; SATA-Obit 75

**Knickerbocker, Diedrich**
See Irving, Washington

**Knight, Etheridge** 1931-1991 . **CLC 40; BLC 2; DAM POET; PC 14**
See also BW 1, 3; CA 21-24R; 133; CANR 23, 82; DLB 41; MTCW 2; RGAL

**Knight, Sarah Kemble** 1666-1727 ......... **LC 7**
See also DLB 24, 200

**Knister, Raymond** 1899-1932 ......... **TCLC 56**
See also CA 186; DLB 68; RGEL

**Knowles, John** 1926-2001 . **CLC 1, 4, 10, 26; DA; DAC; DAM MST, NOV**
See also AAYA 10; BPFB 2; BYA 3; CA 17-20R; CANR 40, 74, 76; CDALB 1968-1988; CN; DLB 6; EXPN; MTCW 1, 2; NFS 2; RGAL; SATA 8, 89; YAW

**Knox, Calvin M.**
See Silverberg, Robert

**Knox, John** c. 1505-1572 .................... **LC 37**
See also DLB 132

**Knye, Cassandra**
See Disch, Thomas M(ichael)

**Koch, C(hristopher) J(ohn)** 1932- .... **CLC 42**
See also CA 127; CANR 84; CN

**Koch, Christopher**
See Koch, C(hristopher) J(ohn)

**Koch, Kenneth** 1925- .... **CLC 5, 8, 44; DAM POET**
See also CA 1-4R; CAD; CANR 6, 36, 57, 97; CD; CP; DLB 5; INT CANR-36; MTCW 2; SATA 65; WP

**Kochanowski, Jan** 1530-1584 ............. **LC 10**
See also RGWL

**Kock, Charles Paul de** 1794-1871 . **NCLC 16**

**Koda Rohan**
See Koda Shigeyuki

**Koda Shigeyuki** 1867-1947 ............. **TCLC 22**
See also CA 121; 183; DLB 180

**Koestler, Arthur** 1905-1983 ... **CLC 1, 3, 6, 8, 15, 33**
See also BRWS 1; CA 1-4R; 109; CANR 1, 33; CDBLB 1945-1960; DLBY 83; MTCW 1, 2; RGEL

**Kogawa, Joy Nozomi** 1935- ...... **CLC 78, 129; DAC; DAM MST, MULT**
See also CA 101; CANR 19, 62; CN; CWP; FW; MTCW 2; NFS 3; SATA 99

**Kohout, Pavel** 1928- ......................... **CLC 13**
See also CA 45-48; CANR 3

**Koizumi, Yakumo**
See Hearn, (Patricio) Lafcadio (Tessima Carlos)

**Kolmar, Gertrud** 1894-1943 ........... **TCLC 40**
See also CA 167

**Komunyakaa, Yusef** 1947- ......... **CLC 86, 94; BLCS**
See also AFAW 2; CA 147; CANR 83; CP; CSW; DLB 120; PFS 5; RGAL

**Konrad, George**
See Konrad, Gyorgy
See also CWW 2

**Konrad, Gyorgy** 1933- ............. **CLC 4, 10, 73**
See also Konrad, George
See also CA 85-88; CANR 97; CWW 2; DLB 232

**Konwicki, Tadeusz** 1926- ........ **CLC 8, 28, 54, 117**
See also CA 101; CAAS 9; CANR 39, 59; CWW 2; DLB 232; IDFW 3; MTCW 1

**Koontz, Dean R(ay)** 1945- .... **CLC 78; DAM NOV, POP**
See also AAYA 9, 31; BEST 89:3, 90:2; CA 108; CANR 19, 36, 52, 95; CMW; CPW; DA3; HGG; MTCW 1; SATA 92; SFW; YAW

**Kopernik, Mikolaj**
See Copernicus, Nicolaus

**Kopit, Arthur (Lee)** 1937- ..... **CLC 1, 18, 33; DAM DRAM**
See also AITN 1; CA 81-84; CABS 3; CD; DFS 7; DLB 7; MTCW 1; RGAL

**Kops, Bernard** 1926- .......................... **CLC 4**
See also CA 5-8R; CANR 84; CBD; CN; CP; DLB 13

**Kornbluth, C(yril) M.** 1923-1958 .... **TCLC 8**
See also CA 105; 160; DLB 8; SFW

**Korolenko, V. G.**
See Korolenko, Vladimir Galaktionovich

**Korolenko, Vladimir**
See Korolenko, Vladimir Galaktionovich

**Korolenko, Vladimir G.**
See Korolenko, Vladimir Galaktionovich

**Korolenko, Vladimir Galaktionovich** 1853-1921 ................................ **TCLC 22**
See also CA 121

**Korzybski, Alfred (Habdank Skarbek)** 1879-1950 ................................ **TCLC 61**
See also CA 123; 160

**Kosinski, Jerzy (Nikodem)** 1933-1991 .... **CLC 1, 2, 3, 6, 10, 15, 53, 70; DAM NOV**
See also AMWS 7; BPFB 2; CA 17-20R; 134; CANR 9, 46; DA3; DLB 2; DLBY 82; HGG; MTCW 1, 2; NFS 12; RGAL

**Kostelanetz, Richard (Cory)** 1940- .. **CLC 28**
See also CA 13-16R; CAAS 8; CANR 38, 77; CN; CP

**Kotlowitz, Robert** 1924- ..................... **CLC 4**
See also CA 33-36R; CANR 36

**Kotzebue, August (Friedrich Ferdinand) von** 1761-1819 ................................ **NCLC 25**
See also DLB 94

**Kotzwinkle, William** 1938- ...... **CLC 5, 14, 35**
See also BPFB 2; CA 45-48; CANR 3, 44, 84; CLR 6; DLB 173; FANT; MAICYA; SATA 24, 70; SFW; YAW

**Kowna, Stancy**
See Szymborska, Wislawa

**Kozol, Jonathan** 1936- ....................... **CLC 17**
See also CA 61-64; CANR 16, 45, 96

**Kozoll, Michael** 1940(?)- .................... **CLC 35**

**Kramer, Kathryn** 19(?)- ..................... **CLC 34**

**Kramer, Larry** 1935- .. **CLC 42; DAM POP; DC 8**
See also CA 124; 126; CANR 60; GLL 1

**Krasicki, Ignacy** 1735-1801 ............... **NCLC 8**

**Krasinski, Zygmunt** 1812-1859 ........ **NCLC 4**
See also RGWL

**Kraus, Karl** 1874-1936 ....................... **TCLC 5**
See also CA 104; DLB 118

**Kreve (Mickevicius), Vincas** 1882-1954 ................................ **TCLC 27**
See also CA 170; DLB 220

**Kristeva, Julia** 1941- .................. **CLC 77, 140**
See also CA 154; CANR 99; DLB 242; FW

**Kristofferson, Kris** 1936- ................. **CLC 26**
See also CA 104

**Krizanc, John** 1956- ........................... **CLC 57**
See also CA 187

**Krleza, Miroslav** 1893-1981 ........ **CLC 8, 114**
See also CA 97-100; 105; CANR 50; DLB 147; EW; RGWL

**Kroetsch, Robert** 1927- . **CLC 5, 23, 57, 132; DAC; DAM POET**
See also CA 17-20R; CANR 8, 38; CCA 1; CN; CP; DLB 53; MTCW 1

**Kroetz, Franz**
See Kroetz, Franz Xaver
**Kroetz, Franz Xaver** 1946- ............... **CLC 41**
See also CA 130
**Kroker, Arthur (W.)** 1945- ............... **CLC 77**
See also CA 161
**Kropotkin, Peter (Aleksieevich)**
1842-1921 ................................. **TCLC 36**
See also CA 119
**Krotkov, Yuri** 1917-1981 ................... **CLC 19**
See also CA 102
**Krumb**
See Crumb, R(obert)
**Krumgold, Joseph (Quincy)**
1908-1980 ..................................... **CLC 12**
See also BYA 1, 2; CA 9-12R; 101; CANR 7; MAICYA; SATA 1, 48; SATA-Obit 23; YAW
**Krumwitz**
See Crumb, R(obert)
**Krutch, Joseph Wood** 1893-1970 ..... **CLC 24**
See also ANW; CA 1-4R; 25-28R; CANR 4; DLB 63, 206
**Krutzch, Gus**
See Eliot, T(homas) S(tearns)
**Krylov, Ivan Andreevich**
1768(?)-1844 ............................. **NCLC 1**
See also DLB 150
**Kubin, Alfred (Leopold Isidor)**
1877-1959 ................................. **TCLC 23**
See also CA 112; 149; DLB 81
**Kubrick, Stanley** 1928-1999 ............. **CLC 16**
See also AAYA 30; CA 81-84; 177; CANR 33; DLB 26; TCLC 112
**Kueng, Hans** 1928-
See Kung, Hans
See also CA 53-56; CANR 66; MTCW 1, 2
**Kumin, Maxine (Winokur)** 1925- ..... **CLC 5, 13, 28; DAM POET; PC 15**
See also AITN 2; AMWS 4; ANW; CA 1-4R; CAAS 8; CANR 1, 21, 69; CP; CWP; DA3; DLB 5; EXPP; MTCW 1, 2; PAB; SATA 12
**Kundera, Milan** 1929- . **CLC 4, 9, 19, 32, 68, 115, 135; DAM NOV; SSC 24**
See also AAYA 2; BPFB 2; CA 85-88; CANR 19, 52, 74; CWW 2; DA3; DLB 232; EW; MTCW 1, 2; RGSF; SSFS 10
**Kunene, Mazisi (Raymond)** 1930- ... **CLC 85**
See also BW 1, 3; CA 125; CANR 81; DLB 117
**Kung, Hans** ........................................ **CLC 130**
See also Kueng, Hans
**Kunikida, Doppo** 1869(?)-1908 ....... **TCLC 99**
See also DLB 180
**Kunitz, Stanley (Jasspon)** 1905- .. **CLC 6, 11, 14, 148; PC 19**
See also AMWS 3; CA 41-44R; CANR 26, 57, 98; CP; DA3; DLB 48; INT CANR-26; MTCW 1, 2; PFS 11; RGAL
**Kunze, Reiner** 1933- .......................... **CLC 10**
See also CA 93-96; CWW 2; DLB 75
**Kuprin, Aleksander Ivanovich**
1870-1938 ................................... **TCLC 5**
See also CA 104; 182
**Kureishi, Hanif** 1954(?)- ........... **CLC 64, 135**
See also CA 139; CBD; CD; CN; DLB 194, 245; GLL 2; IDFW 4; WLIT 4
**Kurosawa, Akira** 1910-1998 .... **CLC 16, 119; DAM MULT**
See also AAYA 11; CA 101; 170; CANR 46
**Kushner, Tony** 1957(?)- .......... **CLC 81; DAM DRAM; DC 10**
See also AMWS 9; CA 144; CAD; CANR 74; CD; DA3; DFS 5; DLB 228; GLL 1; LAIT 5; MTCW 2; RGAL
**Kuttner, Henry** 1915-1958 ............... **TCLC 10**
See also CA 107; 157; DLB 8; FANT; SFW

**Kuzma, Greg** 1944- ............................. **CLC 7**
See also CA 33-36R; CANR 70
**Kuzmin, Mikhail** 1872(?)-1936 ...... **TCLC 40**
See also CA 170
**Kyd, Thomas** 1558-1594 .......... **LC 22; DAM DRAM; DC 3**
See also BRW 1; DLB 62; IDTP; RGEL; TEA; WLIT 3
**Kyprianos, Iossif**
See Samarakis, Antonis
**La Bruyere, Jean de** 1645-1696 ......... **LC 17**
See also EW; GFL Beginnings to 1789
**Lacan, Jacques (Marie Emile)**
1901-1981 ................................... **CLC 75**
See also CA 121; 104
**Laclos, Pierre Ambroise Francois**
1741-1803 ................................. **NCLC 4, 87**
See also EW; GFL Beginnings to 1789; RGWL
**Lacolere, Francois**
See Aragon, Louis
**La Colere, Francois**
See Aragon, Louis
**La Deshabilleuse**
See Simenon, Georges (Jacques Christian)
**Lady Gregory**
See Gregory, Lady Isabella Augusta (Persse)
**Lady of Quality, A**
See Bagnold, Enid
**La Fayette, Marie-(Madelaine Pioche de la Vergne)** 1634-1693 ......................... **LC 2**
See also GFL Beginnings to 1789; RGWL
**Lafayette, Rene**
See Hubbard, L(afayette) Ron(ald)
**La Fontaine, Jean de** 1621-1695 ......... **LC 50**
See also EW; GFL Beginnings to 1789; MAICYA; RGWL; SATA 18
**Laforgue, Jules** 1860-1887 . **NCLC 5, 53; PC 14; SSC 20**
See also EW; GFL 1789 to the Present; RGWL
**Lagerkvist, Paer (Fabian)**
1891-1974 ...... **CLC 7, 10, 13, 54; DAM DRAM, NOV**
See also Lagerkvist, Par
See also CA 85-88; 49-52; DA3; EW; MTCW 1, 2
**Lagerkvist, Par** ................................ **SSC 12**
See also Lagerkvist, Paer (Fabian)
See also MTCW 2; RGSF; RGWL
**Lagerloef, Selma (Ottiliana Lovisa)**
1858-1940 ................................. **TCLC 4, 36**
See also Lagerlof, Selma (Ottiliana Lovisa)
See also CA 108; MTCW 2; SATA 15
**Lagerlof, Selma (Ottiliana Lovisa)**
See Lagerloef, Selma (Ottiliana Lovisa)
See also CLR 7; SATA 15
**La Guma, (Justin) Alex(ander)**
1925-1985 .......... **CLC 19; BLCS; DAM NOV**
See also AFW; BW 1, 3; CA 49-52; 118; CANR 25, 81; DLB 117, 225; MTCW 1, 2; WLIT 2
**Laidlaw, A. K.**
See Grieve, C(hristopher) M(urray)
**Lainez, Manuel Mujica**
See Mujica Lainez, Manuel
See also HW 1
**Laing, R(onald) D(avid)** 1927-1989 . **CLC 95**
See also CA 107; 129; CANR 34; MTCW 1
**Lamartine, Alphonse (Marie Louis Prat) de**
1790-1869 . **NCLC 11; DAM POET; PC 16**
See also GFL 1789 to the Present; RGWL
**Lamb, Charles** 1775-1834 ..... **NCLC 10; DA; DAB; DAC; DAM MST; WLC**
See also BRW 4; CDBLB 1789-1832; DLB 93, 107, 163; RGEL; SATA 17

**Lamb, Lady Caroline** 1785-1828 ... **NCLC 38**
See also DLB 116
**Lamming, George (William)** 1927- ... **CLC 2, 4, 66, 144; BLC 2; DAM MULT**
See also BW 2, 3; CA 85-88; CANR 26, 76; DLB 125; MTCW 1, 2
**L'Amour, Louis (Dearborn)**
1908-1988 ...... **CLC 25, 55; DAM NOV, POP**
See also Burns, Tex; Mayo, Jim
See also AAYA 16; AITN 2; BEST 89:2; BPFB 2; CA 1-4R; 125; CANR 3, 25, 40; CPW; DA3; DLB 206; DLBY 80; MTCW 1, 2; RGAL
**Lampedusa, Giuseppe (Tomasi) di**
..................................................... **TCLC 13**
See also Tomasi di Lampedusa, Giuseppe
See also CA 164; DLB 177; EW; MTCW 2; RGWL
**Lampman, Archibald** 1861-1899 ... **NCLC 25**
See also DLB 92; RGEL
**Lancaster, Bruce** 1896-1963 ............. **CLC 36**
See also CA 9-10; CANR 70; CAP 1; SATA 9
**Lanchester, John** ............................... **CLC 99**
See also CA 194
**Landau, Mark Alexandrovich**
See Aldanov, Mark (Alexandrovich)
**Landau-Aldanov, Mark Alexandrovich**
See Aldanov, Mark (Alexandrovich)
**Landis, Jerry**
See Simon, Paul (Frederick)
**Landis, John** 1950- ............................. **CLC 26**
See also CA 112; 122
**Landolfi, Tommaso** 1908-1979 .... **CLC 11, 49**
See also CA 127; 117; DLB 177
**Landon, Letitia Elizabeth**
1802-1838 ................................. **NCLC 15**
See also DLB 96
**Landor, Walter Savage**
1775-1864 ................................. **NCLC 14**
See also BRW 4; DLB 93, 107; RGEL
**Landwirth, Heinz** 1927-
See Lind, Jakov
See also CA 9-12R; CANR 7
**Lane, Patrick** 1939- ... **CLC 25; DAM POET**
See also CA 97-100; CANR 54; CP; DLB 53; INT 97-100
**Lang, Andrew** 1844-1912 ................. **TCLC 16**
See also CA 114; 137; CANR 85; DLB 98, 141, 184; FANT; MAICYA; RGEL; SATA 16
**Lang, Fritz** 1890-1976 ............... **CLC 20, 103**
See also CA 77-80; 69-72; CANR 30
**Lange, John**
See Crichton, (John) Michael
**Langer, Elinor** 1939- ........................ **CLC 34**
See also CA 121
**Langland, William** 1332(?)-1400(?) ... **LC 19; DA; DAB; DAC; DAM MST, POET**
See also BRW 1; DLB 146; RGEL; WLIT 3
**Langstaff, Launcelot**
See Irving, Washington
**Lanier, Sidney** 1842-1881 ..... **NCLC 6; DAM POET**
See also AMWS 1; DLB 64; DLBD 13; EXPP; MAICYA; RGAL; SATA 18
**Lanyer, Aemilia** 1569-1645 ............ **LC 10, 30**
See also DLB 121
**Lao Tzu** c. 6th cent. B.C.-3rd cent. B.C. .................................................. **CMLC 7**
**Lao-Tzu**
See Lao Tzu
**Lapine, James (Elliot)** 1949- ............. **CLC 39**
See also CA 123; 130; CANR 54; INT 130

**Larbaud, Valery (Nicolas)**
1881-1957 .................................. **TCLC 9**
See also CA 106; 152; GFL 1789 to the Present

**Lardner, Ring**
See Lardner, Ring(gold) W(ilmer)
See also BPFB 2; RGAL; RGSF

**Lardner, Ring W., Jr.**
See Lardner, Ring(gold) W(ilmer)

**Lardner, Ring(gold) W(ilmer)**
1885-1933 .............. **TCLC 2, 14; SSC 32**
See also Lardner, Ring
See also AMW; CA 104; 131; CDALB 1917-1929; DLB 11, 25, 86, 171; DLBD 16; MTCW 1, 2

**Laredo, Betty**
See Codrescu, Andrei

**Larkin, Maia**
See Wojciechowska, Maia (Teresa)

**Larkin, Philip (Arthur)** 1922-1985 ... **CLC 3, 5, 8, 9, 13, 18, 33, 39, 64; DAB; DAM MST, POET; PC 21**
See also BRWS 1; CA 5-8R; 117; CANR 24, 62; CDBLB 1960 to Present; DA3; DLB 27; MTCW 1, 2; PFS 3, 4, 12; RGEL

**Larra (y Sanchez de Castro), Mariano Jose de** 1809-1837 ........................... **NCLC 17**

**Larsen, Eric** 1941- .............................. **CLC 55**
See also CA 132

**Larsen, Nella** 1893-1963 .... **CLC 37; BLC 2; DAM MULT**
See also AFAW 1, 2; BW 1; CA 125; CANR 83; DLB 51; FW

**Larson, Charles R(aymond)** 1938- ... **CLC 31**
See also CA 53-56; CANR 4

**Larson, Jonathan** 1961-1996 ............. **CLC 99**
See also AAYA 28; CA 156

**Las Casas, Bartolome de** 1474-1566 . **LC 31; HLC**
See also Casas, Bartolome de las
See also LAW

**Lasch, Christopher** 1932-1994 ........ **CLC 102**
See also CA 73-76; 144; CANR 25; DLB 246; MTCW 1, 2

**Lasker-Schueler, Else** 1869-1945 ... **TCLC 57**
See also CA 183; DLB 66, 124

**Laski, Harold J(oseph)** 1893-1950 . **TCLC 79**
See also CA 188

**Latham, Jean Lee** 1902-1995 ............. **CLC 12**
See also AITN 1; BYA 1; CA 5-8R; CANR 7, 84; CLR 50; MAICYA; SATA 2, 68; YAW

**Latham, Mavis**
See Clark, Mavis Thorpe

**Lathen, Emma** ...................................... **CLC 2**
See also Hennissart, Martha; Latsis, Mary J(ane)
See also BPFB 2; CMW

**Lathrop, Francis**
See Leiber, Fritz (Reuter, Jr.)

**Latsis, Mary J(ane)** 1927(?)-1997
See Lathen, Emma
See also CA 85-88; 162; CMW

**Lattimore, Richmond (Alexander)**
1906-1984 ..................................... **CLC 3**
See also CA 1-4R; 112; CANR 1

**Laughlin, James** 1914-1997 ............. **CLC 49**
See also CA 21-24R; 162; CAAS 22; CANR 9, 47; CP; DLB 48; DLBY 96, 97

**Laurence, (Jean) Margaret (Wemyss)**
1926-1987 . **CLC 3, 6, 13, 50, 62; DAC; DAM MST; SSC 7**
See also BRW 13; CA 5-8R; 121; CANR 33; DLB 53; FW; MTCW 1, 2; NFS 11; RGEL; RGSF; SATA-Obit 50; TCWW 2

**Laurent, Antoine** 1952- ..................... **CLC 50**

**Lauscher, Hermann**
See Hesse, Hermann

**Lautreamont** 1846-1870 .. **NCLC 12; SSC 14**
See also GFL 1789 to the Present; RGWL

**Laverty, Donald**
See Blish, James (Benjamin)

**Lavin, Mary** 1912-1996 . **CLC 4, 18, 99; SSC 4**
See also CA 9-12R; 151; CANR 33; CN; DLB 15; FW; MTCW 1; RGEL; RGSF

**Lavond, Paul Dennis**
See Kornbluth, C(yril) M.; Pohl, Frederik

**Lawler, Raymond Evenor** 1922- ....... **CLC 58**
See also CA 103; CD; RGEL

**Lawrence, D(avid) H(erbert Richards)**
1885-1930 .... **TCLC 2, 9, 16, 33, 48, 61, 93; DA; DAB; DAC; DAM MST, NOV, POET; SSC 4, 19; WLC**
See also Chambers, Jessie
See also BPFB 2; BRW 7; CA 104; 121; CDBLB 1914-1945; DA3; DLB 10, 19, 36, 98, 162, 195; EXPP; EXPS; LAIT 2, 3; MTCW 1, 2; PFS 6; RGEL; RGSF; SSFS 2, 6; WLIT 4; WP

**Lawrence, T(homas) E(dward)**
1888-1935 ............................. **TCLC 18**
See also Dale, Colin
See also BRWS 2; CA 115; 167; DLB 195

**Lawrence of Arabia**
See Lawrence, T(homas) E(dward)

**Lawson, Henry (Archibald Hertzberg)**
1867-1922 ................. **TCLC 27; SSC 18**
See also CA 120; 181; DLB 230; RGEL; RGSF

**Lawton, Dennis**
See Faust, Frederick (Schiller)

**Laxness, Halldor** .............................. **CLC 25**
See also Gudjonsson, Halldor Kiljan
See also EW; RGWL

**Layamon** fl. c. 1200- ....................... **CMLC 10**
See also DLB 146; RGEL

**Laye, Camara** 1928-1980 ... **CLC 4, 38; BLC 2; DAM MULT**
See also AFW; BW 1; CA 85-88; 97-100; CANR 25; MTCW 1, 2; WLIT 2

**Layton, Irving (Peter)** 1912- ....... **CLC 2, 15; DAC; DAM MST, POET**
See also CA 1-4R; CANR 2, 33, 43, 66; CP; DLB 88; MTCW 1, 2; PFS 12; RGEL

**Lazarus, Emma** 1849-1887 ............... **NCLC 8**

**Lazarus, Felix**
See Cable, George Washington

**Lazarus, Henry**
See Slavitt, David R(ytman)

**Lea, Joan**
See Neufeld, John (Arthur)

**Leacock, Stephen (Butler)**
1869-1944 ............ **TCLC 2; DAC; DAM MST; SSC 39**
See also CA 104; 141; CANR 80; DLB 92; MTCW 2; RGEL; RGSF

**Lead, Jane Ward** 1623-1704 ................ **LC 72**
See also DLB 131

**Lear, Edward** 1812-1888 ................ **NCLC 3**
See also BRW 5; CLR 1, 75; DLB 32, 163, 166; MAICYA; RGEL; SATA 18, 100; WP

**Lear, Norman (Milton)** 1922- ........... **CLC 12**
See also CA 73-76

**Leautaud, Paul** 1872-1956 ............. **TCLC 83**
See also DLB 65; GFL 1789 to the Present

**Leavis, F(rank) R(aymond)**
1895-1978 ..................................... **CLC 24**
See also BRW 7; CA 21-24R; 77-80; CANR 44; DLB 242; MTCW 1, 2; RGEL

**Leavitt, David** 1961- ..... **CLC 34; DAM POP**
See also CA 116; 122; CANR 50, 62, 101; CPW; DA3; DLB 130; GLL 1; INT 122; MTCW 2

**Leblanc, Maurice (Marie Emile)**
1864-1941 .................... **TCLC 49**
See also CA 110; CMW

**Lebowitz, Fran(ces Ann)** 1951(?)- ... **CLC 11, 36**
See also CA 81-84; CANR 14, 60, 70; INT CANR-14; MTCW 1

**Lebrecht, Peter**
See Tieck, (Johann) Ludwig

**le Carre, John** ............... **CLC 3, 5, 9, 15, 28**
See also Cornwell, David (John Moore)
See also AAYA 42; BEST 89:4; BPFB 2; BRWS 2; CDBLB 1960 to Present; CMW; CN; CPW; DLB 87; MSW; MTCW 2; RGEL

**Le Clezio, J(ean) M(arie) G(ustave)**
1940- ............................................. **CLC 31**
See also CA 116; 128; DLB 83; GFL 1789 to the Present; RGSF

**Leconte de Lisle, Charles-Marie-Rene**
1818-1894 .................................. **NCLC 29**
See also EW; GFL 1789 to the Present

**Le Coq, Monsieur**
See Simenon, Georges (Jacques Christian)

**Leduc, Violette** 1907-1972 ................. **CLC 22**
See also CA 13-14; 33-36R; CANR 69; CAP 1; GFL 1789 to the Present; GLL 1

**Ledwidge, Francis** 1887(?)-1917 .... **TCLC 23**
See also CA 123; DLB 20

**Lee, Andrea** 1953- ... **CLC 36; BLC 2; DAM MULT**
See also BW 1, 3; CA 125; CANR 82

**Lee, Andrew**
See Auchincloss, Louis (Stanton)

**Lee, Chang-rae** 1965- ....................... **CLC 91**
See also CA 148; CANR 89

**Lee, Don L.** .......................................... **CLC 2**
See also Madhubuti, Haki R.

**Lee, George W(ashington)**
1894-1976 ......... **CLC 52; BLC 2; DAM MULT**
See also BW 1; CA 125; CANR 83; DLB 51

**Lee, (Nelle) Harper** 1926- . **CLC 12, 60; DA; DAB; DAC; DAM MST, NOV; WLC**
See also AAYA 13; AMWS 8; BPFB 2; BYA 3; CA 13-16R; CANR 51; CDALB 1941-1968; CSW; DA3; DLB 6; EXPN; LAIT 3; MTCW 1, 2; NFS 2; SATA 11; WYA; YAW

**Lee, Helen Elaine** 1959(?)- ................. **CLC 86**
See also CA 148

**Lee, John** ............................................. **CLC 70**

**Lee, Julian**
See Latham, Jean Lee

**Lee, Larry**
See Lee, Lawrence

**Lee, Laurie** 1914-1997 ............. **CLC 90; DAB; DAM POP**
See also CA 77-80; 158; CANR 33, 73; CP; CPW; DLB 27; MTCW 1; RGEL

**Lee, Lawrence** 1941-1990 ................. **CLC 34**
See also CA 131; CANR 43

**Lee, Li-Young** 1957- ............................ **PC 24**
See also CA 153; CP; DLB 165; PFS 11

**Lee, Manfred B(ennington)**
1905-1971 ..................................... **CLC 11**
See also Queen, Ellery
See also CA 1-4R; 29-32R; CANR 2; CMW; DLB 137

**Lee, Shelton Jackson** 1957(?)- ....... **CLC 105; BLCS; DAM MULT**
See also Lee, Spike
See also BW 2, 3; CA 125; CANR 42

**Lee, Spike**
See Lee, Shelton Jackson
See also AAYA 4, 29

**Lee, Stan** 1922- ................................. **CLC 17**
See also AAYA 5; CA 108; 111; INT 111

**Lee, Tanith** 1947- .................... **CLC 46**
See also AAYA 15; CA 37-40R; CANR 53, 102; FANT; SATA 8, 88; SFW; YAW

**Lee, Vernon** ...................... **TCLC 5; SSC 33**
See also Paget, Violet
See also DLB 57, 153, 156, 174, 178; GLL 1

**Lee, William**
See Burroughs, William S(eward)
See also GLL 1

**Lee, Willy**
See Burroughs, William S(eward)
See also GLL 1

**Lee-Hamilton, Eugene (Jacob)**
1845-1907 ..................... **TCLC 22**
See also CA 117

**Leet, Judith** 1935- .................... **CLC 11**
See also CA 187

**Le Fanu, Joseph Sheridan**
1814-1873 ..... **NCLC 9, 58; DAM POP; SSC 14**
See also CMW; DA3; DLB 21, 70, 159, 178; HGG; RGEL; RGSF; SUFW

**Leffland, Ella** 1931- ..................... **CLC 19**
See also CA 29-32R; CANR 35, 78, 82; DLBY 84; INT CANR-35; SATA 65

**Leger, Alexis**
See Leger, (Marie-Rene Auguste) Alexis Saint-Leger

**Leger, (Marie-Rene Auguste) Alexis Saint-Leger** 1887-1975 .. **CLC 4, 11, 46; DAM POET; PC 23**
See also Saint-John Perse
See also CA 13-16R; 61-64; CANR 43; MTCW 1

**Leger, Saintleger**
See Leger, (Marie-Rene Auguste) Alexis Saint-Leger

**Le Guin, Ursula K(roeber)** 1929- ..... **CLC 8, 13, 22, 45, 71, 136; DAB; DAC; DAM MST, POP; SSC 12**
See also AAYA 9, 27; AITN 1; BPFB 2; BYA 5, 8, 11; CA 21-24R; CANR 9, 32, 52, 74; CDALBS 1968-1988; CLR 3, 28; CN; CPW; DA3; DLB 8, 52; EXPS; FANT; FW; INT CANR-32; JRDA; LAIT 5; MAICYA; MTCW 1, 2; NFS 6, 9; SATA 4, 52, 99; SCFW; SFW; SSFS 2; SUFW; WYA; YAW

**Lehmann, Rosamond (Nina)**
1901-1990 ..................... **CLC 5**
See also CA 77-80; 131; CANR 8, 73; DLB 15; MTCW 2; RGEL; RHW

**Leiber, Fritz (Reuter, Jr.)**
1910-1992 ..................... **CLC 25**
See also BPFB 2; CA 45-48; 139; CANR 2, 40, 86; DLB 8; FANT; HGG; MTCW 1, 2; SATA 45; SATA-Obit 73; SCFW 2; SFW; SUFW

**Leibniz, Gottfried Wilhelm von**
1646-1716 ..................... **LC 35**
See also DLB 168

**Leimbach, Martha** 1963-
See Leimbach, Marti
See also CA 130

**Leimbach, Marti** ..................... **CLC 65**
See also Leimbach, Martha

**Leino, Eino** ..................... **TCLC 24**
See also Loennbohm, Armas Eino Leopold

**Leiris, Michel (Julien)** 1901-1990 ..... **CLC 61**
See also CA 119; 128; 132; GFL 1789 to the Present

**Leithauser, Brad** 1953- ..................... **CLC 27**
See also CA 107; CANR 27, 81; CP; DLB 120

**Lelchuk, Alan** 1938- ..................... **CLC 5**
See also CA 45-48; CAAS 20; CANR 1, 70; CN

**Lem, Stanislaw** 1921- ...... **CLC 8, 15, 40, 149**
See also CA 105; CAAS 1; CANR 32; CWW 2; MTCW 1; SCFW 2; SFW

**Lemann, Nancy** 1956- ..................... **CLC 39**
See also CA 118; 136

**Lemonnier, (Antoine Louis) Camille**
1844-1913 ..................... **TCLC 22**
See also CA 121

**Lenau, Nikolaus** 1802-1850 ........... **NCLC 16**

**L'Engle, Madeleine (Camp Franklin)**
1918- ..................... **CLC 12; DAM POP**
See also AAYA 28; AITN 2; BPFB 2; BYA 2, 4, 5, 7; CA 1-4R; CANR 3, 21, 39, 66; CLR 1, 14, 57; CPW; CWRI; DA3; DLB 52; JRDA; MAICYA; MTCW 1, 2; SAAS 15; SATA 1, 27, 75; SFW; WYA; YAW

**Lengyel, Jozsef** 1896-1975 ................. **CLC 7**
See also CA 85-88; 57-60; CANR 71; RGSF

**Lenin** 1870-1924
See Lenin, V. I.
See also CA 121; 168

**Lenin, V. I.** ..................... **TCLC 67**
See also Lenin

**Lennon, John (Ono)** 1940-1980 .. **CLC 12, 35**
See also CA 102; SATA 114

**Lennox, Charlotte Ramsay**
1729(?)-1804 ..................... **NCLC 23**
See also DLB 39; RGEL

**Lentricchia, Frank (Jr.)** 1940- .......... **CLC 34**
See also CA 25-28R; CANR 19; DLB 246

**Lenz, Gunter** ..................... **CLC 65**

**Lenz, Siegfried** 1926- ............ **CLC 27; SSC 33**
See also CA 89-92; CANR 80; CWW 2; DLB 75; RGSF; RGWL

**Leon, David**
See Jacob, (Cyprien-)Max

**Leonard, Elmore (John, Jr.)** 1925- . **CLC 28, 34, 71, 120; DAM POP**
See also AAYA 22; AITN 1; BEST 89:1, 90:4; BPFB 2; CA 81-84; CANR 12, 28, 53, 76, 96; CMW; CN; CPW; DA3; DLB 173, 226; INT CANR-28; MSW; MTCW 1, 2; RGAL; TCWW 2

**Leonard, Hugh** ..................... **CLC 19**
See Byrne, John Keyes
See also CBD; DLB 13

**Leonov, Leonid (Maximovich)**
1899-1994 ..................... **CLC 92; DAM NOV**
See also CA 129; CANR 74, 76; MTCW 1, 2

**Leopardi, Giacomo** 1798-1837 ..... **NCLC 22; PC 37**
See also EW; RGWL; WP

**Le Reveler**
See Artaud, Antonin (Marie Joseph)

**Lerman, Eleanor** 1952- ..................... **CLC 9**
See also CA 85-88; CANR 69

**Lerman, Rhoda** 1936- ..................... **CLC 56**
See also CA 49-52; CANR 70

**Lermontov, Mikhail Yuryevich**
1814-1841 ................. **NCLC 5, 47; PC 18**
See also DLB 205; EW; RGWL

**Leroux, Gaston** 1868-1927 ............. **TCLC 25**
See also CA 108; 136; CANR 69; CMW; SATA 65

**Lesage, Alain-Rene** 1668-1747 ........ **LC 2, 28**
See also EW; GFL Beginnings to 1789; RGWL

**Leskov, N(ikolai) S(emenovich)** 1831-1895
See Leskov, Nikolai (Semyonovich)

**Leskov, Nikolai (Semyonovich)**
1831-1895 ................. **NCLC 25; SSC 34**
See also Leskov, N(ikolai) S(emenovich)
See also DLB 238

**Leskov, Nikolai Semenovich**
See Leskov, Nikolai (Semyonovich)

**Lesser, Milton**
See Marlowe, Stephen

**Lessing, Doris (May)** 1919- ... **CLC 1, 2, 3, 6, 10, 15, 22, 40, 94; DA; DAB; DAC; DAM MST, NOV; SSC 6; WLCS**
See also AFW; BRWS 1; CA 9-12R; CAAS 14; CANR 33, 54, 76; CD; CDBLB 1960 to Present; CN; DA3; DLB 15, 139; DLBY 85; EXPS; FW; LAIT 4; MTCW 1, 2; RGEL; RGSF; SFW; SSFS 1, 12; WLIT 2, 4

**Lessing, Gotthold Ephraim** 1729-1781 . **LC 8**
See also DLB 97; EW; RGWL

**Lester, Richard** 1932- ..................... **CLC 20**

**Levenson, Jay** ..................... **CLC 70**

**Lever, Charles (James)**
1806-1872 ..................... **NCLC 23**
See also DLB 21; RGEL

**Leverson, Ada** 1865(?)-1936(?) ....... **TCLC 18**
See also Elaine
See also CA 117; DLB 153; RGEL

**Levertov, Denise** 1923-1997 .. **CLC 1, 2, 3, 5, 8, 15, 28, 66; DAM POET; PC 11**
See also AMWS 3; CA 1-4R; 178; 163; CAAE 178; CAAS 19; CANR 3, 29, 50; CDALBS; CP; CWP; DLB 5, 165; EXPP; FW; INT CANR-29; MTCW 1, 2; PAB; PFS 7; RGAL; WP

**Levi, Jonathan** ..................... **CLC 76**

**Levi, Peter (Chad Tigar)**
1931-2000 ..................... **CLC 41**
See also CA 5-8R; 187; CANR 34, 80; CP; DLB 40

**Levi, Primo** 1919-1987 . **CLC 37, 50; SSC 12**
See also CA 13-16R; 122; CANR 12, 33, 61, 70; DLB 177; MTCW 1, 2; RGWL; TCLC 109

**Levin, Ira** 1929- .......... **CLC 3, 6; DAM POP**
See also CA 21-24R; CANR 17, 44, 74; CMW; CN; CPW; DA3; HGG; MTCW 1, 2; SATA 66; SFW

**Levin, Meyer** 1905-1981 .......... **CLC 7; DAM POP**
See also AITN 1; CA 9-12R; 104; CANR 15; DLB 9, 28; DLBY 81; SATA 21; SATA-Obit 27

**Levine, Norman** 1924- ..................... **CLC 54**
See also CA 73-76; CAAS 23; CANR 14, 70; DLB 88

**Levine, Philip** 1928- .. **CLC 2, 4, 5, 9, 14, 33, 118; DAM POET; PC 22**
See also AMWS 5; CA 9-12R; CANR 9, 37, 52; CP; DLB 5; PFS 8

**Levinson, Deirdre** 1931- ..................... **CLC 49**
See also CA 73-76; CANR 70

**Levi-Strauss, Claude** 1908- ................. **CLC 38**
See also CA 1-4R; CANR 6, 32, 57; DLB 242; GFL 1789 to the Present; MTCW 1, 2

**Levitin, Sonia (Wolff)** 1934- ............... **CLC 17**
See also AAYA 13; CA 29-32R; CANR 14, 32, 79; CLR 53; JRDA; MAICYA; SAAS 2; SATA 4, 68, 119; YAW

**Levon, O. U.**
See Kesey, Ken (Elton)

**Levy, Amy** 1861-1889 ..................... **NCLC 59**
See also DLB 156, 240

**Lewes, George Henry** 1817-1878 ... **NCLC 25**
See also DLB 55, 144

**Lewis, Alun** 1915-1944 ....... **TCLC 3; SSC 40**
See also BRW 7; CA 104; 188; DLB 20, 162; PAB; RGEL

**Lewis, C. Day**
See Day Lewis, C(ecil)

**Lewis, C(live) S(taples)** 1898-1963 .... **CLC 1, 3, 6, 14, 27, 124; DA; DAB; DAC; DAM MST, NOV, POP; WLC**
See also AAYA 3, 39; BPFB 2; BRWS 3; CA 81-84; CANR 33, 71; CDBLB 1945-1960; CLR 3, 27; CWRI; DA3; DLB 15,

100, 160; FANT; JRDA; MAICYA; MTCW 1, 2; RGEL; SATA 13, 100; SCFW; SFW; SUFW; WCH; WYA; YAW

**Lewis, Cecil Day**
See Day Lewis, C(ecil)

**Lewis, Janet** 1899-1998 ............... **CLC 41**
See also Winters, Janet Lewis
See also CA 9-12R; 172; CANR 29, 63; CAP 1; CN; DLBY 87; RHW; TCWW 2

**Lewis, Matthew Gregory**
1775-1818 ............... **NCLC 11, 62**
See also DLB 39, 158, 178; HGG; RGEL; SUFW

**Lewis, (Harry) Sinclair** 1885-1951 . **TCLC 4, 13, 23, 39; DA; DAB; DAC; DAM MST, NOV; WLC**
See also AMW; BPFB 2; CA 104; 133; CDALB 1917-1929; DA3; DLB 9, 102; DLBD 1; LAIT 3; MTCW 1, 2; RGAL

**Lewis, (Percy) Wyndham**
1884(?)-1957 ....... **TCLC 2, 9, 104; SSC 34**
See also BRW 7; CA 104; 157; DLB 15; FANT; MTCW 2; RGEL

**Lewisohn, Ludwig** 1883-1955 ......... **TCLC 19**
See also CA 107; DLB 4, 9, 28, 102

**Lewton, Val** 1904-1951 ................. **TCLC 76**
See also IDFW 3, 4

**Leyner, Mark** 1956- .......................... **CLC 92**
See also CA 110; CANR 28, 53; DA3; MTCW 2

**Lezama Lima, Jose** 1910-1976 .... **CLC 4, 10, 101; DAM MULT; HLCS 2**
See also CA 77-80; CANR 71; DLB 113; HW 1, 2; LAW; RGWL

**L'Heureux, John (Clarke)** 1934- ...... **CLC 52**
See also CA 13-16R; CANR 23, 45, 88; DLB 244

**Liddell, C. H.**
See Kuttner, Henry

**Lie, Jonas (Lauritz Idemil)**
1833-1908(?) ........................... **TCLC 5**
See also CA 115

**Lieber, Joel** 1937-1971 ........................ **CLC 6**
See also CA 73-76; 29-32R

**Lieber, Stanley Martin**
See Lee, Stan

**Lieberman, Laurence (James)**
1935- ....................................... **CLC 4, 36**
See also CA 17-20R; CANR 8, 36, 89; CP

**Lieh Tzu** fl. 7th cent. B.C.-5th cent. B.C. ........................................... **CMLC 27**

**Lieksman, Anders**
See Haavikko, Paavo Juhani

**Li Fei-kan** 1904-
See Pa Chin
See also CA 105

**Lifton, Robert Jay** 1926- ................... **CLC 67**
See also CA 17-20R; CANR 27, 78; INT CANR-27; SATA 66

**Lightfoot, Gordon** 1938- ................... **CLC 26**
See also CA 109

**Lightman, Alan P(aige)** 1948- ........... **CLC 81**
See also CA 141; CANR 63

**Ligotti, Thomas (Robert)** 1953- ...... **CLC 44; SSC 16**
See also CA 123; CANR 49; HGG

**Li Ho** 791-817 ......................................... **PC 13**

**Liliencron, (Friedrich Adolf Axel) Detlev von** 1844-1909 ........................... **TCLC 18**
See also CA 117

**Lilly, William** 1602-1681 ..................... **LC 27**

**Lima, Jose Lezama**
See Lezama Lima, Jose

**Lima Barreto, Afonso Henrique de**
1881-1922 ............................ **TCLC 23**
See also CA 117; 181; LAW

**Lima Barreto, Afonso Henriques de**
See Lima Barreto, Afonso Henrique de

**Limonov, Edward** 1944- .................... **CLC 67**
See also CA 137

**Lin, Frank**
See Atherton, Gertrude (Franklin Horn)

**Lincoln, Abraham** 1809-1865 ......... **NCLC 18**
See also LAIT 2

**Lind, Jakov** ............... **CLC 1, 2, 4, 27, 82**
See also Landwirth, Heinz
See also CAAS 4

**Lindbergh, Anne (Spencer) Morrow**
1906-2001 ................ **CLC 82; DAM NOV**
See also BPFB 2; CA 17-20R; 193; CANR 16, 73; MTCW 1, 2; SATA 33; SATA-Obit 125

**Lindsay, David** 1878(?)-1945 .......... **TCLC 15**
See also CA 113; 187; FANT; SFW

**Lindsay, (Nicholas) Vachel**
1879-1931 . **TCLC 17; DA; DAC; DAM MST, POET; PC 23; WLC**
See also AMWS 1; CA 114; 135; CANR 79; CDALB 1865-1917; DA3; DLB 54; EXPP; RGAL; SATA 40; WP

**Linke-Poot**
See Doeblin, Alfred

**Linney, Romulus** 1930- ....................... **CLC 51**
See also CA 1-4R; CAD; CANR 40, 44, 79; CD; CSW; RGAL

**Linton, Eliza Lynn** 1822-1898 ....... **NCLC 41**
See also DLB 18

**Li Po** 701-763 ....................... **CMLC 2; PC 29**
See also WP

**Lipsius, Justus** 1547-1606 ..................... **LC 16**

**Lipsyte, Robert (Michael)** 1938- ...... **CLC 21; DA; DAC; DAM MST, NOV**
See also AAYA 7; CA 17-20R; CANR 8, 57; CLR 23; JRDA; LAIT 5; MAICYA; SATA 5, 68, 113; WYA; YAW

**Lish, Gordon (Jay)** 1934- ... **CLC 45; SSC 18**
See also CA 113; 117; CANR 79; DLB 130; INT 117

**Lispector, Clarice** 1925(?)-1977 ....... **CLC 43; HLCS 2; SSC 34**
See also CA 139; 116; CANR 71; DLB 113; DNFS; FW; HW 2; LAW; RGSF; RGWL; WLIT 1

**Littell, Robert** 1935(?)- ....................... **CLC 42**
See also CA 109; 112; CANR 64; CMW

**Little, Malcolm** 1925-1965
See Malcolm X
See also BW 1, 3; CA 125; 111; CANR 82; DA; DA3; DAB; DAC; DAM MST, MULT; MTCW 1, 2

**Littlewit, Humphrey Gent.**
See Lovecraft, H(oward) P(hillips)

**Litwos**
See Sienkiewicz, Henryk (Adam Alexander Pius)

**Liu, E.** 1857-1909 ............................ **TCLC 15**
See also CA 115; 190

**Lively, Penelope (Margaret)** 1933- .. **CLC 32, 50; DAM NOV**
See also BPFB 2; CA 41-44R; CANR 29, 67, 79; CLR 7; CN; CWRI; DLB 14, 161, 207; FANT; JRDA; MAICYA; MTCW 1, 2; SATA 7, 60, 101

**Livesay, Dorothy (Kathleen)**
1909-1996 . **CLC 4, 15, 79; DAC; DAM MST, POET**
See also AITN 2; CA 25-28R; CAAS 8; CANR 36, 67; DLB 68; FW; MTCW 1; RGEL

**Livy** c. 59B.C.-c. 12 ....................... **CMLC 11**
See also AW 2; DLB 211; RGWL

**Lizardi, Jose Joaquin Fernandez de**
1776-1827 ............................ **NCLC 30**
See also LAW

**Llewellyn, Richard**
See Llewellyn Lloyd, Richard Dafydd Vivian
See also DLB 15

**Llewellyn Lloyd, Richard Dafydd Vivian**
1906-1983 ............................ **CLC 7, 80**
See also Llewellyn, Richard
See also CA 53-56; 111; CANR 7, 71; SATA 11; SATA-Obit 37

**Llosa, (Jorge) Mario (Pedro) Vargas**
See Vargas Llosa, (Jorge) Mario (Pedro)
See also LAIT 5

**Lloyd, Manda**
See Mander, (Mary) Jane

**Lloyd Webber, Andrew** 1948-
See Webber, Andrew Lloyd
See also AAYA 1; CA 116; 149; DAM DRAM; SATA 56

**Llull, Ramon** c. 1235-c. 1316 ........ **CMLC 12**

**Lobb, Ebenezer**
See Upward, Allen

**Locke, Alain (Le Roy)** 1886-1954 . **TCLC 43; BLCS**
See also BW 1, 3; CA 106; 124; CANR 79; DLB 51; RGAL

**Locke, John** 1632-1704 .................... **LC 7, 35**
See also DLB 101; RGEL; WLIT 3

**Locke-Elliott, Sumner**
See Elliott, Sumner Locke

**Lockhart, John Gibson** 1794-1854 .. **NCLC 6**
See also DLB 110, 116, 144

**Lockridge, Ross (Franklin), Jr.**
1914-1948 ............................ **TCLC 111**
See also CA 108; 145; CANR 79; DLB 143; DLBY 80; RGAL; RHW

**Lodge, David (John)** 1935- ...... **CLC 36, 141; DAM POP**
See also BEST 90:1; BRWS 4; CA 17-20R; CANR 19, 53, 92; CN; CPW; DLB 14, 194; INT CANR-19; MTCW 1, 2

**Lodge, Thomas** 1558-1625 ................. **LC 41**
See also DLB 172; RGEL

**Loewinsohn, Ron(ald William)**
1937- ....................................... **CLC 52**
See also CA 25-28R; CANR 71

**Logan, Jake**
See Smith, Martin Cruz

**Logan, John (Burton)** 1923-1987 ........ **CLC 5**
See also CA 77-80; 124; CANR 45; DLB 5

**Lo Kuan-chung** 1330(?)-1400(?) ......... **LC 12**

**Lombard, Nap**
See Johnson, Pamela Hansford

**Lomotey (editor), Kofi** ..................... **CLC 70**

**London, Jack** ........ **TCLC 9, 15, 39; SSC 4; WLC**
See also London, John Griffith
See also AAYA 13; AITN 2; AMW; BPFB 2; BYA 4, 13; CDALB 1865-1917; DLB 8, 12, 78, 212; EXPS; LAIT 3; NFS 8; RGAL; RGSF; SATA 18; SSFS 7; TCWW 2

**London, John Griffith** 1876-1916
See London, Jack
See also AMW; CA 110; 119; CANR 73; DA; DA3; DAB; DAC; DAM MST, NOV; JRDA; MAICYA; MTCW 1, 2; SFW; TUS; WYA; YAW

**Long, Emmett**
See Leonard, Elmore (John, Jr.)

**Longbaugh, Harry**
See Goldman, William (W.)

**Longfellow, Henry Wadsworth**
1807-1882 .. **NCLC 2, 45, 101, 103; DA; DAB; DAC; DAM MST, POET; PC 30; WLCS**
See also AMW; CDALB 1640-1865; DA3; DLB 1, 59, 235; EXPP; PAB; PFS 2, 7; RGAL; SATA 19; WP

**Longinus** c. 1st cent. - .................. **CMLC 27**
  See also AW 2; DLB 176
**Longley, Michael** 1939- .................... **CLC 29**
  See also CA 102; CP; DLB 40
**Longus** fl. c. 2nd cent. - .................. **CMLC 7**
**Longway, A. Hugh**
  See Lang, Andrew
**Lonnrot, Elias** 1802-1884 ............... **NCLC 53**
  See also EFS 1
**Lonsdale, Roger** ed. ......................... **CLC 65**
**Lopate, Phillip** 1943- ...................... **CLC 29**
  See also CA 97-100; CANR 88; DLBY 80; INT 97-100
**Lopez, Barry (Holstun)** 1945- ........... **CLC 70**
  See also AAYA 9; ANW; CA 65-68; CANR 7, 23, 47, 68, 92; INT CANR-7, -23; MTCW 1; RGAL; SATA 67
**Lopez Portillo (y Pacheco), Jose** 1920- ................................................ **CLC 46**
  See also CA 129; HW 1
**Lopez y Fuentes, Gregorio** 1897(?)-1966 ................................. **CLC 32**
  See also CA 131; HW 1
**Lorca, Federico Garcia**
  See Garcia Lorca, Federico
  See also DFS 4; RGWL; WP
**Lord, Bette Bao** 1938- ............. **CLC 23; AAL**
  See also BEST 90:3; BPFB 2; CA 107; CANR 41, 79; INT CA-107; SATA 58
**Lord Auch**
  See Bataille, Georges
**Lord Byron**
  See Byron, George Gordon (Noel)
  See also PAB; WP
**Lorde, Audre (Geraldine)** 1934-1992 ... **CLC 18, 71; BLC 2; DAM MULT, POET; PC 12**
  See also Domini, Rey
  See also AFAW 1; BW 1, 3; CA 25-28R; 142; CANR 16, 26, 46, 82; DA3; DLB 41; FW; MTCW 1, 2; RGAL
**Lord Houghton**
  See Milnes, Richard Monckton
**Lord Jeffrey**
  See Jeffrey, Francis
**Loreaux, Nichol** ................................. **CLC 65**
**Lorenzini, Carlo** 1826-1890
  See Collodi, Carlo
  See also MAICYA; SATA 29, 100
**Lorenzo, Heberto Padilla**
  See Padilla (Lorenzo), Heberto
**Loris**
  See Hofmannsthal, Hugo von
**Loti, Pierre** ........................................ **TCLC 11**
  See also Viaud, (Louis Marie) Julien
  See also DLB 123; GFL 1789 to the Present
**Lou, Henri**
  See Andreas-Salome, Lou
**Louie, David Wong** 1954- .................. **CLC 70**
  See also CA 139
**Louis, Father M.**
  See Merton, Thomas
**Lovecraft, H(oward) P(hillips)** 1890-1937 ...... **TCLC 4, 22; DAM POP; SSC 3**
  See also AAYA 14; BPFB 2; CA 104; 133; DA3; HGG; MTCW 1, 2; RGAL; SCFW; SFW; SUFW
**Lovelace, Earl** 1935- ........................... **CLC 51**
  See also BW 2; CA 77-80; CANR 41, 72; CD; CN; DLB 125; MTCW 1
**Lovelace, Richard** 1618-1657 ............... **LC 24**
  See also BRW 2; DLB 131; EXPP; PAB; RGEL
**Lowell, Amy** 1874-1925 .... **TCLC 1, 8; DAM POET; PC 13**
  See also AMW; CA 104; 151; DLB 54, 140; EXPP; MAWW; MTCW 2; RGAL

**Lowell, James Russell** 1819-1891 ... **NCLC 2, 90**
  See also AMWS 1; CDALB 1640-1865; DLB 1, 11, 64, 79, 189, 235; RGAL
**Lowell, Robert (Traill Spence, Jr.)** 1917-1977 .... **CLC 1, 2, 3, 4, 5, 8, 9, 11, 15, 37, 124; DA; DAB; DAC; DAM MST, NOV; PC 3; WLC**
  See also AMW; CA 9-12R; 73-76; CABS 2; CANR 26, 60; CDALBS; DA3; DLB 5, 169; MTCW 1, 2; PAB; PFS 6, 7; RGAL; WP
**Lowenthal, Michael (Francis)** 1969- ................................................ **CLC 119**
  See also CA 150
**Lowndes, Marie Adelaide (Belloc)** 1868-1947 ................................. **TCLC 12**
  See also CA 107; CMW; DLB 70; RHW
**Lowry, (Clarence) Malcolm** 1909-1957 ............. **TCLC 6, 40; SSC 31**
  See also BPFB 2; BRWS 3; CA 105; 131; CANR 62; CDBLB 1945-1960; DLB 15; MTCW 1, 2; RGEL
**Lowry, Mina Gertrude** 1882-1966
  See Loy, Mina
  See also CA 113
**Loxsmith, John**
  See Brunner, John (Kilian Houston)
**Loy, Mina** ..... **CLC 28; DAM POET; PC 16**
  See also Lowry, Mina Gertrude
  See also DLB 4, 54
**Loyson-Bridet**
  See Schwob, Marcel (Mayer Andre)
**Lucan** 39-65 .................................... **CMLC 33**
  See also AW 2; DLB 211; EFS 2; RGWL
**Lucas, Craig** 1951- ............................. **CLC 64**
  See also CA 137; CAD; CANR 71; CD; GLL 2
**Lucas, E(dward) V(errall)** 1868-1938 ................................. **TCLC 73**
  See also CA 176; DLB 98, 149, 153; SATA 20
**Lucas, George** 1944- .......................... **CLC 16**
  See also AAYA 1, 23; CA 77-80; CANR 30; SATA 56
**Lucas, Hans**
  See Godard, Jean-Luc
**Lucas, Victoria**
  See Plath, Sylvia
**Lucian** c. 125-c. 180 ......................... **CMLC 32**
  See also AW 2; DLB 176; RGWL
**Lucretius** c. 94B.C.-c. 49B.C. ............ **CMLC 48**
  See also AW 2; DLB 211; EFS 2; RGWL
**Ludlam, Charles** 1943-1987 ........ **CLC 46, 50**
  See also CA 85-88; 122; CAD; CANR 72; 86
**Ludlum, Robert** 1927-2001 ....... **CLC 22, 43; DAM NOV, POP**
  See also AAYA 10; BEST 89:1, 90:3; BPFB 2; CA 33-36R; 195; CANR 25, 41, 68; CMW; CPW; DA3; DLBY 82; MSW; MTCW 1, 2
**Ludwig, Ken** ................................... **CLC 60**
  See also CA 195; CAD
**Ludwig, Otto** 1813-1865 .................... **NCLC 4**
  See also DLB 129
**Lugones, Leopoldo** 1874-1938 ....... **TCLC 15; HLCS 2**
  See also CA 116; 131; HW 1; LAW
**Lu Hsun** ............................ **TCLC 3; SSC 20**
  See also Shu-Jen, Chou
**Lukacs, George** .................................. **CLC 24**
  See also Lukacs, Gyorgy (Szegeny von)
**Lukacs, Gyorgy (Szegeny von)** 1885-1971
  See Lukacs, George
  See also CA 101; 29-32R; CANR 62; DLB 242; EW; MTCW 2

**Luke, Peter (Ambrose Cyprian)** 1919-1995 .................................. **CLC 38**
  See also CA 81-84; 147; CANR 72; CBD; CD; DLB 13
**Lunar, Dennis**
  See Mungo, Raymond
**Lurie, Alison** 1926- ............. **CLC 4, 5, 18, 39**
  See also BPFB 2; CA 1-4R; CANR 2, 17, 50, 88; CN; DLB 2; MTCW 1; SATA 46, 112
**Lustig, Arnost** 1926- ........................... **CLC 56**
  See also AAYA 3; CA 69-72; CANR 47, 102; CWW 2; DLB 232; SATA 56
**Luther, Martin** 1483-1546 ................ **LC 9, 37**
  See also DLB 179; EW; RGWL
**Luxemburg, Rosa** 1870(?)-1919 ..... **TCLC 63**
  See also CA 118
**Luzi, Mario** 1914- .............................. **CLC 13**
  See also CA 61-64; CANR 9, 70; CWW 2; DLB 128
**L'vov, Arkady** ................................... **CLC 59**
**Lyly, John** 1554(?)-1606 ........... **LC 41; DAM DRAM; DC 7**
  See also BRW 1; DLB 62, 167; RGEL
**L'Ymagier**
  See Gourmont, Remy(-Marie-Charles) de
**Lynch, David (K.)** 1946- .................... **CLC 66**
  See also CA 124; 129
**Lynch, James**
  See Andreyev, Leonid (Nikolaevich)
**Lyndsay, Sir David** 1485-1555 ............. **LC 20**
  See also RGEL
**Lynn, Kenneth S(chuyler)** 1923-2001 ................................... **CLC 50**
  See also CA 1-4R; CANR 3, 27, 65
**Lynx**
  See West, Rebecca
**Lyons, Marcus**
  See Blish, James (Benjamin)
**Lyotard, Jean-Francois** 1924-1998 ................................. **TCLC 103**
  See also DLB 242
**Lyre, Pinchbeck**
  See Sassoon, Siegfried (Lorraine)
**Lytle, Andrew (Nelson)** 1902-1995 ... **CLC 22**
  See also CA 9-12R; 150; CANR 70; CN; CSW; DLB 6; DLBY 95; RGAL; RHW
**Lyttelton, George** 1709-1773 ................ **LC 10**
  See also RGEL
**Lytton of Knebworth**
  See Bulwer-Lytton, Edward (George Earle Lytton)
**Maas, Peter** 1929-2001 ...................... **CLC 29**
  See also CA 93-96; INT CA-93-96; MTCW 2
**Macaulay, Catherine** 1731-1791 .......... **LC 64**
  See also DLB 104
**Macaulay, (Emilie) Rose** 1881(?)-1958 ........................ **TCLC 7, 44**
  See also CA 104; DLB 36; RGEL; RHW
**Macaulay, Thomas Babington** 1800-1859 ................................... **NCLC 42**
  See also BRW 4; CDBLB 1832-1890; DLB 32, 55; RGEL
**MacBeth, George (Mann)** 1932-1992 ................................. **CLC 2, 5, 9**
  See also CA 25-28R; 136; CANR 61, 66; DLB 40; MTCW 1; PFS 8; SATA 4; SATA-Obit 70
**MacCaig, Norman (Alexander)** 1910-1996 ............ **CLC 36; DAB; DAM POET**
  See also BRWS 6; CA 9-12R; CANR 3, 34; CP; DLB 27; RGEL
**MacCarthy, Sir (Charles Otto) Desmond** 1877-1952 ................................ **TCLC 36**
  See also CA 167

**MacDiarmid, Hugh** .... CLC 2, 4, 11, 19, 63; PC 9
See also Grieve, C(hristopher) M(urray)
See also CDBLB 1945-1960; DLB 20; RGEL

**MacDonald, Anson**
See Heinlein, Robert A(nson)

**Macdonald, Cynthia** 1928- ......... CLC 13, 19
See also CA 49-52; CANR 4, 44; DLB 105

**MacDonald, George** 1824-1905 ....... TCLC 9, 113
See also BYA 5; CA 106; 137; CANR 80; CLR 67; DLB 18, 163, 178; FANT; MAICYA; RGEL; SATA 33, 100; SFW

**Macdonald, John**
See Millar, Kenneth

**MacDonald, John D(ann)** 1916-1986 .. CLC 3, 27, 44; DAM NOV, POP
See also BPFB 2; CA 1-4R; 121; CANR 1, 19, 60; CMW; CPW; DLB 8; DLBY 86; MSW; MTCW 1, 2; SFW

**Macdonald, John Ross**
See Millar, Kenneth

**Macdonald, Ross** ..... CLC 1, 2, 3, 14, 34, 41
See also Millar, Kenneth
See also AMWS 4; BPFB 2; DLBD 6; MSW; RGAL

**MacDougal, John**
See Blish, James (Benjamin)

**MacDougal, John**
See Blish, James (Benjamin)

**MacDowell, John**
See Parks, Tim(othy Harold)

**MacEwen, Gwendolyn (Margaret)** 1941-1987 ............................ CLC 13, 55
See also CA 9-12R; 124; CANR 7, 22; DLB 53; SATA 50; SATA-Obit 55

**Macha, Karel Hynek** 1810-1846 .... NCLC 46

**Machado (y Ruiz), Antonio** 1875-1939 ................................... TCLC 3
See also CA 104; 174; DLB 108; EW; HW 2; RGWL

**Machado de Assis, Joaquim Maria** 1839-1908 ..... TCLC 10; BLC 2; HLCS 2; SSC 24
See also CA 107; 153; CANR 91; LAW; RGSF; RGWL; WLIT 1

**Machen, Arthur** ................. TCLC 4; SSC 20
See also Jones, Arthur Llewellyn
See also CA 179; DLB 36, 156, 178; RGEL

**Machiavelli, Niccolo** 1469-1527 ..... LC 8, 36; DA; DAB; DAC; DAM MST; WLCS
See also EW; LAIT 1; NFS 9; RGWL

**MacInnes, Colin** 1914-1976 .......... CLC 4, 23
See also CA 69-72; 65-68; CANR 21; DLB 14; MTCW 1, 2; RGEL; RHW

**MacInnes, Helen (Clark)** 1907-1985 ........ CLC 27, 39; DAM POP
See also BPFB 2; CA 1-4R; 117; CANR 1, 28, 58; CMW; CPW; DLB 87; MSW; MTCW 1, 2; SATA 22; SATA-Obit 44

**Mackenzie, Compton (Edward Montague)** 1883-1972 ................................. CLC 18
See also CA 21-22; 37-40R; CAP 2; DLB 34, 100; RGEL

**Mackenzie, Henry** 1745-1831 ........ NCLC 41
See also DLB 39; RGEL

**Mackintosh, Elizabeth** 1896(?)-1952
See Tey, Josephine
See also CA 110; CMW

**MacLaren, James**
See Grieve, C(hristopher) M(urray)

**Mac Laverty, Bernard** 1942- ............. CLC 31
See also CA 116; 118; CANR 43, 88; CN; INT CA-118; RGSF

**MacLean, Alistair (Stuart)** 1922(?)-1987 .. CLC 3, 13, 50, 63; DAM POP
See also CA 57-60; 121; CANR 28, 61; CMW; CPW; MTCW 1; SATA 23; SATA-Obit 50; TCWW 2

**Maclean, Norman (Fitzroy)** 1902-1990 .... CLC 78; DAM POP; SSC 13
See also CA 102; 132; CANR 49; CPW; DLB 206; TCWW 2

**MacLeish, Archibald** 1892-1982 ... CLC 3, 8, 14, 68; DAM POET
See also AMW; CA 9-12R; 106; CAD; CANR 33, 63; CDALBS; DLB 4, 7, 45; DLBY 82; EXPP; MTCW 1, 2; PAB; PFS 5; RGAL

**MacLennan, (John) Hugh** 1907-1990 . CLC 2, 14, 92; DAC; DAM MST
See also CA 5-8R; 142; CANR 33; DLB 68; MTCW 1, 2; RGEL

**MacLeod, Alistair** 1936- ........ CLC 56; DAC; DAM MST
See also CA 123; CCA 1; DLB 60; MTCW 2; RGSF

**Macleod, Fiona**
See Sharp, William
See also RGEL

**MacNeice, (Frederick) Louis** 1907-1963 ......... CLC 1, 4, 10, 53; DAB; DAM POET
See also BRW 7; CA 85-88; CANR 61; DLB 10, 20; MTCW 1, 2; RGEL

**MacNeill, Dand**
See Fraser, George MacDonald

**Macpherson, James** 1736-1796 ........... LC 29
See also Ossian
See also DLB 109; RGEL

**Macpherson, (Jean) Jay** 1931- .......... CLC 14
See also CA 5-8R; CANR 90; CP; CWP; DLB 53

**Macrobius** fl. 430- .......................... CMLC 48

**MacShane, Frank** 1927-1999 ............. CLC 39
See also CA 9-12R; 186; CANR 3, 33; DLB 111

**Macumber, Mari**
See Sandoz, Mari(e Susette)

**Madach, Imre** 1823-1864 ................ NCLC 19

**Madden, (Jerry) David** 1933- ........ CLC 5, 15
See also CA 1-4R; CAAS 3; CANR 4, 45; CN; CSW; DLB 6; MTCW 1

**Maddern, Al(an)**
See Ellison, Harlan (Jay)

**Madhubuti, Haki R.** 1942- . CLC 6, 73; BLC 2; DAM MULT, POET; PC 5
See also Lee, Don L.
See also BW 2, 3; CA 73-76; CANR 24, 51, 73; CP; CSW; DLB 5, 41; DLBD 8; MTCW 2; RGAL

**Maepenn, Hugh**
See Kuttner, Henry

**Maepenn, K. H.**
See Kuttner, Henry

**Maeterlinck, Maurice** 1862-1949 ... TCLC 3; DAM DRAM
See also CA 104; 136; CANR 80; DLB 192; EW; GFL 1789 to the Present; RGWL; SATA 66

**Maginn, William** 1794-1842 ............. NCLC 8
See also DLB 110, 159

**Mahapatra, Jayanta** 1928- .... CLC 33; DAM MULT
See also CA 73-76; CAAS 9; CANR 15, 33, 66, 87; CP

**Mahfouz, Naguib (Abdel Aziz Al-Sabilgi)** 1911(?)-
See Mahfuz, Najib (Abdel Aziz al-Sabilgi)
See also BEST 89:2; CA 128; CANR 55, 101; CWW 2; DA3; DAM NOV; MTCW 1, 2; RGWL; SSFS 9

**Mahfuz, Najib (Abdel Aziz al-Sabilgi)** ............................................ CLC 52, 55
See also Mahfouz, Naguib (Abdel Aziz Al-Sabilgi)
See also AFW; DLBY 88; RGSF; WLIT 2

**Mahon, Derek** 1941- ......................... CLC 27
See also BRWS 6; CA 113; 128; CANR 88; CP; DLB 40

**Maiakovskii, Vladimir**
See Mayakovski, Vladimir (Vladimirovich)
See also IDTP; RGWL

**Mailer, Norman** 1923- ... CLC 1, 2, 3, 4, 5, 8, 11, 14, 28, 39, 74, 111; DA; DAB; DAC; DAM MST, NOV, POP
See also AAYA 31; AITN 2; AMW; BPFB 2; CA 9-12R; CABS 1; CANR 28, 74, 77; CDALB 1968-1988; CN; CPW; DA3; DLB 2, 16, 28, 185; DLBD 3; DLBY 80, 83; MTCW 1, 2; NFS 10; RGAL

**Maillet, Antonine** 1929- ..... CLC 54, 118; DAC
See also CA 115; 120; CANR 46, 74, 77; CCA 1; CWW 2; DLB 60; INT 120; MTCW 2

**Mais, Roger** 1905-1955 ..................... TCLC 8
See also BW 1, 3; CA 105; 124; CANR 82; DLB 125; MTCW 1; RGEL

**Maistre, Joseph** 1753-1821 ............. NCLC 37
See also GFL 1789 to the Present

**Maitland, Frederic William** 1850-1906 ................................. TCLC 65

**Maitland, Sara (Louise)** 1950- .......... CLC 49
See also CA 69-72; CANR 13, 59; FW

**Major, Clarence** 1936- . CLC 3, 19, 48; BLC 2; DAM MULT
See also AFAW 2; BW 2, 3; CA 21-24R; CAAS 6; CANR 13, 25, 53, 82; CN; CP; CSW; DLB 33; MSW

**Major, Kevin (Gerald)** 1949- . CLC 26; DAC
See also AAYA 16; CA 97-100; CANR 21, 38; CLR 11; DLB 60; INT CANR-21; JRDA; MAICYA; SATA 32, 82; WYA; YAW

**Maki, James**
See Ozu, Yasujiro

**Malabaila, Damiano**
See Levi, Primo

**Malamud, Bernard** 1914-1986 .. CLC 1, 2, 3, 5, 8, 9, 11, 18, 27, 44, 78, 85; DA; DAB; DAC; DAM MST, NOV, POP; SSC 15; WLC
See also AAYA 16; AMWS 1; BPFB 2; CA 5-8R; 118; CABS 1; CANR 28, 62; CDALB 1941-1968; CPW; DA3; DLB 2, 28, 152; DLBY 80, 86; EXPS; LAIT 4; MTCW 1, 2; NFS 4, 9; RGAL; RGSF; SSFS 8, 13

**Malan, Herman**
See Bosman, Herman Charles; Bosman, Herman Charles

**Malaparte, Curzio** 1898-1957 ........ TCLC 52

**Malcolm, Dan**
See Silverberg, Robert

**Malcolm X** .... CLC 82, 117; BLC 2; WLCS
See also Little, Malcolm
See also LAIT 5

**Malherbe, Francois de** 1555-1628 ......... LC 5
See also GFL Beginnings to 1789

**Mallarme, Stephane** 1842-1898 ....... NCLC 4, 41; DAM POET; PC 4
See also EW; GFL 1789 to the Present; RGWL

**Mallet-Joris, Francoise** 1930- .......... **CLC 11**
See also CA 65-68; CANR 17; DLB 83; GFL 1789 to the Present

**Malley, Ern**
See McAuley, James Phillip

**Mallowan, Agatha Christie**
See Christie, Agatha (Mary Clarissa)

**Maloff, Saul** 1922- ................................. **CLC 5**
See also CA 33-36R

**Malone, Louis**
See MacNeice, (Frederick) Louis

**Malone, Michael (Christopher)** 1942- ................................................ **CLC 43**
See also CA 77-80; CANR 14, 32, 57

**Malory, Sir Thomas** 1410(?)-1471(?) . **LC 11; DA; DAB; DAC; DAM MST; WLCS**
See also BRW 1; CDBLB Before 1660; DLB 146; EFS 2; RGEL; SATA 59; SATA-Brief 33; SUFW; WLIT 3

**Malouf, (George Joseph) David** 1934- .................................... **CLC 28, 86**
See also CA 124; CANR 50, 76; CN; CP; MTCW 2

**Malraux, (Georges-)Andre** 1901-1976 ........ **CLC 1, 4, 9, 13, 15, 57; DAM NOV**
See also BPFB 2; CA 21-22; 69-72; CANR 34, 58; CAP 2; DA3; DLB 72; EW; GFL 1789 to the Present; MTCW 1, 2; RGWL

**Malzberg, Barry N(athaniel)** 1939- ... **CLC 7**
See also CA 61-64; CAAS 4; CANR 16; CMW; DLB 8; SFW

**Mamet, David (Alan)** 1947- .. **CLC 9, 15, 34, 46, 91; DAM DRAM; DC 4**
See also AAYA 3; CA 81-84; CABS 3; CANR 15, 41, 67, 72; CD; DA3; DFS 2, 3, 6, 12; DLB 7; IDFW 4; MTCW 1, 2; RGAL

**Mamoulian, Rouben (Zachary)** 1897-1987 .................................... **CLC 16**
See also CA 25-28R; 124; CANR 85

**Mandelshtam, Osip**
See Mandelstam, Osip (Emilievich)
See also RGWL

**Mandelstam, Osip (Emilievich)** 1891(?)-1943(?) ........ **TCLC 2, 6; PC 14**
See also Mandelstam, Osip
See also CA 104; 150; EW; MTCW 2

**Mander, (Mary) Jane** 1877-1949 ... **TCLC 31**
See also CA 162; RGEL

**Mandeville, John** fl. 1350- ............. **CMLC 19**
See also DLB 146

**Mandiargues, Andre Pieyre de** ....... **CLC 41**
See also Pieyre de Mandiargues, Andre
See also DLB 83

**Mandrake, Ethel Belle**
See Thurman, Wallace (Henry)

**Mangan, James Clarence** 1803-1849 ................................ **NCLC 27**
See also RGEL

**Maniere, J.-E.**
See Giraudoux, Jean(-Hippolyte)

**Mankiewicz, Herman (Jacob)** 1897-1953 ................................ **TCLC 85**
See also CA 120; 169; DLB 26; IDFW 3, 4

**Manley, (Mary) Delariviere** 1672(?)-1724 ............................ **LC 1, 42**
See also DLB 39, 80; RGEL

**Mann, Abel**
See Creasey, John

**Mann, Emily** 1952- ................................ **DC 7**
See also CA 130; CAD; CANR 55; CD; CWD

**Mann, (Luiz) Heinrich** 1871-1950 ... **TCLC 9**
See also CA 106; 164, 181; DLB 66, 118; EW; RGWL

**Mann, (Paul) Thomas** 1875-1955 ... **TCLC 2, 8, 14, 21, 35, 44, 60; DA; DAB; DAC; DAM MST, NOV; SSC 5; WLC**
See also BPFB 2; CA 104; 128; DA3; DLB 66; EW; GLL 1; MTCW 1, 2; RGSF; RGWL; SSFS 4, 9

**Mannheim, Karl** 1893-1947 ............. **TCLC 65**

**Manning, David**
See Faust, Frederick (Schiller)
See also TCWW 2

**Manning, Frederic** 1887(?)-1935 ... **TCLC 25**
See also CA 124

**Manning, Olivia** 1915-1980 .......... **CLC 5, 19**
See also CA 5-8R; 101; CANR 29; FW; MTCW 1; RGEL

**Mano, D. Keith** 1942- ..................... **CLC 2, 10**
See also CA 25-28R; CAAS 6; CANR 26, 57; DLB 6

**Mansfield, Katherine** ............ **TCLC 2, 8, 39; DAB; SSC 9, 23, 38; WLC**
See also Beauchamp, Kathleen Mansfield
See also BPFB 2; BRW 7; DLB 162; EXPS; FW; GLL 1; RGEL; RGSF; SSFS 2, 8, 10, 11

**Manso, Peter** 1940- ............................ **CLC 39**
See also CA 29-32R; CANR 44

**Mantecon, Juan Jimenez**
See Jimenez (Mantecon), Juan Ramon

**Mantel, Hilary (Mary)** 1952- .......... **CLC 144**
See also CA 125; CANR 54, 101; CN; RHW

**Manton, Peter**
See Creasey, John

**Man Without a Spleen, A**
See Chekhov, Anton (Pavlovich)

**Manzoni, Alessandro** 1785-1873 ... **NCLC 29, 98**
See also EW; RGWL

**Map, Walter** 1140-1209 ................. **CMLC 32**

**Mapu, Abraham (ben Jekutiel)** 1808-1867 ................................ **NCLC 18**

**Mara, Sally**
See Queneau, Raymond

**Marat, Jean Paul** 1743-1793 ................. **LC 10**

**Marcel, Gabriel Honore** 1889-1973 . **CLC 15**
See also CA 102; 45-48; MTCW 1, 2

**March, William** 1893-1954 ............. **TCLC 96**

**Marchbanks, Samuel**
See Davies, (William) Robertson
See also CCA 1

**Marchi, Giacomo**
See Bassani, Giorgio

**Marcus Aurelius**
See Aurelius, Marcus
See also AW 2

**Marguerite**
See de Navarre, Marguerite

**Marguerite de Navarre**
See de Navarre, Marguerite
See also RGWL

**Margulies, Donald** 1954- ................... **CLC 76**
See also DFS 13; DLB 228

**Marie de France** c. 12th cent. - ..... **CMLC 8; PC 22**
See also DLB 208; FW; RGWL

**Marie de l'Incarnation** 1599-1672 ....... **LC 10**

**Marier, Captain Victor**
See Griffith, D(avid Lewelyn) W(ark)

**Mariner, Scott**
See Pohl, Frederik

**Marinetti, Filippo Tommaso** 1876-1944 ................................ **TCLC 10**
See also CA 107; DLB 114; EW

**Marivaux, Pierre Carlet de Chamblain de** 1688-1763 ............................ **LC 4; DC 7**
See also GFL Beginnings to 1789; RGWL

**Markandaya, Kamala** .................. **CLC 8, 38**
See also Taylor, Kamala (Purnaiya)
See also BYA 13

**Markfield, Wallace** 1926- ................... **CLC 8**
See also CA 69-72; CAAS 3; CN; DLB 2, 28

**Markham, Edwin** 1852-1940 .......... **TCLC 47**
See also CA 160; DLB 54, 186; RGAL

**Markham, Robert**
See Amis, Kingsley (William)

**Marks, J**
See Highwater, Jamake (Mamake)

**Marks-Highwater, J**
See Highwater, Jamake (Mamake)

**Markson, David M(errill)** 1927- ....... **CLC 67**
See also CA 49-52; CANR 1, 91; CN

**Marley, Bob** ...................................... **CLC 17**
See also Marley, Robert Nesta

**Marley, Robert Nesta** 1945-1981
See Marley, Bob
See also CA 107; 103

**Marlowe, Christopher** 1564-1593 ....... **LC 22, 47; DA; DAB; DAC; DAM DRAM, MST; DC 1; WLC**
See also BRW 1; CDBLB Before 1660; DA3; DFS 1, 5, 13; DLB 62; EXPP; RGEL; WLIT 3

**Marlowe, Stephen** 1928- ................... **CLC 70**
See also Queen, Ellery
See also CA 13-16R; CANR 6, 55; CMW; SFW

**Marmontel, Jean-Francois** 1723-1799 .. **LC 2**

**Marquand, John P(hillips)** 1893-1960 ................................ **CLC 2, 10**
See also AMW; BPFB 2; CA 85-88; CANR 73; CMW; DLB 9, 102; MTCW 2; RGAL

**Marques, Rene** 1919-1979 ..... **CLC 96; DAM MULT; HLC 2**
See also CA 97-100; 85-88; CANR 78; DLB 113; HW 1, 2; LAW; RGSF

**Marquez, Gabriel (Jose) Garcia**
See Garcia Marquez, Gabriel (Jose)

**Marquis, Don(ald Robert Perry)** 1878-1937 ................................ **TCLC 7**
See also CA 104; 166; DLB 11, 25; RGAL

**Marric, J. J.**
See Creasey, John
See also MSW

**Marryat, Frederick** 1792-1848 ........ **NCLC 3**
See also DLB 21, 163; RGEL

**Marsden, James**
See Creasey, John

**Marsh, Edward** 1872-1953 ............. **TCLC 99**

**Marsh, (Edith) Ngaio** 1899-1982 ....... **CLC 7, 53; DAM POP**
See also CA 9-12R; CANR 6, 58; CMW; CPW; DLB 77; MSW; MTCW 1, 2; RGEL

**Marshall, Garry** 1934- ....................... **CLC 17**
See also AAYA 3; CA 111; SATA 60

**Marshall, Paule** 1929- .. **CLC 27, 72; BLC 3; DAM MULT; SSC 3**
See also AFAW 1, 2; BPFB 2; BW 2, 3; CA 77-80; CANR 25, 73; CN; DA3; DLB 33, 157, 227; MTCW 1, 2; RGAL

**Marshallik**
See Zangwill, Israel

**Marsten, Richard**
See Hunter, Evan

**Marston, John** 1576-1634 ........ **LC 33; DAM DRAM**
See also BRW 2; DLB 58, 172; RGEL

**Martha, Henry**
See Harris, Mark

**Marti (y Perez), Jose (Julian)** 1853-1895 ...... **NCLC 63; DAM MULT; HLC 2**
See also HW 2; LAW; RGWL; WLIT 1

**Martial** c. 40-c. 104 ............ **CMLC 35; PC 10**
See also AW 2; DLB 211; RGWL

**Martin, Ken**
See Hubbard, L(afayette) Ron(ald)

**Martin, Richard**
See Creasey, John

**Martin, Steve** 1945- .......................... **CLC 30**
See also CA 97-100; CANR 30, 100; MTCW 1

**Martin, Valerie** 1948- ......................... **CLC 89**
See also BEST 90:2; CA 85-88; CANR 49, 89

**Martin, Violet Florence**
1862-1915 ................................. **TCLC 51**

**Martin, Webber**
See Silverberg, Robert

**Martindale, Patrick Victor**
See White, Patrick (Victor Martindale)

**Martin du Gard, Roger**
1881-1958 ................................. **TCLC 24**
See also CA 118; CANR 94; DLB 65; GFL 1789 to the Present; RGWL

**Martineau, Harriet** 1802-1876 ....... **NCLC 26**
See also DLB 21, 55, 159, 163, 166, 190; FW; RGEL; YABC 2

**Martines, Julia**
See O'Faolain, Julia

**Martinez, Enrique Gonzalez**
See Gonzalez Martinez, Enrique

**Martinez, Jacinto Benavente y**
See Benavente (y Martinez), Jacinto

**Martinez de la Rosa, Francisco de Paula**
1787-1862 ................................ **NCLC 102**

**Martinez Ruiz, Jose** 1873-1967
See Azorin; Ruiz, Jose Martinez
See also CA 93-96; HW 1

**Martinez Sierra, Gregorio**
1881-1947 ................................... **TCLC 6**
See also CA 115

**Martinez Sierra, Maria (de la O'LeJarraga)**
1874-1974 ................................... **TCLC 6**
See also CA 115

**Martinsen, Martin**
See Follett, Ken(neth Martin)

**Martinson, Harry (Edmund)**
1904-1978 .................................. **CLC 14**
See also CA 77-80; CANR 34

**Marut, Ret**
See Traven, B.

**Marut, Robert**
See Traven, B.

**Marvell, Andrew** 1621-1678 .. **LC 4, 43; DA; DAB; DAC; DAM MST, POET; PC 10; WLC**
See also BRW 2; CDBLB 1660-1789; DLB 131; EXPP; PFS 5; RGEL; WP

**Marx, Karl (Heinrich)** 1818-1883 . **NCLC 17**
See also DLB 129

**Masaoka, Shiki** ................................ **TCLC 18**
See also Masaoka, Tsunenori

**Masaoka, Tsunenori** 1867-1902
See Masaoka, Shiki
See also CA 117; 191

**Masefield, John (Edward)**
1878-1967 ..... **CLC 11, 47; DAM POET**
See also CA 19-20; 25-28R; CANR 33; CAP 2; CDBLB 1890-1914; DLB 10, 19, 153, 160; EXPP; FANT; MTCW 1, 2; PFS 5; RGEL; SATA 19

**Maso, Carole** 19(?)- .......................... **CLC 44**
See also CA 170; GLL 2; RGAL

**Mason, Bobbie Ann** 1940- ... **CLC 28, 43, 82; SSC 4**
See also AAYA 5, 42; AMWS 8; BPFB 2; CA 53-56; CANR 11, 31, 58, 83; CDALBS; CN; CSW; DA3; DLB 173; DLBY 87; EXPS; INT CANR-31; MTCW 1, 2; NFS 4; RGAL; RGSF; SSFS 3,8; YAW

**Mason, Ernst**
See Pohl, Frederik

**Mason, Hunni B.**
See Sternheim, (William Adolf) Carl

**Mason, Lee W.**
See Malzberg, Barry N(athaniel)

**Mason, Nick** 1945- ............................ **CLC 35**

**Mason, Tally**
See Derleth, August (William)

**Mass, Anna** ...................................... **CLC 59**

**Mass, William**
See Gibson, William

**Massinger, Philip** 1583-1640 ............... **LC 70**
See also DLB 58; RGEL

**Master Lao**
See Lao Tzu

**Masters, Edgar Lee** 1868-1950 ....... **TCLC 2, 25; DA; DAC; DAM MST, POET; PC 1, 36; WLCS**
See also AMWS 1; CA 104; 133; CDALB 1865-1917; DLB 54; EXPP; MTCW 1, 2; RGAL; WP

**Masters, Hilary** 1928- ......................... **CLC 48**
See also CA 25-28R; CANR 13, 47, 97; CN; DLB 244

**Mastrosimone, William** 19(?)- .......... **CLC 36**
See also CA 186; CAD; CD

**Mathe, Albert**
See Camus, Albert

**Mather, Cotton** 1663-1728 .................. **LC 38**
See also AMWS 2; CDALB 1640-1865; DLB 24, 30, 140; RGAL

**Mather, Increase** 1639-1723 ................. **LC 38**
See also DLB 24

**Matheson, Richard (Burton)** 1926- .. **CLC 37**
See also AAYA 31; CA 97-100; CANR 88, 99; DLB 8, 44; HGG; INT 97-100; SCFW 2; SFW

**Mathews, Harry** 1930- ................... **CLC 6, 52**
See also CA 21-24R; CAAS 6; CANR 18, 40, 98; CN

**Mathews, John Joseph** 1894-1979 .. **CLC 84; DAM MULT**
See also CA 19-20; 142; CANR 45; CAP 2; DLB 175; NNAL

**Mathias, Roland (Glyn)** 1915- .......... **CLC 45**
See also CA 97-100; CANR 19, 41; CP; DLB 27

**Matsuo Basho** 1644-1694 ......... **LC 62; DAM POET; PC 3**
See also Basho, Matsuo
See also PFS 2, 7

**Mattheson, Rodney**
See Creasey, John

**Matthews, (James) Brander**
1852-1929 ................................. **TCLC 95**
See also DLB 71, 78; DLBD 13

**Matthews, Greg** 1949- ........................ **CLC 45**
See also CA 135

**Matthews, William (Procter III)**
1942-1997 ................................... **CLC 40**
See also AMWS 9; CA 29-32R; 162; CAAS 18; CANR 12, 57; CP; DLB 5

**Matthias, John** 1941- ............................ **CLC 9**
See also CA 33-36R; CANR 56; CP

**Matthiessen, F(rancis) O(tto)**
1902-1950 ................................. **TCLC 100**
See also CA 185; DLB 63

**Matthiessen, Peter** 1927- ... **CLC 5, 7, 11, 32, 64; DAM NOV**
See also AAYA 6, 40; AMWS 5; ANW; BEST 90:4; BPFB 2; CA 9-12R; CANR 21, 50, 73, 100; CN; DA3; DLB 6, 173; MTCW 1, 2; SATA 27

**Maturin, Charles Robert**
1780(?)-1824 .............................. **NCLC 6**
See also DLB 178; HGG; RGEL

**Matute (Ausejo), Ana Maria** 1925- .. **CLC 11**
See also CA 89-92; MTCW 1; RGSF

**Maugham, W. S.**
See Maugham, W(illiam) Somerset

**Maugham, W(illiam) Somerset**
1874-1965 ... **CLC 1, 11, 15, 67, 93; DA; DAB; DAC; DAM DRAM, MST, NOV; SSC 8; WLC**
See also BPFB 2; BRW 6; CA 5-8R; 25-28R; CANR 40; CDBLB 1914-1945; CMW; DA3; DLB 10, 36, 77, 100, 162, 195; LAIT 3; MTCW 1, 2; RGEL; RGSF; SATA 54

**Maugham, William Somerset**
See Maugham, W(illiam) Somerset

**Maupassant, (Henri Rene Albert) Guy de**
1850-1893 . **NCLC 1, 42, 83; DA; DAB; DAC; DAM MST; SSC 1; WLC**
See also DA3; DLB 123; EW; EXPS; GFL 1789 to the Present; LAIT 2; RGSF; RGWL; SSFS 4; SUFW; TWA

**Maupin, Armistead (Jones, Jr.)**
1944- ............................. **CLC 95; DAM POP**
See also CA 125; 130; CANR 58, 101; CPW; DA3; GLL 1; INT 130; MTCW 2

**Maurhut, Richard**
See Traven, B.

**Mauriac, Claude** 1914-1996 ................ **CLC 9**
See also CA 89-92; 152; CWW 2; DLB 83; GFL 1789 to the Present

**Mauriac, Francois (Charles)**
1885-1970 .......... **CLC 4, 9, 56; SSC 24**
See also CA 25-28; CAP 2; DLB 65; EW; GFL 1789 to the Present; MTCW 1, 2; RGWL

**Mavor, Osborne Henry** 1888-1951
See Bridie, James
See also CA 104

**Maxwell, William (Keepers, Jr.)**
1908-2000 .................................. **CLC 19**
See also AMWS 8; CA 93-96; 189; CANR 54, 95; CN; DLBY 80; INT CA-93-96

**May, Elaine** 1932- .............................. **CLC 16**
See also CA 124; 142; CAD; CWD; DLB 44

**Mayakovski, Vladimir (Vladimirovich)**
1893-1930 ............................. **TCLC 4, 18**
See also Maiakovskii, Vladimir; Mayakovsky, Vladimir
See also CA 104; 158; EW; MTCW 2; SFW

**Mayakovsky, Vladimir**
See Mayakovski, Vladimir (Vladimirovich)
See also WP

**Mayhew, Henry** 1812-1887 ............. **NCLC 31**
See also DLB 18, 55, 190

**Mayle, Peter** 1939(?)- .......................... **CLC 89**
See also CA 139; CANR 64

**Maynard, Joyce** 1953- ........................ **CLC 23**
See also CA 111; 129; CANR 64

**Mayne, William (James Carter)**
1928- ........................................... **CLC 12**
See also AAYA 20; CA 9-12R; CANR 37, 80, 100; CLR 25; FANT; JRDA; MAI-CYA; SAAS 11; SATA 6, 68, 122; YAW

**Mayo, Jim**
See L'Amour, Louis (Dearborn)
See also TCWW 2

**Maysles, Albert** 1926- ........................ **CLC 16**
See also CA 29-32R

**Maysles, David** 1932-1987 ................ **CLC 16**
See also CA 191

**Mazer, Norma Fox** 1931- ................... **CLC 26**
See also AAYA 5, 36; BYA 1, 8; CA 69-72; CANR 12, 32, 66; CLR 23; JRDA; MAI-CYA; SAAS 1; SATA 24, 67, 105; YAW

**Mazzini, Giuseppe** 1805-1872 ........ **NCLC 34**

**McAlmon, Robert (Menzies)**
1895-1956 .................................. **TCLC 97**
See also CA 107; 168; DLB 4, 45; DLBD 15; GLL 1

**McAuley, James Phillip** 1917-1976 .. **CLC 45**
See also CA 97-100; RGEL

**McBain, Ed**
See Hunter, Evan
See also MSW

**McBrien, William (Augustine)** 1930- ............................................. **CLC 44**
See also CA 107; CANR 90

**McCabe, Patrick** 1955- ..................... **CLC 133**
See also CA 130; CANR 50, 90; CN; DLB 194

**McCaffrey, Anne (Inez)** 1926- ......... **CLC 17; DAM NOV, POP**
See also AAYA 6, 34; AITN 2; BEST 89:2; BPFB 2; BYA 5; CA 25-28R; CANR 15, 35, 55, 96; CLR 49; CPW; DA3; DLB 8; JRDA; MAICYA; MTCW 1, 2; SAAS 11; SATA 8, 70, 116; SFW; WYA; YAW

**McCall, Nathan** 1955(?)- ..................... **CLC 86**
See also BW 3; CA 146; CANR 88

**McCann, Arthur**
See Campbell, John W(ood, Jr.)

**McCann, Edson**
See Pohl, Frederik

**McCarthy, Charles, Jr.** 1933-
See McCarthy, Cormac
See also CANR 42, 69, 101; CN; CPW; CSW; DA3; DAM POP; MTCW 2

**McCarthy, Cormac** ........ **CLC 4, 57, 59, 101**
See also McCarthy, Charles, Jr.
See also AAYA 41; AMWS 8; BPFB 2; CA 13-16R; CANR 10; DLB 6, 143; MTCW 2; TCWW 2

**McCarthy, Mary (Therese)** 1912-1989 .. **CLC 1, 3, 5, 14, 24, 39, 59; SSC 24**
See also AMW; BPFB 2; CA 5-8R; 129; CANR 16, 50, 64; DA3; DLB 2; DLBY 81; FW; INT CANR-16; MAWW; MTCW 1, 2; RGAL

**McCartney, (James) Paul** 1942- . **CLC 12, 35**
See also CA 146

**McCauley, Stephen (D.)** 1955- .......... **CLC 50**
See also CA 141

**McClaren, Peter** ...................... **CLC 70**

**McClure, Michael (Thomas)** 1932- ... **CLC 6, 10**
See also CA 21-24R; CAD; CANR 17, 46, 77; CD; CP; DLB 16; WP

**McCorkle, Jill (Collins)** 1958- ........... **CLC 51**
See also CA 121; CSW; DLB 234; DLBY 87

**McCourt, Frank** 1930- ..................... **CLC 109**
See also CA 157; CANR 97; NCFS 1

**McCourt, James** 1941- ........................ **CLC 5**
See also CA 57-60; CANR 98

**McCourt, Malachy** 1932- ................. **CLC 119**

**McCoy, Horace (Stanley)** 1897-1955 ................................. **TCLC 28**
See also CA 108; 155; CMW; DLB 9

**McCrae, John** 1872-1918 ................ **TCLC 12**
See also CA 109; DLB 92; PFS 5

**McCreigh, James**
See Pohl, Frederik

**McCullers, (Lula) Carson (Smith)** 1917-1967 .... **CLC 1, 4, 10, 12, 48, 100; DA; DAB; DAC; DAM MST, NOV; SSC 9, 24; WLC**
See also AAYA 21; AMW; BPFB 2; CA 5-8R; 25-28R; CABS 1, 3; CANR 18; CDALB 1941-1968; DA3; DFS 5; DLB 2, 7, 173, 228; EXPS; FW; GLL 1; LAIT 3, 4; MAWW; MTCW 1, 2; NFS 6; RGAL; RGSF; SATA 27; SSFS 5; YAW

**McCulloch, John Tyler**
See Burroughs, Edgar Rice

**McCullough, Colleen** 1938(?)- .......... **CLC 27, 107; DAM NOV, POP**
See also AAYA 36; BPFB 2; CA 81-84; CANR 17, 46, 67, 98; CPW; DA3; MTCW 1, 2; RHW

**McDermott, Alice** 1953- .................... **CLC 90**
See also CA 109; CANR 40, 90

**McElroy, Joseph** 1930- ................... **CLC 5, 47**
See also CA 17-20R; CN

**McEwan, Ian (Russell)** 1948- .... **CLC 13, 66; DAM NOV**
See also BEST 90:4; BRWS 4; CA 61-64; CANR 14, 41, 69, 87; CN; DLB 14, 194; HGG; MTCW 1, 2; RGSF

**McFadden, David** 1940- .................... **CLC 48**
See also CA 104; CP; DLB 60; INT 104

**McFarland, Dennis** 1950- .................. **CLC 65**
See also CA 165

**McGahern, John** 1934- ... **CLC 5, 9, 48; SSC 17**
See also CA 17-20R; CANR 29, 68; CN; DLB 14, 231; MTCW 1

**McGinley, Patrick (Anthony)** 1937- . **CLC 41**
See also CA 120; 127; CANR 56; INT 127

**McGinley, Phyllis** 1905-1978 ............. **CLC 14**
See also CA 9-12R; 77-80; CANR 19; CWRI; DLB 11, 48; PFS 9, 13; SATA 2, 44; SATA-Obit 24

**McGinniss, Joe** 1942- ......................... **CLC 32**
See also AITN 2; BEST 89:2; CA 25-28R; CANR 26, 70; CPW; DLB 185; INT CANR-26

**McGivern, Maureen Daly**
See Daly, Maureen

**McGrath, Patrick** 1950- .................... **CLC 55**
See also CA 136; CANR 65; CN; DLB 231; HGG

**McGrath, Thomas (Matthew)** 1916-1990 ..... **CLC 28, 59; DAM POET**
See also CA 9-12R; 132; CANR 6, 33, 95; MTCW 1; SATA 41; SATA-Obit 66

**McGuane, Thomas (Francis III)** 1939- .................... **CLC 3, 7, 18, 45, 127**
See also AITN 2; BPFB 2; CA 49-52; CANR 5, 24, 49, 94; CN; DLB 2, 212; DLBY 80; INT CANR-24; MTCW 1; TCWW 2

**McGuckian, Medbh** 1950- .... **CLC 48; DAM POET; PC 27**
See also BRWS 5; CA 143; CP; CWP; DLB 40

**McHale, Tom** 1942(?)-1982 ............. **CLC 3, 5**
See also AITN 1; CA 77-80; 106

**McIlvanney, William** 1936- ................ **CLC 42**
See also CA 25-28R; CANR 61; CMW; DLB 14, 207

**McIlwraith, Maureen Mollie Hunter**
See Hunter, Mollie
See also SATA 2

**McInerney, Jay** 1955- .... **CLC 34, 112; DAM POP**
See also AAYA 18; BPFB 2; CA 116; 123; CANR 45, 68; CN; CPW; DA3; INT 123; MTCW 2

**McIntyre, Vonda N(eel)** 1948- .......... **CLC 18**
See also CA 81-84; CANR 17, 34, 69; MTCW 1; SFW; YAW

**McKay, Claude** ........ **TCLC 7, 41; BLC 3; DAB; PC 2**
See also McKay, Festus Claudius
See also AFAW 1, 2; DLB 4, 45, 51, 117; EXPP; GLL 2; LAIT 3; PAB; PFS 4; RGAL; WP

**McKay, Festus Claudius** 1889-1948
See McKay, Claude
See also BW 1, 3; CA 104; 124; CANR 73; DA; DAC; DAM MST, MULT, NOV, POET; MTCW 1, 2; WLC

**McKuen, Rod** 1933- ........................ **CLC 1, 3**
See also AITN 1; CA 41-44R; CANR 40

**McLoughlin, R. B.**
See Mencken, H(enry) L(ouis)

**McLuhan, (Herbert) Marshall** 1911-1980 ............................. **CLC 37, 83**
See also CA 9-12R; 102; CANR 12, 34, 61; DLB 88; INT CANR-12; MTCW 1, 2

**McMillan, Terry (L.)** 1951- .... **CLC 50, 61, 112; BLCS; DAM MULT, NOV, POP**
See also AAYA 21; BPFB 2; BW 2, 3; CA 140; CANR 60; CPW; DA3; MTCW 2; RGAL; YAW

**McMurtry, Larry (Jeff)** 1936- .. **CLC 2, 3, 7, 11, 27, 44, 127; DAM NOV, POP**
See also AAYA 15; AITN 2; AMWS 5; BEST 89:2; BPFB 2; CA 5-8R; CANR 19, 43, 64, 103; CDALB 1968-1988; CN; CPW; CSW; DA3; DLB 2, 143; DLBY 80, 87; MTCW 1, 2; RGAL; TCWW 2

**McNally, T. M.** 1961- ........................ **CLC 82**

**McNally, Terrence** 1939- ... **CLC 4, 7, 41, 91; DAM DRAM**
See also CA 45-48; CAD; CANR 2, 56; CD; DA3; DLB 7; GLL 1; MTCW 2

**McNamer, Deirdre** 1950- .................. **CLC 70**

**McNeal, Tom** ................................ **CLC 119**

**McNeile, Herman Cyril** 1888-1937
See Sapper
See also CA 184; CMW; DLB 77

**McNickle, (William) D'Arcy** 1904-1977 .......... **CLC 89; DAM MULT**
See also CA 9-12R; 85-88; CANR 5, 45; DLB 175, 212; NNAL; RGAL; SATA-Obit 22

**McPhee, John (Angus)** 1931- ............. **CLC 36**
See also AMWS 3; ANW; BEST 90:1; CA 65-68; CANR 20, 46, 64, 69; CPW; DLB 185; MTCW 1, 2

**McPherson, James Alan** 1943- .. **CLC 19, 77; BLCS**
See also BW 1, 3; CA 25-28R; CAAS 17; CANR 24, 74; CN; CSW; DLB 38, 244; MTCW 1, 2; RGAL; RGSF

**McPherson, William (Alexander)** 1933- ................................................. **CLC 34**
See also CA 69-72; CANR 28; INT CANR-28

**McTaggart, J. McT. Ellis**
See McTaggart, John McTaggart Ellis

**McTaggart, John McTaggart Ellis** 1866-1925 ............................. **TCLC 105**
See also CA 120

**Mead, George Herbert** 1873-1958 . **TCLC 89**

**Mead, Margaret** 1901-1978 ............... **CLC 37**
See also AITN 1; CA 1-4R; 81-84; CANR 4; DA3; FW; MTCW 1, 2; SATA-Obit 20

**Meaker, Marijane (Agnes)** 1927-
See Kerr, M. E.
See also CA 107; CANR 37, 63; INT 107; JRDA; MAICYA; MTCW 1; SATA 20, 61, 99; SATA-Essay 111; YAW

**Medoff, Mark (Howard)** 1940- ... **CLC 6, 23; DAM DRAM**
See also AITN 1; CA 53-56; CAD; CANR 5; CD; DFS 4; DLB 7; INT CANR-5

**Medvedev, P. N.**
See Bakhtin, Mikhail Mikhailovich

**Meged, Aharon**
See Megged, Aharon

**Meged, Aron**
See Megged, Aharon

**Megged, Aharon** 1920- ........................ **CLC 9**
See also CA 49-52; CAAS 13; CANR 1

**Mehta, Ved (Parkash)** 1934- ............. **CLC 37**
See also CA 1-4R; CANR 2, 23, 69; MTCW 1

**Melanter**
See Blackmore, R(ichard) D(oddridge)

**Melies, Georges** 1861-1938 ............. **TCLC 81**
**Melikow, Loris**
  See Hofmannsthal, Hugo von
**Melmoth, Sebastian**
  See Wilde, Oscar (Fingal O'Flahertie Wills)
**Meltzer, Milton** 1915- ...................... **CLC 26**
  See also AAYA 8; BYA 2, 6; CA 13-16R; CANR 38, 92; CLR 13; DLB 61; JRDA; MAICYA; SAAS 1; SATA 1, 50, 80; SATA-Essay 124; YAW
**Melville, Herman** 1819-1891 ..... **NCLC 3, 12, 29, 45, 49, 91, 93; DA; DAB; DAC; DAM MST, NOV; SSC 1, 17, 46; WLC**
  See also AAYA 25; AMW; AMWR 1; CDALB 1640-1865; DA3; DLB 3, 74; EXPN; EXPS; LAIT 1, 2; NFS 7, 9; RGAL; RGSF; SATA 59; SSFS 3
**Membreno, Alejandro** ...................... **CLC 59**
**Menander** c. 342B.C.-c. 293B.C. ... **CMLC 9; DAM DRAM; DC 3**
  See also AW 1; DLB 176; RGWL
**Menchu, Rigoberta** 1959-
  See also CA 175; DNFS; HLCS 2; WLIT 1
**Mencken, H(enry) L(ouis)** 1880-1956 ................................. **TCLC 13**
  See also AMW; CA 105; 125; CDALB 1917-1929; DLB 11, 29, 63, 137, 222; MTCW 1, 2; RGAL
**Mendelsohn, Jane** 1965- ...................... **CLC 99**
  See also CA 154; CANR 94
**Mercer, David** 1928-1980 ........ **CLC 5; DAM DRAM**
  See also CA 9-12R; 102; CANR 23; CBD; DLB 13; MTCW 1; RGEL
**Merchant, Paul**
  See Ellison, Harlan (Jay)
**Meredith, George** 1828-1909 .. **TCLC 17, 43; DAM POET**
  See also CA 117; 153; CANR 80; CDBLB 1832-1890; DLB 18, 35, 57, 159; RGEL
**Meredith, William (Morris)** 1919- .... **CLC 4, 13, 22, 55; DAM POET; PC 28**
  See also CA 9-12R; CAAS 14; CANR 6, 40; CP; DLB 5
**Merezhkovsky, Dmitry Sergeyevich** 1865-1941 ................................. **TCLC 29**
  See also CA 169
**Merimee, Prosper** 1803-1870 ... **NCLC 6, 65; SSC 7**
  See also DLB 119, 192; EW; EXPS; GFL 1789 to the Present; RGSF; RGWL; SSFS 8
**Merkin, Daphne** 1954- ...................... **CLC 44**
  See also CA 123
**Merlin, Arthur**
  See Blish, James (Benjamin)
**Merrill, James (Ingram)** 1926-1995 .. **CLC 2, 3, 6, 8, 13, 18, 34, 91; DAM POET; PC 28**
  See also AMWS 3; CA 13-16R; 147; CANR 10, 49, 63; DA3; DLB 5, 165; DLBY 85; INT CANR-10; MTCW 1, 2; PAB; RGAL
**Merriman, Alex**
  See Silverberg, Robert
**Merriman, Brian** 1747-1805 .......... **NCLC 70**
**Merritt, E. B.**
  See Waddington, Miriam
**Merton, Thomas** 1915-1968 ..... **CLC 1, 3, 11, 34, 83; PC 10**
  See also AMWS 8; CA 5-8R; 25-28R; CANR 22, 53; DA3; DLB 48; DLBY 81; MTCW 1, 2
**Merwin, W(illiam) S(tanley)** 1927- .... **CLC 1, 2, 3, 5, 8, 13, 18, 45, 88; DAM POET**
  See also AMWS 3; CA 13-16R; CANR 15, 51; CP; DA3; DLB 5, 169; INT CANR-15; MTCW 1, 2; PAB; PFS 5; RGAL
**Metcalf, John** 1938- ............. **CLC 37; SSC 43**
  See also CA 113; CN; DLB 60; RGSF

**Metcalf, Suzanne**
  See Baum, L(yman) Frank
**Mew, Charlotte (Mary)** 1870-1928 .. **TCLC 8**
  See also CA 105; 189; DLB 19, 135; RGEL
**Mewshaw, Michael** 1943- ...................... **CLC 9**
  See also CA 53-56; CANR 7, 47; DLBY 80
**Meyer, Conrad Ferdinand** 1825-1905 ................................. **NCLC 81**
  See also DLB 129; EW; RGWL
**Meyer, Gustav** 1868-1932
  See Meyrink, Gustav
  See also CA 117; 190
**Meyer, June**
  See Jordan, June
  See also GLL 2
**Meyer, Lynn**
  See Slavitt, David R(ytman)
**Meyers, Jeffrey** 1939- ...................... **CLC 39**
  See also CA 73-76; CAAE 186; CANR 54, 102; DLB 111
**Meynell, Alice (Christina Gertrude Thompson)** 1847-1922 ............... **TCLC 6**
  See also CA 104; 177; DLB 19, 98; RGEL
**Meyrink, Gustav** ................................. **TCLC 21**
  See also Meyer, Gustav
  See also DLB 81
**Michaels, Leonard** 1933- .... **CLC 6, 25; SSC 16**
  See also CA 61-64; CANR 21, 62; CN; DLB 130; MTCW 1
**Michaux, Henri** 1899-1984 ........... **CLC 8, 19**
  See also CA 85-88; 114; GFL 1789 to the Present; RGWL
**Micheaux, Oscar (Devereaux)** 1884-1951 ................................. **TCLC 76**
  See also BW 3; CA 174; DLB 50; TCWW 2
**Michelangelo** 1475-1564 ...................... **LC 12**
**Michelet, Jules** 1798-1874 ...................... **NCLC 31**
  See also EW; GFL 1789 to the Present
**Michels, Robert** 1876-1936 .............. **TCLC 88**
**Michener, James A(lbert)** 1907(?)-1997 ......... **CLC 1, 5, 11, 29, 60, 109; DAM NOV, POP**
  See also AAYA 27; AITN 1; BEST 90:1; BPFB 2; CA 5-8R; 161; CANR 21, 45, 68; CN; CPW; DA3; DLB 6; MTCW 1, 2; RHW
**Mickiewicz, Adam** 1798-1855 .. **NCLC 3, 101**
  See also EW; RGWL
**Middleton, Christopher** 1926- .......... **CLC 13**
  See also CA 13-16R; CANR 29, 54; DLB 40
**Middleton, Richard (Barham)** 1882-1911 ................................. **TCLC 56**
  See also CA 187; DLB 156; HGG
**Middleton, Stanley** 1919- ............... **CLC 7, 38**
  See also CA 25-28R; CAAS 23; CANR 21, 46, 81; CN; DLB 14
**Middleton, Thomas** 1580-1627 ........... **LC 33; DAM DRAM, MST; DC 5**
  See also BRW 2; DLB 58; RGEL
**Migueis, Jose Rodrigues** 1901- ......... **CLC 10**
**Mikszath, Kalman** 1847-1910 ........ **TCLC 31**
  See also CA 170
**Miles, Jack** ...................... **CLC 100**
**Miles, Josephine (Louise)** 1911-1985 .. **CLC 1, 2, 14, 34, 39; DAM POET**
  See also CA 1-4R; 116; CANR 2, 55; DLB 48
**Militant**
  See Sandburg, Carl (August)
**Mill, Harriet (Hardy) Taylor** 1807-1858 ................................. **NCLC 102**
  See also FW
**Mill, John Stuart** 1806-1873 .... **NCLC 11, 58**
  See also CDBLB 1832-1890; DLB 55, 190; FW 1; RGEL

**Millar, Kenneth** 1915-1983 ... **CLC 14; DAM POP**
  See also Macdonald, Ross
  See also CA 9-12R; 110; CANR 16, 63; CMW; CPW; DA3; DLB 2, 226; DLBD 6; DLBY 83; MTCW 1, 2
**Millay, E. Vincent**
  See Millay, Edna St. Vincent
**Millay, Edna St. Vincent** 1892-1950 ........ **TCLC 4, 49; DA; DAB; DAC; DAM MST, POET; PC 6; WLCS**
  See also Boyd, Nancy
  See also AMW; CA 104; 130; CDALB 1917-1929; DA3; DLB 45; EXPP; MAWW; MTCW 1, 2; PAB; PFS 3; RGAL; WP
**Miller, Arthur** 1915- ...... **CLC 1, 2, 6, 10, 15, 26, 47, 78; DA; DAB; DAC; DAM DRAM, MST; DC 1; WLC**
  See also AAYA 15; AITN 1; AMW; CA 1-4R; CABS 3; CAD; CANR 2, 30, 54, 76; CD; CDALB 1941-1968; DA3; DFS 1, 3; DLB 7; LAIT 4; MTCW 1, 2; RGAL; WYAS 1
**Miller, Henry (Valentine)** 1891-1980 ... **CLC 1, 2, 4, 9, 14, 43, 84; DA; DAB; DAC; DAM MST, NOV; WLC**
  See also AMW; BPFB 2; CA 9-12R; 97-100; CANR 33, 64; CDALB 1929-1941; DA3; DLB 4, 9; DLBY 80; MTCW 1, 2; RGAL
**Miller, Jason** 1939(?)-2001 ................... **CLC 2**
  See also AITN 1; CA 73-76; CAD; DFS 12; DLB 7
**Miller, Sue** 1943- ........... **CLC 44; DAM POP**
  See also BEST 90:3; CA 139; CANR 59, 91; DA3; DLB 143
**Miller, Walter M(ichael, Jr.)** 1923-1996 ............................... **CLC 4, 30**
  See also BPFB 2; CA 85-88; DLB 8; SCFW; SFW
**Millett, Kate** 1934- ........................... **CLC 67**
  See also AITN 1; CA 73-76; CANR 32, 53, 76; DA3; FW; GLL 1; MTCW 1, 2
**Millhauser, Steven (Lewis)** 1943- .... **CLC 21, 54, 109**
  See also CA 110; 111; CANR 63; CN; DA3; DLB 2; FANT; INT CA-111; MTCW 2
**Millin, Sarah Gertrude** 1889-1968 ... **CLC 49**
  See also CA 102; 93-96; DLB 225
**Milne, A(lan) A(lexander)** 1882-1956 ..... **TCLC 6, 88; DAB; DAC; DAM MST**
  See also BRWS 5; CA 104; 133; CLR 1, 26; CMW; CWRI; DA3; DLB 10, 77, 100, 160; FANT; MAICYA; MTCW 1, 2; RGEL; SATA 100; WCH; YABC 1
**Milner, Ron(ald)** 1938- ....... **CLC 56; BLC 3; DAM MULT**
  See also AITN 1; BW 1; CA 73-76; CAD; CANR 24, 81; CD; DLB 38; MTCW 1
**Milnes, Richard Monckton** 1809-1885 ................................. **NCLC 61**
  See also DLB 32, 184
**Milosz, Czeslaw** 1911- ...... **CLC 5, 11, 22, 31, 56, 82; DAM MST, POET; PC 8; WLCS**
  See also CA 81-84; CANR 23, 51, 91; CWW 2; DA3; EW; MTCW 1, 2; RGWL
**Milton, John** 1608-1674 .......... **LC 9, 43; DA; DAB; DAC; DAM MST, POET; PC 19, 29; WLC**
  See also BRW 2; CDBLB 1660-1789; DA3; DLB 131, 151; EFS 1; EXPP; LAIT 1; PAB; PFS 3; RGEL; WLIT 3; WP
**Min, Anchee** 1957- ........................... **CLC 86**
  See also CA 146; CANR 94

**Minehaha, Cornelius**
See Wedekind, (Benjamin) Frank(lin)

**Miner, Valerie** 1947- .................. **CLC 40**
See also CA 97-100; CANR 59; FW; GLL 2

**Minimo, Duca**
See D'Annunzio, Gabriele

**Minot, Susan** 1956- ..................... **CLC 44**
See also AMWS 6; CA 134; CN

**Minus, Ed** 1938- .......................... **CLC 39**
See also CA 185

**Miranda, Javier**
See Bioy Casares, Adolfo
See also CWW 2

**Miranda, Javier**
See Bioy Casares, Adolfo

**Mirbeau, Octave** 1848-1917 ........... **TCLC 55**
See also DLB 123, 192; GFL 1789 to the Present

**Miro (Ferrer), Gabriel (Francisco Victor)**
1879-1930 ........................... **TCLC 5**
See also CA 104; 185

**Misharin, Alexandr** ....................... **CLC 59**

**Mishima, Yukio** ... **CLC 2, 4, 6, 9, 27; DC 1; SSC 4**
See Hiraoka, Kimitake
See also BPFB 2; DLB 182; GLL 1; MTCW 2; RGSF; RGWL; SSFS 5

**Mistral, Frederic** 1830-1914 ........... **TCLC 51**
See also CA 122; GFL 1789 to the Present

**Mistral, Gabriela**
See Godoy Alcayaga, Lucila
See also LAW; RGWL; WP

**Mistry, Rohinton** 1952- ......... **CLC 71; DAC**
See also CA 141; CANR 86; CCA 1; CN; SSFS 6

**Mitchell, Clyde**
See Ellison, Harlan (Jay); Silverberg, Robert

**Mitchell, James Leslie** 1901-1935
See Gibbon, Lewis Grassic
See also CA 104; 188; DLB 15

**Mitchell, Joni** 1943- ...................... **CLC 12**
See also CA 112; CCA 1

**Mitchell, Joseph (Quincy)**
1908-1996 ............................ **CLC 98**
See also CA 77-80; 152; CANR 69; CN; CSW; DLB 185; DLBY 96

**Mitchell, Margaret (Munnerlyn)**
1900-1949 . **TCLC 11; DAM NOV, POP**
See also AAYA 23; BPFB 2; BYA 1; CA 109; 125; CANR 55, 94; CDALBS; DA3; DLB 9; LAIT 2; MTCW 1, 2; NFS 9; RGAL; RHW; WYAS 1; YAW

**Mitchell, Peggy**
See Mitchell, Margaret (Munnerlyn)

**Mitchell, S(ilas) Weir** 1829-1914 .... **TCLC 36**
See also CA 165; DLB 202; RGAL

**Mitchell, W(illiam) O(rmond)**
1914-1998 .. **CLC 25; DAC; DAM MST**
See also CA 77-80; 165; CANR 15, 43; CN; DLB 88

**Mitchell, William** 1879-1936 .......... **TCLC 81**

**Mitford, Mary Russell** 1787-1855 ... **NCLC 4**
See also DLB 110, 116; RGEL

**Mitford, Nancy** 1904-1973 ............. **CLC 44**
See also CA 9-12R; DLB 191; RGEL

**Miyamoto, (Chujo) Yuriko**
1899-1951 ........................... **TCLC 37**
See also CA 170, 174; DLB 180

**Miyazawa, Kenji** 1896-1933 .......... **TCLC 76**
See also CA 157

**Mizoguchi, Kenji** 1898-1956 .......... **TCLC 72**
See also CA 167

**Mo, Timothy (Peter)** 1950(?)- ... **CLC 46, 134**
See also CA 117; CN; DLB 194; MTCW 1; WLIT 4

**Modarressi, Taghi (M.)** 1931-1997 ... **CLC 44**
See also CA 121; 134; INT 134

**Modiano, Patrick (Jean)** 1945- ......... **CLC 18**
See also CA 85-88; CANR 17, 40; CWW 2; DLB 83

**Moerck, Paal**
See Roelvaag, O(le) E(dvart)

**Mofolo, Thomas (Mokopu)**
1875(?)-1948 .. **TCLC 22; BLC 3; DAM MULT**
See also AFW; CA 121; 153; CANR 83; DLB 225; MTCW 2; WLIT 2

**Mohr, Nicholasa** 1938- .......... **CLC 12; DAM MULT; HLC 2**
See also AAYA 8; CA 49-52; CANR 1, 32, 64; CLR 22; DLB 145; HW 1, 2; JRDA; LAIT 5; RGAL; SAAS 8; SATA 8, 97; SATA-Essay 113; YAW

**Mojtabai, A(nn) G(race)** 1938- ..... **CLC 5, 9, 15, 29**
See also CA 85-88; CANR 88

**Moliere** 1622-1673 .......... **LC 10, 28, 64; DA; DAB; DAC; DAM DRAM, MST; DC 13; WLC**
See also DA3; DFS 13; EW; GFL Beginnings to 1789; RGWL

**Molin, Charles**
See Mayne, William (James Carter)

**Molina, Tirso de** 1580(?)-1648 .... **LC 72; DC 13; HLCS 2**
See also Tirso de Molina

**Molnar, Ferenc** 1878-1952 .. **TCLC 20; DAM DRAM**
See also CA 109; 153; CANR 83; DLB 215; RGWL

**Momaday, N(avarre) Scott** 1934- ...... **CLC 2, 19, 85, 95; DA; DAB; DAC; DAM MST, MULT, NOV, POP; PC 25; WLCS**
See also AAYA 11; AMWS 4; ANW; BPFB 2; CA 25-28R; CANR 14, 34, 68; CDALBS; CN; CPW; DA3; DLB 143, 175; EXPP; INT CANR-14; LAIT 4; MTCW 1, 2; NFS 10; NNAL; PFS 2, 11; RGAL; SATA 48; SATA-Brief 30; WP; YAW

**Monette, Paul** 1945-1995 .............. **CLC 82**
See also CA 139; 147; CN; GLL 1

**Monroe, Harriet** 1860-1936 ............ **TCLC 12**
See also CA 109; DLB 54, 91

**Monroe, Lyle**
See Heinlein, Robert A(nson)

**Montagu, Elizabeth** 1720-1800 ......... **NCLC 7**
See also FW

**Montagu, Mary (Pierrepont) Wortley**
1689-1762 ..................... **LC 9, 57; PC 16**
See also DLB 95, 101; RGEL

**Montagu, W. H.**
See Coleridge, Samuel Taylor

**Montague, John (Patrick)** 1929- ...... **CLC 13, 46**
See also CA 9-12R; CANR 9, 69; CP; DLB 40; MTCW 1; PFS 12; RGEL

**Montaigne, Michel (Eyquem) de**
1533-1592 ......... **LC 8; DA; DAB; DAC; DAM MST; WLC**
See also EW; GFL Beginnings to 1789; RGWL

**Montale, Eugenio** 1896-1981 ... **CLC 7, 9, 18; PC 13**
See also CA 17-20R; 104; CANR 30; DLB 114; EW; MTCW 1; RGWL

**Montesquieu, Charles-Louis de Secondat**
1689-1755 ..................... **LC 7, 69**
See also EW; GFL Beginnings to 1789

**Montessori, Maria** 1870-1952 ...... **TCLC 103**
See also CA 115; 147

**Montgomery, (Robert) Bruce** 1921(?)-1978
See Crispin, Edmund
See also CA 179; 104; CMW

**Montgomery, L(ucy) M(aud)**
1874-1942 ......... **TCLC 51; DAC; DAM MST**
See also AAYA 12; BYA 1; CA 108; 137; CLR 8; DA3; DLB 92; DLBD 14; JRDA; MAICYA; MTCW 2; RGEL; SATA 100; WYA; YABC 1

**Montgomery, Marion H., Jr.** 1925- .... **CLC 7**
See also AITN 1; CA 1-4R; CANR 3, 48; CSW; DLB 6

**Montgomery, Max**
See Davenport, Guy (Mattison, Jr.)

**Montherlant, Henry (Milon) de**
1896-1972 ..... **CLC 8, 19; DAM DRAM**
See also CA 85-88; 37-40R; DLB 72; EW; GFL 1789 to the Present; MTCW 1

**Monty Python**
See Chapman, Graham; Cleese, John (Marwood); Gilliam, Terry (Vance); Idle, Eric; Jones, Terence Graham Parry; Palin, Michael (Edward)
See also AAYA 7

**Moodie, Susanna (Strickland)**
1803-1885 .............................. **NCLC 14**
See also DLB 99

**Moody, Hiram F. III** 1961-
See Moody, Rick
See also CA 138; CANR 64

**Moody, Rick** .............................. **CLC 147**
See also Moody, Hiram F. III

**Moody, William Vaughan**
1869-1910 ............................. **TCLC 105**
See also CA 110; 178; DLB 7, 54; RGAL

**Mooney, Edward** 1951-
See Mooney, Ted
See also CA 130

**Mooney, Ted** ..................... **CLC 25**
See also Mooney, Edward

**Moorcock, Michael (John)** 1939- ...... **CLC 5, 27, 58**
See also Bradbury, Edward P.
See also AAYA 26; CA 45-48; CAAS 5; CANR 2, 17, 38, 64; CN; DLB 14, 231; FANT; MTCW 1, 2; SATA 93; SFW; SUFW

**Moore, Brian** 1921-1999 ... **CLC 1, 3, 5, 7, 8, 19, 32, 90; DAB; DAC; DAM MST**
See also Bryan, Michael
See also CA 1-4R; 174; CANR 1, 25, 42, 63; CCA 1; CN; FANT; MTCW 1, 2; RGEL

**Moore, Edward**
See Muir, Edwin
See also RGEL

**Moore, G. E.** 1873-1958 ................ **TCLC 89**

**Moore, George Augustus**
1852-1933 ................... **TCLC 7; SSC 19**
See also BRW 6; CA 104; 177; DLB 10, 18, 57, 135; RGEL; RGSF

**Moore, Lorrie** ....................... **CLC 39, 45, 68**
See also Moore, Marie Lorena
See also DLB 234

**Moore, Marianne (Craig)**
1887-1972 .... **CLC 1, 2, 4, 8, 10, 13, 19, 47; DA; DAB; DAC; DAM MST, POET; PC 4; WLCS**
See also AMW; CA 1-4R; 33-36R; CANR 3, 61; CDALB 1929-1941; DA3; DLB 45; DLBD 7; EXPP; MAWW; MTCW 1, 2; PAB; RGAL; SATA 20; WP

**Moore, Marie Lorena** 1957-
See Moore, Lorrie
See also CA 116; CANR 39, 83; CN; DLB 234

**Moore, Thomas** 1779-1852 .............. **NCLC 6**
See also DLB 96, 144; RGEL

**Moorhouse, Frank** 1938- ................... **SSC 40**
See also CA 118; CANR 92; CN; RGSF

**Mora, Pat(ricia)** 1942-
See also CA 129; CANR 57, 81; CLR 58; DAM MULT; DLB 209; HLC 2; HW 1, 2; SATA 92

**Moraga, Cherrie** 1952- ........ **CLC 126; DAM MULT**
See also CA 131; CANR 66; DLB 82; FW; GLL 1; HW 1, 2

**Morand, Paul** 1888-1976 .... **CLC 41; SSC 22**
See also CA 184; 69-72; DLB 65

**Morante, Elsa** 1918-1985 ............. **CLC 8, 47**
See also CA 85-88; 117; CANR 35; DLB 177; MTCW 1, 2; RGWL

**Moravia, Alberto** ........ **CLC 2, 7, 11, 27, 46; SSC 26**
See Pincherle, Alberto
See also DLB 177; EW; MTCW 2; RGSF; RGWL

**More, Hannah** 1745-1833 .............. **NCLC 27**
See also DLB 107, 109, 116, 158; RGEL

**More, Henry** 1614-1687 ...................... **LC 9**
See also DLB 126

**More, Sir Thomas** 1478-1535 ........ **LC 10, 32**
See also BRWS 7; RGEL

**Moreas, Jean** ............................. **TCLC 18**
See also Papadiamantopoulos, Johannes
See also GFL 1789 to the Present

**Morgan, Berry** 1919- ......................... **CLC 6**
See also CA 49-52; DLB 6

**Morgan, Claire**
See Highsmith, (Mary) Patricia
See also GLL 1

**Morgan, Edwin (George)** 1920- ...... **CLC 31**
See also CA 5-8R; CANR 3, 43, 90; CP; DLB 27

**Morgan, (George) Frederick** 1922- .. **CLC 23**
See also CA 17-20R; CANR 21; CP

**Morgan, Harriet**
See Mencken, H(enry) L(ouis)

**Morgan, Jane**
See Cooper, James Fenimore

**Morgan, Janet** 1945- ......................... **CLC 39**
See also CA 65-68

**Morgan, Lady** 1776(?)-1859 ........... **NCLC 29**
See also DLB 116, 158; RGEL

**Morgan, Robin (Evonne)** 1941- .......... **CLC 2**
See also CA 69-72; CANR 29, 68; FW; GLL 2; MTCW 1; SATA 80

**Morgan, Scott**
See Kuttner, Henry

**Morgan, Seth** 1949(?)-1990 ............... **CLC 65**
See also CA 185; 132

**Morgenstern, Christian (Otto Josef Wolfgang)** 1871-1914 ................ **TCLC 8**
See also CA 105; 191

**Morgenstern, S.**
See Goldman, William (W.)

**Mori, Rintaro**
See Mori Ogai
See also CA 110

**Moricz, Zsigmond** 1879-1942 ......... **TCLC 33**
See also CA 165

**Morike, Eduard (Friedrich)** 1804-1875 .................... **NCLC 10**
See also DLB 133; RGWL

**Mori Ogai** 1862-1922 ..................... **TCLC 14**
See Ogai
See also CA 164; DLB 180; TWA

**Moritz, Karl Philipp** 1756-1793 ........... **LC 2**
See also DLB 94

**Morland, Peter Henry**
See Faust, Frederick (Schiller)

**Morley, Christopher (Darlington)** 1890-1957 .............................. **TCLC 87**
See also CA 112; DLB 9; RGAL

**Morren, Theophil**
See Hofmannsthal, Hugo von

**Morris, Bill** 1952- ............................. **CLC 76**

**Morris, Julian**
See West, Morris L(anglo)

**Morris, Steveland Judkins** 1950(?)-
See Wonder, Stevie
See also CA 111

**Morris, William** 1834-1896 .............. **NCLC 4**
See also BRW 5; CDBLB 1832-1890; DLB 18, 35, 57, 156, 178, 184; FANT; RGEL; SFW; SUFW

**Morris, Wright** 1910-1998 .. **CLC 1, 3, 7, 18, 37**
See also AMW; CA 9-12R; 167; CANR 21, 81; CN; DLB 2, 206; DLBY 81; MTCW 1, 2; RGAL; TCLC 107; TCWW 2

**Morrison, Arthur** 1863-1945 ......... **TCLC 72; SSC 40**
See also CA 120; 157; CMW; DLB 70, 135, 197; RGEL

**Morrison, Chloe Anthony Wofford**
See Morrison, Toni

**Morrison, James Douglas** 1943-1971
See Morrison, Jim
See also CA 73-76; CANR 40

**Morrison, Jim** ................................. **CLC 17**
See also Morrison, James Douglas

**Morrison, Toni** 1931- . **CLC 4, 10, 22, 55, 81, 87; BLC 3; DA; DAB; DAC; DAM MST, MULT, NOV, POP**
See also AAYA 1, 22; AFAW 1, 2; AMWS 3; BPFB 2; BW 2, 3; CA 29-32R; CANR 27, 42, 67; CDALB 1968-1988; CN; CPW; DA3; DLB 6, 33, 143; DLBY 81; EXPN; FW; LAIT 2, 4; MAWW; MTCW 1, 2; NFS 1, 6, 8; RGAL; RHW; SATA 57; SSFS 5; YAW

**Morrison, Van** 1945- ........................ **CLC 21**
See also CA 116; 168

**Morrissy, Mary** 1958- ....................... **CLC 99**

**Mortimer, John (Clifford)** 1923- ..... **CLC 28, 43; DAM DRAM, POP**
See also CA 13-16R; CANR 21, 69; CD; CDBLB 1960 to Present; CMW; CN; CPW; DA3; DLB 13, 245; INT CANR-21; MSW; MTCW 1, 2; RGEL

**Mortimer, Penelope (Ruth)** 1918-1999 ................................... **CLC 5**
See also CA 57-60; 187; CANR 45, 88; CN

**Morton, Anthony**
See Creasey, John

**Morton, Thomas** 1579(?)-1647(?) ........ **LC 72**
See also DLB 24; RGEL

**Mosca, Gaetano** 1858-1941 ............ **TCLC 75**

**Mosher, Howard Frank** 1943- ......... **CLC 62**
See also CA 139; CANR 65

**Mosley, Nicholas** 1923- ................. **CLC 43, 70**
See also CA 69-72; CANR 41, 60; CN; DLB 14, 207

**Mosley, Walter** 1952- ........... **CLC 97; BLCS; DAM MULT, POP**
See also AAYA 17; BPFB 2; BW 2; CA 142; CANR 57, 92; CMW; CPW; DA3; MSW; MTCW 2

**Moss, Howard** 1922-1987 ...... **CLC 7, 14, 45, 50; DAM POET**
See also CA 1-4R; 123; CANR 1, 44; DLB 5

**Mossgiel, Rab**
See Burns, Robert

**Motion, Andrew (Peter)** 1952- ......... **CLC 47**
See also BRWS 7; CA 146; CANR 90; CP; DLB 40

**Motley, Willard (Francis)** 1912-1965 ................................ **CLC 18**
See also BW 1; CA 117; 106; CANR 88; DLB 76, 143

**Motoori, Norinaga** 1730-1801 ........ **NCLC 45**

**Mott, Michael (Charles Alston)** 1930- ................................. **CLC 15, 34**
See also CA 5-8R; CAAS 7; CANR 7, 29

**Mountain Wolf Woman** 1884-1960 .. **CLC 92**
See also CA 144; CANR 90; NNAL

**Moure, Erin** 1955- ............................. **CLC 88**
See also CA 113; CP; CWP; DLB 60

**Mowat, Farley (McGill)** 1921- ......... **CLC 26; DAC; DAM MST**
See also AAYA 1; BYA 2; CA 1-4R; CANR 4, 24, 42, 68; CLR 20; CPW; DLB 68; INT CANR-24; JRDA; MAICYA; MTCW 1, 2; SATA 3, 55; YAW

**Mowatt, Anna Cora** 1819-1870 ..... **NCLC 74**
See also RGAL

**Moyers, Bill** 1934- ............................ **CLC 74**
See also AITN 2; CA 61-64; CANR 31, 52

**Mphahlele, Es'kia**
See Mphahlele, Ezekiel
See also AFW; DLB 125, 225; RGSF; SSFS 11

**Mphahlele, Ezekiel** 1919- ........ **CLC 25, 133; BLC 3; DAM MULT**
See also Mphahlele, Es'kia
See also BW 2, 3; CA 81-84; CANR 26, 76; CN; DA3; DLB 225; MTCW 2; SATA 119

**Mqhayi, S(amuel) E(dward) K(rune Loliwe)** 1875-1945 ...... **TCLC 25; BLC 3; DAM MULT**
See also CA 153; CANR 87

**Mrozek, Slawomir** 1930- ............... **CLC 3, 13**
See also CA 13-16R; CAAS 10; CANR 29; CWW 2; DLB 232; MTCW 1

**Mrs. Belloc-Lowndes**
See Lowndes, Marie Adelaide (Belloc)

**M'Taggart, John M'Taggart Ellis**
See McTaggart, John McTaggart Ellis

**Mtwa, Percy** (?)- ............................... **CLC 47**

**Mueller, Lisel** 1924- ........ **CLC 13, 51; PC 33**
See also CA 93-96; CP; DLB 105; PFS 9, 13

**Muir, Edwin** 1887-1959 ............... **TCLC 2, 87**
See also Moore, Edward
See also BRWS 6; CA 104; 193; DLB 20, 100, 191; RGEL

**Muir, John** 1838-1914 ..................... **TCLC 28**
See also AMWS 9; ANW; CA 165; DLB 186

**Mujica Lainez, Manuel** 1910-1984 ... **CLC 31**
See also Lainez, Manuel Mujica
See also CA 81-84; 112; CANR 32; HW 1

**Mukherjee, Bharati** 1940- ........ **CLC 53, 115; AAL; DAM NOV; SSC 38**
See also BEST 89:2; CA 107; CANR 45, 72; CN; DLB 60; DNFS; FW; MTCW 1, 2; RGAL; RGSF; SSFS 7

**Muldoon, Paul** 1951- ....... **CLC 32, 72; DAM POET**
See also BRWS 4; CA 113; 129; CANR 52, 91; CP; DLB 40; INT 129; PFS 7

**Mulisch, Harry** 1927- ....................... **CLC 42**
See also CA 9-12R; CANR 6, 26, 56

**Mull, Martin** 1943- ........................... **CLC 17**
See also CA 105

**Muller, Wilhelm** ............................. **NCLC 73**

**Mulock, Dinah Maria**
See Craik, Dinah Maria (Mulock)
See also RGEL

**Munford, Robert** 1737(?)-1783 ............. **LC 5**
See also DLB 31

**Mungo, Raymond** 1946- .................... **CLC 72**
See also CA 49-52; CANR 2

**Munro, Alice** 1931- ..... **CLC 6, 10, 19, 50, 95; DAC; DAM MST, NOV; SSC 3; WLCS**
See also AITN 2; BPFB 2; CA 33-36R; CANR 33, 53, 75; CCA 1; CN; DA3; DLB 53; MTCW 1, 2; RGEL; RGSF; SATA 29; SSFS 5, 13

**Munro, H(ector) H(ugh)** 1870-1916
See Saki
See also CA 104; 130; CDBLB 1890-1914; DA; DA3; DAB; DAC; DAM MST, NOV; DLB 34, 162; EXPS; MTCW 1, 2; RGEL; WLC

**Murakami, Haruki** 1949- ................ **CLC 150**
See also CA 136, 165; CANR 102; DLB 182; MJW; SFW

**Murasaki, Lady**
See Murasaki Shikibu

**Murasaki Shikibu** 978(?)-1026(?) ... **CMLC 1**
See also EFS 2; RGWL

**Murdoch, (Jean) Iris** 1919-1999 ... **CLC 1, 2, 3, 4, 6, 8, 11, 15, 22, 31, 51; DAB; DAC; DAM MST, NOV**
See also BRWS 1; CA 13-16R; 179; CANR 8, 43, 68, 103; CDBLB 1960 to Present; CN; DA3; DLB 14, 194, 233; INT CANR-8; MTCW 1, 2; RGEL; WLIT 4

**Murfree, Mary Noailles** 1850-1922 ... **SSC 22**
See also CA 122; 176; DLB 12, 74; RGAL

**Murnau, Friedrich Wilhelm**
See Plumpe, Friedrich Wilhelm

**Murphy, Richard** 1927- ..................... **CLC 41**
See also BRWS 5; CA 29-32R; CP; DLB 40

**Murphy, Sylvia** 1937- ........................ **CLC 34**
See also CA 121

**Murphy, Thomas (Bernard)** 1935- ... **CLC 51**
See also CA 101

**Murray, Albert L.** 1916- .................... **CLC 73**
See also BW 2; CA 49-52; CANR 26, 52, 78; CSW; DLB 38

**Murray, Judith Sargent** 1751-1820 ..................... **NCLC 63**
See also DLB 37, 200

**Murray, Les(lie Allan)** 1938- ........... **CLC 40; DAM POET**
See also BRWS 7; CA 21-24R; CANR 11, 27, 56, 103; CP; RGEL

**Murry, J. Middleton**
See Murry, John Middleton

**Murry, John Middleton** 1889-1957 ..................... **TCLC 16**
See also CA 118; DLB 149

**Musgrave, Susan** 1951- ................ **CLC 13, 54**
See also CA 69-72; CANR 45, 84; CCA 1; CP; CWP

**Musil, Robert (Edler von)** 1880-1942 ............... **TCLC 12, 68; SSC 18**
See also CA 109; CANR 55, 84; DLB 81, 124; EW; MTCW 2; RGSF; RGWL

**Muske, Carol** ..................... **CLC 90**
See also Muske-Dukes, Carol (Anne)

**Muske-Dukes, Carol (Anne)** 1945-
See Muske, Carol
See also CA 65-68; CANR 32, 70; CWP

**Musset, (Louis Charles) Alfred de** 1810-1857 ..................... **NCLC 7**
See also DLB 192; EW; GFL 1789 to the Present; RGWL; TWA

**Mussolini, Benito (Amilcare Andrea)** 1883-1945 ..................... **TCLC 96**
See also CA 116

**My Brother's Brother**
See Chekhov, Anton (Pavlovich)

**Myers, L(eopold) H(amilton)** 1881-1944 ..................... **TCLC 59**
See also CA 157; DLB 15; RGEL

**Myers, Walter Dean** 1937- ..... **CLC 35; BLC 3; DAM MULT, NOV**
See also AAYA 4, 23; BW 2; BYA 6, 8, 11; CA 33-36R; CANR 20, 42, 67; CLR 4, 16, 35; DLB 33; INT CANR-20; JRDA; LAIT 5; MAICYA; MAICYAS; MTCW 2; SAAS 2; SATA 41, 71, 109; SATA-Brief 27; YAW

**Myers, Walter M.**
See Myers, Walter Dean

**Myles, Symon**
See Follett, Ken(neth Martin)

**Nabokov, Vladimir (Vladimirovich)** 1899-1977 ....... **CLC 1, 2, 3, 6, 8, 11, 15, 23, 44, 46, 64; DA; DAB; DAC; DAM MST, NOV; SSC 11; WLC**
See also AMW; AMWR 1; BPFB 2; CA 5-8R; 69-72; CANR 20, 102; CDALB 1941-1968; DA3; DLB 2, 244; DLBD 3; DLBY 80, 91; EXPS; MTCW 1, 2; NFS 9; RGAL; RGSF; SSFS 6; TCLC 108

**Naevius** c. 265B.C.-201B.C. ........... **CMLC 37**
See also DLB 211

**Nagai, Kafu** ................ **TCLC 51**
See also Nagai, Sokichi
See also DLB 180

**Nagai, Sokichi** 1879-1959
See Nagai, Kafu
See also CA 117

**Nagy, Laszlo** 1925-1978 ....................... **CLC 7**
See also CA 129; 112

**Naidu, Sarojini** 1879-1949 .............. **TCLC 80**
See also RGEL

**Naipaul, Shiva(dhar Srinivasa)** 1945-1985 ....... **CLC 32, 39; DAM NOV**
See also CA 110; 112; 116; CANR 33; DA3; DLB 157; DLBY 85; MTCW 1, 2

**Naipaul, V(idiadhar) S(urajprasad)** 1932- ........ **CLC 4, 7, 9, 13, 18, 37, 105; DAB; DAC; DAM MST, NOV; SSC 38**
See also BPFB 2; BRWS 1; CA 1-4R; CANR 1, 33, 51, 91; CDBLB 1960 to Present; CN; DA3; DLB 125, 204, 206; DLBY 85; MTCW 1, 2; RGEL; RGSF; WLIT 4

**Nakos, Lilika** 1899(?)- ........................ **CLC 29**

**Narayan, R(asipuram) K(rishnaswami)** 1906-2001 .... **CLC 7, 28, 47, 121; DAM NOV; SSC 25**
See also BPFB 2; CA 81-84; CANR 33, 61; CN; DA3; DNFS; MTCW 1, 2; RGEL; RGSF; SATA 62; SSFS 5

**Nash, (Frediric) Ogden** 1902-1971 . **CLC 23; DAM POET; PC 21**
See also CA 13-14; 29-32R; CANR 34, 61; CAP 1; DLB 11; MAICYA; MTCW 1, 2; RGAL; SATA 2, 46; TCLC 109; WP

**Nashe, Thomas** 1567-1601(?) ............... **LC 41**
See also DLB 167; RGEL

**Nathan, Daniel**
See Dannay, Frederic

**Nathan, George Jean** 1882-1958 .... **TCLC 18**
See also Hatteras, Owen
See also CA 114; 169; DLB 137

**Natsume, Kinnosuke** 1867-1916
See Natsume, Soseki
See also CA 104

**Natsume, Soseki** ........................ **TCLC 2, 10**
See also Natsume, Kinnosuke
See also CA 195; DLB 180; RGWL

**Natti, (Mary) Lee** 1919-
See Kingman, Lee
See also CA 5-8R; CANR 2

**Naylor, Gloria** 1950- .... **CLC 28, 52; BLC 3; DA; DAC; DAM MST, MULT, NOV, POP; WLCS**
See also AAYA 6, 39; AFAW 1, 2; AMWS 8; BW 2, 3; CA 107; CANR 27, 51, 74; CN; CPW; DA3; DLB 173; FW; MTCW 1, 2; NFS 4, 7; RGAL

**Neff, Debra** ........................ **CLC 59**

**Neihardt, John Gneisenau** 1881-1973 ........................ **CLC 32**
See also CA 13-14; CANR 65; CAP 1; DLB 9, 54; LAIT 2

**Nekrasov, Nikolai Alekseevich** 1821-1878 ........................ **NCLC 11**

**Nelligan, Emile** 1879-1941 .............. **TCLC 14**
See also CA 114; DLB 92

**Nelson, Willie** 1933- ........................... **CLC 17**
See also CA 107

**Nemerov, Howard (Stanley)** 1920-1991 ........ **CLC 2, 6, 9, 36; DAM POET; PC 24**
See also AMW; CA 1-4R; 134; CABS 2; CANR 1, 27, 53; DLB 5, 6; DLBY 83; INT CANR-27; MTCW 1, 2; PFS 10; RGAL

**Neruda, Pablo** 1904-1973 .. **CLC 1, 2, 5, 7, 9, 28, 62; DA; DAB; DAC; DAM MST, MULT, POET; HLC 2; PC 4; WLC**
See also CA 19-20; 45-48; CAP 2; DA3; DNFS; HW 1; LAW; MTCW 1, 2; PFS 11; RGWL; WLIT 1; WP

**Nerval, Gerard de** 1808-1855 ... **NCLC 1, 67; PC 13; SSC 18**
See also EW; GFL 1789 to the Present; RGSF; RGWL

**Nervo, (Jose) Amado (Ruiz de)** 1870-1919 ................ **TCLC 11; HLCS 2**
See also CA 109; 131; HW 1; LAW

**Nessi, Pio Baroja y**
See Baroja (y Nessi), Pio

**Nestroy, Johann** 1801-1862 ............ **NCLC 42**
See also DLB 133; RGWL

**Netterville, Luke**
See O'Grady, Standish (James)

**Neufeld, John (Arthur)** 1938- ........... **CLC 17**
See also AAYA 11; CA 25-28R; CANR 11, 37, 56; CLR 52; MAICYA; SAAS 3; SATA 6, 81; YAW

**Neumann, Alfred** 1895-1952 ......... **TCLC 100**
See also CA 183; DLB 56

**Neumann, Ferenc**
See Molnar, Ferenc

**Neville, Emily Cheney** 1919- ............. **CLC 12**
See also BYA 2; CA 5-8R; CANR 3, 37, 85; JRDA; MAICYA; SAAS 2; SATA 1; YAW

**Newbound, Bernard Slade** 1930-
See Slade, Bernard
See also CA 81-84; CANR 49; CD; DAM DRAM

**Newby, P(ercy) H(oward)** 1918-1997 ......... **CLC 2, 13; DAM NOV**
See also CA 5-8R; 161; CANR 32, 67; CN; DLB 15; MTCW 1; RGEL

**Newcastle**
See Cavendish, Margaret Lucas

**Newlove, Donald** 1928- ........................ **CLC 6**
See also CA 29-32R; CANR 25

**Newlove, John (Herbert)** 1938- ......... **CLC 14**
See also CA 21-24R; CANR 9, 25; CP

**Newman, Charles** 1938- .................. **CLC 2, 8**
See also CA 21-24R; CANR 84; CN

**Newman, Edwin (Harold)** 1919- ....... **CLC 14**
See also AITN 1; CA 69-72; CANR 5

**Newman, John Henry** 1801-1890 . **NCLC 38, 99**
See also BRWS 7; DLB 18, 32, 55; RGEL

**Newton, (Sir) Isaac** 1642-1727 ...... **LC 35, 52**

**Newton, Suzanne** 1936- ..................... **CLC 35**
See also BYA 7; CA 41-44R; CANR 14; JRDA; SATA 5, 77

**New York Dept. of Ed.** ..................... **CLC 70**

**Nexo, Martin Andersen** 1869-1954 ........................ **TCLC 43**
See also DLB 214

**Nezval, Vitezslav** 1900-1958 .......... **TCLC 44**
See also CA 123

**Ng, Fae Myenne** 1957(?)- ................. **CLC 81**
See also CA 146

**Ngema, Mbongeni** 1955- ................. **CLC 57**
See also BW 2; CA 143; CANR 84; CD

**Ngugi, James T(hiong'o)** ......... **CLC 3, 7, 13**
See also Ngugi wa Thiong'o

**Ngugi wa Thiong'o** 1938- .. **CLC 36; BLC 3; DAM MULT, NOV**
See also Ngugi, James T(hiong'o)
See also AFW; BW 2; CA 81-84; CANR 27, 58; DLB 125; DNFS; MTCW 1, 2; RGEL

**Nichol, B(arrie) P(hillip)** 1944-1988 . **CLC 18**
See also CA 53-56; DLB 53; SATA 66

**Nichols, John (Treadwell)** 1940- ....... **CLC 38**
See also CA 9-12R; CAAE 190; CAAS 2; CANR 6, 70; DLBY 82; TCWW 2

**Nichols, Leigh**
See Koontz, Dean R(ay)

**Nichols, Peter (Richard)** 1927- .... **CLC 5, 36, 65**
See also CA 104; CANR 33, 86; CBD; CD; DLB 13, 245; MTCW 1

**Nicholson, Linda ed.** .......................... **CLC 65**

**Ni Chuilleanain, Eilean** 1942- .............. **PC 34**
See also CA 126; CANR 53, 83; CP; CWP; DLB 40

**Nicolas, F. R. E.**
See Freeling, Nicolas

**Niedecker, Lorine** 1903-1970 ..... **CLC 10, 42; DAM POET**
See also CA 25-28; CAP 2; DLB 48

**Nietzsche, Friedrich (Wilhelm)** 1844-1900 .................... **TCLC 10, 18, 55**
See also CA 107; 121; DLB 129; EW; RGWL

**Nievo, Ippolito** 1831-1861 ............... **NCLC 22**

**Nightingale, Anne Redmon** 1943-
See Redmon, Anne
See also CA 103

**Nightingale, Florence** 1820-1910 ... **TCLC 85**
See also CA 188; DLB 166

**Nik. T. O.**
See Annensky, Innokenty (Fyodorovich)

**Nin, Anais** 1903-1977 .... **CLC 1, 4, 8, 11, 14, 60, 127; DAM NOV, POP; SSC 10**
See also AITN 2; BPFB 2; CA 13-16R; 69-72; CANR 22, 53; DLB 2, 4, 152; GLL 2; MAWW; MTCW 1, 2; RGAL; RGSF

**Nishida, Kitaro** 1870-1945 ............... **TCLC 83**

**Nishiwaki, Junzaburo** 1894-1982 ........ **PC 15**
See also Nishiwaki, Junzaburo
See also CA 194; 107; MJW

**Nishiwaki, Junzaburo** 1894-1982
See Nishiwaki, Junzaburo
See also CA 194

**Nissenson, Hugh** 1933- .................. **CLC 4, 9**
See also CA 17-20R; CANR 27; CN; DLB 28

**Niven, Larry** ................................... **CLC 8**
See also Niven, Laurence Van Cott
See also AAYA 27; BPFB 2; BYA 10; DLB 8; SCFW 2

**Niven, Laurence Van Cott** 1938-
See Niven, Larry
See also CA 21-24R; CAAS 12; CANR 14, 44, 66; CPW; DAM POP; MTCW 1, 2; SATA 95; SFW

**Nixon, Agnes Eckhardt** 1927- .......... **CLC 21**
See also CA 110

**Nizan, Paul** 1905-1940 .................... **TCLC 40**
See also CA 161; DLB 72; GFL 1789 to the Present

**Nkosi, Lewis** 1936- ... **CLC 45; BLC 3; DAM MULT**
See also BW 1, 3; CA 65-68; CANR 27, 81; CBD; CD; DLB 157, 225

**Nodier, (Jean) Charles (Emmanuel)** 1780-1844 ................. **NCLC 19**
See also DLB 119; GFL 1789 to the Present

**Noguchi, Yone** 1875-1947 ................ **TCLC 80**

**Nolan, Christopher** 1965- ................ **CLC 58**
See also CA 111; CANR 88

**Noon, Jeff** 1957- ............................. **CLC 91**
See also CA 148; CANR 83; SFW

**Norden, Charles**
See Durrell, Lawrence (George)

**Nordhoff, Charles (Bernard)** 1887-1947 ................. **TCLC 23**
See also CA 108; DLB 9; LAIT 1; RHW 1; SATA 23

**Norfolk, Lawrence** 1963- .................... **CLC 76**
See also CA 144; CANR 85; CN

**Norman, Marsha** 1947- ......... **CLC 28; DAM DRAM; DC 8**
See also CA 105; CABS 3; CAD; CANR 41; CD; CSW; CWD; DFS 2; DLBY 84; FW

**Normyx**
See Douglas, (George) Norman

**Norris, (Benjamin) Frank(lin, Jr.)** 1870-1902 ............ **TCLC 24; SSC 28**
See also AMW; BPFB 2; CA 110; 160; CDALB 1865-1917; DLB 12, 71, 186; NFS 12; RGAL; TCWW 2; TUS

**Norris, Leslie** 1921- ............................ **CLC 14**
See also CA 11-12; CANR 14; CAP 1; CP; DLB 27

**North, Andrew**
See Norton, Andre

**North, Anthony**
See Koontz, Dean R(ay)

**North, Captain George**
See Stevenson, Robert Louis (Balfour)

**North, Milou**
See Erdrich, Louise

**Northrup, B. A.**
See Hubbard, L(afayette) Ron(ald)

**North Staffs**
See Hulme, T(homas) E(rnest)

**Norton, Alice Mary**
See Norton, Andre
See also MAICYA; SATA 1, 43

**Norton, Andre** 1912- ........................ **CLC 12**
See also Norton, Alice Mary
See also AAYA 14; BPFB 2; BYA 4, 10, 12; CA 1-4R; CANR 68; CLR 50; DLB 8, 52; JRDA; MTCW 1; SATA 91; YAW

**Norton, Caroline** 1808-1877 ........... **NCLC 47**
See also DLB 21, 159, 199

**Norway, Nevil Shute** 1899-1960
See Shute, Nevil
See also CA 102; 93-96; CANR 85; MTCW 2; RHW; SFW

**Norwid, Cyprian Kamil** 1821-1883 ............................ **NCLC 17**

**Nosille, Nabrah**
See Ellison, Harlan (Jay)

**Nossack, Hans Erich** 1901-1978 ......... **CLC 6**
See also CA 93-96; 85-88; DLB 69

**Nostradamus** 1503-1566 ...................... **LC 27**

**Nosu, Chuji**
See Ozu, Yasujiro

**Notenburg, Eleanora (Genrikhovna) von**
See Guro, Elena

**Nova, Craig** 1945- ........................ **CLC 7, 31**
See also CA 45-48; CANR 2, 53

**Novak, Joseph**
See Kosinski, Jerzy (Nikodem)

**Novalis** 1772-1801 ........................... **NCLC 13**
See also DLB 90; EW; RGWL

**Novis, Emile**
See Weil, Simone (Adolphine)

**Nowlan, Alden (Albert)** 1933-1983 . **CLC 15; DAC; DAM MST**
See also CA 9-12R; CANR 5; DLB 53; PFS 12

**Noyes, Alfred** 1880-1958 ...... **TCLC 7; PC 27**
See also CA 104; 188; DLB 20; EXPP; FANT; PFS 4; RGEL

**Nunn, Kem** ....................................... **CLC 34**
See also CA 159

**Nwapa, Flora** 1931-1993 .... **CLC 133; BLCS**
See also BW 2; CA 143; CANR 83; CWRI; DLB 125; WLIT 2

**Nye, Robert** 1939- . **CLC 13, 42; DAM NOV**
See also CA 33-36R; CANR 29, 67; CN; CP; CWRI; DLB 14; FANT; HGG; MTCW 1; RHW; SATA 6

**Nyro, Laura** 1947-1997 ..................... **CLC 17**
See also CA 194

**Oates, Joyce Carol** 1938- .. **CLC 1, 2, 3, 6, 9, 11, 15, 19, 33, 52, 108, 134; DA; DAB; DAC; DAM MST, NOV, POP; SSC 6; WLC**
See also AAYA 15; AITN 1; AMWS 2; BEST 89:2; BPFB 2; BYA 11; CA 5-8R; CANR 25, 45, 74; CDALB 1968-1988; CN; CP; CPW; CWP; DA3; DLB 2, 5, 130; DLBY 81; EXPS; FW; HGG; INT CANR-25; LAIT 4; MAWW; MTCW 1, 2; NFS 8; RGAL; RGSF; SSFS 1, 8

**O'Brien, Darcy** 1939-1998 .................. **CLC 11**
See also CA 21-24R; 167; CANR 8, 59

**O'Brien, E. G.**
See Clarke, Arthur C(harles)

**O'Brien, Edna** 1936- ...... **CLC 3, 5, 8, 13, 36, 65, 116; DAM NOV; SSC 10**
See also BRWS 5; CA 1-4R; CANR 6, 41, 65, 102; CDBLB 1960 to Present; CN; DA3; DLB 14, 231; FW; MTCW 1, 2; RGSF; WLIT 4

**O'Brien, Fitz-James** 1828-1862 ..... **NCLC 21**
See also DLB 74; RGAL

**O'Brien, Flann** .......... **CLC 1, 4, 5, 7, 10, 47**
See also O Nuallain, Brian
See also BRWS 2; DLB 231; RGEL

**O'Brien, Richard** 1942- ..................... **CLC 17**
See also CA 124

**O'Brien, (William) Tim(othy)** 1946- . **CLC 7, 19, 40, 103; DAM POP**
See also AAYA 16; AMWS 5; CA 85-88; CANR 40, 58; CDALBS; CN; CPW; DA3; DLB 152; DLBD 9; DLBY 80; MTCW 2; RGAL

**Obstfelder, Sigbjoern** 1866-1900 .... **TCLC 23**
See also CA 123

**O'Casey, Sean** 1880-1964 .... **CLC 1, 5, 9, 11, 15, 88; DAB; DAC; DAM DRAM, MST; DC 12; WLCS**
See also BRW 7; CA 89-92; CANR 62; CBD; CDBLB 1914-1945; DA3; DLB 10; MTCW 1, 2; RGEL; WLIT 4

**O'Cathasaigh, Sean**
See O'Casey, Sean

**Occom, Samson** 1723-1792 .................. **LC 60**
See also DLB 175; NNAL

**Ochs, Phil(ip David)** 1940-1976 ........ **CLC 17**
See also CA 185; 65-68

**O'Connor, Edwin (Greene)** 1918-1968 ............................... **CLC 14**
See also CA 93-96; 25-28R

**O'Connor, (Mary) Flannery** 1925-1964 .... **CLC 1, 2, 3, 6, 10, 13, 15, 21, 66, 104; DA; DAB; DAC; DAM MST, NOV; SSC 1, 23; WLC**
See also AAYA 7; AMW; BPFB 3; CA 1-4R; CANR 3, 41; CDALB 1941-1968; DA3; DLB 2, 152; DLBD 12; DLBY 80; EXPS; LAIT 5; MAWW; MTCW 1, 2; NFS 3; RGAL; RGSF; SSFS 2, 7, 10

**O'Connor, Frank** ............ **CLC 23; SSC 5**
See also O'Donovan, Michael John
See also DLB 162; RGSF; SSFS 5

**O'Dell, Scott** 1898-1989 .................. **CLC 30**
See also AAYA 3; BPFB 3; BYA 1, 2, 3, 5; CA 61-64; 129; CANR 12, 30; CLR 1, 16; DLB 52; JRDA; MAICYA; SATA 12, 60; YAW

**Odets, Clifford** 1906-1963 ..... **CLC 2, 28, 98; DAM DRAM; DC 6**
See also AMWS 2; CA 85-88; CAD; CANR 62; DFS 3; DLB 7, 26; MTCW 1, 2; RGAL

**O'Doherty, Brian** 1934- ................ **CLC 76**
See also CA 105

**O'Donnell, K. M.**
See Malzberg, Barry N(athaniel)

**O'Donnell, Lawrence**
See Kuttner, Henry

**O'Donovan, Michael John** 1903-1966 ............................ **CLC 14**
See also O'Connor, Frank
See also CA 93-96; CANR 84

**Oe, Kenzaburo** 1935- .......... **CLC 10, 36, 86; DAM NOV; SSC 20**
See also CA 97-100; CANR 36, 50, 74; DA3; DLB 182; DLBY 94; MTCW 1, 2

**Oe Kenzaburo**
See Oe, Kenzaburo
See also CWW; EWL; MJW; RGSF; RGWL

**O'Faolain, Julia** 1932- .... **CLC 6, 19, 47, 108**
See also CA 81-84; CAAS 2; CANR 12, 61; CN; DLB 14, 231; FW; MTCW 1; RHW

**O'Faolain, Sean** 1900-1991 ...... **CLC 1, 7, 14, 32, 70; SSC 13**
See also CA 61-64; 134; CANR 12, 66; DLB 15, 162; MTCW 1, 2; RGEL; RGSF

**O'Flaherty, Liam** 1896-1984 ....... **CLC 5, 34; SSC 6**
See also CA 101; 113; CANR 35; DLB 36, 162; DLBY 84; MTCW 1, 2; RGEL; RGSF; SSFS 5

**Ogai**
See Mori Ogai
See also MJW

**Ogilvy, Gavin**
See Barrie, J(ames) M(atthew)

**O'Grady, Standish (James)** 1846-1928 ................................ **TCLC 5**
See also CA 104; 157

**O'Grady, Timothy** 1951- ................... **CLC 59**
See also CA 138

**O'Hara, Frank** 1926-1966 ....... **CLC 2, 5, 13, 78; DAM POET**
See also CA 9-12R; 25-28R; CANR 33; DA3; DLB 5, 16, 193; MTCW 1, 2; PFS 8; 12; RGAL; WP

**O'Hara, John (Henry)** 1905-1970 . **CLC 1, 2, 3, 6, 11, 42; DAM NOV; SSC 15**
See also AMW; BPFB 3; CA 5-8R; 25-28R; CANR 31, 60; CDALB 1929-1941; DLB 9, 86; DLBD 2; MTCW 1, 2; NFS 11; RGAL; RGSF

**O Hehir, Diana** 1922- ...................... **CLC 41**
See also CA 93-96

**Ohiyesa** 1858-1939
See Eastman, Charles A(lexander)

**Okigbo, Christopher (Ifenayichukwu)** 1932-1967 ... **CLC 25, 84; BLC 3; DAM MULT, POET; PC 7**
See also AFW; BW 1, 3; CA 77-80; CANR 74; DLB 125; MTCW 1, 2; RGEL

**Okri, Ben** 1959- ............................... **CLC 87**
See also AFW; BRWS 5; BW 2, 3; CA 130; 138; CANR 65; CN; DLB 157, 231; INT CA-138; MTCW 2; RGSF; WLIT 2

**Olds, Sharon** 1942- ... **CLC 32, 39, 85; DAM POET; PC 22**
See also CA 101; CANR 18, 41, 66, 98; CP; CPW; CWP; DLB 120; MTCW 2

**Oldstyle, Jonathan**
See Irving, Washington

**Olesha, Iurii**
See Olesha, Yuri (Karlovich)
See also RGWL

**Olesha, Yuri (Karlovich)** 1899-1960 .. **CLC 8**
See also Olesha, Iurii
See also CA 85-88; EW

**Oliphant**
See Oliphant, Margaret (Oliphant Wilson)
See also SUFW

**Oliphant, Laurence** 1829(?)-1888 .. **NCLC 47**
See also DLB 18, 166

**Oliphant, Margaret (Oliphant Wilson)** 1828-1897 ........... **NCLC 11, 61; SSC 25**
See also Oliphant
See also DLB 18, 159, 190; HGG; RGEL; RGSF; SUFW

**Oliver, Mary** 1935- ................. **CLC 19, 34, 98**
See also AMWS 7; CA 21-24R; CANR 9, 43, 84, 92; CP; CWP; DLB 5, 193

**Olivier, Laurence (Kerr)** 1907-1989 . **CLC 20**
See also CA 111; 150; 129

**Olsen, Tillie** 1912- ............... **CLC 4, 13, 114; DA; DAB; DAC; DAM MST; SSC 11**
See also BYA 11; CA 1-4R; CANR 1, 43, 74; CDALBS; CN; DA3; DLB 28, 206; DLBY 80; EXPS; FW; MTCW 1, 2; RGAL; RGSF; SSFS 1

**Olson, Charles (John)** 1910-1970 .. **CLC 1, 2, 5, 6, 9, 11, 29; DAM POET; PC 19**
See also AMWS 2; CA 13-16; 25-28R; CABS 2; CANR 35, 61; CAP 1; DLB 5, 16, 193; MTCW 1, 2; RGAL; WP

**Olson, Toby** 1937- .............................. **CLC 28**
See also CA 65-68; CANR 9, 31, 84; CP

**Olyesha, Yuri**
See Olesha, Yuri (Karlovich)

**Omar Khayyam**
See Khayyam, Omar
See also RGWL

**Ondaatje, (Philip) Michael** 1943- .... **CLC 14, 29, 51, 76; DAB; DAC; DAM MST; PC 28**
See also CA 77-80; CANR 42, 74; CN; CP; DA3; DLB 60; MTCW 2; PFS 8

**Oneal, Elizabeth** 1934-
See Oneal, Zibby
See also CA 106; CANR 28, 84; MAICYA; SATA 30, 82; YAW

**Oneal, Zibby** ............................ **CLC 30**
See also Oneal, Elizabeth
See also AAYA 5, 41; BYA 13; CLR 13; JRDA

**O'Neill, Eugene (Gladstone)** 1888-1953 ........ **TCLC 1, 6, 27, 49; DA; DAB; DAC; DAM DRAM, MST; WLC**
See also AITN 1; AMW; CA 110; 132; CAD; CDALB 1929-1941; DA3; DFS 9, 11, 12; DLB 7; LAIT 3; MTCW 1, 2; RGAL

**Onetti, Juan Carlos** 1909-1994 ... **CLC 7, 10; DAM MULT, NOV; HLCS 2; SSC 23**
See also CA 85-88; 145; CANR 32, 63; DLB 113; HW 1, 2; LAW; MTCW 1, 2; RGSF

**O Nuallain, Brian** 1911-1966
See O'Brien, Flann
See also CA 21-22; 25-28R; CAP 2; DLB 231; FANT

**Ophuls, Max** 1902-1957 .................. **TCLC 79**
See also CA 113

**Opie, Amelia** 1769-1853 .................. **NCLC 65**
See also DLB 116, 159; RGEL

**Oppen, George** 1908-1984 ..... **CLC 7, 13, 34; PC 35**
See also CA 13-16R; 113; CANR 8, 82; DLB 5, 165; TCLC 107

**Oppenheim, E(dward) Phillips** 1866-1946 ................................ **TCLC 45**
See also CA 111; CMW; DLB 70

**Opuls, Max**
See Ophuls, Max

**Origen** c. 185-c. 254 ....................... **CMLC 19**

**Orlovitz, Gil** 1918-1973 ................... **CLC 22**
See also CA 77-80; 45-48; DLB 2, 5

**Orris**
See Ingelow, Jean

**Ortega y Gasset, Jose** 1883-1955 ... **TCLC 9; DAM MULT; HLC 2**
See also CA 106; 130; EW; HW 1, 2; MTCW 1, 2

**Ortese, Anna Maria** 1914- ................ **CLC 89**
See also DLB 177

**Ortiz, Simon J(oseph)** 1941- . **CLC 45; DAM MULT, POET; PC 17**
See also AMWS 4; CA 134; CANR 69; CP; DLB 120, 175; EXPP; NNAL; PFS 4; RGAL

**Orton, Joe** ................... **CLC 4, 13, 43; DC 3**
See also Orton, John Kingsley
See also BRWS 5; CBD; CDBLB 1960 to Present; DFS 3, 6; DLB 13; GLL 1; MTCW 2; RGEL; WLIT 4

**Orton, John Kingsley** 1933-1967
See Orton, Joe
See also CA 85-88; CANR 35, 66; DAM DRAM; MTCW 1, 2

**Orwell, George** ......... **TCLC 2, 6, 15, 31, 51; DAB; WLC**
See also Blair, Eric (Arthur)
See also BPFB 3; BRW 7; BYA 5; CDBLB 1945-1960; CLR 68; DLB 15, 98, 195; EXPN; LAIT 4, 5; NFS 3, 7; RGEL; SCFW 2; SFW; SSFS 4; WLIT 4; YAW

**Osborne, David**
See Silverberg, Robert

**Osborne, George**
See Silverberg, Robert

**Osborne, John (James)** 1929-1994 .... **CLC 1, 2, 5, 11, 45; DA; DAB; DAC; DAM DRAM, MST; WLC**
See also BRWS 1; CA 13-16R; 147; CANR 21, 56; CDBLB 1945-1960; DFS 4; DLB 13; MTCW 1, 2; RGEL

**Osborne, Lawrence** 1958- ................ **CLC 50**
See also CA 189

**Osbourne, Lloyd** 1868-1947 ........... **TCLC 93**

**Oshima, Nagisa** 1932- ........................ **CLC 20**
See also CA 116; 121; CANR 78

**Oskison, John Milton** 1874-1947 .. **TCLC 35; DAM MULT**
See also CA 144; CANR 84; DLB 175; NNAL

**Ossian** c. 3rd cent. - ........................ **CMLC 28**
See also Macpherson, James

**Ossoli, Sarah Margaret (Fuller)** 1810-1850 ............................. **NCLC 5, 50**
See also Fuller, Margaret; Fuller, Sarah Margaret
See also CDALB 1640-1865; DLB 1, 59, 73, 183, 223, 239; FW; SATA 25

**Ostriker, Alicia (Suskin)** 1937- ........ **CLC 132**
See also CA 25-28R; CAAS 24; CANR 10, 30, 62, 99; CWP; DLB 120; EXPP

**Ostrovsky, Alexander** 1823-1886 .. **NCLC 30, 57**

**Otero, Blas de** 1916-1979 ................... **CLC 11**
See also CA 89-92; DLB 134

**Otto, Rudolf** 1869-1937 .................. **TCLC 85**

**Otto, Whitney** 1955- ......................... **CLC 70**
See also CA 140**

**Ouida** .................................................. **TCLC 43**
See also De La Ramee, (Marie) Louise
See also DLB 18, 156; RGEL

**Ouologuem, Yambo** 1940- ............... **CLC 146**
See also CA 111; 176

**Ousmane, Sembene** 1923- ... **CLC 66; BLC 3**
See also Sembene, Ousmane
See also BW 1, 3; CA 117; 125; CANR 81; CWW 2; MTCW 1

**Ovid** 43B.C.-17 . **CMLC 7; DAM POET; PC 2**
See also AW 2; DA3; DLB 211; RGWL; WP

**Owen, Hugh**
See Faust, Frederick (Schiller)

**Owen, Wilfred (Edward Salter)** 1893-1918 ........ **TCLC 5, 27; DA; DAB; DAC; DAM MST, POET; PC 19; WLC**
See also BRW 6; CA 104; 141; CDBLB 1914-1945; DLB 20; EXPP; MTCW 2; PFS 10; RGEL; WLIT 4

**Owens, Rochelle** 1936- ......................... **CLC 8**
See also CA 17-20R; CAAS 2; CAD; CANR 39; CD; CP; CWD; CWP

**Oz, Amos** 1939- ...... **CLC 5, 8, 11, 27, 33, 54; DAM NOV**
See also CA 53-56; CANR 27, 47, 65; CWW 2; MTCW 1, 2; RGSF

**Ozick, Cynthia** 1928- .......... **CLC 3, 7, 28, 62; DAM NOV, POP; SSC 15**
See also AMWS 5; BEST 90:1; CA 17-20R; CANR 23, 58; CN; CPW; DA3; DLB 28, 152; DLBY 82; EXPS; INT CANR-23; MTCW 1, 2; RGAL; RGSF; SSFS 3, 12

**Ozu, Yasujiro** 1903-1963 .................... **CLC 16**
See also CA 112

**Pacheco, C.**
See Pessoa, Fernando (Antonio Nogueira)

**Pacheco, Jose Emilio** 1939-
See also CA 111; 131; CANR 65; DAM MULT; HLC 2; HW 1, 2; RGSF

**Pa Chin** ................................................. **CLC 18**
See also Li Fei-kan

**Pack, Robert** 1929- ............................ **CLC 13**
See also CA 1-4R; CANR 3, 44, 82; CP; DLB 5; SATA 118

**Padgett, Lewis**
See Kuttner, Henry

**Padilla (Lorenzo), Heberto** 1932-2000 ............................. **CLC 38**
See also AITN 1; CA 123; 131; 189; HW 1

**Page, Jimmy** 1944- ............................... **CLC 12**

**Page, Louise** 1955- .............................. **CLC 40**
See also CA 140; CANR 76; CBD; CD; CWD; DLB 233

**Page, P(atricia) K(athleen)** 1916- ...... **CLC 7, 18; DAC; DAM MST; PC 12**
See also Cape, Judith
See also CA 53-56; CANR 4, 22, 65; CP; DLB 68; MTCW 1; RGEL

**Page, Stanton**
See Fuller, Henry Blake

**Page, Stanton**
See Fuller, Henry Blake

**Page, Thomas Nelson** 1853-1922 ....... **SSC 23**
See also CA 118; 177; DLB 12, 78; DLBD 13; RGAL

**Pagels, Elaine Hiesey** 1943- ............ **CLC 104**
See also CA 45-48; CANR 2, 24, 51; FW

**Paget, Violet** 1856-1935
See Lee, Vernon
See also CA 104; 166; GLL 1; HGG

**Paget-Lowe, Henry**
See Lovecraft, H(oward) P(hillips)

**Paglia, Camille (Anna)** 1947- ........... **CLC 68**
See also CA 140; CANR 72; CPW; FW; GLL 2; MTCW 2

**Paige, Richard**
See Koontz, Dean R(ay)

**Paine, Thomas** 1737-1809 ............... **NCLC 62**
See also AMWS 1; CDALB 1640-1865; DLB 31, 43, 73, 158; LAIT 1; RGAL; RGEL

**Pakenham, Antonia**
See Fraser, (Lady) Antonia (Pakenham)

**Palamas, Kostes** 1859-1943 ............... **TCLC 5**
See also CA 105; 190; RGWL

**Palazzeschi, Aldo** 1885-1974 ............. **CLC 11**
See also CA 89-92; 53-56; DLB 114

**Pales Matos, Luis** 1898-1959
See Pales Matos, Luis
See also HLCS 2; HW 1; LAW

**Paley, Grace** 1922- ........... **CLC 4, 6, 37, 140; DAM POP; SSC 8**
See also AMWS 6; CA 25-28R; CANR 13, 46, 74; CN; CPW; DA3; DLB 28; EXPS; FW; INT CANR-13; MAWW; MTCW 1, 2; RGAL; RGSF; SSFS 3

**Palin, Michael (Edward)** 1943- ......... **CLC 21**
See also Monty Python
See also CA 107; CANR 35; SATA 67

**Palliser, Charles** 1947- ....................... **CLC 65**
See also CA 136; CANR 76; CN

**Palma, Ricardo** 1833-1919 .............. **TCLC 29**
See also CA 168; LAW

**Pancake, Breece Dexter** 1952-1979
See Pancake, Breece D'J
See also CA 123; 109

**Pancake, Breece D'J** ......................... **CLC 29**
See also Pancake, Breece Dexter
See also DLB 130

**Panchenko, Nikolai** ........................... **CLC 59**

**Pankhurst, Emmeline (Goulden)** 1858-1928 .............................. **TCLC 100**
See also CA 116; FW

**Panko, Rudy**
See Gogol, Nikolai (Vasilyevich)

**Papadiamantis, Alexandros** 1851-1911 ................................. **TCLC 29**
See also CA 168

**Papadiamantopoulos, Johannes** 1856-1910
See Moreas, Jean
See also CA 117

**Papini, Giovanni** 1881-1956 ............ **TCLC 22**
See also CA 121; 180

**Paracelsus** 1493-1541 .......................... **LC 14**
See also DLB 179

**Parasol, Peter**
See Stevens, Wallace

**Pardo Bazan, Emilia** 1851-1921 ........ **SSC 30**
See also FW; RGSF; RGWL

**Pareto, Vilfredo** 1848-1923 ............. **TCLC 69**
See also CA 175

**Paretsky, Sara** 1947- .. **CLC 135; DAM POP**
See also AAYA 30; BEST 90:3; CA 125; 129; CANR 59, 95; CMW; CPW; DA3; INT CA-129; MSW; RGAL

**Parfenie, Maria**
See Codrescu, Andrei

**Parini, Jay (Lee)** 1948- ............... **CLC 54, 133**
See also CA 97-100; CAAS 16; CANR 32, 87

**Park, Jordan**
See Kornbluth, C(yril) M.; Pohl, Frederik

**Park, Robert E(zra)** 1864-1944 ..... **TCLC 73**
See also CA 122; 165

**Parker, Bert**
See Ellison, Harlan (Jay)

**Parker, Dorothy (Rothschild)** 1893-1967 .... **CLC 15, 68; DAM POET; PC 28; SSC 2**
See also AMWS 9; CA 19-20; 25-28R; CAP 2; DA3; DLB 11, 45, 86; EXPP; FW; MAWW; MTCW 1, 2; RGAL; RGSF

**Parker, Robert B(rown)** 1932- ........ **CLC 27; DAM NOV, POP**
See also AAYA 28; BEST 89:4; BPFB 3; CA 49-52; CANR 1, 26, 52, 89; CMW; CPW; INT CANR-26; MSW; MTCW 1

**Parkin, Frank** 1940- ........................... **CLC 43**
See also CA 147

**Parkman, Francis, Jr.** 1823-1893 .. **NCLC 12**
See also AMWS 2; DLB 1, 30, 186, 235; RGAL

**Parks, Gordon (Alexander Buchanan)** 1912- ............. **CLC 1, 16; BLC 3; DAM MULT**
See also AAYA 36; AITN 2; BW 2, 3; CA 41-44R; CANR 26, 66; DA3; DLB 33; MTCW 2; SATA 8, 108

**Parks, Tim(othy Harold)** 1954- ...... **CLC 147**
See also CA 126; 131; CANR 77; DLB 231; INT CA-131

**Parmenides** c. 515B.C.-c. 450B.C. ................................... **CMLC 22**
See also DLB 176

**Parnell, Thomas** 1679-1718 .................. **LC 3**
See also DLB 94; RGEL

**Parra, Nicanor** 1914- ...... **CLC 2, 102; DAM MULT; HLC 2**
See also CA 85-88; CANR 32; CWW 2; HW 1; LAW; MTCW 1

**Parra Sanojo, Ana Teresa de la** 1890-1936
See de la Parra, (Ana) Teresa (Sonojo)
See also HLCS 2; LAW

**Parrish, Mary Frances**
See Fisher, M(ary) F(rances) K(ennedy)

**Parshchikov, Aleksei** ......................... **CLC 59**

**Parson**
See Coleridge, Samuel Taylor

**Parson Lot**
See Kingsley, Charles

**Parton, Sara Payson Willis** 1811-1872 ............................... **NCLC 86**
See also DLB 43, 74, 239

**Partridge, Anthony**
See Oppenheim, E(dward) Phillips

**Pascal, Blaise** 1623-1662 ...................... **LC 35**
See also EW; GFL Beginnings to 1789; RGWL

**Pascoli, Giovanni** 1855-1912 .......... **TCLC 45**
See also CA 170; EW

**Pasolini, Pier Paolo** 1922-1975 .. **CLC 20, 37, 106; PC 17**
See also CA 93-96; 61-64; CANR 63; DLB 128, 177; MTCW 1; RGWL

**Pasquini**
See Silone, Ignazio

**Pastan, Linda (Olenik)** 1932- .......... **CLC 27; DAM POET**
See also CA 61-64; CANR 18, 40, 61; CP; CSW; CWP; DLB 5; PFS 8

**Pasternak, Boris (Leonidovich)** 1890-1960 ........ **CLC 7, 10, 18, 63; DA; DAB; DAC; DAM MST, NOV, POET; PC 6; SSC 31; WLC**
See also BPFB 3; CA 127; 116; DA3; EW; MTCW 1, 2; RGSF; RGWL; WP

**Patchen, Kenneth** 1911-1972 .. **CLC 1, 2, 18; DAM POET**
See also CA 1-4R; 33-36R; CANR 3, 35; DLB 16, 48; MTCW 1; RGAL

**Pater, Walter (Horatio)** 1839-1894 . **NCLC 7, 90**
See also BRW 5; CDBLB 1832-1890; DLB 57, 156; RGEL

**Paterson, A(ndrew) B(arton)** 1864-1941 ............................. **TCLC 32**
See also CA 155; DLB 230; RGEL; SATA 97

**Paterson, Katherine (Womeldorf)**
1932- .................... **CLC 12, 30**
See also AAYA 1, 31; BYA 1, 2, 7; CA 21-24R; CANR 28, 59; CLR 7, 50; CWRI; DLB 52; JRDA; LAIT 4; MAICYA; MAICYAS; MTCW 1; SATA 13, 53, 92; WYA; YAW

**Patmore, Coventry Kersey Dighton**
1823-1896 ........................ **NCLC 9**
See also DLB 35, 98; RGEL

**Paton, Alan (Stewart)** 1903-1988 ...... **CLC 4, 10, 25, 55, 106; DA; DAB; DAC; DAM MST, NOV; WLC**
See also AAYA 26; AFW; BPFB 3; BRWS 2; BYA 1; CA 13-16; 125; CANR 22; CAP 1; DA3; DLB 225; DLBD 17; EXPN; LAIT 4; MTCW 1, 2; NFS 3, 12; RGEL; SATA 11; SATA-Obit 56; WLIT 2

**Paton Walsh, Gillian** 1937- ............... **CLC 35**
See also Paton Walsh, Jill; Walsh, Jill Paton
See also AAYA 11; CANR 38, 83; CLR 2, 65; DLB 161; JRDA; MAICYA; SAAS 3; SATA 4, 72, 109; YAW

**Paton Walsh, Jill**
See Paton Walsh, Gillian
See also BYA 1, 8

**Patton, George S(mith), Jr.**
1885-1945 ........................ **TCLC 79**
See also CA 189

**Paulding, James Kirke** 1778-1860 ... **NCLC 2**
See also DLB 3, 59, 74; RGAL

**Paulin, Thomas Neilson** 1949-
See Paulin, Tom
See also CA 123; 128; CANR 98; CP

**Paulin, Tom** ........................ **CLC 37**
See also Paulin, Thomas Neilson
See also DLB 40

**Pausanias** c. 1st cent. - .................. **CMLC 36**

**Paustovsky, Konstantin (Georgievich)**
1892-1968 ........................ **CLC 40**
See also CA 93-96; 25-28R

**Pavese, Cesare** 1908-1950 .. **TCLC 3; PC 13; SSC 19**
See also CA 104; 169; DLB 128, 177; EW; RGSF; RGWL

**Pavic, Milorad** 1929- ........................ **CLC 60**
See also CA 136; CWW 2; DLB 181

**Pavlov, Ivan Petrovich** 1849-1936 . **TCLC 91**
See also CA 118; 180

**Payne, Alan**
See Jakes, John (William)

**Paz, Gil**
See Lugones, Leopoldo

**Paz, Octavio** 1914-1998 . **CLC 3, 4, 6, 10, 19, 51, 65, 119; DA; DAB; DAC; DAM MST, MULT, POET; HLC 2; PC 1; WLC**
See also CA 73-76; 165; CANR 32, 65; CWW 2; DA3; DLBY 90, 98; DNFS; HW 1, 2; LAW; MTCW 1, 2; RGWL; SSFS 13; WLIT 1

**p'Bitek, Okot** 1931-1982 .... **CLC 96; BLC 3; DAM MULT**
See also AFW; BW 2, 3; CA 124; 107; CANR 82; DLB 125; MTCW 1, 2; RGEL; WLIT 2

**Peacock, Molly** 1947- ........................ **CLC 60**
See also CA 103; CAAS 21; CANR 52, 84; CP; CWP; DLB 120

**Peacock, Thomas Love**
1785-1866 ........................ **NCLC 22**
See also BRW 4; DLB 96, 116; RGEL; RGSF

**Peake, Mervyn** 1911-1968 ............ **CLC 7, 54**
See also CA 5-8R; 25-28R; CANR 3; DLB 15, 160; FANT; MTCW 1; RGEL; SATA 23; SFW

**Pearce, Philippa** ........................ **CLC 21**
See also Christie, (Ann) Philippa
See also BYA 5; CLR 9; DLB 161; MAICYA; SATA 1, 67

**Pearl, Eric**
See Elman, Richard (Martin)

**Pearson, T(homas) R(eid)** 1956- ........ **CLC 39**
See also CA 120; 130; CANR 97; CSW; INT 130

**Peck, Dale** 1967- ........................ **CLC 81**
See also CA 146; CANR 72; GLL 2

**Peck, John (Frederick)** 1941- ............ **CLC 3**
See also CA 49-52; CANR 3, 100; CP

**Peck, Richard (Wayne)** 1934- ........... **CLC 21**
See also AAYA 1, 24; BYA 1, 6, 8, 11; CA 85-88; CANR 19, 38; CLR 15; INT CANR-19; JRDA; MAICYA; SAAS 2; SATA 18, 55, 97; SATA-Essay 110; WYA; YAW

**Peck, Robert Newton** 1928- .... **CLC 17; DA; DAC; DAM MST**
See also AAYA 3; BYA 1, 6; CA 81-84, 182; CAAE 182; CANR 31, 63; CLR 45; JRDA; LAIT 3; MAICYA; SAAS 1; SATA 21, 62, 111; SATA-Essay 108; YAW

**Peckinpah, (David) Sam(uel)**
1925-1984 ........................ **CLC 20**
See also CA 109; 114; CANR 82

**Pedersen, Knut** 1859-1952
See Hamsun, Knut
See also CA 104; 119; CANR 63; MTCW 1, 2

**Peeslake, Gaffer**
See Durrell, Lawrence (George)

**Peguy, Charles (Pierre)**
1873-1914 ........................ **TCLC 10**
See also CA 107; 193; GFL 1789 to the Present

**Peirce, Charles Sanders**
1839-1914 ........................ **TCLC 81**
See also CA 194

**Pellicer, Carlos** 1900(?)-1977
See also CA 153; 69-72; HLCS 2; HW 1

**Pena, Ramon del Valle y**
See Valle-Inclan, Ramon (Maria) del

**Pendennis, Arthur Esquir**
See Thackeray, William Makepeace

**Penn, William** 1644-1718 ................... **LC 25**
See also DLB 24

**PEPECE**
See Prado (Calvo), Pedro

**Pepys, Samuel** 1633-1703 ..... **LC 11, 58; DA; DAB; DAC; DAM MST; WLC**
See also BRW 2; CDBLB 1660-1789; DA3; DLB 101; RGEL; WLIT 3

**Percy, Thomas** 1729-1811 ............... **NCLC 95**
See also DLB 104

**Percy, Walker** 1916-1990 ....... **CLC 2, 3, 6, 8, 14, 18, 47, 65; DAM NOV, POP**
See also AMWS 3; BPFB 3; CA 1-4R; 131; CANR 1, 23, 64; CPW; CSW; DA3; DLB 2; DLBY 80, 90; MTCW 1, 2; RGAL

**Percy, William Alexander**
1885-1942 ........................ **TCLC 84**
See also CA 163; MTCW 2

**Perec, Georges** 1936-1982 ......... **CLC 56, 116**
See also CA 141; DLB 83; GFL 1789 to the Present

**Pereda (y Sanchez de Porrua), Jose Maria de** 1833-1906 ........................ **TCLC 16**
See also CA 117

**Pereda y Porrua, Jose Maria de**
See Pereda (y Sanchez de Porrua), Jose Maria de

**Peregoy, George Weems**
See Mencken, H(enry) L(ouis)

**Perelman, S(idney) J(oseph)**
1904-1979 .. **CLC 3, 5, 9, 15, 23, 44, 49; DAM DRAM; SSC 32**
See also AITN 1, 2; BPFB 3; CA 73-76; 89-92; CANR 18; DLB 11, 44; MTCW 1, 2; RGAL

**Peret, Benjamin** 1899-1959 .... **TCLC 20; PC 33**
See also CA 117; 186; GFL 1789 to the Present

**Peretz, Isaac Loeb** 1851(?)-1915 ... **TCLC 16; SSC 26**
See also CA 109

**Peretz, Yitzhok Leibush**
See Peretz, Isaac Loeb

**Perez Galdos, Benito** 1843-1920 ... **TCLC 27; HLCS 2**
See also CA 125; 153; EW; HW 1; RGWL

**Peri Rossi, Cristina** 1941-
See also CA 131; CANR 59, 81; DLB 145; HLCS 2; HW 1, 2

**Perlata**
See Peret, Benjamin

**Perloff, Marjorie G(abrielle)**
1931- ........................ **CLC 137**
See also CA 57-60; CANR 7, 22, 49

**Perrault, Charles** 1628-1703 ... **LC 2, 56; DC 12**
See also BYA 4; GFL Beginnings to 1789; MAICYA; RGWL; SATA 25

**Perry, Anne** 1938- ........................ **CLC 126**
See also CA 101; CANR 22, 50, 84; CMW; CN; CPW

**Perry, Brighton**
See Sherwood, Robert E(mmet)

**Perse, St.-John**
See Leger, (Marie-Rene Auguste) Alexis Saint-Leger

**Perutz, Leo(pold)** 1882-1957 .......... **TCLC 60**
See also CA 147; DLB 81

**Peseenz, Tulio F.**
See Lopez y Fuentes, Gregorio

**Pesetsky, Bette** 1932- ........................ **CLC 28**
See also CA 133; DLB 130

**Peshkov, Alexei Maximovich** 1868-1936
See Gorky, Maxim
See also CA 105; 141; CANR 83; DA; DAC; DAM DRAM, MST, NOV; MTCW 2

**Pessoa, Fernando (Antonio Nogueira)**
1898-1935 ....... **TCLC 27; DAM MULT; HLC 2; PC 20**
See also CA 125; 183; EW; RGWL; WP

**Peterkin, Julia Mood** 1880-1961 ...... **CLC 31**
See also CA 102; DLB 9

**Peters, Joan K(aren)** 1945- ............... **CLC 39**
See also CA 158

**Peters, Robert L(ouis)** 1924- ............... **CLC 7**
See also CA 13-16R; CAAS 8; CP; DLB 105

**Petofi, Sandor** 1823-1849 ............... **NCLC 21**
See also RGWL

**Petrakis, Harry Mark** 1923- ............... **CLC 3**
See also CA 9-12R; CANR 4, 30, 85; CN

**Petrarch** 1304-1374 ............ **CMLC 20; DAM POET; PC 8**
See also DA3; EW; RGWL

**Petronius** c. 20-66 ........................ **CMLC 34**
See also AW 2; DLB 211; RGWL

**Petrov, Evgeny** ........................ **TCLC 21**
See also Kataev, Evgeny Petrovich

**Petry, Ann (Lane)** 1908-1997 ... **CLC 1, 7, 18**
See also AFAW 1, 2; BPFB 3; BW 1, 3; BYA 2; CA 5-8R; 157; CAAS 6; CANR 4, 46; CLR 12; CN; DLB 76; JRDA; LAIT 1; MAICYA; MAICYAS; MTCW 1; RGAL; SATA 5; SATA-Obit 94; TCLC 112

**Petursson, Halligrimur** 1614-1674 ........ **LC 8**
**Peychinovich**
  See Vazov, Ivan (Minchov)
**Phaedrus** c. 15B.C.-c. 50 ................ **CMLC 25**
  See also DLB 211
**Phelps (Ward), Elizabeth Stuart**
  See Phelps, Elizabeth Stuart
  See also FW
**Phelps, Elizabeth Stuart**
  1844-1911 .............................. **TCLC 113**
  See also Dickinson, Mrs. Herbert Ward
  See also DLB 74
**Philips, Katherine** 1632-1664 ............... **LC 30**
  See also DLB 131; RGEL
**Philipson, Morris H.** 1926- ................ **CLC 53**
  See also CA 1-4R; CANR 4
**Phillips, Caryl** 1958- . **CLC 96; BLCS; DAM MULT**
  See also BRWS 5; BW 2; CA 141; CANR 63; CBD; CD; CN; DA3; DLB 157; MTCW 2; WLIT 4
**Phillips, David Graham**
  1867-1911 ................................ **TCLC 44**
  See also CA 108; 176; DLB 9, 12; RGAL
**Phillips, Jack**
  See Sandburg, Carl (August)
**Phillips, Jayne Anne** 1952- ........ **CLC 15, 33, 139; SSC 16**
  See also BPFB 3; CA 101; CANR 24, 50, 96; CN; CSW; DLBY 80; INT CANR-24; MTCW 1, 2; RGAL; RGSF; SSFS 4
**Phillips, Richard**
  See Dick, Philip K(indred)
**Phillips, Robert (Schaeffer)** 1938- .... **CLC 28**
  See also CA 17-20R; CAAS 13; CANR 8; DLB 105
**Phillips, Ward**
  See Lovecraft, H(oward) P(hillips)
**Piccolo, Lucio** 1901-1969 ................... **CLC 13**
  See also CA 97-100; DLB 114
**Pickthall, Marjorie L(owry) C(hristie)**
  1883-1922 ................................ **TCLC 21**
  See also CA 107; DLB 92
**Pico della Mirandola, Giovanni**
  1463-1494 ................................ **LC 15**
**Piercy, Marge** 1936- .... **CLC 3, 6, 14, 18, 27, 62, 128; PC 29**
  See also BPFB 3; CA 21-24R; CAAE 187; CAAS 1; CANR 13, 43, 66; CN; CP; CWP; DLB 120, 227; EXPP; FW; MTCW 1, 2; PFS 9; SFW
**Piers, Robert**
  See Anthony, Piers
**Pieyre de Mandiargues, Andre** 1909-1991
  See Mandiargues, Andre Pieyre de
  See also CA 103; 136; CANR 22, 82; GFL 1789 to the Present
**Pilnyak, Boris** 1894-1938 . **TCLC 23; SSC 48**
  See also Vogau, Boris Andreyevich
**Pinchback, Eugene**
  See Toomer, Jean
**Pincherle, Alberto** 1907-1990 .... **CLC 11, 18; DAM NOV**
  See also Moravia, Alberto
  See also CA 25-28R; 132; CANR 33, 63; MTCW 1
**Pinckney, Darryl** 1953- ..................... **CLC 76**
  See also BW 2, 3; CA 143; CANR 79
**Pindar** 518(?)B.C.-438(?)B.C. ........ **CMLC 12; PC 19**
  See also AW 1; DLB 176; RGWL
**Pineda, Cecile** 1942- .......................... **CLC 39**
  See also CA 118; DLB 209
**Pinero, Arthur Wing** 1855-1934 ... **TCLC 32; DAM DRAM**
  See also CA 110; 153; DLB 10; RGEL

**Pinero, Miguel (Antonio Gomez)**
  1946-1988 .............................. **CLC 4, 55**
  See also CA 61-64; 125; CAD; CANR 29, 90; HW 1
**Pinget, Robert** 1919-1997 ....... **CLC 7, 13, 37**
  See also CA 85-88; 160; CWW 2; DLB 83; GFL 1789 to the Present
**Pink Floyd**
  See Barrett, (Roger) Syd; Gilmour, David; Mason, Nick; Waters, Roger; Wright, Rick
**Pinkney, Edward** 1802-1828 ............. **NCLC 31**
**Pinkwater, Daniel Manus** 1941- ....... **CLC 35**
  See also Pinkwater, Manus
  See also AAYA 1; BYA 9; CA 29-32R; CANR 12, 38, 89; CLR 4; CSW; FANT; JRDA; MAICYA; SAAS 3; SATA 46, 76, 114; SFW; YAW
**Pinkwater, Manus**
  See Pinkwater, Daniel Manus
  See also SATA 8
**Pinsky, Robert** 1940- ......... **CLC 9, 19, 38, 94, 121; DAM POET; PC 27**
  See also AMWS 6; CA 29-32R; CAAS 4; CANR 58, 97; CP; DA3; DLBY 82, 98; MTCW 2; RGAL
**Pinta, Harold**
  See Pinter, Harold
**Pinter, Harold** 1930- .. **CLC 1, 3, 6, 9, 11, 15, 27, 58, 73; DA; DAB; DAC; DAM DRAM, MST; DC 15; WLC**
  See also BRWS 1; CA 5-8R; CANR 33, 65; CBD; CD; CDBLB 1960 to Present; DA3; DFS 3, 5, 7; DLB 13; IDFW 3, 4; MTCW 1, 2; RGEL
**Piozzi, Hester Lynch (Thrale)**
  1741-1821 ............................... **NCLC 57**
  See also DLB 104, 142
**Pirandello, Luigi** 1867-1936 ...... **TCLC 4, 29; DA; DAB; DAC; DAM DRAM, MST; DC 5; SSC 22; WLC**
  See also CA 104; 153; CANR 103; DFS 4, 9; EW; MTCW 2; RGSF; RGWL
**Pirsig, Robert M(aynard)** 1928- ... **CLC 4, 6, 73; DAM POP**
  See also CA 53-56; CANR 42, 74; CPW 1; DA3; MTCW 1, 2; SATA 39
**Pisarev, Dmitry Ivanovich**
  1840-1868 ............................... **NCLC 25**
**Pix, Mary (Griffith)** 1666-1709 ............. **LC 8**
  See also DLB 80
**Pixerecourt, (Rene Charles) Guilbert de**
  1773-1844 ............................... **NCLC 39**
  See also DLB 192; GFL 1789 to the Present
**Plaatje, Sol(omon) T(shekisho)**
  1878-1932 ................. **TCLC 73; BLCS**
  See also BW 2, 3; CA 141; CANR 79; DLB 225
**Plaidy, Jean**
  See Hibbert, Eleanor Alice Burford
**Planche, James Robinson**
  1796-1880 ................................ **NCLC 42**
  See also RGEL
**Plant, Robert** 1948- ............................ **CLC 12**
**Plante, David (Robert)** 1940- ...... **CLC 7, 23, 38; DAM NOV**
  See also CA 37-40R; CANR 12, 36, 58, 82; CN; DLBY 83; INT CANR-12; MTCW 1
**Plath, Sylvia** 1932-1963 ..... **CLC 1, 2, 3, 5, 9, 11, 14, 17, 50, 51, 62, 111; DA; DAB; DAC; DAM MST, POET; PC 1, 37; WLC**
  See also AAYA 13; AMWS 1; BPFB 3; CA 19-20; CANR 34, 101; CAP 2; CDALB 1941-1968; DA3; DLB 5, 6, 152; EXPN; EXPP; FW; LAIT 4; MAWW; MTCW 1, 2; NFS 1; PAB; PFS 1; RGAL; SATA 96; WP; YAW

**Plato** c. 428B.C.-347B.C. ......... **CMLC 8; DA; DAB; DAC; DAM MST; WLCS**
  See also AW 1; DA3; DLB 176; LAIT 1; RGWL
**Platonov, Andrei**
  See Klimentov, Andrei Platonovich
**Platt, Kin** 1911- ................................. **CLC 26**
  See also AAYA 11; CA 17-20R; CANR 11; JRDA; SAAS 17; SATA 21, 86
**Plautus** c. 254B.C.-c. 184B.C. ...... **CMLC 24; DC 6**
  See also AW 1; DLB 211; RGWL
**Plick et Plock**
  See Simenon, Georges (Jacques Christian)
**Plieksans, Janis**
  See Rainis, Janis
**Plimpton, George (Ames)** 1927- ....... **CLC 36**
  See also AITN 1; CA 21-24R; CANR 32, 70, 103; DLB 185, 241; MTCW 1, 2; SATA 10
**Pliny the Elder** c. 23-79 ................. **CMLC 23**
  See also DLB 211
**Plomer, William Charles Franklin**
  1903-1973 .............................. **CLC 4, 8**
  See also AFW; CA 21-22; CANR 34; CAP 2; DLB 20, 162, 191, 225; MTCW 1; RGEL; RGSF; SATA 24
**Plotinus** 204-270 ............................ **CMLC 46**
  See also DLB 176
**Plowman, Piers**
  See Kavanagh, Patrick (Joseph)
**Plum, J.**
  See Wodehouse, P(elham) G(renville)
**Plumly, Stanley (Ross)** 1939- ............. **CLC 33**
  See also CA 108; 110; CANR 97; CP; DLB 5, 193; INT 110
**Plumpe, Friedrich Wilhelm**
  1888-1931 ................................ **TCLC 53**
  See also CA 112
**Po Chu-i** 772-846 ............................ **CMLC 24**
**Poe, Edgar Allan** 1809-1849 ..... **NCLC 1, 16, 55, 78, 94, 97; DA; DAB; DAC; DAM MST, POET; PC 1; SSC 1, 22, 34, 35; WLC**
  See also AAYA 14; AMW; BPFB 3; BYA 5, 11; CDALB 1640-1865; CMW; DA3; DLB 3, 59, 73, 74; EXPP; EXPS; HGG; LAIT 2; MSW; PAB; PFS 1, 3, 9; RGAL; RGSF; SATA 23; SFW; SSFS 2, 4, 7, 8; WP
**Poet of Titchfield Street, The**
  See Pound, Ezra (Weston Loomis)
**Pohl, Frederik** 1919- ........... **CLC 18; SSC 25**
  See also AAYA 24; CA 61-64; CAAE 188; CAAS 1; CANR 11, 37, 81; CN; DLB 8; INT CANR-11; MTCW 1, 2; SATA 24; SCFW 2; SFW
**Poirier, Louis** 1910-
  See Gracq, Julien
  See also CA 122; 126; CWW 2
**Poitier, Sidney** 1927- ......................... **CLC 26**
  See also BW 1; CA 117; CANR 94
**Polanski, Roman** 1933- ..................... **CLC 16**
  See also CA 77-80
**Poliakoff, Stephen** 1952- ................... **CLC 38**
  See also CA 106; CBD; CD; DLB 13
**Police, The**
  See Copeland, Stewart (Armstrong); Summers, Andrew James; Sumner, Gordon Matthew
**Polidori, John William** 1795-1821 . **NCLC 51**
  See also DLB 116; HGG
**Pollitt, Katha** 1949- ..................... **CLC 28, 122**
  See also CA 120; 122; CANR 66; MTCW 1, 2
**Pollock, (Mary) Sharon** 1936- ......... **CLC 50; DAC; DAM DRAM, MST**
  See also CA 141; DLB 60

**Polo, Marco** 1254-1324 .................. **CMLC 15**
**Polonsky, Abraham (Lincoln)**
   1910-1999 ...................... **CLC 92**
   See also CA 104; 187; DLB 26; INT 104
**Polybius** c. 200B.C.-c. 118B.C. ...... **CMLC 17**
   See also AW 1; DLB 176; RGWL
**Pomerance, Bernard** 1940- ... **CLC 13; DAM DRAM**
   See also CA 101; CAD; CANR 49; CD; DFS 9; LAIT 2
**Ponge, Francis** 1899-1988 . **CLC 6, 18; DAM POET**
   See also CA 85-88; 126; CANR 40, 86; GFL 1789 to the Present; RGWL
**Poniatowska, Elena** 1933- ... **CLC 140; DAM MULT; HLC 2**
   See also CA 101; CANR 32, 66; DLB 113; HW 1, 2; WLIT 1
**Pontoppidan, Henrik** 1857-1943 .... **TCLC 29**
   See also CA 170
**Poole, Josephine** ................... **CLC 17**
   See also Helyar, Jane Penelope Josephine
   See also SAAS 2; SATA 5
**Popa, Vasko** 1922-1991 .................. **CLC 19**
   See also CA 112; 148; DLB 181; RGWL
**Pope, Alexander** 1688-1744 ...... **LC 3, 58, 60, 64; DA; DAB; DAC; DAM MST, POET; PC 26; WLC**
   See also BRW 3; CDBLB 1660-1789; DA3; DLB 95, 101; EXPP; PAB; PFS 12; RGEL; WLIT 3; WP
**Popov, Yevgeny** ...................... **CLC 59**
**Porter, Connie (Rose)** 1959(?)- ......... **CLC 70**
   See also BW 2, 3; CA 142; CANR 90; SATA 81
**Porter, Gene(va Grace) Stratton** .. **TCLC 21**
   See also Stratton-Porter, Gene(va Grace)
   See also BPFB 3; CA 112; CWRI; RHW
**Porter, Katherine Anne** 1890-1980 ... **CLC 1, 3, 7, 10, 13, 15, 27, 101; DA; DAB; DAC; DAM MST, NOV; SSC 4, 31, 43**
   See also AAYA 42; AITN 2; AMW; BPFB 3; CA 1-4R; 101; CANR 1, 65; CDALBS; DA3; DLB 4, 9, 102; DLBD 12; DLBY 80; EXPS; LAIT 3; MAWW; MTCW 1, 2; RGAL; RGSF; SATA 39; SATA-Obit 23; SSFS 1, 8, 11
**Porter, Peter (Neville Frederick)**
   1929- ................ **CLC 5, 13, 33**
   See also CA 85-88; CP; DLB 40
**Porter, William Sydney** 1862-1910
   See Henry, O.
   See also CA 104; 131; CDALB 1865-1917; DA; DA3; DAB; DAC; DAM MST; DLB 12, 78, 79; MTCW 1, 2; YABC 2
**Portillo (y Pacheco), Jose Lopez**
   See Lopez Portillo (y Pacheco), Jose
**Portillo Trambley, Estela** 1927-1998
   See Trambley, Estela Portillo
   See also CANR 32; DAM MULT; DLB 209; HLC 2; HW 1
**Posse, Abel** ......................... **CLC 70**
**Post, Melville Davisson**
   1869-1930 .................. **TCLC 39**
   See also CA 110; CMW
**Potok, Chaim** 1929- ... **CLC 2, 7, 14, 26, 112; DAM NOV**
   See also AAYA 15; AITN 1, 2; BPFB 3; BYA 1; CA 17-20R; CANR 19, 35, 64, 98; CN; DA3; DLB 28, 152; EXPN; INT CANR-19; LAIT 4; MTCW 1, 2; NFS 4; SATA 33, 106; YAW
**Potter, Dennis (Christopher George)**
   1935-1994 ............. **CLC 58, 86, 123**
   See also CA 107; 145; CANR 33, 61; CBD; DLB 233; MTCW 1

**Pound, Ezra (Weston Loomis)**
   1885-1972 .. **CLC 1, 2, 3, 4, 5, 7, 10, 13, 18, 34, 48, 50, 112; DA; DAB; DAC; DAM MST, POET; PC 4; WLC**
   See also AMW; AMWR 1; CA 5-8R; 37-40R; CANR 40; CDALB 1917-1929; DA3; DLB 4, 45, 63; DLBD 15; EFS 2; EXPP; MTCW 1, 2; PAB; PFS 2, 8; RGAL; WP
**Povod, Reinaldo** 1959-1994 ................ **CLC 44**
   See also CA 136; 146; CANR 83
**Powell, Adam Clayton, Jr.**
   1908-1972 ......... **CLC 89; BLC 3; DAM MULT**
   See also BW 1, 3; CA 102; 33-36R; CANR 86
**Powell, Anthony (Dymoke)**
   1905-2000 ............ **CLC 1, 3, 7, 9, 10, 31**
   See also BRW 7; CA 1-4R; 189; CANR 1, 32, 62; CDBLB 1945-1960; CN; DLB 15; MTCW 1, 2; RGEL
**Powell, Dawn** 1897-1965 ................. **CLC 66**
   See also CA 5-8R; DLBY 97
**Powell, Padgett** 1952- ........................ **CLC 34**
   See also CA 126; CANR 63, 101; CSW; DLB 234
**Powell, (Oval) Talmage** 1920-2000
   See Queen, Ellery
   See also CA 5-8R; CANR 2, 80
**Power, Susan** 1961- ........................... **CLC 91**
   See also CA 160; NFS 11
**Powers, J(ames) F(arl)** 1917-1999 ..... **CLC 1, 4, 8, 57; SSC 4**
   See also CA 1-4R; 181; CANR 2, 61; CN; DLB 130; MTCW 1; RGAL; RGSF
**Powers, John J(ames)** 1945-
   See Powers, John R.
   See also CA 69-72
**Powers, John R.** .................... **CLC 66**
   See also Powers, John J(ames)
**Powers, Richard (S.)** 1957- ................ **CLC 93**
   See also AMWS 9; BPFB 3; CA 148; CANR 80; CN
**Pownall, David** 1938- ........................ **CLC 10**
   See also CA 89-92, 180; CAAS 18; CANR 49, 101; CBD; CD; CN; DLB 14
**Powys, John Cowper** 1872-1963 ... **CLC 7, 9, 15, 46, 125**
   See also CA 85-88; DLB 15; FANT; MTCW 1, 2; RGEL
**Powys, T(heodore) F(rancis)**
   1875-1953 ...................... **TCLC 9**
   See also CA 106; 189; DLB 36, 162; FANT; RGEL; SUFW
**Prado (Calvo), Pedro** 1886-1952 ... **TCLC 75**
   See also CA 131; HW 1; LAW
**Prager, Emily** 1952- ........................... **CLC 56**
**Pratt, E(dwin) J(ohn)**
   1883(?)-1964 ........ **CLC 19; DAC; DAM POET**
   See also CA 141; 93-96; CANR 77; DLB 92; RGEL
**Premchand** ..................................... **TCLC 21**
   See also Srivastava, Dhanpat Rai
**Preussler, Otfried** 1923- ..................... **CLC 17**
   See also CA 77-80; SATA 24
**Prevert, Jacques (Henri Marie)**
   1900-1977 ............................ **CLC 15**
   See also CA 77-80; 69-72; CANR 29, 61; GFL 1789 to the Present; IDFW 3, 4; MTCW 1; RGWL; SATA-Obit 30
**Prevost, (Antoine Francois)**
   1697-1763 ............................ **LC 1**
   See also EW; GFL Beginnings to 1789; RGWL

**Price, (Edward) Reynolds** 1933- ... **CLC 3, 6, 13, 43, 50, 63; DAM NOV; SSC 22**
   See also AMWS 6; CA 1-4R; CANR 1, 37, 57, 87; CN; CSW; DLB 2, 218; INT CANR-37
**Price, Richard** 1949- ...................... **CLC 6, 12**
   See also CA 49-52; CANR 3; DLBY 81
**Prichard, Katharine Susannah**
   1883-1969 ................................ **CLC 46**
   See also CA 11-12; CANR 33; CAP 1; MTCW 1; RGEL; RGSF; SATA 66
**Priestley, J(ohn) B(oynton)**
   1894-1984 .......... **CLC 2, 5, 9, 34; DAM DRAM, NOV**
   See also BRW 7; CA 9-12R; 113; CANR 33; CDBLB 1914-1945; DA3; DLB 10, 34, 77, 100, 139; DLBY 84; MTCW 1, 2; RGEL; SFW
**Prince** 1958(?)- ................................ **CLC 35**
**Prince, F(rank) T(empleton)** 1912- .. **CLC 22**
   See also CA 101; CANR 43, 79; CP; DLB 20
**Prince Kropotkin**
   See Kropotkin, Peter (Alekseevich)
**Prior, Matthew** 1664-1721 ...................... **LC 4**
   See also DLB 95; RGEL
**Prishvin, Mikhail** 1873-1954 .......... **TCLC 75**
**Pritchard, William H(arrison)**
   1932- ................................ **CLC 34**
   See also CA 65-68; CANR 23, 95; DLB 111
**Pritchett, V(ictor) S(awdon)**
   1900-1997 ........ **CLC 5, 13, 15, 41; DAM NOV; SSC 14**
   See also BPFB 3; BRWS 3; CA 61-64; 157; CANR 31, 63; CN; DA3; DLB 15, 139; MTCW 1, 2; RGEL; RGSF
**Private 19022**
   See Manning, Frederic
**Probst, Mark** 1925- ........................... **CLC 59**
   See also CA 130
**Prokosch, Frederic** 1908-1989 ....... **CLC 4, 48**
   See also CA 73-76; 128; CANR 82; DLB 48; MTCW 2
**Propertius, Sextus** c. 50B.C.-c.
   16B.C. ............................. **CMLC 32**
   See also AW 2; DLB 211; RGWL
**Prophet, The**
   See Dreiser, Theodore (Herman Albert)
**Prose, Francine** 1947- ........................ **CLC 45**
   See also CA 109; 112; CANR 46, 95; DLB 234; SATA 101
**Proudhon**
   See Cunha, Euclides (Rodrigues Pimenta) da
**Proulx, Annie**
   See Proulx, E(dna) Annie
**Proulx, E(dna) Annie** 1935- .. **CLC 81; DAM POP**
   See also AMWS 7; BPFB 3; CA 145; CANR 65; CN; CPW 1; DA3; MTCW 2
**Proust,**
   **(Valentin-Louis-George-Eugene-)Marcel**
   1871-1922 . **TCLC 7, 13, 33; DA; DAB; DAC; DAM MST, NOV; WLC**
   See also BPFB 3; CA 104; 120; DA3; DLB 65; EW; GFL 1789 to the Present; MTCW 1, 2; RGWL
**Prowler, Harley**
   See Masters, Edgar Lee
**Prus, Boleslaw** 1845-1912 ............... **TCLC 48**
   See also RGWL
**Pryor, Richard (Franklin Lenox Thomas)**
   1940- ................................ **CLC 26**
   See also CA 122; 152
**Przybyszewski, Stanislaw**
   1868-1927 .................. **TCLC 36**
   See also CA 160; DLB 66

**Pteleon**
See Grieve, C(hristopher) M(urray)
See also DAM POET

**Puckett, Lute**
See Masters, Edgar Lee

**Puig, Manuel** 1932-1990 .... **CLC 3, 5, 10, 28, 65, 133; DAM MULT; HLC 2**
See also BPFB 3; CA 45-48; CANR 2, 32, 63; DA3; DLB 113; DNFS; GLL 1; HW 1, 2; LAW; MTCW 1, 2; RGWL; WLIT 1

**Pulitzer, Joseph** 1847-1911 ............. **TCLC 76**
See also CA 114; DLB 23

**Purchas, Samuel** 1577(?)-1626 ............. **LC 70**
See also DLB 151

**Purdy, A(lfred) W(ellington)**
1918-2000 ........ **CLC 3, 6, 14, 50; DAC; DAM MST, POET**
See also CA 81-84; 189; CAAS 17; CANR 42, 66; CP; DLB 88; PFS 5; RGEL

**Purdy, James (Amos)** 1923- .... **CLC 2, 4, 10, 28, 52**
See also AMWS 7; CA 33-36R; CAAS 1; CANR 19, 51; CN; DLB 2; INT CANR-19; MTCW 1; RGAL

**Pure, Simon**
See Swinnerton, Frank Arthur

**Pushkin, Alexander (Sergeyevich)**
1799-1837 . **NCLC 3, 27, 83; DA; DAB; DAC; DAM DRAM. MST, POET; PC 10; SSC 27; WLC**
See also DA3; DLB 205; EW; EXPS; RGSF; RGWL; SATA 61; SSFS 9

**P'u Sung-ling** 1640-1715 ....... **LC 49; SSC 31**

**Putnam, Arthur Lee**
See Alger, Horatio, Jr.

**Puzo, Mario** 1920-1999 ........ **CLC 1, 2, 6, 36, 107; DAM NOV, POP**
See also BPFB 3; CA 65-68; 185; CANR 4, 42, 65, 99; CN; CPW; DA3; DLB 6; MTCW 1, 2; RGAL

**Pygge, Edward**
See Barnes, Julian (Patrick)

**Pyle, Ernest Taylor** 1900-1945
See Pyle, Ernie
See also CA 115; 160

**Pyle, Ernie** ....................................... **TCLC 75**
See also Pyle, Ernest Taylor
See also DLB 29; MTCW 2

**Pyle, Howard** 1853-1911 ................. **TCLC 81**
See also BYA 2, 4; CA 109; 137; CLR 22; DLB 42, 188; DLBD 13; LAIT 1; MAICYA; SATA 16, 100. YAW

**Pym, Barbara (Mary Crampton)**
1913-1980 ............... **CLC 13, 19, 37, 111**
See also BPFB 3; BRWS 7; CA 13-14; 97-100; CANR 13, 34; CAP 1; DLB 14, 207; DLBY 87; MTCW 1, 2; RGEL

**Pynchon, Thomas (Ruggles, Jr.)**
1937- ...... **CLC 2, 3, 6, 9, 11, 18, 33, 62, 72, 123; DA; DAB; DAC; DAM MST, NOV, POP; SSC 14; WLC**
See also AMWS 2; BEST 90:2; BPFB 3; CA 17-20R; CANR 22, 46, 73; CN; CPW 1; DA3; DLB 2, 173; MTCW 1, 2; RGAL; SFW; TUS

**Pythagoras** c. 582B.C.-c. 507B.C. . **CMLC 22**
See also DLB 176

**Q**
See Quiller-Couch, Sir Arthur (Thomas)

**Qian Zhongshu**
See Ch'ien Chung-shu

**Qroll**
See Dagerman, Stig (Halvard)

**Quarrington, Paul (Lewis)** 1953- ..... **CLC 65**
See also CA 129; CANR 62, 95

**Quasimodo, Salvatore** 1901-1968 ..... **CLC 10**
See also CA 13-16; 25-28R; CAP 1; DLB 114; EW; MTCW 1; RGWL

**Quay, Stephen** 1947- .......................... **CLC 95**
See also CA 189

**Quay, Timothy** 1947- ........................ **CLC 95**
See also CA 189

**Queen, Ellery** ................................. **CLC 3, 11**
See also Dannay, Frederic; Davidson, Avram (James); Deming, Richard; Fairman, Paul W.; Flora, Fletcher; Hoch, Edward D(entinger); Kane, Henry; Lee, Manfred B(ennington); Marlowe, Stephen; Powell, (Oval) Talmage; Sheldon, Walter J(ames); Sturgeon, Theodore (Hamilton); Tracy, Don(ald Fiske); Vance, John Holbrook
See also BPFB 3; CMW; MSW; RGAL

**Queen, Ellery, Jr.**
See Dannay, Frederic; Lee, Manfred B(ennington)

**Queneau, Raymond** 1903-1976 ..... **CLC 2, 5, 10, 42**
See also CA 77-80; 69-72; CANR 32; DLB 72; EW; GFL 1789 to the Present; MTCW 1, 2; RGWL

**Quevedo, Francisco de** 1580-1645 ....... **LC 23**

**Quiller-Couch, Sir Arthur (Thomas)**
1863-1944 ................. **TCLC 53**
See also CA 118; 166; DLB 135, 153, 190; HGG; RGEL; SUFW

**Quin, Ann (Marie)** 1936-1973 ............. **CLC 6**
See also CA 9-12R; 45-48; DLB 14, 231

**Quinn, Martin**
See Smith, Martin Cruz

**Quinn, Peter** 1947- ........................... **CLC 91**

**Quinn, Simon**
See Smith, Martin Cruz

**Quintana, Leroy V.** 1944- ..................... **PC 36**
See also CA 131; CANR 65; DAM MULT; DLB 82; HLC 2; HW 1, 2

**Quiroga, Horacio (Sylvestre)**
1878-1937 ....... **TCLC 20; DAM MULT; HLC 2**
See also CA 117; 131; HW 1; LAW; MTCW 1; RGSF; WLIT 1

**Quoirez, Francoise** 1935- ..................... **CLC 9**
See also Sagan, Francoise
See also CA 49-52; CANR 6, 39, 73; CWW 2; MTCW 1, 2

**Raabe, Wilhelm (Karl)** 1831-1910 . **TCLC 45**
See also CA 167; DLB 129

**Rabe, David (William)** 1940- .. **CLC 4, 8, 33; DAM DRAM**
See also CA 85-88; CABS 3; CAD; CANR 59; CD; DFS 3, 8, 13; DLB 7, 228

**Rabelais, Francois** 1494-1553 ........ **LC 5, 60; DA; DAB; DAC; DAM MST; WLC**
See also EW; GFL Beginnings to 1789; RGWL

**Rabinovitch, Sholem** 1859-1916
See Aleichem, Sholom
See also CA 104

**Rabinyan, Dorit** 1972- ..................... **CLC 119**
See also CA 170

**Rachilde**
See Vallette, Marguerite Eymery

**Racine, Jean** 1639-1699 . **LC 28; DAB; DAM MST**
See also DA3; EW; GFL Beginnings to 1789; RGWL

**Radcliffe, Ann (Ward)** 1764-1823 ... **NCLC 6, 55, 106**
See also DLB 39, 178; HGG; RGEL; SUFW; WLIT 3

**Radclyffe-Hall, Marguerite**
See Hall, (Marguerite) Radclyffe

**Radiguet, Raymond** 1903-1923 ...... **TCLC 29**
See also CA 162; DLB 65; GFL 1789 to the Present; RGWL

**Radnoti, Miklos** 1909-1944 ............. **TCLC 16**
See also CA 118; RGWL

**Rado, James** 1939- ............................. **CLC 17**
See also CA 105

**Radvanyi, Netty** 1900-1983
See Seghers, Anna
See also CA 85-88; 110; CANR 82

**Rae, Ben**
See Griffiths, Trevor

**Raeburn, John (Hay)** 1941- ............... **CLC 34**
See also CA 57-60

**Ragni, Gerome** 1942-1991 ................. **CLC 17**
See also CA 105; 134

**Rahv, Philip** ......................................... **CLC 24**
See also Greenberg, Ivan
See also DLB 137

**Raimund, Ferdinand Jakob**
1790-1836 ................................... **NCLC 69**
See also DLB 90

**Raine, Craig (Anthony)** 1944- .. **CLC 32, 103**
See also CA 108; CANR 29, 51, 103; CP; DLB 40; PFS 7

**Raine, Kathleen (Jessie)** 1908- ...... **CLC 7, 45**
See also CA 85-88; CANR 46; CP; DLB 20; MTCW 1; RGEL

**Rainis, Janis** 1865-1929 .................. **TCLC 29**
See also CA 170; DLB 220

**Rakosi, Carl** ........................................ **CLC 47**
See also Rawley, Callman
See also CAAS 5; CP; DLB 193

**Ralegh, Sir Walter**
See Raleigh, Sir Walter
See also BRW 1; RGEL; WP

**Raleigh, Richard**
See Lovecraft, H(oward) P(hillips)

**Raleigh, Sir Walter** 1554(?)-1618 ....... **LC 31, 39; PC 31**
See also Ralegh, Sir Walter
See also CDBLB Before 1660; DLB 172; EXPP; TEA

**Rallentando, H. P.**
See Sayers, Dorothy L(eigh)

**Ramal, Walter**
See de la Mare, Walter (John)

**Ramana Maharshi** 1879-1950 ....... **TCLC 84**

**Ramoacn y Cajal, Santiago**
1852-1934 ................................. **TCLC 93**

**Ramon, Juan**
See Jimenez (Mantecon), Juan Ramon

**Ramos, Graciliano** 1892-1953 ........ **TCLC 32**
See also CA 167; HW 2; LAW; WLIT 1

**Rampersad, Arnold** 1941- ................. **CLC 44**
See also BW 2, 3; CA 127; 133; CANR 81; DLB 111; INT 133

**Rampling, Anne**
See Rice, Anne
See also GLL 2

**Ramsay, Allan** 1686(?)-1758 ................. **LC 29**
See also DLB 95; RGEL

**Ramsay, Jay**
See Campbell, (John) Ramsey

**Ramuz, Charles-Ferdinand**
1878-1947 ................................ **TCLC 33**
See also CA 165

**Rand, Ayn** 1905-1982 ...... **CLC 3, 30, 44, 79; DA; DAC; DAM MST, NOV, POP; WLC**
See also AAYA 10; AMWS 4; BPFB 3; BYA 12; CA 13-16R; 105; CANR 27, 73; CDALBS; CPW; DA3; DLB 227; MTCW 1, 2; NFS 10; RGAL; SFW; YAW

**Randall, Dudley (Felker)** 1914-2000 . **CLC 1, 135; BLC 3; DAM MULT**
See also BW 1, 3; CA 25-28R; 189; CANR 23, 82; DLB 41; PFS 5

**Randall, Robert**
See Silverberg, Robert

**Ranger, Ken**
See Creasey, John

**Ransom, John Crowe** 1888-1974 .. **CLC 2, 4, 5, 11, 24; DAM POET**
See also AMW; CA 5-8R; 49-52; CANR 6, 34; CDALBS; DA3; DLB 45, 63; EXPP; MTCW 1, 2; RGAL

**Rao, Raja** 1909- ..... **CLC 25, 56; DAM NOV**
See also CA 73-76; CANR 51; CN; MTCW 1, 2; RGEL; RGSF

**Raphael, Frederic (Michael)** 1931- ... **CLC 2, 14**
See also CA 1-4R; CANR 1, 86; CN; DLB 14

**Ratcliffe, James P.**
See Mencken, H(enry) L(ouis)

**Rathbone, Julian** 1935- ..................... **CLC 41**
See also CA 101; CANR 34, 73

**Rattigan, Terence (Mervyn)** 1911-1977 ............ **CLC 7; DAM DRAM**
See also BRWS 7; CA 85-88; 73-76; CBD; CDBLB 1945-1960; DFS 8; DLB 13; IDFW 3, 4; MTCW 1, 2; RGEL

**Ratushinskaya, Irina** 1954- ............ **CLC 54**
See also CA 129; CANR 68; CWW 2

**Raven, Simon (Arthur Noel)** 1927-2001 .................................. **CLC 14**
See also CA 81-84; CANR 86; CN

**Ravenna, Michael**
See Welty, Eudora

**Rawley, Callman** 1903-
See Rakosi, Carl
See also CA 21-24R; CANR 12, 32, 91

**Rawlings, Marjorie Kinnan** 1896-1953 .................................. **TCLC 4**
See also AAYA 20; ANW; BPFB 3; BYA 3; CA 104; 137; CANR 74; CLR 63; DLB 9, 22, 102; DLBD 17; JRDA; MAICYA; MTCW 2; RGAL; SATA 100; YABC 1; YAW

**Ray, Satyajit** 1921-1992 .. **CLC 16, 76; DAM MULT**
See also CA 114; 137

**Read, Herbert Edward** 1893-1968 ..... **CLC 4**
See also BRW 6; CA 85-88; 25-28R; DLB 20, 149; PAB; RGEL

**Read, Piers Paul** 1941- ............ **CLC 4, 10, 25**
See also CA 21-24R; CANR 38, 86; CN; DLB 14; SATA 21

**Reade, Charles** 1814-1884 .......... **NCLC 2, 74**
See also DLB 21; RGEL

**Reade, Hamish**
See Gray, Simon (James Holliday)

**Reading, Peter** 1946- .......................... **CLC 47**
See also CA 103; CANR 46, 96; CP; DLB 40

**Reaney, James** 1926- .. **CLC 13; DAC; DAM MST**
See also CA 41-44R; CAAS 15; CANR 42; CD; CP; DLB 68; RGEL; SATA 43

**Rebreanu, Liviu** 1885-1944 ............ **TCLC 28**
See also CA 165; DLB 220

**Rechy, John (Francisco)** 1934- ...... **CLC 1, 7, 14, 18, 107; DAM MULT; HLC 2**
See also CA 5-8R; CAAE 195; CAAS 4; CANR 6, 32, 64; CN; DLB 122; DLBY 82; HW 1, 2; INT CANR-6; RGAL

**Redcam, Tom** 1870-1933 ................. **TCLC 25**

**Reddin, Keith** .................................. **CLC 67**
See also CAD

**Redgrove, Peter (William)** 1932- . **CLC 6, 41**
See also BRWS 6; CA 1-4R; CANR 3, 39, 77; CP; DLB 40

**Redmon, Anne** .................................. **CLC 22**
See also Nightingale, Anne Redmon
See also DLBY 86

**Reed, Eliot**
See Ambler, Eric

**Reed, Ishmael** 1938- .. **CLC 2, 3, 5, 6, 13, 32, 60; BLC 3; DAM MULT**
See also AFAW 1, 2; BPFB 3; BW 2, 3; CA 21-24R; CANR 25, 48, 74; CN; CP; CSW; DA3; DLB 2, 5, 33, 169, 227; DLBD 8; MSW; MTCW 1, 2; PFS 6; RGAL; TCWW 2

**Reed, John (Silas)** 1887-1920 ........... **TCLC 9**
See also CA 106; 195

**Reed, Lou** ..................................... **CLC 21**
See also Firbank, Louis

**Reese, Lizette Woodworth** 1856-1935 . **PC 29**
See also CA 180; DLB 54

**Reeve, Clara** 1729-1807 ................... **NCLC 19**
See also DLB 39; RGEL

**Reich, Wilhelm** 1897-1957 .............. **TCLC 57**

**Reid, Christopher (John)** 1949- ....... **CLC 33**
See also CA 140; CANR 89; CP; DLB 40

**Reid, Desmond**
See Moorcock, Michael (John)

**Reid Banks, Lynne** 1929-
See Banks, Lynne Reid
See also CA 1-4R; CANR 6, 22, 38, 87; CLR 24; JRDA; MAICYA; SATA 22, 75, 111; YAW

**Reilly, William K.**
See Creasey, John

**Reiner, Max**
See Caldwell, (Janet Miriam) Taylor (Holland)

**Reis, Ricardo**
See Pessoa, Fernando (Antonio Nogueira)

**Remarque, Erich Maria** 1898-1970 ... **CLC 21; DA; DAB; DAC; DAM MST, NOV**
See also AAYA 27; BPFB 3; CA 77-80; 29-32R; DA3; DLB 56; EXPN; LAIT 3; MTCW 1, 2; NFS 4; RGWL

**Remington, Frederic** 1861-1909 ..... **TCLC 89**
See also CA 108; 169; DLB 12, 186, 188; SATA 41

**Remizov, A.**
See Remizov, Aleksei (Mikhailovich)

**Remizov, A. M.**
See Remizov, Aleksei (Mikhailovich)

**Remizov, Aleksei (Mikhailovich)** 1877-1957 .................................. **TCLC 27**
See also CA 125; 133

**Renan, Joseph Ernest** 1823-1892 .. **NCLC 26**
See also GFL 1789 to the Present

**Renard, Jules** 1864-1910 ................. **TCLC 17**
See also CA 117; GFL 1789 to the Present

**Renault, Mary** ........... **CLC 3, 11, 17**
See also Challans, Mary
See also BPFB 3; BYA 2; DLBY 83; GLL 1; LAIT 1; MTCW 2; RGEL; RHW

**Rendell, Ruth (Barbara)** 1930- . **CLC 28, 48; DAM POP**
See also Vine, Barbara
See also BPFB 3; CA 109; CANR 32, 52, 74; CN; CPW; DLB 87; INT CANR-32; MSW; MTCW 1, 2

**Renoir, Jean** 1894-1979 ................... **CLC 20**
See also CA 129; 85-88

**Resnais, Alain** 1922- ......................... **CLC 16**

**Reverdy, Pierre** 1889-1960 ................ **CLC 53**
See also CA 97-100; 89-92; GFL 1789 to the Present

**Rexroth, Kenneth** 1905-1982 .... **CLC 1, 2, 6, 11, 22, 49, 112; DAM POET; PC 20**
See also CA 5-8R; 107; CANR 14, 34, 63; CDALB 1941-1968; DLB 16, 48, 165, 212; DLBY 82; INT CANR-14; MTCW 1, 2; RGAL

**Reyes, Alfonso** 1889-1959 .. **TCLC 33; HLCS 2**
See also CA 131; HW 1; LAW

**Reyes y Basoalto, Ricardo Eliecer Neftali**
See Neruda, Pablo

**Reymont, Wladyslaw (Stanislaw)** 1868(?)-1925 ............................ **TCLC 5**
See also CA 104

**Reynolds, Jonathan** 1942- ............. **CLC 6, 38**
See also CA 65-68; CANR 28

**Reynolds, Joshua** 1723-1792 ............. **LC 15**
See also DLB 104

**Reynolds, Michael S(hane)** 1937-2000 .................................. **CLC 44**
See also CA 65-68; 189; CANR 9, 89, 97

**Reznikoff, Charles** 1894-1976 ............ **CLC 9**
See also CA 33-36; 61-64; CAP 2; DLB 28, 45; WP

**Rezzori (d'Arezzo), Gregor von** 1914-1998 .................................. **CLC 25**
See also CA 122; 136; 167

**Rhine, Richard**
See Silverstein, Alvin; Silverstein, Virginia B(arbara Opshelor)

**Rhodes, Eugene Manlove** 1869-1934 .................................. **TCLC 53**

**R'hoone**
See Balzac, Honore de

**Rhys, Jean** 1894(?)-1979 ....... **CLC 2, 4, 6, 14, 19, 51, 124; DAM NOV; SSC 21**
See also BRWS 2; CA 25-28R; 85-88; CANR 35, 62; CDBLB 1945-1960; DA3; DLB 36, 117, 162; DNFS; MTCW 1, 2; RGEL; RGSF; RHW

**Ribeiro, Darcy** 1922-1997 ................. **CLC 34**
See also CA 33-36R; 156

**Ribeiro, Joao Ubaldo (Osorio Pimentel)** 1941- .................................... **CLC 10, 67**
See also CA 81-84

**Ribman, Ronald (Burt)** 1932- ............. **CLC 7**
See also CA 21-24R; CAD; CANR 46, 80; CD

**Ricci, Nino** 1959- ............................. **CLC 70**
See also CA 137; CCA 1

**Rice, Anne** 1941- .. **CLC 41, 128; DAM POP**
See also Rampling, Anne
See also AAYA 9; AMWS 7; BEST 89:2; BPFB 3; CA 65-68; CANR 12, 36, 53, 74, 100; CN; CPW; CSW; DA3; GLL 2; HGG; MTCW 2; YAW

**Rice, Elmer (Leopold)** 1892-1967 ...... **CLC 7, 49; DAM DRAM**
See also CA 21-22; 25-28R; CAP 2; DFS 12; DLB 4, 7; MTCW 1, 2; RGAL

**Rice, Tim(othy Miles Bindon)** 1944- ........................................ **CLC 21**
See also CA 103; CANR 46; DFS 7

**Rich, Adrienne (Cecile)** 1929- ... **CLC 3, 6, 7, 11, 18, 36, 73, 76, 125; DAM POET; PC 5**
See also AMWS 1; CA 9-12R; CANR 20, 53, 74; CDALBS; CP; CSW; CWP; DA3; DLB 5, 67; EXPP; FW; MAWW; MTCW 1, 2; PAB; RGAL; WP

**Rich, Barbara**
See Graves, Robert (von Ranke)

**Rich, Robert**
See Trumbo, Dalton

**Richard, Keith** ............................... **CLC 17**
See also Richards, Keith

**Richards, David Adams** 1950- .......... **CLC 59; DAC**
See also CA 93-96; CANR 60; DLB 53

**Richards, I(vor) A(rmstrong)** 1893-1979 .............................. **CLC 14, 24**
See also BRWS 2; CA 41-44R; 89-92; CANR 34, 74; DLB 27; MTCW 2; RGEL

**Richards, Keith** 1943-
See Richard, Keith
See also CA 107; CANR 77

**Richardson, Anne**
See Roiphe, Anne (Richardson)

**Richardson, Dorothy Miller**
1873-1957 ................................ **TCLC 3**
See also CA 104; 192; DLB 36; FW; RGEL

**Richardson (Robertson), Ethel Florence Lindesay** 1870-1946
See Richardson, Henry Handel
See also CA 105; 190; DLB 230; RHW

**Richardson, Henry Handel** ............. **TCLC 4**
See Richardson (Robertson), Ethel Florence Lindesay
See also DLB 197; RGEL; RGSF

**Richardson, John** 1796-1852 ........ **NCLC 55; DAC**
See also CCA 1; DLB 99

**Richardson, Samuel** 1689-1761 ...... **LC 1, 44; DA; DAB; DAC; DAM MST, NOV; WLC**
See also BRW 3; CDBLB 1660-1789; DLB 39; RGEL; WLIT 3

**Richler, Mordecai** 1931-2001 .... **CLC 3, 5, 9, 13, 18, 46, 70; DAC; DAM MST, NOV**
See also AITN 1; CA 65-68; CANR 31, 62; CCA 1; CLR 17; CWRI; DLB 53; MAICYA; MTCW 1, 2; RGEL; SATA 44, 98; SATA-Brief 27

**Richter, Conrad (Michael)**
1890-1968 ................................ **CLC 30**
See also AAYA 21; BYA 2; CA 5-8R; 25-28R; CANR 23; DLB 9, 212; LAIT 1; MTCW 1, 2; RGAL; SATA 3; TCWW 2; YAW

**Ricostranza, Tom**
See Ellis, Trey

**Riddell, Charlotte** 1832-1906 ......... **TCLC 40**
See also CA 165; DLB 156

**Ridge, John Rollin** 1827-1867 ...... **NCLC 82; DAM MULT**
See also CA 144; DLB 175; NNAL

**Ridgeway, Jason**
See Marlowe, Stephen

**Ridgway, Keith** 1965- ...................... **CLC 119**
See also CA 172

**Riding, Laura** ................................ **CLC 3, 7**
See also Jackson, Laura (Riding)
See also RGAL

**Riefenstahl, Berta Helene Amalia** 1902-
See Riefenstahl, Leni
See also CA 108

**Riefenstahl, Leni** ........................... **CLC 16**
See also Riefenstahl, Berta Helene Amalia

**Riffe, Ernest**
See Bergman, (Ernst) Ingmar

**Riggs, (Rolla) Lynn** 1899-1954 ..... **TCLC 56; DAM MULT**
See also CA 144; DLB 175; NNAL

**Riis, Jacob A(ugust)** 1849-1914 ..... **TCLC 80**
See also CA 113; 168; DLB 23

**Riley, James Whitcomb**
1849-1916 ........ **TCLC 51; DAM POET**
See also CA 118; 137; MAICYA; RGAL; SATA 17

**Riley, Tex**
See Creasey, John

**Rilke, Rainer Maria** 1875-1926 .. **TCLC 1, 6, 19; DAM POET; PC 2**
See also CA 104; 132; CANR 62, 99; DA3; DLB 81; EW; MTCW 1, 2; RGWL; WP

**Rimbaud, (Jean Nicolas) Arthur**
1854-1891 . **NCLC 4, 35, 82; DA; DAB; DAC; DAM MST, POET; PC 3; WLC**
See also DA3; EW; GFL 1789 to the Present; RGWL; TWA; WP

**Rinehart, Mary Roberts**
1876-1958 ................................ **TCLC 52**
See also BPFB 3; CA 108; 166; RGAL; RHW

**Ringmaster, The**
See Mencken, H(enry) L(ouis)

**Ringwood, Gwen(dolyn Margaret) Pharis**
1910-1984 ................................ **CLC 48**
See also CA 148; 112; DLB 88

**Rio, Michel** 19(?)- ........................... **CLC 43**

**Ritsos, Giannes**
See Ritsos, Yannis

**Ritsos, Yannis** 1909-1990 ........ **CLC 6, 13, 31**
See also CA 77-80; 133; CANR 39, 61; EW; MTCW 1; RGWL

**Ritter, Erika** 1948(?)- ...................... **CLC 52**
See also CD; CWD

**Rivera, Jose Eustasio** 1889-1928 ... **TCLC 35**
See also CA 162; HW 1, 2; LAW

**Rivera, Tomas** 1935-1984
See also CA 49-52; CANR 32; DLB 82; HLCS 2; HW 1; RGAL; TCWW 2; WLIT 1

**Rivers, Conrad Kent** 1933-1968 ......... **CLC 1**
See also BW 1; CA 85-88; DLB 41

**Rivers, Elfrida**
See Bradley, Marion Zimmer
See also GLL 1

**Riverside, John**
See Heinlein, Robert A(nson)

**Rizal, Jose** 1861-1896 ...................... **NCLC 27**

**Roa Bastos, Augusto (Antonio)**
1917- .... **CLC 45; DAM MULT; HLC 2**
See also CA 131; DLB 113; HW 1; LAW; RGSF; WLIT 1

**Robbe-Grillet, Alain** 1922- .... **CLC 1, 2, 4, 6, 8, 10, 14, 43, 128**
See also BPFB 3; CA 9-12R; CANR 33, 65; DLB 83; EW; GFL 1789 to the Present; IDFW 3, 4; MTCW 1, 2; RGWL

**Robbins, Harold** 1916-1997 .... **CLC 5; DAM NOV**
See also BPFB 3; CA 73-76; 162; CANR 26, 54; DA3; MTCW 1, 2

**Robbins, Thomas Eugene** 1936-
See Robbins, Tom
See also CA 81-84; CANR 29, 59, 95; CN; CPW; CSW; DA3; DAM NOV, POP; MTCW 1, 2

**Robbins, Tom** ........................... **CLC 9, 32, 64**
See also Robbins, Thomas Eugene
See also AAYA 32; BEST 90:3; BPFB 3; DLBY 80; MTCW 2

**Robbins, Trina** 1938- ........................ **CLC 21**
See also CA 128

**Roberts, Charles G(eorge) D(ouglas)**
1860-1943 ................................ **TCLC 8**
See also CA 105; 188; CLR 33; CWRI; DLB 92; RGEL; RGSF; SATA 88; SATA-Brief 29

**Roberts, Elizabeth Madox**
1886-1941 ................................ **TCLC 68**
See also CA 111; 166; CWRI; DLB 9, 54, 102; RGAL; RHW; SATA 33; SATA-Brief 27

**Roberts, Kate** 1891-1985 ................... **CLC 15**
See also CA 107; 116

**Roberts, Keith (John Kingston)**
1935-2000 ................................ **CLC 14**
See also CA 25-28R; CANR 46; SFW

**Roberts, Kenneth (Lewis)**
1885-1957 ................................ **TCLC 23**
See also CA 109; DLB 9; RGAL; RHW

**Roberts, Michele (Brigitte)** 1949- ...... **CLC 48**
See also CA 115; CANR 58; CN; DLB 231; FW

**Robertson, Ellis**
See Ellison, Harlan (Jay); Silverberg, Robert

**Robertson, Thomas William**
1829-1871 ....... **NCLC 35; DAM DRAM**
See also Robertson, Tom

**Robertson, Tom**
See Robertson, Thomas William
See also RGEL

**Robeson, Kenneth**
See Dent, Lester

**Robinson, Edwin Arlington**
1869-1935 ..... **TCLC 5, 101; DA; DAC; DAM MST, POET; PC 1, 35**
See also AMW; CA 104; 133; CDALB 1865-1917; DLB 54; EXPP; MTCW 1, 2; PAB; PFS 4; RGAL; WP

**Robinson, Henry Crabb**
1775-1867 ................................ **NCLC 15**
See also DLB 107

**Robinson, Jill** 1936- ......................... **CLC 10**
See also CA 102; INT 102

**Robinson, Kim Stanley** 1952- ........... **CLC 34**
See also AAYA 26; CA 126; CN; SATA 109; SFW

**Robinson, Lloyd**
See Silverberg, Robert

**Robinson, Marilynne** 1944- ............... **CLC 25**
See also CA 116; CANR 80; CN; DLB 206

**Robinson, Smokey** ........................... **CLC 21**
See also Robinson, William, Jr.

**Robinson, William, Jr.** 1940-
See Robinson, Smokey
See also CA 116

**Robison, Mary** 1949- .................. **CLC 42, 98**
See also CA 113; 116; CANR 87; CN; DLB 130; INT 116; RGSF

**Rod, Edouard** 1857-1910 ................ **TCLC 52**

**Roddenberry, Eugene Wesley** 1921-1991
See Roddenberry, Gene
See also CA 110; 135; CANR 37; SATA 45; SATA-Obit 69

**Roddenberry, Gene** ........................... **CLC 17**
See also Roddenberry, Eugene Wesley
See also AAYA 5; SATA-Obit 69

**Rodgers, Mary** 1931- ........................ **CLC 12**
See also BYA 5; CA 49-52; CANR 8, 55, 90; CLR 20; CWRI; INT CANR-8; JRDA; MAICYA; SATA 8

**Rodgers, W(illiam) R(obert)**
1909-1969 ................................ **CLC 7**
See also CA 85-88; DLB 20; RGEL

**Rodman, Eric**
See Silverberg, Robert

**Rodman, Howard** 1920(?)-1985 ........ **CLC 65**
See also CA 118

**Rodman, Maia**
See Wojciechowska, Maia (Teresa)

**Rodo, Jose Enrique** 1871(?)-1917
See also CA 178; HLCS 2; HW 2; LAW

**Rodolph, Utto**
See Ouologuem, Yambo

**Rodriguez, Claudio** 1934-1999 ......... **CLC 10**
See also CA 188; DLB 134

**Rodriguez, Richard** 1944-
See also CA 110; CANR 66; DAM MULT; DLB 82; HLC 2; HW 1, 2; LAIT 5; WLIT 1

**Roelvaag, O(le) E(dvart)**
1876-1931 ................................ **TCLC 17**
See also Rolvaag, O(le) E(dvart)
See also CA 117; 171; DLB 9

**Roethke, Theodore (Huebner)**
1908-1963 ......... **CLC 1, 3, 8, 11, 19, 46, 101; DAM POET; PC 15**
See also AMW; CA 81-84; CABS 2; CDALB 1941-1968; DA3; DLB 5, 206; EXPP; MTCW 1, 2; PAB; PFS 3; RGAL; WP

**Rogers, Samuel** 1763-1855 ............. **NCLC 69**
See also DLB 93; RGEL

**Rogers, Thomas Hunton** 1927- ......... **CLC 57**
See also CA 89-92; INT 89-92

**Rogers, Will(iam Penn Adair)**
1879-1935 ... **TCLC 8, 71; DAM MULT**
See also CA 105; 144; DA3; DLB 11; MTCW 2; NNAL

**Rogin, Gilbert** 1929- .......................... **CLC 18**
See also CA 65-68; CANR 15
**Rohan, Koda**
See Koda Shigeyuki
**Rohlfs, Anna Katharine Green**
See Green, Anna Katharine
**Rohmer, Eric** ................................ **CLC 16**
See also Scherer, Jean-Marie Maurice
**Rohmer, Sax** ................................. **TCLC 28**
See also Ward, Arthur Henry Sarsfield
See also DLB 70; MSW
**Roiphe, Anne (Richardson)** 1935- .. **CLC 3, 9**
See also CA 89-92; CANR 45, 73; DLBY 80; INT 89-92
**Rojas, Fernando de** 1475-1541 ........... **LC 23; HLCS 1**
See also RGWL
**Rojas, Gonzalo** 1917-
See also HLCS 2; HW 2
**Rojas, Gonzalo** 1917-
See also CA 178; HLCS 2
**Rolfe, Frederick (William Serafino Austin Lewis Mary)** 1860-1913 ......... **TCLC 12**
See also Corvo, Baron
See also CA 107; DLB 34, 156; RGEL
**Rolland, Romain** 1866-1944 ........... **TCLC 23**
See also CA 118; DLB 65; GFL 1789 to the Present; RGWL
**Rolle, Richard** c. 1300-c. 1349 ...... **CMLC 21**
See also DLB 146; RGEL
**Rolvaag, O(le) E(dvart)**
See Roelvaag, O(le) E(dvart)
See also DLB 212; NFS 5; RGAL
**Romain Arnaud, Saint**
See Aragon, Louis
**Romains, Jules** 1885-1972 ................... **CLC 7**
See also CA 85-88; CANR 34; DLB 65; GFL 1789 to the Present; MTCW 1
**Romero, Jose Ruben** 1890-1952 .... **TCLC 14**
See also CA 114; 131; HW 1; LAW
**Ronsard, Pierre de** 1524-1585 . **LC 6, 54; PC 11**
See also EW; GFL Beginnings to 1789; RGWL
**Rooke, Leon** 1934- . **CLC 25, 34; DAM POP**
See also CA 25-28R; CANR 23, 53; CCA 1; CPW
**Roosevelt, Franklin Delano** 1882-1945 ................................ **TCLC 93**
See also CA 116; 173; LAIT 3
**Roosevelt, Theodore** 1858-1919 ..... **TCLC 69**
See also CA 115; 170; DLB 47, 186
**Roper, William** 1498-1578 .................... **LC 10**
**Roquelaure, A. N.**
See Rice, Anne
**Rosa, Joao Guimaraes** 1908-1967 ... **CLC 23; HLCS 1**
See also Guimaraes Rosa, Joao
See also CA 89-92; DLB 113; WLIT 1
**Rose, Wendy** 1948- .. **CLC 85; DAM MULT; PC 13**
See also CA 53-56; CANR 5, 51; CWP; DLB 175; NNAL; PFS 13; RGAL; SATA 12
**Rosen, R. D.**
See Rosen, Richard (Dean)
**Rosen, Richard (Dean)** 1949- ........... **CLC 39**
See also CA 77-80; CANR 62; CMW; INT CANR-30
**Rosenberg, Isaac** 1890-1918 ........... **TCLC 12**
See also BRW 6; CA 107; 188; DLB 20; PAB; RGEL
**Rosenblatt, Joe** ................................ **CLC 15**
See also Rosenblatt, Joseph
**Rosenblatt, Joseph** 1933-
See Rosenblatt, Joe
See also CA 89-92; CP; INT 89-92

**Rosenfeld, Samuel**
See Tzara, Tristan
**Rosenstock, Sami**
See Tzara, Tristan
**Rosenstock, Samuel**
See Tzara, Tristan
**Rosenthal, M(acha) L(ouis)** 1917-1996 ................................ **CLC 28**
See also CA 1-4R; 152; CAAS 6; CANR 4, 51; CP; DLB 5; SATA 59
**Ross, Barnaby**
See Dannay, Frederic
**Ross, Bernard L.**
See Follett, Ken(neth Martin)
**Ross, J. H.**
See Lawrence, T(homas) E(dward)
**Ross, John Hume**
See Lawrence, T(homas) E(dward)
**Ross, Martin** 1862-1915
See Martin, Violet Florence
See also DLB 135; GLL 2; RGEL; RGSF
**Ross, (James) Sinclair** 1908-1996 ... **CLC 13; DAC; DAM MST; SSC 24**
See also CA 73-76; CANR 81; CN; DLB 88; RGEL; RGSF; TCWW 2
**Rossetti, Christina (Georgina)** 1830-1894 . **NCLC 2, 50, 66; DA; DAB; DAC; DAM MST, POET; PC 7; WLC**
See also BRW 5; BYA 4; DA3; DLB 35, 163, 240; EXPP; MAICYA; PFS 10; RGEL; SATA 20; WCH
**Rossetti, Dante Gabriel** 1828-1882 . **NCLC 4, 77; DA; DAB; DAC; DAM MST, POET; WLC**
See also BRW 5; CDBLB 1832-1890; DLB 35; EXPP; RGEL
**Rossner, Judith (Perelman)** 1935- . **CLC 6, 9, 29**
See also AITN 2; BEST 90:3; BPFB 3; CA 17-20R; CANR 18, 51, 73; CN; DLB 6; INT CANR-18; MTCW 1, 2
**Rostand, Edmond (Eugene Alexis)** 1868-1918 ........ **TCLC 6, 37; DA; DAB; DAC; DAM DRAM, MST; DC 10**
See also CA 104; 126; DA3; DFS 1; DLB 192; LAIT 1; MTCW 1
**Roth, Henry** 1906-1995 ...... **CLC 2, 6, 11, 104**
See also AMWS 9; CA 11-12; 149; CANR 38, 63; CAP 1; CN; DA3; DLB 28; MTCW 1, 2; RGAL
**Roth, (Moses) Joseph** 1894-1939 ... **TCLC 33**
See also CA 160; DLB 85
**Roth, Philip (Milton)** 1933- ... **CLC 1, 2, 3, 4, 6, 9, 15, 22, 31, 47, 66, 86, 119; DA; DAB; DAC; DAM MST, NOV, POP; SSC 26; WLC**
See also AMWS 3; BEST 90:3; BPFB 3; CA 1-4R; CANR 1, 22, 36, 55, 89; CDALB 1968-1988; CN; CPW 1; DA3; DLB 2, 28, 173; DLBY 82; MTCW 1, 2; RGAL; RGSF; SSFS 12
**Rothenberg, Jerome** 1931- ............... **CLC 6, 57**
See also CA 45-48; CANR 1; CP; DLB 5, 193
**Rotter, Pat ed.** ................................ **CLC 65**
**Roumain, Jacques (Jean Baptiste)** 1907-1944 ...... **TCLC 19; BLC 3; DAM MULT**
See also BW 1; CA 117; 125
**Rourke, Constance (Mayfield)** 1885-1941 ................................ **TCLC 12**
See also CA 107; YABC 1
**Rousseau, Jean-Baptiste** 1671-1741 ...... **LC 9**
**Rousseau, Jean-Jacques** 1712-1778 .... **LC 14, 36; DA; DAB; DAC; DAM MST; WLC**
See also DA3; EW; GFL Beginnings to 1789; RGWL
**Roussel, Raymond** 1877-1933 ........ **TCLC 20**
See also CA 117; GFL 1789 to the Present

**Rovit, Earl (Herbert)** 1927- ................ **CLC 7**
See also CA 5-8R; CANR 12
**Rowe, Elizabeth Singer** 1674-1737 ..... **LC 44**
See also DLB 39, 95
**Rowe, Nicholas** 1674-1718 ................ **LC 8**
See also DLB 84; RGEL
**Rowlandson, Mary** 1637(?)-1678 ......... **LC 66**
See also DLB 24, 200; RGAL
**Rowley, Ames Dorrance**
See Lovecraft, H(oward) P(hillips)
**Rowling, J(oanne) K.** 1966(?)- ........... **CLC 137**
See also AAYA 34; BYA 13; CA 173; CLR 66; SATA 109
**Rowson, Susanna Haswell** 1762(?)-1824 ................ **NCLC 5, 69**
See also DLB 37, 200; RGAL
**Roy, Arundhati** 1960(?)- .................. **CLC 109**
See also CA 163; CANR 90; DLBY 97
**Roy, Gabrielle** 1909-1983 ........... **CLC 10, 14; DAB; DAC; DAM MST**
See also CA 53-56; 110; CANR 5, 61; CCA 1; DLB 68; MTCW 1; RGWL; SATA 104
**Royko, Mike** 1932-1997 ................... **CLC 109**
See also CA 89-92; 157; CANR 26; CPW
**Rozanov, Vassili** 1856-1919 ........... **TCLC 104**
**Rozewicz, Tadeusz** 1921- ...... **CLC 9, 23, 139; DAM POET**
See also CA 108; CANR 36, 66; CWW 2; DA3; DLB 232; MTCW 1, 2
**Ruark, Gibbons** 1941- ......................... **CLC 3**
See also CA 33-36R; CAAS 23; CANR 14, 31, 57; DLB 120
**Rubens, Bernice (Ruth)** 1923- .... **CLC 19, 31**
See also CA 25-28R; CANR 33, 65; CN; DLB 14, 207; MTCW 1
**Rubin, Harold**
See Robbins, Harold
**Rudkin, (James) David** 1936- ........... **CLC 14**
See also CA 89-92; CBD; CD; DLB 13
**Rudnik, Raphael** 1933- ....................... **CLC 7**
See also CA 29-32R
**Ruffian, M.**
See Hasek, Jaroslav (Matej Frantisek)
**Ruiz, Jose Martinez** ......................... **CLC 11**
See also Martinez Ruiz, Jose
**Rukeyser, Muriel** 1913-1980 . **CLC 6, 10, 15, 27; DAM POET; PC 12**
See also AMWS 6; CA 5-8R; 93-96; CANR 26, 60; DA3; DLB 48; FW; GLL 2; MTCW 1, 2; PFS 10; RGAL; SATA-Obit 22
**Rule, Jane (Vance)** 1931- .................. **CLC 27**
See also CA 25-28R; CAAS 18; CANR 12, 87; CN; DLB 60; FW
**Rulfo, Juan** 1918-1986 ....... **CLC 8, 80; DAM MULT; HLC 2; SSC 25**
See also CA 85-88; 118; CANR 26; DLB 113; HW 1, 2; LAW; MTCW 1, 2; RGSF; RGWL; WLIT 1
**Rumi, Jalal al-Din** 1207-1273 ....... **CMLC 20**
See also RGWL; WP
**Runeberg, Johan** 1804-1877 ........... **NCLC 41**
**Runyon, (Alfred) Damon** 1884(?)-1946 .......................... **TCLC 10**
See also CA 107; 165; DLB 11, 86, 171; MTCW 2; RGAL
**Rush, Norman** 1933- ......................... **CLC 44**
See also CA 121; 126; INT 126
**Rushdie, (Ahmed) Salman** 1947- .... **CLC 23, 31, 55, 100; DAB; DAC; DAM MST, NOV, POP; WLCS**
See also BEST 89:3; BPFB 3; BRWS 4; CA 108; 111; CANR 33, 56; CN; CPW 1; DA3; DLB 194; FANT; INT CA-111; MTCW 1, 2; RGEL; RGSF; WLIT 4
**Rushforth, Peter (Scott)** 1945- .......... **CLC 19**
See also CA 101

**Ruskin, John** 1819-1900 ............... **TCLC 63**
  See also BRW 5; BYA 5; CA 114; 129; CDBLB 1832-1890; DLB 55, 163, 190; RGEL; SATA 24
**Russ, Joanna** 1937- ............................. **CLC 15**
  See also BPFB 3; CA 5-28R; CANR 11, 31, 65; CN; DLB 8; FW; GLL 1; MTCW 1; SCFW 2; SFW
**Russell, George William** 1867-1935
  See Baker, Jean H.
  See also CA 104; 153; CDBLB 1890-1914; DAM POET; RGEL
**Russell, Jeffrey Burton** 1934- ........... **CLC 70**
  See also CA 25-28R; CANR 11, 28, 52
**Russell, (Henry) Ken(neth Alfred)**
  1927- ............................................. **CLC 16**
  See also CA 105
**Russell, William Martin** 1947- ......... **CLC 60**
  See also CA 164; DLB 233
**Rutherford, Mark** ............................ **TCLC 25**
  See also White, William Hale
  See also DLB 18; RGEL
**Ruyslinck, Ward** ............................... **CLC 14**
  See also Belser, Reimond Karel Maria de
**Ryan, Cornelius (John)** 1920-1974 ..... **CLC 7**
  See also CA 69-72; 53-56; CANR 38
**Ryan, Michael** 1946- .......................... **CLC 65**
  See also CA 49-52; DLBY 82
**Ryan, Tim**
  See Dent, Lester
**Rybakov, Anatoli (Naumovich)**
  1911-1998 ............................... **CLC 23, 53**
  See also CA 126; 135; 172; SATA 79; SATA-Obit 108
**Ryder, Jonathan**
  See Ludlum, Robert
**Ryga, George** 1932-1987 ....... **CLC 14; DAC; DAM MST**
  See also CA 101; 124; CANR 43, 90; CCA 1; DLB 60
**S. H.**
  See Hartmann, Sadakichi
**S. S.**
  See Sassoon, Siegfried (Lorraine)
**Saba, Umberto** 1883-1957 ............... **TCLC 33**
  See also CA 144; CANR 79; DLB 114; RGWL
**Sabatini, Rafael** 1875-1950 ............. **TCLC 47**
  See also BPFB 3; CA 162; RHW
**Sabato, Ernesto (R.)** 1911- ........ **CLC 10, 23; DAM MULT; HLC 2**
  See also CA 97-100; CANR 32, 65; DLB 145; HW 1, 2; LAW; MTCW 1, 2
**Sa-Carniero, Mario de** 1890-1916 . **TCLC 83**
**Sacastru, Martin**
  See Bioy Casares, Adolfo
**Sacastru, Martin**
  See Bioy Casares, Adolfo
  See also CWW 2
**Sacher-Masoch, Leopold von**
  1836(?)-1895 ............................... **NCLC 31**
**Sachs, Marilyn (Stickle)** 1927- ........ **CLC 35**
  See also AAYA 2; BYA 6; CA 17-20R; CANR 13, 47; CLR 2; JRDA; MAICYA; SAAS 2; SATA 3, 68; SATA-Essay 110; WYA; YAW
**Sachs, Nelly** 1891-1970 ................ **CLC 14, 98**
  See also CA 17-18; 25-28R; CANR 87; CAP 2; MTCW 2; RGWL
**Sackler, Howard (Oliver)**
  1929-1982 ..................................... **CLC 14**
  See also CA 61-64; 108; CAD; CANR 30; DLB 7
**Sacks, Oliver (Wolf)** 1933- ............... **CLC 67**
  See also CA 53-56; CANR 28, 50, 76; CPW; DA3; INT CANR-28; MTCW 1, 2
**Sadakichi**
  See Hartmann, Sadakichi

**Sade, Donatien Alphonse Francois**
  1740-1814 ............................... **NCLC 3, 47**
  See also EW; GFL Beginnings to 1789; RGWL
**Sadoff, Ira** 1945- ................................. **CLC 9**
  See also CA 53-56; CANR 5, 21; DLB 120
**Saetone**
  See Camus, Albert
**Safire, William** 1929- ........................ **CLC 10**
  See also CA 17-20R; CANR 31, 54, 91
**Sagan, Carl (Edward)** 1934-1996 .... **CLC 30, 112**
  See also AAYA 2; CA 25-28R; 155; CANR 11, 36, 74; CPW; DA3; MTCW 1, 2; SATA 58; SATA-Obit 94
**Sagan, Francoise** ............ **CLC 3, 6, 9, 17, 36**
  See also Quoirez, Francoise
  See also CWW 2; DLB 83; GFL 1789 to the Present; MTCW 2
**Sahgal, Nayantara (Pandit)** 1927- .... **CLC 41**
  See also CA 9-12R; CANR 11, 88; CN
**Said, Edward W.** 1935- ..................... **CLC 123**
  See also CA 21-24R; CANR 45, 74; DLB 67; MTCW 2
**Saint, H(arry) F.** 1941- ....................... **CLC 50**
  See also CA 127
**St. Aubin de Teran, Lisa** 1953-
  See Teran, Lisa St. Aubin de
  See also CA 118; 126; CN; INT 126
**Saint Birgitta of Sweden** c.
  1303-1373 .................................. **CMLC 24**
**Sainte-Beuve, Charles Augustin**
  1804-1869 .................................. **NCLC 5**
  See also EW; GFL 1789 to the Present
**Saint-Exupery, Antoine (Jean Baptiste Marie Roger) de** 1900-1944 .... **TCLC 2, 56; DAM NOV; WLC**
  See also BPFB 3; BYA 3; CA 108; 132; CLR 10; DA3; DLB 72; EW; GFL 1789 to the Present; LAIT 3; MAICYA; MTCW 1, 2; RGWL; SATA 20
**St. John, David**
  See Hunt, E(verette) Howard, (Jr.)
**St. John, J. Hector**
  See Crevecoeur, Michel Guillaume Jean de
**Saint-John Perse**
  See Leger, (Marie-Rene Auguste) Alexis Saint-Leger
  See also EW; GFL 1789 to the Present; RGWL
**Saintsbury, George (Edward Bateman)**
  1845-1933 ............................... **TCLC 31**
  See also CA 160; DLB 57, 149
**Sait Faik** ............................................. **TCLC 23**
  See also Abasiyanik, Sait Faik
**Saki** ...................................... **TCLC 3; SSC 12**
  See also Munro, H(ector) H(ugh)
  See also BRWS 6; LAIT 2; MTCW 2; RGEL; SSFS 1
**Sakutaro, Hagiwara**
  See Hagiwara, Sakutaro
**Sala, George Augustus** 1828-1895 . **NCLC 46**
**Saladin** 1138-1193 ........................... **CMLC 38**
**Salama, Hannu** 1936- ....................... **CLC 18**
**Salamanca, J(ack) R(ichard)** 1922- .. **CLC 4, 15**
  See also CA 25-28R; CAAE 193
**Salas, Floyd Francis** 1931-
  See also CA 119; CAAS 27; CANR 44, 75, 93; DAM MULT; DLB 82; HLC 2; HW 1, 2; MTCW 2
**Sale, J. Kirkpatrick**
  See Sale, Kirkpatrick
**Sale, Kirkpatrick** 1937- ..................... **CLC 68**
  See also CA 13-16R; CANR 10
**Salinas, Luis Omar** 1937- ..... **CLC 90; DAM MULT; HLC 2**
  See also CA 131; CANR 81; DLB 82; HW 1, 2

**Salinas (y Serrano), Pedro**
  1891(?)-1951 ............................. **TCLC 17**
  See also CA 117; DLB 134
**Salinger, J(erome) D(avid)** 1919- .. **CLC 1, 3, 8, 12, 55, 56, 138; DA; DAB; DAC; DAM MST, NOV, POP; SSC 2, 28; WLC**
  See also AAYA 2, 36; AMW; BPFB 3; CA 5-8R; CANR 39; CDALB 1941-1968; CLR 18; CN; CPW 1; DA3; DLB 2, 102, 173; EXPN; LAIT 4; MAICYA; MTCW 1, 2; NFS 1; RGAL; RGSF; SATA 67; WYA; YAW
**Salisbury, John**
  See Caute, (John) David
**Salter, James** 1925- ................. **CLC 7, 52, 59**
  See also AMWS 9; CA 73-76; DLB 130
**Saltus, Edgar (Everton)** 1855-1921 . **TCLC 8**
  See also CA 105; DLB 202; RGAL
**Saltykov, Mikhail Evgrafovich**
  1826-1889 ................................. **NCLC 16**
  See also DLB 238:
**Saltykov-Shchedrin, N.**
  See Saltykov, Mikhail Evgrafovich
**Samarakis, Antonis** 1919- ................. **CLC 5**
  See also CA 25-28R; CAAS 16; CANR 36
**Sanchez, Florencio** 1875-1910 ........ **TCLC 37**
  See also CA 153; HW 1; LAW
**Sanchez, Luis Rafael** 1936- .............. **CLC 23**
  See also CA 128; DLB 145; HW 1; WLIT 1
**Sanchez, Sonia** 1934- .... **CLC 5, 116; BLC 3; DAM MULT; PC 9**
  See also BW 2, 3; CA 33-36R; CANR 24, 49, 74; CLR 18; CP; CSW; CWP; DA3; DLB 41; DLBD 8; MAICYA; MTCW 1, 2; SATA 22; WP
**Sand, George** 1804-1876 ..... **NCLC 2, 42, 57; DA; DAB; DAC; DAM MST, NOV; WLC**
  See also DA3; DLB 119, 192; EW; FW; GFL 1789 to the Present; RGWL
**Sandburg, Carl (August)** 1878-1967 . **CLC 1, 4, 10, 15, 35; DA; DAB; DAC; DAM MST, POET; PC 2; WLC**
  See also AAYA 24; AMW; BYA 1, 3; CA 5-8R; 25-28R; CANR 35; CDALB 1865-1917; CLR 67; DA3; DLB 17, 54; EXPP; LAIT 2; MAICYA; MTCW 1, 2; PAB; PFS 3, 6, 12; RGAL; SATA 8; WCH; WP; WYA
**Sandburg, Charles**
  See Sandburg, Carl (August)
**Sandburg, Charles A.**
  See Sandburg, Carl (August)
**Sanders, (James) Ed(ward)** 1939- ... **CLC 53; DAM POET**
  See also CA 13-16R; CAAS 21; CANR 13, 44, 78; CP; DLB 16
**Sanders, Lawrence** 1920-1998 ......... **CLC 41; DAM POP**
  See also BEST 89:4; BPFB 3; CA 81-84; 165; CANR 33, 62; CMW; CPW; DA3; MTCW 1
**Sanders, Noah**
  See Blount, Roy (Alton), Jr.
**Sanders, Winston P.**
  See Anderson, Poul (William)
**Sandoz, Mari(e Susette)** 1900-1966 .. **CLC 28**
  See also CA 1-4R; 25-28R; CANR 17, 64; DLB 9, 212; LAIT 2; MTCW 1, 2; SATA 5; TCWW 2
**Saner, Reg(inald Anthony)** 1931- ....... **CLC 9**
  See also CA 65-68; CP
**Sankara** 788-820 ............................. **CMLC 32**
**Sannazaro, Jacopo** 1456(?)-1530 ........... **LC 8**
  See also RGWL

**Sansom, William** 1912-1976 .......... **CLC 2, 6; DAM NOV; SSC 21**
See also CA 5-8R; 65-68; CANR 42; DLB 139; MTCW 1; RGEL; RGSF

**Santayana, George** 1863-1952 ........ **TCLC 40**
See also AMW; CA 115; 194; DLB 54, 71, 246; DLBD 13; RGAL

**Santiago, Danny** ................................. **CLC 33**
See also James, Daniel (Lewis)
See also DLB 122

**Santmyer, Helen Hooven** 1895-1986 ........................................ **CLC 33**
See also CA 1-4R; 118; CANR 15, 33; DLBY 84; MTCW 1; RHW

**Santoka, Taneda** 1882-1940 ............. **TCLC 72**

**Santos, Bienvenido N(uqui)** 1911-1996 ........... **CLC 22; DAM MULT**
See also CA 101; 151; CANR 19, 46; RGAL

**Sapir, Edward** 1884-1939 ............. **TCLC 108**
See also DLB 92

**Sapper** ............................................. **TCLC 44**
See also McNeile, Herman Cyril

**Sapphire**
See Sapphire, Brenda

**Sapphire, Brenda** 1950- ...................... **CLC 99**

**Sappho** fl. 6256th cent. B.C.- ............. **CMLC 3; DAM POET; PC 5**
See also DA3; DLB 176; RGWL; WP

**Saramago, Jose** 1922- ...... **CLC 119; HLCS 1**
See also CA 153; CANR 96

**Sarduy, Severo** 1937-1993 ........... **CLC 6, 97; HLCS 2**
See also CA 89-92; 142; CANR 58, 81; CWW 2; DLB 113; HW 1, 2; LAW

**Sargeson, Frank** 1903-1982 ............... **CLC 31**
See also CA 25-28R; 106; CANR 38, 79; GLL 2; RGEL; RGSF

**Sarmiento, Domingo Faustino** 1811-1888
See also HLCS 1; LAW; WLIT 1

**Sarmiento, Felix Ruben Garcia**
See Dario, Ruben

**Saro-Wiwa, Ken(ule Beeson)** 1941-1995 ................................. **CLC 114**
See also BW 2; CA 142; 150; CANR 60; DLB 157

**Saroyan, William** 1908-1981 ... **CLC 1, 8, 10, 29, 34, 56; DA; DAB; DAC; DAM DRAM, MST, NOV; SSC 21; WLC**
See also CA 5-8R; 103; CAD; CANR 30; CDALBS; DA3; DLB 7, 9, 86; DLBY 81; LAIT 4; MTCW 1, 2; RGAL; RGSF; SATA 23; SATA-Obit 24

**Sarraute, Nathalie** 1900-1999 .... **CLC 1, 2, 4, 8, 10, 31, 80**
See also BPFB 3; CA 9-12R; 187; CANR 23, 66; CWW 2; DLB 83; EW; GFL 1789 to the Present; MTCW 1, 2; RGWL

**Sarton, (Eleanor) May** 1912-1995 ..... **CLC 4, 14, 49, 91; DAM POET**
See also AMWS 8; CA 1-4R; 149; CANR 1, 34, 55; CN; CP; DLB 48; DLBY 81; FW; INT CANR-34; MTCW 1, 2; RGAL; SATA 36; SATA-Obit 86

**Sartre, Jean-Paul** 1905-1980 . **CLC 1, 4, 7, 9, 13, 18, 24, 44, 50, 52; DA; DAB; DAC; DAM DRAM, MST, NOV; DC 3; SSC 32; WLC**
See also CA 9-12R; 97-100; CANR 21; DA3; DFS 5; DLB 72; EW; GFL 1789 to the Present; MTCW 1, 2; RGSF; RGWL; SSFS 9

**Sassoon, Siegfried (Lorraine)** 1886-1967 .... **CLC 36, 130; DAB; DAM MST, NOV, POET; PC 12**
See also BRW 6; CA 104; 25-28R; CANR 36; DLB 20, 191; DLBD 18; MTCW 1, 2; PAB; RGEL

**Satterfield, Charles**
See Pohl, Frederik

**Satyremont**
See Peret, Benjamin

**Saul, John (W. III)** 1942- ...... **CLC 46; DAM NOV, POP**
See also AAYA 10; BEST 90:4; CA 81-84; CANR 16, 40, 81; CPW; HGG; SATA 98

**Saunders, Caleb**
See Heinlein, Robert A(nson)

**Saura (Atares), Carlos** 1932-1998 ..... **CLC 20**
See also CA 114; 131; CANR 79; HW 1

**Sauser-Hall, Frederic** 1887-1961 ...... **CLC 18**
See also Cendrars, Blaise
See also CA 102; 93-96; CANR 36, 62; MTCW 1

**Saussure, Ferdinand de** 1857-1913 ................................. **TCLC 49**
See also DLB 242

**Savage, Catharine**
See Brosman, Catharine Savage

**Savage, Thomas** 1915- ...................... **CLC 40**
See also CA 126; 132; CAAS 15; CN; INT 132; TCWW 2

**Savan, Glenn** (?)- ................................. **CLC 50**

**Sayers, Dorothy L(eigh)** 1893-1957 ....... **TCLC 2, 15; DAM POP**
See also BPFB 3; BRWS 3; CA 104; 119; CANR 60; CDBLB 1914-1945; CMW; DLB 10, 36, 77, 100; MSW; MTCW 1, 2; RGEL; SSFS 12

**Sayers, Valerie** 1952- .................. **CLC 50, 122**
See also CA 134; CANR 61; CSW

**Sayles, John (Thomas)** 1950- . **CLC 7, 10, 14**
See also CA 57-60; CANR 41, 84; DLB 44

**Scammell, Michael** 1935- .................. **CLC 34**
See also CA 156

**Scannell, Vernon** 1922- ...................... **CLC 49**
See also CA 5-8R; CANR 8, 24, 57; CP; CWRI; DLB 27; SATA 59

**Scarlett, Susan**
See Streatfeild, (Mary) Noel

**Scarron** 1847-1910
See Mikszath, Kalman

**Schaeffer, Susan Fromberg** 1941- ..... **CLC 6, 11, 22**
See also CA 49-52; CANR 18, 65; CN; DLB 28; MTCW 1, 2; SATA 22

**Schama, Simon (Michael)** 1945- ..... **CLC 150**
See also BEST 89:4; CA 105; CANR 39, 91

**Schary, Jill**
See Robinson, Jill

**Schell, Jonathan** 1943- ...................... **CLC 35**
See also CA 73-76; CANR 12

**Schelling, Friedrich Wilhelm Joseph von** 1775-1854 ................................. **NCLC 30**
See also DLB 90

**Scherer, Jean-Marie Maurice** 1920-
See Rohmer, Eric
See also CA 110

**Schevill, James (Erwin)** 1920- ........... **CLC 7**
See also CA 5-8R; CAAS 12; CAD; CD

**Schiller, Friedrich von** 1759-1805 .............. **NCLC 39, 69; DAM DRAM; DC 12**
See also DLB 94; EW; RGWL

**Schisgal, Murray (Joseph)** 1926- ....... **CLC 6**
See also CA 21-24R; CAD; CANR 48, 86; CD

**Schlee, Ann** 1934- ............................ **CLC 35**
See also CA 101; CANR 29, 88; SATA 44; SATA-Brief 36

**Schlegel, August Wilhelm von** 1767-1845 ................................. **NCLC 15**
See also DLB 94; RGWL

**Schlegel, Friedrich** 1772-1829 ........ **NCLC 45**
See also DLB 90; EW; RGWL

**Schlegel, Johann Elias (von)** 1719(?)-1749 ................................. **LC 5**

**Schlesinger, Arthur M(eier), Jr.** 1917- ......................................... **CLC 84**
See also AITN 1; CA 1-4R; CANR 1, 28, 58; DLB 17; INT CANR-28; MTCW 1, 2; SATA 61

**Schmidt, Arno (Otto)** 1914-1979 ...... **CLC 56**
See also CA 128; 109; DLB 69

**Schmitz, Aron Hector** 1861-1928
See Svevo, Italo
See also CA 104; 122; MTCW 1

**Schnackenberg, Gjertrud (Cecelia)** 1953- ......................................... **CLC 40**
See also CA 116; CANR 100; CP; CWP; DLB 120; PFS 13

**Schneider, Leonard Alfred** 1925-1966
See Bruce, Lenny
See also CA 89-92

**Schnitzler, Arthur** 1862-1931 . **TCLC 4; SSC 15**
See also CA 104; DLB 81, 118; EW; RGSF; RGWL

**Schoenberg, Arnold Franz Walter** 1874-1951 ................................. **TCLC 75**
See also CA 109; 188

**Schonberg, Arnold**
See Schoenberg, Arnold Franz Walter

**Schopenhauer, Arthur** 1788-1860 .. **NCLC 51**
See also DLB 90; EW

**Schor, Sandra (M.)** 1932(?)-1990 ..... **CLC 65**
See also CA 132

**Schorer, Mark** 1908-1977 .................... **CLC 9**
See also CA 5-8R; 73-76; CANR 7; DLB 103

**Schrader, Paul (Joseph)** 1946- .......... **CLC 26**
See also CA 37-40R; CANR 41; DLB 44

**Schreiner, Olive (Emilie Albertina)** 1855-1920 ................................. **TCLC 9**
See also AFW; BRWS 2; CA 105; 154; DLB 18, 156, 190, 225; FW; RGEL; WLIT 2

**Schulberg, Budd (Wilson)** 1914- .. **CLC 7, 48**
See also BPFB 3; CA 25-28R; CANR 19, 87; CN; DLB 6, 26, 28; DLBY 81

**Schulman, Arnold**
See Trumbo, Dalton

**Schulz, Bruno** 1892-1942 .. **TCLC 5, 51; SSC 13**
See also CA 115; 123; CANR 86; MTCW 2; RGSF; RGWL

**Schulz, Charles M(onroe)** 1922-2000 ........................................ **CLC 12**
See also AAYA 39; CA 9-12R; 187; CANR 6; INT CANR-6; SATA 10; SATA-Obit 118

**Schumacher, E(rnst) F(riedrich)** 1911-1977 ........................................ **CLC 80**
See also CA 81-84; 73-76; CANR 34, 85

**Schuyler, James Marcus** 1923-1991 .. **CLC 5, 23; DAM POET**
See also CA 101; 134; DLB 5, 169; INT 101; WP

**Schwartz, Delmore (David)** 1913-1966 ... **CLC 2, 4, 10, 45, 87; PC 8**
See also AMWS 2; CA 17-18; 25-28R; CANR 35; CAP 2; DLB 28, 48; MTCW 1, 2; PAB; RGAL

**Schwartz, Ernst**
See Ozu, Yasujiro

**Schwartz, John Burnham** 1965- ....... **CLC 59**
See also CA 132

**Schwartz, Lynne Sharon** 1939- ........ **CLC 31**
See also CA 103; CANR 44, 89; MTCW 2

**Schwartz, Muriel A.**
See Eliot, T(homas) S(tearns)

**Schwarz-Bart, Andre** 1928- ............ **CLC 2, 4**
See also CA 89-92

**Schwarz-Bart, Simone** 1938- . **CLC 7; BLCS**
See also BW 2; CA 97-100

**Schwitters, Kurt (Hermann Edward Karl Julius)** 1887-1948 .......... **TCLC 95**
See also CA 158

**Schwob, Marcel (Mayer Andre)** 1867-1905 ................. **TCLC 20**
See also CA 117; 168; DLB 123; GFL 1789 to the Present

**Sciascia, Leonardo** 1921-1989 .. **CLC 8, 9, 41**
See also CA 85-88; 130; CANR 35; DLB 177; MTCW 1; RGWL

**Scoppettone, Sandra** 1936- ............... **CLC 26**
See also Early, Jack
See also AAYA 11; BYA 8; CA 5-8R; CANR 41, 73; GLL 1; SATA 9, 92; YAW

**Scorsese, Martin** 1942- ................ **CLC 20, 89**
See also AAYA 38; CA 110; 114; CANR 46, 85

**Scotland, Jay**
See Jakes, John (William)

**Scott, Duncan Campbell** 1862-1947 ....... **TCLC 6; DAC**
See also CA 104; 153; DLB 92; RGEL

**Scott, Evelyn** 1893-1963 .................... **CLC 43**
See also CA 104; 112; CANR 64; DLB 9, 48; RHW

**Scott, F(rancis) R(eginald)** 1899-1985 ................. **CLC 22**
See also CA 101; 114; CANR 87; DLB 88; INT CA-101; RGEL

**Scott, Frank**
See Scott, F(rancis) R(eginald)

**Scott, Joan** ......................... **CLC 65**

**Scott, Joanna** 1960- ............................ **CLC 50**
See also CA 126; CANR 53, 92

**Scott, Paul (Mark)** 1920-1978 ...... **CLC 9, 60**
See also BRWS 1; CA 81-84; 77-80; CANR 33; DLB 14, 207; MTCW 1; RGEL; RHW

**Scott, Sarah** 1723-1795 ......................... **LC 44**
See also DLB 39

**Scott, Sir Walter** 1771-1832 .... **NCLC 15, 69; DA; DAB; DAC; DAM MST, NOV, POET; PC 13; SSC 32; WLC**
See also AAYA 22; BRW 4; BYA 2; CD-BLB 1789-1832; DLB 93, 107, 116, 144, 159; HGG; LAIT 1; RGEL; RGSF; SSFS 10; SUFW; WLIT 3; YABC 2

**Scribe, (Augustin) Eugene** 1791-1861 ..... **NCLC 16; DAM DRAM; DC 5**
See also DLB 192; GFL 1789 to the Present; RGWL

**Scrum, R.**
See Crumb, R(obert)

**Scudery, Madeleine de** 1607-1701 .. **LC 2, 58**
See also GFL Beginnings to 1789

**Scum**
See Crumb, R(obert)

**Scumbag, Little Bobby**
See Crumb, R(obert)

**Seabrook, John**
See Hubbard, L(afayette) Ron(ald)

**Sealy, I(rwin) Allan** 1951- ................. **CLC 55**
See also CA 136; CN

**Search, Alexander**
See Pessoa, Fernando (Antonio Nogueira)

**Sebastian, Lee**
See Silverberg, Robert

**Sebastian Owl**
See Thompson, Hunter S(tockton)

**Sebestyen, Ouida** 1924- ..................... **CLC 30**
See also AAYA 8; BYA 7; CA 107; CANR 40; CLR 17; JRDA; MAICYA; SAAS 10; SATA 39; YAW

**Secundus, H. Scriblerus**
See Fielding, Henry

**Sedges, John**
See Buck, Pearl S(ydenstricker)

**Sedgwick, Catharine Maria** 1789-1867 ........................ **NCLC 19, 98**
See also DLB 1, 74, 239, 243; RGAL

**Seelye, John (Douglas)** 1931- ............... **CLC 7**
See also CA 97-100; CANR 70; INT 97-100; TCWW 2

**Seferiades, Giorgos Stylianou** 1900-1971
See Seferis, George
See also CA 5-8R; 33-36R; CANR 5, 36; MTCW 1

**Seferis, George** ............................ **CLC 5, 11**
See also Seferiades, Giorgos Stylianou
See also EW; RGWL

**Segal, Erich (Wolf)** 1937- . **CLC 3, 10; DAM POP**
See also BEST 89:1; BPFB 3; CA 25-28R; CANR 20, 36, 65; CPW; DLBY 86; INT CANR-20; MTCW 1

**Seger, Bob** 1945- ................................. **CLC 35**

**Seghers, Anna** ............................ **CLC 7**
See also Radvanyi, Netty
See also DLB 69

**Seidel, Frederick (Lewis)** 1936- ........ **CLC 18**
See also CA 13-16R; CANR 8, 99; CP; DLBY 84

**Seifert, Jaroslav** 1901-1986 .. **CLC 34, 44, 93**
See also CA 127; DLB 215; MTCW 1, 2

**Sei Shonagon** c. 966-1017(?) ........... **CMLC 6**

**Sejour, Victor** 1817-1874 ................... **DC 10**
See also DLB 50

**Sejour Marcou et Ferrand, Juan Victor**
See Sejour, Victor

**Selby, Hubert, Jr.** 1928- ........ **CLC 1, 2, 4, 8; SSC 20**
See also CA 13-16R; CANR 33, 85; CN; DLB 2, 227

**Selzer, Richard** 1928- ......................... **CLC 74**
See also CA 65-68; CANR 14

**Sembene, Ousmane**
See Ousmane, Sembene
See also AFW; CWW 2; WLIT 2

**Senancour, Etienne Pivert de** 1770-1846 ................. **NCLC 16**
See also DLB 119; GFL 1789 to the Present

**Sender, Ramon (Jose)** 1902-1982 ...... **CLC 8; DAM MULT; HLC 2**
See also CA 5-8R; 105; CANR 8; HW 1; MTCW 1; RGWL

**Seneca, Lucius Annaeus** c. 4B.C.-c. 65 ........... **CMLC 6; DAM DRAM; DC 5**
See also AW 2; DLB 211; RGWL

**Senghor, Leopold Sedar** 1906- ......... **CLC 54, 130; BLC 3; DAM MULT, POET; PC 25**
See also AFW; BW 2; CA 116; 125; CANR 47, 74; DNFS; GFL 1789 to the Present; MTCW 1, 2

**Senna, Danzy** 1970- ......................... **CLC 119**
See also CA 169

**Serling, (Edward) Rod(man)** 1924-1975 ................. **CLC 30**
See also AAYA 14; AITN 1; CA 162; 57-60; DLB 26; SFW

**Serna, Ramon Gomez de la**
See Gomez de la Serna, Ramon

**Serpieres**
See Guillevic, (Eugene)

**Service, Robert**
See Service, Robert W(illiam)
See also BYA 4; DAB; DLB 92

**Service, Robert W(illiam)** 1874(?)-1958 ....... **TCLC 15; DA; DAC; DAM MST, POET; WLC**
See also Service, Robert
See also CA 115; 140; CANR 84; PFS 10; RGEL; SATA 20

**Seth, Vikram** 1952- .......... **CLC 43, 90; DAM MULT**
See also CA 121; 127; CANR 50, 74; CN; CP; DA3; DLB 120; INT 127; MTCW 2

**Seton, Cynthia Propper** 1926-1982 .. **CLC 27**
See also CA 5-8R; 108; CANR 7

**Seton, Ernest (Evan) Thompson** 1860-1946 ................. **TCLC 31**
See also ANW; BYA 3; CA 109; CLR 59; DLB 92; DLBD 13; JRDA; SATA 18

**Seton-Thompson, Ernest**
See Seton, Ernest (Evan) Thompson

**Settle, Mary Lee** 1918- ................. **CLC 19, 61**
See also BPFB 3; CA 89-92; CAAS 1; CANR 44, 87; CN; CSW; DLB 6; INT 89-92

**Seuphor, Michel**
See Arp, Jean

**Sevigne, Marie (de Rabutin-Chantal)** 1626-1696 ............................ **LC 11**
See also GFL Beginnings to 1789

**Sewall, Samuel** 1652-1730 .................... **LC 38**
See also DLB 24; RGAL

**Sexton, Anne (Harvey)** 1928-1974 ..... **CLC 2, 4, 6, 8, 10, 15, 53, 123; DA; DAB; DAC; DAM MST, POET; PC 2; WLC**
See also AMWS 2; CA 1-4R; 53-56; CABS 2; CANR 3, 36; CDALB 1941-1968; DA3; DLB 5, 169; EXPP; FW; MAWW; MTCW 1, 2; PAB; PFS 4; RGAL; SATA 10

**Shaara, Jeff** 1952- ............................. **CLC 119**
See also CA 163

**Shaara, Michael (Joseph, Jr.)** 1929-1988 ............... **CLC 15; DAM POP**
See also AITN 1; BPFB 3; CA 102; 125; CANR 52, 85; DLBY 83

**Shackleton, C. C.**
See Aldiss, Brian W(ilson)

**Shacochis, Bob** ............................. **CLC 39**
See also Shacochis, Robert G.

**Shacochis, Robert G.** 1951-
See Shacochis, Bob
See also CA 119; 124; CANR 100; INT 124

**Shaffer, Anthony (Joshua)** 1926- ...... **CLC 19; DAM DRAM**
See also CA 110; 116; CBD; CD; DFS 13; DLB 13

**Shaffer, Peter (Levin)** 1926- .. **CLC 5, 14, 18, 37, 60; DAB; DAM DRAM, MST; DC 7**
See also BRWS 1; CA 25-28R; CANR 25, 47, 74; CBD; CD; CDBLB 1960 to Present; DA3; DFS 5, 13; DLB 13, 233; MTCW 1, 2; RGEL

**Shakey, Bernard**
See Young, Neil

**Shalamov, Varlam (Tikhonovich)** 1907(?)-1982 ................ **CLC 18**
See also CA 129; 105; RGSF

**Shamlu, Ahmad** 1925-2000 ............... **CLC 10**
See also CWW 2

**Shammas, Anton** 1951- ..................... **CLC 55**

**Shandling, Arline**
See Berriault, Gina

**Shange, Ntozake** 1948- .... **CLC 8, 25, 38, 74, 126; BLC 3; DAM DRAM, MULT; DC 3**
See also AAYA 9; AFAW 1, 2; BW 2; CA 85-88; CABS 3; CAD; CANR 27, 48, 74; CD; CP; CWD; CWP; DA3; DFS 2, 11; DLB 38; FW; LAIT 5; MTCW 1, 2; NFS 11; RGAL; YAW

**Shanley, John Patrick** 1950- ............. **CLC 75**
See also CA 128; 133; CAD; CANR 83; CD

**Shapcott, Thomas W(illiam)** 1935- .. **CLC 38**
See also CA 69-72; CANR 49, 83, 103; CP

**Shapiro, Jane** .................. **CLC 76**
**Shapiro, Karl (Jay)** 1913-2000 ...... **CLC 4, 8, 15, 53; PC 25**
  See also AMWS 2; CA 1-4R; 188; CAAS 6; CANR 1, 36, 66; CP; DLB 48; EXPP; MTCW 1, 2; PFS 3; RGAL
**Sharp, William** 1855-1905 ............. **TCLC 39**
  See also Macleod, Fiona
  See also CA 160; DLB 156; RGEL
**Sharpe, Thomas Ridley** 1928-
  See Sharpe, Tom
  See also CA 114; 122; CANR 85; CN; DLB 231; INT 122
**Sharpe, Tom** ........................... **CLC 36**
  See also Sharpe, Thomas Ridley
  See also DLB 14
**Shatrov, Mikhail** ..................... **CLC 59**
**Shaw, Bernard**
  See Shaw, George Bernard
  See also BW 1; MTCW 2
**Shaw, G. Bernard**
  See Shaw, George Bernard
**Shaw, George Bernard** 1856-1950 .. **TCLC 3, 9, 21, 45; DA; DAB; DAC; DAM DRAM, MST; WLC**
  See also Shaw, Bernard
  See also BRW 6; CA 104; 128; CDBLB 1914-1945; DA3; DFS 1, 3, 6, 11; DLB 10, 57, 190; LAIT 3; MTCW 1, 2; RGEL; WLIT 4
**Shaw, Henry Wheeler** 1818-1885 .. **NCLC 15**
  See also DLB 11; RGAL
**Shaw, Irwin** 1913-1984 .......... **CLC 7, 23, 34; DAM POP**
  See also AITN 1; BPFB 3; CA 13-16R; 112; CANR 21; CDALB 1941-1968; CPW; DLB 6, 102; DLBY 84; MTCW 1, 21
**Shaw, Robert** 1927-1978 .................... **CLC 5**
  See also AITN 1; CA 1-4R; 81-84; CANR 4; DLB 13, 14
**Shaw, T. E.**
  See Lawrence, T(homas) E(dward)
**Shawn, Wallace** 1943- ...................... **CLC 41**
  See also CA 112; CAD; CD
**Shchedrin, N.**
  See Saltykov, Mikhail Evgrafovich
**Shea, Lisa** 1953- ............................ **CLC 86**
  See also CA 147
**Sheed, Wilfrid (John Joseph)** 1930- . **CLC 2, 4, 10, 53**
  See also CA 65-68; CANR 30, 66; CN; DLB 6; MTCW 1, 2
**Sheldon, Alice Hastings Bradley** 1915(?)-1987
  See Tiptree, James, Jr.
  See also CA 108; 122; CANR 34; INT 108; MTCW 1
**Sheldon, John**
  See Bloch, Robert (Albert)
**Sheldon, Walter J(ames)** 1917-1996
  See Queen, Ellery
  See also AITN 1; CA 25-28R; CANR 10
**Shelley, Mary Wollstonecraft (Godwin)** 1797-1851 ........ **NCLC 14, 59, 103; DA; DAB; DAC; DAM MST, NOV; WLC**
  See also AAYA 20; BPFB 3; BRW 3; BRWS 3; BYA 5; CDBLB 1789-1832; DA3; DLB 110, 116, 159, 178; EXPN; HGG; LAIT 1; NFS 1; RGEL; SATA 29; SCFW; SFW; WLIT 3
**Shelley, Percy Bysshe** 1792-1822 .. **NCLC 18, 93; DA; DAB; DAC; DAM MST, POET; PC 14; WLC**
  See also BRW 4; CDBLB 1789-1832; DA3; DLB 96, 110, 158; EXPP; PAB; PFS 2; RGEL; WLIT 3; WP
**Shepard, Jim** 1956- .......................... **CLC 36**
  See also CA 137; CANR 59; SATA 90

**Shepard, Lucius** 1947- ..................... **CLC 34**
  See also CA 128; 141; CANR 81; HGG; SCFW 2; SFW
**Shepard, Sam** 1943- .... **CLC 4, 6, 17, 34, 41, 44; DAM DRAM; DC 5**
  See also AAYA 1; AMWS 3; CA 69-72; CABS 3; CAD; CANR 22; CD; DA3; DFS 3,6,7; DLB 7, 212; IDFW 3, 4; MTCW 1, 2; RGAL
**Shepherd, Michael**
  See Ludlum, Robert
**Sherburne, Zoa (Lillian Morin)** 1912-1995 .................................. **CLC 30**
  See also AAYA 13; CA 1-4R; 176; CANR 3, 37; MAICYA; SAAS 18; SATA 3; YAW
**Sheridan, Frances** 1724-1766 .................. **LC 7**
  See also DLB 39, 84
**Sheridan, Richard Brinsley** 1751-1816 ........... **NCLC 5, 91; DA; DAB; DAC; DAM DRAM, MST; DC 1; WLC**
  See also BRW 3; CDBLB 1660-1789; DFS 4; DLB 89; RGEL; WLIT 3
**Sherman, Jonathan Marc** ................. **CLC 55**
**Sherman, Martin** 1941(?)- ................. **CLC 19**
  See also CA 116; 123; CANR 86
**Sherwin, Judith Johnson**
  See Johnson, Judith (Emlyn)
  See also CANR 85; CP; CWP
**Sherwood, Frances** 1940- .................. **CLC 81**
  See also CA 146
**Sherwood, Robert E(mmet)** 1896-1955 ......... **TCLC 3; DAM DRAM**
  See also CA 104; 153; CANR 86; DFS 11; DLB 7, 26; IDFW 3, 4; RGAL
**Shestov, Lev** 1866-1938 ................... **TCLC 56**
**Shevchenko, Taras** 1814-1861 ........ **NCLC 54**
**Shiel, M(atthew) P(hipps)** 1865-1947 ................................ **TCLC 8**
  See also Holmes, Gordon
  See also CA 106; 160; DLB 153; HGG; MTCW 2; SFW; SUFW
**Shields, Carol** 1935- ....... **CLC 91, 113; DAC**
  See also AMWS 7; CA 81-84; CANR 51, 74, 98; CCA 1; CN; CPW; DA3; MTCW 2
**Shields, David** 1956- ...................... **CLC 97**
  See also CA 124; CANR 48, 99
**Shiga, Naoya** 1883-1971 ..... **CLC 33; SSC 23**
  See also CA 101; 33-36R; DLB 180; MJW
**Shilts, Randy** 1951-1994 ................... **CLC 85**
  See also AAYA 19; CA 115; 127; 144; CANR 45; DA3; GLL 1; INT 127; MTCW 2
**Shimazaki, Haruki** 1872-1943
  See Shimazaki Toson
  See also CA 105; 134; CANR 84
**Shimazaki Toson** ...................... **TCLC 5**
  See also Shimazaki, Haruki
  See also DLB 180
**Sholokhov, Mikhail (Aleksandrovich)** 1905-1984 ............... **CLC 7, 15**
  See also CA 101; 112; MTCW 1, 2; RGWL; SATA-Obit 36
**Shone, Patric**
  See Hanley, James
**Shreve, Susan Richards** 1939- .......... **CLC 23**
  See also CA 49-52; CAAS 5; CANR 5, 38, 69, 100; MAICYA; SATA 46, 95; SATA-Brief 41
**Shue, Larry** 1946-1985 .......... **CLC 52; DAM DRAM**
  See also CA 145; 117; DFS 7
**Shu-Jen, Chou** 1881-1936
  See Lu Hsun
  See also CA 104
**Shulman, Alix Kates** 1932- ........... **CLC 2, 10**
  See also CA 29-32R; CANR 43; FW; SATA 7

**Shuster, Joe** 1914-1992 ..................... **CLC 21**
**Shute, Nevil** ..................... **CLC 30**
  See also Norway, Nevil Shute
  See also BPFB 3; MTCW 2; NFS 9
**Shuttle, Penelope (Diane)** 1947- .......... **CLC 7**
  See also CA 93-96; CANR 39, 84, 92; CP; CWP; DLB 14, 40
**Sidney, Mary** 1561-1621 ................. **LC 19, 39**
**Sidney, Sir Philip** 1554-1586 ........ **LC 19, 39; DA; DAB; DAC; DAM MST, POET; PC 32**
  See also BRW 1; CDBLB Before 1660; DA3; DLB 167; EXPP; PAB; RGEL; TEA; WP
**Siegel, Jerome** 1914-1996 ................. **CLC 21**
  See also CA 116; 169; 151
**Siegel, Jerry**
  See Siegel, Jerome
**Sienkiewicz, Henryk (Adam Alexander Pius)** 1846-1916 ................................ **TCLC 3**
  See also CA 104; 134; CANR 84; RGSF; RGWL
**Sierra, Gregorio Martinez**
  See Martinez Sierra, Gregorio
**Sierra, Maria (de la O'LeJarraga) Martinez**
  See Martinez Sierra, Maria (de la O'LeJarraga)
**Sigal, Clancy** 1926- ......................... **CLC 7**
  See also CA 1-4R; CANR 85; CN
**Sigourney, Lydia Howard (Huntley)** 1791-1865 ............................ **NCLC 21, 87**
  See also DLB 1, 42, 73, 239, 243
**Siguenza y Gongora, Carlos de** 1645-1700 ...................... **LC 8; HLCS 2**
  See also LAW
**Sigurjonsson, Johann** 1880-1919 ... **TCLC 27**
  See also CA 170
**Sikelianos, Angelos** 1884-1951 ...... **TCLC 39; PC 29**
  See also RGWL
**Silkin, Jon** 1930-1997 .................. **CLC 2, 6, 43**
  See also CA 5-8R; CAAS 5; CANR 89; CP; DLB 27
**Silko, Leslie (Marmon)** 1948- ..... **CLC 23, 74, 114; DA; DAC; DAM MST, MULT, POP; SSC 37; WLCS**
  See also AAYA 14; AMWS 4; ANW; BYA 12; CA 115; 122; CANR 45, 65; CN; CP; CPW 1; CWP; DA3; DLB 143, 175; EXPP; EXPS; LAIT 4; MTCW 2; NFS 4; NNAL; PFS 9; RGAL; RGSF; SSFS 4, 8, 10, 11
**Sillanpaa, Frans Eemil** 1888-1964 ... **CLC 19**
  See also CA 129; 93-96; MTCW 1
**Sillitoe, Alan** 1928- .. **CLC 1, 3, 6, 10, 19, 57, 148**
  See also AITN 1; BRWS 5; CA 9-12R; CAAE 191; CAAS 2; CANR 8, 26, 55; CDBLB 1960 to Present; CN; DLB 14, 139; MTCW 1, 2; RGEL; RGSF; SATA 61
**Silone, Ignazio** 1900-1978 ................... **CLC 4**
  See also CA 25-28; 81-84; CANR 34; CAP 2; EW; MTCW 1; RGSF; RGWL
**Silone, Ignazione**
  See Silone, Ignazio
**Silver, Joan Micklin** 1935- ................. **CLC 20**
  See also CA 114; 121; INT 121
**Silver, Nicholas**
  See Faust, Frederick (Schiller)
  See also TCWW 2
**Silverberg, Robert** 1935- ........... **CLC 7, 140; DAM POP**
  See also AAYA 24; BPFB 3; BYA 7, 9; CA 1-4R; 186; CAAE 186; CAAS 5; CANR 1, 20, 36, 85; CLR 59; CN; CPW; DLB 8; INT CANR-20; MAICYA; MTCW 1, 2; SATA 13, 91; SATA-Essay 104; SCFW 2; SFW

**Silverstein, Alvin** 1933- .................... **CLC 17**
See also CA 49-52; CANR 2; CLR 25; JRDA; MAICYA; SATA 8, 69, 124

**Silverstein, Virginia B(arbara Opshelor)** 1937- ............................................ **CLC 17**
See also CA 49-52; CANR 2; CLR 25; JRDA; MAICYA; SATA 8, 69, 124

**Sim, Georges**
See Simenon, Georges (Jacques Christian)

**Simak, Clifford D(onald)** 1904-1988 . **CLC 1, 55**
See also CA 1-4R; 125; CANR 1, 35; DLB 8; MTCW 1; SATA-Obit 56; SFW

**Simenon, Georges (Jacques Christian)** 1903-1989 .......... **CLC 1, 2, 3, 8, 18, 47; DAM POP**
See also BPFB 3; CA 85-88; 129; CANR 35; CMW; DA3; DLB 72; DLBY 89; EW; GFL 1789 to the Present; MSW; MTCW 1, 2; RGWL

**Simic, Charles** 1938- .... **CLC 6, 9, 22, 49, 68, 130; DAM POET**
See also AMWS 8; CA 29-32R; CAAS 4; CANR 12, 33, 52, 61, 96; CP; DA3; DLB 105; MTCW 2; PFS 7; RGAL; WP

**Simmel, Georg** 1858-1918 ............... **TCLC 64**
See also CA 157

**Simmons, Charles (Paul)** 1924- ........ **CLC 57**
See also CA 89-92; INT 89-92

**Simmons, Dan** 1948- .... **CLC 44; DAM POP**
See also AAYA 16; CA 138; CANR 53, 81; CPW; HGG

**Simmons, James (Stewart Alexander)** 1933- ............................................ **CLC 43**
See also CA 105; CAAS 21; CP; DLB 40

**Simms, William Gilmore** 1806-1870 .................................. **NCLC 3**
See also DLB 3, 30, 59, 73; RGAL

**Simon, Carly** 1945- ........................... **CLC 26**
See also CA 105

**Simon, Claude** 1913-1984 . **CLC 4, 9, 15, 39; DAM NOV**
See also CA 89-92; CANR 33; DLB 83; EW; GFL 1789 to the Present; MTCW 1

**Simon, Myles**
See Follett, Ken(neth Martin)

**Simon, (Marvin) Neil** 1927- ... **CLC 6, 11, 31, 39, 70; DAM DRAM; DC 14**
See also AAYA 32; AITN 1; AMWS 4; CA 21-24R; CANR 26, 54, 87; CD; DA3; DFS 2, 6, 12; DLB 7; LAIT 4; MTCW 1, 2; RGAL

**Simon, Paul (Frederick)** 1941(?)- ..... **CLC 17**
See also CA 116; 153

**Simonon, Paul** 1956(?)- ..................... **CLC 30**

**Simonson, Rick ed.** ........................... **CLC 70**

**Simpson, Harriette**
See Arnow, Harriette (Louisa) Simpson

**Simpson, Louis (Aston Marantz)** 1923- .......... **CLC 4, 7, 9, 32, 149; DAM POET**
See also AMWS 9; CA 1-4R; CAAS 4; CANR 1, 61; CP; DLB 5; MTCW 1, 2; PFS 7, 11; RGAL

**Simpson, Mona (Elizabeth)** 1957- ... **CLC 44, 146**
See also CA 122; 135; CANR 68, 103; CN

**Simpson, N(orman) F(rederick)** 1919- ............................................ **CLC 29**
See also CA 13-16R; CBD; DLB 13; RGEL

**Sinclair, Andrew (Annandale)** 1935- . **CLC 2, 14**
See also CA 9-12R; CAAS 5; CANR 14, 38, 91; CN; DLB 14; FANT; MTCW 1

**Sinclair, Emil**
See Hesse, Hermann

**Sinclair, Iain** 1943- ........................... **CLC 76**
See also CA 132; CANR 81; CP; HGG

**Sinclair, Iain MacGregor**
See Sinclair, Iain

**Sinclair, Irene**
See Griffith, D(avid Lewelyn) W(ark)

**Sinclair, Mary Amelia St. Clair** 1865(?)-1946
See Sinclair, May
See also CA 104; HGG; RHW

**Sinclair, May** ............... **TCLC 3, 11**
See also Sinclair, Mary Amelia St. Clair
See also CA 166; DLB 36, 135; RGEL

**Sinclair, Roy**
See Griffith, D(avid Lewelyn) W(ark)

**Sinclair, Upton (Beall)** 1878-1968 ..... **CLC 1, 11, 15, 63; DA; DAB; DAC; DAM MST, NOV; WLC**
See also AMWS 5; BPFB 3; BYA 2; CA 5-8R; 25-28R; CANR 7; CDALB 1929-1941; DA3; DLB 9; INT CANR-7; LAIT 3; MTCW 1, 2; NFS 6; RGAL; SATA 9; YAW

**Singer, Isaac**
See Singer, Isaac Bashevis

**Singer, Isaac Bashevis** 1904-1991 .. **CLC 1, 3, 6, 9, 11, 15, 23, 38, 69, 111; DA; DAB; DAC; DAM MST, NOV; SSC 3; WLC**
See also AAYA 32; AITN 1, 2; AMW; BPFB 3; BYA 1, 4; CA 1-4R; 134; CANR 1, 39; CDALB 1941-1968; CLR 1; CWRI; DA3; DLB 6, 28, 52; DLBY 91; EXPS; HGG; JRDA; LAIT 3; MAICYA; MTCW 1, 2; RGAL; RGSF; SATA 3, 27; SATA-Obit 68; SSFS 2, 12

**Singer, Israel Joshua** 1893-1944 .... **TCLC 33**
See also CA 169

**Singh, Khushwant** 1915- ................... **CLC 11**
See also CA 9-12R; CAAS 9; CANR 6, 84; CN; RGEL

**Singleton, Ann**
See Benedict, Ruth (Fulton)

**Sinjohn, John**
See Galsworthy, John

**Sinyavsky, Andrei (Donatevich)** 1925-1997 ....................................... **CLC 8**
See also Tertz, Abram
See also CA 85-88; 159

**Sirin, V.**
See Nabokov, Vladimir (Vladimirovich)

**Sissman, L(ouis) E(dward)** 1928-1976 ....................................... **CLC 9, 18**
See also CA 21-24R; 65-68; CANR 13; DLB 5

**Sisson, C(harles) H(ubert)** 1914- ........ **CLC 8**
See also CA 1-4R; CAAS 3; CANR 3, 48, 84; CP; DLB 27

**Sitwell, Dame Edith** 1887-1964 ..... **CLC 2, 9, 67; DAM POET; PC 3**
See also BRW 7; CA 9-12R; CANR 35; CDBLB 1945-1960; DLB 20; MTCW 1, 2; RGEL

**Siwaarmill, H. P.**
See Sharp, William

**Sjoewall, Maj** 1935- .......................... **CLC 7**
See also Sjowall, Maj
See also CA 65-68; CANR 73

**Sjowall, Maj**
See Sjoewall, Maj
See also BPFB 3; CMW 1; MSW

**Skelton, John** 1460(?)-1529 ..... **LC 71; PC 25**
See also BRW 1; RGEL

**Skelton, Robin** 1925-1997 ................. **CLC 13**
See also Zuk, Georges
See also AITN 2; CA 5-8R; 160; CAAS 5; CANR 28, 89; CCA 1; CP; DLB 27, 53

**Skolimowski, Jerzy** 1938- .................. **CLC 20**
See also CA 128

**Skram, Amalie (Bertha)** 1847-1905 .................................. **TCLC 25**
See also CA 165

**Skvorecky, Josef (Vaclav)** 1924- ...... **CLC 15, 39, 69; DAC; DAM NOV**
See also CA 61-64; CAAS 1; CANR 10, 34, 63; DA3; DLB 232; MTCW 1, 2

**Slade, Bernard** ........................ **CLC 11, 46**
See also Newbound, Bernard Slade
See also CAAS 9; CCA 1; DLB 53

**Slaughter, Carolyn** 1946- ................... **CLC 56**
See also CA 85-88; CANR 85; CN

**Slaughter, Frank G(ill)** 1908-2001 ... **CLC 29**
See also AITN 2; CA 5-8R; CANR 5, 85; INT CANR-5; RHW

**Slavitt, David R(ytman)** 1935- ...... **CLC 5, 14**
See also CA 21-24R; CAAS 3; CANR 41, 83; CP; DLB 5, 6

**Slesinger, Tess** 1905-1945 ................ **TCLC 10**
See also CA 107; DLB 102

**Slessor, Kenneth** 1901-1971 .............. **CLC 14**
See also CA 102; 89-92; RGEL

**Slowacki, Juliusz** 1809-1849 ............ **NCLC 15**

**Smart, Christopher** 1722-1771 .. **LC 3; DAM POET; PC 13**
See also DLB 109; RGEL

**Smart, Elizabeth** 1913-1986 ............. **CLC 54**
See also CA 81-84; 118; DLB 88

**Smiley, Jane (Graves)** 1949- ...... **CLC 53, 76, 144; DAM POP**
See also AMWS 6; BPFB 3; CA 104; CANR 30, 50, 74, 96; CN; CPW 1; DA3; DLB 227, 234; INT CANR-30

**Smith, A(rthur) J(ames) M(arshall)** 1902-1980 ...................... **CLC 15; DAC**
See also CA 1-4R; 102; CANR 4; DLB 88; RGEL

**Smith, Adam** 1723-1790 ...................... **LC 36**
See also DLB 104; RGEL

**Smith, Alexander** 1829-1867 .......... **NCLC 59**
See also DLB 32, 55

**Smith, Anna Deavere** 1950- ............... **CLC 86**
See also CA 133; CANR 103; CD; DFS 2

**Smith, Betty (Wehner)** 1904-1972 .... **CLC 19**
See also BPFB 3; BYA 3; CA 5-8R; 33-36R; DLBY 82; LAIT 3; RGAL; SATA 6

**Smith, Charlotte (Turner)** 1749-1806 .................................. **NCLC 23**
See also DLB 39, 109; RGEL

**Smith, Clark Ashton** 1893-1961 ........ **CLC 43**
See also CA 143; CANR 81; FANT; HGG; MTCW 2; SFW

**Smith, Dave** ................ **CLC 22, 42**
See also Smith, David (Jeddie)
See also CAAS 7; DLB 5

**Smith, David (Jeddie)** 1942-
See Smith, Dave
See also CA 49-52; CANR 1, 59; CP; CSW; DAM POET

**Smith, Florence Margaret** 1902-1971
See Smith, Stevie
See also CA 17-18; 29-32R; CANR 35; CAP 2; DAM POET; MTCW 1, 2

**Smith, Iain Crichton** 1928-1998 ....... **CLC 64**
See also CA 21-24R; 171; CN; CP; DLB 40, 139; RGSF

**Smith, John** 1580(?)-1631 ...................... **LC 9**
See also DLB 24, 30; TUS

**Smith, Johnston**
See Crane, Stephen (Townley)

**Smith, Joseph, Jr.** 1805-1844 ......... **NCLC 53**

**Smith, Lee** 1944- .......................... **CLC 25, 73**
See also CA 114; 119; CANR 46; CSW; DLB 143; DLBY 83; INT CA-119; RGAL

**Smith, Martin**
See Smith, Martin Cruz

**Smith, Martin Cruz** 1942- .... **CLC 25; DAM MULT, POP**
See also BEST 89:4; BPFB 3; CA 85-88; CANR 6, 23, 43, 65; CMW; CPW; HGG; INT CANR-23; MTCW 2; NNAL; RGAL

**Smith, Mary-Ann Tirone** 1944- ........ **CLC 39**
See also CA 118; 136

**Smith, Patti** 1946- ........................... **CLC 12**
See also CA 93-96; CANR 63

**Smith, Pauline (Urmson)**
1882-1959 ............................ **TCLC 25**
See also DLB 225

**Smith, Rosamond**
See Oates, Joyce Carol

**Smith, Sheila Kaye**
See Kaye-Smith, Sheila

**Smith, Stevie** ......... **CLC 3, 8, 25, 44; PC 12**
See also Smith, Florence Margaret
See also BRWS 2; DLB 20; MTCW 2; PAB; PFS 3; RGEL

**Smith, Wilbur (Addison)** 1933- ........ **CLC 33**
See also CA 13-16R; CANR 7, 46, 66; CPW; MTCW 1, 2

**Smith, William Jay** 1918- ................... **CLC 6**
See also CA 5-8R; CANR 44; CP; CSW; CWRI; DLB 5; MAICYA; SAAS 22; SATA 2, 68

**Smith, Woodrow Wilson**
See Kuttner, Henry

**Smolenskin, Peretz** 1842-1885 ....... **NCLC 30**

**Smollett, Tobias (George)** 1721-1771 ... **LC 2, 46**
See also BRW 3; CDBLB 1660-1789; DLB 39, 104; RGEL

**Snodgrass, W(illiam) D(e Witt)**
1926- .......... **CLC 2, 6, 10, 18, 68; DAM POET**
See also AMWS 6; CA 1-4R; CANR 6, 36, 65, 85; CP; DLB 5; MTCW 1, 2; RGAL

**Snow, C(harles) P(ercy)** 1905-1980 ... **CLC 1, 4, 6, 9, 13, 19; DAM NOV**
See also BRW 7; CA 5-8R; 101; CANR 28; CDBLB 1945-1960; DLB 15, 77; DLBD 17; MTCW 1, 2; RGEL

**Snow, Frances Compton**
See Adams, Henry (Brooks)

**Snyder, Gary (Sherman)** 1930- . **CLC 1, 2, 5, 9, 32, 120; DAM POET; PC 21**
See also AMWS 8; ANW; CA 17-20R; CANR 30, 60; CP; DA3; DLB 5, 16, 165, 212, 237; MTCW 2; PFS 9; RGAL; WP

**Snyder, Zilpha Keatley** 1927- ........... **CLC 17**
See also AAYA 15; BYA 1; CA 9-12R; CANR 38; CLR 31; JRDA; MAICYA; SAAS 2; SATA 1, 28, 75, 110; SATA-Essay 112; YAW

**Soares, Bernardo**
See Pessoa, Fernando (Antonio Nogueira)

**Sobh, A.**
See Shamlu, Ahmad

**Sobol, Joshua** .................................. **CLC 60**
See also CWW 2

**Socrates** 470B.C.-399B.C. .............. **CMLC 27**

**Soderberg, Hjalmar** 1869-1941 ...... **TCLC 39**
See also RGSF

**Sodergran, Edith (Irene)**
See Soedergran, Edith (Irene)
See also RGWL

**Soedergran, Edith (Irene)**
1892-1923 ............................. **TCLC 31**
See also Sodergran, Edith (Irene)
See also EW

**Softly, Edgar**
See Lovecraft, H(oward) P(hillips)

**Softly, Edward**
See Lovecraft, H(oward) P(hillips)

**Sokolov, Raymond** 1941- .................... **CLC 7**
See also CA 85-88

**Sokolov, Sasha** ................................. **CLC 59**

**Solo, Jay**
See Ellison, Harlan (Jay)

**Sologub, Fyodor** ............................... **TCLC 9**
See also Teternikov, Fyodor Kuzmich

**Solomon, Northup** 1808-1863 ...... **NCLC 105**

**Solomons, Ikey Esquir**
See Thackeray, William Makepeace

**Solomos, Dionysios** 1798-1857 ....... **NCLC 15**

**Solwoska, Mara**
See French, Marilyn

**Solzhenitsyn, Aleksandr I(sayevich)**
1918- .. **CLC 1, 2, 4, 7, 9, 10, 18, 26, 34, 78, 134; DA; DAB; DAC; DAM MST, NOV; SSC 32; WLC**
See also AITN 1; BPFB 3; CA 69-72; CANR 40, 65; DA3; EW; EXPS; LAIT 4; MTCW 1, 2; NFS 6; RGSF; RGWL; SSFS 9

**Somers, Jane**
See Lessing, Doris (May)

**Somerville, Edith** 1858-1949 .......... **TCLC 51**
See also DLB 135; RGEL; RGSF

**Somerville & Ross**
See Martin, Violet Florence; Somerville, Edith

**Sommer, Scott** 1951- .......................... **CLC 25**
See also CA 106

**Sondheim, Stephen (Joshua)** 1930- . **CLC 30, 39, 147; DAM DRAM**
See also AAYA 11; CA 103; CANR 47, 67; LAIT 4

**Song, Cathy** 1955- ............................. **PC 21**
See also CA 154; CWP; DLB 169; EXPP; FW; PFS 5

**Sontag, Susan** 1933- .... **CLC 1, 2, 10, 13, 31, 105; DAM POP**
See also AMWS 3; CA 17-20R; CANR 25, 51, 74, 97; CN; CPW; DA3; DLB 2, 67; MAWW; MTCW 1, 2; RGAL; RHW; SSFS 10

**Sophocles** 496(?)B.C.-406(?)B.C. .... **CMLC 2, 47; DA; DAB; DAC; DAM DRAM, MST; DC 1; WLCS**
See also AW 1; DA3; DFS 1, 4, 8; DLB 176; LAIT 1; RGWL

**Sordello** 1189-1269 ......................... **CMLC 15**

**Sorel, Georges** 1847-1922 ............... **TCLC 91**
See also CA 118; 188

**Sorel, Julia**
See Drexler, Rosalyn

**Sorokin, Vladimir** ............................ **CLC 59**

**Sorrentino, Gilbert** 1929- .. **CLC 3, 7, 14, 22, 40**
See also CA 77-80; CANR 14, 33; CN; CP; DLB 5, 173; DLBY 80; INT CANR-14

**Soto, Gary** 1952- .................... **CLC 32, 80; DAM MULT; HLC 2; PC 28**
See also AAYA 10, 37; BYA 11; CA 119; 125; CANR 50, 74; CLR 38; CP; DLB 82; EXPP; HW 1, 2; INT JRDA; MTCW 2; PFS 7; RGAL; SATA 80, 120; YAW

**Soupault, Philippe** 1897-1990 ........... **CLC 68**
See also CA 116; 147; 131; GFL 1789 to the Present

**Souster, (Holmes) Raymond** 1921- .... **CLC 5, 14; DAC; DAM POET**
See also CA 13-16R; CAAS 14; CANR 13, 29, 53; CP; DA3; DLB 88; RGEL; SATA 63

**Southern, Terry** 1924(?)-1995 ............ **CLC 7**
See also BPFB 3; CA 1-4R; 150; CANR 1, 55; CN; DLB 2; IDFW 3, 4

**Southey, Robert** 1774-1843 ........ **NCLC 8, 97**
See also BRW 4; DLB 93, 107, 142; RGEL; SATA 54

**Southworth, Emma Dorothy Eliza Nevitte**
1819-1899 ................................ **NCLC 26**
See also DLB 239

**Souza, Ernest**
See Scott, Evelyn

**Soyinka, Wole** 1934- .... **CLC 3, 5, 14, 36, 44; BLC 3; DA; DAB; DAC; DAM DRAM, MST, MULT; DC 2; WLC**
See also AFW; BW 2, 3; CA 13-16R; CANR 27, 39, 82; CD; CN; CP; DA3; DFS 10; DLB 125; MTCW 1, 2; RGEL; WLIT 2

**Spackman, W(illiam) M(ode)**
1905-1990 ................................. **CLC 46**
See also CA 81-84; 132

**Spacks, Barry (Bernard)** 1931- ........ **CLC 14**
See also CA 154; CANR 33; CP; DLB 105

**Spanidou, Irini** 1946- ......................... **CLC 44**
See also CA 185

**Spark, Muriel (Sarah)** 1918- ..... **CLC 2, 3, 5, 8, 13, 18, 40, 94; DAB; DAC; DAM MST, NOV; SSC 10**
See also BRWS 1; CA 5-8R; CANR 12, 36, 76, 89; CDBLB 1945-1960; CN; CP; DA3; DLB 15, 139; FW; INT CANR-12; LAIT 4; MTCW 1, 2; RGEL; WLIT 4; YAW

**Spaulding, Douglas**
See Bradbury, Ray (Douglas)

**Spaulding, Leonard**
See Bradbury, Ray (Douglas)

**Spelman, Elizabeth** ......................... **CLC 65**

**Spence, J. A. D.**
See Eliot, T(homas) S(tearns)

**Spencer, Elizabeth** 1921- ................. **CLC 22**
See also CA 13-16R; CANR 32, 65, 87; CN; CSW; DLB 6; MTCW 1; RGAL; SATA 14

**Spencer, Leonard G.**
See Silverberg, Robert

**Spencer, Scott** 1945- ......................... **CLC 30**
See also CA 113; CANR 51; DLBY 86

**Spender, Stephen (Harold)**
1909-1995 ........ **CLC 1, 2, 5, 10, 41, 91; DAM POET**
See also BRWS 2; CA 9-12R; 149; CANR 31, 54; CDBLB 1945-1960; CP; DA3; DLB 20; MTCW 1, 2; PAB; RGEL

**Spengler, Oswald (Arnold Gottfried)**
1880-1936 ............................... **TCLC 25**
See also CA 118; 189

**Spenser, Edmund** 1552(?)-1599 ...... **LC 5, 39; DA; DAB; DAC; DAM MST, POET; PC 8; WLC**
See also BRW 1; CDBLB Before 1660; DA3; DLB 167; EFS 2; EXPP; PAB; RGEL; WLIT 3; WP

**Spicer, Jack** 1925-1965 .......... **CLC 8, 18, 72; DAM POET**
See also CA 85-88; DLB 5, 16, 193; GLL 1; WP

**Spiegelman, Art** 1948- ...................... **CLC 76**
See also AAYA 10; CA 125; CANR 41, 55, 74; MTCW 2; SATA 109; YAW

**Spielberg, Peter** 1929- ........................ **CLC 6**
See also CA 5-8R; CANR 4, 48; DLBY 81

**Spielberg, Steven** 1947- .................... **CLC 20**
See also AAYA 8, 24; CA 77-80; CANR 32; SATA 32

**Spillane, Frank Morrison** 1918-
See Spillane, Mickey
See also CA 25-28R; CANR 28, 63; DA3; DLB 226; MTCW 1, 2; SATA 66

**Spillane, Mickey** ........................... **CLC 3, 13**
See also Spillane, Frank Morrison
See also BPFB 3; CMW; DLB 226; MSW; MTCW 2

**Spinoza, Benedictus de** 1632-1677 .. **LC 9, 58**

**Spinrad, Norman (Richard)** 1940- ... **CLC 46**
See also BPFB 3; CA 37-40R; CAAS 19; CANR 20, 91; DLB 8; INT CANR-20; SFW

**Spitteler, Carl (Friedrich Georg)**
1845-1924 .................... **TCLC 12**
See also CA 109; DLB 129

**Spivack, Kathleen (Romola Drucker)**
1938- ................................. **CLC 6**
See also CA 49-52

**Spoto, Donald** 1941- .................... **CLC 39**
See also CA 65-68; CANR 11, 57, 93

**Springsteen, Bruce (F.)** 1949- .......... **CLC 17**
See also CA 111

**Spurling, Hilary** 1940- ................ **CLC 34**
See also CA 104; CANR 25, 52, 94

**Spyker, John Howland**
See Elman, Richard (Martin)

**Squires, (James) Radcliffe**
1917-1993 ............................. **CLC 51**
See also CA 1-4R; 140; CANR 6, 21

**Srivastava, Dhanpat Rai** 1880(?)-1936
See Premchand
See also CA 118

**Stacy, Donald**
See Pohl, Frederick

**Stael**
See Stael-Holstein, Anne Louise Germaine Necker
See also RGWL

**Stael, Germaine de** ................ **NCLC 91**
See also Stael-Holstein, Anne Louise Germaine Necker
See also DLB 119, 192; FW; GFL 1789 to the Present

**Stael-Holstein, Anne Louise Germaine Necker** 1766-1817 .................... **NCLC 3**
See also Stael; Stael, Germaine de
See also EW; TWA

**Stafford, Jean** 1915-1979 .. **CLC 4, 7, 19, 68; SSC 26**
See also CA 1-4R; 85-88; CANR 3, 65; DLB 2, 173; MTCW 1, 2; RGAL; RGSF; SATA-Obit 22; TCWW 2

**Stafford, William (Edgar)**
1914-1993 .. **CLC 4, 7, 29; DAM POET**
See also CA 5-8R; 142; CAAS 3; CANR 5, 22; DLB 5, 206; EXPP; INT CANR-22; PFS 2, 8; RGAL; WP

**Stagnelius, Eric Johan** 1793-1823 . **NCLC 61**

**Staines, Trevor**
See Brunner, John (Kilian Houston)

**Stairs, Gordon**
See Austin, Mary (Hunter)
See also TCWW 2

**Stairs, Gordon** 1868-1934
See Austin, Mary (Hunter)

**Stalin, Joseph** 1879-1953 ................ **TCLC 92**

**Stancykowna**
See Szymborska, Wislawa

**Stannard, Martin** 1947- .................... **CLC 44**
See also CA 142; DLB 155

**Stanton, Elizabeth Cady**
1815-1902 ............................. **TCLC 73**
See also CA 171; DLB 79; FW

**Stanton, Maura** 1946- ........................ **CLC 9**
See also CA 89-92; CANR 15; DLB 120

**Stanton, Schuyler**
See Baum, L(yman) Frank

**Stapledon, (William) Olaf**
1886-1950 .............................. **TCLC 22**
See also CA 111; 162; DLB 15; SFW

**Starbuck, George (Edwin)**
1931-1996 ............ **CLC 53; DAM POET**
See also CA 21-24R; 153; CANR 23

**Stark, Richard**
See Westlake, Donald E(dwin)

**Staunton, Schuyler**
See Baum, L(yman) Frank

**Stead, Christina (Ellen)** 1902-1983 ... **CLC 2, 5, 8, 32, 80**
See also BRWS 4; CA 13-16R; 109; CANR 33, 40; FW; MTCW 1, 2; RGEL; RGSF

**Stead, William Thomas**
1849-1912 ............................. **TCLC 48**
See also CA 167

**Stebnitsky, M.**
See Leskov, Nikolai (Semyonovich)

**Steele, Sir Richard** 1672-1729 .............. **LC 18**
See also BRW 3; CDBLB 1660-1789; DLB 84, 101; RGEL; WLIT 3

**Steele, Timothy (Reid)** 1948- .............. **CLC 45**
See also CA 93-96; CANR 16, 50, 92; CP; DLB 120

**Steffens, (Joseph) Lincoln**
1866-1936 ............................. **TCLC 20**
See also CA 117

**Stegner, Wallace (Earle)** 1909-1993 .. **CLC 9, 49, 81; DAM NOV; SSC 27**
See also AITN 1; AMWS 4; ANW; BEST 90:3; BPFB 3; CA 1-4R; 141; CAAS 9; CANR 1, 21, 46; DLB 9, 206; DLBY 93; MTCW 1, 2; RGAL; TCWW 2

**Stein, Gertrude** 1874-1946 .... **TCLC 1, 6, 28, 48; DA; DAB; DAC; DAM MST, NOV, POET; PC 18; SSC 42; WLC**
See also AMW; CA 104; 132; CDALB 1917-1929; DA3; DLB 4, 54, 86, 228; DLBD 15; EXPS; GLL 1; MAWW; MTCW 1, 2; RGAL; RGSF; SSFS 5; WP

**Steinbeck, John (Ernst)** 1902-1968 ... **CLC 1, 5, 9, 13, 21, 34, 45, 75, 124; DA; DAB; DAC; DAM DRAM, MST, NOV; SSC 11, 37; WLC**
See also AAYA 12; AMW; BPFB 3; BYA 2, 3, 13; CA 1-4R; 25-28R; CANR 1, 35; CDALB 1929-1941; DA3; DLB 7, 9, 212; DLBD 2; EXPS; LAIT 3; MTCW 1, 2; NFS 1, 5, 7; RGAL; RGSF; RHW; SATA 9; SSFS 3, 6; TCWW 2; WYA; YAW

**Steinem, Gloria** 1934- .................... **CLC 63**
See also CA 53-56; CANR 28, 51; DLB 246; FW; MTCW 1, 2

**Steiner, George** 1929- .. **CLC 24; DAM NOV**
See also CA 73-76; CANR 31, 67; DLB 67; MTCW 1, 2; SATA 62

**Steiner, K. Leslie**
See Delany, Samuel R(ay), Jr.

**Steiner, Rudolf** 1861-1925 .............. **TCLC 13**
See also CA 107

**Stendhal** 1783-1842 ......... **NCLC 23, 46; DA; DAB; DAC; DAM MST, NOV; SSC 27; WLC**
See also DA3; DLB 119; EW; GFL 1789 to the Present; RGWL

**Stephen, Adeline Virginia**
See Woolf, (Adeline) Virginia

**Stephen, Sir Leslie** 1832-1904 ........ **TCLC 23**
See also BRW 5; CA 123; DLB 57, 144, 190

**Stephen, Sir Leslie**
See Stephen, Sir Leslie

**Stephen, Virginia**
See Woolf, (Adeline) Virginia

**Stephens, James** 1882(?)-1950 .......... **TCLC 4**
See also CA 104; 192; DLB 19, 153, 162; FANT; RGEL

**Stephens, Reed**
See Donaldson, Stephen R(eeder)

**Steptoe, Lydia**
See Barnes, Djuna
See also GLL 1

**Sterchi, Beat** 1949- ........................... **CLC 65**

**Sterling, Brett**
See Bradbury, Ray (Douglas); Hamilton, Edmond

**Sterling, Bruce** 1954- .......................... **CLC 72**
See also CA 119; CANR 44; SCFW 2; SFW

**Sterling, George** 1869-1926 ............ **TCLC 20**
See also CA 117; 165; DLB 54

**Stern, Gerald** 1925- .................... **CLC 40, 100**
See also AMWS 9; CA 81-84; CANR 28, 94; CP; DLB 105; RGAL

**Stern, Richard (Gustave)** 1928- ... **CLC 4, 39**
See also CA 1-4R; CANR 1, 25, 52; CN; DLBY 87; INT CANR-25

**Sternberg, Josef von** 1894-1969 ....... **CLC 20**
See also CA 81-84

**Sterne, Laurence** 1713-1768 .. **LC 2, 48; DA; DAB; DAC; DAM MST, NOV; WLC**
See also BRW 3; CDBLB 1660-1789; DLB 39; RGEL

**Sternheim, (William Adolf) Carl**
1878-1942 ............................... **TCLC 8**
See also CA 105; 193; DLB 56, 118; RGWL

**Stevens, Mark** 1951- ......................... **CLC 34**
See also CA 122

**Stevens, Wallace** 1879-1955 ....... **TCLC 3, 12, 45; DA; DAB; DAC; DAM MST, POET; PC 6; WLC**
See also AMW; AMWR 1; CA 104; 124; CDALB 1929-1941; DA3; DLB 54; EXPP; MTCW 1, 2; PAB; PFS 13; RGAL; WP

**Stevenson, Anne (Katharine)** 1933- .. **CLC 7, 33**
See also BRWS 6; CA 17-20R; CAAS 9; CANR 9, 33; CP; CWP; DLB 40; MTCW 1; RHW

**Stevenson, Robert Louis (Balfour)**
1850-1894 . **NCLC 5, 14, 63; DA; DAB; DAC; DAM MST, NOV; SSC 11; WLC**
See also AAYA 24; BPFB 3; BRW 5; BYA 1, 2, 4, 13; CDBLB 1890-1914; CLR 10, 11; DA3; DLB 18, 57, 141, 156, 174; DLBD 13; HGG; JRDA; LAIT 1, 3; MAICYA; NFS 11; RGEL; RGSF; SATA 100; SUFW; WCH; WLIT 4; WYA; YABC 2; YAW

**Stewart, J(ohn) I(nnes) M(ackintosh)**
1906-1994 .................... **CLC 7, 14, 32**
See also Innes, Michael
See also CA 85-88; 147; CAAS 3; CANR 47; CMW; MTCW 1, 2

**Stewart, Mary (Florence Elinor)**
1916- ................ **CLC 7, 35, 117; DAB**
See also AAYA 29; BPFB 3; CA 1-4R; CANR 1, 59; CMW; CPW; FANT; RHW; SATA 12; YAW

**Stewart, Mary Rainbow**
See Stewart, Mary (Florence Elinor)

**Stifle, June**
See Campbell, Maria

**Stifter, Adalbert** 1805-1868 .. **NCLC 41; SSC 28**
See also DLB 133; RGSF; RGWL

**Still, James** 1906-2001 ...................... **CLC 49**
See also CA 65-68; 195; CAAS 17; CANR 10, 26; CSW; DLB 9; SATA 29

**Sting** 1951-
See Sumner, Gordon Matthew
See also CA 167

**Stirling, Arthur**
See Sinclair, Upton (Beall)

**Stitt, Milan** 1941- ............................... **CLC 29**
See also CA 69-72

**Stockton, Francis Richard** 1834-1902
See Stockton, Frank R.
See also CA 108; 137; MAICYA; SATA 44; SFW

**Stockton, Frank R.** ........................ **TCLC 47**
See also Stockton, Francis Richard
See also BYA 4, 13; DLB 42, 74; DLBD 13; EXPS; SATA-Brief 32; SSFS 3

**Stoddard, Charles**
See Kuttner, Henry

**Stoker, Abraham** 1847-1912
  See Stoker, Bram
  See also CA 105; 150; DA; DA3; DAC; DAM MST, NOV; HGG; SATA 29
**Stoker, Bram** ............ **TCLC 8; DAB; WLC**
  See also Stoker, Abraham
  See also AAYA 23; BPFB 3; BRWS 3; BYA 5; CDBLB 1890-1914; DLB 36, 70, 178; RGEL; WLIT 4
**Stolz, Mary (Slattery)** 1920- ............. **CLC 12**
  See also AAYA 8; AITN 1; CA 5-8R; CANR 13, 41; JRDA; MAICYA; SAAS 3; SATA 10, 71; YAW
**Stone, Irving** 1903-1989 . **CLC 7; DAM POP**
  See also AITN 1; BPFB 3; CA 1-4R; 129; CAAS 3; CANR 1, 23; CPW; DA3; INT CANR-23; MTCW 1, 2; RHW; SATA 3; SATA-Obit 64
**Stone, Oliver (William)** 1946- ............ **CLC 73**
  See also AAYA 15; CA 110; CANR 55
**Stone, Robert (Anthony)** 1937- ... **CLC 5, 23, 42**
  See also AMWS 5; BPFB 3; CA 85-88; CANR 23, 66, 95; CN; DLB 152; INT CANR-23; MTCW 1
**Stone, Zachary**
  See Follett, Ken(neth Martin)
**Stoppard, Tom** 1937- ... **CLC 1, 3, 4, 5, 8, 15, 29, 34, 63, 91; DA; DAB; DAC; DAM DRAM, MST; DC 6; WLC**
  See also BRWS 1; CA 81-84; CANR 39, 67; CBD; CD; CDBLB 1960 to Present; DA3; DFS 2,5,8,11, 13; DLB 13, 233; DLBY 85; MTCW 1, 2; RGEL; WLIT 4
**Storey, David (Malcolm)** 1933- . **CLC 2, 4, 5, 8; DAM DRAM**
  See also BRWS 1; CA 81-84; CANR 36; CBD; CD; CN; DLB 13, 14, 207, 245; MTCW 1; RGEL
**Storm, Hyemeyohsts** 1935- ..... **CLC 3; DAM MULT**
  See also CA 81-84; CANR 45; NNAL
**Storm, Theodor** 1817-1888 .................. **SSC 27**
  See also RGSF; RGWL
**Storm, (Hans) Theodor (Woldsen)**
  1817-1888 .................. **NCLC 1; SSC 27**
  See also DLB 129; EW
**Storni, Alfonsina** 1892-1938 . **TCLC 5; DAM MULT; HLC 2; PC 33**
  See also CA 104; 131; HW 1; LAW
**Stoughton, William** 1631-1701 ............ **LC 38**
  See also DLB 24
**Stout, Rex (Todhunter)** 1886-1975 ..... **CLC 3**
  See also AITN 2; BPFB 3; CA 61-64; CANR 71; CMW; MSW; RGAL
**Stow, (Julian) Randolph** 1935- ... **CLC 23, 48**
  See also CA 13-16R; CANR 33; CN; MTCW 1; RGEL
**Stowe, Harriet (Elizabeth) Beecher**
  1811-1896 ....... **NCLC 3, 50; DA; DAB; DAC; DAM MST, NOV; WLC**
  See also AMWS 1; CDALB 1865-1917; DA3; DLB 1, 12, 42, 74, 189, 239, 243; EXPN; JRDA; LAIT 2; MAICYA; NFS 6; RGAL; YABC 1
**Strabo** c. 64B.C.-c. 25 .................... **CMLC 37**
  See also DLB 176
**Strachey, (Giles) Lytton**
  1880-1932 .................. **TCLC 12**
  See also BRWS 2; CA 110; 178; DLB 149; DLBD 10; MTCW 2
**Strand, Mark** 1934- ......... **CLC 6, 18, 41, 71; DAM POET**
  See also AMWS 4; CA 21-24R; CANR 40, 65, 100; CP; DLB 5; PAB; PFS 9; RGAL; SATA 41
**Stratton-Porter, Gene(va Grace)** 1863-1924
  See Porter, Gene(va Grace) Stratton
  See also ANW; CA 137; DLB 221; DLBD 14; MAICYA; SATA 15

**Straub, Peter (Francis)** 1943- . **CLC 28, 107; DAM POP**
  See also BEST 89:1; BPFB 3; CA 85-88; CANR 28, 65; CPW; DLBY 84; HGG; MTCW 1, 2
**Strauss, Botho** 1944- .......................... **CLC 22**
  See also CA 157; CWW 2; DLB 124
**Streatfeild, (Mary) Noel**
  1897(?)-1986 ....................... **CLC 21**
  See also CA 81-84; 120; CANR 31; CLR 17; CWRI; DLB 160; MAICYA; SATA 20; SATA-Obit 48
**Stribling, T(homas) S(igismund)**
  1881-1965 ......................... **CLC 23**
  See also CA 189; 107; CMW; DLB 9; RGAL
**Strindberg, (Johan) August**
  1849-1912 ........ **TCLC 1, 8, 21, 47; DA; DAB; DAC; DAM DRAM, MST; WLC**
  See also CA 104; 135; DA3; DFS 4, 9; EW; MTCW 2; RGWL
**Stringer, Arthur** 1874-1950 ............ **TCLC 37**
  See also CA 161; DLB 92
**Stringer, David**
  See Roberts, Keith (John Kingston)
**Stroheim, Erich von** 1885-1957 ..... **TCLC 71**
**Strugatskii, Arkadii (Natanovich)**
  1925-1991 ............................ **CLC 27**
  See also CA 106; 135; SFW
**Strugatskii, Boris (Natanovich)**
  1933- .................................... **CLC 27**
  See also CA 106; SFW
**Strummer, Joe** 1953(?)- ...................... **CLC 30**
**Strunk, William, Jr.** 1869-1946 ...... **TCLC 92**
  See also CA 118; 164
**Stryk, Lucien** 1924- ............................ **PC 27**
  See also CA 13-16R; CANR 10, 28, 55; CP
**Stuart, Don A.**
  See Campbell, John W(ood, Jr.)
**Stuart, Ian**
  See MacLean, Alistair (Stuart)
**Stuart, Jesse (Hilton)** 1906-1984 ... **CLC 1, 8, 11, 14, 34; SSC 31**
  See also CA 5-8R; 112; CANR 31; DLB 9, 48, 102; DLBY 84; SATA 2; SATA-Obit 36
**Stubblefield, Sally**
  See Trumbo, Dalton
**Sturgeon, Theodore (Hamilton)**
  1918-1985 ............................ **CLC 22, 39**
  See also Queen, Ellery
  See also BPFB 3; BYA 9, 10; CA 81-84; 116; CANR 32, 103; DLB 8; DLBY 85; HGG; MTCW 1, 2; SCFW; SFW; SUFW
**Sturges, Preston** 1898-1959 ............ **TCLC 48**
  See also CA 114; 149; DLB 26
**Styron, William** 1925- ..... **CLC 1, 3, 5, 11, 15, 60; DAM NOV, POP; SSC 25**
  See also AMW; BEST 90:4; BPFB 3; CA 5-8R; CANR 6, 33, 74; CDALB 1968-1988; CN; CPW; CSW; DA3; DLB 2, 143; DLBY 80; INT CANR-6; LAIT 2; MTCW 1, 2; NCFS 1; RGAL; RHW
**Su, Chien** 1884-1918
  See Su Man-shu
  See also CA 123
**Suarez Lynch, B.**
  See Bioy Casares, Adolfo; Borges, Jorge Luis
**Suassuna, Ariano Vilar** 1927-
  See also CA 178; HLCS 1; HW 2; LAW
**Suckling, Sir John** 1609-1642 ............... **PC 30**
  See also BRW 2; DAM POET; DLB 58, 126; EXPP; PAB; RGEL
**Suckow, Ruth** 1892-1960 .................... **SSC 18**
  See also CA 193; 113; DLB 9, 102; RGAL; TCWW 2
**Sudermann, Hermann** 1857-1928 .. **TCLC 15**
  See also CA 107; DLB 118

**Sue, Eugene** 1804-1857 ..................... **NCLC 1**
  See also DLB 119
**Sueskind, Patrick** 1949- ..................... **CLC 44**
  See also Suskind, Patrick
**Sukenick, Ronald** 1932- ........ **CLC 3, 4, 6, 48**
  See also CA 25-28R; CAAS 8; CANR 32, 89; CN; DLB 173; DLBY 81
**Suknaski, Andrew** 1942- ..................... **CLC 19**
  See also CA 101; CP; DLB 53
**Sullivan, Vernon**
  See Vian, Boris
**Sully Prudhomme, Rene-Francois-Armand**
  1839-1907 ........................... **TCLC 31**
  See also GFL 1789 to the Present
**Su Man-shu** ......................................... **TCLC 24**
  See also Su, Chien
**Summerforest, Ivy B.**
  See Kirkup, James
**Summers, Andrew James** 1942- ........ **CLC 26**
**Summers, Andy**
  See Summers, Andrew James
**Summers, Hollis (Spurgeon, Jr.)**
  1916- ............................................ **CLC 10**
  See also CA 5-8R; CANR 3; DLB 6
**Summers, (Alphonsus Joseph-Mary Augustus) Montague**
  1880-1948 ............................ **TCLC 16**
  See also CA 118; 163
**Sumner, Gordon Matthew** ............... **CLC 26**
  See also Sting
**Surtees, Robert Smith** 1805-1864 .. **NCLC 14**
  See also DLB 21; RGEL
**Susann, Jacqueline** 1921-1974 ............. **CLC 3**
  See also AITN 1; BPFB 3; CA 65-68; 53-56; MTCW 1, 2
**Su Shi**
  See Su Shih
  See also RGWL
**Su Shih** 1036-1101 ......................... **CMLC 15**
  See also Su Shi
**Suskind, Patrick**
  See Sueskind, Patrick
  See also BPFB 3; CA 145; CWW 2
**Sutcliff, Rosemary** 1920-1992 ........ **CLC 26; DAB; DAC; DAM MST, POP**
  See also AAYA 10; BYA 1, 4; CA 5-8R; 139; CANR 37; CLR 1, 37; CPW; JRDA; MAICYA; MAICYAS; RHW; SATA 6, 44, 78; SATA-Obit 73; YAW
**Sutro, Alfred** 1863-1933 .................... **TCLC 6**
  See also CA 105; 185; DLB 10; RGEL
**Sutton, Henry**
  See Slavitt, David R(ytman)
**Suzuki, D. T.**
  See Suzuki, Daisetz Teitaro
**Suzuki, Daisetz T.**
  See Suzuki, Daisetz Teitaro
**Suzuki, Daisetz Teitaro**
  1870-1966 ............................ **TCLC 109**
  See also CA 121; 111; MTCW 1, 2
**Suzuki, Teitaro**
  See Suzuki, Daisetz Teitaro
**Svevo, Italo** ................. **TCLC 2, 35; SSC 25**
  See also Schmitz, Aron Hector
  See also EW; RGWL
**Swados, Elizabeth (A.)** 1951- ............ **CLC 12**
  See also CA 97-100; CANR 49; INT 97-100
**Swados, Harvey** 1920-1972 ................. **CLC 5**
  See also CA 5-8R; 37-40R; CANR 6; DLB 2
**Swan, Gladys** 1934- ........................... **CLC 69**
  See also CA 101; CANR 17, 39
**Swanson, Logan**
  See Matheson, Richard (Burton)

**Swarthout, Glendon (Fred)**
1918-1992 .................................. **CLC 35**
See also CA 1-4R; 139; CANR 1, 47; LAIT 5; SATA 26; TCWW 2; YAW

**Sweet, Sarah C.**
See Jewett, (Theodora) Sarah Orne

**Swenson, May** 1919-1989 ...... **CLC 4, 14, 61, 106; DA; DAB; DAC; DAM MST, POET; PC 14**
See also AMWS 4; CA 5-8R; 130; CANR 36, 61; DLB 5; EXPP; GLL 2; MTCW 1, 2; SATA 15; WP

**Swift, Augustus**
See Lovecraft, H(oward) P(hillips)

**Swift, Graham (Colin)** 1949- ......... **CLC 41, 88**
See also BRWS 5; CA 117; 122; CANR 46, 71; CN; DLB 194; MTCW 2; RGSF

**Swift, Jonathan** 1667-1745 ..... **LC 1, 42; DA; DAB; DAC; DAM MST, NOV, POET; PC 9; WLC**
See also AAYA 41; BRW 3; BYA 5; CDBLB 1660-1789; CLR 53; DA3; DLB 39, 95, 101; EXPN; LAIT 1; NFS 6; RGEL; SATA 19; WLIT 3

**Swinburne, Algernon Charles**
1837-1909 ........ **TCLC 8, 36; DA; DAB; DAC; DAM MST, POET; PC 24; WLC**
See also BRW 5; CA 105; 140; CDBLB 1832-1890; DA3; DLB 35, 57; PAB; RGEL

**Swinfen, Ann** ................................... **CLC 34**

**Swinnerton, Frank Arthur**
1884-1982 .................................. **CLC 31**
See also CA 108; DLB 34

**Swithen, John**
See King, Stephen (Edwin)

**Sylvia**
See Ashton-Warner, Sylvia (Constance)

**Symmes, Robert Edward**
See Duncan, Robert (Edward)

**Symonds, John Addington**
1840-1893 ................................. **NCLC 34**
See also DLB 57, 144

**Symons, Arthur** 1865-1945 ............. **TCLC 11**
See also CA 107; 189; DLB 19, 57, 149; RGEL

**Symons, Julian (Gustave)**
1912-1994 ........................ **CLC 2, 14, 32**
See also CA 49-52; 147; CAAS 3; CANR 3, 33, 59; CMW; DLB 87, 155; DLBY 92; MSW; MTCW 1

**Synge, (Edmund) J(ohn) M(illington)**
1871-1909 . **TCLC 6, 37; DAM DRAM; DC 2**
See also BRW 6; CA 104; 141; CDBLB 1890-1914; DLB 10, 19; RGEL; WLIT 4

**Syruc, J.**
See Milosz, Czeslaw

**Szirtes, George** 1948- ........................ **CLC 46**
See also CA 109; CANR 27, 61; CP

**Szymborska, Wislawa** 1923- ............. **CLC 99**
See also CA 154; CANR 91; CWP; CWW 2; DA3; DLB 232; DLBY 96; MTCW 2

**T. O., Nik**
See Annensky, Innokenty (Fyodorovich)

**Tabori, George** 1914- ......................... **CLC 19**
See also CA 49-52; CANR 4, 69; CBD; CD; DLB 245

**Tagore, Rabindranath** 1861-1941 ... **TCLC 3, 53; DAM DRAM, POET; PC 8; SSC 48**
See also CA 104; 120; DA3; MTCW 1, 2; RGEL; RGSF; RGWL

**Taine, Hippolyte Adolphe**
1828-1893 ................................... **NCLC 15**
See also EW; GFL 1789 to the Present

**Talese, Gay** 1932- ............................... **CLC 37**
See also AITN 1; CA 1-4R; CANR 9, 58; DLB 185; INT CANR-9; MTCW 1, 2

**Tallent, Elizabeth (Ann)** 1954- ......... **CLC 45**
See also CA 117; CANR 72; DLB 130

**Tally, Ted** 1952- ................................. **CLC 42**
See also CA 120; 124; CAD; CD; INT 124

**Talvik, Heiti** 1904-1947 ................... **TCLC 87**

**Tamayo y Baus, Manuel**
1829-1898 ..................................... **NCLC 1**

**Tammsaare, A(nton) H(ansen)**
1878-1940 ................................... **TCLC 27**
See also CA 164; DLB 220

**Tam'si, Tchicaya**
See Tchicaya, Gerald Felix

**Tan, Amy (Ruth)** 1952- .... **CLC 59, 120, 151; AAL; DAM MULT, NOV, POP**
See also AAYA 9; BEST 89:3; BPFB 3; CA 136; CANR 54; CDALBS; CN; CPW 1; DA3; DLB 173; EXPN; FW; LAIT 5; MTCW 2; NFS 1; RGAL; SATA 75; SSFS 9; YAW

**Tandem, Felix**
See Spitteler, Carl (Friedrich Georg)

**Tanizaki, Jun'ichiro** 1886-1965 ... **CLC 8, 14, 28; SSC 21**
See also CA 93-96; 25-28R; DLB 180; MJW; MTCW 2; RGSF; RGWL

**Tanner, William**
See Amis, Kingsley (William)

**Tao Lao**
See Storni, Alfonsina

**Tarantino, Quentin (Jerome)**
1963- ........................................ **CLC 125**
See also CA 171

**Tarassoff, Lev**
See Troyat, Henri

**Tarbell, Ida M(inerva)** 1857-1944 . **TCLC 40**
See also CA 122; 181; DLB 47

**Tarkington, (Newton) Booth**
1869-1946 ..................................... **TCLC 9**
See also BPFB 3; BYA 3; CA 110; 143; CWRI; DLB 9, 102; MTCW 2; RGAL; SATA 17

**Tarkovsky, Andrei (Arsenyevich)**
1932-1986 ..................................... **CLC 75**
See also CA 127

**Tartt, Donna** 1964(?)- ......................... **CLC 76**
See also CA 142

**Tasso, Torquato** 1544-1595 .................... **LC 5**
See also EFS 2; EW; RGWL

**Tate, (John Orley) Allen** 1899-1979 .. **CLC 2, 4, 6, 9, 11, 14, 24**
See also AMW; CA 5-8R; 85-88; CANR 32; DLB 4, 45, 63; DLBD 17; MTCW 1, 2; RGAL; RHW

**Tate, Ellalice**
See Hibbert, Eleanor Alice Burford

**Tate, James (Vincent)** 1943- ..... **CLC 2, 6, 25**
See also CA 21-24R; CANR 29, 57; CP; DLB 5, 169; PFS 10; RGAL; WP

**Tauler, Johannes** c. 1300-1361 ...... **CMLC 37**
See also DLB 179

**Tavel, Ronald** 1940- ............................. **CLC 6**
See also CA 21-24R; CAD; CANR 33; CD

**Taviani, Paolo** 1931- ........................... **CLC 70**
See also CA 153

**Taylor, Bayard** 1825-1878 ............... **NCLC 89**
See also DLB 3, 189; RGAL

**Taylor, C(ecil) P(hilip)** 1929-1981 .... **CLC 27**
See also CA 25-28R; 105; CANR 47; CBD

**Taylor, Edward** 1642(?)-1729 ..... **LC 11; DA; DAB; DAC; DAM MST, POET**
See also AMW; DLB 24; EXPP; RGAL

**Taylor, Eleanor Ross** 1920- ................. **CLC 5**
See also CA 81-84; CANR 70

**Taylor, Elizabeth** 1932-1975 ..... **CLC 2, 4, 29**
See also CA 13-16R; CANR 9, 70; DLB 139; MTCW 1; RGEL; SATA 13

**Taylor, Frederick Winslow**
1856-1915 ................................. **TCLC 76**
See also CA 188

**Taylor, Henry (Splawn)** 1942- .......... **CLC 44**
See also CA 33-36R; CAAS 7; CANR 31; CP; DLB 5; PFS 10

**Taylor, Kamala (Purnaiya)** 1924-
See Markandaya, Kamala
See also CA 77-80; CN

**Taylor, Mildred D(elois)** 1943- .......... **CLC 21**
See also AAYA 10; BW 1; BYA 3, 8; CA 85-88; CANR 25; CLR 9, 59; CSW; DLB 52; JRDA; LAIT 3; MAICYA; SAAS 5; SATA 15, 70; WYA; YAW

**Taylor, Peter (Hillsman)** 1917-1994 .. **CLC 1, 4, 18, 37, 44, 50, 71; SSC 10**
See also AMWS 5; BPFB 3; CA 13-16R; 147; CANR 9, 50; CSW; DLBY 81, 94; EXPS; INT CANR-9; MTCW 1, 2; RGSF; SSFS 9

**Taylor, Robert Lewis** 1912-1998 ....... **CLC 14**
See also CA 1-4R; 170; CANR 3, 64; SATA 10

**Tchekhov, Anton**
See Chekhov, Anton (Pavlovich)

**Tchicaya, Gerald Felix** 1931-1988 .. **CLC 101**
See also CA 129; 125; CANR 81

**Tchicaya U Tam'si**
See Tchicaya, Gerald Felix

**Teasdale, Sara** 1884-1933 .... **TCLC 4; PC 31**
See also CA 104; 163; DLB 45; GLL 1; RGAL; SATA 32

**Tegner, Esaias** 1782-1846 ................. **NCLC 2**

**Teilhard de Chardin, (Marie Joseph) Pierre**
1881-1955 ................................... **TCLC 9**
See also CA 105; GFL 1789 to the Present

**Temple, Ann**
See Mortimer, Penelope (Ruth)

**Tennant, Emma (Christina)** 1937- .. **CLC 13, 52**
See also CA 65-68; CAAS 9; CANR 10, 38, 59, 88; CN; DLB 14; SFW

**Tenneshaw, S. M.**
See Silverberg, Robert

**Tennyson, Alfred** 1809-1892 ... **NCLC 30, 65; DA; DAB; DAC; DAM MST, POET; PC 6; WLC**
See also BRW 4; CDBLB 1832-1890; DA3; DLB 32; EXPP; PAB; PFS 1, 2, 4, 11; RGEL; WLIT 4; WP

**Teran, Lisa St. Aubin de** ................... **CLC 36**
See also St. Aubin de Teran, Lisa

**Terence** c. 184B.C.-c. 159B.C. ....... **CMLC 14; DC 7**
See also AW 1; DLB 211; RGWL

**Teresa de Jesus, St.** 1515-1582 ............. **LC 18**

**Terkel, Louis** 1912-
See Terkel, Studs
See also CA 57-60; CANR 18, 45, 67; DA3; MTCW 1, 2

**Terkel, Studs** ....................................... **CLC 38**
See also Terkel, Louis
See also AAYA 32; AITN 1; MTCW 2

**Terry, C. V.**
See Slaughter, Frank G(ill)

**Terry, Megan** 1932- .............. **CLC 19; DC 13**
See also CA 77-80; CABS 3; CAD; CANR 43; CD; CWD; DLB 7; GLL 2

**Tertullian** c. 155-c. 245 .................. **CMLC 29**

**Tertz, Abram**
See Sinyavsky, Andrei (Donatevich)
See also CWW 2; RGSF

**Tesich, Steve** 1943(?)-1996 .......... **CLC 40, 69**
See also CA 105; 152; CAD; DLBY 83

**Tesla, Nikola** 1856-1943 ................. **TCLC 88**

**Teternikov, Fyodor Kuzmich** 1863-1927
See Sologub, Fyodor
See also CA 104

**Tevis, Walter** 1928-1984 ..................... **CLC 42**
See also CA 113; SFW

**Tey, Josephine** ........................... **TCLC 14**
See also Mackintosh, Elizabeth
See also DLB 77; MSW

**Thackeray, William Makepeace**
1811-1863 ...... **NCLC 5, 14, 22, 43; DA; DAB; DAC; DAM MST, NOV; WLC**
See also BRW 5; CDBLB 1832-1890; DA3; DLB 21, 55, 159, 163; RGEL; SATA 23; WLIT 3

**Thakura, Ravindranatha**
See Tagore, Rabindranath

**Thames, C. H.**
See Marlowe, Stephen

**Tharoor, Shashi** 1956- ........................ **CLC 70**
See also CA 141; CANR 91; CN

**Thelwell, Michael Miles** 1939- .......... **CLC 22**
See also BW 2; CA 101

**Theobald, Lewis, Jr.**
See Lovecraft, H(oward) P(hillips)

**Theocritus** c. 310B.C.- ..................... **CMLC 45**
See also AW 1; DLB 176; RGWL

**Theodorescu, Ion N.** 1880-1967
See Arghezi, Tudor
See also CA 116

**Theriault, Yves** 1915-1983 .... **CLC 79; DAC; DAM MST**
See also CA 102; CCA 1; DLB 88

**Theroux, Alexander (Louis)** 1939- .... **CLC 2, 25**
See also CA 85-88; CANR 20, 63; CN

**Theroux, Paul (Edward)** 1941- ...... **CLC 5, 8, 11, 15, 28, 46; DAM POP**
See also AAYA 28; AMWS 8; BEST 89:4; BPFB 3; CA 33-36R; CANR 20, 45, 74; CDALBS; CN; CPW 1; DA3; DLB 2; HGG; MTCW 1, 2; RGAL; SATA 44, 109

**Thesen, Sharon** 1946- ....................... **CLC 56**
See also CA 163; CP; CWP

**Thevenin, Denis**
See Duhamel, Georges

**Thibault, Jacques Anatole Francois**
1844-1924
See France, Anatole
See also CA 106; 127; DA3; DAM NOV; MTCW 1, 2

**Thiele, Colin (Milton)** 1920- ............. **CLC 17**
See also CA 29-32R; CANR 12, 28, 53; CLR 27; MAICYA; SAAS 2; SATA 14, 72, 125; YAW

**Thomas, Audrey (Callahan)** 1935- .... **CLC 7, 13, 37, 107; SSC 20**
See also AITN 2; CA 21-24R; CAAS 19; CANR 36, 58; CN; DLB 60; MTCW 1; RGSF

**Thomas, Augustus** 1857-1934 ......... **TCLC 97**

**Thomas, D(onald) M(ichael)** 1935- . **CLC 13, 22, 31, 132**
See also BPFB 3; BRWS 4; CA 61-64; CAAS 11; CANR 17, 45, 75; CDBLB 1960 to Present; CN; CP; DA3; DLB 40, 207; HGG; INT CANR-17; MTCW 1, 2; SFW

**Thomas, Dylan (Marlais)**
1914-1953 ...... **TCLC 1, 8, 45, 105; DA; DAB; DAC; DAM DRAM, MST, POET; PC 2; SSC 3, 44; WLC**
See also BRWS 1; CA 104; 120; CANR 65; CDBLB 1945-1960; DA3; DLB 13, 20, 139; EXPP; LAIT 3; MTCW 1, 2; PAB; PFS 1, 3, 8; RGEL; RGSF; SATA 60; WLIT 4; WP

**Thomas, (Philip) Edward**
1878-1917 ........ **TCLC 10; DAM POET**
See also CA 106; 153; DLB 98; RGEL

**Thomas, Joyce Carol** 1938- .............. **CLC 35**
See also AAYA 12; BW 2, 3; CA 113; 116; CANR 48; CLR 19; DLB 33; INT CA-116; JRDA; MAICYA; MTCW 1, 2; SAAS 7; SATA 40, 78, 123; YAW

**Thomas, Lewis** 1913-1993 ................. **CLC 35**
See also ANW; CA 85-88; 143; CANR 38, 60; MTCW 1, 2

**Thomas, M. Carey** 1857-1935 ........ **TCLC 89**
See also FW

**Thomas, Paul**
See Mann, (Paul) Thomas

**Thomas, Piri** 1928- ............ **CLC 17; HLCS 2**
See also CA 73-76; HW 1

**Thomas, R(onald) S(tuart)**
1913-2000 . **CLC 6, 13, 48; DAB; DAM POET**
See also CA 89-92; 189; CAAS 4; CANR 30; CDBLB 1960 to Present; CP; DLB 27; MTCW 1; RGEL

**Thomas, Ross (Elmore)** 1926-1995 .. **CLC 39**
See also CA 33-36R; 150; CANR 22, 63; CMW

**Thompson, Francis (Joseph)**
1859-1907 .................................. **TCLC 4**
See also BRW 5; CA 104; 189; CDBLB 1890-1914; DLB 19; RGEL; TEA

**Thompson, Francis Clegg**
See Mencken, H(enry) L(ouis)

**Thompson, Hunter S(tockton)**
1939- .. **CLC 9, 17, 40, 104; DAM POP**
See also BEST 89:1; BPFB 3; CA 17-20R; CANR 23, 46, 74, 77; CPW; CSW; DA3; DLB 185; MTCW 1, 2

**Thompson, James Myers**
See Thompson, Jim (Myers)

**Thompson, Jim (Myers)**
1906-1977(?) ................................ **CLC 69**
See also BPFB 3; CA 140; CMW; CPW; DLB 226; MSW

**Thompson, Judith** ............................. **CLC 39**
See also CWD

**Thomson, James** 1700-1748 ... **LC 16, 29, 40; DAM POET**
See also BRWS 3; DLB 95; RGEL

**Thomson, James** 1834-1882 .......... **NCLC 18; DAM POET**
See also DLB 35; RGEL

**Thoreau, Henry David** 1817-1862 .. **NCLC 7, 21, 61; DA; DAB; DAC; DAM MST; PC 30; WLC**
See also AAYA 42; AMW; ANW; BYA 3; CDALB 1640-1865; DA3; DLB 1, 223; LAIT 2; RGAL

**Thorndike, E. L.**
See Thorndike, Edward L(ee)

**Thorndike, Edward L(ee)**
1874-1949 ................................ **TCLC 107**
See also CA 121

**Thornton, Hall**
See Silverberg, Robert

**Thucydides** c. 455B.C.-c. 395B.C. . **CMLC 17**
See also AW 1; DLB 176; RGWL

**Thumboo, Edwin Nadason** 1933- ........ **PC 30**
See also CA 194

**Thurber, James (Grover)**
1894-1961 ........ **CLC 5, 11, 25, 125; DA; DAB; DAC; DAM DRAM, MST, NOV; SSC 1, 47**
See also AMWS 1; BPFB 3; BYA 5; CA 73-76; CANR 17, 39; CDALB 1929-1941; CWRI; DA3; DLB 4, 11, 22, 102; EXPS; FANT; LAIT 3; MAICYA; MTCW 1, 2; RGAL; RGSF; SATA 13; SSFS 1, 10; SUFW

**Thurman, Wallace (Henry)**
1902-1934 ........ **TCLC 6; BLC 3; DAM MULT**
See also BW 1, 3; CA 104; 124; CANR 81; DLB 51

**Tibullus** c. 54B.C.-c. 18B.C. .......... **CMLC 36**
See also AW 2; DLB 211; RGWL

**Ticheburn, Cheviot**
See Ainsworth, William Harrison

**Tieck, (Johann) Ludwig**
1773-1853 .............. **NCLC 5, 46; SSC 31**
See also DLB 90; EW; RGSF; RGWL; SUFW

**Tiger, Derry**
See Ellison, Harlan (Jay)

**Tilghman, Christopher** 1948(?)- ....... **CLC 65**
See also CA 159; CSW; DLB 244

**Tillich, Paul (Johannes)**
1886-1965 .................................... **CLC 131**
See also CA 5-8R; 25-28R; CANR 33; MTCW 1, 2

**Tillinghast, Richard (Williford)**
1940- ............................................. **CLC 29**
See also CA 29-32R; CAAS 23; CANR 26, 51, 96; CP; CSW

**Timrod, Henry** 1828-1867 .............. **NCLC 25**
See also DLB 3; RGAL

**Tindall, Gillian (Elizabeth)** 1938- ....... **CLC 7**
See also CA 21-24R; CANR 11, 65; CN

**Tiptree, James, Jr.** ..................... **CLC 48, 50**
See also Sheldon, Alice Hastings Bradley
See also DLB 8; SFW

**Tirso de Molina**
See Molina, Tirso de
See also RGWL

**Titmarsh, Michael Angelo**
See Thackeray, William Makepeace

**Tocqueville, Alexis (Charles Henri Maurice Clerel Comte) de** 1805-1859 .. **NCLC 7, 63**
See also EW; GFL 1789 to the Present

**Tolkien, J(ohn) R(onald) R(euel)**
1892-1973 .. **CLC 1, 2, 3, 8, 12, 38; DA; DAB; DAC; DAM MST, NOV, POP; WLC**
See also AAYA 10; AITN 1; BPFB 3; BRWS 2; CA 17-18; 45-48; CANR 36; CAP 2; CDBLB 1914-1945; CLR 56; CPW 1; CWRI; DA3; DLB 15, 160; EFS 2; FANT; JRDA; LAIT 1; MAICYA; MTCW 1, 2; NFS 8; RGEL; SATA 2, 32, 100; SATA-Obit 24; SFW; SUFW; WCH; WYA; YAW

**Toller, Ernst** 1893-1939 .................. **TCLC 10**
See also CA 107; 186; DLB 124; RGWL

**Tolson, M. B.**
See Tolson, Melvin B(eaunorus)

**Tolson, Melvin B(eaunorus)**
1898(?)-1966 ........ **CLC 36, 105; BLC 3; DAM MULT, POET**
See also AFAW 1, 2; BW 1, 3; CA 124; 89-92; CANR 80; DLB 48, 76; RGAL

**Tolstoi, Aleksei Nikolaevich**
See Tolstoy, Alexey Nikolaevich

**Tolstoi, Lev**
See Tolstoy, Leo (Nikolaevich)
See also RGSF; RGWL

**Tolstoy, Alexey Nikolaevich**
1882-1945 .................................. **TCLC 18**
See also CA 107; 158; SFW

**Tolstoy, Leo (Nikolaevich)**
1828-1910 .. **TCLC 4, 11, 17, 28, 44, 79; DA; DAB; DAC; DAM MST, NOV; SSC 9, 30, 45; WLC**
See also Tolstoi, Lev
See also CA 104; 123; DA3; DLB 238; EFS 2; EW; EXPS; IDTP; LAIT 2; NFS 10; SATA 26; SSFS 5

**Tolstoy, Count Leo**
See Tolstoy, Leo (Nikolaevich)
**Tomasi di Lampedusa, Giuseppe** 1896-1957
See Lampedusa, Giuseppe (Tomasi) di
See also CA 111
**Tomlin, Lily** ................................. **CLC 17**
See also Tomlin, Mary Jean
**Tomlin, Mary Jean** 1939(?)-
See Tomlin, Lily
See also CA 117
**Tomlinson, (Alfred) Charles** 1927- .... **CLC 2, 4, 6, 13, 45; DAM POET; PC 17**
See also CA 5-8R; CANR 33; CP; DLB 40
**Tomlinson, H(enry) M(ajor)**
1873-1958 ........................... **TCLC 71**
See also CA 118; 161; DLB 36, 100, 195
**Tonson, Jacob**
See Bennett, (Enoch) Arnold
**Toole, John Kennedy** 1937-1969 ..... **CLC 19, 64**
See also BPFB 3; CA 104; DLBY 81; MTCW 2
**Toomer, Eugene**
See Toomer, Jean
**Toomer, Eugene Pinchback**
See Toomer, Jean
**Toomer, Jean** 1892-1967 .... **CLC 1, 4, 13, 22; BLC 3; DAM MULT; PC 7; SSC 1, 45; WLCS**
See also AFAW 1, 2; AMWS 3, 9; BW 1; CA 85-88; CDALB 1917-1929; DA3; DLB 45, 51; EXPP; EXPS; MTCW 1, 2; NFS 11; RGAL; RGSF; SSFS 5
**Toomer, Nathan Jean**
See Toomer, Jean
**Toomer, Nathan Pinchback**
See Toomer, Jean
**Torley, Luke**
See Blish, James (Benjamin)
**Tornimparte, Alessandra**
See Ginzburg, Natalia
**Torre, Raoul della**
See Mencken, H(enry) L(ouis)
**Torrence, Ridgely** 1874-1950 .......... **TCLC 97**
See also DLB 54
**Torrey, E(dwin) Fuller** 1937- ............ **CLC 34**
See also CA 119; CANR 71
**Torsvan, Ben Traven**
See Traven, B.
**Torsvan, Benno Traven**
See Traven, B.
**Torsvan, Berick Traven**
See Traven, B.
**Torsvan, Berwick Traven**
See Traven, B.
**Torsvan, Bruno Traven**
See Traven, B.
**Torsvan, Traven**
See Traven, B.
**Tourneur, Cyril** 1575(?)-1626 .. **LC 66; DAM DRAM**
See also BRW 2; DLB 58; RGEL
**Tournier, Michel (Edouard)** 1924- .... **CLC 6, 23, 36, 95**
See also CA 49-52; CANR 3, 36, 74; DLB 83; GFL 1789 to the Present; MTCW 1, 2; SATA 23
**Tournimparte, Alessandra**
See Ginzburg, Natalia
**Towers, Ivar**
See Kornbluth, C(yril) M.
**Towne, Robert (Burton)** 1936(?)- ...... **CLC 87**
See also CA 108; DLB 44; IDFW 3, 4
**Townsend, Sue** ................................ **CLC 61**
See also Townsend, Susan Elaine
See also AAYA 28; CBD; CWD; SATA 55, 93; SATA-Brief 48

**Townsend, Susan Elaine** 1946-
See Townsend, Sue
See also CA 119; 127; CANR 65; CD; CPW; DAB; DAC; DAM MST; INT 127; YAW
**Townshend, Peter (Dennis Blandford)**
1945- ................................. **CLC 17, 42**
See also CA 107
**Tozzi, Federigo** 1883-1920 ............. **TCLC 31**
See also CA 160
**Tracy, Don(ald Fiske)** 1905-1970(?)
See Queen, Ellery
See also CA 1-4R; 176; CANR 2
**Traill, Catharine Parr** 1802-1899 .. **NCLC 31**
See also DLB 99
**Trakl, Georg** 1887-1914 ....... **TCLC 5; PC 20**
See also CA 104; 165; EW; MTCW 2; RGWL
**Transtroemer, Tomas (Goesta)**
1931- ............. **CLC 52, 65; DAM POET**
See also CA 117; 129; CAAS 17
**Transtromer, Tomas Gosta**
See Transtroemer, Tomas (Goesta)
**Traven, B.** 1882(?)-1969 ................ **CLC 8, 11**
See also CA 19-20; 25-28R; CAP 2; DLB 9, 56; MTCW 1; RGAL
**Trediakovsky, Vasilii Kirillovich**
1703-1769 ...................................... **LC 68**
See also DLB 150
**Treitel, Jonathan** 1959- ..................... **CLC 70**
**Trelawny, Edward John**
1792-1881 ................................. **NCLC 85**
See also DLB 110, 116, 144
**Tremain, Rose** 1943- ......................... **CLC 42**
See also CA 97-100; CANR 44, 95; CN; DLB 14; RGSF; RHW
**Tremblay, Michel** 1942- ............ **CLC 29, 102; DAC; DAM MST**
See also CA 116; 128; CCA 1; CWW 2; DLB 60; GLL 1; MTCW 1, 2
**Trevanian** ............................................. **CLC 29**
See also Whitaker, Rod(ney)
**Trevor, Glen**
See Hilton, James
**Trevor, William** .. **CLC 7, 9, 14, 25, 71, 116; SSC 21**
See also Cox, William Trevor
See also BRWS 4; CBD; DLB 14, 139; MTCW 2; RGEL; RGSF; SSFS 10
**Trifonov, Iurii (Valentinovich)**
See Trifonov, Yuri (Valentinovich)
See also RGWL
**Trifonov, Yuri (Valentinovich)**
1925-1981 ................................. **CLC 45**
See also Trifonov, Iurii (Valentinovich)
See also CA 126; 103; MTCW 1
**Trilling, Diana (Rubin)** 1905-1996 . **CLC 129**
See also CA 5-8R; 154; CANR 10, 46; INT CANR-10; MTCW 1, 2
**Trilling, Lionel** 1905-1975 ....... **CLC 9, 11, 24**
See also AMWS 3; CA 9-12R; 61-64; CANR 10; DLB 28, 63; INT CANR-10; MTCW 1, 2; RGAL
**Trimball, W. H.**
See Mencken, H(enry) L(ouis)
**Tristan**
See Gomez de la Serna, Ramon
**Tristram**
See Housman, A(lfred) E(dward)
**Trogdon, William (Lewis)** 1939-
See Heat-Moon, William Least
See also CA 115; 119; CANR 47, 89; CPW; INT CA-119
**Trollope, Anthony** 1815-1882 .... **NCLC 6, 33, 101; DA; DAB; DAC; DAM MST, NOV; SSC 28; WLC**
See also BRW 5; CDBLB 1832-1890; DA3; DLB 21, 57, 159; RGEL; RGSF; SATA 22

**Trollope, Frances** 1779-1863 .......... **NCLC 30**
See also DLB 21, 166
**Trotsky, Leon** 1879-1940 ................. **TCLC 22**
See also CA 118; 167
**Trotter (Cockburn), Catharine**
1679-1749 ........................................ **LC 8**
See also DLB 84
**Trotter, Wilfred** 1872-1939 ............. **TCLC 97**
**Trout, Kilgore**
See Farmer, Philip Jose
**Trow, George W. S.** 1943- .................. **CLC 52**
See also CA 126; CANR 91
**Troyat, Henri** 1911- ........................... **CLC 23**
See also CA 45-48; CANR 2, 33, 67; GFL 1789 to the Present; MTCW 1
**Trudeau, G(arretson) B(eekman)** 1948-
See Trudeau, Garry B.
See also CA 81-84; CANR 31; SATA 35
**Trudeau, Garry B.** ............................. **CLC 12**
See also Trudeau, G(arretson) B(eekman)
See also AAYA 10; AITN 2
**Truffaut, Francois** 1932-1984 ... **CLC 20, 101**
See also CA 81-84; 113; CANR 34
**Trumbo, Dalton** 1905-1976 ............... **CLC 19**
See also CA 21-24R; 69-72; CANR 10; DLB 26; IDFW 3, 4; YAW
**Trumbull, John** 1750-1831 ............. **NCLC 30**
See also DLB 31; RGAL
**Trundlett, Helen B.**
See Eliot, T(homas) S(tearns)
**Truth, Sojourner** 1797(?)-1883 ....... **NCLC 94**
See also DLB 239; FW; LAIT 2
**Tryon, Thomas** 1926-1991 ........... **CLC 3, 11; DAM POP**
See also AITN 1; BPFB 3; CA 29-32R; 135; CANR 32, 77; CPW; DA3; HGG; MTCW 1
**Tryon, Tom**
See Tryon, Thomas
**Ts'ao Hsueh-ch'in** 1715(?)-1763 ............. **LC 1**
**Tsushima, Shuji** 1909-1948
See Dazai Osamu
See also CA 107
**Tsvetaeva (Efron), Marina (Ivanovna)**
1892-1941 ................ **TCLC 7, 35; PC 14**
See also CA 104; 128; CANR 73; EW; MTCW 1, 2; RGWL
**Tuck, Lily** 1938- ................................. **CLC 70**
See also CA 139; CANR 90
**Tu Fu** 712-770 .......................................... **PC 9**
See also Du Fu
See also DAM MULT; WP
**Tunis, John R(oberts)** 1889-1975 ..... **CLC 12**
See also BYA 1; CA 61-64; CANR 62; DLB 22, 171; JRDA; MAICYA; SATA 37; SATA-Brief 30; YAW
**Tuohy, Frank** ..................................... **CLC 37**
See also Tuohy, John Francis
See also DLB 14, 139
**Tuohy, John Francis** 1925-
See Tuohy, Frank
See also CA 5-8R; 178; CANR 3, 47; CN
**Turco, Lewis (Putnam)** 1934- ..... **CLC 11, 63**
See also CA 13-16R; CAAS 22; CANR 24, 51; CP; DLBY 84
**Turgenev, Ivan** 1818-1883 ....... **NCLC 21, 37; DA; DAB; DAC; DAM MST, NOV; DC 7; SSC 7; WLC**
See also DFS 6; DLB 238; EW; RGSF; RGWL
**Turgenev, Ivan Sergeevich**
See Turgenev, Ivan
**Turgot, Anne-Robert-Jacques**
1727-1781 ...................................... **LC 26**
**Turner, Frederick** 1943- ..................... **CLC 48**
See also CA 73-76; CAAS 10; CANR 12, 30, 56; DLB 40

**Tutu, Desmond M(pilo)** 1931- ......... **CLC 80; BLC 3; DAM MULT**
See also BW 1, 3; CA 125; CANR 67, 81

**Tutuola, Amos** 1920-1997 ...... **CLC 5, 14, 29; BLC 3; DAM MULT**
See also AFW; BW 2, 3; CA 9-12R; 159; CANR 27, 66; CN; DA3; DLB 125; DNFS; MTCW 1, 2; RGEL; WLIT 2

**Twain, Mark** .... **TCLC 6, 12, 19, 36, 48, 59; SSC 34; WLC**
See also Clemens, Samuel Langhorne
See also AAYA 20; AMW; BPFB 3; BYA 2, 3, 11; CLR 58, 60, 66; DLB 11, 12, 23, 64, 74; EXPN; EXPS; FANT; LAIT 2; NFS 1, 6; RGAL; RGSF; SFW; SSFS 1, 7; YAW

**Tyler, Anne** 1941- . **CLC 7, 11, 18, 28, 44, 59, 103; DAM NOV, POP**
See also AAYA 18; AMWS 4; BEST 89:1; BPFB 3; BYA 12; CA 9-12R; CANR 11, 33, 53; CDALBS; CN; CPW; CSW; DLB 6, 143; DLBY 82; EXPN; MAWW; MTCW 1, 2; NFS 2, 7, 10; RGAL; SATA 7, 90; YAW

**Tyler, Royall** 1757-1826 ..................... **NCLC 3**
See also DLB 37; RGAL

**Tynan, Katharine** 1861-1931 ............ **TCLC 3**
See also CA 104; 167; DLB 153, 240; FW

**Tyutchev, Fyodor** 1803-1873 .......... **NCLC 34**

**Tzara, Tristan** 1896-1963 ...... **CLC 47; DAM POET; PC 27**
See also CA 153; 89-92; MTCW 2

**Uhry, Alfred** 1936- .. **CLC 55; DAM DRAM, POP**
See also CA 127; 133; CAD; CD; CSW; DA3; DFS 11; INT 133

**Ulf, Haerved**
See Strindberg, (Johan) August

**Ulf, Harved**
See Strindberg, (Johan) August

**Ulibarri, Sabine R(eyes)** 1919- ........ **CLC 83; DAM MULT; HLCS 2**
See also CA 131; CANR 81; DLB 82; HW 1, 2; RGSF

**Unamuno (y Jugo), Miguel de** 1864-1936 ..... **TCLC 2, 9; DAM MULT, NOV; HLC 2; SSC 11**
See also CA 104; 131; CANR 81; DLB 108; EW; HW 1, 2; MTCW 1, 2; RGSF; RGWL

**Undercliffe, Errol**
See Campbell, (John) Ramsey

**Underwood, Miles**
See Glassco, John

**Undset, Sigrid** 1882-1949 ........ **TCLC 3; DA; DAB; DAC; DAM MST, NOV; WLC**
See also CA 104; 129; DA3; EW; FW; MTCW 1, 2; RGWL

**Ungaretti, Giuseppe** 1888-1970 ... **CLC 7, 11, 15**
See also CA 19-20; 25-28R; CAP 2; DLB 114; EW; RGWL

**Unger, Douglas** 1952- ......................... **CLC 34**
See also CA 130; CANR 94

**Unsworth, Barry (Forster)** 1930- .... **CLC 76, 127**
See also BRWS 7; CA 25-28R; CANR 30, 54; CN; DLB 194

**Updike, John (Hoyer)** 1932- . **CLC 1, 2, 3, 5, 7, 9, 13, 15, 23, 34, 43, 70, 139; DA; DAB; DAC; DAM MST, NOV, POET, POP; SSC 13, 27; WLC**
See also AAYA 36; AMW; AMWR 1; BPFB 3; BYA 12; CA 1-4R; CABS 1; CANR 4, 33, 51, 94; CDALB 1968-1988; CN; CP; CPW 1; DA3; DLB 2, 5, 143, 227; DLBD 3; DLBY 80, 82, 97; EXPP; HGG; MTCW 1, 2; NFS 12; RGAL; RGSF; SSFS 3

**Upshaw, Margaret Mitchell**
See Mitchell, Margaret (Munnerlyn)

**Upton, Mark**
See Sanders, Lawrence

**Upward, Allen** 1863-1926 ................ **TCLC 85**
See also CA 117; 187; DLB 36

**Urdang, Constance (Henriette)** 1922-1996 ................................. **CLC 47**
See also CA 21-24R; CANR 9, 24; CP; CWP

**Uriel, Henry**
See Faust, Frederick (Schiller)

**Uris, Leon (Marcus)** 1924- .......... **CLC 7, 32; DAM NOV, POP**
See also AITN 1, 2; BEST 89:2; BPFB 3; CA 1-4R; CANR 1, 40, 65; CN; CPW 1; DA3; MTCW 1, 2; SATA 49

**Urista, Alberto H.** 1947- ...................... **PC 34**
See also Alurista
See also CA 45-48, 182; CANR 2, 32; HLCS 1; HW 1

**Urmuz**
See Codrescu, Andrei

**Urquhart, Guy**
See McAlmon, Robert (Menzies)

**Urquhart, Jane** 1949- ............. **CLC 90; DAC**
See also CA 113; CANR 32, 68; CCA 1

**Usigli, Rodolfo** 1905-1979
See also CA 131; HLCS 1; HW 1; LAW

**Ustinov, Peter (Alexander)** 1921- ....... **CLC 1**
See also AITN 1; CA 13-16R; CANR 25, 51; CBD; CD; DLB 13; MTCW 2

**U Tam'si, Gerald Felix Tchicaya**
See Tchicaya, Gerald Felix

**U Tam'si, Tchicaya**
See Tchicaya, Gerald Felix

**Vachss, Andrew (Henry)** 1942- ....... **CLC 106**
See also CA 118; CANR 44, 95; CMW

**Vachss, Andrew H.**
See Vachss, Andrew (Henry)

**Vaculik, Ludvik** 1926- ......................... **CLC 7**
See also CA 53-56; CANR 72; CWW 2; DLB 232

**Vaihinger, Hans** 1852-1933 ............. **TCLC 71**
See also CA 116; 166

**Valdez, Luis (Miguel)** 1940- .. **CLC 84; DAM MULT; DC 10; HLC 2**
See also CA 101; CAD; CANR 32, 81; CD; DFS 5; DLB 122; HW 1; LAIT 4

**Valenzuela, Luisa** 1938- ............ **CLC 31, 104; DAM MULT; HLCS 2; SSC 14**
See also CA 101; CANR 32, 65; CWW 2; DLB 113; FW; HW 1, 2; LAW; RGSF

**Valera y Alcala-Galiano, Juan** 1824-1905 ................................ **TCLC 10**
See also CA 106

**Valery, (Ambroise) Paul (Toussaint Jules)** 1871-1945 ... **TCLC 4, 15; DAM POET; PC 9**
See also CA 104; 122; DA3; EW; GFL 1789 to the Present; MTCW 1, 2; RGWL

**Valle-Inclan, Ramon (Maria) del** 1866-1936 ......... **TCLC 5; DAM MULT; HLC 2**
See also CA 106; 153; CANR 80; DLB 134; EW; HW 2; RGSF; RGWL

**Vallejo, Antonio Buero**
See Buero Vallejo, Antonio

**Vallejo, Cesar (Abraham)** 1892-1938 .. **TCLC 3, 56; DAM MULT; HLC 2**
See also CA 105; 153; HW 1; LAW; RGWL

**Valles, Jules** 1832-1885 .................... **NCLC 71**
See also DLB 123; GFL 1789 to the Present

**Vallette, Marguerite Eymery** 1860-1953 ................................. **TCLC 67**
See also CA 182; DLB 123, 192

**Valle Y Pena, Ramon del**
See Valle-Inclan, Ramon (Maria) del

**Van Ash, Cay** 1918- .......................... **CLC 34**

**Vanbrugh, Sir John** 1664-1726 ......... **LC 21; DAM DRAM**
See also BRW 2; DLB 80; IDTP; RGEL

**Van Campen, Karl**
See Campbell, John W(ood, Jr.)

**Vance, Gerald**
See Silverberg, Robert

**Vance, Jack** ........................................ **CLC 35**
See also Vance, John Holbrook
See also DLB 8; SCFW 2

**Vance, John Holbrook** 1916-
See Queen, Ellery; Vance, Jack
See also CA 29-32R; CANR 17, 65; CMW; FANT; MTCW 1; SFW

**Van Den Bogarde, Derek Jules Gaspard Ulric Niven** 1921-1999 .............. **CLC 14**
See also CA 77-80; 179; DLB 19

**Vandenburgh, Jane** ............................ **CLC 59**
See also CA 168

**Vanderhaeghe, Guy** 1951- ................. **CLC 41**
See also BPFB 3; CA 113; CANR 72

**van der Post, Laurens (Jan)** 1906-1996 ................................... **CLC 5**
See also AFW; CA 5-8R; 155; CANR 35; CN; DLB 204; RGEL

**van de Wetering, Janwillem** 1931- ... **CLC 47**
See also CA 49-52; CANR 4, 62, 90; CMW

**Van Dine, S. S.** ................................ **TCLC 23**
See also Wright, Willard Huntington
See also MSW

**Van Doren, Carl (Clinton)** 1885-1950 ................................ **TCLC 18**
See also CA 111; 168

**Van Doren, Mark** 1894-1972 ........ **CLC 6, 10**
See also CA 1-4R; 37-40R; CANR 3; DLB 45; MTCW 1, 2; RGAL

**Van Druten, John (William)** 1901-1957 ................................. **TCLC 2**
See also CA 104; 161; DLB 10; RGAL

**Van Duyn, Mona (Jane)** 1921- ...... **CLC 3, 7, 63, 116; DAM POET**
See also CA 9-12R; CANR 7, 38, 60; CP; CWP; DLB 5

**Van Dyne, Edith**
See Baum, L(yman) Frank

**van Itallie, Jean-Claude** 1936- ............. **CLC 3**
See also CA 45-48; CAAS 2; CAD; CANR 1, 48; CD; DLB 7

**van Ostaijen, Paul** 1896-1928 ........ **TCLC 33**
See also CA 163

**Van Peebles, Melvin** 1932- ........... **CLC 2, 20; DAM MULT**
See also BW 2, 3; CA 85-88; CANR 27, 67, 82

**van Schendel, Arthur(-Francois-Emile)** 1874-1946 ................................ **TCLC 56**

**Vansittart, Peter** 1920- ...................... **CLC 42**
See also CA 1-4R; CANR 3, 49, 90; CN; RHW

**Van Vechten, Carl** 1880-1964 ........... **CLC 33**
See also AMWS 2; CA 183; 89-92; DLB 4, 9, 51; RGAL

**van Vogt, A(lfred) E(lton)** 1912-2000 . **CLC 1**
See also BPFB 3; BYA 13; CA 21-24R; 190; CANR 28; DLB 8; SATA 14; SATA-Obit 124; SCFW; SFW

**Varda, Agnes** 1928- ........................... **CLC 16**
See also CA 116; 122

**Vargas Llosa, (Jorge) Mario (Pedro)** 1936- ..... **CLC 3, 6, 9, 10, 15, 31, 42, 85; DA; DAB; DAC; DAM MST, MULT, NOV; HLC 2**
See also Llosa, (Jorge) Mario (Pedro) Vargas
See also BPFB 3; CA 73-76; CANR 18, 32, 42, 67; DA3; DLB 145; DNFS; HW 1, 2; LAW; MTCW 1, 2; RGWL; WLIT 1

**Vasiliu, George**
See Bacovia, George
**Vasiliu, Gheorghe**
See Bacovia, George
See also CA 123; 189
**Vassa, Gustavus**
See Equiano, Olaudah
**Vassilikos, Vassilis** 1933- ............... **CLC 4, 8**
See also CA 81-84; CANR 75
**Vaughan, Henry** 1621-1695 ................ **LC 27**
See also BRW 2; DLB 131; PAB; RGEL
**Vaughn, Stephanie** ........................... **CLC 62**
**Vazov, Ivan (Minchov)** 1850-1921 . **TCLC 25**
See also CA 121; 167; DLB 147
**Veblen, Thorstein B(unde)**
1857-1929 ................................ **TCLC 31**
See also AMWS 1; CA 115; 165; DLB 246
**Vega, Lope de** 1562-1635 .... **LC 23; HLCS 2**
See also EW; RGWL
**Vendler, Helen (Hennessy)** 1933- ... **CLC 138**
See also CA 41-44R; CANR 25, 72; MTCW 1, 2
**Venison, Alfred**
See Pound, Ezra (Weston Loomis)
**Verdi, Marie de**
See Mencken, H(enry) L(ouis)
**Verdu, Matilde**
See Cela, Camilo Jose
**Verga, Giovanni (Carmelo)**
1840-1922 ................... **TCLC 3; SSC 21**
See also CA 104; 123; CANR 101; EW; RGSF; RGWL
**Vergil** 70B.C.-19B.C. ........ **CMLC 9, 40; DA; DAB; DAC; DAM MST, POET; PC 12; WLCS**
See also Virgil
See also AW 2; DA3; DLB 211; EFS 1
**Verhaeren, Emile (Adolphe Gustave)**
1855-1916 ................................ **TCLC 12**
See also CA 109; GFL 1789 to the Present
**Verlaine, Paul (Marie)** 1844-1896 .. **NCLC 2, 51; DAM POET; PC 2, 32**
See also EW; GFL 1789 to the Present; RGWL
**Verne, Jules (Gabriel)** 1828-1905 ... **TCLC 6, 52**
See also AAYA 16; BYA 4; CA 110; 131; DA3; DLB 123; GFL 1789 to the Present; JRDA; LAIT 2; MAICYA; RGWL; SATA 21; SCFW; SFW; WCH
**Verus, Marcus Annius**
See Aurelius, Marcus
**Very, Jones** 1813-1880 ...................... **NCLC 9**
See also DLB 1, 243; RGAL
**Vesaas, Tarjei** 1897-1970 .................. **CLC 48**
See also CA 190; 29-32R; EW
**Vialis, Gaston**
See Simenon, Georges (Jacques Christian)
**Vian, Boris** 1920-1959 ........................ **TCLC 9**
See also CA 106; 164; DLB 72; GFL 1789 to the Present; MTCW 2; RGWL
**Viaud, (Louis Marie) Julien** 1850-1923
See Loti, Pierre
See also CA 107
**Vicar, Henry**
See Felsen, Henry Gregor
**Vicker, Angus**
See Felsen, Henry Gregor
**Vidal, Gore** 1925- ...... **CLC 2, 4, 6, 8, 10, 22, 33, 72, 142; DAM NOV, POP**
See also Box, Edgar
See also AITN 1; AMWS 4; BEST 90:2; BPFB 3; CA 5-8R; CAD; CANR 13, 45, 65, 100; CD; CDALBS; CN; CPW; DA3; DFS 2; DLB 6, 152; INT CANR-13; MTCW 1, 2; RGAL; RHW

**Viereck, Peter (Robert Edwin)**
1916- ................................. **CLC 4; PC 27**
See also CA 1-4R; CANR 1, 47; CP; DLB 5; PFS 9
**Vigny, Alfred (Victor) de**
1797-1863 . **NCLC 7, 102; DAM POET; PC 26**
See also DLB 119, 192; EW; GFL 1789 to the Present; RGWL
**Vilakazi, Benedict Wallet**
1906-1947 ................................ **TCLC 37**
See also CA 168
**Villa, Jose Garcia** 1914-1997 ............... **PC 22**
See also AAL; CA 25-28R; CANR 12; EXPP
**Villarreal, Jose Antonio** 1924-
See also CA 133; CANR 93; DAM MULT; DLB 82; HLC 2; HW 1; LAIT 4; RGAL
**Villaurrutia, Xavier** 1903-1950 ....... **TCLC 80**
See also CA 192; HW 1; LAW
**Villehardouin, Geoffroi de**
1150(?)-1218(?) ........................ **CMLC 38**
**Villiers de l'Isle Adam, Jean Marie Mathias Philippe Auguste** 1838-1889 ... **NCLC 3; SSC 14**
See also DLB 123; GFL 1789 to the Present; RGSF
**Villon, Francois** 1431-1463(?) . **LC 62; PC 13**
See also DLB 208; EW; RGWL
**Vine, Barbara** ................................... **CLC 50**
See also Rendell, Ruth (Barbara)
See also BEST 90:4
**Vinge, Joan (Carol) D(ennison)**
1948- ................................ **CLC 30; SSC 24**
See also AAYA 32; BPFB 3; CA 93-96; CANR 72; SATA 36, 113; SFW; YAW
**Viola, Herman J(oseph)** 1938- .......... **CLC 70**
See also CA 61-64; CANR 8, 23, 48, 91
**Violis, G.**
See Simenon, Georges (Jacques Christian)
**Viramontes, Helena Maria** 1954-
See also CA 159; DLB 122; HLCS 2; HW
**Virgil**
See Vergil
See also LAIT 1; RGWL; WP
**Visconti, Luchino** 1906-1976 ............. **CLC 16**
See also CA 81-84; 65-68; CANR 39
**Vittorini, Elio** 1908-1966 ......... **CLC 6, 9, 14**
See also CA 133; 25-28R; EW; RGWL
**Vivekananda, Swami** 1863-1902 .... **TCLC 88**
**Vizenor, Gerald Robert** 1934- ....... **CLC 103; DAM MULT**
See also CA 13-16R; CAAS 22; CANR 5, 21, 44, 67; DLB 175, 227; MTCW 2; NNAL; TCWW 2
**Vizinczey, Stephen** 1933- .................. **CLC 40**
See also CA 128; CANR 1; INT 128
**Vliet, R(ussell) G(ordon)**
1929-1984 ................................. **CLC 22**
See also CA 37-40R; 112; CANR 18
**Vogau, Boris Andreyevich** 1894-1937(?)
See Pilnyak, Boris
See also CA 123
**Vogel, Paula A(nne)** 1951- ................. **CLC 76**
See also CA 108; CD; RGAL
**Voigt, Cynthia** 1942- ......................... **CLC 30**
See also AAYA 3, 30; BYA 1, 3, 6, 7, 8; CA 106; CANR 18, 37, 40, 94; CLR 13, 48; INT CANR-18; JRDA; LAIT 5; MAICYA; MAICYAS; SATA 48, 79, 116; SATA-Brief 33; YAW
**Voigt, Ellen Bryant** 1943- ................. **CLC 54**
See also CA 69-72; CANR 11, 29, 55; CP; CSW; CWP; DLB 120
**Voinovich, Vladimir (Nikolaevich)**
1932- ................................ **CLC 10, 49, 147**
See also CA 81-84; CAAS 12; CANR 33, 67; MTCW 1

**Vollmann, William T.** 1959- .. **CLC 89; DAM NOV, POP**
See also CA 134; CANR 67; CPW; DA3; MTCW 2
**Voloshinov, V. N.**
See Bakhtin, Mikhail Mikhailovich
**Voltaire** 1694-1778 ............ **LC 14; DA; DAB; DAC; DAM DRAM, MST; SSC 12; WLC**
See also BYA 13; DA3; EW; GFL Beginnings to 1789; NFS 7; RGWL
**von Aschendrof, Baron Ignatz** 1873-1939
See Ford, Ford Madox
**von Daeniken, Erich** 1935- ................ **CLC 30**
See also AITN 1; CA 37-40R; CANR 17, 44
**von Daniken, Erich**
See von Daeniken, Erich
**von Hartmann, Eduard**
1842-1906 ................................ **TCLC 96**
**von Hayek, Friedrich August**
See Hayek, F(riedrich) A(ugust von)
**von Heidenstam, (Carl Gustaf) Verner**
See Heidenstam, (Carl Gustaf) Verner von
**von Heyse, Paul (Johann Ludwig)**
See Heyse, Paul (Johann Ludwig von)
**von Hofmannsthal, Hugo**
See Hofmannsthal, Hugo von
**von Horvath, Odon**
See Horvath, Odon von
**von Horvath, Odon**
See Horvath, Odon von
**von Horvath, Oedoen**
See Horvath, Odon von
See also CA 184
**von Liliencron, (Friedrich Adolf Axel) Detlev**
See Liliencron, (Friedrich Adolf Axel) Detlev von
**Vonnegut, Kurt, Jr.** 1922- . **CLC 1, 2, 3, 4, 5, 8, 12, 22, 40, 60, 111; DA; DAB; DAC; DAM MST, NOV, POP; SSC 8; WLC**
See also AAYA 6; AITN 1; AMWS 2; BEST 90:4; BPFB 3; BYA 3; CA 1-4R; CANR 1, 25, 49, 75, 92; CDALB 1968-1988; CN; CPW 1; DA3; DLB 2, 8, 152; DLBD 3; DLBY 80; EXPN; EXPS; LAIT 4; MTCW 1, 2; NFS 3; RGAL; SCFW; SFW; SSFS 5; TUS; YAW
**Von Rachen, Kurt**
See Hubbard, L(afayette) Ron(ald)
**von Rezzori (d'Arezzo), Gregor**
See Rezzori (d'Arezzo), Gregor von
**von Sternberg, Josef**
See Sternberg, Josef von
**Vorster, Gordon** 1924- ....................... **CLC 34**
See also CA 133
**Vosce, Trudie**
See Ozick, Cynthia
**Voznesensky, Andrei (Andreievich)**
1933- ........ **CLC 1, 15, 57; DAM POET**
See also CA 89-92; CANR 37; CWW 2; MTCW 1
**Waddington, Miriam** 1917- ............... **CLC 28**
See also CA 21-24R; CANR 12, 30; CCA 1; CP; DLB 68
**Wagman, Fredrica** 1937- ..................... **CLC 7**
See also CA 97-100; INT 97-100
**Wagner, Linda W.**
See Wagner-Martin, Linda (C.)
**Wagner, Linda Welshimer**
See Wagner-Martin, Linda (C.)
**Wagner, Richard** 1813-1883 ............. **NCLC 9**
See also DLB 129; EW
**Wagner-Martin, Linda (C.)** 1936- .... **CLC 50**
See also CA 159

**Wagoner, David (Russell)** 1926- .... **CLC 3, 5, 15; PC 33**
See also AMWS 9; CA 1-4R; CAAS 3; CANR 2, 71; CN; CP; DLB 5; SATA 14; TCWW 2

**Wah, Fred(erick James)** 1939- ......... **CLC 44**
See also CA 107; 141; CP; DLB 60

**Wahloo, Per** 1926-1975 ........................ **CLC 7**
See also BPFB 3; CA 61-64; CANR 73; CMW 1; MSW

**Wahloo, Peter**
See Wahloo, Per

**Wain, John (Barrington)** 1925-1994 . **CLC 2, 11, 15, 46**
See also CA 5-8R; 145; CAAS 4; CANR 23, 54; CDBLB 1960 to Present; DLB 15, 27, 139, 155; MTCW 1, 2

**Wajda, Andrzej** 1926- ........................ **CLC 16**
See also CA 102

**Wakefield, Dan** 1932- ........................... **CLC 7**
See also CA 21-24R; CAAS 7; CN

**Wakoski, Diane** 1937- ...... **CLC 2, 4, 7, 9, 11, 40; DAM POET; PC 15**
See also CA 13-16R; CAAS 1; CANR 9, 60; CP; CWP; DLB 5; INT CANR-9; MTCW 2

**Wakoski-Sherbell, Diane**
See Wakoski, Diane

**Walcott, Derek (Alton)** 1930- .... **CLC 2, 4, 9, 14, 25, 42, 67, 76; BLC 3; DAB; DAC; DAM MST, MULT, POET; DC 7**
See also BW 2; CA 89-92; CANR 26, 47, 75, 80; CBD; CD; CP; DA3; DLB 117; DLBY 81; DNFS; EFS 1; MTCW 1, 2; PFS 6; RGEL

**Waldman, Anne (Lesley)** 1945- .......... **CLC 7**
See also CA 37-40R; CAAS 17; CANR 34, 69; CP; CWP; DLB 16

**Waldo, E. Hunter**
See Sturgeon, Theodore (Hamilton)

**Waldo, Edward Hamilton**
See Sturgeon, Theodore (Hamilton)

**Walker, Alice (Malsenior)** 1944- ... **CLC 5, 6, 9, 19, 27, 46, 58, 103; BLC 3; DA; DAB; DAC; DAM MST, MULT, NOV, POET, POP; PC 30; SSC 5; WLCS**
See also AAYA 3, 33; AFAW 1, 2; AMWS 3; BEST 89:4; BPFB 3; BW 2, 3; CA 37-40R; CANR 9, 27, 49, 66, 82; CDALB 1968-1988; CN; CPW; CSW; DA3; DLB 6, 33, 143; EXPN; EXPS; FW; INT CANR-27; LAIT 3; MAWW; MTCW 1, 2; NFS 5; RGAL; RGSF; SATA 31; SSFS 2, 11; YAW

**Walker, David Harry** 1911-1992 ....... **CLC 14**
See also CA 1-4R; 137; CANR 1; CWRI; SATA 8; SATA-Obit 71

**Walker, Edward Joseph** 1934-
See Walker, Ted
See also CA 21-24R; CANR 12, 28, 53; CP

**Walker, George F.** 1947- . **CLC 44, 61; DAB; DAC; DAM MST**
See also CA 103; CANR 21, 43, 59; CD; DLB 60

**Walker, Joseph A.** 1935- ....... **CLC 19; DAM DRAM, MST**
See also BW 1, 3; CA 89-92; CAD; CANR 26; CD; DFS 12; DLB 38

**Walker, Margaret (Abigail)** 1915-1998 .......... **CLC 1, 6; BLC; DAM MULT; PC 20**
See also AFAW 1, 2; BW 2, 3; CA 73-76; 172; CANR 26, 54, 76; CN; CP; CSW; DLB 76, 152; EXPP; FW; MTCW 1, 2; RGAL; RHW

**Walker, Ted** ........................................... **CLC 13**
See also Walker, Edward Joseph
See also DLB 40

**Wallace, David Foster** 1962- ..... **CLC 50, 114**
See also CA 132; CANR 59; DA3; MTCW 2

**Wallace, Dexter**
See Masters, Edgar Lee

**Wallace, (Richard Horatio) Edgar** 1875-1932 ................................ **TCLC 57**
See also CA 115; CMW; DLB 70; MSW; RGEL

**Wallace, Irving** 1916-1990 ........... **CLC 7, 13; DAM NOV, POP**
See also AITN 1; BPFB 3; CA 1-4R; 132; CAAS 1; CANR 1, 27; CPW; INT CANR-27; MTCW 1, 2

**Wallant, Edward Lewis** 1926-1962 ... **CLC 5, 10**
See also CA 1-4R; CANR 22; DLB 2, 28, 143; MTCW 1, 2; RGAL

**Wallas, Graham** 1858-1932 ............ **TCLC 91**

**Walley, Byron**
See Card, Orson Scott

**Walpole, Horace** 1717-1797 ................. **LC 49**
See also BRW 3; DLB 39, 104; HGG; RGEL

**Walpole, Hugh (Seymour)** 1884-1941 ................................. **TCLC 5**
See also CA 104; 165; DLB 34; HGG; MTCW 2; RGEL; RHW

**Walser, Martin** 1927- ......................... **CLC 27**
See also CA 57-60; CANR 8, 46; CWW 2; DLB 75, 124

**Walser, Robert** 1878-1956 .... **TCLC 18; SSC 20**
See also CA 118; 165; CANR 100; DLB 66

**Walsh, Gillian Paton**
See Paton Walsh, Gillian

**Walsh, Jill Paton** ................................. **CLC 35**
See also Paton Walsh, Gillian
See also CLR 2, 65

**Walter, Villiam Christian**
See Andersen, Hans Christian

**Walton, Izaak** 1593-1683 ...................... **LC 72**
See also BRW 2; CDBLB Before 1660; DLB 151; RGEL

**Wambaugh, Joseph (Aloysius, Jr.)** 1937- ....... **CLC 3, 18; DAM NOV, POP**
See also AITN 1; BEST 89:3; BPFB 3; CA 33-36R; CANR 42, 65; CMW; CPW 1; DA3; DLB 6; DLBY 83; MSW; MTCW 1, 2

**Wang Wei** 699(?)-761(?) ........................ **PC 18**

**Ward, Arthur Henry Sarsfield** 1883-1959
See Rohmer, Sax
See also CA 108; 173; CMW; HGG

**Ward, Douglas Turner** 1930- ............ **CLC 19**
See also BW 1; CA 81-84; CAD; CANR 27; CD; DLB 7, 38

**Ward, E. D.**
See Lucas, E(dward) V(errall)

**Ward, Mrs. Humphry** 1851-1920
See Ward, Mary Augusta
See also RGEL

**Ward, Mary Augusta** 1851-1920 ... **TCLC 55**
See also Ward, Mrs. Humphry
See also DLB 18

**Ward, Peter**
See Faust, Frederick (Schiller)

**Warhol, Andy** 1928(?)-1987 ................ **CLC 20**
See also AAYA 12; BEST 89:4; CA 89-92; 121; CANR 34

**Warner, Francis (Robert le Plastrier)** 1937- ............................................ **CLC 14**
See also CA 53-56; CANR 11

**Warner, Marina** 1946- ......................... **CLC 59**
See also CA 65-68; CANR 21, 55; CN; DLB 194

**Warner, Rex (Ernest)** 1905-1986 ...... **CLC 45**
See also CA 89-92; 119; DLB 15; RGEL; RHW

**Warner, Susan (Bogert)** 1819-1885 ................................. **NCLC 31**
See also DLB 3, 42, 239

**Warner, Sylvia (Constance) Ashton**
See Ashton-Warner, Sylvia (Constance)

**Warner, Sylvia Townsend** 1893-1978 ................. **CLC 7, 19; SSC 23**
See also BRWS 7; CA 61-64; 77-80; CANR 16, 60; DLB 34, 139; FANT; FW; MTCW 1, 2; RGEL; RGSF; RHW

**Warren, Mercy Otis** 1728-1814 ..... **NCLC 13**
See also DLB 31, 200; RGAL

**Warren, Robert Penn** 1905-1989 .. **CLC 1, 4, 6, 8, 10, 13, 18, 39, 53, 59; DA; DAB; DAC; DAM MST, NOV, POET; PC 37; SSC 4; WLC**
See also AITN 1; AMW; BPFB 3; BYA 1; CA 13-16R; 129; CANR 10, 47; CDALB 1968-1988; DA3; DLB 2, 48, 152; DLBY 80, 89; INT CANR-10; MTCW 1, 2; RGAL; RGSF; RHW; SATA 46; SATA-Obit 63; SSFS 8

**Warshofsky, Isaac**
See Singer, Isaac Bashevis

**Warton, Thomas** 1728-1790 ..... **LC 15; DAM POET**
See also DLB 104, 109; RGEL

**Waruk, Kona**
See Harris, (Theodore) Wilson

**Warung, Price** ..................................... **TCLC 45**
See also Astley, William
See also RGEL

**Warwick, Jarvis**
See Garner, Hugh
See also CCA 1

**Washington, Alex**
See Harris, Mark

**Washington, Booker T(aliaferro)** 1856-1915 ...... **TCLC 10; BLC 3; DAM MULT**
See also BW 1; CA 114; 125; DA3; LAIT 2; RGAL; SATA 28

**Washington, George** 1732-1799 ........... **LC 25**
See also DLB 31

**Wassermann, (Karl) Jakob** 1873-1934 ................................. **TCLC 6**
See also CA 104; 163; DLB 66

**Wasserstein, Wendy** 1950- .. **CLC 32, 59, 90; DAM DRAM; DC 4**
See also CA 121; 129; CABS 3; CAD; CANR 53, 75; CD; CWD; DA3; DFS 5; DLB 228; FW; INT 129; MTCW 2; SATA 94

**Waterhouse, Keith (Spencer)** 1929- . **CLC 47**
See also CA 5-8R; CANR 38, 67; CBD; CN; DLB 13, 15; MTCW 1, 2

**Waters, Frank (Joseph)** 1902-1995 .. **CLC 88**
See also CA 5-8R; 149; CAAS 13; CANR 3, 18, 63; DLB 212; DLBY 86; RGAL; TCWW 2

**Waters, Mary C.** ............................... **CLC 70**

**Waters, Roger** 1944- ........................... **CLC 35**

**Watkins, Frances Ellen**
See Harper, Frances Ellen Watkins

**Watkins, Gerrold**
See Malzberg, Barry N(athaniel)

**Watkins, Paul** 1964- ............................ **CLC 55**
See also CA 132; CANR 62, 98

**Watkins, Vernon Phillips** 1906-1967 ................................... **CLC 43**
See also CA 9-10; 25-28R; CAP 1; DLB 20; RGEL

**Watson, Irving S.**
See Mencken, H(enry) L(ouis)

**Watson, John H.**
See Farmer, Philip Jose

**Watson, Richard F.**
See Silverberg, Robert

**Waugh, Auberon (Alexander)**
1939-2001 .................... **CLC 7**
See also CA 45-48; 192; CANR 6, 22, 92; DLB 14, 194

**Waugh, Evelyn (Arthur St. John)**
1903-1966 .. **CLC 1, 3, 8, 13, 19, 27, 44, 107; DA; DAB; DAC; DAM MST, NOV, POP; SSC 41; WLC**
See also BPFB 3; BRW 7; CA 85-88; 25-28R; CANR 22; CDBLB 1914-1945; DA3; DLB 15, 162, 195; MTCW 1, 2; RGEL; RGSF; WLIT 4

**Waugh, Harriet** 1944- ....................... **CLC 6**
See also CA 85-88; CANR 22

**Ways, C. R.**
See Blount, Roy (Alton), Jr.

**Waystaff, Simon**
See Swift, Jonathan

**Webb, Beatrice (Martha Potter)**
1858-1943 ........................ **TCLC 22**
See also CA 117; 162; DLB 190; FW

**Webb, Charles (Richard)** 1939- ......... **CLC 7**
See also CA 25-28R

**Webb, James H(enry), Jr.** 1946- ...... **CLC 22**
See also CA 81-84

**Webb, Mary Gladys (Meredith)**
1881-1927 ........................ **TCLC 24**
See also CA 182; 123; DLB 34; FW

**Webb, Mrs. Sidney**
See Webb, Beatrice (Martha Potter)

**Webb, Phyllis** 1927- .......................... **CLC 18**
See also CA 104; CANR 23; CCA 1; CP; CWP; DLB 53

**Webb, Sidney (James)** 1859-1947 .. **TCLC 22**
See also CA 117; 163; DLB 190

**Webber, Andrew Lloyd** ................... **CLC 21**
See also Lloyd Webber, Andrew
See also DFS 7

**Weber, Lenora Mattingly**
1895-1971 ........................... **CLC 12**
See also CA 19-20; 29-32R; CAP 1; SATA 2; SATA-Obit 26

**Weber, Max** 1864-1920 ................... **TCLC 69**
See also CA 109; 189

**Webster, John** 1580(?)-1634(?) .. **LC 33; DA; DAB; DAC; DAM DRAM, MST; DC 2; WLC**
See also BRW 2; CDBLB Before 1660; DLB 58; IDTP; RGEL; WLIT 3

**Webster, Noah** 1758-1843 ................ **NCLC 30**
See also DLB 1, 37, 42, 43, 73, 243

**Wedekind, (Benjamin) Frank(lin)**
1864-1918 ......... **TCLC 7; DAM DRAM**
See also CA 104; 153; DLB 118; EW; RGWL

**Wehr, Demaris** .................................. **CLC 65**

**Weidman, Jerome** 1913-1998 ............. **CLC 7**
See also AITN 2; CA 1-4R; 171; CAD; CANR 1; DLB 28

**Weil, Simone (Adolphine)**
1909-1943 ........................... **TCLC 23**
See also CA 117; 159; EW; FW; GFL 1789 to the Present; MTCW 2

**Weininger, Otto** 1880-1903 ............. **TCLC 84**

**Weinstein, Nathan**
See West, Nathanael

**Weinstein, Nathan von Wallenstein**
See West, Nathanael

**Weir, Peter (Lindsay)** 1944- .............. **CLC 20**
See also CA 113; 123

**Weiss, Peter (Ulrich)** 1916-1982 .. **CLC 3, 15, 51; DAM DRAM**
See also CA 45-48; 106; CANR 3; DFS 5; DLB 69, 124; RGWL

**Weiss, Theodore (Russell)** 1916- ... **CLC 3, 8, 14**
See also CA 9-12R; CAAE 189; CAAS 2; CANR 46, 94; CP; DLB 5

**Welch, (Maurice) Denton**
1915-1948 ........................ **TCLC 22**
See also CA 121; 148; RGEL

**Welch, James** 1940- ..... **CLC 6, 14, 52; DAM MULT, POP**
See also CA 85-88; CANR 42, 66; CN; CP; CPW; DLB 175; NNAL; RGAL; TCWW 2

**Weldon, Fay** 1931- . **CLC 6, 9, 11, 19, 36, 59, 122; DAM POP**
See also BRWS 4; CA 21-24R; CANR 16, 46, 63, 97; CDBLB 1960 to Present; CN; CPW; DLB 14, 194; FW; HGG; INT CANR-16; MTCW 1, 2; RGEL; RGSF

**Wellek, Rene** 1903-1995 ................... **CLC 28**
See also CA 5-8R; 150; CAAS 7; CANR 8; DLB 63; INT CANR-8

**Weller, Michael** 1942- .................. **CLC 10, 53**
See also CA 85-88; CAD; CD

**Weller, Paul** 1958- ............................. **CLC 26**

**Wellershoff, Dieter** 1925- ................... **CLC 46**
See also CA 89-92; CANR 16, 37

**Welles, (George) Orson** 1915-1985 .. **CLC 20, 80**
See also AAYA 40; CA 93-96; 117

**Wellman, John McDowell** 1945-
See Wellman, Mac
See also CA 166; CD

**Wellman, Mac** ..................................... **CLC 65**
See also Wellman, John McDowell; Wellman, John McDowell
See also CAD; RGAL

**Wellman, Manly Wade** 1903-1986 ... **CLC 49**
See also CA 1-4R; 118; CANR 6, 16, 44; FANT; SATA 6; SATA-Obit 47; SFW

**Wells, Carolyn** 1869(?)-1942 .......... **TCLC 35**
See also CA 113; 185; CMW; DLB 11

**Wells, H(erbert) G(eorge)**
1866-1946 . **TCLC 6, 12, 19; DA; DAB; DAC; DAM MST, NOV; SSC 6; WLC**
See also AAYA 18; BPFB 3; BRW 6; CA 110; 121; CDBLB 1914-1945; CLR 64; DA3; DLB 34, 70, 156, 178; EXPS; HGG; LAIT 3; MTCW 1, 2; RGEL; RGSF; SATA 20; SCFW; SFW; SSFS 3; SUFW; WCH; WLIT 4; YAW

**Wells, Rosemary** 1943- ...................... **CLC 12**
See also AAYA 13; BYA 7, 8; CA 85-88; CANR 48; CLR 16, 69; CWRI; MAICYA; SAAS 1; SATA 18, 69, 114; YAW

**Welsh, Irvine** 1958- ......................... **CLC 144**
See also CA 173

**Welty, Eudora** 1909-2001 .... **CLC 1, 2, 5, 14, 22, 33, 105; DA; DAB; DAC; DAM MST, NOV; SSC 1, 27; WLC**
See also AMW; AMWR 1; BPFB 3; CA 9-12R; CABS 1; CANR 32, 65; CDALB 1941-1968; CN; CSW; DA3; DLB 2, 102, 143; DLBD 12; DLBY 87; EXPS; HGG; LAIT 3; MAWW; MTCW 1, 2; RGAL; RGSF; RHW; SSFS 2, 10

**Wen I-to** 1899-1946 ........................ **TCLC 28**

**Wentworth, Robert**
See Hamilton, Edmond

**Werfel, Franz (Viktor)** 1890-1945 ... **TCLC 8**
See also CA 104; 161; DLB 81, 124; RGWL

**Wergeland, Henrik Arnold**
1808-1845 ........................ **NCLC 5**

**Wersba, Barbara** 1932- ................... **CLC 30**
See also AAYA 2, 30; BYA 6, 12, 13; CA 29-32R, 182; CAAE 182; CANR 16, 38; CLR 3; DLB 52; JRDA; MAICYA; SAAS 2; SATA 1, 58; SATA-Essay 103; YAW

**Wertmueller, Lina** 1928- ................... **CLC 16**
See also CA 97-100; CANR 39, 78

**Wescott, Glenway** 1901-1987 .. **CLC 13; SSC 35**
See also CA 13-16R; 121; CANR 23, 70; DLB 4, 9, 102; RGAL

**Wesker, Arnold** 1932- ... **CLC 3, 5, 42; DAB; DAM DRAM**
See also CA 1-4R; CAAS 7; CANR 1, 33; CBD; CD; CDBLB 1960 to Present; DLB 13; MTCW 1; RGEL

**Wesley, Richard (Errol)** 1945- ............ **CLC 7**
See also BW 1; CA 57-60; CAD; CANR 27; CD; DLB 38

**Wessel, Johan Herman** 1742-1785 ........ **LC 7**

**West, Anthony (Panther)**
1914-1987 ....................... **CLC 50**
See also CA 45-48; 124; CANR 3, 19; DLB 15

**West, C. P.**
See Wodehouse, P(elham) G(renville)

**West, Cornel (Ronald)** 1953- ......... **CLC 134; BLCS**
See also CA 144; CANR 91; DLB 246

**West, Delno C(loyde), Jr.** 1936- ........ **CLC 70**
See also CA 57-60

**West, Dorothy** 1907-1998 ............. **TCLC 108**
See also BW 2; CA 143; 169; DLB 76

**West, (Mary) Jessamyn** 1902-1984 ... **CLC 7, 17**
See also CA 9-12R; 112; CANR 27; DLB 6; DLBY 84; MTCW 1, 2; RHW; SATA-Obit 37; YAW

**West, Morris L(anglo)** 1916-1999 ..... **CLC 6, 33**
See also BPFB 3; CA 5-8R; 187; CANR 24, 49, 64; CN; CPW; MTCW 1, 2

**West, Nathanael** 1903-1940 ....... **TCLC 1, 14, 44; SSC 16**
See also AMW; BPFB 3; CA 104; 125; CDALB 1929-1941; DA3; DLB 4, 9, 28; MTCW 1, 2; RGAL

**West, Owen**
See Koontz, Dean R(ay)

**West, Paul** 1930- ...................... **CLC 7, 14, 96**
See also CA 13-16R; CAAS 7; CANR 22, 53, 76, 89; CN; DLB 14; INT CANR-22; MTCW 2

**West, Rebecca** 1892-1983 ... **CLC 7, 9, 31, 50**
See also BPFB 3; BRWS 3; CA 5-8R; 109; CANR 19; DLB 36; DLBY 83; FW; MTCW 1, 2; RGEL

**Westall, Robert (Atkinson)**
1929-1993 ................................. **CLC 17**
See also AAYA 12; BYA 2, 6, 7, 8, 9; CA 69-72; 141; CANR 18, 68; CLR 13; FANT; JRDA; MAICYA; MAICYAS; SAAS 2; SATA 23, 69; SATA-Obit 75; WYA; YAW

**Westermarck, Edward** 1862-1939 . **TCLC 87**

**Westlake, Donald E(dwin)** 1933- ........ **CLC 7, 33; DAM POP**
See also BPFB 3; CA 17-20R; CAAS 13; CANR 16, 44, 65, 94; CMW; CPW; INT CANR-16; MSW; MTCW 2

**Westmacott, Mary**
See Christie, Agatha (Mary Clarissa)

**Weston, Allen**
See Norton, Andre

**Wetcheek, J. L.**
See Feuchtwanger, Lion

**Wetering, Janwillem van de**
See van de Wetering, Janwillem

**Wetherald, Agnes Ethelwyn**
1857-1940 ........................ **TCLC 81**
See also DLB 99

**Wetherell, Elizabeth**
See Warner, Susan (Bogert)

**Whale, James** 1889-1957 .............. **TCLC 63**
**Whalen, Philip** 1923- .................. **CLC 6, 29**
   See also CA 9-12R; CANR 5, 39; CP; DLB 16; WP
**Wharton, Edith (Newbold Jones)**
   1862-1937 ........ **TCLC 3, 9, 27, 53; DA; DAB; DAC; DAM MST, NOV; SSC 6; WLC**
   See also AAYA 25; AMW; AMWR 1; BPFB 3; CA 104; 132; CDALB 1865-1917; DA3; DLB 4, 9, 12, 78, 189; DLBD 13; EXPS; HGG; LAIT 2, 3; MAWW; MTCW 1, 2; NFS 5, 11; RGAL; RGSF; RHW; SSFS 6, 7; SUFW
**Wharton, James**
   See Mencken, H(enry) L(ouis)
**Wharton, William (a pseudonym)** . **CLC 18, 37**
   See also CA 93-96; DLBY 80; INT 93-96
**Wheatley (Peters), Phillis**
   1753(?)-1784 ...... **LC 3, 50; BLC 3; DA; DAC; DAM MST, MULT, POET; PC 3; WLC**
   See also AFAW 1, 2; CDALB 1640-1865; DA3; DLB 31, 50; EXPP; PFS 13; RGAL
**Wheelock, John Hall** 1886-1978 ....... **CLC 14**
   See also CA 13-16R; 77-80; CANR 14; DLB 45
**White, Babington**
   See Braddon, Mary Elizabeth
**White, E(lwyn) B(rooks)**
   1899-1985 . **CLC 10, 34, 39; DAM POP**
   See also AITN 2; AMWS 1; CA 13-16R; 116; CANR 16, 37; CDALBS; CLR 1, 21; CPW; DA3; DLB 11, 22; FANT; MAICYA; MTCW 1, 2; RGAL; SATA 2, 29, 100; SATA-Obit 44
**White, Edmund (Valentine III)**
   1940- ............. **CLC 27, 110; DAM POP**
   See also AAYA 7; CA 45-48; CANR 3, 19, 36, 62; CN; DA3; DLB 227; MTCW 1, 2
**White, Hayden V.** 1928- ................. **CLC 148**
   See also CA 128; DLB 246
**White, Patrick (Victor Martindale)**
   1912-1990 ...... **CLC 3, 4, 5, 7, 9, 18, 65, 69; SSC 39**
   See also BRWS 1; CA 81-84; 132; CANR 43; MTCW 1; RGEL; RGSF; RHW
**White, Phyllis Dorothy James** 1920-
   See James, P. D.
   See also CA 21-24R; CANR 17, 43, 65; CMW; CN; CPW; DA3; DAM POP; MTCW 1, 2
**White, T(erence) H(anbury)**
   1906-1964 ................................ **CLC 30**
   See also AAYA 22; BPFB 3; BYA 4, 5; CA 73-76; CANR 37; DLB 160; FANT; JRDA; LAIT 1; MAICYA; RGEL; SATA 12; SUFW; YAW
**White, Terence de Vere** 1912-1994 ... **CLC 49**
   See also CA 49-52; 145; CANR 3
**White, Walter**
   See White, Walter F(rancis)
   See also BLC; DAM MULT
**White, Walter F(rancis)**
   1893-1955 ................................ **TCLC 15**
   See also White, Walter
   See also BW 1; CA 115; 124; DLB 51
**White, William Hale** 1831-1913
   See Rutherford, Mark
   See also CA 121; 189
**Whitehead, Alfred North**
   1861-1947 ................................ **TCLC 97**
   See also CA 117; 165; DLB 100
**Whitehead, E(dward) A(nthony)**
   1933- ............................................ **CLC 5**
   See also CA 65-68; CANR 58; CD
**Whitemore, Hugh (John)** 1936- ....... **CLC 37**
   See also CA 132; CANR 77; CBD; CD; INT CA-132

**Whitman, Sarah Helen (Power)**
   1803-1878 ................................ **NCLC 19**
   See also DLB 1, 243
**Whitman, Walt(er)** 1819-1892 .. **NCLC 4, 31, 81; DA; DAB; DAC; DAM MST, POET; PC 3; WLC**
   See also AAYA 42; AMW; AMWR 1; CDALB 1640-1865; DA3; DLB 3, 64, 224; EXPP; LAIT 2; PAB; PFS 2, 3, 13; RGAL; SATA 20; WP; WYAS 1
**Whitney, Phyllis A(yame)** 1903- ....... **CLC 42; DAM POP**
   See also AAYA 36; AITN 2; BEST 90:3; CA 1-4R; CANR 3, 25, 38, 60; CLR 59; CMW; CPW; DA3; JRDA; MAICYA; MTCW 2; RHW; SATA 1, 30; YAW
**Whittemore, (Edward) Reed (Jr.)**
   1919- .......................................... **CLC 4**
   See also CA 9-12R; CAAS 8; CANR 4; CP; DLB 5
**Whittier, John Greenleaf**
   1807-1892 ........................... **NCLC 8, 59**
   See also AMWS 1; DLB 1, 243; RGAL
**Whittlebot, Hernia**
   See Coward, Noel (Peirce)
**Wicker, Thomas Grey** 1926-
   See Wicker, Tom
   See also CA 65-68; CANR 21, 46
**Wicker, Tom** ........................................ **CLC 7**
   See also Wicker, Thomas Grey
**Wideman, John Edgar** 1941- ...... **CLC 5, 34, 36, 67, 122; BLC 3; DAM MULT**
   See also AFAW 1, 2; BPFB 4; BW 2, 3; CA 85-88; CANR 14, 42, 67; CN; DLB 33, 143; MTCW 2; RGAL; RGSF; SSFS 6, 12
**Wiebe, Rudy (Henry)** 1934- .. **CLC 6, 11, 14, 138; DAC; DAM MST**
   See also CA 37-40R; CANR 42, 67; CN; DLB 60; RHW
**Wieland, Christoph Martin**
   1733-1813 ................................ **NCLC 17**
   See also DLB 97; EW; RGWL
**Wiene, Robert** 1881-1938 ............... **TCLC 56**
**Wieners, John** 1934- ............................ **CLC 7**
   See also CA 13-16R; CP; DLB 16; WP
**Wiesel, Elie(zer)** 1928- ........ **CLC 3, 5, 11, 37; DA; DAB; DAC; DAM MST, NOV; WLCS**
   See also AAYA 7; AITN 1; CA 5-8R; CAAS 4; CANR 8, 40, 65; CDALBS; DA3; DLB 83; DLBY 87; INT CANR-8; LAIT 4; MTCW 1, 2; NFS 4; SATA 56; YAW
**Wiggins, Marianne** 1947- .................. **CLC 57**
   See also BEST 89:3; CA 130; CANR 60
**Wiggs, Susan** .................................... **CLC 70**
**Wight, James Alfred** 1916-1995
   See Herriot, James
   See also CA 77-80; CPW; SATA 55; SATA-Brief 44; YAW
**Wilbur, Richard (Purdy)** 1921- ..... **CLC 3, 6, 9, 14, 53, 110; DA; DAB; DAC; DAM MST, POET**
   See also AMWS 3; CA 1-4R; CABS 2; CANR 2, 29, 76, 93; CDALBS; CP; DLB 5, 169; EXPP; INT CANR-29; MTCW 1, 2; PAB; PFS 11, 12; RGAL; SATA 9, 108; WP
**Wild, Peter** 1940- ............................... **CLC 14**
   See also CA 37-40R; CP; DLB 5
**Wilde, Oscar (Fingal O'Flahertie Wills)**
   1854(?)-1900 .... **TCLC 1, 8, 23, 41; DA; DAB; DAC; DAM DRAM, MST, NOV; SSC 11; WLC**
   See also BRW 5; CA 104; 119; CDBLB 1890-1914; DA3; DFS 4, 8, 9; DLB 10, 19, 34, 57, 141, 156, 190; EXPS; FANT; RGEL; RGSF; SATA 24; SSFS 7; SUFW; TEA; WCH; WLIT 4

**Wilder, Billy** .......................... **CLC 20**
   See also Wilder, Samuel
   See also DLB 26
**Wilder, Samuel** 1906-
   See Wilder, Billy
   See also CA 89-92
**Wilder, Stephen**
   See Marlowe, Stephen
**Wilder, Thornton (Niven)**
   1897-1975 .. **CLC 1, 5, 6, 10, 15, 35, 82; DA; DAB; DAC; DAM DRAM, MST, NOV; DC 1; WLC**
   See also AAYA 29; AITN 2; AMW; CA 13-16R; 61-64; CAD; CANR 40; CDALBS; DA3; DFS 1, 4; DLB 4, 7, 9, 228; DLBY 97; LAIT 3; MTCW 1, 2; RGAL; RHW; WYAS 1
**Wilding, Michael** 1942- ..................... **CLC 73**
   See also CA 104; CANR 24, 49; CN; RGSF
**Wiley, Richard** 1944- ......................... **CLC 44**
   See also CA 121; 129; CANR 71
**Wilhelm, Kate** ..................................... **CLC 7**
   See also Wilhelm, Katie (Gertrude)
   See also AAYA 20; CAAS 5; DLB 8; INT CANR-17; SCFW 2
**Wilhelm, Katie (Gertrude)** 1928-
   See Wilhelm, Kate
   See also CA 37-40R; CANR 17, 36, 60, 94; MTCW 1; SFW
**Wilkins, Mary**
   See Freeman, Mary E(leanor) Wilkins
**Willard, Nancy** 1936- ..................... **CLC 7, 37**
   See also BYA 5; CA 89-92; CANR 10, 39, 68; CLR 5; CWP; CWRI; DLB 5, 52; FANT; MAICYA; MTCW 1; SATA 37, 71; SATA-Brief 30
**William of Ockham** 1290-1349 ..... **CMLC 32**
**Williams, Ben Ames** 1889-1953 ...... **TCLC 89**
   See also CA 183; DLB 102
**Williams, C(harles) K(enneth)**
   1936- .... **CLC 33, 56, 148; DAM POET**
   See also CA 37-40R; CAAS 26; CANR 57; CP; DLB 5
**Williams, Charles**
   See Collier, James Lincoln
**Williams, Charles (Walter Stansby)**
   1886-1945 ............................. **TCLC 1, 11**
   See also CA 104; 163; DLB 100, 153; FANT; RGEL; SUFW
**Williams, (George) Emlyn**
   1905-1987 .......... **CLC 15; DAM DRAM**
   See also CA 104; 123; CANR 36; DLB 10, 77; MTCW 1
**Williams, Hank** 1923-1953 ............. **TCLC 81**
**Williams, Hugo** 1942- ....................... **CLC 42**
   See also CA 17-20R; CANR 45; CP; DLB 40
**Williams, J. Walker**
   See Wodehouse, P(elham) G(renville)
**Williams, John A(lfred)** 1925- ...... **CLC 5, 13; BLC 3; DAM MULT**
   See also AFAW 2; BW 2, 3; CA 53-56; CAAE 195; CAAS 3; CANR 6, 26, 51; CN; CSW; DLB 2, 33; INT CANR-6; RGAL; SFW
**Williams, Jonathan (Chamberlain)**
   1929- .......................................... **CLC 13**
   See also CA 9-12R; CAAS 12; CANR 8; CP; DLB 5
**Williams, Joy** 1944- .......................... **CLC 31**
   See also CA 41-44R; CANR 22, 48, 97
**Williams, Norman** 1952- .................. **CLC 39**
   See also CA 118
**Williams, Sherley Anne** 1944-1999 . **CLC 89; BLC 3; DAM MULT, POET**
   See also AFAW 2; BW 2, 3; CA 73-76; 185; CANR 25, 82; DLB 41; INT CANR-25; SATA 78; SATA-Obit 116

**Williams, Shirley**
See Williams, Sherley Anne

**Williams, Tennessee** 1914-1983 . **CLC 1, 2, 5, 7, 8, 11, 15, 19, 30, 39, 45, 71, 111; DA; DAB; DAC; DAM DRAM, MST; DC 4; WLC**
See also AAYA 31; AITN 1, 2; AMW; CA 5-8R; 108; CABS 3; CAD; CANR 31; CDALB 1941-1968; DA3; DFS 1, 3, 7, 12; DLB 7; DLBD 4; DLBY 83; GLL 1; LAIT 4; MTCW 1, 2; RGAL

**Williams, Thomas (Alonzo)** 1926-1990 .................................. **CLC 14**
See also CA 1-4R; 132; CANR 2

**Williams, William C.**
See Williams, William Carlos

**Williams, William Carlos** 1883-1963 .... **CLC 1, 2, 5, 9, 13, 22, 42, 67; DA; DAB; DAC; DAM MST, POET; PC 7; SSC 31**
See also AMW; AMWR 1; CA 89-92; CANR 34; CDALB 1917-1929; DA3; DLB 4, 16, 54, 86; EXPP; MTCW 1, 2; PAB; PFS 1, 6, 11; RGAL; RGSF; WP

**Williamson, David (Keith)** 1942- ..... **CLC 56**
See also CA 103; CANR 41; CD

**Williamson, Ellen Douglas** 1905-1984
See Douglas, Ellen
See also CA 17-20R; 114; CANR 39

**Williamson, Jack** ................................ **CLC 29**
See also Williamson, John Stewart
See also CAAS 8; DLB 8; SCFW 2

**Williamson, John Stewart** 1908-
See Williamson, Jack
See also CA 17-20R; CANR 23, 70; SFW

**Willie, Frederick**
See Lovecraft, H(oward) P(hillips)

**Willingham, Calder (Baynard, Jr.)** 1922-1995 .................................. **CLC 5, 51**
See also CA 5-8R; 147; CANR 3; CSW; DLB 2, 44; IDFW 3, 4; MTCW 1

**Willis, Charles**
See Clarke, Arthur C(harles)

**Willy**
See Colette, (Sidonie-Gabrielle)

**Willy, Colette**
See Colette, (Sidonie-Gabrielle)
See also GLL 1

**Wilson, A(ndrew) N(orman)** 1950- .. **CLC 33**
See also BRWS 6; CA 112; 122; CN; DLB 14, 155, 194; MTCW 2

**Wilson, Angus (Frank Johnstone)** 1913-1991 . **CLC 2, 3, 5, 25, 34; SSC 21**
See also BRWS 1; CA 5-8R; 134; CANR 21; DLB 15, 139, 155; MTCW 1, 2; RGEL; RGSF

**Wilson, August** 1945- ... **CLC 39, 50, 63, 118; BLC 3; DA; DAB; DAC; DAM DRAM, MST, MULT; DC 2; WLCS**
See also AAYA 16; AFAW 2; AMWS 8; BW 2, 3; CA 115; 122; CAD; CANR 42, 54, 76; CD; DA3; DFS 3, 7; DLB 228; LAIT 4; MTCW 1, 2; RGAL

**Wilson, Brian** 1942- ............................ **CLC 12**

**Wilson, Colin** 1931- ....................... **CLC 3, 14**
See also CA 1-4R; CAAS 5; CANR 1, 22, 33, 77; CMW; CN; DLB 14, 194; HGG; MTCW 1; SFW

**Wilson, Dirk**
See Pohl, Frederik

**Wilson, Edmund** 1895-1972 .. **CLC 1, 2, 3, 8, 24**
See also AMW; CA 1-4R; 37-40R; CANR 1, 46; DLB 63; MTCW 1, 2; RGAL

**Wilson, Ethel Davis (Bryant)** 1888(?)-1980 ....... **CLC 13; DAC; DAM POET**
See also CA 102; DLB 68; MTCW 1; RGEL

**Wilson, Harriet**
See Wilson, Harriet E. Adams
See also DLB 239

**Wilson, Harriet E. Adams** 1827(?)-1863(?) ........ **NCLC 78; BLC 3; DAM MULT**
See also Wilson, Harriet
See also DLB 50, 243

**Wilson, John** 1785-1854 .................... **NCLC 5**

**Wilson, John (Anthony) Burgess** 1917-1993
See Burgess, Anthony
See also CA 1-4R; 143; CANR 2, 46; DA3; DAC; DAM NOV; MTCW 1, 2

**Wilson, Lanford** 1937- ........... **CLC 7, 14, 36; DAM DRAM**
See also CA 17-20R; CABS 3; CAD; CANR 45, 96; CD; DFS 4, 9, 12; DLB 7

**Wilson, Robert M.** 1944- ................. **CLC 7, 9**
See also CA 49-52; CAD; CANR 2, 41; CD; MTCW 1

**Wilson, Robert McLiam** 1964- ......... **CLC 59**
See also CA 132

**Wilson, Sloan** 1920- .......................... **CLC 32**
See also CA 1-4R; CANR 1, 44; CN

**Wilson, Snoo** 1948- ........................... **CLC 33**
See also CA 69-72; CBD; CD

**Wilson, William S(mith)** 1932- ......... **CLC 49**
See also CA 81-84

**Wilson, (Thomas) Woodrow** 1856-1924 ............................... **TCLC 79**
See also CA 166; DLB 47

**Wilson and Warnke eds.** .................. **CLC 65**

**Winchilsea, Anne (Kingsmill) Finch** 1661-1720
See Finch, Anne
See also RGEL

**Windham, Basil**
See Wodehouse, P(elham) G(renville)

**Wingrove, David (John)** 1954- ......... **CLC 68**
See also CA 133; SFW

**Winnemucca, Sarah** 1844-1891 .... **NCLC 79; DAM MULT**
See also DLB 175; NNAL; RGAL

**Winstanley, Gerrard** 1609-1676 .......... **LC 52**

**Wintergreen, Jane**
See Duncan, Sara Jeannette

**Winters, Janet Lewis** ......................... **CLC 41**
See also Lewis, Janet
See also DLBY 87

**Winters, (Arthur) Yvor** 1900-1968 .... **CLC 4, 8, 32**
See also AMWS 2; CA 11-12; 25-28R; CAP 1; DLB 48; MTCW 1; RGAL

**Winterson, Jeanette** 1959- .... **CLC 64; DAM POP**
See also BRWS 4; CA 136; CANR 58; CN; CPW; DA3; DLB 207; FANT; FW; GLL 1; MTCW 2; RHW

**Winthrop, John** 1588-1649 ................. **LC 31**
See also DLB 24, 30

**Wirth, Louis** 1897-1952 .................... **TCLC 92**
See also CA 159

**Wiseman, Frederick** 1930- ................ **CLC 20**
See also CA 159

**Wister, Owen** 1860-1938 ................... **TCLC 21**
See also BPFB 3; CA 108; 162; DLB 9, 78, 186; RGAL; SATA 62; TCWW 2

**Witkacy**
See Witkiewicz, Stanislaw Ignacy

**Witkiewicz, Stanislaw Ignacy** 1885-1939 ................................ **TCLC 8**
See also CA 105; 162; DLB 215; EW; RGWL; SFW

**Wittgenstein, Ludwig (Josef Johann)** 1889-1951 ............................... **TCLC 59**
See also CA 113; 164; MTCW 2

**Wittig, Monique** 1935(?)- .................. **CLC 22**
See also CA 116; 135; CWW 2; DLB 83; FW; GLL 1

**Wittlin, Jozef** 1896-1976 ..................... **CLC 25**
See also CA 49-52; 65-68; CANR 3

**Wodehouse, P(elham) G(renville)** 1881-1975 .... **CLC 1, 2, 5, 10, 22; DAB; DAC; DAM NOV; SSC 2**
See also AITN 2; BRWS 3; CA 45-48; 57-60; CANR 3, 33; CDBLB 1914-1945; CPW 1; DA3; DLB 34, 162; MTCW 1, 2; RGEL; RGSF; SATA 22; SSFS 10; TCLC 108

**Woiwode, L.**
See Woiwode, Larry (Alfred)

**Woiwode, Larry (Alfred)** 1941- ... **CLC 6, 10**
See also CA 73-76; CANR 16, 94; CN; DLB 6; INT CANR-16

**Wojciechowska, Maia (Teresa)** 1927- ............................................. **CLC 26**
See also AAYA 8; BYA 3; CA 9-12R; 183; CAAE 183; CANR 4, 41; CLR 1; JRDA; MAICYA; SAAS 1; SATA 1, 28, 83; SATA-Essay 104; YAW

**Wojtyla, Karol**
See John Paul II, Pope

**Wolf, Christa** 1929- ....... **CLC 14, 29, 58, 150**
See also CA 85-88; CANR 45; CWW 2; DLB 75; FW; MTCW 1; RGWL

**Wolfe, Gene (Rodman)** 1931- ........... **CLC 25; DAM POP**
See also AAYA 35; CA 57-60; CAAS 9; CANR 6, 32, 60; CPW; DLB 8; FANT; MTCW 2; SATA 118; SCFW 2; SFW

**Wolfe, George C.** 1954- ........ **CLC 49; BLCS**
See also CA 149; CAD; CD

**Wolfe, Thomas (Clayton)** 1900-1938 ...... **TCLC 4, 13, 29, 61; DA; DAB; DAC; DAM MST, NOV; SSC 33; WLC**
See also AMW; BPFB 3; CA 104; 132; CANR 102; CDALB 1929-1941; DA3; DLB 9, 102; DLBD 2, 16; DLBY 85, 97; MTCW 1, 2; RGAL

**Wolfe, Thomas Kennerly, Jr.** 1930- ................... **CLC 147; DAM POP**
See also Wolfe, Tom
See also CA 13-16R; CANR 9, 33, 70; DA3; DLB 185; INT CANR-9; MTCW 1, 2; TUS

**Wolfe, Tom** ............... **CLC 1, 2, 9, 15, 35, 51**
See also Wolfe, Thomas Kennerly, Jr.
See also AAYA 8; AITN 2; AMWS 3; BEST 89:1; BPFB 3; CN; CPW; CSW; DLB 152; LAIT 5; RGAL

**Wolff, Geoffrey (Ansell)** 1937- .......... **CLC 41**
See also CA 29-32R; CANR 29, 43, 78

**Wolff, Sonia**
See Levitin, Sonia (Wolff)

**Wolff, Tobias (Jonathan Ansell)** 1945- ................................ **CLC 39, 64**
See also AAYA 16; AMWS 7; BEST 90:2; BYA 12; CA 114; 117; CAAS 22; CANR 54, 76, 96; CN; CSW; DA3; DLB 130; INT CA-117; MTCW 2; RGAL; RGSF; SSFS 4, 11

**Wolfram von Eschenbach** c. 1170-c. 1220 .................................... **CMLC 5**
See also DLB 138; EW; RGWL

**Wolitzer, Hilma** 1930- ........................ **CLC 17**
See also CA 65-68; CANR 18, 40; INT CANR-18; SATA 31; YAW

**Wollstonecraft, Mary** 1759-1797 ..... **LC 5, 50**
See also BRWS 3; CDBLB 1789-1832; DLB 39, 104, 158; FW; LAIT 1; RGEL; WLIT 3

**Wonder, Stevie** ................................. **CLC 12**
See also Morris, Steveland Judkins

**Wong, Jade Snow** 1922- .................... **CLC 17**
See also CA 109; CANR 91; SATA 112

**Woodberry, George Edward** 1855-1930 ............................... **TCLC 73**
See also CA 165; DLB 71, 103

**Woodcott, Keith**
See Brunner, John (Kilian Houston)

**Woodruff, Robert W.**
See Mencken, H(enry) L(ouis)

**Woolf, (Adeline) Virginia**
1882-1941 .. **TCLC 1, 5, 20, 43, 56, 101; DA; DAB; DAC; DAM MST, NOV; SSC 7; WLC**
See also BPFB 3; BRW 7; CA 104; 130; CANR 64; CDBLB 1914-1945; DA3; DLB 36, 100, 162; DLBD 10; EXPS; FW; LAIT 3; MTCW 1, 2; NCFS 2; NFS 8, 12; RGEL; RGSF; SSFS 4, 12; WLIT 4

**Woollcott, Alexander (Humphreys)**
1887-1943 ................................. **TCLC 5**
See also CA 105; 161; DLB 29

**Woolrich, Cornell** ............................ **CLC 77**
See also Hopley-Woolrich, Cornell George
See also MSW

**Woolson, Constance Fenimore**
1840-1894 ............................... **NCLC 82**
See also DLB 12, 74, 189, 221; RGAL

**Wordsworth, Dorothy** 1771-1855 .. **NCLC 25**
See also DLB 107

**Wordsworth, William** 1770-1850 .. **NCLC 12, 38; DA; DAB; DAC; DAM MST, POET; PC 4; WLC**
See also BRW 4; CDBLB 1789-1832; DA3; DLB 93, 107; EXPP; PAB; PFS 2; RGEL; WLIT 3; WP

**Wotton, Sir Henry** 1568-1639 .............. **LC 68**
See also DLB 121; RGEL

**Wouk, Herman** 1915- ... **CLC 1, 9, 38; DAM NOV, POP**
See also BPFB 2, 3; CA 5-8R; CANR 6, 33, 67; CDALBS; CN; CPW; DA3; DLBY 82; INT CANR-6; LAIT 4; MTCW 1, 2; NFS 7

**Wright, Charles (Penzel, Jr.)** 1935- .. **CLC 6, 13, 28, 119, 146**
See also AMWS 5; CA 29-32R; CAAS 7; CANR 23, 36, 62, 88; CP; DLB 165; DLBY 82; MTCW 1, 2; PFS 10

**Wright, Charles Stevenson** 1932- ... **CLC 49; BLC 3; DAM MULT, POET**
See also BW 1; CA 9-12R; CANR 26; CN; DLB 33

**Wright, Frances** 1795-1852 ............ **NCLC 74**
See also DLB 73

**Wright, Frank Lloyd** 1867-1959 .... **TCLC 95**
See also AAYA 33; CA 174

**Wright, Jack R.**
See Harris, Mark

**Wright, James (Arlington)**
1927-1980 ........ **CLC 3, 5, 10, 28; DAM POET; PC 36**
See also AITN 2; AMWS 3; CA 49-52; 97-100; CANR 4, 34, 64; CDALBS; DLB 5, 169; EXPP; MTCW 1, 2; PFS 7, 8; RGAL; WP

**Wright, Judith (Arundell)**
1915-2000 ................. **CLC 11, 53; PC 14**
See also CA 13-16R; 188; CANR 31, 76, 93; CP; CWP; MTCW 1, 2; PFS 8; RGEL; SATA 14; SATA-Obit 121

**Wright, L(aurali) R.** 1939- ................ **CLC 44**
See also CA 138; CMW

**Wright, Richard (Nathaniel)**
1908-1960 .... **CLC 1, 3, 4, 9, 14, 21, 48, 74; BLC 3; DA; DAB; DAC; DAM MST, MULT, NOV; SSC 2; WLC**
See also AAYA 5, 42; AFAW 1, 2; AMW; BPFB 3; BW 1; BYA 2; CA 108; CANR 64; CDALB 1929-1941; DA3; DLB 76, 102; DLBD 2; EXPN; LAIT 3, 4; MTCW 1, 2; NCFS 1; NFS 1, 7; RGAL; RGSF; SSFS 3, 9; YAW

**Wright, Richard B(ruce)** 1937- .......... **CLC 6**
See also CA 85-88; DLB 53

**Wright, Rick** 1945- ............................. **CLC 35**

**Wright, Rowland**
See Wells, Carolyn

**Wright, Stephen** 1946- ....................... **CLC 33**

**Wright, Willard Huntington** 1888-1939
See Van Dine, S. S.
See also CA 115; 189; CMW; DLBD 16

**Wright, William** 1930- ....................... **CLC 44**
See also CA 53-56; CANR 7, 23

**Wroth, Lady Mary** 1587-1653(?) ........ **LC 30**
See also DLB 121

**Wu Ch'eng-en** 1500(?)-1582(?) ............. **LC 7**

**Wu Ching-tzu** 1701-1754 ..................... **LC 2**

**Wurlitzer, Rudolph** 1938(?)- .... **CLC 2, 4, 15**
See also CA 85-88; CN; DLB 173

**Wyatt, Sir Thomas** c. 1503-1542 . **LC 70; PC 27**
See also BRW 1; DLB 132; EXPP; RGEL; TEA

**Wycherley, William** 1640-1716 ...... **LC 8, 21; DAM DRAM**
See also BRW 2; CDBLB 1660-1789; DLB 80; RGEL

**Wylie, Elinor (Morton Hoyt)**
1885-1928 ...................... **TCLC 8; PC 23**
See also AMWS 1; CA 105; 162; DLB 9, 45; EXPP; RGAL

**Wylie, Philip (Gordon)** 1902-1971 ... **CLC 43**
See also CA 21-22; 33-36R; CAP 2; DLB 9; SFW

**Wyndham, John** ............................ **CLC 19**
See also Harris, John (Wyndham Parkes Lucas) Beynon
See also SCFW 2

**Wyss, Johann David Von**
1743-1818 ................................ **NCLC 10**
See also JRDA; MAICYA; SATA 29; SATA-Brief 27

**Xenophon** c. 430B.C.-c. 354B.C. ... **CMLC 17**
See also AW 1; DLB 176; RGWL

**Yakumo Koizumi**
See Hearn, (Patricio) Lafcadio (Tessima Carlos)

**Yamamoto, Hisaye** 1921- ........ **SSC 34; AAL; DAM MULT**
See also LAIT 4

**Yanez, Jose Donoso**
See Donoso (Yanez), Jose

**Yanovsky, Basile S.**
See Yanovsky, V(assily) S(emenovich)

**Yanovsky, V(assily) S(emenovich)**
1906-1989 ........................ **CLC 2, 18**
See also CA 97-100; 129

**Yates, Richard** 1926-1992 ......... **CLC 7, 8, 23**
See also CA 5-8R; 139; CANR 10, 43; DLB 2, 234; DLBY 81, 92; INT CANR-10

**Yeats, W. B.**
See Yeats, William Butler

**Yeats, William Butler** 1865-1939 .... **TCLC 1, 11, 18, 31, 93; DA; DAB; DAC; DAM DRAM, MST, POET; PC 20; WLC**
See also BRW 6; CA 104; 127; CANR 45; CDBLB 1890-1914; DA3; DLB 10, 19, 98, 156; EXPP; MTCW 1, 2; PAB; PFS 1, 2, 5, 7, 13; RGEL; WLIT 4; WP

**Yehoshua, A(braham) B.** 1936- .. **CLC 13, 31**
See also CA 33-36R; CANR 43, 90; RGSF

**Yellow Bird**
See Ridge, John Rollin

**Yep, Laurence Michael** 1948- ........... **CLC 35**
See also AAYA 5, 31; BYA 7; CA 49-52; CANR 1, 46, 92; CLR 3, 17, 54; DLB 52; FANT; JRDA; MAICYA; MAICYAS; SATA 7, 69, 123; WYA; YAW

**Yerby, Frank G(arvin)** 1916-1991 . **CLC 1, 7, 22; BLC 3; DAM MULT**
See also BPFB 3; BW 1, 3; CA 9-12R; 136; CANR 16, 52; DLB 76; INT CANR-16; MTCW 1; RGAL; RHW

**Yesenin, Sergei Alexandrovich**
See Esenin, Sergei (Alexandrovich)

**Yevtushenko, Yevgeny (Alexandrovich)**
1933- .. **CLC 1, 3, 13, 26, 51, 126; DAM POET**
See also Evtushenko, Evgenii Aleksandrovich
See also CA 81-84; CANR 33, 54; CWW 2; MTCW 1

**Yezierska, Anzia** 1885(?)-1970 .......... **CLC 46**
See also CA 126; 89-92; DLB 28, 221; FW; MTCW 1; RGAL

**Yglesias, Helen** 1915- ..................... **CLC 7, 22**
See also CA 37-40R; CAAS 20; CANR 15, 65, 95; CN; INT CANR-15; MTCW 1

**Yokomitsu, Riichi** 1898-1947 .......... **TCLC 47**
See also CA 170

**Yonge, Charlotte (Mary)**
1823-1901 ................................. **TCLC 48**
See also CA 109; 163; DLB 18, 163; RGEL; SATA 17; WCH

**York, Jeremy**
See Creasey, John

**York, Simon**
See Heinlein, Robert A(nson)

**Yorke, Henry Vincent** 1905-1974 ..... **CLC 13**
See also Green, Henry
See also CA 85-88; 49-52

**Yosano Akiko** 1878-1942 .... **TCLC 59; PC 11**
See also CA 161

**Yoshimoto, Banana** ......................... **CLC 84**
See also Yoshimoto, Mahoko
See also NFS 7

**Yoshimoto, Mahoko** 1964-
See Yoshimoto, Banana
See also CA 144; CANR 98

**Young, Al(bert James)** 1939- . **CLC 19; BLC 3; DAM MULT**
See also BW 2, 3; CA 29-32R; CANR 26, 65; CN; CP; DLB 33

**Young, Andrew (John)** 1885-1971 ...... **CLC 5**
See also CA 5-8R; CANR 7, 29; RGEL

**Young, Collier**
See Bloch, Robert (Albert)

**Young, Edward** 1683-1765 ............... **LC 3, 40**
See also DLB 95; RGEL

**Young, Marguerite (Vivian)**
1909-1995 ................................. **CLC 82**
See also CA 13-16; 150; CAP 1; CN

**Young, Neil** 1945- ............................ **CLC 17**
See also CA 110; CCA 1

**Young Bear, Ray A.** 1950- ...... **CLC 94; DAM MULT**
See also CA 146; DLB 175; NNAL

**Yourcenar, Marguerite** 1903-1987 ... **CLC 19, 38, 50, 87; DAM NOV**
See also BPFB 3; CA 69-72; CANR 23, 60, 93; DLB 72; DLBY 88; EW; GFL 1789 to the Present; GLL 1; MTCW 1, 2; RGWL

**Yuan, Chu** 340(?)B.C.-278(?)B.C. . **CMLC 36**

**Yurick, Sol** 1925- ................................ **CLC 6**
See also CA 13-16R; CANR 25; CN

**Zabolotsky, Nikolai Alekseevich**
1903-1958 ................................. **TCLC 52**
See also CA 116; 164

**Zagajewski, Adam** 1945- ...................... **PC 27**
See also CA 186; DLB 232

**Zalygin, Sergei** -2000 ........................ **CLC 59**

**Zamiatin, Evgenii**
See Zamyatin, Evgeny Ivanovich
See also RGSF; RGWL

**Zamiatin, Yevgenii**
See Zamyatin, Evgeny Ivanovich

**Zamora, Bernice (B. Ortiz)** 1938- .. **CLC 89; DAM MULT; HLC 2**
See also CA 151; CANR 80; DLB 82; HW 1, 2

**Zamyatin, Evgeny Ivanovich**
1884-1937 .............................. **TCLC 8, 37**
See also Zamiatin, Evgenii
See also CA 105; 166; EW; SFW

**Zangwill, Israel** 1864-1926 ... **TCLC 16; SSC 44**
See also CA 109; 167; CMW; DLB 10, 135, 197; RGEL

**Zappa, Francis Vincent, Jr.** 1940-1993
See Zappa, Frank
See also CA 108; 143; CANR 57

**Zappa, Frank** ...................................... **CLC 17**
See also Zappa, Francis Vincent, Jr.

**Zaturenska, Marya** 1902-1982 ..... **CLC 6, 11**
See also CA 13-16R; 105; CANR 22

**Zeami** 1363-1443 ...................................... **DC 7**
See also RGWL

**Zelazny, Roger (Joseph)** 1937-1995 . **CLC 21**
See also AAYA 7; BPFB 3; CA 21-24R; 148; CANR 26, 60; CN; DLB 8; FANT; MTCW 1, 2; SATA 57; SATA-Brief 39; SCFW; SFW; SUFW

**Zhdanov, Andrei Alexandrovich**
1896-1948 .................................. **TCLC 18**
See also CA 117; 167

**Zhukovsky, Vasily (Andreevich)**
1783-1852 ................................. **NCLC 35**
See also DLB 205

**Ziegenhagen, Eric** ............................. **CLC 55**

**Zimmer, Jill Schary**
See Robinson, Jill

**Zimmerman, Robert**
See Dylan, Bob

**Zindel, Paul** 1936- ..... **CLC 6, 26; DA; DAB; DAC; DAM DRAM, MST, NOV; DC 5**
See also AAYA 2, 37; BYA 2, 3, 8, 11; CA 73-76; CAD; CANR 31, 65; CD; CDALBS; CLR 3, 45; DA3; DFS 12; DLB 7, 52; JRDA; LAIT 5; MAICYA; MTCW 1, 2; SATA 16, 58, 102; YAW

**Zinov'Ev, A. A.**
See Zinoviev, Alexander (Aleksandrovich)

**Zinoviev, Alexander (Aleksandrovich)**
1922- .......................................... **CLC 19**
See also CA 116; 133; CAAS 10

**Zoilus**
See Lovecraft, H(oward) P(hillips)

**Zola, Emile (Edouard Charles Antoine)**
1840-1902 ........ **TCLC 1, 6, 21, 41; DA; DAB; DAC; DAM MST, NOV; WLC**
See also CA 104; 138; DA3; DLB 123; EW; GFL 1789 to the Present; IDTP; RGWL

**Zoline, Pamela** 1941- ........................ **CLC 62**
See also CA 161; SFW

**Zoroaster** 628(?)B.C.-551(?)B.C. ... **CMLC 40**

**Zorrilla y Moral, Jose** 1817-1893 .... **NCLC 6**

**Zoshchenko, Mikhail (Mikhailovich)**
1895-1958 ................. **TCLC 15; SSC 15**
See also CA 115; 160; RGSF

**Zuckmayer, Carl** 1896-1977 ............. **CLC 18**
See also CA 69-72; DLB 56, 124; RGWL

**Zuk, Georges**
See Skelton, Robin
See also CCA 1

**Zukofsky, Louis** 1904-1978 ... **CLC 1, 2, 4, 7, 11, 18; DAM POET; PC 11**
See also AMWS 3; CA 9-12R; 77-80; CANR 39; DLB 5, 165; MTCW 1; RGAL

**Zweig, Paul** 1935-1984 ................ **CLC 34, 42**
See also CA 85-88; 113

**Zweig, Stefan** 1881-1942 ................. **TCLC 17**
See also CA 112; 170; DLB 81, 118

**Zwingli, Huldreich** 1484-1531 ............. **LC 37**
See also DLB 179

# Literary Criticism Series
# Cumulative Topic Index

This index lists all topic entries in Gale's *Classical and Medieval Literature Criticism, Contemporary Literary Criticism, Literature Criticism from 1400 to 1800, Nineteenth-Century Literature Criticism,* and *Twentieth-Century Literary Criticism.*

**The Aesopic Fable** LC 51: 1-100
   The British Aesopic Fable, 1-54
   The Aesopic Tradition in Non-English-Speaking Cultures, 55-66
   Political Uses of the Aesopic Fable, 67-88
   The Evolution of the Aesopic Fable, 89-99

**Age of Johnson** LC 15: 1-87
   Johnson's London, 3-15
   aesthetics of neoclassicism, 15-36
   "age of prose and reason," 36-45
   clubmen and bluestockings, 45-56
   printing technology, 56-62
   periodicals: "a map of busy life," 62-74
   transition, 74-86

**Age of Spenser** LC 39: 1-70
   Overviews, 2-21
   Literary Style, 22-34
   Poets and the Crown, 34-70

**AIDS in Literature** CLC 81: 365-416

**Alcohol and Literature** TCLC 70: 1-58
   overview, 2-8
   fiction, 8-48
   poetry and drama, 48-58

**American Abolitionism** NCLC 44: 1-73
   overviews, 2-26
   abolitionist ideals, 26-46
   the literature of abolitionism, 46-72

**American Autobiography** TCLC 86: 1-115
   overviews, 3-36
   American authors and autobiography, 36-82
   African-American autobiography, 82-114

**American Black Humor Fiction** TCLC 54: 1-85
   characteristics of black humor, 2-13
   origins and development, 13-38
   black humor distinguished from related literary trends, 38-60
   black humor and society, 60-75
   black humor reconsidered, 75-83

**American Civil War in Literature** NCLC 32: 1-109
   overviews, 2-20
   regional perspectives, 20-54
   fiction popular during the war, 54-79
   the historical novel, 79-108

**American Frontier in Literature** NCLC 28: 1-103
   definitions, 2-12
   development, 12-17
   nonfiction writing about the frontier, 17-30
   frontier fiction, 30-45
   frontier protagonists, 45-66
   portrayals of Native Americans, 66-86
   feminist readings, 86-98
   twentieth-century reaction against frontier literature, 98-100

**American Humor Writing** NCLC 52: 1-59
   overviews, 2-12
   the Old Southwest, 12-42
   broader impacts, 42-5
   women humorists, 45-58

*American Mercury,* **The** TCLC 74: 1-80

**American Popular Song, Golden Age of** TCLC 42: 1-49
   background and major figures, 2-34
   the lyrics of popular songs, 34-47

**American Proletarian Literature** TCLC 54: 86-175
   overviews, 87-95
   American proletarian literature and the American Communist Party, 95-111
   ideology and literary merit, 111-7
   novels, 117-36
   Gastonia, 136-48
   drama, 148-54
   journalism, 154-9
   proletarian literature in the United States, 159-74

**American Romanticism** NCLC 44: 74-138
   overviews, 74-84
   sociopolitical influences, 84-104
   Romanticism and the American frontier, 104-15
   thematic concerns, 115-37

**American Western Literature** TCLC 46: 1-100
   definition and development of American Western literature, 2-7
   characteristics of the Western novel, 8-23
   Westerns as history and fiction, 23-34
   critical reception of American Western literature, 34-41
   the Western hero, 41-73
   women in Western fiction, 73-91
   later Western fiction, 91-9

**American Writers in Paris** TCLC 98: 1-156
   overviews and general studies, 2-155

**Anarchism** NCLC 84: 1-97
   overviews and general studies, 2-23
   the French anarchist tradition, 23-56
   Anglo-American anarchism, 56-68
   anarchism: incidents and issues, 68-97

**Animals in Literature** TCLC 106: 1-120
   overviews and general studies, 2-8
   animals in American literature, 8-45
   animals in Canadian literature, 45-57
   animals in European literature, 57-100
   animals in Latin American literature, 100-06
   animals in women's literature, 106-20

**The Apocalyptic Movement** TCLC 106: 121-69

**Aristotle** CMLC 31:1-397
   philosophy, 3-100
   poetics, 101-219
   rhetoric, 220-301
   science, 302-397

**Art and Literature** TCLC 54: 176-248
   overviews, 176-93
   definitions, 193-219
   influence of visual arts on literature, 219-31
   spatial form in literature, 231-47

**Arthurian Literature** CMLC 10: 1-127
   historical context and literary beginnings, 2-27
   development of the legend through Malory, 27-64
   development of the legend from Malory to the Victorian Age, 65-81
   themes and motifs, 81-95
   principal characters, 95-125

**Arthurian Revival** NCLC 36: 1-77
   overviews, 2-12
   Tennyson and his influence, 12-43
   other leading figures, 43-73
   the Arthurian legend in the visual arts, 73-6

**Australian Literature** TCLC 50: 1-94
   origins and development, 2-21
   characteristics of Australian literature, 21-33
   historical and critical perspectives, 33-41
   poetry, 41-58
   fiction, 58-76
   drama, 76-82
   Aboriginal literature, 82-91

**Beat Generation, Literature of the** TCLC 42: 50-102
   overviews, 51-9
   the Beat generation as a social phenomenon, 59-62
   development, 62-5

Beat literature, 66-96
   influence, 97-100

**The Bell Curve Controversy** CLC 91: 281-330

*Bildungsroman* **in Nineteenth-Century Literature** NCLC 20: 92-168
   surveys, 93-113
   in Germany, 113-40
   in England, 140-56
   female *Bildungsroman,* 156-67

**Bloomsbury Group** TCLC 34: 1-73
   history and major figures, 2-13
   definitions, 13-7
   influences, 17-27
   thought, 27-40
   prose, 40-52
   and literary criticism, 52-4
   political ideals, 54-61
   response to, 61-71

**The Blues in Literature** TCLC 82: 1-71

**Bly, Robert,** *Iron John: A Book about Men and Men's Work* CLC 70: 414-62

**The Book of J** CLC 65: 289-311

**British Ephemeral Literature** LC 59: 1-70
   overviews, 1-9
   broadside ballads, 10-40
   chapbooks, jestbooks, pamphlets, and newspapers, 40-69

**Buddhism and Literature** TCLC 70: 59-164
   eastern literature, 60-113
   western literature, 113-63

**Businessman in American Literature** TCLC 26: 1-48
   portrayal of the businessman, 1-32
   themes and techniques in business fiction, 32-47

**The Calendar** LC 55: 1-92
   overviews, 2-19
   measuring time, 19-28
   calendars and culture, 28-60
   calendar reform, 60-92

**Catholicism in Nineteenth-Century American Literature** NCLC 64: 1-58
   overviews, 3-14
   polemical literature, 14-46
   Catholicism in literature, 47-57

**Celtic Mythology** CMLC 26: 1-111
   overviews, 2-22
   Celtic myth as literature and history, 22-48
   Celtic religion: Druids and divinities, 48-80
   Fionn MacCuhaill and the Fenian cycle, 80-111

**Celtic Twilight See Irish Literary Renaissance**

**Chartist Movement and Literature, The** NCLC 60: 1-84
   overview: nineteenth-century working-class fiction, 2-19
   Chartist fiction and poetry, 19-73
   the Chartist press, 73-84

**Children's Literature, Nineteenth-Century** NCLC 52: 60-135
   overviews, 61-72
   moral tales, 72-89
   fairy tales and fantasy, 90-119
   making men/making women, 119-34

**Christianity in Twentieth-Century Literature** TCLC 110: 1-79
   overviews and general studies, 2-31
   Christianity in twentieth-century fiction, 31-78

**The City and Literature** TCLC 90: 1-124
   Overviews, 2-9
   The City in American Literature, 9-86
   The City in European Literature, 86-124

**Civic Critics, Russian** NCLC 20: 402-46
   principal figures and background, 402-9
   and Russian Nihilism, 410-6
   aesthetic and critical views, 416-45

**The Cockney School** NCLC 68: 1-64
   overview, 2-7
   *Blackwood's Magazine* and the contemporary critical response, 7-24
   the political and social import of the Cockneys and their critics, 24-63

**Colonial America: The Intellectual Background** LC 25: 1-98
   overviews, 2-17
   philosophy and politics, 17-31
   early religious influences in Colonial America, 31-60
   consequences of the Revolution, 60-78
   religious influences in post-revolutionary America, 78-87
   colonial literary genres, 87-97

**Colonialism in Victorian English Literature** NCLC 56: 1-77
   overviews, 2-34
   colonialism and gender, 34-51
   monsters and the occult, 51-76

**Columbus, Christopher, Books on the Quincentennial of His Arrival in the New World** CLC 70: 329-60

**Comic Books** TCLC 66: 1-139
   historical and critical perspectives, 2-48
   superheroes, 48-67
   underground comix, 67-88
   comic books and society, 88-122
   adult comics and graphic novels, 122-36

**Connecticut Wits** NCLC 48: 1-95
   general overviews, 2-40
   major works, 40-76
   intellectual context, 76-95

**Crime in Literature** TCLC 54: 249-307
   evolution of the criminal figure in literature, 250-61
   crime and society, 261-77
   literary perspectives on crime and punishment, 277-88
   writings by criminals, 288-306

**The Crusades** CMLC 38: 1-144
   history of the Crusades, 3-60
   literature of the Crusades, 60-116
   the Crusades and the people: attitudes and influences, 116-44

**Cyberpunk** TCLC 106: 170-366
   overviews and general studies, 171-88
   feminism and cyberpunk, 188-230
   history and cyberpunk, 230-70
   sexuality and cyberpunk, 270-98
   social issues and cyberpunk, 299-366

**Czechoslovakian Literature of the Twentieth Century** TCLC 42:103-96
   through World War II, 104-35
   de-Stalinization, the Prague Spring, and contemporary literature, 135-72
   Slovak literature, 172-85
   Czech science fiction, 185-93

**Dadaism** TCLC 46: 101-71
   background and major figures, 102-16
   definitions, 116-26
   manifestos and commentary by Dadaists, 126-40
   theater and film, 140-58
   nature and characteristics of Dadaist writing, 158-70

**Darwinism and Literature** NCLC 32: 110-206
   background, 110-31
   direct responses to Darwin, 131-71
   collateral effects of Darwinism, 171-205

**Death in American Literature** NCLC 92: 1-170
   overviews, 2-32
   death in the works of Emily Dickinson, 32-72
   death in the works of Herman Melville, 72-101
   death in the works of Edgar Allan Poe, 101-43
   death in the works of Walt Whitman, 143-70

**Death in Nineteenth-Century British Literature** NCLC 68: 65-142
   overviews, 66-92
   responses to death, 92-102
   feminist perspectives, 103-17
   striving for immortality, 117-41

**Death in Literature** TCLC 78:1-183
   fiction, 2-115
   poetry, 115-46
   drama, 146-81

**de Man, Paul, Wartime Journalism of** CLC 55: 382-424

**Detective Fiction, Nineteenth-Century** NCLC 36: 78-148
   origins of the genre, 79-100
   history of nineteenth-century detective fiction, 101-33
   significance of nineteenth-century detective fiction, 133-46

**Detective Fiction, Twentieth-Century** TCLC 38: 1-96
   genesis and history of the detective story, 3-22
   defining detective fiction, 22-32
   evolution and varieties, 32-77
   the appeal of detective fiction, 77-90

**Dime Novels** NCLC 84: 98-168
   overviews and general studies, 99-123
   popular characters, 123-39
   major figures and influences, 139-52
   socio-political concerns, 152-167

**Disease and Literature** TCLC 66: 140-283
   overviews, 141-65
   disease in nineteenth-century literature, 165-81
   tuberculosis and literature, 181-94
   women and disease in literature, 194-221
   plague literature, 221-53
   AIDS in literature, 253-82

**The Double in Nineteenth-Century Literature** NCLC 40: 1-95
   genesis and development of the theme, 2-15
   the double and Romanticism, 16-27
   sociological views, 27-52
   psychological interpretations, 52-87
   philosophical considerations, 87-95

**Dramatic Realism** NCLC 44: 139-202
   overviews, 140-50
   origins and definitions, 150-66
   impact and influence, 166-93
   realist drama and tragedy, 193-201

**Drugs and Literature** TCLC 78: 184-282
   overviews, 185-201
   pre-twentieth-century literature, 201-42
   twentieth-century literature, 242-82

**Eastern Mythology** CMLC 26: 112-92
   heroes and kings, 113-51
   cross-cultural perspective, 151-69
   relations to history and society, 169-92

**Eighteenth-Century British Periodicals** LC 63: 1-123
   rise of periodicals, 2-31
   impact and influence of periodicals, 31-64
   periodicals and society, 64-122

# LITERARY CRITICISM SERIES — CUMULATIVE TOPIC INDEX

**Electronic "Books": Hypertext and Hyperfiction** CLC 86: 367-404
- books vs. CD-ROMS, 367-76
- hypertext and hyperfiction, 376-95
- implications for publishing, libraries, and the public, 395-403

**Eliot, T. S., Centenary of Birth** CLC 55: 345-75

**Elizabethan Drama** LC 22: 140-240
- origins and influences, 142-67
- characteristics and conventions, 167-83
- theatrical production, 184-200
- histories, 200-12
- comedy, 213-20
- tragedy, 220-30

**Elizabethan Prose Fiction** LC 41: 1-70
- overviews, 1-15
- origins and influences, 15-43
- style and structure, 43-69

**Enclosure of the English Common** NCLC 88: 1-57
- overviews, 1-12
- early reaction to enclosure, 12-23
- nineteenth-century reaction to enclosure, 23-56

**The Encyclopedists** LC 26: 172-253
- overviews, 173-210
- intellectual background, 210-32
- views on esthetics, 232-41
- views on women, 241-52

**English Caroline Literature** LC 13: 221-307
- background, 222-41
- evolution and varieties, 241-62
- the Cavalier mode, 262-75
- court and society, 275-91
- politics and religion, 291-306

**English Decadent Literature of the 1890s** NCLC 28: 104-200
- fin de siècle: the Decadent period, 105-19
- definitions, 120-37
- major figures: "the tragic generation," 137-50
- French literature and English literary Decadence, 150-7
- themes, 157-61
- poetry, 161-82
- periodicals, 182-96

**English Essay, Rise of the** LC 18: 238-308
- definitions and origins, 236-54
- influence on the essay, 254-69
- historical background, 269-78
- the essay in the seventeenth century, 279-93
- the essay in the eighteenth century, 293-307

**English Mystery Cycle Dramas** LC 34: 1-88
- overviews, 1-27
- the nature of dramatic performances, 27-42
- the medieval worldview and the mystery cycles, 43-67
- the doctrine of repentance and the mystery cycles, 67-76
- the fall from grace in the mystery cycles, 76-88

**The English Realist Novel, 1740-1771** LC 51: 102-98
- Overviews, 103-22
- From Romanticism to Realism, 123-58
- Women and the Novel, 159-175
- The Novel and Other Literary Forms, 176-197

**English Revolution, Literature of the** LC 43: 1-58
- overviews, 2-24
- pamphlets of the English Revolution, 24-38
- political Sermons of the English Revolution, 38-48
- poetry of the English Revolution, 48-57

**English Romantic Hellenism** NCLC 68: 143-250
- overviews, 144-69
- historical development of English Romantic Hellenism, 169-91
- influence of Greek mythology on the Romantics, 191-229
- influence of Greek literature, art, and culture on the Romantics, 229-50

**English Romantic Poetry** NCLC 28: 201-327
- overviews and reputation, 202-37
- major subjects and themes, 237-67
- forms of Romantic poetry, 267-78
- politics, society, and Romantic poetry, 278-99
- philosophy, religion, and Romantic poetry, 299-324

**The Epistolary Novel** LC 59: 71-170
- overviews, 72-96
- women and the Epistolary novel, 96-138
- principal figures: Britain, 138-53
- principal figures: France, 153-69

**Espionage Literature** TCLC 50: 95-159
- overviews, 96-113
- espionage fiction/formula fiction, 113-26
- spies in fact and fiction, 126-38
- the female spy, 138-44
- social and psychological perspectives, 144-58

**European Debates on the Conquest of the Americas** LC 67: 1-129
- overviews, 3-56
- major Spanish figures, 56-98
- English perceptions of Native Americans, 98-129

**European Romanticism** NCLC 36: 149-284
- definitions, 149-77
- origins of the movement, 177-82
- Romantic theory, 182-200
- themes and techniques, 200-23
- Romanticism in Germany, 223-39
- Romanticism in France, 240-61
- Romanticism in Italy, 261-4
- Romanticism in Spain, 264-8
- impact and legacy, 268-82

**Existentialism and Literature** TCLC 42: 197-268
- overviews and definitions, 198-209
- history and influences, 209-19
- Existentialism critiqued and defended, 220-35
- philosophical and religious perspectives, 235-41
- Existentialist fiction and drama, 241-67

**Familiar Essay** NCLC 48: 96-211
- definitions and origins, 97-130
- overview of the genre, 130-43
- elements of form and style, 143-59
- elements of content, 159-73
- the Cockneys: Hazlitt, Lamb, and Hunt, 173-91
- status of the genre, 191-210

**The Faust Legend** LC 47: 1-117

**Fear in Literature** TCLC 74: 81-258
- overviews, 81
- pre-twentieth-century literature, 123
- twentieth-century literature, 182

**Feminism in the 1990s: Commentary on Works by Naomi Wolf, Susan Faludi, and Camille Paglia** CLC 76: 377-415

**Feminist Criticism in 1990** CLC 65: 312-60

**Fifteenth-Century English Literature** LC 17: 248-334
- background, 249-72
- poetry, 272-315
- drama, 315-23
- prose, 323-33

**Film and Literature** TCLC 38: 97-226
- overviews, 97-119
- film and theater, 119-34
- film and the novel, 134-45
- the art of the screenplay, 145-66
- genre literature/genre film, 167-79
- the writer and the film industry, 179-90
- authors on film adaptations of their works, 190-200
- fiction into film: comparative essays, 200-23

**Finance and Money as Represented in Nineteenth-Century Literature** NCLC 76: 1-69
- historical perspectives, 2-20
- the image of money, 20-37
- the dangers of money, 37-50
- women and money, 50-69

**Folklore and Literature** TCLC 86: 116-293
- overviews, 118-144
- Native American literature, 144-67
- African-American literature, 167-238
- Folklore and the American West, 238-57
- Modern and postmodern literature, 257-91

**Food in Literature** TCLC 114: 1-133
- Food and Children's Literature, 2-14
- Food as a Literary Device, 14-32
- Rituals Invloving Food, 33-45
- Food and Social and Ethnic Identity, 45-90
- Women's Relationship with Food, 91-132

**French Drama in the Age of Louis XIV** LC 28: 94-185
- overview, 95-127
- tragedy, 127-46
- comedy, 146-66
- tragicomedy, 166-84

**French Enlightenment** LC 14: 81-145
- the question of definition, 82-9
- Le siècle des lumières, 89-94
- women and the salons, 94-105
- censorship, 105-15
- the philosophy of reason, 115-31
- influence and legacy, 131-44

**French New Novel** TCLC 98: 158-234
- overviews and general studies, 158-92
- influences, 192-213
- themes, 213-33

**French Realism** NCLC 52: 136-216
- origins and definitions, 137-70
- issues and influence, 170-98
- realism and representation, 198-215

**French Revolution and English Literature** NCLC 40: 96-195
- history and theory, 96-123
- romantic poetry, 123-50
- the novel, 150-81
- drama, 181-92
- children's literature, 192-5

**Futurism, Italian** TCLC 42: 269-354
- principles and formative influences, 271-9
- manifestos, 279-88
- literature, 288-303
- theater, 303-19
- art, 320-30
- music, 330-6
- architecture, 336-9
- and politics, 339-46
- reputation and significance, 346-51

**Gaelic Revival** See **Irish Literary Renaissance**

**Gates, Henry Louis, Jr., and African-American Literary Criticism** CLC 65: 361-405

**Gay and Lesbian Literature** CLC 76: 416-39

**German Exile Literature** TCLC 30: 1-58
- the writer and the Nazi state, 1-10

definition of, 10-4
life in exile, 14-32
surveys, 32-50
Austrian literature in exile, 50-2
German publishing in the United States, 52-7

**German Expressionism** TCLC 34: 74-160
history and major figures, 76-85
aesthetic theories, 85-109
drama, 109-26
poetry, 126-38
film, 138-42
painting, 142-7
music, 147-53
and politics, 153-8

**The Gilded Age** NCLC 84: 169-271
popular themes, 170-90
Realism, 190-208
Aestheticism, 208-26
socio-political concerns, 226-70

*Glasnost* **and Contemporary Soviet Literature** CLC 59: 355-97

**Gothic Novel** NCLC 28: 328-402
development and major works, 328-34
definitions, 334-50
themes and techniques, 350-78
in America, 378-85
in Scotland, 385-91
influence and legacy, 391-400

**The Governess in Nineteenth-Century Literature** NCLC 104: 1-131
overviews and general studies, 3-28
social roles and economic conditions, 28-86
fictional governesses, 86-131

**Graphic Narratives** CLC 86: 405-32
history and overviews, 406-21
the "Classics Illustrated" series, 421-2
reviews of recent works, 422-32

**Graveyard Poets** LC 67: 131-212
origins and development, 131-52
major figures, 152-75
major works, 175-212

**Greek Historiography** CMLC 17: 1-49

**Greek Mythology** CMLC 26: 193-320
overviews, 194-209
origins and development of Greek mythology, 209-29
cosmogonies and divinities in Greek mythology, 229-54
heroes and heroines in Greek mythology, 254-80
women in Greek mythology, 280-320

**Harlem Renaissance** TCLC 26: 49-125
principal issues and figures, 50-67
the literature and its audience, 67-74
theme and technique in poetry, fiction, and drama, 74-115
and American society, 115-21
achievement and influence, 121-2

**Havel, Václav, Playwright and President** CLC 65: 406-63

**Historical Fiction, Nineteenth-Century** NCLC 48: 212-307
definitions and characteristics, 213-36
Victorian historical fiction, 236-65
American historical fiction, 265-88
realism in historical fiction, 288-306

**Holocaust and the Atomic Bomb: Fifty Years Later** CLC 91: 331-82
the Holocaust remembered, 333-52
Anne Frank revisited, 352-62
the atomic bomb and American memory, 362-81

**Holocaust Denial Literature** TCLC 58: 1-110
overviews, 1-30
Robert Faurisson and Noam Chomsky, 30-52
Holocaust denial literature in America, 52-71
library access to Holocaust denial literature, 72-5
the authenticity of Anne Frank's diary, 76-90
David Irving and the "normalization" of Hitler, 90-109

**Holocaust, Literature of the** TCLC 42: 355-450
historical overview, 357-61
critical overview, 361-70
diaries and memoirs, 370-95
novels and short stories, 395-425
poetry, 425-41
drama, 441-8

**Homosexuality in Nineteenth-Century Literature** NCLC 56: 78-182
defining homosexuality, 80-111
Greek love, 111-44
trial and danger, 144-81

**Hungarian Literature of the Twentieth Century** TCLC 26: 126-88
surveys of, 126-47
*Nyugat* and early twentieth-century literature, 147-56
mid-century literature, 156-68
and politics, 168-78
since the 1956 revolt, 178-87

**Hysteria in Nineteenth-Century Literature** NCLC 64: 59-184
the history of hysteria, 60-75
the gender of hysteria, 75-103
hysteria and women's narratives, 103-57
hysteria in nineteenth-century poetry, 157-83

**Imagism** TCLC 74: 259-454
history and development, 260
major figures, 288
sources and influences, 352
Imagism and other movements, 397
influence and legacy, 431

**Incest in Nineteenth-Century American Literature** NCLC 76: 70-141
overview, 71-88
the concern for social order, 88-117
authority and authorship, 117-40

**Incest in Victorian Literature** NCLC 92: 172-318
overviews, 173-85
novels, 185-276
plays, 276-84
poetry, 284-318

**Indian Literature in English** TCLC 54: 308-406
overview, 309-13
origins and major figures, 313-25
the Indo-English novel, 325-55
Indo-English poetry, 355-67
Indo-English drama, 367-72
critical perspectives on Indo-English literature, 372-80
modern Indo-English literature, 380-9
Indo-English authors on their work, 389-404

**The Industrial Revolution in Literature** NCLC 56: 183-273
historical and cultural perspectives, 184-201
contemporary reactions to the machine, 201-21
themes and symbols in literature, 221-73

**The Irish Famine as Represented in Nineteenth-Century Literature** NCLC 64: 185-261
overviews, 187-98
historical background, 198-212
famine novels, 212-34
famine poetry, 234-44
famine letters and eye-witness accounts, 245-61

**Irish Literary Renaissance** TCLC 46: 172-287
overview, 173-83
development and major figures, 184-202
influence of Irish folklore and mythology, 202-22
Irish poetry, 222-34
Irish drama and the Abbey Theatre, 234-56
Irish fiction, 256-86

**Irish Nationalism and Literature** NCLC 44: 203-73
the Celtic element in literature, 203-19
anti-Irish sentiment and the Celtic response, 219-34
literary ideals in Ireland, 234-45
literary expressions, 245-73

**Irish Novel, The** NCLC 80: 1-130
overviews, 3-9
principal figures, 9-22
peasant and middle class Irish novelists, 22-76
aristocratic Irish and Anglo-Irish novelists, 76-129

**Israeli Literature** TCLC 94: 1-137
overviews, 2-18
Israeli fiction, 18-33
Israeli poetry, 33-62
Israeli drama, 62-91
women and Israeli literature, 91-112
Arab characters in Israeli literature, 112-36

**Italian Futurism** *See* **Futurism, Italian**

**Italian Humanism** LC 12: 205-77
origins and early development, 206-18
revival of classical letters, 218-23
humanism and other philosophies, 224-39
humanism and humanists, 239-46
the plastic arts, 246-57
achievement and significance, 258-76

**Italian Romanticism** NCLC 60: 85-145
origins and overviews, 86-101
Italian Romantic theory, 101-25
the language of Romanticism, 125-45

**Jacobean Drama** LC 33: 1-37
the Jacobean worldview: an era of transition, 2-14
the moral vision of Jacobean drama, 14-22
Jacobean tragedy, 22-3
the Jacobean masque, 23-36

**Jazz and Literature** TCLC 102: 3-124

**Jewish-American Fiction** TCLC 62: 1-181
overviews, 2-24
major figures, 24-48
Jewish writers and American life, 48-78
Jewish characters in American fiction, 78-108
themes in Jewish-American fiction, 108-43
Jewish-American women writers, 143-59
the Holocaust and Jewish-American fiction, 159-81

**Journals of Lewis and Clark, The** NCLC 100: 1-88
overviews, 4-30
journal-keeping methods, 30-46
Fort Mandan, 46-51
the Clark journal, 51-65
the journals as literary texts, 65-87

**Knickerbocker Group, The** NCLC 56: 274-341
  overviews, 276-314
  Knickerbocker periodicals, 314-26
  writers and artists, 326-40

**Lake Poets, The** NCLC 52: 217-304
  characteristics of the Lake Poets and their works, 218-27
  literary influences and collaborations, 227-66
  defining and developing Romantic ideals, 266-84
  embracing Conservatism, 284-303

**Larkin, Philip, Controversy** CLC 81: 417-64

**Latin American Literature, Twentieth-Century** TCLC 58: 111-98
  historical and critical perspectives, 112-36
  the novel, 136-45
  the short story, 145-9
  drama, 149-60
  poetry, 160-7
  the writer and society, 167-86
  Native Americans in Latin American literature, 186-97

**The Levellers** LC 51: 200-312
  overviews, 201-29
  principal figures, 230-86
  religion, political philosophy, and pamphleteering, 287-311

**Literature and Millenial Lists** CLC 119: 431-67
  The Modern Library list, 433
  The Waterstone list, 438-439

**Literature of the American Cowboy** NCLC 96: 1-60
  overview, 3-20
  cowboy fiction, 20-36
  cowboy poetry and songs, 36-59

**Literature of the California Gold Rush** NCLC 92: 320-85
  overviews, 322-24
  early California Gold Rush fiction, 324-44
  Gold Rush folklore and legend, 344-51
  the rise of Western local color, 351-60
  social relations and social change, 360-385

**Madness in Nineteenth-Century Literature** NCLC 76: 142-284
  overview, 143-54
  autobiography, 154-68
  poetry, 168-215
  fiction, 215-83

**Madness in Twentieth-Century Literature** TCLC 50: 160-225
  overviews, 161-71
  madness and the creative process, 171-86
  suicide, 186-91
  madness in American literature, 191-207
  madness in German literature, 207-13
  madness and feminist artists, 213-24

**Magic Realism** TCLC 110: 80-327
  overviews and general studies, 81-94
  magic realism in African literature, 95-110
  magic realism in American literature, 110-32
  magic realism in Canadian literature, 132-46
  magic realism in European literature, 146-66
  magic realism in Asian literature, 166-79
  magic realism in Latin-American literature, 179-223
  magic realism in Israeli literature and the novels of Salman Rushdie, 223-38
  magic realism in literature written by women, 239-326

**The Masque** LC 63: 124-265
  development of the masque, 125-62
  sources and structure, 162-220
  race and gender in the masque, 221-64

**Medical Writing** LC 55: 93-195
  colonial America, 94-110
  enlightenment, 110-24
  medieval writing, 124-40
  sexuality, 140-83
  vernacular, 185-95

**Memoirs of Trauma** CLC 109: 419-466
  overview, 420
  criticism, 429

**Metaphysical Poets** LC 24: 356-439
  early definitions, 358-67
  surveys and overviews, 367-92
  cultural and social influences, 392-406
  stylistic and thematic variations, 407-38

**Modern Essay, The** TCLC 58: 199-273
  overview, 200-7
  the essay in the early twentieth century, 207-19
  characteristics of the modern essay, 219-32
  modern essayists, 232-45
  the essay as a literary genre, 245-73

**Modern Irish Literature** TCLC 102: 125-321
  overview, 129-44
  dramas, 144-70
  fiction, 170-247
  poetry, 247-321

**Modern Japanese Literature** TCLC 66: 284-389
  poetry, 285-305
  drama, 305-29
  fiction, 329-61
  western influences, 361-87

**Modernism** TCLC 70: 165-275
  definitions, 166-184
  Modernism and earlier influences, 184-200
  stylistic and thematic traits, 200-229
  poetry and drama, 229-242
  redefining Modernism, 242-275

**Muckraking Movement in American Journalism** TCLC 34: 161-242
  development, principles, and major figures, 162-70
  publications, 170-9
  social and political ideas, 179-86
  targets, 186-208
  fiction, 208-19
  decline, 219-29
  impact and accomplishments, 229-40

**Multiculturalism in Literature and Education** CLC 70: 361-413

**Music and Modern Literature** TCLC 62: 182-329
  overviews, 182-211
  musical form/literary form, 211-32
  music in literature, 232-50
  the influence of music on literature, 250-73
  literature and popular music, 273-303
  jazz and poetry, 303-28

**Native American Literature** CLC 76: 440-76

**Natural School, Russian** NCLC 24: 205-40
  history and characteristics, 205-25
  contemporary criticism, 225-40

**Naturalism** NCLC 36: 285-382
  definitions and theories, 286-305
  critical debates on Naturalism, 305-16
  Naturalism in theater, 316-32
  European Naturalism, 332-61
  American Naturalism, 361-72
  the legacy of Naturalism, 372-81

**Negritude** TCLC 50: 226-361
  origins and evolution, 227-56
  definitions, 256-91
  Negritude in literature, 291-343
  Negritude reconsidered, 343-58

**New Criticism** TCLC 34: 243-318
  development and ideas, 244-70
  debate and defense, 270-99
  influence and legacy, 299-315

**The New World in Renaissance Literature** LC 31: 1-51
  overview, 1-18
  utopia vs. terror, 18-31
  explorers and Native Americans, 31-51

**New York Intellectuals and *Partisan Review*** TCLC 30: 117-98
  development and major figures, 118-28
  influence of Judaism, 128-39
  *Partisan Review*, 139-57
  literary philosophy and practice, 157-75
  political philosophy, 175-87
  achievement and significance, 187-97

***The New Yorker*** TCLC 58: 274-357
  overviews, 274-95
  major figures, 295-304
  *New Yorker* style, 304-33
  fiction, journalism, and humor at *The New Yorker*, 333-48
  the new *New Yorker*, 348-56

**Newgate Novel** NCLC 24: 166-204
  development of Newgate literature, 166-73
  *Newgate Calendar*, 173-7
  Newgate fiction, 177-95
  Newgate drama, 195-204

**Nigerian Literature of the Twentieth Century** TCLC 30: 199-265
  surveys of, 199-227
  English language and African life, 227-45
  politics and the Nigerian writer, 245-54
  Nigerian writers and society, 255-62

**Nihilism and Literature** TCLC 110: 328-93
  overviews and general studies, 328-44
  European and Russian nihilism, 344-73
  nihilism in the works of Albert Camus, Franz Kafka, and John Barth, 373-92

**Nineteenth-Century Captivity Narratives** NCLC 80:131-218
  overview, 132-37
  the political significance of captivity narratives, 137-67
  images of gender, 167-96
  moral instruction, 197-217

**Nineteenth-Century Native American Autobiography** NCLC 64: 262-389
  overview, 263-8
  problems of authorship, 268-81
  the evolution of Native American autobiography, 281-304
  political issues, 304-15
  gender and autobiography, 316-62
  autobiographical works during the turn of the century, 362-88

**Nineteenth-Century Euro-American Literary Representations of Native Americans** NCLC 104: 132-264
  overviews and general studies, 134-53
  Native American history, 153-72
  the Indians of the Northeast, 172-93
  the Indians of the Southeast, 193-212
  the Indians of the West, 212-27
  Indian-hater fiction, 227-43
  the Indian as exhibit, 243-63

**Norse Mythology** CMLC 26: 321-85
  history and mythological tradition, 322-44
  Eddic poetry, 344-74
  Norse mythology and other traditions, 374-85

**Northern Humanism** LC 16: 281-356
  background, 282-305
  precursor of the Reformation, 305-14

the Brethren of the Common Life, the Devotio Moderna, and education, 314-40
the impact of printing, 340-56

**Novel of Manners, The** NCLC 56: 342-96
social and political order, 343-53
domestic order, 353-73
depictions of gender, 373-83
the American novel of manners, 383-95

**Nuclear Literature: Writings and Criticism in the Nuclear Age** TCLC 46: 288-390
overviews, 290-301
fiction, 301-35
poetry, 335-8
nuclear war in Russo-Japanese literature, 338-55
nuclear war and women writers, 355-67
the nuclear referent and literary criticism, 367-88

**Occultism in Modern Literature** TCLC 50: 362-406
influence of occultism on literature, 363-72
occultism, literature, and society, 372-87
fiction, 387-96
drama, 396-405

**Opium and the Nineteenth-Century Literary Imagination** NCLC 20:250-301
original sources, 250-62
historical background, 262-71
and literary society, 271-9
and literary creativity, 279-300

**Orientalism** NCLC 96: 149-364
overviews, 150-98
Orientalism and imperialism, 198-229
Orientalism and gender, 229-59
Orientalism and the nineteenth-century novel, 259-321
Orientalism in nineteenth-century poetry, 321-63

**The Oxford Movement** NCLC 72: 1-197
overviews, 2-24
background, 24-59
and education, 59-69
religious responses, 69-128
literary aspects, 128-178
political implications, 178-196

**The Parnassian Movement** NCLC 72: 198-241
overviews, 199-231
and epic form, 231-38
and positivism, 238-41

**Pastoral Literature of the English Renaissance** LC 59: 171-282
overviews, 172-214
principal figures of the Elizabethan period, 214-33
principal figures of the later Renaissance, 233-50
pastoral drama, 250-81

**Periodicals, Nineteenth-Century British** NCLC 24: 100-65
overviews, 100-30
in the Romantic Age, 130-41
in the Victorian era, 142-54
and the reviewer, 154-64

**Plath, Sylvia, and the Nature of Biography** CLC 86: 433-62
the nature of biography, 433-52
reviews of *The Silent Woman,* 452-61

**Political Theory from the 15th to the 18th Century** LC 36: 1-55
Overview, 1-26
Natural Law, 26-42
Empiricism, 42-55

**Polish Romanticism** NCLC 52: 305-71
overviews, 306-26
major figures, 326-40
Polish Romantic drama, 340-62
influences, 362-71

**Politics and Literature** TCLC 94: 138-61
overviews, 139-96
Europe, 196-226
Latin America, 226-48
Africa and the Caribbean, 248-60

**Popular Literature** TCLC 70: 279-382
overviews, 280-324
"formula" fiction, 324-336
readers of popular literature, 336-351
evolution of popular literature, 351-382

**The Portrayal of Jews in Nineteenth-Century English Literature** NCLC 72: 242-368
overviews, 244-77
Anglo-Jewish novels, 277-303
depictions by non-Jewish writers, 303-44
Hebraism versus Hellenism, 344-67

**The Portrayal of Mormonism** NCLC 96: 61-148
overview, 63-72
early Mormon literature, 72-100
Mormon periodicals and journals, 100-10
women writers, 110-22
Mormonism and nineteenth-century literature, 122-42
Mormon poetry, 142-47

**Postcolonialism** TCLC 114: 134-239
Overviews and General Studies, 135-153
African Postcolonial Writing, 153-72
Asian/Pacific Literature, 172-78
Postcolonial Literary Theory, 178-213
Postcolonial Women's Writing, 213-38

**Postmodernism** TCLC 90:125-307
Overview, 126-166
Criticism , 166-224
Fiction, 224-282
Poetry, 282-300
Drama, 300-307

**Pre-Raphaelite Movement** NCLC 20: 302-401
overview, 302-4
genesis, 304-12
*Germ* and *Oxford and Cambridge Magazine,* 312-20
Robert Buchanan and the "Fleshly School of Poetry," 320-31
satires and parodies, 331-4
surveys, 334-51
aesthetics, 351-75
sister arts of poetry and painting, 375-94
influence, 394-9

**Pre-romanticism** LC 40: 1-56
overviews, 2-14
defining the period, 14-23
new directions in poetry and prose, 23-45
the focus on the self, 45-56

**Pre-Socratic Philosophy** CMLC 22: 1-56
overviews, 3-24
the Ionians and the Pythagoreans, 25-35
Heraclitus, the Eleatics, and the Atomists, 36-47
the Sophists, 47-55

**Protestant Reformation, Literature of the** LC 37: 1-83
overviews, 1-49
humanism and scholasticism, 49-69
the reformation and literature, 69-82

**Psychoanalysis and Literature** TCLC 38: 227-338
overviews, 227-46
Freud on literature, 246-51
psychoanalytic views of the literary process, 251-61
psychoanalytic theories of response to literature, 261-88

psychoanalysis and literary criticism, 288-312
psychoanalysis as literature/literature as psychoanalysis, 313-34

**The Quarrel between the Ancients and the Moderns** LC 63: 266-381
overviews, 267-301
Renaissance origins, 301-32
Quarrel between the Ancients and the Moderns in France, 332-58
Battle of the Books in England, 358-80

**Rap Music** CLC 76: 477-50

**Renaissance Natural Philosophy** LC 27: 201-87
cosmology, 201-28
astrology, 228-54
magic, 254-86

**Representations of the Devil in Nineteenth-Century Literature** NCLC 100: 89-223
overviews, 90-115
the Devil in American fiction, 116-43
English Romanticism: the satanic school, 143-89
Luciferian discourse in European literature, 189-222

**Restoration Drama** LC 21: 184-275
general overviews, 185-230
Jeremy Collier stage controversy, 230-9
other critical interpretations, 240-75

**Revising the Literary Canon** CLC 81: 465-509

**Revising the Literary Canon** TCLC 114: 240-84
Overviews and General Studies, 241-85
Canon Change in American Literature, 285-339
Gender and the Literary Canon, 339-59
Minority and Third-World Literature and the Canon, 359-84

**Revolutionary Astronomers** LC 51: 314-65
Overviews, 316-25
Principal Figures, 325-51
Revolutionary Astronomical Models, 352-64

**Robin Hood, Legend of** LC 19: 205-58
origins and development of the Robin Hood legend, 206-20
representations of Robin Hood, 220-44
Robin Hood as hero, 244-56

**Rushdie, Salman,** *Satanic Verses* **Controversy** CLC 55: 214-63; 59:404-56

**Russian Nihilism** NCLC 28: 403-47
definitions and overviews, 404-17
women and Nihilism, 417-27
literature as reform: the Civic Critics, 427-33
Nihilism and the Russian novel: Turgenev and Dostoevsky, 433-47

**Russian Thaw** TCLC 26: 189-247
literary history of the period, 190-206
theoretical debate of socialist realism, 206-11
*Novy Mir,* 211-7
*Literary Moscow,* 217-24
Pasternak, *Zhivago,* and the Nobel Prize, 224-7
poetry of liberation, 228-31
Brodsky trial and the end of the Thaw, 231-6
achievement and influence, 236-46

**Salem Witch Trials** LC 38: 1-145
overviews, 2-30
historical background, 30-65
judicial background, 65-78
the search for causes, 78-115
the role of women in the trials, 115-44

**Salinger, J. D., Controversy Surrounding** *In Search of J. D. Salinger* CLC 55: 325-44

**Science and Modern Literature** TCLC 90: 308-419
  Overviews, 295-333
  Fiction, 333-95
  Poetry, 395-405
  Drama, 405-19

**Science in Nineteenth-Century Literature** NCLC 100: 224-366
  overviews, 225-65
  major figures, 265-336
  sociopolitical concerns, 336-65

**Science Fiction, Nineteenth-Century** NCLC 24: 241-306
  background, 242-50
  definitions of the genre, 251-56
  representative works and writers, 256-75
  themes and conventions, 276-305

**Scottish Chaucerians** LC 20: 363-412

**Scottish Poetry, Eighteenth-Century** LC 29: 95-167
  overviews, 96-114
  the Scottish Augustans, 114-28
  the Scots Vernacular Revival, 132-63
  Scottish poetry after Burns, 163-66

**Sea in Literature, The** TCLC 82: 72-191
  drama, 73-9
  poetry, 79-119
  fiction, 119-91

**Sea in Nineteenth-Century English and American Literature, The** NCLC 104: 265-362
  overviews and general studies, 267-306
  major figures in American sea fiction— Cooper and Melville, 306-29
  American sea poetry and short stories, 329-45
  English sea literature, 345-61

**Sensation Novel, The** NCLC 80: 219-330
  overviews, 221-46
  principal figures, 246-62
  nineteenth-century reaction, 262-91
  feminist criticism, 291-329

**Sentimental Novel, The** NCLC 60: 146-245
  overviews, 147-58
  the politics of domestic fiction, 158-79
  a literature of resistance and repression, 179-212
  the reception of sentimental fiction, 213-44

**Sex and Literature** TCLC 82: 192-434
  overviews, 193-216
  drama, 216-63
  poetry, 263-87
  fiction, 287-431

**Sherlock Holmes Centenary** TCLC 26: 248-310
  Doyle's life and the composition of the Holmes stories, 248-59
  life and character of Holmes, 259-78
  method, 278-79
  Holmes and the Victorian world, 279-92
  Sherlockian scholarship, 292-301
  Doyle and the development of the detective story, 301-07
  Holmes's continuing popularity, 307-09

**The Silver Fork Novel** NCLC 88: 58-140
  criticism, 59-139

**Slave Narratives, American** NCLC 20: 1-91
  background, 2-9
  overviews, 9-24
  contemporary responses, 24-7
  language, theme, and technique, 27-70
  historical authenticity, 70-5
  antecedents, 75-83
  role in development of Black American literature, 83-8

**The Slave Trade in British and American Literature** LC 59: 283-369
  overviews, 284-91
  depictions by white writers, 291-331
  depictions by former slaves, 331-67

**Social Conduct Literature** LC 55: 196-298
  overviews, 196-223
  prescriptive ideology in other literary forms, 223-38
  role of the press, 238-63
  impact of conduct literature, 263-87
  conduct literature and the perception of women, 287-96
  women writing for women, 296-98

**Socialism** NCLC 88: 141-237
  origins, 142-54
  French socialism, 154-83
  Anglo-American socialism, 183-205
  Socialist-Feminism, 205-36

**Spanish Civil War Literature** TCLC 26: 311-85
  topics in, 312-33
  British and American literature, 333-59
  French literature, 359-62
  Spanish literature, 362-73
  German literature, 373-75
  political idealism and war literature, 375-83

**Spanish Golden Age Literature** LC 23: 262-332
  overviews, 263-81
  verse drama, 281-304
  prose fiction, 304-19
  lyric poetry, 319-31

**Spasmodic School of Poetry** NCLC 24: 307-52
  history and major figures, 307-21
  the Spasmodics on poetry, 321-7
  *Firmilian* and critical disfavor, 327-39
  theme and technique, 339-47
  influence, 347-51

**Sports in Literature** TCLC 86: 294-445
  overviews, 295-324
  major writers and works, 324-402
  sports, literature, and social issues, 402-45

**Steinbeck, John, Fiftieth Anniversary of** *The Grapes of Wrath* CLC 59: 311-54

**Sturm und Drang** NCLC 40: 196-276
  definitions, 197-238
  poetry and poetics, 238-58
  drama, 258-75

**Supernatural Fiction in the Nineteenth Century** NCLC 32: 207-87
  major figures and influences, 208-35
  the Victorian ghost story, 236-54
  the influence of science and occultism, 254-66
  supernatural fiction and society, 266-86

**Supernatural Fiction, Modern** TCLC 30: 59-116
  evolution and varieties, 60-74
  "decline" of the ghost story, 74-86
  as a literary genre, 86-92
  technique, 92-101
  nature and appeal, 101-15

**Surrealism** TCLC 30: 334-406
  history and formative influences, 335-43
  manifestos, 343-54
  philosophic, aesthetic, and political principles, 354-75
  poetry, 375-81
  novel, 381-6
  drama, 386-92
  film, 392-8
  painting and sculpture, 398-403
  achievement, 403-5

**Symbolism, Russian** TCLC 30: 266-333
  doctrines and major figures, 267-92
  theories, 293-8
  and French Symbolism, 298-310
  themes in poetry, 310-4
  theater, 314-20
  and the fine arts, 320-32

**Symbolist Movement, French** NCLC 20: 169-249
  background and characteristics, 170-86
  principles, 186-91
  attacked and defended, 191-7
  influences and predecessors, 197-211
  and Decadence, 211-6
  theater, 216-26
  prose, 226-33
  decline and influence, 233-47

**Television and Literature** TCLC 78: 283-426
  television and literacy, 283-98
  reading vs. watching, 298-341
  adaptations, 341-62
  literary genres and television, 362-90
  television genres and literature, 390-410
  children's literature/children's television, 410-25

**Theater of the Absurd** TCLC 38: 339-415
  "The Theater of the Absurd," 340-7
  major plays and playwrights, 347-58
  and the concept of the absurd, 358-86
  theatrical techniques, 386-94
  predecessors of, 394-402
  influence of, 402-13

**Tin Pan Alley** *See* **American Popular Song, Golden Age of**

**Tobacco Culture** LC 55: 299-366
  social and economic attitudes toward tobacco, 299-344
  tobacco trade between the old world and the new world, 344-55
  tobacco smuggling in Great Britain, 355-66

**Transcendentalism, American** NCLC 24: 1-99
  overviews, 3-23
  contemporary documents, 23-41
  theological aspects of, 42-52
  and social issues, 52-74
  literature of, 74-96

**Travel Writing in the Nineteenth Century** NCLC 44: 274-392
  the European grand tour, 275-303
  the Orient, 303-47
  North America, 347-91

**Travel Writing in the Twentieth Century** TCLC 30: 407-56
  conventions and traditions, 407-27
  and fiction writing, 427-43
  comparative essays on travel writers, 443-54

**Tristan and Isolde Legend** CMLC 42: 311-404

**True-Crime Literature** CLC 99: 333-433
  history and analysis, 334-407
  reviews of true-crime publications, 407-23
  writing instruction, 424-29
  author profiles, 429-33

***Ulysses* and the Process of Textual Reconstruction** TCLC 26: 386-416
  evaluations of the new *Ulysses,* 386-94
  editorial principles and procedures, 394-401
  theoretical issues, 401-16

**Utilitarianism** NCLC 84: 272-340
  J. S. Mill's Utilitarianism: liberty, equality, justice, 273-313
  Jeremy Bentham's Utilitarianism: the science of happiness, 313-39

# CUMULATIVE TOPIC INDEX

**Utopianism** NCLC 88: 238-346
    overviews: Utopian literature, 239-59
    Utopianism in American literature, 259-99
    Utopianism in British literature, 299-311
    Utopianism and Feminism, 311-45

**Utopian Literature, Nineteenth-Century** NCLC 24: 353-473
    definitions, 354-74
    overviews, 374-88
    theory, 388-408
    communities, 409-26
    fiction, 426-53
    women and fiction, 454-71

**Utopian Literature, Renaissance** LC 32: 1-63
    overviews, 2-25
    classical background, 25-33
    utopia and the social contract, 33-9
    origins in mythology, 39-48
    utopia and the Renaissance country house, 48-52
    influence of millenarianism, 52-62

**Vampire in Literature** TCLC 46: 391-454
    origins and evolution, 392-412
    social and psychological perspectives, 413-44
    vampire fiction and science fiction, 445-53

**Vernacular Bibles** LC 67: 214-388
    overviews, 215-59
    the English Bible, 259-355
    the German Bible, 355-88

**Victorian Autobiography** NCLC 40: 277-363
    development and major characteristics, 278-88
    themes and techniques, 289-313
    the autobiographical tendency in Victorian prose and poetry, 313-47
    Victorian women's autobiographies, 347-62

**Victorian Fantasy Literature** NCLC 60: 246-384
    overviews, 247-91
    major figures, 292-366
    women in Victorian fantasy literature, 366-83

**Victorian Hellenism** NCLC 68: 251-376
    overviews, 252-78
    the meanings of Hellenism, 278-335
    the literary influence, 335-75

**Victorian Novel** NCLC 32: 288-454
    development and major characteristics, 290-310
    themes and techniques, 310-58
    social criticism in the Victorian novel, 359-97
    urban and rural life in the Victorian novel, 397-406
    women in the Victorian novel, 406-25
    Mudie's Circulating Library, 425-34
    the late-Victorian novel, 434-51

**Vietnamese Literature** TCLC 102: 322-386

**Vietnam War in Literature and Film** CLC 91: 383-437
    overview, 384-8
    prose, 388-412
    film and drama, 412-24
    poetry, 424-35

**Violence in Literature** TCLC 98: 235-358
    overviews and general studies, 236-74
    violence in the works of modern authors, 274-358

**Vorticism** TCLC 62: 330-426
    Wyndham Lewis and Vorticism, 330-8
    characteristics and principles of Vorticism, 338-65
    Lewis and Pound, 365-82
    Vorticist writing, 382-416
    Vorticist painting, 416-26

**Well-Made Play, The** NCLC 80: 331-370
    overviews, 332-45
    Scribe's style, 345-56
    the influence of the well-made play, 356-69

**Women's Autobiography, Nineteenth Century** NCLC 76: 285-368
    overviews, 287-300
    autobiographies concerned with religious and political issues, 300-15
    autobiographies by women of color, 315-38
    autobiographies by women pioneers, 338-51
    autobiographies by women of letters, 351-68

**Women's Diaries, Nineteenth-Century** NCLC 48: 308-54
    overview, 308-13
    diary as history, 314-25
    sociology of diaries, 325-34
    diaries as psychological scholarship, 334-43
    diary as autobiography, 343-8
    diary as literature, 348-53

**Women in Modern Literature** TCLC 94: 262-425
    overviews, 263-86
    American literature, 286-304
    other national literatures, 304-33
    fiction, 333-94
    poetry, 394-407
    drama, 407-24

**Women Writers, Seventeenth-Century** LC 30: 2-58
    overview, 2-15
    women and education, 15-9
    women and autobiography, 19-31
    women's diaries, 31-9
    early feminists, 39-58

**World War I Literature** TCLC 34: 392-486
    overview, 393-403
    English, 403-27
    German, 427-50
    American, 450-66
    French, 466-74
    and modern history, 474-82

**Yellow Journalism** NCLC 36: 383-456
    overviews, 384-96
    major figures, 396-413

**Young Playwrights Festival**
    1988 CLC 55: 376-81
    1989 CLC 59: 398-403
    1990 CLC 65: 444-8

# *CLC* Cumulative Nationality Index

**ALBANIAN**

Kadare, Ismail  52

**ALGERIAN**

Althusser, Louis  106
Camus, Albert  1, 2, 4, 9, 11, 14, 32, 63, 69, 124
Cixous, Helene  92
Cohen-Solal, Annie  50

**AMERICAN**

Abbey, Edward  36, 59
Abbott, Lee K(ittredge)  48
Abish, Walter  22
Abrams, M(eyer) H(oward)  24
Acker, Kathy  45, 111
Adams, Alice (Boyd)  6, 13, 46
Addams, Charles (Samuel)  30
Adler, C(arole) S(chwerdtfeger)  35
Adler, Renata  8, 31
Ai  4, 14, 69
Aiken, Conrad (Potter)  1, 3, 5, 10, 52
Albee, Edward (Franklin III)  1, 2, 3, 5, 9, 11, 13, 25, 53, 86, 113
Alexander, Lloyd (Chudley)  35
Alexie, Sherman (Joseph Jr.)  96
Algren, Nelson  4, 10, 33
Allen, Edward  59
Allen, Paula Gunn  84
Allen, Woody  16, 52
Allison, Dorothy E.  78
Alta  19
Alter, Robert B(ernard)  34
Alther, Lisa  7, 41
Altman, Robert  16, 116
Alvarez, Julia  93
Ambrose, Stephen E(dward)  145
Ammons, A(rchie) R(andolph)  2, 3, 5, 8, 9, 25, 57, 108
L'Amour, Louis (Dearborn)  25, 55
Anaya, Rudolfo A(lfonso)  23, 148
Anderson, Jon (Victor)  9
Anderson, Poul (William)  15
Anderson, Robert (Woodruff)  23
Angell, Roger  26
Angelou, Maya  12, 35, 64, 77
Anthony, Piers  35
Apple, Max (Isaac)  9, 33
Appleman, Philip (Dean)  51
Archer, Jules  12
Arendt, Hannah  66, 98
Arnow, Harriette (Louisa) Simpson  2, 7, 18
Arrick, Fran  30
Arzner, Dorothy  98
Ashbery, John (Lawrence)  2, 3, 4, 6, 9, 13, 15, 25, 41, 77, 125
Asimov, Isaac  1, 3, 9, 19, 26, 76, 92
Attaway, William (Alexander)  92
Auchincloss, Louis (Stanton)  4, 6, 9, 18, 45
Auden, W(ystan) H(ugh)  1, 2, 3, 4, 6, 9, 11, 14, 43, 123
Auel, Jean M(arie)  31, 107

Auster, Paul  47, 131
Bach, Richard (David)  14
Badanes, Jerome  59
Baker, Elliott  8
Baker, Nicholson  61
Baker, Russell (Wayne)  31
Bakshi, Ralph  26
Baldwin, James (Arthur)  1, 2, 3, 4, 5, 8, 13, 15, 17, 42, 50, 67, 90, 127
Bambara, Toni Cade  19, 88
Banks, Russell  37, 72
Baraka, Amiri  1, 2, 3, 5, 10, 14, 33, 115
Barber, Benjamin R.  141
Barbera, Jack (Vincent)  44
Barnard, Mary (Ethel)  48
Barnes, Djuna  3, 4, 8, 11, 29, 127
Barondess, Sue K(aufman)  8
Barrett, Andrea  150
Barrett, William (Christopher)  27
Barth, John (Simmons)  1, 2, 3, 5, 7, 9, 10, 14, 27, 51, 89
Barthelme, Donald  1, 2, 3, 5, 6, 8, 13, 23, 46, 59, 115
Barthelme, Frederick  36, 117
Barzun, Jacques (Martin)  51, 145
Bass, Rick  79, 143
Baumbach, Jonathan  6, 23
Bausch, Richard (Carl)  51
Baxter, Charles (Morley)  45, 78
Beagle, Peter S(oyer)  7, 104
Beattie, Ann  8, 13, 18, 40, 63, 146
Becker, Walter  26
Beecher, John  6
Begiebing, Robert J(ohn)  70
Behrman, S(amuel) N(athaniel)  40
Belitt, Ben  22
Bell, Madison Smartt  41, 102
Bell, Marvin (Hartley)  8, 31
Bellow, Saul  1, 2, 3, 6, 8, 10, 13, 15, 25, 33, 34, 63, 79
Benary-Isbert, Margot  12
Benchley, Peter (Bradford)  4, 8
Benedikt, Michael  4, 14
Benford, Gregory (Albert)  52
Bennett, Jay  35
Benson, Jackson J.  34
Benson, Sally  17
Bentley, Eric (Russell)  24
Berendt, John (Lawrence)  86
Berger, Melvin H.  12
Berger, Thomas (Louis)  3, 5, 8, 11, 18, 38
Bergstein, Eleanor  4
Bernard, April  59
Bernstein, Charles  142,
Berriault, Gina  54, 109
Berrigan, Daniel  4
Berry, Chuck  17
Berry, Wendell (Erdman)  4, 6, 8, 27, 46
Berryman, John  1, 2, 3, 4, 6, 8, 10, 13, 25, 62
Bessie, Alvah  23
Bettelheim, Bruno  79
Betts, Doris (Waugh)  3, 6, 28

Bidart, Frank  33
Birkerts, Sven  116
Bishop, Elizabeth  1, 4, 9, 13, 15, 32
Bishop, John  10
Blackburn, Paul  9, 43
Blackmur, R(ichard) P(almer)  2, 24
Blaise, Clark  29
Blatty, William Peter  2
Blessing, Lee  54
Blish, James (Benjamin)  14
Bloch, Robert (Albert)  33
Bloom, Harold  24, 103
Blount, Roy (Alton) Jr.  38
Blume, Judy (Sussman)  12, 30
Bly, Robert (Elwood)  1, 2, 5, 10, 15, 38, 128
Bochco, Steven  35
Bogan, Louise  4, 39, 46, 93
Bogosian, Eric  45, 141
Bograd, Larry  35
Bonham, Frank  12
Bontemps, Arna(ud Wendell)  1, 18
Booth, Philip  23
Booth, Wayne C(layson)  24
Bottoms, David  53
Bourjaily, Vance (Nye)  8, 62
Bova, Ben(jamin William)  45
Bowers, Edgar  9
Bowles, Jane (Sydney)  3, 68
Bowles, Paul (Frederick)  1, 2, 19, 53
Boyle, Kay  1, 5, 19, 58, 121
Boyle, T(homas) Coraghessan  36, 55, 90
Bradbury, Ray (Douglas)  1, 3, 10, 15, 42, 98
Bradley, David (Henry) Jr.  23, 118
Bradley, John Ed(mund Jr.)  55
Bradley, Marion Zimmer  30
Bradshaw, John  70
Brady, Joan  86
Brammer, William  31
Brancato, Robin F(idler)  35
Brand, Millen  7
Branden, Barbara  44
Branley, Franklyn M(ansfield)  21
Brautigan, Richard (Gary)  1, 3, 5, 9, 12, 34, 42
Braverman, Kate  67
Brennan, Maeve  5
Bridgers, Sue Ellen  26
Brin, David  34
Brodkey, Harold (Roy)  56
Brodsky, Joseph  4, 6, 13, 36, 100
Brodsky, Michael (Mark)  19
Bromell, Henry  5
Broner, E(sther) M(asserman)  19
Bronk, William (M.)  10
Brooks, Cleanth  24, 86, 110
Brooks, Gwendolyn (Elizabeth)  1, 2, 4, 5, 15, 49, 125
Brooks, Mel  12
Brooks, Peter  34
Brooks, Van Wyck  29
Brosman, Catharine Savage  9

Broughton, T(homas) Alan  19
Broumas, Olga  10, 73
Brown, Claude  30
Brown, Dee (Alexander)  18, 47
Brown, Rita Mae  18, 43, 79
Brown, Rosellen  32
Brown, Sterling Allen  1, 23, 59
Brown, (William) Larry  73
Browne, (Clyde) Jackson  21
Browning, Tod  16
Bruccoli, Matthew J(oseph)  34
Bruce, Lenny  21
Bryan, C(ourtlandt) D(ixon) B(arnes)  29
Buchwald, Art(hur)  33
Buck, Pearl S(ydenstricker)  7, 11, 18, 127
Buckley, William F(rank) Jr.  7, 18, 37
Buechner, (Carl) Frederick  2, 4, 6, 9
Bukowski, Charles  2, 5, 9, 41, 82, 108
Bullins, Ed  1, 5, 7
Burke, Kenneth (Duva)  2, 24
Burnshaw, Stanley  3, 13, 44
Burr, Anne  6
Burroughs, William S(eward)  1, 2, 5, 15, 22, 42, 75, 109
Busch, Frederick  7, 10, 18, 47
Bush, Ronald  34
Butler, Octavia E(stelle)  38, 121
Butler, Robert Olen (Jr.)  81
Byars, Betsy (Cromer)  35
Byrne, David  26
Cage, John (Milton Jr.)  41
Cain, James M(allahan)  3, 11, 28
Caldwell, Erskine (Preston)  1, 8, 14, 50, 60
Caldwell, (Janet Miriam) Taylor (Holland)  2, 28, 39
Calisher, Hortense  2, 4, 8, 38, 134
Cameron, Carey  59
Cameron, Peter  44
Campbell, John W(ood Jr.)  32
Campbell, Joseph  69
Campion, Jane  95
Canby, Vincent  13
Canin, Ethan  55
Capote, Truman  1, 3, 8, 13, 19, 34, 38, 58
Capra, Frank  16
Caputo, Philip  32
Card, Orson Scott  44, 47, 50
Carey, Ernestine Gilbreth  17
Carlisle, Henry (Coffin)  33
Carlson, Ron(ald F.)  54
Carpenter, Don(ald Richard)  41
Carr, Caleb  86
Carr, John Dickson  3
Carr, Virginia Spencer  34
Carroll, James P.  38
Carroll, Jim  35, 143
Carruth, Hayden  4, 7, 10, 18, 84
Carson, Rachel Louise  71
Carver, Raymond  22, 36, 53, 55, 126
Casey, John (Dudley)  59
Casey, Michael  2
Casey, Warren (Peter)  12
Cassavetes, John  20
Cassill, R(onald) V(erlin)  4, 23
Cassity, (Allen) Turner  6, 42
Castaneda, Carlos (Cesar Aranha)  12, 119
Castedo, Elena  65
Castillo, Ana (Hernandez Del)  151
Catton, (Charles) Bruce  35
Caunitz, William J.  34
Chabon, Michael  55, 149
Chappell, Fred (Davis)  40, 78
Charyn, Jerome  5, 8, 18
Chase, Mary Ellen  2
Chayefsky, Paddy  23
Cheever, John  3, 7, 8, 11, 15, 25, 64
Cheever, Susan  18, 48
Cheney, Lynne V.  70
Chester, Alfred  49
Childress, Alice  12, 15, 86, 96
Chin, Frank (Chew Jr.)  135
Choi, Susan  119

Chomsky, (Avram) Noam  132
Chute, Carolyn  39
Ciardi, John (Anthony)  10, 40, 44, 129
Cimino, Michael  16
Cisneros, Sandra  69, 118
Clampitt, Amy  32
Clancy, Tom  45, 112
Clark, Eleanor  5, 19
Clark, Walter Van Tilburg  28
Clarke, Shirley  16
Clavell, James (duMaresq)  6, 25, 87
Cleaver, (Leroy) Eldridge  30, 119
Clifton, (Thelma) Lucille  19, 66
Coburn, D(onald) L(ee)  10
Codrescu, Andrei  46, 121
Coen, Ethan  108
Coen, Joel  108
Cohen, Arthur A(llen)  7, 31
Coles, Robert (Martin)  108
Collier, Christopher  30
Collier, James Lincoln  30
Collins, Linda  44
Colter, Cyrus  58
Colum, Padraic  28
Colwin, Laurie (E.)  5, 13, 23, 84
Condon, Richard (Thomas)  4, 6, 8, 10, 45, 100
Connell, Evan S(helby) Jr.  4, 6, 45
Connelly, Marc(us Cook)  7
Conroy, (Donald) Pat(rick)  30, 74
Cook, Robin  14
Cooke, Elizabeth  55
Cook-Lynn, Elizabeth  93
Cooper, J(oan) California  56
Coover, Robert (Lowell)  3, 7, 15, 32, 46, 87
Coppola, Francis Ford  16, 126
Corcoran, Barbara (Asenath)  17
Corman, Cid  9
Cormier, Robert (Edmund)  12, 30
Corn, Alfred (DeWitt III)  33
Corso, (Nunzio) Gregory  1, 11
Costain, Thomas B(ertram)  30
Cowley, Malcolm  39
Cozzens, James Gould  1, 4, 11, 92
Crane, R(onald) S(almon)  27
Crase, Douglas  58
Creeley, Robert (White)  1, 2, 4, 8, 11, 15, 36, 78
Crews, Harry (Eugene)  6, 23, 49
Crichton, (John) Michael  2, 6, 54, 90
Cristofer, Michael  28
Cronenberg, David  143
Crow Dog, Mary (Ellen)  93
Crowley, John  57
Crumb, R(obert)  17
Cryer, Gretchen (Kiger)  21
Cudlip, David R(ockwell)  34
Cummings, E(dward) E(stlin)  1, 3, 8, 12, 15, 68
Cunningham, J(ames) V(incent)  3, 31
Cunningham, Julia (Woolfolk)  12
Cunningham, Michael  34
Currie, Ellen  44
Dacey, Philip  51
Dahlberg, Edward  1, 7, 14
Daitch, Susan  103
Daly, Elizabeth  52
Daly, Maureen  17
Dannay, Frederic  11
Danvers, Dennis  70
Danziger, Paula  21
Davenport, Guy (Mattison Jr.)  6, 14, 38
Davidson, Donald (Grady)  2, 13, 19
Davidson, Sara  9
Davis, Angela (Yvonne)  77
Davis, H(arold) L(enoir)  49
Davison, Peter (Hubert)  28
Dawson, Fielding  6
Deer, Sandra  45
Delany, Samuel R(ay) Jr.  8, 14, 38, 141
Delbanco, Nicholas (Franklin)  6, 13

DeLillo, Don  8, 10, 13, 27, 39, 54, 76, 143
Deloria, Vine (Victor) Jr.  21, 122
Del Vecchio, John M(ichael)  29
de Man, Paul (Adolph Michel)  55
DeMarinis, Rick  54
Demby, William  53
Denby, Edwin (Orr)  48
De Palma, Brian (Russell)  20
Deren, Maya  16, 102
Derleth, August (William)  31
Deutsch, Babette  18
De Vries, Peter  1, 2, 3, 7, 10, 28, 46
Dexter, Pete  34, 55
Diamond, Neil  30
Dick, Philip K(indred)  10, 30, 72
Dickey, James (Lafayette)  1, 2, 4, 7, 10, 15, 47, 109
Dickey, William  3, 28
Dickinson, Charles  49
Didion, Joan  1, 3, 8, 14, 32, 129
Dillard, Annie  9, 60, 115
Dillard, R(ichard) H(enry) W(ilde)  5
Disch, Thomas M(ichael)  7, 36
Dixon, Stephen  52
Dobyns, Stephen  37
Doctorow, E(dgar) L(aurence)  6, 11, 15, 18, 37, 44, 65, 113
Dodson, Owen (Vincent)  79
Doerr, Harriet  34
Donaldson, Stephen R(eeder)  46, 138
Donleavy, J(ames) P(atrick)  1, 4, 6, 10, 45
Donovan, John  35
Doolittle, Hilda  3, 8, 14, 31, 34, 73
Dorn, Edward (Merton)  10, 18
Dorris, Michael (Anthony)  109
Dos Passos, John (Roderigo)  1, 4, 8, 11, 15, 25, 34, 82
Douglas, Ellen  73
Dove, Rita (Frances)  50, 81
Dowell, Coleman  60
Drexler, Rosalyn  2, 6
Drury, Allen (Stuart)  37
Duberman, Martin (Bauml)  8
Dubie, Norman (Evans)  36
Du Bois, W(illiam) E(dward) B(urghardt)  1, 2, 13, 64, 96
Dubus, Andre  13, 36, 97
Duffy, Bruce  50
Dugan, Alan  2, 6
Dumas, Henry L.  6, 62
Duncan, Lois  26
Duncan, Robert (Edward)  1, 2, 4, 7, 15, 41, 55
Dunn, Katherine (Karen)  71
Dunn, Stephen  36
Dunne, John Gregory  28
Durang, Christopher (Ferdinand)  27, 38
Durban, (Rosa) Pam  39
Dworkin, Andrea  43, 123
Dwyer, Thomas A.  114
Dybek, Stuart  114
Dylan, Bob  3, 4, 6, 12, 77
Eastlake, William (Derry)  8
Eberhart, Richard (Ghormley)  3, 11, 19, 56
Eberstadt, Fernanda  39
Eckert, Allan W.  17
Edel, (Joseph) Leon  29, 34
Edgerton, Clyde (Carlyle)  39
Edmonds, Walter D(umaux)  35
Edson, Russell  13
Edwards, Gus  43
Ehle, John (Marsden Jr.)  27
Ehrenreich, Barbara  110
Eigner, Larry  9
Eiseley, Loren Corey  7
Eisenstadt, Jill  50
Eliade, Mircea  19
Eliot, T(homas) S(tearns)  1, 2, 3, 6, 9, 10, 13, 15, 24, 34, 41, 55, 57, 113
Elkin, Stanley L(awrence)  4, 6, 9, 14, 27, 51, 91
Elledge, Scott  34

Elliott, George P(aul)  2
Ellis, Bret Easton  39, 71, 117
Ellison, Harlan (Jay)  1, 13, 42, 139
Ellison, Ralph (Waldo)  1, 3, 11, 54, 86, 114
Ellmann, Lucy (Elizabeth)  61
Ellmann, Richard (David)  50
Elman, Richard (Martin)  19
L'Engle, Madeleine (Camp Franklin)  12
Ephron, Nora  17, 31
Epstein, Daniel Mark  7
Epstein, Jacob  19
Epstein, Joseph  39
Epstein, Leslie  27
Erdman, Paul E(mil)  25
Erdrich, Louise  39, 54, 120
Erickson, Steve  64
Eshleman, Clayton  7
Estleman, Loren D.  48
Eugenides, Jeffrey  81
Everett, Percival L.  57
Everson, William (Oliver)  1, 5, 14
Exley, Frederick (Earl)  6, 11
Ezekiel, Tish O'Dowd  34
Fagen, Donald  26
Fair, Ronald L.  18
Faludi, Susan  140
Fante, John (Thomas)  60
Farina, Richard  9
Farley, Walter (Lorimer)  17
Farmer, Philip Jose  1, 19
Farrell, James T(homas)  1, 4, 8, 11, 66
Fast, Howard (Melvin)  23, 131
Faulkner, William (Cuthbert)  1, 3, 6, 8, 9, 11, 14, 18, 28, 52, 68
Fauset, Jessie Redmon  19, 54
Faust, Irvin  8
Fearing, Kenneth (Flexner)  51
Federman, Raymond  6, 47
Feiffer, Jules (Ralph)  2, 8, 64
Feinberg, David B.  59
Feldman, Irving (Mordecai)  7
Felsen, Henry Gregor  17
Ferber, Edna  18, 93
Ferlinghetti, Lawrence (Monsanto)  2, 6, 10, 27, 111
Ferrigno, Robert  65
Fiedler, Leslie A(aron)  4, 13, 24
Field, Andrew  44
Fierstein, Harvey (Forbes)  33
Fish, Stanley Eugene  142
Fisher, M(ary) F(rances) K(ennedy)  76, 87
Fisher, Vardis (Alvero)  7
Fitzgerald, Robert (Stuart)  39
Flanagan, Thomas (James Bonner)  25, 52
Fleming, Thomas (James)  37
Foote, Horton  51, 91
Foote, Shelby  75
Forbes, Esther  12
Forché, Carolyn (Louise)  25, 83, 86
Ford, John  16
Ford, Richard  46, 99
Foreman, Richard  50
Forman, James Douglas  21
Fornés, María Irene  39, 61
Forrest, Leon (Richard)  4
Fosse, Bob  20
Fox, Paula  2, 8, 121
Fox, William Price (Jr.)  22
Francis, Robert (Churchill)  15
Frank, Elizabeth  39
Fraze, Candida (Merrill)  50
Frazier, Ian  46
Freeman, Judith  55
French, Albert  86
French, Marilyn  10, 18, 60
Friedan, Betty (Naomi)  74
Friedman, B(ernard) H(arper)  7
Friedman, Bruce Jay  3, 5, 56
Frost, Robert (Lee)  1, 3, 4, 9, 10, 13, 15, 26, 34, 44
Frye, (Herman) Northrop  24, 70
Fuchs, Daniel  34

Fuchs, Daniel  8, 22
Fukuyama, Francis  131
Fuller, Charles (H. Jr.)  25
Fulton, Alice  52
Fuson, Robert H(enderson)  70
Fussell, Paul  74
Gaddis, William  1, 3, 6, 8, 10, 19, 43, 86
Gaines, Ernest J(ames)  3, 11, 18, 86
Gaitskill, Mary  69
Gallagher, Tess  18, 63
Gallant, Roy A(rthur)  17
Gallico, Paul (William)  2
Galvin, James  38
Gann, Ernest Kellogg  23
Garcia, Cristina  76
Gardner, Herb(ert)  44
Gardner, John (Champlin) Jr.  2, 3, 5, 7, 8, 10, 18, 28, 34
Garrett, George (Palmer)  3, 11, 51
Garrigue, Jean  2, 8
Gass, William H(oward)  1, 2, 8, 11, 15, 39, 132
Gates, Henry Louis Jr.  65
Gaye, Marvin (Pentz Jr.)  26
Gelbart, Larry (Simon)  21, 61
Gelber, Jack  1, 6, 14, 79
Gellhorn, Martha (Ellis)  14, 60
Gent, Peter  29
George, Jean Craighead  35
Gertler, T.  134
Ghiselin, Brewster  23
Gibbons, Kaye  50, 88, 145
Gibson, William  23
Gibson, William (Ford)  39, 63
Gifford, Barry (Colby)  34
Gilbreth, Frank B(unker) Jr.  17
Gilchrist, Ellen (Louise)  34, 48, 143
Giles, Molly  39
Gilliam, Terry (Vance)  21, 141
Gilroy, Frank D(aniel)  2
Gilstrap, John  99
Ginsberg, Allen  1, 2, 3, 4, 6, 13, 36, 69, 109
Giovanni, Nikki  2, 4, 19, 64, 117
Glasser, Ronald J.  37
Gleick, James (W.)  147
Glück, Louise (Elisabeth)  7, 22, 44, 81
Godwin, Gail (Kathleen)  5, 8, 22, 31, 69, 125
Goines, Donald  80
Gold, Herbert  4, 7, 14, 42
Goldbarth, Albert  5, 38
Goldman, Francisco  76
Goldman, William (W.)  1, 48
Goldsberry, Steven  34
Goodman, Paul  1, 2, 4, 7
Gordon, Caroline  6, 13, 29, 83
Gordon, Mary (Catherine)  13, 22, 128
Gordon, Sol  26
Gordone, Charles  1, 4
Gould, Lois  4, 10
Goyen, (Charles) William  5, 8, 14, 40
Graham, Jorie  48, 118
Grau, Shirley Ann  4, 9, 146
Graver, Elizabeth  70
Gray, Amlin  29
Gray, Francine du Plessix  22
Gray, Spalding  49, 112
Grayson, Richard (A.)  38
Greeley, Andrew M(oran)  28
Green, Hannah  3
Green, Julien  3, 11, 77
Green, Paul (Eliot)  25
Greenberg, Joanne (Goldenberg)  7, 30
Greenberg, Richard  57
Greenblatt, Stephen J(ay)  70
Greene, Bette  30
Greene, Gael  8
Gregor, Arthur  9
Griffin, John Howard  68
Griffin, Peter  39
Grisham, John  84

Grumbach, Doris (Isaac)  13, 22, 64
Grunwald, Lisa  44
Guare, John  8, 14, 29, 67
Gubar, Susan (David)  145
Guest, Barbara  34
Guest, Judith (Ann)  8, 30
Guild, Nicholas M.  33
Gunn, Bill  5
Gurganus, Allan  70
Gurney, A(lbert) R(amsdell) Jr.  32, 50, 54
Gustafson, James M(oody)  100
Guterson, David  91
Guthrie, A(lfred) B(ertram) Jr.  23
Guy, Rosa (Cuthbert)  26
Hacker, Marilyn  5, 9, 23, 72, 91
Hailey, Elizabeth Forsythe  40
Haines, John (Meade)  58
Haldeman, Joe (William)  61
Haley, Alex(ander Murray Palmer)  8, 12, 76
Hall, Donald (Andrew Jr.)  1, 13, 37, 59, 151
Halpern, Daniel  14
Hamill, Pete  10
Hamilton, Edmond  1
Hamilton, Virginia (Esther)  26
Hammett, (Samuel) Dashiell  3, 5, 10, 19, 47
Hamner, Earl (Henry) Jr.  12
Hannah, Barry  23, 38, 90
Hansberry, Lorraine (Vivian)  17, 62
Hansen, Joseph  38
Hanson, Kenneth O(stlin)  13
Hardwick, Elizabeth (Bruce)  13
Harjo, Joy  83
Harlan, Louis R(udolph)  34
Harling, Robert  53
Harmon, William (Ruth)  38
Harper, Michael S(teven)  7, 22
Harris, MacDonald  9
Harris, Mark  19
Harrison, Barbara Grizzuti  144
Harrison, Harry (Max)  42
Harrison, James (Thomas)  6, 14, 33, 66, 143
Harrison, Kathryn  70, 151
Harriss, Will(ard Irvin)  34
Hart, Moss  66
Hartman, Geoffrey H.  27
Haruf, Kent  34
Hass, Robert  18, 39, 99
Haviaras, Stratis  33
Hawkes, John (Clendennin Burne Jr.)  1, 2, 3, 4, 7, 9, 14, 15, 27, 49
Hayden, Robert E(arl)  5, 9, 14, 37
Hayman, Ronald  44
H. D.  3, 8, 14, 31, 34, 73
Hearne, Vicki  56
Hearon, Shelby  63
Heat-Moon, William Least  29
Hecht, Anthony (Evan)  8, 13, 19
Hecht, Ben  8
Heifner, Jack  11
Heilbrun, Carolyn G(old)  25
Heinemann, Larry (Curtiss)  50
Heinlein, Robert A(nson)  1, 3, 8, 14, 26, 55
Heller, Joseph  1, 3, 5, 8, 11, 36, 63
Hellman, Lillian (Florence)  2, 4, 8, 14, 18, 34, 44, 52
Helprin, Mark  7, 10, 22, 32
Hemingway, Ernest (Miller)  1, 3, 6, 8, 10, 13, 19, 30, 34, 39, 41, 44, 50, 61, 80
Hempel, Amy  39
Henley, Beth  23
Hentoff, Nat(han Irving)  26
Herbert, Frank (Patrick)  12, 23, 35, 44, 85
Herbst, Josephine (Frey)  34
Herlihy, James Leo  6
Herrmann, Dorothy  44
Hersey, John (Richard)  1, 2, 7, 9, 40, 81, 97
L'Heureux, John (Clarke)  52

Heyen, William  13, 18
Higgins, George V(incent)  4, 7, 10, 18
Highsmith, (Mary) Patricia  2, 4, 14, 42, 102
Highwater, Jamake (Mamake)  12
Hijuelos, Oscar  65
Hill, George Roy  26
Hillerman, Tony  62
Himes, Chester (Bomar)  2, 4, 7, 18, 58, 108
Hinton, S(usan) E(loise)  30, 111
Hirsch, Edward  31, 50
Hirsch, E(ric) D(onald) Jr.  79
Hoagland, Edward  28
Hoban, Russell (Conwell)  7, 25
Hobson, Laura Z(ametkin)  7, 25
Hochman, Sandra  3, 8
Hoffman, Alice  51
Hoffman, Daniel (Gerard)  6, 13, 23
Hoffman, Stanley  5
Hoffman, William  141
Hoffman, William M(oses)  40
Hogan, Linda  73
Holland, Isabelle  21
Hollander, John  2, 5, 8, 14
Holleran, Andrew  38
Holmes, John Clellon  56
Honig, Edwin  33
Horgan, Paul (George Vincent O'Shaughnessy)  9, 53
Horovitz, Israel (Arthur)  56
Horwitz, Julius  14
Hougan, Carolyn  34
Howard, Maureen  5, 14, 46, 151
Howard, Richard  7, 10, 47
Howe, Fanny (Quincy)  47
Howe, Irving  85
Howe, Susan  72
Howe, Tina  48
Howes, Barbara  15
Hubbard, L(afayette) Ron(ald)  43
Huddle, David  49
Hughart, Barry  39
Hughes, (James) Langston  1, 5, 10, 15, 35, 44, 108
Hugo, Richard F(ranklin)  6, 18, 32
Humphrey, William  45
Humphreys, Josephine  34, 57
Hunt, E(verette) Howard (Jr.)  3
Hunt, Marsha  70
Hunter, Evan  11, 31
Hunter, Kristin (Eggleston)  35
Hurston, Zora Neale  7, 30, 61
Huston, John (Marcellus)  20
Hustvedt, Siri  76
Huxley, Aldous (Leonard)  1, 3, 4, 5, 8, 11, 18, 35, 79
Hwang, David Henry  55
Hyde, Margaret O(ldroyd)  21
Hynes, James  65
Ian, Janis  21
Ignatow, David  4, 7, 14, 40
Ingalls, Rachel (Holmes)  42
Inge, William (Motter)  1, 8, 19
Innaurato, Albert (F.)  21, 60
Irving, John (Winslow)  13, 23, 38, 112
Isaacs, Susan  32
Isler, Alan (David)  91
Ivask, Ivar Vidrik  14
Jackson, Jesse  12
Jackson, Shirley  11, 60, 87
Jacobs, Jim  12
Jacobsen, Josephine  48, 102
Jakes, John (William)  29
Jameson, Fredric  142
Janowitz, Tama  43, 145
Jarrell, Randall  1, 2, 6, 9, 13, 49
Jeffers, (John) Robinson  2, 3, 11, 15, 54
Jen, Gish  70
Jennings, Waylon  21
Jensen, Laura (Linnea)  37
Jin, Xuefei  109

Joel, Billy  26
Johnson, Charles (Richard)  7, 51, 65
Johnson, Denis  52
Johnson, Diane  5, 13, 48
Johnson, Joyce  58
Johnson, Judith (Emlyn)  7, 15
Jones, Edward P.  76
Jones, Gayl  6, 9, 131
Jones, James  1, 3, 10, 39
Jones, LeRoi  1, 2, 3, 5, 10, 14
Jones, Louis B.  65
Jones, Madison (Percy Jr.)  4
Jones, Nettie (Pearl)  34
Jones, Preston  10
Jones, Robert F(rancis)  7
Jones, Thom (Douglas)  81
Jong, Erica  4, 6, 8, 18, 83
Jordan, June  5, 11, 23, 114
Jordan, Pat(rick M.)  37
Just, Ward (Swift)  4, 27
Justice, Donald (Rodney)  6, 19, 102
Kadohata, Cynthia  59, 122
Kahn, Roger  30
Kaletski, Alexander  39
Kallman, Chester (Simon)  2
Kaminsky, Stuart M(elvin)  59
Kanin, Garson  22
Kantor, MacKinlay  7
Kaplan, David Michael  50
Kaplan, James  59
Karl, Frederick R(obert)  34
Katz, Steve  47
Kauffman, Janet  42
Kaufman, Bob (Garnell)  49
Kaufman, George S.  38
Kaufman, Sue  3, 8
Kazan, Elia  6, 16, 63
Kazin, Alfred  34, 38, 119
Keaton, Buster  20
Keene, Donald  34
Keillor, Garrison  40, 115
Kellerman, Jonathan  44
Kelley, William Melvin  22
Kellogg, Marjorie  2
Kemelman, Harry  2
Kennedy, Adrienne (Lita)  66
Kennedy, William  6, 28, 34, 53
Kennedy, X. J.  8, 42
Kenny, Maurice (Francis)  87
Kerouac, Jack  1, 2, 3, 5, 14, 29, 61
Kerr, Jean  22
Kerr, M. E.  12, 35
Kerr, Robert  55
Kerrigan, (Thomas) Anthony  4, 6
Kesey, Ken (Elton)  1, 3, 6, 11, 46, 64
Kesselring, Joseph (Otto)  45
Kessler, Jascha (Frederick)  4
Kettelkamp, Larry (Dale)  12
Keyes, Daniel  80
Kherdian, David  6, 9
Kienzle, William X(avier)  25
Killens, John Oliver  10
Kincaid, Jamaica  43, 68, 137
King, Martin Luther Jr.  83
King, Stephen (Edwin)  12, 26, 37, 61, 113
King, Thomas  89
Kingman, Lee  17
Kingsley, Sidney  44
Kingsolver, Barbara  55, 81, 130
Kingston, Maxine (Ting Ting) Hong  12, 19, 58, 121
Kinnell, Galway  1, 2, 3, 5, 13, 29, 129
Kirkwood, James  9
Kissinger, Henry A(lfred)  137
Kizer, Carolyn (Ashley)  15, 39, 80
Klappert, Peter  57
Klein, Norma  30
Klein, T(heodore) E(ibon) D(onald)  34
Knapp, Caroline  99
Knebel, Fletcher  14
Knight, Etheridge  40
Knowles, John  1, 4, 10, 26

Koch, Kenneth  5, 8, 44
Komunyakaa, Yusef  86, 94
Koontz, Dean R(ay)  78
Kopit, Arthur (Lee)  1, 18, 33
Kosinski, Jerzy (Nikodem)  1, 2, 3, 6, 10, 15, 53, 70
Kostelanetz, Richard (Cory)  28
Kotlowitz, Robert  4
Kotzwinkle, William  5, 14, 35
Kozol, Jonathan  17
Kozoll, Michael  35
Kramer, Kathryn  34
Kramer, Larry  42
Kristofferson, Kris  26
Krumgold, Joseph (Quincy)  12
Krutch, Joseph Wood  24
Kubrick, Stanley  16
Kumin, Maxine (Winokur)  5, 13, 28
Kunitz, Stanley (Jasspon)  6, 11, 14, 148
Kushner, Tony  81
Kuzma, Greg  7
Lancaster, Bruce  36
Landis, John  26
Langer, Elinor  34
Lapine, James (Elliot)  39
Larsen, Eric  55
Larsen, Nella  37
Larson, Charles R(aymond)  31
Lasch, Christopher  102
Latham, Jean Lee  12
Lattimore, Richmond (Alexander)  3
Laughlin, James  49
Lear, Norman (Milton)  12
Leavitt, David  34
Lebowitz, Fran(ces Ann)  11, 36
Lee, Andrea  36
Lee, Chang-rae  91
Lee, Don L.  2
Lee, George W(ashington)  52
Lee, Helen Elaine  86
Lee, Lawrence  34
Lee, Manfred B(ennington)  11
Lee, (Nelle) Harper  12, 60
Lee, Shelton Jackson  105
Lee, Stan  17
Leet, Judith  11
Leffland, Ella  19
Le Guin, Ursula K(roeber)  8, 13, 22, 45, 71, 136
Leiber, Fritz (Reuter Jr.)  25
Leimbach, Marti  65
Leithauser, Brad  27
Lelchuk, Alan  5
Lemann, Nancy  39
Lentricchia, Frank (Jr.)  34
Leonard, Elmore (John Jr.)  28, 34, 71, 120
Lerman, Eleanor  9
Lerman, Rhoda  56
Lester, Richard  20
Levertov, Denise  1, 2, 3, 5, 8, 15, 28, 66
Levi, Jonathan  76
Levin, Ira  3, 6
Levin, Meyer  7
Levine, Philip  2, 4, 5, 9, 14, 33, 118
Levinson, Deirdre  49
Levitin, Sonia (Wolff)  17
Lewis, Janet  41
Leyner, Mark  92
Lieber, Joel  6
Lieberman, Laurence (James)  4, 36
Lifton, Robert Jay  67
Lightman, Alan P(aige)  81
Ligotti, Thomas (Robert)  44
Lindbergh, Anne (Spencer) Morrow  82
Linney, Romulus  51
Lipsyte, Robert (Michael)  21
Lish, Gordon (Jay)  45
Littell, Robert  42
Loewinsohn, Ron(ald William)  52
Logan, John (Burton)  5
Lopate, Phillip  29
Lopez, Barry (Holstun)  70

Lord, Bette Bao 23
Lorde, Audre (Geraldine) 18, 71
Louie, David Wong 70
Lowell, Robert (Traill Spence Jr.) 1, 2, 3, 4, 5, 8, 9, 11, 15, 37, 124
Loy, Mina 28
Lucas, Craig 64
Lucas, George 16
Ludlam, Charles 46, 50
Ludlum, Robert 22, 43
Ludwig, Ken 60
Lurie, Alison 4, 5, 18, 39
Lynch, David (K.) 66
Lynn, Kenneth S(chuyler) 50
Lytle, Andrew (Nelson) 22
Maas, Peter 29
Macdonald, Cynthia 13, 19
MacDonald, John D(ann) 3, 27, 44
MacInnes, Helen (Clark) 27, 39
Maclean, Norman (Fitzroy) 78
MacLeish, Archibald 3, 8, 14, 68
MacShane, Frank 39
Madden, (Jerry) David 5, 15
Madhubuti, Haki R. 6, 73
Mailer, Norman 1, 2, 3, 4, 5, 8, 11, 14, 28, 39, 74, 111
Major, Clarence 3, 19, 48
Malamud, Bernard 1, 2, 3, 5, 8, 9, 11, 18, 27, 44, 78, 85
Malcolm X 82, 117
Maloff, Saul 5
Malone, Michael (Christopher) 43
Malzberg, Barry N(athaniel) 7
Mamet, David (Alan) 9, 15, 34, 46, 91
Mamoulian, Rouben (Zachary) 16
Mano, D. Keith 2, 10
Manso, Peter 39
Margulies, Donald 76
Markfield, Wallace 8
Markson, David M(errill) 67
Marlowe, Stephen 70
Marquand, John P(hillips) 2, 10
Marqués, René 96
Marshall, Garry 17
Marshall, Paule 27, 72
Martin, Steve 30
Martin, Valerie 89
Maso, Carole 44
Mason, Bobbie Ann 28, 43, 82
Masters, Hilary 48
Mastrosimone, William 36
Matheson, Richard (Burton) 37
Mathews, Harry 6, 52
Mathews, John Joseph 84
Matthews, William (Procter III) 40
Matthias, John (Edward) 9
Matthiessen, Peter 5, 7, 11, 32, 64
Maupin, Armistead (Jones Jr.) 95
Maxwell, William (Keepers Jr.) 19
May, Elaine 16
Maynard, Joyce 23
Maysles, Albert 16
Maysles, David 16
Mazer, Norma Fox 26
McBrien, William (Augustine) 44
McCaffrey, Anne (Inez) 17
McCall, Nathan 86
McCarthy, Mary (Therese) 1, 3, 5, 14, 24, 39, 59
McCauley, Stephen (D.) 50
McClure, Michael (Thomas) 6, 10
McCorkle, Jill (Collins) 51
McCourt, James 5
McCourt, Malachy 119
McCullers, (Lula) Carson (Smith) 1, 4, 10, 12, 48, 100
McDermott, Alice 90
McElroy, Joseph 5, 47
McFarland, Dennis 65
McGinley, Phyllis 14
McGinniss, Joe 32
McGrath, Thomas (Matthew) 28, 59

McGuane, Thomas (Francis III) 3, 7, 18, 45, 127
McHale, Tom 3, 5
McInerney, Jay 34, 112
McIntyre, Vonda N(eel) 18
McKuen, Rod 1, 3
McMillan, Terry (L.) 50, 61, 112
McMurtry, Larry (Jeff) 2, 3, 7, 11, 27, 44, 127
McNally, Terrence 4, 7, 41, 91
McNally, T. M. 82
McNamer, Deirdre 70
McNeal, Tom 119
McNickle, (William) D'Arcy 89
McPhee, John (Angus) 36
McPherson, James Alan 19, 77
McPherson, William (Alexander) 34
Mead, Margaret 37
Medoff, Mark (Howard) 6, 23
Mehta, Ved (Parkash) 37
Meltzer, Milton 26
Mendelsohn, Jane 99
Meredith, William (Morris) 4, 13, 22, 55
Merkin, Daphne 44
Merrill, James (Ingram) 2, 3, 6, 8, 13, 18, 34, 91
Merton, Thomas 1, 3, 11, 34, 83
Merwin, W(illiam) S(tanley) 1, 2, 3, 5, 8, 13, 18, 45, 88
Mewshaw, Michael 9
Meyers, Jeffrey 39
Michaels, Leonard 6, 25
Michener, James A(lbert) 1, 5, 11, 29, 60, 109
Miles, Jack 100
Miles, Josephine (Louise) 1, 2, 14, 34, 39
Millar, Kenneth 14
Miller, Arthur 1, 2, 6, 10, 15, 26, 47, 78
Miller, Henry (Valentine) 1, 2, 4, 9, 14, 43, 84
Miller, Jason 2
Miller, Sue 44
Miller, Walter M(ichael Jr.) 4, 30
Millett, Kate 67
Millhauser, Steven (Lewis) 21, 54, 109
Milner, Ron(ald) 56
Miner, Valerie 40
Minot, Susan 44
Minus, Ed 39
Mitchell, Joseph (Quincy) 98
Modarressi, Taghi (M.) 44
Mohr, Nicholasa 12
Mojtabai, A(nn) G(race) 5, 9, 15, 29
Momaday, N(avarre) Scott 2, 19, 85, 95
Monette, Paul 82
Montague, John (Patrick) 13, 46
Montgomery, Marion H. Jr. 7
Moody, Rick 147
Mooney, Ted 25
Moore, Lorrie 39, 45, 68
Moore, Marianne (Craig) 1, 2, 4, 8, 10, 13, 19, 47
Moraga, Cherrie 126
Morgan, Berry 6
Morgan, (George) Frederick 23
Morgan, Robin (Evonne) 2
Morgan, Seth 65
Morris, Bill 76
Morris, Wright 1, 3, 7, 18, 37
Morrison, Jim 17
Morrison, Toni 4, 10, 22, 55, 81, 87
Mosher, Howard Frank 62
Mosley, Walter 97
Moss, Howard 7, 14, 45, 50
Motley, Willard (Francis) 18
Mountain Wolf Woman 92
Moyers, Bill 74
Mueller, Lisel 13, 51
Mull, Martin 17
Mungo, Raymond 72
Murphy, Sylvia 34
Murray, Albert L. 73

Muske, Carol 90
Myers, Walter Dean 35
Nabokov, Vladimir (Vladimirovich) 1, 2, 3, 6, 8, 11, 15, 23, 44, 46, 64
Nash, (Fredric) Ogden 23
Naylor, Gloria 28, 52
Neihardt, John Gneisenau 32
Nelson, Willie 17
Nemerov, Howard (Stanley) 2, 6, 9, 36
Neufeld, John (Arthur) 17
Neville, Emily Cheney 12
Newlove, Donald 6
Newman, Charles 2, 8
Newman, Edwin (Harold) 14
Newton, Suzanne 35
Nichols, John (Treadwell) 38
Niedecker, Lorine 10, 42
Nin, Anaïs 1, 4, 8, 11, 14, 60, 127
Nissenson, Hugh 4, 9
Nixon, Agnes Eckhardt 21
Norman, Marsha 28
Norton, Andre 12
Nova, Craig 7, 31
Nunn, Kem 34
Nyro, Laura 17
Oates, Joyce Carol 1, 2, 3, 6, 9, 11, 15, 19, 33, 52, 108, 134
O'Brien, Darcy 11
O'Brien, (William) Tim(othy) 7, 19, 40, 103
Ochs, Phil(ip David) 17
O'Connor, Edwin (Greene) 14
O'Connor, (Mary) Flannery 1, 2, 3, 6, 10, 13, 15, 21, 66, 104
O'Dell, Scott 30
Odets, Clifford 2, 28, 98
O'Donovan, Michael John 14
O'Grady, Timothy 59
O'Hara, Frank 2, 5, 13, 78
O'Hara, John (Henry) 1, 2, 3, 6, 11, 42
O Hehir, Diana 41
Olds, Sharon 32, 39, 85
Oliver, Mary 19, 34, 98
Olsen, Tillie 4, 13, 114
Olson, Charles (John) 1, 2, 5, 6, 9, 11, 29
Olson, Toby 28
Oppen, George 7, 13, 34
Orlovitz, Gil 22
Ortiz, Simon J(oseph) 45
Ostriker, Alicia (Suskin) 132
Otto, Whitney 70
Owens, Rochelle 8
Ozick, Cynthia 3, 7, 28, 62
Pack, Robert 13
Pagels, Elaine Hiesey 104
Paglia, Camille (Anna) 68
Paley, Grace 4, 6, 37, 140
Palliser, Charles 65
Pancake, Breece D'J 29
Paretsky, Sara 135
Parini, Jay (Lee) 54, 133
Parker, Dorothy (Rothschild) 15, 68
Parker, Robert B(rown) 27
Parks, Gordon (Alexander Buchanan) 1, 16
Pastan, Linda (Olenik) 27
Patchen, Kenneth 1, 2, 18
Paterson, Katherine (Womeldorf) 12, 30
Peacock, Molly 60
Pearson, T(homas) R(eid) 39
Peck, John (Frederick) 3
Peck, Richard (Wayne) 21
Peck, Robert Newton 17
Peckinpah, (David) Sam(uel) 20
Percy, Walker 2, 3, 6, 8, 14, 18, 47, 65
Perelman, S(idney) J(oseph) 3, 5, 9, 15, 23, 44, 49
Perloff, Marjorie G(abrielle) 137
Pesetsky, Bette 28
Peterkin, Julia Mood 31
Peters, Joan K(aren) 39
Peters, Robert L(ouis) 7
Petrakis, Harry Mark 3

Petry, Ann (Lane)  1, 7, 18
Philipson, Morris H.  53
Phillips, Jayne Anne  15, 33, 139
Phillips, Robert (Schaeffer)  28
Piercy, Marge  3, 6, 14, 18, 27, 62, 128
Pinckney, Darryl  76
Pineda, Cecile  39
Pinkwater, Daniel Manus  35
Pinsky, Robert  9, 19, 38, 94, 121
Pirsig, Robert M(aynard)  4, 6, 73
Plante, David (Robert)  7, 23, 38
Plath, Sylvia  1, 2, 3, 5, 9, 11, 14, 17, 50, 51, 62, 111
Platt, Kin  26
Plimpton, George (Ames)  36
Plumly, Stanley (Ross)  33
Pohl, Frederik  18
Poitier, Sidney  26
Pollitt, Katha  28, 122
Polonsky, Abraham (Lincoln)  92
Pomerance, Bernard  13
Porter, Connie (Rose)  70
Porter, Katherine Anne  1, 3, 7, 10, 13, 15, 27, 101
Potok, Chaim  2, 7, 14, 26, 112
Pound, Ezra (Weston Loomis)  1, 2, 3, 4, 5, 7, 10, 13, 18, 34, 48, 50, 112
Povod, Reinaldo  44
Powell, Adam Clayton Jr.  89
Powell, Dawn  66
Powell, Padgett  34
Power, Susan  91
Powers, J(ames) F(arl)  1, 4, 8, 57
Powers, John R.  66
Powers, Richard (S.)  93
Prager, Emily  56
Price, (Edward) Reynolds  3, 6, 13, 43, 50, 63
Price, Richard  6, 12
Prince  35
Pritchard, William H(arrison)  34
Probst, Mark  59
Prokosch, Frederic  4, 48
Prose, Francine  45
Proulx, E(dna) Annie  81
Pryor, Richard (Franklin Lenox Thomas)  26
Purdy, James (Amos)  2, 4, 10, 28, 52
Puzo, Mario  1, 2, 6, 36, 107
Pynchon, Thomas (Ruggles Jr.)  2, 3, 6, 9, 11, 18, 33, 62, 72, 123
Quay, Stephen  95
Quay, Timothy  95
Queen, Ellery  3, 11
Quinn, Peter  91
Rabe, David (William)  4, 8, 33
Rado, James  17
Raeburn, John (Hay)  34
Ragni, Gerome  17
Rahv, Philip  24
Rakosi, Carl  47
Rampersad, Arnold  44
Rand, Ayn  3, 30, 44, 79
Randall, Dudley (Felker)  1, 135
Ransom, John Crowe  2, 4, 5, 11, 24
Raphael, Frederic (Michael)  2, 14
Rechy, John (Francisco)  1, 7, 14, 18, 107
Reddin, Keith  67
Redmon, Anne  22
Reed, Ishmael  2, 3, 5, 6, 13, 32, 60
Reed, Lou  21
Remarque, Erich Maria  21
Rexroth, Kenneth  1, 2, 6, 11, 22, 49, 112
Reynolds, Jonathan  6, 38
Reynolds, Michael S(hane)  44
Reznikoff, Charles  9
Ribman, Ronald (Burt)  7
Rice, Anne  41, 128
Rice, Elmer (Leopold)  7, 49
Rich, Adrienne (Cecile)  3, 6, 7, 11, 18, 36, 73, 76, 125
Richter, Conrad (Michael)  30
Riding, Laura  3, 7

Ringwood, Gwen(dolyn Margaret) Pharis  48
Rivers, Conrad Kent  1
Robbins, Harold  5
Robbins, Trina  21
Robinson, Jill  10
Robinson, Kim Stanley  34
Robinson, Marilynne  25
Robinson, Smokey  21
Robison, Mary  42, 98
Roddenberry, Gene  17
Rodgers, Mary  12
Rodman, Howard  65
Roethke, Theodore (Huebner)  1, 3, 8, 11, 19, 46, 101
Rogers, Thomas Hunton  57
Rogin, Gilbert  18
Roiphe, Anne (Richardson)  3, 9
Rooke, Leon  25, 34
Rose, Wendy  85
Rosen, Richard (Dean)  39
Rosenthal, M(acha) L(ouis)  28
Rossner, Judith (Perelman)  6, 9, 29
Roth, Henry  2, 6, 11, 104
Roth, Philip (Milton)  1, 2, 3, 4, 6, 9, 15, 22, 31, 47, 66, 86, 119
Rothenberg, Jerome  6, 57
Rovit, Earl (Herbert)  7
Royko, Mike  109
Ruark, Gibbons  3
Rudnik, Raphael  7
Rukeyser, Muriel  6, 10, 15, 27
Rule, Jane (Vance)  27
Rush, Norman  44
Russ, Joanna  15
Russell, Jeffrey Burton  70
Ryan, Cornelius (John)  7
Ryan, Michael  65
Sachs, Marilyn (Stickle)  35
Sackler, Howard (Oliver)  14
Sadoff, Ira  9
Safire, William  10
Sagan, Carl (Edward)  30, 112
Said, Edward W.  123
Saint, H(arry) F.  50
Salamanca, J(ack) R(ichard)  4, 15
Sale, Kirkpatrick  68
Salinas, Luis Omar  90
Salinger, J(erome) D(avid)  1, 3, 8, 12, 55, 56, 138
Salter, James  7, 52, 59
Sanchez, Sonia  5, 116
Sandburg, Carl (August)  1, 4, 10, 15, 35
Sanders, (James) Ed(ward)  53
Sanders, Lawrence  41
Sandoz, Mari(e Susette)  28
Saner, Reg(inald Anthony)  9
Santiago, Danny  33
Santmyer, Helen Hooven  33
Santos, Bienvenido N(uqui)  22
Sapphire, Brenda  99
Saroyan, William  1, 8, 10, 29, 34, 56
Sarton, (Eleanor) May  4, 14, 49, 91
Saul, John (W. III)  46
Savage, Thomas  40
Savan, Glenn  50
Sayers, Valerie  50, 122
Sayles, John (Thomas)  7, 10, 14
Schaeffer, Susan Fromberg  6, 11, 22
Schell, Jonathan  35
Schevill, James (Erwin)  7
Schisgal, Murray (Joseph)  6
Schlesinger, Arthur M(eier) Jr.  84
Schnackenberg, Gjertrud (Cecelia)  40
Schor, Sandra (M.)  65
Schorer, Mark  9
Schrader, Paul (Joseph)  26
Schulberg, Budd (Wilson)  7, 48
Schulz, Charles M(onroe)  12
Schuyler, James Marcus  5, 23
Schwartz, Delmore (David)  2, 4, 10, 45, 87
Schwartz, John Burnham  59

Schwartz, Lynne Sharon  31
Scoppettone, Sandra  26
Scorsese, Martin  20, 89
Scott, Evelyn  43
Scott, Joanna  50
Sebestyen, Ouida  30
Seelye, John (Douglas)  7
Segal, Erich (Wolf)  3, 10
Seger, Bob  35
Seidel, Frederick (Lewis)  18
Selby, Hubert Jr.  1, 2, 4, 8
Selzer, Richard  74
Serling, (Edward) Rod(man)  30
Seton, Cynthia Propper  27
Settle, Mary Lee  19, 61
Sexton, Anne (Harvey)  2, 4, 6, 8, 10, 15, 53, 123
Shaara, Michael (Joseph Jr.)  15
Shacochis, Bob  39
Shange, Ntozake  8, 25, 38, 74, 126
Shanley, John Patrick  75
Shapiro, Jane  76
Shapiro, Karl (Jay)  4, 8, 15, 53
Shaw, Irwin  7, 23, 34
Shawn, Wallace  41
Shea, Lisa  86
Sheed, Wilfrid (John Joseph)  2, 4, 10, 53
Shepard, Jim  36
Shepard, Lucius  34
Shepard, Sam  4, 6, 17, 34, 41, 44
Sherburne, Zoa (Lillian Morin)  30
Sherman, Jonathan Marc  55
Sherman, Martin  19
Shields, Carol  91, 113
Shields, David  97
Shilts, Randy  85
Shreve, Susan Richards  23
Shue, Larry  52
Shulman, Alix Kates  2, 10
Shuster, Joe  21
Siegel, Jerome  21
Sigal, Clancy  7
Silko, Leslie (Marmon)  23, 74, 114
Silver, Joan Micklin  20
Silverberg, Robert  7, 140
Silverstein, Alvin  17
Silverstein, Virginia B(arbara Opshelor)  17
Simak, Clifford D(onald)  1, 55
Simic, Charles  6, 9, 22, 49, 68, 130
Simmons, Charles (Paul)  57
Simmons, Dan  44
Simon, Carly  26
Simon, (Marvin) Neil  6, 11, 31, 39, 70
Simon, Paul (Frederick)  17
Simpson, Louis (Aston Marantz)  4, 7, 9, 32, 149
Simpson, Mona (Elizabeth)  44, 146
Sinclair, Upton (Beall)  1, 11, 15, 63
Singer, Isaac Bashevis  1, 3, 6, 9, 11, 15, 23, 38, 69, 111
Sissman, L(ouis) E(dward)  9, 18
Slaughter, Frank G(ill)  29
Slavitt, David R(ytman)  5, 14
Smiley, Jane (Graves)  53, 76, 144
Smith, Anna Deavere  86
Smith, Betty (Wehner)  19
Smith, Clark Ashton  43
Smith, Dave  22, 42
Smith, Lee  25, 73
Smith, Martin Cruz  25
Smith, Mary-Ann Tirone  39
Smith, Patti  12
Smith, William Jay  6
Snodgrass, W(illiam) D(e Witt)  2, 6, 10, 18, 68
Snyder, Gary (Sherman)  1, 2, 5, 9, 32, 120
Snyder, Zilpha Keatley  17
Sokolov, Raymond  7
Sommer, Scott  25
Sondheim, Stephen (Joshua)  30, 39, 147
Sontag, Susan  1, 2, 10, 13, 31, 105
Sorrentino, Gilbert  3, 7, 14, 22, 40

Soto, Gary  32, 80
Southern, Terry  7
Spackman, W(illiam) M(ode)  46
Spacks, Barry (Bernard)  14
Spanidou, Irini  44
Spencer, Elizabeth  22
Spencer, Scott  30
Spicer, Jack  8, 18, 72
Spiegelman, Art  76
Spielberg, Peter  6
Spielberg, Steven  20
Spinrad, Norman (Richard)  46
Spivack, Kathleen (Romola Drucker)  6
Spoto, Donald  39
Springsteen, Bruce (F.)  17
Squires, (James) Radcliffe  51
Stafford, Jean  4, 7, 19, 68
Stafford, William (Edgar)  4, 7, 29
Stanton, Maura  9
Starbuck, George (Edwin)  53
Steele, Timothy (Reid)  45
Stegner, Wallace (Earle)  9, 49, 81
Steinbeck, John (Ernst)  1, 5, 9, 13, 21, 34, 45, 75, 124
Steinem, Gloria  63
Steiner, George  24
Sterling, Bruce  72
Stern, Gerald  40, 100
Stern, Richard (Gustave)  4, 39
Sternberg, Josef von  20
Stevens, Mark  34
Stevenson, Anne (Katharine)  7, 33
Still, James  49
Stitt, Milan  29
Stolz, Mary (Slattery)  12
Stone, Irving  7
Stone, Oliver (William)  73
Stone, Robert (Anthony)  5, 23, 42
Storm, Hyemeyohsts  3
Stout, Rex (Todhunter)  3
Strand, Mark  6, 18, 41, 71
Straub, Peter (Francis)  28, 107
Stribling, T(homas) S(igismund)  23
Stuart, Jesse (Hilton)  1, 8, 11, 14, 34
Sturgeon, Theodore (Hamilton)  22, 39
Styron, William  1, 3, 5, 11, 15, 60
Sukenick, Ronald  3, 4, 6, 48
Summers, Hollis (Spurgeon Jr.)  10
Susann, Jacqueline  3
Swados, Elizabeth (A.)  12
Swados, Harvey  5
Swan, Gladys  69
Swarthout, Glendon (Fred)  35
Swenson, May  4, 14, 61, 106
Talese, Gay  37
Tallent, Elizabeth (Ann)  45
Tally, Ted  42
Tan, Amy (Ruth)  59, 120, 151
Tartt, Donna  76
Tate, James (Vincent)  2, 6, 25
Tate, (John Orley) Allen  2, 4, 6, 9, 11, 14, 24
Tavel, Ronald  6
Taylor, Eleanor Ross  5
Taylor, Henry (Splawn)  44
Taylor, Mildred D(elois)  21
Taylor, Peter (Hillsman)  1, 4, 18, 37, 44, 50, 71
Taylor, Robert Lewis  14
Terkel, Studs  38
Terry, Megan  19
Tesich, Steve  40, 69
Tevis, Walter  42
Theroux, Alexander (Louis)  2, 25
Theroux, Paul (Edward)  5, 8, 11, 15, 28, 46
Thomas, Audrey (Callahan)  7, 13, 37, 107
Thomas, Joyce Carol  35
Thomas, Lewis  35
Thomas, Piri  17
Thomas, Ross (Elmore)  39
Thompson, Hunter S(tockton)  9, 17, 40, 104

Thompson, Jim (Myers)  69
Thurber, James (Grover)  5, 11, 25, 125
Tilghman, Christopher  65
Tillich, Paul (Johannes)  131
Tillinghast, Richard (Williford)  29
Tiptree, James Jr.  48, 50
Tolson, Melvin B(eaunorus)  36, 105
Tomlin, Lily  17
Toole, John Kennedy  19, 64
Toomer, Jean  1, 4, 13, 22
Torrey, E(dwin) Fuller  34
Towne, Robert (Burton)  87
Traven, B.  8, 11
Trevanian  29
Trilling, Diana (Rubin)  129
Trilling, Lionel  9, 11, 24
Trow, George W. S.  52
Trudeau, Garry B.  12
Trumbo, Dalton  19
Tryon, Thomas  3, 11
Tuck, Lily  70
Tunis, John R(oberts)  12
Turco, Lewis (Putnam)  11, 63
Turner, Frederick  48
Tyler, Anne  7, 11, 18, 28, 44, 59, 103
Uhry, Alfred  55
Ulibarrí, Sabine R(eyes)  83
Unger, Douglas  34
Updike, John (Hoyer)  1, 2, 3, 5, 7, 9, 13, 15, 23, 34, 43, 70, 139
Urdang, Constance (Henriette)  47
Uris, Leon (Marcus)  7, 32
Vachss, Andrew (Henry)  106
Valdez, Luis (Miguel)  84
Van Ash, Cay  34
Vance, Jack  35
Vandenburgh, Jane  59
Van Doren, Mark  6, 10
Van Duyn, Mona (Jane)  3, 7, 63, 116
Van Peebles, Melvin  2, 20
Van Vechten, Carl  33
Vaughn, Stephanie  62
Vendler, Helen (Hennessy)  138
Vidal, Gore  2, 4, 6, 8, 10, 22, 33, 72, 142
Viereck, Peter (Robert Edwin)  4
Vinge, Joan (Carol) D(ennison)  30
Viola, Herman J(oseph)  70
Vizenor, Gerald Robert  103
Vliet, R(ussell) G(ordon)  22
Vogel, Paula A(nne)  76
Voigt, Cynthia  30
Voigt, Ellen Bryant  54
Vollmann, William T.  89
Vonnegut, Kurt Jr.  1, 2, 3, 4, 5, 8, 12, 22, 40, 60, 111
Wagman, Fredrica  7
Wagner-Martin, Linda (C.)  50
Wagoner, David (Russell)  3, 5, 15
Wakefield, Dan  7
Wakoski, Diane  2, 4, 7, 9, 11, 40
Waldman, Anne (Lesley)  7
Walker, Alice (Malsenior)  5, 6, 9, 19, 27, 46, 58, 103
Walker, Joseph A.  19
Walker, Margaret (Abigail)  1, 6
Wallace, David Foster  50, 114
Wallace, Irving  7, 13
Wallant, Edward Lewis  5, 10
Wambaugh, Joseph (Aloysius Jr.)  3, 18
Ward, Douglas Turner  19
Warhol, Andy  20
Warren, Robert Penn  1, 4, 6, 8, 10, 13, 18, 39, 53, 59
Wasserstein, Wendy  32, 59, 90
Waters, Frank (Joseph)  88
Watkins, Paul  55
Webb, Charles (Richard)  7
Webb, James H(enry) Jr.  22
Weber, Lenora Mattingly  12
Weidman, Jerome  7
Weiss, Theodore (Russell)  3, 8, 14
Welch, James  6, 14, 52

Wellek, Rene  28
Weller, Michael  10, 53
Welles, (George) Orson  20, 80
Wellman, Mac  65
Wellman, Manly Wade  49
Wells, Rosemary  12
Welty, Eudora  1, 2, 5, 14, 22, 33, 105
Wersba, Barbara  30
Wescott, Glenway  13
Wesley, Richard (Errol)  7
West, Cornel (Ronald)  134
West, Delno C(loyde) Jr.  70
West, (Mary) Jessamyn  7, 17
West, Paul  7, 14, 96
Westlake, Donald E(dwin)  7, 33
Whalen, Philip  6, 29
Wharton, William (a pseudonym)  18, 37
Wheelock, John Hall  14
White, Edmund (Valentine III)  27, 110
White, E(lwyn) B(rooks)  10, 34, 39
White, Hayden V.  148
Whitney, Phyllis A(yame)  42
Whittemore, (Edward) Reed (Jr.)  4
Wicker, Tom  7
Wideman, John Edgar  5, 34, 36, 67, 122
Wieners, John  7
Wiesel, Elie(zer)  3, 5, 11, 37
Wiggins, Marianne  57
Wilbur, Richard (Purdy)  3, 6, 9, 14, 53, 110
Wild, Peter  14
Wilder, Billy  20
Wilder, Thornton (Niven)  1, 5, 6, 10, 15, 35, 82
Wiley, Richard  44
Wilhelm, Kate  7
Willard, Nancy  7, 37
Williams, C(harles) K(enneth)  33, 56, 148
Williams, John A(lfred)  5, 13
Williams, Jonathan (Chamberlain)  13
Williams, Joy  31
Williams, Norman  39
Williams, Sherley Anne  89
Williams, Tennessee  1, 2, 5, 7, 8, 11, 15, 19, 30, 39, 45, 71, 111
Williams, Thomas (Alonzo)  14
Williams, William Carlos  1, 2, 5, 9, 13, 22, 42, 67
Williamson, Jack  29
Willingham, Calder (Baynard Jr.)  5, 51
Wilson, August  39, 50, 63, 118
Wilson, Brian  12
Wilson, Edmund  1, 2, 3, 8, 24
Wilson, Lanford  7, 14, 36
Wilson, Robert M.  7, 9
Wilson, Sloan  32
Wilson, William S(mith)  49
Winters, (Arthur) Yvor  4, 8, 32
Winters, Janet Lewis  41
Wiseman, Frederick  20
Wodehouse, P(elham) G(renville)  1, 2, 5, 10, 22
Woiwode, Larry (Alfred)  6, 10
Wojciechowska, Maia (Teresa)  26
Wolfe, Gene (Rodman)  25
Wolfe, George C.  49
Wolfe, Thomas Kennerly Jr.  147
Wolff, Geoffrey (Ansell)  41
Wolff, Tobias (Jonathan Ansell)  39, 64
Wolitzer, Hilma  17
Wonder, Stevie  12
Wong, Jade Snow  17
Woolrich, Cornell  77
Wouk, Herman  1, 9, 38
Wright, Charles (Penzel Jr.)  6, 13, 28, 119, 146
Wright, Charles Stevenson  49
Wright, James (Arlington)  3, 5, 10, 28
Wright, Richard (Nathaniel)  1, 3, 4, 9, 14, 21, 48, 74
Wright, Stephen  33
Wright, William  44
Wurlitzer, Rudolph  2, 4, 15

Wylie, Philip (Gordon) 43
Yates, Richard 7, 8, 23
Yep, Laurence Michael 35
Yerby, Frank G(arvin) 1, 7, 22
Yglesias, Helen 7, 22
Young, Al(bert James) 19
Young, Marguerite (Vivian) 82
Young Bear, Ray A. 94
Yurick, Sol 6
Zamora, Bernice (B. Ortiz) 89
Zappa, Frank 17
Zaturenska, Marya 6, 11
Zelazny, Roger (Joseph) 21
Ziegenhagen, Eric 55
Zindel, Paul 6, 26
Zoline, Pamela 62
Zukofsky, Louis 1, 2, 4, 7, 11, 18
Zweig, Paul 34, 42

## ANTIGUAN

Edwards, Gus 43
Kincaid, Jamaica 43, 68, 137

## ARGENTINIAN

Bioy Casares, Adolfo 4, 8, 13, 88
Borges, Jorge Luis 1, 2, 3, 4, 6, 8, 9, 10, 13, 19, 44, 48, 83
Cortázar, Julio 2, 3, 5, 10, 13, 15, 33, 34, 92
Costantini, Humberto 49
Dorfman, Ariel 48, 77
Guevara, Che 87
Guevara (Serna), Ernesto 87
Mujica Lainez, Manuel 31
Puig, Manuel 3, 5, 10, 28, 65, 133
Sabato, Ernesto (R.) 10, 23
Valenzuela, Luisa 31, 104

## ARMENIAN

Mamoulian, Rouben (Zachary) 16

## AUSTRALIAN

Anderson, Jessica (Margaret) Queale 37
Astley, Thea (Beatrice May) 41
Brinsmead, H(esba) F(ay) 21
Buckley, Vincent (Thomas) 57
Buzo, Alexander (John) 61
Carey, Peter 40, 55, 96
Clark, Mavis Thorpe 12
Clavell, James (duMaresq) 6, 25, 87
Courtenay, Bryce 59
Davison, Frank Dalby 15
Elliott, Sumner Locke 38
FitzGerald, Robert D(avid) 19
Greer, Germaine 131
Grenville, Kate 61
Hall, Rodney 51
Hazzard, Shirley 18
Hope, A(lec) D(erwent) 3, 51
Hospital, Janette Turner 42, 145
Jolley, (Monica) Elizabeth 46
Jones, Rod 50
Keneally, Thomas (Michael) 5, 8, 10, 14, 19, 27, 43, 117
Koch, C(hristopher) J(ohn) 42
Lawler, Raymond Evenor 58
Malouf, (George Joseph) David 28, 86
Matthews, Greg 45
McAuley, James Phillip 45
McCullough, Colleen 27, 107
Murray, Les(lie Allan) 40
Porter, Peter (Neville Frederick) 5, 13, 33
Prichard, Katharine Susannah 46
Shapcott, Thomas W(illiam) 38
Slessor, Kenneth 14
Stead, Christina (Ellen) 2, 5, 8, 32, 80
Stow, (Julian) Randolph 23, 48
Thiele, Colin (Milton) 17
Weir, Peter (Lindsay) 20
West, Morris L(anglo) 6, 33

White, Patrick (Victor Martindale) 3, 4, 5, 7, 9, 18, 65, 69
Wilding, Michael 73
Williamson, David (Keith) 56
Wright, Judith (Arundell) 11, 53

## AUSTRIAN

Adamson, Joy(-Friederike Victoria) 17
Bachmann, Ingeborg 69
Bernhard, Thomas 3, 32, 61
Bettelheim, Bruno 79
Frankl, Viktor E(mil) 93
Gregor, Arthur 9
Handke, Peter 5, 8, 10, 15, 38, 134
Hochwaelder, Fritz 36
Jandl, Ernst 34
Lang, Fritz 20, 103
Lind, Jakov 1, 2, 4, 27, 82
Perloff, Marjorie G(abrielle) 137
Sternberg, Josef von 20
Wellek, Rene 28
Wilder, Billy 20

## BARBADIAN

Brathwaite, Edward (Kamau) 11
Clarke, Austin C(hesterfield) 8, 53
Kennedy, Adrienne (Lita) 66
Lamming, George (William) 2, 4, 66, 144

## BELGIAN

Crommelynck, Fernand 75
Ghelderode, Michel de 6, 11
Lévi-Strauss, Claude 38
Mallet-Joris, Françoise 11
Michaux, Henri 8, 19
Sarton, (Eleanor) May 4, 14, 49, 91
Simenon, Georges (Jacques Christian) 1, 2, 3, 8, 18, 47
van Itallie, Jean-Claude 3
Yourcenar, Marguerite 19, 38, 50, 87

## BOTSWANAN

Head, Bessie 25, 67

## BRAZILIAN

Amado, Jorge 13, 40, 106
Boff, Leonardo (Genezio Darci) 70
Cabral de Melo Neto, Joao 76
Castaneda, Carlos (Cesar Aranha) 12, 119
Dourado, (Waldomiro Freitas) Autran 23, 60
Drummond de Andrade, Carlos 18
Lispector, Clarice 43
Ribeiro, Darcy 34
Ribeiro, Joao Ubaldo (Osorio Pimentel) 10, 67
Rosa, Joao Guimaraes 23

## BULGARIAN

Bagryana, Elisaveta 10
Belcheva, Elisaveta 10
Canetti, Elias 3, 14, 25, 75, 86
Kristeva, Julia 77, 140

## CAMEROONIAN

Beti, Mongo 27

## CANADIAN

Acorn, Milton 15
Aquin, Hubert 15
Atwood, Margaret (Eleanor) 2, 3, 4, 8, 13, 15, 25, 44, 84, 135
Avison, Margaret 2, 4, 97
Barfoot, Joan 18
Bellow, Saul 1, 2, 3, 6, 8, 10, 13, 15, 25, 33, 34, 63, 79
Berton, Pierre (Francis Demarigny) 104
Birney, (Alfred) Earle 1, 4, 6, 11
Bissett, Bill 18

Blais, Marie-Claire 2, 4, 6, 13, 22
Blaise, Clark 29
Bowering, George 15, 47
Bowering, Marilyn R(uthe) 32
Brossard, Nicole 115
Buckler, Ernest 13
Buell, John (Edward) 10
Callaghan, Morley Edward 3, 14, 41, 65
Campbell, Maria 85
Carrier, Roch 13, 78
Child, Philip 19, 68
Chislett, (Margaret) Anne 34
Clarke, Austin C(hesterfield) 8, 53
Cohen, Leonard (Norman) 3, 38
Cohen, Matt(hew) 19
Coles, Don 46
Cook, Michael 58
Cooper, Douglas 86
Coupland, Douglas 85, 133
Craven, Margaret 17
Cronenberg, David 143
Davies, (William) Robertson 2, 7, 13, 25, 42, 75, 91
de la Roche, Mazo 14
Donnell, David 34
Ducharme, Rejean 74
Dudek, Louis 11, 19
Egoyan, Atom 151
Engel, Marian 36
Everson, R(onald) G(ilmour) 27
Faludy, George 42
Ferron, Jacques 94
Finch, Robert (Duer Claydon) 18
Findley, Timothy 27, 102
Fraser, Sylvia 64
Frye, (Herman) Northrop 24, 70
Gallant, Mavis 7, 18, 38
Garner, Hugh 13
Gilmour, David 35
Glassco, John 9
Gotlieb, Phyllis Fay (Bloom) 18
Govier, Katherine 51
Gunnars, Kristjana 69
Gustafson, Ralph (Barker) 36
Haig-Brown, Roderick (Langmere) 21
Hailey, Arthur 5
Harris, Christie (Lucy) Irwin 12
Hébert, Anne 4, 13, 29
Highway, Tomson 92
Hillis, Rick 66
Hine, (William) Daryl 15
Hodgins, Jack 23
Hood, Hugh (John Blagdon) 15, 28
Hyde, Anthony 42
Jacobsen, Josephine 48, 102
Jiles, Paulette 13, 58
Johnston, George (Benson) 51
Jones, D(ouglas) G(ordon) 10
Kelly, M(ilton) T(errence) 55
King, Thomas 89
Kinsella, W(illiam) P(atrick) 27, 43
Klein, A(braham) M(oses) 19
Kogawa, Joy Nozomi 78, 129
Krizanc, John 57
Kroetsch, Robert 5, 23, 57, 132
Kroker, Arthur (W.) 77
Lane, Patrick 25
Laurence, (Jean) Margaret (Wemyss) 3, 6, 13, 50, 62
Layton, Irving (Peter) 2, 15
Levine, Norman 54
Lightfoot, Gordon 26
Livesay, Dorothy (Kathleen) 4, 15, 79
MacEwen, Gwendolyn (Margaret) 13, 55
MacLennan, (John) Hugh 2, 14, 92
MacLeod, Alistair 56
Macpherson, (Jean) Jay 14
Maillet, Antonine 54, 118
Major, Kevin (Gerald) 26
McFadden, David 48
McLuhan, (Herbert) Marshall 37, 83
Metcalf, John 37

Mistry, Rohinton  71
Mitchell, Joni  12
Mitchell, W(illiam) O(rmond)  25
Moore, Brian  1, 3, 5, 7, 8, 19, 32, 90
Morgan, Janet  39
Moure, Erin  88
Mowat, Farley (McGill)  26
Mukherjee, Bharati  53, 115
Munro, Alice  6, 10, 19, 50, 95
Musgrave, Susan  13, 54
Newlove, John (Herbert)  14
Nichol, B(arrie) P(hillip)  18
Nowlan, Alden (Albert)  15
Ondaatje, (Philip) Michael  14, 29, 51, 76
Page, P(atricia) K(athleen)  7, 18
Pollock, (Mary) Sharon  50
Pratt, E(dwin) J(ohn)  19
Purdy, A(lfred) W(ellington)  3, 6, 14, 50
Quarrington, Paul (Lewis)  65
Reaney, James  13
Ricci, Nino  70
Richards, David Adams  59
Richler, Mordecai  3, 5, 9, 13, 18, 46, 70
Ringwood, Gwen(dolyn Margaret) Pharis  48
Ritter, Erika  52
Rooke, Leon  25, 34
Rosenblatt, Joe  15
Ross, (James) Sinclair  13
Roy, Gabrielle  10, 14
Rule, Jane (Vance)  27
Ryga, George  14
Scott, F(rancis) R(eginald)  22
Shields, Carol  91, 113
Skelton, Robin  13
Skvorecky, Josef (Vaclav)  15, 39, 69
Slade, Bernard  11, 46
Smart, Elizabeth  54
Smith, A(rthur) J(ames) M(arshall)  15
Souster, (Holmes) Raymond  5, 14
Suknaski, Andrew  19
Theriault, Yves  79
Thesen, Sharon  56
Thomas, Audrey (Callahan)  7, 13, 37, 107
Thompson, Judith  39
Tremblay, Michel  29, 102
Urquhart, Jane  90
Vanderhaeghe, Guy  41
van Vogt, A(lfred) E(lton)  1
Vizinczey, Stephen  40
Waddington, Miriam  28
Wah, Fred(erick James)  44
Walker, David Harry  14
Walker, George F.  44, 61
Webb, Phyllis  18
Wiebe, Rudy (Henry)  6, 11, 14, 138
Wilson, Ethel Davis (Bryant)  13
Wright, L(aurali) R.  44
Wright, Richard B(ruce)  6
Young, Neil  17

## CHILEAN

Alegria, Fernando  57
Allende, Isabel  39, 57, 97
Donoso (Yañez), José  4, 8, 11, 32, 99
Dorfman, Ariel  48, 77
Neruda, Pablo  1, 2, 5, 7, 9, 28, 62
Parra, Nicanor  2, 102

## CHINESE

Chang, Jung  71
Ch'ien Chung-shu  22
Ding Ling  68
Lord, Bette Bao  23
Mo, Timothy (Peter)  46, 134
Pa Chin  18
Peake, Mervyn  7, 54
Wong, Jade Snow  17

## COLOMBIAN

García Márquez, Gabriel (Jose)  2, 3, 8, 10, 15, 27, 47, 55, 68

## CONGOLESE

Tchicaya, Gerald Felix  101

## CUBAN

Arenas, Reinaldo  41
Cabrera Infante, G(uillermo)  5, 25, 45, 120
Calvino, Italo  5, 8, 11, 22, 33, 39, 73
Carpentier (y Valmont), Alejo  8, 11, 38, 110
Fornés, María Irene  39, 61
Garcia, Cristina  76
Guevara, Che  87
Guillén, Nicol´s (Cristobal)  48, 79
Lezama Lima, Jose  4, 10, 101
Padilla (Lorenzo), Heberto  38
Sarduy, Severo  6, 97

## CZECH

Friedlander, Saul  90
Havel, Vaclav  25, 58, 65, 123
Holub, Miroslav  4
Hrabal, Bohumil  13, 67
Klima, Ivan  56
Kohout, Pavel  13
Kundera, Milan  4, 9, 19, 32, 68, 115, 135
Lustig, Arnost  56
Seifert, Jaroslav  34, 44, 93
Skvorecky, Josef (Vaclav)  15, 39, 69
Vaculik, Ludvik  7

## DANISH

Abell, Kjeld  15
Bodker, Cecil  21
Dreyer, Carl Theodor  16
Hoeg, Peter  95

## DOMINICAN REPUBLICAN

Alvarez, Julia  93

## DUTCH

Bernhard, Thomas  3, 32, 61
de Hartog, Jan  19
Mulisch, Harry  42
Ruyslinck, Ward  14
van de Wetering, Janwillem  47

## EGYPTIAN

Chedid, Andree  47

## ENGLISH

Ackroyd, Peter  34, 52, 140
Adams, Douglas (Noel)  27, 60
Adams, Richard (George)  4, 5, 18
Adcock, Fleur  41
Aickman, Robert (Fordyce)  57
Aiken, Joan (Delano)  35
Aldington, Richard  49
Aldiss, Brian W(ilson)  5, 14, 40
Allingham, Margery (Louise)  19
Almedingen, E. M.  12
Alvarez, A(lfred)  5, 13
Ambler, Eric  4, 6, 9
Amis, Kingsley (William)  1, 2, 3, 5, 8, 13, 40, 44, 129
Amis, Martin (Louis)  4, 9, 38, 62, 101
Anderson, Lindsay (Gordon)  20
Anthony, Piers  35
Archer, Jeffrey (Howard)  28
Arden, John  6, 13, 15
Armatrading, Joan  17
Arthur, Ruth M(abel)  12
Arundel, Honor (Morfydd)  17
Atkinson, Kate  99
Auden, W(ystan) H(ugh)  1, 2, 3, 4, 6, 9, 11, 14, 43, 123

Ayckbourn, Alan  5, 8, 18, 33, 74
Ayrton, Michael  7
Bagnold, Enid  25
Bailey, Paul  45
Bainbridge, Beryl (Margaret)  4, 5, 8, 10, 14, 18, 22, 62, 130
Ballard, J(ames) G(raham)  3, 6, 14, 36, 137
Banks, Lynne Reid  23
Barker, Clive  52
Barker, George Granville  8, 48
Barker, Howard  37
Barker, Pat(ricia)  32, 94, 146
Barnes, Julian (Patrick)  42, 141
Barnes, Peter  5, 56
Barrett, (Roger) Syd  35
Bates, H(erbert) E(rnest)  46
Beer, Patricia  58
Bennett, Alan  45, 77
Berger, John (Peter)  2, 19
Berkoff, Steven  56
Bermant, Chaim (Icyk)  40
Betjeman, John  2, 6, 10, 34, 43
Billington, (Lady) Rachel (Mary)  43
Binyon, T(imothy) J(ohn)  34
Blunden, Edmund (Charles)  2, 56
Bolt, Robert (Oxton)  14
Bond, Edward  4, 6, 13, 23
Booth, Martin  13
Bowen, Elizabeth (Dorothea Cole)  1, 3, 6, 11, 15, 22, 118
Bowie, David  17
Boyd, William  28, 53, 70
Bradbury, Malcolm (Stanley)  32, 61
Bragg, Melvyn  10
Braine, John (Gerard)  1, 3, 41
Brenton, Howard  31
Brittain, Vera (Mary)  23
Brooke-Rose, Christine  40
Brookner, Anita  32, 34, 51, 136
Brophy, Brigid (Antonia)  6, 11, 29, 105
Brunner, John (Kilian Houston)  8, 10
Bunting, Basil  10, 39, 47
Burgess, Anthony  1, 2, 4, 5, 8, 10, 13, 15, 22, 40, 62, 81, 94
Byatt, A(ntonia) S(usan Drabble)  19, 65, 136
Caldwell, (Janet Miriam) Taylor (Holland)  2, 28, 39
Campbell, (John) Ramsey  42
Carter, Angela (Olive)  5, 41, 76
Causley, Charles (Stanley)  7
Caute, (John) David  29
Chambers, Aidan  35
Chaplin, Charles Spencer  16
Chapman, Graham  21
Chatwin, (Charles) Bruce  28, 57, 59
Chitty, Thomas Willes  11
Christie, Agatha (Mary Clarissa)  1, 6, 8, 12, 39, 48, 110
Churchill, Caryl  31, 55
Clark, (Robert) Brian  29
Clarke, Arthur C(harles)  1, 4, 13, 18, 35, 136
Cleese, John (Marwood)  21
Colegate, Isabel  36
Comfort, Alex(ander)  7
Compton-Burnett, I(vy)  1, 3, 10, 15, 34
Cooney, Ray  62
Copeland, Stewart (Armstrong)  26
Cornwell, David (John Moore)  9, 15
Costello, Elvis  21
Coward, Noel (Peirce)  1, 9, 29, 51
Creasey, John  11
Crispin, Edmund  22
Dabydeen, David  34
D'Aguiar, Fred  145
Dahl, Roald  1, 6, 18, 79
Daryush, Elizabeth  6, 19
Davie, Donald (Alfred)  5, 8, 10, 31
Davies, Rhys  23
Day Lewis, C(ecil)  1, 6, 10
Deighton, Len  4, 7, 22, 46

Delaney, Shelagh  29
Dennis, Nigel (Forbes)  8
Dickinson, Peter (Malcolm)  12, 35
Drabble, Margaret  2, 3, 5, 8, 10, 22, 53, 129
Duffy, Maureen  37
du Maurier, Daphne  6, 11, 59
Durrell, Lawrence (George)  1, 4, 6, 8, 13, 27, 41
Dyer, Geoff  149
Eagleton, Terence (Francis)  63, 132
Edgar, David  42
Edwards, G(erald) B(asil)  25
Eliot, T(homas) S(tearns)  1, 2, 3, 6, 9, 10, 13, 15, 24, 34, 41, 55, 57, 113
Elliott, Janice  47
Ellis, A. E.  7
Ellis, Alice Thomas  40
Empson, William  3, 8, 19, 33, 34
Enright, D(ennis) J(oseph)  4, 8, 31
Ewart, Gavin (Buchanan)  13, 46
Fairbairns, Zoe (Ann)  32
Farrell, J(ames) G(ordon)  6
Feinstein, Elaine  36
Fenton, James Martin  32
Ferguson, Niall  134
Fielding, Helen  146
Figes, Eva  31
Fisher, Roy  25
Fitzgerald, Penelope  19, 51, 61, 143
Fleming, Ian (Lancaster)  3, 30
Follett, Ken(neth Martin)  18
Forester, C(ecil) S(cott)  35
Forster, E(dward) M(organ)  1, 2, 3, 4, 9, 10, 13, 15, 22, 45, 77
Forster, Margaret  149
Forsyth, Frederick  2, 5, 36
Fowles, John (Robert)  1, 2, 3, 4, 6, 9, 10, 15, 33, 87
Francis, Dick  2, 22, 42, 102
Fraser, Antonia (Pakenham)  32, 107
Fraser, George MacDonald  7
Frayn, Michael  3, 7, 31, 47
Freeling, Nicolas  38
Fry, Christopher  2, 10, 14
Fugard, Sheila  48
Fuller, John (Leopold)  62
Fuller, Roy (Broadbent)  4, 28
Gardam, Jane  43
Gardner, John (Edmund)  30
Garfield, Leon  12
Garner, Alan  17
Garnett, David  3
Gascoyne, David (Emery)  45
Gee, Maggie (Mary)  57
Gerhardie, William Alexander  5
Gilliatt, Penelope (Ann Douglass)  2, 10, 13, 53
Glanville, Brian (Lester)  6
Glendinning, Victoria  50
Gloag, Julian  40
Godden, (Margaret) Rumer  53
Golding, William (Gerald)  1, 2, 3, 8, 10, 17, 27, 58, 81
Graham, Winston (Mawdsley)  23
Graves, Richard Perceval  44
Graves, Robert (von Ranke)  1, 2, 6, 11, 39, 44, 45
Gray, Simon (James Holliday)  9, 14, 36
Green, Henry  2, 13, 97
Greene, Graham (Henry)  1, 3, 6, 9, 14, 18, 27, 37, 70, 72, 125
Griffiths, Trevor  13, 52
Grigson, Geoffrey (Edward Harvey)  7, 39
Gunn, Thom(son William)  3, 6, 18, 32, 81
Haig-Brown, Roderick (Langmere)  21
Hailey, Arthur  5
Hall, Rodney  51
Hamburger, Michael (Peter Leopold)  5, 14
Hamilton, (Anthony Walter) Patrick  51
Hampton, Christopher (James)  4
Hare, David  29, 58, 136

Harris, (Theodore) Wilson  25
Harrison, Tony  43, 129
Hartley, L(eslie) P(oles)  2, 22
Harwood, Ronald  32
Hastings, Selina  44
Hawking, Stephen W(illiam)  63, 105
Headon, (Nicky) Topper  30
Heppenstall, (John) Rayner  10
Hibbert, Eleanor Alice Burford  7
Hill, Geoffrey (William)  5, 8, 18, 45
Hill, Susan (Elizabeth)  4, 113
Hinde, Thomas  6, 11
Hitchcock, Alfred (Joseph)  16
Hocking, Mary (Eunice)  13
Holden, Ursula  18
Holdstock, Robert P.  39
Hollinghurst, Alan  55, 91
Hooker, (Peter) Jeremy  43
Hopkins, John (Richard)  4
Household, Geoffrey (Edward West)  11
Howard, Elizabeth Jane  7, 29
Hughes, David (John)  48
Hughes, Richard (Arthur Warren)  1, 11
Hughes, Ted  2, 4, 9, 14, 37, 119
Huxley, Aldous (Leonard)  1, 3, 4, 5, 8, 11, 18, 35, 79
Idle, Eric  21
Ingalls, Rachel (Holmes)  42
Isherwood, Christopher (William Bradshaw)  1, 9, 11, 14, 44
Ishiguro, Kazuo  27, 56, 59, 110
Jacobson, Dan  4, 14
Jagger, Mick  17
James, C(yril) L(ionel) R(obert)  33
James, P. D.  18, 46, 122
Jellicoe, (Patricia) Ann  27
Jennings, Elizabeth (Joan)  5, 14, 131
Jhabvala, Ruth Prawer  4, 8, 29, 94, 138
Johnson, B(ryan) S(tanley William)  6, 9
Johnson, Pamela Hansford  1, 7, 27
Johnson, Paul (Bede)  147
Jolley, (Monica) Elizabeth  46
Jones, David (Michael)  2, 4, 7, 13, 42
Jones, Diana Wynne  26
Jones, Mervyn  10, 52
Jones, Mick  30
Josipovici, Gabriel (David)  6, 43
Kavan, Anna  5, 13, 82
Kaye, M(ary) M(argaret)  28
Keates, Jonathan  34
King, Francis (Henry)  8, 53, 145
Kirkup, James  1
Koestler, Arthur  1, 3, 6, 8, 15, 33
Kops, Bernard  4
Kureishi, Hanif  64, 135
Lanchester, John  99
Larkin, Philip (Arthur)  3, 5, 8, 9, 13, 18, 33, 39, 64
Leavis, F(rank) R(aymond)  24
Lee, Laurie  90
Lee, Tanith  46
Lehmann, Rosamond (Nina)  5
Lennon, John (Ono)  12, 35
Lessing, Doris (May)  1, 2, 3, 6, 10, 15, 22, 40, 94
Levertov, Denise  1, 2, 3, 5, 8, 15, 28, 66
Levi, Peter (Chad Tigar)  41
Lewis, C(live) S(taples)  1, 3, 6, 14, 27, 124
Lively, Penelope (Margaret)  32, 50
Lodge, David (John)  36, 141
Loy, Mina  28
Luke, Peter (Ambrose Cyprian)  38
MacInnes, Colin  4, 23
Mackenzie, Compton (Edward Montague)  18
Macpherson, (Jean) Jay  14
Maitland, Sara (Louise)  49
Manning, Olivia  5, 19
Mantel, Hilary (Mary)  144
Masefield, John (Edward)  11, 47
Mason, Nick  35

Maugham, W(illiam) Somerset  1, 11, 15, 67, 93
Mayle, Peter  89
Mayne, William (James Carter)  12
McEwan, Ian (Russell)  13, 66
McGrath, Patrick  55
Mercer, David  5
Middleton, Christopher  13
Middleton, Stanley  7, 38
Mitford, Nancy  44
Mo, Timothy (Peter)  46, 134
Moorcock, Michael (John)  5, 27, 58
Mortimer, John (Clifford)  28, 43
Mortimer, Penelope (Ruth)  5
Mosley, Nicholas  43, 70
Mott, Michael (Charles Alston)  15, 34
Murdoch, (Jean) Iris  1, 2, 3, 4, 6, 8, 11, 15, 22, 31, 51
Naipaul, V(idiadhar) S(urajprasad)  4, 7, 9, 13, 18, 37, 105
Newby, P(ercy) H(oward)  2, 13
Nichols, Peter (Richard)  5, 36, 65
Noon, Jeff  91
Norfolk, Lawrence  76
Nye, Robert  13, 42
O'Brien, Richard  17
O'Faolain, Julia  6, 19, 47, 108
Olivier, Laurence (Kerr)  20
Orton, Joe  4, 13, 43
Osborne, John (James)  1, 2, 5, 11, 45
Osborne, Lawrence  50
Page, Jimmy  12
Page, Louise  40
Page, P(atricia) K(athleen)  7, 18
Palin, Michael (Edward)  21
Parkin, Frank  43
Parks, Tim(othy Harold)  147
Paton Walsh, Gillian  35
Paulin, Tom  37
Peake, Mervyn  7, 54
Perry, Anne  126
Phillips, Caryl  96
Pinter, Harold  1, 3, 6, 9, 11, 15, 27, 58, 73
Plant, Robert  12
Poliakoff, Stephen  38
Potter, Dennis (Christopher George)  58, 86, 123
Powell, Anthony (Dymoke)  1, 3, 7, 9, 10, 31
Pownall, David  10
Powys, John Cowper  7, 9, 15, 46, 125
Priestley, J(ohn) B(oynton)  2, 5, 9, 34
Prince, F(rank) T(empleton)  22
Pritchett, V(ictor) S(awdon)  5, 13, 15, 41
Pym, Barbara (Mary Crampton)  13, 19, 37, 111
Quin, Ann (Marie)  6
Raine, Craig (Anthony)  32, 103
Raine, Kathleen (Jessie)  7, 45
Rathbone, Julian  41
Rattigan, Terence (Mervyn)  7
Raven, Simon (Arthur Noel)  14
Read, Herbert Edward  4
Read, Piers Paul  4, 10, 25
Reading, Peter  47
Redgrove, Peter (William)  6, 41
Reid, Christopher (John)  33
Rendell, Ruth (Barbara)  28, 48
Rhys, Jean  2, 4, 6, 14, 19, 51, 124
Rice, Tim(othy Miles Bindon)  21
Richard, Keith  17
Richards, I(vor) A(rmstrong)  14, 24
Roberts, Keith (John Kingston)  14
Roberts, Michele (Brigitte)  48
Rowling, J(oanne) K.  137
Rudkin, (James) David  14
Rushdie, (Ahmed) Salman  23, 31, 55, 100
Rushforth, Peter (Scott)  19
Russell, (Henry) Ken(neth Alfred)  16
Russell, William Martin  60
Sacks, Oliver (Wolf)  67
Sansom, William  2, 6

Sassoon, Siegfried (Lorraine) **36, 130**
Scammell, Michael **34**
Scannell, Vernon **49**
Schama, Simon (Michael) **150**
Schlee, Ann **35**
Schumacher, E(rnst) F(riedrich) **80**
Scott, Paul (Mark) **9, 60**
Shaffer, Anthony (Joshua) **19**
Shaffer, Peter (Levin) **5, 14, 18, 37, 60**
Sharpe, Tom **36**
Shaw, Robert **5**
Sheed, Wilfrid (John Joseph) **2, 4, 10, 53**
Shute, Nevil **30**
Shuttle, Penelope (Diane) **7**
Silkin, Jon **2, 6, 43**
Sillitoe, Alan **1, 3, 6, 10, 19, 57, 148**
Simonon, Paul **30**
Simpson, N(orman) F(rederick) **29**
Sinclair, Andrew (Annandale) **2, 14**
Sinclair, Iain **76**
Sisson, C(harles) H(ubert) **8**
Sitwell, Edith **2, 9, 67**
Slaughter, Carolyn **56**
Smith, Stevie **3, 8, 25, 44**
Snow, C(harles) P(ercy) **1, 4, 6, 9, 13, 19**
Spender, Stephen (Harold) **1, 2, 5, 10, 41, 91**
Spurling, Hilary **34**
Stannard, Martin **44**
Stewart, J(ohn) I(nnes) M(ackintosh) **7, 14, 32**
Stewart, Mary (Florence Elinor) **7, 35, 117**
Stoppard, Tom **1, 3, 4, 5, 8, 15, 29, 34, 63, 91**
Storey, David (Malcolm) **2, 4, 5, 8**
Streatfeild, (Mary) Noel **21**
Strummer, Joe **30**
Summers, Andrew James **26**
Sumner, Gordon Matthew **26**
Sutcliff, Rosemary **26**
Swift, Graham (Colin) **41, 88**
Swinfen, Ann **34**
Swinnerton, Frank Arthur **31**
Symons, Julian (Gustave) **2, 14, 32**
Szirtes, George **46**
Taylor, Elizabeth **2, 4, 29**
Tennant, Emma (Christina) **13, 52**
Teran, Lisa St. Aubin de **36**
Thomas, D(onald) M(ichael) **13, 22, 31, 132**
Tindall, Gillian (Elizabeth) **7**
Tolkien, J(ohn) R(onald) R(euel) **1, 2, 3, 8, 12, 38**
Tomlinson, (Alfred) Charles **2, 4, 6, 13, 45**
Townshend, Peter (Dennis Blandford) **17, 42**
Treitel, Jonathan **70**
Tremain, Rose **42**
Tuohy, Frank **37**
Turner, Frederick **48**
Unsworth, Barry (Forster) **76, 127**
Ustinov, Peter (Alexander) **1**
Van Den Bogarde, Derek Jules Gaspard Ulric Niven **14**
Vansittart, Peter **42**
Wain, John (Barrington) **2, 11, 15, 46**
Walker, Ted **13**
Walsh, Jill Paton **35**
Warner, Francis (Robert le Plastrier) **14**
Warner, Marina **59**
Warner, Rex (Ernest) **45**
Warner, Sylvia Townsend **7, 19**
Waterhouse, Keith (Spencer) **47**
Waters, Roger **35**
Waugh, Auberon (Alexander) **7**
Waugh, Evelyn (Arthur St. John) **1, 3, 8, 13, 19, 27, 44, 107**
Waugh, Harriet **6**
Webber, Andrew Lloyd **21**
Weldon, Fay **6, 9, 11, 19, 36, 59, 122**
Weller, Paul **26**
Wesker, Arnold **3, 5, 42**
West, Anthony (Panther) **50**
West, Paul **7, 14, 96**
West, Rebecca **7, 9, 31, 50**
Westall, Robert (Atkinson) **17**
White, Patrick (Victor Martindale) **3, 4, 5, 7, 9, 18, 65, 69**
White, T(erence) H(anbury) **30**
Whitehead, E(dward) A(nthony) **5**
Whitemore, Hugh (John) **37**
Wilding, Michael **73**
Williams, Hugo **42**
Wilson, A(ndrew) N(orman) **33**
Wilson, Angus (Frank Johnstone) **2, 3, 5, 25, 34**
Wilson, Colin **3, 14**
Wilson, Snoo **33**
Wingrove, David (John) **68**
Winterson, Jeanette **64**
Wodehouse, P(elham) G(renville) **1, 2, 5, 10, 22**
Wright, Rick **35**
Wyndham, John **19**
Yorke, Henry Vincent **13**
Young, Andrew (John) **5**

## ESTONIAN

Ivask, Ivar Vidrik **14**

## FIJI ISLANDER

Prichard, Katharine Susannah **46**

## FILIPINO

Santos, Bienvenido N(uqui) **22**

## FINNISH

Haavikko, Paavo Juhani **18, 34**
Salama, Hannu **18**
Sillanpaa, Frans Eemil **19**

## FRENCH

Adamov, Arthur **4, 25**
Anouilh, Jean (Marie Lucien Pierre) **1, 3, 8, 13, 40, 50**
Aragon, Louis **3, 22**
Audiberti, Jacques **38**
Aymé, Marcel (Andre) **11**
Barthes, Roland (Gérard) **24, 83**
Barzun, Jacques (Martin) **51, 145**
Bataille, Georges **29**
Baudrillard, Jean **60**
Beauvoir, Simone (Lucie Ernestine Marie Bertrand) de **1, 2, 4, 8, 14, 31, 44, 50, 71, 124**
Beckett, Samuel (Barclay) **1, 2, 3, 4, 6, 9, 10, 11, 14, 18, 29, 57, 59, 83**
Blanchot, Maurice **135**
Bonnefoy, Yves **9, 15, 58**
Bresson, Robert **16**
Breton, Andre **2, 9, 15, 54**
Butor, Michel (Marie Francois) **1, 3, 8, 11, 15**
Camus, Albert **1, 2, 4, 9, 11, 14, 32, 63, 69, 124**
Carrere, Emmanuel **89**
Cayrol, Jean **11**
Chabrol, Claude **16**
Char, Rene(-Emile) **9, 11, 14, 55**
Chedid, Andree **47**
Cixous, Helene **92**
Clair, Rene **20**
Cocteau, Jean (Maurice Eugene Clement) **1, 8, 15, 16, 43**
Cousteau, Jacques-Yves **30**
del Castillo, Michel **38**
Derrida, Jacques **24, 87**
Destouches, Louis-Ferdinand **9, 15**
Duhamel, Georges **8**
Duras, Marguerite **3, 6, 11, 20, 34, 40, 68, 100**
Ernaux, Annie **88**
Federman, Raymond **6, 47**
Foucault, Michel **31, 34, 69**
Fournier, Pierre **11**
Francis, Claude **50**
Gallo, Max Louis **95**
Gary, Romain **25**
Gascar, Pierre **11**
Genet, Jean **1, 2, 5, 10, 14, 44, 46**
Giono, Jean **4, 11**
Godard, Jean-Luc **20**
Goldmann, Lucien **24**
Gontier, Fernande **50**
Gray, Francine du Plessix **22**
Green, Julien **3, 11, 77**
Guillevic, (Eugene) **33**
Ionesco, Eugene **1, 4, 6, 9, 11, 15, 41, 86**
Japrisot, Sebastien **90**
Jouve, Pierre Jean **47**
Kristeva, Julia **77, 140**
Lacan, Jacques (Marie Emile) **75**
Laurent, Antoine **50**
Le Clézio, J(ean) M(arie) G(ustave) **31**
Leduc, Violette **22**
Leger, (Marie-Rene Auguste) Alexis Saint-Leger **4, 11, 46**
Leiris, Michel (Julien) **61**
Lévi-Strauss, Claude **38**
Mallet-Joris, Françoise **11**
Malraux, (Georges-)AndréU **1, 4, 9, 13, 15, 57**
Mandiargues, Andre Pieyre de **41**
Marcel, Gabriel Honore **15**
Mauriac, Claude **9**
Mauriac, Francois (Charles) **4, 9, 56**
Merton, Thomas **1, 3, 11, 34, 83**
Modiano, Patrick (Jean) **18**
Montherlant, Henry (Milon) de **8, 19**
Morand, Paul **41**
Nin, Anaïs **1, 4, 8, 11, 14, 60, 127**
Perec, Georges **56, 116**
Pinget, Robert **7, 13, 37**
Ponge, Francis **6, 18**
Poniatowska, Elena **140**
Prévert, Jacques (Henri Marie) **15**
Queneau, Raymond **2, 5, 10, 42**
Quoirez, Francoise **9**
Renoir, Jean **20**
Resnais, Alain **16**
Reverdy, Pierre **53**
Rio, Michel **43**
Robbe-Grillet, Alain **1, 2, 4, 6, 8, 10, 14, 43, 128**
Rohmer, Eric **16**
Romains, Jules **7**
Sachs, Nelly **14, 98**
Sarraute, Nathalie **1, 2, 4, 8, 10, 31, 80**
Sartre, Jean-Paul **1, 4, 7, 9, 13, 18, 24, 44, 50, 52**
Sauser-Hall, Frederic **18**
Schwarz-Bart, Andre **2, 4**
Schwarz-Bart, Simone **7**
Simenon, Georges (Jacques Christian) **1, 2, 3, 8, 18, 47**
Simon, Claude **4, 9, 15, 39**
Soupault, Philippe **68**
Steiner, George **24**
Tournier, Michel (Edouard) **6, 23, 36, 95**
Troyat, Henri **23**
Truffaut, Francois **20, 101**
Tuck, Lily **70**
Tzara, Tristan **47**
Varda, Agnes **16**
Wittig, Monique **22**
Yourcenar, Marguerite **19, 38, 50, 87**

## FRENCH GUINEAN

Damas, Leon-Gontran **84**

# CUMULATIVE NATIONALITY INDEX

## GERMAN

Amichai, Yehuda  9, 22, 57, 116
Arendt, Hannah  66, 98
Arp, Jean  5
Becker, Jurek  7, 19
Benary-Isbert, Margot  12
Bienek, Horst  7, 11
Boell, Heinrich (Theodor)  2, 3, 6, 9, 11, 15, 27, 32, 72
Buchheim, Lothar-Guenther  6
Bukowski, Charles  2, 5, 9, 41, 82, 108
Eich, Guenter  15
Ende, Michael (Andreas Helmuth)  31
Enzensberger, Hans Magnus  43
Fassbinder, Rainer Werner  20
Figes, Eva  31
Grass, Guenter (Wilhelm)  1, 2, 4, 6, 11, 15, 22, 32, 49, 88
Habermas, Juergen  104
Hamburger, Michael (Peter Leopold)  5, 14
Handke, Peter  5, 8, 10, 15, 38, 134
Heidegger, Martin  24
Herzog, Werner  16
Hesse, Hermann  1, 2, 3, 6, 11, 17, 25, 69
Heym, Stefan  41
Hildesheimer, Wolfgang  49
Hochhuth, Rolf  4, 11, 18
Hofmann, Gert  54
Jhabvala, Ruth Prawer  4, 8, 29, 94, 138
Johnson, Uwe  5, 10, 15, 40
Juenger, Ernst  125
Kissinger, Henry A(lfred)  137
Kroetz, Franz Xaver  41
Kunze, Reiner  10
Lenz, Siegfried  27
Levitin, Sonia (Wolff)  17
Mueller, Lisel  13, 51
Nossack, Hans Erich  6
Preussler, Otfried  17
Remarque, Erich Maria  21
Riefenstahl, Leni  16
Sachs, Nelly  14, 98
Schmidt, Arno (Otto)  56
Schumacher, E(rnst) F(riedrich)  80
Seghers, Anna  7
Strauss, Botho  22
Sueskind, Patrick  44
Tillich, Paul (Johannes)  131
Walser, Martin  27
Weiss, Peter (Ulrich)  3, 15, 51
Wellershoff, Dieter  46
Wolf, Christa  14, 29, 58, 150
Zuckmayer, Carl  18

## GHANIAN

Armah, Ayi Kwei  5, 33, 136

## GREEK

Broumas, Olga  10, 73
Elytis, Odysseus  15, 49, 100
Haviaras, Stratis  33
Karapanou, Margarita  13
Nakos, Lilika  29
Ritsos, Yannis  6, 13, 31
Samarakis, Antonis  5
Seferis, George  5, 11
Spanidou, Irini  44
Vassilikos, Vassilis  4, 8

## GUADELOUPEAN

Condé, Maryse  52, 92
Schwarz-Bart, Simone  7

## GUATEMALAN

Asturias, Miguel Ángel  3, 8, 13

## GUINEAN

Laye, Camara  4, 38

## GUYANESE

Dabydeen, David  34
Harris, (Theodore) Wilson  25

## HAITIAN

Danticat, Edwidge  94, 139

## HUNGARIAN

Faludy, George  42
Koestler, Arthur  1, 3, 6, 8, 15, 33
Konrád, György  4, 10, 73
Lengyel, József  7
Lukacs, George  24
Nagy, Laszlo  7
Szirtes, George  46
Tabori, George  19
Vizinczey, Stephen  40

## ICELANDIC

Gunnars, Kristjana  69

## INDIAN

Alexander, Meena  121
Ali, Ahmed  69
Anand, Mulk Raj  23, 93
Desai, Anita  19, 37, 97
Ezekiel, Nissim  61
Ghosh, Amitav  44
Mahapatra, Jayanta  33
Mehta, Ved (Parkash)  37
Mistry, Rohinton  71
Mukherjee, Bharati  53, 115
Narayan, R(asipuram) K(rishnaswami)  7, 28, 47, 121
Rao, Raja  25, 56
Ray, Satyajit  16, 76
Rushdie, (Ahmed) Salman  23, 31, 55, 100
Sahgal, Nayantara (Pandit)  41
Sealy, I(rwin) Allan  55
Seth, Vikram  43, 90
Singh, Khushwant  11
Tharoor, Shashi  70
White, T(erence) H(anbury)  30

## IRANIAN

Modarressi, Taghi (M.)  44
Shamlu, Ahmad  10

## IRISH

Banville, John  46, 118
Beckett, Samuel (Barclay)  1, 2, 3, 4, 6, 9, 10, 11, 14, 18, 29, 57, 59, 83
Behan, Brendan  1, 8, 11, 15, 79
Blackwood, Caroline  6, 9, 100
Boland, Eavan (Aisling)  40, 67, 113
Bowen, Elizabeth (Dorothea Cole)  1, 3, 6, 11, 15, 22, 118
Boyle, Patrick  19
Brennan, Maeve  5
Brown, Christy  63
Carroll, Paul Vincent  10
Clarke, Austin  6, 9
Colum, Padraic  28
Cox, William Trevor  9, 14, 71
Day Lewis, C(ecil)  1, 6, 10
Dillon, Eilis  17
Donleavy, J(ames) P(atrick)  1, 4, 6, 10, 45
Doyle, Roddy  81
Durcan, Paul  43, 70
Friel, Brian  5, 42, 59, 115
Gébler, Carlo (Ernest)  39
Hanley, James  3, 5, 8, 13
Hart, Josephine  70
Heaney, Seamus (Justin)  5, 7, 14, 25, 37, 74, 91
Johnston, Jennifer (Prudence)  7, 150
Jordan, Neil (Patrick)  110
Kavanagh, Patrick (Joseph)  22
Keane, Molly  31
Kiely, Benedict  23, 43
Kinsella, Thomas  4, 19, 138
Lavin, Mary  4, 18, 99
Leonard, Hugh  19
Longley, Michael  29
Mac Laverty, Bernard  31
MacNeice, (Frederick) Louis  1, 4, 10, 53
Mahon, Derek  27
McCabe, Patrick  133
McGahern, John  5, 9, 48
McGinley, Patrick (Anthony)  41
McGuckian, Medbh  48
Montague, John (Patrick)  13, 46
Moore, Brian  1, 3, 5, 7, 8, 19, 32, 90
Morrison, Van  21
Morrissy, Mary  99
Muldoon, Paul  32, 72
Murphy, Richard  41
Murphy, Thomas (Bernard)  51
Nolan, Christopher  58
O'Brien, Edna  3, 5, 8, 13, 36, 65, 116
O'Casey, Sean  1, 5, 9, 11, 15, 88
O'Doherty, Brian  76
O'Faolain, Julia  6, 19, 47, 108
O'Faolain, Sean  1, 7, 14, 32, 70
O'Flaherty, Liam  5, 34
Paulin, Tom  37
Rodgers, W(illiam) R(obert)  7
Simmons, James (Stewart Alexander)  43
Trevor, William  7, 9, 14, 25, 71, 116
White, Terence de Vere  49
Wilson, Robert McLiam  59

## ISRAELI

Agnon, S(hmuel) Y(osef Halevi)  4, 8, 14
Amichai, Yehuda  9, 22, 57, 116
Appelfeld, Aharon  23, 47
Bakshi, Ralph  26
Friedlander, Saul  90
Grossman, David  67
Kaniuk, Yoram  19
Levin, Meyer  7
Megged, Aharon  9
Oz, Amos  5, 8, 11, 27, 33, 54
Shammas, Anton  55
Sobol, Joshua  60
Yehoshua, A(braham) B.  13, 31

## ITALIAN

Antonioni, Michelangelo  20, 144
Bacchelli, Riccardo  19
Bassani, Giorgio  9
Bertolucci, Bernardo  16
Bufalino, Gesualdo  74
Buzzati, Dino  36
Calasso, Roberto  81
Calvino, Italo  5, 8, 11, 22, 33, 39, 73
De Sica, Vittorio  20
Eco, Umberto  28, 60, 142
Fallaci, Oriana  11, 110
Fellini, Federico  16, 85
Fo, Dario  32, 109
Gadda, Carlo Emilio  11
Ginzburg, Natalia  5, 11, 54, 70
Giovene, Andrea  7
Landolfi, Tommaso  11, 49
Levi, Primo  37, 50
Luzi, Mario  13
Montale, Eugenio  7, 9, 18
Morante, Elsa  8, 47
Moravia, Alberto  2, 7, 11, 27, 46
Ortese, Anna Maria  89
Palazzeschi, Aldo  11
Pasolini, Pier Paolo  20, 37, 106
Piccolo, Lucio  13
Pincherle, Alberto  11, 18
Quasimodo, Salvatore  10
Ricci, Nino  70
Sciascia, Leonardo  8, 9, 41
Silone, Ignazio  4
Ungaretti, Giuseppe  7, 11, 15

Visconti, Luchino **16**
Vittorini, Elio **6, 9, 14**
Wertmueller, Lina **16**

## JAMAICAN

Bennett, Louise (Simone) **28**
Cliff, Jimmy **21**
Cliff, Michelle **120**
Marley, Bob **17**
Thelwell, Michael Miles **22**

## JAPANESE

Abe, Kōbō **8, 22, 53, 81**
Enchi, Fumiko (Ueda) **31**
Endo, Shusaku **7, 14, 19, 54, 99**
Ibuse, Masuji **22**
Ichikawa, Kon **20**
Ishiguro, Kazuo **27, 56, 59, 110**
Kawabata, Yasunari **2, 5, 9, 18, 107**
Kurosawa, Akira **16, 119**
Murakami, Haruki **150**
Ōe, Kenzaburō **10, 36, 86**
Oshima, Nagisa **20**
Ozu, Yasujiro **16**
Shiga, Naoya **33**
Tanizaki, Jun'ichiro **8, 14, 28**
Whitney, Phyllis A(yame) **42**
Yoshimoto, Banana **84**

## KENYAN

Ngugi, James T(hiong'o) **3, 7, 13**
Ngũgĩ wa Thiong'o **36**

## MALIAN

Ouologuem, Yambo **146**

## MARTINICAN

Césaire, Aimé (Fernand) **19, 32, 112**
Fanon, Frantz **74**
Glissant, Edouard **10, 68**

## MEXICAN

Arreola, Juan José **147**
Castellanos, Rosario **66**
Esquivel, Laura **141**
Fuentes, Carlos **3, 8, 10, 13, 22, 41, 60, 113**
Ibarguengoitia, Jorge **37**
Lopez Portillo (y Pacheco), Jose **46**
Lopez y Fuentes, Gregorio **32**
Paz, Octavio **3, 4, 6, 10, 19, 51, 65, 119**
Poniatowska, Elena **140**
Rulfo, Juan **8, 80**

## MOROCCAN

Arrabal, Fernando **2, 9, 18, 58**

## NEW ZEALANDER

Adcock, Fleur **41**
Ashton-Warner, Sylvia (Constance) **19**
Baxter, James K(eir) **14**
Campion, Jane **95**
Gee, Maurice (Gough) **29**
Grace, Patricia Frances **56**
Hilliard, Noel (Harvey) **15**
Hulme, Keri **39, 130**
Ihimaera, Witi **46**
Marsh, (Edith) Ngaio **7, 53**
Sargeson, Frank **31**

## NICARAGUAN

Alegria, Claribel **75**
Cardenal, Ernesto **31**

## NIGERIAN

Achebe, (Albert) Chinua(lumogu) **1, 3, 5, 7, 11, 26, 51, 75, 127**
Clark Bekederemo, J(ohnson) P(epper) **38**

Ekwensi, Cyprian (Odiatu Duaka) **4**
Emecheta, (Florence Onye) Buchi **14, 48, 128**
Nwapa, Flora **133**
Okigbo, Christopher (Ifenayichukwu) **25, 84**
Okri, Ben **87**
Saro-Wiwa, Ken(ule Beeson) **114**
Soyinka, Wole **3, 5, 14, 36, 44**
Tutuola, Amos **5, 14, 29**

## NORTHERN IRISH

Deane, Seamus (Francis) **122**
Simmons, James (Stewart Alexander) **43**
Wilson, Robert McLiam **59**

## NORWEGIAN

Friis-Baastad, Babbis Ellinor **12**
Heyerdahl, Thor **26**
Vesaas, Tarjei **48**

## PAKISTANI

Ali, Ahmed **69**
Ghose, Zulfikar **42**

## PARAGUAYAN

Roa Bastos, Augusto (Antonio) **45**

## PERUVIAN

Allende, Isabel **39, 57, 97**
Arguedas, Jose Maria **10, 18**
Goldemberg, Isaac **52**
Vargas Llosa, (Jorge) Mario (Pedro) **3, 6, 9, 10, 15, 31, 42, 85**

## POLISH

Agnon, S(hmuel) Y(osef Halevi) **4, 8, 14**
Becker, Jurek **7, 19**
Bermant, Chaim (Icyk) **40**
Bienek, Horst **7, 11**
Brandys, Kazimierz **62**
Dabrowska, Maria (Szumska) **15**
Gombrowicz, Witold **4, 7, 11, 49**
Herbert, Zbigniew **9, 43**
John Paul II, Pope **128**
Kieslowski, Krzysztof **120**
Konwicki, Tadeusz **8, 28, 54, 117**
Kosinski, Jerzy (Nikodem) **1, 2, 3, 6, 10, 15, 53, 70**
Lem, Stanislaw **8, 15, 40, 149**
Milosz, Czeslaw **5, 11, 22, 31, 56, 82**
Mrozek, Slawomir **3, 13**
Polanski, Roman **16**
Rozewicz, Tadeusz **9, 23, 139**
Singer, Isaac Bashevis **1, 3, 6, 9, 11, 15, 23, 38, 69, 111**
Skolimowski, Jerzy **20**
Szymborska, Wislawa **99**
Wajda, Andrzej **16**
Wittlin, Jozef **25**
Wojciechowska, Maia (Teresa) **26**

## PORTUGUESE

Migueis, Jose Rodrigues **10**
Saramago, José **119**

## PUERTO RICAN

Ferré, Rosario **139**
Marqués, René **96**
Piñero, Miguel (Antonio Gomez) **4, 55**
Sánchez, Luis Rafael **23**

## ROMANIAN

Celan, Paul **10, 19, 53, 82**
Cioran, E(mil) M. **64**
Codrescu, Andrei **46, 121**
Ionesco, Eugene **1, 4, 6, 9, 11, 15, 41, 86**
Rezzori (d'Arezzo), Gregor von **25**

Tzara, Tristan **47**
Wiesel, Elie(zer) **3, 5, 11, 37**

## RUSSIAN

Aitmatov, Chingiz (Torekulovich) **71**
Akhmadulina, Bella Akhatovna **53**
Akhmatova, Anna **11, 25, 64, 126**
Aksyonov, Vassily (Pavlovich) **22, 37, 101**
Aleshkovsky, Yuz **44**
Almedingen, E. M. **12**
Asimov, Isaac **1, 3, 9, 19, 26, 76, 92**
Bakhtin, Mikhail Mikhailovich **83**
Bitov, Andrei (Georgievich) **57**
Brodsky, Joseph **4, 6, 13, 36, 100**
Deren, Maya **16, 102**
Ehrenburg, Ilya (Grigoryevich) **18, 34, 62**
Eliade, Mircea **19**
Gary, Romain **25**
Goldberg, Anatol **34**
Grade, Chaim **10**
Grossman, Vasily (Semenovich) **41**
Iskander, Fazil **47**
Kabakov, Sasha **59**
Kaletski, Alexander **39**
Krotkov, Yuri **19**
Leonov, Leonid (Maximovich) **92**
Limonov, Edward **67**
Nabokov, Vladimir (Vladimirovich) **1, 2, 3, 6, 8, 11, 15, 23, 44, 46, 64**
Olesha, Yuri (Karlovich) **8**
Pasternak, Boris (Leonidovich) **7, 10, 18, 63**
Paustovsky, Konstantin (Georgievich) **40**
Rahv, Philip **24**
Rand, Ayn **3, 30, 44, 79**
Ratushinskaya, Irina **54**
Rybakov, Anatoli (Naumovich) **23, 53**
Sarraute, Nathalie **1, 2, 4, 8, 10, 31, 80**
Shalamov, Varlam (Tikhonovich) **18**
Shatrov, Mikhail **59**
Sholokhov, Mikhail (Aleksandrovich) **7, 15**
Sinyavsky, Andrei (Donatevich) **8**
Solzhenitsyn, Aleksandr I(sayevich) **1, 2, 4, 7, 9, 10, 18, 26, 34, 78, 134**
Strugatskii, Arkadii (Natanovich) **27**
Strugatskii, Boris (Natanovich) **27**
Tarkovsky, Andrei (Arsenyevich) **75**
Trifonov, Yuri (Valentinovich) **45**
Troyat, Henri **23**
Voinovich, Vladimir (Nikolaevich) **10, 49, 147**
Voznesensky, Andrei (Andreievich) **1, 15, 57**
Yanovsky, V(assily) S(emenovich) **2, 18**
Yevtushenko, Yevgeny (Alexandrovich) **1, 3, 13, 26, 51, 126**
Yezierska, Anzia **46**
Zaturenska, Marya **6, 11**
Zinoviev, Alexander (Aleksandrovich) **19**

## SALVADORAN

Alegria, Claribel **75**
Argueta, Manlio **31**

## SCOTTISH

Banks, Iain M(enzies) **34**
Brown, George Mackay **5, 48, 100**
Cronin, A(rchibald) J(oseph) **32**
Dunn, Douglas (Eaglesham) **6, 40**
Graham, W(illiam) S(idney) **29**
Gray, Alasdair (James) **41**
Grieve, C(hristopher) M(urray) **11, 19**
Hunter, Mollie **21**
Jenkins, (John) Robin **52**
Kelman, James **58, 86**
Laing, R(onald) D(avid) **95**
MacBeth, George (Mann) **2, 5, 9**
MacCaig, Norman (Alexander) **36**
MacInnes, Helen (Clark) **27, 39**
MacLean, Alistair (Stuart) **3, 13, 50, 63**
McIlvanney, William **42**

Morgan, Edwin (George) 31
Smith, Iain Crichton 64
Spark, Muriel (Sarah) 2, 3, 5, 8, 13, 18, 40, 94
Taylor, C(ecil) P(hilip) 27
Walker, David Harry 14
Welsh, Irvine 144
Young, Andrew (John) 5

## SENEGALESE

Ousmane, Sembene 66
Senghor, Leopold Sedar 54, 130

## SOMALIAN

Farah, Nuruddin 53, 137

## SOUTH AFRICAN

Abrahams, Peter (Henry) 4
Breytenbach, Breyten 23, 37, 126
Brink, Andre (Philippus) 18, 36, 106
Brutus, Dennis 43
Coetzee, J(ohn) M(ichael) 23, 33, 66, 117
Courtenay, Bryce 59
Fugard, (Harold) Athol 5, 9, 14, 25, 40, 80
Fugard, Sheila 48
Gordimer, Nadine 3, 5, 7, 10, 18, 33, 51, 70, 123
Harwood, Ronald 32
Head, Bessie 25, 67
Hope, Christopher (David Tully) 52
Kunene, Mazisi (Raymond) 85
La Guma, (Justin) Alex(ander) 19
Millin, Sarah Gertrude 49
Mphahlele, Ezekiel 25, 133
Mtwa, Percy 47
Ngema, Mbongeni 57
Nkosi, Lewis 45
Paton, Alan (Stewart) 4, 10, 25, 55, 106
Plomer, William Charles Franklin 4, 8
Prince, F(rank) T(empleton) 22
Smith, Wilbur (Addison) 33
Tolkien, J(ohn) R(onald) R(euel) 1, 2, 3, 8, 12, 38
Tutu, Desmond M(pilo) 80
van der Post, Laurens (Jan) 5
Vorster, Gordon 34

## SPANISH

Alberti, Rafael 7
Alfau, Felipe 66
Almodovar, Pedro 114
Alonso, Damaso 14
Arrabal, Fernando 2, 9, 18, 58
Benet, Juan 28
Buero Vallejo, Antonio 15, 46, 139
Bunuel, Luis 16, 80
Casona, Alejandro 49
Castedo, Elena 65
Cela, Camilo José 4, 13, 59, 122
Cernuda (y Bidón), Luis 54
del Castillo, Michel 38
Delibes, Miguel 8, 18
Espriu, Salvador 9
Gironella, José María 11
Gomez de la Serna, Ramon 9
Goytisolo, Juan 5, 10, 23, 133
Guillén, Jorge 11
Matute (Ausejo), Ana Maria 11
Otero, Blas de 11
Rodriguez, Claudio 10
Ruiz, Jose Martinez 11
Saura (Atares), Carlos 20
Sender, Ramon (Jose) 8

## SRI LANKAN

Gunesekera, Romesh 91

## ST. LUCIAN

Walcott, Derek (Alton) 2, 4, 9, 14, 25, 42, 67, 76

## SWEDISH

Beckman, Gunnel 26
Bergman, (Ernst) Ingmar 16, 72
Ekeloef, (Bengt) Gunnar 27
Johnson, Eyvind (Olof Verner) 14
Lagerkvist, Paer (Fabian) 7, 10, 13, 54
Martinson, Harry (Edmund) 14
Sjoewall, Maj 7
Spiegelman, Art 76
Transtroemer, Tomas (Goesta) 52, 65
Wahlöö, Per 7
Weiss, Peter (Ulrich) 3, 15, 51

## SWISS

Canetti, Elias 3, 14, 25, 75, 86
Duerrenmatt, Friedrich 1, 4, 8, 11, 15, 43, 102
Frisch, Max (Rudolf) 3, 9, 14, 18, 32, 44
Hesse, Hermann 1, 2, 3, 6, 11, 17, 25, 69
King, Francis (Henry) 8, 53, 145
Kung, Hans 130
Pinget, Robert 7, 13, 37
Sauser-Hall, Frederic 18
Sterchi, Beat 65
von Daeniken, Erich 30

## TRINIDADIAN

Guy, Rosa (Cuthbert) 26
James, C(yril) L(ionel) R(obert) 33
Lovelace, Earl 51
Naipaul, Shiva(dhar Srinivasa) 32, 39
Naipaul, V(idiadhar) S(urajprasad) 4, 7, 9, 13, 18, 37, 105
Rampersad, Arnold 44

## TURKISH

Hikmet, Nazim 40
Kemal, Yashar 14, 29
Seferis, George 5, 11

## UGANDAN

p'Bitek, Okot 96

## URUGUAYAN

Galeano, Eduardo (Hughes) 72
Onetti, Juan Carlos 7, 10

## WELSH

Abse, Dannie 7, 29
Arundel, Honor (Morfydd) 17
Clarke, Gillian 61
Dahl, Roald 1, 6, 18, 79
Davies, Rhys 23
Francis, Dick 2, 22, 42, 102
Hughes, Richard (Arthur Warren) 1, 11
Humphreys, Emyr Owen 47
Jones, David (Michael) 2, 4, 7, 13, 42
Jones, Terence Graham Parry 21
Levinson, Deirdre 49
Llewellyn Lloyd, Richard Dafydd Vivian 7, 80
Mathias, Roland (Glyn) 45
Norris, Leslie 14
Roberts, Kate 15
Rubens, Bernice (Ruth) 19, 31
Thomas, R(onald) S(tuart) 6, 13, 48
Watkins, Vernon Phillips 43
Williams, (George) Emlyn 15

## YUGOSLAVIAN

Andrić, Ivo 8
Cosic, Dobrica 14
Kisha, Danilo 57
Krlezha, Miroslav 8, 114
Pavic, Milorad 60
Popa, Vasko 19
Simic, Charles 6, 9, 22, 49, 68, 130
Tesich, Steve 40, 69

# CLC-151 Title Index

*The Adjuster* (Egoyan) **151**:126-30, 132, 134, 136, 139-41, 145, 147, 150-53, 156, 161, 167, 173
"Again, Like Before" (Castillo) **151**:47
"The Alligator Bride" (Hall) **151**:196
*Andrew the Lion Farmer* (Hall) **151**:182
"Another Elegy" (Hall) **151**:200-02
"The Antihero" (Castillo) **151**:5-7, 34-5
"Apples" (Hall) **151**:196
*Bach Cello Suite #4: Sarabande* (Egoyan) **151**:175
"Baseball and the Meaning of Life" (Hall) **151**:200-02, 208
"A Beard for a Blue Pantry" (Hall) **151**:224
*Before My Time* (Howard) **151**:275
*The Best American Poetry 1989* (Hall) **151**:193
*The Binding Chair* (Harrison) **151**:257
*Bridgeport Bus* (Howard) **151**:261, 269-70, 272, 275, 283
"By Way of Acknowledgment" (Castillo) **151**:47
*Calendar* (Egoyan) **151**:129-30, 134, 136, 139, 141-42, 146-47, 150, 152-53, 161, 166-67
"El Chicle" (Castillo) **151**:104
"A Christmas Gift for the President of the United States, Chicano Poets and a Marxist or Two" (Castillo) **151**:11, 20, 102
"Christmas Snow" (Hall) **151**:187
"Christmas Story of the Golden Cockroach" (Castillo) **151**:48
"Conversations with an Absent Lover on a Beachless Afternoon" (Castillo) **151**:48
"A Counter-Revolutionary Proposition" (Castillo) **151**:3-4
"Crawfish Love" (Castillo) **151**:65
"Daddy with Chesterfields in a Rolled Up Sleeve" (Castillo) **151**:11
"Daylilies on the Hill" (Hall) **151**:208
*Death to the Death of Poetry* (Hall) **151**:204, 206, 208
*Dr. Ox's Experiment* (Egoyan) **151**:155, 175
"Eating the Pig" (Hall) **151**:192
"Electra Currents" (Castillo) **151**:11
"Elegy for Wesley Wells" (Hall) **151**:207
*Elsewhereless* (Egoyan) **151**:155, 175
"Encuentros" (Castillo) **151**:11
"Esta mano" (Castillo) **151**:20
"Exile" (Hall) **151**:195
*Exiles and Marriages* (Hall) **151**:207, 214
*Exotica* (Egoyan) **151**:132-37, 139, 142-48, 150, 152-57, 159, 161, 165-67, 173
*Expensive Habits* (Howard) **151**:262-63, 269, 275, 285
*Exposure* (Harrison) **151**:238-43, 249, 251
"Extra Innings" (Hall) **151**:201
*Facts of Life* (Howard) **151**:262, 269-70, 272, 275-76, 278, 280-81
*Family Viewing* (Egoyan) **151**:122-29, 134, 136, 139-40, 142, 147-49, 151-52, 154, 161, 166, 173-74
*Felicia's Journey* (Egoyan) **151**:155, 168-76
"The Figure of the Woods" (Hall) **151**:187
"First Inning" (Hall) **151**:200

"For Jean Rhys" (Castillo) **151**:11
"Foreign Market" (Castillo) **151**:47
"Four Classic Texts" (Hall) **151**:181-82, 188, 190
*Goddess of the Americas: Writings on the Virgin of Guadalupe* (Castillo) **151**:46, 74, 76, 103
"Gold" (Hall) **151**:196
*Grace Abounding* (Howard) **151**:275, 285
*Gross Misconduct* (Egoyan) **151**:135, 152
*The Happy Man* (Hall) **151**:181-82, 193, 197-98, 204, 213
"Her Long Illness" (Hall) **151**:223
*Here at Eagle Pond* (Hall) **151**:200, 213
*Howard in Particular* (Egoyan) **151**:136
"I Am the Daughter / Mother Who Has Learned" (Castillo) **151**:20
*I Ask the Impossible* (Castillo) **151**:104
*The Ideal Bakery* (Hall) **151**:187
"An Idyll" (Castillo) **151**:5-7
"If Not for the Blessing of a Son" (Castillo) **151**:48, 65
"In My Country" (Castillo) **151**:20
"In the Beginning There Was Eva" (Castillo) **151**:110
"In the One Day" (Hall) **151**:182
*In This Quarter* (Egoyan) **151**:124
"Internal and External Forms" (Hall) **151**:196
*The Invitation* (Castillo) **151**:3-5, 7, 30, 37, 45
"Je Suis Une Table" (Hall) **151**:195
*The Joy Luck Club* (Tan) **151**:294-352
"Juan in a Million" (Castillo) **151**:45
"Kicking the Leaves" (Hall) **151**:192, 197
*Kicking the Leaves* (Hall) **151**:181, 191, 193, 197-98, 204, 213
"The Kiss" (Hall) **151**:195-96
*The Kiss: A Memoir* (Harrison) **151**:246-57
"A Kiss Errant" (Castillo) **151**:47, 65
*The Kitchen God's Wife* (Tan) **151**:334
"Last Days" (Hall) **151**:223
*Letters* (Castillo)
  See *The Mixquiahuala Letters*
"Life After Jane" (Hall) **151**:217
*Life Work* (Hall) **151**:201-03, 207-09, 212
"A Lifetime" (Castillo) **151**:47,65
"Loca Santa" (Castillo) **151**:34
"The Long River" (Hall) **151**:191, 196
"Loverboys" (Castillo) **151**:45
*Loverboys* (Castillo) **151**:45-8, 103
*A Lover's Almanac* (Howard) **151**:281-85, 287, 289-90, 292
"La Macha" (Castillo) **151**:115
*Massacre of the Dreamers: Essays on Xicanisma* (Castillo) **151**:30-1, 33, 36, 46, 48-9, 51, 70, 72, 83, 101-03, 107-08, 110
"Me and Baby" (Castillo) **151**:20
"Mi Comadre Me Aconseja" (Castillo) **151**:11
"La Miss Rose" (Castillo) **151**:47-8
*The Mixquiahuala Letters* (Castillo) **151**:3-9, 13-15, 17-25, 30-3, 37, 45-6, 48-9, 52-3, 57-8, 60-4, 83-4, 86-7, 100-02
*Mujeres No Son Rosas* (Castillo) **151**:3, 5, 30-1, 37, 40, 45

"The Museum of Clear Ideas" (Hall) **151**:200-02, 204, 208, 212-13, 219
*The Museum of Clear Ideas* (Hall) **151**:201
*My Daughter, My Son, The Eagle, The Dove* (Castillo) **151**:46, 100, 103
*My Father Was a Toltec and Selected Poems, 1973-1988* (Castillo) **151**:11, 18-20, 30, 37, 101-03
*My Father Was a Toltec: New and Collected Poems* (Castillo) **151**:30, 45
*Natural History* (Howard) **151**:264, 267-68, 270-77, 282-83, 285
*Next of Kin* (Egoyan) **151**:124, 127, 131-36, 138-41, 144-47, 150, 152, 154, 161, 166, 173
"1934" (Hall) **151**:195
"1975" (Castillo) **151**:3-4
*Not a Word about Nightingales* (Howard) **151**:275
"Not just Because My Husband Said?" (Castillo) **151**:35
"A Note on This Poem" (Hall) **151**:187
*Old and New Poems* (Hall) **151**:193-99, 209, 213, 216
*The Old Life* (Hall) **151**:204, 212, 223
*The One Day: A Poem in Three Parts* (Hall) **151**:181, 185, 187, 189-92, 197-99, 204-05, 208-13, 215
*Open House* (Egoyan) **151**:131
*Otro Canto* (Castillo) **151**:3-5, 0, 30, 45
"Pastoral" (Hall) **151**:188-89, 210
*Peel My Love Like an Onion* (Castillo) **151**:46, 91-2, 101, 103
"Poetry and Ambition" (Hall) **151**:185
"The Poetry Notebook: Two" (Hall) **151**:193, 197
*Poison* (Harrison) **151**:243-45, 257
"The Porcelain Couple" (Hall) **151**:224
"Praise for Death" (Hall) **151**:198
*Principal Products of Portugal* (Hall) **151**:205-06
"Prophecy" (Hall) **151**:188, 191, 197
*Remembering Poets: Reminiscences and Opinions* (Hall) **151**:200
*A Roof of Tiger Lilies* (Hall) **151**:213
"Rusticus" (Hall) **151**:180
*Salome* (Egoyan) **151**:155, 175
*Sapogonia: An Anti-Romance in 3/8 Meter* (Castillo) **151**:18-20, 30, 33-5, 37-8, 40-3, 45, 84, 86-7, 92-3, 95, 101-02
"Saturdays" (Castillo) **151**:11
"The Ship Pounding" (Hall) **151**:224
"Shrubs Burnt Away" (Hall) **151**:181-82, 197
*So Far From God* (Castillo) **151**:22-4, 30, 33-5, 37, 44-6, 65-70, 72, 76-8, 83, 86-7, 91, 101-02, 104, 107-08, 110, 112, 114-17
*Speaking Parts* (Egoyan) **151**:123-32, 134, 136, 139-40, 145, 147, 150-51, 153-54, 174
*String Too Short to Be Saved* (Hall) **151**:180, 216
"Subtitles" (Castillo) **151**:47
*The Sweet Hereafter* (Egoyan) **151**:147-51, 153-68, 170-74, 176

# TITLE INDEX

*Their Ancient Glittering Eyes: Remembering Poets and More Poets* (Hall) **151**:200
*Thicker Than Water* (Harrison) **151**:238-41, 245-46, 248-49, 251, 256-57
"Third Inning" (Hall) **151**:200
*This Bridge Called My Back: Writings by Radical Women of Color* (Castillo) **151**:107
"This Poem" (Hall) **151**:192
*A Thousand Orange Trees* (Harrison) **151**:245, 249, 257
"To Build a House" (Hall) **151**:189-90
"Tomás de Utrera's First Day of Spring" (Castillo) **151**:20
"The Town of Hill" (Hall) **151**:196
"Traficante, Too" (Castillo) **151**:11
"Trees" (Hall) **151**:205
"Tubes" (Hall) **151**:192
"Twelve Seasons" (Hall) **151**:197
"Vatolandia" (Castillo) **151**:47
"We Would Like You to Know" (Castillo) **151**:10, 20
*The Weather for Poetry* (Hall) **151**:206
"Weeds and Peonies" (Hall) **151**:221
"Who Was Juana Gallo?" (Castillo) **151**:47-8, 65
"La Wild Woman" (Castillo) **151**:103
"Without" (Hall) **151**:224
*Without* (Hall) **151**:212, 214, 221, 223-24
"Woman of Marrakech" (Castillo) **151**:11
*Women Are Not Roses* (Castillo)
    See *Mujeres No Son Rosas*
*Writing Well* (Hall) **151**:184, 213
"Zoila Lopez" (Castillo) **151**:36